Handbook of Computer Networks and Cyber Security

Brij B. Gupta • Gregorio Martinez Perez
Dharma P. Agrawal • Deepak Gupta
Editors

Handbook of Computer Networks and Cyber Security

Principles and Paradigms

 Springer

Editors
Brij B. Gupta
Department of Computer Engineering
National Institute
of Technology Kurukshetra
Kurukshetra, India

Gregorio Martinez Perez
Department of Computer Science
University of Murcia
Catedrático de Universidad
Murcia, Spain

Dharma P. Agrawal
Department of Electrical Engineering
and Computer Science
University of Cincinnati
Cincinnati, USA

Deepak Gupta
LoginRadius Inc.
Vancouver, BC, Canada

ISBN 978-3-030-22279-6   ISBN 978-3-030-22277-2   (eBook)
https://doi.org/10.1007/978-3-030-22277-2

This Springer imprint is published by the registered company Springer Nature Switzerland AG.
The registered company address is: Gewerbestrasse 11, 6330 Cham, Switzerland

Dedicated to my wife, **Varsha Gupta***, and daughter,* **Prisha Gupta***, for their constant support during the course of this handbook*
                    —B. B. Gupta

Dedicated to my wife, **Raquel***, and son,* **Izan***, for their constant support during the course of this handbook*
                    —Gregorio Martinez Perez

Dedicated to my wife, **Purnima Agrawal***, for her constant support during the course of this handbook*
                    —Dharma P. Agrawal

Dedicated to my family for their constant support during the course of this handbook
                    —Deepak Gupta

Preface

Computers have become an integrated part of the modern world and are being extensively used for storing and retrieving information. Business organizations are becoming more productive and efficient with the use of Internet-based applications. A significant rise in their use can be seen for personal purposes as they provide speedy and accurate solution for performing a variety of tasks.

However, the vast amount of data and information that is being stored and communicated among these computing devices is usually of confidential nature which requires high-end protection from the adversarial attacks. Cyberattacks have become a crucial concern for the economies across the globe. Hence, it has become inevitable to establish adequate security measures to safeguard the sensitive information and security critical systems and to identify and evaluate the underlying factors influencing their development.

This handbook contains chapters dealing with different aspects of computer networks and cybersecurity. These include:

- Fundamentals, overviews, and trends of computer networks and cybersecurity
- Security and privacy in ad hoc networks, e-services, mobile systems, wireless sensor networks, smart grid and distributed generation systems, social applications and networks, industrial systems, pervasive/ubiquitous computing, ambient intelligence, cloud computing, and e-services
- Security and privacy of robotic systems and Web service
- Cyber risk and vulnerability assessment for cybercrime
- Cybercrime and warfare
- Cyber threat analysis and modelling
- IoT threat analysis and modelling
- Human factors in security and privacy
- Cyber forensic tools, techniques, and analysis
- Visual analytics for cybersecurity
- Cybersecurity testbeds, tools, and methodologies
- Active and passive cyber defense techniques
- Critical infrastructure protection

- Intrusion detection and prevention
- Botnet detection and mitigation
- Biometric security and privacy
- Human factors in security and privacy
- Cybercrime and warfare,
- Cryptography, stenography, and cryptosystems
- Honeypots and security
- Security policies and access control
- Network security and management
- Wireless security
- Bluetooth, Wi-Fi, WiMAX, and LTE security
- Infrared communication security
- Cyber threats, implications, and their defense
- Security standards and law
- Security modelling

Specifically, this handbook contains discussion on the following:

- An Investigation Study of Privacy Preservation in Cloud
- Security Frameworks in Mobile Cloud Computing
- Latest Quantitative Security Risk Analysis Models for Information Systems with Respect to Cloud Computing
- AckIBE-Based Secure Cloud Data Management Framework
- Machine Learning Solution for Security-Cognizant Data Placement on Cloud Platforms
- Threats Behind Default Configurations of Network Devices: Local Network Attacks and Their Countermeasures
- Security and Privacy issues in Wireless Sensor and Body Area Networks
- Security in Underwater Wireless Sensor Networks
- Security Issues in Cognitive Radio Ad Hoc Networks
- Security and Privacy in Social Networks: Data and Structural Anonymity
- SOI FinFET for Computer Networks and Cybersecurity Systems
- Software-Defined Networking as an Innovative Approach to Computer Networks
- Software-Defined Network (SDN) Data Plane Security: Issues, Solutions, and Future Directions
- Survey on DDoS Attacks, Techniques, and Solutions in Software-Defined Network
- Classification of Cooperative Distributed Denial-of-Service (DDoS) Defense Schemes
- Epidemic Modelling for the Spread of Bots Through DDoS Attack in E-Commerce Network
- Physical Unclonable Functions (puf)-Based Security in IoT: Key Challenges and Solutions
- Fog Computing: Applications and Secure Data Aggregation
- A Comprehensive Review of Distributed Denial-of-Service (DDoS) Attacks in Fog Computing Environment

- Secure Machine Learning Scenario from Big Data in Cloud Computing via Internet of Things Network
- Heterogeneous-Internet of Vehicles (IoV) Communication in the Twenty-First Century: A Comprehensive Study
- A Review on Security and Privacy in Mobile Systems
- Investigation of Security Issues and Promising Solution in Distributed Systems Monitoring
- An Analysis of Provable Security Frameworks for RFID Security
- Computational Techniques for Real-Time Credit Card Fraud Detection
- Security and privacy in Industrial System
- Privacy Preservation of Electronic Health Record: Current Status and Future Direction
- QKD Protocols' Security Between Theory and Engineering Implementation
- Survey of Security and Privacy Issues on Biometric System
- Design of a Fingerprint-Based Session Key Generation and Secure Communication Establishment Protocol
- Trees, Cryptosignatures, and Cyberspace Mobile Agent Interfaces
- Permutation-Substitution-Based Image Encryption Algorithms Using Pseudo Random Number Generators
- Recent Trends in Document Authentication Using Text Steganography
- Machine Learning-Based Intrusion Detection Techniques
- Feature Selection Using Machine Learning to Classify a Malware
- DeepDGA-MINet: Cost-Sensitive Deep Learning-Based Framework for Handling Multiclass Imbalanced DGA Detection
- ABFT: Analytics to Uplift Big Social Events Using Forensic Tools
- HackIt: A Real-Time Simulation Tool for Studying Real-World Cyberattacks in the Laboratory

Kurukshetra, India   Brij B. Gupta
Murcia, Spain   Gregorio Martinez Perez
Cincinnati, OH, USA   Dharma P. Agrawal
Vancouver, BC, Canada   Deepak Gupta
December 2019

Acknowledgment

Many people have contributed greatly to this *Handbook of Computer Networks and Cyber Security Principles and Paradigms*. We, the editors, would like to acknowledge all of them for their valuable help and generous ideas in improving the quality of this handbook. With our feelings of gratitude, we would like to introduce them in turn. The first mention is the authors and reviewers of each chapter of this handbook. Without their outstanding expertise, constructive reviews, and devoted effort, this comprehensive handbook would become something without contents. The second mention is the Springer publisher staff, especially Susan Lagerstrom-Fife, Senior Publishing Editor, and her team for their constant encouragement, continuous assistance, and untiring support. Without their technical support, this handbook would not be completed. The third mention is our family for being the source of continuous love, unconditional support, and prayers not only for this work but throughout our life. Last but far from least, we express our heartfelt thanks to the Almighty for bestowing over us the courage to face the complexities of life and complete this work.

Contents

About the Editors

Brij B. Gupta received his PhD from Indian Institute of Technology Roorkee, India, in the area of Information and Cybersecurity. In 2009, he was selected for Canadian Commonwealth Scholarship Award by the Government of Canada. He has published more than 250 research papers in international journals and conferences of high repute including IEEE, Elsevier, ACM, Springer, Wiley, Taylor & Francis, Inderscience, etc. He has visited several countries, i.e., Canada, Japan, Australia, China, Spain, Hong Kong, Italy, Malaysia, Macau, etc., to present his research work. His biography was selected and published in the 30th edition of *Marquis Who's Who in the World*, 2012. In addition, he has been selected to receive "2017 Albert Nelson Marquis Lifetime Achievement Award" by *Marquis Who's Who in the World*, USA. He also received Sir Visvesvaraya Young Faculty Research Fellowship Award in 2017 from the Ministry of Electronics and Information Technology, Government of India. Recently, he has been awarded with "2018 Best Faculty Award for Research Activities" and "2018 Best Faculty Award for Project and Laboratory Development" from the National Institute of Technology, Kurukshetra, India. He is also working as principal investigator of various R&D projects sponsored by various funding agencies of the Government of India. He serves as associate editor of *IEEE Transactions on Industrial Informatics* and *IEEE Access* and executive editor of *IJITCA* and Inderscience, respectively. Moreover, he also leads the *International Journal of Cloud Applications and Computing* (IJCAC), IGI Global, USA, as editor-in-chief. He also serves as reviewer for various journals of IEEE, Springer, Wiley, Taylor & Francis, etc. He also served as TPC chair of the 2018 IEEE INFOCOM: CCSNA, USA. He is senior member of IEEE; member of ACM, SIGCOMM, SDIWC, Internet Society, and the Institute of Nanotechnology; and life member of the International Association of Engineers (IAENG) and the International Association of Computer Science and Information Technology (IACSIT). He was also visiting researcher with Yamaguchi University, Japan (2015 and 2018); Deakin University, Australia (2017); and Swinburne University of Technology, Australia (2018). At present, he is working as assistant professor in the Department of Computer Engineering, National Institute of Technology, Kurukshetra, India. His research interest includes information security, cybersecurity, mobile/smartphone, cloud computing, web security, intrusion detection, computer networks, and phishing.

Gregorio Martinez Perez received his PhD in Computer Science at the University of Murcia (Spain). In 1997, he started working in the Computer Service of the same university on various projects on end-user products related to security and networking, and in 2014, he was appointed as full professor in the same department. His scientific activity is mainly devoted to cybersecurity, privacy, and 5G networking, including security considerations, management models, network slicing, and communication architectures. He is also working on the design and autonomic monitoring of real-time and critical applications and systems. He is working on different national (14 in the last decade) and European IST research projects (11 in the last decade) related to these topics, being principal investigator in most of them. He has published more than 160 papers in national and international conference proceedings, magazines, and journals. He has been guest editing more than 30 special issues in different journals and magazines in the last few years. He is member of the editorial board of 16 journals, most of them related to the topics being covered in this handbook. He has already supervised ten PhD students, several of them recognized with honors. He is currently the deputy director for Knowledge Transfer of the University of Murcia.

Dharma P. Agrawal is the Ohio Board of Regents distinguished professor and the founding director for the Center for Distributed and Mobile Computing in the Department of Electrical Engineering and Computing Systems. He has been a faculty member at the ECE Department, Carnegie Mellon University (on sabbatical leave); NC State University, Raleigh; and Wayne State University. His current research interests include applications of sensor networks in monitoring patients with Parkinson's disease and neurosis, fitness of athletes' personal wellness, and firefighters' physical condition in action, efficient and secured communication in sensor networks, secured group communication in vehicular networks, the use of femtocells in LTE technology and interference issues, heterogeneous wireless networks, and resource allocation and security in mesh networks for 4G technology. His recent contribution in the form of a coauthored introductory textbook entitled *Introduction to Wireless and Mobile Systems*, 4th edition, has been widely accepted throughout the world. The book has been reprinted both in China and India and translated into Korean and Chinese languages. His coauthored book entitled *Ad hoc and Sensor Networks*, 2nd edition, has been published in spring of 2011. A coedited book, entitled *Encyclopedia on Ad Hoc and Ubiquitous Computing*, has been published by the World Scientific, and coauthored books entitled *Wireless Sensor Networks: Deployment Alternatives and Analytical Modeling*; *Innovative Approaches to Spectrum Selection, Sensing, On-Demand Medium Access in Hetero-geneous Multihop Networks*; and *Spectrum Sharing in Cognitive Radio Networks* have been published by Lambert Academic. He is a founding editorial board member of *International Journal of Distributed Sensor Networks*, *International Journal of Ad Hoc and Ubiquitous Computing (IJAHUC)*, *Ad Hoc & Sensor Wireless Networks*, and *Journal of Information Assurance and Security (JIAS)*. He has served as an editor of the IEEE *Computer Magazine* and the *IEEE Transactions on Computers, Journal of Parallel and Distributed Computing,* and *International Journal of High Speed Computing.* He has been the program chair and general chair for numerous international conferences and meetings. He has received numerous certificates from the IEEE Computer Society. He was awarded a *Third Millennium Medal* by the IEEE for his outstanding contributions. He has delivered keynote speech at 34 different international conferences. He has published over 655 papers and has given 52 different tutorials and extensive training courses in various conferences in the USA and numerous institutions in Taiwan, Korea, Jordan, UAE, Malaysia, and India in the areas of ad hoc and sensor networks and mesh networks, including security issues. He has graduated 72 PhD and 58 MS students. He has been named as an ISI Highly Cited Researcher and is a fellow of the IEEE, the ACM, the AAAS, and the World Innovation Foundation and a recent recipient of 2008 IEEE CS Harry Goode Award. Recently, in June 2011, he was selected as the Best Mentor for Doctoral Students at the University of Cincinnati. Recently, he has been inducted as a charter fellow of the National Academy of Inventors. He has also been elected a fellow of the IACSIT (International Association of Computer Science and Information Technology), 2013.

Deepak Gupta received his Master of Science degree from Illinois Institute of Technology, Chicago, USA, in the area of Computer Forensics and Cybersecurity with a specialization in Voice Over Internet Protocol (VOIP). As an undergraduate student, he became certified on the major networking platforms, first as a CCNA (Cisco Certified Network Administrator) and then as a MCP (Microsoft Certified Professional) which would come to serve him well in his professional life. As a graduate student, he continued to challenge himself by working on a number of research papers and projects related to computer network security and forensics research, including the topics of multi-boot computer systems with change of boot loader and MP3 steganography. He also developed and furthered his interest in VOIP technology by working on and leading research projects with Bell Labs, a prominent VOIP research lab based in Chicago. He also wrote research papers in this field on the topics of P2P communication and SIP protocols which won him the Best Student VOIP Project Award in 2007. Over the last 10 years of professional experience, he has gained a broad range of experience in computer security and technology that spans multiple fields and industries. After graduating with distinction with an MS in Computer Science, he went on to work for Sageworks, a financial software company based in Raleigh, NC. There, among other things, he developed a centralized integration process for core banking platforms that would allow customers to easily port and map their data to the central banking database. Deepak is a product visionary who founded a web agency and two other startups as a software entrepreneur to help businesses to simplify their user communication. It was during this time that his passion for innovation and entrepreneurship led him to found LoginRadius, a costumer identity and access management (CIAM) SaaS platform that helps businesses improve and optimize their customer experience by creating unified digital identities across multiple touch points, where he remains today as co-founder and CTO. At LoginRadius, he makes use of his expertise in security and forensics to innovate and improve how identity services are delivered and secured in the cloud identity space and helps businesses deliver social media integrations by a simplified REST API. Currently, LoginRadius is a leading provider of cloud-based CIAM solutions for mid-to-large-sized companies, and the platform serves over 3000 businesses with a monthly reach of 850 million users worldwide. The company has been named as an industry leader in the CIAM space by Gartner, Forrester, KuppingerCole, and Computer Weekly. Deepak is also passionate about helping businesses improve and optimize their customer experience. He lives and breathes this topic with customers everyday by helping them think through questions such as how do users interact with their website, how to simplify the customer's experience (via single sign-on, one touch login, etc.), and how to keep the customer's data secure. He is active member of the IEEE, ACM, OpenID Foundation, Cloud Security Alliance (CSA), and other tech communities. He is doing his current research in machine learning, artificial intelligence, and blockchain technologies. Web: www.guptadeepak.com, www.loginradius.com

Chapter 1
Security Frameworks in Mobile Cloud Computing

Chaitanya Vemulapalli, Sanjay Kumar Madria, and Mark Linderman

Abstract The concept of mobile cloud computing (MCC) combines mobile computing with cloud resources, and therefore, has opened up new directions in the field of mobile computing. Cloud resources can help in overcoming the memory, energy, and other computing resource limitations of mobile devices. Thus, the mobile cloud computing applications can address some of the resource constraint issues by offloading tasks to cloud servers. Despite these advantages, mobile cloud computing is still not widely adopted due to various challenges associated with security in mobile cloud computing framework including issues of privacy, access control, service level agreements, interoperability, charging model, etc. In this chapter, we focus on the challenges associated with security in mobile cloud computing, and key features required in a security framework for MCC. Initially, we describe key architectures pertaining to various applications of mobile cloud computing, and later, we discuss few security frameworks proposed for MCC in terms of handling privacy, security, and attacks.

Keywords Mobile cloud computing · Security · Mobile computing · Location Based services

1 Introduction

Mobile computing is becoming part of everyday life with wireless communication becoming ubiquitous. The technological advancement in mobile devices and invention of smart phones has taken the usage of mobile phones from the conventional use of voice communication to more now as the computing device. Incorporation

C. Vemulapalli · S. K. Madria (✉)
Missouri University of Science and Technology, Rolla, MO, USA
e-mail: sv2v7@mst.edu; madrias@mst.edu

M. Linderman
AFRL, Information Directorate, Rome, NY, USA
e-mail: mark.linderman@us.af.mil

© Springer Nature Switzerland AG 2020
B. B. Gupta et al. (eds.), *Handbook of Computer Networks and Cyber Security*,
https://doi.org/10.1007/978-3-030-22277-2_1

of sophisticated features like in-built camera, GPS, multimedia capabilities, etc. gave additional functionalities to the mobile devices. The range of functions that can be performed by mobile devices is the main driving force behind the growth of mobile computing. All these advanced features increase the software and processing overhead in mobile devices. Moreover, the advancement of software in mobile devices is happening at a more rapid pace compared to advancement in mobile hardware. Users are not able to fully exploit these advanced features due to hardware limitations of the mobile devices such as limited processing capabilities, insufficient storage, limited battery backup, etc.

In the last decade, with access to Internet becoming more and more ubiquitous, connecting to a cloud server via Internet from a mobile device is no longer a difficult proposition. This stimulated a new idea of using cloud resources for the processing and storage requirements of mobile device and gave rise to the new computing paradigm of mobile cloud computing. In this paradigm, to overcome the above said hardware limitations of mobile devices, storage tasks, communication, and computation intensive tasks are offloaded to cloud servers instead of performing them in mobile devices itself. The mobile devices will retain only thin client for user interface or display of results. Examples of such thin clients include mobile apps like YouTube, Facebook, etc.

Usage of smart phones and mobile cloud computing is also increasing at a rapid pace. According to ABI Research (Allied Business Intelligence, Inc.), a market intelligence company, the number of mobile cloud computing subscribers worldwide grew from 42.8 million subscribers in 2008 to over 100 million in 2014 [13]. Another study by Juniper Research said that the market of cloud-based mobile applications grew by about 88% from $400 million in 2009 to $9.5 billion in 2014 [23]. It was reported that more than 240 million of mobile cloud computing (MCC) customers will use cloud services with an earning revenue of 5.2 billion dollars in 2015. Gartner forecasts that global mobile phone shipments will increase 1.6% in 2018, with total mobile phone sales amounting to almost 1.9 billion units. In 2019, it will grow by 5% year over year. This growth in mobile cloud computing has opened up the possibility of enhancing applications like location-based services, information sharing, etc.

Use of mobile cloud computing in disaster recovery and emergency service has also been described in [26]. Though the concept of using cloud resources has made the mobile computing more useful and empowered it to perform any task without limitations, the security and privacy issues associated with cloud computing are deterring the large scale adoption of mobile cloud computing applications. In despite of efforts devoted in research both in industry and in academia, there are a number of loopholes in the security policies of mobile cloud computing. According to surveys [2, 27], 74% of IT executives are not interested to adopt cloud services due to security issues and risks associated with it. Some secondary limitations like limited processing power, low storage are mentioned as obstacles for computationally intensive and storage demanding applications on a mobile platform. The major data security risks such as data loss, data breach, and data privacy result from the fact that mobile users' data is stored and processed in clouds that are located at the service providers' end.

Rest of this chapter is organized as follows: In Sect. 2, we initially describe some of the architectures of mobile cloud computing proposed by researchers. In Sect. 3, we discuss the importance of security in mobile cloud computing and the security aspects that are necessary in MCC. In Sect. 4, we provide a review of the security frameworks proposed in the literature for authentication, privacy, secure storage, and secure computing. In Sect. 5, we discuss attacks, risk assessment, and vulnerability in mobile clouds. Section 6 is the discussion section comparing different techniques. And, finally, Sect. 7 concludes this chapter.

2 Architecture of Mobile Cloud Computing

Since the demand for smartphones and tablets is constantly increasing, manufacturers of these devices are improving the technology and usability of devices. It is because of handy shape and size, mobile devices are being used to perform most tasks that a desktop or laptop computer is currently used for. These devices can also connect to the resources of cloud computing called mobile cloud computing (MCC) which has increased the challenges due to the security loopholes. Mobile cloud computing is relatively a new computing paradigm and the basic general idea behind an architecture of mobile cloud computing involves mobile devices, mobile network, and cloud servers. Mobile devices access the Internet using wireless network, and through the Internet communicate with the cloud servers.

Figure 1.1 depicts a general architecture of mobile cloud computing. Though this is a basic architecture of mobile cloud computing, various other versions of mobile cloud computing architectures have been proposed based on the applications. Many of the services available under conventional cloud computing are also available for mobile computing. These include Data storage as a Service (DaaS), Communication as a Service (CaaS), Security as a Service (SecaaS), Software as a Service (SaaS), etc.

One of the main applications of mobile cloud computing already being widely used is data storage in cloud. Here, authorized users are allocated storage space in the cloud servers. In this architecture, data files such as images, videos, and other personal files are uploaded to the cloud server to overcome the storage limitations in mobile devices and give the flexibility of accessing the files anytime and from anywhere. Mobile apps like Dropbox, iCloud, SkyDrive, etc. are few such examples.

Another important type of usage or application of mobile cloud computing is where communication and computation are offloaded to the cloud. Figure 1.2 gives a pictorial representation of the architecture associated with this type of service/application of MCC. In this architecture, virtual smart phone devices are setup in the cloud to which the physical devices can connect and offload their tasks. These are called by different names such as virtual images [3], extended semi shadow images (ESSI) [11], etc., by different authors but the underlying idea is the same, i.e., having virtual machines in the cloud server. In this chapter, we use the term virtual image to describe these virtual machines in the cloud. These virtual images can be full or partial images. Virtual images are free of any physical

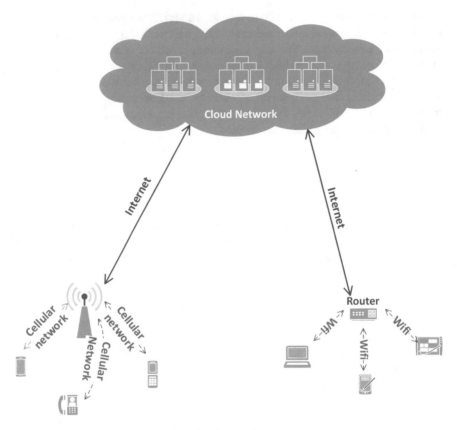

Fig. 1.1 General architecture of mobile cloud computing

limitations that are synonymous with physical mobile devices such as limited battery power and limited processing capabilities. Moreover, users can allocate/configure these virtual images as per requirement. Mobile devices connect to their respective virtual images in the cloud through the Internet from available wireless networks. Mobile devices connect to the nearby access points through wireless communication and access points are connected to cloud servers via the Internet in various ways with fixed network used at some point in the network. The mobile devices are connected to virtual images in the cloud using a secure communication channel through the Internet. The two main operations that result in high battery consumption in a mobile device are computing and communication tasks. The mobile devices can offload high CPU consumption tasks to the virtual image in cloud since it possesses more powerful computing resources and no battery limitation. Similarly, communication among physical mobile devices is affected by many factors such as mobility, range, battery power, and other environmental factors. Offloading the communication tasks to their virtual counter parts in the cloud can help in overcoming these factors since virtual images are fully connected and do not possess any battery limitations.

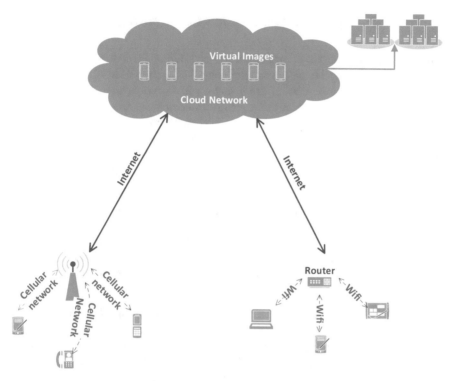

Fig. 1.2 Architecture of mobile cloud computing with virtual images

Olafare et al. [20] performed a research focused on the security challenges and possible solutions in MCC. They proposed the adoption of applications on the mobile device which keep a check on amount of information third-party applications can have access to. In addition, the validity and authenticity of third-party application needs to be checked before installing. Also, the third-party application signature or certificate needs to be checked in order to ensure that the updated version signature matches the original signature of the third-party application. The authors further discussed MCC models/architectures with security components to counter attacks. It is also being suggested to use SSL certificate for the security of communication channel. Without using SSL, it is easy for an attacker to bridge the data transmission and act as a cloud server to tamper the data. Using SSL, when the user starts using the cloud services, data sent to the user is an SSL encrypted data. The key for decryption of the data is sent to the user over a personal email account. The authors then classified the security threats into three major categories: mobile device threats, threats to the cloud (cloud computing), and network threats. For each category of security issues that are related to MCC, the author has designed a framework/architecture with security components.

3 Security Aspects of Mobile Cloud Computing

Most of the applications of mobile cloud computing involve exchange of data with cloud servers which are beyond the control of mobile users. This information may also include private data of users such as his location, usage details, etc. So it is very important to protect this user information from adversary. Since cloud provider is also a third party, it can also be considered as a potential adversary. The security requirements in MCC may slightly vary with the application but the basic and mandatory aspects of security in mobile cloud computing would be (1) authentication, (2) data integrity and confidentiality, and (3) privacy.

Authentication In mobile cloud computing, mobile users utilize the cloud resources for their storage needs, offloading computation and communication tasks. Since cloud servers will be used by number of users, there should be an authentication mechanism between mobile users and the cloud. In another architecture of MCC mentioned earlier, virtualization is used and virtual images are maintained in the cloud. This architecture requires added authentication mechanism between virtual images.

Data Integrity and Confidentiality One of the main applications of cloud computing is to use cloud resources for storing users' data. This is one of the major advantages of mobile cloud computing. Usually, mobile devices have limited storage capacity. In order to overcome this limitation, files are offloaded to the cloud servers so that they can be accessed from anywhere and at any time. But the cloud servers are not in the control of mobile users, and hence, cloud service providers could also be potential adversary. Therefore, efficient encryption mechanisms must be in place to preserve the confidentiality and integrity of the files stored in the cloud servers. Moreover, there should be provision for users to verify the integrity of files at any instant of time.

Privacy In mobile cloud computing, mobile users constantly communicate with cloud servers to access their resources. In this process, privacy of the mobile user needs to be protected from the cloud service provider as well. In some applications like location-based services using mobile cloud computing, this is more important as the user location information should be protected from other entities.

4 Security Frameworks for Mobile Cloud Computing

4.1 Authentication Frameworks for Mobile Cloud Computing

A Framework of Authentication in the Cloud for Mobile Users In the paper [7], the authors address the issue of device authentication in mobile cloud computing using policy based authentication. The proposed scheme uses the implicit authentication and trustcube. Unlike traditional authentication mechanisms which are based on aspects like what you have, what you know, and what you are, implicit authentication is based on what you do. By this users are identified by their habits, as opposed to their belongings, memorized data, and biometrics. Implicit authentication can be implemented in various ways like IP address, device profiles, etc. However, in this scheme, they use implicit authentication based on mobile data such as calling patterns, short messages (SMS) activity, website accesses, and location information which is automatically available with the network operators/carriers. This kind of implicit authentication gives an added security by protecting against unwanted access from stolen handsets. Implicit authentication is a statistical test and works based on comparison with threshold values. Based on the observed behavior of the users with mobile data, probabilistic authentication scores are calculated and assigned to client devices. The proposed authentication framework compares the calculated authentic score with the threshold values to verify whether the device is with legitimate user or not. The threshold value and amount of uncertainty allowed is dependent on the type of the application.

Figure 1.3 depicts the block diagram of the proposed framework. It has four main components: (a) client device, (b) data aggregator, (c) authentication engine, (d) authentication consumer. Client devices are the mobile devices on which the user performs his daily actions. The data aggregator constantly collects data on

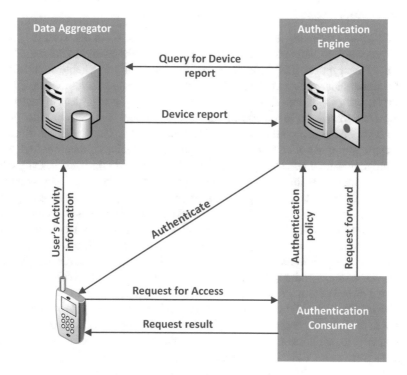

Fig. 1.3 Main components of the MCC framework and their interactions

context and action from the client devices. The authentication engine will obtain this information from data aggregator or from client device directly and the corresponding authentication policies from authentication consumer. Based on the results from the authentication engine, the authentication consumer responds to the clients' request.

Prior to the authentication process, authentication consumer prepares the list of access requests that require authentication. A policy is determined for each of the request and registered with the authentication engine. Each policy consists of at least three parts: the access request, the information to be collected from the client devices or data aggregator for this access request, and a policy rule. The policy rules consist of integrity check rules on the platform and environment, a threshold value for the authentication score, and the alternate authentication method if the authentication score is less than a threshold value. After the policy is registered with the authentication engine, when the authentication consumer receives an access request, it redirects the request to the authentication engine. Authentication engine obtains the required client info from the data aggregator or the client itself and then applies the authentication rule in the policy and determines the authentication result and sends this back to the authentication consumer. If the authentication result is successful, the authentication consumer will service the request. The proposed framework can also be scaled to large number of users by using multiple instances of authentication service within the cloud on demand.

Feasibility of Deploying Biometric Encryption in MCC In the work [31], Zhao et al. proposed an authentication framework for mobile cloud environment using biometric encryption (BE). Biometric encryption is more reliable compared to conventional security systems based on secret key due to its features that are difficult to forget, lose, share, and forge. The science of using physiological or behavioral features of human such as fingerprint, iris, face, signature, voice, etc. to identify him or her is called biometric identification. Combination of this biometric identification and cryptography is called biometric encryption. It combines biometrics and secret key, and they cannot be achieved in the templates stored in the system. Only when a living biometric feature was proposed to the system, the secret key would be generated. There are three encryption system models based on biometric encryption. First is the key release model in which the biometric feature and secret key are superposed to be the biometric feature template. Secret key is released only when the biometric feature matches. Second is the key binding model in which biometric feature and key materials are combined to be the biometric feature templates in encryption scheme. Third model is the key generation model in which secret key is extracted directly from the signal instead of from the external input.

The architecture of the proposed framework is depicted in Fig. 1.4. In the proposed framework, a separate cloud authentication center (CAC) is established to relieve the application server from the burden of analyzing and verifying requests from users. CAC is assumed to be a trusted party. Initially, BE application developers register their products in the platform when they are released. This informs the required parameters, including the category of the application, biometric

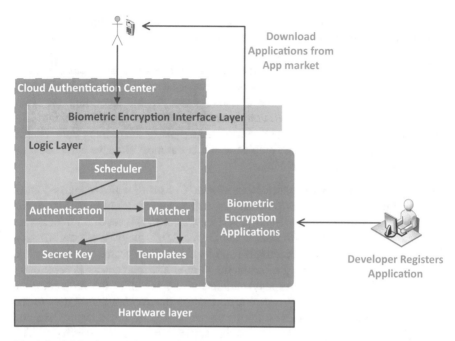

Fig. 1.4 Mobile cloud platform architecture for authentication using biometric encryption

features requested, security level, etc. These applications are downloaded by the users from app repository in the platform. Before a user can begin using the applications, a record containing his biometric features must be created on the platform and this is done through a specific interface. Application accomplishes this by calling BE module on the mobile device. CAC is the core component for the architecture. It schedules requests from clients, matches the submitted biometric data with the original ones, and also manages the biometric feature templates and secret keys. It makes the authorization for all the applications and users. Overall, the CAC analyzes the biometric data sent by applications and sends the result to application servers.

A Framework for Secure Mobile Cloud Computing The authors of this paper [25] discuss the use of biometric authentication framework to access the cloud. Biometric authentication supplies a bigger measure of protection and accuracy compared to other authentication methods with low hardware costs and secure entry. Biometric is the most effective method to authenticate the users and to protect them from illegal and unauthorized customers. The preprocessing steps and algorithms for extracting the features, and matching of the biometrics traits are discussed in detail. The authentication of fingerprint password is done over web-based services within cloud computing. The two phases discussed are biometric authentication framework enrollment and verification. The matching algorithm steps include comparing the input images with the template images. Template images are collected during the enrollment which are then compared with input images during the recognition phase. This phase decides if the input image and template image match or not. The authors proposed a novel matching score algorithm for considering features of biometrics. It is a combination of strong and weak classifiers which combines the matching scores of each subsystem to find multiple matching scores which are then sent to the decision phase. In this algorithm, the weak classifier is called for each iteration in order to generate a weak ranking. The matching algorithm decides to underline diverse parts of the training data. Hence, it was concluded that biometric authentication is the most effective authentication method as the fingerprints are unique.

Middleware Layer for Authenticating Mobile Consumers of Amazon S3 Data
In [18], Lomotey and Deters proposed an authentication framework for mobile consumers of Amazon Simple Storage Service (Amazon S3) based on middleware oriented framework called MiLAMob and OAuth 2.0. Usually, to access Amazon S3, users have to provide credentials such as access key, secret access key, and a signature which is not very efficient for mobile environment as it contributes to HTTP traffic in request response architecture. Generating the hash message authentication code (HMAC) signature in mobile device also contributes to the computation overhead. Moreover, storing an access key Id, secret access key, and HMAC signature in mobile device is another security issue since the device can fall into wrong hands at any moment. The proposed framework overcomes these issues by introducing a middleware which handles the security and data request issues with Amazon S3 on behalf of the user. Architecture of the proposed framework shown in [18] is illustrated in Fig. 1.5.

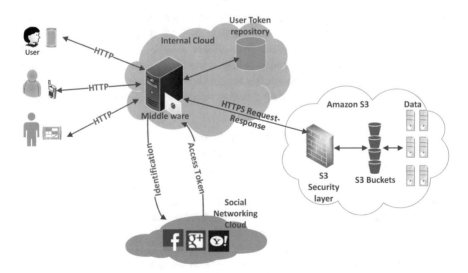

Fig. 1.5 Framework for authentication using middleware-layer for MCC

The proposed MiLAMob framework contains four major components. They are (1) mobile platform, (2) middleware, (3) the social networking platform, and (4) Amazon S3. For mobile platform, the framework advocates usage of mobile web frameworks approach rather than native approach mainly for the reason that it allows users to use heterogeneous mobile devices rather than being confined to a single mobile provider. The middleware is core of MiLAMob framework with three interfaces connected to mobile participants, social networking cloud, and Amazon S3. When a user wants to access Amazon S3, he/she first connects to middleware through publicly available URI. Middleware redirects the user to an authentication page where the user can chose a preferred authentication method. It could be either a personal login or through available social media like Facebook login, Google login, etc. If the user chooses to authenticate using Google credentials, then he is redirected to Google login page where he enters his id and password. After successful authentication, the middleware receives the users' security tokens and based on that it retrieves the user's Amazon S3 security credentials from its repository. The middleware then sends the request over HTTPS to Amazon S3 authentication system. If the request passes the authentication test, middleware retrieves the requested object and sends it to the mobile user. In this mechanism, user only interacts with middleware or social network media and Amazon S3 component is hidden from the user. Mobile users have no knowledge about Amazon S3 security tokens. Due to this, unauthorized use of system is prevented to some extent. Though this middleware component can be hosted on any public domain cloud, this paper advocates to host it on a private cloud to have full control of security issues. Incorporating authentication using social network media is the distinguishing feature of MiLAMob framework and it facilitates business-to-business (B2B) and business-to-consumer (B2C) support. Thus, by allowing user to authenticate using personal login or social network media, MiLAMob framework facilitates what is referred to as hybrid authentication mechanism.

Context Awareness Architecture in MCC Most of the authentication frameworks try to authenticate the device rather than the actual user and device may be lost or go into wrong hands very easily. This is an important issue when it comes to mobile devices. In order to overcome this issue, in [32], Zhou et al. proposed an authentication framework based on context aware data. Context aware data includes phone records, calendar, GPS applications, and battery data. Most of the other implicit authentication frameworks previously proposed take only time factor into consideration and does not take the periodic activities into consideration. The proposed context awareness architecture (CAA) in mobile cloud computing proposed in [32] is illustrated in Fig. 1.6.

The proposed CAA architecture primarily consists of three entities, namely the mobile client, cloud services, and CAA protocol. The mobile client/device has context aware data for mobile devices and corresponding protocol as the two major components. Decision-making device calculates the similarity of users recent behavior and activities with respect to the context awareness algorithm and then compares with the data in users characteristics database. It then passes the calculated

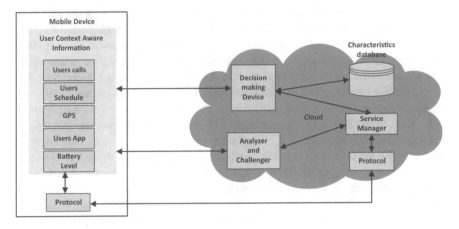

Fig. 1.6 Context aware architecture for authentication in MCC

similarity to the service manager. Service manager is the main component of this architecture. Based on the results provided by decision-making device, the service manager decides whether to allow the users to use the resources or to throw challenges through the Analyzer and Challenger. It also performs the task for formulating and implementing the new protocol and deciding whether to take the users frequent activities into users characteristics database. Data received by Analyzer and Challenger is divided into three kinds: high risk, medium danger, and low risk. If the received data is completely different from the one in characteristics database, then it is considered as high risk and the user is asked to enter a PIN code. If the user fails to enter the correct PIN code, he is denied access to the resources. In the medium danger condition, the user is asked to enter date of birth or a special phone number. In the low risk case, the user need not enter any further information for authentication and this reduces the explicit input of data. The user context data accepted by service manager as that of correct users is stored in users characteristic database for future authentication.

Consolidated Identity Management System for Secure MCC Security is the major obstacle while using the cloud server. In the survey conducted by the authors [14], it was noticed that more than 66% of the users tend to store personal identifiable information (PII) in unprotected text files, cookies, or applications. Mobile devices could be lost or stolen and compromised. These facts related to mobile devices make them attractive targets to obtain unauthorized access by intruders. In order to support the legitimate access process over the clouds, third-party identity management systems (IDMs) have been proposed. The access management systems depend on IDMs for identity generation, authentication, and authorization. However, IDMs are vulnerable to attacks which lead authors to introduce new IDM architecture dubbed consolidated IDM (CIDM) which countermeasures these vulnerabilities. It includes separating the credentials and distributing them over all the IDMs, adding second layer of authentication by allowing user to respond to human-based challenge–response and securing the communication link among cloud service provider and CIDM. A set of experiments were conducted over the IDMs and CIDMs and it was observed that the security provided by CIDM outperforms compared to the security provided by the current IDM systems. Also, it has less energy and communication overhead compared to the current IDM systems.

Identity Management Protocol for Secure MCC With increase in the use of mobile cloud computing, there is an increase in number of applications provided by the SP (service providers) which is causing traffic overload problems. This needs excessive network maintenance, creating an imbalance between profit and investment. The increasing number of mobile users has also caused identity management problems, which according to authors can be solved by using improved IDM3G protocol along with an additional authentication management protocol. The requirements for IDs include not just clarity for users, but also support for multiple IDs and maintaining anonymity and privacy. Interoperability, efficient management, and certification management are discussed in [22] which are considered to be the key network issues. The proposed method maintains the mobile operators (MOs) and constructs a trusted base with cross certification between service providers and MOs. It depends on public key infrastructure (PKI) to enable mutual dependence-based communication and ID management by service providers. It uses IDM which reduces the authentication steps leading to improvement in mobile network bandwidth and availability. The IDM protocol also maximizes the load balancing to cope with social engineering attacks and to reduce network cost. It maintains transparency, confidentiality, and ID management in mobile network. The new method when compared to existing IDM3G has minimum MOs data throughput and overall network cost and improved MOs availability in mobile networks.

4.2   Privacy Preserving Security Frameworks for MCC

Security Framework of Group Location-Based MCC Chen et al. [5] proposed a scheme to preserve the identity of user accessing location-based services. They proposed a security scheme that uses location-based group scheduling service called *JOIN* [16] to address this security problem. The architecture of the proposed framework [5] is illustrated in Fig. 1.7.

The *JOIN* system has three main components: (a) mobile devices/mobile users, (b) JOIN server, and (c) cloud database. *JOIN* server stores user data, friends around mobile user, and also handles the authentication of users. On the other hand, location information, services, and information about devices are stored in cloud database. Initially, the user gets registered with the *JOIN* system to start using its services. The mobile device transmits user identification, password, group name, and a key (K_A) to $JOIN$ server for registration. The key (K_A) is generated by applying a hash function on the international mobile subscriber identity $(IMSI)$. $(K_A) = H(IMSI)$. The *JOIN* server stores this information and generates a

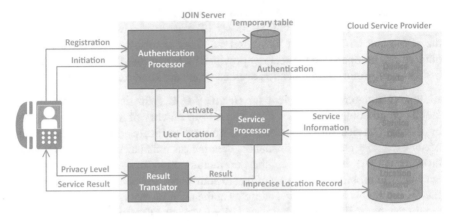

Fig. 1.7 Components of the proposed framework and their interactions

key (K_B) by using hash function on the concatenated string of ID and (K_A). $K_B = H(ID\|K_A)$. K_B and group name are then stored on cloud database for user authentication. When a user wants to use the *JOIN* services, he logs in using the ID and password. Then, in order to start an activity, the user transmits K_A, group name, and location information to *JOIN* server. Upon receiving this information, the *JOIN* server regenerates K'_B by hashing the ID and K_A used by the user. $K'_B = H(ID\|K_A)$. This newly generated key is compared with the K_B stored in cloud database. Upon successful verification, a request is sent to all other members of the same group. All the group members respond with their respective K_A, group name, and location information. *JOIN* server authenticates each of these users as mentioned above and generates a list of friends using temporary table and list of points of interests using the cloud database near the mobile users location. This information is then encrypted using advanced standard algorithm (E) with initiator key (K_B). $C = E_{K_B}(Data)$ and transmitted to the initiator. The initiator then computes the key K_B using self ID and K_A and uses that to decrypt (D) the encrypted data (C), $Data = D_{K_B}(C)$. Thus, in this scheme the identity of user accessing the location-based system (LBS) is protected by applying hash function on the $IMSI$ to generate K_A.

In-Device Spatial Cloaking for Mobile User Privacy Assisted by the Cloud In the paper [28], Wang et al. proposed a framework to protect the privacy of mobile user in location-based services. The overall architecture of the proposed scheme is illustrated in Fig. 1.8.

In this scheme, the spatial space is hierarchically decomposed into h levels with each level having 4^h grid cells [1]. The entire system area is represented by the root at level zero. At each subsequent level, based on each grid cell in the upper level is subdivided into four child cells. In this scheme, two cells having same parent and residing in same row are termed as horizontal neighbors (C_H) and two cells having same parent and present in same column are termed as vertical neighbors (C_V).

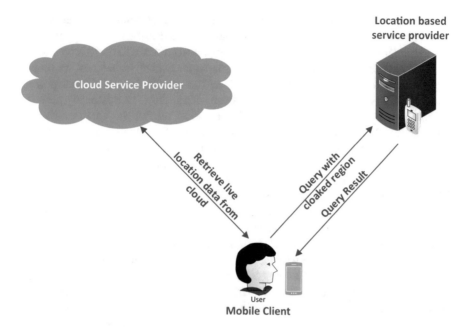

Fig. 1.8 Architecture of privacy scheme for MCC

Historical data of each grid cell is maintained by the cloud service provider. When the mobile client wants to access LBS, it requests for the information on live users in four child grid cells corresponding to its current grid cell position (C). If it is less than the threshold (k), the number of live users is calculated according to the equation:

$$Sum(S) = Live\ No\ of\ Users\ in\ C_C + Live\ No\ of\ Users(C_H \| C_V)$$

where C_C is the number of live users in child grid cell containing the request issuer.

If this sum value is greater than threshold k, the generalized spatial region is generated based on C_C, and (C_H or C_V) anyone having a live number of user less than k. If S is less than k, the current grid cell is considered as a generalized spatial region. If the C_C containing the request issuer has more than k live users, C_C becomes the new current cell. The same process is repeated on the new current cell until the bottom level of grid is reached or the child grid cell is found having a live number of users less than k. The process of obtaining live users information from cloud service provider increases the latency and communication overhead. To reduce these affects, an optimizing cloaked algorithm is also proposed in this paper. This algorithm uses the historical information of live users in each grid cell stored in the cloud service provider. User location privacy is protected as the condition imposed on C_H or C_V provides anonymity to the request issuer's cell.

Protecting User Identity with Dynamic Credential and Mobility User identity verification is a crucial part of overall security of the system. Usually, in cloud computing identity verification is done using password or digital certificates which may be hacked by an adversary using some sophisticated techniques. In mobile environment this is a more serious threat as the mobile devices do not possess enough resources to run sophisticated security algorithms. In this paper [29], the authors proposed a dynamic credential generation mechanism for user identity verification. They propose to create a new kind of credential called dynamic credential as the identity proof by using the randomness in communication between cloud and user, like the mobility of the user. This dynamic user credentials change frequently based on the communication between cloud and the user. According to the authors, this dynamic credential provides more security than conventional credential management methods against attackers that can fake or steal the credential. In the first type of conventional credential management system such as using passwords to access the cloud, the credential does not change for a long time. So, if the attacker manages to steal the credential once, he will have access to the data for a very long time until the credential is changed again by the user. In another conventional credential management method, user is forced to change the credential periodically, for example, digital certificates. But even in this, once the attacker manages to fake or steal the credential, the time span would be long enough to launch an attack before user is forced to change the credential. On the other hand, in the proposed scheme, dynamic credential changes constantly based on user-cloud communications.

According to the proposed scheme, the messages exchanged between user and cloud are transformed into dynamic secrets. Users dynamic secret (S_U) is constantly updated by XOR operation of existing secret and the message (M_i) transmitted ($S_U = S_U \oplus M_i$). Similarly, dynamic secret (S_C) of the cloud is also constantly updated by XOR operation with the message (M_i) transmitted. A packet counter N is updated with update of dynamic secrets ($N = N+1$). A mobile user requests for a new data channel when he wants to start a new communication or when he changes the base stations. A threshold value denoted as $N_{threshold}$ is determined based on how frequently the user wants to change the credential. Each time the mobile user requests for new data channel from base station or number of packets exchanged reached a threshold, dynamic credentials (S) are updated. The dynamic credentials are updated as $S = S \oplus H(S_U \| S_C)$, where $\|$ is the concatenation operation. The values of S_U, S_C, and N are set to zero. Due to the constant change in credentials dynamically, the possibility of an attacker recovering user credential and using it successfully is very less.

Thus, any information loss will deprive the attacker of a valid credential at the time of launching the attack and this is the main strength of the proposed scheme. Unreliability of wireless communication with implicit information loss provides protection against attacker tapping on wireless signals. Similarly, the mobility of the user provides protection against attacker tapping on base stations as he has to predict user's movements and place tapping in every possible base station on user's path which is not practical. Even if the attacker manages to know the dynamic credential $S(t)$ for all t and performs spoofing or message injection attacks, it would be self-evident as it causes de-synchronization between user and cloud dynamic credentials. This scheme is also light weight and does not cause any overhead to mobile clients as it involves only bit-wise-XOR and hash functions.

Privacy Protection for Mobile Cloud Data Using Network Coding   In this paper [6], the mobile data is collected and analyzed using big data analytics in order to understand and predict each individual behaviors. This information provides a great commercial potential for mobile cloud services. However, to keep the collected individual information secured is a new challenge. The huge computing power of intruders and the un-trustedness of cloud servers are pronounced to be the primary reasons of security breach. Using current security techniques has proved loopholes which will lead to a number of new challenges in protecting mobile privacy. In order to defend against malicious attackers with huge computing power in outsourced database (ODB), the authors proposed an unconditionally secure network coding based pseudonym scheme. The authors did a background study of other privacy methods, namely location privacy protection and system security model for group LBS using ODB. Though these methods may seem very effective, the hackers still have succeeded in breaking the security provided by aforementioned methods. The international mobile subscriber identity (IMSI) based group security (IGS) algorithm is further discussed in detail. The privacy analysis gives a solid proof of how the proposed scheme is unconditionally secure and it can simultaneously defend against attackers from both outside and inside. The results discussed show that the proposed network coding not only exhibits better delay performance, but also provides lower energy consumption compared to other methods.

The authors of this paper suggested an enhanced secure pseudonym scheme to protect the privacy of mobile cloud data, unconditionally secure lightweight network coding pseudonym scheme to face the huge computing power challenge, and two-tier network coding to solve privacy issue of untrusted cloud server issue. The international mobile subscriber identity (IMSI) based group security(IGS) algorithm is further discussed in detail. A two-tier coding includes generating Key_A for authenticating a legal customer's identity, and Key_B (pseudonym) for protecting customer's private data. If Key_A is certificated, the server generates Key_B using Key_A as input which then activates the login processor. The general information flows of privacy preserved LBS are described in this paper. The privacy analysis gives a solid proof of how the proposed scheme is unconditionally secure and it can simultaneously defend against attackers from both outside and inside. The results discussed show that the proposed network coding not only exhibits better delay performance, but also provides lower energy consumption compared to other methods.

4.3   Secure Data Storage Frameworks for MCC

Secure Data Service Mechanism in MCC The secure data service scheme proposed by Jia et al. [13] outsources data and security management to cloud. In this scheme, users have the flexibility to move the data and data sharing overhead to cloud without any information disclosure. Their scheme consists of three main entities, namely data owner, data sharer, and cloud service provider (CSP). Secure data service is achieved by using identity based encryption and proxy re-encryption. Identity based encryption is based on bilinear mapping.

$$e : G_1 \times G_1 \rightarrow G_T \tag{1.1}$$

The above equation defines a bilinear equation having bilinearity, computability, and non-degeneracy properties. Here, G_1 and G_T are the multiplicative cyclic groups with prime order q and g is the generator of G_1. This scheme uses two hash functions, which are

$$H_1 : \{0, 1\}^* \rightarrow G_1, \tag{1.2}$$

$$H_2 : G_T \rightarrow G_1 \tag{1.3}$$

In the proxy re-encryption scheme, a semi-trusted proxy transforms ciphertext encrypted with owner public key into another ciphertext encrypted with requester public key.

The proposed scheme consists of six algorithms used in each of the six phases. The six phases are setup phase, key generation phase, encryption phase, re-encryption key generation phase, re-encryption phase, and decryption phase. Each stage is explained below:

Setup Phase—$Setup(1^\lambda)$ This is the first stage of the scheme where master secret key (MSK) and system parameters are generated based on the given security parameter (λ). System parameters (P_{sys}) include G_1, G_T, g, g_s, and $MSK = s$. The system parameters are public and they are distributed among all users, whereas the master secret key is kept private and known only to the authority.

Key Generation Phase—$KeyGen(ID_O, P_{sys}, MSK)$ In this phase, the mobile users register with the system and obtain a secret key SK. This is generated to the users based on their identity (ID_O) using MSK and H_1, where (ID_O) is user identity of the data owner.

$$SK_{ID_O} = H_1(ID_O)^s, where\ ID_O \in \{0, 1\}^* \tag{1.4}$$

Encryption Phase—$Encrypt(P_{sys}, ID_O, m)$ In the encryption phase, the data file F is divided into n chunks as $F = (m_1, m_2, \ldots m_n)$. Encrypt algorithm is run for each chunk m_i and $M_i = (g_r, m_i.e(g^s, H_1((ID_O)^r)))$, where $r \in Z_q^*$ is generated. Finally, the data owner uploads the encrypted version of the data file $F' = (M_1, M_2, \ldots M_n)$ to the cloud.

$$IBE_{ID_O}(m_i) = (g_r, m_i.e(g^s, H_1((ID_O)^r))) \tag{1.5}$$

Re-encryption Key Generation Phase—RKGen$(P_{sys}, SK_{ID_O}, ID_O, ID_R)$ In this phase, the RKGen algorithm generates re-encryption key $RK_{ID_O \rightarrow ID_R}$ which is transferred to the cloud. Cloud uses it to permit the authorized user to decrypt the ciphertext using his own secret key. ID_R is identity of the requester.

$$RK_{ID_O \rightarrow ID_R} = (H_1(ID_O)^{-s}, IBE_{ID_R}(X)) where X \in G_T \tag{1.6}$$

Re-encryption Phase—Reencrypt$(P_{sys}, RK_{ID_O \rightarrow ID_R}, C_{ID_O})$. Here, the cipher-text encrypted using owner public key is transformed into ciphertext encrypted with requester public key. Using this algorithm, the re-encryption key generated in the previous stage $(RK_{ID_O \rightarrow ID_R})$ and the ciphertext for ID_O (C_{ID_O}) are used to generate ciphertext for ID_R (C_{ID_R}) as follows:

$$
\begin{aligned}
&C_{ID_R} = (c_1, c_2, c_3); \\
&where \ c_1 = g^r; \\
&c_2 = m * e(g^r, H_2(X)); \\
&c_3 = IBE_{ID_R}(X)
\end{aligned} \tag{1.7}
$$

Decryption Phase—Decrypt$(P_{sys}, SK_{ID_R}, C_{ID_R})$ This is the final phase of secure data service scheme, where the cloud server verifies the requester's re-encryption key and sends the re-encrypted file. The decrypt algorithm decrypts the ciphertext C_{ID_R} using SK_{ID_R} and retrieves the original message m_i.

$$m_i = \frac{c_2}{e(c_1, H_2(x))} \tag{1.8}$$

As the transformation of ciphertext has taken place in re-encryption stage, the requester can decrypt the file without the involvement of the data owner. In this way, the requester gets the entire file $F = (m_1, m_2, \ldots .m_n)$.

Efficient and Secure Data Storage Operations for MCC In [34], Zhou and Huang proposed a privacy preserving cipher policy attribute-based encryption $(PP\text{-}CP\text{-}ABE)$ scheme based on bilinear mapping, access tree, and secret shar-ing scheme. The architecture for the proposed scheme is illustrated in Fig. 1.9. This scheme mainly consists of five entities, namely data owner (DO), data requester/receiver (DR), encryption service provider (ESP), decryption service provider (DSP), and cloud service provider (CSP). The DO and DR store and retrieve data from cloud, respectively. But, computation intensive tasks like

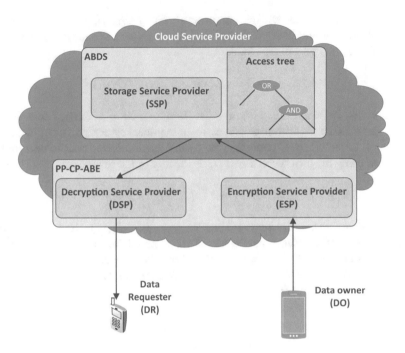

Fig. 1.9 System architecture for the secure data storage framework

encryption and decryption operations are outsourced to CSP. When the data owner wants to upload a file to cloud, ESP encrypts the file without having knowledge about the security keys, and when the data requester/receiver wants to retrieve the file, it is decrypted by the DSP without any data contents being revealed to it. The CSP is used to store encrypted data. This scheme also consists of a trusted authority (TA) which is responsible for generating and distributing keys among data owners.

Access policy tree is constructed with the help of internal nodes and leaf nodes. The leaf nodes represent the attributes associated with DO, while internal node represents the logic gates (e.g., AND or OR). Bilinear mapping function for the scheme is defined as

$$e : G_0 \times G_0 \to G_1 \tag{1.9}$$

where G_0 and G_1 are the two multiplicative cyclic groups with large prime order p. Pairing also has the bilinearity property:

$$e(P^a, Q^b) = e(P, Q)^{ab} \forall P, Q \in G_0, \forall a, b \in Z_p^* \tag{1.10}$$

This scheme consists of the following phases:

Setup Phase In this phase, the trusted authority (TA) chooses a bilinear map

$$e : G_0 \times G_0 \to G_1 \tag{1.11}$$

of prime order p with generator g. TA then randomly selects $\alpha, \beta \in Z_p$ and constructs the public parameters PK which is known to everyone and the master key MK known only to itself. The generation of PK and MK is shown below:

$$PK = (G_1, g, h = g^\beta, f = g^{1/\beta}, e(g, g)^\alpha) \tag{1.12}$$

$$MK = (\beta, g^\alpha) \tag{1.13}$$

Registration Phase Users need to register with trusted authority TA to get private keys. Trusted authority authenticates the users based on their attributes (S) and generates a private key to each of the users.

$$SK = \{D = g^{(\alpha+\gamma)/\beta}, \forall j \in S : D_j = g^r . H(j)^{r_j}, D'_j = g^{r_j}\} \tag{1.14}$$

where $r \in Z_p$, S represents user attributes, $r_j \in Z_p, and \ j \in S$.

Encryption Phase Before the data owner can start outsourcing computation of encryption, the DO needs to specify the data access tree (DAT). The DAT is divided into two sub-trees DAT_{DO} and DAT_{ESP}, where DAT_{DO} is DO controlled data access policy and DAT_{ESP} is cloud controlled data access policy.

$$DAT = DAT_{DO} \wedge DAT_{ESP} \tag{1.15}$$

Here, $\wedge$ represents a logical AND gate and depends on the root node of DAT. The DAT_{DO} normally contains one attribute. The DO randomly creates a one degree polynomial $(q_r(x))$ and generates secrets $s = q_r(0), s_1 = q_r(1), and \ s_2 = q_r(2)$. The DO sends DAT_{ESP} and s_1 to ESP. The ESP runs $Encrypt(s_1, T_{ESP})$ algorithm to generate temporal cipher (CT) on the basis of received information as depicted in the following equations:

$$CT_{ESP} = \{\forall y \in Y_{ESP} : C_y = g^{q_y(0)}, C'_y = H(att(y))^{q_y(0)}\} \tag{1.16}$$

where Y_{ESP} is the set of leaf nodes in T_{ESP}

$$q_y(0) = q_{parent(y)} * (index(y)) \tag{1.17}$$

where $q_{root}(0) = s_1$ in case of DAT_{ESP} and Y_{ESP} represents the set of leaf nodes in DAT_{ESP}, att(y) returns the attributes associated with the leaf node y, and index(y) returns the unique index associated with each node.

In the meantime, DO completes the encryption process using s and s_2.

$$CT_{DO} = \{\forall y \in Y_{DO} : C_y = g^{q_y(0)}, C'_y = H(att(y))^{q_y(0)}\} \tag{1.18}$$

$$C = Me(g, g)^{\alpha s}, C = h^S \tag{1.19}$$

where M is a message and e represents the bilinear mapping. DO sends CT_{DO} $\hat{C}$ and C to ESP. The ESP generates the ciphertext on the basis of received information.

$$CT = \{DAT = DAT_{ESP} \wedge DAT_{DO}; \hat{C} = Me(g,g)^{\alpha s};$$

$$C = h^s; \forall y \in Y_{DO} \bigcup DAT_{ESP} C_y = g^{q_y(0)}, \qquad (1.20)$$

$$C'_y = H(att(y))^{q_y(0)}\}$$

Decryption Phase In this phase, the computation required for decrypting is offloaded to decryption service provider (DSP) by data receiver/requester. Without revealing private key information, DO blinds the private key with the help of random number $t \in Z_p$.

$$D^t = g^{t(\alpha+r))/\beta} \qquad (1.21)$$

$$SK_B = \{D_B = g^{t(\alpha+r)/\beta}, \forall j \in S : D_j = g^r.H(j)^{rj}, D'_j = g^{rj}\} \qquad (1.22)$$

DSP uses the blinded key on encrypted file to generate a raw file. DO converts the raw file into the original file with acceptable processing and storage overhead. Detailed decryption process can be found in the paper [34].

Secure Cloud Storage for Data Archive of Smart Phones Secure cloud storage scheme for convenient data archive of smart phones proposed by Hsueh et al. [10] ensures the security and integrity of mobile users' files stored on cloud servers. The architecture of the proposed framework is illustrated in Fig. 1.10. This scheme mainly consists of four entities, namely mobile device which utilizes cloud services, certification authority which is responsible for mobile devices authentication, telecommunication module for generating and tracking mobile device password, and cloud service provider (CSP). In this paper, the authors assume that the secret key SK, public key (PK), and session key (SEK) are securely distributed among all mobile devices, the telecommunication module, and certification authority. The steps involved in the proposed scheme are explained below:

Registration Stage—Step 1 The mobile user has to register with the telecommunication module via the certification authority to use the services offered by the cloud. The registration request from a mobile device to the certificate authority is represented as:

$$MD \rightarrow CA : E_{PK_{TE}}(MU, NO, TK), U_n, S_{SK_{MU}}(H(MU, NO)),$$

$$H(MU, NO), Apply \qquad (1.23)$$

where MU represents the mobile user, NO represents the user's phone number, TK is the combination of the phone number (NO) and cloud service password (CPW), U_n is the randomly generated number, H is a standard hash function, $E_{PK_{TE}}$

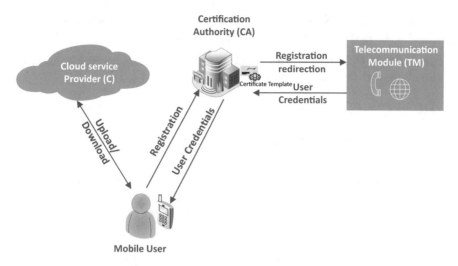

Fig. 1.10 Architecture for the secure data archive in cloud

represents encryption with the public key (PK) of telecommunication module (TE), and $S_{SK_{MU}}$ is a signature for the mobile user using a cryptographic function on the passed value and secret key (SK) of the mobile device. Signature is used to determine the legitimacy of the action and random number is used as proof of identity of the mobile user.

***Registration Stage**—Step 2* After receiving the message from the mobile device, the certification authority validates the authenticity of the message with the help of received signature. If the message is from a valid user, certification authority sends the following message to telecommunication module:

$$ CA \rightarrow TE : E_{PK_{TE}}(MU, NO, TK), U_n, S_{SK_{CA}}(H(MU, NO)), Apply \quad (1.24) $$

where $S_{SK_{CA}}$ is the signature of certification authority using cryptographic function on the passed value and secret key (SK).

***Registration Stage**—Step 3* Upon receiving the above mentioned communication from certification authority, the telecommunication module generates the cloud service password CPW and transmits it to certification authority to be passed on to mobile user.

$$ TE \rightarrow CA : E_{PK_{MU}}(MU, NO, U_n, E_{TK}(CPW)) \quad (1.25) $$

***Registration Stage**—Step 4* Certification authority switches to pass on the cloud service password from telecommunication module to mobile device.

$$ CA \rightarrow MU : E_{PK_{MU}}(MU, NO, U_n, E_{TK}(CPW)) \quad (1.26) $$

Registration Stage—Step 5 The received cloud service password (CPW) is extracted and stored in phone memory to access cloud services.

Upload Stage Uploading data to cloud is a single step process in which mobile user uploads the data to cloud by encrypting it with session key (SEK).

$$MU \rightarrow Cloud : CPW, MU, E_{SEK}(Data), S_{MU}(H(MU||SV||E_{SEK}(Data)) \tag{1.27}$$

where SEK is the session key, SV is the secret value, and S_{MU} is the signature of the mobile user.

Download Stage—Step 1 In order to download the file, mobile user sends the required information such as cloud service password, hash function, etc. The cloud can verify that the source of mobile user is correct using the hash function in the request.

$$MU \rightarrow Cloud : CPW, MU, H(MU||SV) \tag{1.28}$$

Download Stage—Step 2 After verification, the cloud returns the user's personal data to the mobile device.

$$Cloud \rightarrow MU : E_{SEK}(Data), H(E_{SEK}(Data||SV) \tag{1.29}$$

The authors also explained the steps involved in synchronization and sharing of the data using the proposed scheme in [10].

Energy-Efficient Incremental Integrity for Securing Storage in MCC In the paper [12], Itani et al. addressed the issue of verifying the integrity of the data files stored in cloud servers. Their idea is to design secure data structures using the concepts of incremental cryptography and trusted computing which protect user documents with less energy consumption from mobile clients and also support dynamic data operations. As incremental cryptography, they proposed to use set of HMAC functions that supports the incremental update property. This means that if a message having a MAC value is updated by inserting/deleting a block of data, the incremental function can securely generate an updated MAC value using only the inserted/deleted block and old MAC value. According to this scheme, there are mainly three components: (1) mobile client which makes use of MCC services, (2) cloud service provider like Amazon, Google, etc. that provides cloud services, and (3) a trusted third party which sets up a set of secure cryptographic coprocessors in the cloud. Every coprocessor may be associated with more than one mobile clients and distributes a secret key (K_S) to each of the mobile clients. The entire system operation can be described as a three step process. Each of the three steps are described below:

(1) Initialization Step In this step, if a file F_i is being moved to cloud, an incremental MAC, MAC_{F_i} is calculated for it using the shared secret key K_S. This MAC value MAC_{F_i} is stored in mobile client itself and the files are moved to cloud servers.

(2) Data Update Step File update can be done mainly using three dynamic operations: (a) file creation, (b) file block insertion, and (c) file block deletion. Other file update operations such as block replacement and block movement can be performed using earlier mentioned insertion and deletion operations. In file creation operation, to protect the integrity of the newly created file F_{K+1}, MAC value $MAC_{F_{K+1}}$ is computed using the shared secret key K_S. The computed MAC value is stored locally in mobile client, and the file is transferred to the cloud. In file block insertion operation when the mobile client requests for the file F_i to which the block update is to be performed, the cloud sends a copy of the file to mobile client and another one to crypto coprocessor. Upon receiving the file F_i, crypto coprocessor computes the incremental MAC, MAC'_{F_i} for the file and transmits to the mobile client. Upon receiving the file to be updated F_i and MAC'_{F_i} from crypto coprocessor, mobile client verifies the integrity by comparing the received MAC value with the stored MAC value MAC_{F_i}. If the MAC values match, then block is inserted at the required location in the file and MAC_{F_i} is updated by applying incremental MAC operation on the inserted block only using old MAC value and the shared secret key K_S. The file block deletion operation is similar to insertion operation with only difference being MAC updated dependent on deleted block and the old MAC value.

(3) The Data Verification Step The mobile client can verify its files stored in the cloud at any time. The key advantage of the proposed scheme is that this integrity verification can be performed by mobile clients without incurring the overhead of files download or integrity verification. For integrity verification of collection of files or whole file system in the cloud, mobile client first sends a request to crypto coprocessor. Crypto coprocessor then successively retrieves the files from the cloud, generates their incremental MACs using shared secret key K_S, and transmits them to the mobile client. The mobile client then compares the received MACs and stored MACs to verify the integrity of the files.

4.4 Security Frameworks for Computation Using MCC

Securing Authentication and Trusted Migration of Weblets in the Cloud with Reduced Traffic A mechanism for securing communication among the Weblets in elastics applications using mobile cloud computing is proposed in [21]. In the proposed security framework, the authors tried to accomplish three security objectives with respect to elastic applications in MCC. For an elastic application, Weblets can be running either in mobile device or cloud or in both. The location where a Weblet is launched is decided by device elasticity manager (DEM) and cloud elasticity services (CES). Weblets might be migrated from cloud to device or vice versa based on computation they perform and the application. In some applications, Weblets launched in cloud and mobile devices may work independently and in other applications, they might be working in concurrence to accomplish the task based on requirement. First is to provide secure migration of Weblets between cloud and device. Second one is to enable better authentication of the Weblets and the third objective is to manage the traffic in the communication channel between cloud and device. The ideas to accomplish the three objectives are discussed below:

Secure Migration of Weblets Using SSH Protocol To ensure secure migration of Weblets, communication channel between mobile device and cloud is set up using tunneling mechanism with secure shell protocol (SSH) that employs public/private key authentication to verify the end nodes. Initially, the firewall of the mobile device is tunneled by http tunneling at port 80 which is a universally opened port. Next, communication channel is established between mobile device and cloud using SSH protocol on port 22 to form the tunnel. Initially, a request is sent from the mobile device to the cloud to establish the tunnel via Internet. Then the transport layer protocol authenticates. Transport protocol component of SSH acknowledges mobile device with the cloud and user authentication protocol part of SSH acknowledges cloud with device information. After successful verification at both ends, tunnel is established and connection protocol part of SSH multiplexes it into a logical link. Figure 1.11 illustrates the proposed secure tunnel establishment between mobile device and cloud network.

Better Authentication Using SFTP Protocol Weblets are subjected to secure file transfer protocol (SFTP) to have additional layer of security around it. As part of this, Weblets are encrypted after entering the tunnel for transmission. Since, SFTP also works with port 22, another tunneling in the firewall would not be required. Every Weblet transmission is associated with a user authentication key and host authentication key. User authentication key in the Weblet is to prove their genuine mobile location and host authentication key is transmitted to the cloud before Weblet transmission is started. It ensures that each Weblets reaches their correct cloud virtual network and it is changed frequently by SSH. SFTP together with SSH ensures secure migration and authentication of the Weblets.

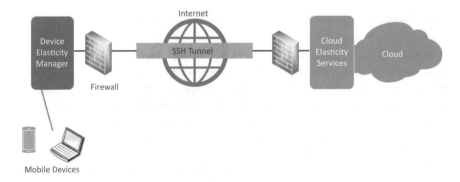

Fig. 1.11 Secure communication channel between mobile device and cloud

Reducing Traffic in Channel with Back Pressure Technique The authors propose to use the backpressure technique of fluids in the communication channel to manage traffic in the communication channel. If the traffic increases, the back pressure technique backs up the Weblets towards the Weblets' origin which could be either mobile device or cloud based on the direction of migration. Once the traffic reduces, the channel releases the back pressure to transmit the Weblets.

Secure Cloud Framework for Mobile Computing and Communication Using MobiCloud Huang et al. [11] proposed a new MCC framework which is a new service oriented model of mobile ad hoc networks (MANET). In this model, each mobile node is termed as service node which may provide or consume a service. Service includes sensing services, storage services, or computation services. This framework is close to the architecture described earlier in the architecture section where there are virtual images of mobile phones stored in the cloud to offload some of the tasks performed by physical devices. In this model, these are termed as extended semi shadow images (ESSI). These could be a partial clone, an exact clone, or an image of device having extended functionality. The communication channels between mobile node and ESSI is through a secure connection like SSL, IPsec, etc. The architecture of MobiCloud as shown in [11] is illustrated in Fig. 1.12.

In this architecture, information flow and data access control are isolated by creating multiple virtual domains using network virtualization service called

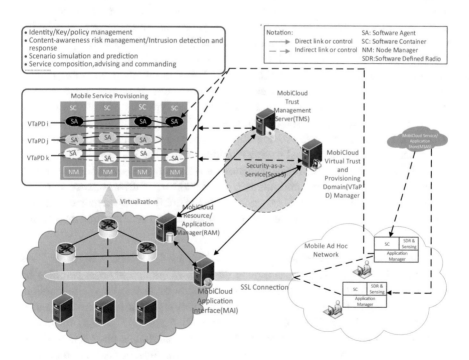

Fig. 1.12 MobiCloud architecture

VTaPD. This is created using programmable routers [17]. MobiCloud Application Interface (MAI) plays the key role on the server side. It is responsible for the services used by mobile devices and also provides interfaces for: (a) MobiCloud Virtual and Provisioning Domain manager ($VTaPD$) module, (b) resource and application manager module. All the nodes in a particular $VTaPD$ have the complete routing information of that particular $VTaPD$. On the device side, link between mobile device and cloud services is achieved through software agent. A single software agent may be running on a mobile device as well as on a cloud platform also. Under the supervision of application manager, a mobile device can access multiple cloud services or MANETs with the help of multiple software agents. Sensor manager is responsible for collection of sensing information such as battery status, location information, etc. from the mobile nodes and node manager handles the loading and unloading of software agents on ESSI. Each $VTaPD$ is associated with multiple software agents that may belong to different $ESSI$. The $VTaPD$ manager decides on the intrusion detection and risk management by collecting sensing information from mobile device. The trust management server module handles the key management, data access management, and user-centric identity management.

In this scheme, the authors used the attribute based key management which uses multiple attributes to identify an entity. When compared with the asymmetric encryption technique where attributes are considered as public keys and trusted authority generates the corresponding private keys. Only difference being the private keys are not generated from large prime number but instead from descriptive terms. The private keys are securely distributed to mobile devices by the trust management server module. The attribute based identity management scheme defines point of network presence ($PoNP$). The line radiating from the $PoNP$ shows the relationship of mobile users to various counter parties. Each $PoNP$ is a combination of type, value, and attributes. The type consists of: (a) identity issuer, (b) private key issuer, and (c) validation period. The PoNP may have multiple attributes. Each attribute is the combination of type and value. The default $PoNP$ is associated with each individual having a unique value. The uniqueness is achieved by applying a publicly known hash function on some uniquely identifiable attribute of the mobile user (e.g., passport number, email address, or driver license identity). Multiple $PoNPs$ or attributes are used to define the publicly known native identities for the device. These identities are used for authentication, authorization, and access control.

Securing Elastic Applications on Mobile Devices for Cloud Computing As mentioned in the first section, computation tasks of mobile devices can also be offloaded to cloud servers to achieve fast processing or save battery consumption, etc. In this paper, the authors tried to address various security issues associated with elastic mobile application. Zhang et al. [30] proposed a design for elastic devices which are resource constrained devices such as mobile phones augmented with cloud-based functionalities. They proposed framework for elastic applications that can run efficiently on resource constrained devices by transparently making

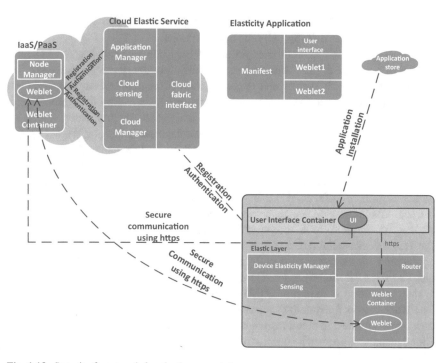

Fig. 1.13 Security framework for elastic computation

use of cloud resources whenever needed. Basically, an elastic application consists of one or more Weblets, each of which can be launched on a device or cloud or migrated to cloud based on requirement and also communicate with each other. They also discussed the security requirements in such a model and proposed security framework for elastic mobile applications in cloud environment.

Figure 1.13 illustrates the architecture of the proposed security framework in elastic applications as shown in [30].

On the Device Side Key components on the device side include (1) device elasticity manager, (2) router, (3) sensing collector. Device elasticity manager (DEM) takes care of the application launch configuration and run time adjustments. Configuration includes Weblet location, selection of communication paths, etc. It also maintains a cost model and optimizer based on which configuration settings of the application are decided. Router module keeps track of the location of Weblets and makes the location of Weblets transparent to users. Sensing module maintains the information regarding device utilization and shares the same with DEM when required.

On Cloud Side In the cloud, we have the cloud elastic service (CES) that consists of: (a) cloud manager that maintains each Weblets resource utilization details like memory used, bandwidth consumed, and computation. (b) Application manager that is responsible for installation and maintenance of elastic application in the cloud.

(c) Sensing module that monitors failures and resource availability. Resource usage within cloud node is monitored by the node manager.

In this paper, the authors tried to address various security issues associated with elastic mobile applications. For each application, the developer calculates the $SHA1$ value of each Weblet and stores it in Java like application package. Only authenticated users can install the applications. While installing the application in device or cloud, the installer re-computes the hash value and compares it with the stored hash value for integrity verification. A Weblet session key and Weblet session secret are generated by DEM. The scheme also described the authentication process among Weblets. During application launch, the keys are distributed to all Weblets that belong to an application. Initially, the Weblet generates a hash-based message authentication code ($HMAC$) using nonce, source Weblet ID, destination Weblet ID, and Weblet session secret. This along with the original message is sent to the destination Weblet. Upon receiving the message, destination Weblet recalculates the $HMAC$ using the received message and own session secret key. This value is compared with the received $HMAC$ in order to authenticate the Weblet. This paper also describes the secure process to migrate a Weblet from device to the cloud. When Weblet migration is required, DEM sends a request to Weblet to stop executing. The Weblet saves the running state and session secret and returns to DEM which in turn sends a request to cloud manager using the cloud fabric interface for migration. Cloud manager allocates resources to migrated Weblet and starts the execution from last saved state.

SMOC: A Secure Mobile Cloud Computing Platform Mobile offloading is a new concept that is been used ubiquitously. Hao et al. [8] suggested to run an operating system of mobile device and arbitrary applications on a cloud-based virtual machine. It leverages the hardware virtualization functionality on the smart mobile device. The authors provided two design fundamentals in detail. First sharing a resource platform so that an application running can freely migrate between the user's mobile device and a backend cloud server. A special file system extension was designed to enable free migration. Second, hardware virtualization technology, which isolates the data from the local mobile device operating system is used to protect user data. The authors introduced two client programs of which one is depicted as input proxy responsible for capturing the user's input before passing them to the guest OS and sending it to the VM so that guest OS cannot learn anything about the user's input. On the other hand, the guest OS is the location where app's output is rendered. Even the compromised VM cannot affect other apps and data. The user can also delete the compromised VM afterwards. The user response time can be improved, and the device energy consumption can be reduced if heavy computational processes can be moved from mobile device to the cloud VM. It also has security advantages. The platform design is discussed in detail in this paper. In conclusion, the authors say that they successfully implemented a prototype of the suggested platform using off-the-shelf hardware. The platform is then observed to be efficient, practical, and secure.

5 Attack, Risk Assessment, and Verifiability in Mobile Clouds

Cyberattack Detection in MCC Using a Deep Learning Approach Mobile cloud computing (MCC) is an emerging architecture which provides a myriads of benefits because of which it has become a soft target for cyber threats in the mobile cloud environment. In this paper [19], the authors proposed a framework with an advanced detection mechanism developed from deep learning technique. It allows to detect various attacks with high accuracy. They also have discussed the limitations of intrusion detection approaches used by other researchers. In the system model proposed by the authors, when the request is sent from a mobile user to the system, it goes through attack detection module which has various functions to detect the attack. Every request is verified carefully by comparing with the current database and/or sending to security service providers for double-checking. If the request identified as harmless, it is treated normally, whereas in other case, the request is treated as malicious and attack defend function works on the request to implement prompt security policies in order to prevent the spread as well as impacts of this attack.

The authors explained deep learning model for cyberattack detection and explained how the learning model detects cyberattacks in the cloud system. The learning model detects cyberattacks in the cloud system. It consists of two phases, namely feature analysis and learning process. Different types of malicious packets may have special features usually discrete from normal requests. These special features will be used to differentiate the malicious requests from the normal requests. The deep training is implemented using the set of simple sub-models which are learned sequentially. The non-linear transformation is used to obtain sensible set of weights. These training weights decide if the request is malicious or harmless. The authors discussed dataset collection and evaluation methods to evaluate the experimental results. It was observed that the proposed method can achieve high accuracy in detecting cyberattacks, and outperform other existing machine learning methods. In addition, they have emphasized the stability, efficiency, flexibility, and robustness of the deep learning model which can be applied to many mobile cloud applications.

A Stochastic Programming Approach for Risk Management in MCC Mobile cloud computing (MCC) is an emerging platform because using cloud computing technology, mobile applications can be performed more efficiently, thereby generating huge profits for mobile users as well as cloud service providers. Although there are many security solutions implemented to detect and prevent cyberattacks, achieving complete security is still nearly impossible. The cyber insurance is an emerging alternative to address and manage cyber risks. Under cyber insurance coverage, cloud service provider (CSP) losses will be covered partially or fully by the cyber insurance provider (IP). However, cyber insurance is not always the best solution of the variety of attacks and CSP's limited budget. The authors of this paper [9] discuss the advanced risk management strategies to minimize losses caused by cyberattacks, to select appropriate security solutions, software/hardware implementation and insurance policies, to deal with different types of attacks. They developed a dynamic framework based on stochastic programming approach for the risk management problem in mobile cloud environment. The sole purpose of the framework is to find the optimal trade-off among security policies, insurance policies, and countermeasures under uncertainty of cyberattacks and their losses such that the expected total cost of the cloud service provider is minimized. The framework suggested consists of two decision stages for CSP. In the first stage, the CSP has to decide how much it should invest to buy security packages to prevent cyberattacks and how much it should spend to buy insurance packages to cover losses caused by the attacks. To address the multi-stage optimization problem under uncertainty of attacks and a limited budget, the authors adopt the stochastic programming method to find optimal budget allocation policies for the CSP.

Secure and Verifiable Outsourcing of Exponentiation Operations for MCC
Cloud computing allows the end users to securely access the shared pool of resources such as computational power and storage. Among all the computation types, modular exponentiation and scalar multiplication on elliptic curves in finite group is a widely used cryptosystem. It includes large integers, making it expensive for mobile phones. Outsourcing the exponentiation operation to cloud server is a cheap option but not secure. Kai et al. have introduced a secure outsourcing scheme (ExpSOS) [33] which requires limited number of modular multiplications at local mobile environment. The procedure depends on secure disguising procedure that maps the integers in the group which maps into another larger group so that cloud can carry out the computation in larger group keeping data secure. The end-user can recover the result back from the result returned by the cloud. The authors assumed that for the end-user, exponentiation operations are operated in the integer ring modulo N, where N is not necessarily a prime number. They multiplied N by a randomly selected large prime p and define $L = pN$ as a part of secure disguising procedure. Then k was selected such that $1 \leq k \leq p - 1$. $y = x + kN \pmod{L}$ was computed, where x is input to cloud. It is hard to determine which point x is mapped to, without the knowledge of k. The algorithm for the ExpSOS protocol under honest but-curious single-server (HCS) model is discussed in detail in this paper. They considered secure outsourcing as two building blocks to implement scalar multiplication, point addition, and point doubling. The ExpSOS is then analyzed by the authors for the necessary properties of a result verification scheme through some counterexamples and security complexity analysis is done over it. It was then concluded that ExpSOS enables end users to outsource the computation of exponentiation to a single untrusted server at the cost of only a few multiplications and it can provide different security levels at the cost of different computational overhead. ExpSOS also provides a secure verification scheme with probability approximately 1 to ensure that the mobile end users do always receive a valid result.

A Practical, Secure, and Verifiable Cloud Computing for Mobile Systems It is known that providing data to the cloud service provider in plaintext may lead to loss of data privacy. Premnath et al. [24] combined the secure multiparty computation protocol and the garbled circuit design with the cryptographically secure pseudorandom number generation method, which enables cloud to perform any arbitrary computation on encrypted data. In this method, with private pseudorandom bit sequences and Boolean circuit, the servers create garbled circuit. The servers create the garbled circuit as $GC = GC1 \oplus GC2 \oplus GC3 \oplus \ldots \oplus GCn$ by performing an XOR operation on the shares obtained by local computations over private pseudorandom bit sequences and the Boolean circuit of the servers. With the use of these garbled inputs, another server executes garbled circuit to give garbled outputs.

In this process, the client sets servers and sends desired computation and seed value to each server. Each server creates a Boolean circuit which corresponds to the requested computation. Each server generates a private pseudorandom bit sequence using seed value. Using the semantics for the pair of garbled values, the client translates these garbled values into plaintext bits to recover the result of the requested computation. The client checks garbled output for each output wire matches with garbled values that it computed on its own. The system assures privacy of the mobile clients' data. It can enable oblivious evaluation of any arbitrary function on a third-party cloud server. It was also observed that it requires very little computation and communication participation from the mobile client to achieve secure and verifiable computing capability with this method. This method is also useful to detect a cheating evaluator if it provides output without performing any computation.

Deep Learning for Secure Mobile Edge Computing Mobile edge computing (MEC) is the most efficient approach for enabling cloud-computing capabilities over cellular networks. However, security is increasingly becoming a challenging issue in MEC-based applications. In this paper [4], the authors proposed a deep-learning-based model in order to detect security threats and malicious attacks incorporating the location information into the detection framework. The model uses unsupervised learning to automate the detection process at the edge of a cellular network. It includes feature preprocessing engine and malicious application detection engine. In the feature preprocessing engine, APK files were unpacked and the feature elements that will be used as the input of the malicious application detection engine were extracted. The two-dimensional array of bits was created based on which kind the feature element falls into. The malicious application detection engine includes first unsupervised pre-training with unlabeled samples and second, supervised fine-tuning with labeled samples.

The deep learning architecture has a multi-layer stack of modules to compute the non-linear input–output mapping. The automated learning of the features using a general-purpose learning algorithm is the key advantage of deep learning. In case of non-linear and complicated relations between features and malicious applications, the output layer of the malicious application detection engine was used as the input of the SoftMax function to represent a categorical distribution. They compared the performance of the proposed model with four widely adopted machine learning algorithms, namely Support Vector Machine, Decision Tree, Random Forest, and

SoftMax Regression. The strengths of the proposed model are discussed in detail. It was also observed that the size of the training dataset plays an important role in improving the accuracy of the deep-learning-based detection method. The authors concluded that on average the accuracy of the proposed deep-learning-based model is more compared to other four detection methods.

6 Summary and Discussion

Table 1.1 gives a cumulative picture of various security frameworks discussed in this chapter and the main ideas behind their security mechanism. In addition, we provide an executive summary and discuss some of the possible research ideas for future in reference to the work discussed in this chapter.

In [7] proposed by Chow et al., secure authentication is achieved by using implicit authentication mechanism. Observable user information is collected and stored on data aggregator after hashing at the mobile client to preserve the privacy of the users. The authentication engine makes use of this information for implicit authentication and generates result for authentication consumer. But this requires frequent application of hash function by the mobile client each time the user related information is transferred to the data aggregator. This may result in computation overhead on the mobile device. The proposed idea of using biometric information along with encryption or secret key for authentication by Zhao et al. in [31] could be feasible to implement in future as biometric sensors can be accommodated in the mobile devices. But as of date not many mobile devices are equipped with biometric sensors to implement the proposed framework. On top of it, there are certain pitfalls with biometric features as well. They are prone to problems like false acceptance, nearest impostors attack, change in fingerprint with age, etc. Secure storage of biometric information is also a challenge. Moreover, biometric science is still developing and challenges associated with using biometric encryption still needs an in-depth research. Another authentication framework [32] proposed by Zhou et al. is similar to the scheme proposed in [7]. But this one could be more secure than [7] since this considers more parameters like periodic events, spatial information, and others also while building the context aware data for a particular user. But in this scheme also the process of updating the context data of the user in the cloud could cause communication and computation overhead for the devices. The authors [25] discuss how biometric is the most effective method to authenticate the users and to protect from illegal and unauthorized customers. However, the authors have not implemented or simulated the log files based on their scheme. Also, they need to redesign policies for accessing log record as they will presumably be utilized to discover unapproved endeavors to get to data by outsiders, the cloud supplier, or any gatecrashers. In the other authentication framework [18] proposed by Lomotey el al., the authors propose to use a middleware layer having interface with social media network to handle authentication with Amazon S3 on behalf of mobile device. But this scheme again has the drawback of using id and password

Table 1.1 Cumulative study of the proposed frameworks

Paper title	Security issue addressed	Main idea
Authentication in the clouds: a framework and its application to mobile users [7]	Authentication between mobile client and cloud	Implicit authentication
Feasibility of deploying biometric encryption in mobile cloud computing [31]	Authentication in mobile cloud computing	Combination of biometric identification and secret key called biometric encryption
A framework for secure mobile cloud computing [25]	Biometric authentication	Preprocessing steps and algorithms for extracting the features and matching the biometrics trait
The context awareness architecture in mobile cloud computing [32]	Authentication of user in mobile cloud computing	Using context aware computing
Consolidated identity management system for secure mobile cloud computing [14]	Securing lost, stolen, or compromised personal identifiable information	Architecture dubbed consolidated identity management system (CIDM) which countermeasures the vulnerabilities to personal identifiable information
Improved identity management protocol for secure mobile cloud computing [22]	User ID management and security problems	Using improved IDM3G protocol along with an additional authentication management protocol
Middleware-layer for authenticating mobile consumers of Amazon S3 data [18]	Authentication of mobile consumers for Amazon S3	MiLaMob framework, social network media, and hybrid authentication mechanism
Securing authentication and trusted migration of Weblets in the cloud with reduced traffic [21]	Secure migration of Weblets in elastic application using MCC	Secure shell protocol, secure file transfer protocol, and back pressure technique
MobiCloud: building secure cloud framework for mobile computing and communication [11]	Proposed MobiCloud framework and addressed relevant security issues	Network virtualization service, attribute based key management
Securing elastic applications on mobile devices for cloud computing [30]	Secure installation, migration, authentication, and authorization of Weblets in elastic applications	Hash function for installation, shared session, and secret keys for authentication and migration. Application session keys and application session secrets for authorization
SMOC: a secure mobile cloud computing platform [8]	Security against untrusted applications	Sharing a resource platform and hardware virtualization technology
Mobility can help: protect user identity with dynamic credential [29]	Identity protection/privacy protection	Uses randomness in user-cloud communication to generate dynamic credentials

(continued)

Table 1.1 (continued)

Paper title	Security issue addressed	Main idea
Privacy protection for mobile cloud data: a network coding approach [6]	Huge computing power challenge and privacy issue of untrusted cloud server	Development of unconditionally secure network coding based pseudonym scheme
A security framework of group location-based mobile applications in cloud computing [5]	Identity or privacy protection	Hash function on IMSI number of mobile client
In-device spatial cloaking for mobile user privacy assisted by the cloud [28]	Privacy protection	Spatial cloaking
Efficient and secure data storage operations for mobile cloud computing [34]	Security of data stored in cloud	Privacy preserving CP-ABE based on bilinear mapping access policy tree and secret sharing scheme and attribute based data storage scheme
Secure cloud storage for convenient data archive of smart phones [10]	Security and integrity of data stored in cloud	Uses the standard cryptographic functions
SDSM: a secure data service mechanism in mobile cloud computing [13]	Secure data storage and data sharing in cloud	Bilinear mapping based identity based encryption and proxy re-encryption
Energy-efficient incremental integrity for securing storage in mobile cloud computing [12]	Enables verification of integrity of files stored in the cloud	Incremental cryptography and trusted computing
A deep learning approach for cyberattack detection in mobile cloud computing [19]	Data integrity, users confidentiality, service availability	Detect and isolate cyber threats using advanced detection mechanism based on deep learning approach
A stochastic programming approach for risk management in mobile cloud computing [9]	Software and hardware implementation and insurance policies	Stochastic programming approach to minimize the expected total loss for the cloud service provider
Secure and verifiable outsourcing of exponentiation operations for mobile cloud computing [33]	Secure outsourcing of exponentiation operations to one single untrusted server	Secure outsourcing disguising scheme (ExpSOS) which requires limited number of modular multiplications at local mobile environment
A practical, secure, and verifiable cloud computing for mobile systems [24]	Data privacy	Combination of secure multiparty computation protocol and the garbled circuit design with the cryptographically secure pseudorandom number generation
Deep learning for secure mobile edge computing [4]	Security of mobile edge computing	Deep-learning (unsupervised learning) based model to detect security threats and malicious attacks using location information

to initially identify with the middleware. So if the attacker can get the user id and password through phishing or other social engineering attacks, he can get access to the user's social media (if the user uses social media to identify himself to the middleware) and also the data stored in Amazon S3.

The authors in [14] introduced a new IDM architecture dubbed consolidated IDM (CIDM) which countermeasures possible vulnerabilities. But the authors have not investigated the possibilities, consequences, and countermeasures of cloud provider compromise through, for example, tampered binaries, injected malicious code, or malicious insiders. Also, the authors have failed to investigate the issue of inadequate dynamic federation and agile mechanisms in current IDM systems which is an architectural concern and should be addressed at the design level. The proposed method in [22] maintains the mobile operators (MO) and constructs a trusted base with cross certification between service providers and MO. While it depends on public key infrastructure (PKI) to enable mutual dependence-based communication and ID management by service providers, the authors have not evaluated the context of DoS attack which should be conducted continually and additional studies of the PGP algorithm are needed. In security schemes presented for computation using MCC, the security scheme proposed in [21] by Panneerselvam et al. is based on the idea of establishing a tunnel using secure shell protocol and secure file transfer protocols for secure migration of Weblets from mobile to cloud and vice versa. Though the scheme is straightforward and feasible, it requires an additional task of constant monitoring of the tunnel since attackers can use the tunnel to bypass the firewall on either side. MobiCloud framework proposed by Huang et al. in [11] is showed to enhance the MANET functionality. But in the proposed security mechanism the authors did not consider the trustworthiness of the cloud node. Mobile user information should also be securely stored in the cloud. An elastic mobile cloud application model was proposed by Zhang et al. in [30]. They also proposed security framework for the same which includes secure installation, secure migration of Weblets, authentication between the Weblets and authorization of Weblets. Though the proposed scheme ensures secure installation, it does not mention about the security threat to Weblets after installation of Weblet in the cloud. If an attacker can modify the code of the Weblet in the cloud, then it can result in configuration change of DEM and CES.

In the security schemes presented for privacy preservation, the security scheme proposed by Chen et al. [5] to preserve the privacy of LBS users is based on the idea of using hashed IMSI number. But if the IMSI number is stolen from the legitimate user, the entire system fails. Another privacy preserving scheme discussed in this paper was proposed by Xiao et al. [29]. It is based on the concept of dynamic credentials where the credentials are constantly changed based on the communication between user and the cloud. But in this scheme, the cloud which is also a third party is assumed to be trusted entity which is a very strong assumption. In another privacy preserving scheme, Wang et al. [28] proposed a privacy preserving framework for location-based services using mobile cloud computing. But the accuracy of the proposed mechanism is dependent on historical lower bound of the number of users in each grid cell. This is because it predicts number of users in each grid cell based on the historical data that may be wrong at that instant of time which in turn results in privacy loss. The enhancing secure pseudonym scheme to protect the privacy of mobile cloud data and unconditionally secure lightweight network coding pseudonym scheme [6] will face the huge computing power challenge as well as two-tier network coding challenge to solve privacy issue of untrusted cloud server.

Coming to the secure storage frameworks, Jia et al. [13] proposed a secure data storage scheme which is based on proxy re-encryption and identity based encryption. This scheme is designed to offload most of the security tasks to cloud, the mobile users have to perform cryptographic operations before uploading file to cloud which require considerable amount of energy. Moreover, utilizing cloud resources for all the cryptographic computation may increase the usage charges to the user. Zhou and Huang [34] also proposed a security framework based on privacy preserving CP-ABE and attribute based data storage scheme. The underlying CP-ABE scheme is proven to have linearly increasing ciphertext with increase in attributes. As the proposed scheme also involves a kind of CP-ABE, it also suffers from the same drawback. Another work proposed by Hsueh et al. [10] used standard asymmetric encryption techniques to encrypt the files and then stores them on the cloud servers. But due to this process, the computation overhead in the mobile devices increases. The security framework proposed by Itani et al. [12] provides a way for mobile user to verify the integrity of files stored in the cloud. This scheme is based on the incremental cryptography and trusted computing. The proposed security framework is clearly energy efficient mainly for two reasons. First, due to use of incremental MAC, computation overhead on the mobile client is greatly reduced as we need not compute the hash value for whole file every time it is updated. Second, while verifying the integrity of the file(s), the mobile client just need to compare MAC values as the task of computing MAC value for file(s) is done by crypto coprocessor. But the proposed scheme only provides a way to verify the integrity of the file stored in the cloud. It does not protect the files from being modified or unauthorized access, as files are directly moved to cloud and in cloud computing environment, cloud service provider is also a third party and can be a potential adversary.

The authors in [19] proposed a deep learning model for cyberattack detection but have not implemented on real devices and evaluated the accuracy of the model on the real time basis. Also, they have not evaluated the energy consumption and detection time of the deep learning model and compared with other methods. The authors of this paper [9] discuss the advanced risk management strategies to minimize losses caused by cyberattacks to select appropriate security solutions, software/hardware implementation, and insurance policies to deal with different types of attacks. However, they have not studied the relation between security and insurance providers through bundling strategies and matching theory. In addition, they agree that they have not investigated the relation between a direct loss and its indirect losses. The paper [33] suggested ExpSOS scheme with the security parameter, which is cost-aware in that it can provide different security levels at the cost of different computational overhead. Hence, it is difficult to provide the cost of entire process beforehand. The authors [24] suggested to use private pseudorandom bit sequences and Boolean circuit that the servers use to create garbled circuit. This method preserves the privacy of the client data even if the evaluating server colludes with all but one of the cloud servers that participated in the creation of the garbled circuit. In this paper [4], the authors proposed a deep-learning-based model in order to detect security threats and malicious attacks incorporating the location information into the detection framework. However, the critical challenge is handling streaming and fast-moving input data and to use these data to train the deep-learning-based model.

Mobile cloud computing is inherited from cloud computing and hence many of the security issues in cloud computing also exist in mobile cloud computing. MCC also has an added constraint of limited computational resources at the mobile device end that needs to be considered while designing the security frameworks. Hence, some of the security frameworks that work well with cloud computing may not be applicable to MCC. Lightweight frameworks are needed for mobile cloud computing. All the frameworks we discussed in this chapter perform the CPU intensive tasks in the cloud to avoid overhead in the mobile devices. Cryptographic functions like hashing, other high computation tasks are designed to be offloaded to the cloud. Cloud services are mostly charged based on usage so this concept of offload computation tasks actually becomes a trade-off between energy saved at the device side and expenses paid for the cloud usage.

7 Conclusion

Mobile cloud computing (MCC) provides mobile users with a rich resource functionality despite the restricted resources in their mobile devices. In this chapter, initially, we discussed the importance of different mobile cloud computing frameworks and their implicit advantages. Next, we described the key architectures of the mobile cloud computing, and key aspects of security in mobile cloud computing environment. Next, we reviewed some of the security frameworks proposed for mobile cloud computing. Privacy is a significant challenge in using mobile cloud-based services, particularly when processing mobile users' data or applications and when shifting them from mobile devices to heterogeneous distributed cloud servers located at multiple locations. Thus, next, privacy issues and some solutions in mobile cloud computing domain have been discussed. We also discussed secure storage for mobile cloud as well as secure computing ideas for mobile cloud computing. Later, we provided a discussion section where after providing a summary, we contrasted different schemes and compared them with possible future work. Thus, this chapter will serve as a good review of the security work in MCC for those who are targeting research and building applications in this area.

References

1. Aref, W. G., & Samet, H. (1990). Efficient processing of window queries in the pyramid data structure. In *Proceedings of the Ninth ACM SIGACT-SIGMOD-SIGART Symposium on Principles of Database Systems, PODS '90* (pp. 265–272). New York: ACM. https://doi.org/10.1145/298514.298579
2. Buyya, R., Yeo, C. S., Venugopal, S., Broberg, J., & Brandic, I. (2009). Cloud computing and emerging it platforms: Vision, hype, and reality for delivering computing as the 5th utility. *Future Generation Computer Systems, 25*(6), 599–616. https://doi.org/10.1016/j.future.2008.12.001
3. Chen, E., & Itoh, M. (2010). Virtual smartphone over IP. In *IEEE International Symposium on a World of Wireless Mobile and Multimedia Networks (WoWMoM), 2010* (pp. 1–6). https://doi.org/10.1109/WOWMOM.2010.5534992
4. Chen, Y., Zhang, Y., & Maharjan, S. (2017). Deep learning for secure mobile edge computing. arXiv preprint arXiv:1709.08025.
5. Chen, Y. J., & Wang, L. C. (2011). A security framework of group location-based mobile applications in cloud computing. In *40th International Conference on Parallel Processing Workshops (ICPPW), 2011* (pp. 184–190). https://doi.org/10.1109/ICPPW.2011.6
6. Chen, Y.-J., & Wang, L.-C. (2017). Privacy protection for mobile cloud data: A network coding approach. arXiv preprint arXiv:1701.07075.
7. Chow, R., Jakobsson, M., Masuoka, R., Molina, J., Niu, Y., Shi, E., et al. (2010). Authentication in the clouds: A framework and its application to mobile users. In *Proceedings of the 2010 ACM Workshop on Cloud Computing Security Workshop, CCSW '10* (pp. 1–6). New York: ACM. https://doi.org/10.1145/1866835.1866837
8. Hao, Z., Tang, Y., Zhang, Y., Novak, E., Carter, N., & Li, Q. (2015). SMOC: A secure mobile cloud computing platform. In *IEEE Conference on Computer Communications (INFOCOM)*. Piscataway: IEEE.
9. Hoang, D. T., Niyato, D., Wang, P., Wang, S. S., Nguyen, D., & Dutkiewicz, E. (2018). A stochastic programming approach for risk management in mobile cloud computing. In *Wireless Communications and Networking Conference (WCNC), 2018*. Piscataway: IEEE.
10. Hsueh, S. C., Lin, J. Y., & Lin, M. Y. (2011). Secure cloud storage for convenient data archive of smart phones. In *IEEE 15th International Symposium on Consumer Electronics (ISCE), 2011* (pp. 156–161). https://doi.org/10.1109/ISCE.2011.5973804
11. Huang, D., Zhang, X., Kang, M., & Luo, J. (2010). MobiCloud: Building secure cloud framework for mobile computing and communication. In *Fifth IEEE International Symposium on Service Oriented System Engineering (SOSE), 2010* (pp. 27–34). https://doi.org/10.1109/SOSE.2010.20
12. Itani, W., Kayssi, A., & Chehab, A. (2010). Energy-efficient incremental integrity for securing storage in mobile cloud computing. In *International Conference on Energy Aware Computing (ICEAC), 2010* (pp. 1–2). https://doi.org/10.1109/ICEAC.2010.5702296
13. Jia, W., Zhu, H., Cao, Z., Wei, L., & Lin, X. (2011). SDSM: A secure data service mechanism in mobile cloud computing. In *IEEE Conference on Computer Communications Workshops (INFOCOM WKSHPS), 2011* (pp. 1060–1065). https//doi.org/10.1109/INFCOMW.2011.5928784
14. Khalil, I., Khreishah, A., & Azeem, M. (2014). Consolidated identity management system for secure mobile cloud computing. *Computer Networks, 65*, 99–110.
15. Khan, A. N., Mat Kiah, M. L., Khan, S. U., & Madani, S. A. (2013). Towards secure mobile cloud computing: A survey. *Future Generation Computer Systems, 29*(5), 1278–1299. https://doi.org/10.1016/j.future.2012.08.003
16. Lee, Y., Wang, L., & Gau, R. (2010). Implementation issues of location-based group scheduling for cloud applications. In *IEEE VTS Asia Pacific Wireless Communications Symposium Conference (APWCS 2010)*.

17. Lockwood, J., McKeown, N., Watson, G., Gibb, G., Hartke, P., Naous, J., et al. (2007). NetFPGA–An open platform for gigabit-rate network switching and routing. In *IEEE International Conference on Microelectronic Systems Education, 2007. MSE '07* (pp. 160–161). https://doi.org/10.1109/MSE.2007.69

18. Lomotey, R. K., & Deters, R. (2013). Middleware-layer for authenticating mobile consumers of amazon s3 data*. In *Proceedings of the 2013 IEEE International Conference on Cloud Engineering, IC2E '13* (pp. 108–113). Washington: IEEE Computer Society. https://doi.org/10.1109/IC2E.2013.10

19. Nguyen, K. K., Hoang, D. T., Niyato, D., Wang, P., & Dutkiewicz, E. (2018). Cyberattack detection in mobile cloud computing: A deep learning approach. In *Wireless Communications and Networking Conference (WCNC)*, Piscataway: IEEE.

20. Olafare, O., Parhizkar, H., & Vem, S. (2015). A new secure mobile cloud architecture. arXiv preprint arXiv:1504.07563.

21. Panneerselvam, J., Sotiriadis, S., Bessis, N., & Antonopoulos, N. (2012). Securing authentication and trusted migration of weblets in the cloud with reduced traffic. In *Third International Conference on Emerging Intelligent Data and Web Technologies (EIDWT), 2012* (pp. 316–319). https://doi.org/10.1109/EIDWT.2012.20

22. Park, I.-S., Lee, Y.-D., & Jeong, J. (2013). Improved identity management protocol for secure mobile cloud computing. In *46th Hawaii International Conference on System Sciences (HICSS), 2013*. Piscataway: IEEE.

23. Perez, S. (2010). Mobile cloud computing: $9.5 billion by 2014.

24. Premnath, S. N., & Zygmunt, J. H. (2014). A practical, secure, and verifiable cloud computing for mobile systems. *Procedia Computer Science, 34*, 474–483.

25. Ramavathu, L., Bairam, M., & Manchala, S. (2017). A framework for secure mobile cloud computing. In *Proceedings of the First International Conference on Computational Intelligence and Informatics*. Singapore: Springer.

26. Satyanarayanan, M. (2010). Mobile computing: The next decade. In *Proceedings of the 1st ACM Workshop on Mobile Cloud Computing & Services: Social Networks and Beyond, MCS '10, pp. 5:1–5:6*. New York: ACM. https://doi.org/10.1145/1810931.1810936

27. Subashini, S., & Kavitha, V. (2011). Review: A survey on security issues in service delivery models of cloud computing. *Journal of Network and Computer Applications, 34*(1), 1–11. https://doi.org/10.1016/j.jnca.2010.07.006

28. Wang, S., & Wang, X. (2010). In-device spatial cloaking for mobile user privacy assisted by the cloud. In *Eleventh International Conference on Mobile Data Management (MDM)* (pp. 381–386). https://doi.org/10.1109/MDM.2010.82

29. Xiao, S., & Gong, W. (2010). Mobility can help: Protect user identity with dynamic credential. In *Eleventh International Conference on Mobile Data Management (MDM)* (pp. 378–380). https://doi.org/10.1109/MDM.2010.73

30. Zhang, X., Schiffman, J., Gibbs, S., Kunjithapatham, A., & Jeong, S. (2009). Securing elastic applications on mobile devices for cloud computing. In *Proceedings of the 2009 ACM Workshop on Cloud Computing Security, CCSW '09* (pp. 127–134). New York: ACM. https://doi.org/10.1145/1655008.1655026

31. Zhao, K., Jin, H., Zou, D., Chen, G., & Dai, W. (2013). Feasibility of deploying biometric encryption in mobile cloud computing. In *8th ChinaGrid Annual Conference (ChinaGrid), 2013* (pp. 28–33). https://doi.org/10.1109/ChinaGrid.2013.10

32. Zhou, J., Chen, J., Li, L., & Zhang, Z. (2012). The context awareness architecture in mobile cloud computing. In *Fifth International Symposium on Computational Intelligence and Design (ISCID)* (Vol. 1, pp. 302–305). https://doi.org/10.1109/ISCID.2012.83

33. Zhou, K., Afifi, M. H., & Ren, J. (2017). ExpSOS: Secure and verifiable outsourcing of exponentiation operations for mobile cloud computing. *IEEE Transactions on Information Forensics and Security, 12*(11), 2518–2531.

34. Zhou, Z., & Huang, D. (2012). Efficient and secure data storage operations for mobile cloud computing. In *8th International Conference on Network and Service Management (CNSM) and 2012 Workshop on Systems Virtualization Management (SVM)* (pp. 37–45).

Chapter 2
An Investigation Study of Privacy Preserving in Cloud Computing Environment

Ahmed M. Manasrah, M. A. Shannaq, and M. A. Nasir

Abstract Cloud computing allows users with limited resources to farm out their data to the cloud for computation, bandwidth, storage, and services on a pay-per-use basis. Consequently, researchers worldwide are trying to address issues related to the user's data privacy through proposing various methods such as outsourcing data in an encrypted form. However, encrypting data will conceal the relationships between data. Moreover, due to the voluminous data at the data centers, designing an efficient and reliable online-encrypted text-based searching scheme is challenging. Therefore, this paper surveys the state of the art on the data privacy preserving over the cloud through analyzing and discussing the various privacy-preserving methods that were proposed to sustain the privacy of the user's data. The pros and cons of the surveyed approaches are drawn in comparison with each other. Finally, the results are consolidated and the issues to be addressed in the future are concluded for the advancements in cloud data privacy preserving.

Keywords Cloud computing · Cloud storage · Privacy preserving

1 Introduction

The establishment of cloud has brought tremendous benefits to users and enterprises. The idea behind the establishment of the cloud is to allocate ubiquitous, on-demand access to processing resources and data storage to computers and other devices to store and process their data at a third-party data centers that might be located outside their premises. The allocated on-demand resources can be invoked and revoked with

A. M. Manasrah (✉)
Computer and Information Science Department, Higher Colleges of Technology, Sharjah, UAE

Computer Sciences Department, Yarmouk University, Irbid, Jordan
e-mail: amanasrah@hct.ac.ae; ahmad.a@yu.edu.jo

M. A. Shannaq · M. A. Nasir
Computer Sciences Department, Yarmouk University, Irbid, Jordan

© Springer Nature Switzerland AG 2020
B. B. Gupta et al. (eds.), *Handbook of Computer Networks and Cyber Security*,
https://doi.org/10.1007/978-3-030-22277-2_2

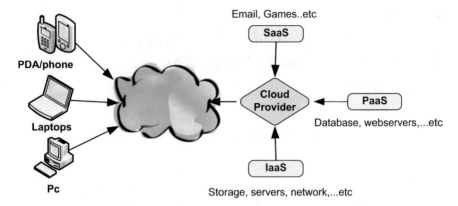

Fig. 2.1 Cloud component, typically Infrastructure as a Service (IaaS), Software as a Service (SaaS) or Platform as a Service (PaaS) [1]

minimal administration efforts. The shared resources aim to provide coherence and economy of scale, such as the utilities over the networks (electricity, gas, water, etc.). Therefore, companies and enterprises can avoid different infrastructure costs and focus more on their business and productivity.

A cloud provider (or cloud service providers or CSPs) offers some cloud computing components (see Fig. 2.1) on a "pay as you go or pay per use" basis. This may lead to high charges if the cloud-pricing model is not well adapted by the administrators.

With the constant growth in demand for cloud computing, the cloud provider might not meet the different organizations legal need while they need to contemplate the benefits of using the cloud against its risks. For instance, the control of the back-end infrastructure is limited only to the CSP. Moreover, CSPs often decide on the usage and management policies, which might abate the cloud user's ability over their deployment. Cloud users are also restricted with certain control and management policies of their applications, data and services, such as allocating certain amount of bandwidth for each customer and are often shared among other cloud users. Cloud computing involves constraints that make the progress in cloud computing services challenging; these constraints are consolidated in Table 2.1.

The reliance of the cloud computing usage by organizations and users has taken a long time since the time cloud computing came into existence. The reason behind this delay in adopting cloud computing is the security concerns because IT security is challenging even under the best of circumstances. Typically, the cloud environments are likely to have strong security measures deployed at their infrastructures. However, companies and organizations are of more concern of security at the CSP.

The CSP might not be able to meet the regulatory requirement of a company or organization. For instance, a law that allows the government to get at the data in secret is a demotivating factor for foreign companies to store their data inside such countries. Other countries may have even more rigorous government-access rules.

Table 2.1 Cloud computing constraints and challenges

Constraint/Challenge	Description
Naming heterogeneity	When the customers and the cloud service providers, using different names to identify attributes
Multi-occupancy	Allows multi-occupants to have an isolated environment for each one in terms of (CPU, memory, and network) in the same physical machine
Virtualization	Allows multi-occupants to execute their applications on the same physical environment, but separately
Forward secrecy	Old security keys cannot be accessed by any group member
Backward secrecy	Future generated keys should not be accessible to previous group members hence, cloud data is only accessible to privileged users
Searchable encryption	Encrypted cloud data should be searchable without decrypting the data neither the query and the returned records satisfy the search query

Typically, in the cloud environment, the data are processed or stored at data centers that are located far away from the organization city or country. Therefore, losing the control of the data is a security risk to most of the world organizations because in this case, someone else is controlling the data (i.e., the CSP). The concern is even amplified with free CSPs especially that SCPs can delete the outsourced data if they believe that the data violating some service terms [2–4]. Even though the demand for cloud computing is increasing, the concerns about users' data privacy are also increasing and formidable. Therefore, another set of issues concerning the advances in the field of privacy preserving for users' identity and their data also exists and acts as a barrier in this regard as shown in Table 2.2. Unfortunately, providing and preserving data privacy in the cloud have not been fully developed yet, and still require extra efforts in order to achieve successful results. Therefore, addressing all these issues could assist in designing novel privacy-preserving searching mechanisms over encrypted cloud data that are secure against intruders or attackers. Such designs could be a mark of success in the preservation of privacy in Cloud Computing.

In this paper, the issues related to cloud data privacy preserving are addressed. Various existing approaches related to data encryption concerning cloud data privacy preserving are discussed. After studying the existing approaches, issues and challenges are pointed out. To the best of our knowledge, this is the first survey that shortlist the issues and challenges of users and data privacy preserving over the cloud along the various possible solutions for the future researches.

2   Privacy-Preserving Methods

Various efforts have been made to address the preservation of data privacy over the cloud. This paper analyzes some of those efforts and provides a brief overview to the most known approaches in the field. This paper therefore classifies the privacy-preserving approaches in cloud computing into five broad categories as illustrated in Fig. 2.2.

Table 2.2 Privacy-preserving issues and challenges

Issue	Challenge
Insufficient control	The data are stored and processed in the cloud out of the data owner control
Lack of training and expertise	The constant change and complexity of the cloud environments forces the data owners to provide special expertise to manage the different cloud technologies. Therefore, recruiting and training talents are the barriers against implementing cloud strategies
Information disclosure	Since sensitive information and user's data move across the cloud, does the CSPs disclose any information to governments
Unauthorized storage/usage	Backups should not reveal neither it is possible to access and retrieve Sensitive information should not be accessed or revealed from Backups
Uncontrolled data proliferation	The data flow in the cloud should not be predictable neither controllable
Dynamic provision	The dynamic nature of the cloud should always keep the privacy of the data and their owners unclear, even for a legally responsible entity
Data accessibility, transfer and retention [5]	How the data on cloud are being accessed, destructed and by whom?
Location of data	The physical location of the storage servers may have legal implications (such as Jurisdiction issues)
Data security and disclosure of breaches	How the customer's data being protected by the CSPs. Does the CSP alert customers when cloud security is breached?
Addressing transborder data flow restriction [6]	Does the CSP adopt an international regulatory and compliance laws and rules? How the data protection across different regulatory and legal jurisdictions is maintained?

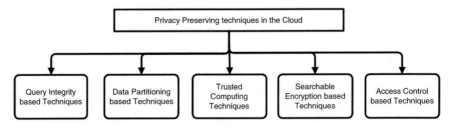

Fig. 2.2 Categories of privacy-preserving techniques in cloud computing

The following subsections examine most of the known cloud-based privacy-preserving methodologies and analyze these methodologies in terms of their pros and cons in comparison with each other.

3   Searchable Encryption-Based Techniques

Generally, IT managers and even individuals are likely to be cautious of delegating the control of their data to outside service providers because information stored at a third party may have weaker privacy protections than information in the possession of the creator of the information. Moreover, the outside provider has the right to change their underlying technology without their customer's consent, which may cause issues related to performance, and latency [4, 7]. Traditionally, data privacy is preserved by cryptographic primitives by the side of unique and secure identities for the queries and their responses jointly with usage/access rights policies. However, searching over the encrypted data is a formidable mission. Moreover, users normally lose control over their encrypted outsourced data in a tradeoff relation to their security and privacy preservation of the outsourced data. However, considering the diverse types of data that can be stored in the cloud and the user's demand for the data safety, preserving the data privacy in the cloud becomes even more challenging [8].

For instance, looking for certain data that are stored in an encrypted form in the cloud, one may need to download all encrypted data, and then decrypts and searches them. However, it is not efficient neither convenient especially with huge encrypted data or a resource constraint devices. Alternatively, the user may require sending his private key to the cloud server to perform the decryption and searching procedures on his behalf. However, sending the private key to the cloud server may cause serious issues with data files integrity and secrecy [9–13]. Therefore, to ensure the privacy of the outsourced data, different searchable encryption-based systems have been proposed. These searchable encryption-based systems entail encrypting the data by the data owner before outsourcing it to the cloud with the ability to search and retrieve relevant data through a keyword search or ranked keyword search techniques. These searchable encryption schemes can be divided into three categories: Symmetric-key based techniques, Fuzzy-searchable based techniques, and Public-key based techniques as portrayed in Fig. 2.3.

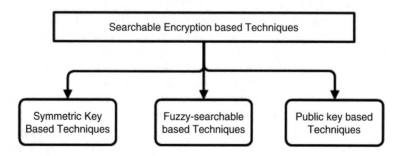

Fig. 2.3 Taxonomy of searchable encryption-based techniques

3.1 Symmetric-Key Based Techniques

The symmetric-key encryption system allows a data owner to outsource his data, encrypted with a symmetric encryption-based techniques (i.e., stream cipher), to untrusted locations over the cloud. The encrypted outsourced data are still searchable for relevant files by means of a trapdoor (i.e., a keyword) that is generated via the data owner private key. The generated trapdoor will be transferred to the server to search for a matched encrypted data with the trapdoor. In this regards, Song, Wagner [14] introduced an encryption and a searching technique over encrypted data with sequential scanning. The authors construct a special two-layered encryption technique that allows searching over cipher-texts without disclosing any sensitive information to the server. The authors proposed to encrypt each word separately assuming that each word has the same length, and then compute the bitwise exclusive or (XOR) with a special sequence of pseudorandom bits inside the plain text. To carry out the search, the data owner must create a private key (k_i) that is corresponded to the locations of the searched word (W_i). The generated private key is then XORed with the cipher-text $(C_i \oplus W_i)$ to extract a corresponding structure that is in the form $\langle s, F_{ki}(s) \rangle$ where (s) is some pseudorandom sequence values generated using some stream cipher, and $F_{ki}(s)$ is a pseudorandom function. In this technique, the complexity of encrypting the data and searching for a specific keyword over the encrypted data increases at most linearly with the size of the files collection and the data length. For instance, for a document of length (n) words, the encryption and the searching algorithms require $O(n)$ stream and block cipher operations. However, the proposed technique leaks important information about the documents using any statistical techniques. To handle the variable length words, Goh [15] developed a semantic secure indexes model to prevent leaking any sensitive or statistical information of the outsourced documents against adaptive chosen keyword attacks. The proposed model constructs an index for each document based on pseudo-random functions used as hash functions, and Bloom filters (BF) as a document word index. The word in this model is represented in an index by a codeword for each document which is derived through applying the pseudorandom function once with the word as input and another with a unique document identifier. The non-standard use of the pseudorandom function is to prevent correlation attacks. To search over encrypted documents for the word (y), the user should compute the trapdoor $T_y \leftarrow$ Trapdoor $\left(K_{\text{priv}}, I_{D_i} \right)$ for the word (y), where (K_{priv}) is the master private key, (D_i) is a unique document identifier, and I_{D_i} is the index for each document (D_i). The trapdoor (T_y) is then send to the server where the encrypted documents and the corresponding BF index $I_{D_i} = (D_i, \text{BF})$ existed. The server tests for a match with the documents through the function SearchIndex $\left(T_y, I_{D_i} \right)$. The BF is represented as an array of bits initially set to 0, and a set of hash functions to mark a set element as 1 of some array positions. To verify if an element belongs to the BF array, the hash values for this element are computed to identify the corresponding array positions. If any of the bits at these positions is 0, then the element is not in the set. This technique provides O (1) search time complexity per document and can handle variable length words. However, this scheme only supports exact match queries.

Similarly, Chang and Mitzenmacher [16] built a dictionary-based keyword index for each document based on pseudo-random functions. The authors aim to mask a dictionary keyword index for each file using pseudo-random bits to be kept at a remote server. On the other hand, the users can easily retrieve certain files using a short seed that enables the server to unmask selective parts of the index. For each file, an index is created as a set of linked lists, each linked list is associated with a list of keywords in the dictionary of the corresponding file. Initially, all values are set to 0, then if the document m_j contains the keyword w_i, its index position $I_j[P_s(i)]$ is set to 1. The users compute a secrete value r_i using a mapping function F where, $r_i = F_r(i)$, $i \in [2^d]$. For each document, a masking index string M_j is created through a document mapping function G, such that $M_j[i] = I_j[i] \oplus G_{ri}(j)$. The documents are then encrypted using an encryption algorithm and the encrypted documents are outsourced to the cloud along with the corresponding index mask string M_j. Two secrets keys (s) and (r) along with the dictionary are kept at the user's device. Since the authors presume that the data owners are using mobile devices with limited bandwidth and storage space, their solution incur minimum overhead in terms of bandwidth and storage. The search time for this approach is O(n/p), where (n) is the size of the documents collection and (p) is the number of cores. However, this scheme supports an exact single keyword match queries.

To improve the efficiency and the security to a higher degree compared to the previous schemes and to support multi-user environments, Curtmola, Garay [17] proposed a searchable broadcast encryption scheme. The proposed searchable symmetric encryption (SSE-1 and SSE-2) is based on an index per document. The user that owns the data can grant/revoke privileges to authorized users to access/query the outsourced data. In this schema, the proposed index has an array that holds a collection of linked list for documents identifier containing a keyword $D(w_i)$ in an encrypted form and a look-up table to trace and decrypt the first elements of each list in the array. The nodes of the linked list L_i are the document identifiers $D(w_i)$ that contain the keyword w_i. The array locations are the nodes of all L_i in a scrambled way. The lookup table (T) entries on the other hand are the keywords w_i index in the array and the decryption key of the first element in L_i. Both the array and the lookup table are encrypted and kept at the server along with the encrypted files. However, if a position in the array is known along with first node encryption key, one can trace and decrypt the other nodes of L_i which correspond to the document identifiers $D(w_i)$. In this schema, the server complexity is constant per document with the searched word, and the overall complexity for each query is proportional to the number of documents that have the searched single word. The computation and the storage complexity at the user side is O(1) and the search time for the server is optimal, but the update of the index is inefficient. Similarly, Chase and Kamara [18] considered stronger security definitions to produce schema that is efficient, associative, and adaptively secure in structured data. The authors of this schema proposed an encryption model for structured data like social networks, images, maps, location information, etc. and, at the same time, the proposed structured data can be privately queried. The focus of this scheme is to build a structured encryption algorithm that is searchable using specific query token if the secrete key is known. The structured data encryption algorithm operates over a labeled data that has a label (L) and a sequence of data items (m) (i.e., connecting a set of keywords to each data item). For each keyword (w), an array is initiated to hold a pointer j from the pseudo-random permutation set $G_K(L(w))$ and the semi-private item v_i. In this schema, the dictionary was implemented based on hash tables which makes this schema yields an optimal search time $O(|I|)$. However, the encrypted index can be very large. Similarly, van Liesdonk et al. [19] proposed a schema to deal with adaptive security based on one index per keyword to support efficient search and updates of the documents stored at a CSP server. Their proposed scheme converts each distinct keyword into a searchable representation of the form $S_W = (f_{kf}(w), m(I_w), R(w))$ that can be tracked by the trapdoor $T_w = (f_{k_f}(w), R'(w))$ with the ability to efficiently update the searchable representation whenever needed. $f_{k_f}(w)$ is a pseudorandom function that identifies S_W, $m(I_w)$ is a masking function for the collection of documents IDs that contains the keyword (w), $R(w)$ and $R'(w)$ are the associated unmasking functions. In case $f_{k_f}(w)$ is found, the server sends back the encrypted data items with the matched IDs in I_w to the client. Even though this schema uses only a simple primitive like pseudo-random functions, but it still obliges for two rounds of communication to generate, update the index, and to search for the documents. Finally, the proposed schema may produce a very large encrypted index. Kurosawa and Ohtaki [20] proposed a schema that is slightly stronger than Curtmola et al. [17]. They proposed a verifiable searchable symmetric encryption scheme that is universally composable (i.e., Protocols security is preserved even if arbitrarily composed with other instances of the same or other protocols) [21] and reliable against active adversaries or malicious servers. They address the issue of an active adversary who might forge the encrypted files to make the retrieving of the files incorrect. The proposed schema is translated to a client/server protocol. The protocol has two phases: (1) the store phase which is executed once by the client to compute $(I, C) \leftarrow Enc(Gen(1^k), D, W)$, where I is an encrypted index of the keywords W, C is the encrypted documents D, and the $Gen(1^k)$ is the secrete key. (2) The search phase which is executed many times by the server to compute $(C(w), Tag) \leftarrow Search(I, C, Trpdr(K, w))$, where $C(w)$ is a ciphertext of D, $t(w) \leftarrow Trpdr(K, w)$ is a trapdoor generated by the client in response to a keyword w query and Tag is $MAC(K, m)$ a tag generation algorithm for a message m encrypted using the key K. If the client receives $(\tilde{C}(w), Tag)$ from the server, the client verifies the validity of the received Tags the Tag Accept/Reject $\leftarrow Verify(K, Trpdr(K, w), \tilde{C}(w), Tag)$. The client decrypts the files if the verification functions returns accept. The proposed scheme consists of six polynomial time algorithms and requires a linear searching time, but supports only single-keyword search.

None of the previous schemes is explicitly dynamic with the ability to add, delete, and update files efficiently. Therefore, Kamara and Papamanthou [22] proposed to extend the inverted index approach proposed in Curtmola and Garay [17] and construct a new sublinear-time schema that is secure against adaptive chosen keyword attacks. The proposed schema has reduced index sizes with the ability to add/delete files efficiently. Therefore, they added three extra encrypted data structure, namely search array, search table (i.e., dictionary), and a deletion array that can be used by the server to monitor the search array positions in case of an update. They used a homomorphic encryption scheme to encrypt the node's pointers. To modify the pointer without ever having to decrypt the node, they used a private-key encryption scheme which consists of XORing the message with two pseudo-random functions. Finally, they added a free list that can be used by the server to determine the free locations to add new files. The proposed dynamic index-based schemes are a tuple of nine polynomial-time algorithms. The client generates a secret key $K \leftarrow \text{Gen}(1^k)$ to be used for the files (D) encryption to produce an encrypted index I and a sequence of ciphertexts C $(I, C) \leftarrow (K, D)$. In order for the client to search for a keyword, the client builds a search token $\tau_s \leftarrow \text{SrchToken}(K, w)$. The client can also request to add or delete a file (f) through generating add $(\tau_a, C_f) \leftarrow \text{AddToken}(K, f)$ or delete $\tau_a \leftarrow \text{DelToken}(K, f)$ tokens. The clients also can issue a search request $I_w \leftarrow \text{Search}(I, C, \tau_s)$ with the encrypted index I, a sequence of ciphertexts C and a search token τ_s to retrieve a sequence of files identifiers $I_w \subset C$. In this schema, the searching time for the server is linear (by using a hash table) which is optimal, but this approach is very complex and difficult to implement.

Moreover, the search procedure cannot be parallelized on the server because they represent a T-set as a linked list. As a result, Kamara and Papamanthou [23] improved the efficiency further through proposing a new dynamic and highly parallelizable sub-linear searchable symmetric encryption scheme based on the multi-core architectures. In this schema, they used a new tree-based multi-map data structure which they call a keyword red-black tree (KRB). The KRB tree is a dynamic data structure that is similar to an inverted index but can be used to answer multi-map queries efficiently. The KRB allows both keyword-based search and file-based search operations. This schema is useful for handling updates efficiently. The parallel search is executed similar to the binary trees, where the first processor searches for a specific keyword at the root of the tree. The tree will be divided into two sub-trees, the first processor continues with one sub-tree while another processor is assigned to the other sub-tree. The set of keywords are kept in a keyword hash table as a tuple (key, value) with a key of exponential size and the value is an encryption of a Boolean value. This approach yields very efficient schemes in less than the optimal sequential search time, and allows efficient updates, but this scheme is designed only for single keyword Boolean search, that means whether or not the keyword exists. A complete comparison of all the schemes can be found in Table 2.3 and Table 2.4.

Although these searchable symmetric encryption techniques allow a user to search securely over encrypted data through keywords, the main disadvantage with these techniques is that they support only exact keyword searches. Consequently, this reduces the system efficiency because the search complexity will be the number of distinct keywords in the document collection. Another approach to solve such problems are the Fuzzy-Searchable Encryption based systems.

Table 2.3 Comparison of several symmetric-key encryption schemes

Scheme	Dynamism	Search time	Index size
Song et al. [14]	Static	$O(n/p)$	N/A
Goh [15]	Dynamic	$O(n/p)$	$O(n)$
Chang and Mitzenmacher [16]	Static	$O(n)$	$O(mn)$
Curtmola et al. [17]	Static	$O(r)$	$O(m+n)$
van Liesdonk et al. [19]	Dynamic	$O(r)$	$O(mn)$
Chase and Kamara [18]	Static	$O(r)$	$O(mn)$
Kurosawa and Ohtaki [20]	Static	$O(n)$	$O(mn)$
Kamara et al. [22]	Dynamic	$O(r)$	$O(m+n)$
Kamara and Papamanthou [23]	Dynamic	$O((r/p)\log n)$	$O(mn)$

Where n is the size of the document collection, r the number of documents containing keyword **w**, m the size of the keywords space, and p the number of cores

Table 2.4 Comparison of several symmetric-key encryption schemes

Scheme	Description	Main drawbacks
Song et al. [14]	A technique for searching in encrypted data with sequential scanning by using a special two-layered encryption construct that allows searching the cipher-texts	It leaks important information about the documents using statistical techniques, and only works with words of the same length
Goh [15]	An efficient secure index construction based on pseudo-random functions and Bloom filters	Supports only exact match queries
Chang and Mitzenmacher [16]	A dictionary-based keyword index for each document based on pseudo-random functions	Supports only exact match queries
Curtmola et al. [17]	A solution for the multi-user problem based on broadcast encryption	Updates to the index are inefficient
Kamara et al. [22]	An efficient, associative, and adaptively secure schema based on creating a model for structured data	The encrypted index can be very large
van Liesdonk et al. [19]	Two schemes based on one index per keyword to support efficient search and updates of the database	The encrypted index can be very large
Kurosawa and Ohtaki [20]	A verifiable searchable symmetric encryption scheme that is universally composable	Supports only single-keyword search
Kamara et al. [22]	A new schema that achieves the properties based on the inverted index approach [17]	Complex and difficult to implement
Kamara and Papamanthou [23]	A new dynamic and sub-linear searchable symmetric encryption scheme that is highly parallelizable based on the multi-core architectures	Single keyword Boolean search

3.2   *Fuzzy-Searchable Encryption*

Fuzzy keyword search returns the matching files to the users' searching inputs that even matched exactly to a set of predefined keywords or the closest possible matching files based on keyword similarity semantics, because fuzzy keyword search can tolerate minor typos and formatting inconsistencies [24]. In this regards, Adjedj et al. [25] described a way to solve the issue of preserving privacy in a biometric identification system using a fuzzy search scheme. They used symmetric searchable encryption (SSE) which allows a client to encrypt the data in such a way that these data can still be searched to achieve reasonable computational costs for each identification request. In this schema, they combined SSE and locality-sensitive hashing (LSH). The main purpose of using LSH is to make outputs the same result for near points and a different result for distant points by using a matching algorithm which computes a similarity score between the two points. By using SSE architecture, the secret keys are stored on the client side but not on the database side (i.e., server side stores the encrypted data without secret keys). This will ensure the privacy of the stored data, but it is unsuitable for many applications, such as when data are frequently updated or streaming.

In an attempt to tolerate minor typos and formatting inconsistencies, Li et al. [24] realized that depending on a spell checker mechanism does not address the problem (i.e., mistyped words or two valid words typed interchangeably) due to the extra communication cost with the users to identify the correct words. Therefore, they proposed the first solution for effective fuzzy keyword search over encrypted cloud data. They constructed a wildcard-based fuzzy set $S_{w_i,d} = \left\{ S'_{w_i,0}, S'_{w_i,1}, \ldots, S'_{w_i,d} \right\}$ with edit distance d for each keyword $w_i \in W$ before building the index. The $S'_{w_i,\tau}$ denotes the set of words w'_i with τ wildcards representing the edit operations on $w_i \in W$. This technique can deal with minor typo errors when users type in query keywords through using the edit distance to quantify keyword similarity through semantic keyword with edit distance d $= 1$ from w_i. That is, all the words that are satisfying the similarity criteria $ed\left(w_i, w'_i\right) \leq$ d are listed. The index $\left\{ \left(\left\{ T_{w'_i} \right\} w'_i \in S_{w_i,d}, Enc\left(sk, FID_{w_i} \| w_i \right) \right) \right\}$ $w_i \in W$ with the set of encrypted files IDs (FID_{w_i}) that contain the keyword w_i is built and a trapdoor set $\left\{ T_{w'_i} \right\}$ is computed for each word$w' \in S_{w_i,d}$. The index and the encrypted files are then outsourced to the cloud server for storage. The secret key sk is shared between the data owner and authorized users. To search for a keyword w with a private key k, the authorized user computes the trapdoor set $\left\{ T_{w'_i} \right\}$ $w' \in S_{w,k}$ and send to the server. The server then compares the request with the index table and returns all possible encrypted file identifiers$\left\{ Enc\left(sk, FID_{w_i} \| w_i \right) \right\}$. The size of the index $S_{w_i,d}$ with a keyword length of l and edit distance of d is $O(l^d)$. This schema is secure and privacy preserving, but it is only applicable to strings under edit distance, and fuzzy sets may become too big with longer words, which necessitates issuing large trapdoors sets. Therefore, Kuzu et al. [26] described an efficient similarity search over the encrypted data based on the locality sensitive hashing (LSH) which is the nearest neighbor algorithm for index creation and the bloom filter (BF) for translation of strings, to provide a more generic solution and to utilize the distinct similarity search contexts. Similar features are put into one bucket with high probability due to the property of LSH while not similar features are kept into different buckets. This schema embeds the query string into the BF and represented as a set of n-grams. Each n-gram is then subject to a hash function and the corresponding bit locations are set to 1. They use a publicly available typo-generator which produces a variety of spelling errors to check if the keywords contain typographical errors, and to measure the Jaccard distance between the encodings of the original and perturbed versions, to determine distance thresholds for their Fuzzy Search scheme. In this schema, one round is needed for a limited number of data items with large set of features, and two rounds are needed if the number of data items is huge, but it introduce a certain degree of false positive rate in the searching results.

However, a semi-honest-but-curious cloud server might save its computation or download bandwidth through executing only a fraction of the search operation honestly and return a fraction of the search results honestly as well. Therefore, a verifiable scheme is needed to ensure that the user can verify the correctness and the completeness of the search results. In this regards, Wang et al. [27] proposed a new efficient and verifiable fuzzy keyword search (VFKS) scheme over the encrypted data in cloud computing to return the closest possible results based on similarity semantics. They use a wildcard-based fuzzy keyword set and the BF to enable a fuzzy keyword search over encrypted data and maintain keyword privacy and the verifiability of the search result. Their approach consists of the algorithms (Keygen, Buildindex, trapdoor, search, Verify). In which the Keygen algorithm $(sk, sk') \leftarrow (\text{Keygen}(1^k))$ executed by the data owner with a security parameter k to produce the secrete key (sk) to generate the index and the document encryption key (sk') used to decrypt the document. The Buildindex algorithm $G_W \leftarrow \text{Buildindex}(sk, W)$ executed by the data owner to create the index G_W, i.e., a symbol-based tree using the secrete key (sk) and the distinct keyword set of the documents collection D.

The symbol-based index tree G_W and the encrypted documents are outsourced to the cloud server. The user can generate a trapdoor set $\{T_{\omega'}\}\omega' \in S_{\omega,d} \leftarrow \text{trapdoor}(sk, S_{\omega,d})$ for all wildcard-based fuzzy keywords $S_{\omega_i,d} = \left\{S'_{\omega_i,0}, S'_{\omega_i,1}, \ldots, S'_{\omega_i,d}\right\}$ of the keyword ω' with edit distance $ed(\omega, \omega') < d$. The server executes the search algorithm (flag, ID_ω, proof) $\leftarrow \text{Search}(G_W, \{T_{\omega'}\})$ upon receiving the user trapdoor set $\{T_{\omega'}\}$ to search for the document with keyword ω and return the document identifier ID_ω, true and a proof if document existed otherwise false, and a proof. The user executes (true/false) $\leftarrow \text{Verify}(T_\omega, (\text{flag}, ID_\omega, \text{proof}))$ to verify whether the server is honest or not over the search result (flag, ID_ω, proof) and outputs true if the server honestly search, otherwise false is returned. They utilized the well-known multi-way tree to store the fuzzy keyword set over a predefined symbol set, which might grow in size if the keyword length is huge. This schema is secure and privacy preserving, while supporting efficient verifiability

Table 2.5 Comparison of several Fuzzy-searchable encryption schemes

Scheme	Description	Main drawbacks
Adjedj et al. [25]	A way of solving the issue of preserving privacy in a biometric identification system based on a fuzzy search scheme	Unsuitable for many applications when data are frequently updated or streaming
Li et al. [24]	The first solution for effective fuzzy keyword search over encrypted cloud data based on a fuzzy set for the keywords before building the index	Has a long word which necessitates performing large trapdoors
Kuzu et al. [26]	An efficient similarity search over the encrypted data based on LSH and BF	Introduces a certain degree of false positive rate in the searching
Lu [28]	A privacy-preserving search logarithm over the encrypted data to support a range of queries based on Logarithmic Search on Encrypted Data	The indexing information makes it as vulnerable as order-preserving encryption
Wang et al. [27]	A new efficient and verifiable fuzzy keyword search based on the method of wildcard-based fuzzy keyword set and the BF	The same key is used to encrypt and decrypt the data

of the searching result. However, this schema focuses on key word search but does not consider a phrase search. Moreover, the index generation is handled by the data owner, which means that the owner might abandon the exact keyword index constructed before and generate a specialized fuzzy-keyword index for fuzzy search, hence wasting much more computation and storage resources (Table 2.5).

All these previous techniques are based on symmetric key encryption, in which the same key is used to encrypt and decrypt the data. To enable an authorized user to access the encrypted data, the data owner must share this key. By sharing this key, unauthorized users can also use this key to access the encrypted data.

3.3 Public-Key Encryption

A searchable symmetric key-based encryption schema are valid for users owning the data and wish to upload it to a third-party and untrusted server (i.e., cloud server). On the other hand, there are cases when the outsourced data (medical data, stock quotes, emails, etc.) are public and uploaded by different owners and the user is not aware of it, at the same time, the user wishes to retrieve certain files without revealing to the server which file he wants. The public-key encryption with keyword search is the solution for such cases. The public-key encryption uses two different keys, private and a public key. The private key is given by the data owner to the users and the public key is given to the server in this context as illustrated in Fig. 2.4.

The first searchable encryption scheme using a public key system was proposed in [29]. This scheme can be extended to handle range, subset, and conjunctive

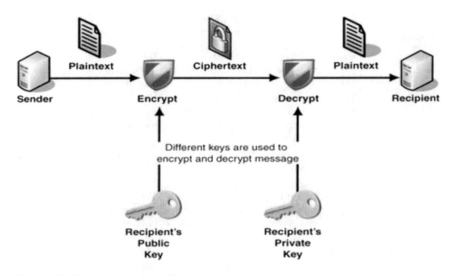

Fig. 2.4 Public-key encryption architecture

queries. It also hides the attributes for messages that match a query. They use identity-based encryption (IBE), in which the keyword acts as the identity. The proposed searchable public-key encryption consists of four polynomial time randomized algorithms (KeyGen, PEKS, Trapdoor, Test). The data owner generates his public/private key pair using the algorithm $(A_{pub}, A_{priv}) \leftarrow$ KeyGen(s) over a security parameter s. In order to search for any keyword W, the user generates a trapdoor $T_W \leftarrow$ Trapdoor(A_{priv}, W) using their private key A_{priv} for certain keywords W. The server determines whether a document contains one of the keywords W specified by the users (yes $\|W = W'\|$ no $\|W \neq W'\|) \leftarrow$ Test(A_{pub}, S, T_W) through the received Trapdoor T_W, the given public key A_{pub} and a searchable encryption $S = PEKS(A_{pub}, W')$. The proposed scheme has two constructions for 12public-key searchable encryption: (1) An efficient construction based on a variant of the Diffie–Hellman (BDH) assumption by building a non-interactive searchable encryption scheme from a bilinear map. They have proved that this scheme is semantically secure against a chosen keyword attack in the random oracle model based on the difficulty of the bilinear Diffie–Hellman problem. (2) A limited construction using any trapdoor permutation, which is less efficient because this construction assumes that, general trapdoor permutations assuming that the total number of keywords the user wishes to search for is bounded by some polynomial function in the security parameter. They can reduce the size of the public file by allowing the user to re-use individual public keys for different keywords. In this schema, the searching time is linear, but Public key solutions are usually computationally expensive. Furthermore, the keyword privacy cannot be protected in the public key setting, since the server could encrypt any keyword with a public key and then use the received trapdoor to evaluate the ciphertext. Finally, the proposed constructions are applicable to searching on a small number of keywords rather than an entire file.

Bellare et al. [30] proposed a deterministic searchable public-key encryption scheme. The main idea in this technique is to associate a tag with a plaintext, which can be computed by the client to form a particular query $F(pk, x_1)$ and by the server from a ciphertext that encrypts it $G(pk, c)$. They can then use this tag (i.e. the output of the polynomial time algorithms F, G) to create a tree-based index that can be used for searching. Since searchable tags are deterministic, the server can organize them in a sorted system and match the minimum logarithmic time. The proposed scheme consists of three polynomial time algorithms $AE = (K, E, D)$. This schema is t-efficiently searchable encryption where $t(.) < 1 \; \forall \; x_i \in Ptsp(k)$, $Ptsp(k)$ is the plaintext space and the probability $F(pk, x_1) = G(pk, c) = 1$ over $(pk, sk) \leftarrow K(1^k)$ and $c \leftarrow E(pk, x_1)$. This technique is a combination of any public-key encryption scheme and any deterministic hash function and so this scheme is secure, but they have left without solution the problem of finding standard model schemes. The issue of this proposed approach is that it only provides privacy to text drawn from a space of large min-entropy.

A range of queries over multiple attributes in the public key settings have been studied in the herein cited study [31]. They proposed an encryption scheme called Multi-dimensional Range Query over Encrypted Data (MRQED) that allows a network gateway to encrypt summaries of network flows before submitting them to the cloud. The proposed scheme was proven with the network audit logs. An authority can release a public key to an auditor to decrypt flows within certain ranges only. The proposed scheme operates over a tuple of flow features (t, a, p) representing the flow timestamp range $t \in [t_1, t_2]$, the flow source address range $a \in [a_1, a_2]$ and the destination flow port number range $p \in [p_1, p_2]$. Their proposed range queries imply $(t \geq t_1) \wedge (a = a_1) \wedge (p_1 \leq p \leq p_2)$ where all flows (t, a, p) within the defined range can be decrypted with the provided decryption key without revealing the other flow attribute values nor issuing huge number of keys. The proposed schema consists of four polynomial-time algorithms $(Setup(k, L_\Delta), Encrypt(PK, X, Msg), DeriveKey(PK, DK, B), QeurtyDecrypt$ $(PK, SK, C))$ in which the setup algorithm $(PK, SK) \leftarrow Setup(k, L_\Delta)$ over a security parameter k and a point in lattice L_Δ (represents a tuple as a point in L_Δ) produces a public key PK and a private key SK. The gateway encrypts the pair $(Msg., X)$ that consists of an arbitrary string representing the entire flow summary and a point X in a multi-dimensional space representing the attributes using the public key PK to produce the ciphertext $C \leftarrow Encrypt(PK, X, Msg)$. The authority derives a decryption key $DK \leftarrow DeriveKey(PK, SK, B)$ for a hyper-rectangle B in L_Δ (i.e., test whether a point X falls inside it) using the public and the private key pair (PK, SK). Finally, an auditor can decrypt (plaintext/null) $\leftarrow QeurtyDecrypt(PK, DK, C)$ relevant flows using the provided key pair (PK, DK) over the retrieved ciphertext C. However, in this schema, each flow is represented as a hyper-rectangle B in L_Δ. This requires issuing one pair of keys for each flow, having a huge number of flows would require a huge number of key pair pools.

Liu et al. [32] proposed an Efficient Privacy Preserving Keyword Search Scheme (EPPKS) in cloud computing, which reduces a client's computational overhead by allowing the cloud service provider to participate partially in the decipherment process while protecting the data and the queries privacy. The proposed schema does not require a private key transmission; to make it suitable for the cloud environment. This schema consists of the following seven randomized polynomial time algorithms EPPKS = (Keygen, EMBEnc, KWEnc, TCompute, Test, Decrypt, Recovery). The user and the service provider execute the Keygen function to produce public/private key pair. For the user U, he executes $U : (U_{pub}, U_{priv}) \leftarrow$ Keygen(k_1) over a sufficiently large security parameter k_1 to produce his key pair (U_{pub}, U_{priv}). Similarly, the service provider S executes $S : (S_{pub}, S_{priv}) \leftarrow$ Keygen(k_2) over a sufficiently large security parameter k_2 to produce his public/private key pair (S_{pub}, S_{priv}). The user encrypts the data using his public key and the service provider private key to produce the message m ciphertext $C_m \leftarrow$ EMBEnc(U_{pub}, S_{priv}, m). The keywords are also encrypted before outsourcing the data to the service provider using the user public key $C_{W_i} \leftarrow$ KWEnc (U_{pub}, W_i). In order to retrieve a file with keywords W_j, the user executes $T_{W_j} \leftarrow$ TCompute (U_{priv}, W_j) and sends it to the CSP. The CSP on the other hand executes $\left(W_i \overset{?}{=} W_j\right) \leftarrow$ KWTest $(U_{pub}, C_{W_i}, T_{W_j})$ to determine whether a given file has the keyword W_j. An intermediate result C_ρ will be calculated by the CSP before returning the matching file to the user as a result of executing $C_\rho \leftarrow$ PDecrypt(S_{priv}, U_{pub}, C_m). Upon receiving the files, the user executes $m \leftarrow$ Re $coery(U_{priv}, C_m, C_\rho)$. This schema supports multiple keyword searching on the encrypted data and it is semantically secure, because the service provider could search in the encrypted files efficiently without leaking any information, but there is a big challenge if the user requires the service provider to provide the computational service.

All these schemes achieve good security and privacy but they require high computations and memory of the end-devices during the encryption and decryption process. Moreover, these schemes provide unsearchable encryption, but do not fit well for less powerful client devices, which have only limited bandwidth, CPU, and memory as discussed in [33]. Table 2.6 consolidates the various public key-based privacy-preserving approaches advantage and their shortcomings.

Among the different available solutions that aim to design operations compatible with data encryptions while preserving the privacy of the data outsourced to the cloud, Searchable Encryption (SE) schemes seem to allow a curious party to carry out searches on encrypted cloud data without having to decrypt it, hence maintaining its privacy. Table 2.7 summarizes the advantages and the disadvantages of the common searchable encryption schemes in cloud computing.

4   Conclusion and Future Work

While data encryption seems to be the right countermeasure to prevent privacy violations, classical encryption mechanisms fall short of meeting the privacy requirements in the cloud setting. Typical cloud storage systems also provide basic operations on stored data such as statistical data analysis, logging and searching

Table 2.6 Comparison of several public-key encryption schemes

Scheme	Description	Main drawbacks
Boneh et al. [29]	The first scheme to use a public key system based on identity-based encryption	Keyword privacy is not protected in the public key setting
Bellare et al. [30]	A deterministic searchable public-key encryption scheme based on associating a tag with a plaintext	Cannot find a standard model schemes
Katz et al. [34]	The first notion of predicate encryption based on IBS, hidden vector encryption (HVE) and attribute-based encryption	This scheme is only proven to be selectively secure and no delegation functionality is provided
Attrapadung and Libert [35]	A protocol based on functional encryption and public key schemes using Inner Product Encryption	Cannot be proven fully secure under some natural assumptions
Liu et al. [33]	A SPKS scheme for cloud storage services based on enabling cloud service providers to participate in the decryption process partially	It may disclose information to CSP to participate in the decryption process

Table 2.7 Comparison of searchable encryption schemes in cloud computing

	Advantages	Disadvantages
Symmetric-key encryption	• The private keys are used in symmetric-key encryption and are resistant to external attacks • Simple to generate keys • Symmetric-key encryption algorithms require low computing power to be created	• The same key is used to encrypt and decrypt the data and by sharing this key, unauthorized users can access the encrypted data • The private key must be exchanged in a secure manner • Every participant must have an identical private key • Symmetric-key encryption supports only exact keyword search
Fuzzy-searchable encryption	Enhances system usability by returning the matching files or the closest possible matching files based on keyword similarity semantics	The same key is used to encrypt and decrypt the data. Through sharing this key, unauthorized users can access the encrypted data
Public-key encryption	The unique private and public keys are provided for each user, which will allow them to perform secure exchanges of information	• Generating the keys is expensive • Public-key encryption algorithms require more computational cost than Symmetric-key encryption

and these operations would not be feasible if the data were encrypted using classical encryption algorithms. Among various solutions aiming at designing operations that would be compatible with data encryption, Searchable Encryption (SE) schemes allow a potentially curious party to perform searches on encrypted data without having to decrypt it. SE seems a suitable approach to solve the data privacy problem in the cloud setting. A further challenge is raised by SE in the multi-user setting, whereby each user may have access to a set of encrypted data segments stored by a number of different users. Multi-user searchable encryption schemes allow a user to search through several data segments based on some search rights granted by the owners of those segments. Privacy requirements in this setting are manifold, and not only the confidentiality of the data segments but also the privacy of the queries should be ensured against intruders and potentially malicious CSP. Recently, few research efforts came up with multi-user keyword search schemes meeting these privacy requirements, either through some key sharing among users or based on a Trusted Third Party (TTP).

These studies provide limited keyword search functionality for cloud storage services. Thus, service providers must implement a complete secure search scheme to promote their services. This study proposes a scheme for performing ranked multikeyword searches with fault tolerance in cloud storage systems. The proposed scheme uses similar keyword sets to perform a similarity search, and a secure k-nearest neighbor (kNN) scheme to perform a ranked multikeyword search. Moreover, the proposed scheme is fault tolerant to account for cloud users inputting an incorrect keyword, and still involves performing a file search. When the files are located, they are assigned an associated correlation value.

References

1. Manasrah, A. M., Smadi, T., & ALmomani, A. (2016). A variable service broker routing policy for data center selection in cloud analyst. *Journal of King Saud University-Computer and Information Sciences, 29*(3), 365–377.
2. Zhang, H., et al. (2015). Towards privacy preserving publishing of set-valued data on hybrid cloud. *Cloud Computing, IEEE Transactions on, 99*, 1–1.
3. Wagle, D. M. (2014). Comparative study of privacy preservation and access control of cloud data. *International Journal of Engineering Research & Technology (IJERT), 3*(11), 165–174.
4. Nabeel, M., & Bertino, E. (2014). Privacy preserving delegated access control in public clouds. *Knowledge and Data Engineering, IEEE Transactions on, 26*(9), 2268–2280.
5. AlSudiari, M. A., & Vasista, T. (2012). Cloud computing and privacy regulations: An exploratory study on issues and implications. *Advanced Computing, 3*(2), 159.
6. Seddon, J. J., & Currie, W. L. (2013). Cloud computing and trans-border health data: Unpacking US and EU healthcare regulation and compliance. *Health Policy and Technology, 2*(4), 229–241.
7. Dong, X., et al. (2014). Achieving an effective, scalable and privacy-preserving data sharing service in cloud computing. *Computers & Security, 42*, 151–164.
8. Joseph, N. M., Daniel, E., & Vasanthi, N. (2013). Survey on privacy-preserving methods for storage in cloud computing. In: *Amrita International Conference of Women in Computing*.
9. Jogade, S., Sharma, R., & Kadam, R. (2014). Partitioning data and domain integrity checking for storage-improving cloud storage security using data partitioning technique. *International Journal of Emerging Research in Management & Technology, 3*(3), 133–137.
10. Chen, F., & Liu, A. X. (2014). Privacy and integrity preserving multi-dimensional range queries for cloud computing. In *Networking Conference, 2014 IFIP*. IEEE.
11. Ku, W.-S., et al. (2013). A query integrity assurance scheme for accessing outsourced spatial databases. *GeoInformatica, 17*(1), 97–124.

12. Hu, L., et al. (2013). Spatial query integrity with Voronoi neighbors. *Knowledge and Data Engineering, IEEE Transactions on, 25*(4), 863–876.
13. Naruchitparames, J., & Güneş, M. H. (2011). Enhancing data privacy and integrity in the cloud. In *High Performance Computing and Simulation (HPCS), 2011 International Conference on.* IEEE.
14. Song, D. X., Wagner, D., & Perrig, A. (2000). Practical techniques for searches on encrypted data. In *Security and Privacy, 2000. S&P 2000. Proceedings 2000 IEEE Symposium on.* IEEE.
15. Goh, E.-J. (2003). *Secure indexes for efficient searching on encrypted compressed data* (Technical report 2003/216, Cryptology ePrint archive, 2003). http://eprint.iacr.org/2003/216
16. Chang, Y.-C., & Mitzenmacher, M. (2005). Privacy preserving keyword searches on remote encrypted data. In *Applied cryptography and network security.* Berlin: Springer.
17. Curtmola, R., et al. (2006) Searchable symmetric encryption: Improved definitions and efficient constructions. In *Proceedings of the 13th ACM Conference on Computer and Communications Security.* ACM.
18. Chase, M., & Kamara, S. (2010). Structured encryption and controlled disclosure. In *Advances in cryptology-ASIACRYPT 2010* (pp. 577–594). Berlin: Springer.
19. van Liesdonk, P., et al. (2010). Computationally efficient searchable symmetric encryption. In *Secure data management* (pp. 87–100). Berlin: Springer.
20. Kurosawa, K., & Ohtaki, Y. (2012). UC-secure searchable symmetric encryption. In *Financial cryptography and data security* (pp. 285–298). Berlin: Springer.
21. Canetti, R. (2001). Universally composable security: A new paradigm for cryptographic protocols. In *Foundations of Computer Science, 2001. Proceedings. 42nd IEEE Symposium on.* IEEE.
22. Kamara, S., Papamanthou, C., & Roeder, T. (2012). Dynamic searchable symmetric encryption. In *Proceedings of the 2012 ACM Conference on Computer and Communications Security.* ACM.
23. Kamara, S., & Papamanthou, C. (2013). Parallel and dynamic searchable symmetric encryption. In *Financial cryptography and data security* (pp. 258–274). Berlin: Springer.
24. Li, J., et al. (2010). Fuzzy keyword search over encrypted data in cloud computing. In *INFOCOM, 2010 Proceedings IEEE.* IEEE.
25. Adjedj, M., et al. (2009). Biometric identification over encrypted data made feasible. In *Information systems security* (pp. 86–100). Berlin: Springer.
26. Kuzu, M., Islam, M. S., & Kantarcioglu, M. (2012). Efficient similarity search over encrypted data. In *Data Engineering (ICDE), 2012 IEEE 28th International Conference on.* IEEE.
27. Wang, J., et al. (2012). A new efficient verifiable fuzzy keyword search scheme. *JoWUA, 3*(4), 61–71.
28. Lu, Y. (2012). Privacy-preserving logarithmic-time search on encrypted data in cloud. In *NDSS.*
29. Boneh, D., et al. (2004). Public key encryption with keyword search. In *Advances in cryptology-Eurocrypt 2004.* Berlin: Springer.
30. Bellare, M., Boldyreva, A., & O'Neill, A. (2007). Deterministic and efficiently searchable encryption. In *Advances in cryptology-CRYPTO 2007* (pp. 535–552). Berlin: Springer.
31. Shi, E., et al. (2007). Multi-dimensional range query over encrypted data. In *SP'07, IEEE Symposium on.* IEEE.
32. Liu, Q., Wang, G., & Wu, J. (2009). An efficient privacy preserving keyword search scheme in cloud computing. In *Computational Science and Engineering, 2009. CSE'09. International Conference on.* IEEE.
33. Liu, Q., Wang, G., & Wu, J. (2012). Secure and privacy preserving keyword searching for cloud storage services. *Journal of Network and Computer Applications, 35*(3), 927–933.
34. Katz, J., Sahai, A., & Waters, B. (2008). Predicate encryption supporting disjunctions, polynomial equations, and inner products. In *Advances in cryptology–EUROCRYPT 2008* (pp. 146–162). Berlin: Springer.
35. Attrapadung, N., & Libert, B. (2010). Functional encryption for inner product: Achieving constant-size ciphertexts with adaptive security or support for negation. In *Public key cryptography–PKC 2010* (pp. 384–402). Berlin: Springer.

Chapter 3
Towards New Quantitative Cybersecurity Risk Analysis Models for Information Systems: A Cloud Computing Case Study

Mouna Jouini and Latifa Ben Arfa Rabai

Abstract The objective of this chapter is to propose new quantitative models to assess security threats of information systems. We adopt methods for assessing the failure cost due to security breakdowns. In fact, the importance of quantifying security risk continues to grow as individuals, enterprises, and governments become increasingly reliant on information systems. Moreover, nowadays security of these deployed systems has suffered because they lack significant security measures and accurate information security risk assessment which is considered as an ongoing process of discovering, correcting, and preventing security problems by providing appropriate levels of security for information systems. In this context, we define economic security risk models to help managers to assess accurately the security threats: the internal mean failure cost and the external mean failure cost, respectively, MFCint and MFCext, which studied the threat space and identified the source of threats space risk by estimating their costs. Moreover, we define the mean failure cost extension (MFCE) model which is based on our hybrid threat classification model.

Keywords Cloud computing · Security quantification · Economic security models · Threats · Security requirements · Components · Stakeholders

M. Jouini (✉)
Strategies for Modelling and ARtificial inTelligence Research Laboratory (SMART Lab), Higher Institute of Management, University of Tunis, Tunis, Tunisia

L. Ben Arfa Rabai
Strategies for Modelling and ARtificial inTelligence Research Laboratory (SMART Lab), Higher Institute of Management, University of Tunis, Tunis, Tunisia

College of Business, University of Buraimi, Al Buraimi, Sultanate Oman

© Springer Nature Switzerland AG 2020
B. B. Gupta et al. (eds.), *Handbook of Computer Networks and Cyber Security*,
https://doi.org/10.1007/978-3-030-22277-2_3

63

1 Introduction

Organizations, governments, and individuals are facing many information security risks. These risks can cause serious damages that might lead to significant financial losses, breach of the confidentiality of sensitive information, or loss of integrity or availability of sensitive data. In fact, the financial (or economic) security threat loss to organizations could be significant. Recent literature has also documented significant costs related to information systems security breaches. For example, the 2015 Global State of Information Security Survey [2] reveals that a huge heists of consumer data were also reported in South Korea, where 105 million payment card accounts were exposed in a security breach in 2015. The survey compared also the security incidents cost in small and large organizations. In fact, it claimed that small organizations proved the exception in discovering compromises. That is to say companies with revenues of less than $100 million detected 5% fewer incidents this year (in 2014) compared to 2009. However, larger companies have seen a huge increase in the numbers of incidents between 2009 and 2014. In fact, the number of incidents detected by medium size and large organizations (those with revenues of $100 million to $1 billion) jumped by 64% between 2009 and 2014.

Due to serious impacts of security threats, managers must find ways to retrieve and understand threats sources so as to mitigate them. To facilitate effective protection of information systems, we propose in this chapter two economic security risk models that estimate security threats failure of information system.

The chapter addresses quantitative cybersecurity models based on our threats classification models defined in our previous work [22] in order to accurately assess threats breaches. In fact, information system threat classifications help system managers to build their organizations' information systems with less vulnerabilities and implement information security strategies and thus protect their assets from these threats. The first model assesses security risk and let managers identifying the source of space intrusion (either internal or external) to propose appropriate counter measure to mitigate them. The second model is based on our threats classification model that allows studying the threats class impact instead of a threat impact as a threat varies over time. Furthermore, we illustrate the use of our quantitative security analysis model on Cloud Computing (CC) system.

This chapter is organized as follows: The first section presents the context of our chapter. The second section presents the motivation of our work. The third section shows an overview of Cloud Computing environment. The fourth section presents an economic cybersecurity model based on a threat source criterion that we called the internal mean failure cost model (MFC_{int}) and external mean failure cost model (MFC_{ext}). In addition, we provide a new method to validate our security risk models and illustrate their use using a Cloud Computing application. The fifth section introduces the mean failure cost extension (MFCE) model. Also, we validate the MFCE model and show an illustration on practical application of this model.

2 Motivation: Quantitative Cybersecurity Risk Assessment Models

To make effective security decisions, managers need to assess or estimate the cybersecurity breaches of the system and well characterize it. There are many measures in literature to support the analysis of how well a system meets its security objectives [4, 18, 20, 23, 40], and [21]. Several economic security risk assessment models exist in literature. We can cite, for example, the mean failure cost (MFC) model [3] that quantifies the security of information systems that we will present in this section.

2.1 Related Work

Although the ability of existing models to estimate the security breaches due to security threats and vulnerabilities may suffer from several limitations which motivate researchers to develop more models. Basically, there are two security risk analyses or risk assessment approaches: Qualitative and Quantitative methods that we are interested in this work.

Quantitative methods [5, 8, 9, 13, 14, 28, 33, 36, 37, 42], and [7] allow the definition of the consequences of security risks occurrence in a quantitative way. In fact, they estimate the costs in numerical values and hence give an accurate estimation of it. For example, the mean time to failure (MTTF) quantifies the failure rate of the system and the MFC model gives the cost per system stakeholder due to security breaches. However, the existing method analysis results are not precise and are even confusing. In fact, quantitative measures must depend on the scope and accuracy of defined measurement scale. Therefore, they fail to present accurate costs and precise results. On the other side, the analysis results must be enriched by qualitative descriptions to be more precise and comprehensive [5].

For example, in [28], the authors propose a SAEM method which is a cost–benefit analysis process for analyzing security design decisions based on the comparison of a "threat index." The authors in [12] propose security ontology for organizing knowledge on threats, safeguards, and assets. This work constructs classification for each of these groups and creates a method for quantitative risk analysis, using its own framework. The work does not use known standards or guidelines as an input for its evaluation model, so desired mechanisms and countermeasures have to be defined in the process of risk analysis. The ENISA report [13] also provided an approach for risk assessment based on the estimation of risk levels on ISO/IEC 27005:2008. Security risk would be high if both the probability of the event and its impact are high. The assessment provided is semi-quantitative, as it uses value ranges for both event probability and impact, but does not consider their combined influence in a quantitative manner. Bojanc and Jerman suggested in [33] a model that evaluates the information assets, their vulnerability, and the threats to information assets. The values of the risk parameters are the basis for selecting the appropriate risk treatment and the evaluation of the various security measures that reduce security risks. Singh and Joshi proposed in [36] a risk assessment framework for University computing environment that reduces the security risk breach. The model supports three phase activities, the first phase assesses the threats and vulnerabilities in order to identify the weak point in educational environment, the second phase focuses on the highest risk and creates actionable remediation plan, the third phase of risk assessment model recognizes the vulnerability management compliance requirement in order to improve University's security position.

Yang et al. propose in [8] a measurement and assessment model of Cloud Computing based on Markov chain to describe random risk environment. The model used information entropy to measure risk, effectively reduced the existing subjective factors in the assessment process, provided a practical and reliable method for risk management decisions. Finally, Cayirci and de Oliveira introduce in [7] a quantitative security risk assessment model based on cloud service providers' performance history. The model addresses provider and consumer concerns by relying on trusted third parties to collect soft and hard trust data elements, allowing for continuous risk monitoring in the cloud.

We notice that the existing quantitative security risk models reflect the loss risk of the whole system and they ignore the variance stakes among different stakeholders. In fact, the operation of a system involves many stakeholders, who have different cares (stakes). These models ignore others factors like *the failure cost with respect to requirements, the variability of system threats*. Nevertheless, the mean failure cost (MFC) considers many factors that we will enumerate in the next section.

2.2 Mean Failure Cost Model (MFC): A Quantitative Cybersecurity Risk Assessment Model

The MFC [3] represents a stochastic model that quantifies this random variable in terms of financial loss per unit of operation time (e.g., $/h) due to security threats. It represents for each stakeholder the amount of loss that results from security threats and system vulnerabilities. The MFC varies by stakeholder and takes into account the variance of the stakes that a stakeholder has in meeting each security requirement. The infrastructure in question reflects the values that stakeholders have in each security requirement, the dependency of security requirements on the operation of architectural components, and the impact that security threats have on these components.

The MFC process proceeds in four steps:

- Generation of Stakes Matrix (ST) which represents the cost that each stakeholder would lose if the system failed to meet a security requirement of the system.
- Generation of Dependency Matrix (DP) which represents how to estimate the probability that a particular security requirement is violated in the course of operating the system for some period of time.

- Generation of Impact Matrix (IM) which determines which threats affect which components and assesses the likelihood of success of each threat in light of perpetrator behavior and possible countermeasures.
- Generation of the Threat Vector (PT) which represents the probability that a threat materializes during unitary period of operation.

The mean failure cost is defined by the following formula:

$$MFC = ST \circ DP \circ IM \circ PT \tag{3.1}$$

We will propose in this chapter two new models extension of the mean failure model (MFC). In fact, the MFC model considers the following characteristics:

- It quantifies the cost in terms of financial loss per unit of operation time (dollars per hour).
- It quantifies the impact of failures: it provides cost as a result of security attacks. It offers decision support for security countermeasure design.
- It distinguishes between stakeholders: it provides cost for each system's stakeholder as a result of a security failure.
- It distinguishes between specification components: it considers that each system has many security requirements that represent concerns of the stakeholders.

However, the MFC model does not consider any classification threats and does not take into account any threat perspective either. In fact, such results take a global view at the threats targeting an information system which leads to inaccurate results.

2.3 Mean Failure Cost (MFC) Limits

Security threats may be originating from within or from outside threats that may be manifested, as well, via a threat agent using a particular penetration technique to cause dangerous effects [10, 29], and [22]. Thus, managers need to know and find threats that influence their assets and identify their impact to determine what they need to do to prevent attacks by selecting appropriate countermeasures. Then, they need to evaluate the extent of the damage caused by these threats.

Therefore, it is necessary to have an understanding of the threats and the vulnerabilities. Security threats can be observed and classified in different ways by considering different dimensions or classes of the system like its source code, attacker's motivation or its users, or their roles.

On the other hand, understanding and identifying the threats represent the first step in building a secure system. Indeed, to identify threats and evaluate existing control techniques, it is important to understand well security threat and especially security sources [1, 2, 6, 21, 22, 34], and [35]. Threats classification allows better identifying of threats characteristics and thus an accurate estimation of security risks. For example, if you know that there is a risk that someone could order products from your company but then repudiate receiving the shipment, you should ensure that you accurately identify the purchaser and then log all critical events during the delivery process [34]. Moreover, prior work has been based on the assumption that similar systems tend to produce similar vulnerabilities. For example, the kinds of vulnerabilities in a Windows operating system might be similar to those in the Linux operating system because both operating systems exhibit similar basic functionality [17].

Therefore, threats classification is an important task in security risk assessment models to assess accurately risks. After studying the MFC model in previous section, we notice that this model does not include threat classes and more especially it includes the following shortcomings:

- Security threats are evolutive and variable over time and have several characteristics, and in PT vector, there is no logical or hierarchical structure between the different catalogued threats as they are not based on a particular attribute to classify them.
- Underestimation of the MFC: In fact, in the threat vector PT, the term used to define the threat can be ambiguous (do not include threats classes); this can lead to an overlap between the various threats, i.e., each threat may belong to several classes at once and thus it is computed many times, so we have an underestimation of the mean failure cost.
- Managers cannot identify the source of threats risks in order to suggest appropriate countermeasures.
- The MFC is blind towards the structure and the dimensions of security threats. It considers that any failure due to a threat is a failure with respect to the whole specification. But stakeholders may have different stakes in different security threats dimensions and perspectives which are not reflected in the MFC.

We aim in this chapter to propose three cybersecurity metrics that overcome the limits of the mean failure cost model (MFC). We propose new metrics that take into account security threat dimensions or criteria that give accurate security risk assessment. The proposed models will be applied to a practical case study, namely a Cloud Computing system.

3 Cloud Computing Environments

Cloud Computing is the result of Information and Communication Technology (ICT) evolution. In fact, it is based on several technologies like virtualization, distributed systems, web service oriented architecture, service flows and workflows, and web 2.0. Two major events triggered the spread of Cloud Computing in 2006. The first was the announcement of a new business model, "Cloud Computing," by Google CEO Eric Schmidt.

Cloud Computing is a system that enabling access to remotely hosted data and computation resources from anywhere. In the same year, Amazon.com announced one of themost important Cloud Computing services till date called Elastic Cloud Computing (EC2) [12].

The National Institute of Standards and Technology defines Cloud Computing as "a model which grants convenient, on demand network access to a shared pool of configurable computing resources (e.g., networks, servers, storage, applications, and services) that can be rapidly provisioned and released with minimal management effort or service provider interaction" [26], and [27].

Cloud Computing plays an important role in many recent critical applications, such as astronomy, weather forecasting, and financial applications.

3.1 Cloud Computing Architecture

The Cloud Computing Architecture of a Cloud Computing system is the structure of the system which includes cloud resources, services, middleware, software components, and the relationships between them [4, 18], and [23]. It is composed mainly of two parts: the front end and the back end connecting to each other through the Internet. The front end is the side of the computer user or client including the client's computer and the application required to access to the Cloud Computing system. The back end is the "cloud" section of the system which includes the various physical/virtual computers, servers, software, and data storage systems. Figure 3.1 summarizes the proposed Cloud Computing architecture [4, 18], and [23].

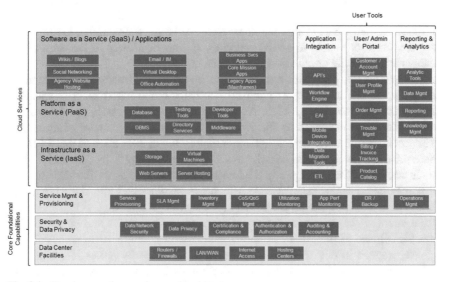

Fig. 3.1 Cloud computing services and architecture

Cloud Computing providers can offer services at different layers:

- Infrastructure as a Service (IaaS): This layer provides the basic computing infrastructure of servers, processing, storage, networks where the consumer is able to deploy and run arbitrary software, which can include operating systems and applications.
- Platform as a Service (PaaS): This layer provides a platform upon which applications can be written or deployed.
- Software as a Service (SaaS): This layer delivers applications through a web browser to thousands of customers without having to be installed on their computers.

3.2 Cloud Computing Security Issues

In the last few years, the Cloud Computing reveals a remarkable potential to provide on-demand services to users with greater flexibility in a cost-effective manner. While moving towards the concept of on-demand service, resource pooling, shifting everything on the distributive environment, security is the major obstacle for this new dreamed vision of computing capability. In fact, users' data are stored outside the cloud in data centers where risks out number rewards. In fact, customers' data in the Cloud are stored on multiple third-party servers and thus it is not cared by the user and no one knows where exactly data are saved. Among these we mention the loss of control and the loss of security [22, 24, 30, 36, 38, 41], and [39]. Indeed, by trusting critical data to a service provider (externalization of service), a user (whether an individual or an organization) takes risks with the availability, confidentiality, and integrity of this data. For example, availability may be affected if the subscriber's data is unavailable when needed (due, for example, to a denial of service attack or merely to a loss) and integrity may be affected if the subscriber's data is inadvertently or maliciously damaged or destroyed.

Many surveys deal with security risks in Cloud environment. For example, according to a Forbes' report published in 2015, cloud based security spending is expected to increase by 42%. According to another research, the IT security expenditure had increased to 79.1% by 2015, showing an increase of more than 10% each year. International Data Corporation (IDC) in 2011 showed that 74.6% of enterprise customers ranked security as a major challenge [15, 16, 38], and [11].

In addition, Cloud Computing is based on several technologies like virtualization that may cause major security risks which can be classified into three categories like virtual machine modification, denial of service, monitoring virtual machines from host (MVM), communications between virtual machines and host (CBVH), etc. [4, 18], and [23].

We propose in this section classification of CC security issues into nine sub-categories [19], which include: virtualization security issues, business services continuity, management interfaces risks, privacy issues, data location, data breaches, accountability problems, multi-tenancy problem, and regulation and governance problem.

Security Issues in Virtualization Cloud Computing architecture is based on many virtualization components such as hypervisor and virtual machine. Hypervisor is a controller known also as virtual machine manager (VMM), which allows multiple operating systems to be run on a system at a time. Since multiple operating systems may be running on a single hardware platform, it is not possible to keep track of all such systems and hence maintaining the security of the operating systems is difficult. In this case, guest system can run malicious code on the machine system and bring the system down or take full control of the system and block access to other guest operating systems [22], and [41]. Malicious insiders are very serious attacks; hence, it presents an opportunity for an adversary to harvest confidential data or gain complete control over the Cloud services with little or no risk of detection [22, 41], and [11].

Business Services Continuity One more availability problem in CC environment is distributed denial of service (DDoS) attacks. Attackers make use of large botnets (zombies) to reduce the profits of SaaS providers by DDoS by making their services unavailable [13]. Furthermore, a major risk to services continuity in the Cloud Computing environment is loss of internet connectivity (that could occur due to some circumstances like natural disasters) as Cloud businesses are dependent on the internet access to their information. In addition, there are also concerns that the seizure of a data hosting server by law enforcement agencies may result in the unnecessary interruption or cessation of unrelated services whose data are stored on the same physical machine. This resulted in the unintended consequence of disrupting the continuity of businesses whose data and information are hosted on the seized hardware.

Management Interfaces Risks Cloud Computing providers expose a set of software interfaces that customers use to manage and interact with Cloud services (like provisioning, management, orchestration, and monitoring). The customer management interfaces of public Cloud providers are Internet accessible and mediate access to larger sets of resources and therefore pose an increased risk especially when combined with remote access and web browser vulnerabilities [13]. Unauthorized access to the management interface is therefore an especially relevant vulnerability for Cloud systems. These interfaces must be designed to protect against both accidental and malicious attempts because they allow authentication and access control to encryption and activity monitoring that depend directly on the security and availability of general Cloud services [11].

Data Breaches Cloud Computing system allows the storage of customer data in different ways. In fact, data in Cloud systems travel in clusters, in virtual machines, in databases, or into third-party storages, which increase the risk of information leak and data corruption. Indeed, operations in data centers might lead to information leak caused, for example, by a customer's information being mistaken by another's.

Furthermore, most of the Cloud providers instead of acquiring a server try to rent a server from other service providers because they are cost affective and flexible for operation. This gives a high possibility for malicious insiders to steal customers' data from the external server [12, 22], and [41].

Compliance and Governance As security in Cloud Computing systems presents a big challenge, cloud vendor has to provide some assurance in service level agreements (SLA) to convince the customer on security issues. The SLA illustrates different security levels and tries to make the customer understand the security policies that are being implemented. Customers may also in the SLA indicate its expectations in terms of security for these types of systems. Providers must deliver a comprehensive list of regulations that govern the system and associated services and how compliance with these items is executed [22], and [11]. However, the SLA may not offer a promise to provide such services on the part of the Cloud provider which can create several security breaches (for example, meet privacy and confidentiality needs) for many reasons. In fact, Cloud providers cannot give evidence of their own conformity with the relevant requirements and do not permit external audit by the Cloud customer and/or security certifications [11, 22, 41], and [13].

In addition, a more serious problem is that there is no way to specify the policies on how sensitive data are shared, treated, and located among Cloud service providers. In fact, information is routinely leaked with poor data management practices. Cloud service providers must ensure, for example, the data security in natural disasters. Indeed, there are certain legal issues entangled with Cloud security as well, because there are certain laws that Cloud service providers should comply with and these laws vary from country to country which may cause data replication across multiple sites.

Access Problem: Data Location Cloud Computing environments suffer from lack of transparency since customer' data are located in Cloud provider data centers and anywhere in the world, and hence are out of the customer's control which leads to many problems [11, 22, 32, 41] and [13]. In fact, the user space may be shared across applications that can lead to data replication, making mapping of users and their privileges a complicated task. This, also, requires the user to remember multiple accounts/passwords and maintain them which may entail forgetting them in many cases. Indeed, by using the Cloud, users need to look at who (their role and their privileges, etc.) is managing (get access to) their data (when they release the information into the Cloud for processing) and what types of controls are applied to these individuals [11, 31], and [16].

Data breaches present a crucial problem for organizations. For example: many organizations such as financial institutions, health care providers, and government agencies are legally required to protect their data from compromise due to the sensitivity of their information. Generally, these organizations are required to manage and maintain their own datacenters with stringent physical and logical protection mechanisms ensuring that their data remain protected. These organizations simply cannot utilize Cloud Computing in a generic manner due to the inherent risk of data compromise from systems they do not control.

Privacy Issues Privacy problems in Cloud Computing environments come from many reasons. First, Cloud Computing customer's data and especially personal information can be breached more easily than if stored in users' machines. In fact, customer's data are stored in services provider's data centers and thus it is not guaranteed if the providers will protect their data and especially their personal information. Indeed, as most of the servers are external, the provider should make sure who is accessing the data and who is maintaining the server to protect the customer's personal information. Also, in the shared infrastructure, customers' private information risk more potential unauthorized access and exposure [22, 41], and [13].

Moreover, privacy problems for organizations stem from the diversity of privacy regulations from country to country. In fact, data in Cloud system are stored anywhere and user cannot guess if you are violating privacy regulations in the countries where you operate [22, 41], and [13]. Indeed, there is a need for approaches to label directly the data with security and privacy policies that would travel with sensitive data from one provider to another so that the proper technical controls can be employed by various Cloud providers to protect the data [32]. Data are prone in this case to many attacks like: sniffing, spoofing, man-in-the-middle attacks, side channel, and replay attacks and so in some cases the CP does not guarantee respect for the confidentiality or the nondisclosure of information [13].

Isolation Failure (Multi-Tenancy Problem) Multi-tenancy and shared resources (computing capacity, storage, network, memory, routing, etc.) represent main characteristics of Cloud Computing environments. There is a risk of failure of deferent mechanisms between different tenants of the shared infrastructure due to principally hypervisor vulnerability. In fact, infrastructure as a service (IaaS) Cloud layer relies on architectural designs where physical resources are shared by multiple virtual machines and therefore multiple customers. In fact, resource sharing means that malicious activities (spamming, port scanning, etc.) carried out by one tenant may affect and get access to another tenant host [13].

Accountability Problems Accountability has to do with keeping track of actions that are related to security actions and responsibilities [41]. It aims to give tracking evidence on user behaviors and system status, which can also be used in system performance analysis or intrusion detection purposes.

As security is the most concern for Cloud Computing adoption, we propose in this chapter secutiy metrics to quantify cybersecurity risk in order to let managers to select appropriate countermeasures.

4 MFC_{ext} and MFC_{int}: New Quantitative Security Risk Assessment Models

In this section, we illustrate an extension of the MFC model [3] by suggesting a classification of the identified threats to propose two types of measures: The Internal MFC (MFC_{int}) and the External MFC (MFC_{ext}) in order to know the source of threats shaped information systems and especially the Cloud Computing systems to take appropriate security strategies or mitigate their effects.

4.1   Security Threat Space Intrusion

Threat source or threat space intrusion represents a primordial criterion for identifying threat source in order to take appropriate security decisions. For the purpose of our system, we propose to classify the threat space into subspaces according to a model of three dimensions labeled Internal, External, and InternalExternal. This classification allows to localize the origin (or source) of a threat. In fact, threat is caused either from within an organization, system, or/and architecture or from an external point of origin [18].

4.1.1   Internal Threats

Internal threats occur when someone has authorized access to the network with either an account on a server or physical access to the network. A threat can be internal to the organization as the result of employee action or failure of an organization process [18].

Regarding internal attacks, we can cite theft of proprietary information, accidental or non-malicious breaches, sabotage, fraud, and eavesdropping/snooping as instances of insider threats.

4.1.2   External Threats

External threats can arise from individuals or organizations working outside of a company. They do not have authorized access to the computer systems or network. They work their way into a network mainly from the Internet or dialup access servers. The most obvious external threats to computer systems and the resident data are natural disasters like hurricanes, fires, floods, and earthquakes. External attacks occur through connected networks (wired and wireless), physical intrusion, or a partner network [18].

Lacey et al. provide an updated profile of sophisticated outside attacks which can compromise the security of Mobile Ad hoc Network (MANET) [25]. They include eavesdropping, routing table overflow, routing cache poisoning, routing maintenance, data forwarding, wormhole, sinkhole, byzantine, selfish nodes, external denial of service, internal denial of service, spoofing, Sybil, badmouthing, viruses, and flattering.

4.1.3   Internal/External Threats

Internal/external threats take place when someone having authorized access to the network (for example, an employee of the organization) causes external threats to the system [18].

4.2 MFC_{ext} and MFC_{int}: The Proposed Model

The threats vector is a vector of probabilities of attack to the system during a time unit. These threats, as we said above, come from external or internal boundaries of the system. This classification lets us to propose two new extension of the threat vector (PT) of the MFC metric. Consequently, there will be two extensions measures of the mean failure cost (MFC). We can calculate the external mean failure cost MFCext and the internal mean failure cost MFCint. Depending on the attack space vector AS, the new MFC formula will be

$$MFC_{ext} = ST \circ DP \circ IM \circ PT \circ AS_{ext} \tag{3.2}$$

and

$$MFC_{int} = ST \circ DP \circ IM \circ PT \circ AS_{int} \tag{3.3}$$

AS_{int} and AS_{ext} are two vectors having the same dimension of the threat vector PT containing the probability values of threat related to intrusion types (internal or external). Figure 3.2 shows AS_{int} and AS_{ext} structures.

These new extensions of MFC model improve analysis of the vulnerability of the system. They allow specifying the nature of security solution that minimizes the mean failure cost.

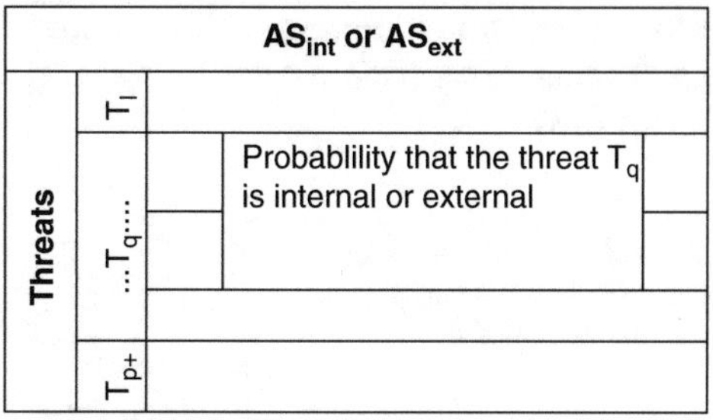

Fig. 3.2 Space intrusion vector

4.3 Illustration of the Cybersecurity Model: A Cloud Computing System

In this section, we illustrate the use of the MFC_{int} and the MFC_{ext} in a Cloud Computing system [4]. We identify, hence, the threats intrusion space in Cloud system through the extension mentioned above.

We identify, firstly, the security requirements, the stakeholders and their stakes in meeting these requirements, the architectural components, and the security threats that affect the Cloud Computing system. Then, we fill the matrixes ST, DP, ICM, CM, and PT using empirical data from [38] to obtain the following MFCext and MFCint vectors.

We consider four classes of stakeholders (as described in Sect. 3) in this case study, namely: a Cloud Computing provider (PR), a corporate subscriber (CS), a governmental subscriber (GS), and an individual subscriber (IS).

As for security requirements, we identify seven generic security requirements classified based on the levels of criticality of data as shown in our previous work [4], and [23], namely:

- Availability of critical data (AVC),
- Availability of archival data (AVA),
- Integrity of critical data (INC),
- Integrity of archival data (INA),
- Confidentiality of classified data (CC),
- Confidentiality of proprietary data (CP), and
- Confidentiality of public data (CB).

Based on a quantification of these stakes in terms of thousands of dollars ($K) per hours of operation, we produce the following stakes matrix ST as shown in Table 3.1.

Based on the Cloud Computing system architecture defined in our previous work [4], and [18], we generate the dependency matrix shown in Table 3.2. We consider that the Cloud Computing system components include: a browser (Br), a proxy server (Prx), a router/firewall (R/F), a load balancer (LB), a web server (WS), an application server (AS), a database server (DS), a backup server (BS), and a storage server (SS).

Table 3.1 Matrix of stakes: cost of failing a security requirement in $K/h

	Security requirements						
	AVC	AVA	INC	INA	CC	CP	CB
Stakeholders							
PR	500	90	800	150	1500	1200	120
CS	150	40	220	80	250	180	60
GS	60	20	120	50	2500	30	12
IS	0.050	0.015	0.300	0.200	0.300	0.100	0.010

Table 3.2 Dependency matrix

	Components									
	Br	R/F	LB	WS	AS	DB	BS	SS	NoF	
Security requirements										
AVC	0.14	0.14	0.14	0.14	0.06	0.04	0.14	0.06	0.14	0
AVA	0.16	0.16	0.16	0.16	0.07	0.05	0.05	0.03	0.16	0
INC	0.03	0.03	0.2	0.2	0.09	0.03	0.2	0.02	0.2	0
INA	0.04	0.04	0.32	0.32	0.14	0.04	0.04	0.01	0.32	0
CB	0.1	0.03	0.23	0.23	0.1	0.1	0.1	0.01	0.1	0
CP	0.1	0.03	0.23	0.23	0.1	0.1	0.1	0.01	0.1	0
CC	0.1	0.03	0.23	0.23	0.1	0.1	0.1	0.01	0.1	0

Table 3.3 Probability of threat space intrusion

Threats	Probability outsider committed	Probability insider committed
(MVM)	1	0
(BVH)	1	0
(VMm)	0.6	0.4
(VMS)	1	0
VMM)	0.5	0.5
(VMC)	0.5	0.5
VMM)	0.6	0.4
(DoS)	0.136	0.864
(FA)	1	0
(DL)	0.8	0.2
(MI)	0	1
(ASTH)	1	0
(ANU)	0	1
(IAI)	0.8	0.2

Using empirical data from [3], we can decompose the probability of event threat committed in two complementary probabilities (outsider/insider system committed) as shown in Table 3.3.

We have catalogued fourteen distinct types of threats (Table 3.5). To compute the MFC_{ext} and the MFC_{int} we need to know the probability of the attack for each threat during 1 h. Also, we need to fill the values of impact matrix IM. The IM matrix relates component failure to security threats; specifically, it represents the probability of failure of components given that some security threat has materialized.

Tables 3.4 and 3.5 represent the impact matrix and the threat vector.

Thus, we compute the mean failure cost of external threats (see Table 3.6) and the mean failure cost of internal threats (see Table 3.7) using the formulas presented above. Entries of these three matrices and the two vectors come from our empirical study [3] which has an immense source of references.

Table 3.4 Impact matrix

Components	Threats														
	MVH	CVH	VMm	VMS	MVV	VMC	VMM	DoS	FA	DL	MI	ASTH	ANU	IAI	NoT
Brws	0	0	0	0	0	0	0	0.02	0.01	0	0.03	0.02	0	0.03	0
Prox	0.01	0.05	0	0.01	0.01	0.05	0.05	0.02	0.01	0	0.005	0.02	0.01	0	0
R/FW	0.03	0.05	0.033	0.03	0.03	0.05	0.05	0.06	0.04	0	0.005	0.02	0.01	0.01	0
LB	0.02	0.003	0	0.01	0.02	0.003	0.003	0.06	0.04	0	0.005	0.02	0.01	0.01	0
WS	0.03	0.003	0.033	0	0.03	0.003	0.003	0.02	0.04	0	0.01	0.02	0.01	0.01	0
AS	0.02	0.003	0.033	0.06	0.02	0.003	0.003	0.036	0.04	0	0.05	0.02	0.01	0.07	0
DBS	0.001	0	0.033	0.04	0.001	0	0	0.036	0.04	0.05	0.03	0.02	0.01	0.06	0
BS	0.001	0	0	0.04	0.001	0	0	0.036	0.04	0.05	0.03	0.02	0.01	0.06	0
SS	0.04	0.05	0	0.04	0.04	0.05	0.05	0.036	0.04	0.05	0.03	0.02	0.01	0.06	0
NoF	0.06	0.04	0.03	0.03	0.06	0.04	0.04	0.01	0.02	0.01	0.02	0.05	0.06	0.005	1

Table 3.5 Threat vector

Threats	Probability
Monitoring virtual machines from host (MVM)	8.063×10^{-4}
Communications between virtual machines and host (CBVH)	8.063×10^{-4}
Virtual machine modification (VMm)	8.063×10^{-4}
Placement of malicious VM images on physical systems (VMS)	8.063×10^{-4}
Monitoring VMs from other VM (MVV)	40.31×10^{-4}
Communication between VMs (VMC)	40.31×10^{-4}
Virtual machine mobility (VMM)	40.31×10^{-4}
Denial of service (DoS)	14.39×10^{-4}
Flooding attacks (FA)	56.44×10^{-4}
Data loss or leakage (DL)	5.75×10^{-4}
Malicious insiders (MI)	6.623×10^{-4}
Account, service, and traffic hijacking (ASTH)	17.277×10^{-4}
Abuse and nefarious use of Cloud Computing (ANU)	17.277×10^{-4}
Insecure application programming interfaces (IAI)	29.026×10^{-4}
No threats (NoT)	0.9682

Table 3.6 The MFC of external threats

Stakeholders	MFC_{ext}($K/h)
PR	10.61051
CS	2.46562
GS	6.278502
IS	0.002382

Table 3.7 The MFC of internal threats

Stakeholders	MFC_{int}($K/h)
PR	4.5932
CS	1.07261
GS	2.7060
IS	0.001035

Computing the new values of the MFC extensions can give us the critical space of intrusion. In our case, we can adapt some solutions like adding more firewalls, proxy servers, and antivirus servers. In fact, the MFCext values for Cloud systems are more significant compared to the MFCint values and hence the Cloud security risks come mainly from external threats.

The MFC_{ext} and the MFC_{int} give the critical threats space to help managers to take the appropriate countermeasures. They improve the analysis of the system vulnerability. They specify the type of solution to minimize the average cost of failure. In fact, using the threat classification source dimension, they allow identifying the source of the threats space (either internal or external source) to let managers concentrate on the intrusion space having the higher mean failure costs. However, this quantification is not sufficient since threats have several dimensions like motivation and intention that we must take into account. Therefore, these models do not provide accurate estimation of costs resulting from threats breaches.

4.4   Validation of the MFC_{int} and the MFC_{ext}

System stakeholders seek secure information systems to reduce cost and protect their assets from damage and ensure the confidentiality, availability, and the integrity of information. To help stakeholders, the MFC metric gives a quantitative value of security system without any qualification as the security quantification did not allow deciding whether the system is secured or not. The question for all stakeholders is whether their system is secure or not.

For this purpose, we propose to find an interval that classifies the security of information systems. Thus, we propose to find lower and upper bounds of this interval which present, respectively, the mean failure cost for a 100% secure and a 100% unsecure system. In fact, the lower bound Blow represents a secure system with the minimum cost and the upper bound Bupp represents an unsecure system with a maximum cost. Therefore, we say that a system is secure if its MFC is lower than the average between the upper bound and the lower bound, that is, if the $MFC < ([Blow + Bupp]/2)$ and the system is not secure if $MFC > ([Blow + Bupp]/2)$. Finally, we proceed to the classification of our MFC as secure or not.

Assuming that the system is secure, the probabilities of system components failure are very low see null. For this goal, we modify the impact threat classes matrix ICM as follows: we put 0 for lines, 1 at the last column, and the last line is made complementary to the columns and the equilibrium of the line. For an unsecure system, we make the reverse of founded bounds.

We compute, finally, the lower bound vector of mean failure costs and the upper bound vector of MFC as shown in Tables 3.8 and 3.9, using our new formula.

To validate our MFC external vector (MFC_{ext}) and the MFC internal vector (MFC_{int}) presented in Tables 3.10 and 3.11 for Cloud Computing system, we propose to evaluate the stakeholders' security costs in order to decide if this system is secure or not.

Table 3.8 MFC_{ext} lower bound

Stakeholders	MFC_{ext} ($K/h)
PR	14.92
CS	3.222
GS	10.38
IS	0.0032

Table 3.9 MFC_{ext} upper bound

Stakeholders	MFC_{ext} ($K/h)
PR	4400.5
CS	1001.6
GS	2805.5
IS	1.029

Table 3.10 MFC_{int} lower bound

Stakeholders	MFC_{int} ($K/h)
PR	12.899
CS	2.759
GS	9.120
IS	0.0027

Table 3.11 MFC_{int} upper bound

Stakeholders	MFC_{int} ($K/h)
PR	4260.564
CS	969.749
GS	2716.285
IS	0.9969

For the MFC external model, we notice that for each stakeholder the MFCext value is lower than $([Blow + Bupp]/2)$ $(MFC_{ext} < [Blow + Bupp]/2)$; thus, the system is secure. For the MFCint vector, for each stakeholder we notice as well that MFCint value is lower than $([Blow + Bupp]/2)$ $(MFC_{int} < [Blow + Bupp]/2)$; thus, the system is secure. Thus, we can deduce that Cloud Computing environment is a secure system.

In addition to the contribution of the application of MFC model, we can say that in certain level of Cloud Computing services like the infrastructure as a service layer (IaaS), it is very difficult to specify a threat in a system component because we can find a large number of components, in this layer, so it can be better to associate a class of threats rather than a specific threat for each component. Indeed, as countermeasures, one solution will solve several problems rather than one problem.

4.5 MFC_{ext} and MFC_{int} Limits and Advantages

The MFCext and MFCint models present several advantages. In fact, they can identify the source of the most severe threats causing risk to let managers take the necessary countermeasures against this intrusion space. So, these models take into account the source criterion of security threats.

As these models do not take into account all threats characteristics and just consider one criterion which does not accurately describe a security threat (the source of a threat), they do not give accurate values on the cost of security failure.

On the other hand, the considered criteria are based on a binary classification (internal or external), while threat sources may include three subclasses. Subsequently, these models do not illustrate accurate estimation of security failure cost values. In addition, the underestimation of security threat risk presented does not let managers propose adequate security strategies to mitigate the risk.

5 The MFC Extension Model (MFCE)

In the next section, we will suggest two cybersecurity measures in order to better quantify system threats using the source dimension of security threats. In this section, we propose a new cybersecurity metric referred to as mean failure cost extension (MFCE), based on threats classification and especially on the hybrid threat classification (HTC) model [22]. We, then, illustrate this infrastructure by means of a Cloud Computing application.

5.1 The MFCE Model

In order to improve the estimation of the costs due to security breakdowns, we propose a quantitative security threats model based on our threats classification (HTC) [22]. We propose a security solution per threat class. For this reason, we propose a novel model in which we focus on refining the estimation of the impact matrix IM and the threat vector PT of the mean failure cost (MFC) model introduced in Sect. 3. We call this model the MFC extension model (MFCE) [18]. Our cybersecurity model allows studying the impact of a whole class of threats rather than a mere threat. Indeed, threats are variable in time and security solutions change over time. The basic idea is to consider a class of threats, try to find solutions to this class, and consider the probability that a class is present will be the average of the probabilities of present threats in this class threats in order to achieve a certain stability of this class in time. This allows converging towards a stability of existence of a class [18].

For the impact matrix IM, we generate two matrices: the new impact matrix IMC and the threat classes matrix CM, as shown in Figs. 3.3 and 3.4. Thus, the MFC extension (MFCE) has the following new formula:

$$MFCE = ST \circ DP \circ ICM \circ CM \circ PT \tag{3.4}$$

The MFCE model represents a cybersecurity metric as a decision-making technique to derive relevant decision-making security solutions. This quantitative

Fig. 3.3 The impact threat classes matrix structure

ICM	Threat classes			
	Cl1	... Clr...		Cls+1
Components				
C1				
...		Prob that Component Ck		
Ch		fails once threat Class Clr has materialized		
Ch+1				

Fig. 3.4 The threat classes
matrix structure

CM	Threats			
	T1	...Tq ...		Tp+1
Threats classes				
Cl1				
... Clr		Prob of having Class Clr once Threat Tq has materialized		
Cls+1				

decision-making metric allows selecting countermeasures per threats class rather than a threat to better study and identify security threats.

5.2 Illustration of the MFC Extension Model: Cloud Computing System

We illustrate in this section the application of our new cybersecurity metric (MFC extension model) on the same computing system in order to compare the derived results.

We identify, firstly, the security requirements, the stakeholders and their stakes in meeting these requirements, the architectural components, and the security threats that affect the Cloud Computing system. Then, we used the matrixes ST, DP, and PT defined in the previous section. These matrices are shown in Tables 3.1, 3.2, and 3.5.

5.2.1 The Impact Threats Classes Matrix

The following step in our model is to derive the impact threat classes matrix, i.e., the derivation of the set of threat classes we wish to consider in our system. We applied our hybrid threat classification presented in previous work [22] on this case study to generate threat classes. In fact, we proposed in earlier work [22] a dynamic and multidimensional threat classification model that allows better defining and articulating of threat characteristics [18]. The model contains the following criteria:

- Threat source: Origin of threat either internal or external.
- Threat agents: Agents that cause threats that can be human, accidental environmental or technological.
- Security threat motivation: Goal of attackers on a system which can be malicious or non-malicious.
- Security threat intention: The intent of the human who caused the threat that is intentional or accidental.

Thus, the classes we have are presented in Table 3.12.

Table 3.12 Security threat classes for Cloud Computing system

Security threat	Classes description
IHMA	Insider human malicious accidental threat
IHMI	Insider human malicious intentional threat
IHNMA	Insider human non-malicious accidental threat
IHNMI	Insider human non-malicious intentional threat
OHMA	Outsider human malicious accidental threat
OHMI	Outsider human malicious intentional threat
OHNMA	Outsider human non-malicious accidental threat
OHNMI	Outsider human non-malicious intentional threat
EV	Environmental threat
IT	Insider technological threat
OT	Outsider technological threat

Components in a system may fail to meet security requirements due to malicious activity when a threat class is materialized. The ICM matrix represents eleven columns, one for each threat class plus one for the absence of threats classes (NoC), and ten rows, one for each component plus one for the event that no component has failed during one period of time (NoF). The impact threats classes matrix is given in Table 3.13 [18].

5.2.2 The Threat Classes Matrix

The threat classes matrix (Table 3.14) shows that each security threat belongs at most to one threat class, that is, each threat has its proper characteristics. In CM matrix, columns represent security threats (the last column represents the absence of threat (NoT)), rows represent threat classes, and a cell CM(q, s) represents the probability of having Class Clr once Threat Tq has materialized: if a class defines n threats, then this is 1/n and 0 if it is outside.

We have catalogued fourteen distinct types of threats and eleven threat classes. To compute the MFC extension (MFCE), we need to know the probability of the attack class for each threat during 1 h. We need also to fill the values in Table 3.14, they come from our empirical study [3].

Using the four Matrices (stakes, dependency, impact threat classes, and threat classes) and the threat classes vector, we can compute the vector of mean failure costs extension (Table 3.15) for each stakeholder of Cloud Computing system using the formula:

$$MFCE = ST \circ DP \circ ICM \circ CM \circ PT \tag{3.5}$$

The MFC vector is shown in Table 3.15.

Table 3.13 Impact threat classes matrix

Components	Threats classes											
	IHMA	IHMI	IHNMA	OHMA	OHMI	OHNMA	OHNMI	EV	ASTH	IT	OT	NoT
Brws	0.011	0.03	0.005	0.015	0.04	0.027	0.02	0.013	0.01	0.03	0.03	0.769
Prox	0.011	0.03	0.005	0.015	0.04	0.027	0.02	0.013	0.01	0.03	0.03	0.769
R/FW	0.011	0.03	0.005	0.015	0.04	0.027	0.02	0.013	0.01	0.03	0.03	0.769
LB	0.011	0.03	0.005	0.015	0.04	0.027	0.02	0.013	0.01	0.03	0.03	0.769
WS	0.011	0.03	0.005	0.015	0.04	0.027	0.02	0.013	0.01	0.03	0.03	0.769
AS	0.011	0.03	0.005	0.015	0.04	0.027	0.02	0.013	0.01	0.03	0.03	0.769
DBS	0.011	0.03	0.005	0.015	0.04	0.027	0.02	0.013	0.01	0.03	0.03	0.769
BS	0.011	0.03	0.005	0.015	0.04	0.027	0.02	0.013	0.01	0.03	0.03	0.769
SS	0.011	0.03	0.005	0.015	0.04	0.027	0.02	0.013	0.01	0.03	0.03	0.769
NoF	0.09	0.08	0.09	0.09	0.08	0.08	0.09	0.09	0.09	0.08	0.08	0.06

Table 3.14 Threat classes matrix

Threats	MVH	CVH	VMm	VMS	MVV	VMC	VMM	DoS	FA	DL	MI	ASTH	ANU	IAI	NoT
Threats classes															
IHMA	0	0	0	0	0	0	0	0	0	0	0	0	0	0	1
IHMI	0	0	0	0	0	0	0	0.33	0	0	0.33	0	0.33	0	0
IHNMA	0	0	0	0	0	0	0	0	0	0	0	0	0	0	1
IHNMI	0	0	0	0	0	0	0	0	0	0	0	0	0	0	1
OHMA	0.5	0	0	0	0	0	0	0	0	0	0	0	0	0.5	0
OHMI	0.25	0.25	0	0	0	0	0	0	0	0.25	0	0.25	0	0	0
OHNMA	0	0	0	0	0	0	0	0	0	0	0	0	0	0	1
OHNMI	0	0	0	0	0	0	0	0	0	0	0	0	0	0	1
EV	0	0	0	0	0	0	0	0	0	1	0	0	0	0	0
IT	0	0	0	0	0.5	0.5	0	0	0	0	0	0	0	0	0
OT	0	0	0	0.5	0	0.5	0	0	0	0	0	0	0	0	0
NoC	0.05	0.083	0.13	0.05	0.05	0.05	0.13	0.08	0	0.083	0.08	0.083	0.08	0.05	0

Table 3.15 Stakeholder
mean failure cost extension

Stakeholders	MFCE ($K/h)
PR	280.551
CS	63.856
GS	178.863
IS	0.065

Table 3.16 MFC lower
bound

Stakeholders	MFC ($K/h)
PR	8.018
CS	1.824
GS	5.111
IS	0.001

Table 3.17 MFC upper
bound

Stakeholders	MFC ($K/h)
PR	1923.666
CS	437.846
GS	1226.416
IS	0.065

5.3 Validation of the MFCE Model

Using the same method presented in the previous section, we calculate the upper and the lower bounds for the mean failure cost extension (MFCE) model.

Assuming that the system is secure, the probabilities of failure of system components are very low see null. For this goal, we modify the impact threat classes matrix ICM as follows: we put 0 for lines, 1 at the last column, and the last line is made complementary to the columns and the equilibrium of the line. For an unsecure system, we make the reverse of founded bounds.

We compute, finally, the lower bound vector of mean failure costs and the upper bound vector of MFC as shown in Tables 3.16 and 3.17, using our new formula.

To validate our MFC extension vector (MFCE) presented in Table 3.15 for Cloud Computing system, we propose to evaluate the stakeholders' security costs in order to decide if this system is secure or not. As we notice that the MFC values for Cloud Computing system are lower than the average of the MFC bounds for each stakeholder presented in Tables 3.16 and 3.17, so we can say that Cloud Computing environment is a secure system.

6 Conclusion

Security represents a major problem for information systems and organizations must estimate costs due to security breaches. Security risks are caused by various inter-related internal and external factors. A security vulnerability could also propagate and escalate through the causal chains of risk factors via multiple paths, leading to different system security risks. In order to estimate threats risks we propose three models that are based on threats classification. The MFC_{int} and the MFC_{ext} are based on the threat source dimension to identify the source of threat space. The MFCE enables a system's stakeholders to quantify the risks they take with the security of their assets and it is based on the HTC model. In addition, we propose to qualify security breaches costs by suggesting a cost interval to classify the security quantification for information system to decide whether the system is secure or not. These security analysis models enable organizations to predict the financial costs to lose due to threats breaches, which is validated via a case study.

We envision to develop an extendable quantitative security risk assessment model that considers several threats dimensions to give more accurate security loss values.

References

1. AhmadKhan, M. (2016). A survey of security issues for cloud computing. *Journal of Network and Computer Applications, 71*, 11–29.
2. Applegate, D. S., & Stavrou, A. (2013). Towards a cyber conflict taxonomy. In *5th International Conference on Cyber Conflict*.
3. Ben Aissa, A., Abercrombie, R. K., Sheldon, F. T., & Mili, A. (2010). Quantifying security threats and their potential impact: A case study. *Innovation in Systems and Software Engineering, 6*(4), 269–281.
4. Ben Arfa, L., Jouini, M., Ben Aissa, A., & Mili, A. (2013). A cybersecurity model in cloud computing environments. *Journal of King Saud University Computer and Information Sciences, 25*(1), 63–75.
5. Boehme, R., & Nowey, T. (2008). Economic security metrics. In E. Irene, F. Felix, & R. Ralf (Eds.), *Dependability metrics* (Vol. 4909, pp. 176–187).
6. Bompard, E., Huang, T., Wu, Y., & Cremenescu, M. (2013). Classification and trend analysis of threats origins to the security of power systems. *Electrical Power and Energy Systems, 50*, 50–64.
7. Cayirci, E., & de Oliveira, A. S. (2018). Modelling trust and risk for cloud services. *Journal of Cloud Computing, 7*(1), 14.
8. Cayirci, E., Garaga, A., De Oliveira, A. S., & Roudier, Y. (2016). A risk assessment model for selecting cloud service providers. *Journal of Cloud Computing, 5*(1), 14.
9. Chanchala, J., & Singh, U. K. (2016). Quantitative information security risk assessment model for university computing environment. In *International Conference on Information Technology (ICIT)*.
10. Chandran, S., Hrudya, P., & Poornachandran, P. (2015). An efficient classification model for detecting advanced persistent threat. In *International Conference on Advances in Computing, Communications and Informatics (ICACCI)*.
11. Cloud Security Alliance. (2018). *The treacherous - Top threats to cloud computing + industry insights*.
12. Demchenko, Y., Gommans, L., de Laat, C., & Oudenaarde, B. (2005). Web services and grid security vulnerabilities and threats analysis and model. In *Proceedings of 6th IEEE/ACM International Workshop on Grid Computing*.
13. ENSIA. (2010). Report on cloud computing security risk assessment. http://www.enisa.europa.eu/act/rm/files/deliverables/cloudcomputing-risk-assessment

14. Feng, N., Wang, H. J., & Li, M. (2013). A security risk analysis model for information systems: Causal relationships of risk factors and vulnerability propagation analysis. *Information Sciences, 256*, 57–73.
15. Gens, F. (2011). *New IDC IT cloud services survey: Top benefits and challenges. IDC eXchange 2011*. http://blogs.idc.com/ie/?p=730
16. Gururaj, R., Iftikhar, M., & Khan, F. A. (2017). A comprehensive survey on security in cloud computing. In *International Workshop on Cyber Security and Digital Investigation (CSDI)* (Vol. 110, pp. 465–472).
17. Igure, V., & Williams, R. (2008). Taxonomies of attacks and vulnerabilities in computer systems. *Communications Surveys & Tutorials, 10*(1), 6–19.
18. Jouini, M., Ben Aissa, A., Ben Arfa, L., & Mili, A. (2012). Towards quantitative measures of information security: A cloud computing case study. *International Journal of Cyber Security and Digital Forensics, 1*(3), 265–279.
19. Jouini, M., & Ben Arfa, L. (2014). Surveying and analyzing security problems in cloud computing environments. In *Tenth International Conference on Computational Intelligence and Security, CIS 2014* (pp. 689–693).
20. Jouini, M., & Ben Arfa, L. (2016). Comparative study of information security risk assessment models for cloud computing systems. In *The 6th International Symposium on Frontiers in Ambient and Mobile Systems (FAMS 2016)* (Vol. 83, pp. 1084–1089)
21. Jouini, M., & Ben Arfa, L. (2018). Threats classification: State of the art. In *Computer systems and software engineering: Concepts, methodologies, tools, and applications* (pp. 1851–1876). Hershey: IGI Global.
22. Jouini, M., Ben Arfa, L., & Ben Aissa, A. (2014). Classification of security threats in information systems. *Procedia Computer Science, 32*, 489–496. ANT/SEIT 2014.
23. Jouini, M., Ben Arfa, L., Ben Aissa, A., & Mili, A. (2012). An economic model of security threats for cloud computing systems. In *Proceedings of International Conference on Cyber Security, Cyber Warfare and Digital Forensic (CyberSec)* (pp. 100–105).
24. Kumar, P. R., Raj, P. H., & Jelciana, P. (2018). Exploring data security issues and solutions in cloud computing. In *International Conference on Smart Computing and Communications (ICSCC2017)* (Vol. 125, pp. 691–697).
25. Lacey, T. H., Mills, R. F., Mullins, B. E., Raines, R. A., Oxley, M. E., & Rogers, S. K. (2011). RIPsec - Using reputation based multilayer security to protect MANETs. *Computers and Security, 31*(1), 122–136.
26. Mell, P., & Grance, T. (2009). Effectively and securely using the cloud computing paradigm. In *ACM Cloud Computing Security Workshop*.
27. Mell, P., & Grance, T. (2011). *The NIST Definition of Cloud Computing*. NIST Special Publication 800-145. Gaithersburg: National Institute of Standards and Technology.
28. Ming-Chang, L. (2014). Information security risk analysis methods and research trends: AHP and fuzzy comprehensive method. *International Journal of Computer Science & Information Technology, 6*, 29–45.
29. Mohammed, A., Abdullah, A., Phu, D., & Bala, S. (2012). Information security threats classification pyramid. In *Proceedings of IEEE 24th International Conference on Advanced Information Networking and Applications Workshops (WAINA)* (pp. 208–221).
30. M'rhaoaurh, I., Okar, C., Namir, A., & Chafiq, N. (2018). Challenges of cloud computing use: A systematic literature review. In *MATEC Web of Conferences 200* (00007).
31. Ramadianti, N., Medard, P., & Mganga, C. (2011). *Enhancing information security in cloud computing services using SLA based metrics*. School of Computing Blekinge Institute of Technology SE-371 79 Karlskrona Sweden, Master's Thesis.
32. Ravi Kumar, P., Herbert Rajb, P., & Jelcianac, P. (2018). Exploring data security issues and solutions in cloud computing. In *6th International Conference on Smart Computing and Communications* (Vol. 125, pp. 691–697).
33. Rok, B., & Bork, J. (2013). A quantitative model for information security risk management. *Engineering Management Journal, 25*, 25–37.

34. Shiu, S., Baldwin, A., Beres, Y., Mont, M. C., & Duggan, G. (2011). Economic methods and decision-making by security professionals. In *The Tenth Workshop on the Economics of Information Security (WEIS)*.
35. Singh, A., & Chatterjee, K. (2017). Cloud security issues and challenges: A survey. *Journal of Network and Computer Applications, 79*, 88–115.
36. Singh, S., Jeong, Y., & Park, J. H. (2016). A survey on cloud computing security: Issues, threats, and solutions. *Journal of Network and Computer Applications, 75*, 200–222.
37. Speaks, S. (2010). Reliability and MTBF overview. *Vicor Reliability Engineering*.
38. Stergiou, C., Psannis, K. E., Kim, B., & Gupta, B. (2018). Secure integration of IoT and cloud computing. *Future Generation Computer Systems, 78*, 964–975.
39. Subramanian, N., & Jeyaraj, N. (2018). Recent security challenges in cloud computing. *Computers & Electrical Engineering, 71*, 28–42.
40. The Center for Internet Security (CIS). (2009). The CIS Security Metrics v1.0.0.
41. Wooley, P. S. (2011). *Identifying cloud computing security risks*. Technical report, 7 University of Oregon Eugene.
42. Yang, M., Jiang, R., Gao, T., Xie, W., & Wang, J. (2018). Research on cloud computing security risk assessment based on information entropy and Markov chain. *IJ Network Security, 20*(4), 664–673.

Chapter 4
A Novel AckIBE-Based Secure Cloud Data Management Framework

Dharavath Ramesh and Syam Kumar Pasupuleti

Abstract A smart grid of cloud includes various operations and other measures like smart meters, smart appliances, and renewable energy efficiency resources. The primary issues of this grid are how to manage various kinds of front-end devices such as smart meters and power assets efficiently and also, to efficiently process an enormous amount of data of participating devices. Since the cloud environment possesses various properties like scalability, cost saving, energy saving, and flexibility, it can serve as an efficient entrant to face these issues and challenges. This chapter introduces a more secure smart cloud computing framework-based AckIBE for data management, which we term as *"Smart-Model."* The aim is to construct a hierarchical structure of homogeneous and heterogeneous cloud centers that delivers various types of computing services to support big data analysis and information management. Furthermore, we introduce a security-related solution based on acknowledgment identity-based encryption (*AckIBE*), signature and proxy re-encryption to face critical security issues of the proposed framework. Additionally, we introduce acknowledgments sent by the end-user to the provider to ensure that the data have been received by the end-user and not lost in the environment of cloud communication.

Keywords Cloud data · Secure management · Smart model · Identity-based encryption

D. Ramesh (✉)
Department of Computer Science and Engineering, Indian Institute of Technology (ISM),
Dhanbad, Jharkhand, India
e-mail: ramesh.d.in@ieee.org

S. K. Pasupuleti
Department of Computer Science and Engineering, Institute for Development and Research in
Banking Technology, Hyderabad, India
e-mail: psyamkumar@idrbt.ac.in

© Springer Nature Switzerland AG 2020   91
B. B. Gupta et al. (eds.), *Handbook of Computer Networks and Cyber Security*,
https://doi.org/10.1007/978-3-030-22277-2_4

1   Introduction

While comparing traditional power grids with smart grids, it is found that smart grid models ensure improvement in terms of reliability, substantiality, and efficiency of computing services [1]. Although smart grids provide various advantages to electrical-related grids, their inclusion and accuracy is limited to smaller locations. Various challenges and issues recommend that smart grids to be deployed in larger capacities. Information management is concerned with the management of gathering, storing, and processing the information [2–4]. At the same time, there is needed to handle and manage large quantities of data that contain the selection, deployment, and inclusion of the data, monitoring the data, and analysis of the data of smart cloud models. Big data in the smart cloud models are created from several sources. These sources can be utilization activities of the users; phase-wise data used for storage and retrievals; data on energy consumption used by various smart location meters; management, maintenance, and control over the data. Other parameters also include network-related data acquired by operational devices such as servers and virtual machines, not directly obtained through the measurement but widely used in decision making.

The measurement of big data in terms of power utilities is increasing exponentially. By the year 2020, it is estimated that the number of smart operational meters of various cloud models of various continents will reach 650 million, whereas China is predicted to install about 450 million smart operational meters by that date. Smart grids usually require real-time processing, any delay in which may lead to a serious consequence in the whole system.

1.1   Support of Cloud Computing

Cloud computing has various advantages such as energy efficiency, scalability, flexibility, agility, and cost saving [5]. This has made it a significant model of computing in the near future. The cloud in the form of smart models addresses the issue of large-scale information and also responsible for a high energy and cost saving platform. This is due to (1) high scalability in order to deal with the amount of information being processed and (2) efficient utilization of resources in the corresponding data centers. Cloud environment also yields faster computation, efficient storage, and distributed computing facility to manage the big data. To process the potential of big data, there is a need to acquire new data analysis algorithms and approaches to manage the growth of enormous unexpected data. With the help of under managed cloud infrastructure, a service provider can provide better, cheaper, and more reliable cloud services to the consumers and end-users. Some of the related properties of operational grid and some cloud models in the form of smart-cloud models are analyzed to validate the relationship between them [6]. Motivated by the work presented in [27], in this paper, we propose a secure

Smart Cloud Framework (i.e., Smart Model) based AckIBE in the management of big data in homogeneous and heterogeneous cloud data centers. This chapter has threefold contributions:

- Introduction of smart-model: A framework based on cloud computing to perform information management of big data in the form of smart models that gives reasonable scalability as well as security.
- An identity-based encryption-based security solution is introduced for the proposed smart-model of IBE and identity-based proxy re-encryption to provide secure communication.
- We further introduce acknowledgments as AckIBE and show how messages along with signatures and the acknowledgments are sent in a hierarchical cloud environment from one level to another.

The rest of this chapter is organized as follows. Section 2 reviews the related work. Sections 3 and 4 present the proposed Smart-Model with possible security solutions. In a particular manner, Sect. 3 emphasizes the proposed methodology of Smart-Model architecture while Sect. 4 emphasizes related solutions based on AckIBE. Section 5 illustrates the security solutions and Sect. 6 presents the related schemes for secure framework. Finally, Sect. 7 demonstrates the security analysis followed by conclusions and future scope in Sect. 8.

2   Related Literature

2.1   Security Approaches of Smart Model

Smart model management of information generally consists of three main tasks, namely gathering, processing, and storing of information. For gathering of information, since smart models accumulate huge information from different kinds of devices located at different locations; several solutions have been introduced to address this challenge [2, 4, 10]. To manage the challenge of interoperability, a proposal to standardize the data structures is used in smart grids is proposed [11].

Since the deployment in smart grid is large, it suffers from several security vulnerabilities [24]. Authors of [12–15] introduced different methodologies to acquire the security challenges with respect to the processing of information of smart meters. Wei et al. [17] respectively proposed to protect smart model against cyber-attacks. Zhang et al. [16] proposed frameworks of security which are used in controlling the consistency of the security requirements of all the components of smart model. An authentication approach using digital signatures and time stamps is proposed by Rogers et al. [18]. As discussed in [8, 19, 20], identity-based cryptography is considered as a good candidate for secure cloud computing.

Authors of [21, 22, 28–30] introduced various security architectures for efficient cloud data storage. A methodology proposed in [25] discusses identity-based signature (IB-S) schemes in the non-hierarchical-based environment of cloud. The work proposed in [26] constructs an agreement protocol named IB-key in the environment of general grid computation whereas the proposed work provides security based on IB-encryption/signature and IB proxy re-encryption schemes to the proposed model.

3 Basic IB Schemes

There are two different blocks in cryptography for the security of the Smart-Model, namely identity-based encryption (IB-E) and identity-based signature schemes (IB-S) which are available. Li et al. [25] proposed identity-based cryptography to remove the need to check whether the certificates are valid in the traditional public_key scenario. In the scheme of IB-E, the generator of the key named private_key (PKG) with a reliable party firstly produces secret key called master_key (mk) and a related parameter known as params.

The private keys are distributed in the form of digital certificates which are issued in normal public key schemes. The PKG authenticates users and then sends them the private keys with respect to their identities. Any sender who possesses IDrec enciphers an original plain-text PT(M) into a ciphertext C by executing the Encrypt algorithm. When ciphertext C is obtained, the receiver deciphers C by executing the decryption algorithm taking input as the KIDrec, the private key received from the party PKG.

Similarly, the description of an identity-based signature scheme [8] is proposed as follows. As soon as the signer provides user identity IDsig, the party computes the private_key as KIDsig with respect to the IDsig by executing the extraction algorithm taking input as the secret master key mk. By executing the sign algorithm, the signer signs with PT(M) to obtain a corresponding signature using KIDsig. Both the IB-E and IB-S does not use digital certificates, but provide certification for the each user. The user, who registered his/her identity and received his/her private key can only decrypt using the decryption procedure or create a valid signature. The signature scheme IB-S had already been proposed by Shamir [8], but the practical realization of IB-E was achieved in [7]. Hierarchical identity-based cryptography is the extension of identity-based cryptography [23] in such a manner that the root PKG delegates private key generation and identity authentication to other users that act as lower-level PKGs.

3.1 Other IB Schemes

The process of proxy re-encryption makes a proxy to change the ciphertext created using the public key of Alice in such a way that the changed ciphertext can be deciphered using the private key of another party Bob. Ateniese et al. [20] introduced the first fully functioning proxy re-encryption scheme. After Ateniese et al.'s work, numerous proxy re-encryption schemes with different functionalities have been introduced. Ramesh et al. proposed an e-Stream-based secure dynamic updation policy for secure cloud storage. In this, the authors examined a stream cipher called ChaCha20 to provide the security for efficient data storage dynamically [21]. Xiaming Hu et al. proposed Secure and Efficient Identity-Based Proxy Signature Scheme in the Standard Model Based on Computational Diffie–Hellman Problem on proxy signature scheme [22].

4 Secure Smart Model

In this section, we illustrate the system construction with its architecture, component views, and flow of information management. Smart-Model denotes a framework that provides scalable, flexible, and secured transformation of data designed for smart-models and uses cloud computing technology. Here, we have adopted an idea to construct the model in three different layers of hierarchy as: Top-Cloud, Regional-Cloud, and End-user levels. The first and second level consists of cloud computing centers whereas the last level consists of end-user intelligent devices. The cloud at the topmost level takes the charge of managing and handling the participated devices and collection of data at various regional cloud centers. On the other side, the regional cloud computing devices handle lower hierarchical level located front-end intelligent devices, which are at a level lower than the computing entities (centers) of regional cloud (i.e., Homogeneous region) with the data transmitted from participating devices. Since smart grids are sensitive and needed strict protection, information leakage of any kind should be prevented in smart grids else it may lead to fatal consequences. In this framework, we further introduce a security solution in the form of IB-Encryption, Signature, and IB proxy re-encryption schemes [7–9]. The advantage of using identity-based encryption over traditional public key encryption scheme is that the former uses identities instead of digital certificate which depend upon public key infrastructure.

This saves the resource utilization for performing computation and resolve scalability problems. Also, in order to ensure that data reach the destined receiver and not get lost in the large cloud environment, we introduce acknowledgment to be sent by receivers to the senders. These acknowledgments are also sent in an encrypted form on receiving the acknowledgment the senders decrypt it and gets the concerned information. The architecture used is drawn in Fig. 4.1.

4.1 Smart-Model: System Architecture

In this section, we brief about the proposed architecture. The overview of the proposed model is shown in Fig. 4.2. This model includes a constructed grid, which

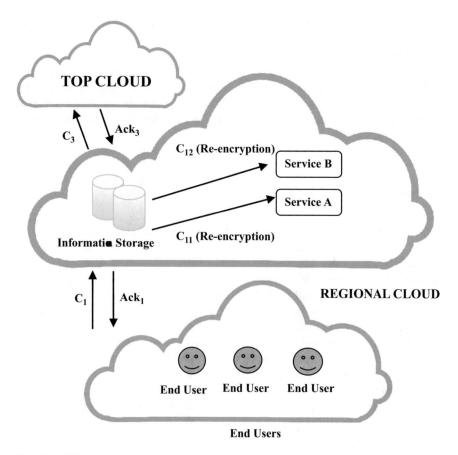

Fig. 4.1 Architecture used in the system

is partitioned into segmented regions. A cloud computing center handles these regions. The computing center is arranged and managed either by public or private cloud offerings. The basic functionality of any regional center is to handle end-user devices which are situated in the same locality (i.e., corresponding region) and also to give a primary level of processing of data that comes from the participated active devices. The main computing center at the top level is responsible to manage and process the suitable information data for the participated grids. And also, the center is responsible for the deployment of the following services that fall under cloud computing.

Infrastructure-as-a-Service (IaaS) This service is provided with on-demand basis, which makes resources available to all the applications and services deployed. The basic functionalities of management in the proposed model such as collection of data, processing, and storage are managed under this service.

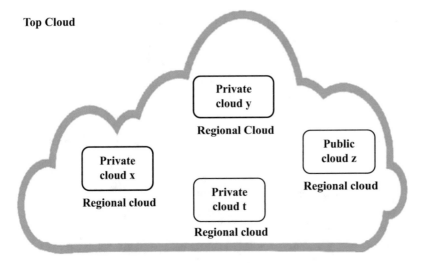

Fig. 4.2 Architecture of the smart frame

Software-as-a-Service (SaaS) This service deploys the required services of a smart model at the top of the system. For example, required services that enable customers to save and optimize their usage of energy [20], e.g., GPM.

Platform-as-a-Service (PaaS) This service offers different tools and library functions responsible for the development of cloud computing services and applications. Since there are numerous applications which are required to support various security offerings to permit legal interceptions, it is convenient to have platform-as-a-service that has these inbuilt requirements for the implementation of the applications.

Data-as-a-Service (DaaS) For providing relevant information for statistics purpose, DaaS can be deployed. Smart grid data are usually enormously large in amount. It serves beneficial to provide such statistics services for service users.

4.2   Component Views

In this framework, we propose four basic functional clusters as follows. These types of services are illustrated in Fig. 4.3.

Information Storage All the information on smart grid collected from front-end intelligent devices like smart meters, etc., are kept in main storage, which are developed to get information from various modes of transportation with the help of wired channel as well as wireless channel. The related statistics exist in the corresponding cluster.

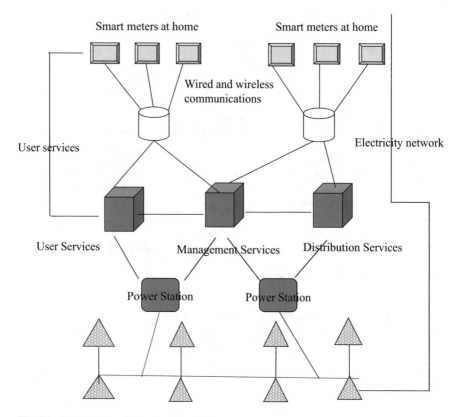

Fig. 4.3 Functionality of cloud service clusters

User Services All the services that an electricity consumer uses fall under this service. The examples include monitoring, controlling, and optimizing the use of their electric utilization. This sort of service includes most of the SaaS and also PaaS that provides libraries for user services.

Control and Management Services All services with respect to system management like governance service, monitor, task scheduling, and security fall under this category.

Electricity Distribution Services The services related to electricity distribution fall under this category. Examples include optimization service, measuring quality of service measurement, services pertaining to distribution.

4.3 Flow of Information Management

As smart grids are supposed to handle the enormous amount of data, it is challenging to efficiently manage the information flows in the system. In our proposed Smart-Model, a centralized service is suggested to manage the flow of information. The required inputs are taken from the clusters which are in service and other statistics such as size of the data and the time at which the data are entered into the cluster. Taking these inputs, the service creates a basic schedule of information flow. The schedule gives the description of the beginning and end of information flows and also how their processing is done (i.e., type of operations used on the flows with their locations). For execution, participated centers with their corresponding clusters need to go through the schedules.

It is important to notice that since the amount of information and related requests in the model may vary time by time, every flow has got an elapsed time. Once this elapsed time expires, a new schedule has to be inclined and sent to the participating centers again. A related smart model flow is shown in Fig. 4.4.

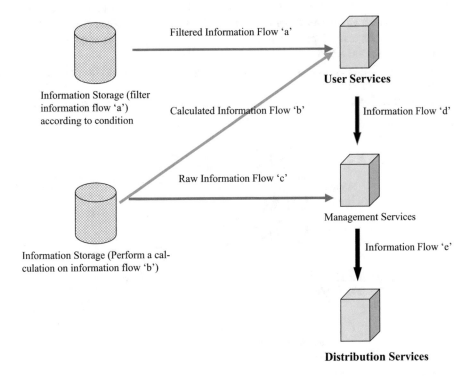

Fig. 4.4 Flow of information schedule

5 Security Solutions for Smart Model

5.1 Model Description

In this section, we assume the following parameters while realizing the security framework. The working of this framework is illustrated in Fig. 4.5 in the form of proxy re-encryption methodology.

- There exists a generator of private PKG that issues private keys for the entities participating in the hierarchy whenever they register. It is assumed that the party PKG is responsible and possesses the capacity for maintaining the Smart-Model generally at different levels with reliable credentials.
- Unique strings are used as IDs to identify the existing cloud at the top level and end-users assigned. These are used as either to encrypt the original message or to verify the signature.
- Every participating entity receives its related private key based on the identity which can decipher the ciphertext that includes the confidential data.
- Every participating entity sends an encrypted data to the entity that is participating its peer level. So, the end-user can send the data to the regional cloud entities. Similarly, the entities present in the regional cloud are able to send encrypted data to the cloud existing at a higher level.
- Every participating entity authenticates shared data through its private key received from PKG.
- Every level, which receives the data, can send the acknowledgment to the sender.

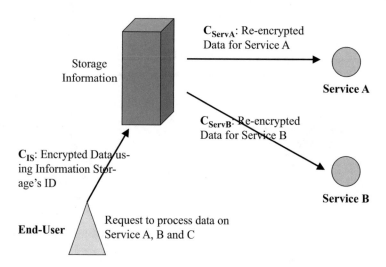

Fig. 4.5 Proxy re-encryption

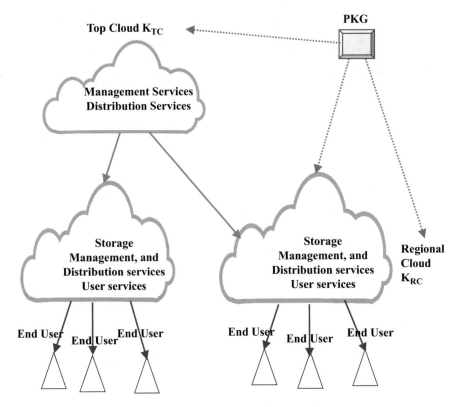

Fig. 4.6 Hierarchical architecture

Based on the above assumptions, we construct the architecture as depicted in Fig. 4.6. The hierarchy of the top cloud contains distribution services, management services, and power stations. The top cloud manages the regional clouds. These regional clouds contain basic user services and storages of information. Below regional clouds, there exists a lower hierarchy of smart (intelligent) end-user devices.

5.2 Key Generation

Setup With the help of a parameter γ, the *PKG* produces a secret key, also known as master key *mkey* and a parameters' set *params*. This *params* is distributed to end-users and all the clouds.

Extract_TCKey: After getting the identity TC of top cloud, the party PKG produces a private key K_{TC}, in correspondence with the identity TC by executing *Extract()*, the extraction algorithm of the private key in which TC is taken as input. It is represented as:

$$K_{TC} \leftarrow \text{Extract\_TCKey} \,(params, mkey, TC)$$

Extract_ISKey: After getting a IS as Information Storage's identity, the PKG produces a private key K_{IS}, with the identity of IS by executing the extraction algorithm of private key *Extract()* in which IS is taken as input. It is represented as:

$$K_{IS} \leftarrow \text{Extract\_ISKey} \,(params, mkey, IS)\,.$$

Extract_ServiceKey: After getting Service A's identity *ServA* in the regional cloud, the PKG produces a key K_{ServA} as private key in correspondence with the identity *ServA* by executing *Extract()*, the extraction algorithm of the private key in which *ServA* is taken as input. It is represented as:

$$K_{ServA} \leftarrow \text{Extract\_ServiceKey} \,(params, mkey, ServA)\,.$$

Extract_EUKey: After getting the identity EU of top cloud, the party PKG produces a private key K_{EU} in correspondence with the identity EU by executing *Extract()*, the extraction algorithm of private key in which EU is taken as input. It is represented as:

$$K_{EU} \leftarrow \text{Extract\_EUKey} \,(params, mkey, EU)\,.$$

5.2.1   Encryption to Top Cloud

a) *Encrypt_to_TC*: Any information storage can encipher M, an original message into a ciphertext C_{TC} by executing *Encrypt()*, the IBE encryption algorithm taking input as Information Storage's identity TC and params. We represent the encryption as follows:

$$C_{IS} \leftarrow \text{Encrypt\_to\_TC} \,(params, TC, M)\,.$$

b) *Decrypt_TC*: The top cloud deciphers the obtained C (Ciphertext) to deciphered message *M* by executing *Decrypt IBE decryption algorithm* with the key K_{TC} generated in correspondence with the information storage's identity *TC*. The decryption is presented as follows:

$$M \leftarrow \text{Decrypt\_TC} \,(params, K_{TC,}\, C_{TC})\,.$$

5.2.2   Encryption to IS

(a) *Encrypt_to_IS*: Any end-user can encipher M into a ciphertext C_{IS} by executing *Encrypt()*, the *IBE encryption algorithm* taking input as identity IS of Information Storage and params. We represent the encryption as follows:

$$C_{IS} \leftarrow \text{Encrypt\_to\_IS } (params, IS, M)$$

(b) *Decrypt_IS*: Any regional cloud can decipher the obtained ciphertext C to M by executing IBE decryption algorithm with its private key K_{IS} in correspondence with its identity IS. This represents the decryption as follows:

$$M \leftarrow \text{Decrypt\_IS} \left(params, K_{IS}, C_{IS}\right)$$

5.2.3   Proxy Re-encryption

(a) *RencKGen*: The storage of regional cloud produces a re-encryption key $\text{RencK}_{IS} \rightarrow_{ServA}$ by taking input as K_{IS}, the self-private key, IS, ServA. This is represented as:

$$\text{RencK}_{IS} \rightarrow_{ServA} \leftarrow \text{RencKGen} \left(K_{IS}, IS, ServA\right)$$

(b) *Re_encrypt*: The ciphertext C_{IS} is re-encrypted with the help of the re-encryption key $\text{RencK}_{IS} \rightarrow_{ServA}$ and receives a ciphertext C_{ServA}. This process is represented by $C_{ServA} \leftarrow \text{Re\_encrypt } (\text{RenK}_{IS->ServA}, C_{IS})$.
(c) *Decrypt_Service*: The service A deciphered ciphertext C_{ServA} with the help of its private key K_{ServA}. It is represented as $M \leftarrow \text{Decrypt\_Service}(K_{ServA}, C_{ServA})$.

5.2.4   Signature Generation by Top Cloud

(a) *Sign_TC*: Any user at end level is able to produce a signature δ for the original message (M) with the help of the private key K_{IS} with respect to its identity TC. This is represented as follows: $\delta \leftarrow \text{Sign\_TC}(params, K_{IS}, M)$.
(b) *Verify_TC*: Verification of the signature δ of message M with the help of identity of the end-user and parameter *params*. This is represented by $w \leftarrow \text{Verify\_TC}(params, IS, \delta, M)$. The result w denotes *"acceptance"* or *"rejection."* Verification of the signatures produced by a service in a regional cloud is done in a similar manner.

5.2.5 Signature Generation in Regional Cloud

(a) *Sign_IS*: End-user produces a signature δ for the original message M with the help of the key generated as K_{IS} with respect to its identity IS. This is represented as follows:

$$\delta \leftarrow \text{Sign\_IS} \left(params, K_{IS,} M \right).$$

(b) *Verify_IS*: Verification of the signature δ of message M with the help of identity of the end-user and parameter params. This is represented by d ←Verify_IS(params, IS, δ,M). Verification of the signatures produced by a service is done in a similar manner.

5.2.6 Signature Generation by End-Users

(a) *Sign_EU*: End-user produces a signature δ for the original message M with the help of the key K_{ServA} with respect to its identity EU. This is represented as follows:

$$\delta \leftarrow \text{Sign\_EU} \left(params, K_{EU,} M \right).$$

(b) *Verify_EU*: Verification of the signature δ of message M with the help of identity of the end-user and parameter *params*. This is represented by d ←Verify_EU(params, EU, δ,M). The result d is either "accept" or "reject."

Acknowledgment by the Regional Cloud Any level, whether topmost cloud, regional cloud or the end-user can send the acknowledgment to any sender level. It is also sent in an encrypted form so that the recipient can decrypt it. The same encryption procedure is used.

6 Schemes for Secure Framework

The framework discussed below uses an IBE scheme [6] and identity-based proxy re-encryption scheme [1]. Both the schemes use a bilinear pairing $e: G \times G \rightarrow G_T$. Here, the groups G and G_T are of prime order, which has the following properties:

- Bilinear: $\forall r, s \in Z_p^*$, $e(g^r, h^s) = e(g, h)^{rs}$.
- Non-degeneracy: It follows: $e(g, h) \neq 1$.
- Practically, e must be computable.

6.1   Confidentiality

The below-mentioned parameters propagate the knowledge of generating keys.

- *Key_Setup*: The group *PKG* produces G and G_T of order p as a prime and an admissible pairing e: $G \times G \rightarrow G_T$, a generator $g \in G$ and a hash function H_1: $\{0,1\}_* \rightarrow G$ and H_2:$G_T \rightarrow \{0,1\}^n$ for a positive integer n where n is the size of the plaintext. We then take random a where $a \in g^u$. The top cloud sets secret master key $mkey = u$ and a set of public parameters $params = (G,G_T,e,g,a,H_1,H_2)$. The parameter *params* is distributed to top, regional, and end-users by *PKG*.
- *Extract_TC_Key*: After getting the identity of top cloud TC, the PKG calculates $H1(TC)^u \in G$ and returns the private key $\boldsymbol{K}_{TC} = H1(TC)^u$.
- *Extract_IS_Key*: After getting the top cloud's identity IS, the PKG calculates H1 $(IS)^u \in G$ and returns the private key $\boldsymbol{K}_{IS} = H1(TC)^u$.
- *Extract_Service_Key*: After getting the top cloud's identity ServA, the PKG calculates H1 $(ServA)^u \in G$ and returns the private key $\boldsymbol{K}_{ServA} = H1(ServA)^u$.
- *Extract_User_Key*: After getting a user's identity EU, the PKG calculates H1 $(EU)^u \in G$ and returns the private key $\boldsymbol{K}_{EU} = H1(EU)^u$.

6.1.1   Encryption to Top Cloud

- *Extract_to_TC*: A regional cloud entity can encipher an original message M with the help of *params* parameter and the identity TC of top cloud using following calculations. Take random value v where, $v \in Z_p$. Calculate C1 $= g^v$ and C2 $=$ M. e(a, H1(TC))^u. Later, we get output ciphertext as $C_{TC} = (C1,C2)$.
- *Decrypt_TC*: With the help of private key $\boldsymbol{K}_{TC} = H1(TC)^v$, the top cloud can decrypt a received ciphertext $C_{TC} = (C1,C2)$ into M, where M $=$ C2/(e(C1, $\boldsymbol{K}_{TC}$)).

6.1.2   Encryption to Information Storage

- *Extract_to_IS*: Any regional cloud entity can encipher an original message M with the help of the top cloud's identity TC and parameter params and using following calculations. Take random value v where, $v \in Z_p$. Calculate C1$=g^v$ and C2 $=$ M. e(a, H1(TC))^v. Later, we get output ciphertext as $C_{IS} = (C1, C2)$.
- *Decrypt_IS*: With the private key $\boldsymbol{K}_{IS} = H1(IS)^v$, the top cloud can decrypt a received ciphertext $C_{IS} = (C1,C2)$ into M, where M $=$ C2/(e(C1, $\boldsymbol{K}_{IS}$)).

6.1.3   Proxy Re-encryption to Information Storage

- *RenKGen*: A Re-encryption key is received by an information storage possessing identity as IS by calculating $RenK_{IS->ServA} = (RK_1, RK_2, RK_3)$. Here we

compute $RK_1 = g^x$ and $RK_2 = L.e(a, H_1(ServA))^x$ and $RK_3 = K_{IS}^{-1}.H_2(T)$. We take random $x \in Z_p$. and $L \in G_T$.
- *Re_encrypt*: We have the Re-encryption key $RenK_{IS->ServA} = (RK_1, RK_2, RK_3)$. The ciphertext $C_{IS} = (C1, C2)$ is re-encrypted by service A and a new ciphertext is calculated as $C_{ServA} = (C1, C2, e(C1, RK3), RK1, RK2)$.
- *Decrypt_Service*: Let $C_{servA} = (C_1', C_2', RK_1', RK_2') = (C1, C2.e(C1, RK3), RK_1, RK_2)$.

Since we have $K_{servA} = H1(ServA)^u$, the service A calculates $L = RK_2' / e(K_{servA}, RK_1')$. Later, we calculate $M = C_2' / e(C_1', H_2(L))$.

6.2 Authentication Service

Following is the description of the IBS scheme that makes use of IBS scheme Gentry and Silverberg has drawn from bilinear pairings.

Key Generation Another hash function represented as $H_2 : \{0,1\}^* \rightarrow G$ will be used in the signature generation. We have a master key of PKG as u_0 and a public parameter's set params $= (G, GT, e, g0, b, H1, H2)$. Here, we take $b = g_0^{u0}$ as random. We have similar computations of extraction of key to regional cloud and top cloud as that of scheme of IBE.

6.2.1 Signature Generation by End-User Cloud

Sign_EU Every regional cloud computes a signature ∂ for the M with the help of its private key $K_{TC} (= \boldsymbol{K} = g_1^{u0})$. First, calculate $g_1 = H_1(EU) \in G$ and $g_M = H_1(EU, M) \in G$. Then choose w randomly as $w \in Z_p$, and calculate $\partial_1 = \boldsymbol{K} . g_M^w$ and $\partial_2 = g_0^w$. Later, we get signature $\partial = (\partial 1, \partial 2)$ as the output.

Verify_EU Any participating entity can perform verification of the signature ∂ for the message M with the help of the params parameters and EU, the identity of the top cloud. For verification a verifier checks whether $e(g_0, \partial_1) = e(b, g_1) e(\partial_2, g_M)$.

7 Security Analysis

The IBE scheme's correctness can be proven easily. The proof of the scheme is as follows. Let $C_{ServA} = (C_1', C_2', RK_1', RK_2') = (C_1, C_2, e(C_1, RK3), RK_1, RK_2)$.

$$RK_2'/e\left(K_{servA}, RK_1'\right) = RK_2'/e\left(H_1(ServA)^u, RK_1\right)$$
$$= L.e(u, H_1(ServA))^x/e\left(H_1(ServA)^u, RK_1\right)$$
$$= L.e(g^u, H_1(ServA))^x/e\left(H_1(ServA)^u, RK_1\right)$$
$$= L.e\left(H_1(ServA)^u, g^x\right)/e\left(H_1(ServA)^u, RK_1\right)$$
$$= L.$$

$$C_2'/e\left(C_1', H_2(L)\right) = C_2.e(C_1, RK_3)/e(C_1, H_2(L))$$
$$= C_2.e\left(C_1, K_{IS}^{-1}.H_2(L)\right)/e(C_1, H_2(L))$$
$$= C_2.e\left(C_1, K_{IS}^{-1}\right)$$
$$= M.e(a, H_1(IS))^v.e\left(C_1, K_{IS}^{-1}\right)$$
$$= M.e\left(g^v, H_1(IS)^u\right).e\left(C_1, K_{IS}^{-1}\right)$$
$$= M.$$

The validity of the verification algorithm of the signature scheme can be proved as:

$$e(g_0, \partial_1) = e\left(g_0, K.g_M^w\right)$$
$$= e((g_0, K) \cdot e\left(g_0, g_M^w\right)$$
$$= e(g_0, g_1^{u_0})e\left(g_0^w, g_M\right)$$
$$= e\left(g_0^{u_0}, g_1\right)e\left(g_0^w, g_M\right)$$
$$= e(b, g_1)\ e(\partial_2, g_M)$$

7.1 Customized Platform

We provide a particularstate of the transition through the usage of the platform. We have participated entities as Top cloud, entities in the Regional Cloud and end-user. The scenario shows private key generation of the entities, Signature Generation and Encryption, Decryption and Signature Verification, Acknowledgment sent by a sender and received by the receiver. Let the confidential message be *"SM8||75KW||Kolkata."* The scenario is represented in Fig. 4.7, in the below manner.

8 Conclusions and Future Scope

This chapter introduces a secure framework (i.e., smart model) which is a general framework used for managing big data information in smart grids. The proposed framework is based on cloud computing technology and is formulated at three levels of hierarchy, i.e., top, regional, and end-user levels. The top cloud manages the

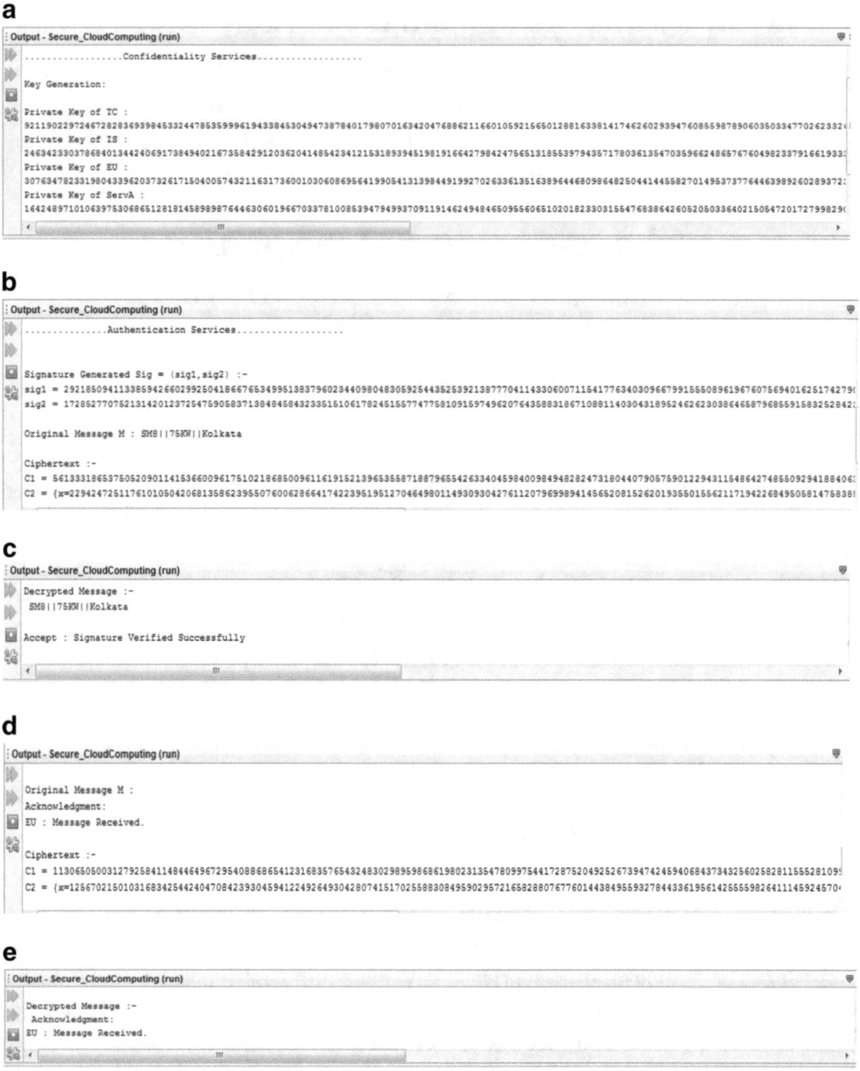

a

b

c

d

e

Fig. 4.7 Basic Operations of the model. (**a**) Registration of entities in Regional Cloud, Top Cloud, End-user, Service A. (**b**) Signature Generation and Encryption by the sender. (**c**) Decryption and Signature Verification by the receiver. (**d**) Acknowledgment Sent by the receiver to the sender. (**e**) Acknowledgment received by the sender. (**a**) *First step*: The entities of two clouds and end-user are registered and their private keys are generated. (**b**) *Second step*: In the second step: The meter of the smart_model uses the regional center identity to encipher its confidential message with respect to the daily consumption of electricity. Along with this, a signature is also generated based on IBS scheme and both the encrypted message (ciphertext) and the signature are sent to the Regional center (server). (**c**) *Third step*: The received message is decrypted by the regional center using its generated private key and also verified for authentication using a verification process of IBS scheme. (**d**) *Fourth step*: The regional center sends an encrypted acknowledgment to the sender (here smart meter). The encryption and decryption process is done by using the same IBE scheme. (**e**) *Fifth step:* The smart meter receives the acknowledgment by decrypting the received data

regional cloud whereas every regional cloud handles data got from various front-end intelligent devices. Since the cloud environment needs a security solution, two strategies named identity-based cryptography and identity-based proxy re-encryption have been provided. Thus, the proposed security framework is scalable, flexible, and secure. Additionally, we applied acknowledgment scheme so that the sender receives the feedback from the destined receiver to ensure that the data is not lost and has been delivered successfully. We have also described the architecture showing that how entities in regional cloud, top cloud, and end-user interact and transfer confidential data, signature, and acknowledgment within the system.

The efficiency of this framework can be further extended by using Identity-Based proxy signature scheme in the standard model based on the Computational Diffie Hellman Problem. This provides tight security reduction and more complete security, including resisting the delegator attack. It has more efficient performance and less computational cost than other similar existing schemes. Also, apart from this scheme, Identity-based Conditional Proxy Re-encryption can be used. This scheme is secure against the chosen ciphertext and identity attack in the random oracle model.

Acknowledgment This work is supported by the Indian Institute of Technology (ISM), Dhanbad, Govt. of India. The authors wish to express their gratitude and heartiest thanks to the Department of Computer Science and Engineering, Indian Institute of Technology (ISM), Dhanbad, India for providing their research support.

References

1. Farhangi, H. (2010). The path of the smart grid. *IEEE Power and Energy Magazine, 8*(1), 18.
2. Bojkovic, Z., & Bakmaz, B. (2012). Smart grid communications architecture: a survey and challenges. In *Proceedings of the 11th International Conference on Applied Computer and Applied Computational Science (ACACOS)* (pp. 83–89).
3. McDaniel, P., & McLaughlin, S. (2009). Security and privacy challenges in the smart grid. *IEEE Security and Privacy, 7*(3), 75–77.
4. Fan, Z., Kulkarni, P., Gormus, S., Efthymiou, C., Kalogridis, G., Sooriyabandara, M., et al. (2013). Smart grid communications: overview of research challenges, solutions, and standardization activities. *IEEE Communications Surveys and Tutorials, 15*(1), 21–38.
5. Mell, P., & Grance, T. (2011). The NIST definition of cloud computing.
6. Rusitschka, S., Eger, K., & Gerdes, C. (2010). Smart grid data cloud: a model for utilizing cloud computing in the smart grid domain. In: *Smart Grid Communications (SmartGridComm), 2010 First IEEE International Conference on* (pp. 483–488). IEEE.
7. Boneh, D., & Franklin, M. (2001). Identity-based encryption from the Weil pairing. In *Annual International Cryptology Conference* (pp. 213–229). Berlin: Springer.
8. Shamir, A. (1984). Identity-based cryptosystems and signature schemes. In *Workshop on the theory and application of cryptographic techniques* (pp. 47–53). Berlin: Springer.
9. Green, M., & Ateniese, G. (2007). Identity-based proxy re-encryption. In *Applied cryptography and network security* (pp. 288–306). Berlin: Springer.
10. Wang, W., Xu, Y., & Khanna, M. (2011). A survey on the communication architectures in smart grid. *Computer Networks, 55*(15), 3604–3629.
11. Dinh, H. T., Lee, C., Niyato, D., & Wang, P. (2013). A survey of mobile cloud computing: architecture, applications, and approaches. *Wireless Communications and Mobile Computing, 13*(18), 1587–1611.

12. Efthymiou, C., & Kalogridis, G. (2010). Smart grid privacy via anonymization of smart metering data. In *Smart Grid Communications (SmartGridComm), 2010 First IEEE International Conference on* (pp. 238–243). IEEE.
13. Kalogridis, G., Efthymiou, C., Denic, S. Z., Lewis, T. A., & Cepeda, R. (2010). Privacy for smart meters: towards undetectable appliance load signatures. In: *Smart Grid Communications (SmartGridComm), 2010 First IEEE International Conference on* (pp. 232–237). IEEE.
14. Li, H., Mao, R., Lai, L., & Qiu, R. C. (2010). Compressed meter reading for delay-sensitive and secure load report in smart grid. In: *Smart Grid Communications (SmartGridComm), 2010 First IEEE International Conference on* (pp. 114–119). IEEE.
15. Chu, C. K., Liu, J. K., Wong, J. W., Zhao, Y., & Zhou, J. (2013). Privacy-preserving smart metering with regional statistics and personal enquiry services. In *Proceedings of the 8th ACM SIGSAC Symposium on Information, Computer and Communications Security* (pp. 369–380). ACM.
16. Zhang, T., Lin, W., Wang, Y., Deng, S., Shi, C., & Chen, L. (2010). The design of information security protection framework to support smart grid. In *Power System Technology (POWERCON), 2010 International Conference on* (pp. 1–5), IEEE.
17. Wei, D., Lu, Y., Jafari, M., Skare, P., & Rohde, K. (2010). An integrated security system of protecting smart grid against cyber-attacks. In *Innovative smart grid technologies (ISGT), 2010* (pp. 1–7). IEEE.
18. Rogers, K. M., Klump, R., Khurana, H., Aquino-Lugo, A. A., & Overbye, T. J. (2010). An authenticated control framework for distributed voltage support on the smart grid. *IEEE Transactions on Smart Grid, 1*(1), 40–47.
19. Liang, K., Liu, J. K., Wong, D. S., & Susilo, W. (2014). An efficient cloud-based revocable identity-based proxy re-encryption scheme for public clouds data sharing. In *European symposium on research in computer security* (pp. 257–272). Cham: Springer.
20. Ateniese, G., Fu, K., Green, M., & Hohenberger, S. (2006). Improved proxy re-encryption schemes with applications to secure distributed storage. *ACM Transactions on Information and System Security (TISSEC), 9*(1), 1–30.
21. Ramesh, D., Mishra, R., & Edla, D. R. (2017). Secure data storage in cloud: an e-stream cipher-based secure and dynamic updation policy. *Arabian Journal for Science and Engineering, 42*(2), 873–883.
22. Hu, X., Zhang, X., Wang, J., Xu, H., Tan, W., & Yang, Y. (2017). Secure and efficient identity-based proxy signature scheme in the standard model based on computational Diffie–Hellman problem. *Arabian Journal for Science and Engineering, 42*(2), 639–649.
23. Gentry, C., & Silverberg, A. (2002). Hierarchical ID-based cryptography. In *International conference on the theory and application of cryptology and information security* (pp. 548–566). Berlin, Heidelberg: Springer.
24. Khurana, H., Hadley, M., Lu, N., & Frincke, D. A. (2010). Smart-grid security issues. *IEEE Security and Privacy, 8*(1), 81–85.
25. Li, H., Dai, Y., Tian, L., & Yang, H. (2009). Identity-based authentication for cloud computing. In *IEEE international conference on cloud computing* (pp. 157–166). Berlin: Springer.
26. Lim, H. W., & Paterson, K. G. (2005). Identity-based cryptography for grid security. In *e-Science and Grid Computing, 2005. First International Conference on* (10 pp). IEEE.
27. Baek, J., Vu, Q. H., Liu, J. K., Huang, X., & Xiang, Y. (2015). A secure cloud computing based framework for big data information management of smart grid. *IEEE Transactions on Cloud Computing, 3*(2), 233–244.
28. Ramesh, D., Mishra, R., & Pandit, A. K. (2018). An efficient stream cipher based secure and dynamic updation method for cloud data centre. In *International Conference on Soft Computing Systems* (pp. 505–516). Springer, Singapore.
29. Ramesh, D., Mishra, R., & Nayak, B. S. (2016). Cha-Cha 20: stream cipher based encryption for cloud data centre. In *Proceedings of the Second International Conference on Information and Communication Technology for Competitive Strategies*, ACM, 40
30. Ramesh, D., & Priya, R. (2016). Multi-authority scheme based CP-ABE with attribute revocation for cloud data storage. In *Microelectronics, Computing and Communications (MicroCom), 2016 International Conference on* (pp. 1–4). IEEE

Chapter 5
A Practicable Machine Learning Solution for Security-Cognizant Data Placement on Cloud Platforms

Rahul Vishwanath Kale, Bharadwaj Veeravalli, and Xiaoli Wang

Abstract While designing data placement strategies for cloud storage platforms, data security and data retrieval time are two equally important parameters that determine the quality of data placement. As these two parameters are generally mutually conflicting, it is imperative that we need to strike a balance between data security and retrieval time to assure the quality-of-service promised by the network/cloud service provider. To guarantee the data integrity of data stored on the network storage nodes in case of any threats or cyberattacks, the placement strategy should be adaptable to incorporate the threat characteristics. This is achieved by integrating machine intelligence to the network prone to attacks to identify the most vulnerable threat type for each node. This objective forms an imperative addendum to the attack resilient and retrieval time trade-off strategy (ARRT) strategy proposed in the literature to deploy as a practicable solution for a service provider. A set of Pareto-optimal solutions which strikes a balance between retrieval time and security based on inherent network properties by ARRT will be our initial condition for our machine learning model in this work. We take a radically different approach in which we attempt to identify the most vulnerable threat type for each node in the recommended Pareto-optimal solutions to minimize data loss through appropriate refinement of the existing data placement. This is achieved by supplementing the evolutionary algorithm with a machine learning model and we refer to this integrated and complete approach as security-cognizant data placement (SDP) strategy. In this study, based on the relevant performance metric that includes data integrity which is a measure of robustness, we evaluate and quantify our performance through rigorous discrete event simulations on arbitrary cloud topologies and demonstrate the impact of a neural network in delivering a superior performance.

R. V. Kale (✉) · B. Veeravalli
Department of Electrical and Computer Engineering, National University of Singapore, Singapore, Singapore
e-mail: elekrv@nus.edu.sg; elebv@nus.edu.sg

X. Wang
School of Computer Science and Technology, Xidian University, Xi'an, China
e-mail: wangxiaoli@mail.xidian.edu.cn

© Springer Nature Switzerland AG 2020
B. B. Gupta et al. (eds.), *Handbook of Computer Networks and Cyber Security*,
https://doi.org/10.1007/978-3-030-22277-2_5

Keywords Security · Retrieval time · Data placement · Machine learning

1 Introduction

With data-driven applications on the rise, fast and secure storage space is need of the
hour. Usefulness of such applications is usually characterized by the efficiency with
which it can obtain the accurate outcome. Customer data based financial systems,
sensor data-driven Internet of Things (IoT) based systems, driverless autonomous
vehicles in smart city initiatives rely on continuous processing of large amount of
data. Due to the sensitivity of information handled by these systems and the overall
concerns regarding security and privacy of cloud storage solutions, organizations
take a more cautious approach for entrusting cloud storage as viable choice for
their sensitive data. On the other hand, the data handled by large-scale applications
demands a scalable storage system with quick response time.

Strategic data placement can be effective in simultaneously addressing both of
the issues, time performance and data security, by striking a trade-off between them.
The cloud service provider (CSP) can implement these strategic data placements
through a data placement decision unit (as shown in Fig. 5.1) such that elite
customers can be assured maximum security for their stored data as per their
service agreement. Data fragmentation [5, 9, 12, 14] is a popular technique used to
achieve data security by splitting the file in smaller chunks of data and distributing
it over the network. Fragmentation ensures that even if the attacker gets hold of
a single fragment of data, no meaningful information is divulged. To improve
the data retrieval time, data replication [2, 4, 16, 18] is one of the widely used
techniques. By distributing multiple copies of the same data within the network, data
retrieval time can be reduced as there are more potential sites to retrieve the data.
Recent studies [8, 10, 13, 17, 20, 21] in cloud storage security and performance
improvement address these two problems individually. Strategically combining
the data fragmentation and data replication can assist in addressing both the data
security and retrieval time concerns simultaneously albeit with trade-offs among the

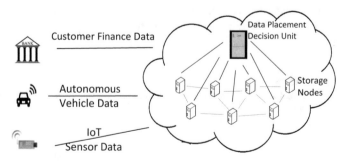

Fig. 5.1 System overview

two. Cyberattacks such as Trojans, Denial of Service (DoS), Distributed Denial of Service (DDoS), Packet Forging Attacks, Application Layer Attacks, Fingerprinting Attacks [7, 11] can lead to data compromise or data loss on a cloud storage system.

Each storage node on the cloud may host multiple applications and hence each node is susceptible to various kinds of threats and vulnerabilities. The information about the most likely threat on each node within given data placement solution, based on the applications hosted on the nodes as well as the historical information regarding the attacks on the network, may assist in improving overall security and quality of the data placement solution. The attack information can be obtained through logs in the network [1]. To identify the most potential threat for a given node, machine learning techniques can be quite useful. Machine learning approaches [3, 6, 22] can be used to classify the nodes in different threat categories depending on the applications hosted on the node and frequency of application-based attacks. They can be trained using attack graphs or attack models [24] designed to target a particular application or vulnerability. By using machine learning techniques, system can be made scalable and can be effectively applied to various cloud topologies. Such scalable and adaptive data placement strategies can be useful for addressing cloud storage security concerns in smart city applications [15, 26].

Our recent work reported in [25] conclusively demonstrated that ARRT, which obtains a set of Pareto-optimal solutions, offers users a balance between desired security and the retrieval time. We further assess the suggested placements using machine learning approaches, to assist in deciding placement of individual data chunks for improving the security. Although our solutions guarantee minimum retrieval time and maximum security level, the proposed scheme needs to be adaptable to maintain the data integrity in case of any threats. Only then the entire strategy would be a practicable approach. Hence, to make the study complete, our contributions in the paper are as follows:

- We attempt to use machine learning to classify the most vulnerable threat type for each node in the recommended placement solutions.
- We will present the types of features used to train the neural network as well as the overall strategy followed in the design.
- We evaluate the proposed strategy through extensive discrete event simulation model on cloud storage systems.

To the best of our literature knowledge, this study is one of its first kind to use a machine learning approach that takes into account attack characteristics explicitly for simultaneously optimizing the time and security performances.

The rest of the paper is organized as follows: In Sect. 2, we explore different technologies that are related to data security and time performance on cloud-based systems. In Sect. 3, we formulate the problem to be addressed and describe the system. In Sect. 4, we describe the neural network used to identify the most vulnerable threat type for each node. We illustrate the effectiveness of the proposed SDP strategy in Sect. 5 before concluding the paper in Sect. 6.

2 Related Work

Strategies for optimal data placement addressing data security and data retrieval problems have been extensively investigated in the literature.

Boru et al. in [2] utilize data replication in datacenters to improve the overall quality-of-service (QoS) by reducing the network delays and bandwidth usage with special focus on optimizing the energy efficiency. Data replication was effectively used to address key issues such as data availability, response time, and network congestion. Data replication is used for performance enhancement in [16] through combination of two strategies, first strategy to improve the QoS and second to minimize the replication number and cost. The authors in [4] present a policy for data replication specifically on a computational cloud environment which improves availability of the access to the data files and therefore improves the overall fault tolerance. These strategies which focus on improving the retrieval time performance by replication do not address the data security issue arising from additional data copies. Mansouri proposed new replica replacement approach to improve execution performance, network usage, replication frequency in data grids to maintain QoS while considering the security factors in [18]. The dynamic replica management approach selects a replica based on factors such as previous replica access, replica size, number of accesses, and security attributes to maintain response time and security. However, the solution suggested with this strategy does not provide users a choice to select a data placement solution that satisfies their time and security requirements, which is an important consideration of our proposed SDP strategy. Hudic et al. in [9] propose a data fragmentation approach to provide security and confidentiality for data stored on cloud platforms by classifying the data according to user requirements into different confidentiality levels to utilize selective encryption, thereby making this approach comparatively efficient to general data fragmentation and encryption. Work in [5] proposes enhanced data fragmentation technique to maintain data confidentiality even when data dependency exists among the data fragments. The information leakage issue is addressed by representing and solving the problem of minimum and closed fragments as constraint satisfaction problem. Data fragmentation is used to ensure sufficient data separation to avoid full encryption and to provide extra secrecy for distributed storage systems in [12]. However, these strategies do not take data retrieval time into consideration as additional overhead is involved in combining the data fragments. For cloud servers, different data fragmentation techniques such as simple fragmentation, predefined pattern, random pattern, encryption with random pattern were compared in [14] based on their worst case execution times for different file formats. Thus, we can strategically fuse data fragmentation and data replication in our proposed SDP to address both data security and retrieval time concerns simultaneously.

The data placement problem for geographically distributed cloud storage environment is addressed in [21] by proposing a data placement, using mixed integer linear programming, to reduce overall cost while satisfying the performance and latency constraints. Khalajzadeh et al. in [13] propose a graph-partitioning based approach to optimize social media data placement to minimize data storage cost fulfilling the required latency requirement. However, these approaches do not address the data security aspect for the recommended data placement solution. Data placement strategy proposed in [8] utilizes data replication to improve the performance of an Infrastructure as a Service (IaaS) cloud system by replicating smaller partitions, instead of entire dataset, over the entire network. This proposed strategy improves the robustness of workload misprediction and reduces the storage requirements; however, it does not address the security issue arising due to data replication. The authors in [10] propose a data placement strategy focusing on minimization of storage cost in collaborative cloud storage environment satisfying the scientific user requirements, data size, and other dependencies. This integer linear programming model provides cost-efficiency but fails to address the issue of data security. Matt et al. presented a heuristic optimization approach in [20] to suggest a data placement solution in a cloud-based storage system. This approach provides storage cost reduction and latency optimization while satisfying the QoS constraints by monitoring data access patterns to arrive at the optimized solution. Data security for intermediate data generated in a scientific workflow is addressed by data placement algorithm based on ant colony optimization in [17]. The algorithm identifies data centers ensuring maximum data security for intermediate data in terms of data confidentiality, data integrity, and authentication access. However, data retrieval time aspect is not addressed in strategy formulation.

Machine learning techniques are utilized in different applications for cybersecurity. Various machine learning based methods such as artificial neural network (ANN), Bayesian network, clustering, decision trees, evolutionary computation, support vector machine, hidden Markov model(HMM), etc. are suggested in [3] for cybersecurity intrusion detection. The authors have also provided a comprehensive list of datasets for training the machine learning models for intrusion detection at different network levels. An intrusion detection system (IDS) presented in [6] uses an ANN to analyze the collected information of an IoT system to identify a DoS attack. Internet packet traces were used to train the ANN and the performance was validated using a simulated IoT network. Saied et al. in [22] utilized ANN to identify and protect against known and unknown DDoS attacks using the network traffic characteristic features that differentiate DDoS attack traffic and genuine traffic. Using both old and up-to-date pattern datasets for training the ANN, the algorithm was implemented in real physical environments to accurately detect DDoS attack with a limitation of DDoS attacks involving encrypted packet headers. Thus machine learning techniques such as ANN can be quite useful in cybersecurity applications. Unlike the recent data placement strategies which target either data security or time performance individually, our SDP-recommended data placement refined using machine learning provides optimized time performance with enhanced data security by ensuring data integrity and data availability [19] in case of cyberattacks. The authors in [26] emphasize that sensitive user identity data from transportation, healthcare systems, intelligent surveillance systems within smart city needs to be safeguarded against information compromise and privacy leakage through unauthorized access and cyberattacks. However computational overhead involved in ensuring the data security poses a major challenge in increasing the overall efficiency as massive data processing is required in smart city applications. Li et al. in [15] present a mobile-cloud framework to address the user privacy leakage in smart cities by preventing the data overcollection. The active approach aims to maximize releasing user operation pressure and completely mitigate the data overcollection problem. However, the impact on time performance due to the implementation of this framework was not considered. Thus utilizing data placement strategies that focus on both retrieval time performance and data security for cloud storage platforms such as SDP can be quite advantageous even for smart city applications.

3 Problem Formulation and Data Placement Optimization Model

3.1 Problem Description

As mentioned in the introduction, in this paper, we attempt to incorporate learning ability in the system to enhance the data placement quality by clearly capturing attack characteristics. For the sake of continuity, we now present only the problem formulation and give the ARRT algorithm used in this paper from our earlier works. Interested readers may refer to the finer details in [25].

We consider a cloud storage system consisting of N storage nodes, denoted as $V = \{v_1, v_2, \cdots, v_N\}$. A symmetric matrix $E = (e_{ij})_{N \times N}$ represents the connections among N nodes, where a physical link connecting v_i and v_j nodes is indicated by $e_{ij} = e_{ji} = 1$, whereas $e_{ij} = e_{ji} = 0$ means that there is no direct connection between the nodes v_i and v_j. The topology of the system can be denoted as a graph $G(V, E)$, where V and E are the sets of vertices (storage nodes) and edges (connection links), respectively.

The volume of data D is divided into n chunks where α_i with $i = 1, 2, \cdots, n$ denote the size of i-th chunk. Let $H = (h_{ij})_{n \times m}$ denote a data placement solution, where $h_{ij} \in H$ represents the j-th copy of the i-th chunk stores on the h_{ij}-th node and m denotes the total number of data copies.

Suppose there are r_{ij} number of read requests submitted from access point v_i for data chunk α_j, where $r_{ij} \neq 0$.

Based on actual large-scale cloud platforms, the access points/nodes and storage nodes in the system are part of different levels of architecture. Let the total number of requests from node v_i for chunk α_j be r_{ij}, where $i = 1, \cdots, N$ and $j = 1, \cdots, n$. Given a data placement solution H and a set of reading requests $(r_{ij})_{N \times n}$, we can obtain its corresponding retrieval time $T(H)$ and security factor $S(H)$ (to be defined later in this section). Now, the impending challenging issue is searching for an optimal $H^\star$ that minimizes data retrieval time while providing maximum security level. We address this problem by first formulating the objective functions of $T(H)$ and $S(H)$, on the basis of which we shall establish a multi-objective optimization model.

3.2   Retrieval Time

We assume that, when a read request comes, all the chunks of a file need to be retrieved. The total time required for data retrieval will be equal to the time taken to retrieve all of the required chunks, which can be represented by

$$T(H) = \sum_{i=1}^{N}\sum_{j=1}^{n} T_{ij}(H) = \sum_{i=1}^{N}\sum_{j=1}^{n} \left(r_{ij} \times \alpha_j \times z_{i,t_{ij}}\right), \tag{5.1}$$

where N is the total number of nodes in a system that can be regarded as access points, while n is the total number of chunks.

3.3   Security Factor

In a given network $G = (V, E)$, the betweenness centrality of node v_i is defined as

$$c_i = \sum_{\substack{j=1, \\ j\neq i}}^{N-1} \sum_{\substack{k=j+1, \\ k\neq i}}^{N} \frac{S_{jk}(v_i)}{S_{jk}}. \tag{5.2}$$

Here, N is the number of nodes in network G, S_{jk} is the total number of shortest paths between nodes v_j and v_k, and $S_{jk}(v_i)$ indicates the number of shortest paths between nodes v_j and v_k that pass along node v_i.

The vulnerability of nodes storing the data is largely influenced by two factors—first is the extent of possible data loss due to attack on a single node storing the data; the other is the geodesic distance between any two nodes that both store a data chunk. Based on this fact, security factor $S(H)$ will be given by

$$S(H) = Ad(H) \times \frac{1}{Ac(H)}, \tag{5.3}$$

where the average geodesic distance of $Ad(H)$ can be computed as

$$Ad(H) = \frac{\sum_{i=1}^{n\times m}\sum_{j=1}^{n\times m} d_{q_i,q_j}}{(n \times m)(n \times m - 1)/2}. \tag{5.4}$$

The average centrality $Ac(H)$ is given by

$$Ac(H) = \frac{\sum_{i=1}^{n}\sum_{j=1}^{m} c_{h_{ij}}}{n \times m} = \frac{\sum_{k=1}^{n\times m} c_{q_k}}{n \times m}. \tag{5.5}$$

Note that the security level function $S(H)$ is to be maximized, so it is equivalent to minimizing its reciprocal $1/S(H)$, hereafter referred to as "inverse of security."

3.4   Multi-Objective Optimization Model

With the objective functions of retrieval time and security level given in (5.1) and (5.3), respectively, here, we build a multi-objective optimization model for optimal data placement on cloud storage systems.

$$
\begin{cases}
\min T(H) = \min_H \sum_{i=1}^{N} \sum_{j=1}^{n} \left(r_{ij} \times \alpha_j \times z_{i,t_{ij}} \right), \\[2mm]
\min \dfrac{1}{S(H)} = \min_H \dfrac{(n \times m - 1) \sum_{k=1}^{n \times m} c_{q_k}}{2 \sum_{i=1}^{n \times m} \sum_{j=1}^{n \times m} d_{q_i,q_j}},
\end{cases}
$$

where

1. $H = \{h_{ij} \mid i = 1, 2, \cdots, n, \; j = 1, 2, \cdots, m\}$ with $h_{ij} \in \{1, 2, \cdots, N\}$.
2. $q_k = h_{ij}$, where $k = (i - 1) \times m + j, i = 1, 2, \cdots, n$, and $j = 1, 2, \cdots, m$.

Subject to: $\forall i, j \in \{1, 2, \cdots, n \times m\}, q_i \neq q_j$.

3.5   Multi-Objective Optimization Algorithm

Since the two objectives in the proposed model conflict each other, there does not typically exist a feasible solution that minimizes both $T(H)$ and $1/S(H)$ simultaneously. The best trade-offs among conflicting objectives can be defined in terms of Pareto optimality [23]. In our proposed approach ARRT, we encode an individual as a feasible data placement solution directly. That is, an individual H is an $n \times m$ matrix, where $h_{ij} \in H$ represents that the j-th copy of the i-th chunk stored on the h_{ij}-th storage node. A feasible individual H should satisfy that $h_{ij} \in \{1, 2, \cdots, N\}$ and there should not be any identical elements in H.

3.5.1   Crossover

In ARRT, we first adopt two-point crossover on parents H^1 and H^2 to produce two infeasible offsprings O^1 and O^2 and then fix them based on a mapping relationship between H^1 and H^2. This procedure is given in [25] as crossover operator.

3.5.2   Local Search Procedure

In order to improve convergence speed of the proposed algorithm ARRT, we introduce a local search operator in local search algorithm, which consists of two sub-algorithms—algorithm for optimization of retrieval time and algorithm for optimization of security level, all of which are referred in [25].

3.5.3   Complete Framework of Algorithm ARRT

Let $\lambda^1, \cdots, \lambda^L$ be a set of evenly spread weight vectors in the objective space and $x^1 = (x_1^1, x_2^1)$ and $x^2 = (x_1^2, x_2^2)$ be the boundary reference points found till now in the evolutionary process, where x_1^1 and x_2^2 are the minimum values of the first and the second objective functions found so far, respectively, while x_2^1 and x_1^2 are the maximum values of the second and the first objective functions in the current population. The problem of obtaining the PF of the proposed model can be decomposed into L scalar optimization subproblems by using the normalized Tchebycheff approach [27]. Thus the objective function of the i-th subproblem with $i = 1, \cdots, L$ is given by

$$g(H\lambda^i, x^1, x^2) = max \left\{ \frac{\lambda_1^i |T(H) - x_1^1|}{x_1^2 - x_1^1}, \ \frac{\lambda_2^i |1/S(H) - x_2^2|}{x_2^1 - x_2^2} \right\}.$$

The proposed ARRT minimizes all these L objective functions simultaneously. The framework is described in Algorithm 1.

3.6   Proposed Security-Cognizant Data Placement (SDP) Strategy

The SDP strategy to obtain the data placement recommendation with enhanced security proposed in this paper is as shown in Fig. 5.2. The general description of each component shown in Fig. 5.2 is as follows:

– **Cloud/network graph**: The cloud storage system consisting of a set of storage nodes is modeled as a network graph.
– **Attack resilient and retrieval time trade-off strategy (ARRT)**: ARRT strategy takes into consideration inherent network properties such as betweenness centrality, link speeds, node storage capacity, internode separation, etc. to obtain a set of data placement solutions providing a trade-off between data retrieval time and data security.

Algorithm 1 Attack resilient and retrieval time trade-off strategy (ARRT)

Input: The number of the subproblems: L, a uniformly spread of L weight vectors: $\lambda^1, \cdots, \lambda^L$, the number of neighborhood of each weight vector: Nb, mutation probability: pr_m, a stopping criterion.

Output: Pareto Front.

1: **(Initialization):** Compute the Euclidean distances between any two weight vectors in $\{\lambda^1, \cdots, \lambda^L\}$ to obtain the Nb closest neighbors, denoted as $B(i)$, for each weight vector λ^i with $i = 1, 2, \cdots, L$. Randomly generate L individuals according to the encoding scheme as an initial population $\{H^1, \cdots, H^L\}$. For each individual H^i, calculate $T(H^i)$ by (5.1) and security level $S(H^i)$ by (5.3). Initialize reference points x^1 and x^2 as $x_1^1 = x_1^2 = \infty$ and $x_2^1 = x_2^2 = -\infty$. Let the generation number $t = 0$.
   //**Evolution:**

2: **for** $i = 1, 2, \cdots, L$ **do**

3: **(Crossover):** Randomly select two indexes p and q from $B(i)$, and then apply crossover operator given by Crossover Algorithm [25] on H^p and H^q to generate two new offsprings O^1 and O^2.

4: **(Mutation):** Apply mutation operator on O^1 and O^2 with mutation probability pr_m to generate O^3 and O^4.

5: **(Local Search):** Apply local search operator given by Local Search Algorithm [25] on O^3 and O^4 to produce four improved offsprings O^5, O^6, O^7, and O^8.

6: **(Update):** For each newly generated offspring $O \in \{O^5, O^6, O^7, O^8\}$, firstly update reference points x^1 and x^2, and then for each $j \in B(i)$, if $g(O\lambda^j, x^1, x^2) < g(H^j\lambda^j, x^1, x^2)$, set $H^j = O$.

7: **end for**

8: **Stopping Criteria:**

   – If the termination condition does not hold, then go to **step 2**; otherwise, find out all non-dominated solutions in the current population and output the Pareto Front.

- **Placement recommendations based on inherent network properties**: ARRT recommends a Pareto-optimal set of placement solutions, each solution consists of number of nodes dependent on number of chunks and number of replicas.

- **Network attack information**: The network attack information comprises of different types of threats based on the applications hosted and attack history for each node. This information can be obtained using the logs in the system [1]. The network attack information will be updated periodically and hence it can be considered as dynamic factor useful for improving the security.

- **Neural network**: The neural network utilizes dynamic network properties, such as frequency of the attacks of each threat type and types of applications hosted on each node, during its training phase. The training data required for the neural network will be generated using attack model described in Sect. 4. The machine learning model used for identification of threat type will be multilayer perceptron (MLP) with single hidden layer and logistic sigmoid function as activation function. MLP follows the process of supervised learning through backpropagation.

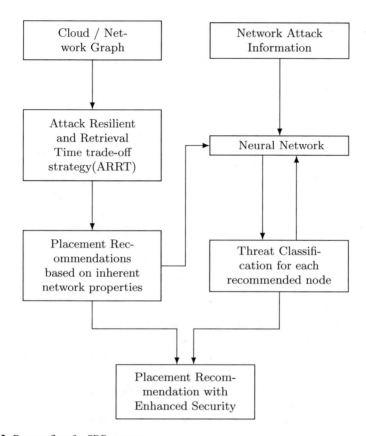

Fig. 5.2 Process flow for SDP strategy

- **Threat classification for each recommended node**: Using the neural network, each node from the recommended placement solution will be classified into its most vulnerable threat type. It will help in enhancing overall security of the data placement solution, also serving as an input to adjust the weights during the learning phase.
- **Placement recommendation with enhanced security**: This is the final output of the system. By using the combination of recommended placements and the additional information, CSP can precisely select a particular node to place the data chunk so as to maximize the data security within the placement. By avoiding the replica placement of same data chunk on nodes with same vulnerability, CSP can minimize the data loss in case of a cyberattack.

4 Machine Learning for Enhanced Security

4.1 Threat Types

Different applications will be hosted on each node in the given cloud network.
Each application may be susceptible to different kinds of threats. Consider a cloud
network that hosts a set of applications denoted by A and vulnerable to threat
types denoted by T such that $A = \{a_1, a_2, \cdots, a_n\}$ and $T = \{t_1, t_2, \cdots, t_n\}$,
where $a_1, a_2, \cdots, a_n$ represent the applications and $t_1, t_2, \cdots, t_n$ represent the
threat types. Here we assume that not all nodes will host all the applications. CSPs
or network administrators can safeguard against either individual applications or
individual threats, i.e., they can follow either software-focused approach or threat-
focused approach for protection against network cyberattacks as described in [1].
Consider one such example of threat-focused approach shown in Fig. 5.3. Threat
type t_1 can be potentially used to affect applications a_1, a_3, and a_4 and hence nodes
hosting any of these applications are vulnerable to threat type t_1. Therefore, in order
to protect against threat type t_1, all nodes hosting any of these applications need to
be safeguarded.

In software-focused approach, as an example shown in Fig. 5.4, application a_1 is
vulnerable to threat types t_1, t_2, and t_3. Assume there is another application a_2 which
is vulnerable to threat types t_2, t_5, and t_6. Therefore, if a node hosts both applications
a_1 and a_2, it can be exploited using any one of the threat types $t_1, t_2, t_3, t_5,$ or t_6.

Depending on the applications hosted on the node and the frequency of attacks
exploiting a particular threat type, we can identify the most vulnerable threat type
for that particular node. This information will be used to enhance the security of
data placement.

Fig. 5.3 Threat focused approach

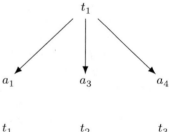

Fig. 5.4 Software focused approach

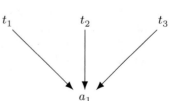

4.2 Machine Learning Model

4.2.1 Motivation

In order to identify the most likely threat type for each storage node, different parameters or features (described in Sect. 4.2.2) for each node need to be evaluated. If new storage nodes are added in the network or as the new threat types are being detected within the network, the underlying threat identification system must be updated without incurring additional overheads through any complex computational procedure. To achieve this sophisticated near real-time requirement, it is only a learning entity that can automate this process. This means it will utilize the relevant threat information periodically or as and when required, in its learning process. Different cloud topologies are adopted by different CSPs according to their preference and available resources and hence the likely threat identification system should be deployable irrespective of the topology adopted. Machine learning based implementation will be able to ensure the versatility of system as its design is independent of network topology. Thus, there is a clear motivation to augment a neural network to achieve the above-mentioned requirements.

4.2.2 General Description

The machine learning model used for the identification of most vulnerable threat type will be multilayer perceptron. The features or inputs to the neural network will be as follows:

- **Applications hosted on the node:** There is one input corresponding to each application available on the network. If that application is hosted on the node, then value of input corresponding to that application will be 1 else it will be 0. Even though each application can be susceptible to different vulnerabilities, there may be a case where two more applications are vulnerable to same threat type. In such a case, that node will be most likely to be exploited using that particular threat type. Therefore, it is important to know the applications hosted on each node. For example, if the number of different applications hosted on the network is 4, then $A = \{a_1, a_2, a_3, a_4\}$ and each node will have four inputs corresponding to the number of applications hosted on the network. Suppose, a particular node hosts only a_1 and a_2, the input values or feature values of application inputs corresponding to a_1 and a_2 will be 1, whereas same for a_3 and a_4 will be 0 for this node.
- **Frequency of attacks exploiting the threats:** Only knowing the applications hosted on a particular node is insufficient to determine the correct threat type that it is most vulnerable to. Attackers tend to exploit certain threat types by repeatedly targeting the same vulnerability over a period of time. Therefore, it is essential to know attack frequency exploiting each threat type on a particular node. Nodes hosting the same applications, but having different attack history

information may be vulnerable to different threat type, which is a key point in using these frequencies as input features for machine learning. There will be one input each corresponding to the frequency of attacks for each threat type. In order to normalize frequency input within the range 0–1, attack frequency bins are created. The feature value is incremented in steps of 0.2 corresponding to number of attacks.

Note that the inputs or features are selected in such a way that, for each detection of attack on a node, features related to only that node need to be updated. In this way, during each update, write operations are kept to a minimum.

4.2.3 Attack Model and Training Data

To generate the training data required to train the neural network, an attack model was designed and implemented to obtain threat labels corresponding to the node feature set. We generate an attack model that fully adheres to situations wherein a node is subject to application-based attacks as exemplified in [7]. Thus, as with real-life scenario, the system trained using this particular attack model will be able to maintain the data integrity and prevent the data loss due to application-based attacks. While designing the attack model, to capture real-life scenarios, following assumptions and ideas were used to generate realistic quality training data.

- Not all the nodes will host all the applications. Therefore it is less likely that entire network will be disrupted in offering the service to clients.
- Hosted applications and the corresponding threats to potentially exploit them are known to the network administrator or CSP.
- For selecting a node to attack for a given threat type, we select the nodes which host more number of applications exploitable using that threat type.
- If certain vulnerabilities need to be exploited using repeated attacks, we increase the attack frequency feature value appropriately.
- Update the attack frequency feature values and corresponding threat type label of the node after the attack.

We use the above methodology to generate training data described in Sect. 5.

For the system hosting six different application with three possible vulnerabilities, the performance of the neural network trained using this attack model is shown in Table 5.1. The overall accuracy of the system was found to be about 80%.

Table 5.1 Performance of neural network

Threat types	Precision	Recall	F1-score
0	0.78	0.75	0.76
1	0.81	0.81	0.81
2	0.82	0.83	0.83

4.2.4   Utilization of Output

The output of neural network will classify each placement node in one of the k threat types such that $t_k \in T$ described earlier in Sect. 4.1. Depending on the replication factor m and the number of data chunks n in each file, we will have total P number of nodes in each of the placement solution where $P = m * n$.

Depending on the distribution of applications within the network, since only a fraction of P nodes will belong to the same threat type, the quality of data placement can be identified and key decisions regarding more secure placement can be taken using this fraction. Let F be defined as the ratio of maximum number of nodes belonging to the same threat type to the total number of nodes in the placement solution. Therefore, this fraction F can be mathematically represented as

$$F = \max(N_{t_k})/P,$$

where N_{t_k} is the number of nodes belonging to threat type t_k for each $t_k \in T$.

For a data placement to be safe against a particular cyberattack, there needs to be at least one copy of each data chunk available for retrieval. Suppose data chunk k and its replicas k_1 and k_2 are placed on nodes with vulnerable threat type t_1. If the network is attacked targeting the threat type t_1, all the copies of a data chunk k are lost and entire data can no longer be retrieved which will result in a complete data loss for that particular file. Therefore if more than $(m-1) * n$ number of nodes belong to same threat type t_k in a given data placement solution, that placement will result in data loss, if the system is attacked by exploiting threat type t_k. Hence, in order for the placement to be safe, we need $F \leq (m-1)/m$. When F satisfies this condition, at least two replicas of each chunk can be placed on nodes with different threat types, thereby safeguarding against complete data loss and preserving the data integrity. We evaluate the influence of this factor F on data placement and integrity through rigorous discrete event simulations in the next section.

5   Experiments and Performance Evaluation

We conducted extensive performance evaluation studies on cloud platforms. For previously proposed ARRT strategy [25] performance evaluation, the sizes of data chunks were randomly chosen between from 150 to 300 units. The transmission time between a pair of nodes for a unit size of data was normalized according to the network specification.

For the sake of continuity, we present a typical output obtained through ARRT in Fig. 5.5 [25].

Each point in the graph refers to a placement solution consisting of number of nodes equal to product of replication factor and number of data chunks for the file. To demonstrate how robust each set of placements would be, against an attack in terms of the number of storage nodes that can get compromised yet assuring the data integrity, we carried out an extensive discrete event simulation.

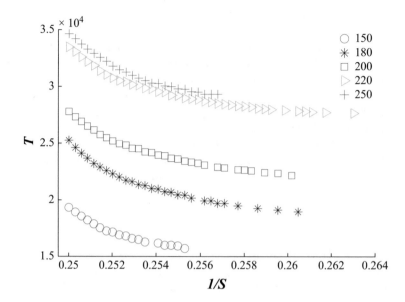

Fig. 5.5 Output of ARRT

Based on the methodology described in Sect. 4 on our attack model, we generated a total of 7000 attack events on a network of size comprising 200 nodes. In our evaluation, similar to a real-life scenario, an attack on a node implies that the attacked node is unavailable for communication/storage and hence the data on the attacked node is no longer available for retrieval. We define the robustness factor as the percentage of attacks sustained successfully by preserving at least one copy of all the chunks for retrieval. This robustness factor will serve as a metric for the comparison between placements suggested by ARRT and SDP. The number of nodes attacked in each case belongs to the same threat type and hence maximum number of nodes that can be attacked in each scenario will be equal to $F * P$. For this experiment, we fixed the value of replication factor m as 3 and number of chunks n was set to 10. ARRT strategy solution corresponds to random distribution of data chunks and their replicas over the set of nodes recommended as the data placement solution. On the other hand, for SDP strategy, the data chunks and their corresponding replicas are placed according to output obtained from neural network as described in Sect. 4 instead of random distribution over the same set of nodes as ARRT strategy. We now demonstrate the influence of machine learning approach in improving the robustness of data placement solution using different range of F values which helps to determine the quality of the data placement.

1. $F \leq 1/m$

For a small value of F, specifically less than or equal to $1/m$, the data placement quality is good as evident from Fig. 5.6. In this example, at most ten nodes belong to

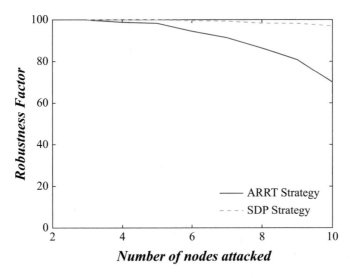

Fig. 5.6 Robustness comparison for $F \leq 1/m$

the same threat type and hence for small number of nodes attacked, ARRT strategy performs reasonably well. However, as the number of attacked nodes increases, robustness of ARRT placement gradually starts decreasing. On the other hand, in case of solution provided by SDP, the robustness is significantly high and consistent. The information provided by the learning model in SDP regarding threat types of each node can be effectively used to avoid placing replicas of same data chunk on nodes with same threat type. Such data placement is more likely when the applications hosted are well distributed over the network so that less number nodes will have same type of vulnerability.

2. $1/m < F \leq (m-1)/m$

The quality of data placements with $1/m < F \leq (m-1)/m$ is not as good as previous case; however, it is still within the limit for a potentially safe data placement. In our example, in the worst case scenario, there could be up to 20 nodes that belong to the same threat type and hence when compromised can result in data loss for ARRT placement. As shown in Fig. 5.7, for ARRT placement, as number of attacked nodes increases beyond 10, the robustness starts to deteriorate rapidly as with high number of nodes susceptible to same threat type, ARRT placements tend to place all replicas of same data chunks on similar nodes, thereby affecting the robustness of the placement solution. Since F is still within the safety limit, the robustness of more secure data placements suggested with the help of SDP remains consistently superior than ARRT as shown in Fig. 5.7. Such a value of F may occur on networks where the distribution of applications is inconsistent, thereby resulting in many nodes being susceptible to same threat types.

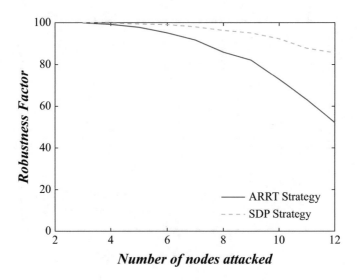

Fig. 5.7 Robustness comparison for $1/m < F \leq (m-1)/m$

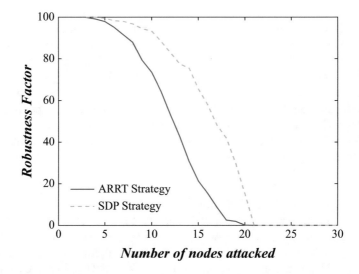

Fig. 5.8 Robustness comparison for $F > (m-1)/m$

3. $F > (m-1)/m$

In order for the placement to be completely safe, F needs to be less than or equal to $(m-1)/m$ as established in Sect. 4. However, if F is greater than $(m-1)/m$, the quality of that data placement solution decreases rapidly as evident from Fig. 5.8. This is an example of poor and inadvertent distribution of applications, which should be avoided by the CSP to provide reliable quality-of-service. If many similar applications are hosted on most of the nodes in the network, it could lead to a major disruption if attacker exploits that particular vulnerability, thereby resulting in disjoint network scenario. It may be noted that data placement assisted by SDP delivers superior performance than ARRT placement (when the number of attacked nodes is less than 20 in our experiment). However, robustness performance of data placements suggested by both strategies decreases sharply with increasing number of attacked nodes as shown in Fig. 5.8. This clearly justifies the fact that, in order for the data placement to be safe and reliable, F should remain within the acceptable limit.

6 Conclusions

Data security and retrieval time are two key performance metrics for every storage system. Specifically on cloud platforms, due to constant threat of cyberattacks, data security needs are to be given special attention. In this paper, we enhanced a multi-objective optimization data placement strategy which strikes a trade-off between data security and retrieval time. This is achieved by augmenting the fundamental ARRT algorithm with an artificial intelligence paradigm to significantly improve the data integrity and security, thus making the entire strategy a practicable approach. As an example, we considered application-based attack types in our simulations and specifically designed a training model that enables a neural network to learn the threat features which will be used to classify as per the most vulnerable threat types. Our proposed SDP approach assists the service provider in refining the data placements nodes suggested earlier by ARRT, thereby enhancing the robustness and quality-of-service to the users. To the best of our literature knowledge, the study presented here is the first-of-its-kind to demonstrate the impact of a neural network for large-scale networked storage systems that simultaneously considers data security and data retrieval time. Although this study serves as a clear demonstration of what a machine learning model could promise to enhance the performance, as an immediate extension, one could use other learning models such as SVM/rule-based techniques to further optimize the performance.

Acknowledgements The NUS authors would like to thank the funding support by MOE Tier-1 grant no. R-263-000-C14-112 in carrying out this project. The third author would like to thank the funding support by NNSF, China (No.61402350, No.61472297, and No.61572391) and CSC, China.

References

1. Awan, M. S. K., Burnap, P., & Rana, O. (2016). Identifying cyber risk hotspots: A framework for measuring temporal variance in computer network risk. *Computers & Security, 57*, 31–46.
2. Boru, D., Kliazovich, D., Granelli, F., Bouvry, P., & Zomaya, A. Y. (2015). Energy-efficient data replication in cloud computing datacenters. *Cluster Computing, 18*(1), 385–402.

3. Buczak, A. L., & Guven, E. (2016). A survey of data mining and machine learning methods for cyber security intrusion detection. *IEEE Communications Surveys & Tutorials, 18*(2), 1153–1176.
4. da Silva, G. H. G., Holanda, M., & Araujo, A. (2016). Data replication policy in a cloud computing environment. In *11th Iberian Conference on Information Systems and Technologies (CISTI), 2016* (pp. 1–6). Piscataway: IEEE.
5. di Vimercati, S. D. C., Foresti, S., Jajodia, S., Livraga, G., Paraboschi, S., & Samarati, P. (2014). Fragmentation in presence of data dependencies. *IEEE Transactions on Dependable and Secure Computing, 11*(6), 510–523.
6. Hodo, E., Bellekens, X., Hamilton, A., Dubouilh, P. L., Iorkyase, E., Tachtatzis, C., et al. (2016). Threat analysis of IoT networks using artificial neural network intrusion detection system. In *International Symposium on Networks, Computers and Communications (ISNCC), 2016* (pp. 1–6). Piscataway: IEEE.
7. Hoque, N., Bhuyan, M. H., Baishya, R. C., Bhattacharyya, D. K., & Kalita, J. K. (2014). Network attacks: Taxonomy, tools and systems. *Journal of Network and Computer Applications, 40*, 307–324.
8. Hsu, C. J., Freeh, V. W., & Villanustre, F. (2017). Trilogy: Data placement to improve performance and robustness of cloud computing. In *2017 IEEE International Conference on Big Data* (pp. 2442–2451). Piscataway: IEEE.
9. Hudic, A., Islam, S., Kieseberg, P., Rennert, S., & Weippl, E. R. (2013) Data confidentiality using fragmentation in cloud computing. *International Journal of Pervasive Computing and Communications, 9*(1), 37–51.
10. Ikken, S., Renault, É., Barkat, A., Tari, A., & Kechad, T. (2017). Cost-efficient big intermediate data placement in a collaborative cloud storage environment. In *IEEE 19th International Conference on High Performance Computing and Communications; IEEE 15th International Conference on Smart City; IEEE 3rd International Conference on Data Science and Systems (HPCC/SmartCity/DSS), 2017* (pp. 514–521). Piscataway: IEEE.
11. Kale, R.V., Veeravalli, B., & Wang, X. (2017). Design and performance characterization of practically realizable graph-based security aware algorithms for hierarchical and non-hierarchical cloud architectures. In *International Conference on Frontier Computing* (pp. 392–402). Singapore: Springer,
12. Kapusta, K., & Memmi, G. (2015). Data protection by means of fragmentation in distributed storage systems. In *International Conference on Protocol Engineering (ICPE) and International Conference on New Technologies of Distributed Systems (NTDS), 2015* (pp. 1–8). Piscataway: IEEE.
13. Khalajzadeh, H., Yuan, D., Grundy, J., & Yang, Y. (2017). Cost-effective social network data placement and replication using graph-partitioning. In *IEEE International Conference on Cognitive Computing (ICCC), 2017* (pp. 64–71). Piscataway: IEEE.
14. Lentini, S., Grosso, E., & Masala, G. L. (2018). A comparison of data fragmentation techniques in cloud servers. In *International Conference on Emerging Internetworking, Data & Web Technologies* (pp. 560–571). Cham: Springer.
15. Li, Y., Dai, W., Ming, Z., & Qiu, M. (2016). Privacy protection for preventing data over-collection in smart city. *IEEE Transactions on Computers, 65*(5), 1339–1350.
16. Lin, J. W., Chen, C. H., & Chang, J. M. (2013). QoS-aware data replication for data-intensive applications in cloud computing systems. *IEEE Transactions on Cloud Computing, 1*(1), 101–115.
17. Liu, W., Peng, S., Du, W., Wang, W., & Zeng, G. S. (2014). Security-aware intermediate data placement strategy in scientific cloud workflows. *Knowledge and Information Systems, 41*(2), 423–447.
18. Mansouri, N. (2016). QDR: A QoS-aware data replication algorithm for data grids considering security factors. *Cluster Computing, 19*(3), 1071–1087.
19. Mansouri, Y., Toosi, A. N., & Buyya, R. (2017). Data storage management in cloud environments: Taxonomy, survey, and future directions. *ACM Computing Surveys (CSUR), 50*(6), 91.

20. Matt, J., Waibel, P., & Schulte, S. (2017). Cost-and latency-efficient redundant data storage in the cloud. In *IEEE 10th International Conference on Service-Oriented Computing and Applications (SOCA), 2017* (pp. 164–172). Piscataway: IEEE.
21. Oh, K., Chandra, A., & Weissman, J. (2017). Trips: Automated multi-tiered data placement in a geo-distributed cloud environment. In *Proceedings of the 10th ACM International Systems and Storage Conference* (p. 12). New York: ACM.
22. Saied, A., Overill, R. E., & Radzik, T. (2016). Detection of known and unknown DDoS attacks using artificial neural networks. *Neurocomputing, 172*, 385–393.
23. Seada, H., & Deb, K. (2016). A unified evolutionary optimization procedure for single, multiple, and many objectives. *IEEE Transactions on Evolutionary Computation, 20*(3), 358–369.
24. Sen, A., & Madria, S. (2016). Risk assessment in a sensor cloud framework using attack graphs. *IEEE Transactions on Services Computing, 10*, 942–955.
25. Wang, X., Vishwanath, K. R., & Veeravalli, B. (2017). Simultaneous optimization of user-centric security-conscious data storage on cloud platforms. In *IEEE 42nd Local Computer Networks (LCN)* (pp. 223–226).
26. Zhang, K., Ni, J., Yang, K., Liang, X., Ren, J., & Shen, X. S. (2017). Security and privacy in smart city applications: Challenges and solutions. *IEEE Communications Magazine, 55*(1), 122–129.
27. Zhang, Q., & Li, H. (2007). Moea/d: A multiobjective evolutionary algorithm based on decomposition. *IEEE Transactions on Evolutionary Computation, 11*(6), 712–731.

Chapter 6
Threats Behind Default Configurations of Network Devices: Wired Local Network Attacks and Their Countermeasures

A. Vázquez-Ingelmo, Á. M. Moreno-Montero, and F. J. García-Peñalvo

Abstract Network devices not only allow users to build powerful local networks but also to protect them, their data, and their communications from unwanted intruders. However, it is important to give special attention to security within local networks, since internal attacks could be catastrophic for users. Internal security can be overlooked once the belief that all efforts and resources should be focused on protecting users from external intruders has been established. That belief is dangerous since it can foster the misconfiguration of internal network devices, providing a network infrastructure based on weak settings. This chapter should serve as a summary of a series of local network attacks as well as their countermeasures through the right configuration of the network devices. The attacks will be presented through a set of practical scenarios emulated on GNS3 to clarify their impact and consequences. Also, countermeasures will be discussed to illustrate their impact on networks and the advantages and disadvantages of their application.

Keywords LAN · Security · LAN attacks · GNS3 · Network devices

1 Introduction

Network devices are increasingly sophisticating their features to provide a better quality of service (QoS), performance, scalability, and, of course, to strengthen security regarding network access and communications. These devices not only

A. Vázquez-Ingelmo (✉) · F. J. García-Peñalvo
GRIAL Research Group, Department of Computers and Automatics, University of Salamanca, Salamanca, Spain
e-mail: andreavazquez@usal.es; fgarcia@usal.es

Á. Moreno-Montero
Department of Computers and Automatics, University of Salamanca, Salamanca, Spain
e-mail: amoreno@usal.es

© Springer Nature Switzerland AG 2020   133
B. B. Gupta et al. (eds.), *Handbook of Computer Networks and Cyber Security*,
https://doi.org/10.1007/978-3-030-22277-2_6

allow users to build powerful local area networks (LANs) but also to protect them, their data, and their connections from unwanted intruders.

By introducing highly manageable devices in local networks, personnel in charge of communications can design advanced topologies to support complex requirements regarding connections and data flows. However, the possibility of configuring large sets of features may lead to the miss of interesting or even essential functionalities. What is more, having so many options to configure can be overwhelming, ending up in focusing on configuring just a minimal set of basic features. A basic configuration may be seen as enough for networks with a low volume of requirements, but local protection is an aspect that must not be neglected.

Local networks contain personal computers, shared resources, and many data flows; and these data flows could contain valuable information given the widespread use of cloud computing [1] or the Internet-of-Things [2], for example. Protecting all these elements from external attackers is essential, either through cryptography [3, 4] or through powerful firewalls. However, focusing all concerns on external protection may overlook the security inside the local network. Local network protection is also crucial; there are many attack vectors within local networks that can be easily exploited by attackers if they have access to the local infrastructure, and it is not always possible to trust all the internal users of a local network. For that reason, ignoring LAN protection could be catastrophic.

Attacks originated within local networks target at accessing critical resources, at obtaining personal information like passwords and even target at denying services. Installing network devices as configurable switches and routers can add security layers in contrast with hub-connected networks or networks based on basic switches, where access may be even easier.

That is why network devices, besides being their productivity limited when not leveraged, could be even a threat. Delivered from manufacturers, these devices usually come with a set of default settings seeking to ease the plugging and launch of the network infrastructure. These settings may compromise the network and generate security holes. It is a trivial task for an attacker to research the default settings of the network devices and exploit their vulnerabilities to bypass a network's defenses.

For these reasons, it is important for administrators and users to check and test the default settings of newly introduced network devices before their actual deployment. It is also crucial to know about potential attacks within LANs and understand proper network devices' configurations, their functionalities, and their benefits.

This chapter aims to present a summary of the most common and dangerous LAN attack vectors that take advantage of network infrastructures' settings. Every attack's theoretical foundation will be described to subsequently show the behavior of the network under each attack and their effects through practical scenarios.

Practical network scenarios allow consolidating knowledge by having a broader view of what is happening on different elements of the network infrastructure and to face real-world challenges. However, the resources (mainly referring to physical network devices) can be limited when facing these challenges; the variety of possible topologies and settings to be studied makes the utilization of practical scenarios for exploring these concepts a complex approach, as advanced network devices are not always affordable and building a variety of real topologies is time-consuming.

However, it is possible to rely on some software solutions to address these issues. Network simulators and emulators provide reliable features to build virtual network infrastructures and explore the communications and interactions of their devices in-depth. In particular, GNS3 (https://www.gns3.com/) [5] is a network emulator that offers a vast set of possibilities regarding the deployment of virtual network infrastructures. By designing different topologies, a collection of scenarios can be established to test the effects of LAN attacks within a safe environment.

To complete every simulated scenario, a set of countermeasures for every attack will be presented by explaining the concepts behind the mitigation techniques as well as the advantages and disadvantages of applying the countermeasure.

It is essential to take into account that not any countermeasure for an attack is the most suitable for a specific infrastructure. Some kinds of countermeasures mess with the overall capabilities of the networks, like their scalability, flexibility, or performance. There is not a global right solution for each attack. Administrators should discuss which defense fits best with their network requirements.

The rest of this chapter is structured as follows. Section 2 describes the background in which the work is framed, as well as the functionalities and benefits of the available network simulators and emulators, introducing the tool used in this chapter for emulating scenarios: GNS3. This section also points out the existing applications of network simulators and network emulators for computer networking training courses. In Sect. 4, a set of significant network attacks are explained and executed within emulated network topologies, to introduce their countermeasures subsequently. Section 5 discusses the LAN vulnerabilities previously presented and the viability of their mitigation techniques. Finally, the conclusions of this chapter can be found in Sect. 6.

2 Background

2.1 Local Network Vulnerabilities

Local network attacks are the most effective manner to compromise personal communications [6]. LAN wired technologies like Ethernet are popular [7] because of their simplicity and their easy configuration, but this simplicity has a price; functionality and self-configuration are priorities over security, provoking the emergence of vulnerabilities that can be exploited through attack vectors.

Network protocols were mainly designed to be functional, scalable, and efficient, overlooking security aspects [6, 8]. However, the continuous increase of communications and data flows (and their worth) has encouraged the emergence of attackers driven by the goal of stealing valuable and personal information. Having access to a weakly configured wired LAN, an intruder could gain access to sensible data, deny local services, and even penetrate legitimate personal computers connected to the network [9].

The belief that all efforts and resources should be focused on protecting users from external intruders is dangerous since it can foster the establishment of weak settings on internal network devices; delegating all of the infrastructure's protection on border firewalls. Of course, this external protection is crucial, but it cannot be the only concern for network administrators.

The transition from hub-connected Ethernet networks to switched Ethernet networks can raise the overall security, by having a dedicated segment for each host and reducing the shared segments that devices such as hubs provoked. However, switches are not a full solution for protecting wired networks; in fact, they open up space for more vulnerabilities if not correctly configured. The ease of deployment of network devices and their instantaneous functionality can relegate to a second place an in-depth configuration.

Knowing about network security is not only a task of advanced administrators; any individual in charge of network infrastructure, no matter its dimension, should be aware of the configuration of their devices, focusing on security. That is why it is important to educate not only administrators but also users on security concepts. Understanding vulnerabilities and attack techniques, as well as their consequences, are essential to avoid the most important security threats.

LAN attacks involve different methods to compromise communications, but they mostly take advantage of the standard operation of network protocols, mainly at the link layer (the second layer of the OSI model). Attacks such as ARP and DHCP poisoning, Man in the Middle (MITM), session hijacking, resource exhaustion, VLAN hopping, among many more, are simple, dangerous, and popular methods for compromising Ethernet segments, as previous surveys on LAN security have pointed out [10].

Other resources, like Cisco certifications such as CCNA (Cisco Certified Network Associate) that not only validate a series of associate-level contents in computer networking areas such as routing, switching, wireless, among others but also in the security field, exemplifies different attack vectors that can be executed on LANs [11].

These resources have been consulted to select the most significant scenarios regarding LAN security and replicate them through network emulators, with the goal of obtaining a summary with a practical approach of the most dangerous wired LAN vulnerabilities and security solutions.

2.2 *Network Simulators and Emulators*

As it has been introduced, network simulators and network emulators provide a solution for training, avoiding the necessity of purchasing physical resources, which are likely to be costly. Simulators and emulators mainly differ on the strategy to replicate the behavior of the target; on the one hand, simulators model and implement this behavior to be available in a virtual environment, and on the other hand, emulators enable a system to execute the binary images of another system, allowing the host system to behave exactly like the original would act under any circumstances.

Relying on simulation software enables freedom regarding the exploration of different topologies. These tools reliably imitate real hardware, being the behavior of the devices almost as seen in real-world scenarios. Monitoring the network is also easier and more intuitive, being one of the most valuable benefits of simulating network scenarios; by controlling all the devices through a single tool, users are allowed to have a full and detailed view of the infrastructure and its connections, with also the possibility of easily capturing and inspecting the transmitted packets through the different links between devices. This feature makes debugging more intuitive by deeply understanding how data flows work in different situations.

However, there are some drawbacks; although network simulators provide the functionalities to generate complex topologies, it is important to take into account that performance and some compelling features of the virtual infrastructure might be limited by the machine in which the network devices are being simulated. But the major drawback comes from the fact that some functionalities might not be implemented within the simulation software, and some behaviors might not be exactly as in reality, which may generate confusion around the concepts seen through the simulations.

On the other hand, network emulators provide all the benefits listed before, but they rely on real-world operating system (OS) images, allowing the emulation of the target hardware functionalities on another independent hardware platform. These features make the emulated scenarios more real since the functionalities of the devices are only limited by their OS image features.

There exist different tools for simulating and emulating network devices and for building topologies with them. However, two particular tools stand out: Cisco Packet Tracer (a network simulator) and GNS3 (a network emulator).

Cisco Packet Tracer (CPT) is a command-line interface level simulation tool developed by Cisco Systems as a part of their Networking Academy [12]. Through a graphical interface, CPT allows users to build virtual network topologies and explore them as well as their data flows. Their functions, however, are limited to a set of features.

Moreover, GNS3 is a network simulator that provides an environment with almost no limitations regarding the functions of the devices [5]. To emulate the devices, users must have original Cisco Internetwork Operating System (IOS) images [13]. GNS3 supports any command or parameter that the selected Cisco IOS supports [14]. Also, GNS3 also supports the virtualization and the connection to networks of hosts with different operating systems through virtualization software such as VMware [15] or VirtualBox [16].

2.3   Computer Networking Training Based on Virtual Scenarios

Training based on practical scenarios in computer networking areas has already been used. Given the abstract and highly theoretical concepts behind computer networking, the necessity of applying practical approaches to understand this field profoundly is plausible [17]. Network simulators/emulators provide safe environments to explore and experience the workflow of network protocols and the behavior of the devices composing the infrastructure under different conditions.

Using simulation tools as Cisco Packet Tracer or emulation tools like GNS3 has proved to be beneficial to foster knowledge acquisition about computer networking [17–25]. That is why these tools can be seen useful not only to introduce network security and vulnerability concepts but also to raise awareness about the hazards of misconfigurations in local networks and consolidate knowledge regarding the protection of wired LANs.

3   Materials and Methods

For this chapter, GNS3 has been selected as the tool for emulating the scenarios, given the fact that the attack vectors that will be described rely on specific tools that cannot be found on CPT. This condition makes it necessary to virtualize hosts with these tools and malicious exploits installed on their operating systems. In other words, it is necessary to connect virtualized hosts to the simulated networks, which is one of the features of GNS3, as already explained before. Also, the choice of an emulator over a simulator brings the scenarios closer to reality.

The scenarios will be based on Cisco devices, meaning that the syntax of the executed commands will follow the corresponding Cisco IOS rules. Nevertheless, the theoretical foundation in which the scenarios will be framed is not linked to a specific operating system. These scenarios will be preconfigured to count with the DHCP protocol, avoiding the static configuration of IP addresses every time the scenario is used.

The Cisco appliances used to emulate the network equipment throughout this chapter are:

- Routers: Cisco 7200 appliance (*c7200-adventerprisek9-mz.124-24.T5.image*)
- Switches: Cisco IOSvL2 appliance (*vios_l2-adventerprisek9-m.03.2017.qcow2*)

Also, VMware has been selected as the virtualization software for emulating hosts. The operating system for the hosts was Kali Linux (64-bit, 2018.3 version), given its suite of tools for penetrating and exploiting vulnerabilities.

In respect of the tools used for compromising the virtual topologies, the following have been selected taking into account their purpose, and they will be described when they are to be used in the scenarios:

- *Dsniff* tool suite
- *Macof*
- *Arpsoof (Dsniff* tool suite)
- *Ettercap*
- *Yersinia*
- *Icmpush*
- *Hping3*
- *dhcpx*

The selected scenarios will be presented incrementally following a simplified version (5-layer version) of the OSI model [26], omitting the session and presentation layers, starting from the link layer and finishing at the application layer. However, a section focused on the security of the network devices themselves is first presented to address threats on the access of these essential elements.

The choice of attacks to be presented is based on security surveys [10] and other resources such as Cisco guides and courses [11, 27, 28].

4 Local Network Attacks

This section covers a set of practical scenarios with different goals. Through these topologies, different attack vectors can be explored in detail, as well as the solutions or countermeasures to mitigate them.

4.1 Device Security

Network devices are the foundation of any network infrastructure. They can be managed and configured to fit into different requirements. These devices are delivered with factory settings that most of the times are enough to initiate a functional network infrastructure. However, these settings, as will be presented throughout this chapter, default settings are not recommended because of their capacity of generating security holes.

To modify the devices' default settings, personnel in charge of the network need to access the equipment and execute the necessary commands to achieve desired configurations.

Access to these devices must be restricted to prevent unwanted intruders from modifying established settings. Also, device settings should be protected from reading; although writing privileges were thoroughly safeguarded, knowing the exact configuration of the network infrastructure opens up a whole world of possibilities for an attacker, being able to research vulnerabilities or security holes on the current settings to subsequently exploit them without the necessity of modifying any network configuration.

For these reasons, it is important to count on robust device configurations regarding its access policy and privileges [29]. Otherwise, an attacker could compromise the established network security policy.

In this subsection, some general guidelines to harden the network devices to avoid unwanted accesses to these critical elements are presented. The following security measures compose a simple outline of tasks to be done to ensure the network devices' protection; however, there exist more advanced features like the AAA framework, monitoring, access control lists (ACLs), etc., to add more security layers that are out of the scope of this chapter [30].

4.1.1 Global Protection

By default, accessing the privileged level of a device to start their configuration is straightforward, since this privileged mode is not protected. These issues, of course, need to be addressed to avoid unwanted users to modify the configuration of the devices.

One of the first tasks regarding the security of the network is to protect the privileged level by configuring a password. The following snippet shows an example of configuration:

```
Device(config)# enable secret <pass>
 Device(config)# login block-for <b_seconds> attempts <num> within
    <a_seconds>
```

The previous snippet configures a password to access the privileged level and also configures different parameters. The login process will be blocked during <b_seconds> if a <num> of wrong access attempts have been detected within <a_seconds>.

This configuration is essential and should be among the first configuration commands fired on newly installed devices. The "block-for" action prevents malicious attacks such as *DoS flooding attacks* that take advantage of the behavior of the device when processing the login functionality: by flooding the device with a vast amount of login petitions, it could be possible to drain its resources, provoking a system crash.

Other attacks that this configuration could prevent are the so-called "dictionary attacks" [31]. These attacks seek for gaining privilege access and compromise the devices. A dictionary attack is a process that uses random combinations of usernames and passwords until the right one is found by automating the attack through scripts, generally. That is why blocking the connection when some failed login attempts have been detected is essential.

Finally, although the blocking policy and passwords have been set, the lasts are stored in plain text by default. Password encryption must be enabled to modify this dangerous behavior.

4.1.2   Console Connections

Sometimes, factory settings only allow the devices' first-time connections through a physical port (such as the console port) until remote connections are configured. These devices can be protected by default usernames and passwords. Default passwords must be modified, since the username/password pair for a particular device can be quickly discovered after a fast search on the Internet, meaning that any user with bad intentions could access the network infrastructure.

To address this simple but dangerous vulnerability, it is necessary to change the default login data or to protect the console lines if not even default login credentials are set.

This protection is achieved through the following lines.

```
Device(config)# line console 0
 Device(config-line)# password <pass>
 Device(config-line)# exec-timeout <minutes>
 Device(config-line)# login
```

These commands specify that the access through the console port will be protected by the defined password. Also, an inactivity timeout could be defined to deactivate the line once the time has expired. Finally, it is essential to specify that the password check will be done at login. After these commands are fired, next time someone tries to access a device, a login page will be prompted.

4.1.3   Remote Connections

On the other hand, network devices allow the possibility to access them remotely, which is more useful as it does not require a physical connection to the devices. However, there are some considerations regarding remote connections.

The default protocol to perform these connections is generally Telnet [32], which is by nature insecure given its lack of encryption regarding its communications. An attacker could sniff the network traffic and perform malicious actions to compromise the devices' configurations. That is why remote connections should be made through a more secure protocol, such as SSH [33], which allow encrypted connections.

To utilize SSH as the protocol to execute remote connections, it is important first to generate a pair of RSA keys and then prevent non-SSH connections under VTY lines.

```
Device(config)# line vty 0 <num>
 Device(config-line)# transport input ssh
```

It is also possible to define access control lists (ACLs) to have more fine-grained protection on these lines and avoid unwanted hosts even to try to establish a connection. Network administrators should ensure that no connections to the devices are made through insecure protocols, and perform the required actions to limit the access.

4.2   Link Layer

Link layer attacks need special attention; not only because of their nature but also because they allow attackers to perform more elaborated attacks, being the basis of profoundly harmful exploits [34].

These attacks focus on layer two devices (bridges, 2-layer switches, etc.). Switches are a useful manner of segmenting local area networks and therefore, to provide an extra layer of security by having a dedicated segment for each machine connected to these devices.

However, to provide their functionality, switches rely on some techniques that are not entirely secure, opening up security holes when leveraged by attackers. The key concept behind switches is their content addressable memory tables (CAM tables, also known as MAC address table).

To prevent these devices from acting like hubs (i.e., flooding all traffic through all the connected ports, which is hugely insecure since any connected device could sniff network traffic not intended for them), switches store a correspondence between the MAC address and the source port of the incoming data frames. By storing these pair of values, switches can forward the network traffic uniquely to the port in which the receiver is connected, avoiding forwarding data systematically through all links, and therefore, segmenting the local network.

The MAC/port correspondence is stored in the switches' CAM tables. Thus, attackers mainly focus on how to corrupt these correspondences to being able to sniff traffic that was not intended for them. As it will be described, a switch's CAM table corruption is extremely dangerous, being the basis of Man in the Middle (MitM) and spoofing attacks.

On the other hand, a popular and essential layer two protocol is also on the focus of intruders: the address resolution protocol [35]. This protocol allows hosts to know the IP/MAC addresses correspondence of another device to initiate a communication. By forging data frames with a fake address correspondence, an attacker can poison the devices' ARP tables, taking advantage of this situation, as it will be detailed on the spoofing attacks Sect. 4.2.2.

Finally, although trivial, another type of attack can compromise a switch's behavior: the CAM overflow attack, which is focused on the resource exhaustion of the switches. To end this section, a highly valuable layer two feature will be addressed: the virtual local area networks (VLANs).

4.2.1   Spoofing Attacks

Spoofing attacks aim at forging network data frames to impersonate legitimate hosts [36], as their name suggests. The power of these attacks comes from the design and nature of the ARP protocol and the possibility of forging fake network data frames.

The ARP protocol is based on ARP request messages that request information about the MAC address of a particular IP address. These messages are broadcasted, and the target host would respond with an ARP reply if their IP address is the one the sender was looking for.

The main issue comes from the fact that the ARP protocol is stateless, and a host could send gratuitous ARP replies (i.e., ARP replies that do not answer a previous ARP request). By forging these ARP replies, an intruder could "poison" the ARP caches or the CAM tables of the network devices, being capable of sniffing the victim's network traffic.

This simple workflow can lead to dangerous attack vectors such as the Man In The Middle (MITM) attack and the port stealing attack, which will be illustrated in the following subsection.

Man in the Middle (MITM)

The idea behind the MITM attacks is basically that the attacker is situated in the middle of a communication, generally a victim host and the LAN default gateway [37]. To achieve this situation, an attacker can take advantage of the aforementioned gratuitous ARP reply messages. As pointed out in [6], any network element must accept an ARP reply although not requested.

The workflow of this attack is executed as follows:

1. The attacker identifies the two communication sides (i.e., the two victims) that will be compromised. It is among these two sides in which the attacker will be logically situated to be capable of sniffing all their associated traffic.
2. The attacker forges an ARP reply message containing a fake MAC/IP correspondence. The correspondence will take the attacker's MAC address and the first victim's IP to build a fake match of MAC/IP addresses. This ARP reply message should be sent to the second victim to poison its ARP table.
3. The second step is repeated, but in this case, the correspondence will take the attacker's MAC address and the second victim's IP. This new forged ARP reply should be sent to the first victim.
4. The first victim will send network packets to the legitimate IP address (i.e., the second victim's IP address), but the Ethernet frame will contain the attacker MAC address so that the network frames will arrive at the malicious host.
5. The malicious host will inspect the data, driven by its purpose, and then will forward the original packet to the legitimate host (i.e., the second victim).
6. The second victim will receive the packet as if nothing happened.
7. This attack works on both ways, so the second victim's packets will also be intercepted and forwarded by the attacker.

The attacker generally put itself in the middle of a victim host and the LAN's default router to intercept all of the communications of the victim, as shown in Fig. 6.1.

Let's consider the scenario in Fig. 6.2 to illustrate the workflow of the MITM attack.

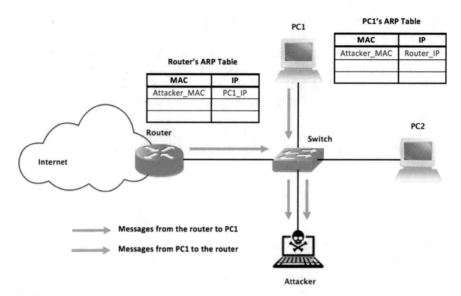

Fig. 6.1 Effects of a MITM attack

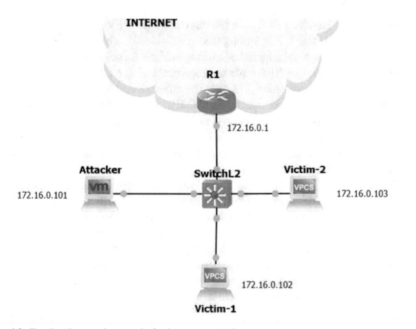

Fig. 6.2 Emulated network scenario for layer two attacks

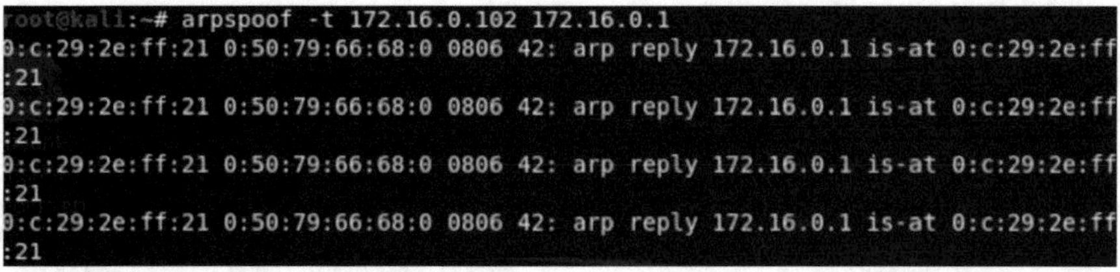

```
root@kali:~# arpspoof -t 172.16.0.102 172.16.0.1
0:c:29:2e:ff:21 0:50:79:66:68:0 0806 42: arp reply 172.16.0.1 is-at 0:c:29:2e:ff
:21
0:c:29:2e:ff:21 0:50:79:66:68:0 0806 42: arp reply 172.16.0.1 is-at 0:c:29:2e:ff
:21
0:c:29:2e:ff:21 0:50:79:66:68:0 0806 42: arp reply 172.16.0.1 is-at 0:c:29:2e:ff
:21
0:c:29:2e:ff:21 0:50:79:66:68:0 0806 42: arp reply 172.16.0.1 is-at 0:c:29:2e:ff
:21
```

Fig. 6.3 ARP spoofing attack. The attacker is continuously sending ARP reply messages with fake information

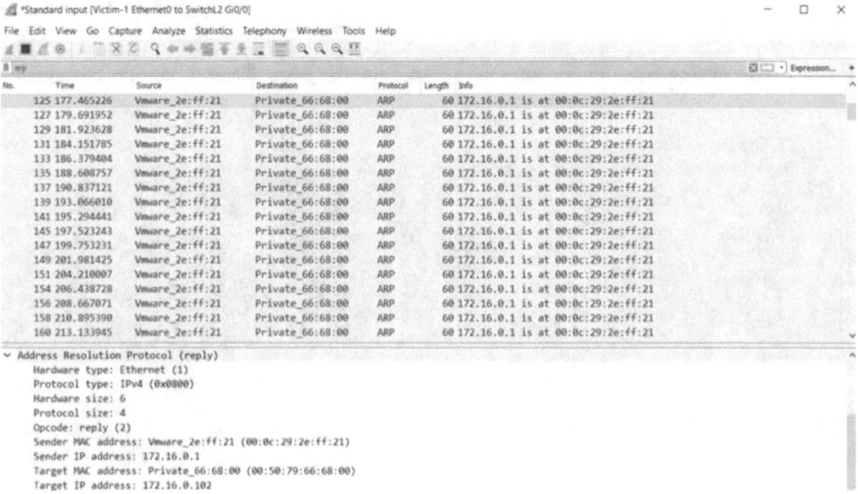

Fig. 6.4 Traffic through the victim and the switch link

At first, the attacker is unable to sniff Victim-1 traffic, due to the network segmentation occasioned by the switch. By executing the ping command and Wireshark on the different links, it is clear that messages generated by Victim-1 (and their responses) can only be sniffed through the link connecting the victim to the switch.

The attacker executes the *arpspoof* command (Fig. 6.3), which sends gratuitous ARP replies with a fake correspondence of IP/MAC addresses. In this case, the attacker wants to make believe the victim that the host with the IP address 172.16.0.1 (i.e., the default router) has the MAC corresponding to the attacker.

While the attacking is executing, it is possible to see how the victim is receiving several ARP reply messages with fake information (Fig. 6.4).

If the attack is executed in both ways (making believe the router that the victim's IP address corresponds with the attacker MAC address), the intruder could be able to sniff all the communications between two devices.

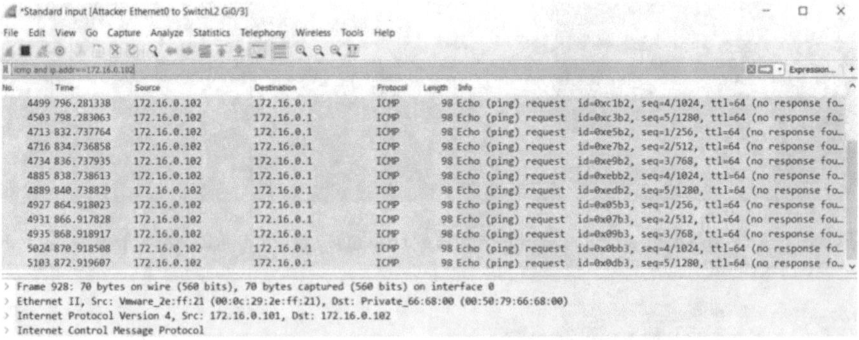

Fig. 6.5 The network capture on the link of the attacker shows that the attacker is receiving messages from the victim intended to the router

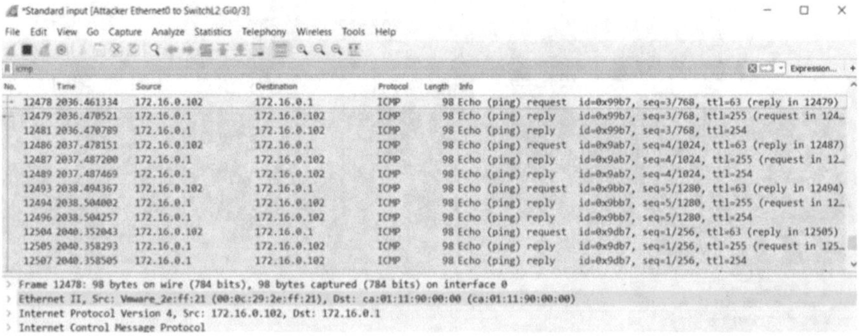

Fig. 6.6 Successful MITM attack; the messages are reaching both the victim and the router, but the attacker is in the middle of the communication

Executing the initial ping in this situation shows that, effectively, traffic goes from the victim to the attacker first. However, the ICMP messages never reach the router, because the malicious host has not enabled IP forwarding, so it discards the messages (Fig. 6.5).

To complete the attack, the malicious host needs to enable the IP forwarding option to process the received messages and forward it to the original destination. Also, it is necessary to disable the ICMP Redirect option, to avoid the intruder from sending ICMP Redirect messages (which could make the attack very verbose due to the continuous redirections).

By executing once again the ping from the victim to the router, it is clear to observe the success of the attack (Fig. 6.6) due to the ARP tables' poisoning: in the router's ARP table, the hardware address associated to the 172.16.0.102 address (the victim) is the attacker's MAC address (Fig. 6.7), and vice versa for the victim's ARP table (Fig. 6.8).

```
R1#show arp
Protocol  Address          Age (min)  Hardware Addr   Type   Interface
Internet  172.16.0.1          -       ca01.1190.0000  ARPA   FastEthernet0/0
Internet  172.16.0.101        0       000c.292e.ff21  ARPA   FastEthernet0/0
Internet  172.16.0.102        0       000c.292e.ff21  ARPA   FastEthernet0/0
Internet  172.16.0.103        31      0050.7966.6801  ARPA   FastEthernet0/0
```

Fig. 6.7 Router's poisoned ARP table. The associated MAC address to the 172.16.0.102 IP address is the attacker's one

```
VPCS> arp

00:0c:29:2e:ff:21   172.16.0.1 expires in 119 seconds
```

Fig. 6.8 Victim's poisoned ARP table. The associated MAC address to the 172.16.0.1 IP address is the attacker's one

Port Stealing

Port stealing is another way of sniffing legitimate traffic not intended for the malicious receiver. This attack also takes advantage of the ARP protocol behavior.

The workflow of the port stealing attack is as follows [38, 39]:

1. The attacker identifies the victim's MAC address.
2. The attacker continually floods the network with forged network frames with the victim's MAC address as the source.
3. By continuously flooding the network with these messages, the switch will map the victim's MAC address to the port behind the attacker is connected.
4. The switch will forward the frames intended to the victim through the attacker's port (since the last message with the victim's MAC address as the source came from that port), being the intruder able to sniff the victim's messages. In other words, the attacker has "stolen" the victim's port (Fig. 6.9).

The previous scenario will be used to illustrate this attack. By using *Ettercap,* it is possible to steal a switch's port straightforward. *Ettercap* fakes the source of the gratuitous ARP and puts the victims' MAC addresses to force the switch to learn that these addresses are behind the attacker port.

The effect of this attack is the same as in the previous scenario. The intruder is now able to sniff the communications between the victims. In the CAM table of the switch, it is possible to see how the different victims' MAC addresses have been mapped to the attacker's port (Fig. 6.10).

Countermeasures

On the one hand, the security measures could be passive. Passive techniques involve monitoring the network traffic and checking for MAC and IP addresses

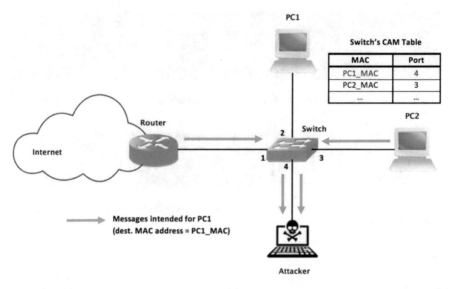

Fig. 6.9 Effects of the port stealing attack

```
Switch#show mac address-table
          Mac Address Table
-------------------------------------------------------------

Vlan     Mac Address        Type           Ports
----     -----------        ----           -----
   1     000c.292e.ff21     DYNAMIC        Gi0/3
   1     0050.7966.6800     DYNAMIC        Gi0/3
   1     0050.7966.6801     DYNAMIC        Gi0/3
   1     0c7a.8560.8001     DYNAMIC        Gi0/3
   1     ca01.1190.0000     DYNAMIC        Gi0/2
```

Fig. 6.10 Switch's poisoned CAM table; different MAC addresses have been mapped to the same port (Gi0/3).

inconsistencies. The main drawback of this solution is the time lag when trying to detect suspicious behaviors [40], as it could be too late once the attack has been identified, and damage could be already done even if the danger has been mitigated.

Active techniques, on the other hand, involve some methods present in most manageable switches (Cisco, Netgear, and Juniper, among others). The Dynamic ARP Inspection (DAI) method is one of the most powerful and flexible functionalities of manageable switches to offer protection against this kind of attacks.

A switch with the DAI feature enabled intercepts all ARP messages received through untrusted ports and verifies that the MAC/IP correspondence is legit. To validate these correspondences, the switch uses a DHCP snooping database in which

```
Switch#show ip dhcp snooping binding
MacAddress            IpAddress       Lease(sec)  Type           VLAN  Interface
------------------    -----------     ----------  ------------   ----  ------------------
00:0C:29:2E:FF:21     172.16.0.103    86351       dhcp-snooping  1     GigabitEthernet0/3
00:50:79:66:68:00     172.16.0.101    86284       dhcp-snooping  1     GigabitEthernet0/0
00:50:79:66:68:01     172.16.0.102    86389       dhcp-snooping  1     GigabitEthernet0/1
Total number of bindings: 3
```

Fig. 6.11 Switch's DHCP snooping database

the MAC/IP addresses obtained via DHCP are stored (Fig. 6.11). It is also possible to use ACLs to verify these correspondences, but DHCP snooping is recommended.

Once the *ip dhcp snooping* functionality has been set, it is necessary to mark as "trusted" the port to which the legitimate DHCP server is connected.

After activating the DHCP snooping and ARP inspection features (marking all ports as untrusted to ensure frame validation before forwarding them), the attacker is not able anymore to perform ARP spoofing techniques to poison the devices' ARP tables since the switch is rejecting any untrusted packet (i.e., any packet with a MAC/IP correspondence not stored in the DHCP snooping binding database).

MAC Flooding Attacks

As explained before, ARP replies can be forged and sent gratuitously. This opens up another attack vector focused on overflowing layer two devices. By continuously flooding the network with fake ARP replies at a high rate, the CAM table of these devices will always be full.

This attack could provoke two different behaviors on switches, depending on the implementation. On the one hand, if the switch's CAM table full, it could not map any other MAC/IP correspondence, causing legitimate frames to be dropped. The CAM table overflow then develops into a denial of service attack, preventing authorized users to send their messages. On the other hand, another dangerous behavior could be provoked on switches by the MAC flooding attack, as it can be seen in Fig. 6.12, when a CAM table overflow is successful, the switch could revert its mode to a broadcast mode, meaning that the switch will lose its network segmenting benefits by behaving like a hub.

Let us consider the previous scenario. Through the *macof* tool, the attacker forges random messages with random MAC addresses to overflow the switch's CAM table. A successful attack would populate this table until no more space is available.

The effect of this attack, as aforementioned, is that the switch will start acting like a hub, forwarding every Ethernet frame through all its port and losing its segmentation functionality.

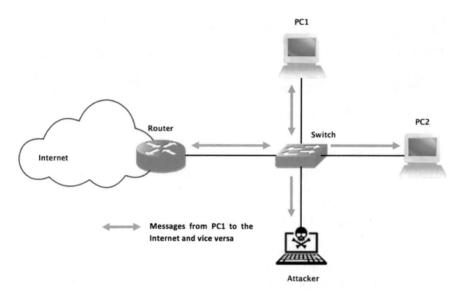

Fig. 6.12 Switch behaving like a hub when its CAM table has been overflown

```
*Oct 13 10:40:48.752: %PM-4-ERR_DISABLE: psecure-violation error detected on Gi0/3, putting Gi0/3 in err-disab
le state
*Oct 13 10:40:48.755: %PORT_SECURITY-2-PSECURE_VIOLATION: Security violation occurred, caused by MAC address
224.50a8.14c8 on port GigabitEthernet0/3.
*Oct 13 10:40:49.755: %LINEPROTO-5-UPDOWN: Line protocol on Interface GigabitEthernet0/3, changed state to dow
n
*Oct 13 10:40:50.754: %LINK-3-UPDOWN: Interface GigabitEthernet0/3, changed state to down
Switch#
```

Fig. 6.13 Security violation and automatic shutdown of the switch's port

Countermeasures

The port security feature can be used as the countermeasure for MAC flooding attacks. This feature enables the administrators to determine a limit of the number of different MAC addresses allowed behind a port. It also lets the administrator select the action to take under attack, being possible to even shutdown the origin of the attack.

For example, by adding the *shutdown* policy on violation to the emulated switch, the attacker is not able to continue sending messages, as the port has been shut down (Fig. 6.13).

With the *protect* and *restrict* policies, the port is still up, but it does not accept any packets from not trusted MAC addresses (i.e., MAC addresses found after the violation error has been detected). This is achieved by configuring the first MAC addresses found behind a port as STATIC (Fig. 6.14) and not accepting any message through that port that does not come from that MAC address.

It is possible to observe how the attacker has automatically lost the connection after trying to execute the attack (Fig. 6.15).

```
Switch#show mac address-table
            Mac Address Table
-----------------------------------------------------------

Vlan      Mac Address          Type          Ports
----      -----------          --------      ------
   1      9224.50a8.14c8       STATIC        Gi0/3
   1      ca01.1190.0000       DYNAMIC       Gi0/2
Total Mac Addresses for this criterion: 2
```

Fig. 6.14 Switch's CAM table with the port-security restrict policy

```
root@kali:~# ping 172.16.0.1
PING 172.16.0.1 (172.16.0.1) 56(84) bytes of data.
From 172.16.0.101 icmp_seq=1 Destination Host Unreachable
From 172.16.0.101 icmp_seq=2 Destination Host Unreachable
From 172.16.0.101 icmp_seq=3 Destination Host Unreachable
From 172.16.0.101 icmp_seq=4 Destination Host Unreachable
From 172.16.0.101 icmp_seq=5 Destination Host Unreachable
```

Fig. 6.15 The attacker is not able to communicate after enabling the port security feature

By configuring port security, network administrators can be unburdened from manually shutting down ports after anomalies are found.

4.2.2 Virtual Local Area Networks (VLANs)

Virtual Local Area Networks are a useful manner of adding more segmentation to a LAN by defining virtual networks on top of the physical infrastructure. Configuring VLANs is seen as a good security practice since each VLAN will behave as an individual LAN from a logical point of view. For example, an attacker in a particular VLAN could not perform a MITM attack on hosts connected to a different VLAN.

However, there are some default settings that need to be addressed to avoid vulnerabilities regarding this mechanism [41, 42].

Trunk Ports

Trunk ports allow savings regarding the ports used for switches' interconnection. By defining a trunk port, all of the configured VLANs traffic will flow through a single port. To identify which VLAN each data frame belongs to, switches rely on the IEEE 802.1Q protocol [43].

However, there is a dangerous Cisco default setting regarding trunk ports that could allow an intruder with access to a malicious switch to obtain a trunk port,

Table 6.1 Link type regarding the working mode between two switches' ports

Local/remote port mode	Dynamic auto	Dynamic desirable	Trunk	Access
Dynamic auto	Access	Trunk	Trunk	Access
Dynamic desirable	Trunk	Trunk	Trunk	Access
Trunk	Trunk	Trunk	Trunk	Limited
Access	Access	Access	Limited	Access

being capable of receiving all the traffic from all VLANs, and, therefore, bypassing the VLAN security layer. The dynamic trunk protocol [44] allows switches to negotiate trunk ports on between two switches automatically. To do so, the network administrators can configure the working mode of a port with different values. When a switch discovers another switch, based on these values, the negotiation can change a port to a trunk port automatically. The correspondence of the working mode values, as indicated in [45], can be consulted in Table 6.1.

The previous table illustrates the capability of an attacker with access to a local switch to tune the working mode of its switch to automatically change the working method of the remote switch port to operate as a trunk port.

Native VLAN

The native VLAN is the VLAN used for trunk ports, and it is the solution for interconnecting switches that do not support the 802.1Q protocol with switches that do support it. Therefore, the native VLAN does not need to be tagged with the corresponding VLAN identifier.

Factory settings on some switches define the native VLAN as the VLAN 1, and it is by default the VLAN which all the switch's ports belong. This vulnerability can be exploited by an attacker since it allows the execution of the *double-tagging attack* [10].

The double-tagging attack is performed in four steps (Fig. 6.16):

1. The attacker identifies the VLAN to which the victim is connected.
2. An attacker connects to a switch through a port that belongs to the native VLAN and sends a frame tagged with two VLAN identifiers: the native VLAN identifier and the victim's VLAN identifier.
3. The switch receives the frame and inspects the tags, stripping the native VLAN tag. As the native VLAN frames do not need to be tagged, the switch forwards the frame through its trunk ports now with only the second introduced tag by the attacker.
4. The next switch that receives the frame inspects the tag and forwards it to the corresponding VLAN, reaching a host that should not have been reached by the attacker (since they did not belong to the same VLAN).

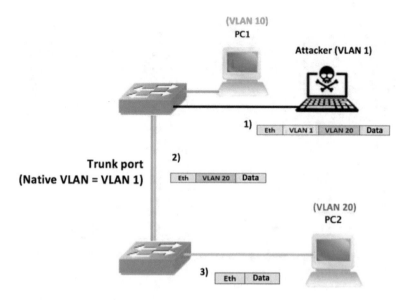

Fig. 6.16 VLAN hopping through the double-tagging technique

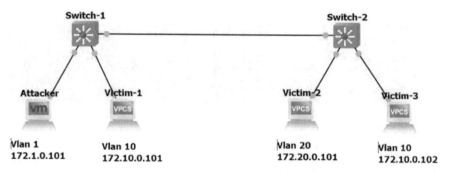

Fig. 6.17 A scenario with pre-configured VLANs and default settings

Using the scenario in Fig. 6.17, the attacker objective is to communicate with hosts that are not on the same VLAN (which is at first, not possible).

Using Yersinia, the attacker sends DTP messages to the switch to negotiate the working mode of the port (Fig. 6.18). Given the fact that the default mode is "dynamic auto", the attacker can obtain the trunk port by using a "dynamic desirable" or "trunk" configuration (as seen in Table 6.1).

It is possible to observe by showing the status of the switch's interfaces that the attack has succeeded: The Gi0/1 interface (which the attacker is connected to) is now marked as a trunk link (Fig. 6.19).

The attacker now can forge Ethernet frames with the target VLAN identifier and communicate with the victim (Fig. 6.20).

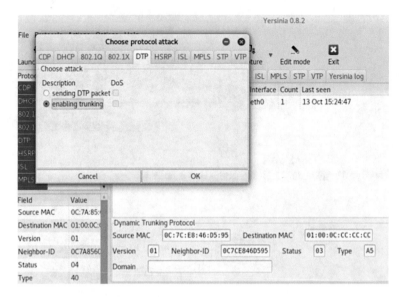

Fig. 6.18 Using Yersinia to obtain a trunk link with a switch

```
Switch#show int status

Port        Name              Status        Vlan      Duplex    Speed Type
Gi0/0                         connected     trunk     a-full    auto  RJ45
Gi0/1                         connected     trunk     a-full    auto  RJ45
Gi0/2                         connected     10        a-full    auto  RJ45
Gi0/3                         connected     1         a-full    auto  RJ45
```

Fig. 6.19 Successful DTP attack

```
*Standard input [Switch-1 Gi0/1 to Attacker Ethernet0]                                                  —    □    ×
File  Edit  View  Go  Capture  Analyze  Statistics  Telephony  Wireless  Tools  Help

icmp                                                                                    ⊠ ⊡ ▾ Expression...  +
No.      Time           Source            Destination       Protocol  Length  Info
     106 53.008800      172.10.0.200      172.10.0.102      ICMP          56  Echo (ping) request  id=0x0042, seq=66/16896, ttl=64 (no response fo..
     311 156.363083     172.10.0.200      172.10.0.102      ICMP          56  Echo (ping) request  id=0x0042, seq=66/16896, ttl=64 (no response fo..
     316 159.542506     172.10.0.200      172.10.0.102      ICMP          56  Echo (ping) request  id=0x0042, seq=66/16896, ttl=64 (no response fo..
```

Fig. 6.20 The victim is receiving messages from an attacker located in a different VLAN

On the other hand, since the attacker is connected to the VLAN 1, which is, by default, the native VLAN used on trunk ports, it could also perform a double tagging attack with Yersinia (Fig. 6.21).

The switch will strip the native VLAN tag and send the victim the forged message, being the VLAN hopping successfully due to the switches' default settings.

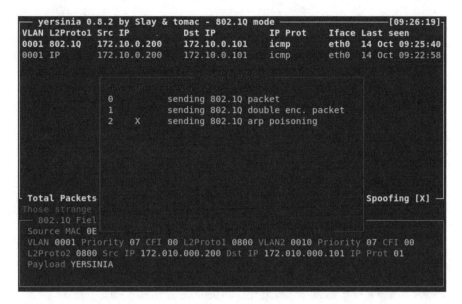

```
┌── yersinia 0.8.2 by Slay & tomac - 802.1Q mode ──────────────[09:26:19]┐
│VLAN L2Protol Src IP          Dst IP           IP Prot    Iface Last seen│
│0001 802.1Q   172.10.0.200    172.10.0.101     icmp       eth0  14 Oct 09:25:40│
│0001 IP       172.10.0.200    172.10.0.101     icmp       eth0  14 Oct 09:22:58│
│                                                                        │
│                                                                        │
│            0            sending 802.1Q packet                          │
│            1            sending 802.1Q double enc. packet              │
│            2    X        sending 802.1Q arp poisoning                  │
│                                                                        │
│                                                                        │
│                                                                        │
│                                                                        │
│                                                                        │
│─ Total Packets                                     Spoofing [X] ─│
│Those strange                                                           │
│── 802.1Q Fiel                                                          │
│Source MAC 0E                                                           │
│VLAN 0001 Priority 07 CFI 00 L2Protol 0800 VLAN2 0010 Priority 07 CFI 00│
│L2Proto2 0800 Src IP 172.010.000.200 Dst IP 172.010.000.101 IP Prot 01  │
│Payload YERSINIA                                                        │
└────────────────────────────────────────────────────────────────────────┘
```

Fig. 6.21 Using Yersinia to send a double-tagged frame. The first frame will have the VLAN identifier = 1, and the second tag the target VLAN (in this case, the VLAN with id = 10)

Countermeasures

In this case, the countermeasures are straightforward. It is possible to deactivate the DTP protocol in all ports to mitigate the trunk port (i.e., configuring the *switchport nonegotiate* policy). In case of needing to define these type of ports, it is recommended to do it manually, constituting a less flexible but more secure practice.

On the other hand, to prevent double-tagging attacks, the native VLAN should be changed to a different VLAN not used to connect hosts. This action ensures that the native VLAN is exclusively used for trunk ports, overriding the dangerous VLAN 1 default setting.

4.3 Network Layer

Network layer attacks are focused on layer three devices, especially routers (but also hosts). Primarily, layer three attacks look for compromising routing tables to spoof IP addresses. Routing tables are crucial resources within this layer; the routing capabilities of layer-3 devices are supported by previously learned routes.

Some protocols at the network layer that support the Internet protocol (IP) could be leveraged to compromise the security of a LAN. The Internet Control Message Protocol (ICMP) is one of these protocols: it provides the capability to send error messages or operational information to monitor the communications [46]. ICMP messages are useful, but in particular situations, messages like the ICMP Redirect type, could be used to poison the devices' routing tables with fake information.

However, at this level, there are also other vulnerabilities that can lead to denial of service attacks if the routers' default settings are not checked and modified accordingly, and these vulnerabilities need equal attention.

4.3.1 Spoofing Attacks Based on ICMP

ICMP Redirect messages are useful to speed the process of finding the most efficient route to a particular destination. If a network relies on two gateways and one of the routers is the default gateway, any host will first send every message to this particular router.

However, after inspecting the packet's destination, the default gateway can determine if that route is the shortest path to the target network. If that is not the case, the default router will then send an ICMP Redirect message to inform the sender that the best route to reach the destination is through the another LAN's gateway. The subsequent messages sent to the destination network will be routed by the secondary gateway, as it will be more efficient. This behavior is achieved by modifying the sender's routing table through the ICMP Redirect message [47].

An attacker could forge ICMP Redirect messages to fake their content and make believe a host that the default gateway has changed to perform a MITM attack (Fig. 6.22).

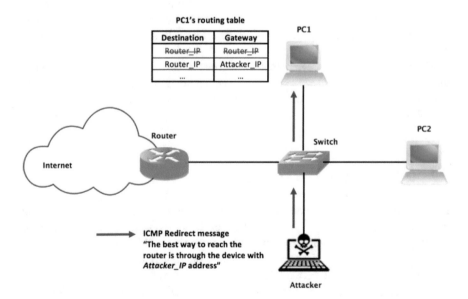

Fig. 6.22 Performing a MITM attack through ICMP redirect messages.

```
root@debian:~# route -nC
Kernel IP routing cache
Source           Destination      Gateway          Flags Metric Ref     Use Iface
0.0.0.0          255.255.255.255  255.255.255.255  bl    0      0         1 lo
172.16.0.101     172.16.0.102     172.16.0.102     il    0      0         1 lo
172.16.0.1       172.16.0.102     172.16.0.102     il    0      0         8 lo
0.0.0.0          255.255.255.255  255.255.255.255  bl    0      0         0 lo
0.0.0.0          255.255.255.255  255.255.255.255  bl    0      0         0 lo
root@debian:~#
```

Fig. 6.23 Victim host's routing table under normal circumstances

Fig. 6.24 Spoofed ICMP redirect messages forged by the attacker

```
root@debian:~# route -nC
Kernel IP routing cache
Source           Destination      Gateway          Flags Metric Ref     Use Iface
172.16.0.102     172.16.0.101     172.16.0.101           0      0         1 eth0
172.16.0.102     172.16.0.101     172.16.0.101           0      0        61 eth0
0.0.0.0          255.255.255.255  255.255.255.255  bl    0      0         5 lo
0.0.0.0          255.255.255.255  255.255.255.255  bl    0      0        10 lo
172.16.0.101     172.16.0.102     172.16.0.102     il    0      0        75 lo
172.16.0.1       172.16.0.102     172.16.0.102     il    0      0       356 lo
172.16.0.102     172.16.0.1       172.16.0.101           0      0       360 eth0
```

Fig. 6.25 Poisoned routing table. The poisoned route to the gateway is highlighted within the rectangle

This procedure will be described following the first scenario used in the layer 2 section (Fig. 6.2). At first, the victim's routing table is legit, and the gateway for default destinations is the legitimate router (Fig. 6.23).

The attacker forges an ICMP Redirect message to modify the victim's routing table. To do so, using *icmpush* [48, 49], the intruder announces that the best next hop to reach the router is the attacker itself (Fig. 6.24).

If the victim is vulnerable (i.e., the acceptance of ICMP Redirect messages is enabled), its routing table will be compromised. Indeed, the routing table (Fig. 6.25) shows how the victim will now send first to the attacker (172.16.0.101) the messages intended to the router (172.16.0.1).

The attacker could be able to sniff the victim's traffic under these circumstances.

Countermeasures

Some devices accept ICMP redirect messages by default, which, as it has been observed, could lead to a MITM attack. The countermeasures for this attack are trivial. Every device should be configured to reject any ICMP redirect message.

However, if the ICMP redirect functionality is required within a LAN, the devices must only accept these messages from legitimate sources (i.e., the trusted LAN gateways).

4.3.2 Flooding Attacks

As seen in other scenarios, no device is completely protected against denial of service vulnerabilities. At this level, a very simple attack can compromise the resources of a whole LAN: the *smurf* attack. This attack utilizes ICMP echo request messages [50] and targets at big LANs to overflow the victim's system.

The *smurf* attack workflow is straightforward (Fig. 6.26):

1. The attacker forges an ICMP echo request message with the victim's IP as the source and the broadcast address of a big LAN as the destination.
2. If the destination LAN is vulnerable, every connected host will answer the echo request sending an ICMP echo reply message to the victim's IP address.
3. The victim will receive a vast quantity of messages that could overload the system.

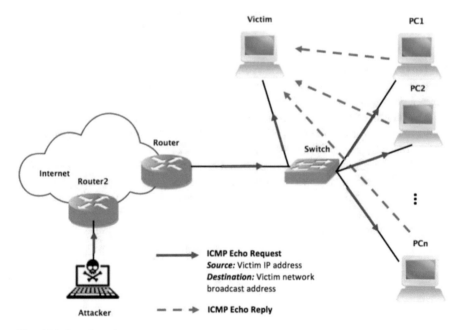

Fig. 6.26 Smurf attack

The drawback of attempting to perform this attack is that nowadays is difficult to find a big enough LAN with this vulnerability. Given the necessity of a big LAN, this attack cannot be easily reproduced in a virtual environment, as it would consume a lot of resources.

Countermeasures

By simply deactivating the directed broadcast feature, it is possible to deny the application of this attack. This is currently the default behavior [51], but it is important to check and understand the damages that can cause a misconfiguration of this option.

4.4 Transport Layer

Transport layer attacks are more focused on exhaustion and denial of service of the network devices. Among the protocols on this layer, the two most popular transport protocols are located: TCP and UDP protocols.

TCP and UDP protocols provide an exploitable context to perform DoS attacks [52]. As it has been previously pointed out, flooding a network is a simple but effective manner to overload its systems and provoke catastrophic damage, so it is necessary to understand the possible security measures that can be taken to prevent DoS attacks.

4.4.1 UDP Flooding Attack

As its name suggests, the procedure for executing this attack is straightforward: flooding a network with UDP packets directed to random ports at a high rate. By performing this attack, the victim device must:

- Check if any application is listening through that port
- If that is not the case, the victim must build an ICMP destination unreachable message and send it to the source of the UDP packet (which is probably a fake IP address to avoid the attack turning against the intruder)

The network will then be flooded with the UDP packets and the ICMP messages, besides the CPU burden provoked on the victim device that could make the system freeze (Fig. 6.27).

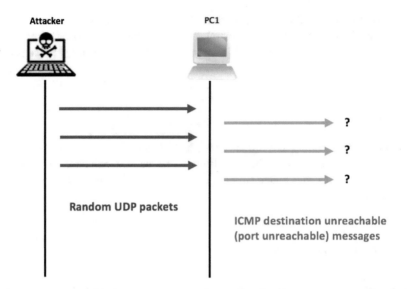

Fig. 6.27 UDP flooding attack

```
CPU utilization for five seconds: 0%/0%; one minute: 1%; five minutes: 0%
 PID QTy       PC Runtime (ms)    Invoked   uSecs    Stacks TTY Process
   1 Cwe 60798288         0           2        0 5452/6000   0 Chunk Manager
   2 Csp 60780774         0          40        0 2528/3000   0 Load Meter
   3 Mwe 62877EA4         0           1        0 5636/6000   0 chkpt message ha
```

Fig. 6.28 Normal CPU load

No.	Time	Source	Destination	Protocol	Length	Info
3991	176.089902	172.16.0.103	172.16.0.1	UDP	60	2962 → 0 Len=0
3992	176.091399	172.16.0.103	172.16.0.1	UDP	60	2963 → 0 Len=0
3993	176.093396	172.16.0.1	172.16.0.103	ICMP	70	Destination unreachable (Port unreachable)
3994	176.093396	172.16.0.1	172.16.0.103	ICMP	70	Destination unreachable (Port unreachable)
3995	176.102882	172.16.0.103	172.16.0.1	UDP	60	2964 → 0 Len=0
3996	176.103880	172.16.0.1	172.16.0.103	ICMP	70	Destination unreachable (Port unreachable)
3997	176.103880	172.16.0.1	172.16.0.103	ICMP	70	Destination unreachable (Port unreachable)
3998	176.104379	172.16.0.103	172.16.0.1	UDP	60	2965 → 0 Len=0
3999	176.111865	172.16.0.103	172.16.0.1	UDP	60	2966 → 0 Len=0
4000	176.112863	172.16.0.103	172.16.0.1	UDP	60	2967 → 0 Len=0
4001	176.114361	172.16.0.1	172.16.0.103	ICMP	70	Destination unreachable (Port unreachable)
4002	176.114361	172.16.0.1	172.16.0.103	ICMP	70	Destination unreachable (Port unreachable)
4003	176.123839	172.16.0.103	172.16.0.1	UDP	60	2968 → 0 Len=0
4004	176.124838	172.16.0.1	172.16.0.103	ICMP	70	Destination unreachable (Port unreachable)
4005	176.124838	172.16.0.1	172.16.0.103	ICMP	70	Destination unreachable (Port unreachable)
4006	176.124838	172.16.0.103	172.16.0.1	UDP	60	2969 → 0 Len=0
4007	176.131326	172.16.0.103	172.16.0.1	UDP	60	2970 → 0 Len=0
4008	176.132827	172.16.0.103	172.16.0.1	UDP	60	2971 → 0 Len=0
4009	176.135321	172.16.0.1	172.16.0.103	ICMP	70	Destination unreachable (Port unreachable)
4010	176.135321	172.16.0.1	172.16.0.103	ICMP	70	Destination unreachable (Port unreachable)
4011	176.142309	172.16.0.103	172.16.0.1	UDP	60	2972 → 0 Len=0

Fig. 6.29 Traffic capture between the router and the switch during the UDP flooding attack

To describe this attack, the previous scenario (Fig. 6.2) has been used. At first, the router's CPU (which will be the victim in this case) shows a normal CPU load for the initial situation with no traffic (Fig. 6.28).

```
CPU utilization for five seconds: 99%/100%; one minute: 53%; five minutes: 15%
  PID QTy       PC Runtime (ms)     Invoked    uSecs     Stacks TTY Process
    1 Cwe 60798288            0          2        0 5452/6000    0 Chunk Manager
    2 Csp 60780774            8        114       70 2528/3000    0 Load Meter
    3 Mwe 62877EA4            0          1        0 5636/6000    0 chkpt message ha
```

Fig. 6.30 Effect of the flooding attack on the CPU load

```
R1(config)#ip access-list extended no-flood-UDP
R1(config-ext-nacl)#permit udp any any
R1(config-ext-nacl)#class-map UDP
R1(config-cmap)#match access-group name no-flood-UDP
R1(config-cmap)#policy-map 1
R1(config-pmap)#class UDP
R1(config-pmap-c)#police 10000 conform-action transmit exceed-action drop
R1(config-pmap-c-police)#exit
R1(config-pmap-c)#control-plane
R1(config-cp)#service-policy input 1
R1(config-cp)#end
R1#
```

Fig. 6.31 The configuration of a policy to limit the input packet rate

Through this practical scenario, the attacker is focused on compromise the router's functionalities by increasing its CPU load to its limit. With the *hping3* tool, it is possible to perform a UDP flood attack. Once the attack has started, the traffic captures show how the attack is working (Fig. 6.29): the router is continuously sending ICMP destination unreachable messages to the attacker's defined destination (in this case, the machine with IP address 172.16.0.103) due to the random ports specified in the malicious UDP messages.

It can be observed that the router's CPU is overloaded by the show processes command. This attack could lead to a DoS situation, forcing the router to drop legitimate packets due to its high CPU utilization (Fig. 6.30).

Countermeasures

These attacks can be prevented by implementing a traffic policy to limit the rate [53] of received UDP packets, to protect the devices from UDP flooding.

If the UDP traffic is limited to a 10000 bytes/s (the ideal value might vary depending on the network infrastructure), the CPU of the router will no longer be overloaded, as it discards any packet that violates the policy (Fig. 6.31).

In this case, it can be observed that, under the same attack, the router's CPU has less load than when the policy was not deployed, and does not reach the 100% of its capacities (Fig. 6.32).

```
CPU utilization for five seconds: 66%/100%; one minute: 33%; five minutes: 19%
 PID QTy        PC Runtime (ms)    Invoked   uSecs    Stacks TTY Process
   1 Cwe 60798288            0         2        0 5452/6000   0 Chunk Manager
   2 Csp 60780774           20       191      104 2528/3000   0 Load Meter
   3 Mwe 62877EA4            0         1        0 5636/6000   0 chkpt message ha
```

Fig. 6.32 CPU load while the attack is executed after implementing the policy

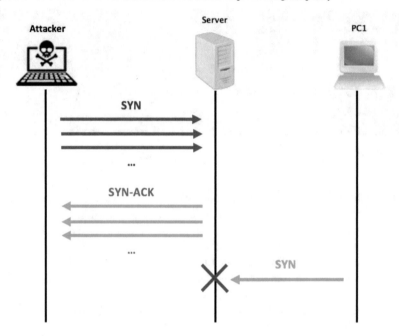

Fig. 6.33 TCP SYN flooding attack

4.4.2 TCP SYN Flooding Attack

The basis of this attack is similar to the previous flooding attacks, but in this case, the attacker takes advantage of the TCP protocol workflow, especially of the TCP SYN message.

By continually sending TCP SYN messages to the target device, but never responding to the corresponding TCP SYN-ACK messages, the victim will be setting aside the resources to establish the connections in vain (Fig. 6.33). The attacker can monopolize all of the victim's resources, being impossible for a legitimate user to create an actual connection (i.e., denying the service of the victim).

To describe this attack, the same scenario as in the UDP flooding attack is used. In this case, the victim is a host with a default Apache server deployed. If another host tries to access the website, the default homepage is displayed without any trouble (Fig. 6.34).

It works!

This is the default web page for this server.

The web server software is running but no content has been added, yet.

Fig. 6.34 Accessing a web server under normal circumstances

No.	Time	Source	Destination	Protocol	Length	Info
21433	1566.157755	175.132.244.46	172.16.0.102	TCP	60	40488 → 80 [SYN] Seq=0 Win=337 Len=0
21434	1566.158248	175.132.244.46	172.16.0.102	TCP	60	52296 → 80 [SYN] Seq=0 Win=1161 Len=0
21435	1566.158754	175.132.244.46	172.16.0.102	TCP	60	[TCP Port numbers reused] 14592 → 80 [SYN] Seq=0 Win=3646 Len=0
21436	1566.159253	175.132.244.46	172.16.0.102	TCP	60	23342 → 80 [SYN] Seq=0 Win=1476 Len=0
21437	1566.159751	175.132.244.46	172.16.0.102	TCP	60	21449 → 80 [SYN] Seq=0 Win=3103 Len=0
21438	1566.160752	175.132.244.46	172.16.0.102	TCP	60	52457 → 80 [SYN] Seq=0 Win=2550 Len=0
21439	1566.161261	175.132.244.46	172.16.0.102	TCP	60	[TCP Port numbers reused] 11692 → 80 [SYN] Seq=0 Win=1959 Len=0
21440	1566.162241	175.132.244.46	172.16.0.102	TCP	60	17781 → 80 [SYN] Seq=0 Win=3222 Len=0
21441	1566.163255	175.132.244.46	172.16.0.102	TCP	60	[TCP Port numbers reused] 28675 → 80 [SYN] Seq=0 Win=435 Len=0
21442	1566.163742	175.132.244.46	172.16.0.102	TCP	60	48694 → 80 [SYN] Seq=0 Win=305 Len=0
21443	1566.164755	175.132.244.46	172.16.0.102	TCP	60	34610 → 80 [SYN] Seq=0 Win=2315 Len=0
21444	1566.165236	175.132.244.46	172.16.0.102	TCP	60	[TCP Port numbers reused] 33197 → 80 [SYN] Seq=0 Win=1949 Len=0
21445	1566.166240	175.132.244.46	172.16.0.102	TCP	60	10523 → 80 [SYN] Seq=0 Win=1260 Len=0
21446	1566.167232	175.132.244.46	172.16.0.102	TCP	60	7268 → 80 [SYN] Seq=0 Win=2378 Len=0

Fig. 6.35 TCP SYN flooding attack; TCP SYN messages are continuously being sent to the web server

The attacker performs the TCP SYN flood attack through *metasploit*'s TCP module. As it can be seen, the execution of the attack provokes several TCP traffic (Fig. 6.35).

Under these circumstances, the server cannot accept any new connection due to the consumption of its resources. If a host tries to reaccess the server, it will not be able to establish the connection.

Countermeasures

There are different measures to prevent this attack. By configuring the TCP-intercept feature, the gateway can determine if a connection is going to be established or if it is a potential TCP SYN attack. With this functionality enabled, the routers manage half-opened connections, preventing the servers from consuming resources until the TCP ACK message is received by the router, forwarding it finally to the server when the connection has proved to be legit. The router discards half-opened connections that are not acknowledged within a defined time interval.

However, if the attacker is inside the LAN (as in the previous scenario), the protection should be introduced in the server. A firewall could be configured, as well as the SYN cookie protection [54].

4.5 Application Layer

This final section will provide an overview of how low-level attacks could compromise essential services such as the DHCP protocol. Other application layer services could be compromised with malicious intentions, like the HTTP/HTTPS protocol or the DNS protocol, but given their complexity and extension, attacks over these protocols are out of the scope of this chapter.

4.5.1 Attacks on the DHCP Protocol

The Dynamic Host Configuration Protocol (DHCP) [55] allow hosts to automatically configure their network parameters (such as a valid IP address, the default router IP address, the DNS servers' addresses, etc.) by following the client-server model. The hosts will try to negotiate the parameters by discovering the configured DHCP servers on the LAN after exchanging a series of messages.

The dependency on this crucial service is also a target for attackers. The denominated DHCP Starvation attack followed by the use of a rogue DHCP server [56] could make the target hosts trust the information given from the malicious server to become victims of MITM attacks, among others.

Attackers can exploit the DHCP as follows:

1. By flooding the network with several DHCP requests originated from spoofed MAC addresses, an attacker could end with all of the available IP addresses.
2. If the previous step is successful, then any legitimate host would be able to obtain an IP address (becoming a DoS attack at this stage).
3. The attacker is then able to use a malicious DHCP server configured to provide harmful network parameters given its purpose.

For instance, if the attacker configures the default router DHCP parameter to aim at a malicious host's IP address, a MITM attack could be performed, since all the messages that the victims' would send outside the LAN would be processed by the attacker first (Fig. 6.36).

Using the same scenario as in the layer 2 section (Fig. 6.2), the attacker can use a tool like *dhcpx* to perform a DHCP starvation attack.

The tool is in charge of sending several DHCP request messages to lease all the available IP addresses. The DHCP server will receive these requests and assign the IP addresses accordingly until it runs out of available IP addresses (Fig. 6.37).

It is possible to see the effects of the attack by observing the DHCP binding table (Fig. 6.38) on the victim DHCP server (in this case, the router). The table shows several IP bindings with random MAC addresses forged by the attacker.

After executing this attack, a legitimate host is unable to obtain its network parameters due to the several IP bindings on the server, provoking a DoS situation.

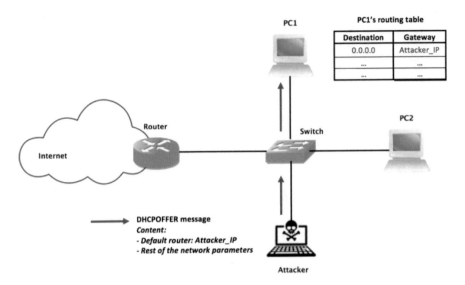

Fig. 6.36 DHCP rogue attack

Fig. 6.37 DHCP Starvation attack; several DHCP request messages flood the network to saturate the DHCP service

IP address	Client-ID/ Hardware address/ User name	Lease expiration	Type
172.16.0.101	000c.292e.ff21	Oct 16 2018 09:33 AM	Automatic
172.16.0.102	0100.5079.6668.00	Oct 16 2018 09:34 AM	Automatic
172.16.0.103	000c.29c1.6997	Oct 16 2018 09:36 AM	Automatic
172.16.0.104	0100.5079.6668.01	Oct 16 2018 09:44 AM	Automatic
172.16.0.105	0165.3c22.fb77.63	Oct 15 2018 09:50 AM	Automatic
172.16.0.106	017e.c9d9.5b9f.84	Oct 15 2018 09:51 AM	Automatic
172.16.0.107	0102.423d.947b.72	Oct 15 2018 09:51 AM	Automatic
172.16.0.108	017d.05d5.f831.ec	Oct 15 2018 09:51 AM	Automatic

Bindings from all pools not associated with VRF:

Fig. 6.38 DHCP binding table of the victim server

If the starvation attack succeeded, the attacker now can develop a rogue DHCP server on the network and provide forged network parameters (for instance, putting itself as the default gateway to perform a MITM attack, as shown in Fig. 6.39).

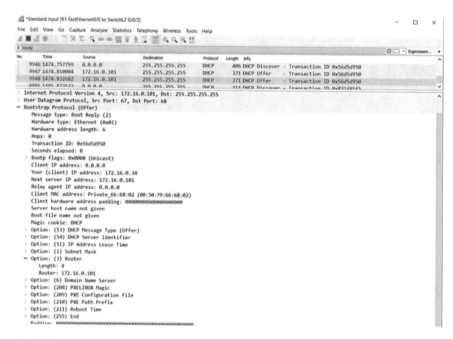

Fig. 6.39 The rogue DHCP server is offering malicious network parameters. The router IP address corresponds to the attacker

```
Switch(config)#int gi0/3
Switch(config-if)#switchport port-security
Switch(config-if)#switchport port-security maximum 4
Switch(config-if)#switchport port-security violation shutdown
Switch(config-if)#
```

Fig. 6.40 The configuration of port-security to mitigate DHCP starvation attacks

Countermeasures

The countermeasures for the presented DHCP attacks are similar to the ARP spoofing ones. The reason is that the attacker needs to spoof MAC addresses to make believe the DHCP server that there are several hosts asking for network parameters. If port-security is configured to limit the different number MAC addresses behind a port, the attack will be unsuccessful.

To prove this technique with an example, a limit of four MAC addresses is established behind the attacker port (Fig. 6.40).

It is possible to check that, although the attacker is performing the attack, the switch only allowed the first four DHCP requests, rejecting any new message from a different MAC address. The DHCP binding table shows how only four IP addresses have been leased (Fig. 6.41), as specified in the port-security policy.

The DHCP snooping technology also prevents devices attached to untrusted ports to deploy rogue DHCP servers. By declaring as untrusted any port that is not

```
R1#sh ip dhcp binding
Bindings from all pools not associated with VRF:
IP address          Client-ID/              Lease expiration        Type
                    Hardware address/
                    User name
172.16.0.101        000c.292e.ff21          Oct 17 2018 09:30 AM    Automatic
172.16.0.102        013c.82bd.3d7a.41       Oct 16 2018 09:36 AM    Automatic
172.16.0.103        013b.d184.6a37.bc       Oct 17 2018 09:31 AM    Automatic
172.16.0.104        0162.b74c.dce0.fd       Oct 17 2018 09:31 AM    Automatic
R1#
```

Fig. 6.41 DHCP binding table under the DHCP starvation attack

connected to the legitimate DHCP server(s), the switches will not forward DHCP offers coming from them. As can be observed, although the attacker is continuously sending malicious DHCP offer messages, the victims are not receiving any of them since the switch is intercepting them because they come from an untrusted port.

5   Discussion

The addressed network attacks focused on wired LAN vulnerabilities. These attacks are considered one of the most effective manners of stealing information or compromise communications. As it has been demonstrated, there are several methods to exploit LAN vulnerabilities, being simple but powerful techniques.

LAN vulnerabilities can be easily exploited when network devices are not correctly configured. It is important to rely on devices that are easy to deploy, but their security settings cannot be overlooked in favor of instant functionality.

The link layer section is this chapter's broadest section regarding vulnerabilities and security issues. Link layer attacks exploit low-level vulnerabilities and allow attackers to exploit this level's weaknesses, providing the basis to execute more advanced attacks. That is why link layer protection is crucial, and it is essential to know how default settings can compromise this vital layer in the protocol's stack.

The attacks based on the ARP protocol, for example, can poison the ARP tables of the devices to make them believe fake MAC/IP addresses correspondences to perform MITM attacks and steal confidential information subsequently. By configuring measures such as Dynamic ARP Inspection on layer-2 devices, these are the ones in charge of shutting down these type of attacks, unburdening higher layer devices (like legitimate hosts) of this responsibility.

Flooding attacks are present almost at every layer. These attacks, focused on provoking a denial of services, are difficult to prevent without limiting some of the network capabilities (as seen in the UDP flooding countermeasures, where it is necessary to establish a traffic limit rate to avoid the DoS attack). Packet filtering also can mess with network performance by having to examine every packet before actually processing it.

At the application level, the DHCP starvation and rogue techniques have been addressed. There are more vulnerable applications at this level, but DHCP is an essential network service. If compromised, the hosts could be left offline until the service is restored since they have not a valid IP address configured. As already presented before, an attacker could take advantage of this situation and perform DoS attacks or introduce a fake DHCP server to spoof the network information.

Through the scenarios, it has been possible to notice that the selected network attacks are focused on intercepting communications (e.g., by performing MITM attacks through several techniques) or denying them (DoS attacks). Nowadays, information is an essential asset for companies, institutions and, of course, for regular users. Passwords, files, personal data, etc., are the intruders' awards when an attack is successful. For this reason, attackers look for compromising communications by spoofing legitimate addresses, poisoning the devices' network information and so on.

The countermeasures described throughout this chapter help to prevent these attacks by configuring the network devices adequately. However, security measures come with a cost. Not every countermeasure fit the established network requirements. As seen in the previous scenarios, some of these configurations could lead to lack of flexibility in the network infrastructure, for example, by configuring static IP/MAC addresses correspondence. That is why it is necessary to configure these measures regarding the required security level. Some network infrastructures are less concerned about flexibility and performance, and need more robust security barriers and vice versa. It is crucial to understand the managed network infrastructure and its purpose before start configuring the devices.

By presenting these vulnerabilities through practical scenarios, it has been possible to have a broad and realistic view of the consequences that these attacks can have. In this chapter, the selected scenarios have used Cisco devices. Some of these devices count on specific functionalities. However, it is easy to extrapolate the content of the scenarios to other networking operating systems. It is the responsibility of the network administrators to know their specific infrastructure and to be aware of the factory settings of their particular devices to act accordingly.

The described attacks are only a small set of the potential vulnerabilities on a wired LAN. Having a general understanding of network vulnerabilities and being informed continuously about new attack vectors are essential tasks to keep a network infrastructure safe.

6 Conclusions

A set of network attacks have been presented through virtualized and scenarios with the GNS3 emulation software. Knowing and understanding how attackers take advantage of vulnerabilities of the network infrastructure is essential for any network administrator, but also for an end-user to prevent compromised actions. By using network emulators, administrators can replicate attacks putting themselves in the attacker role, providing them a powerful tool to simulate security policies before they are established.

This chapter has addressed the most popular and dangerous network attacks organized by following the OSI model structure. However, overall device configurations have also been explained since these elements usually have fragile security settings when delivered from manufacturers, such as the lack of protection of the administrative access.

On the link layer section, some techniques to compromise switches and their protocols have been described. Flooding attacks aim at overflowing the switches' CAM tables and spoofing attacks aim at "stealing" MAC addresses of other legitimate hosts. The link layer level counts on features like VLANs, but a proper configuration is needed to avoid unwanted vulnerabilities to be exploited, such as the management of trunk ports or double-tagging attacks.

On the network layer section spoofing and flooding, attacks have also been addressed, being the target at this level the routing tables of the devices. Attackers take advantage of layer three protocols such as ICMP to poison these tables with fake or malicious routes.

On the transport layer, the main focus is put in exhausting the devices' resources to provoke a denial of service. In this case, the TCP and UDP workflows are exploited to increase the CPU usage until reaching the devices' limit, provoking system crashes.

Finally, DHCP protocol vulnerabilities have been presented at the application layer section. Attacks at this level seek to compromise high-level services like DHCP to perform MITM attacks or sniff the victims' traffic.

The emulation environment (GNS3) has provided a safe and useful context to perform and understand the previous attacks and vulnerabilities freely, as well as to show how these attacks can be prevented or mitigated through the configuration of proper parameters on the network devices' settings.

Future work lines would involve the completion of this chapter with more content at different levels (attacks on the spanning tree protocol, routing protocols' vulnerabilities, attacks on the IPv6 protocol, TCP session hijacking, DNS vulnerabilities, firewall configurations, etc.) and new scenarios to understand the new concepts.

Acknowledgment This research work has been supported by the Spanish *Ministry of Education and Vocational Training* under a FPU fellowship (FPU17/03276).

References

1. Ko, H., Mesicek, L., Choi, J., Choi, J., & Hwang, S. (2018). A study on secure contents strategies for applications with DRM on cloud computing. *International Journal of Cloud Applications, 8*(1), 143–153.
2. Tewari, A., & Gupta, B. (2018). Security, privacy and trust of different layers in Internet-of-Things (IoTs) framework. *Future Generation Computer Systems*. https://doi.org/10.1016/j.future.2018.04.027

3. Gupta, B., Agrawal, D. P., & Yamaguchi, S. (2016). *Handbook of research on modern cryptographic solutions for computer and cyber security*. Pennsylvania: IGI Global.
4. Gupta, B. B. (2018). *Computer and cyber security: principles, algorithm, applications, and perspectives*. Boca Raton: CRC Press.
5. Welsh, C. (2013). *GNS3 network simulation guide*. Birmingham: Packt.
6. García Rambla, J. L. (2012). *Ataques en redes de datos IPv4 e IPv6* (p. 272). Madrid, Spain: 0xWORD.
7. Sommer, J., et al. (2010). Ethernet–a survey on its fields of application. *IEEE Communications Surveys Tutorials, 12*(2), 263–284.
8. Metcalfe, R. M., & Boggs, D. R. (1976). Ethernet: distributed packet switching for local computer networks. *Communications of the ACM, 19*(7), 395–404.
9. Mitnick, K. D., & Simon, W. L. (2009). *The art of intrusion: the real stories behind the exploits of hackers, intruders and deceivers*. Hoboken, NJ: Wiley.
10. Kiravuo, T., Sarela, M., & Manner, J. (2013). A survey of Ethernet LAN security. *IEEE Communications Surveys Tutorials, 15*(3), 1477–1491.
11. Santos, O., & Stuppi, J. (2015). *CCNA security 210–260 official cert guide*. Indianapolis,IN: Cisco Press.
12. Cisco Packet Tracer. (2009). *Cisco networking academy*. San Jose, CA: Cisco Systems.
13. Dooley, K., & Brown, I. (2006). *Cisco IOS cookbook: Field-tested solutions to Cisco router problems*. Sebastopol, CA: O'Reilly Media.
14. Sun, L., Wu, J., Zhang, Y., & Yin, H. (2013). Comparison between physical devices and simulator software for Cisco network technology teaching. In *Computer Science and Education (ICCSE), 2013 8th International Conference on* (pp. 1357–1360). IEEE.
15. Walters, B. (1999). VMware virtual platform. *Linux Journal, 1999*(63es), 6.
16. Oracle, V. M. (2015). *VirtualBox*. https://www.virtualbox.org/
17. Zhang, Y., Liang, R., & Ma, H. (2012). Teaching innovation in computer network course for undergraduate students with packet tracer. *IERI Procedia, 2*, 504–510.
18. Janitor, J., Jakab, F., & Kniewald, K. (2010). Visual learning tools for teaching/learning computer networks: Cisco networking academy and packet tracer. In: *2010 Sixth International Conference on Networking and Services* (pp. 351–355). IEEE.
19. Moreno-Montero, Á. M., & Retorillo-Manzano, D. (2017). Design and deployment of hands-on network lab experiments for computer science engineers. *International Journal of Engineering Education, 33*, 855–864.
20. Archana, C. (2015). Analysis of RIPv2, OSPF, EIGRP Configuration on router Using CISCO Packet tracer. *International Journal of Engineering Science Innovative Technology, 4*(2), 215–222.
21. Makasiranondh, W., Maj, S. P., & Veal, D. (2010). Pedagogical evaluation of simulation tools usage in network technology education. *World Transactions on Engineering Technology Education, 8*(3), 321–326.
22. Wang, Y., & Wang, J. (2010). Use gns3 to simulate network laboratory. *Computer Programming Skills Maintenance, 12*, 046.
23. Gil, P., Garcia, G. J., Delgado, A., Medina, R. M., Calderon, A., & Marti, P. (2014). Computer networks virtualization with GNS3: Evaluating a solution to optimize resources and achieve a distance learning. In *Frontiers in Education Conference (FIE), 2014 IEEE* (pp. 1–4). IEEE.
24. Faxun, L. (2010). The application of GNS3 in network experiments. *Computer Telecommunication, 10*, 032.
25. PENG, C.-y., & LIU, B. (2010). Application of GNS3 at computer network teaching [J]. *Theory Research, 20*, 136.
26. Zimmermann, H. (1980). OSI reference model–The ISO model of architecture for open systems interconnection. *IEEE Transactions on Communications, 28*(4), 425–432.
27. Boyles, T. (2010). *CCNA security study guide: exam 640-553*. Hoboken, NJ: Wiley.
28. Dubrawsky, I. (2004). *Safe layer 2 security in-depth*. White paper, San Jose, CA: Cisco Inc.

29. Cisco Systems. (2008). *Cisco IOS security configuration guide*. Retrieved from https://www.cisco.com/c/en/us/td/docs/ios/security/configuration/guide/12_4/sec_12_4_book.pdf
30. Paquet, C. (2009). *Implementing Cisco IOS network security (IINS)*. Indianapolis, Indiana: Cisco Press.
31. Vykopal, J., Plesnik, T., & Minarik, P. (2009). Network-based dictionary attack detection. In *Future Networks, 2009 International Conference on* (pp. 23–27). IEEE.
32. Postel, J., & Reynolds, J. K. (1983). *Telnet protocol specification (RFC 854)*. Retrieved from https://tools.ietf.org/html/rfc854
33. Ylonen, T., & Lonvick, C. (2005). *The secure shell (SSH) protocol architecture (RFC 4251)*. Retrieved from https://tools.ietf.org/html/rfc4251
34. Bhaiji, Y. (2007). *Understanding, preventing, and defending against layer 2 attacks*. Retrieved from http://www.nanog.org/meetings/nanog42/presentations/Bhaiji_Layer_2_Attacks.pdf
35. Plummer, D. (1982). *Ethernet address resolution protocol: Or converting network protocol addresses to 48. bit Ethernet address for transmission on Ethernet hardware (RFC 826)*. Retrieved from https://tools.ietf.org/html/rfc826
36. Whalen, S. (2001). *An introduction to ARP spoofing*. Retrieved from http://node99.org/projects/arpspoof
37. Wagner, R. (2001). *Address resolution protocol spoofing and man-in-the-middle attacks*. The SANS Institute.
38. Spangler, R. (2003). Packet sniffing on layer 2 switched local area networks. *Packetwatch Research*, 1–5.
39. Ornaghi, A., & Valleri, M. (2003). Man in the middle attacks. In *Blackhat Conference Europe*.
40. Ramachandran, V., & Nandi, S. (2005). Detecting ARP spoofing: An active technique. In: *International Conference on Information Systems Security* (pp. 239–250). Berlin: Springer.
41. Convery, S. (2002). *Hacking layer 2: Fun with Ethernet switches*. Retrieved from https://www.blackhat.com/presentations/bh-usa-02/bh-us-02-convery-switches.pdf.
42. Altunbasak, H., Krasser, S., Owen, H. L., Grimminger, J., Huth, H.-P., & Sokol, J. (2005). Securing layer 2 in local area networks. In: *International conference on networking* (pp. 699–706). Berlin: Springer.
43. IEEE. (2018). IEEE standard for local and metropolitan area network-bridges and bridged networks. *IEEE Std 802.1Q-2018 (Revision of IEEE Std 802.1Q-2014)*, 1-1993. https://doi.org/10.1109/IEEESTD.2018.8403927
44. Annaamalai, A., & Mahajan, U. (2002). *Dynamic trunk protocol*. Google Patents
45. Cisco Networking Academy. (2014). *Dynamic trunking protocol (3.2.3) > Cisco Networking Academy's Introduction to VLANs*. Retrieved from http://www.ciscopress.com/articles/article.asp?p=2181837&seqNum=8
46. Postel, J. (1981). *Internet control message protocol (RFC 792)*. Retrieved from https://tools.ietf.org/html/rfc792
47. Low, C. (2001). *ICMP attacks illustrated*. SANS Institute. Retrieved from https://www.sans.org/reading-room/whitepapers/threats/icmp-attacks-illustrated-477
48. Serrano-Marín, J. D. (2018). *Implementación de un sistema de detección/prevención de intrusiones*. Jaén: Universidad de Jaén
49. Ramakrishna, P., & Maarof, M. (2002). Detection and prevention of active sniffing on routing protocol. In: *SCOReD 2002. Student Conference on Research and Development* (pp. 498–501). IEEE.
50. Kumar, S. (2007). Smurf-based distributed denial of service (DDoS) attack amplification in internet. In: *Internet Monitoring and Protection, 2007. ICIMP 2007. Second International Conference on* (pp. 25–25). IEEE.
51. Senie, D. (1999). *Changing the default for directed broadcasts in routers (RFC 2644)*. Retrieved from https://tools.ietf.org/html/rfc2644
52. Mirkovic, J., & Reiher, P. (2004). A taxonomy of DDoS attack and DDoS defense mechanisms. *ACM SIGCOMM Computer Communication Review, 34*(2), 39–53.

53. Cisco. (2014). *Comparing traffic policing and traffic shaping for bandwidth limiting*. Retrieved from https://www.cisco.com/c/en/us/support/docs/quality-of-service-qos/qos-policing/19645-policevsshape.html
54. Eddy, W. (2007). *TCP SYN flooding attacks and common mitigations, 2070-1721*. https://www.rfc-editor.org/rfc/rfc4987.txt
55. Droms, R. (1997). *Dynamic host configuration protocol, 2070-1721*. http://www.rfc-editor.org/info/rfc2131
56. Daş, R., Karabade, A., & Tuna, G. (2015). Common network attack types and defense mechanisms. In: *Signal Processing and Communications Applications Conference (SIU), 2015 23th* (pp. 2658–2661). IEEE.

Chapter 7
Security and Privacy Issues in Wireless Sensor and Body Area Networks

Moumita Roy, Chandreyee Chowdhury, and Nauman Aslam

Abstract Advancements in wireless communication and availability of miniaturized, battery powered micro electronics devices have revolutionized the trend of computation and communication activities to the generation of smart computing where spatially distributed autonomous devices with sensors forming wireless sensor network (WSN) are utilized to measure physical or environmental conditions. WSNs have emerged as one of the most interesting areas of research due to its diverse application areas such as healthcare, utilities, remote monitoring, smart cities, and smart home which not only perform effective monitoring but also improve quality of living. Even the sensor nodes can be strategically placed in, on, or around human body to measure vital physiological parameters as well. Such sensor network which is formed over human body is termed as wireless body area network (WBAN) which could be beneficial for numerous applications such as eldercare, detection of chronic diseases, sports, and military. Hence, both network applications deal with sensitive data which requires utmost security and privacy. Thus, the security and privacy issues and challenges related to WSN and WBAN along with the defense measures in place should be studied in detail which not only is beneficial for effective application but also will motivate the researcher to find their own path for exercising better protection/defense. Accordingly, in this chapter a brief overview of both networks is presented along with their inherent characteristics, and the need for security and privacy in either networks is illustrated as well. Besides, study has been made regarding potential threats to security and privacy in both networks and existing measures to handle these issues. Finally the open research challenges are identified to draw the attention of the researcher to investigate further in this field.

Keywords WSN · WBAN · Security · Privacy

M. Roy · C. Chowdhury (✉)
Jadavpur University, Kolkata, India

N. Aslam
Northumbria University, Newcastle upon Tyne, UK
e-mail: nauman.aslam@northumbria.ac.uk

© Springer Nature Switzerland AG 2020
B. B. Gupta et al. (eds.), *Handbook of Computer Networks and Cyber Security*,
https://doi.org/10.1007/978-3-030-22277-2_7

1 Introduction

Developments and technological advancements in wireless communication have initiated the era of smart computing. Rather than super-computing devices, lightweight battery driven consumer electronic devices with sensing and communication capabilities have become affordable today. These devices can be deployed to monitor and control a wide range of phenomena including remote events to daily life activities. These devices are commonly known as sensors that can be deployed spatially over the region where the activities need to be monitored. For example, if the temperature of a power plant needs to be monitored, sensors are to be strategically placed at various locations of the power plant. These distributed autonomous sensors form a wireless sensor network (WSN) [11, 41] where the nodes cooperate among themselves to report their sensed readings to a remote station. Thus, if any sensor node reports a high/low temperature value, users sitting at a remote place may get an alert and may take measures accordingly. In this way, the sensor nodes are utilized to measure physical or environmental conditions such as monitoring forest fire, wild habitats, earthquakes, or even health of bridges.

On the other hand, the advent of small bio-sensors that can either be worn as watches or bracelets or be implanted such as a pacemaker, the concept of wireless body area network (WBAN) [35, 43] is seeded. Such networks can measure body vitals at regular intervals while maintaining the convenience of the user. The users may carry out their daily activities and enjoy the comfort of staying at their homes while these sensors collect their body vitals and report to a medical center. Hence, WBAN can be viewed as a variant of WSN where the network is deployed in/on or around human body. Though sensing and communication are the two key elements for both these networks and hence they share many similarities, there are some significant differences too. Most importantly, in most of these cases, such networks lose their significance if security and privacy issues are not diligently handled. Consequently, this chapter first provides an overview of both WSN and WBAN followed by a brief discussion on the privacy and security issues in Sect. 3 through 5. Existing solutions to these issues and associated deployment hurdles are also presented in the subsequent section (Sect. 6). Potential applications of WSN and WBAN and their security and privacy requirements are also discussed in Sect. 7. This is followed by a discussion of the pertinent research issues. Finally, the chapter concludes in Sect. 9.

2 Overview of Wireless Sensor and Body Area Networks

WSNs have emerged as one of the most interesting areas of research due to its diverse application domains such as healthcare, utilities, remote monitoring, smart cities, and smart home which not only perform effective monitoring but also improve quality of living [35]. WSN is a collection of small sensor nodes that are deployed over a region where a physical phenomenon is to be detected, monitored, or tracked. The sensors could be deployed over a controlled environment where monitoring or surveillance is critical or in an uncontrolled environment where security for sensor networks is utmost important [61]. Each sensor node consists of four subsystems, namely power supply, sensing, processing, and communication subsystem [6, 35]. Additionally, a sensor node may also have actuators, positioning modules, etc. The sensor nodes are often referred to as "motes" where low power and high frequency transceivers are implemented on chips and digital circuits tend to shrink and be fabricated densely [6]. The nodes sense data and send it to a base station (also called sink) via other nodes.

Vast literature could be found on WSN routing [36, 52], that is, how a sensor node finds suitable path to send a packet to sink. Works can also be found on clustering nodes in WSN [4, 31], energy harvesting [48, 58], and MAC layer communication issues [18, 51]. Few WSN deployments are also reported recently [20, 56].

Now-a-days, smartphones present an interesting combination of sensing, computation, and communication facilities. Additionally, its wide availability and usage make it a viable device for novel application development. These phones can connect through Bluetooth to the bio-sensor nodes to collect body vitals from them and may send the information to a remote server through the Internet. Even the accelerometer sensor of smartphone can itself act as a wearable body sensor to collect data about user's postures to detect activities including fall. Thus, WSN is no longer a way of monitoring remote applications only. The miniaturized, ultra-low power bio-sensor nodes, and wide availability of smartphones paved the way for wireless body area networks (WBAN), a variant of WSN that is increasingly getting importance for smart healthcare. WBAN has immense potential to be used in not only medical internet of things (IoT) applications but also for sports, entertainment, and smart home. Even with availability of the bio-sensor nodes, a patient need not visit a medical facility for checkup when symptoms appear, but can opt for proactive medical supervision. WBAN enables a person to be under constant medical supervision at free-living conditions even residing at home [9]. This is a convenient and important option for effective treatment of chronic diseases and eldercare today.

2.1 Network Architecture

WBAN has evolved as an application area of WSN over human body and thus the basic architecture of both networks is quite similar as well. The sensor networks communication architecture [49] is shown in Fig. 7.1. The sensor nodes are generally scattered over the region where some phenomena are to be reported. Each of these scattered sensor nodes has the capabilities to collect data and route the data to the sink as well as the end users. Data can be routed to the end user by a multi-hop infrastructureless architecture through the sink via Internet or satellite as shown in Fig. 7.1.

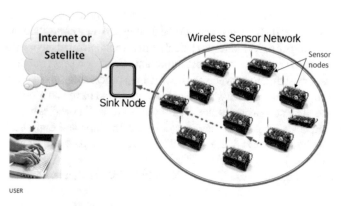

Fig. 7.1 Architecture of WSN

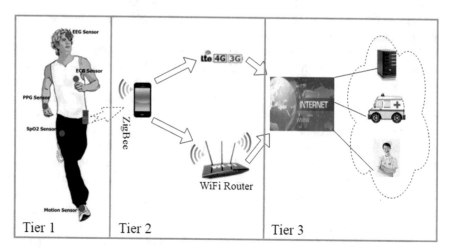

Fig. 7.2 Three tier architecture of WBAN

Similarly, the health monitoring system which can be regarded as an application of WSN is based on three tier architecture [42] as shown in Fig. 7.2. Tier 1 focuses on network formation among bio-sensor nodes together with a network coordinator or the sink (which could be a smart handheld such as smartphone) where the sensor nodes collect health parameters and communicate to the sink; tier 2 includes wireless technologies such as WLAN or GPRS so that the sink of tier 1 could communicate the health data to the remote medical server located at tier 3 to be analyzed by medical professionals.

Both networks comprise of battery-powered devices thus subject to bounded lifetime. Lifetime could be measured in days, months, or even years. For instance, in case of implanted nodes in WBAN such as pacemakers require at least 5 years of lifetime [43]. Besides, the storage capacity of each node in both networks is limited and the nodes having low computational capabilities [3]. Hence, complex computational approach to address different issues in both networks such as routing [34, 43], reliability analysis [11], and security [39, 44] is usually avoided. However, there are few dissimilarities between these resource constraint networks (i.e., WSN and WBAN) as well. The comparative study [3] between WSN and WBAN is listed in Table 7.1. The sensors exploited in WSN are generally multi-function devices which are designed to be applied in large range network. Besides, the nodes in WSN are subject to movements that result from environmental influences (such as wind or water) or the sensors may be attracted to or carried by mobile entities, or this may be a desired property of the system [41]. The cost sensitive network formation ensures reliability using redundant devices to collect data at the desired location. For example, sensor networks exploited in military application are based on the dense deployment of disposable and low-cost sensor nodes such that destruction of some nodes by hostile actions does not affect the overall throughput [2]. The nodes are deployed following random distribution and point to point communication between nodes take place in WSN. Unlike WSN, the nodes in WBAN are usually single function devices designed to be applied in small range of network (i.e., in, on, or around human body). The nodes in WBAN are placed over human body at specified locations and thus the relative node movements subject to posture change. In addition, the electro-magnetic radiation results due to communication between bio-sensor devices are absorbed by human tissue which is measured in terms of specific absorption rate (SAR) [35]. Several health hazards [35] may take place if regulatory limit of SAR [9] is violated. However, both networks deal with sensitive information depending on their use particularly when it is directly related to human subjects (i.e., in case of WBAN). Hence, both networks require security component to prevent misuse of the technology, although the security aspects could be distinct according to the applicability.

2.2 Performance Metric

System performance of both WSN and WBAN can be measured from different aspects as shown in Fig. 7.3. Applications of both networks have environmental, economic, and social impact on the measurable output [26]. When the focus is on to build a network of resource constraint nodes in order to monitor the environment, the expected outcome is evaluated in terms of energy efficiency and network lifetime such that the resource utilization gets maximized. However, when the feasibility of the system is analyzed in related to economic perspective, the performance of the system is assessed with respect to cost saving operation and maintenance such as overhead cost, reliability, and mean time to failure (MTTF). While considering the social aspect of the applications of WSN as well as WBAN, the goal of these technologies is to improve quality of living. Thus, acceptability of such systems is related to user satisfaction and cost-benefit analysis. However, the performance of each individual perspective when combined with other gives the system a new dimension. For instance, the social impact of the system together with economic

Table 7.1 Comparison between WSN and WBAN

Features	WSN	WBAN
Similarities		
Limited resources	Subject to limited energy (in terms of limited battery power) and storage capacity and low computational capabilities	Subject to limited energy (in terms of limited battery power) and storage capacity and low computational capabilities
Differences		
Sensor/actuator	Multifunction device	Single function device
	Rare or slow movement	Fast relative movement
	Designed to be applied in large range network	Designed to be applied in small range network
	Lifetime is measured in months generally less than 10 years	Lifetime is measured in days; however, in case of implanted sensor it could be less than 10 years
	Cost sensitive	Safety is must (i.e., low SAR) and quality is important
Dependability	Redundancy-based reliability	Reliability is prime requirement
	Expected QoS	Guaranteed QoS
	Security is important	Security is must
Network	Large-scale hierarchical network	Small-scale network usually follows star topology although multi-hop topology is sometimes preferred to restrict energy consumption
	Redundancy in device	Redundancy in device is avoided
	Usually random node distribution	Usually nodes are placed at specified locations in, on, or around human body
Traffic	Burst (dominant) or periodical	Periodical (dominant) or burst
	Uni-directional or bi-directional traffic	Uni-directional traffic from sensor to sink
	M:1 or point to point communication	Generally M:1 communication
Channel	ISM band is utilized	Specific medical channel, ISM band
	Obstacle is unknown	Obstacle is mainly body surface or through body

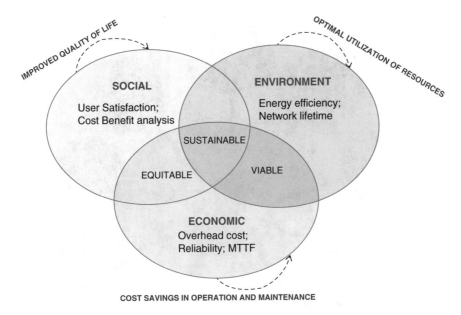

Fig. 7.3 The notion of measuring system performance for both WSN and WBAN

outcome makes the system equitable whereas performance measured in economic and environment point of view makes the system viable. Nevertheless, when all three notions of measuring system performance are integrated sustainable system is obtained.

3   Security Threats in WSN and WBAN

Security is prime concern to any system for effective functioning particularly when it involves wireless technologies. Security is a concept similar to the safety of the system as a whole [3, 32, 45]. Both WSN and WBAN are prone to inherent security challenges that are associated with wireless communications. The basic security requirements [8, 28, 53, 59] related to both networks (illustrated in Fig. 7.4) are as follows.

- **Availability:** This ensures the desired network services are available at right time even in the presence of denial of service attack [59].
- **Data authentication:** This ensures the communication from one node to another is genuine and an adversary cannot masquerade as trusted node.
- **Data confidentiality:** This ensures the given message should only get understood by the intended recipient.

Fig. 7.4 Security requirements in WSN and WBAN

- **Data integrity:** This ensures the message sent by the sender must not get modified on the way before reaching at the receiver.
- **Data freshness:** This ensures that the data is recent and an adversary cannot replay an old message.
- **Secure localization:** Sensor network applications often exploit geographical information of nodes. This security requirement ensures the location information of nodes should not get revealed to the attacker.
- **Flexibility:** This ensures that the network will be used in different scenarios where environmental circumstances, hazards, and mission may change frequently.
- **Robustness:** This ensures that the network should be robust across various security attacks. However, if any attack takes place, its impact should be less.
- **Time synchronization:** Most sensor network applications rely on some form of time synchronization. For instance, a sensor node's radio may often be turned off for some duration to preserve energy resource.

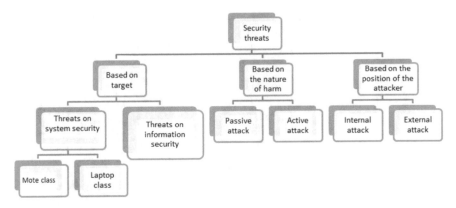

Fig. 7.5 Categorization of security threats in WSN and WBAN

- **Self organization:** WSNs are also ad-hoc networks having flexibility and extensible properties. In WSN, every sensor node is independent and flexible enough to be self-organizing and self-healing according to the situations.

The broadcast nature of wireless communication together with unguided transmission medium brings with it a host of security threats in both networks. The potential threats in both networks are categorized in different ways as shown in Fig. 7.5. First categorization is made based on the target where the adversary attempts to do harm and accordingly imposes threats on system security or information security [3]. Denial of service, impersonations are examples of attacks on system security whereas data modification, eavesdropping, and replaying are examples of attacks on information security. Denial of service (DoS) [28, 47] is a type of attack where the attacker attempts to prevent the legitimate nodes in the network to get service. When an adversary eavesdrops identity information of a trusted node and uses this information to cheat other nodes in the network, the attack is called impersonation [3, 28]. In data modification attack [3, 28] the attacker can delete or replace part or all of eavesdropped information and the modified information is sent back to original receiver to accomplish some illegal purpose. However, in eavesdropping [3] any opponent can intercept radio communications between the wireless nodes freely and easily (due to open nature of wireless medium) to steal data for malicious acts. The attacker can even resend a piece of valid information (obtained through eavesdropping) to original receiver after a while to achieve same purpose in different case. This form of attack is termed as replay attack [3, 28]. However, the threats on system security could be further classified as mote class attack and laptop class attack [59]. In mote class attack [59] an adversary launches attack on WSN exploiting few nodes with similar capabilities to the network nodes whereas in laptop class attack [59] makes use of more powerful devices such as laptop to attack a WSN. Nevertheless, system threats could be further classified based on the intensity of the harm, i.e., passive attack and active attack [3, 59]. Active attacks are more harmful as compared to passive counter

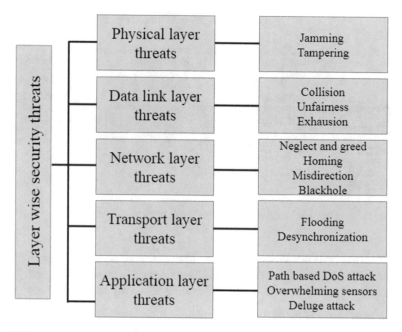

Fig. 7.6 Layer-wise security threats in WBAN

parts. For instance, eavesdropping or monitoring packet exchanges in WSN by a
malicious node are examples of passive attack whereas active attacks involve some
modifications of data as well as injection of false data. Besides, the system threats
could be categorized based on the position of the adversary, i.e., internal attack
and external attack [59]. External attack belongs to a node which is not part of the
WSN but internal attack takes place when a legitimate node exhibits unintended
or unauthorized behavior. Few attacks are occurred at different layers as well thus
require to be handled differently at each layer. For instance, DoS attacks in WSN
could take place in physical layer in the form of jamming or tampering, at link
layer in terms of collision, exhaustion, or unfairness, at network layer it could be
neglect and greed, homing, misdirection, black holes and in transport layer this
attack could be performed by malicious flooding and desynchronization [37]. Layer-
wise security attacks are listed in Fig. 7.6.

Physical Layer Physical layer of WSN as well as WBAN is responsible for
frequency selection, carrier frequency generation, signal detection, modulation, and
data encryption [59]. Here, vulnerabilities could occur in the following form.

– **Jamming [59]:** This type of attack interferes the radio frequencies used by the
  nodes in the network. A jamming source could disrupt the entire network or
  smaller portion of the network.

- **Tampering [59]:** In this type of attack, an attacker can extract sensitive information such as cryptographic keys or other data from the victim node if it get access to that node.

Data Link Layer Data link layer of WSN as well as WBAN is responsible for multiplexing of data streams, data frame detection, medium access, and error control [59]. Here, vulnerabilities could occur in the following form. This layer ensures reliable point to point or point to multi-point connections. Here, potential security threats take place in the following manner.

- **Collision [59]:** Collision occurs when two or more nodes attempt to transmit on the same frequency at the same time.
- **Unfairness [59]:** Unfairness can be regarded as a weak form of DoS attack where the adversary creates unfairness in the network by exploiting collision and exhaustion attacks.
- **Exhaustion [59]:** Repeated collision could be exploited by the attacker to create resource exhaustion.

Network Layer Network layer of WSN as well as WBAN is responsible for routing data from source to destination [8, 59]. Here, vulnerabilities could occur in the following form.

- **Neglect and greed [53]:** This attack occurs when a packet travels in between nodes from sender to destination. The malicious node can force multi-hopping in the network either by splashing some packets or by misdirecting towards wrong a node. Hence, this attack disturbs the network activities of the adjoining nodes.
- **Homing [8]:** In this type of attack search is carried out in the ongoing data traffic to identify the cluster head or key manager that have the capability to terminate the entire network.
- **Misdirection [8]:** In this attack, the attacker misdirects data traffic.
- **Hello flood attack [8]:** In this type of attack, a single malicious node sends a useless message which is then replayed by the attacker to generate high traffic thus the channel gets congested.
- **Selective forwarding [8]:** In this type of attack a compromised node only sends data to the selected few nodes instead of all the nodes. This selected recipients list is made according to the interests of the attacker to achieve his malicious objective.
- **Sybil attack [8]:** Here, the attacker replicates a single node and represents it with multiple identities to the other nodes in the network.
- **Wormhole attack [8]:** This attack causes relocation of data packets through tunneling over a link of low latency.
- **Black hole [53]:** This attack is also referred to as sink holes that launches the attack through building a covenant node seems to be very attractive (i.e., it promotes zero-cost routes to neighboring nodes with respect to the routing algorithm). Accordingly, this causes maximum traffic to flow towards these fake nodes. Thus, nodes adjoining to these malicious nodes collide for immense bandwidth leading to resource contention and message destruction.

- **Acknowledgement flooding [8]:** In this attack, a malicious node spoofs the acknowledgements to provide false information to the destined neighboring nodes.

Transport Layer Transport layer of WSN as well as WBAN is responsible for managing end to end connections [59]. Here, the vulnerabilities could be as follows.

- **Flooding [59]:** In this type of attack, an attacker repeatedly makes new connection requests until the resources required by each connection are exhausted or reach a maximum limit and thus in either case further legitimate requests get ignored.
- **Desynchronization [59]:** Desynchronization causes disruption of an existing connection where an attacker may degrade or even prevent the ability of the end hosts to successfully exchange data. Consequently, the energy is wasted instead by attempting in order to recover from errors which never really existed.

Application Layer Application layer of WSN as well as WBAN carries out the responsibility of traffic management. Besides, this layer also acts as the provider of software for different applications that translates data into a comprehensible form or helps in collection of information by sending queries [8]. Here the following vulnerabilities could take place.

- **Path-based DoS attack [8]:** In this type of attack an attacker creates a huge traffic in the route towards base station.
- **Overwhelming sensors [53]:** In this attack an attacker attempts to overwhelm network nodes with sensor stimuli that causes the network to forward large volumes of traffic to a base station. Hence, network bandwidth is consumed in this attack and node energy is drained. However, it is effective only when particular sensor readings (for example, motion detection or heat signatures) trigger communications instead when sensor readings are sent at fixed intervals.
- **Deluge (reprogramming) attack [53]:** Protocols such as TinyOS's Deluge network-programming system enable remotely reprogram nodes in deployed networks. Most of these systems, including Deluge, are designed to be used in a trustworthy environment. If the reprogramming process isn't secure, an intruder can hijack this process and take control of large portions of a network.

4 Similarities and Differences Between WSN and WBAN with Respect to Security Issues

WSN and WBAN applications deal with sensitive data and thus security is prime requirement in both networks to protect the system from getting misused by the adversary having malicious intention. The network activities take place through wireless medium in both cases. Hence, both WSNs and WBANs are prone to security threats related to shared broadcast medium [3]. In addition, the lightweight security measures having low computation and communication overhead are desirable to enhance security in the resource constraint networks like WSN and WBAN. However, there are some key differences between these two networks as illustrated earlier (in Sect. 2) and therefore the security techniques designed for WSN may not be applied to build up security in WBAN applications. Since WSN is a large network deployed over large region as compared to WBAN, the sensor nodes in WSN may easily got tampered by the adversary. In addition, clustering could be an overhead for WBAN and thus unlike WSN cluster-based security solutions cannot be applied to WBAN. Moreover, security solutions designed for WBAN must not violate the regulatory limit of SAR. Most importantly, WBAN involves human subjects thus security is utmost important otherwise it could be misused by a person with detrimental objectives and even it could be life threatening as well.

5 Privacy Issues of WSN and WBAN

Privacy is a key issue to be handled in any system that deals with sensitive information. Privacy is concerned about who can access the information [3]. Privacy issues may arise due to many reasons such as personal belief, social and cultural environment, and other general public/private causes citeal2012security. Both WSN and WBAN deal with sensitive information related to physical phenomena or human health, hence privacy is a prime aspect that regulates the acceptability of such system by the people. Health related data are always private in nature and hence sending data out from a patient through wireless media in case of WBAN applications imposes serious threats to privacy of an individual [3]. Even it could be life threatening for an individual if this information is misused by people with harmful intentions. Some of the major aspects to be addressed before deployment of WBAN applications in order to guarantee privacy are where the health data should be stored, who can view the patient's medical record, who will be responsible for maintaining these data in case any emergency arises, and so on. Most importantly, it is to be taken into account that whether the data are obtained with the consent of the person or without it due to the requirement by the system so that the misuse of this private information could be prevented.

The privacy measures [3] must include the following before widespread deployment of the WBAN applications.

- All communications over wireless networks and Internet are required to be encrypted so that these do not give any meaningful information other than the intended recipients.
- It is also essential that individual user should not be identified unless there is a need.
- Another important measure is to create awareness among general public regarding technology along with security and privacy issues and their implications in

order to make balanced judgments concerning the extent to which it may have a negative impact on their own standards of privacy.

6 Existing Security and Privacy Solutions for WSN and WBAN

There are many security mechanisms designed primarily to be applied in generic WSN. However, very few of them could be applied readily to WBAN as well with low power computation [25].

6.1 IEEE 802.11 Security Solutions

The IEEE 802.1X standard defines the standard for port-based network access control to provide compatible authentication and authorization mechanisms for devices interconnected by various 802 LANs [10]. The standard could also be used to distribute security keys for 802.11 wireless LANs (WLANs) [19] that enables public key authentication and encryption between access points (APs) and mobile nodes (MNs). WLAN [19] defines two types of authentication mechanisms which are open system authentication and shared system authentication. In 802.1X, the port denotes the association between MN and AP. The 802.1X authentication system consists of three main components which are supplicant, authenticator, and authentication server (AS) [10]. A supplicant is usually an MN which is requesting WLAN access whereas an authenticator represents the network access server (NAS). In 802.11 AP serves as NAS. A RADIUS server is commonly exploited as the authentication server, although other types of AAA servers such as diameter could also act as the authentication server. The authentication server might be physically integrated into an AP in case of IEEE 802.11 standard.

6.2 IEEE 802.15.6 Security Solutions

The IEEE 802.15.6 is the latest international standard for WBAN which aims to provide an international standard for low-power, short-range, and extremely reliable wireless communication for use in close proximity to, or inside, a human body (but not limited to humans) [57]. A vast range of data rates is supported in IEEE 802.15.6 standard for different applications. This standard targets to cover both medical and non-medical applications with different requirements. The security structure of the IEEE 802.15.6 standard includes several states, procedures, and protocols [57]. A security association in the IEEE 802.15.6 standard is defined as a procedure to identify a node and a hub to each other, to establish a new master key (MK) shared between them, or to activate an existing MK pre-shared between them. Five protocols are included in the security association in the IEEE 802.15.6 standard which are a non-cryptographic protocol for activating a pre-shared MK, and four key exchange protocols for generating a new MK. The generated/activated MK is then utilized through another protocol for creating of a pairwise temporal key (PTK) which will work as the session key for data security. A protocol is also defined in the standard for the security disassociation procedure as well where after its successful execution, the participants will delete the MK and PTK. The standard includes both authenticated key exchange (AKE) and password-based AKE (PAKE) protocols. A strong cryptographic session key is established between legitimate participants in an authenticated manner using AKE whereas PAKE protocols allow an authenticated key establishment based on a pre-shared human-memorable password.

6.3   IEEE 802.15.4 Security Solutions

The IEEE 802.15.4 standard (for wearable body sensor nodes) has different security modes [25, 46] that can be built on WBANs. The IEEE 802.15.4 defines low-power standard which are designed for low data rate wireless personal area networks (WPANs). This standard specifies the physical and media access control layers, which focus on low-cost and low-speed ubiquitous communication between devices. IEEE 802.15.4 standard is very close to WBANs because it supports low data rate applications having low cost of power consumption. The standard is employed by many designers and researchers in order to develop protocols and mechanisms for WBANs. The IEEE 802.15.4 security suits are categorized into null, encryption only (AES-CTR), authentication only (AES-CBC-MAC), and encryption and authentication (AESCCM) suites. Different security modes and their descriptions are listed in Table 7.2.

6.3.1   AES-CTR

Confidentiality in AES-CTR [25] is protected using advance encryption standard (AES) block cipher with counter mode (CTR) which is also known as integer counter mode. Here, the plaintext (PT) is broken into 16-byte blocks $PT_1, PT_2, ..., PT_n$. The sender j computes the cipher text by $CT_j = PT_j XORK_{en}(C_j)$, where CT_j denotes the encrypted text or cipher text, PT_j represents the data block, and $K_{en}(C_j)$ gives the encryption key of the counter C_j. The receiver decodes the cipher text using the formula $PT_j = CT_j XORK_{en}(C_j)$. The encryption and decryption processes are illustrated in Fig. 7.7.

Table 7.2 Different security modes in IEEE 802.15.4 standard

Security modes	Description
Null	No security is provided in this mode
AES-CTR	This security mode provides advance encryption standard (AES) with counter mode (CTR)
AES-CBC-MAC-128	Authentication and message integrity protection are provided here using advance encryption standard (AES) with cipher block chaining (CBC) and 128 bit message authentication code (MAC)
AES-CBC-MAC-64	Authentication and message integrity protection are provided here using advance encryption standard (AES) with cipher block chaining (CBC) and 64 bit message authentication code (MAC)
AES-CBC-MAC-32	Authentication and message integrity protection are provided here using advance encryption standard (AES) with cipher block chaining (CBC) and 32 bit message authentication code (MAC)
AES-CCM-128	This security mode provides high level security by first applying integrity protection using cipher block chaining (CBC) with 128 bit message authentication code (MAC) and then encrypting data payload and MAC by employing AES-CTR mode
AES-CCM-64	This security mode provides high level security by first applying integrity protection using cipher block chaining (CBC) with 64 bit message authentication code (MAC) and then encrypting data payload and MAC by employing AES-CTR mode
AES-CCM-32	This security mode provides high level security by first applying integrity protection using cipher block chaining (CBC) with 32 bit message authentication code (MAC) and then encrypting data payload and MAC by employing AES-CTR mode

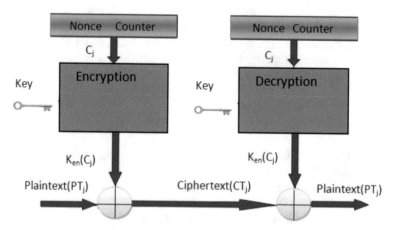

Fig. 7.7 CTR encryption and decryption processes

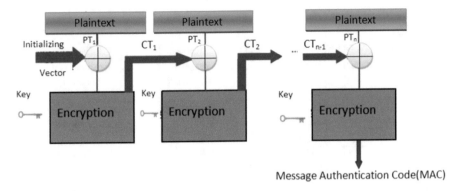

Fig. 7.8 CBC-MAC operation

6.3.2   AES-CBC-MAC

In AES-CBC-MAC [25], authentication and message integrity are provided using a cipher-block chaining message authentication code (CBC-MAC). According to CBC-MAC, an n block message $PT = PT_1, PT_2 \ldots, PT_n$ is authenticated among the parties who share a secret key for the block cipher. The sender can compute either of the 4, 8, or 16 byte message authentication code (MAC). However, the MAC can only be computed by parties having the symmetric key. Here, the plaintext is XORed with the previous cipher text until the final MAC is created where the cipher texts are generated by $CT_j = K_{en}(PT_j XOR CT_{j-1})$ and plaintexts can be generated from the cipher text by $PT_j = K_{de}(CT_j) XOR CT_{j-1}$. The sender appends the plaintext data with the computed MAC. The receiver then verifies the integrity by computing its own MAC and comparing it with the received MAC. The receiver accepts the packet only if both MACs are equal. The block diagram of CBC-MAC operation is illustrated in Fig. 7.8.

6.3.3   AES-CCM

This security suite includes both data integrity and encryption [25] and thus provides high level security. Here, integrity is protected over the header and data payload using CBC-MAC mode and then the data payload is encrypted using AES-CTR mode.

6.4   Existing Research Works

Existing research works that present security solutions for WSN and WBAN are listed according to timeline in Table 7.3. These research works primar-

Table 7.3 Researches on existing security and privacy solutions

Year	Research work	Network	Security mechanism	Threats handled	Performance metric
2008	[29]	WSN	Variation of strong password-based solutions	Threats to user authentication	Computational load, communication cost
2009	[30]	WSN	Secure and energy efficient clustered routing protocol	Usual attacks in WSN	Network lifetime, energy efficiency
2010	[60]	WSN	Key management scheme using hash function	Effect of compromised sensor nodes	Network resilience
2011	[14]	WSN	Symmetric cryptography	Threats to authentication	Energy consumption, scalability
	[46]	WBAN	Null, encryption only (AES-CTR), authentication only (AES-CBC-MAC), and encryption and authentication (AES-CCM)	Threats to eavesdropping, data modification and authentication	Corrupted slots in contention free period, bandwidth utilization, probability of failed guaranteed time slots
2012	[16]	WSN	Lightweight polynomial-based key management protocol	Common attacks to WSN such as node clone, impersonation	Computation and communication overhead
2013	[39]	WBAN	Biometric-based security	Threats to data authentication	Computational complexity, power efficiency
	[4]	WBAN	Cluster-based security mechanism	Spoofed, altered, replayed routing information, selective forwarding, sinkhole, sybil, wormhole attack	Lifetime, energy efficiency
2014	[27]	WSN	Multipath routing	Black hole attacks	Throughput, delay, packet loss
2015	[5]	WSN	Lightweight trust-based routing protocol	Different types of malicious threats	Packet delivery ratio, network lifetime, end to end delay, memory, and energy consumption
2016	[15]	WSN	Energy efficient encryption method	Brute force attack, HELLO flood attack, selective forwarding attack, and compromised cluster head attack	Network lifetime, energy consumption

(continued)

Table 7.3 (continued)

Year	Research work	Network	Security mechanism	Threats handled	Performance metric
2017	[24]	WSN	Payload-based mutual authentication	Network attacks such as replay, resource exhaustion, sybil	Energy consumption, network throughput
	[44]	WBAN	Secure lightweight routing strategy	Blackhole attack	Packet delivery ratio, energy consumption, ratio of false negatives
	[21]	WBAN	Anonymous authentication	Threats to authentication and modification	
2018	[7]	WSN	Certificate-based authentication	Threats to gateway authentication	
	[50]	WBAN	Multilayer authentication protocol and secure session key generation method	Threats to authentication	

ily focus on designing lightweight security techniques [16] to be applied in resource-constrained networks (such as WSN and WBAN) over the years. In [16], lightweight polynomial-based key management (LPKM) scheme has been proposed for distributed WSNs. Different types of keys are established by the sensor nodes to bootstrap trust and secure one-to-one and one-to-many communications in a flexible, reliable, and non-interactive way. The threat model includes most common attacks to WSNs such as node clone attacks, and node impersonation attacks. Besides, LPKM can tolerate dynamic network topology and incurs little computational and communication overhead. In [29], two simple user authentication protocols for WSN are proposed which are variations of a strong password-based solutions. Here, performance is measured in terms of computational load, communication cost, and security of the proposed protocols. Security threats to authentication are mostly handled in this work. A collaborative lightweight trust (CLT) based routing protocol for WSN has been proposed in [5] that incurs minimal overhead in regard to memory and energy consumption. The protocol does not use promiscuous mode of operation to monitor the neighboring nodes for trust assessment, instead it employs a novel trust counselor that monitors and warns the neighboring nodes whose trust falls below a warning threshold. A sensor node is notified with a warning message to rectify the packet forwarding behavior in order to improve its trust relationship with its neighbors. Performance of CLT protocol is measured by theoretical analysis and simulation in terms of packet delivery ratio, network lifetime, end-to-end delay, memory, and energy consumption. Existing literature [14, 60] identifies key distribution in shared broadcast medium is the major concern in employing cryptography-based security solutions. In [60], a novel key management scheme called SKM has been proposed for sequence-based key management in WSNs. Here, sensor nodes are pre-distributed with the first term and the recursive formula of a numerical sequence. Accordingly, the two tiny pre-distributed information ensure the establishment of pairwise keys between each sensor node with its neighbors after its deployment with a small amount of computation. The efficiency of SKM is obtained through security analysis. Whereas in [14] a lightweight authentication model has been presented for wireless sensor networks. The model is composed of a key management scheme based on the use of simple symmetric cryptographic primitives with very low computational requirements and an authentication protocol. In [24], a lightweight payload-based mutual authentication scheme for a cluster-based hierarchical WSN has been designed. Here, the proposed scheme operates in two steps. First step includes election of an optimal percentage of cluster heads which are then authenticated and allowed to communicate with neighboring nodes. In the next step, each cluster head that acts in a role of server authenticates the nearby nodes for cluster formation. The proposed scheme has been validated using various simulation metrics such as energy consumption, network throughput. Although different security mechanisms have been designed to ensure authentication and protect data integrity, the techniques devised for WSN cannot readily be applied to WBAN as well due to their inherent differences. In [44], an energy efficient lightweight mechanism has been proposed to be applied in WBAN that prevents malicious intruders from dropping data packets or forwarding fake data. The mechanism has been experimented with adhoc on-demand distance vector (AODV) protocol though it can work with any other reactive WBAN routing protocol. Effectiveness of the protocol is evaluated in detecting malicious nodes with low overhead. In [39], the use of biometric characteristics is explored in securing data communication within WBAN and minimizing computational complexity as well as power efficiency. Here, hybrid authentication model is exploited as a conceptual framework for the system. In this work, the framework requires a unique feature of human body regarded as the authentication identity, while the other techniques use hardware and software to achieve the same purpose. In [4], an energy-efficient key management scheme for WBANs has been proposed that takes into account available resources of a node during the whole life cycle of key management. The proposed scheme is a cluster-based hybrid security framework that provides support for both intra-WBAN and inter-WBAN communications. Here, use of multiple clusters gives impact on energy efficiency. Security of the cluster formation process is implemented using electrocardiogram (EKG)-based key agreement scheme. Both preloading of keys and physiological value-based generated keys are exploited in this hybrid key management technique. Highly dynamic and random EKG values of the human body are used here for pairwise key generation and refreshment. The performance of the proposed cluster-based key management scheme is evaluated in terms of energy efficiency and network lifetime. However, for a small network consists of 15 to 20 nodes (standard network size for WBAN [35]) clustering could be an overhead. Exiting security solutions designed for both WSN and WBAN mostly cover threats to authentication and data integrity. Hence, a comprehensive solution is still to be designed to address all other potential threats as well and to obtain a secure and optimal scheme for either networks. Thus, security and privacy in WSN and WBAN have been part of the active research over the years and will remain in the forthcoming time-frame as well.

7 Potential Applications

WSN applications in diverse domain can be broadly categorized according to their prime objective of deployment as shown in Fig. 7.9. A taxonomy of representative WSN applications is presented in Fig. 7.9. As depicted in the figure, the leading application domains of WSNs include environment, military and surveillance, health (body area networks), industry and agriculture, and urbanization and infrastructure [40]. WSN applications are generally of two types: monitoring and tracking. Remote monitoring is one of the primary concerns of WSN applications where environmental phenomenon or human activities are remotely supervised. In a number of applications, sensor nodes are often deployed in remote areas for monitoring natural phenomena like rain-forest and/or biodiversity monitoring [13], forest fire detection or surveillance [2]. In these applications, nodes are deployed at random (dropped from a vehicle, etc.) or are strategically placed. Such nodes remain more or less static throughout their lifetime though the connectivity varies due to node failure, communication failure, limited hardware resource, and environmental factors which are external to the system. It is mentioned in [13] that sensor networks for such applications are typically deployed in small scale and/or only for a short period of time. One of the major points of concern for this is system reliability [11]. It is not possible to come over and fix the faulty nodes at regular intervals. Security is another major concern for these networks particularly various forms of DoS attacks.

Security is even more important when WSNs are deployed in habitable areas for surveillance and/or infrastructure monitoring. One of the interesting applications in

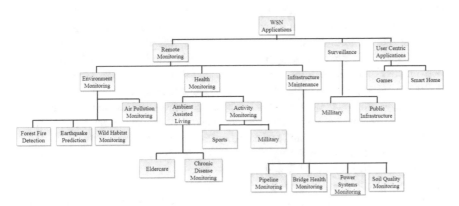

Fig. 7.9 Diverse application areas of WSN

military is military operations involving force protection with unattended ground sensors formed into intelligent networks around forward operating bases [40]. Networked mines called self-healing mine fields that automatically rearrange themselves to ensure optimal coverage are another interesting example. VigilNet (VigilNet. http://www.cs.virginia.edu/wsn/vigilnet/) presents an integrated sensor network system for energy-efficient surveillance missions. Encryption is a widely used mechanism to ensure data privacy and integrity. But even in such cases, tampering a node may divulge the security key information and/or traffic can also be rerouted. However, shared key cryptography [14] may make this kind of attacks difficult to launch. Application layer attacks, as detailed in Sect. 3, can also be launched especially when WSNs are used for surveillance. Ensuring precision and thereby reducing the false positive events is a major challenge in surveillance applications to encourage wide adoption of such prediction measures.

However, WSNs also find applications in sports, entertainment, medical applications, and smart home, where in addition to placing ambient sensors (temperature sensor, proximity sensor, etc.), the sensor nodes are also strategically placed in, on, or around human body to measure vital physiological parameters forming WBAN [35] over human body. WBANs are exploited for developing several applications related to remote healthcare, ambient assisted living even in user centric applications such as gaming and smart home as is summarized in Fig. 7.10. Human activity recognition has garnered a great research interest in recent years [3]. However, the use of WSN in healthcare applications is growing in fast pace where remote medical supervision could be beneficial for eldercare, detection of chronic diseases, etc. With ambient assisted living applications, the aged people can feel more independent in performing everyday activities. For instance, the ironHand project ((2016). D3.3.4 Glove Integrated Prototype (Fourth Iteration). [Online]. Available: http://www.ironhand.eu/) aims to facilitate elders with poor hand grips to continue with their daily work. The idea is to build a robotic glove that can add strengthen the grip for users with impaired hand function. Different accelerometers, muscle sensors (EMG sensor), and infrared sensors (IR sensor) are used in the gloves to capture the tension of muscle, which generates variable length data [33].

WBAN is also applied to monitor the practice of a player as well as his/her fitness in sports like hammer throwing, swimming, water volleyball, cricket, football, etc. [17]. Analyzing sensing data, specialized measures can be taken to improve their performance and maintaining their health. For water sports like swimming and water volleyball, the wearable sensors also change their communication mediums, i.e., from air to water or vice versa due to the movement of body. Hence such applications require not only water resistant case to place the sensors but also smart MAC protocols to tackle change of communication medium on the fly.

It is predicted that WBANs can be used in disaster rescue or emergency response like fire rescue [33] and flood rescue. In disaster rescue, body sensors would broadcast distress signals which can be received by rescue devices, or may get relayed or delivered by neighboring BANs (R. Huang and L. Chu, "Disaster rescue mode for body area networks," U.S. Patent 9 247 375, Jan. 26, 2016. [Online]. Available: https://www.google.ch/patents/US9247375). This adds an important dimension of WBAN applications which not only requires intra-BAN

Fig. 7.10 Diverse application areas of WBAN

but also inter-BAN communication ability in cross-medium. In such applications, different kind of sensors like temperature sensors, multimedia sensors, etc., along with GPS are used. Thus, the data size differs for each type of sensors. In the flood rescue response, sensors may use both water and air as the propagation medium thus requiring smart MAC protocols as well.

In all these applications sensors are either placed in, on, or around human body or they gather data about user behavior. Thus humans are closely related to the system. Hence, these applications call for security issues. For instance, data integrity is a critical requirement for WBAN applications as wrong information about body vitals of an individual could lead to wrong treatment and consequently, fatal consequences. Data privacy is also very important for these applications as sensitive data about user behavior, their daily lifestyles could be divulged and may pose to be a social threat. Even, any information or misinformation about player's fitness may ruin their reputation. Thus, WSN and hence WBAN applications should be made increasingly secure in order to guarantee precision and durability of the monitoring applications for which they are deployed. As more and more parties are getting involved with such applications, stringent privacy norms should also be set.

8 Open Research Issues

Now-a-days, sensors have become the eye of IoT-based applications [1]. Sensing and communications go hand-in-hand to solve a plethora of problems for smart city applications [22]. But rather than placing sensors at a remote location such as forest fire monitoring, WSNs are increasingly placed in habitable areas, such as city wide air pollution monitoring systems. Presently, sensors are also designed to have some capability of energy harvesting. Thus, with proximity to the sensor deployment and increase of interested parties, maintaining data confidentiality and integrity is becoming harder day-by-day. Intelligent noise removal techniques can also be employed as today's sensors have some computation power. Crowdsourcing is emerging as a new technique for collecting data using the smartphone sensors carried by the citizens [12]. Smart home, smart building [38], and assisted living are important applications where sensing data are used to improve the quality of life of citizens. However, this calls for many important concerns from citizen's point of view, including sharing of personal data such as user location and ambient sound. Sharing of these data can raise significant concerns about security and user privacy [55]. As stated in [23], sensing and sourcing applications potentially collect sensitive sensor data pertaining to individuals that can be used to detect behavioral patterns of individuals. For example, GPS sensor readings can be used to proactively predict traffic congestion levels and/or anomalies in a given community, but at the same time these can be used to infer private information like movement trajectory of an individual, routes they take during their daily commutes, as well as their home and work locations [12]. Thus security and privacy issues of WSNs are even more pertinent for today's sensors that are deployed in habitable areas and are collecting data on urban lifestyle.

Sensors, especially bio-sensors are also worn by citizens and they also pose significant security and privacy challenges that only a few existing solutions could address. Currently, WBANs involve homecare, especially, eldercare and hospital environment scenarios. In homecare and hospital scenarios, body sensors are in direct communication range of the sink, and they do not require to route packets. But only sometimes they require to send data through maximum 2 hops [42]. Thus few literature could be found on routing attacks such as selective forwarding, wormhole and sinkhole attacks in the intra-BAN level of WBANs. However, in the near future, with the deployment of mobile networks, WBANs can play a critical role in treatment of victims in disaster events. In disaster scenarios, body sensors might need to send their data through other devices outside their immediate radio range. Therefore, routing protocols with strong security features will become a crucial service for effective end-to-end communications in the intra-BAN level of WBANs. Intruders may launch denial of service attacks by causing inter-BAN interference and thereby blocking all data traffic from reaching the sink.

The second issue that definitely will become more important in near future is lack of cohesive policy sets to protect the patient's privacy. As WBANs become ubiquitous, more parties such as pharmacies and insurance companies will be involved in the system. Therefore, patient related data will be accessed by more parties, and more attacks on patient privacy are possible that may affect their social lives as well. Thus, privacy attacks may pose to be a major obstacle to growth and development of this technology and may hinder wide adoption of it. If current and future privacy issues are not well formulated, WBAN may remain only as a research prototype. In new set of policies, all possible future parties and privacy threads associated with them should be considered so that all involved parties find it difficult to abuse from patient data.

The next generation of WSNs and hence WBANs could benefit from the advantage of cloud computing technology. Combining mobile cloud computing with sensors wide applications and business models are beginning to emerge [54]. With the support of mobile cloud computing, the deployment of innovative healthcare monitoring applications with richer multimedia contents is now technically feasible but more reliable quality of service and more types of convergence services are needed. This combination will require new security threads [54]. The growth of sensing technology not only for WBANs but for many other variants of WSNs is rapid and fast thus needing suitable updation of current security and privacy issues. New points of concern will be raised in this area in the near future, in this section we just mentioned a few of them.

9 Conclusions

This chapter presents a thorough study on the security and privacy issues of WSN and WBAN. At the beginning, the networks are studied in detail along with their characteristics, architecture, performance metrics, applications and accordingly a comparative analysis has been made as well. After that the key requirements for security and privacy in both networks are illustrated. A categorization of the potential threats to both networks has also been made to get insight of the attacks such as their origin, nature, and objective. Next, the existing measures are studied accordingly. Finally, the open research challenges are identified to motivate the researchers for further investigation in those areas.

References

1. Adat, V., & Gupta, B. (2018). Security in internet of things: Issues, challenges, taxonomy, and architecture. *Telecommunication Systems, 67*(3), 423–441.
2. Akyildiz, I. F., Su, W., Sankarasubramaniam, Y., & Cayirci, E. (2002). Wireless sensor networks: A survey. *Computer Networks, 38*(4), 393–422.
3. Al Ameen, M., Liu, J., & Kwak, K. (2012). Security and privacy issues in wireless sensor networks for healthcare applications. *Journal of Medical Systems, 36*(1), 93–101.
4. Ali, A., & Khan, F. A. (2013). Energy-efficient cluster-based security mechanism for intra-WBAN and inter-WBAN communications for healthcare applications. *EURASIP Journal on Wireless Communications and Networking, 2013*(1), 216.
5. Anita, X., Bhagyaveni, M. A., & Manickam, J. M. L. (2015). Collaborative lightweight trust management scheme for wireless sensor networks. *Wireless Personal Communications, 80*(1), 117–140.
6. Arampatzis, T., Lygeros, J., & Manesis, S. (2005). A survey of applications of wireless sensors and wireless sensor networks. In *Proceedings of the 2005 IEEE International Symposium on Mediterranean Conference on Control and Automation, Intelligent Control* (pp. 719–724). Piscataway: IEEE.

7. Bicket, J., Rowson, J. M., & Phillips, C. (2018). Authentication of a gateway device in a sensor network. US Patent App. 10/085,149.
8. Borgohain, T., Kumar, U., & Sanyal, S. (2015). Survey of security and privacy issues of internet of things. arXiv preprint arXiv:1501.02211.
9. Cavallari, R., Martelli, F., Rosini, R., Buratti, C., & Verdone, R. (2014). A survey on wireless body area networks: Technologies and design challenges. *IEEE Communications Surveys & Tutorials, 16*(3), 1635–1657.
10. Chen, J. C., Jiang, M. C., & Liu, Y. W. (2005). Wireless lan security and IEEE 802.11 i. *IEEE Wireless Communications, 12*(1), 27–36.
11. Chowdhury, C., Aslam, N., Ahmed, G., Chattapadhyay, S., Neogy, S., & Zhang, L. (2018). Novel algorithms for reliability evaluation of remotely deployed wireless sensor networks. *Wireless Personal Communications, 98*(1), 1331–1360.
12. Chowdhury, C., & Roy, S. (2017). Mobile crowdsensing for smart cities. In *Smart cities: Foundations, principles, and applications* (pp. 125–154). Hoboken: Wiley.
13. Corke, P., Wark, T., Jurdak, R., Hu, W., Valencia, P., & Moore, D. (2010). Environmental wireless sensor networks. *Proceedings of the IEEE, 98*(11), 1903–1917.
14. Delgado-Mohatar, O., Fúster-Sabater, A., & Sierra, J. M. (2011). A light-weight authentication scheme for wireless sensor networks. *Ad Hoc Networks, 9*(5), 727–735.
15. Elhoseny, M., Yuan, X., El-Minir, H., & Riad, A. (2016). An energy efficient encryption method for secure dynamic WSN. *Security and Communication Networks, 9*(13), 2024–2031.
16. Fan, X., & Gong, G. (2012). LPKM: A lightweight polynomial-based key management protocol for distributed wireless sensor networks. In *International Conference on Ad Hoc Networks* (pp. 180–195). Berlin: Springer.
17. Fu, Y., & Liu, J. (2013). Monitoring system for sports activities using body area networks. In *Proceedings of the 8th International Conference on Body Area Networks* (pp. 408–413).
18. Gungor, V. C., & Hancke, G. P. (2009). Industrial wireless sensor networks: Challenges, design principles, and technical approaches. *IEEE Transactions on Industrial Electronics, 56*(10), 4258–4265.
19. Gupta, B. B. (2018). *Computer and cyber security: Principles, algorithm, applications, and perspectives*. Boca Raton: CRC Press.
20. Halder, S., Ghosal, A., & Bit, S. D. (2011). A pre-determined node deployment strategy to prolong network lifetime in wireless sensor network. *Computer Communications, 34*(11), 1294–1306.
21. He, D., Zeadally, S., Kumar, N., & Lee, J. H. (2017). Anonymous authentication for wireless body area networks with provable security. *IEEE Systems Journal, 11*(4), 2590–2601.
22. Hossain, M. S., Muhammad, G., Abdul, W., Song, B., & Gupta, B. (2018). Cloud-assisted secure video transmission and sharing framework for smart cities. *Future Generation Computer Systems, 83*, 596–606.
23. Huang, K. L., Kanhere, S., & Hu, W. (2010). Are you contributing trustworthy data? The case for a reputation system in participatory sensing. In *Proceedings of the 13th ACM International Conference on Modeling, Analysis, and Simulation of Wireless and Mobile Systems (MSWIM'10)* (pp. 14–22). New York: ACM.
24. Jan, M., Nanda, P., Usman, M., & He, X. (2017). PAWN: A payload-based mutual authentication scheme for wireless sensor networks. *Concurrency and Computation: Practice and Experience, 29*(17), e3986.
25. Javadi, S. S., & Razzaque, M. (2013). Security and privacy in wireless body area networks for health care applications. In *Wireless networks and security* (pp. 165–187). Berlin: Springer.
26. Kallio, J., & Koivusaari, J. (2016). WSN related requirement analysis towards sustainable building automation operations and maintenance. In *Ubiquitous computing and ambient intelligence* (pp. 212–217). Berlin: Springer.
27. Khan, K., & Goodridge, W. (2014). Impact of multipath routing on WSN security attacks. *International Journal of Intelligent Systems and Applications, 6*(6), 72.
28. Kompara, M., & Hölbl, M. (2018). Survey on security in intra-body area network communication. *Ad Hoc Networks, 70*, 23–43.

29. Lee, T. H. (2008). Simple dynamic user authentication protocols for wireless sensor networks. In *Second International Conference on Sensor Technologies and Applications, 2008. SENSOR-COMM'08* (pp. 657–660). Piscataway: IEEE.

30. Liu, Q., & Wang, P. K. (2009). Secure and energy-efficient clustered routing protocol for wireless sensor networks [j]. *Computer Simulation, 4,* 041.

31. Liu, X., Cao, J., Lai, S., Yang, C., Wu, H., & Xu, Y. L. (2011). Energy efficient clustering for WSN-based structural health monitoring. In *Proceedings IEEE INFOCOM, 2011* (pp. 2768–2776). Piscataway: IEEE.

32. Mainanwal, V., Gupta, M., & Upadhayay, S. K. (2015) A survey on wireless body area network: Security technology and its design methodology issue. In *2015 International Conference on Innovations in Information, Embedded and Communication Systems (ICIIECS)* (pp. 1–5). Piscataway: IEEE.

33. Maitra, T., & Roy, S. (2018). Research challenges in ban due to the mixed WSN features: Some perspectives and future directions. *IEEE Sensors Journal, 17*(17), 5759–5766.

34. Movassaghi, S., Abolhasan, M., & Lipman, J. (2013). A review of routing protocols in wireless body area networks. *Journal of Networks, 8*(3), 559–575.

35. Movassaghi, S., Abolhasan, M., Lipman, J., Smith, D., & Jamalipour, A. (2014). Wireless body area networks: A survey. *IEEE Communications Surveys & Tutorials, 16*(3), 1658–1686.

36. Pantazis, N. A., Nikolidakis, S. A., & Vergados, D. D. (2013). Energy-efficient routing protocols in wireless sensor networks: A survey. *IEEE Communications Surveys & Tutorials, 15*(2), 551–591.

37. Pathan, A. S. K., Lee, H. W., & Hong, C. S. (2006). Security in wireless sensor networks: Issues and challenges. In *The 8th International Conference on Advanced Communication Technology, ICACT 2006* (Vol. 2, 6 pp.). Piscataway: IEEE.

38. Plageras, A. P., Psannis, K. E., Stergiou, C., Wang, H., & Gupta, B. B. (2018). Efficient IoT-based sensor big data collection–processing and analysis in smart buildings. *Future Generation Computer Systems, 82,* 349–357.

39. Ramli, S. N., Ahmad, R., Abdollah, M. F., & Dutkiewicz, E. (2013). A biometric-based security for data authentication in wireless body area network (WBAN). In *15th International Conference on Advanced Communication Technology (ICACT)* (pp. 998–1001). Piscataway: IEEE.

40. Rawat, P., Singh, K. D., Chaouchi, H., & Bonnin, J. M. (2014). Wireless sensor networks: Recent developments and potential synergies. *The Journal of Supercomputing, 68*(1), 1–48.

41. Romer, K., & Mattern, F. (2004). The design space of wireless sensor networks. *IEEE Wireless Communications, 11*(6), 54–61.

42. Roy, M., Chowdhury, C., & Aslam, N. (2017). Designing 2-hop interference aware energy efficient routing (hier) protocol for wireless body area networks. In *International Conference on Communication Systems and Networks* (pp. 262–283). Berlin: Springer.

43. Roy, M., Chowdhury, C., & Aslam, N. (2017). Designing an energy efficient WBAN routing protocol. In *9th International Conference on Communication Systems and Networks (COMSNETS)* (pp. 298–305). Piscataway: IEEE.

44. Roy, M., Chowdhury, C., Kundu, A., & Aslam, N. (2017). Secure lightweight routing (SLR) strategy for wireless body area networks. In *IEEE International Conference on Advanced Networks and Telecommunications Systems (ANTS)* (pp. 1–4). Piscataway: IEEE.

45. Roy, M., Chowdhury, C., & Neogy, S. (2014). Developing secured manet using trust. In *Fourth International Conference on Advances in Computing and Communications (ICACC)* (pp. 183–186). Piscataway: IEEE.

46. Saleem, S., Ullah, S., & Kwak, K. S. (2011). A study of IEEE 802.15. 4 security framework for wireless body area networks. *Sensors, 11*(2), 1383–1395.

47. Saleem, S., Ullah, S., & Yoo, H. S. (2009). On the security issues in wireless body area networks. *International Journal of Digital Content Technology and Its Applications, 3*(3), 178–184.

48. Seah, W. K., Eu, Z. A., & Tan, H. P. (2009). Wireless sensor networks powered by ambient energy harvesting (WSN-heap)-survey and challenges. In *1st International Conference on*

Wireless Communication, Vehicular Technology, Information Theory and Aerospace & Electronic Systems Technology. Wireless VITAE 2009 (pp. 1–5). Piscataway: IEEE.
49. Senouci, M. R., Mellouk, A., Senouci, M. A., & Oukhellou, L. (2014). Belief functions in telecommunications and network technologies: An overview. *Annals of Telecommunications, 69*(3–4), 135–145.
50. Shen, J., Chang, S., Shen, J., Liu, Q., & Sun, X. (2018). A lightweight multi-layer authentication protocol for wireless body area networks. *Future Generation Computer Systems, 78,* 956–963.
51. Sheng, Z., Yang, S., Yu, Y., Vasilakos, A., Mccann, J., & Leung, K. (2013). A survey on the IETF protocol suite for the internet of things: Standards, challenges, and opportunities. *IEEE Wireless Communications, 20*(6), 91–98.
52. Singh, S. K., Singh, M., & Singh, D. K. (2010). Routing protocols in wireless sensor networks– a survey. *International Journal of Computer Science & Engineering Survey, 1*(2), 63–83.
53. Singla, A., & Sachdeva, R. (2013). Review on security issues and attacks in wireless sensor networks. *International Journal of Advanced Research in Computer Science and Software Engineering, 3*(4), 529–534.
54. Stergiou, C., Psannis, K. E., Kim, B. G., & Gupta, B. (2018). Secure integration of IoT and cloud computing. *Future Generation Computer Systems, 78,* 964–975.
55. Tewari, A., & Gupta, B. (2018, in press). Security, privacy and trust of different layers in internet-of-things (IoTs) framework. *Future Generation Computer Systems.* https://doi.org/10.1016/j.future.2018.04.027
56. Tiegang, F., Guifa, T., & Limin, H. (2014). Deployment strategy of wsn based on minimizing cost per unit area. *Computer Communications, 38,* 26–35.
57. Toorani, M. (2016). Security analysis of the IEEE 802.15. 6 standard. *International Journal of Communication Systems, 29*(17), 2471–2489.
58. Vullers, R. J., Van Schaijk, R., Visser, H. J., Penders, J., & Van Hoof, C. (2010). Energy harvesting for autonomous wireless sensor networks. *IEEE Solid-State Circuits Magazine, 2*(2), 29–38.
59. Wang, Y., Attebury, G., & Ramamurthy, B. (2006). A survey of security issues in wireless sensor networks. *IEEE Communications Surveys & Tutorials, 8,* 2–23.
60. Zhang, T., & Qu, H. (2010). A lightweight key management scheme for wireless sensor networks. In *Second International Workshop on Education Technology and Computer Science (ETCS)* (Vol. 1, pp. 272–275). Piscataway: IEEE.
61. Zia, T., & Zomaya, A. (2006). Security issues in wireless sensor networks. In *Proceedings of the International Conference on Systems and Networks Communications (ICSNC 2006)* (p. 40). Piscataway: IEEE.

Chapter 8
Preventing Security and Privacy Attacks in WBANs

Avani Vyas and Sujata Pal

Abstract Sensors and radio channels have made remote health monitoring easier with the use of wireless body area networks (WBANs). WBANs use bio-sensors, implanted on/inside the human body, to collect real-time health readings. These sensors collect data wirelessly and then send it to medical server via wireless communication channels. Human health readings are of great importance and wireless channels are not always secure. This makes security and privacy disquiet in WBANs. Sensor nodes are the most common target of an intruder in WBANs. Intruder can also attack the communication channels and medical server of WBANs. Therefore, WBAN needs prevention while sending sensed information to the health care monitoring system. We also need to maintain confidentiality while transmitting the data to the server. In this chapter, we discuss various types of possible attacks in WBANs and summarized different lightweighted security methods proposed for resource constraint WBANs. We thoroughly explained how channel characteristics and human body features could be exploited to identify intruder in WBANs without using complex encryption. Additionally, the chapter briefly review methods for generating symmetric keys and exchanging messages over insecure channels in cloud assisted WBANs.

Keywords Security and privacy · Link fingerprints · Attacks · Encryption methods · Secure key exchange methods

1 Introduction

From the past few years, wearable body sensors are in fashion for health monitoring, fitness training, and sports applications. Companies are introducing smart devices with embedded wearable sensors to increase health awareness among people

A. Vyas · S. Pal (✉)
Department of Computer Science and Engineering, Indian Institute of Technology Ropar, Rupnagar, India
e-mail: 2017csz0007@iitrpr.ac.in; Sujata@iitrpr.ac.in

© Springer Nature Switzerland AG 2020
B. B. Gupta et al. (eds.), *Handbook of Computer Networks and Cyber Security*,
https://doi.org/10.1007/978-3-030-22277-2_8

[13, 14, 40]. WBAN helps in collecting health readings of a patient from his home. **Insulin pumps** are used widely for monitoring the glucose level of human body. These pumps are programmed to induce and adjust the dosage level of insulin in case of deficiency. **Implantable cardioverter defibrillators (ICDs)** are used as pacemakers for heart patients. ICDs are programmable and controlled remotely through the radio channels. The authorities program ICDs to generate electric shocks in case of slow heartbeat. Corporate companies provide many other remote monitoring facilities for patient.[1]

The contribution of technology towards improving the lifestyle of a human can also be used as a direct tool to harm the patient. The risk of security increases with the interoperability of network devices. Experiments have revealed that insulin pumps can be hacked and dosage levels can be modified [11]. The wireless link used between a device and a remote terminal is vulnerable to hacking and hence makes insulin pump insecure. Tests on pacemakers by Halperin et al. [16] revealed that pacemakers are exposed to various radio-attacks. The planned radio-attacks were able to decode the patient's name, his medical history, type, and ID of ICD and changed the settings of ICD as well. Hence, the person using a pacemaker is directly under the risk of losing privacy and integrity of data.

These loopholes ignited research towards meeting security and privacy requirements in WBANs. WBAN is an application of IoT in the field of healthcare. The layered IoT architecture has different security requirements at different layers [1, 15, 38]. Javadi and Razzaque [19] discussed various security risks possible at physical, data link, network, and transport layer in WBANs. However, they did not address the solutions provided to meet the requirements of security and privacy in WBANs. Figure 8.1 summarizes different techniques discussed in this chapter for maintaining the security and privacy of WBANs.

1.1 Security Threats in WBANs

Similar to other wireless networks, WBAN is also prone to privacy and security risks [23]. The role of privacy in WBAN is to keep the medical status of the patient confidential, whereas security prevents spoofing of physical nodes and channel used for intra-BAN and inter-BAN communication. *Intra-BAN communication* in WBANs refers to the communication between sensor nodes and the coordinator, whereas *inter-BAN communication* is the communication between two or more BANs implanted on different bodies. In intra-BAN communication, an intruder can induce wrong readings by imitating himself as a valid node. WBANs also support

---

[1]https://mhealthintelligence.com/news/top-10-remote-patient-monitoring-solutions-for-hospitals.

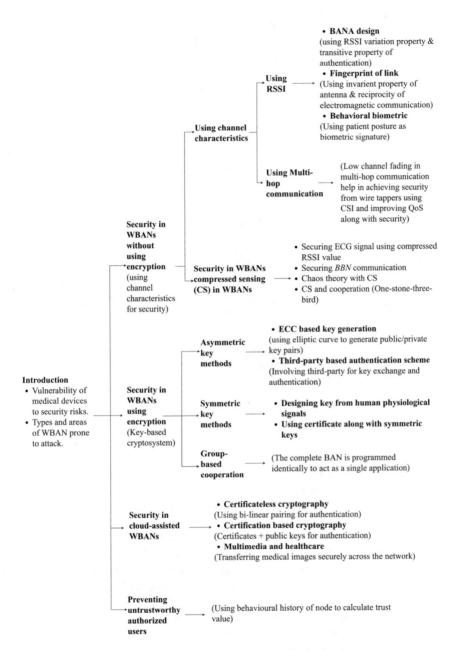

Fig. 8.1 Overview of the security preserving methods discussed in the chapter

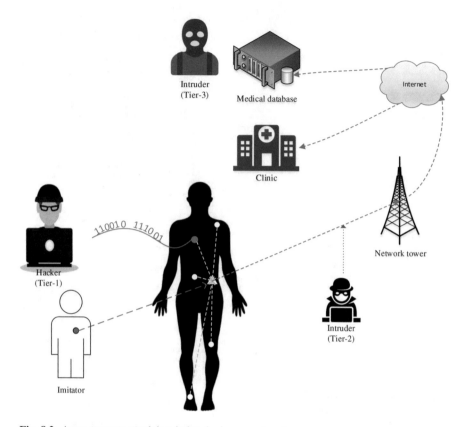

Fig. 8.2 Areas prone to attack in wireless body area networks

inter-BAN communication for relaying data towards medical servers. The inter-BAN communication is an open field for intruders where an intruder can act as a false BAN network to support relaying and can get readings of another person.

WBAN follows the three-tier architecture consisting of PAN (personal area network) at tier-1, LAN (local area network) at tier-2, and WAN (wide area network) at tier-3. Nodes in WBANs are placed at human body which collect health readings and transmit to the coordinator node, also referred as the hub or base station. Sensor nodes, medical server/local server, and channels are attacked by the intruder in WBANs, as shown in Fig. 8.2 [3, 28]. An attack can be a passive or active attack. Under passive attack, an attacker does not make changes to data, whereas active attack causes modifications in the data. Table 8.1 gives an overview of areas prone to security attacks and types of attacks possible and WBAN. Different types of attack in WBANs are discussed below:

– *Fabrication attack:* Medical details of the patient must be accessible to verified persons only. Every person registers himself for getting an authority to access the medical status of a patient. The person can be a doctor, nurse, family member, or

Table 8.1 Security attacks in WBANs

Area under attack	Type of attack Active	Passive	Name of attack	Risk
Sensor node	✓	–	Fabrication	Authentication
	–	✓	Eavesdropping	Confidentiality
Medical server	✓	–	Modification	Integrity
	–	✓	Eavesdropping	Confidentiality
Channel	✓	–	Jamming, tunneling	DoS, integrity
	–	✓	Eavesdropping	Confidentiality

a trustworthy friend. Under fabrication attack, an unauthorized person manages to get access to private details of the patient. The fabrication attack causes *authorization* risk.

- *Masquerade attack:* Masquerade attack occurs when a stranger node imitates itself as a part of the WBAN. In Fig. 8.2, the imitator can send his heartbeat rate instead of patient's and thus misguiding the medical team. The masquerade attack risks *authenticity* of collected medical readings.
- *Eavesdropping:* Eavesdropping is a passive attack which causes a breach of confidentiality. An eavesdropper sits silently and overhears the ongoing communication. The patient is not always comfortable in sharing the medical detail with everyone. For example, the AIDS report of the patient can be the confidential document which he will never want to expose to others. The unwanted access to this info via the communication channel or compromised sensor node will breach *confidentiality* of the health status of a patient.
- *Modification attack:* A doctor must get accurate medical details to ensure the correct diagnosis of the patient. However, due to the lack of security, the data may get compromised and an intruder can make changes in medical readings. This type of attack is termed as modification attack and causes the loss of *integrity*.
- *Other attacks:* Other possible types of attack are denial of service (DoS), jamming, and tunneling attacks. These attacks may prevent reaching medical services to patients (Table 8.1).

The medical data is of high importance. WBANs must be resilient to attacks discussed previously. Methods are required to detect intruders at tier-1 who are trying to pose themselves as legitimate members. Sharing of medical reports over the wireless channel at tier-2 must also be made secure. Another requirement is to design lightweighted security mechanisms to achieve security and privacy in resource constraint WBANs. Further sections discuss how intruder detection at tier-1 is possible in WBANs using human body and channel characteristics, and how security at tier-2 is provided to secure the communication over the channel.

2   Security Without Encryption in WBANs

The interoperability of devices used in WBAN gives an opportunity to exploit multiple properties of the network to enable secure communications. Literature suggests many encryption/decryption techniques. However, they are not suitable for resource constraint WBANs, especially intra-WBAN communication. Security in WBANs has been made possible by utilizing channel characteristics and network properties.

2.1   Techniques Using Channel Characteristics

Channel state information (CSI) describes characteristics of the physical layer, such as channel fading model, shadowing effect, and outage probability. The quality of the signal received is highly dependent on CSI and distance between two communicating parties. Jakes fading model [18] says that the range of good communication is up to the distance half of the channel wavelength. The channel beyond the distance greater than the wavelength is treated as independent. Hence researchers found CSI useful and utilized it to design various secure communication techniques in WBANs. These methods can successfully detect the intruder and fraudery data received at the coordinator.

2.1.1   Exploiting Received Signal Strength Indicator to Design Fingerprint

Received signal strength indicator (RSSI) measures the strength of the signal received at the receiver side, subject to channel characteristics. With the increasing distance of communication, RSSI drops. Nodes in intra-WBAN are implanted at few centimeters distance from each other. All the nodes belonging to the same intra-WBAN have same CSI and almost similar distance, hence similar RSSI value at the hub. This gave rise to *RSSI variation property* which states that RSSI variation of nodes implanted on the same body is relatively less when compared to the RSSI variation of off-body communication. In off-body communication one of the two communicating nodes is present outside the body at some distance. It is possible to identify the intruder using RSSI because he will have different CSI and hence different RSSI. In the preceding paragraphs we discussed few techniques which use RSSI and CSI to achieve security in WBANs.

- **Body Area Network Authentication (BANA Design)**
  Traditional key exchange cryptography techniques of wireless sensor networks
  (WSNs) cannot provide the required level of authorization in WBANs. Moreover, traditional cryptography techniques use extra hardware. In response, Shi
  et al. proposed a new authorization mechanism named BANA for achieving
  authorization in WBANs without adding hardware complexity [34, 35]. They
  exploited *RSSI variation property* and *transitive property of authentication* to
  design BANA. The *transitive property of authentication* is used to provide
  authentication in multi-hop connections. *Transitive property of authentication*
  states that if A authenticates B and B authenticates C, then A can also trust C.
  Shi et al. conducted an experiment to prove the RSSI variation property. They
  implanted five nodes on a person and collected RSSI for all nodes. They placed a
  transceiver at some distance from the body to create an off-body communication.
  RSSI for nodes communicating on different channels (off-body) was highly
  vacillating, whereas nodes communicating on the similar channel (on-body) were
  having stable RSSI. The similar observation followed for LOS (line of sight) and
  non-LOS communication, respectively. The non-LOS had more RSSI variation
  than the LOS communication. LOS and non-LOS communication are defined
  as:

  - *LOS communication:* In LOS communication of WBANs, two communicat-
    ing nodes are positioned on the same side of the human body. For example,
    one node is on the chest and other on the knee of a human.
  - *Non-LOS communication:* In non-LOS of WBANs, the two communicating
    nodes are on the opposite side of the human body. For example, one node is
    on the chest and other node is on left hip of a human.

BANA Design The control unit (CU) of BAN such as coordinator broadcasts
and asks sensor nodes to send messages continuously till the coherence time
of the channel. *Coherence time* of the channel is the time for which there is
negligible change in characteristics of the received signal. The sensor node
chooses a random time after which it starts message transmission. At the end
of the coherence period, CU calculates the average of received RSSI for each
node, called as average received variation (ARV). CU uses k-means clustering to
classify nodes into two groups based on their ARV. The node having low ARV
is added to authenticated node group, otherwise node is included in the rejected
group. If node present outside the body participates in BANA's authentication
process, then ARV value for that will be high and hence will be prevented from
entering into the network. Due to high ARV this method mistakenly reject non-
LOS legitimate sensor nodes as well. This fault is conquered by utilizing the

transitive property of authentication. The non-LOS communication is supported using multi-hop path communication. Nodes on multi-hop path trust their peer which implies trust between the original message generator and receiving nodes. However, due to transitive property, spoofing a single node will compromise the whole network.

– **Fingerprints of Link**

The diagnosis and output of WBAN systems is dependent on data submitted by body sensors. The importance of medical data is of great importance so there must exist trust mechanism to authenticate the sensors who are submitting the data. Ali et al. [2] used *invariant property of antenna* and link characteristics (*reciprocity property of electromagnetic communication*) to create link fingerprints. The link fingerprint is designed to guarantee the authenticity of the originator of readings. *Invariant property of antenna* states, identical antennas transmit identical signals. *Reciprocity property of electromagnetic communication* states that signals traveling on similar channel will experience same type of channel loss. These link fingerprints are difficult to forge because the wireless link characteristics change with little change in channel parameters such as distance, wavelength, and channel fading model. Therefore, any imitator, as shown in Fig. 8.2 trying to send his heart readings would have different channel loss and can be identified easily. This methodology will prevent man-in-middle attack.

To prevent the authentication attack, both the users Alice and Bob encrypt their link fingerprints and submit it to the victor. Alice and Bob do not communicate directly instead, they share their key with the Victor. Victor authenticates every ongoing communication between the two users, using saved fingerprint, and is capable of finding the faulty communicator. Whenever the Eve would try to interfere with ongoing communication between Alice and Bob, change in link characteristic will occur which would be identified by the Victor. In order to test the proposed approach authors attached one sensor on the Alice and another on Bob. They considered Bob's sensor as a base station. Sensors used contain same type of antenna. They coded RSSI value as a link fingerprint. The experiment concluded that there was a high correlation between the RSSI value of Alice and Bob, which makes it suitable to use as link fingerprint. However, the method does not provide confidentiality if eavesdropper cracks the key shared between users and Victor.

– **Behavioral Biometric**

Body movement causes change in the path of communication of sensor nodes in BANs. The distance between the nodes in intra-BAN changes with the change in human posture. This effects the RSSI of a signal received at the hub. This RSSI value is used to create biometric for every human posture. Zhao et al. [47]

defined behavioral biometric as the average of RSSI values received from all nodes at the hub. The average RSSI value is then used to create fingerprint. For example, posture of a patient measuring his body temperature using thermometer will give different average RSSI value than the patient who is taking pills. The fingerprints are then used to provide authentication in WBANs. This approach divides the network into three regions, namely trusted, limited-trusted, and non-trusted regions. Wearable bio-sensors (WBs) are considered into the non-trusted region initially. The base station along with collecting data from WBs is also acting as the authentication node (AN). The AN is considered into limited-trusted region as it is approachable to attackers.

As soon as a WB is introduced in the network, it is authenticated by the AN using the following steps: WB pings "Hello" to AN and AN also acknowledges with a "Hello" message. On receiving an acknowledgment, WB replies with a non-private message which is used by AN to extract RSSI from the signal and forms the fingerprint of the channel. The fingerprint is then compared against the stored authenticated ID (designed by averaging the RSSI value of authenticated nodes) for verification. A match adds the node in the network. Authors claim that the proposed method is resilient to active and passive attacks due to the use of low bandwidth for communication. In order to eavesdrop the conversation or to act as a legitimate user, the intruder has to be present closer to the user. They assumed that an eavesdropper cannot be present that close to the patient. Moreover, they claimed that it is difficult to attain the behavioral fingerprints of the authenticated user.

2.1.2 Exploiting Multi-Hop Communications

Apart from the star topology, WBANs also support multi-hop communication. The channel used for communication in WBANs is lossy and is subjected to various attenuation and path loss effects. Multi-hop communication helps in preserving the quality of information by preventing a signal from traveling long distances. *Diversity combining techniques* at the sink helps in extracting best quality signal from all receiving signals. *Diversity combining techniques* are used at the receiver side to combine multiple signals. These signals are received from different communication channels with different CSI.

Niu et al. [29] used multi-hop communication to exploit physical characteristics of the channel to achieve secrecy in WBANs. They claimed that, due to low channel fading in multi-hop communication, the data rate on the main link is high and is difficult to tap by the intruder.

Wire tappers break the channel and harm the confidentiality and integrity of the ongoing communication. The physical layer characteristics can be exploited to perform healthy communication in the presence of wire tappers. The following physical layer characteristics can be used to spot wire tappers in the network [27]:

- The channel of communication is different for legitimate nodes and wire tappers, hence different CSI of legitimate nodes and wire tappers.
- Transmitter is aware of CSI of all legitimate and wiretap channels.
- The legitimate channel is modeled with log-normal fading and the wiretap channel is modeled using Rayleigh fading.
- Slotted ALOHA is used as a channel allocation protocol.

Secrecy outage probability (SOP) matrix is used to measure the level of secrecy. The signal traveling over a channel is expected to suffer from attenuation and channel fading. The SOP measures the amount of channel fading allowed for prescribed level of secrecy. The signal to noise ratio (SNR) of the signal received at the receiver must be high for the good quality communication. The use of multi-hop relaying with spatial-diversity combining techniques shortens the path of communication and helps in preserving the SNR value. *Diversity combining techniques* at the sink are used to extract the best quality signal among all the receiving signals. The wire tapper is expected to have low quality of communication and hence would be easy to recognize.

Moosavi and Bui favored the use of multi-hop relaying to meet the SOP requirements. However, multi-hop relaying induces delay and effects QoS. To achieve quality, they calculated the load at each node using *traffic distribution* (inter-arrival rate of packets), *transmission time distribution* (time needed by slotted ALOHA to transmit packet), and service time distribution (time needed until the successful delivery of the message). The queuing delay and service are used to approximate the end-to-end latency of the packet. The approximated end-to-end delay is supposed to be less than the defined threshold for better QoS. In order to exploit the advantage of multi-hop relaying while preserving QoS, they build Nash equilibrium-based topology using multi-hop topology formation game (MTFG). In MTFG, topology is built using a cost function made up of SOP and QoS. Hence they achieved security along with QoS requirement.

2.2 *Augmenting Security with Compressed Sensing*

Compressed sensing is a tool used by energy-constrained communication networks to preserve energy. Compressed sensing facilitates sampling of the sensed signal at rate lower than the Nyquist sampling rate [32]. It helps in reducing the amount of data sent on the channel. Nyquist sampling rate states that in order to reconstruct the original signal at the receiver side, the sampling rate of the signal must be twice the maximum frequency of the signal.

Compressed Sensing (CS) Compressed sensing is used to reduce the size of the communication message when the signal transmitted by the sender to receiver is sparse [9]. The sparsity of the signal is obtained by multiplying it with the suitable transformation basis. Let $\hat{x}$ be the sparse matrix which is used to define sparsity of the original signal x as per Eq. (8.1).

$$x = \Psi.\hat{x} \tag{8.1}$$

where Ψ is a transform basis, i.e., DFT or wavelet transformation. The input signal x is projected by a measurement matrix Φ on the output signal y as per Eq. (8.2).

$$y = \Phi.x = \Phi.\Psi.\hat{x} \tag{8.2}$$

Measurement matrix defines the number of measurement to be taken from the sparse signal x. The number of measurements m is calculated as per Eq. (8.3), where constant $c > 0$, n is the number of observations, and k is the sparsity of x.

$$m > c.k.\log(\frac{n}{k}) \tag{8.3}$$

As a result, the output signal y contains measurements of non-zero elements in sparse matrix. The focus on sensing only the subsamples (y) achieves compression in the sensed data. At the receiver side, it is possible to recover x from the received signal y using similar measurement matrix Φ.

CS can be used to reduce the network overhead caused by complex security methods by reducing the size of encrypted message. Following method describes how compressed RSSI values are used by Dautov and Tsouri [8] to secure the ECG signal.

The RSSI value of the signal is grouped and maintained in sequences of size m. The average of all the RSSI values is then subtracted from every value. The authors named this process as "distillation." The distilled values are then passed through the linear feedback shift register (LFSR). The LFSR acts as an encoder and secures data by shuffling the bits. The message generated by the LFSR is appended with the suitable number of zeros. This process is repeated L times resulting into L matrices. These matrices are then linearly combined to compress them into a single matrix. The ECG signal x generated by a sensor node is then multiplied with this matrix to encrypt the signal. The method proposed ensures security from an intruder as it is difficult for an intruder to generate the same set of RSSI values. Error estimation in message recovery at the receiver side is done using root mean square error (RMSE), relative error (RE), and similarity coefficient (SC). The simulated results concluded that error in the reconstructed signal kept on increasing with the increasing distance of the intruder.

Peng et al. [30] made similar attempt for encrypting data in body-to-body networks. ***Body-to-body network (BBN)*** is the communication network between two nodes belonging to separate BANs. In resource constraint BANs, benefits from

BBN are achieved by sharing resources across the network, for relaying data towards the destination. However, it is apprehensive to transfer confidential data through other networks. Peng et al. used BBN to achieve multiple benefits while serving WBAN applications. They assumed information to be transmitted is in the form of an image. In order to provide security to the data traveling across the networks, they proposed chaotic compressive sensing (CCS). CCS is the combination of the chaos theory and CS. The measurement matrix used in compression is treated as an encryption key.

Chaos Theory Chaos theory is the study of unpredictable behavior of dynamic networks governed by the deterministic laws [10]. "A chaotic sequence is pseudo-random and finite" [30].

Decompression of the received signal to get original signal x at receiver side needs measurement matrix. The message in BBN follows inter-BAN path so it is not secure to send measurement matrix for every message to every receiver. Moreover, storing huge measurement matrix consumes large memory. Peng et al. resolved both security and memory requirement issues using chaos theory. The pseudo-random generators of chaos theory helped in generating different measurement matrices for different users. Since the chaos theory is deterministic, sharing a seed of pseudo-random generator with receiver will make it possible to recover measurement matrix without consuming extra memory. The performance of CCS was tested on a popular image "Lena" in MATLAB. CCS successfully encrypted the image and recovered at receiver side with high entropy. However, CCS shares seed of encryption matrix (i.e., measurement matrix) over the insecure channel. Wire tapper can easily invade the ongoing communication using this seed.

One-Stone-Three-Bird [45] is another combination of compressed sensing and security using cooperation. BAN need a lightweight and secure aggregation methods for transmission of medical images over the network. *One-stone-three-bird* compresses a medical image to 20% of the original size. Authors claim that this reduction in size is possible with the use of compressed sensing. A sensor node, "*sensor*" captures multiple medical images. These images are then transferred to the next neighboring hop, "*next*" in intra-BAN. The sensor "*next*" randomly generates measurement matrix and also finds sparsity of all received images. Each sparse image is then multiplied with the measurement matrix and forwarded to the sink node, "$sink_{intra}$". The sink node aggregates all the received images and then sends an aggregated image to the next hop of inter-BAN. Finally the sink at receiver, "$sink_{final}$" decompress the image using the orthogonal matching pursuit [39]. *One-stone-three-bird* uses cooperation between the generator of the message and its next neighboring hop *next*. However, the technique requires a pre-trusted partner who can spend his energy for compression of images generated by his neighbor node.

3 Secure Key Exchange Methods in WBANs for Encryption-Based Cryptosystem

Key exchange cryptographic techniques are used widely to provide secure communication between parties communicating from distance. Key management is an energy consuming task. Cooperation has made it possible to use key encryption in energy-constrained intra-WBANs, by distributing the load of key management across the network members. The group-based cooperation discussed in Sect. 3.3 explains one such instance of group key management.

There are two types of key encryption techniques, asymmetric and symmetric. In asymmetric key encryption methods, a pair of public and private keys is used for encryption and decryption, respectively. A message encrypted using a public key can be decrypted using the corresponding private key only. In symmetric key encryption, communicating parties use single key for encrypting and decrypting the packet. The challenge in key-based encryption is to distribute keys between the communicating parties securely. The symmetric key agreement is subjected to very popular problem in cryptography, called man-in-middle attack.

Use of certification along with public/private key pair adds an extra layer of security. Certificate helps in validating the other party by authenticating the public key. Hence, both the certificate and private key together are needed to decrypt the information in certification-based cryptosystems [48]. On the other hand, there exist certificateless public key cryptographic (CL-PKC) techniques. In CL-PKC, third trusted party, for example, network manager, authenticates the public key rather than using certificates. CL-PKC technique prevented the need of managing certificates. The problem of key distribution is solved by generating keys at either ends with an agreement. This prevents the need of sharing keys over an insecure channel.

3.1 Asymmetric Key Generation Methods

Public keys are freely available for every party in asymmetric encryption. Asymmetric keys are used to make digital signatures and hence are very useful in preventing *repudiation attacks*. In WBANs, repudiation occurs when a patient denies after submitting the health data. Similarly, doctor can also misbehave and claim that he has not given particular prescriptions to the patient. Asymmetric key distribution is not that much challenging as symmetric key distribution. Elliptical curve cryptosystem (ECC) is used widely in asymmetric cryptosystem for generating public private key pairs.

3.1.1 ECC-Based Key Generation

ECC method is most commonly used in public-key cryptography. ECC helps in generating public/private key pairs which are difficult to decode. ECC is based on elliptic curve discrete logarithm problem (ECDLP) which states that it is difficult to find the discrete logarithm of a random elliptic curve. Public key is generated from ECC using the following procedure:

$$Q = k.p \in E(f_p) \tag{8.4}$$

Given an elliptic curve $E(f_p)$ and a base point $P \in E(f_p)$, there exists an order k which is used to calculate other point Q on the curve. The two communicating parties, P_1 and P_2 choose an order k randomly at both sides and name it $k1$ and $k2$, respectively. P_1 uses $k1$ as its private and P_2 uses $k2$ as its private key. Given a predefined point P the two parties calculate their public keys, $Q1$ and $Q2$ using Eq. (8.4), respectively. For an attacker it is difficult to compute the private key, k using the public key, Q and random point, P.

3.1.2 Third-Party-Based Authentication Scheme Using Asymmetric Keys

Authentication in WBANs can also be achieved using a third-party. This third-party is trustworthy and authenticates messages exchanged between the sender and the receiver. Third-party-based authentication can also provide anonymity to the user over an insecure channel. One such approach is given by Liu et al. [25]. They involved network manager (NM) as a third trusted party. The new WBAN device such as PDA, mobile, and the new user is registered to the NM before starting functioning. The algorithm steps are performed as follows:

- The NM generates its public and private keys. Private key is any key belonging to the set of integers. Public key is generated using Eq. (8.4).
- Similar to NM, signer generates his private key and labels it as a partial private key. The public key is generated using partial private key on Eq. (8.4) and is named as partial public key.
- The other half of the private key is generated by the NM on request from the user using user's private key and hash value of user's public key and user identification.

  The NM then generates the key pair which is used to secure future communication. The key generated by the procedure is user specific for every WBAN application which prevents interference. The method is proved secure by conducting the theoretical analysis and simulations. However, key maintenance is the overhead in the suggested approach. The number of keys increases with the increase in the application. Moreover, in emergency situations, dependency on a single key can cause delay in necessary treatments. The other improvements over certificateless authentication scheme by Liu et al. [25] are suggested in [44, 46].

3.2 Symmetric Key Generation Methods

This section describes two methods that can be used to generate symmetric keys at the two ends securely. The first method describes use of a human-based physiological signal for generating a secure key in WBANs and the second method discusses the use of ECC to generate symmetric keys.

3.2.1 Physiological Signal-Based Key Generation

Venkatasubramanian et al. [41] proposed a physiological signal-based key agreement (PSKA) key exchange algorithm to support secure communication in WBANs. Physiological signals are unique and vary temporally [42]. Hence, the dynamicity of physiological signals makes them suitable to use as a cryptography key. In PSKA only the nodes which are implanted on the human body know the physiological signal of that body. Thus, node outside the body cannot decode the key designed using particular human physiological signal. Moreover, the dependability of physiological signal on the BAN user ensures different key for the different subject.

PSKA uses *Fuzzy vault* scheme in symmetric key-based encryption to communicate secret key. Fuzzy vault uses a polynomial of order v and a vector of features which is generated by legitimate nodes belonging to the BAN. The order of the polynomial and parameters used to generate feature vector are pre-informed to the nodes. Fuzzy vault generates output Y in the form of a set (vault). Each element of the set X consists of a pair of a single feature vector and its value when mapped into polynomial function. In order to increase security of message *chaff* values are added to X. *Chaff* values are the randomly generated set of points. Hence, the output set X consists of feature pairs and *chaff* values. At the receiver side, feature vectors are generated using same parameters as used by the sender. About polynomial, receiver knows its order only, not the exact polynomial. He interprets a polynomial and generates his own vault Y. Pairs generated in Y are then matched with the received vault X. If sufficient pairs are not matched, then receiver changes the coefficients of the polynomial. The coefficient, for which sufficient pairs of Y match with the received vault X, is treated as a symmetric key.

PSKA prevents man-in-middle attack because nodes not belonging to similar BAN cannot generate same set of physiological signal vector and hence cannot generate similar set of vault. In worst case, even if feature vector gets compromised, then also an intruder cannot overhear complete communication because physiological signals vary with the time which would change the feature vector. PSKA enables real-time security. The *chaff* points added make it more difficult for the strange entity to figure out the non-chaff pairs.

3.2.2 Certification-Based Authentication Scheme Using Symmetric Keys

An early detection of heart stroke or drowsiness can help in reducing road accidents. The use of body area network (BAN) can prevent the rate of road accidents. BAN can provide assistance in driving if it is possible to detect the current health status of the driver. The vehicular resources are utilized and the electronic control unit (ECU) of the vehicle is used as a hub. The ECU collects and processes the data, and provides feedback to the driver. Wang et al. [43] defined an authentication and encryption module which can be used together or individually to provide secure communication.

Certificate validation method provided by IEEE 802.15.6 is used for authentication. The certificate of new node is validated by the ECU. First the certificate is tested and validated. Then the node is provided with the username and password. Password is validated by following challenge-response authentication. Whenever a new node (having username and password) tries to enter into the network, it comes across a challenge. A challenge could be the biometric data collected by the nodes. In response, the new node generates a 256-bit secret key using secure hash algorithm-256 (SHA-256), known by the trusted members only. The response is generated by the hub also and is matched with the response received from the new node.

After authentication, data is further secured using symmetric key encryption technique. To generate the symmetric key at both ends they followed the following procedure. Using ECC, first both parties generate their public/private key pairs and exchange public keys. Let say $k1$ and $k2$ are the private keys and Q1 and Q2 are the corresponding public keys.

$$K1 \times Q2 = k1 \times (k2 \times P) = k2 \times (k1 \times P) = k2 \times Q1 \qquad (8.5)$$

According to Eq. (8.5) both sides have same value (R.H.S = L.H.S). The private key and received public keys are then used to generate the symmetric key. Public keys are generated at the two communicating ends using ECC. To share the keys between the two communicating parties elliptic-curve Diffie–Hellman (ECDH) key agreement protocol is used [5]. Once a symmetric key is generated AES is used for encryption/decryption of the data in future communication.

3.3 Group-Based Cooperation

In group-based cooperation, all the sensors of a WBAN are programmed identically and form a virtual group (VG) for accomplishing a single application. The members of this single application work together to make the network more efficient. Group-based symmetric key generation solution has been proposed to prevent interception attack in WBANs [24]. The key is generated by the coordinator node using RSSI values of all its VG members. Authors exploited the reciprocity property of the

RSSI to get the symmetric key at both the ends (sender and receiver). As this is a symmetric key algorithm, the new node willing to join the existing VG must have the key to communicate with all the group members. Authors claim that granting complete responsibility of symmetric key generation to the coordinator of the VG only will consume more resources. They suggested distribution of the key generation burden among all the group members. The VG is assigned a multicast address, the new node probes message on this multicast address which is received by all the members of the VG. In response, the existing members find the RSSI value of the received signal from the new member and acknowledge the probe message. From the acknowledged message new node gets the RSSI value of all the members of the group and uses it to generate the key.

On the other hand, the group members forward the saved RSSI value (extracted from the probe message sent by the new node) to the coordinator node. The coordinator and new node has the same set of values to generate a symmetric key due to reciprocity property of the RSSI value. The proposed idea prevented individual communication between a new node and VG members and hence preserved energy. The evaluation setup consisted of 4 MICAz motes using Zigbee for communication with low powered antenna. The method experimented on the setup concluded that it is difficult for an eavesdropper to get all the RSSI values to generate a similar key.

4   Security in Cloud Assisted WBANs

Continuous patient monitoring generates huge traffic, which needs high storage, efficient resources, and quick responses. Cloud computing has made it possible to provide low cost and quick services in WBANs. The sensed data is passed to the cloud, where it is pre-processed and stored to provide the required services. Figure 8.3 shows the cloud assisted WBANs (CAWBANs) architecture. A person with sensors on his body can be present anywhere, at home or in office. The coordinator node attached to human body collects and transfers the sensed data to the cloud via cellular network. Doctors as well as patient can access the stored information from the cloud.

Clouds are configured with high processing machines and data storages. Cloud helps in increasing performance of resource constraint WBANs by providing extra processing capabilities. Mobile cloud computing (MCC) increases the accessibility of data for doctors and family members [36]. Clouds can be programmed to induce self decision-making capabilities in the network. However, a successful attack on cloud can cause serious damage to multiple users. Stergiou et al. [37] discussed various security issues related to MCC and integration of cloud to IoT. Following paragraphs discuss different methods needed to preserve privacy and security in CAWBAN.

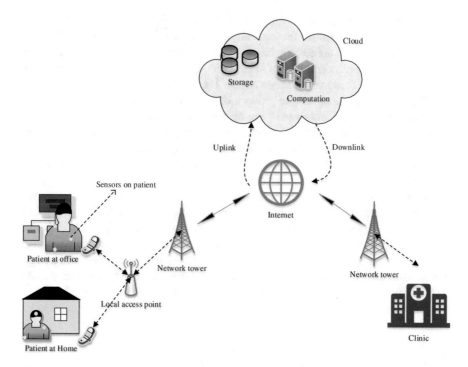

Fig. 8.3 Architecture of cloud assisted wireless body area networks

4.1 Certificateless Cryptography Technique for CAWBANs

In this section we discuss how CAWBANs provide anonymity to users, authenticity at the cloud server and prevent repudiation attack without using certificates with encryption keys. We discuss a method by Shen et al. [33] which uses hash value of user ID instead of his actual ID to provide anonymity to the user. In their model, they considered three entities, namely users, NM, and cloud server (CSr). NM is assumed to be the trusted party and CSr is also supposed to be registered to the NM before providing services. The lightweight certificate less security protocol consists of three phases: initialization, registration, and authentication.

– *Initialization:* In this phase, NM publishes necessary parameters named *params*. *Params* are used by the NM and users to generate public/private key pair using ECC. The public key Q is generated using Eq. (8.4). The order k used to generate the public key Q is treated as a private key. Here k is labeled as s for the NM and s_U for users. Private keys s and s_U are chosen randomly from the cyclic group mentioned in *params*. The CSr also generates his public/private key pair using the same method.

– *Registration:* After initialization, each user registers itself to the NM. The NM is supposed to get user id ID_U in advance. The user who wants to get registered sends the hash value of his ID and public key Q_U to the NM. The NM uses this hash value to verify the existence of user in his database. Once user is verified, he is assigned an index number and signature. Similarly, the CSr is also verified against its stored ID ID_C by the NM. The index number of the user is then verified by the CSr and if successful, user is added to the CSr database.

- *Authentication:* A user sends service request to the CSr. The service request contains the current time stamp t_C, hashed public key, and coded index number. Upon receiving request, the CSr authenticates the user by decoding his hashed index number and matches it with the entry saved in his database during the registration phase. The embedded time stamp of the request message helps in identifying invalid requests. Once the user is labeled as legitimate, the CSr generates a session key and message authentication code for the further communication. Authentication code contains the session key and hash value computed by applying hash function on the public key of the user Q_U, current time stamp t_C, and a value $T1$ generated using Eq. (8.4), where k is chosen randomly from the cyclic group mentioned in *params*. On receiving the request response, user decodes the session key.

Pairing-Based Cryptography Pairing-based cryptography can also be used to maintain security of the data stored in the cloud [7]. In *pairing-based cryptography*, numbers from additive cyclic groups are paired together to generate a number belonging to the multiplicative cyclic group. A pairing-map function is given by $G1 \times G1 \rightarrow G2$. It is assumed that patient, doctor, and cloud will get their asymmetric key pair from key generation center (KGC). To maintain privacy, they used asymmetric key pairs. A patient uses his mobile device to upload medical reports collected by the attached body sensors, on the cloud. Patient encrypts his health data using his public key. Hence, no other person other than the patient can read patient's reports, as it needs the private key to unlock the message. For authentication between the two parties which could be the cloud and patient or the cloud and doctor, symmetric key encryption method is used. Both the communicating parties calculate session key at their respective ends using the following steps:

- A patient (or doctor) creates a message containing bilinear pairing of the private key of the patient (or doctor) and the public key of the cloud and current time stamp. The message is then encrypted using the public key of the cloud and is communicated to the cloud along with the identity of a patient (or doctor).
- On receiving the message, cloud decrypts the message using his private key and compares the current time stamp with the time stamp extracted from the received message. The time stamp confirmation prevents replay attacks.
- Cloud uses bilinear pairing on the received public key of the patient (or doctor) and his secret key. The result of the pairing is then compared with the bilinear pairing value extracted from the received message.
- Both sender and receiver calculate session key using a similar hash function on paired value. Now, both the parties can encrypt their messages using the session key as a symmetric key.

This method prevents multiple attacks, such as man-in-middle attack and replay attack. However, the patient has to provide his private key to the doctor to unlock the reports uploaded on the cloud by the patient. There is no mechanism of renewing a private key of the patient, which means once a key is compromised it can be misused continuously.

4.2 Certification-Based Cryptography Techniques in CAWBANs

Chebyshev chaotic maps are used to generate public key and certificates [22]. User registers himself to the medical cloud center C and in return C provides certificate to user using Chebyshev chaotic maps. Whenever a patient wants to contact to a doctor remotely, the communication between the patient and the doctor is authenticated by the cloud. Patient initiates the communication and sends his identity along with name of the doctor's identity to the cloud and doctor. In this message patient appends session key, certificate, public key, and current time stamps. On receiving a request from the patient, doctor generates same set of messages and sends it to the cloud and patient. Now cloud has received certificates from both the patient and doctor. Cloud authenticates the parties and replies back to both the parties. The patient and doctor holding each other's public key can now generate a session key to secure further communication. This method prevents many attacks. However, the session key does not change in the second message. Hence once a session key is revealed, the intruder impersonate himself as a legitimate user.

4.3 Cloud Computing and Multimedia for Healthcare

IoT along with the functionality of cloud computing supported the growth of smart cities [31]. Smart monitoring of the patient in the era of IoT has become possible in various ways. Multimedia in the form of video surveillance is exploited well to remain updated with the activities of the patient. Video surveillance generates data in bulk which is compressed and transmitted across the networks. The multimedia data also need security while traveling across the channels. Memos et al. [26] proposed a secure routing scheme in the smart city environment which claims to secure the identity, route, and location of the sensor node. A packet in this multi-hop routing is always forwarded to a trustworthy node in the neighbor. If no trustworthy node is found in the neighborhood, then node will not forward its packet. The header of the forwarded packet is changed at each hop due to routing decision at each step. The recalculation of packet header at each hop ensures the safety of the packet. The intruder must get sync with the changing header to spoof the packet which is difficult.

A watermark generated from the signature of the user can also be used to prevent the repudiation attack [17]. Key frames are extracted from the video using genetic algorithm (GA) and are split into RGB components. The selection of key frames helps in reducing the size of a video. The watermark as a signature is then inserted at random parts of each component. This generates a watermarked video which is then posted on the public cloud. The integrity of the video content is maintained by securing the signatures, i.e., the watermark, with key encryption. Intruder cannot directly copy the watermark as it is encrypted.

5 Preventing Untrustworthy Authorized Users

Methods discussed so far are concerned about preventing unauthorized access to the data. However, there exists a possibility that the attacker is present inside the network only, i.e., the untrustworthy authorized user. Trust management is possible through various ways such as trust-based routing scheme [12] and trust-based data access [4, 6, 21]. For trust-based routing, all the possible paths are ranked according to the trust value of nodes constituting the path. Similarly, trust-based assessment grants access to sensitive information after calculating the trust value only. For trust management mechanism, reward and punishment feedbacks are used. For example, Boukerche and Ren [6] used reward and punishment method to evaluate the trust measure of nodes. Nodes which cooperate in forwarding data securely are rewarded. On the other hand, mischievous nodes are punished for misbehaving. If the level of trust degrades, then node can also be moved out of the network. Kaur and Sood [20] designed a mechanism to provide security at medical database. All the authorized parties are assigned trust score using three factors: the first factor is the count of evil deeds committed by a node in past, the second is internal factor including feedback from direct neighbors, and the third is external factor which includes feedback from third parties.

6 Open Issues

After several solutions proposed to achieve security and privacy in WBANs, there exist issues which are not completely resolved.

- **Flexibility:** In WBANs, authorization may keep on changing according to the requirement and thus need to be flexible. For example, a nurse having authorization of a particular WBAN may change her job. Now new nurse wanted to access this WBAN this flexibility is not provided by the existing methods.
- **Handling emergency:** Most of the methods assign control of data access to patient in order to preserve the privacy. However, in case of emergency patient cannot share his BAN access with family members or other new doctors. For

example, the approach by Chen et al. [7] allows only patient to unlock his report. In such scenarios some backups for emergency situations are needed.

- **Interference:** WBANs support inter-WBAN communication to increase the throughput and optimize energy utilization. However, routing data through other network challenges security and privacy. Inter-WBAN communication highly suffers from signal interference. The security and privacy aspects in interference are still not addressed in the literature.
- **Single point failure:** Cloud technology has helped in increasing processing capability and storage of WBANs. However, in CAWBANs cloud can be aimed as the single point failure. Existing security mechanisms are not resilient to this failure.
- **Trust issues:** Existing methods focus on identifying intruder in the network. The cases where culprit exists inside the network are still unexplored. All the methods assume coordinator as a trustworthy party, failure of which is still an open problem.
- **Energy aspects:** Implanted nodes in WBANs are not rechargeable. It is very difficult for nano devices to hold sufficient energy in them to increase the lifetime of the network. Cryptosystem at sensors level increases burden on these devices. Hence, there is always a scope of energy efficient lightweighted security and privacy preserving methods that helps in improving WBANs services further.

7 Conclusion

Next generation medical services are introduced with the aim of improving lifestyle and health aspects. The medical services provided at home manage to preserve time compared to the traditional visits to health experts. WBAN handles emergency situations and provides instant diagnosis. Medical readings of a patient are sensitive information so security and privacy of data is an important factor in WBANs. In this chapter, we discussed various types of attacks possible in three-tier architecture of WBANs. The discussion about commercial health devices concluded that these devices are not ready to fight against security and privacy attacks. We explained how lightweighted security mechanisms are established to provide security in resource deficient WBANs. Following this we briefly review the use of channel and human body characteristics to build link fingerprints and secure the communication. The cloud-based CAWBANs improved the functionality of WBANs, while at the same time it introduced another feasible zone prone to attacks. We discussed how certificateless and certification-based cryptography methods are used to secure communication over cloud in WBANs. The chapter also provides small discussion on how to secure medical images and videos when transmitted across the network. We listed existing open issues in WBANs for future work to provide ubiquitous secure wireless health services.

References

1. Adat, V., & Gupta, B. (2018). Security in internet of things: Issues, challenges, taxonomy, and architecture. *Telecommunication Systems, 67*(3), 423–441.
2. Ali, S. T., Sivaraman, V., Ostry, D., Tsudik, G., & Jha, S. (2014). Securing first-hop data provenance for bodyworn devices using wireless link fingerprints. *IEEE Transactions on Information Forensics and Security, 9*(12), 2193–2204.
3. Al-Janabi, S., Al-Shourbaji, I., Shojafar, M., & Shamshirband, S. (2017). Survey of main challenges (security and privacy) in wireless body area networks for healthcare applications. *Egyptian Informatics Journal, 18*(2), 113–122.
4. Athanasiou, G., Fengou, M. A., Beis, A., & Lymberopoulos, D. (2015). A trust assessment mechanism for ubiquitous healthcare environment employing cloud theory. In *2015 37th Annual International Conference of the IEEE Engineering in Medicine and Biology Society (EMBC)* (pp. 1405–1408). Piscataway: IEEE.
5. Barker, E., Johnson, D., & Smid, M. (2006). *Recommendation for pair-wise key establishment schemes using discrete logarithm cryptography*. National Institute of Standards and Technology.
6. Boukerche, A., & Ren, Y. (2009). A secure mobile healthcare system using trust-based multicast scheme. *IEEE Journal on Selected Areas in Communications, 27*(4), 387–399.
7. Chen, C. L., Yang, T. T., & Shih, T. F. (2014). A secure medical data exchange protocol based on cloud environment. *Journal of Medical Systems, 38*(9), 112.
8. Dautov, R., & Tsouri, G. R. (2016). Securing while sampling in wireless body area networks with application to electrocardiography. *IEEE Journal of Biomedical and Health Informatics, 20*(1), 135–142.
9. Donoho, D. L. (2006). Compressed sensing. *IEEE Transactions on Information Theory, 52*(4), 1289–1306.
10. Ekeland, I. (1998). What is chaos theory? *Review (Fernand Braudel Center), 21*(2), 137–150. http://www.jstor.org/stable/40241422
11. Finkle, J. (2016). *J&J warns diabetic patients: Insulin pump vulnerable to hacking*. Reuters Published October 4
12. Gao, Y., & Liu, W. (2015). A security routing model based on trust for medical sensor networks. In *IEEE International Conference on Communication Software and Networks (ICCSN)* (pp. 405–408). Piscataway: IEEE.
13. Goode, L. (2013). Comparing wearables: Fitbit flex vs. jawbone up and more. http://allthingsd.com/20130715/fitbit-flex-vs-jawbone-up-and-more-a-wearables-comparison/
14. Goode, L. (2018). Apple watch's update adds heart-monitoring capabilities. https://www.wired.com/story/apple-watch-series-4/
15. Gupta, B. B. (2018). *Computer and cyber security: Principles, Algorithm, applications, and perspectives*. Boca Raton: CRC Press.
16. Halperin, D., Heydt-Benjamin, T. S., Ransford, B., Clark, S. S., Defend, B., Morgan, W., et al. (2008). Pacemakers and implantable cardiac defibrillators: Software radio attacks and zero-power defenses. In *IEEE Symposium on Security and Privacy, SP 2008* (pp. 129–142). Piscataway: IEEE.
17. Hossain, M. S., Muhammad, G., Abdul, W., Song, B., & Gupta, B. (2018). Cloud-assisted secure video transmission and sharing framework for smart cities. *Future Generation Computer Systems, 83*, 596–606.
18. Jakes, W. C., & Cox, D. C. (1994). *Microwave mobile communications*. Piscataway: IEEE Press.
19. Javadi, S. S., & Razzaque, M. (2013). Security and privacy in wireless body area networks for health care applications. In *Wireless networks and security* (pp. 165–187). Berlin: Springer.
20. Kaur, N., & Sood S. K. (2018). A trustworthy system for secure access to patient centric sensitive information. *Telematics and Informatics, 35*(4), 790–800.

21. Kraounakis, S., Demetropoulos, I. N., Michalas, A., Obaidat, M. S., Sarigiannidis, P. G., & Louta, M. D. (2015). A robust reputation-based computational model for trust establishment in pervasive systems. *IEEE Systems Journal, 9*(3), 878–891.
22. Li, C. T., Lee, C. C., & Weng, C. Y. (2016). A secure cloud-assisted wireless body area network in mobile emergency medical care system. *Journal of Medical Systems, 40*(5), 117.
23. Li, M., Lou, W., & Ren, K. (2010). Data security and privacy in wireless body area networks. *IEEE Wireless Communications, 17*(1), 51–58.
24. Li, Z., Wang, H., & Fang, H. (2017). Group-based cooperation on symmetric key generation for wireless body area networks. *IEEE Internet of Things Journal, 4*(6), 1955–1963.
25. Liu, J., Zhang, Z., Chen, X., & Kwak, K. S. (2014). Certificateless remote anonymous authentication schemes for wireless body area networks. *IEEE Transactions on Parallel and Distributed Systems, 25*(2), 332–342.
26. Memos, V. A., Psannis, K. E., Ishibashi, Y., Kim, B. G., & Gupta, B. B. (2018). An efficient algorithm for media-based surveillance system (EAMSuS) in IoT smart city framework. *Future Generation Computer Systems, 83*, 619–628.
27. Moosavi, H., & Bui, F. M. (2016). Delay-aware optimization of physical layer security in multi-hop wireless body area networks. *IEEE Transactions on Information Forensics and Security, 11*(9), 1928–1939.
28. Movassaghi, S., Abolhasan, M., Lipman, J., Smith, D., & Jamalipour, A. (2014). Wireless body area networks: A survey. *IEEE Communications Surveys & Tutorials, 16*(3), 1658–1686.
29. Niu, H., Sun, L., Ito, M., & Sezaki, K. (2014). Secure transmission through multihop relaying in wireless body area networks. In *IEEE 3rd Global Conference on Consumer Electronics (GCCE)* (pp. 395–396). Piscataway: IEEE.
30. Peng, H., Tian, Y., Kurths, J., Li, L., Yang, Y., & Wang, D. (2017). Secure and energy-efficient data transmission system based on chaotic compressive sensing in body-to-body networks. *IEEE Transactions on Biomedical Circuits and Systems, 11*(3), 558–573.
31. Plageras, A. P., Psannis, K. E., Stergiou, C., Wang, H., & Gupta, B. B. (2018). Efficient IoT-based sensor big data collection–processing and analysis in smart buildings. *Future Generation Computer Systems, 82*, 349–357.
32. Rani, M., Dhok, S., & Deshmukh, R. (2018). A systematic review of compressive sensing: Concepts, implementations and applications. *IEEE Access, 6*, 4875–4894.
33. Shen, J., Chang, S., Shen, J., Liu, Q., & Sun, X. (2018). A lightweight multi-layer authentication protocol for wireless body area networks. *Future Generation Computer Systems, 78*, 956–963.
34. Shi, L., Li, M., & Yu, S. (2012). BANA: Body area network authentication exploiting channel characteristics. In *5th ACM Conference on Security and Privacy in Wireless and Mobile Networks (WiSec'12)*.
35. Shi, L., Li, M., Yu, S., & Yuan, J. (2013). BANA: Body area network authentication exploiting channel characteristics. *IEEE Journal on Selected Areas in Communications, 31*(9), 1803–1816.
36. Stergiou, C., & Psannis, K. E. (2017). Recent advances delivered by mobile cloud computing and internet of things for big data applications: A survey. *International Journal of Network Management, 27*(3), e1930.
37. Stergiou, C., Psannis, K. E., Kim, B. G., & Gupta, B. (2018). Secure integration of IoT and cloud computing. *Future Generation Computer Systems, 78*, 964–975.
38. Tewari, A., & Gupta, B. (2018). Security, privacy and trust of different layers in internet-of-things (IoTs) framework. Future Generation Computer Systems
39. Tropp, J. A., & Gilbert, A. C. (2007). Signal recovery from random measurements via orthogonal matching pursuit. *IEEE Transactions on Information Theory, 53*(12), 4655–4666.
40. Umpierrez, G. E., & Klonoff, D. C. (2018). Diabetes technology update: Use of insulin pumps and continuous glucose monitoring in the hospital. *Diabetes Care, 41*(8), 1579–1589.
41. Venkatasubramanian, K. K., Banerjee, A., & Gupta, S. K. S. (2010). PSKA: Usable and secure key agreement scheme for body area networks. *IEEE Transactions on Information Technology in Biomedicine, 14*(1), 60–68.

42. Venkatasubramanian, K. K., & Gupta, S. K. (2010). Physiological value-based efficient usable security solutions for body sensor networks. *ACM Transactions on Sensor Networks, 6*(4), 31.
43. Wang, J., Han, K., Alexandridis, A., Zilic, Z., Pang, Y., Wu, W., et al. (2018). A novel security scheme for body area networks compatible with smart vehicles. *Computer Networks, 143*, 74–81.
44. Wang, C., & Zhang, Y. (2015). New authentication scheme for wireless body area networks using the bilinear pairing. *Journal of Medical Systems, 39*(11), 136.
45. Wang, L., Li, L., Li, J., Li, J., Gupta, B. B., & Liu, X. (2018). Compressive sensing of medical images with confidentially homomorphic aggregations. *IEEE Internet of Things Journal, 6*, 1402–1409.
46. Zhao, Z. (2014). An efficient anonymous authentication scheme for wireless body area networks using elliptic curve cryptosystem. *Journal of Medical Systems, 38*(2), 13.
47. Zhao, N., Ren, A., Rehman, M. U., Zhang, Z., Yang, X., & Hu, F. (2016). Biometric behavior authentication exploiting propagation characteristics of wireless channel. *IEEE Access, 4*, 4789–4796.
48. Zhou, C., & Cui, Z. (2016). Certificate-based signature scheme in the standard model. *IET Information Security, 11*(5), 256–260.

Chapter 9
Underwater Wireless Sensor Networks

Usha Jain and Muzzammil Hussain

Abstract In this chapter, we will provide the brief introduction of wireless sensor networks (WSNs) and the detailed introduction of underwater wireless sensor networks (UWSNs). We define the basic issues and different applications related to UWSNs. This chapter provides the description about the difference between the terrestrial WSNs and UWSNs. Later, we discuss the different task of the sensor nodes and deployment architecture of the UWSNs. We elaborate the factors that affect UWSNs design as well as communication architecture of the UWSNs. Here, we explain security issues and provide the detailed description of TCP/IP protocol stack. Later, we define all the protocols for secure communication in UWSNs. One important aspect of this chapter is the study of different simulation tools. We pull together all of the content on simulation of the UWSNs. Finally, we conclude the chapter.

Keywords Underwater wireless sensor networks (UWSNs) · Sensor node · Security attacks · Security protocols · Simulation · Emulation

1 Introduction

A large number of sensor nodes with limited resources and one or more base stations comprise wireless sensor networks (WSNs). Sensor networks are only the reason for revolutionizing the different areas of industry and science. The use of sensor nodes emerges in many more applications like industrial (machine surveillance), underwater, structural monitoring, habitat monitoring of microorganisms, intelligent buildings, facility management, disaster relief operations, medical and health care, agriculture, and many more. Sensor nodes observe the near objects or environments, and report to the base station about the change in observations.

U. Jain (✉) · M. Hussain
Department of Computer Science and Engineering, Central University of Rajasthan, Ajmer, India
e-mail: 2014phdcse03@curaj.ac.in

© Springer Nature Switzerland AG 2020   227
B. B. Gupta et al. (eds.), *Handbook of Computer Networks and Cyber Security*,
https://doi.org/10.1007/978-3-030-22277-2_9

Wireless sensor networks help in detecting and controlling the critical situations. These networks facilitate many more application areas and try to explore many new ones; but this depends on many characteristic requirements like type of service, quality of service (QoS), faulty tolerance, span time, scalability, flexibility, maintainability, and security [1]. For realizing these characteristic requirements, some mechanisms have been designed such as multihop wireless communication, energy efficient operations, auto configuration, data centric, locality, collaboration, and in-network processing [1].

Wireless sensor networks are different from mobile ad hoc NETworks (MANETs). An ad hoc network is developed for a specific requirement of the application and it is free from the infrastructure. MANET is an ad hoc network with mobility of the sensor nodes and wireless communications in multihop architecture. WSNs are associated with such kind of applications where it is impractical to arrive at the location of the network deployment. The lifetime of the sensor node is the lifetime of the network. In WSNs, once the node runs out of battery or failed due to any reason, it is very difficult in the replacement of the battery or charging of the battery in such a hostile environment. But, in MANETs, the terminal can have more energy with large or powerful battery. WSNs can perform many activities together such as communication, sensing, and computation. This network supports different densities of the network (sparse and dense deployment of the sensor nodes). However, MANETs are unable to handle such kind of the diversity in the deployment of the network. WSNs can easily handle the abrupt changes in the observation, from inactivity to high activity and can help in managing and controlling in the critical situation. While MANETs are used to handle the situation with a specific traffic over the channel in a well-defined manner. WSNs support the scalability of the network from hundreds to thousands or more. On the other hand, it is difficult in case of MANETs. Self-configuration is a common characteristic of the wireless sensor networks and mobile ad hoc networks. But, WSNs strictly follow self-configuration characteristic due to the adequate connectivity of the network and maintaining the trade-offs in energy. WSNs' protocols are data centric where MANETs are not related to data centricity because this network does not follow the redundant deployment. The mobility in WSNs is due to the movement of the sensor nodes according to the specific requirement of the application. The sensor node can be mobile in two situations in WSNs. First, when the sink node is mobile and second, when a node can be used to detect and sense the intrusion inside the network and it has to raise the alarm or send an alert to the base station [2]. However, sensor nodes can dynamically move from one place to another in MANETs.

2 Underwater Wireless Sensor Networks

Underwater wireless sensor networks (UWSNs) are a class of wireless sensor networks in which sensor nodes are placed underwater to study the different areas such as marine life, climate change, natural disasters, and many more others. Sensor nodes are deployed in shallow or deep water to observe the changes and these nodes transmit the report of changes to the sink nodes. There is a need of an efficient communication among underwater devices to make these applications feasible. UWSNs suffer from different challenges like limited bandwidth, more propagation delay, limited battery power, high bit error rate, and others. These networks have more probability of failure because of battery life of sensor nodes and acoustic signal communication [3].

Underwater wireless sensor networks can consist of three types of sensor node: static nodes, semi-static nodes and mobile nodes [4]. Static sensor nodes are anchored to the dock, buoys, or the bottom of the ocean. Semi-static sensor nodes are used for monitoring for a short duration; it may be hours or some days. These nodes are hanged with the buoys and placed by the ship temporarily. Static and semi-static deployment of sensor nodes are mainly energy constrained. Mobile sensor nodes are attached with vehicles like as autonomous underwater vehicles (AUVs), remotely operated vehicles (ROVs), and other underwater vehicles. Mobile nature of sensor nodes helps in covering maximum area in underwater but it raises the problem of network connectivity and localization of nodes. The sensor nodes that are connected with AUVs, suffers less from energy constraint. Sensor nodes in underwater networks are deployed to monitor the changes over a given area [4].

Deployment of sensor networks in underwater environment affects from density of the networks, coverage of the sensor nodes, and number of the sensor nodes. In underwater networks scenario, deployment should be sparse, have good range of connectivity, and deploy a smaller number of nodes [4].

The designing of the UWSNs has some major challenges such as limited bandwidth, impaired channel due to fading and multipath, high propagation delay, high bit error rate, and limited battery power; and sensors are prone of fouling and corrosion [5]. Some disadvantages of underwater communication are as follows:

- When it is needed to buffer the data (before dropping the data) for a long duration, it requires more storage.
- The sink node regularly transmits an enquiry message, if it does not receive any message from other nodes or base station. The regular transmission of enquiry messages raise the problem of power consumption.

2.1 Applications of UWSNs

Deployment of sensor nodes depend upon the applications. UWSNs should be self-organized and self-configurable to adopt the changes in oceanic environment. These characteristics help in performing collaborative tasks of surveillance over a given area. These features explore different applications of underwater wireless sensor networks. The range of applications of UWSNs consists of environment monitoring, exploration monitoring, disaster detection and prevention, undersea navigation, tactical surveillance, mine reconnaissance, and sampling of ocean (Fig. 9.1).

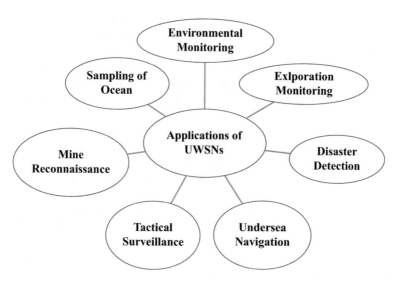

Fig. 9.1 Different applications of underwater wireless sensor networks

- Environment Monitoring: Underwater wireless sensor networks perform monitoring of pollution, currents, winds, biological changes, marine lives of microorganism, and fishes. It helps in understanding of changes of climate and its effect on marine and coastal life. It also provides information of the effect of human activities on ecosystem of underwater area. It helps in prediction of changes in water quality and its effect upon human beings and underwater creatures.
- Exploration Monitoring: Oilfields and reservoirs can be monitored or detected with the help of underwater wireless sensor networks. It can help in the exploration of valuable minerals from the sea or ocean.
- Disaster Detection and Prevention: By calculating the seismic activity, sensor nodes can provide information about tsunami or seaquakes. This information helps in preventing the major losses [6, 7].
- Undersea Navigation: Sensor nodes help in the identification of rocks, hazards of drowning collapse, position of dock, and detection of sandbank in shallow water.
- Tactical Surveillance: Underwater wireless sensor networks can be used in intrusion detection, surveillance, and reconnaissance. It can help in detecting autonomous underwater vehicles (AUV's), submarines, frigates, and short delivery vehicles [8].
- Mine Reconnaissance: Sensor nodes can help in the detection of change on seabed and mine like objects with the help of autonomous underwater vehicles.
- Sampling of Ocean: With the help of underwater wireless sensor networks, we can find out the idiosyncratic oceanic environment.

Table 9.1 Difference between UWSNs and terrestrial WSNs

Parameters	Underwater wireless sensor networks (UWSNs)	Terrestrial wireless sensor networks (WSNs)
Deployment	Sparsely	Densely
Communication Medium	acoustic or optical	radio
Bandwidth	Low	High
Delay	High	Comparatively less
Power	More	Less
Topology	Highly dynamic	Static or dynamic
Quality of link	High possibility of bit error rate and packet loss	Less
Mobility	Less predictable	Predictable
Memory	More memory (with data caching) due to intermittent nature of UWSNs	Very limited storage
Spatial correlation	Rarely correlated due to more distance between sensor nodes	Highly correlated
Cost	Expensive due to extra protection and complex transceiver	Relatively cheaper

3   Difference Between Terrestrial WSNs and UWSNs

Underwater wireless sensor networks are a set of large number of sensor nodes that are connected to sink(s) to report the changes in deep oceans. Underwater wireless sensor networks have higher probability of link interruption from UWSNs [3, 9]. Comparison table between UWSNs and terrestrial WSNs is as given in Table 9.1. The three primary aspects of link interruption in UWSNs are as follows:

- Network Structure: Due to energy exhaustion or changes in network topology, it is common in UWSNs that sensor node becomes unresponsive or it may be failed. Besides, UWSNs depends upon acoustic medium. Therefore, the variations in communication range affects negatively on the topology generation of the network.
- Underwater Environment: Sound waves of passing ships or creatures in the ocean, and tides or currents in the ocean can create a disturbance in acoustic channel.
- Channel Characteristic Limitations: UWSNs suffers from more transmission delay because of low transmission rate.

4   Underwater Sensor Node

In the previous sections, we have discussed the brief introduction of UWSNs and the basic difference between terrestrial WSNs and UWSNs. In this section, we describe the internal architecture of the sensor node that helps in acoustic communication and define the tasks of underwater sensor node [10]. Underwater sensor node comprises of six parts:

- Controller/CPU: It is responsible for the processing of the data received form sensor nodes and this stored data is used to analyze the situation. It decides what action should be taken, when and where the data should be sent. It is the core unit of the sensor node's architecture.
- Memory: This component is used to store the program and the key values that are used in communication. Different memory types may be used to store the received data.
- Sensor/Actuator and Interface Circuitry: Sensor nodes are used to sense the physical environment and works as an interface that observe the real world. Actuators are responsible for initiating appropriate action after receiving the observed data from the sensor nodes. Interface circuitry is used to make a proper medium for maintaining the data assistance between controller and sensor.
- Acoustic Modem: Physical data are converted in acoustic signal with the help of acoustic modem. After conversion of the signal, it can easily be transmitted over the channel.
- Power Supply: Cabled charging is unavailable in underwater environment. Rechargeable battery or solar cells can be equipped with sensor node. The life of a network depends on the life of the sensor nodes. Therefore, energy saving mechanisms would be used in UWSNs.

5 Communication Architecture for Underwater Wireless Sensor Networks

In this section, we elaborate the communication architecture of the underwater sensor networks. The deployment topology of the network is helpful in determining the energy consumption, and capacity of the network. For the reliable communication in the UWSNs, the topology of the network should be optimized after the deployment. Underwater communication is expensive because the devices that are employed in the communication have high cost. The architecture of the UWSNs can be of three types:

- *Static 2-D UWSNs for Ocean Bottom Monitoring:* In this type of architecture, sensor nodes are deployed on the bottom of the ocean or on seabed. Underwater sink connects with the sensor nodes via acoustic signals. Underwater sink has two transceivers: (a) Horizontal transceiver (used for communication between sink and sensor nodes) and (b) Vertical transceiver (used for communicating with the surface station). The communication between underwater sink and sensor nodes may be commands by the sinks and observed data by the sensor nodes. Surface stations are connected with the surface sinks or onshore sinks through radio frequency signal or satellite transmitter. This architecture helps in underwater environmental monitoring. Energy is the main resource constraint in any kind of WSNs; therefore, the communication would be in such a manner that will reduce the energy consumption and signaling overhead in an excessive amount. Multihop communication in UWSNs can increase the network capacity and reduce the energy consumption with the help of intermediate nodes. However, this multihop communication increases the overhead of routing [11].

- *Static 3-D UWSNs for Ocean Column Monitoring:* This architecture is constituted by sensor nodes whose height from the bottom is controlled by the different techniques such as sensor nodes can be attached with the floating buoys etc. These techniques of deploying the sensor nodes may create some destruction in ship navigation. Sensor nodes can be detected or captured by the enemies and enemies can reprogram the sensor nodes. However, some major challenges with 3-D architecture are the effect of ocean currents on the depth, sensing coverage area, and communication coverage of the senor node [8].
- *3-D UWSNs with AUVs:* Fixed portion of the network is constituted of sensor nodes and mobile portion is composed of autonomous underwater vehicles. This architecture enhances the abilities of the underwater networks to study or control the different situations. The concept of adaptive sampling and self-configuration is most recommended in mobile nature of UWSNs. Due to the scarcity of energy resources, AUVs can use solar energy to endurance of the network. This architecture helps in the study of exploration, environmental monitoring, and tactical surveillance. From the objective of the exploration, oceanographic instruments (like gliders or drifters) are employed. Gliders and drifters are battery powered underwater vehicles that report about the abrupt changes to the onshore station and receives the operational command from the station [11, 12].

6   Secure Communication in UWSNs

Recently, secure communication is an open research issue in UWSNs, because of its unique characteristics. A protocol stack has been defined for the support of UWSNs that helps in understanding their features and singularities. As similar to the terrestrial WSNs, the protocol stack for UWSNs consists of five layers: Physical layer, Data link layer, Network layer, Transport layer, and Application layer [1, 3]. The physical layer handles the selection of frequency, generation of carrier frequencies, detection of signals, modulation, and encryption of data. The data link layer is liable for data multiplexing, frame detection, medium access control, and error detection, and ensures proper connectivity of the network. The network layer is responsible for data-centric approach, and power efficient routing of the data at minimum cost. The transport layer is responsible for controlling the congestion over the channel, reliable communication and proper data flow. The application layer handles the different application software that are developed on the basis of sensing tasks.

Different management planes have been associated to the layer of the protocol stack. These planes are power management, mobility management, task management, quality of service (QoS) management, and security management. The power management plane ensures the minimum power consumption, and manages the functionality of the sensor node to maintain the energy level of the node. The mobility management plane is responsible for detecting and managing the mobility of the sensor nodes and this helps in maintaining the routing data to the sink. The task management plane regularizes the sensing tasks of sensor nodes, and sensor nodes with more residual energy perform the observation and the remaining nodes are focused on data routing and aggregation. QoS management plane is responsible for fault tolerance, optimization of performance, and controlling the errors. Security management deals with access control, authentication, authorization, integrity, confidentiality, and others.

UWSNs suffer from different security attacks due to its large scale and sparse deployment. There is a possibility of attacks on two places: sensor nodes and protocols of networks. Attacks on sensor nodes are less probable because of its sparse deployment and it is very difficult to capture or compromise many nodes in UWSNs. Attacks on protocols are of destructive nature for different layers of network architecture. These types of attacks can compromise whole communication network. Further, we will discuss secure protocols for communication with respect to UWSNs.

In this section, we will discuss the functioning of each layer of the protocol stack briefly and describe the possible security attacks at each layer.

6.1 Physical Layer

In terrestrial WSNs, electromagnetic waves are used for communication, but the use of electromagnetic wave in UWSNs is infeasible. UWSNs suffer from the problem of absorption and dispersion of all electromagnetic frequencies. Hence, the acoustic communication is the most preferable option of communication in UWSNs [13].

The characteristics of UWSNs are only the reason for the development of underwater modems. The underwater modem is designed on the basis of noncoherent frequency shift keying (FSK). The noncoherent schemes have high efficiency in terms of power and low efficiency in terms of bandwidth. This feature of noncoherent modulation scheme proves it inapplicable for multiuser networks [14].

Thus, coherent modulation schemes may be applicable due to the characteristics as long-range communication, and high throughput system. As the powerful digital processing came in existence, phase shift keying (PSK) and quadrature amplitude modulation (QAM) techniques can be applied.

The intermediate solution of noncoherent and fully coherent schemes is differential phase shift keying (DPSK) with proper bandwidth utilization. The DPSK increases the requirement of carrier phase tracking, then it increases the probability of the error in modulation.

The orthogonal frequency division multiplexing (OFDM) is a spread spectrum mechanism that is a suitable solution for UWSNs. In OFDM, signals are transmitted over sub-carriers. OFDM performs better in case of multipath environments and noise spreading over the bandwidth.

Channel estimation helps in efficient communication process in UWSNs. Packet probing is an efficient way for channel estimation; meanwhile, it increases the communication overhead, energy consumption and reduces the capacity of the channel [13, 14].

Secure Communication in Physical Layer The unique characteristics of UWSNs make it vulnerable to security attack. Jamming is a Denial of Service (DoS) attack in physical layer. In jamming attack, an attacker node means jammer node disrupts the communication by sending the unwanted signals on same frequency band. However, UWSNs suffer with limited bandwidth. Hence, UWSNs are vulnerable to jamming attack.

The solutions for jamming attack in UWSNs must be different from the existing solutions in terrestrial WSNs. In 2012, Underwater Jamming Detection Protocol was defined to detect the jamming attack. At the same time, this protocol tries to mitigate this attack [15]. The three phases of the proposed protocol are neighbor discovery, jamming detection, and jammed mapping area. In this protocol, irrelevant packets are injected at high rate to block the channel. The packet delivery ratio, total amount of energy consumption, and packet sending ratio are used to detect the jamming attack in the detection phase. However, in case of channel interruption, the above-discussed metrices cannot be verified. Secondly, this protocol uses exact location of the sensor nodes, which is impractical in terms of UWSNs. Hence, this Underwater Jamming Detection Protocol is not efficiently applicable in UWSNs.

The authors classified the attacker nodes in two categories [16]: the first type of attacker node is dummy signal jammer, which is unknown about the network structure; and the second type of attacker node is deceptive jammer, which pretends as the legitimated nodes and knows about the network protocols. This protocol can harm the network easily and tries to degrade the performance of the network.

The friendly jamming can also be used to detect the unwanted eavesdropping over the channel by the means of Jamming through Analog Network Coding (J-ANC). Artificial noise is mixed with the legitimate link. So, the eavesdropper is unable to decode the received packet easily.

On the basis of the nature of the jammer node, jamming attack can be categorized as three types: (1) Continuous Jamming: Attacker node transmits unwanted packet regularly and tries to exhaust full energy. (2) Pulsed Jamming: Jammer node works alternatively with the legitimate node in both of the mode (sleeping and working mode). Jammer node conserves its energy and interrupts the communication randomly. (3) Reactive Jamming: Jammer node and legitimate node work in same mode at the same time. When the legitimate node sends the packet, at the same time attacker node starts to interrupt the transmission by sending useless packets.

6.2   Data Link Layer

UWSNs have some distinctive features like limited bandwidth and high latency. These features pose more challenges in medium access control in UWSNs. Frequency division multiple access (FDMA) is inapplicable for underwater communication due to channel fading and limited bandwidth. Time division multiple access (TDMA) works efficiently with long-time guard and this long-time guard helps in managing propagation delay and its variance in acoustic channel. Carrier sense multiple access (CSMA) tries to avoid collision in transmission at both of the side sender and receiver. At the receiver side, an additional guard time is added to manage propagation delay within the network. Hence, we can argue that CSMA is not suitable for UWSNs [17].

The contention window-based techniques are also not applicable in UWSNs. The reasons behind inapplicability of these techniques are the delay generated by RTS/CTS control packets, carrier sensed idle due to large propagation delay in acoustic channel and the unpredictability of time of start and finish.

The objective of designing access schemes for UWSNs is avoiding the collision and maximizing the efficiency of the network in acoustic channel. Some existing mechanisms use the sleep and awake time to avoid energy consumption. But, deployment of underwater sensor node is sparse, and then these mechanisms are not applicable in acoustic communication.

Code division multiple access (CDMA) is an applicable technique in UWSNs, because it reduces packet retransmission rate and resolves the problem of selective fading of the frequency generated by the multipath nature of acoustic communication. Rake filters are used to avoid the effect of multipath at receiver side.

Direct sequence spread spectrum CDMA (DSSS CDMA) is an efficient mechanism that can be easily adoptable in case of underwater medium access control. It supports high transmission rate and deals with multiple quality of service requirements. DSSS CDMA works efficiently for shallow water communication due to the Doppler and multipath. In this technique, it is difficult to maintain synchronization among the stations with high delay spread [18].

A multicluster protocol is designed for efficient communication over acoustic signals. Autonomous underwater vehicles join the cluster, and each cluster uses TDMA with long-time guards to preclude the propagation delay. Separate spreading codes of each cluster avoid the interference [19].

Because multipath fading and path loss affects the underwater acoustic communication, it is necessary to manage the bit error rate with error control functionalities. Automatic request repeat (ARQ) technique suffers from high delay, more energy consumption, and overheads of packet retransmission. It is efficient to employ forward error correction (FEC) technique in UWSNs. This technique introduces the redundant bits to avoid bit errors in transmission. Both sender and receiver may suffer from energy drain by finding the redundant bits in the messages. Due to the limited availability of the bandwidth, it is possible to choose redundant bits dynamically on the basis of the available bandwidth measurements in underwater acoustic channel.

Secure Medium Access in Data Link Layer Sensor node can access wireless medium in an efficient manner with the help of data link layer protocols that enable proper time synchronization between sensor nodes. This medium access control layer (MAC) layer manages the sleep and wakeup time of the sensor nodes. WATER is water-quality monitoring sensor network with time synchronization which finds out the detached timestamp data. The timestamp of two neighbor nodes are correlated and on the basis of this correlation, anyone can find out the outlier timestamp data. But, this WATER is not appropriate for dynamic UWSNs because there is a deficiency of the outlier data of neighbor node due to its sparse deployment and high packet drop rate. Another scheme is secure vertical and horizontal synchronization (SVHS) which provides both vertical and horizontal time synchronization.

CLUSS is a cluster-based secure synchronization scheme for UWSNs [20]. The three phases of CLUSS protocol are authentication, intercluster synchronization, and intracluster synchronization. In this protocol, the time accuracy is maintained by proper propagation delay of uplink and downlink. This protocol is energy efficient, time synchronized protocol with very few synchronization errors. With the limited resources, time synchronization should be developed with minimum overhead of computation and communication.

6.3 Network Layer

A path from source node to the destination node is provided by the network layer. Network layer handles the issue of long propagation delay. The routing protocols are divided into three types: proactive routing protocols, reactive routing protocols, and geographical routing protocols.

Proactive Routing Protocols The information of routing is maintained in routing table, each and every time, when the topology is changed, automatically routing table is modified and the information of the modification is broadcasted to all other registered nodes of the network. However, it is not necessary in acoustic communication. Hence, proactive protocols are not applicable in UWSNs [21].

Reactive Routing Protocols In this type of the protocols, sensor node starts to find the route to a destination when it is required. Once, a path is discovered, it is kept secure until it is not required. Like proactive routing protocols, reactive protocols also suffered from overhead of signaling. Due to the high latency, path establishment procedure is not easy. Hence, it is not suitable for UWSNs [22].

Geographical Routing Protocols The location of the sensor node must be known in these types of routing protocols. For the localization of the sensor node, it is necessary to be time synchronized communication among the sensor nodes. For this reason, these protocols are unsuitable in UWSNs.

In 2001, a routing protocol is discussed, in which there is a central authority that works as a manager. The manager maintains the network topology, flow of communication, and manages the resources of the network. This protocol avoids the congestion and maintains the quality of services [23].

A multihop routing protocol based on acoustic propagation model is proposed that conserves the energy in UWSNs [24]. The routes are discovered with the help of neighboring information collected by all the nodes.

The routing protocol for UWSNs may be designed for minimizing the communication and signaling overhead; and it can provide optimal performance with minimum path delay, and preserve energy resources.

Secure Routing in Network Layer The designing of the routing protocols is based on the node's nature. Underwater sensor nodes are mobile. Due to their mobility, the topology of the network changes frequently. Therefore, it is not possible to adopt same routing protocol of terrestrial WSNs in underwater communication. The possible security attacks in network layer are flooding, sinkhole, blackhole, and Sybil wormhole attacks. A distributed visualization of wormhole attack mechanism (Dis-VoW) can detect the wormhole attack using distortion in length of the edges and angles with the neighbor nodes [25]. But, Dis-VoW is not suitable for highly dense UWSNs.

A mechanism, wormhole-resilient secure neighbor discovery (WSND) is proposed that is based on the direction of arrival (DoA) in UWSNs [26]. It is quite easier to implement because there is no need of accurate time of synchronization and it is based on the approximation of the acoustic signals.

The authors present a protocol suite for routing with cryptographic primitives (SRCP) for mobile and fixed sensor nodes in UWSNs. This protocol provides the confidentiality and integrity of UWSNs communication.

6.4 Transport Layer

The responsibility of transport layer includes congestion control and flow control. The designed protocol for transport layer cannot be applicable as it is in UWSNs. In this section, we discuss the challenges for the development of the transport layer protocol.

In terrestrial WSNs, when multiple nodes report about an abrupt change, then it is considered as an event. If a single node reports about the change, it is not considered as an event. This type of event detection may lead to resource wastage, so it is not recommendable in UWSNs. The transport layer protocols are not only required for reliable data transmission, but also for congestion control and flow control in UWSNs. When the network devices try to avoid the overloaded data transmission, it is called flow control, but, when the network prevents the congestion by the abundant amount of data, then it is called congestion control.

The existing TCP are inapplicable in UWSNs, since the flow control in transport layer is based on the accurate estimation of the round-trip time. The rate-based transport protocols are unsuitable for acoustic communication environment, since these mechanisms depend on the feedback control messages. The event-to-sink reliable transport (ESRT) protocol is defined to attain efficient detection of the event with minimum consumption of the power [27]. The sensor nodes are sparsely deployed in underwater environment. Hence, the readings of the underwater nodes are significantly different from each other. The protocol designed for transport layer should be adoptable as the new requirements introduced by the applications.

Reliable Data Transmission in Transport Layer In transport layer, user datagram protocol (UDP) and transmission control protocol (TCP) are two protocols for end-to-end reliable communication and flow control [28]. UDP is unsuitable for UWSNs because it ensures the data transmission in connection-oriented manner. Hence, TCP is applicable in case of UWSNs. Secure data transmission can be assured in two methods: Encryption of data and authentication. In end-to-end authentication protocol for UWSNs, digital signature is used to authenticate, then a secret symmetric key is used to encrypt the whole data that is transmitted over the channel [29].

The authors present a key generation system that is efficient for UWSNs [30]. The key generator system generates a key after analyzing the characteristic of the acoustic channel. Hence, the system is only vulnerable to an attacker, if he/she knows the location of the deep fades.

6.5 Application Layer

The application layer protocols are unexplored research area for UWSNs. The objectives of the application layer are providing the information of lower layers transparently to the management applications, give a language to enquire the UWSNs, and allocate tasks and report about the incidents [31].

Secure Application Layer The secure practical application is the main problem of the application layer. Secure localization is the primary problem in many applications like tactical surveillance, environment monitoring, and others in UWSNs.

The trust-based secure localization algorithm (SLTM) is a beta distribution-based trust model which is used to find legitimate beacon node [32]. To improve the trust, a trust filter mechanism is employed to decrease the instability of the underwater communication medium. However, it is not suitable for UWSNs due to its consideration of static nodes in underwater environment. It is impossible to direct the use of terrestrial WSNs trust model in UWSNs. For UWSNs, an efficient trust model must be developed to resist the different security attacks.

7 Simulation Tools for UWSNs

For UWSNs, the deployment of the testbed is really very expensive, since it involves
the complete network structure and communication links to validate a designed
mechanism. In this section, we will provide detailed information of available
tools of simulation and emulation in UWSNs. Simulator is an analysis tool that
is used to set a testbed for validating the designed mechanism. According to the
specific applications of UWSNs, simulation and emulation play an important role
to understand the functioning of the designed mechanism. Simulators are used for
testing and validating of the software or testing in real-time scenario and emulators
are also used for verifying and validating the designed protocol without the actual
deployment of the network [33–35] (Fig. 9.2).

- SUNSET is a simulation, emulation and real-time testing tool that is used for
  analyzing UWSNs. It is more flexible and efficient because it provides the facility
  of real-time scheduler. It deals with five acoustic modems and different sensor
  nodes. Interference model, debug module, packet conversion modules, and utility
  modules are incorporated with this SUNSET. The information of delay in packet
  transmission is provided with the help of timing module. This simulation tool
  helps in eliminating the distance between actual result and simulation.
- DESERT stands for DEsign, Simulate, Emulate, and Realize Testbeds that is
  developed with NS-Miracle framework. This tool is used to design cross-layer
  protocol by supporting application layer, transport layer through the lower layer
  of the protocol stack. It has mobility supporting module. uwcbr and uwvbr are
  two modules of application layer to handle flow of traffic. uwudp and uwtcp are
  two modules of transport layer to provide error and flow control and liable for
  multiplexing and demultiplexing. Three routing protocols are defined in network
  layer. Six MAC protocols are provided in data link layer. However, it does not
  provide better results in experiments.
- SUNRISE is designed from NS-Miracle framework to sense, monitor, and
  actuate for UWSNs. It enables scalability and analysis of the data. It helps in

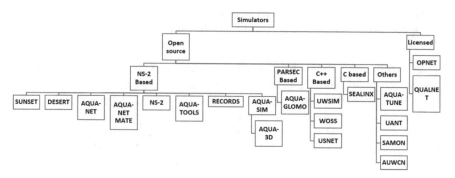

Fig. 9.2 Different simulators for underwater wireless sensor networks

maintaining security and privacy in underwater acoustic communication. However, robot for the underwater application suffers from the battery constrained.

- RECORDS is a framework of remote control in UWSNs. Transmission of remote command becomes possible in multihop communication in the network. It is only designed for static UWSNs [36].
- AQUA-NET is a simulation tool that is designed for protocol stack architecture. It works for embedded systems. It enables optimization of cross-layered architecture.
- AQUA-3D is a robust animator that can analyze the trace files efficiently in UWSNs. It provides prefect visualization of nodes, events, and different objects. There is less probability of compatibility with many simulators for UWSNs.
- SEALINX supports hardware with simultaneous running of modems. It flexibly provides cross-layer communication. It does not support customized the network layer protocol.
- AQUA-SIM is a simulator based on NS-2 that is an open source. Aqua-Sim handles the collision between the packets, propagation model. It contains flexibility and fidelity for UWSNs.
- AQUA-NET MATE is a simulator with virtual channel modem that supports acoustic communication of underwater networks. It supports real-time features and protocol stack layers.
- NS-2 is an open source simulation tool that supports discrete events and it helps in simulation of different protocol. It enables the designing, testing, and validity of the new protocols. It has supported with network animator (NAM) to visualize the connectivity of the medium and nodes' mobility. Sometimes, results obtained by the NS-2 are not enough appropriate as the results of other simulators such as OPNET, OMNET++ and many more.
- UWSIM is a simulator for underwater sensor networks that supports simulation of AUVs. It manages the major challenges like limited bandwidth, frequency, energy resources, and storage capacity of UWSNs properly.
- AQUA-GLOMOSIM simulates the protocols of network layer and physical layer in acoustic communication. Aqua-Glomosim is the upgraded version of Aqua-Glomo. It supports the mobility of the sensor nodes.
- AQUA-TOOLS is a toolkit for channel and physical layer operations in underwater communication. It handles physical layer, data link layer, network layer protocols, and energy constraints.
- WOSS stands for World Ocean Simulation System. It is a simulator that uses Bellhop ray tracing for propagation effects in acoustic communication. It contains full database of the environmental parameters of the world. It simulates the sparsely deployed network that is a complex process.
- USNet is an underwater sensor simulation tool that enables 3-d deployment of the acoustic communication network. This simulation tool deals with threads that can manage many tasks in parallel manner. It simulates the hierarchical architecture of the sensor networks.
- QUAL-NET is a very efficient simulation tool that facilitates simulation by testing, planning, and validating the communication pattern in any type of the

network. It consists of five components that are QualNet Architect (tool for visualization), QualNet Analyzer (Statistical tool for performance analysis of the network), QualNet Packet tracer (analyzer for packet tracing), QualNet File editor, QualNet Command-line Interface. It supports parallel processing and localization of the sensor nodes. It has inbuilt random waypoint mobility model. It is hard to simulate UWSNs in QualNet due to the modeling of characteristics and channel properties of the acoustic communication.

- AQUA-TUNE is a simulator for UWSNs that supports all of the protocol stack. It can set a testbed from 70 h to many days and there is no need for the battery recharging.
- UANT simulates the change in the acoustic channel because it is an underwater acoustic networking simulator. It only deals with two layer that are data link layer and physical layer. It works efficiently in underwater acoustic environment. It was designed with the help of TinyOS and TOSSIM.
- OPNET stands for optimized network engineering tool which can be employed in industrial application for simulation purpose. It supports wireless communication with scalability and customized wireless communication with graphical user interface (GUI) for both 32-bit and 64-bit system. It provides the ability of capturing and visualizing the data flow.
- SAMON simulates the unmanned vehicles by intelligent control. It is a mobile network simulator testbed for sampling in the ocean. It works very efficiently so that the result of simulation and the real-time testing is approximately same. It is very expensive so that it cannot be used in educational purpose.
- AUWCN is an acoustic underwater channel and network simulation tool that works on the physical layer to validate the designed scheme for underwater acoustic channel. It employs Bellhop ray tracing to simulate the physical medium in acoustic communication. It supports the mobility of the sensor node and implements different effects such as Doppler effect, attenuation, and shadow zones.

8 Open Research Issues

As discussed in Sect. 6, UWSNs are vulnerable to different security attacks like jamming, wormhole, Sybil, and many more. To ensure the security of the network, many mechanisms have been proposed for UWSNs. The designed security mechanism does not consider the mobility of the underwater sensor nodes. The protocols are designed on the basis of six aspects: methodology, attacks, node's mobility, energy, outcomes, and challenges. The unique characteristics of UWSNs are responsible for the energy drain, high communication, and computational overheads. For designing an efficient and secure communication protocol, the below mentioned requirements should be considered:

- Security: Security is the major concern in communication. The transmitted data should not be modified by the attacker. It ensures that the transmitted data should be received by only authorized user. As UWSNs are the data centric network, the designed protocol ensures the confidentiality and integrity of the data. Communication should be taken place between two legitimate entities of the network.
- Robustness: The network ensures the proper connectivity and workability in case of any kind of attacks. At the same time, it should efficiently detect the attacker node or try to eliminate it from the network.
- Energy Efficiency: The life of the sensor node is the life of the network. The life of the node depends on the battery of the node. The energy efficient communication protocol maintains the life of the network with the proper communication among mobile nodes.
- Lightweight Protocol: The UWSNs suffers from limited resources in terms of energy, memory, storage, and communication bandwidth. The designed protocol should not be dependent on hardware and software.

9 Conclusion

In this chapter, we have given a brief introduction of wireless sensor networks and detailed introduction of underwater wireless sensor networks. We discussed the difference between the terrestrial WSNs and UWSNs and major challenges in the designing of the UWSNs. We described the deployment architectures of the UWSNs. The protocol stack and secure communication protocols in each layer have been discussed in detail for UWSNs. The simulation and emulation tools have been described properly for the UWSNs. The main objective of this chapter is to encourage the researchers for the development of new efficient and secure communication techniques for communication in underwater environment. This chapter will help in understanding the concept of UWSNs.

References

1. Akyildiz, I. F., Su, W., Sankarasubramaniam, Y., & Cayirci, E. (2002). Wireless sensor networks: A survey. *Computer Networks, 38*(4), 393–422.
2. Yick, J., Mukherjee, B., & Ghosal, D. (2008). Wireless sensor network survey. *Computer Networks, 52*(12), 2292–2330.
3. Akyildiz, I. F., Pompili, D., & Melodia, T. (2005). Underwater acoustic sensor networks: Research challenges. *Ad Hoc Networks, 3*(3), 257–279.
4. Heidemann, J., Stojanovic, M., & Zorzi, M. (2012). Underwater sensor networks: Applications, advances and challenges. *Philosophical Transactions of the Royal Society A: Mathematical, Physical and Engineering Sciences, 370*(1958), 158–175.

5. Proakis, J. G., Sozer, E. M., Rice, J. A., & Stojanovic, M. (2001). Shallow water acoustic networks. *IEEE Communications Magazine, 39*(11), 114–119.
6. Soreide, N. N., Woody, C. E., & Holt, S. M. (2001). Overview of ocean based buoys and drifters: Present applications and future needs. In *OCEANS, 2001. MTS/IEEE Conference and Exhibition* (Vol. 4, pp. 2470–2472). Piscataway: IEEE.
7. Cayirci, E., Tezcan, H., Dogan, Y., & Coskun, V. (2006). Wireless sensor networks for underwater surveillance systems. *Ad Hoc Networks, 4*(4), 431–446.
8. Codiga, D. L., Rice, J. A., & Baxley, P. A. (2004). Networked acoustic modems for real-time data delivery from distributed subsurface instruments in the coastal ocean: Initial system development and performance. *Journal of Atmospheric and Oceanic Technology, 21*(2), 331–346.
9. Howe, B. M., & McGinnis, T. (2004, April). Sensor networks for cabled ocean observatories. In *UT'04. 2004 International Symposium on Underwater Technology* (pp. 113–120). Piscataway: IEEE.
10. Sozer, E. M., Stojanovic, M., & Proakis, J. G. (2000). Underwater acoustic networks. *IEEE Journal of Oceanic Engineering, 25*(1), 72–83.
11. Hinchey, M. (2004). Development of a small autonomous underwater drifter. In *Proceedings of IEEE NECECÕ04*.
12. Stojanovic, M., Catipovic, J. A., & Proakis, J. G. (1994). Phase-coherent digital communications for underwater acoustic channels. *IEEE Journal of Oceanic Engineering, 19*(1), 100–111.
13. Karn, P. (1990, September). MACA-a new channel access method for packet radio. In *ARRL/CRRL Amateur Radio 9th Computer Networking Conference* (Vol. 140, pp. 134–140).
14. Misra, S., Dash, S., Khatua, M., Vasilakos, A. V., & Obaidat, M. S. (2012). Jamming in underwater sensor networks: Detection and mitigation. *IET Communications, 6*(14), 2178–2188.
15. Zuba, M., Shi, Z., Peng, Z., & Cui, J. H. (2011, December). Launching denial-of-service jamming attacks in underwater sensor networks. In *Proceedings of the Sixth ACM International Workshop on Underwater Networks* (p. 12). New York: ACM.
16. Freitag, L., Stojanovic, M., Grund, M., & Singh, S. (2002, March). Acoustic communications for regional undersea observatories. In *Proceedings of oceanology international* (pp. 5–8).
17. Freitag, L., Stojanovic, M., Singh, S., & Johnson, M. (2001). Analysis of channel effects on direct-sequence and frequency-hopped spread-spectrum acoustic communication. *IEEE Journal of Oceanic Engineering, 26*(4), 586–593.
18. Kalofonos, D. N., Stojanovic, M., & Proakis, J. G. (2003). Performance of adaptive MC-CDMA detectors in rapidly fading Rayleigh channels. *IEEE Transactions on Wireless Communications, 2*(2), 229–239.
19. Salva-Garau, F., & Stojanovic, M. (2003, September). Multi-cluster protocol for ad hoc mobile underwater acoustic networks. In *OCEANS 2003. Proceedings* (Vol. 1, pp. 91–98). Piscataway: IEEE.
20. Xu, M., Liu, G., Zhu, D., & Wu, H. (2014). A cluster-based secure synchronization protocol for underwater wireless sensor networks. *International Journal of Distributed Sensor Networks, 10*(4), 398610.
21. Jacquet, P., Muhlethaler, P., Clausen, T., Laouiti, A., Qayyum, A., & Viennot, L. (2001). Optimized link state routing protocol for ad hoc networks. In *Multi Topic Conference, 2001. IEEE INMIC 2001. Proceedings IEEE International Technology for the 21st Century* (pp. 62–68). Piscataway: IEEE.
22. Johnson, D. B., Maltz, D. A., & Broch, J. (2001). DSR: The dynamic source routing protocol for multi-hop wireless ad hoc networks. *Ad Hoc Networking, 5*, 139–172.
23. Bose, P., Morin, P., Stojmenović, I., & Urrutia, J. (2001). Routing with guaranteed delivery in ad hoc wireless networks. *Wireless Networks, 7*(6), 609–616.
24. Xie, G. G., & Gibson, J. H. (2001). A network layer protocol for UANs to address propagation delay induced performance limitations. In *OCEANS, 2001. MTS/IEEE Conference and Exhibition* (Vol. 4, pp. 2087–2094). Piscataway: IEEE.

25. Wang, W., Kong, J., Bhargava, B., & Gerla, M. (2008). Visualisation of wormholes in underwater sensor networks: A distributed approach. *International Journal of Security and Networks, 3*(1), 10–23.
26. WANG, R., & ZHANG, Y. (2010). Wormhole-resilient secure neighbor discovery in underwater acoustic networks. *IEEE Transaction on Aerospace and Electronic Systems, 33*(3), 1500–1506.
27. Akan, Ö. B., & Akyildiz, I. F. (2005). Event-to-sink reliable transport in wireless sensor networks. *IEEE/ACM Transactions on Networking (TON), 13*(5), 1003–1016.
28. Dini, G., & Lo Duca, A. (2012). A secure communication suite for underwater acoustic sensor networks. *Sensors, 12*(11), 15133–15158.
29. Souza, E., Wong, H. C., Cunha, ´i., Loureiro, A. A., Vieira, L. F. M., & Oliveira, L. B. (2013, July). End-to-end authentication in under-water sensor networks. In *Computers and Communications (ISCC), 2013 IEEE Symposium on* (pp. 000299–000304). Piscataway: IEEE.
30. Liu, Y., Jing, J., & Yang, J. (2008, October). Secure underwater acoustic communication based on a robust key generation scheme. In *2008 9th International Conference on Signal Processing. ICSP 2008* (pp. 1838–1841). Piscataway: IEEE.
31. Zhang, Y., Jin, Z. G., Luo, Y. M., & Du, X. (2013). Node secure localization algorithm in underwater sensor network based on trust mechanism. *Journal of Computer Applications, 33*(5), 1208–1211.
32. Han, G., Jiang, J., Shu, L., Niu, J., & Chao, H. C. (2014). Management and applications of trust in Wireless Sensor Networks: A survey. *Journal of Computer and System Sciences, 80*(3), 602–617.
33. Egea-Lopez, E., Vales-Alonso, J., Martinez-Sala, A. S., Pavon-Marino, P., & García-Haro, J. (2005, July). Simulation tools for wireless sensor networks. In *Summer simulation multiconference, SPECTS* (pp. 2–9).
34. Korkalainen, M., Sallinen, M., Kärkkäinen, N., & Tukeva, P. (2009, April). Survey of wireless sensor networks simulation tools for demanding applications. In *Fifth International Conference on Networking and Services, 2009. ICNS'09* (pp. 102–106). Piscataway: IEEE.
35. Neves, P. A. C. S., Fonsec, J., & Rodrigue, J. J. P. C. (2007, March). Simulation tools for wireless sensor networks in medicine: A comparative study. In *International Joint Conference on Biomedical Engineering Systems and Technologies, Funchal, Madeira-Portugal* (Vol. 2016).
36. Toso, G., Calabrese, I., Casari, P., & Zorzi, M. (2014, June). RECORDS: A remote control framework for underwater networks. In *2014 13th Annual Mediterranean Ad Hoc Networking Workshop (MED-HOC-NET)* (pp. 111–118). Piscataway: IEEE.

Chapter 10
Security Issues in Cognitive Radio Ad Hoc Networks

Mahendra Kumar Murmu and Awadhesh Kumar Singh

Abstract The cognitive radio network (CRN) is an interesting variant of opportunistic networks. It is gaining steep popularity due to its peculiar capability in mitigating spectrum scarcity problem. Due to the same reason it has different security challenges than other wireless and opportunistic networks, in particular. The chapter accounts security-related research issues, domains of study, security implications and various approaches proposed in the literature to handle them. In the interest of space, the illustration provides crisp summary of the topic instead of exhaustive presentation.

Keywords CRAHNs · Security · Threats · Attack · QoS

1 Introduction

1.1 Background

The widespread availability of affordable wireless devices has led to notable growth and popularity of wireless networks. Thus, the numbers of wireless applications and their size as well as complexity are consistently increasing and consequently the rise in demand for wireless spectrum too. On the contrary, according to FCC (Federal Communications Commission), a US-based spectrum regulation agency reports 15–85% of assigned spectrum is suffering from underutilization due to sporadic and geographical variations [1]. Therefore, it is the need of the hour to exploit the available spectrum intelligently. The cognitive radio network (CRN) has emerged as a solution to the problem. It uses dynamic spectrum allocation (DSA) methodology [2] and software-defined radio (SDR) to allow wireless devices to switch from one frequency band to another at marginal cost, and the wireless

M. K. Murmu (✉) · A. K. Singh
Department of Computer Engineering, National Institute of Technology, Kurukshetra,
Haryana, India

© Springer Nature Switzerland AG 2020
B. B. Gupta et al. (eds.), *Handbook of Computer Networks and Cyber Security*,
https://doi.org/10.1007/978-3-030-22277-2_10

spectrum is utilized opportunistically. To implement it there are four basic steps, namely, spectrum sensing, spectrum management, spectrum sharing and spectrum mobility. The nodes in CRNs are of two types: primary user (PU) that owns the spectrum and secondary user (SU) that uses it, opportunistically. Therefore, the SU node needs to be aware of the behavioural activity of the primary user in order to form a reasonably stable network [3]. The CRN is alternatively called cognitive radio ad hoc network (CRAHN) or cognitive radio mobile ad hoc network [4, 5].

The CRAHN is a type of wireless network. Therefore, several security concerns in CRAHNs are similar to the security concerns in other computer networks [6–9]. However, the additional communication complexity, due to asynchronous sensing, optimization of cooperative sensing, localization, joint spectrum decision, reconfiguration framework, etc., and the security vulnerabilities in CRAHNs are a bit different.

The chapter presents security issues in the decentralized architecture where the SU nodes are communicating with each other in ad hoc manner. The physical specification of these types of network can be found in IEEE 802.11 b/c/g/f/h [10–14] and IEEE 802.16 [15]. The SU node performs various operations (e.g. spectrum sensing, spectrum sharing, spectrum mobility and spectrum management) collaboratively. The architecture also encompasses the coexistence of single or multiple wireless networks operating in different unlicensed bands. The CRAHN inherits general features, from mobile ad hoc network (MANET), such as lack of central control, node mobility, dynamic topology, wireless connectivity, etc.; however, the features like spectrum mobility and limited authorization are specific to CRAHN that have distinguishable security implications. For example, the effective channel utilization by a CRAHN node may be compromised by frequent interference from licensed users that may lead to malfunction or compromised system performance, and the network may be subjected to congestion, interference and jamming [1, 4].

1.2 Cognitive Radio Ad Hoc Networks

The CRAHNs may be viewed in two parts, as shown in Fig. 10.1. The primary network consists of three categories: licensed-I, licensed-II and unlicensed band. The network over unused band of PU(s) is referred as xG ad hoc network, also called CRAHN [1, 4, 16]. The CRAHNs consist of a collection of autonomous SU nodes. The SU node is equipped with cognitive as well as reconfiguration capability. The cognitive capability handles spectrum sensing and spectrum mobility and the spectrum reconfiguration capability handles spectrum sharing and spectrum management. Due to sensing ability, a node learns about the environment, finds spectrum holes and records it. The set of channel(s) available at SU is called the local channel set (LCS). If any pair of SUs has sensed a common channel, it is called common control channel (CCC) and the cumulative set of channels sensed by all participating SUs is called global channel set (GCS). The SUs are capable enough to take a decision on the basis of their local observation(s). The dotted

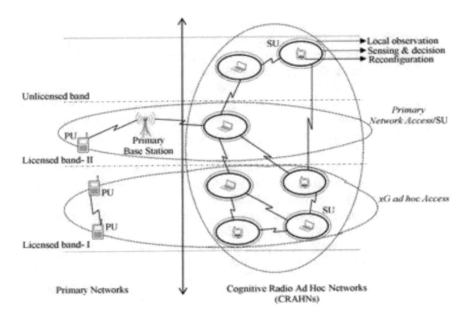

Fig. 10.1 Architecture block diagram of CRAHNs

circle around the SU node represents the range for local observation. The bold circle denotes the range of learning and decision making on the basis of local observations. The SU node is equipped with a reconfiguration device to adopt the environment. Due to autonomous behaviour, the SU node lacks complete topological information. This may result in collision with other SUs as well as PU. Therefore, the SU nodes cooperate and collaborate in order to form a network. In a connected component, the SU nodes may observe spectrum holes from one or more radio environment(s). Similarly, an SU belonging to one network may be connected to another SU that may belong to another network.

The connected SU nodes employ basic operations in the following manner in CRAHNs:

- *Spectrum sensing*: The spectrum sensing states that the devices are capable to sense their radio environments and choose the most suitable band and switch to the best available transmission mode (e.g. modulation type) in the free band [1]. The SU node performs sensing operation individually or cooperatively to detect the PU transmission. The sensing parameters of SU include the channel detection time, sensing band and channel move time. An SU may rely on a weak portion of PU band or free band. In spectrum sensing, the focus of the research has been transmission-based detection, cooperative detection and interference-based detection [1]. The primary objective of using these techniques is to detect the interference with PU. The signal transmitted by SU should not interfere with PU. Due to arbitrary appearance of PU, the SU nodes need to find spectrum holes in opportunistic manner.

- *Spectrum analysis*: Spectrum analysis deals with the identification of the capacity of spectrum holes. The secondary user analyses various characteristics of the network such as capacity, bit error rate and latency to achieve highly reliable as well as spectral efficient communication. The spectrum characterization is affected by several factors such as interference, path loss, wireless link error, link layer delay and hidden terminal problem [4]. However, most disastrous is the arbitrary appearances of PU in the networks. In such case, the SU node may share their information within connected component and find suitable alternate spectrum.
- *Spectrum decision*: The spectrum decision refers to the selection of most appropriate spectrum hole for transmission. It may be taken by a single secondary user or output by several cooperating SU nodes. The spectrum decision process comprises of spectrum characterization, spectrum selection and reconfiguration [1]. Once network characteristics have been analysed, the SU node reconfigures the spectrum operating frequency with the most suitable spectrum hole. In cooperative spectrum decision, the intended spectrum switching may be done *a priori* on the basis of feedback information received from SU neighbours.

1.3   Application of CRAHNs

Recently, the cognitive radio network has drawn the attention of the research community because it supports many interesting applications [17]; refer to Fig. 10.2. Like other ad hoc networks, CRAHN can be used in diverse areas, such as military, personal, commercial and emergency. However, some key applications of CRAHNs include the following:

- *Defence services*: The CRAHN was initially tested in military defence laboratory in USA. Spectrum mobility is a fundamental property of CRAHNs that enhances information security inherently. However, in other ad hoc networks forced spectrum mobility needs to be implemented in order to improve security in walky-talky, wars, terrorist attacks, sensors and other strategic applications.
- *Commercial application*: The CRAHNs have been tested for TV band as major commercial usage. The CRAHN has become a fundamental building block in 4G, LTE and advanced networks that cater pervasive computing environments. The network supports cognitive users seamlessly and ubiquitously to execute applications and to communicate with other users in an anytime anywhere manner.
- *Cellular services*: The CRAHN is useful in providing mobile services due to its capability to operate, on any network and over any service, despite service and network being non-cognitive. The number of subscribers, supported by a cell, can be increased using CRAHNs. Further, CRAHNs enhance the quality of communication over cellular services.

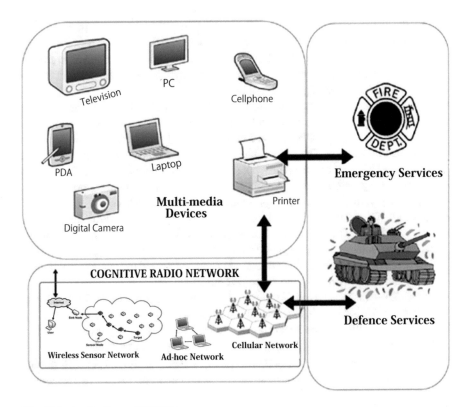

Fig. 10.2 Applications of CRAHNs

- *Emergency services*: The CRAHNs can be used to address traffic burst at disaster and rescue sites during flood, earthquake, volcanic eruption and mining.

1.4   Research Issues in CRAHNs

The following are the major research issues in cognitive radio networks [1, 4, 18]:

- *Security*: The cognitive radio nodes are connected through unused channels in the network. The wireless media is shared and thus the operational environment is unsecure. Also, it faces physical vulnerability that raises multiple security concerns in cognitive radio networks.
- *Quality of services*: The CRAHN falls in the category of opportunistic networks. The network components are required to be active for a sufficiently long time to guarantee the quality of service requirements. The QoS requirements are quantified in terms of reliability, delay, jitter and QoS-aware routing.

- *Mobility*: There are two types of mobility in CRAHN: node mobility and spectrum mobility. The SU nodes take mobility-related decisions on the basis of self-intelligence. They look for resources in the radio environment to form a network. The spectrum mobility causes further dynamism in the network due to forced channel switching by SU nodes.
- *Medium access*: The cognitive radio network is a collection of secondary user nodes. Any two nodes are neighbours iff they exist within their communication range and are tuned on at least one common channel. The nodes may be deployed arbitrarily in a region. The prime source of interference is the presence of licensed user. In addition, there are many other types of interferences that affect overall system throughput, e.g. distributed operations, hidden terminals, exposed nodes, access delay, real-time traffic support and resource reservation.
- *Routing*: The available bandwidth capacity is finite and various applications compete for it. The selection of appropriate radio resource from the available list is appreciable to accomplish the transmission. Some highlights need to be taken care of. Therefore, few entities need careful consideration, e.g. bandwidth utilization, error handling and resource constraint.
- *Data dissemination model*: Spectrum accessibility is affected by licensed user in both variants of the CRAHN, i.e. underlay as well as overlay network. The poor accessibility of the spectrum increases latency that may adversely affect robustness, efficiency, scalability, security and group management.
- *Topology*: Due to node and spectrum mobility, CRAHN suffers frequent topology changes that amount to unpredictability of node location, computational latency, termination detection, etc.
- *Interference*: The interference in CRAHN is not only due to licensed user, it is also caused by environmental conditions, terrestrial situations and many other factors.

The above-listed issues adversely affect the performance of CRAHN. However, the distributed services running on CRAHN are expected to guarantee some desired level of performance and efficiency.

1.5 General Security Objectives

The objective of security is to improve network effectiveness and reliability by preserving information while performing transmission on the fly. In general, the communication systems-based CR technology must validate the communication security requirements [10–12, 15, 19, 20], such as *data confidentiality, privacy, integrity, availability, identification, registration, authentication, authorization, access control* and *non-repudiation*. The *confidentiality* ensures that the network data is strongly protected from malicious user and cannot be read by unauthorized users. *Integrity* refers to the SU node detecting any intentional or unintentional changes to the original data made by the malicious user in transit. *Availability* ensures that SU nodes and individuals can access spectrum holes when need be. *Access control* defines the spectrum holes that are available to the unlicensed user for their opportunistic use. If the licensed user appears, the unlicensed user needs to compromise with its network control. *Identification* ensures that an SU user/device must allow to participate with its tamper-proof identification. Identification of node or resources, i.e. channel, data and message, must be protected through robust keying mechanism. *Authentication* is used to prevent unauthorized users to access spectrum holes. *Authorization* states that though PU node influence the network control policy, the SU nodes have the permission to control the network access in opportunistic manner which is described by the level of authorization for each entity. *Non-repudiation* allows either the sender or receiver of the SU node to deny a transmitted message. An interruption of malicious user may misguide the SU node and hence deny transmitting of messages, since it has already been received [21].

However, the details of the security requirements of CRAHNs have been included in a separate section.

The rest of the chapter is organized as follows. Section 2 describes security background of CRAHNs. Section 3 explains various types of attacks in CRAHNs. Section 4 presents modern security approaches and we conclude the chapter in Sect. 5.

2   The Security Background

2.1   Domains of Security Study in CRAHN

In cognitive radio networks, a selfish or malicious user may modify the air interface to mimic a primary user or secondary user. It can mislead a legitimate node during spectrum sensing, spectrum sharing, spectrum mobility and spectrum management. The CRAHNs can be segregated into the following domain on the basis of their security requirements [22–29]:

- *The physical network boundaries*: It is the study of configuration of physical network, i.e. spectrum holes with the SU devices. The available WANs and LANs must support and use the wireless specification of 802.22 and 802.11 b/c/g/f/h and IEEE 802.16 that provide the cognitive radio functionalities.
- *The liabilities areas*: The traditional insurance policies cover general failures in wireless networks. However, CRAHN may suffer new failures, unwanted risks, threats or attacks during operational transmissions. This study identifies additional liabilities to frame the policy that can ensure effective utilization of cognitive radio ad hoc networks.
- *The functionalities fields*: It is the study of data networking and the software that separates and abstracts the elements defined by software-defined radio (SDR)-equipped system. The objective is to disallow the malicious programmed module to interfere with the original results.

- *The criticality of applications and data*: It deals with the effective utilization of networks and wireless WANs or LANs in all areas of applications. However, due to additional challenges in CRN, the communications become tedious. Therefore, the issues related to the transmission need further study to frame an effective utilization policy.
- *Potential geographical limits*: The geographical variation limits the potential of network usage. The CRAHN may be deployed in some critical terrain that may adversely affect the reliability and imposed new geographical limits. The study of these varieties helps in defining the new usage potential and applicability.
- *Traffic and capacity needs/availability*: It is the study of performance or measures of network availability. It helps in accounting the consistent volume of data transmission.
- *Continuity and recovery needs*: It is the study of failure-free system design. Though it is difficult to achieve, a better resource management and resilient backup mechanism are useful to achieve design objectives.
- *Business application domain*: It is the study of application areas. The efficient and effective utilization of spectrum may scale up the reachability and widen the network application area.
- *Business support domain*: It is the study of ACID (atomicity, consistency, isolation and durability) property while performing business transactions in CRAHNs.
- *Development and testing domains*: It deals with the quantification of possible test spaces (e.g. learning parameters, essential testing knowledge) within the system that ensure desired outputs with minimal resources. Furthermore, the optimum learning for spectrum selection and testing knowledge reduces redundancy and decreases the risk probability in the connected component.
- *Production domains*: It is the study of compatibility and feasibility with other platforms. The interoperability-related issues are more challenging in CRAHNs [30].
- *Alarm management domain*: It is the study to identify distinguishing events in the process of learning and reconfiguration. It is important to maintain the system integrity in transit. Better alarm management reduces the network as well as system delay and also it can minimize the risk factor in CRAHNs.
- *Managerial and administrative responsibilities*: The information security managers are responsible to protect user data from security breaches. The suitably well-drafted guidelines and designed security protocols may ensure information safety and avoid severe failure(s).

2.2 Classical Security Method

The basic security model of CRAHN is illustrated in Fig. 10.3. The security effectiveness of the network can be estimated in terms of security capacity. The security capacity reduces due to attacks in the networks. It may be of two kinds

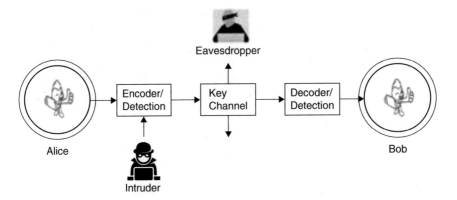

Fig. 10.3 Security model in CRAHNs

such as active attack and passive attack. Assume Alice and Bob are the two entities, i.e. transmitter and receiver, respectively, where secure transmission is going on. The transreceiver may be a legitimate user, e.g. secondary user or primary user. The attacker may try to modify the original information in transit. We denote Intruder and Eavesdropper as the active and passive attacker, respectively, in the figure. A legitimate user is required to transmit information using encrypted key(s). The receiver decrypts the information using the decryption key [31]. If the shared encryption key is known to all the recipients, it is called public key encryption, and if it is known only to the intended user, it is called private key encryption. The key(s) are used to validate the user. Every authorized recipient (secondary user) must be capable enough to synchronize and demodulate the original signal.

2.3   The Security Requirements in CRAHNs

The security requirements in CRAHNs [10–12, 15, 19, 20] are follows:

- *Confidentiality*: It assures that a legitimate SU node has the authority to access the spectrum holes provided there is no PU interference. To achieve this objective, SU needs to pass through a verification procedure that identifies the data transmission participants uniquely. Similarly, the channel identification procedure uses keys to protect it from an unauthorized user [10, 11, 19].
- *Integrity*: A false signal generated by a malicious user on a particular channel may misguide an SU node. The malicious user may hold that channel for a while and modify the original data. In the network, both the parties, i.e. *sender* and *receiver*, may use a robust keying mechanism to protect the data [10, 11, 19].
- *Availability*: A malicious user may attempt to mislead the PU as well as SU by keeping spectrum holes continuously in busy state. Therefore, SU nodes need to

apply an appropriate sensing mechanism so that it can identify the interference caused due to malicious user [10, 11, 19].

- *Access control*: The SU node has temporary access over some control channels in the network. The SU node may apply a robust keying mechanism (e.g. *key management*) to protect control channels from possible threats. The mechanism ensures access to control channels in case of possible attack on the network resources [10, 20].
- *Identification*: Most of the networks use standard naming convention (e.g. *barcode*) to uniquely identify an SU node and channel. A tamper-proof mechanism may be used to protect various entities and the keys can be shared among legitimate participants [20].
- *Authentication*: An SU node needs to perform careful analysis of signals. It must be capable enough to protect its available spectrum hole from the noise injected by the attacker(s). A robust encryption-decryption method may be used to protect data from unauthorized access [15].
- *Authorization*: The SU nodes must have recent updates about the radio environment and behavioural activity of PU nodes. Using authorization key, the SU node controls the spectrum access within their connected component. Every legitimate user must have freedom to access all kinds of resources [15].
- *Non-repudiation*: The interference from a malicious user may mislead SU nodes by pretending that a message has already been received and hence there is no need to transmit it [20].

2.4 Security Issues in CRAHNs

The SDR-equipped secondary user node is capable enough to implement various radio functionalities like modulation/demodulation, signal generation, signal processing and signal coding. It is embedded in software and therefore it provides the highest degree of flexibility and reconfiguration capability for channel assignment and to adjust the transmission parameters to cater various communication services. The devices are intelligent enough to learn the radio environment during the window of opportunity to access the spectrum holes. The security issues [31] in CRAHN may be classified in the following categories:

- *High priority to primary user signals*: The licensed user signal has the highest priority to avoid interference in it. CRAHN is a distributed structure where SU nodes are connected using unused spectrum owned by the primary user. Due to stringent sensitivity of the licensed user, an unlicensed one has several sensing methods such as matched filter detection, energy-based and cyclostationary feature detection. In matched filter detection, PU signal such as the modulation type and order, the pulse shape and the packet format is known to the SU user. It performs better because the PU information is accurate and thus requires less time to achieve high processing gain. In energy detector, the SU node does not have a priori knowledge about the PU signals. If licensed user appears, the SU node avoids the interference by selecting the noise floor as thresholds. However, the technique performs weak for spread spectrum signal. The cyclostationary feature detection uses advanced filtering to detect PU signals. The CRN network is under opportunistic category and thus it may suffer high unreliability [3, 32, 33].

- *Arbitrary behaviour of primary user*: Generally, there is lack of knowledge about PU behaviour in the environment. The interference model only provides the feedback to minimize the interference, not the location information of the primary user. In the literature, there are some methods available to handle the localization problem. However, there is no significant progress on this front. The mobile licensed users arbitrarily grab the spectrum in time, space and frequency domain, and consequently the networks may be interrupted or disconnected prematurely affecting the QoS requirements adversely [19].

- *Hidden terminal problem*: In CRAHNs, the SU nodes cooperatively interact with each other. The licensed user is either skipped or the SU node rarely bothers about its location information. The SU node detects PU availability on the basis of local observation of licensed user-transmitted signals. By default, weak signal is assumed to be interfered one. The SUs are assigned three distinct bands such as control, data channel and busy tone band. It is configured in such a way so that the data transmission can take place only after control is established. In the open environment the spectrum may be affected due to reasons like environmental and terrestrial situation or unwanted objects. This also creates communication interference between the SUs or with the licensed fusion centre [13].

- *Asynchronous sensing*: The SU nodes must have high accuracy sensing capability so that it can sustain the PU interference in the first place as well as detect interference due to other temporal variations. Also, the SU node should be able to detect interference due to other SUs [13].

- *Synchronization requirement*: The CRAHNs consist of a collection of autonomous SU nodes. Every node relies on spectrum holes on the radio environment. Once the unused spectrum is found, the SU node needs synchronization in terms of node activities and channel allocation to accomplish communication or computations. If PU appears, the requirement of time synchronization may play a decisive role. In centralized CRN, the sensing results are relayed to the base station which aggregates and determines the presence of PU transmissions. On the other hand, in decentralized networks, the SU nodes cooperatively maintain and share their sensing-related information among themselves to aggregate and determine the presence of PU transmissions. The latency of PU detection is a key concern. As soon as the PU is detected, the SU node must notify their neighbours in order to ensure the application continuity. In a decentralized system, despite an SU being out of sync with other SUs, the rest of the SUs would detect the energy transmitted from the out of sync one and forward the information to a local coordinator [2].

- *Opportunistic spectrum access*: Generally, the CRAHNs exist for a short span of time because it is highly dependent on the licensed user activity. An SU node may be misguided due to bad functional or non-functional system design. As a result, the window of opportunity to access the spectrum hole is inefficiently utilized [2].

- *Lack of CCC*: Once the SU wakes up, it initiates search for control channels across the entire spectral band. However, a malicious user may engage control channel intentionally. Thus, the SU nodes may not find the spectrum holes and the whole network may collapse [4].
- *Selfish behaviour of a node*: Sometimes, the malicious entities may tend to occupy extra bandwidth and other resources or may block other nodes from acquiring specific resources. The strict control over such selfish act of malicious users is also a challenge in CRAHN [31].

2.5   Generic Security Challenges in CRAHNs

The network security is an important challenge in cognitive radio ad hoc networks [16, 21]. In general, most of the security challenges are found related to the physical, data link and network layer. Therefore, numerous approaches exist in the literature. However, another higher-layer security challenge is an open research problem. The security attacks in CRAHNs have been categorized according to layers as follows:

A. Physical layer

The physical layer security challenges listed in the literature [22, 23, 34] are as follows:

- *Legitimate user emulation attack (LUEA)*: The unauthorized user transmits special signals and pretends as an authorized SU node on the channels which are not being used by the licensed user. An attacker node disallows the legitimate SU node the spectrum access.
- *Learning attack (LA)*: The SU nodes adjust learning parameters in the radio environment. The SU has the right to maximize the data transfer rate and also it may enhance the level of security in the network. The unauthorized user may feed false learning parameters to the legitimate SU node, and therefore, an authorized SU node may start transmission on the false channel.
- *Jamming attack (JA)*: The attacker may generate high-frequency signal and they may flood a single or multiple channels. Consequently, the ongoing communication on that channel is interrupted. This type of attacks can be easily detected by the SU node.
- *Eavesdropping (ED)*: The malicious node continuously senses the radio environment for available spectrum holes. After detection, the attacker will increase the secrecy among PU from the legitimate user or reduce the frequency due to listening secret information while transmission is in progress.

B. Link Layer

The link layer-related security challenge can be found in [12, 27].

- *Channel jamming (CJ)*: If a malicious user occupies the channel and prevents the PU from receiving control message, it is called channel jamming. The attacker interrupts the PU, uses all the channels and hence blocks the services. The types of jammers are as follows: deceptive jammer, constant jammer, random jammer and reactive jammer.
- *Denial of services (DoS)*: An attacker may reduce the channel utilization and copy the MAC control frames by launching of DoS attack on the common control channel. The PU finds the channel busy and consequently denies channel access for transmission of data.
- *Collision attacks (CA)*: A malicious node may send collision attack on the CCC and disregard MAC specifications. The attacker may transmit the noise packets on CCC which causes collision with other legitimate users transmitting on that channel. The receiver node may be misguided due to incorrect signal.

C. Network Layer

The network layer-related security challenges have been illustrated in [24, 25].

- *HELLO flood attack (HFA)*: The attacker may communicate to all other SU nodes in the connected component using HELLO beacons. The attacker may easily misguide the legitimate SU nodes.
- *Sybil attack (SybA)*: The attacker may influence the network using sybil attack that hides the SU nodes' identities. The attacker may send signal to PU and alter the decision-making process. This may result in inefficient channel access in CRAHNs.
- *Ripple effect attack (REA)*: When the spectrum hole is switched to SU, the legitimate user would transfer flawed information with it which leads to disordered state. This type of attack is called REP attack. The attack may alter the actual energy consumption and elongate the time to operate; consequently, the sensing result is affected.

D. Cross-Layer

The cross-layer security challenges are detailed in [26].

- *Lion attacks (LnA)*: The lion attack is observed when, namely, primary user emulation attacks (PUEA) target the physical layer that causes logical disconnection of TCP link with the SU node. It may increase packet loss. Therefore, we may arise for packet retransmission either due to time out or if due to distorted connections.
- *Routing information jamming (RIJ)*: When the SU nodes share routing information among themselves, a handoff may be required to continue transmission. During this phase, the attacker may stimulate the spectrum handoff and stop reconfiguration.
- *Small back-off window attacks (SBW)*: The malicious node may influence the SU to decrease its window size. This may adversely affect the storage capacity of SUs leading to reduced throughput.

3   Attacks in CRAHNs

Unlike other wireless networks, the CRAHNs are vulnerable to many types of attacks especially during the sensing phase. Broadly, the attacks in CRAHN are classified into two categories: *active* and *passive*. An attack is called active if an SU node behaves as attacker to affect the network security, for example, if a malicious user has successfully decrypted the identification key of a legitimate SU node and took authorization control to misguide other SUs. Similarly, a malicious node may emulate as PU, while other SUs are not able to detect it. On the other hand, an attack is called passive one if the attacker's intent is to affect a network node to deviate from specified behaviour. The passive attack should be handled proactively as it may block a passive attacker from switching to an active one; in case, it has intent. Because the extent of damage caused by passive attacker may be ignorable during sensing decision, it may not be ignorable in case of active one.

The design of a proactive assessment mechanism, which avoids an attacker to switch its state from passive to active, is an open research problem. An inefficient proactive assessment may pop up many issues related to spectrum sensing, sharing, mobility and management. Thus, the objective of application requirements must be well charted so that the SU may apply an appropriate sensing method that may help in taking interference preventive decisions. In CRAHN, the attackers have been classified into three categories: malicious users, greedy users and unintentionally behaving user. The malicious users may send false observations in order to mystify other SUs that may trigger band evacuation by legitimate SUs or cause interference to PUs. The greedy users monopolize specific bands by reporting continuous occupancy by incumbent signals. The unintentionally misbehaving users may supply false observations about band availability due to some hardware malfunction or software bug.

There are three types of attacks that are specific to CRAHN, namely, primary user emulation attacks [32], spectrum sense data falsification attacks (SSDFA) and beacon falsification attacks (BFA). The PUEAs are localization-related attacks where an SU node may have been misguided by the malicious user due to false sensing results, for example, emission of signal from the PU node. It is a physical layer-related attack. The SSDFA-type attack may interfere an ongoing communication between a pair SU by an unauthorized user.

A jamming attack or congestion attack may affect a channel by a malicious user. It is a link layer-related attack. The BFA is related with the beacon authentication schemes where an unauthorized user may generate a beacon signal and claim itself as legitimate one. A malicious user may generate a false alarm to conflict legitimate user for their spectrum resource. The attacker behaviour may further be classified in the following categories, like misbehaving, selfish, cheating and malicious. The misbehaving user does not abide by the rules set by the network authority. The selfish user wants to hold the network resources for its own use and it does not concern about other network users whether they benefit from the network. The cheating user does not share correct information about the network resources that are needed to ensure desired quality of service (QoS). The malicious users purposefully target the network to degrade the QoS as well as network efficiency.

4   The Security Approaches

- *Spectrum-aware approach (SAA)*: Spectrum mobility is one of the unique features in CRAHNs. The mobile SU node dynamically adjusts the tuning parameter using the functional operations such as spectrum sensing, spectrum mobility, spectrum sharing and spectrum management. The SU node needs to work upon cross-layer methodology approach and incorporate spectrum mobility in order to exchange state information during communication. Therefore, the behavioural analysis of the spectrum by learning [15, 20] may be helpful to protect information from possible attack.
- *Hammer model framework (HMF)*: The SU node suffers from network jamming [35], alteration of channel information, masquerading of a PU, masquerading of SU, etc. In such a case, efficiency of channel utilization may be degraded. This type of threats is related to the denial of service attack. The hammer model framework [15] has been used to prevent information from DoS-related threats.
- *Propagation-based methodology (PBM)*: The CRAHNs is a highly dynamic network. Due to its spectral variations, the CR technology enormously opens up a large portion of the spectrum access opportunity for communication. Every portion of the band has a sufficient spectrum agility for communication. However, it may adversely affect the communication as it is difficult to detect PU appearance. The hidden terminal problem may arise very frequently. The proposed method [30] suggests to monitor the spectrum at runtime that maps the spectrum in 'multidimensional' space and frequency domain in order to predict with high accuracy. The model reduces the chances of possible threats from malicious users.
- *Robust security model (RSM)*: In CRAHNs, the SU nodes cooperate and collaborate to communicate with each other [14]. Therefore, a reliable and robust security protocol needs to be designed in order to increase the effectiveness of the network. The protocols aware of Byzantine generals' problem [36] may be a rightful approach to achieve robustness. Such design protocols have been used to provide fault tolerance in distributed system and can be used to enhance reliability of cognitive radio ad hoc networks. The design approach [20] may provide security solutions against attackers in cognitive radio ad hoc networks as well.
- *Selfish attack detection methods (COOPON)*: The cognitive radio nodes in COOPON [14] may detect the attacks of selfish SUs toward multiple channel access using cooperation of other legitimate neighbouring SUs. In CRAHNs, the participating SUs exchange the sensed channel information among them. If any receiver SU finds discrepancy of figure in its neighbourhood, it considers SU as attacker in the network.

- *Distance analysis method (DAM)*: The SU node measures the distance metrics and accesses that information cooperatively in the connected component. The data manager accounts trusted value using collected distance information [37]. If the SU node finds any discrepancy, it considers the neighbouring node as malicious in CRAHNs.
- *Strategic surveillance (SS)*: The strategic surveillance [33] refers to the strategic analysis of interaction between defender and attackers through network manager. The manager strategically observes the behavioural activity of attackers and forces the attacker to commit on strategic line.
- *Location-based defence (LocDef)* method [3]: The method relies on sharing and comparing the estimated localization information with the already known location information of PU. If the SU node finds any mismatch in the estimated value, it notifies the node as malicious.

5 Conclusions

The CRAHN is significantly different from other wireless networks, and due to its tremendous application potential, it is evolving as the technology of future. Although the objective of the chapter was to account the security issues in CRAHNs, the illustration is helpful for beginners in setting their future research goals on security vulnerability in order to enhance effectiveness and reliability of CRAHNs. Furthermore, the content is intended to trigger the reader to develop insight about network vulnerability, security requirements and implications and to invent new approaches that may combat various types of adversaries that target CRAHNs.

References

1. Akyildiz, I. F., Lee, W. Y., Vuran, M. C., & Mohanty, S. (2006). NeXt generation/dynamic spectrum access/cognitive radio wireless networks: A survey. *Computer Networks, 50*(13), 2127–2159.
2. Granelli, F., Pawelczak, P., Prasad, R. V., Subbalakshmi, K. P., Chandramouli, R., Hoffmeyer, J. A., & Berger, H. S. (2010). Standardization and research in cognitive and dynamic spectrum access networks: IEEE SCC41 efforts and other activities. *IEEE Communications Magazine, 48*(1), 71.
3. Orumwense, E. F., Oyerinde, O., & Mneney, S. H. (2017). Improved cooperative spectrum sensing under primary user emulation attacks in cognitive radio networks. *Journal of Engineering Research, 5*(3), 1–18.
4. Akyildiz, I. F., Lee, W. Y., & Chowdhury, K. R. (2009). CRAHNs: Cognitive radio ad hoc networks. *Ad Hoc Networks, 7*(5), 810–836.
5. Mansoor, N., Islam, A. M., Zareei, M., Baharun, S., Wakabayashi, T., & Komaki, S. (2015). Cognitive radio ad-hoc network architectures: A survey. *Wireless Personal Communications, 81*(3), 1117–1142.

6. Gupta, B. B., Agrawal, D. P., & Yamaguchi, S. (2016). *Handbook of research on modern cryptographic solutions for computer and cyber security*. Pennsylvania: IGI Global. https://doi.org/10.4018/978-1-5225-0105-3.

7. Ko, H., Mesicek, L., Choi, J., Choi, J., & Hwang, S. (2018). A study on secure contents strategies for applications with DRM on cloud computing. *International Journal of Cloud Applications and Computing (IJCAC), 8*(1), 143–153. https://doi.org/10.4018/IJCAC.2018010107.

8. Wang, L., Li, L., Li, J., Li, J., Gupta, B. B., & Liu, X. (2018). Compressive sensing of medical images with confidentially homomorphic aggregations. *IEEE IoT Journal, 6*, 1402. https://doi.org/10.1109/JIOT.2018.2844727.

9. Gupta, B. B., Agrawal, D. P., & Wang, H. (2018). *Computer and cyber security: Principles, algorithm, applications, and perspectives* (p. 666). Boca Raton, FL: CRC Press, Taylor & Francis.

10. Fragkiadakis, A. G., Tragos, E. Z., & Askoxylakis, I. G. (2013). A survey on security threats and detection techniques in cognitive radio networks. *IEEE Communications Surveys and Tutorials, 15*(1), 428–445.

11. Holcomb, S., & Rawat, D. B. (2016, March). Recent security issues on cognitive radio networks: A survey. In *SoutheastCon* (pp. 1–6). Piscataway, NJ: IEEE.

12. Salameh, H. B., Almajali, S., Ayyash, M., & Elgala, H. (2018). Spectrum assignment in cognitive radio networks for internet-of-things delay-sensitive applications under jamming attacks. *IEEE Internet of Things Journal, 5*, 1904.

13. Yucek, T., & Arslan, H. (2009). A survey of spectrum sensing algorithms for cognitive radio applications. *IEEE Communications Surveys and Tutorials, 11*(1), 116–130.

14. Jo, M., Han, L., Kim, D., & In, H. P. (2013). Selfish attacks and detection in cognitive radio ad-hoc networks. *IEEE Network, 27*(3), 46–50.

15. Baldini, G., Sturman, T., Biswas, A. R., Leschhorn, R., Godor, G., & Street, M. (2012). Security aspects in software defined radio and cognitive radio networks: A survey and a way ahead. *IEEE Communications Surveys and Tutorials, 14*(2), 355–379.

16. Nagpal, C. K. (2018). A game theory based solution for security challenges in CRNs. *3D Research, 9*(1), 11.

17. Meghanathan, N., & Reddy, Y. B. (2013). *Cognitive radio technology applications for wireless and mobile ad hoc networks*. IGI Global book series in AWTT. https://doi.org/10.4018/978-1-4666-4221-8.

18. Agarwal, S., Shakya, R. K., Singh, Y. N., & Roy, A. (2012). DSAT-MAC: Dynamic slot allocation based TDMA MAC protocol for cognitive radio networks. In *International Conference on Wireless and Optical Communications Networks (WOCN)* (pp. 1–6).

19. Khasawneh, M., & Agarwal, A. (2017). A collaborative approach for monitoring nodes behavior during spectrum sensing to mitigate multiple attacks in cognitive radio networks. *Security and Communication Networks, 2017*, 1.

20. Mathur, C. N., & Subbalakshmi, K. P. (2007). Security issues in cognitive radio networks. In *Cognitive networks: Towards self-aware networks* (pp. 284–293). Hoboken, NJ: Wiley.

21. Akram, M. W., Salman, M., Shah, M. A., & Ahmed, M. M. (2017, September). A review: Security challenges in cognitive radio networks. In *Automation and computing (ICAC)* (pp. 1–6). Piscataway, NJ: IEEE.

22. Ren, K., Zhu, H., Han, Z., & Poovendran, R. (2013). Security in cognitive radio networks. *Proceedings of IEEE Network, 27*, 2–3.

23. Kang, T., & Guo, L. (2015). Physical layer security in cognitive radio based self-organization network. *Mobile Networks and Applications, 20*(4), 459–465.

24. Bouabdellah, M., Kaabouch, N., El Bouanani, F., & Ben-Azza, H. (2018). Network layer attacks and countermeasures in cognitive radio networks: A survey. *Journal of Information Security and Applications, 38*, 40–49.

25. Babu, B. R., Tripathi, M., Gaur, M. S., Gopalani, D., & Jat, D. S. (2015, May). Cognitive radio ad-hoc networks: Attacks and its impact. In *Emerging Trends in Networks and Computer Communications (ETNCC)* (pp. 125–130). IEEE.

26. Hossain, A., & Sarkar, N. I. (2015, November). Cross layer rendezvous in cognitive radio ad-hoc networks. In *Telecommunication Networks and Applications Conference (ITNAC)* (pp. 149–154). IEEE.
27. Soliman, J. N., Mageed, T. A., & El-Hennawy, H. M. (2017, December). Taxonomy of security attacks and threats in cognitive radio networks. In *Electronics, Communications and Computers (JAC-ECC), 2017 Japan-Africa Conference on IEEE* (pp. 127–131).
28. Attar, A., Tang, H., Vasilakos, A. V., Yu, F. R., & Leung, V. C. (2012). A survey of security challenges in cognitive radio networks: Solutions and future research directions. *Proceedings of the IEEE, 100*(12), 3172–3186.
29. Kim, H. (2013). Privacy preserving security framework for cognitive radio networks. *IETE Technical Review, 30*(2), 142–148.
30. Nuallain, E. O. (2008, October). A proposed propagation-based methodology with which to address the hidden node problem and security/reliability issues in cognitive radio. In *Wireless Communications, Networking and Mobile Computing, 2008. WiCOM'08 IEEE* (pp. 1–5).
31. Jianwu, L. I., Zebing, F., Zhiyong, F., & Ping, Z. (2015). A survey of security issues in cognitive radio networks. *China Communications, 12*(3), 132–150.
32. Jiang, Q. M., Chen, H. F., Xie, L., & Wang, K. (2017). On detecting primary user emulation attack using channel impulse response in the cognitive radio network. *Frontiers of Information Technology and Electronic Engineering, 18*(10), 1665–1676.
33. Ta, D. T., Nguyen-Thanh, N., Maillé, P., & Nguyen, V. T. (2018). Strategic surveillance against primary user emulation attacks in cognitive radio networks. *IEEE Transactions on Cognitive Communications and Networking, 4*, 582.
34. Shah, H. A., & Koo, I. (2018). A novel physical layer security scheme in OFDM-based cognitive radio networks. *IEEE Access, 6*, 29486.
35. Ho-Van, K., & Do-Dac, T. (2018). Reliability-security trade-off analysis of cognitive radio networks with jamming and licensed interference. *Wireless Communications and Mobile Computing, 2018*, 1.
36. Lamport, L., Shostak, R., & Pease, M. (1982). The byzantine generals problem. *ACM Transactions on Programming Languages and Systems (TOPLAS), 4*(3), 382–401.
37. Feng, J., Zhang, M., Xiao, Y., & Yue, H. (2018). Securing cooperative spectrum sensing against collusive SSDF attack using XOR distance analysis in cognitive radio networks. *Sensors, 18*(2), 370.

Chapter 11
Security and Privacy in Social Networks: Data and Structural Anonymity

R. Jain, N. Jain, and A. Nayyar

Abstract Social networking has become an inevitable catchline among teenagers as well as today's older generation. In recent years, there has been observed remarkable growth in social networking sites, especially in terms of adaptability as well as popularity both in the media and academia. The information present on social networking sites is used in social, geographic and economic analysis, thereby giving meaningful insights. Although publishing of such analysis may create serious security threats, users sharing personal information on these social platforms may face privacy breach. Various third-party applications are making use of network data for advertisement, academic research and application development which can also raise security and privacy concerns. This chapter has a binary focus towards studying and analysing security and privacy threats prevailing and providing a detailed description regarding solutions that will aid towards sustaining user's privacy and security. Currently, there exist multiple privacy techniques that propose solutions for maintaining user anonymity on online social networks. The chapter also highlights all the available techniques as well as the issue and challenges surrounding their real-world implementation. The goal of such mechanisms is to push deterged data on social platforms, thereby strengthening user privacy despite of the sensitive information shared on online social networks (OSN). While such mechanisms have gathered researcher's attention for their simplicity, their ability to preserve the user's privacy still struggles with regard to preserving useful knowledge contained in it. Thus, anonymization of OSN might lead to certain information loss. This chapter explores multiple data and structural anonymity techniques for modelling, evaluating and managing user's privacy risks cum concerns with respect to online social networks (OSNs).

R. Jain (✉) · N. Jain
Computer Science and Engineering, Bharati Vidyapeeth's College of Engineering, New Delhi, India
e-mail: rachna.jain@bharatividyapeeth.edu; nikita.jain@bharatividyapeeth.edu

A. Nayyar
Graduate School, Duy Tan University, Da Nang, Vietnam
e-mail: anandnayyar@duytan.edu.vn

© Springer Nature Switzerland AG 2020
B. B. Gupta et al. (eds.), *Handbook of Computer Networks and Cyber Security*,
https://doi.org/10.1007/978-3-030-22277-2_11

Keywords Online social networks · Security · Privacy · Threats ·
Anonymization · De-anonymization · Facebook · Twitter · Link prediction

1 Introduction

As there are millions of active users on online social networks, safeguarding personal information about users with proper security and privacy techniques has become a prioritized need. Various techniques have been proposed and applied to ensure data security on social networks. Among those techniques, the most popular algorithm-based technique is "anonymization". Structural, data and edge-based anonymity are broad categories of privacy protection techniques that are being deployed on online social networks to maintain security by remodelling and reorganizing the visualized graph of a specific social network. Several other algorithms based on decentralization and probabilistic variations are also proposed to attenuate shortcomings of anonymization, although these algorithms also have certain limitations in terms of complexity and robustness. Depending on the type of information that needs to be extracted from the social network graph, a variety of anonymization algorithms are implemented. These algorithms are measured in terms of robustness against all sorts of security attacks and thus provide researchers a strong base for improvisations in terms of theory and mathematical formulations.

Today social media platforms are integrating with various third-party applications. Application developers are providing interfaces via which they can access user's personal information. In addition, different public interest-oriented agencies like banking, insurance, transportations and even telecommunications aggregate data professionally by crawling millions of profiles and thereby put the user's privacy on risk. Therefore, there is an appalling need of anonymizing data on network to safeguard confidential and sensitive information. To mitigate the above-stated issue, various third-party applications are being enforced to abide by finer privacy policies. In addition to this, different third-party platforms are being provided by the OSNs to be executed by the users which can limit the transfer of their respective personal data to outside application vendors.

Another solution which helps in maintaining user privacy is prohibiting public profile viewing on social media. However, using such solution defeats the business model on which today's OSNs are running, as public viewing gets them more users for targeted advertisement displays to generate revenues. In order to enhance user experience while maintaining privacy and security of their personal data, OSNs have provided close-grained privacy settings which can be practiced and implemented by every user. Here, users can create a personal-level access control in which they decide what piece of information is to be shared and with whom. This helps a user set a personalized privacy level of their sensitive data. Such privacy control techniques are broadly classified as view-centric, automated and default. These techniques exploit the level of trust a user shares with every relationship he/she poses on social media. A rule-based policy is defined to represent the social knowledge where the respective authorization of the access request is obtained. The privacy is maintained by automatically learning from user preferences or by providing a visual feedback to help user understand these controls better.

The growing structure of online social networks makes them dynamic in nature. A regular evolution of network does add to the privacy breach of a user. Link prediction algorithms are being used to generalize the network by modelling it in the form of graphs. Here, the dynamic nature of the network is visualized by adding more edges and nodes in the graph. Group-based anonymization can be performed along with link predicted graph to provide privacy with less information loss. De-anonymization attacks are being performed in dynamic social networks. Adversary can easily steal the historical data of any user on social networks to learn his/her social relationships thereby making the attack practical. Modelling of social networks into a graph does lead to information loss. Several cost measures have been introduced to measure such loss and determine its impact on data quality. Attackers are also threatening the user privacy by stealing their links in the network. Any information related to his/her local neighbourhood helps the adversary in visualizing a global picture of the link graph. In order to ensure link privacy, OSNs are required to employ limitations on the look-ahead of their interface.

In an age of enduring digitized association, social networking sites have served as one of the means for associating and maintaining relationships. A large number of users around the world are using OSNs like Facebook (most popular social networking service) to connect and associate online actively. In today's world, SNSs are being used as a useful means for producing social stocks. This useful generation of capital thus enables users to create new relationships and elevate their personal network with fresh connections [1]. Having a sound and a large social network can provide network users (i.e. common people, marketers, advertisers) with otherwise unreachable resources, for example, privacy hack of personal information, financial procurement, targeted advertising and psychological well-being [2–4]. The ability of social networks to provide direct as well as indirect benefits has evolved as important research area with respect to expansion and extensions.

In order to evaluate and analyse the evolving nature of a network, researchers in the past have utilized the valuable data contained by some popular social network sites. Consequently, such studies have helped in analysing the development of new equations within a network [5]. Preferential attachment model and common neighbour analysis have been used as a measurement criterion to understand the framework of a network structure as well as the aspects of the user participating online on SNS. The analysis has been further utilized to prognosticate the chance of new link formations. The preferential attachment model by Albert and Barabasi explains that the degree centrality of a node defines the number of relationships in the form of connections; a network participant can serve and is termed as a powerful pioneer tool for forming fresh network relations to the node [6]. In addition to the above, having a common neighbour connection also defines a pair of active network users that are interacting with online common neighbour or a mutual friend and can drive future online relationships between that pair [7]. These models used for prediction take quantitative indicators from a particular framework based on SNS to find and establish connections within a network structure.

However, analysis in the past has indicated that not much attention has been given to categorize the evolving nature of network structure from a socially interactive network viewpoint, although most networks evolve and are formed via socially active network users in both modes: online and offline. Also, current state-of-the-art articles have pointed out the existence of social network interaction as an online notion on SNS of multiple relationships and associations among active network users over a given period of time, which is also based on basic and existing offline interactions. Although previous studies do not consider the mere fact that development of an evolved social network might be associated with some offline interactions among participants apart from just interactions being done actively in a particular online social network, specifically, network relations on Facebook or Twitter, for example, are generally suggested to form some offline acquaintances rather than only through online interactions, as the use of SNS to keep in touch with people whom they already knew has sometimes exceeded the use of SNS to meet new people [8]. The above-discussed social network analysis techniques thus provide an online one-dimensional perspective to predict social network evolution [5].

Information disclosure in context to OSNs has raised serious privacy and security concerns. Some of such incidents have been reported in the past by the news media [9, 10]. Apart from the above coverage, social networks themselves are adding breaches in user privacy by posting anonymized social data serving a fodder to de-anonymization and inference attacks [11]. Additionally, the design and concept of OSN relationships is becoming a successful means for spreading unwanted content also known as spam, malware and phishing attacks. A new range of attacks are being launched from various fake profiles by malicious entities, using impersonated credentials sold in the underground market. This chapter provides a comprehensive review regarding various solutions to privacy and security issues in OSNs' anonymization. Various articles published till date with regard to privacy and security issues primarily focus towards basic issues like privacy preservation over data posted over social networking sites along with some solutions-based methods [12], Sybil attacks mitigation [13], OSN design limitations to ensure security as well as privacy needs [14] or threats in OSNs [15]. This chapter covers the spectrum of security and privacy issues prevailing on OSNs. It further proposes solution towards security and privacy maintenance via improvised and defect attenuated anonymization.

1.1 Contribution

In this chapter, the security and privacy attacks as well as the current solutions being implemented to mitigate such attacks are explored. Security techniques based on anonymization have a strong mathematical base about the network and thus

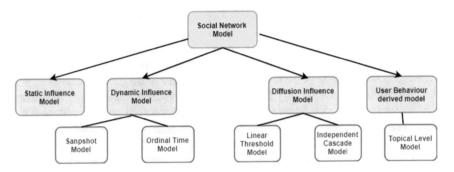

Fig. 11.1 Online social network model

help in mitigating privacy breach. These techniques are compared in terms of information loss, loss of trust and further empirical evaluation. Techniques such as anonymization, generalization, scoring, trust management and privacy control can help in achieving both privacy and security. Here, we explore challenges and propose new research directions for researchers with primary focus to improvise online social network security and privacy.

1.2   Online Social Network Model

Online social network model has been highlighted in Fig. 11.1. The categorization highlighted is based on some inherent properties which today's online social networks should satisfy, such as large-scale implementation, network-based clustering and degree distribution [16].

As shown in Fig. 11.1, social network models are broadly classified into categories like static influence models, dynamic influence models, diffusion influence models and user behaviour-derived model. Static models are the simplest ones. The ease of assess in these models makes the probability of influence unchanged and independent of time. Here, the ongoing snapshot state of the network as well as highly prominent nodes in that state is evaluated [17, 18]. The dynamic influence models, being second category models, take the probability of change in influence over growing time and are termed as dynamic models, although these models are proven to be high on accuracy as they can predict the past record of any particular network and categorize the high affecting data points or nodes for diffused behavioural information, but result in high complexity and cost when tested on large data because of their huge time requirements on such networks.

Another category of social network models is dynamic influence models where the dynamic nature of OSN is incorporated as a base property. These models demonstrate the changing nature of online participation by users. They are further classified as snapshot model, which takes in the user participation at two different snapshots to categorize his/her future participation, while the other model, ordinal time model, evaluates user participation as a function of growing time-based activity [19, 20].

The third category is diffusion influence model. These models are used when binding to behaviour depends on knowing the number of neighbours who projected the similar behaviour. In [21] Domingo and Richardson discussed a framework for the propagation of influence while identifying influential users. A probabilistic model selects the influential users in the context of viral marketing, which is further confirmed via empirical studies. Such models help the attackers in identifying the most active users and use them to publicize a new innovation or a product. More prominently, they tend to impact their friends, as well as friends of friends [22]. Diffusion models are used to optimize marketing decisions. Diffusion models are further classified as linear threshold model proposed by Granovetter [23] which uses a linear threshold approach to capture the influence among evolving social networks and independent cascade model uses a greedy algorithm to incorporate the dynamic nature of social networks apart from just the basic structure of such networks [24].

Lastly, user behaviour-derived models identify social influences among users based on the derivation of actions from other related users.

The evolving nature of social networks can be better understood by models that lead to better inspection of the community structure, social influence, information sensitivity and breach probabilities in these networks. The outcomes of this analysis help in performing various activities around OSN-derived communities such as target-based advertising, information misuse and influence-based security threats.

1.3 Categories of Privacy Breach

Till date, privacy cannot be defined precisely in academia or in government circles. However, many definitions have been cited and given in the past. Privacy initially defined, by Aristotle, is stated as a distinction between political activity as public and family as private [25]. It is also defined as the right an individual or a group of people hold.

In relation to real online social networks, the four causes of privacy breach categorized and discussed are user limitations, design flaws or limitations, implicit flows of information and clash of interests, as shown in Fig. 11.2.

1.3.1 User-Based Limitations

Humans who are the major users of OSNs possess some major limitations and flaws. Because of these flaws they share their aesthetic views or sensitive information on public platforms giving a chance of privacy breach. Users are most likely to post huge amount of information/data on social networks on various occasions, with no concern for results which are: short term as well as long term. Human rationality

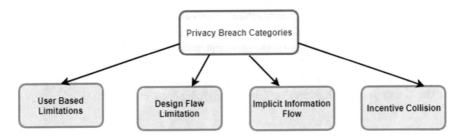

Fig. 11.2 Categories of privacy breach

while making a decision is mostly influenced by the time limit in which one has to make a decision, the data chunk he/she is dealing with, the structure of the data and other cognitive shortcomings of the mind. The causes of a decision resulting in bad privacy made by human beings are derived as (1) compromised rationality and (2) less working memory. Also, it is quite imperative that for a particular user who logs on any OSN, he/she is usually not interested in reading, understanding or analysing after effects of any privacy policy. The common users on OSNs comprise of individuals of different age groups and hence are not much aware of all risks and current ongoing attacks, etc. [26]. A user who is active in any of the OSN and shares his/her personal or related information, is most likely to be distracted psychologically. These distractions make the users compel them to take their privacy for granted and force them to take any decision related to privacy on the basis of limited information. As a result, privacy consciousness gets overlooked by users easily while using OSNs [27]. Inherent trust also leads to privacy breach of personal data.

1.3.2   Design Flaw Limitation

Weak privacy controls form one of the constituents of design limitations and flaws included by the social networks along with the possibility of explicit attacks including cloning attacks. Inability of social networks to provide any authenticity or certification for an account on social platforms leads to mistrust propagation. Despite the stringent privacy policy designed by OSNs, many attackers are still able to easily create fake accounts and impersonate someone else. An attacker can use pictures and videos of the victim or any other personal information on any fake created profile to win over the trust of his friend's connections, thus letting that fake account to enter into their boundary of trust.

Facebook has provided a privilege to every user in which he/she can recover his/her suspended account, although such privileges can be revoked if the attacker associates the victim's account with a newly created dummy account, thereby disassociating the victim's current login email address and the current account. This is also known as "permanent takeover attack" [28]. Facebook can prohibit the syndication of already in-use email addresses with newly created accounts. Adding victims on Facebook and further deactivating their own account is called "deactivated friend attack" [29]. Deactivation which is temporary makes the user invisible for some time. Very minimal privacy settings apply to such deactivated user, i.e. after sometime the attacker span his victims' profiles for all types of updated and personal information after reactivating his account.

1.3.3 Implicit Information Flow

Information leak is termed as implicit when one leak leads to other information leaks. For example, Dey et al. [30] stated that only 1.5% of users reveal their age from a study conducted over 1.47 million Facebook accounts. Using the high school graduation year and friend connections of these users, one would be able to estimate the ages of 84% of these users with a mean error of plus or minus 4 years. Similarly, the user activity related to his/her videos, pages he/she likes and ads clicked by them can lead to implicit information leak that can be misused by any attacker [31]. A similar example on Twitter where particular information can be considered implicit is the tweeting timing activity of a user which can be either in the morning or evening is also a privacy breach [32].

1.3.4 Incentive Collision

Most social networks are being supported by revenue generated from advertisements just like various other web services. This creates a clash of motive between user's rights and advertiser's rights for the service provider. As the service providers are quite dependent on advertiser's money for proper functioning, profit making from any social site has become the need of the hour. Similarly, in the absence of a true user base, not much of the advertiser's money will be generated. Users do not permit other users to access their data. Such permission must happen under a properly formed document, human-readable and in-knowledge consent. Also, users do not wish for their data to be utilized for any purpose they are unaware or in non-agreement to. From a user's point of view, any discrepancy in such agreement and consent terms by the service provider is considered as privacy threat. While for the advertiser, the diversity and large-scale information access is sole need and primary objective for running the business. Such collisions lead to privacy breach from the service provider end.

2 Security in OSN

Users tend to expose some unsafe quantity of information on OSNs which can be identified personally, including physical, psychological, cultural and preferential attributes which are readily available. Various studies also observed that usually most of the users reveal personal opinions and interests and such personal data shared on OSNs makes users vulnerable to different cyber and physical attacks. So, security is the topmost requirement for all OSNs to secure end user's information on public platforms.

2.1 Need of Security

A social network is defined as an ecosystem that comprise of various entities. The entities include users, service providers, advertising groups and the third-party application developers. Users are the one that take services from OSN providers, and service providers are the primary stakeholders of this ecosystem. Here, the users and the service providers both face significant consequences from major security issues. In terms of OSN services, the proper functioning of the service is usually disrupted by security threats and this can also damage the service provider's reputation. In the ecosystem of an OSN, user's interaction with other users and third-party social applications, viewing the advertisements placed by a certain group, also leads to security threats [34]. All these entities can access user's personal information. A classic example of the threat is the ability of any attacker to build user's larger profile by spanning his/her accounts from all social platforms. Researchers have analysed and shown that although OSNs provide simple and new ways to associate with each other, it also gives birth to new domain of innovations and challenges to avoid these threats and concerns caused by OSN. Structural characteristics of social network, understanding user behaviour and investigating traffic activity are some of the areas being focused upon for mitigating the hazards of OSN [33]. One of the critical concerns among researchers in industry is mainly due to the linear rise in OSN and cybercrime therefore making cyber security professionals and academia to work on the same.

2.2 Types of Security Attacks and Threats

Attacks on the OSN, by threatening its core business, have usually targeted the service provider. Distributed denial-of-service (DDoS) attacks have misused OSN's platform to distribute malware and social unwanted data spam. There are various ways by which these attacks can be executed. One of the ways could be where an attacker can get an unauthorized control over a legitimate user account and further use the controlled account to launch a planned and efficient attack. This section enlists various security attacks targeted by attackers to compromise the privacy of end users.

(a) *Sybil attacks*: In this attack, the attacker uses various identities to attack the whole network. For example, Sybil attacks can be used to reconstruct altogether new results in voting applications by changing ranks, bad-mouth an opinion and manipulate some online debates. Sybil attacks have largely targeted the OSNs because of their open architecture. This attack is executed when an adversary generates multiple spurious identities to get private and personal information like full name, SSN and bank details from users [35]. Sybil attacks on social networks are executed on distributed, decentralized systems where lots of personal information are shared publicly and it becomes quite challenging to delete the impact of attack and damage created on the OSN website [36].

(b) *Compromised account-based attacks:* An account that is generated and used by real owners but controlled by attackers is termed as compromised legitimate user account attack [37]. A normal social network usage history and established social connects with evolved network are some common properties of such accounts and thus they cannot be doubted for credibility. They are later used by cyber criminals for doing fraudulent activities.

(c) *Social spam and malware:* Spam is termed as unwanted content for a user over OSN. They are received by users under the name of trust over social platforms. Spam hampers resource sharing and damages online activity between users which include interactions, post sharing or liking as it contributes phishing attacks, unwanted commercial messages and website promotion. OSNs are an easy target used by spammers to spread unwanted content due to inherent trust that lies among online relationships termed as friendship in social context, where this embedded trust drives any legitimate user to view and click posts or view online links shared with user's friends. Malware is informally defined as an amalgamation name for a set of functions that acquire access, hamper system functioning, gain access over personal information or even destroy a computer where the owner is unknown to such damage. OSNs are being enormously exploited for distributing malware, also called as social spam [38].

(d) *Distributed denial-of-service attacks (DDoS).* DDoS is another form of attack, where a particular service is overwhelmingly sent with huge quantity of offensive service request which burden the service and denies the access to it. Evidently, many popular services on OSNs are subject to similar attacks, whenever the OSN user interacts with the malicious application, and unsolicited HTTP requests are produced which practically gets triggered from the targeted user's web browser [39].

(e) *Third-party attacks*: Various third-party applications hosted by OSNs like Facebook and Twitter provide add-on services like ads, gaming apps and dating apps. Some part of personal information from the user profile is required to access all third-party applications. For instance, in Facebook, information like profile picture, name, gender, username and networks becomes openly accessible to all users and thereby becomes available to various such applications [40]. However, some applications enjoy privileges like having access to all of the user's pictures, friend list, messages and news feed (wall). Enabling third-party applications to build and publish their own application on the existing network

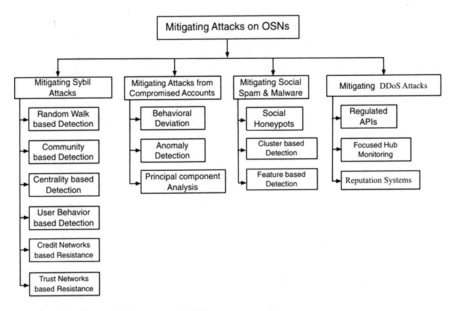

Fig. 11.3 Categories of privacy breach [41]

structure is another facility third-party websites are enjoying and exploiting. Such applications can be malicious or intentional or also seem to be vulnerable and exploited by attackers.

Various mitigating techniques, algorithms and approaches have been proposed and implemented in the past. Figure 11.3 [41] summarizes some of the common mitigation techniques deployed in the past with reference to different attacks.

2.3 Challenges in Threat Resolution

OSN popularity is raising more and more concerns for privacy and security safeguard measures. The evolving nature of OSNs has diverted researchers to look for mitigating techniques regarding every new attack targeted on OSNs. This section gives an overview of open problems which still withstand. The privacy solutions reviewed usually focus on multiple facets of privacy, such as providing visual feedback and granular settings via well-formed and designed user-friendly and informed graphical interface, or fabricating automated or default privacy policies [41, 42]. However, a one-stop privacy solution having all the planes is still a challenge. The third-party platforms which are a need of business for service providers claim to not pass information to other applications. However, that beats the business model idea and thus protecting data from such apps still remains a challenge [43–45]. The open structure of OSN is giving rise to various attacks coming up day by day. Exploring a comprehensive risk assessment and pertaining solutions in context of OSNs can be explored by researchers as potential trackers. Attacks that are intertwined or related can be a challenge for mitigation. Some attacks might be a prerequisite for other attacks. For example, the identity of an individual can be revealed by a de-anonymization attack. The identity can be further misused to employ certain other privacy breach attacks. Researchers still need to explore various scenarios that are synergies of these types of attacks [46, 47].

3 Preserving Privacy and Security

The current assumptions of privacy preservation in relation to the user profiles do not consider the framework ideology of the social network. In this section we discuss various privacy and security preservation techniques.

One of the major solutions in preserving privacy and security of data in OSN is data anonymization. Data anonymization being a complex problem itself mainly focuses on removal of data in order to prohibit adversaries from gaining access to personal data in the form of attribute information while maintaining the usefulness of already public data. Although anonymization is being used for mitigating privacy and security threats, new attacks are being deployed leading to a need in improvement in anonymization.

3.1 Anonymizing User Information

Privacy-preserving techniques were first introduced for user information as a tabular data. With evolution of social media culture, the issues related to online user privacy and security have increased. Researchers tend towards studying anonymization as a privacy-preserving technique usually centred towards social media data. Two types of information disclosure schemes mostly used by attackers are identity disclosure and attribute disclosure attacks.

Definition 1.3.1 [48] *Identity disclosure attack—Given $X = (G, X, J)$, which denotes a current state label of a social network having a graph $G = (V, E)$. Here V depicts a finite group of users, E depicts the social friendships shared by such set of users, an active user's behavioural activity X and a user information J inferred from attributes; the attack that gives a mapping between users from the list having target users V_T and the identities known to them is called identity disclosure attack. Here for each $v \in V_T$, the information that depicts user's social relations and behaviour is already known.*

Definition 1.3.2 [48] *Attribute disclosure attack—Given $X = (G, X, J)$, which denotes a current state label of a social network having a graph $G = (V, E)$. Here V depicts a finite group of users, and E depicts the social friendships shared by* *such set of users, an active user's behavioural activity X and a user information J inferred from attributes; the attack that derives the attributes a_{ir} for all $v \in V_T$ where V_T comprises of all targeted users is called as attribute disclosure attack. Here for each $v \in V_T$, the information that depicts user's social relations and behaviour is already known.*

3.2 k-Anonymity, l-Diversity and t-Closeness

K-anonymity technique anonymizes each specimen point in the dataset such that the particular instance becomes non-differentiable from a minimum of $k - 1$ other specimens in context to specific identifiable user social information which is in the form of attributes. In order to achieve the goal of anonymizing the data via repression or generalization where k-anonymity is protected for every specimen data point in the dataset, some generalizations and repressions are maintained so that the utility of resultant data is maximized [49].

Gagan et al. [48] proved that K-anonymity is an NP-hard problem. To make users indistinguishable from each other, K-anonymity ensures that identification of a user from a minimum of k-1 users having a similar set of features is quite difficult to make. Both users' attributes and structural properties are included in this set of attribute-based features.

Machanacajjhala et al. [50] introduced two attacks, defeating k-anonymity. Homogeneity attack is the first attack, in which the attacker due to lack of diversity of sensitive values in an equivalence class can infer an instance's sensitive attributes. In the second attack the adversary can be attacked via background knowledge access by an attacker which can infer instance's sensitive attributes even when the data is k-anonymized. The background knowledge attack which is the second attack defined here states that the background inform can include either users' friends' or behavioural information. Machanacajjhala et al. [50] also introduced the concept of l-diversity to mitigate above-mentioned attacks. It guarantees that every equivalence class having user attribute-based values derived from personal information is divergent. Formally, l-diversity for a specific set of records is defined as the ability of class to hold at least l well-depicted value for the personal attributes. Entropy l-diversity and recursive (c,l)-diversity are the two instantiations on the concept of diversity.

Distinguishing the propagation of sensitive personal information in the form of attributes from the complete dataset in a given equivalence class is marked as the occurrence of skewed attack. This attack is known as the scenes attack. A new concept of t-closeness based on privacy was introduced by Li et al. [51] where it was stated that there is a striking similarity of how any sensitive information in the form of derived attributes in a particular equivalence class and complete tabular data of user attributes is propagated. In a formal statement, if the distance that lies from the point of propagation of a personal attribute in a particular class to the point of propagation of the attribute in the complete dataset does not exceed a specific limit, then that equivalence class satisfies t-closeness. If all equivalence classes have t-closeness, then the complete dataset is said to have t-closeness.

3.3 Anonymizing Network

In addition to above, another work [52] discussed and identified privacy breach issue based on the social network graph framework. Seed-based or seed-free approaches are two types of attacks based on either a pre-annotated seed user's existence or not. Users with an unclear identity from the attacker are known as seed users.

There are two main steps in seed-based de-anonymization:

Step 1: There is a mapping that is generated between a finite group of seed users belonging to a graph that is already anonymized and the background/auxiliary graph information which is further reiterated.

Step 2: There is a distribution of mapping and de-anonymization from seed users to other set of users.

Seed-free approaches do not require user-related information in the form of a seed set. Other users can be further de-anonymized from such approaches. As a result, they perform with better efficiency and accuracy. One of the recent works in [53] where a de-anonymization algorithm was discussed which defined a new concept of privacy risk measure. Based on entity attribute matching obtained from the heterogeneous network, a set of candidates are chosen for every user in target, where it is again narrowed down to a candidate set of the target user as well as every accounted candidate.

4 Techniques for Data Anonymization: Implementation and Comparisons

This section discusses various proposed and implemented techniques towards data anonymization. The implementation results are also compared.

A de-anonymization approach that maps each pair of users to both background knowledge and anonymized graph based on percolation was proposed by Yartseva and Grossglauser [54]. A phase transition is identified for the seed set size. Here k which is the one and only criterion has been proved to be of a predefined mapping limit which does not need to satisfy a defined threshold number of users in the seed set.

A percolation-based attack was proposed by Korula and Lattanzi [55] that was parallelizable in nature. It initially has previously mapped seed users. Further, the attack breeds by mapping the remaining network, if any two users who have a specific number of mapped neighbours will be further mapped and the improvement is done by adding heuristics based on domain-specific knowledge. Using this approach, it is easy to deal with malicious users as well as fake social relationships in the network.

Ji et al. [56, 57] studied de-anonymizability using seed-based approaches of a social media graph data under both general and specific stochastic model.

Beigi and Liu [58] analysed the issue of user anonymization according to their structural information based on a relation model which is scale-free. The assumption is more realistic as users follow a scale-free degree—distribution. It was shown that any reconstruction of user identification in a given anonymized graph cannot be done based on information of an existing set of seed users. This is due to the inhomogeneities in the user's degree. It is also proved that based on attacker's opinion, as few as n^ϵ seeds are needed in accordance to their degree as well as scale-free property of social network.

Maintenance of trust and privacy being one of the major concerns for users on OSNs have been taken as challenges by various researchers in the past [59, 60]. Such challenges, however, have pointed out the user's likeliness to click unwanted and suspicious links present online like certain advertisements and pages [61]. De-anonymization thus plays a vital role in safeguarding the privacy of user online.

Bringmann et al. [63] also proposed a concept-based approach which utilizes a smaller number of seed nodes (for a random ϵ having a low value) in a graph having n nodes. This is considered as a significant advancement over the existing literature structure that is based on de-anonymization techniques requiring only Θ (n) seeds. Thus, the de-anonymization for privacy preservation is performed in quasilinear time.

Chiasserini et al. [62] included clustering concept in implementing de-anonymization attacks. A variety of clustering categories were used by these attacks. It was analysed and theoretically proved that inclusion of clustering can easily limit the number of seeds in de-anonymization attacks based out of percolation as compared other existing techniques because of its wave-like propagation effect.

Fu et al. [64, 65] used descriptive information, also called as personal information, such as name, gender and birth year, also defined as attributes for de-anonymization. In this, the authors proposed that two users are comparable if their neighbours map to each other. However, how two users are similar mainly relied upon the comparability of neighbours. Therefore, comparability was defined as a recursive problem which can be solved iteratively. The de-anonymization problem was further narrowed down to a simple weighted bipartite graph matching problem to be further investigated using Hungarian algorithm.

Sharad et al. [66] proposed to redesign the problem of graph de-anonymization in social networks as a cognitive problem. 1-hop and 2-hop neighbourhood degree propagation techniques were used by authors to represent users in a graph. Here if neighbourhood of two users maps to each other, then the users itself also map to each other. This approach retrieved structural features of the user's 1-hop and 2-hop neighbourhood from each pair if users were selected by both graphs. In order to acquire degree divergence for both similar and dissimilar user pairs, the machine learning model concept was used. The classifier so built is further trained on these features to predict whether the considered binary pair of nodes is similar to the distinguished ego-nets or not.

5 Evaluation of User Privacy Risk

5.1 Privacy Score Model

Figure 11.4 presents a flow diagram for the privacy scoring model [67]. Using this model, a user can formulate his/her privacy disclosure score based on two major factors: sensitivity and visibility. A potential private information loss can be measured from this score, which is obtained by statistical fuzzy analysis. Previous studies [68, 69] have formulated privacy score on the basis of a single networking site. A dichotomous approach is used in various other scoring models, while a polytomous-based one has proved to be more robust and diverse.

Here the α_j is the sensitivity of each attribute, whereas the $F_{vis}(x)$ is the visibility of every attribute, and the total privacy disclosure score of each user is obtained by privacy disclosure score function given as

$$PDS = \sum_{j=1}^{m} \alpha_j * F_{vis}(x)/m \tag{11.1}$$

Here, j is the jth attribute of the user with m being the number of attributes.

5.2 Algorithm Results: Discussion and Summary

1. It was observed that user inclination towards providing more sensitive information as compared to other attributes was not displayed.
2. Based on the experiments, it was observed that users possibly might disclose their sensitive data such as their email address, current location and interests, while political and religious views were less disclosed.
3. It was noticed that users who had higher affinity to publicize their personal data (can be both sensitive and non-sensitive) possess the highest risk for their privacy breach.

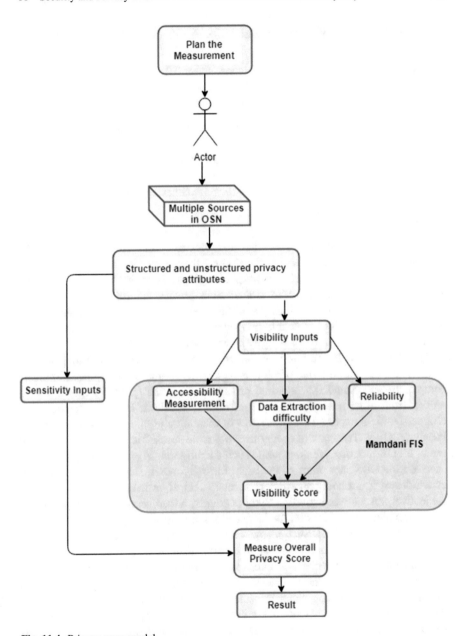

Fig. 11.4 Privacy score model

6   Management of Privacy Settings: Case Studies of OSNs

Four most common social networking sites as of 2018–2019—Facebook, Twitter, Instagram and Snapchat—are explored for their respective privacy settings they offer. Management of privacy setting raises the following research questions:

Q1. What personal attributes can have an influence on information disclosure and privacy settings of SNS users?
Q2. Do users' levels of privacy concern have an effect on the amount of information they disclose in social networking sites?
Q3. Are users aware of privacy policies they are adhering to or agree to?

Twitter gives users a privilege to make tweets "private" which can be viewed by respective user's followers. This being the only privacy setting given has efficiently locked out the general users and other unassociated users. However, major OSN providers such as Facebook and LinkedIn give their respective users a multiplexed and difficult to understand set of privacy controls. Lack of understanding, training and memory makes the effectiveness of such privacy controls weak [4]. These privacy settings must be cautiously analysed and practically implemented, so that the users can be advised to enable privacy settings as soon as they join the social network to address all sorts of security and privacy concerns [70–72].

The most restrictive setting provided by Facebook has been experimented and resulted in flaws from the privacy and security point of view, even if users completely understand the provided privacy settings that probably might not be hidden from other users for any type of breach or attack. In [73], Stutzman and Kramer-Duffield explored the inferences of creating a profile "friends only" on the Facebook OSN. The content of any user's post is accessible to directly connected users. It is further observed that while such a configuration is efficient against other users on the OSN, not much of the users formally use it. However, the researcher concludes of it not being an efficient defence against various other attacks from a subjective perspective, including Sybil accounts, advertisers, applications and the OSN provider itself. In addition, it questions the striking features of the OSN, i.e. friend discovery [74]. Such features have raised a constant concern over cyber privacy and security of an individual on social platforms [75].

Rather than locking one's profile, experiments as well as training have been imparted to users to make them aware regarding how their profile looks on such massive public platforms. Such information helps them better understand about what to share and what not and even with what to access or privacy control. In many social networks, identifying the difference between the visible and hidden data is a complex task in itself. Facebook already has a feature-based functionality that enables users to view their profile from a friend's perspective (directly connected user), or from a non-Facebook user (general users), thus diminishing this difference. This structure enhances the feature functionality, helping the user to get a glimpse of their profile from the viewpoint of a friend of a friend or a Facebook user (unconnected or indirectly connected users).

7 Privacy Preservation in Dynamic Networks

Link prediction has served as an important task of inspecting social networks, which have wide application adoption like information extraction, informatics and other online transaction applications.

OSN has become an integral part of people's life. Various systems like social, biological and informational are using networks to describe relations or links between individuals where the edge represents the former while the nodes represent the latter. Link prediction, therefore, serves an important branch in mining where the prediction is used to predict links between two nodes based on common extracted information and already existing link information.

7.1 Link Prediction

There are various prevailing techniques for link prediction and are categorized as:

- Feature-based classification
- Bayesian probabilistic model
- Probabilistic relational models

The above methods are analysed based on the following parameters:

- Complexity of the model used
- Performance
- How scalable the model is?
- Generalization ability

In this section, we showcase some striking and thoroughly state-of-art discussed link prediction methods based on above categorizations. Their respective strengths and weaknesses are also analysed [76].

7.1.1 Classification Based on Features

Link prediction problem can be modelled as a supervised classification problem in the training interval $[i_0, i_0^{\sim}]$. Here data point is taken as a pair of vertices for a given social network graph, and prediction of any future relation can be made in a test interval $[i_1, i_1^{\sim}]$.

In a formal definition,

A graph G (V, E) with two vertices <x,y>.

Label of the data point <x,y> is $L^{<x, y>}$. Taking interaction as symmetric, i.e. <x,y> and <y,x> represent the same data point or

$$L^{<x,y>} = L^{<y,x>} \tag{11.2}$$

$$L^{<x,y>} \begin{cases} +1, if < x, y > e \ E \\ -1, if < x, y >\notin E \end{cases} \tag{11.3}$$

From the obtained labelled set of data points that are trained based on given classification, a classification model is built to identify the not so known labels of a pair of vertices <x,y> such that <x,y> $\notin$ E for any graph G $\left[i_1, i_1^{\sim} \right]$.

The following tools can be used to solve the above binary classification problem [77]:

- Naïve Bayes
- Neural networks
- Support vector machines
- K-nearest neighbours

The following are the set of features that are obtained from the graph topology to predict links and provide as an input to the classification problem:

• Neighbour-based features

Common Neighbours The size of neighbours in common is termed as [S(u), S(v)] for any given two vertices u and v. The idea of taking common neighbourhood as a feature set is a derivation from the transitive property of the social network graph. Here transitivity is simply defined as, if u is a vertex connected to v and w is also a vertex connected to v, then there is a high chance of u and w being connected. Therefore, as the number of common neighbours increases, the probability of u and w being linked also increases.

Various studies have shown that the existence of any positive correlation between neighbours of u and v at any time t generates a high chance of their collaboration in the near future [78].

Jaccard Coefficient It normalizes the above-obtained common neighbours. Here, it is stated that the chance of selecting a common neighbour of x and y which are any two vertices of a graph is higher, where the selection consists of the unification of neighbour sets of x and y. Thus, a higher coefficient value signifies a high number of neighbours. However, this set of feature selection is weaker as compared to above metrics.

Adamic and Adar [79] Adamic and Adar proposed the similarity score on the basis of commonality between two web pages. This score provided a fair weight to the matching neighbours having a low degree heavily and thus is a more efficient metric.

• Path-based features

Shortest Path Distance The path distance from one node to the other in a social network can formally provide reason behind the formation of a link between them that comes from a mere observation that friend suggestion can come from friends of friend. The probability of such suggestion increases with shorter distance. But, more importantly, due to the small world [80] phenomenon, largely the pair of nodes has less number of vertices in separation. So, the scalability of this feature becomes a huge question. An average rank of 4 among 9 features was obtained and utilized to show how a link can be predicted in a biological co-authorship network by Hasan et al. [81]. Similarly, in [82] a similar low performance was obtained for the same set of features.

Katz Leo Katz proposed this metric in [83]. Being a derived variant of shortest path distance metric, it has a much efficient performance for link prediction. It directly accumulates over all the paths that exist between a pair of vertices u and v. In order to take into account the impact of longer paths in the commonness computation, it exponentially damps the impact of a path by a factor of α [1], where l is the path length. The formally defined equation to calculate the Katz value is as below:

$$katz\,(u,v) = \sum_{l=1}^{\infty} \alpha^l . \mid paths_{u,v}^{<l>} \mid \qquad (11.4)$$

Hitting Time Random walks are a derived concept of graph. A graph having two vertices u and v, the expected number of steps required for a random walk initiated at x to terminate y, defines the hitting time, $H_{u,v}$. Lower hitting time depicts that the nodes share common features, so they have a higher probability of associativity in the future.

For undirected graphs the commute time which is an unsymmetric metric is given as:

$$C_{u,v} = H_{u,v} + H_{u,v} \qquad (11.5)$$

The ease to calculate by performing some trial random walks makes this metric a beneficial one. On the negative aspect, its value can suffer high variance; hence, prediction by this feature can be low [82]. For instance, the hitting time between u and v can be hampered by a vertex w, which is at a distance away from u and v; for instance, if w has high stationary probability, then it could be quite difficult for a random walk to escape from the neighbourhood of w. To eliminate such variation, in this problem we can use random walks with restart, where we periodically reset the random walk by returning to u with a fixed probability α in each step.

7.1.2 Bayesian Probabilistic Model

In this section, prediction models that use Bayesian concepts under supervised learning are discussed. In order to estimate the posterior probability which depicts the probability of vertex pair co-occurrence required for link prediction is the novel concept. The use of score as a feature classification is the advantage of this concept. Various algorithms that have been proposed in the past in this area are by Wang, Satulur and Parthasarathy [84] which uses MRF-based local probabilistic model and by Kashima and Abe [85] which uses a parameterized prediction model. Subsequently, various other features have been used in [84] in order to predict a binary value using a probabilistic method based on several other features.

7.1.3 Probabilistic Relational Model (PRM)

In previous sections, how the feature and path of vertices with attributes have a considerable role in link prediction task was discussed. It is shown in some of the previous optimized algorithms discussed above how various link prediction techniques try to include the certain more attribute properties in the model that predicts with a better performance. However, as these approaches are not generic, it sometimes becomes difficult to apply these in some possible and ideal scenarios. PRM is a tangible tool that models and provides a meticulous method to include vertex as well as edge attribute properties which further provide the joint probability distribution of a set of entities and the links associated with them. By considering the object-relational nature of structured data that captures probabilistic interactions between entities and the links, PRM becomes a beneficial bill. So, it is advisable to use a basic flat model which does not count any such related information. With the two major launched approaches of PRM, one is based on Bayesian networks, which consider direct relation links [86], while the other one is based on relational Markov networks, which consider undirected relation links.

7.2 Link Privacy

In the context of this chapter, social networks are referred as online social networks. Online social sites such as Facebook, Flickr and LinkedIn are included in this context, where users can connect to, or "friend", each other, thus allowing high content-based interactions through activities like joining communities, or other group discussion forums. These sites mainly include various other services that enable users to make profiles and voice personal opinions as well as tastes regarding various units on network through posts and links, such as liking pages and post. Hence, social networks can be viewed as a multimodal graph having multiple entities that include all: users, groups and units. Here a social tie is considered as a link between two individuals. Each individual represented as a node has a profile, where profiles usually have personal information in the form of attributes, such as age, gender and career. There are various link extraction and statistical relational cognitive research communities [87], which analyse the retrieval of interconnected relational data.

There are two types of major links: user-user links and user-group links. Formally, the social network is represented as a graph $G = (U, E_v, H, E_h)$, where U is a set of n nodes which represent user profiles, and v defines the set of properties each node has. A friendship is defined by an edge e_u (u_i, u_j) $\in E_v$ which is a *social link* and depicts a friendship between the nodes u_i and u_j [88]. We use H to denote both fundamental units of social network denoted as socially active groups or any other social information for which users possess certain tastes or opinions, such as fan pages, photos and movies. H is referred here as *affiliation group*. An edge e_h(v_i, h_j) $\in E_h$ represents a particular affiliation link of the membership of data point in network(node) vi to affiliation group h_j [89].

The above-discussed link privacy breaches are described as follows:

7.2.1 Social Link Disclosure

Link disclosure that happens when a relationship that users want to hide from the public is exposed to an adversary where he/she is able to find the existence of a sensitive relationship between two users is called social link disclosure.

In this disclosure, it is assumed that there is a random variable $\hat{e}_{i,j}$ associated with the link relation existence between two nodes v_i and v_j, and an adversary has a model for assigning a probability to $\hat{e}_{i,j}$, $Pr(\hat{e}_{i,j} = true)$: $e_{i,j} \rightarrow R$.

7.2.2 Affiliation Link Disclosure

Affiliation link disclosure is another category where a user that comes from to a particular affiliated set of users can also be a tool to attack sensitive data. Whether two users are attached or affiliated with the same group can also be of a private nature. Usually, it can lead to further information like attribute disclosure, social link disclosure or identity disclosure. Hence, prohibiting affiliations is trivial for preserving the privacy of individuals.

In recent years, social networks are widely used for representing the connectedness between individuals. As time changes the real-time equations between individuals also changes which are not transformed on the social sites, so there exists a privacy breach of individuals in dynamic networks [90, 91]. Retrieving information from a network is an important concern and is inevitable in real-world applications. For example, the recommendation system in YouTube or Amazon aims to predict the interested of potential videos or products; such scenario can be represented by a model having a user-item link prediction problem. The highlighting feature for these applications is how to smartly get information from network structures which is useful and can make wise suggestions [92].

To predict links among users on online social networks, various algorithms have been proposed.

Jyothi et al. [93] proposed the privacy model to preserve the privacy of the published dynamic network, k w-number of mutual friend anonymization. Privacy level is indicated by k and w is the time interval used by adversary to get knowledge about. The k w-NMF algorithm anonymizes each release of network data. This ensures that adversary cannot reidentify the victim even by knowing about each release. A heuristic technique was designed for anonymizing large-scale dynamic networks with limited information distortion. A group sequence table was designed for efficiency evaluation and edge information summarization.

Ahmed et al. [94] have proposed a non-negative matrix factorization (NMF)-based method to predict links in dynamic networks. In this method temporal and structural information is exploited to learn links from social networks. New rules have been designed here for NMF and proved to be converging and congruent.

Li et al. [95] have solved an embedded network problem and focused on modelling the linkage prediction in the dynamic network. A deep dynamic network embedding method has been discussed. The method utilizes the historical information obtained from the network snapshots at past timestamps to learn clear representations of the future network. An objective function, including both network structure and transition, has been used.

7.3 De-Anonymization

The growing and highly penetrating nature of OSN has led to the opportunities for extracting the data that comes from them. Social network data can be provided for open research which can lead to a quantum leap in fields which are diverse as marketing and healthcare. However, with the publishing of data come concerns of privacy. Released information on a public forum is at stake of getting misused. Anonymization is the alteration of data so that private and personal information remains private. De-anonymization is the converse: reidentifying somebody in an anonymized network—or even getting to know something about them that was meant not to be attributable to them. Privacy is typically aided by anonymization, i.e. removing names, addresses, etc.

A mostly used approach in the anonymization of social networks is k-P-anonymization. Before the data is released, any sensitive information associated with individual vertices of the social network graph is suppressed and a sanitized graph that only reveals edge relationships between users is released for data mining purposes. There is now sufficient evidence that it does not. It has been shown that de-anonymization attacks can be used to extract sensitive information about certain users from such an anonymized graph by an adversary whose knowledge is global in nature.

Narayanan and Shmatikov [96] proposed a de-anonymization algorithm based on the network topology. It does not require creation of a large number of dummy "Sybil" nodes and is highly robust to noise and all existing defences and works even when the overlapping between the target network and the adversary's auxiliary information is small.

8 Conclusion

This chapter aims to revisit various security and privacy attacks being employed on OSN in today's world. The current state-of-art discusses about the solutions proposed and implemented to deal with these attacks. Social media sites have provided an easy-to-use platform to a variety of users for sharing their opinions, tastes and personal information (to the access level they permit) globally. However, this privilege comes with its own consequences where a user's security and privacy are at risk and exposed to advertisers, marketers and third-party applications. Hence, apart from proposing new solutions, educating users and making them aware of certain policies they should abide in order to preserve their privacy and security are the need of hour. Apart from the above-mentioned need, this chapter also explores anonymization as another technique that aids in maintaining privacy. Also the chapter is concluded with how links on social sites between users can be predicted thus hampering link privacy. Finally, this article gives new directions for need of progress needed in the field of privacy and security management on OSNs.

References

1. Hsu, C., Wang, C., & Tai, Y. (2011). The closer the relationship, the more the interaction on Facebook? Investigating the case of Taiwan users. *Cyberpsychology, Behavior and Social Networking, 14*(7–8), 473–476.
2. Bourdieu, P., & Wacquant, L. (1992). *An invitation to reflexive sociology* (1st ed.). Chicago: University of Chicago Press.
3. Kane, G., & Alavi, M. (2008). Casting the net: A multimodal network perspective on user-system interactions. *Information Systems Research, 19*(3), 253–272.
4. Ellison, N., Steinfield, C., & Lampe, C. (2007). The benefits of Facebook "Friends:" Social capital and college students' use of online social network sites. *Journal of Computer-Mediated Communication, 12*(4), 1143–1168.
5. Trier, M. (2008). Towards dynamic visualization for understanding evolution of digital communication networks. *Information Systems Research, 19*(3), 335–350.
6. Albert, R., & Barabási, A. (2000). Topology of evolving networks: Local events and universality. *Physical Review Letters, 85*(24), 5234–5237.
7. Newman, M. (2001). Clustering and preferential attachment in growing networks. *Physical Review E, 64*(2), 025102.
8. Carlyne, L., & Kujath, B. (2011). Facebook and MySpace: Complement or substitute for face-to-face interaction? *Cyberpsychology, Behavior and Social Networking, 14*(1–2), 75–78.
9. Dam, W. B. (2009). *School teacher suspended for Facebook gun photo.* http://www.foxnews.com/story/2009/02/05/schoolteacher-suspended-for-facebook-gun-photo/
10. Mail, D. (2011). *Bank worker fired for Facebook post comparing her 7-an-hour wage to Lloyds boss's 4000-an-hour salary.* http://dailym.ai/fjRTlC
11. Narayanan, A., Shi, E., & Rubinstein, B. I. (2011). Link prediction by de-anonymization: How we won the Kaggle social network challenge. In *Proceedings of the 2011 international joint conference on neural networks (IJCNN)* (pp. 1825–1834). New York: IEEE.
12. Zheleva, E., & Getoor, L. (2007). *Privacy in social networks: A survey* (pp. 277–306). New York: Springer.

13. Yu, H. (2011). Sybil defences via social networks: A tutorial and survey. *SIGACT News, 42*(3), 80–101.
14. Zhang, C., Sun, J., Zhu, X., & Fang, Y. (2010). Privacy and security for online social networks: Challenges and opportunities. *IEEE Network, 24*(4), 13–18.
15. Fire, M., Goldschmidt, R., & Elovici, Y. (2014). Online social networks: Threats and solutions. *IEEE Communications Surveys and Tutorials, 16*(4), 2019–2036.
16. Baagyere, E. Y., Qin, Z., Xiong, H., & Zhiguang, Q. (2016). The structural properties of online social networks and their application areas. *IAENG International Journal of Computer Science, 43*(2), 2.
17. Cosley, D., Huttenlocher, D. P., Kleinberg, J. M., Lan, X., & Suri, S. (2010). Sequential influence models in social networks. *ICWSM, 10*, 26.
18. Goyal, A., Bonchi, F., & Lakshmanan, L. V. (2010, February). Learning influence probabilities in social networks. In *Proceedings of the third ACM international conference on web search and data mining* (pp. 241–250). New York: ACM.
19. Backstrom, L., Huttenlocher, D., Kleinberg, J., & Lan, X. (2006, August). Group formation in large social networks: Membership, growth, and evolution. In *Proceedings of the 12th ACM SIGKDD international conference on knowledge discovery and data mining* (pp. 44–54). New York: ACM.
20. Kossinets, G., & Watts, D. J. (2006). Empirical analysis of an evolving social network. *Science, 311*(5757), 88–90.
21. Richardson, M., & Domingos, P. (2002, July). Mining knowledge-sharing sites for viral marketing. In *Proceedings of the eighth ACM SIGKDD international conference on knowledge discovery and data mining* (pp. 61–70). New York: ACM.
22. Domingos, P., & Richardson, M. (2001, August). Mining the network value of customers. In *Proceedings of the seventh ACM SIGKDD international conference on knowledge discovery and data mining* (pp. 57–66). New York: ACM.
23. Granovetter, M. (1978). Threshold models of collective behavior. *American Journal of Sociology, 83*(6), 1420–1443.
24. Kempe, D., Kleinberg, J., & Tardos, É. (2003, August). Maximizing the spread of influence through a social network. In *Proceedings of the ninth ACM SIGKDD international conference on knowledge discovery and data mining* (pp. 137–146). New York: ACM.
25. Privacy: Stanford encyclopedia of philosophy, 2002.
26. Spiekermann, S., Grossklags, J., & Berendt, B. (2001, October). E-privacy in 2nd generation E-commerce: Privacy preferences versus actual behavior. In *Proceedings of the 3rd ACM conference on electronic commerce* (pp. 38–47). New York: ACM.
27. Boshmaf, Y., Muslukhov, I., Beznosov, K., & Ripeanu, M. (2011, December). The socialbot network: When bots socialize for fame and money. In *Proceedings of the 27th annual computer security applications conference* (pp. 93–102). New York: ACM.
28. Bilge, L., Strufe, T., Balzarotti, D., & Kirda, E. (2009, April). All your contacts are belong to us: Automated identity theft attacks on social networks. In *Proceedings of the 18th international conference on World wide web* (pp. 551–560). New York: ACM.
29. Mahmood, S. (2012, November). New privacy threats for Facebook and twitter users. In *2012 Seventh international conference on P2P, parallel, grid, cloud and internet computing (3PGCIC)* (pp. 164–169). New York: IEEE.
30. Dey, R., Tang, C., Ross, K., & Saxena, N. (2012, March). Estimating age privacy leakage in online social networks. In *INFOCOM, 2012 proceedings IEEE* (pp. 2836–2840). New York: IEEE.
31. Chaabane, A., Acs, G., & Kaafar, M. A. (2012, February). You are what you like! Information leakage through users' interests. In *Proceedings of the 19th Annual Network & Distributed System Security Symposium (NDSS)*.
32. Power, R., & Forte, D. (2008). War & peace in cyberspace: Don't Twitter away your organisation's secrets. *Computer Fraud and Security, 2008*(8), 18–20.
33. Wen, S., Haghighi, M. S., Chen, C., Xiang, Y., Zhou, W., & Jia, W. (2015). A sword with two edges: Propagation studies on both positive and negative information in online social networks. *IEEE Transactions on Computers, 64*(3), 640–653.

34. Foster, T. N., & Greene, C. R. (2012). Legal issues of online social networks and the workplace. *Journal of Law, Business and Ethics, 18*, 131.
35. Viswanath, B., Post, A., Gummadi, K. P., & Mislove, A. (2011). An analysis of social network-based sybil defenses. *ACM SIGCOMM Computer Communication Review, 41*(4), 363–374.
36. Danezis, G., & Mittal, P. (2009, February). SybilInfer: Detecting sybil nodes using social networks. In *NDSS* (pp. 1–15).
37. Egele, M., Stringhini, G., Kruegel, C., & Vigna, G. (2013). Compa: Detecting compromised social network accounts. In *Symposium on network and distributed system security (NDSS)*.
38. Heymann, P., Koutrika, G., & Garcia-Molina, H. (2007). Fighting spam on social web sites: A survey of approaches and future challenges. *IEEE Internet Computing, 11*(6), 36–45.
39. Dittrich, D., Reiher, P., & Dietrich, S. (2004). *Internet denial of service: Attack and defense mechanisms*. London: Pearson Education.
40. Huber, M., Mulazzani, M., Weippl, E., Kitzler, G., & Goluch, S. (2011). Friend-in-the-middle attacks: Exploiting social networking sites for spam. *IEEE Internet Computing, 15*(3), 28–34.
41. Cranor, L. F., Guduru, P., & Arjula, M. (2006). User interfaces for privacy agents. *ACM Transactions on Computer-Human Interaction (TOCHI), 13*(2), 135–178.
42. Danezis, G., Domingo-Ferrer, J., Hansen, M., Hoepman, J. H., Metayer, D. L., Tirtea, R., & Schiffner, S. (2015). *Privacy and data protection by design-from policy to engineering*. arXiv preprint arXiv:1501.03726.
43. Gao, H., Hu, J., Huang, T., Wang, J., & Chen, Y. (2011). Security issues in online social networks. *IEEE Internet Computing, 15*(4), 56–63.
44. Guha, S., Tang, K., & Francis, P. (2008, August). NOYB: Privacy in online social networks. In *Proceedings of the first workshop on online social networks* (pp. 49–54). New York: ACM.
45. Debatin, B., Lovejoy, J. P., Horn, A. K., & Hughes, B. N. (2009). Facebook and online privacy: Attitudes, behaviors, and unintended consequences. *Journal of Computer-Mediated Communication, 15*(1), 83–108.
46. Zhou, B., & Pei, J. (2008, April). Preserving privacy in social networks against neighborhood attacks. In *IEEE 24th international conference on data engineering, 2008. ICDE 2008* (pp. 506–515). New York: IEEE.
47. Heatherly, R., Kantarcioglu, M., & Thuraisingham, B. (2013). Preventing private information inference attacks on social networks. *IEEE Transactions on Knowledge and Data Engineering, 25*(8), 1849–1862.
48. Zheleva, E., & Getoor, L. (2011). Privacy in social networks: A survey. In *Social network data analytics* (pp. 277–306). Boston: Springer.
49. Tripathy, B. K., Sishodia, M. S., Jain, S., & Mitra, A. (2014). Privacy and anonymization in social networks. In *Social networking* (pp. 243–270). Cham: Springer.
50. Machanavajjhala, A., Gehrke, J., Kifer, D., & Venkitasubramaniam, M. (2006, April). \ell-Diversity: Privacy beyond\kappa-anonymity. In *22nd International Conference on Data Engineering (ICDE'06)* (p. 24). New York: IEEE.
51. Li, N., Li, T., & Venkatasubramanian, S. (2007, April). T-closeness: Privacy beyond k-anonymity and l-diversity. In *IEEE 23rd international conference on data engineering, 2007. ICDE 2007* (pp. 106–115). New York: IEEE.
52. Backstrom, L., Dwork, C., & Kleinberg, J. (2007, May). Wherefore art thou r3579x?: Anonymized social networks, hidden patterns, and structural steganography. In *Proceedings of the 16th international conference on world wide web* (pp. 181–190). New York: ACM.
53. Zhang, A., Xie, X., Chang, K. C. C., Gunter, C. A., Han, J., & Wang, X. (2014, March). Privacy risk in anonymized heterogeneous information networks. In *EDBT* (pp. 595–606).
54. Yartseva, L., & Grossglauser, M. (2013, October). On the performance of percolation graph matching. In *Proceedings of the first ACM conference on online social networks* (pp. 119–130). New York: ACM.
55. Korula, N., & Lattanzi, S. (2014). An efficient reconciliation algorithm for social networks. *Proceedings of the VLDB Endowment, 7*(5), 377–388.
56. Ji, S., Li, W., Gong, N. Z., Mittal, P., & Beyah, R. A. (2015, February). On your social network de-anonymizablity: Quantification and large scale evaluation with seed knowledge. In *NDSS*.

57. Ji, S., Li, W., Gong, N. Z., Mittal, P., & Beyah, R. A. (2016). Seed based deanonymizability quantification of social networks. *IEEE Transactions on Information Forensics and Security (TIFS), 11*(7), 1398–1411.
58. Beigi, G., & Liu, H. (2018). *Privacy in social media: Identification, mitigation and applications.* arXiv preprint arXiv:1808.02191.
59. Zhang, Z., & Gupta, B. B. (2018). Social media security and trustworthiness: Overview and new direction. *Future Generation Computer Systems, 86,* 914–925.
60. Tucker, C. E. (2014). Social networks, personalized advertising, and privacy controls. *Journal of Marketing Research, 51*(5), 546–562.
61. Neal, Z., Borgatti, S. P., Everett, M. G., & Johnson, J. C. (2013). *Analyzing social networks* (p. 296). Thousand Oaks: Sage. 54.00(paper), 130.00 (cloth).
62. Chiasserini, C. F., Garetto, M., & Leonardi, E. (2018). De-anonymizing clustered social networks by percolation graph matching. *ACM Transactions on Knowledge Discovery from Data (TKDD), 12*(2), 21.
63. Bringmann, K., Friedrich, T., & Krohmer, A. (2018). De-anonymization of heterogeneous random graphs in quasilinear time. *Algorithmica, 80*(11), 3397–3427.
64. Fu, H., Zhang, A., & Xie, X. (2014, April). De-anonymizing social graphs via node similarity. In *Proceedings of the 23rd international conference on world wide web* (pp. 263–264). New York: ACM.
65. Fu, H., Zhang, A., & Xie, X. (2015). Effective social graph deanonymization based on graph structure and descriptive information. *ACM Transactions on Intelligent Systems and Technology (TIST), 6*(4), 49.
66. Sharad, K., & Danezis, G. (2014, November). An automated social graph de-anonymization technique. In *Proceedings of the 13th workshop on privacy in the electronic society* (pp. 47–58). New York: ACM.
67. Aghasian, E., Garg, S., Gao, L., Yu, S., & Montgomery, J. (2017). Scoring users' privacy disclosure across multiple online social networks. *IEEE Access, 5,* 13118–13130.
68. Liu, K., & Terzi, E. (2010). A framework for computing the privacy scores of users in online social networks. *ACM Transactions on Knowledge Discovery from Data (TKDD), 5*(1), 6.
69. Domingo-Ferrer, J. (2010, October). Rational privacy disclosure in social networks. In *International conference on modeling decisions for artificial intelligence* (pp. 255–265). Berlin/Heidelberg: Springer.
70. Tewari, A., & Gupta, B. B. (2018). Security, privacy and trust of different layers in Internet-of-Things (IoTs) framework. *Future Generation Computer Systems.* https://doi.org/10.1016/j.future.2018.04.027.
71. Adat, V., & Gupta, B. B. (2018). Security in Internet of Things: issues, challenges, taxonomy, and architecture. *Telecommunication Systems, 67*(3), 423–441.
72. Gupta, B. B., Gupta, S., & Chaudhary, P. (2017). Enhancing the browser-side context-aware sanitization of suspicious HTML5 code for halting the DOM-based XSS vulnerabilities in cloud. *International Journal of Cloud Applications and Computing (IJCAC), 7*(1), 1–31.
73. Stutzman, F., & Kramer-Duffield, J. (2010, April). Friends only: Examining a privacy-enhancing behavior in Facebook. In *Proceedings of the SIGCHI conference on human factors in computing systems* (pp. 1553–1562). New York: ACM.
74. Pempek, T. A., Yermolayeva, Y. A., & Calvert, S. L. (2009). College students' social networking experiences on Facebook. *Journal of Applied Developmental Psychology, 30*(3), 227–238.
75. Gupta, B. B. (Ed.). (2018). *Computer and cyber security: Principles, algorithm, applications, and perspectives.* New York: CRC Press.
76. Wang, P., Xu, B., Wu, Y., & Zhou, X. (2015). Link prediction in social networks: The state-of-the-art. *Science China Information Sciences, 58*(1), 1–38.
77. Tang, J., Chang, S., Aggarwal, C., & Liu, H. (2015, February). Negative link prediction in social media. In *Proceedings of the eighth ACM international conference on web search and data mining* (pp. 87–96). New York: ACM.

78. Daminelli, S., Thomas, J. M., Durán, C., & Cannistraci, C. V. (2015). Common neighbours and the local-community-paradigm for topological link prediction in bipartite networks. *New Journal of Physics, 17*(11), 113037.
79. Adamic, L. A., & Adar, E. (2003). Friends and neighbors on the web. *Social Networks, 25*(3), 211–230.
80. Watts, D., & Stogatz, S. (1998). Small world. *Nature, 393*, 440–442.
81. Al Hasan, M., Chaoji, V., Salem, S., & Zaki, M. (2006, April). Link prediction using supervised learning. In *SDM06: Workshop on link analysis, counter-terrorism and security.*
82. Liben-Nowell, D., & Kleinberg, J. (2007). The link-prediction problem for social networks. *Journal of the American Society for Information Science and Technology, 58*(7), 1019–1031.
83. Katz, L. (1953). A new status index derived from sociometric analysis. *Psychometrika, 18*(1), 39–43.
84. Wang, C., Satuluri, V., & Parthasarathy, S. (2007, October). Local probabilistic models for link prediction. In *ICDM* (pp. 322–331). New York: IEEE.
85. Kashima, H., & Abe, N. (2006, December). A parameterized probabilistic model of network evolution for supervised link prediction. In *Sixth international conference on data mining, 2006. ICDM'06* (pp. 340–349). New York: IEEE.
86. Taskar, B., Wong, M. F., Abbeel, P., & Koller, D. (2004). Link prediction in relational data. In *Advances in neural information processing systems* (pp. 659–666).
87. Getoor, L., & Diehl, C. P. (2005). Link mining: A survey. *Acm Sigkdd Explorations Newsletter, 7*(2), 3–12.
88. Abawajy, J. H., Ninggal, M. I. H., & Herawan, T. (2016). Privacy preserving social network data publication. *IEEE Communications Surveys and Tutorials, 18*(3), 1974–1997.
89. Veiga, M. H., & Eickhoff, C. (2016). *Privacy leakage through innocent content sharing in online social networks.* arXiv preprint arXiv:1607.02714.
90. Gupta, S., & Gupta, B. B. (2017). Detection, avoidance, and attack pattern mechanisms in modern web application vulnerabilities: Present and future challenges. *International Journal of Cloud Applications and Computing (IJCAC), 7*(3), 1–43.
91. Stergiou, C., Psannis, K. E., Kim, B. G., & Gupta, B. (2018). Secure integration of IoT and cloud computing. *Future Generation Computer Systems, 78*, 964–975.
92. Correa, T., Hinsley, A. W., & De Zuniga, H. G. (2010). Who interacts on the web?: The intersection of users' personality and social media use. *Computers in Human Behavior, 26*(2), 247–253.
93. Jyothi, V., & Kumari, V. V. (2016, August). Privacy preserving in dynamic social networks. In *Proceedings of the international conference on informatics and analytics* (p. 79). New York: ACM.
94. Ahmed, N. M., Chen, L., Wang, Y., Li, B., Li, Y., & Liu, W. (2018). DeepEye: Link prediction in dynamic networks based on non-negative matrix factorization. *Big Data Mining and Analytics, 1*(1), 19–33.
95. Li, T., Zhang, J., Philip, S. Y., Zhang, Y., & Yan, Y. (2018). Deep dynamic network embedding for link prediction. *IEEE Access, 6*, 29219–29230.
96. Narayanan, A., & Shmatikov, V. (2009, May). De-anonymizing social networks. In *30th IEEE symposium on security and privacy, 2009* (pp. 173–187). New York: IEEE.

Chapter 12
SOI FinFET for Computer Networks and Cyber Security Systems

Neeraj Jain and Balwinder Raj

Abstract Today, computer-based systems have become common in everyday life and these systems are used to store leverage information and people are more willing to communicate this sensitive information with the real world. So, computer networks have become the emerging domain for connecting physical devices like home appliances, vehicles, and other embedded electronics, software, actuators, and sensor-based systems, and security of these systems from cyberattacks is essential for secure communication. This results in the easy and safe communication between different entities. So, modern advanced computer systems with efficient integrated transistor technology provide the security and privacy to the computer-based real world. This chapter explores the advanced Silicon-on Insulator Fin Field Effect Transistor (SOI FinFET) technology which is the basic unit of integrated circuit used in every electronic gadget and computer hardware. In this chapter, performance analysis of device-D1 (high-k SOI FinFET structure) is done to implement the efficient computer hardware over a wide temperature range (200–450 K). The attempt is done to find out the ZTC (zero temperature coefficient) biased point of SOI FinFET device to have stable, reliable, and secure systems. The proposed device analysis will provide the hardware design flexibility in the electronic circuits, microprocessors, computer hardware, and thermally stable interfacing components for security applications of information technology.

The potential parameters of device-D1 like A_V (intrinsic gain), g_m (transconductance), V_{EA} (early voltage), g_d (output conductance), I_{off} (off current), I_{on} (on current), I_{on}/I_{off} ratio, C_{gs} (gate-source capacitance), C_{gd} (gate-drain capacitance), f_T (cutoff frequency), and SS (subthreshold slope) are subjected to analysis to evaluate the performance over wide temperature environment. The validation of temperature-based performance of device-D1 gives an opportunity to design numerous analog/RF and digital components in Internet cyber security infrastructure environments.

N. Jain · B. Raj (✉)
Department of Electronics and Communication Engineering, Dr. B. R. Ambedkar National Institute of Technology (NIT), Jalandhar, Punjab, India

© Springer Nature Switzerland AG 2020
B. B. Gupta et al. (eds.), *Handbook of Computer Networks and Cyber Security*,
https://doi.org/10.1007/978-3-030-22277-2_12

Keywords Cyber security · Computer network · SOI FinFET · Temperature · Zero temperature coefficient

1 Introduction

Today, SOI FinFET technology has replaced the conventional transistor technology in almost all nanoelectronic applications. From microprocessor to all system levels, electronic products are integrated with FinFET technology to have advanced functionality and thermal stability over a wide temperature environment. The requirement of low-power, high-performance, and portable consumer products has become the driving force for enhancement in transistor technology. The invention of FinFET technology drastically changes the semiconductor industry life due to 3D (dimensional) quasi-planar nature of geometry [1]. With the development of transistor technology came the advancement and protection from cyberattacks in the computing network [2].

The analog components based on FinFET technology used in sensors (temperature, motion, pressure, shock, proximity, sound, gas, infrared, etc.), amplifiers, signal processors, microcontroller, Internet of Things (IoT), and integrated chips give better technology to computer networks and cyber security applications [3–6]. Therefore, some of the world's top semiconductor chip industries like Cadence and TSMC designed FinFETs at 7-nm technology node for security and high-performance computing platforms, and other industries are further trying to enhance the performance of SOI FinFET by optimizing underlap spacer region at lower technology nodes [7–9].

The SOI high-k FinFET was introduced in the integrated circuits to reduce leakage current which is caused by SCEs and transistor scaling effects [10]. However, there is always a tradeoff among SCEs (short channel effects) and analog/RF performance of FinFET. Further improvement in FinFET structure has been done through SOI layer, high-k spacer, and source/drain engineering techniques [11–13].

According to literature, significant work already proposed with underlap high-k and dual-k spacers to enhance SCEs and analog/RF performances of SOI FinFETs [14, 15]. Similarly, [8, 16] demonstrates the asymmetric dual-k spacers and symmetrical SOI FinFET structures for high-performance application. [17, 18] also elaborated the asymmetrical dual-k spacer SOI FinFET structure for digital SRAM and low-power design applications. Some implementations of high-k SOI FinFETs like oscillators, data converters, RFID (radio frequency identification), mobile phones, and IoT devices make the human life simpler and automated [19–21].

Besides of these, some applications like automobiles, military security, and nuclear sectors require high temperature operated integrated circuits (ICs) and other like medical diagnostic systems and space applications require low temperature based operated equipment. Some industries demand for both high- and low-temperature sustainable ICs for their thermally stable environments [22–24]. FinFETs are the devices which fulfill the requirement of these ICs, and chip industries are now trying to implement the FinFET circuits in all electronic gadgets like computer chips, mobile phones, and sensor-based high-performance security and privacy systems in varying temperature environments [25–31].

2 Reliability and Flexibility Approach of SOI FinFET Towards Security

The performance of computer networks, cyber security operating systems, and a lot of commercial electronic systems varies in different temperature environments due to variation in the performance parameters of its basic transistor parameters. So, having more stability of the mentioned systems against temperature variation, these systems are built by high-k SOI FinFET. The high-k SOI FinFET is more susceptible to temperature variation and provides a more stable analog/RF performance parameter at ZTC biased point. Analog/RF performance parameters are the basic parameters of any electronic system and are evaluated at transistor level. So, this chapter explores and analyzes the performance of high-k SOI FinFET structure and the sensitivity of this structure in temperature range 200–400 K towards analog/RF design is very crucial. So, the investigation is done for ZTC bias point over a wide temperature range through 3D simulations. ZTC bias point is an important parameter which describes the stability of a semiconductor device and shows the negligible variation in current–voltage (I-V) characteristic with temperature. The previous literature work in [32–34] has been done with ZTC bias point for MOSFET stability analysis.

As compared to conventional transistor structure, the high-k SOI FinFET gives better temperature performance at sub-20-nm technology node and enhances the analog and RF performance of complex integrated circuits without increasing the effective chip area. The performance of high-k SOI FinFET is analyzed in terms of I_{on}, I_{off}, I_{on}/I_{off}, SS (subthreshold slope), A_V (intrinsic gain), g_m (transconductance), V_{EA} (early voltage), g_d (output conductance), C_{gs} (gate-source capacitance), C_{gd} (gate-drain capacitance), and f_T (cutoff frequency) performance parameters. Starting with the introduction, Sect. 2 describes reliability and flexibility approach of high-k SOI FinFET. Section 3 gives a detailed design consideration of SOI FinFET structure along with all its structural dimensions, doping concentration, materials involved, and models considered in the 3D simulation process. Section 4 introduces the performance exploration and investigation part of high-k SOI FinFET over a wide temperature range. Section 5 describes the practical aspects of SOI FinFET technology and Sect. 6 presents the conclusion.

3 SOI FinFET Design Consideration and Simulation Setup

The schematic diagram and cross-section view of high-k SOI FinFET structure used for simulation work are shown in Fig. 12.1a, b, respectively. The 3D simulation process is done for 20-nm channel length with high-k spacer region for a given SOI

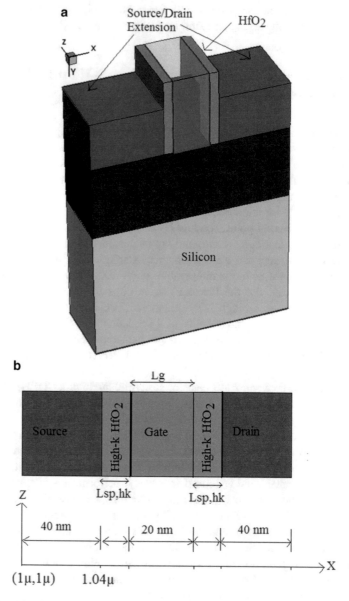

Fig. 12.1 (a) Device-D1 (high-k SOI FinFET) and (b) cross-section of device-D1

FinFET structure, and the source/drain region of this structure is heavily doped as n-type 1×10^{20} cm^{-3} and a lightly doped impurity p-type 1×10^{15} cm^{-3} is used for the channel region. The heavily doped impurities are used for the source/drain region to overcome the mobility degradation which is due to the coulomb charge scattering effect. The $W = (2H_{Fin} + W_{Fin})$ is the total effective width considered

Table 12.1 Dimensional parameters taken for 3D simulation of this work

Parameters	Descriptions (nm)	Device-D1 (nm)
W_{Fin}	Fin width	10
L_g	Gate channel length	20
H_{Fin}	Fin height	26
t_{ox}	Oxide thickness	0.9
BOX	Buried oxide thickness	40
L	Total length of device	110
Lsp,hk	High-k (HfO_2, k = 22) spacer length	5
$W_{s/d}$	Effective width of source/drain	40

for SOI FinFET structure because the effective current component across this width is the sum of all current components along the top surface and sidewalls of Fin at 20-nm node [35, 36]. Metal gate technology is used in SOI FinFET structure because it eliminates the poly gate depletion effect in all semiconductor devices. The length of source/drain is fixed to 40 nm with vertically placed source and drain contacts respectively. Device dimensional parameters of high-k spacer SOI FinFET considered for this 3D simulation work are given in Table 12.1.

Figure 12.1b has cross-section diagram of high-k SOI FinFET in which high-k spacer materials are used for the underlap region both at source and drain side. The use of high-k material in the underlap spacer region increases the I_{on} current or driving capability of the device by optimizing the GIBL (gate-induced barrier lowering) effect with significant reduction of off-state leakage current which results in high signal strength for communication systems. However, the device is compromised with RF performance in terms of cutoff frequency (f_T) due to increased effective gate fringing capacitances which results in slight degradation of circuit-level delay [37].

A lightly doped substrate with concentration of 1×10^{15} cm^{-3} is considered to minimize the random dopant's fluctuation effects in high-k SOI FinFET for detailed performance analysis [38].

The type of spacer and large value of an underlap region in SOI FinFET increase the distributed channel resistance or degradation in I_{on} current, facing the problem of controlling the doping profile. However, these problems are well tackled in [39–41] for MOSFETs. The high-k underlap region at drain side for MOSFETs and degradation in I_{on} can be improved further by introducing the high-k spacer in the underlap region without any significant degradation of output fringing capacitance [42]. So, proper value of high-k spacer region becomes the essential requirement of efficient SOI FinFET design.

The 3D simulation process of high-k SOI FinFET structure is done with the help of Sentaurus TCAD simulator tool [43]. Analog/RF performance of device-D1 is explored for underlap region of 5 nm [44–46] for temperature range of 200–450 K. The metal work function gate is 4.3 eV to have a desired value of threshold voltage. The equivalent oxide thickness (t_{0x}) is taken at a value of 0.9 nm [47–49] with supply voltage V_{DD} of 0.7 V and other simulation environmental parameters are taken according to ITRS (International Technology Roadmap for Semiconductors) report [50]. The simulator validation for FinFET structure is investigated by previously reported results in the literature data of [49]. The models consideration for this reported work are velocity saturation model, field dependent and concentration-dependent mobility that consider the doping models [51]. The Lombardi mobility inversion CVT [52], Auger recombination models with Shockley–Read–Hall (SRH) [52–54], default carrier transport model, and quantum confinement are also considered in the simulation process. The smooth junction meshing and all biasing are done at wide temperature range (200–450 K) to evaluate the performance of SOI FinFET structure.

4 Performance Exploration and Investigation of SOI FinFET

In this section, performance of high-k SOI FinFET (device-D1) in terms of energy (CV^2), intrinsic delay (CV/I), energy-delay product (EDP), power dissipation (PD), subthreshold slope (SS), Q-Factor ($g_{m,max}$/SS), threshold voltage (V_{th}), maximum transconductance (g_{max}), I_{on}, I_{off}, I_{on}/I_{off} ratio, and the analog/RF performance parameters like A_V (intrinsic gain), g_m (transconductance), V_{EA} (early voltage), g_d (output conductance), C_{gs} (gate-source capacitance), C_{gd} (gate-drain capacitance), and f_T (cutoff frequency) are evaluated for various temperature ranges (200–450 K) for the low and high value of drain-source voltages, $V_{DS} = 0.05$ V and $V_{DS} = 0.7$ V, respectively. The temperature variation in the semiconductor device severely affects its electrical characteristic parameters like mobility, subthreshold slope, threshold voltage, leakage current, power dissipation, and intrinsic delay and becomes the major concern in the scaled technology design.

4.1 Electrostatic Performance Evaluation of SOI FinFET

Figure 12.2 shows some electrostatic-dependent performance characteristics of high-k SOI FinFET like SS, I_{on}, I_{off}, and I_{on}/I_{off} ratio with temperature variation at $V_{DS} = 0.05$ V and $V_{DS} = 0.7$ V. It is noticed from Fig. 12.2a that when increasing the temperature, the subthreshold performance of the device degraded due to reduction of I_{on} current both at low and high value of $V_{DS} = 0.05$ V and $V_{DS} = 0.7$ V, respectively. SS is an important parameter which describes the I_{off} leakage current and related with temperature as follows [55].

$$SS\,(mV/decade) \approx 60mV\,\frac{T}{300K} \tag{12.1}$$

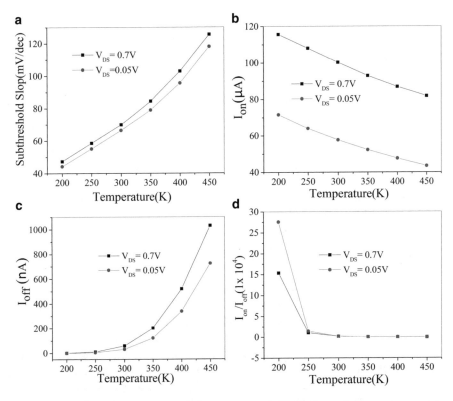

Fig. 12.2 (**a**) SS, (**b**) I_{on} current, (**c**) I_{off} current, and (**d**) I_{on}/I_{off} ratio versus temperature characteristics for high-k SOI FinFET at $V_{DS} = 0.05$ V and $V_{DS} = 0.7$ V

According to Eq. (12.1), at low-temperature range (below 250 K), there is much reduction of SS value that directly reflects the off-state leakage current of the semiconductor device and improvement in I_{off} at lower-temperature range is shown in Fig. 12.2c. So, at low temperature (below 250 K), there is big improvement in I_{on}/I_{off} ratio due to significant reduction of I_{off} current because of the low value of the subthreshold slope (SS) as shown in Fig. 12.2d. High value of I_{on}/I_{off} and low value of I_{off} are desirable for high-speed switching applications.

4.2   Analog Performance Evaluation of SOI FinFET

The I_D (drain current) and g_m (transconductance) against V_{GS} (gate-source) voltage characteristics for various values of temperature range (200–450 K) at $V_{DS} = 0.05$ V and $V_{DS} = 0.7$ V for high-k SOI FinFET are explored in Fig. 12.3a, b, respectively. The drain current as a function of mobility (μ) and threshold voltage (V_{th}) is as follows [56].

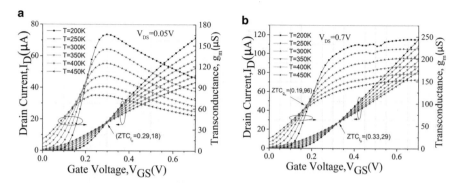

Fig. 12.3 I_D and g_m versus V_{GS} characteristics of high-k SOI FinFET with temperature variation at (**a**) $V_{DS} = 0.05$ V and (**b**) $V_{DS} = 0.7$ V

$$I_D(T) \propto \mu(T)\,[V_{GS} - V_{th}(T)] \qquad (12.2)$$

The mobility term and threshold voltage both are temperature-dependent parameters. The carrier mobility follows the relationship as $\mu(T) = \mu(T_0)(T/T_0)^{-n}$ where the "n" exponent varies at 1.6–2.4 [55]. The threshold voltage of SOI devices follows the inverse temperature characteristics and decreases with increase of temperature [57]. On increasing the temperature, mobility of charge carrier also decreases for SOI FinFET due to lattice scattering effects. So, $\mu(T)$ and $[V_{GS} - V_{th}(T)]$ terms of drain current shown in Eq. (12.2) will show the inverse nature with temperature variation. Upon increasing the temperature, the $\mu(T)$ value decreases which tries to force drain current decrease while the value of $[V_{GS} - V_{th}(T)]$ term increases which tries to force drain current increases. So on increasing the gate bias point, these two effects compensated at a fixed value of the gate to the source voltage (V_{GS}) and the effect of temperature variation at this point can be neglected for evaluating the performance of the SOI device. This fixed value of V_{GS} bias is known as ZTC (zero temperature coefficient) point.

As we observe from the I_D-V_{GS} characteristics shown in Fig. 12.3 that for low and high V_{DS} value below the ZTC_{I_D} point, drain current (I_D) increases with increasing temperature, while above the ZTC_{I_D} point, the nature of drain current becomes opposite. As $V_{GS} < V_{th}$, current mainly flows by diffusion process. So, below the ZTC_{I_D} point, $[V_{GS} - V_{th}(T)]$ becomes the dominating factor as compared to $\mu(T)$ due to more degradation of threshold at high value of temperature. So, drain current increases with increase of temperature value. As $V_{GS} > V_{th}$, the dominating flow of current is by drift process. So, above the ZTC_{I_D} point, $\mu(T)$ decreases with increase of temperature due to more lattice scattering effect and becomes the dominating factor for evaluating the drain current. So, drain current decreases with increase of temperature value.

In Fig. 12.3b, at $V_{DS} = 0.7$ V, we extract the two ZTC points for drain bias and transconductance bias ZTC_{I_D} and ZTC_{g_m}, respectively. Both these ZTC points are important figures of merit for analog circuit design at various temperature values.

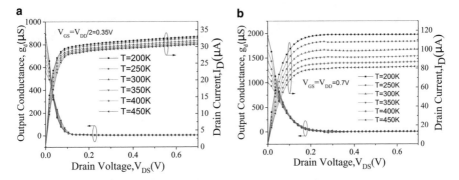

Fig. 12.4 I_D and g_d versus V_{DS} characteristics of high-k SOI FinFET with temperature variation at (**a**) $V_{GS} = 0.35$ V and (**b**) $V_{GS} = 0.7$ V

The ZTC_{I_D} bias point gives the information about constant DC current, while ZTC_{g_m} bias point is used to achieve stable circuit parameters for analog design. Both bias points are affected by the process variation. So, ZTC points are chosen according to the applications. It is noticed from Fig. 12.3b that the extracted value of $ZTC_{g_m} = 0.19V$ and $ZTC_{I_D} = 0.33V$ at $V_{DS} = 0.7$ V. So, below 0.19 V the transconductance (g_m) increases due to degradation of V_{th} upon increasing the temperature, while above 0.19 V the g_m decreases due to reduction of channel mobility by lattice scattering effects upon increasing the temperature.

The output performance characteristics of high-k SOI FinFET, I_D (drain current) and g_d (output conductance) versus V_{DS} (drain to source) voltage at $V_{GS} = 0.35$ V and $V_{GS} = 0.7$ V, are shown in Fig. 12.4a, b, respectively. It is noticed from Fig. 12.4a, b that above the ZTC_{I_D} point, drain current decreases upon increasing the temperature due to the discussed $\mu(T)$ effect with temperature and the opposite nature of the current generated below the ZTC_{I_D}. Low value of g_d is required to improve the intrinsic gain (g_m/g_d) of SOI FinFET device. Further g_d is less sensitive to temperature at $V_{GS} = 0.35$ V compared to $V_{GS} = 0.7$ V at low drain bias point and it can be analyzed from Fig. 12.4.

4.3 RF Performance Evaluation of SOI FinFET

Figure 12.5a, b shows the C_{gs} and C_{gd} capacitances versus V_{GS} characteristics for high-k SOI FinFET at $V_{DS} = 0.05$ V and $V_{DS} = 0.7$ V, respectively. From Fig. 12.5a, it is noticed that at $V_{DS} = 0.05$ V, ZTC for C_{gs} $\left(ZTC_{C_{gs}}\right)$ has a value of 0.192 V and 0.33 V for C_{gd} (ZTC_{Cgd}). Both C_{gs} and C_{gd} increase with increasing temperature below $ZTC_{C_{gs}}$ point, whereas the opposite nature of C_{gs} occurs above the $ZTC_{C_{gs}}$ point. At $V_{DS} = 0.7$ V, there is much variation of C_{gs} and C_{gd} characteristics with V_{GS} over the wide temperature range and no significant ZTC point generated for both C_{gs} and C_{gd} values. This much variation in C_{gs} and C_{gd} characteristics is due

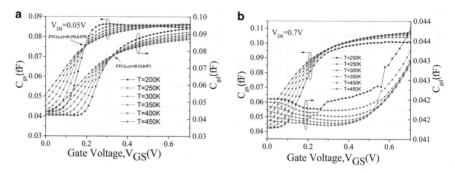

Fig. 12.5 Capacitance C_{gs} and C_{gd} characteristics of high-k SOI FinFET with temperature variation at (**a**) $V_{DS} = 0.05$ V and (**b**) $V_{DS} = 0.7$ V, respectively

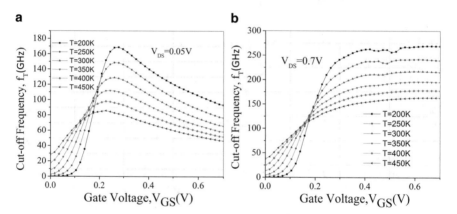

Fig. 12.6 Cutoff frequency (f_T) versus V_{GS} characteristics with temperature variation at (**a**) $V_{DS} = 0.05$ V and (**b**) $V_{DS} = 0.7$ V

to the heating effect generated at drain to source voltage, $V_{DS} = 0.7$ V. So, proper drain bias is important for high-k SOI FinFET to have more thermal stable systems.

Cutoff frequency $f_T = \frac{g_m}{2\pi(C_{gs}+C_{gd})}$ is a desirable parameter for evaluating the RF performance of SOI FinFET. The f_T versus V_{GS} characteristics with temperature variation at $V_{DS} = 0.05$ V and $V_{DS} = 0.7$ V are shown in Fig. 12.6a, b, respectively. It is noticed from Fig. 12.6 that in the weak inversion region, improvement in cutoff frequency (f_T) occurs on increasing the temperature, while the opposite nature of cutoff frequency (f_T) occurs in the strong inversion region. At $V_{DS} = 0.7$ V, above the ZTC point (0.175 V) of f_T, improvement in f_T occurs for low value of temperature due to steep improvement of charge carrier mobility. To have stable RF performance, SOI FinFET structure can be biased at ZTC point which has the value of $V_{GS} = 0.175$ V.

Table 12.2 shows some extracted performance parameters for high-k SOI FinFET for a wide range of temperature at $V_{DS} = 0.7$ V. From the extracted results of Table 12.2, it is noticed that there is improvement in intrinsic delay (CV/I), energy-

Table 12.2 Extracted performance metrics of high-k SOI FinFET for various temperatures at $V_{DS} = 0.7$ V

Temperature (K)	Energy (CV^2) (J) $\times 10^{-17}$	Delay (CV/I) (ps)	EDP (J) $\times 10^{-29}$	PD ($I_{off} * V_{DD}$) (nW)	SS (mV/decade)	I_{on}/I_{off}	V_{th}	$g_{m,max}$ (S) $\times 10^{-4}$	Q-factor ($g_{m,max}/SS$) $\times 10^{-6}$
200	6.80	0.840	5.71	0.528	47.318	1.53×10^5	0.226	2.44	5.16
250	6.89	0.912	6.29	7.05	58.566	1.07×10^4	0.210	2.22	3.79
300	6.91	0.985	6.80	41.0	69.891	1.71×10^3	0.203	2.02	2.89
350	6.90	1.06	7.32	141	84.465	4.60×10^2	0.193	1.83	2.17
400	6.89	1.13	7.81	364	102.959	1.67×10^2	0.181	1.67	1.62
450	6.88	1.20	8.27	721	125.584	7.94×10^1	0.168	1.54	1.23

delay product (EDP), off-state power dissipation (PD = $I_{off}*V_{DD}$), SS value, $g_{m,max}$ (S), I_{on}/I_{off}, and Q-factor ($g_{m,max}/SS$) for low value of temperature. Q-factor and EDP are important figures of merit for circuit applications and these parameters improved due to low value of SS and intrinsic delay at low temperature. The threshold voltage can also be analyzed by extracted results and it decreases with increasing the temperature.

4.4 Extraction of Electrostatic and Analog/RF Performance Parameters

Analog/RF performance parameters like g_m, g_d, A_v (g_m/g_d), V_{EA}, C_{gg}, C_{gs}, C_{gd}, and f_T for high-k SOI FinFET for a wide temperature range (200–450 K) are also evaluated at $V_{DS} = 0.7$ V and shown in Table 12.3. It is noticed from Table 12.3 that there is significant improvement in A_v and much improvement in f_T at lower value of temperature. This improvement is due to increased value of g_m at lower-temperature range.

5 Practical Aspects of SOI FinFET Technology

Today, the world economy directly or indirectly depends on semiconductor industries. In early days, consumer products like mobile phones, cars, watches, and even refrigerators have more power as compared to present products. Now, we are moving fast towards a more connected world, a world of computer networks, Internet of Things and cyber security applications where our consumer appliances are able to communicate each other with more efficient use of energy and other resources with less cost. This is being possible only due to improvement in basic unit (transistor) of chip industries. More numbers of transistors integrated into the chip increase the more functionality of consumer products like mobile phones, tablets, computer peripherals, industrial automation equipment, military, and security applications. More transistors on a single chip can be done with smaller-size transistor with less power consumption, and this can be done by FinFET technology. Chips can perform more and more tasks while becoming smaller at the same time, thus enabling their use in countless devices that improves our lives in multiple ways. So, with this new innovated technology, more advance featured electronic gadgets and industrial automated equipment can be implemented at lower cost in the industries which indirectly reflect the economy of a country.

Table 12.3 Extracted analog/RF performance parameters for high-k SOI FinFET for various temperature values at $V_{DS} = 0.7$ V

Analog/RF extracted performance metrics	Temperature = 200 K	Temperature = 250 K	Temperature = 300 K	Temperature = 350 K	Temperature = 400 K	Temperature = 450 K
g_m (μS)	222	201	179	160	145	132
g_d (μS)	3.25	3.50	3.33	3.17	3.05	2.97
A_V (dB)	36.67	35.18	34.60	34.06	33.51	32.94
V_{EA} (0V)	10.1	9.30	9.56	9.85	10.1	10.3
C_{gg} (aF)	139	141	141	141	141	140
C_{gs} (aF)	96.7	99.0	99.4	99.4	99.3	99.1
C_{gd} (aF)	42.0	41.7	41.6	41.5	41.4	41.4
f_T (GHz)	250	200	202	180	160	149

6 Conclusion

In this chapter, high-k SOI FinFET is explored in terms of performance parameters like intrinsic delay (CV/I), energy-delay product (EDP), off-state power dissipation (PD $= \text{I}_{\text{off}} \cdot \text{V}_{\text{DD}}$), SS value, $\text{g}_{\text{m,max}}$ (S), $\text{I}_{\text{on}}/\text{I}_{\text{off}}$, Q-factor ($\text{g}_{\text{m,max}}/\text{SS}$), and analog/RF parameters like g_{m}, g_{d}, A_{v} ($\text{g}_{\text{m}}/\text{g}_{\text{d}}$), V_{EA}, C_{gg}, C_{gs}, C_{gd}, and f_{T} for a wide temperature range (200–450 K). The analysis is done on the basis of zero temperature coefficient (ZTC) for drain current and transconductance bias point for low- and high-temperature range. Above and below the ZTC point, SOI FinFET has an opposite nature. So, it is concluded that with the help of ZTC point, SOI FinFET can be biased for DC, analog, and RF applications for a wide temperature range and the effect of temperature variation on the performance of device can be minimized at ZTC bias point. So, effective use of FinFET for computer networks, integrated circuits, and cyber security applications improves the performance of chip industries which reflect the economy and business of a country.

References

1. Hisamoto, D., Lee, W. C., Kedzierski, J., Takeuchi, H., Asano, K., Kuo, C., et al. (2000). FinFET-A self-aligned double-gate MOSFET scalable to 20 nm. *IEEE Transactions on Electron Devices, 47*, 2320–2325.
2. Gupta, B., Agrawal, D. P., & Yamaguchi, S. (2016). *Handbook of research on modern cryptographic solutions for computer and cyber security*. Hershey, PA: IGI Global.
3. Ab Malek, M. S. B., Ahmadon, M. A. B., Yamaguchi, S., & Gupta, B. B. (2016). On privacy verification in the IoT service based on PN 2. In *Consumer Electronics 2016 IEEE 5th Global Conference*, IEEE (pp. 1–4).
4. Memos, V. A., Psannis, K. E., Ishibashi, Y., Kim, B.-G., & Gupta, B. B. (2017). An efficient algorithm for media-based surveillance system (EAMSuS) in IoT Smart City framework. *Future Generation Computer Systems, 83*, 619–628.
5. Tewari, A., & Gupta, B. B. (2017). Cryptanalysis of a novel ultra-lightweight mutual authentication protocol for IoT devices using RFID tags. *Journal of Supercomputing, 73*, 1085–1102.
6. Chang, V., Kuo, Y.-H., & Ramachandran, M. (2016). Cloud computing adoption framework: A security framework for business clouds. *Future Generation Computer Systems, 57*, 24–41.
7. Pal, P. K., Kaushik, B. K., & Dasgupta, S. (2013). High-performance and robust SRAM cell based on asymmetric dual-k spacer FinFETs. *IEEE Transactions on Electron Devices, 60*, 3371–3377.
8. Pal, P. K., Kaushik, B. K., & Dasgupta, S. (2014). Investigation of symmetric dual-k spacer trigate FinFETs from delay perspective. *IEEE Transactions on Electron Devices, 61*, 3579–3585.
9. Kumar, S., & Raj, B. (2016). *Simulations and modeling of TFET for low power design* (Handbook of research on computational simulation and modeling in engineering) (pp. 640–667). Hershey, PA: IGI Global.
10. Nowak, E. J., Aller, I., Ludwig, T., Kim, K., Joshi, R. V., Chuang, C.-T., et al. (2004). Turning silicon on its edge [double gate CMOS/FinFET technology]. *IEEE Circuits and Devices Magazine, 20*, 20–31.

11. Kranti, A., & Armstrong, G. A. (2007). Source/drain extension region engineering in FinFETs for low-voltage analog applications. *IEEE Electron Device Letters, 28*, 139–141.
12. Virani, H. G., Adari, R. B. R., & Kottantharayil, A. (2010). Dual-k spacer device architecture for the improvement of performance of silicon n-channel tunnel FETs. *IEEE Transactions on Electron Devices, 57*, 2410–2417.
13. Kumar, S., & Raj, B. (2015). Compact channel potential analytical modeling of DG-TFET based on evanescent-mode approach. *Journal of Computational Electronics, 14*, 820–827.
14. Patil, G. C., & Qureshi, S. (2012). Engineering spacers in dopant-segregated Schottky barrier SOI MOSFET for nanoscale CMOS logic circuits. *Semiconductor Science and Technology, 27*, 045004.
15. Nandi, A., Saxena, A. K., & Dasgupta, S. (2012). Impact of dual-k spacer on analog performance of underlap FinFET. *Microelectronics Journal, 43*, 883–887.
16. Pal, P. K., Kaushik, B. K., & Dasgupta, S. (2015). Asymmetric dual-spacer trigate FinFET device-circuit codesign and its variability analysis. *IEEE Transactions on Electron Devices, 62*, 1105–1112.
17. Jain, N., & Raj, B. (2016). An analog and digital design perspective comprehensive approach on Fin-FET (fin-field effect transistor) technology—A review. *Reviews in Advanced Sciences and Engineering, 5*, 123–137.
18. Goel, A., Gupta, S. K., & Roy, K. (2011). Asymmetric drain spacer extension (ADSE) FinFETs for low-power and robust SRAMs. *IEEE Transactions on Electron Devices, 58*, 296–308.
19. Kumar, S., & Raj, B. (2016). Analysis of I ON and Ambipolar current for dual-material gate-drain overlapped DG-TFET. *Journal of Nanoelectronics and Optoelectronics, 11*, 323–333.
20. Atzori, L., Iera, A., & Morabito, G. (2010). The internet of things: A survey. *Computer Networks, 54*, 2787–2805.
21. Mohanty, S. P. (2015). *Nanoelectronic mixed-signal system design*. New York: McGraw-Hill Education.
22. Jain, A., Sharma, S., & Raj, B. (2016). Design and analysis of high sensitivity photosensor using cylindrical surrounding gate MOSFET for low power sensor applications. *Engineering Science and Technology, 19*, 1864–1870.
23. Kumar, S., & Raj, B. Simulation of nanoscale TFET device structure for low power applications. In *Proceedings of International Conference on Electrical Electronics and Industrial Automation* held on 23rd–24th January 2016. Pattaya, Thailand. ISBN: 9788193137338.
24. Kumar, S., Kumar, S., Karamveer, Kumar, K., & Raj, B. (2016). Analysis of double gate dual material TFET device for low power SRAM cell design. *Quantum Matter, 5*, 762–766.
25. Adat, V., & Gupta, B. B. (2018). Security in internet of things: Issues, challenges, taxonomy, and architecture. *Telecommunication Systems, 67*, 423–441.
26. Stergiou, C., Psannis, K. E., Kim, B.-G., & Gupta, B. (2018). Secure integration of IoT and cloud computing. *Future Generation Computer Systems, 78*, 964–975.
27. Jain, N., & Raj, B. (2018). Capacitance/resistance modeling and analog performance evaluation of 3-D SOI FinFET structure for circuit perspective applications. *World Scientific News, 113*, 194–209.
28. Kumar, S., & Raj, B. (2015). Modeling of DG-tunnel FET for low power VLSI circuit design. In *2015 Eighth International Conference on Contemporary Computing, IEEE* (pp. 455–458).
29. Gupta, B. B. (2018). *Computer and cyber security: Principles, algorithm, applications, and perspectives*. Boca Raton, FL: CRC Press.
30. Ko, H., Mesicek, L., Choi, J., Choi, J., & Hwang, S. (2018). A study on secure contents strategies for applications with DRM on cloud computing. *International Journal of Cloud Applications and Computing, 8*, 143–153.
31. Wang, L., Li, L., Li, J., Li, J., Gupta, B. B., & Liu, X. (2019). Compressive sensing of medical images with confidentially homomorphic aggregations. *IEEE Internet Things Journal, 6*, 1402–1409.
32. Mohapatra, S. K., Pradhan, K. P., & Sahu, P. K. (2015). Temperature dependence inflection point in ultra-thin Si directly on insulator (SDOI) MOSFETs: An influence to key performance metrics. *Superlattices and Microstructures, 78*, 134–143.

33. Singh, S., Raj, B., & Vishvakarma, S. K. (2018). Analytical modeling of split-gate junction-less transistor for a biosensor application. *Sensing and Bio-Sensing Research, 18*, 31–36.
34. Sahu, P. K., Mohapatra, S. K., & Pradhan, K. P. (2015). Zero temperature-coefficient bias point over wide range of temperatures for single- and double-gate UTB-SOI n-MOSFETs with trapped charges. *Materials Science in Semiconductor Processing, 31*, 175–183.
35. Magnone, P., Mercha, A., Subramanian, V., Parvais, P., Collaert, N., Dehan, M., et al. (2009). Matching performance of FinFET devices with fin widths down to 10 nm. *IEEE Electron Device Letters, 30*, 1374.
36. Sharma, S. K., Raj, B., & Khosla, M. (2016). A Gaussian approach for analytical subthreshold current model of cylindrical nanowire FET with quantum mechanical effects. *Microelectronics Journal, 53*, 65–72.
37. Pradhan, K. P., Sahu, P. K., & Mohapatra, S. K. (2015). Analysis of symmetric high-k spacer (SHS) trigate wavy FinFET: A novel device. In *India Conference (INDICON), 2015 Annual IEEE*, IEEE (pp. 1–3).
38. Nowak, E. J. (2002). Maintaining the benefits of CMOS scaling when scaling bogs down. *IBM Journal of Research and Development, 46*, 169–180.
39. Trivedi, V., Fossum, J. G., & Chowdhury, M. M. (2005). Nanoscale FinFETs with gate-source/drain underlap. *IEEE Transactions on Electron Devices, 52*, 56–62.
40. Koley, K., Dutta, A., Syamal, B., Saha, S. K., & Sarkar, C. K. (2013). Subthreshold analog/RF performance enhancement of underlap DG FETs with high-k spacer for low power applications. *IEEE Transactions on Electron Devices, 60*, 63–69.
41. Sachid, A. B., Manoj, C. R., Sharma, D. K., & Rao, V. R. (2008). Gate fringe-induced barrier lowering in underlap FinFET structures and its optimization. *IEEE Electron Device Letters, 29*, 128–130.
42. Goel, A., Gupta, S., Bansal, A., Chiang, M.-H., & Roy, K. (2009). Double-gate MOSFETs with asymmetric drain underlap: A device-circuit co-design and optimization perspective for SRAM. In *2009 Device Res Conf., IEEE* (pp. 57–58).
43. Sentaurus TCAD user's manual. (2009). Synopsys Sentaurus Device (pp. 191–413). Retrieved from http://www.synopsys.com/
44. Mohapatra, S. K., Pradhan, K. P., Singh, D., & Sahu, P. K. (2015). The role of geometry parameters and fin aspect ratio of sub-20nm SOI-FinFET: An analysis towards analog and RF circuit design. *IEEE Transactions on Nanotechnology, 14*, 546–554.
45. Jain, N., & Raj, B. (2017). Impact of underlap spacer region variation on electrostatic and analog performance of symmetrical high-k SOI FinFET at 20 nm channel length. *Journal of Semiconductors, 38*, 122002.
46. Jain, N., & Raj, B. (2018). Analysis and performance exploration of high performance (HfO2) SOI FinFETs over the conventional (Si3 N4) SOI FinFET towards analog/RF design. *Journal of Semiconductors, 39*, 124002.
47. Pradhan, K. P., Mohapatra, S. K., Sahu, P. K., & Behera, D. K. (2014). Impact of high-k gate dielectric on analog and RF performance of nanoscale DG-MOSFET. *Microelectronics Journal, 45*, 144–151.
48. Ho, B., Sun, X., Shin, C., & Liu, T. J. K. (2013). Design optimization of multigate bulk MOSFETs. *IEEE Transactions on Electron Devices, 60*, 28–33.
49. De Andrade, M. G. C., Martino, J. A., Aoulaiche, M., Collaert, N., Simoen, E., & Claeys, C. (2012). Behavior of triple-gate bulk FinFETs with and without DTMOS operation. *Solid State Electronics, 71*, 63–68.
50. ITRS. (2013). International technology roadmap for semiconductors 2013; Executive summary. ITRS [internet], 80. Retrieved from http://www.itrs.net/ITRS
51. Canali, C., Majni, G., Minder, R., & Ottaviani, G. (1975). Electron and hole drift velocity measurements in silicon and their empirical relation to electric field and temperature. *IEEE Transactions on Electron Devices, 22*, 1045–1047.

52. Lombardi, C., Manzini, S., Saporito, A., & Vanzi, M. (1988). A physically based mobility model for numerical simulation of nonplanar devices. *IEEE Transactions on Computer-Aided Design of Integrated Circuits and Systems, 7,* 1164–1171. Retrieved from http://ieeexplore.ieee.org/lpdocs/epic03/wrapper.htm?arnumber=9186.
53. Shockley, W., & Read, W. T. (1952). Statistics of the recombination of holes and electrons. *Physics Review, 87,* 835–842.
54. Hall, R. N. (1952). Electron-hole recombination in germanium. *Physics Review, 87,* 387.
55. Sze, S. M., & Ng, K. K. (2007). *Physics of semiconductor devices* (3rd ed., pp. 164, 682). New York: John Wiley Sons, Inc. Retrieved from http://www.wiley.com/WileyCDA/WileyTitle/productCd-0471143235.html
56. Tan, T. H., & Goel, A. K. (2003). Zero-temperature-coefficient biasing point of a fully-depleted SOI MOSFET. *Microwave and Optical Technology Letters, 37,* 366–370.
57. Groeseneken, G., Colinge, J. P., Maes, H. E., Alderman, J. C., & Holt, S. (1990). Temperature dependence of threshold voltage in thin-film SOI MOSFET's. *IEEE Electron Device Letters, 11,* 329–331.

Chapter 13
Software-Defined Networking: A Novel Approach to Networks

Sumit Badotra and S. N. Panda

Abstract With the rapid change in the network traffic flow, traditional networks need to be innovated. There have been a lot of innovation in devices, application, storage, and computing, but the network remained unrevised. Software-defined networking (SDN) is a new way for the management and operation of networks. With the help of its basic principle of separating the control plane and data plane, it has opened up many ways for revolution in network. A centralized controller in the SDN acts as the vital element. All the information to the data paths or data elements such as network switches/routers is given through southbound application programming interface, and information to the applications such as firewall, load balancer, and business logic is achieved through the northbound application programming interface. The SDN controller is situated in the middle of the architecture in between the network elements and the SDN applications and ultimately makes the flexibility to make many new applications. There are multiple applications which are playing a vital role in networks, but due to the aforementioned challenges in traditional networking, these applications are becoming vendor specific and expensive too. To overcome the situation these applications can be innovated again by using SDN. Although there are many available SDN based applications but in this chapter we are limited to firewall and load balancer. Chapter we will discuss two specific applications as a case of study, which are firewall and load balancer, compare traditional applications and SDN-based applications, and survey and compare related literature.

Keywords Software defined networking · Controller · Control plane · Data plane · Firewall · Load balancer

S. Badotra (✉) · S. N. Panda
Chitkara University Institute of Engineering and Technology, Chitkara University, Rajpura, Punjab, India
e-mail: snpanda@chitkara.edu.in

© Springer Nature Switzerland AG 2020   313
B. B. Gupta et al. (eds.), *Handbook of Computer Networks and Cyber Security*,
https://doi.org/10.1007/978-3-030-22277-2_13

1 Introduction

1.1 Software-Defined Networking

For today's complex networks which are growing rapidly at a very fast pace, programmable networks are the only scopes for meeting up the evolutionary ideas in the field of networking [1]. The needs of today's network are changing dynamically. With the help of separation between network hardware (data plane) and intelligence of the network (control plane), SDN attains the network programmability with the help of separating the network hardware from the intelligence of the network; it permits an easy way of making new applications and also simplifies the working and management of all protocols used in the network [1]. The intelligence of the network (control plane) is also called as SDN controller because it uses the OpenFlow protocol for the purpose of communication, sometimes also known as OpenFlow controller. All the network elements used in the networking are now dumb; no more intelligence resides in them now and used for just simple packet forwarding controlled by southbound interfaces such as ForCES and OpenFlow for the purpose of communication between controller and network devices. From the industry as well as research community, SDN is getting a lot of attention. In spite of the fact that this idea of SDN is new in the field of networking and is an emerging technology, still the rate of its growth is at a very fast pace [1].

In the field of SDN there are still many challenges that need to be addressed. SDN was used for creating and enabling new innovations by transformation and hence making the forwarding plane programmable [2]. The separation of network hardware from the software part of the network devices allows for rapid and easier deployments of new innovations, deploying new applications and simplifying the management of all the protocols needed in handling the network.

Software-defined networking (SDN) is a coming architecture. Architecture of SDN is very powerful, easily manageable, less costly operation and maintenance, and adaptable, hence making it perfectly suitable for the current scenario of networks which are dynamically changing day by day. Programmability in the software part of the network (control plane) is achieved by the SDN [3]. Abstraction of the used infrastructure in the network is also done in SDN. To create all SDN solutions, the OpenFlow protocol is the basis [4].

1.2 Limitations of Other Networking Technologies

The evolution of the Internet has offered a wide variety of distinct services such as online commerce, content delivery IP telephony, and IP-TV. Different types of parameters for such networks are required by these services. Current network is stressed out by this. Accommodation and evolution of new applications and technologies are also very difficult [5].

Traditionally in order to function the network, many network devices such as switches, routers, Network Address Translation (NAT), etc. are used. Manipulation of the traffic is done with these middle boxes which are also called as special device traffic for other purposes as compared to simple packet forwarding. Many complex protocols are contained by these devices [6].

For network administrator it becomes a tedious job to configure these devices individually by using interfaces provided by the different vendors. From vendor to vendor these configuration interfaces are different. Even from one vendor these configuration interfaces sometimes differ [7]. Although there are a number of centralized networking management tools, instead of running on certain centralized networking management tools, most of these devices run at individual level. This causes the slowdown in innovation, increasing the complexity for the management and operation of such networks, and in operating such networks, the capital cost is also increased [4]. Vendor specificity and software bundled with the dedicated hardware and their interfaces is the main problem with traditional networks. Vendors write the lengthy codes and they are very long, and as a result delays are occurring while introducing new features and functions in these networks. Implementing such networks is also very expensive. Control plane and forwarding plane were tightly coupled in traditional networks [3]. In traditional switches between control plane and forwarding plane, there was tight coupling. So, in traditional-type networks, because of this strong coupling between the network hardware (data plane) and intelligence of the network (control plane), introducing the new innovations and functions was very hard. Because of the absence of one common centralized control interface, configuration of traditional type of network devices was also very hard to achieve [8].

Figure 13.1 shows the traditional network architecture. Computer networks are very complex these days. It is even more difficult to manage such networks. Constitution of such computer networks is through various network devices [9].

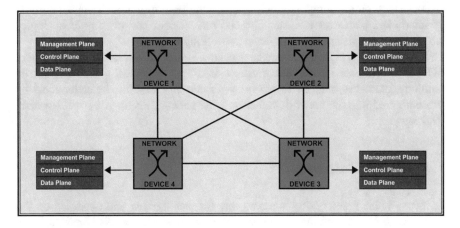

Fig. 13.1 Traditional networks

These network devices can be switches, routers, network address translation (NAT), intrusion detection, intrusion prevention, firewalls, and load balancers. With the help of a complex piece of control code which is further usually proprietary and vendor specific, all of these network devices are run. The network protocols are enabled by the control code that has further taken years for standardization. The configuration to all these network devices individually is done by network administrators by using interfaces provided by the different corresponding vendors. From vendor to vendor these configuration interfaces differ. Even from such one vendor these configuration interfaces sometimes differ [9]. Although there are a number of centralized networking management tools, instead of running on a certain centralized networking management tools, most of these devices run at individual level. Traditional network technology is bottleneck especially for data center administrators. The dynamic nature of requirement of different cloud users has made the job of cloud managers very tedious and time consuming. This causes the slowdown in innovation, increasing complexity for the management for such networks and for operating, and operating such networks capital cost is also increased [10].

1.3 Need of New Architecture

Traditional networks need to be innovated. There have been a lot of innovation in devices, application, storage, and computing, but the network remained unrevised [11]. Traditional networks are comprised of intelligence and data path in themselves only, but as the network is growing in a very fast manner, the number of devices is also increasing, and the structure of the network needs a change. There is a need of such network which can handle the dynamic need and easy manageability of the network [12].

SDN is very much still a research field. In fact, current commercial and let us say "open-source" development driving what is called "software-defined networking" relies heavily on manually configuring orchestration procedures through a number of interlinked platforms to instantiate and run services and overlay technologies which run over existing lowering-level networking technology.

However, SDN, at its truest, predates what we currently see in the market, where SDN in a self-aware sense runs unsupervised and dynamically learns about its topology, resources, and environment. With current SDN this behavior must be preconfigured into the network, rather than the network making its own "learned" decisions.

1.4 SDN Architecture

Software-defined networking is a new way for management and operation on the networks. It has opened up many ways for network revolution. SDN has done the replacement of fixed, complex networks with the dynamic networks which are now programmable. In the field of research, this SDN has redefined the field of both cloud computing and computer networks. This is the biggest revolution that has happened in the field of networking [13].

SDN works on a basic function that separates the network hardware (data plane) from the intelligence of the network (control plane) [14]. With the help of separation (control plane and data plane) in the architecture of SDN it makes the easy development and management of various network devices as well as applications for an administrator. SDN architecture is the future of networking. SDN has made the network programmable. SDN controller or control plane communicates with the network hardware part (data plane) through well-defined application programming interfaces. The most common protocol used for the purpose of communication in SDN is the OpenFlow protocol [15, 16]. The architecture of the SDN is shown in Fig. 13.2.

The OpenFlow paradigm contains three basic parts: pure OpenFlow switch or hybrid switch, SDN controller, and for the purpose of communication a secure connection in between the SDN controller and the OpenFlow switches. An Open-Flow switch maintains a flow table to handle incoming network packets [2]. These OpenFlow switches maintain a flow table to handle particular packets. Each flow table of an OpenFlow switch contains a number of flow table rules in it. Further, each

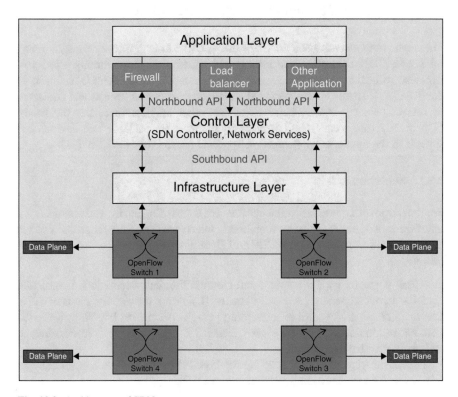

Fig. 13.2 Architecture of SDN

of these flow rules consists of matching fields, actions, and statistics which decides how particularly packets will be handled, and a set of actions are there which help determine the handling of matching packets. In collecting the parameters like how much number of packets is received and the corresponding duration for the traffic flow, these counters are used [17].

OpenFlow switches are used which further separate the forwarding plane of SDN from the control plane. The central plane after separation is called as the control plane, also called SDN controller. It is the main part of SDN architecture. It is the place where the SDN controller resides and hence the whole intelligence of the network [17].

Northbound application programming interface provided the communication channel for the SDN applications to interact with the SDN controller. Northbound application programming interface is used for applications such as creating firewall, load balancer, and NAT applications [4]. The SDN controller interacts with the SDN OpenFlow switches using southbound application programming interface. OpenFlow is the most common protocol used to provide the southbound interfaces [18, 19].

1.5   Components of Software-Defined Networking

The main components used in SDN are southbound application programming interfaces, SDN controller, and northbound application programming interfaces. Efficient utilization of network resources and protocol management is achieved by the SDN [20]. Therefore, the same OpenFlow devices can be used as and converted as firewall, router, or load balancer or any other application as per the needs. SDN architecture is easy, less costly, easily manageable, scalable, and flexible, and support of the dynamically changed networks is provided by the SDN [21].

1.5.1   Southbound API

For the purpose of communication between the forwarding device and controller, an interface is used and is called as southbound interfaces. Two popular protocols used in southbound interfaces are ForCES and OpenFlow and are discussed in detail as follows:

ForCES It stands for Forwarding and Control Element Separation. It basically contains two components, control element (CE) and forwarding element (FE). The main responsibility of the forwarding plane is per packet handling, while the ForCES protocol is used by the control element to instruct the forwarding element on how to forward the packets.

The master/slave model is used by the ForCES protocol. The control element acts as master and forwarding element as slave [22].

OpenFlow The OpenFlow paradigm contains three basic parts: pure OpenFlow switch or hybrid switch, SDN controller, and for the purpose of communication a secure connection in between the SDN controller and the OpenFlow switches. An OpenFlow switch maintains a flow table to handle incoming network packets. These OpenFlow switches maintain a flow table to handle particular packets. Each flow table of an OpenFlow switch contains a number of flow table rules in it. Further, each of these flow rules consists of matching fields, actions, and statistics which decides how particularly packets will handle a set of actions which helps to determine the handling of matching packets. In collecting the parameters like how much number of packets is received and the corresponding duration for the traffic flow, these counters are used [1].

1.5.2 Northbound API

A northbound interface is an interface that provides a communication between the applications and the controller. Another API called a southbound interface is useful in providing a communication channel between the switches or data paths and the SDN controller [23]. By using the northbound interface, anyone can develop network applications like hub, switch, firewall, or load balancer. Northbound applications are placed at the top of the controller. Southbound interfaces such as OpenFlow instruct the switch to perform the functions that are specified in the flow table. With the help of these two APIs (northbound interface and southbound interface), allowance of the network SDN controller communication can be achieved with every network component inside the network [3].

1.5.3 West- and Eastbound API

Westbound Application Programming Interface (API): This interface acts as a channel for providing the interface between SDN management plane and totally different network domains. Network state info and routing choices for every controller are changed through this. Bury domain routing protocols like BGP square measure are used [24].

Eastbound Application Programming Interface (API): Communication is completed from management plane to non-SDN domains. Depending upon the technology utilized in non-SDN domains, its implementation is proportional [24].

2 Background

2.1 History of Programmable Networks

Deploying networks that are easily programmable allows network management innovation and reduces the barriers for deploying new applications and services. Here in the following section, discussion on history of programmable networks is provided.

Active Networks Active networks can be considered as a reasonably good clean slate idea theoretically. In active networks, nodes can perform custom operations on the messages. The active network node receives a code from the user and executes that code when processing their packets. Conventional networks are not easily programmable. It represented a totally new idea to manage the network by using a programming interface that supports the making of many operations. By using active networks, we can easily deploy and experiment with new applications. The main disadvantage of active networks is lack of security [25, 26].

4D Projects 4D consists of infrastructure, discovery plane, decision plane, and dissemination plane. According to the instruction given by the decision plane, the data path moves the packets. The discovery plane collects the information from new elements in the network and sends that information to the decision element so that these elements can be added to the routes. The numbers of decisions are taken by the decision plane that influence the behavior of the networks such as security and load balancer. The dissemination plane gives information to all the elements in the network. But the 4D project suffers from scalability, security, stability, and response time [27, 28].

NETCONF A number of ways are there for the purpose of installation, modification, and deletion of the configuration of network devices used in the networking, and they all are provided by the NETCONF. NETCONF is the best way to reconfigure the devices. The NETCONF allows the native functionality of the device to be mirrored. It reduces implementation costs and allows quick access to new features. NETCONF allows changes in the device [29]. It was regarded as a new way for network management that will handle shortcomings in SNMP. NETCONF-based network cannot be considered as totally programmable because new functionality needs to be created at both manager level and network devices. Its primary function is to aid in automated configuration. It does not enable exact positioning of many brand-new services and applications for networks.

Ethane The Ethane was the immediate predecessor to OpenFlow. Ethane used centralized controller for managing policy and security in the network. The two components of Ethane were SDN controller and switch which use the ethane technology. Ethane is considered as the basis for future work that would lead to software-defined networking [30].

2.2 OpenFlow Protocol

SDN architecture consists of two different application programming interfaces (API): southbound and northbound interfaces. OpenFlow is the most popular southbound API that allows a secure connection between the data plane and control plane.

Working on OpenFlow Protocol In traditional devices, the packet forwarding plane and the control plane are tightly coupled into the same hardware equipment. But in OpenFlow switch these two planes, data planes and control plane, are separated [31]. The data plane component resides on the OpenFlow switch itself, but the control plane is moved to a centralized place called SDN controller. The OpenFlow protocol is used for communication between the controller and switch. OpenFlow protocol defines number of messages, such as modify forwarding table, get stats, send, and send packet-out. Each OpenFlow switch maintains a flow as shown in the figure.

Each flow table contains a number of flow rules. Each flow rule consists of matching fields, actions, and statistics which decide how packets belonging to flow will be handled. When packets arrive at the switch, it is matched against flow table rules. If match is found, appropriate activity is performed that is defined in the flow table of a switch. If a match of the packet is not found, corresponding action is taken as specified in the flow table by the developers. The actions could be dropping that particular packet or sending the network packet to the SDN controller using a secure communication channel [32].

OpenFlow Message Structure The specifications of the OpenFlow make the applications to change the flow table of OpenFlow switches. The OpenFlow paradigm contains three main components: a pure OpenFlow switch or mixed switch, SDN controller, and a safe connection for communication between controller and OpenFlow switch. Switches maintain a flow table to handle particular packets. Each flow table of an OpenFlow switch contains a number of flow table rules in it. Further, each of these flow rules consists of matching fields, actions, and statistics which decide how particular packets will be handled [32].

Each flow entry consists of:

Matching of Incoming Packet Is Achieved Through the Rules These match fields constitute the ingress port, destination Mac address, and destination IP address as shown in Table 13.1 (Fig. 13.3).

Table 13.1 Header fields

Source MAC address
Destination MAC address
Ether type
VLAN priority
VLAN id
Ingress port
Source IP address
Destination IP address
IP TOS bits
IP protocol
Source port
Destination port

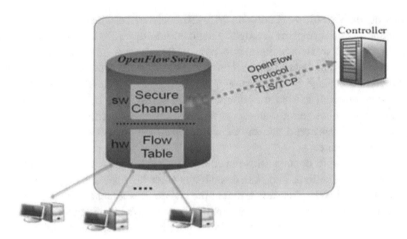

Fig. 13.3 OpenFlow components

Table 13.2 Actions

Action	Description
Forward	Packet is forwarded to a specified port number
Enqueue	Packet forwarding is done thorough queue
Drop	Dropping the packet
Flood	Packet forwarding is done to all ports excluding from the incoming port
Controller	Send packet to controller using secure connection
Modify field	Headers are rewritten
Local	Packet forwarding is done to a local switch using a networking stack

A set of instructions determines how to handle matching packets. Actions can be forward and drop. There are basically three main actions that all OpenFlow switches need to support: forwarding the flow packets out to a specific port so that these network packets can achieve routing within the network; encapsulating and forwarding a network packet to the SDN controller, typically used when there are no matches in the flow table, so the controller can decide on an action; and dropping the flow packets. The OpenFlow protocol also allows for the modification of various header fields of the network such as addresses of source port and destination port [31] (Table 13.2).

Statistics is used to collect parameters like how many numbers of packets are received and duration of traffic flow. Whenever any network packet containing the information comes at the switch, it matches its flow table entries in its flow table [32]. In any case, if the entry of the packet is matched with the existing entries (maintained by the OpenFlow switch), then the appropriate action is taken such as forward, drop. On the other hand, if no match is found, as per the specifications given, corresponding actions are taken. After that the controller comes into action and performs the action such as updating, deleting, or adding flow entries. This process can happen in two ways: reactively or proactively [33].

There are basically two types of OpenFlow switches:

Native They are completely dependent upon the controller instructions for forwarding decisions of packets.

OpenFlow Enabled They have some of their intelligence which resides in them. These OpenFlow switches support the OpenFlow protocol along with traditional switch features.

2.3 Available Versions of OpenFlow Protocol

OpenFlow 1.2 OpenFlow 1.2 was released in December 2011. It has come to include the advanced support for protocol particularly for IPv6. OpenFlow version 1.2 can now match IPv6 source as well as destination addresses, protocol number, flow label number, various ICMPv6 fields, and traffic class. In additional matching capabilities now, vendors have new possibilities to offer or make available OpenFlow by them for support [7].

OpenFlow 1.3 OpenFlow 1.3 introduces new features for monitoring and operations and management (OAM). In a flow table entry, a meter is attached directly and the rate of packets assigned to it is measured by its meter identifier. If a given rate is exceeded with the help of a meter band instead of dropping all those packets from the network, it may optionally choose to recolor all those packets by modifying their differentiated services (DS) field [3]. Thus on OpenFlow 1.3 and later specifications, simple or complex QoS frameworks can be implemented [8].

OpenFlow 1.4 This was released in October 2013. The support for the OpenFlow Extensible Match (OXM) was enhanced by ONF. To the protocol TLV structures for ports, tables, and queues are added. Previously defined hard-coded parts from earlier versions and specifications are now replaced by the newly defined TLV structures. Now it is possible to have the configuration of optical ports. In addition to it, now the control messages in a single message bundle to all the switches can be sent by the controller. There is a minor improvement in group tables and flow eviction on full tables, and a feature of monitoring the traffic flow is also included [7].

3 SDN Controllers

3.1 Introduction

Controller in the SDN acts as the vital element. All the information to the data paths or data elements such as network switches/routers is given through southbound application programming interface and information to the applications such as firewall, load balancer, and business logic is achieved through the northbound application programming interface. The SDN controller is situated in the middle of the architecture in between the network elements and the SDN applications [34]. Whole communication between SDN applications and the network devices will pass through the SDN controller. The configuration of the various network devices is achieved by the SDN controller using the most common protocol called as Open-Flow protocol and hence for the flow of network traffic adopts the optimal network path [35].

Controller Scalability Development of new applications and modifications in the behavior of existing application are much easier with centralized controller. But more requests and events are forwarded to the controller when the size of the network increases, and at particular point, the single SDN controller fails to handle all the requests. The NOX controller is a centralized controller that may be sufficient for a small network, but it could not be sufficient for a large network like data center. We can solve this problem by physically distributing the controller elements while maintaining the global view of the network [36]. Hyper Flow [37] and Kandoo [37] are examples of distributed control planes.

Reactive and Proactive First, in the reactive approach, it states that, whenever a new network traffic packet enters into the OpenFlow switch, the switch performs the searching operation and finds outs any matching field to the corresponding packet. If there is no flow match, the switch immediately sends that particular packet to the SDN controller. A rule is created by the controller in the flow table. It makes better use of the flow table but each flow requires extra time to set up a flow. The downside is that if the connection between controller and switch is lost, the switch has limited functionality [38]. In the proactive approach, SDN controllers prepopulate network traffic rules added into the flow table of an OpenFlow switch, and thus this packet-in event does not happen. Advantages are: no extra time is required to set up a flow, and if connection is lost it does not affect the switches.

3.2   Working of SDN Controller

The SDN controller is a program that is used for manipulation of the network flow tables maintained by the network switches, using the most common protocol called as OpenFlow protocol. The secure connection is used to connect the SDN controller to all OpenFlow switches. Using this secure channel, the controller handles the different switches, send packets to the switches, and receive packets from the switches. Packet forwarding is achieved by these OpenFlow switches and these packets are sent according to the flow rules specified in their corresponding flow tables (Fig. 13.4).

3.3   Various Available SDN Controllers

An SDN controller is also defined as a network operating system (NOS). It allows the abstraction and hence decreasing the complexity of the network is underlying. The main idea was to distinguish between the operating system and network operating system. There is already a significant number of controllers available to choose from: NOX [39], POX [12], Floodlight [40], Ryu [41], OpenDaylight [42], etc. We have decided to use Ryu controller that is written in python language as shown in Fig. 13.2. The information about various controllers, the languages in which they are written, and a brief description are listed in Table 13.3.

Fig. 13.4 SDN controllers

Table 13.3 SDN controllers

Name	Language	Description
Ovs	C	A reference controller. Act as a learning switch
NOX	C++	The first OpenFlow controller
POX	Python	Open-source SDN controller
Beacon	Java	A cross-platform, modular OpenFlow controller
Maestro	Java	Network operating system
Trema	Ruby, C	Used for developing OpenFlow-based controllers
Floodlight	Java	OpenFlow controller that works with OpenFlow switches
FlowVisor	C	Special purpose controller

4 Working of Software-Defined Networking with Mininet

4.1 Introduction

To perform SDN experiment we need some tools. There are a number of options available like emulator and simulator that we can use. Mininet is a system for developing and testing large networks in a single system with limited resources. Mininet is a combination of many applications which further includes many of the advantages of test beds, emulators, and simulators. With the help of this network emulator, we can perform an experiment with large-scale networks having hundreds of hosts and switches. It is cheaper and easily available; configuration can be quickly changed, especially when the performance is being compared with many of the test beds. It establishes easy connection with real-world networks, when compared with the simulator EstiNet [43]. It can accurately simulate thousands of OpenFlow switches, and ns-3 [44] can simulate OpenFlow switches which are configurable and support MPLS extension.

4.2 Working of Mininet

This network emulator permits you to generate a topology of network which constitutes the SDN controllers, OpenFlow switches, hosts which are virtual, and also various links in between them. It provides a very simple, inexpensive, robust networking test beds for developing and testing OpenFlow-based applications. Mininet is also used for creating complex network topologies. We can also create custom topologies according to our needs. It also qualifies a simple Python interface for the purpose of creating a network and its various investigation processes. Creation, modification, and testing SDN-based networks are very easy using Mininet emulator tool [45].

Many supporting features of testbed and simulators are also used in Mininet. When the Mininet emulator tool is compared with real costly hardware testbeds available such as VINI, FIRE, GENI, and Emulab, it is quick, cost-free, and always available to reconfigure. Real, unmodified code is run by Mininet when it is compared with the simulators such as EstiNet and ns-3. Connection with real-world networks is easily achieved. Mininet takes only seconds to boot as compared to full system virtualization which takes a long time to boot. Mininet is used for creating large networks consisting of a large number of switches and hosts; these large networks can also be implemented to real-world networks. It is very easy to install and provides more bandwidth to the network devices attached [46].

4.3 Mininet Commands

- $ sudo mn –h: This is used for displaying a help message describing Mininet's startup option where $ proceeds Linux command that should be typed in root shell prompt.
- $ sudo mn: The default topology is the minimal topology which is a very simple topology that contains OpenFlow switch and 2 hosts. It also creates links between switch and two hosts. This shows the following results:

  ***creating controller
  ***adding controller
  ***adding hosts:
  h1 h2
  ***adding switches:
  s1
  ***adding links:
  (h1,s1) (h2,s1)
  ***configuring hosts
  h1 h2
  ***starting controller
  c0
  ***starting controller
  s1
  ***starting CLI Mininet>

- Mininet>net : This command shows the following results:

  mininet> net
  h1 h1-eth0:s1-eth1 h2 h2-eth0:s1-eth2
  s1 lo: s1-eth1:h1-eth0 s1-eth2:h2-eth0

- Mininet>dump

  This will show switches and hosts listed.
  mininet> dump
  <Host h1: h1-eth0:10.0.0.1 pid=8683>
  <Host h2: h2-eth0:10.0.0.2 pid=8684>

- mininet> nodes

  available nodes are:
  c0 h1 h2 s1
  mininet> pingall
  *** Ping: testing ping reachability
  h1 -> h2 h2 -> h1
  *** Results: 0% dropped (2/2 received)

4.4 Different Topologies Used in Mininet

Mininet can support a number of topologies in which we can also create custom topology, some by default created topologies in Mininet such as single, reversed, minimal, linear, and tree which are discussed below.

Minimal 2 hosts and 1 OpenFlow virtual switch are created in this topology. A link is created in between two hosts and switch which is virtual.

Single This topology contains 1 OpenFlow switch and n number of hosts, and a virtual link is also created between switch and n number of hosts.

Reversed In this topology connection order is reversed as compared to single topology.

Linear In this topology there is a creation of link between the "n" number of OpenFlow switches and "n" number of hosts. A link between host and each switch and among the switches is also created.

Tree "n" levels like tree are contained in this topology and 2 hosts are connected.

4.5 Uses of Mininet

- It is very fast. Creating and starting a basic network takes few seconds.
- You can build custom network topologies. The topology could contain a single switch or thousands of switches representing data center.
- You can run real source code. Any code that can be executed on Linux can also be run on Mininet.
- Mininet can be run on desktop, server, virtual machine (VM), laptop, and in the cloud.
- It is much uncomplicated to use. Mininet experiments can be run and performed by writing simple python scripts.

4.6 Limitations of Mininet

- It forces some resource constraints when run on a single system.
- Applications or an OpenFlow switch that does not support Linux is not able to run in Mininet [46].

  Open vSwitch, Indigo, Pantou, Pica8, and Softswitch are some of the mainly used software switches. Hardware switches which are available are of two types: OpenFlow enabled and native switches. Most SDN controllers such as NOX, POX, Beacon, OpenDaylight, and Maestro support OpenFlow version 1.0 (Table 13.4 and Fig.13.5).

Table 13.4 Hardware and Software Switches

Software switch	Language	Description	Version used
OVS	C/Python	Its source is open and OpenFlow stack which is used as VSwitch in a virtual environment and has been ported to many hardware platforms	V1.0
Indigo	C	Implementation of OpenFlow version that runs on switches used in networking	V1.0
Panton	C	Converts commercial wireless access point or router to OpenFlow-enabled switches	V1.0
Pica8	C	Hardware-independent and Linux-based OpenFlow stack that supports 1.2/1.3 protocols	V1.3
Softswitch	C/C++	It uses the version 1.3 (OpenFlow switch) software—switch implementations	V1.3

Hardware switches		
Company	Version	Model
HP	V1.0	6600,6200zl
Brocade	V1.0	CES 2000 series
Juniper	V1.0	Junos MX series

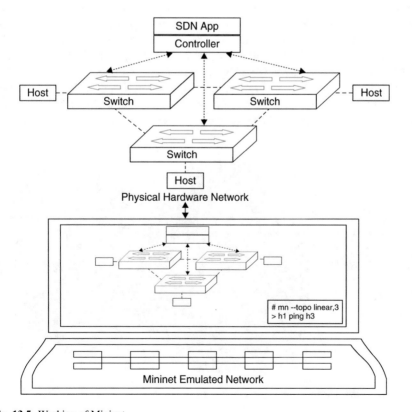

Fig. 13.5 Working of Mininet

5 Comparison of Traditional Applications vs Software-Defined Applications

5.1 Introduction

To block the uncertified access of any intruder either to the network or from the network, a (public network/private network/protected network) security system is used called as firewall. Firewall can be implemented as software firewall and hardware firewall While leaving or entering the network, all packets of data first go through this application where monitoring and examination of each and every packet is done and then of data and drop that packet which does not match with flow rules of firewall. Allowance or rejection of a specific type of information is done by firewall. This information may be contained in an application, a service, or a device. Working of a firewall is as shown in Fig. 13.6.

5.2 Traditional Firewall Introduction

Between a private network and public network, a traditional firewall is placed. Inspections of all outgoing and incoming packets to prevent unauthorized access and attacks are achieved by firewall. Internal users in the network are considered to be trusted users according to the traditional model of security. Internal traffic from internal users is not examined and inspected by firewall. Inspection of such packets of information is not done by firewall. This supposition about trusting internal users is not valid as insiders can too perform attacks and steal useful information. The traditional firewall is placed in between a public network and a private network. The

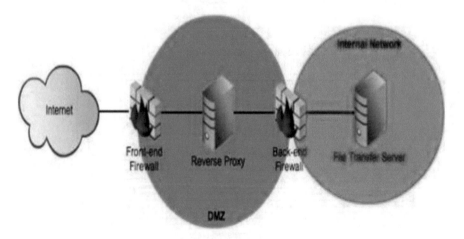

Fig. 13.6 Firewall architecture

traditional firewall uses the allotted network hardware which is very expensive and very complicated to configure. No alternate features or applications can be added in these types of traditional firewalls by the network administrators because of their vendor locked in specificity nature.

Two approaches are there which are used by firewalls in providing security mechanism. In the first approach, all traffic will be denied unless it fulfills certain rules added in the firewall. The second approach follows a firewall allowance of all traffic unless it fulfills certain rules. A firewall filters traffic or allows all traffic depending on which network layer it Operates. A firewall may operate on different layers of the TCP/IP model of the network. The basic operations used by firewalls are given in Fig. 13.7; these operations are followed by firewall while working to secure the network from unauthorized access.

5.3 SDN Firewall Introduction

To overcome the disadvantages of previously developed firewalls, like if they are vendor locked in and use of dedicated hardware, an SDN firewall application can be easily turned into a simple OpenFlow device into a multiple-layer strong firewall. A dedicated network hardware dependency is eliminated and flexibility in configuring the code of firewall is an added feature. With the help of programming conversion, this OpenFlow device into an intelligent firewall has become an easy task. The code of SDN-based firewall can be reconfigured easily. The flow rules are contained inside the flow table, and according to these rules, a custom topology acts like a firewall that restricts the traffic.

5.4 Why SDN Firewall?

In traditional firewall basically, there are two players:

- A Network administrator and another one who has created that firewall. The network administrator (who is actually using the firewall) cannot do modification extension in case of previous firewalls which includes the vendor-specificity firewall which is based on dedicated network hardware used in the networking.
- As per the instructions for configuration is provided by the corresponding vendor of firewall, a network administrator can only go for those configurations in the firewall.
- While on the other hand in SDN, one can create the firewall which is an open-source code. The NA can modify/extend the firewall code. Hardware dependency is removed. Extension in the code can be achieved by just configuring the firewall existing code.

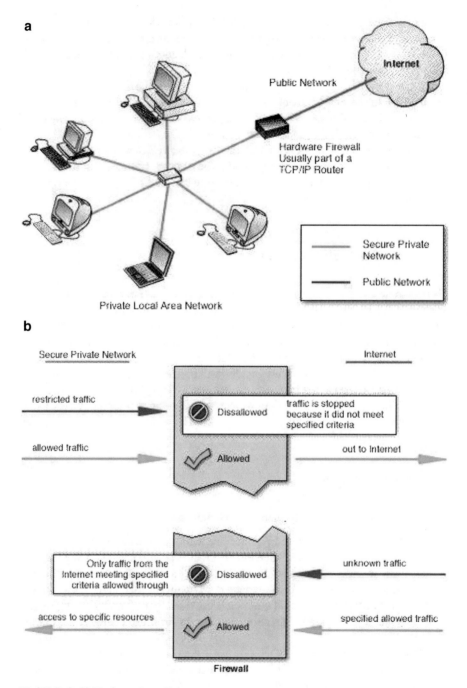

Fig. 13.7 (a, b) Hardware firewall

5.5 Introduction to Load Balancer

With the rapid growth of web applications in the late 1990s, load balancing was used to divide the network load among identical web servers in order to minimize the service time to users and maximize the performance of servers. At that time, techniques such as those based on DNS and adaptive TTL were exploited by enterprise administrators. Today, commercial load balancers are often in use, including in the production network at Arizona State University (ASU). But sometimes there are applications that are not well suited to how the commercial products balance the load. One such application is Rsyslog. This application is in charge of processing syslog packets and writing them into files. It receives its input from Palo Alto firewalls. This firewall generates a wide variety of log messages to alert the network administrator of an existing issue in or a threat to the entire campus network. As can be imagined, the amount and the speed of data that this application generates are huge. The current load balancing solution at ASU is used to spread the load among several Rsyslog servers. The problem is that the existing load balancer does not divide the load equally among the servers because it uses the source IP address to divide the load. Also, it cannot forward the load to one Rsyslog server at a time because there are multiple Palo Alto firewalls and each one of them is mapped to a Rsyslog server.

5.5.1 Need of SDN in Traditional Load Balancer

SDN has the potential to simplify network management and enable innovation in and evolution of computer networks [47]. It is based on the principle of separating the control and data planes. The OpenFlow specification describes the information exchange between the two planes [47]. In this architecture, an OpenFlow switch contains a flow table consisting of flow entries. A flow entry is made up of fields on which incoming packets are matched and actions to be applied upon a match. If there is no match, the packet is forwarded to a controller, which runs a program to handle the packet, and decides whether to insert, delete, or update flow entries in the flow table for subsequent packets matching the same fields. As well, statistics are collected on packets; this information may be used by the controller to make decisions. This allows us to build innovative applications which match with our needs and update them as circumstances change. One such application is load balancing.

Load balancing in enterprise networks is one potential application of OpenFlow. As Wang et al. discuss, they use a binary tree to represent the space of all possible IP addresses [10]. The ith level in the binary tree corresponds to the ith most significant bits of the IP address. The nodes in a subtree correspond to a prefix match on the path from the root to that subtree. Under the assumption that each IP address supplies equal load on the network, a tree representation is effective since at each level the load is distributed equally between the two subtrees. This solution allows fine granularity of load distribution [10].

6 Challenges to SDN

Addressing Dynamic Period of Time Modification The power to alter the provisioning of recent converged infrastructures in minutes and impact multiple devices at an equivalent time could be a game changer, particularly considering that today's relative static environments consider manual configurations. With SDN, new reckon, network, and storage devices and options area unit are straightaway accessible to be used. Once solely running daily checks on what's new in your setting, these dynamic period of time changes mean important gaps in visibility. What's required could be a performance observation answer designed with open arthropod genus. In this fashion you'll integrate directly with SDN systems, listen on the event bus and appearance for brand new devices, services, or changes, and so straightaway modify the infrastructure observation inventory to make sure performance visibility [48].

Accommodating Fast On-Demand Growth The inevitable transaction in demand for brand-new cypher, network, and storage in software-defined infrastructure causes a risk to watching platforms. These solutions should be ready to add watching capability to accommodate the ascension of the infrastructure. If they cannot add further capability on demand, they will quickly become oversubscribed, making performance visibility gaps. Not like bequest infrastructure within the SDN world, we will have multiple overly high topologies running on top of the physical network. Whenever a replacement service starts, it deploys the required virtual infrastructure, and therefore the quantity of monitored parts will grow quickly with accumulated demand—outstripping ancient capability management. The answer is to deploy performance watching at intervals of each physical and virtual appliance. Once further performance management capability is required, spinning up further virtual appliances on demand allows performance [49].

Integrating Service Context Having service context is an expectation today. As a result, performance monitoring needs to be able to listen in context of a particular customer or tenant of the network. Ultimately, users should be able to not only ask about the health and performance of individual devices or links on the network, but also, "How is customer A, HD video service: New York to London, performing?"

This also extends to service topology, meaning the controllers and performance monitoring solutions share the knowledge of physical and logical connectivity of the devices—both physical and virtual—that make up a service, both in real-time and for historical context [48, 49].

7 Application Areas of SDN

OpenFlow switches are general-purpose PC until and unless we insert flow entries in flow tables. These merchant silicon boxes can be converted into a simple hub. Intelligent learning switch, router, and load balancer use a combination of flow entries. The major application areas of SDN are as follows [50, 51]:

SDN Role in the Data Center The technology which is rapidly used in data centers is virtualization. It has not only made a provisioning of server automatic but also much uncomplicated. But the difficulty occurs in network management and technologies used for storing the data. This often leads to the problem of server bottleneck. So, to overcome all the problems software-defined data center (SDDC) will play a key role in moving this infrastructure (used in networking) to more secure and robust condition. To bring each component at equal level, software-defined data center (SDDC) has this basic idea. In creating SDDC, SDN plays an increasing role.

SDN Usage in the LAN and WAN IN LAN and WAN beyond data centers, SDN plays a very vital role. It has become very difficult to manage WAN with the rapid adoption of SAAS but SDN is the solution for it and hence can solve the problem. With the automated provisioning of network resources in SDN, it addresses the important issues in WAN. In LAN, OpenFlow protocol and SDN have radically brought new changes and ultimately allow management in unified wireless and wired, and more security is provided and improves BYOD control.

Role of SDN in Providing Security Enhancement of network security and in accessing the control of network SDN is used. Facilities like providing a higher level of visibility, agility as a result of which there is an increase in the amount of more unevenness in analyzing network traffic packets, network traffic monitoring, and engineering used in handling network traffic are all provided by the SDN.

8 Conclusion

In today's scenario as the network is growing day by day, it further makes the demand of new emerging technology called as SDN. There are heaps of innovation in devices, application, storage, and computing; however, the network remained unaltered. Software package outlined networking could be a new approach for management and operation on the networks. It's displayed in some ways for revolution in network. SDN has done the replacement of fastened, advanced networks with the dynamic networks that are currently programmable and dynamic in nature. Within the field of analysis, this SDN has redefined the sphere of each cloud computing and PC networks. This can be the most important revolution that went on within the field of networking. SDN could be a new approach for planning, building, and operating the networks. It opens the network up for innovation and transformation. The replacement of static, inflexible, and sophisticated networks with networks that are agile, climbable, and innovative is achieved by the SDN. In step with trade folks and analysis students, SDN goes to redefine networking and the cloud world. The fundamental plan behind SDN practicality is to separate network hardware half and therefore the intelligence of the network, making the network programmable. A key entity in SDN design is the controller. A controller within the SDN acts because of an important part. All information or data parts like network switches/routers are given through the southbound application programming interface, and knowledge to the applications like firewall, load balancer, and business logic is achieved through the northbound application programming interface. The SDN controller is settled within the middle of the design in between the network parts, and therefore the SDN applications ultimately make the flexibleness to create several new applications. There is a unit of multiple applications that take an important role in networks; however, thanks to the aforesaid challenges in ancient networking, these applications have become merchant specific and dearly won too. To beat the case, these applications will be innovated once more by victimization SDN. The simple concept that SDN is following is the separation of control plane and data plane; the control plane is the intelligence of the network that instructs the networking devices to forward the network traffic from one place to another, while on the other hand data plane constitutes the dumb networking devices which are used only to carry the traffic as instructed by the centralized SDN controller. With the help of SDN approach in networks the limitations of traditional networks are also vanished. Now, the networks can be managed and programmed and are flexible and more agile. In this chapter we have discussed about SDN, need of SDN in traditional networks, various advantages, and history of programmable networks.

As a point of study, in this chapter comparison between traditional firewall and load balancer with SDN-based firewall and load balancer is presented. However, there are already many firewalls available in the market but they are very expensive. Modification and extendibility of the firewall codes which are vendor specific is the main disadvantage of traditional firewall. Firewall application is used to protect OpenFlow networks where network traffic changes dynamically. The main disadvantage with the traditional firewall is that the network administrator is not able to do the alteration in the firewall code. Modification is done only on the basis of specifications given by the vendor. But by using a programmable SDN firewall application which runs over an OpenFlow-based SDN controller (e.g., Ryu controller), most of the SDN firewall functionalities can be achieved, and hardware dependency is removed and becomes less expensive. Alteration in the codes is only achieved by the specifications provided by the corresponding vendors of the firewall. Using SDN, in this multiple-layer firewall which is an open-source code, the network administrator can modify/extend the firewall code as per the needs. Firewall which uses the OpenFlow protocol also known as programmable firewall attains the programmability by the basic principle of separating the hardware of firewall also called as data plane in SDN and the control software. This SDN-based firewall can be implemented in such a way that it can work on both multiple layers of the TCP/IP model. Another such application is load balancer that is employed as a result of networks that ought to handle a great amount of traffic and serve thousands of shoppers. It's terribly tough for one server to handle such immense load. The answer is to use multiple servers with load balancer acting as a face. The shoppers can send the requests to the load balancer. The load balancer can forward the shopper requests to totally different servers relying upon load equalization strategy. Load balancer use dedicated hardware. That hardware is expensive and inflexible. Currently available load balancers contain few algorithms that can be used. Network administrators cannot create their own algorithms since traditional load balancers are vendor locked and non-programmable. On the other hand, SDN load balancers are programmable and allow you to design and implement your own load balancing strategy. Other advantages of SDN load balancer is we do not need dedicated hardware. The dumb silicon device can be converted to a powerful load balancer by using SDN controllers.

References

1. Xia, W., Wen, Y., Foh, C. H., Niyato, D., & Xie, H. (2015). A survey on software-defined networking. *IEEE Communications Surveys and Tutorials, 17*(1), 27–51.
2. Lantz, B., Heller, B., & McKeown, N. (2010, October). A network in a laptop: Rapid prototyping for software-defined networks. In *Proceedings of the 9th ACM SIGCOMM Workshop on Hot Topics in Networks* (p. 19). New York: ACM.
3. Feamster, N., Rexford, J., & Zegura, E. (2014). The road to SDN: An intellectual history of programmable networks. *ACM SIGCOMM Computer Communication Review, 44*(2), 87–98.
4. Nunes, B. A. A., Mendonca, M., Nguyen, X. N., Obraczka, K., & Turletti, T. (2014). A survey of software-defined networking: Past, present, and future of programmable networks. *IEEE Communications Surveys and Tutorials, 16*(3), 1617–1634.
5. Shenker, S., Casado, M., Koponen, T., & McKeown, N. (2011). The future of networking, and the past of protocols. *Open Networking Summit, 20*, 1–30.
6. McKeown, N., Anderson, T., Balakrishnan, H., Parulkar, G., Peterson, L., Rexford, J., et al. (2008). OpenFlow: Enabling innovation in campus networks. *ACM SIGCOMM Computer Communication Review, 38*(2), 69–74.
7. Fernandez, M. P. (2013, March). Comparing OpenFlow controller paradigms scalability: Reactive and proactive. In *2013 IEEE 27th International Conference on Advanced Information Networking and Applications (AINA)* (pp. 1009–1016). Piscataway: IEEE.
8. Lara, A., Kolasani, A., & Ramamurthy, B. (2014). Network innovation using OpenFlow: A survey. *IEEE Communications Surveys and Tutorials, 16*(1), 493–512.
9. Suzuki, K., Sonoda, K., Tomizawa, N., Yakuwa, Y., Uchida, T., Higuchi, Y., et al. (2014). A survey on OpenFlow technologies. *IEICE Transactions on Communications, 97*(2), 375–386.
10. Wang, R., Butnariu, D., & Rexford, J. (2011). OpenFlow-based server load balancing gone wild. *Hot-ICE, 11*, 12–12.
11. Koerner, M., & Kao, O. (2012, June). Multiple service load-balancing with OpenFlow. In *2012 IEEE 13th International Conference on High Performance Switching and Routing (HPSR)* (pp. 210–214). Piscataway: IEEE.
12. Kaur, S., Singh, J., & Ghumman, N. S. (2014, February). Network programmability using POX controller. In *ICCCS International Conference on Communication, Computing and Systems* (Vol. 138). Piscataway: IEEE.
13. Uppal, H., & Brandon, D. (2010). *OpenFlow based load balancing.* University of Washington. CSE561: Networking. Project Report. Dordrecht: Springer.
14. Shang, Z., Chen, W., Ma, Q., & Wu, B. (2013, November). Design and implementation of server cluster dynamic load balancing based on OpenFlow. In *2013 International Joint Conference on Awareness Science and Technology and Ubi-Media Computing (iCAST-UMEDIA)* (pp. 691–697). Piscataway: IEEE.

15. Ghaffarinejad, A., & Syrotiuk, V. R. (2014, March). Load balancing in a campus network using software defined networking. In *2014 Third GENI Research and Educational Experiment Workshop (GREE)* (pp. 75–76). Piscataway: IEEE.

16. Kaur, K., Singh, J., & Ghumman, N. S. (2014, February). Mininet as software defined networking testing platform. In *International Conference on Communication, Computing and Systems (ICCCS)* (pp. 139–142).

17. Hu, H., Han, W., Ahn, G. J., & Zhao, Z. (2014, August). FLOWGUARD: Building robust firewalls for software-defined networks. In *Proceedings of the Third Workshop on Hot Topics in Software Defined Networking* (pp. 97–102). New York: ACM.

18. Kreutz, D., Ramos, F. M., Verissimo, P. E., Rothenberg, C. E., Azodolmolky, S., & Uhlig, S. (2015). Software-defined networking: A comprehensive survey. *Proceedings of the IEEE, 103*(1), 14–76.

19. Jammal, M., Singh, T., Shami, A., Asal, R., & Li, Y. (2014). Software defined networking: State of the art and research challenges. *Computer Networks, 72*, 74–98.

20. Monaco, M., Michel, O., & Keller, E. (2013, November). Applying operating system principles to SDN controller design. In *Proceedings of the Twelfth ACM Workshop on Hot Topics in Networks* (p. 2). New York: ACM.

21. Bianco, A., Birke, R., Giraudo, L., & Palacin, M. (2010, May). OpenFlow switching: Data plane performance. In *2010 IEEE International Conference on Communications (ICC)* (pp. 1–5). Piscataway: IEEE.

22. Badotra, S., & Singh, J. (2017). A review paper on software defined networking. *International Journal of Advanced Research in Computer Science, 8*(3), 17.

23. Wickboldt, J. A., De Jesus, W. P., Isolani, P. H., Both, C. B., Rochol, J., & Granville, L. Z. (2015). Software-defined networking: Management requirements and challenges. *IEEE Communications Magazine, 53*(1), 278–285.

24. Jarschel, M., Zinner, T., Hoßfeld, T., Tran-Gia, P., & Kellerer, W. (2014). Interfaces, attributes, and use cases: A compass for SDN. *IEEE Communications Magazine, 52*(6), 210–217.

25. Tennenhouse, D. L., Smith, J. M., Sincoskie, W. D., Wetherall, D. J., & Minden, G. J. (1997). A survey of active network research. *IEE Communications Magazine, 35*(1), 80–86.

26. Tennenhouse, D. L., & Wetherall, D. J. (2002). Towards an active network architecture. In *2002 Proceedings DARPA Active Networks Conference and Exposition* (pp. 2–15). Piscataway: IEEE.

27. Caesar, M., Caldwell, D., Feamster, N., Rexford, J., Shaikh, A., & van der Merwe, J. (2005). Design and implementation of a routing control platform. In *Proceedings of the 2nd Conference on Symposium on Networked Systems Design and Implementation* (Vol. 2, pp. 15–28). Berkeley: USENIX Association.

28. Greenberg, A., Hjalmtysson, G., Maltz, D. A., Myers, A., Rexford, J., Xie, G., Yan, H., Zhan, J., & Zhang, H. (2005). A clean slate 4d approach to network control and management. *ACM SIGCOMM Computer Communication Review, 35*(5), 41–54.

29. Enns, R., Bjorklund, M., & Schoenwaelder, J. (2011). *NETCONF configuration protocol.* Fremont: IETF.

30. Casado, M., Freedman, M. J., Pettit, J., Luo, J., McKeown, N., & Shenker, S. (2007). Ethane: Taking control of the enterprise. In *ACM SIGCOMM computer communication review* (Vol. 37, pp. 1–12). New York: ACM.

31. McKeown, N. (2009). Software-defined networking. *INFOCOM Keynote Talk, 17*(2), 30–32.

32. Kloti, R., Kotronis, V., & Smith, P. (2013, October). OpenFlow: A security analysis. In *2013 21st IEEE International Conference on Network Protocols (ICNP)* (pp. 1–6). Piscataway: IEEE.

33. Zhao, D., Zhu, M., & Xu, M. (2014, July). SDWLAN: A flexible architecture of enterprise WLAN for client-unaware fast AP handoff. In *2014 International Conference on Computing, Communication and Networking Technologies (ICCCNT)* (pp. 1–6). Piscataway: IEEE.

34. Dixit, A., Hao, F., Mukherjee, S., Lakshman, T. V., & Kompella, R. (2013, August). Towards an elastic distributed SDN controller. *ACM SIGCOMM Computer Communication Review, 43*(4), 7–12.

35. Shalimov, A., Zuikov, D., Zimarina, D., Pashkov, V., & Smeliansky, R. (2013). Advanced study of SDN/OpenFlow controllers. In *Proceedings of the 9th Central and Eastern European Software Engineering Conference in Russia* (p. 1). New York: ACM.
36. Tootoonchian, A., & Ganjali, Y. (2010). Hyperflow: A distributed control plane for openflow. In *Proceedings of the 2010 Internet Network Management Conference on Research on Enterprise Networking* (p. 3). Berkeley: USENIX Association.
37. Hassas Yeganeh, S., & Ganjali, Y. (2012). Kandoo: A framework for efficient and scalable offloading of control applications. In *Proceedings of the First Workshop on Hot Topics in Software Defined Networks* (pp. 19–24). New York: ACM.
38. Fernandez, M. P. (2013b). Comparing OpenFlow controller paradigms scalability: Reactive and proactive. In *2013 IEEE 27th International Conference on Advanced Information Networking and Applications (AINA)* (pp. 1009–1016). Piscataway: IEEE.
39. Gude, N., Koponen, T., Pettit, J., Pfaff, B., Casado, M., McKeown, N., & Shenker, S. (2008). NOX: Towards an operating system for networks. *ACM SIGCOMM Computer Communication Review, 38*(3), 105–110.
40. Floodlight at http://www.projectfloodlight.org/floodlight/
41. Ryu at https://osrg.github.io/ryu/
42. Badotra, S., & Singh, J. (2017). Open daylight as a controller for software defined networking. *International Journal of Advanced Research in Computer Science, 8*(5), 34.
43. Wang, S. Y., Chou, C. L., & Yang, C. M. (2013). EstiNet OpenFlow network simulator and emulator. *IEEE Communications Magazine, 51*(9), 110–117.
44. Afanasyev, A., Moiseenko, I., & Zhang, L. (2012). *SDN SIM: NDN simulator for NS-3*. Los Angeles: University of California, Tech. Rep, 4.
45. De Oliveira, R. L. S., Schweitzer, C. M., Shinoda, A. A., & Prete, L. R. (2014, June). Using mininet for emulation and prototyping software-defined networks. In *2014 IEEE Colombian Conference on Communications and Computing (COLCOM)* (pp. 1–6). Piscataway: IEEE.
46. Fontes, R. R., Afzal, S., Brito, S. H., Santos, M. A., & Rothenberg, C. E. (2015, November). Mininet-WIFI: Emulating software-defined wireless networks. In *2015 11th International Conference on Network and Service Management (CNSM)* (pp. 384–389). Piscataway: IEEE.
47. Open Networking Foundation. (2018). *OpenFlow switch specifications.* https://www.opennetworking.org/sdn-resources/onf-specifications/openflow
48. Sezer, S., Scott-Hayward, S., Chouhan, P. K., Fraser, B., Lake, D., Finnegan, J., et al. (2013). Are we ready for SDN? Implementation challenges for software-defined networks. *IEEE Communications Magazine, 51*(7), 36–43.
49. Yan, Q., Yu, F. R., Gong, Q., & Li, J. (2016). Software-defined networking (SDN) and distributed denial of service (DDoS) attacks in cloud computing environments: A survey, some research issues, and challenges. *IEEE Communications Surveys and Tutorials, 18*(1), 602–622.
50. Feamster, N., Rexford, J., & Zegura, E. (2013). The road to SDN. *Queue, 11*(12), 20.
51. Scott-Hayward, S., O'Callaghan, G., & Sezer, S. (2013, November). SDN security: A survey. In *2013 EEE SDN for Future Networks and Services (SDN4FNS)* (pp. 1–7). Piscataway: IEEE.

Chapter 14
Software-Defined Network (SDN) Data Plane Security: Issues, Solutions, and Future Directions

Arash Shaghaghi, Mohamed Ali Kaafar, Rajkumar Buyya, and Sanjay Jha

Abstract Software-defined network (SDN) radically changes the network architecture by decoupling the network logic from the underlying forwarding devices. This architectural change rejuvenates the network-layer granting centralized management and reprogrammability of the networks. From a security perspective, SDN separates security concerns into control and data plane, and this architectural recomposition brings up exciting opportunities and challenges. The overall perception is that SDN capabilities will ultimately result in improved security. However, in its raw form, SDN could potentially make networks more vulnerable to attacks and harder to protect. In this paper, we provide a comprehensive review of SDN security domain while focusing on its data plane, which is one of the least explored but most critical aspects in securing this technology. We review the most recent enhancements in SDNs, identify the main vulnerabilities of SDNs, and provide a novel attack taxonomy for SDNs. Thereafter, we provide a comprehensive analysis of challenges involved in protecting SDN data plane and control plane and provide an in-depth look into available solutions with respect to the identified threats and identify their limitations. To highlight the importance of securing the SDN platform,

A. Shaghaghi (✉)
The University of New South Wales (UNSW Sydney), Sydney, NSW, Australia

The University of Melbourne, Parkville, VIC, Australia
e-mail: a.shaghaghi@unsw.edu.au

M. A. Kaafar
CSIRO Data61, Canberra, ACT, Australia

Macquarie University, Sydney, NSW, Australia
e-mail: dali.kaafar@data61.csiro.au

R. Buyya
The University of Melbourne, Parkville, VIC, Australia
e-mail: rbuyya@unimelb.edu.au

S. Jha
The University of New South Wales (UNSW Sydney), Sydney, NSW, Australia
e-mail: sanjay.jha@unsw.edu.au

© Springer Nature Switzerland AG 2020
B. B. Gupta et al. (eds.), *Handbook of Computer Networks and Cyber Security*,
https://doi.org/10.1007/978-3-030-22277-2_14

we also review the numerous security services built on top of this technology. We conclude the paper by offering future research directions.

Keywords Software-defined network (SDN) · Data plane · SDN security · Data plane security

1 Introduction

Traditional IP network devices are purpose-built and application-specific with integrated circuits and chips designed to achieve high throughputs. This "hardware-centric" network model requires network operators to configure each device separately through low-level vendor-specific commands. Hence, in heterogeneous networks, network configuration is tedious, and automatic reconfiguration and response are virtually impossible. Moreover, the data and control plane bundling reduces flexibility, hinders innovation, and slows down the evolution of networking infrastructure. In fact, as shown by recent studies, in the long run, traditional networks are incapable of coping with the increasing demand and continuous expansion in the number of devices and applications brought through advances in Cloud Computing, Internet-of-Things (IoT), and Cyber-Physical Systems [47, 68, 81, 90].

Software-defined network (SDN) is a new network paradigm that decouples the control from data plane in networking devices. This architectural recomposition places the "brain" of the network on a specialized central controller, enabling centralized management and global view of the network. The data plane is composed of "dummy" devices, forwarding packets based on rules specified remotely. These rules may be specified by the application running atop of the controller and triggered according to packet-level extracted information.

SDN's layered architecture follows the "separation-of-concerns" principle [18], which is a fundamental security engineering requirement and is missing in today's Internet architecture. Hence, in theory, SDN lays a solid ground for improving the security of networks, and tremendous efforts have already been made to leverage the capabilities of SDN to enhance security for both network providers and users. The SDN security literature is split into research aiming to secure software-defined network platform itself, solutions attempting to enhance existing network security services (e.g., firewalls), and proposals on creating new security services. In this paper, we take the first direction and our focus is on the security threats associated with data plane of SDNs.

The roadmap ahead is as follows: we start by presenting an overview of SDN architecture and its capabilities, where we also review the latest advances and trends in SDN data plane research. Thereafter, in Sect. 3, we present a security analysis of SDNs followed by a novel taxonomy of attacks against them in Sect. 4. Section 5 presents an overview of SDN security literature, which is then followed by a detailed review of security challenges and available solutions to secure the SDN data plane and control plane in Sects. 6 and 7, respectively. In Sect. 8, we present a categorization and review of the most recent SDN-based security solutions. We devise a set of future research directions in Sect. 9 and conclude the paper in Sect. 10.

2 Software-Defined Network (SDN)

Traditionally, computer networks have been divided into three planes of functionality, namely the management plane, the control plane, and the data plane. In a nutshell, network policies are devised at the management plane and passed to control plane for enforcement and executed at the data plane. Hence, the data plane refers to the network forwarding devices that forward the packets, the control plane represents the protocols used to configure the forwarding tables, and management plane includes the set of software services used to configure the control functionality (e.g., SNMP, NETCONF, etc.). Traditional IP networks follow a "hardware-centric" model where the control and data plane are developed and embedded in the same device by the device vendor. The resulting outcome has been quite effective in terms of network performance and resilience. Nevertheless, this architecture is very resistant to change, slow in adopting innovations, and quite complicated to set up, troubleshoot, and manage.

Software-defined network (SDN) has emerged with its largest special envoy being the loose coupling between the control and data plane. Hence, SDN moves away from a vertical integration of network components to a horizontal one and adds distinctive separate functioning layers for policy definition, enforcement, and implementation. We present an overview of SDN architecture and its main components in Sect. 2.1. Here, we are mostly concerned with SDN's data plane, and in Sect. 2.2 we include a more detailed revision of this layer, where we also discuss the recent trends with stateful data planes.

2.1 Architecture and Main Components

Software-defined Network framework facilitates networks programmability and grants the ability to manage, amend, and control the network behavior dynamically via open interfaces. It enables centralized control of data plane forwarding devices independent of technology used to connect the devices while maintaining live and centralized network-wide view of all the data path elements. SDN enables long-awaited features such as on-demand resource allocation, self-service provisioning, and truly virtualized networking through its intelligent orchestration and provisioning system. The high-level reference SDN architecture promoted by the Open Networking Foundation (ONF) is shown in Fig. 14.1. The architecture is composed of three main layers, namely the data plane, control plane, and application plane. Each layer has its own specific functions and the components that are always present in an SDN deployment include the southbound API, SDN controller (or network

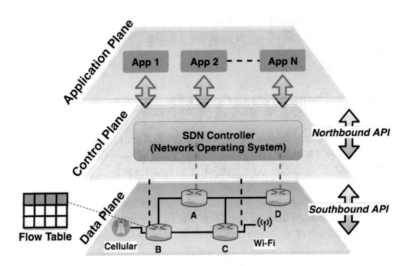

Fig. 14.1 SDN architecture

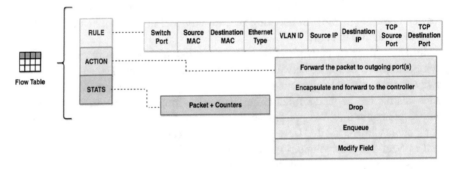

Fig. 14.2 Flow table of an OpenFlow-enabled forwarding device

operating system), northbound API, and network applications. In the following, we present a succinct overview for each of these components through a bottom-up approach. Understanding the core properties of these components play a role when designing solutions to secure the data plane of SDNs.

2.1.1 Data Plane

The data plane is composed of networking equipment such as switches and routers specialized in packet forwarding. However, unlike traditional networks, these are just simple forwarding elements with no embedded intelligence to take autonomous decisions. These devices communicate through standard OpenFlow interfaces with the controller—which ensures configuration and communication compatibility and interoperability among different devices. As shown in Fig. 14.2, an OpenFlow-enabled forwarding device has a forwarding table, which constitutes three parts: (1) rule matching; (2) actions to be executed for matching packets; and (3) counters for matching packet statistics. The rule matching fields include Switch Port, Source MAC, Destination MAC, Ethernet Type, VLAN ID, Source IP, Destination IP, TCP Source Port, TCP Destination Port. A flow rule may be defined as a combination of these fields. The most common actions include: (1) forward the packet to outgoing port(s); (2) encapsulate and forward to controller; (3) drop; (4) enqueue; and (5) modify field. The most common case is to install a default rule to instruct the switch to forward the packet to the controller for a decision.

SDN has enabled the introduction of software switches, which are deemed to be promising solutions for data centers and virtualized network infrastructures [101, 149]. These have been very attractive to data center networks with the most dominant examples being Open vSwitch [102], Switch Light [17], Pica8 [109], Pantou [161], and XorPlus [126].

2.1.2   Southbound API

The southbound API is one of the most critical components of an SDN system, which bridges in-between forwarding devices and the control plane. It enables the controller to control the network behavior by managing flow entries of all underlying switches. The southbound API provides a common interface for the upper layers enabling the controller to use different southbound APIs (e.g., OpenFlow, POF [139], OpFlex [135], and OpenState [16]) and protocol plug-ins to manage existing or new physical or virtual devices (e.g., SNMP, BGP, and NETCONF). These are essential both for backward compatibility and heterogeneity. Therefore, on the data plane, a mix of physical devices, virtual devices (e.g., Open vSwitch, vRouter [133]), and a variety of device interfaces (e.g., OpenFlow, OVSDB [106], OF-Config (OpenFlow Configuration and Management Protocol), NETCONF, and SNMP) can coexist.

Currently, OpenFlow is the most accepted standard for southbound standard. The OpenFlow protocol provides three main types of information to the network operating system (NOS): (1) Packet-In message: whenever a forwarding device does not have a matching flow rule for a packet or there is an explicit rule for a packet specifying this; (2) Event-based messages: each time a link or port change is triggered; and (3) Flow statistics generated by the forwarding devices.

2.1.3   Controller or the Network Operating System

The "brain" of the network, which generates network configurations based on the policies defined by the network operator. It abstracts the lower-level details and makes them available to the application plane through essential services (e.g., network topology, state, device discovery, etc.) and common APIs to developers.

A diverse set of controllers are available each with their own design and architecture. One of the most prevailing factors in differentiating available controllers is as to whether the controller has a centralized or distributed architecture. With a centralized controller, a single entity is responsible to manage all of the forwarding devices. This architecture has two main limitations: (1) single point of failure threat and (2) scaling limitations. The best known centralized controllers that can achieve the level of throughput required by data center networks include NOX-MT [145], Maestro [92], Beacon [37], Ryu NOS [94], and Floodlight [17]. These NOSs employ multi-threaded designs deploying parallel multicore architectures and achieve processing capabilities such as to deal with up to 12 million flows per second [37]. Distributed controllers such as ONOS [15], Onix [65], HyperFlow [144], PANE [40], and DISCO [107] provide much better scaling support and are much more resilient to logical and physical failures by spreading independent controllers across different network segments. Distributed controllers are equipped with east and westbound APIs allowing controllers to exchange data, algorithms for consistency models, and monitoring information. SDNi [162] is an attempt to standardize the east and westbound interface.

A typical SDN controller provides a set of core functionalities including topology manager, stat manager, device manager, notification manager, shortest path forwarding, and security mechanisms. The first four components are self-descriptive in a networked environment and the security mechanisms provide services such as isolation and security enforcement between services and application (e.g., rules generation by low priority services do not overwrite rules created by high priority applications).

2.1.4 Northbound API

Along with the southbound API, the northbound API is one of the key abstractions of SDN. The northbound API is a software ecosystem providing a common interface for developing applications. It abstracts the low-level instruction sets used by southbound interfaces to program the forwarding devices. This application tier often includes global automation and data management applications, as well as providing basic network functions such as data path computation, routing, and security.

Controllers offer quite a broad variety of northbound APIs such as ad hoc and RESTful APIs, multilevel programming interfaces, and file systems. However, as of today, there is no standardization for the northbound API yet. In fact, existing controllers such as Floodlight, Onix, and OpenDaylight [83] implement their own northbound API with different specifications and programming languages. Moreover, SDN programming languages such as Frenetic [43], Nettle [150], NetCore [87], Procera [151], and Pyretic [88] also have their own specification and customization of the northbound API. The lack of a standard API is likely due to the varied nature of applications that can be installed at the application plane (see Sect. 2.1.5), which can include network virtualization schemes, managing cloud computing systems, security application, and other disparate or specialized functions. As an example, work on open northbound APIs is being done for specific vertical applications. OpenStack has developed the Quantum API, which is a vendor-agnostic API for defining logical networks and related network-based services for cloud-based systems. Several vendors have developed plug-ins for Quantum, which has helped it to become the default networking API for OpenStack, one of the largest open source cloud management platforms [63].

2.1.5 Application Plane

The network applications dictate the behavior of the forwarding devices. The applications submit high-level policies to the control plane, which is responsible for enforcing these policies by implementing them as flow rules on network forwarding devices. An SDN application plane consists of one or more network applications (e.g., security, visualization, etc.) that interact with controller(s) to utilize abstract view of the network for their internal decision making processes. An SDN application installed atop of the controller is comprised of an SDN App Logic and A-CPI Driver (used to communicate with the controller) [57].

Many different SDN applications have already been developed, and the current focus is to have an app store support for SDNs [68], where customers can dynamically download and install network apps. Most SDN applications fall into one of the following five categories: traffic engineering, mobility and wireless, measurement and monitoring, security and dependability, and data center networking. There is a category of applications that leverage the SDN capabilities to build solutions that did not exist before. For instance, Policy Enforcement as a Service (PEPS) [123] provides inter-layer and inter-domain access control enabling a "defense-in-depth" protection model, where unsuccessful access requests are dropped before engaging the data provider server. This could potentially be used to build the next generation of firewalls and improve perimeter security against Denial of Service (DoS) attacks. Alternatively, solutions such as AWESoME [146] leverage SDN capabilities to introduce the novel concept of "per service" management allow administrators to manage all traffic of a service comprehensively, i.e., steering all traffic generated by the user accessing a given service, and not just the traffic related to first-party servers. SDN application plane is an ongoing area of research and surveying papers in this area is not within the scope of this paper (see [68] for a detailed survey). Nevertheless, we provide a categorization and a succinct survey of security services that leverage SDN in Sect. 8.

2.2 Latest Advances in SDN Data Plane

The original OpenFlow standard was too restrictive and various proposals have emerged adding extra flexibility to it. They can be categorized in three different directions including (a) adding multiple flow tables to forwarding devices, (b) improving the match rule flexibility, and (c) stateful data planes. While our focus is on the third-case (i.e., stateful SDN data planes), we include a summary of research in the first two cases as well.

2.2.1 Adding Multiple Flow Tables to Forwarding Devices

The single flow table model proposed in original OpenFlow would cause two main problems. First, it would force the developer to deploy OpenFlow rules that combine the Cartesian product of all the required matches. Other than complexity, the exponential increase in the deployed rules would be an extremely inefficient use of flow table capacity, which is typically implemented through the constrained TCAM memory of forwarding devices. Secondly, many applications would benefit from two-stage processing model [99], where packets are first tagged based on some packet characteristics and then matched with rules.

An OpenFlow forwarding devices supporting multiple flow tables (introduced since OpenFlow 1.0 [49]) consist of flow tables composed as a pipeline, where a path through a sequence of flow tables defines how packets should be handled. Proposals have emerged developing advanced hardware solutions enabling a more flexible multiple matching. For instance, reconfigurable match table (RMT) [19] permits flexible mapping, an arbitrary number of match tables having different widths and depths and even supporting matching rules using parameters computers from previous matches.

2.2.2 Improving the Match Rule Flexibility

The first OpenFlow version just matched 12 fields. However, greater matching flexibility was recognized as different network applications at different layers may require the capability to associate actions with different types of matches. Hence, the recent OpenFlow versions add support for more than 40 fields including finer-grained fields such as TCP flags.

2.2.3 Stateful Data Planes

In order to reduce the switch-to-controller signaling and the associated latency issues, recently there have been proposals to introduce some very specific stateful operations into the data plane forwarding devices. One of the most motivational use-cases for this emerging trend is link failure. With the original OpenFlow specification, when a data link fails, the forwarding device should seek instructions from the controller to set up rectifying rules (e.g., forward all traffic to a backup link). In this case, there is a small interval of time when all packets will be lost, and in large networks, the resulting number can be quite large. For instance, for a 100 ms response time from the controller on a 10 Gbps link, it would cause the loss

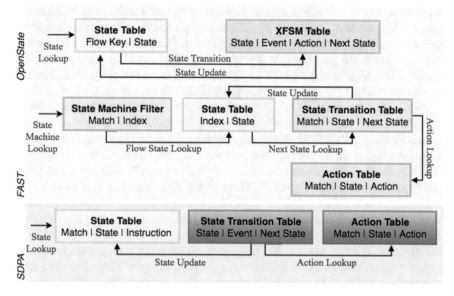

Fig. 14.3 Tables used in OpenState, FAST, and SDPA architectures. Each table is represented as a rectangle containing the table name and the corresponding table columns separated with "|"

of up to 30 million packets. Recent versions of OpenFlow specification introduce optional support for some stateful capabilities—e.g., fast failover, select group type, and synchronized tables for learning type functionalities are available in OpenFlow version 1.5.1 [100].

Up to this date, three proposals have emerged for stateful SDN data planes, which go beyond the basic features introduced with OpenFlow and that require architectural upgrades to be deployed. In general, stateful SDN data plane proposals have three basic principles in common: (1) retaining state information of the flows within forwarding devices, (2) support programmable packet-level state transition in forwarding devices, (3) granting the forwarding devices the permission to update forwarding states based on flow's local state information without requiring them to seek instructions from the SDN controller.

OpenState [16] introduces programmability to SDN's data plane through a special case of eXtended Finite State Machines (XSFM). Each forwarding device keeps two separate tables: state table and XFSM table (see Fig. 14.3). The former stores the current state of the flow based on packets received, which are relevant to that flow. The latter, however, is used to define the rules based on packet's received information. XFSM is modeled as (S, I, O, T), where S is a finite set of states including the start state S_0; I is a finite set of events (inputs); O is a finite set of actions (outputs); and T is a rule (state of transition) that maps ⟨state, event⟩ to ⟨state, action⟩. With OpenState, packet processing in a forwarding device is a three-step process. First, the packet's current state is retrieved from the state table and appended to the packet as a metadata field. If, however, the state table lookup retrieves no match, then the forwarding device assigns "default" state to the incoming packet. Thereafter, the forwarding queries the XFSM table to find the matching rule with ⟨state, event⟩ pair, executes the associated action, and updates the state field of the packet as per the "next-state" field, which is pre-defined in the XFSM table. Finally, the forwarding device's state table is updated based on the "next-state" value retrieved in the previous step for the corresponding flow.

Similar to OpenState, *FAST* [89] also stores pre-installed state machines inside each forwarding device. In FAST, however, each forwarding device could have several instances of the state machine and each is dedicated to a special application. Moreover, instead of two tables used in OpenState, the data plane implements four tables including (1) state machine filter, (2) state table, (3) state transition table, and (4) action table (see Fig. 14.3). There is one state machine filter table for all the instances of the state machine, while each state machine has its own state table, state transition table, and action table. The state machine filter table is used to select the corresponding state machine related to a packet. The state table is a hash table mapping each packet header to a flow state, where each state is stored inside a variable along with its current value—simply put, the state table stores the state information of flows. The forward device uses the state transition table to identify the "next-state" of a packet based on its current state and packet fields. Lastly, the action table specifies the actions that the forwarding device should execute on the packet based on the packet header and its new state.

FAST also upgrades the control plane of an SDN by introducing two new components: (1) a compiler and (2) forwarding device agents. The former being an offline component responsible to translate the state machines into forwarding device agents. The latter, however, are online components, which (1) manage the state machines inside the forwarding devices, (2) perform certain local computations based on the updates received from the forwarding device, (3) manage memory restrictions for confined switches through partial implementation of the state machine inside the forwarding device, and (4) handle communication between the forwarding device and the controllers while updating the controller about the local status of the switch.

Another proposal is *SDPA* [176], which is composed of three main tables including state table, state transition table, and action table (see Fig. 14.3), as well as a state processing module called forwarding processor (FP). The state table has three field values: match, state, and instruction. The "match" value could be any combination of the header fields of the packet, "state" value is the flow's current state, and "instruction" value may be specified either for a "state" or "a packet." Here, the SDN controller communicates with the FP module and initiates the state tables. Moreover, the controller maintains full control and updated information of the state tables via communications with FP either through periodic or specific event updates. With SDPA, when the first packet of a flow is received, the forwarding device sends the packet to the controller, which determines the state table that the corresponding flow state should be stored in. The rest of the packets pertaining to that flow will be processed locally inside the forwarding device without the controller's intervention.

Several different types of applications have already been built atop of the afore-mentioned stateful data plane solutions including HULA [58], port knocking [16], SDN tunneling stateful detection [10], and UDP flooding stateful mitigation[10]. While reviewing each of these solutions is out of scope in this work, we refer the interested reader to [32] for a survey.

3 SDN Security Analysis

3.1 Vulnerability Assessment

Compared to traditional networks, five characteristics of a software-defined network can have the most impact on its security given that they potentially add to the number of vulnerabilities. As illustrated in Fig. 14.4, these characteristics include a cen-tralized controller, open programmable interfaces, forwarding device management protocol, third-party network services, and virtualized logical networks. We provide a succinct summary of these characteristics before analyzing the security of SDNs.

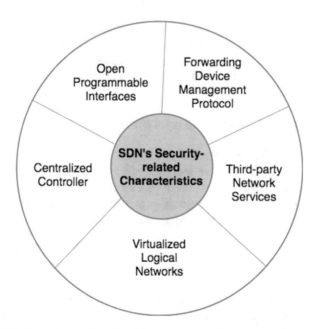

Fig. 14.4 SDN's five main security-related characteristics posing security issues

3.1.1 Centralized Controller

An SDN controller maintains a global view of the network and programs the forwarding devices according to the policies defined at the application plane. While initially controllers were developed as single devices, recently there is more interest in developing distributed controllers with the goal of adjusting to scalability and reliability requirements of real-world deployments. In this case, each set of forwarding devices is assigned to a specific instance of controllers and the controllers follow a master/slave deployment model.

3.1.2 Open Programmable Interfaces

In SDNs, there are three main programmable interfaces: (A) application plane to control plane, (B) east and westbound in the control plane, and (C) control plane to data plane. Compared to traditional networks, these open interfaces are what make an SDN programmable. A, or the northbound API, enables SDN applications to submit policies to the control plane of the network—e.g., REST APIs. B is an interface allowing communication among different inter-connected controllers, which may or may not be running in the same domain. C is the southbound API, which is the most developed and discussed interface in SDNs up to this date. OpenFlow is the agreed standard for the controller to data plane communications, which allows a controller to program a forwarding device irrespective of the underlying hardware or software in the controller or the forwarding device.

3.1.3 Forwarding Device Management Protocol

The forwarding device management protocol along with OpenFlow enables configuration and management of programmable forwarding devices. For instance, the OF-Config protocol may be used to configure an OpenFlow-enabled device as well as multiple logical forwarding devices that may be initiated on top of that device. Another example of this protocol includes the OVSDB [106].

3.1.4 Third-Party Network Services

Similar to a traditional operating system, an SDN controller supports the installation and execution of third-party network services. This allows easy customization, development, and innovation, and reduced costs of proprietary services. Third-party services may communicate with a controller either via internal APIs or open northbound APIs. Moreover, depending on the controller used, applications may be compiled as part of the controller module (e.g., NOX and POX) or may be instantiated at run-time (e.g., OpenDayLight).

3.1.5   Virtualized Logical Networks

Network function virtualization (NFV), created by a consortium of service providers, is tightly coupled with software-defined networks but it does not depend on SDN for its existence. In a nutshell, NFV virtualizes network services, which were previously hardware-based. It focuses on optimizing network services themselves by decoupling network functions (e.g., DNS, caching, etc.).

While independent, the combination of SDN and NFV leads to a greater value and potential. In fact, in many cases, SDN is linked to server virtualization by enabling multiple logical forwarding devices being instantiated over a shared physical device. This potential has already been explored in the literature, and various proposals have emerged [47].

4   Taxonomy of Attacks Against SDNs

Compared to traditional networks, the SDN architecture separates the definition and storage of network policies from their enforcement and implementation. Accordingly, we categorize the attacks targeting SDN's five main components as per their impact on network's policy, enforcement, and implementation. Figure 14.5 illustrates the three main attack types and their relation to SDN's main components. Here, we are focusing on direct associations and potentially, the main motivations of an adversary when targeting any of the SDN's core components. Indeed, attacks against each of the five main components may indirectly fit into all of the three different attack scopes.

4.1   *Implementation Attacks*

Attacks targeting the southbound API and data plane components of a software-defined network are categorized under "implementation attack." Figure 14.6 shows a taxonomy of the main threat vectors associated with this type of attack.

Three different attacks may be used to compromise a data plane including device attack, protocol attack, and side channel attack. A *device attack* refers to all those attacks, where the adversary aims to exploit software or hardware vulnerabilities of an SDN-capable switch to compromise SDN's data plane. In this case, an attacker may target software bugs (e.g., firmware attacks) or hardware features (e.g., TCAM memory) of a forwarding device. For instance, the authors in [175] present an inference attack that using the limited flow table capacity of OpenFlow switches can infer the network parameter (flow table capacity and flow table usage) with relatively high accuracy.

A *protocol attack* refers to attacks targeting the data plane of an SDN by exploiting network protocol vulnerabilities in the forwarding devices (e.g., BGP

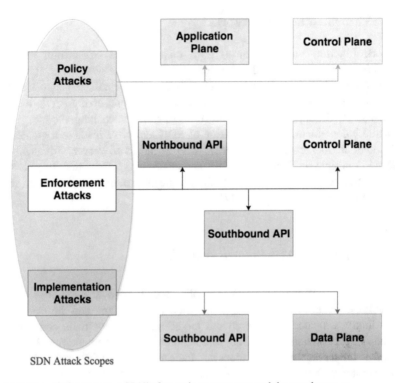

Fig. 14.5 The relation between SDN's five main components and the attack scopes

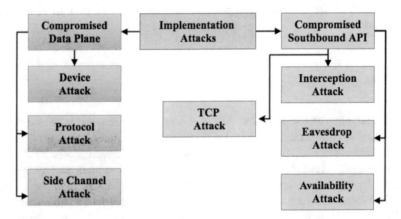

Fig. 14.6 Taxonomy of attack vectors related to "implementation attacks"

attacks). The authors in [64] provide a detailed study of Denial of Service and information disclosure attacks in SDNs, which are exacerbated due to the nature of OpenFlow. As discussed in [163], most OpenFlow-enabled switch models run custom and independent switch firmware implementations with varying capabilities.

For example, the HP 3500 yl and 3800 switch models do not support all of the OpenFlow specified 12-tuple match fields in the hardware (TCAM) flow table. This behavior of the switch firmware may be misused to degrade the overall network performance. For instance, the malicious application could install crafted flow rules that override the existing flow rules (IP matching) with hardware-unsupported match fields (MAC matching) specified. A *side channel attack* in this context refers to the case where an attacker may deduce the forwarding policy of the network just by analyzing the performance metrics of a forwarding device. For example, an input buffer may be used to identify rules, and by analyzing the packet processing times, an attacker could identify the forwarding policy [119].

There are four main attacks against the southbound API of an SDN including interaction, eavesdrop, availability, and TCP attacks. While with an *eavesdrop attack*, the attacker aims to learn about information exchanged between the control and data plane as part of a larger attack plot, in an *interception attack* the attacker's goal is to corrupt the network behavior by modifying the messages being exchanged. For example, the authors in [21] present a man-in-the-middle attack using ARP poisoning to intercept the traffic between a client and an SDN controller. Evidently, such attacks could then be expanded to corrupt the network behavior at a later time. The *availability attack* refers to Denial of Service (DoS) attacks, where the southbound API is flooded with requests causing the network policy implementation to fail. As discussed in [72], attackers can infer flow rules in SDN from probing packets by evaluating the delay time from probing packets and classifying them into classes. Evidently, knowing the reactive rules, attackers can launch DoS attacks by sending numerous rule-matched packets which trigger packet-in packets to overburden the controller.

4.2   Enforcement Attacks

"Enforcement attacks" aim to prevent a software-defined network to properly instruct when, where, and how the policies should be enforced in the network. Hence, attacks targeting the control plane, southbound API, and northbound API may be associated with attacks targeting policy enforcement. Figure 14.7 illustrates a taxonomy of different attack vectors targeting the enforcement of network policies.

Earlier in Sect. 4.1, we denoted different attacks against southbound API. These attacks may also have an adverse impact when it comes to policy enforcement in an SDN as well. For instance, using a man-in-the-middle (MITM) attack, an adversary may alter message exchanges such as *Packet In*[1] message or *Flow-mod*[2] and tamper with the controller's understanding of the requirements of the data plane. As

---

[1] A *Packet In* message is sent by forwarding devices to the controller when a packet does not match any of its flow rules.

[2] A *Flow-mod* message allows the controller to modify the state of an OpenFlow switch.

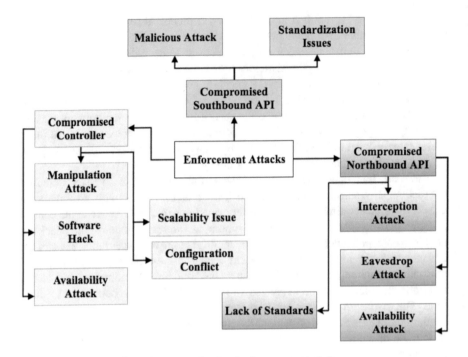

Fig. 14.7 Taxonomy of attack vectors related to "enforcement attacks"

well as malicious attacks, the lack of well-defined standards and constant changes in SDN's southbound API could lead to unwanted, yet malicious involvement in policy enforcement process. For instance, an improperly configured message exchange could lead to invalid or conflicting instructions being set or distributed in the data plane. The authors in [93] analyze the vulnerability of link discovery service in SDN controller showing that the attacker can take advantage of the vulnerability of link discovery service to perform link spoofing attack. The vulnerability exploited in this attack is the lack of a mechanism in SDN controllers to ensure the integrity/origin of LLDP packets.

Similar to SDN's southbound API, the northbound API is susceptible to interception, eavesdrop, and availability attacks. While the nature of both attacks is similar, there are a few key differences: (1) An attacker targeting the northbound API requires higher-level of access to the system and is potentially sitting on the application plane. There may be cases that the applications do not run on the same device and in that case the attack complexity may be reduced as to southbound API (e.g., where the adversary targets the communication link); (2) The impacts of a compromised northbound API are potentially larger given that information exchanged between the control and application plane affect network-wide policies. Unlike southbound API, where OpenFlow is adopted as the standard, the northbound API lacks any standardization. Specifically, each controller has different specifications for the northbound API, and this leads to insecure developments.

Moreover, a poorly designed northbound API could also be exploited by malicious applications to manipulate the behavior of other applications through eviction of active sessions, tampering with control message exchanges, etc.

The third set of attack vectors against policy enforcement originates from the control plane—potentially being the most critical threat against SDNs. Attacks targeting SDN's control plane may be classified into three types: manipulation attack, availability attack, and software hack. *Manipulation attack* refers to any attempt by an adversary to subvert the controllers understanding of the data plane, which ultimately leads to "improper" decision making. For instance, an LLDP (Link Layer Discovery Protocol) related as *Packet In* messages may be used to create fabricated links and network topologies. Similarly, an ARP (Address Resolution Protocol) packet relayed as a *Packet In* message could adversely affect the view of the controller. The authors in [50] propose new SDN-specific attack vectors, host location hijacking attack and link fabrication attack, which can effectively poison the network topology information.

An SDN controller is hosted on a commodity server and may be subject to *software hacks* as any other application. For instance, altering a system variable such as time may effectively turn the controller offline. In the case of *availability attack*, the adversary aims to make the controller unavailable for a certain period of time for part or all of the network. One way to achieve this is for an attacker to flood the controller with *Packet In* messages—given that these are not authenticated.

Scalability and configuration conflicts are also vulnerabilities that may be exploited by opportunistic adversaries. An SDN controller is responsible for all decisions in an SDN. Evidently, a single controller will not scale well for large and dense network with a 10 Gbps link network. As discussed in [5], this may be used to deliver attacks such as saturation and single point of failure. Finally, the combination of a single-domain multiple controllers, multi-tenant controllers, and multiple OpenFlow architectures may lead to configuration conflicts.

4.3 Policy Attacks

"Policy attacks" refer to the threats targeting SDN's ability to define and store proper network policies. As illustrated in Fig. 14.8, an attacker aiming to target network's policy level aims for compromising SDN's control and application planes. By compromising the controller, an attacker could alter the information shared with applications about the network and compromise their decision making. Potentially, this type of attack may be part of a larger stealthy plot to compromise the network status in the long run or to avoid detection by an intrusion detection system—given that with a compromised controller the attacker has almost full access to the network. In alternative scenarios, the adversary's access to the controller may be restricted to certain functions or period of time motivating an attack to the application plane. Evidently, an "honest" configuration conflict in the control plane could also be exploited by an adversary to deliver a "policy attack."

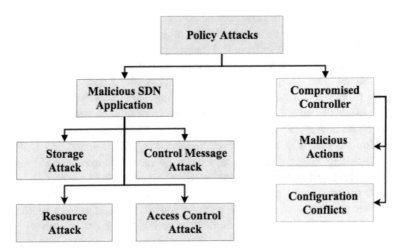

Fig. 14.8 Taxonomy of attack vectors related to "policy attacks"

SDN allows the installation of third-party apps and the current goal is to set up an app store ecosystem for this. Similar to mobile devices, third-party application support adds to the threat vectors against SDNs and ensuring the security and trustworthiness of apps is challenging. As discussed in [118], a major vulnerability that expands the attack surface of compromised applications is that SDN applications are granted complete control and visibility of the network. Hence, a malicious application could use the network state information to manipulate traffic flow for nefarious purposes. Tsou and Monsanto [88, 147] further discuss how nested SDN applications pose dangerous threats at this level.

Generally, attacks targeting SDN's application plane may be categorized into: storage, control message, resource, and access control attacks.

Storage Attack SDN applications are granted access privilege to shared storage. This access may be exploited to manipulate the internal database targeting the network behavior.

Control Message Attack Control messages exchanged between the control and data plane are fundamental for functioning of an SDN. An arbitrary issued control message by an application might be catastrophic. For instance, a malicious application may take down the network by sending control messages modifying or clearing the flow table entries of switches. For instance, as shown in [128] given that there is no restriction for control messages, an SDN application can issue any control messages at any time. A malicious application continuously generates flow rules to consistently fill up the flow table of the switch and the switch cannot handle more flow rules.

Resource Attack Malicious applications may exhaust expensive and critical system resources including memory and CPU, thereby seriously affecting the performance of legitimate applications and the controller itself. Moreover, a malicious SDN application may execute system exit command and dismiss controller instances.

Access Control Attacks A common feature among storage, control message, and resource attacks is access violation. In fact, there is a very limited control in terms of authentication, authorization, and accountability in current controllers. We classify all attacks violating required access authorization as access control attack.

4.3.1 Comparative Analysis

As discussed, attacks targeting an SDN whether falling into implementation, enforcement, or policy category can potentially have devastating impacts. Specifically, compared to traditional networks, attack risks have exacerbated given that an attacker could potentially take down a whole network having compromised any of the main components of an SDN.

Zerkane et al. [168] analyze 114 SDN generic vulnerabilities and compute the severity of these. They conclude that SDN has a lot of vulnerabilities with high and medium severity because of the weaknesses inherited from classical network architecture and due to its specific characteristics. The vulnerabilities related to access control and those affecting availability are categorized as the most severe. Moreover, they also calculate the impacts of the SDN features on security and identify the control plane components with the highest weight given that SDN architecture is based on the separation, the programmability, and the centralization of the control plane. In contrast, application and network element resource have lower intensities because SDN does not affect their designs.

5 An Overview of SDN Security Literature

The SDN security literature may be split into four main directions. First, research aiming to import existing security services to SDNs. For instance, [52, 53, 167] aim to design and develop systematic solutions for building reliable firewalls in SDNs. Second, proposals on how to enhance existing services by leveraging capabilities brought by SDN. As an example, the authors in [164] investigate whether SDN can enhance network security by integrating its capabilities into common security functions. Similarly, solutions such as [1, 98, 156] explore how an SDN can be used to protect networks against malware.

These two directions consisted most of the research in the first few years after SDN's introduction. The recent trend, however, has shifted towards developing innovative security services, which were not feasible to implement before SDN. For instance, using network capabilities to secure Internet-of-Things (IoT) devices (e.g., [96]), smart grid (e.g., [36]), and cloud computing [24]. We will review more examples of SDN-enabled security services in Sect. 8.

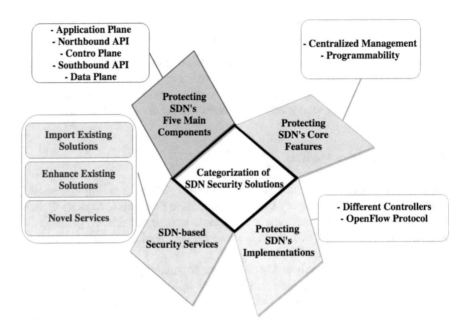

Fig. 14.9 Categorization of SDN security solutions

The fourth direction is research aiming to secure the SDN platform itself, which is a critical requirement and has the most direct impact on SDN's adoption. Recently, this has been an active area of research and various solutions have been proposed to secure SDNs at different layers. Proposals such as [55, 110, 111, 129] aim to design and develop secure controllers (see [117] for a categorization). Another category of research aims to secure the northbound interface of an SDN. For example, [118, 154] introduce a permission system that ensures that controller operations are only made available to the trusted applications. Securing the southbound of an SDN is also an essential requirement. The authors in [14] provide an overview of the vulnerabilities present in the OpenFlow protocol. Accordingly, solutions such as [6, 61, 66, 130] consider different aspects of OpenFlow that pose security challenges and propose solutions. The authors in [163] provide a comprehensive survey of existing SDN attack studies and evaluate the impact of these attacks against published SDN defense solutions.

In general, the focus on the security of a technology itself is very much driven by the adoption rate as many threats are only discovered with increased deployment. Major industry players such as Google and HP [68] have already adopted SDN, which has boosted research in this area even further. Several comprehensive surveys have been published summarizing the ongoing efforts in this area including [7, 68, 119, 121]. Here, as shown in Fig. 14.9, we provide a further categorization of SDN security literature. Out of the four research directions mentioned earlier, all research falling into any of the first three categories is classified as *SDN-based security services*. We categorize research aiming to secure SDN itself into three groups including research aiming to protect (1) SDN's five main components, (2) its core features, and (3) implementations. SDN's core features include centralized management and programmability and various proposals have already been developed to ensure these are protected [119]. SDN's implementation includes securing the different controller platforms, the OpenFlow protocol design and implementations, OpenFlow-enabled devices, and software forwarding devices such as Open vSwitch. An alternative way of decomposing the literature is according to the SDN components that proposals aim to secure. We review solutions proposed to secure the data plane and control plane of SDNs, in Sects. 6 and 7, respectively.

6 Data Plane Security

Network forwarding devices have been a very attractive target for attackers. In fact, given the large amount of information that may be exposed through compromised forwarding devices, resourceful adversaries including intelligence agencies have for long aimed to set up backdoors on them. For instance, Edward Snowden uncovered massive investments by NSA to enable large scale surveillance through core network infrastructure [97, 137]. More recently, the "Vault 7: CIA Hacking Tools" revelations by WikiLeaks [148] disclosed that CIA had actively exploited a common vulnerability in 318 different Cisco routers to carry out surveillance attacks globally. There have also been WikiLeaks' revelations on NSA' upgrading labs tampering with forwarding devices before they are released to the market [108]. However, the attack surface against forwarding devices is not limited to resourceful adversaries. Software and hardware vulnerabilities of the devices [11, 28, 73, 141] and vulnerable implementations of network protocols enable attackers to compromise forwarding devices. For instance, as reported in CVE-2014-9295 [95], a novice hacker could execute arbitrary code on routers simply through crafted packets targeting a specific function of the device.

A compromised forwarding devices may be used to drop or slow down, clone or deviate, inject or forge network traffic to launch attacks targeting the network operator and its users. For instance, the documents disclosed under "Vault 7" revelations indicate that compromised routers may have been used for activities such as data collection, exfiltration (e.g., Operation Aurora [29]), manipulation and modification (insertion of HTML code on webpages), and cover tunneling. A compromised routing system may be also used to bypass firewalls and intrusion prevention systems [38], violating isolation requirements in multi-tenant data centers [60], infiltrate VPNs [70], and more.

In Sect. 4.1, we discussed how a compromised data plane can be used to launch *implementation attacks*. Compared to traditional networks, a compromised forwarding device poses a much higher risk for SDNs. In fact, as discussed in [67], an attacker controlling a forwarding device can potentially take down an SDN entirely. At the same time, SDN also adds to the complications in protecting

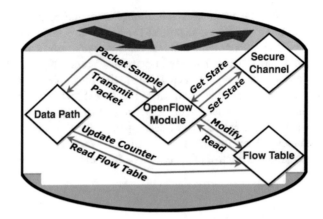

Fig. 14.10 Simplified data flow diagram for an OpenFlow-enabled forwarding device

networks against compromised forwarding devices. For instance, novel attacks such as [69, 143] against the data plane of SDNs were not possible in traditional networks.

Figure 14.10 illustrates a simplified version of a data flow diagram of an OpenFlow-enabled forwarding device. Four main processes are assumed for such a device, (1) Data Path: responsible to perform forwarding task, (2) OpenFlow Module: software running on the device's CPU responsible to coordinate interaction between Data Path, (3) Flow Table, and (4) Secure Channel. The *flow table* contains flow rules for matching L2–4 headers, actions to be invoked on flows, and counters. The *secure channel*, however, is responsible to mediate communication with the controller. The authors in [64] discuss that by using the STRIDE mnemonic and analyzing each component, they have identified this process to be vulnerable to information disclosure, Denial of Service, and tampering attacks. Denial of Service against the flow table refers to the case where an attacker aims to overload the table with flow rules. In an information disclosure attack (see side-channel attacks discussed in Sect. 4.1), the attackers observe the differences in controller response times and derive information about network state such as active flow rules. We define tampering attack as the case an attacker can set up any flow rule on the table and thereby affecting packet forwarding process with full control. Hence, with this updated definition compared to [64], we presume the most dangerous threat to be a tampering attack.

We perceive the following as the main factors complicating protection of the SDN data plane:

– *Incompatibility of the existing solutions:* With the removal of intelligence from the forwarding devices, the defense mechanisms used for traditional networks no longer work in SDNs. In fact, in order to import traditional defenses into SDNs, we would need a fundamental redesign of OpenFlow protocol [82].
– *Unverified reliance of the control plane to the data plane:* SDN controllers rely on *Packet In* messages for their view of the network. However, these messages

are not authenticated or verified. A malicious forwarding device may send forged spoofed messages to subvert the controller view of the network—even with TLS authentication in place. The same vulnerability enables a compromised forwarding device the capability to overload the controller with requests launching a Denial of Service (DoS) attack.

- *Software Switches:* Programmable soft-switches such as Open vSwitches run on top of end host servers. Hence, compared to physical switches, soft-switches are more susceptible to attacks with a comparatively larger attack surface.
- *Stateful SDN forwarding devices:* We have already reviewed stateful SDN switches in Sect. 2.2.c. In general, adding some intelligence and authority to the data plane has performance advantages such as lower latency response to network events and improved fault tolerance through continuation of basic network operations under failing controllers. Furthermore, well-standardized protocols such as for encryption, MAC learning, and codec control message (CCM) exchanges also require some intelligence at data plane. However, these proposals revive some of the vulnerabilities of traditional networks under SDNs.

A relatively sizeable literature aims to protect a data plane against malicious flow rules defined by compromised applications. To this end, solutions such as FortNox [110] enable a NOS to check flow rule contradictions in real-time and authorize applications before granting them the right to update the flow rules. Alternatively, solutions such as FlowChecker [6] and VeriFlow [62] are configuration debugging tools used to identify inconsistencies and faulty flow rules. In order to prevent side-channel attacks, the authors in [138] introduce a timeout proxy on the data plane as an extension to normalize the NOS delay. If the controller fails to respond within a fixed period of time, the timeout proxy replies with default forwarding instructions. Similar other data plane debugging tools are proposed to test whether flow rules at forwarding devices are corresponding to the controller's view [22, 105, 172] or monitor whether the forwarding behaviors of packets are compliant with the control plane policies [169, 170]. However, all of the aforementioned solutions assume forwarding devices are trustworthy and thus, do not work when forwarding devices are compromised. In fact, existing proposals in SDN data plane security have been known to suffer from an inaccurate adversarial model. This limitation directly impacts their adoption and impact. For instance, solutions proposed in [34, 59, 60, 62] assume all, or the majority, of the forwarding devices are trustworthy.

To work in an adversarial setting, path verification tools embed cryptographic information for the controller to verify whether the actual path taken by packets matches with what the controller expects [115]. However, these solutions require extra header space and introduce high bandwidth overhead. In addition, these solutions require the modification of forwarding devices, which adds to the deployment cost. Relevant literature in packet forwarding anomaly detection can be broken down into (1) cryptographic mechanisms, (2) flow statistics, (3) packet probing, and (4) acknowledgment-based mechanisms. Cryptographic mechanisms such as [75, 91] embed signatures in packets and the forwarding devices verify whether the packets have been correctly routed. These approaches suffer from two main limitations for

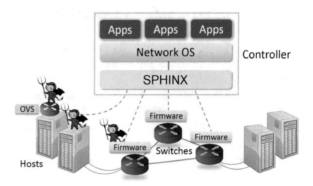

Fig. 14.11 SPHINX architecture

deployment: (1) cryptographic operations incur significant computational overhead and (2) require modification in IP packet formatting. An alternative effective approach to cryptographic solutions is to analyze flow statistics at forwarding device ports (e.g., [12, 77]). However, flow statistic techniques heavily rely on strict time synchronization among forwarding devices, which is hard to achieve in real large-scale networks and are unable to detect packet modification attacks. Packet probing approaches such as [3, 13, 103] sample and analyze probing packets to detect forwarding anomalies. Majority of these solutions are focused on anomaly detection at first and last hops of a network and result in significant communication overhead. Acknowledgment-based solutions such as [74, 78, 173] detect packet dropping through periodical interaction among neighboring forwarding devices. In this case, there is also a significant overhead in computation and storage for forwarding device given that each forwarding device should store the entire forwarding path of flows and collects the acknowledgment packets periodically.

One of the prominent initial attempts to secure the SDN data plane is SPHINX [34]. Proposed in 2015, SPHINX is a framework to detect attacks on network topology and data plane forwarding. SPHINX is one of the very few solutions to secure SDN's data plane that does not assume forwarding devices are trusted. It detects and mitigates attacks originated from malicious forwarding devices through (1) abstracting the network operations with incremental flow graphs and (2) pre-defined security policies specified by its administrator. It also checks for flow consistency throughout a flow path using a similarity index metric, where this metric must be similar for "good" switches on the path. SPHINX architecture is shown in Fig. 14.11—the image is imported from author's published paper.

SPHINX leverages the novel abstraction of flow graphs, which closely approximate the actual network operations, to (a) enable incremental validation of all network updates and constraints, thereby verifying network properties in real-time, and (b) detect both known and potentially unknown security threats to network topology and data plane forwarding without compromising on performance. It analyzes specific OpenFlow control messages to learn new network behavior and metadata for both topological and forwarding state and builds flow graphs for each traffic flow observed in the network. It continuously updates and monitors these flow graphs for permissible changes, and raises alerts if it identifies deviant behavior. SPHINX leverages custom algorithms that incrementally process network updates to determine in real-time if the updates causing deviant behavior should be allowed or not. It also provides a light-weight policy engine that enables administrators to specify expressive policies over network resources and detect security violations.

Based on SPHINX, Shaghaghi et al. [122] propose WedgeTail as the first intrusion prevention system (IPS) for data plane of SDNs. Compared to available solutions, the authors assume a resourceful adversary who may have taken full control over one, or all, of the forwarding devices—i.e., the strongest possible adversary that may exist at the SDN data plane and not assumed in related work. Specifically, the adversary is assumed to be capable of dropping, replaying, misrouting, delaying, and even generating packets (includes both packet modification and fabrication), in random or selective manner over all or part of the traffic. Evidently, the above capabilities grant the adversary the capability to launch attacks against the network hosts, other forwarding devices, or the control plane. The authors in [122] defined WedgeTail as a controller-agnostic IPS designed to "hunt" for forwarding devices failing to process packets as expected. WedgeTail regards packets as "random walkers" [85] in the network and analyzes packet movements as trajectories in a geometric space. By analyzing the expected and actual trajectories of packets, it is capable of automatically localizing malicious forwarding device and identifying the exact malicious behavior (e.g., packet drop, fabrication). WedgeTail response to threats can be programmed using administrator-defined policies. For example, an instant isolation policy may be customized such that: (1) the potentially malicious device is instructed to reset all the flow rules, and (2) the device is re-evaluated at various intervals through the re-iteration of the same packet(s) originally raising suspicion.

In order to make the scanning more efficient and increase the probability of finding malicious devices earlier, WedgeTail begins by prioritizing forwarding for inspection. It adopts unsupervised trajectory sampling [104] to cluster forwarding devices into scanning groups of varying priority depending on the cumulative frequency of occurrence in packet paths traversing the network. To retrieve the expected trajectories, WedgeTail intercepts the relevant OpenFlow messages exchanged between the control and data plane and maintains a virtual replica of the network. This virtual replica is processed by its integrated header space analysis (HSA) [60] component to calculate the expected packet trajectories. The actual packet trajectories are, however, computed by tracking a custom hash of the packet header. Alternatively, if NetSight [48] is deployed, WedgeTail queries for packet history to retrieve the packet trajectory.

More recently, solutions such as FOCES [171] have also been proposed. FOCES captures the correct forwarding behaviors as a linear equation system. Compared to existing verification tools, FOCES detects forwarding anomalies network-wide and not for individual flows without requiring dedicated rules. Furthermore, the authors in [71] propose DYNAPFV, which leverages dynamic packet sampling to verify the integrity of packets on networks while dynamically collecting flow statistics to verify packet forwarding behaviors, and thereby detect attacks violating packet integrity.

7   Control Plane Security

In traditional networks, the control plane is distributed across millions of lines of code and defined across hundreds of RFCs. Hence, the removal of the control plane from the network forwarding devices and implementing it as an external controller in SDNs significantly reduces the complexity of networks, making them simpler and cheaper than traditional networks. However, the SDN controller is an entity, which does not exist in traditional networks and its security requires special consideration. In fact, some of the same arguments complicating the protection of SDN data plane including incompatibility of existing solutions, and unverified reliance of the control plane to the data plane (see Sect. 6) are also applicable when analyzing the security of SDN control plane. The authors in [128] propose a solution that attackers can remotely differentiate between an SDN and a traditional network by analyzing the flow response time. Hence, *security through obscurity*,[3] where one would hope that an attacker cannot differentiate between an SDN and a traditional network is not applicable in this case.

As discussed in Sect. 4.2, attacks against the control plane of a software-defined network can be categorized into manipulation, availability, and software hacks. In this section, we break down these attacks into more specific threat vectors, which we regard as the main challenges in securing the NOS. Figure 14.12 illustrates the main six threat vectors against the network control plane. In the following, we review each of these threat vectors.

1. NOS software attacks: The network operating system is hosted on a commodity server and an attacker can exploit software vulnerabilities to tamper with the functionality of the device. In extreme cases, an attacker can take over the control of the NOS. This is the strongest adversarial setting in an SDN, where the attacker is assumed with full control over the network. However, to the best of our knowledge, the common assumption is that a NOS running on a commodity server is secured through conventional security means (e.g., antivirus) and the majority of the existing solutions aim to detect a NOS that is successfully compromised by an attacker. Recently, Shaghaghi et al. [125] proposed Gwardar with the goal of protecting networks against a compromised NOS. In fact, Gwardar is the first intrusion protection system (IPS) designed to protect an SDN against compromised SDN controllers. The proposed solution builds on capabilities introduced as part of the author's earlier trajectory-based

---

[3]The aphorism "security through obscurity" suggests that hiding information provides some level of security.

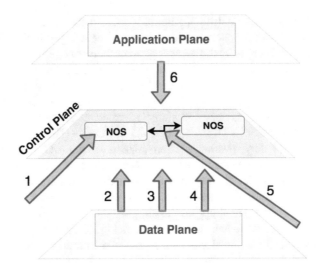

Fig. 14.12 SDN control plane threats

IPS for data plane of SDNs known as WedgeTail [122]. Gwardar retrieves the packet trajectories from the data plane and creates normal models for packet trajectories traversing the network forwarding devices. Gwardar also maintains a virtual replica of the network by intercepting the OpenFlow messages exchanged between the control and data plane. This virtual replica is used to verify the aforementioned normal models. Whenever derivations are detected, Gwardar first performs a trajectory-based inspection of the forwarding devices by employing the attack detection algorithms of Venaticus. For this, it compares the suspicious packet trajectories with the expected ones computed over the virtual replica that it maintains to detect and locate possible malicious forwarding devices. Thereafter, if the anomaly matches the rules specified by the control plane, it inspects the control plane. For this, Gwardar submits flow rules matching the normal set of trajectories to the controller with a high priority and evaluates whether: (a) the controller submits the flow rules correctly to the data plane, and (b) the controller updates the global network view available to applications after these changes. Gwardar detects a compromised NOS when any of the conditions above are invalid. Gwardar may be programmed by its administrator on how to respond to threats. By default, however, it retrieves rules from the most valid virtual replica copy it maintains and applies the valid flow rules to remove the malicious trajectories. In extreme cases, Gwardar may be programmed to take over the network until the NOS has been fixed.

2. DoS attacks: The detachment of the control and data plane in SDNs pushes most of the complexity to the controller. If the controller receives a large number of flow decision requests (*Packet In* messages) this can lead to a bottleneck. Given that these messages are not authenticated, an attacker can leverage the OpenFlow protocol vulnerabilities or send a large number of such packets and execute a

DoS attack against the controller. Alternatively, as discussed in [42], an attacker can send continuous IP packets with random headers to put a NOS into a non-responsive state. Increasing the number of controllers is not effective against DoS attacks by itself since it can lead to cascading failure of controllers [159].

Generally, DoS attacks can be handled by effective and dynamic response methods, which essentially work by monitoring abnormal traffic behaviors and analyzing the flow behaviors and statistics stored in forwarding devices. The authors in [20] present a Distributed Denial of Service (DDoS) flooding attack detection, where they leverage self-organization maps (SOM) to find hidden relations among flows entering into the network to classify network traffic into attack or normal traffic. Their proposed solution requires constant collection and monitoring for required features, which can adversely impact the controller's performance. Hence, [132] propose to simplify this process by sampling traffic on the network for such analyses. The authors in [165] propose an even simpler approach where the controller inserts a flow rule to drop packets as soon as a certain traffic threshold is passed. COFFEE [116] is an alternative OpenFlow-based solution to detect and mitigate botnets. Several other solutions aim to increase the processing power of NOS through distributed architectures such as McNettle [152], DISCO [107], HyperFlow [144] have been proposed in the literature, which are surveyed in [4, 8]. It is important to note that as devastating as a DoS attack can be against a network controller, it does not allow an attacker to gain full unrestricted access to the network—at least, directly and by itself.

3. Spoofing attacks: In order to configure the forwarding devices to provide connectivity among hosts, the NOS must learn the mapping between hosts and switch ports. For this, the controller can instruct the forwarding devices to forward ARP request and unknown packets to itself. The *Packet In* messages retrieved for such packets can then be used to identify which hosts connect to which forwarding device ports. For unknown destination hosts, the controller instructs the forwarding device to flood the packets through a *Packet Out* message. The response from the destination is forwarded to the controller and so, it learns the location of hosts. This learning process is vulnerable to spoofing attacks (e.g., MAC, IP, VLAN tag, etc.) given that it is based on the information provided by forwarding devices and hosts. Further, an attacker can exploit this vulnerability and execute a DoS against the controller by fabricating a large number of packets with arbitrary MAC and IP addresses, which results in a large number of host profiles and controller communications.

In order to prevent ARP spoofing attacks, the authors in [79] introduce a specific component called address resolution mapping (ARM) in the controller to track MAC addresses of authorized hosts. The controller consults with this component and discards ARP responses not verified by ARM. Another requirement to prevent ARP spoofing in OpenFlow is to enable SSL encryption, which is not enabled by default. Furthermore, as discussed in [166], it is also possible to counter ARP spoofing attacks using packet-level information. To mitigate VLAN spoofing, a forwarding device can designate its ports as user-to-network interface (UNI) and network-to-network interface (NNI) and thus, remove VLAN tags in packets received from user-to-network interfaces [2]. To prevent IP spoofing, the authors in [160] propose an OpenFlow virtual source address validation edge (VAVE) embedded into the controller to verify the address of packets without a matching record in the forwarding device's flow table. Feng et al. [39] extended this work, where each forwarding device has a collective view of address assignment and routing (i.e., adding some limited intelligence to the forwarding devices). The authors in [158] introduce software-defined filtering architecture (SEFA), which further extends the VAVE-based approach to IP spoofing. Here, the network forwarding devices are capable of collecting and building flow rules as well as adding filtering rules based on spoofing occurrences.

4. Link Layer Discovery Protocol (LLDP)[4] attacks: To configure the flow tables on forwarding devices, an SDN controller must first learn the network topology using a control protocol such as OpenFlow Discovery Protocol (OFDP) through a boot-up process. For this, the NOS sends an LLDP packet as part of a *Packet Out* message with the output port set to all forwarding devices. The LLDP message is propagated throughout the network with each forwarding devices forwarding the message on all ports and to all neighbors. Each controller receiving an LLDP packet forwards it to the controller through a *Packet In* message, which also includes the port number that received the LLDP packet. In this way, the controller discovers the links between forwarding devices and thus, learning the network topology. Evidently, this process is vulnerable to spoofing attacks, where an attacker can send forged LLDP packets to the controller and deceive its network topology [50]. To mitigate LLDP spoofing attacks, a forwarding device can designate its ports as NNIs and UNIs, and reject LLDP packets received from UNIs [2]. Implementing message authenticity and integrity into LLDP can also mitigate LLDP spoofing attacks.

5. Inter-NOS communication attacks: In order to manage a large network efficiently and avoid the risks of a single point of failure (SPOF),[5] multiple NOSs may be deployed for redundancy or each responsible to govern over a subset of the forwarding devices. In the first case, when an active controller goes down, forwarding devices establish an uplink with the next available controller. For this, a distributed election protocol can be used to elect a master controller, where a slave replica becomes master when the current master fails. Furthermore, controller states must remain consistent among controllers. These communications require an inter-NOS communication channel—also, commonly referred to as east and westbound interface in the literature. An attacker can attack the inter-NOS communications in different ways. For instance, the attacker can manipulate the election process between controllers using spoofing attacks (e.g., a non-NOS involvement in the election protocol). Alternatively, a compromised

---

[4]A link layer protocol used by network devices for advertising their identity, capabilities to neighbors on a LAN segment.

[5]SPOF is a part of a system that upon failure will prevent an entire system from functioning.

controller can manually pick the smallest allowable time to become the next master. In the case of splitting governance over forwarding devices, an attacker could exploit protocol vulnerabilities such as BGP.

The spoofed election messages received from other UNIs can be dropped when the ports that the SDN controller connects to are already known. Otherwise, to prevent an outsider from participating in or tampering with the election process, message origin authentication and integrity need to be implemented for the election protocol and state replication (e.g., using mutually authenticated TLS among the controllers). Similar to other distributed protocols, the communication among the controllers requires additional security mechanisms such as information corroboration, message authentication, and integrity are also needed to mitigate attacks by a malicious controller participating in the election process.

In general, while *spoofing*, *LLDP*, and *inter-NOS communication* attacks are introduced in SDN distributed architecture, defending against them is not specific to SDNs and these attacks are familiar concerns in distributed network systems. Hence, preventing these attacks is mostly an implementation matter where each different controller developers needs to implement best working security mechanisms to prevent them.

6. Attacks by network applications: There are two main challenges in protecting a NOS against malicious applications including implementation of mechanisms to authenticate and authorize them when using controller resources through adequate isolation, audit, and tracking. For instance, the access authorizations required for a network load-balancer are mostly related to network statistics, while an intrusion detection system requires the capability to access the packet headers.

Security-enhanced Floodlight controller (SE-Floodlight) [110] extends the original floodlight controller [17] by adding a secure programmable northbound API, which specifically enforces the privilege separation principle. It also introduces a run-time OpenFlow application verification module for validating the integrity of class modules producing the flow rules. Further, it assigns authorization roles to OpenFlow applications to resolve rule conflicts by comparing the authoritative roles of producers of conflicting rules. SE-Floodlight can also restrict the *Packetout* messages produced by different applications and secure flow rule mediation. PermOF [154] proposes fine-grained permission systems for applications, where a set of permissions (read, notification, write, and system permissions) and isolation mechanisms are used to enforce permission controls. Operation Checkpoint [118] defines a set of permissions to which an application must subscribe to. Furthermore, it introduces a module responsible for implementing the permission checks before authorizing the application commands. Three kinds of problems were indicated in this work: rule conflict detection and correction, application identification, and priority enforcement, which are useful for malicious activity detection and mitigation. Another solution is FRESCO [131], which consists of an application layer and a security enforcement kernel. The former has four main functions including: (a) script-to-module translation, (b) database management, (c) event management, and (d) instance execution. FRESCO also includes a security enforcement kernel to avoid rule conflicts. Several other solutions also aim to secure the NOS against malicious applications, which are surveyed in [7, 68, 119].

8   SDN-Based Security Services

The ability to view network state in real-time, and programmatically control the network behavior, opens up exciting possibilities for network security improvement. For instance, once a DoS attack is detected in the network, a threat mitigation application can dynamically reprogram the forwarding devices at the perimeter of the network to drop the associated traffic. Similarly, if a malware is detected in one segment of a network, the network can instruct forwarding devices to restrict traffic flows to that segment until further analysis. Other solutions leverage the SDN capabilities to offer security as a service. For instance, anonymizing the identity of a user by masking their IPs at network-level as a privacy-enhancing service. Alternatively, sensitive data can be offloaded securely within the organization's network by rerouting associated traffic. These security capabilities can be invoked selectively for specific traffic flows, thereby facilitating an elastic cost model for the value-added services [7]. As mentioned in Sect. 5, developing SDN-based security services is currently an active area of research and an ever increasing number of proposals are emerging. As illustrated in Fig. 14.13, we categorize the existing literature into seven different categories and provide examples for each in the following.

1. *Intrusion Prevention Systems:* SDN facilitates collection of intelligence from different segments of the network in a centralized fashion, which coupled with reprogrammability of the network provides an enhanced platform to design and develop more efficient and effective intrusion detection and prevention systems.

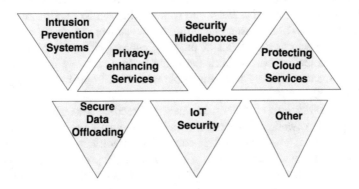

Fig. 14.13 Categorization of SDN-based security services

Here, we review some of the most prominent attempts in this area, which also inspired our proposed solutions in this dissertation.

The authors in [46] combine OpenFlow and sFlow for anomaly detection and mitigation. Their proposed solution has three main modules that continuously interact with each other: (a) the collector, which collects flow statistics through capabilities provided by OpenFlow and sFlow, (b) anomaly detection, which is responsible to analyze the statistics and anomalies, (c) anomaly mitigation, which inserts flow rules in order to mitigate the identified threats. Skowyra et al. [134] introduce a learning intrusion detection system (L-IDS), which utilizes the SDN architecture to detect and react to networks attacks in embedded mobile devices. L-IDS embeds the IDS logic into the network controller and integrates traffic measurement and anomaly detection into forwarding devices. NetFuse [153] is a mechanism to protect OpenFlow-enabled data center networks. NetFuse monitors OpenFlow control messages and uses the read state messages to retrieve active network flows and resource utilization. These are then evaluated using a flow aggregation algorithm to identify the overload flows. Once such a flow is detected, NetFuse dynamically throttles the flow according to rate-limits. The authors in [166] propose OrchSec, which uses multiple diverse controller instances, sFlow for packet-level monitoring, and develop applications for controller (instead of embedding them into it). Another interesting novel solution is Cognition [142]. Cognition leverages SDN capabilities including network-wide view and forwarding device statistics to detect environmental, network configuration, and traffic changes compared to the normal conditions and anticipate potential security threats. The authors in [30] propose NICE, which is an intrusion detection framework for virtual network systems. NICE leverages OpenFlow protocol capabilities to monitor and analyze network traffic. Upon detection of a vulnerability, the suspicious virtual machine (VM) is quarantined and inspected according to pre-defined rules. Similar to the aforementioned solutions, such a dynamic and reconfigurable IDS is hardly feasible in traditional networks. SnortFlow [155] integrates Snort [136] into an OpenFlow-enabled SDN. The SnortFlow server gathers data from Snort agents, evaluates them, and generates the actions, which are submitted to the NOSs (if more than one, the matching NOS is chosen depending on the network segment, where actions should be performed). Mehdi et al. [84] leverage SDN capabilities to bring intrusion detection system from the network core to home networks in order to make it more efficient and compatible with other home network applications such as QoS.

2. *Security Middleboxes:* SDN facilitates redirecting selected network traffic through the network middleboxes, which are typically used to deliver security services. This is a major advantage compared to traditional networks, where this selecting routing was not possible. The authors in [9] propose Slick architecture, where a centralized controller installs and migrates functions onto middleboxes. Here, the network security applications direct the Slick NOS to install functions for routing specific flows. The NOS is then responsible for determining the placement of functions in the middleboxes and establishing the correct paths for

network traffic. Compared to [9], SIMPLE policy enforcement layer proposed in [112] is more practical as it does not tamper with the SDN capabilities or middlebox functionalities. SIMPLE adopts a tag-based packet classification to identify the processing state and tunneling packets between forwarding devices. Note that tag-based mechanisms have a lower processing time compared to hash-based packet classification mechanisms. Liu et al. [76] propose a method to protect against covert channels, where each node in the network has a specified security clearance and the flow rules are specified such that traffic is only routed through the receiver with a security level that is higher than the sender. If lower, then flow is routed through a middlebox for further automated verification. This dynamic and flexible architecture would not have been feasible in traditional networks. Other similar solutions have also emerged leveraging SDN capabilities to enhance network middleboxes, which are surveyed in [120].

3. *Privacy-enhancing Services:* SDN simplifies the deployment of anonymization services given that the controller can dynamically coordinate installation of custom flow rules across the network forwarding devices. Hence, the anonymization is performed online and by the forwarding devices themselves. For instance, the authors in [86] propose AnonyFlow as an anonymization service to prevent IP-based tracking on the Internet. Here, the ISP assigns temporary IPs to users and uses disposable identifiers to user traffic leaving its domain. Jafarian et al. [54] propose OpenFlow Random Host Mutation (OF-RHM), which mutates IP addresses of network hosts randomly in a transparent form. Here, the controller assigns each host a temporary and random virtual IP, where direct access to host using real IP address is restricted to authorized entities only. More recently, [27] leverage SDN capabilities to enhance deployment of Decoy Routing, where the Decoy Routers are managed by the NOS, which is responsible to observe the network traffic to "identify covert signaling by clients who seek Decoy Routing services, decryption and appropriate traffic redirection, identifying maliciously behaving switches, load balancing, and automatic failover" [27].

4. *Protecting Cloud Services:* SDN brings along promising opportunities to research for enhanced security in cloud systems [4]. The authors in [80] propose an SDN facilitated Automated Malware Quarantine (AMQ), where network threats are automatically isolated to limit the associated risks using through a purpose-built SDN applications. Their proposed solution is composed of two main components. First, the Bot Hunter Network Service Module, which detects malware-infected hosts in real-time. Second, the Threat Responder Network Service Module, which is responsible to quarantine and isolate threats from the network. Hence, compared to AMQ in traditional networks, [80] improves response time and removes the need for manual configurations and challenges. CloudWatcher [127] is another solution proposed to improve security of cloud systems by leveraging SDN capabilities. CloudWatcher controls network flow and ensures their inspection by security devices by providing a simple policy scripting language for using these services. It leverages SDN capabilities to dynamically control the network and set up routing flow rules to ensure that flows pass through the specified security services. More recently, Buyya et al.

proposed software-defined clouds (SDC), which facilitates easy reconfiguration and adaptation of physical resources in a cloud infrastructure. Along with numerous operational advantages and efficacy brought forward by SDC, it is assumed that SDC potentially improves the security of cloud services as well [25].

5. *Secure Data Offloading:* SDN allows routing network packets based on the requirements of the applications. This is expected to have considerable impact in computation offloading. Gember et al. [44] propose Enterprise Centering Offloading System (ECOS) as an enterprise solution enabling mobile applications to offload data in accordance to privacy, performance, and energy constraints defined by users. The ECOS-enabled NOS processes the data leveraging idle resources from the enterprise resource pool. Data is classified into user-private, enterprise-private, and no-private, which affects the policies chosen by the NOS. ECOS improves latency up to 94%, saves energy by about 47% and achieves as much as 98% reduction in execution state of mobile applications. ECOS is a great example of leveraging networking capabilities introduced by SDN to address application-layer concerns in a dynamic and flexible way.

6. *IoT Security:* Heterogeneity and scalability are the two main challenges in the security of IoT devices [174]. Leveraging SDN capabilities to address these security challenges is a new area that has been attracting the attention of researchers in the past few years. In the following, we review a few examples and refer the interested reader to [56, 157] for surveys. The authors in [113] propose an identity-based authentication scheme for IoT devices using SDN. In a nutshell, the SDN controller is equipped with a certificate authority responsible to manage all security parameters and authenticating device and gateways through a security protocol. Nobakht et al. [96] leverage SDN's centralized view of the network and reprogrammability and propose a host-based intrusion detection and mitigation framework for IoT devices called IoT-IDM. IoT-IDM is implemented on top of the NOS and upon detection of attacks it instructs the network forwarding devices to avert attack against victim IoT devices. The authors in [26] propose Black SDN for IoT as a solution to mitigate traffic analysis and data gathering by encrypting both packet's payload and header. Bull et al. [23] propose a mechanism to mitigate DDoS attacks using distributed SDN gateways, which monitor the traffic originating from and directed to IoT based devices. Fauzac et al. [41] propose an S-based IoT architecture, where each node in the ad hoc network is viewed as a combination of SDN-enabled forwarding device and legacy host. The security controllers are responsible to monitor traffic and enforce security polices in the ad hoc network. The authors in [114] aim improving the resiliency of IoT communications through SDN's flexible routing, where upon detection of attacks in one network link, the controller activates an alternative new link for the communication.

7. *Other:* SDN capabilities have been found promising in other domains as well. However, these are still emerging areas and dispersed across different domains in the literature. For instance, [31] presents an SDN-driven authentication, authorization, and accounting solution to improve the security of medium-sized

enterprise networks. Alternatively, the authors in [45] leverage SDN capabilities to develop an architecture that enables residential internet customization, which could be used to secure household appliances. Another domain that builds on SDN capabilities is vehicular ad hoc network (VANET). To this end, several proposals have emerged aiming to address the main challenges in VANETs including unbalanced flow traffic among multi-path topology, and inefficient network utilization using SDN. These solutions typically assume a central Road Side Unit Controller (RSUC) that can communicate with data plane elements instructing vehicles and RSUs instruction about the forwarding rules. SDN-enabled VANET has several operational benefits including minimized service latency, improved user experience, and efficient usage of network resources through collision reduction [35]. Moreover, it also improves the resiliency of a VANET through improved mitigation of security breaches including Sink Hole and DDoS attacks.

More recently, Shaghaghi et al. [124] leveraged SDN capabilities and proposed a network-based insider attack resilient framework designed to detect and deter insiders in organizations. Gargoyle introduces a new set of attributes for context analysis called Network Context Attribute (NCA). NCAs are extracted from the device generated network traffic and include information such as the user's device capabilities, security level, network connection type, network status, current and prior interactions with other devices, and suspicious online activities. For instance, Gargoyle detects devices equipped with hacking tools (e.g., port scan, vulnerability scanners), outdated software, unusual behavior (e.g., unusual locations, interactions with devices, etc.), and suspicious browsing history such as accessing blacklisted domains. Gargoyle leverages the capabilities of SDNs and retrieves contextual information by passively analyzing network traffic. This enables Gargoyle to function independent of the user's device integrated sensors and be portable to different organizations deploying SDN with ease and minimum cost. Gargoyle assesses the risk associated with an access request through NCAs and by modeling the user's behavior (both current and historical). As Gargoyle is a network-based solution relying on forwarding devices for context extraction and access enforcement, it has to ensure that the data plane forwarding devices have not been compromised. To achieve this, it integrates reports from WedgeTail [122] when evaluating the trustworthiness of a context. Furthermore, Gargoyle integrates PEPS [123] and can be programmed to apply access restrictions both at host-level and network-level. In fact, Gargoyle's SDN App (GSDN) enhances policy enforcement and facilitates a defense-in-depth protection model. For instance, a suspicious device can be restricted from accessing organization's network until further investigations. Finally, by implementing Function-based Access Control (FBAC)[33], Gargoyle's mobile app (GAPP) can restrict a set of functions for a data requestor depending on perceived trustworthiness of a context.

SDN has also been employed in other domains with the goal of improving efficiency and security including Wireless Local Area Networks (e.g., [51, 140]), smart grid and critical infrastructures (see [36] for a survey).

9 Future Research Directions

Despite the "SDN-boom" in the past few years, this technology is still in its infancy and will only be more secure and reliable with increased adoption and deployment. Specifically, protocols such as OpenFlow and the different NOS platforms are undergoing constant updates, and this makes SDN implementations potentially vulnerable. In summary, our survey of existing solutions designed to protect the control and data plane of SDNs indicates that:

– The majority of existing solutions for the data plane of SDNs are not designed to work within adversarial settings and assume that forwarding devices are trustworthy. On the other hand, solutions assuming otherwise have the following main limitations: substantial processing overhead for the network (e.g., cryptographic solutions), detect threats according to pre-defined rules, are unable to distinguish between specific malicious actions (e.g., packet drop, misroute, etc.), and have limited capability to effectively respond to threats. Recently, solution such as WedgeTail [122] has tried to partially overcome some of these limitations.
– Recent data plane enhancement proposals including stateful data planes (see Sect. 2.2) exacerbate the security challenges in protecting this layer. In a nutshell, stateful data plane proposals suggest the inclusion of switch-level programming abstractions with the goal of adding some form of intelligence into the devices as localized stateful flow processing. However, compared to standard SDN data planes, three main types of vulnerabilities are added with stateful SDN data planes:

  – Unbounded Flow State Memory Allocation: In order to make data planes programmable, each forwarding device must be equipped with memory space to keep track of the state transitions generated by the incoming flows. An attacker may take advantage of the large-in-memory space required for each forwarding device and exhaust the memory of the device.
  – Lack of Authentication Mechanisms in the Data Plane: If independent control functionalities were to be implemented in stateful data planes, then this would require the use of probe message between forwarding devices, or information passing between switches and "piggyback" inside regular traffic packets [32]. Securing inter-forwarding device communications is an important issue, which has almost been ignored in the literature so far. In fact, an attacker may inject fake event/packet into the network impersonating an honest device. Moreover, if the connections are not secured, an attacker may alter the information exchanged between the forwarding devices and change the specific flow states. An attacker could set up fake scenarios, where a link failure has occurred and degrade the network performance.
  – Lack of a Central State Management: State inconsistency is an issue of concern for all distributed systems including inter-linked stateful data planes. However, this is more worrisome in this case given that there exists no central entity to manage the synchronization of states inside the forwarding devices.

Specifically, as state transition is triggered after packets are received, an attacker has the capability to force state transitions pushing the network into an inconsistent state.

On the other hand, the architectural changes introduced with stateful data planes reduce some of the attacks that were possible in traditional SDNs:

- Enforcement Attacks: We defined enforcement attacks in Sect. 4.2. Stateful data planes reduce the required communication between the control and data plane. This improves the resilience of SDN against availability attacks (see Sect. 4.1) by improving its scalability.
- Implementation Attacks: Stateful SDNs mitigate the following vulnerabilities by design: (1) flow information leakage and (2) exhaustible TCAM used for flow tables [32]. In fact, with stateful data planes, the forwarding devices can be programmed to handle incoming flow without the need to contact the controller. Hence, flow information leakage vulnerability is to a large extent less relevant with stateful data plane deployments.

All and all, considering the added number of vulnerabilities introduced with stateful forwarding devices, innovative solutions are required to secure and protect SDNs adopting such devices.

- The majority of existing solutions proposed to secure the NOS are designed to protect it against specific threats (e.g., DoS Attack), which are typically originated from application and data plane. In fact, only a few solutions have been proposed to protect a network against a malicious NOS. Moreover, except Gwardar [125], we are not aware of any other solution designed to detect a NOS that has been successfully compromised and protect a network from it.
- As discussed throughout this paper, the attack surface against forwarding devices has expanded over the last few years. However, today's routing protocols and network troubleshooting tools continue to assume the underlying hardware is trusted. Hence, networks require solutions to automatically detect malicious forwarding devices and protect the network from them irrespective of the cause and independent of underlying software and hardware. Nevertheless, complementary to detection and response is the prediction of attacks. In fact, to the best of our knowledge, there are no solutions in the literature designed to predict attacks targeting SDNs before they actually occur.

10   Summary and Conclusion

In this paper, we presented a comprehensive survey of SDN and its security. We reviewed SDN's architecture and analyzed the security of this emerging technology by identifying the main different threat vectors available to an attacker when attacking a software-defined network. Further, we presented a taxonomy of different attacks with respect to SDN's main components. Thereafter, we highlighted the main challenges complicating the protection of SDN's data and control plane and surveyed existing solutions in the literature. We also provided a categorization of SDN-based security services, which has recently attracted increasing attention in the literature. Finally, we provided a set of suggestions for future research directions in this field.

Acknowledgements We acknowledge the useful comments offered by Sandra Scott-Hayward (Queen's University Belfast, UK) for improving this paper. Arash Shaghaghi acknowledges the Cloud Computing and Distributed Systems Laboratory for hosting his visit at the University of Melbourne, Australia.

References

1. Abaid, Z., Rezvani, M., & Jha, S. (2014). MalwareMonitor: An SDN-based framework for securing large networks. In *Proceedings of the 2014 CoNEXT on Student Workshop* (pp. 40–42). New York, NY: ACM.
2. Abdou, A., Van Oorschot, P. C., & Wan, T. (2018). Comparative analysis of control plane security of SDN and conventional networks. *IEEE Communications Surveys & Tutorials, 20*(4), 3542–3559.
3. Agarwal, K., Rozner, E., Dixon, C., & Carter, J. (2014). SDN traceroute: Tracing SDN forwarding without changing network behavior. In *Proceedings of the Third Workshop on Hot Topics in Software Defined Networking* (pp. 145–150). New York, NY: ACM.
4. Ahmad, I., Namal, S., Ylianttila, M., & Gurtov, A. (2015). Security in software defined networks: A survey. *IEEE Communications Surveys & Tutorials, 17*(4), 2317–2346.
5. Akhunzada, A., Gani, A., Anuar, N. B., Abdelaziz, A., Khan, M. K., Hayat, A., & Khan, S. U. (2016). Secure and dependable software defined networks. *Journal of Network and Computer Applications, 61*, 199–221.
6. Al-Shaer, E., & Al-Haj, S. (2010). FlowChecker: Configuration analysis and verification of federated OpenFlow infrastructures. In *Proceedings of the 3rd ACM Workshop on Assurable and Usable Security Configuration* (pp. 37–44). New York, NY: ACM.
7. Ali, S. T., Sivaraman, V., Radford, A., & Jha, S. (2015). A survey of securing networks using software defined networking. *IEEE Transactions on Reliability, 64*(3), 1086–1097.
8. Alsmadi, I., & Xu, D. (2015). Security of software defined networks: A survey. *Computers & Security, 53*, 79–108.
9. Anwer, M. B., Benson, T., Feamster, N., Levin, D., & Rexford, J. (2013). A slick control plane for network middleboxes. In *Proceedings of the Second ACM SIGCOMM Workshop on Hot Topics in Software Defined Networking* (pp. 147–148). New York, NY: ACM.
10. Arashloo, M. T., Koral, Y., Greenberg, M., Rexford, J., & Walker, D. (2016). SNAP: Stateful network-wide abstractions for packet processing. In *Proceedings of the 2016 Conference on ACM SIGCOMM 2016 Conference* (pp. 29–43). ACM, 2016.
11. Assolini, F. (2012). *The tale of one thousand and one DSL modems.* Kaspersky Lab.
12. Avramopoulos, I., Kobayashi, H., Wang, R., & Krishnamurthy, A. (2004). Highly secure and efficient routing. In *INFOCOM 2004. Twenty-Third Annual Joint Conference of the IEEE Computer and Communications Societies* (Vol. 1). Piscataway, NJ: IEEE.
13. Awerbuch, B., Curtmola, R., Holmer, D., Nita-Rotaru, C., & Rubens, H. (2008). ODSBR: An on-demand secure byzantine resilient routing protocol for wireless ad hoc networks. *ACM Transactions on Information and System Security (TISSEC), 10*(4), 6.

14. Benton, K., Camp, L. J., & Small, C. (2013). OpenFlow vulnerability assessment. In *Proceedings of the Second ACM SIGCOMM Workshop on Hot Topics in Software Defined Networking* (pp. 151–152). New York, NY: ACM.
15. Berde, P., Gerola, M., Hart, J., Higuchi, Y., Kobayashi, M., Koide, T., et al. (2014). ONOS: Towards an open, distributed SDN OS. In *Proceedings of the Third Workshop on Hot Topics in Software Defined Networking* (pp. 1–6). New York, NY: ACM.
16. Bianchi, G., Bonola, M., Capone, A., & Cascone, C. (2014). OpenState: Programming platform-independent stateful OpenFlow applications inside the switch. *ACM SIGCOMM Computer Communication Review, 44*(2), 44–51.
17. Big Switch Networks, Project Floodlight. Retrieved July 1, 2018 from http://www.projectfloodlight.org
18. Bishop, M. A. (2002). *The art and science of computer security*. Reading, MA: Addison-Wesley Longman Publishing.
19. Bosshart, P., Gibb, G., Kim, H.-S., Varghese, G., McKeown, N., Izzard, M., et al. (2013). Forwarding metamorphosis: Fast programmable match-action processing in hardware for SDN. In *ACM SIGCOMM Computer Communication Review* (Vol. 43, pp. 99–110). New York, NY: ACM.
20. Braga, R., de Souza Mota, E., & Passito, A. (2010). Lightweight DDOS flooding attack detection using NOX/OpenFlow. In *2010 IEEE 35th Conference on Local Computer Networks (LCN)* (pp. 408–415). Piscataway, NJ: IEEE.
21. Brooks, M., & Yang, B. (2015). A man-in-the-middle attack against OpenDaylight SDN controller. In *Proceedings of the 4th Annual ACM Conference on Research in Information Technology* (pp. 45–49). New York, NY: ACM.
22. Bu, K., Wen, X., Yang, B., Chen, Y., Li, L. E., & Chen, X. (2016). Is every flow on the right track? Inspect SDN forwarding with RuleScope. In *IEEE INFOCOM 2016-The 35th Annual IEEE International Conference on Computer Communications* (pp. 1–9). Piscataway, NJ: IEEE.
23. Bull, P., Austin, R., Popov, E., Sharma, M., & Watson, R. (2016). Flow based security for IoT devices using an SDN gateway. In *2016 IEEE 4th International Conference on Future Internet of Things and Cloud (FiCloud)* (pp. 157–163). Piscataway, NJ: IEEE.
24. Buyya, R., Calheiros, R. N., Son, J., Dastjerdi, A. V., & Yoon, Y. (2014). Software-defined cloud computing: Architectural elements and open challenges. In *2014 International Conference on Advances in Computing, Communications and Informatics (ICACCI)* (pp. 1–12). Piscataway, NJ: IEEE.
25. Buyya, R., Srirama, S. N., Casale, G., Calheiros, R., Simmhan, Y., Varghese, B., et al. (2017). A manifesto for future generation cloud computing: Research directions for the next decade. *ACM Computing Surveys, 51*(5), 105.
26. Chakrabarty, S., Engels, D. W., & Thathapudi, S. (2015). Black SDN for the internet of things. In *2015 IEEE 12th International Conference on Mobile Ad Hoc and Sensor Systems (MASS)* (pp. 190–198). Piscataway, NJ: IEEE.
27. Chakravarty, S., Naik, V., Acharya, H. B., & Tanwar, C. S. (2015). Towards practical infrastructure for decoy routing (positional paper). In *Proceedings of the Workshop on Security of Emerging Networking Technologies (SENT) Held in Conjunction with 22nd Network and Distributed System Security (NDSS) Symposium. Internet Society.*
28. Chasaki, D., & Wolf, T. (2012). Attacks and defenses in the data plane of networks. *IEEE Transactions on Dependable and Secure Computing, 9*(6), 798–810.
29. Chinese hackers who breached Google gained access to sensitive data, U.S. officials say. Retrieved August 5, 2018 from https://goo.gl/QrP2iV, 2013.
30. Chung, C.-J., Khatkar, P., Xing, T., Lee, J., & Huang, D. (2013). Nice: Network intrusion detection and countermeasure selection in virtual network systems. *IEEE Transactions on Dependable and Secure Computing, 10*(4), 198–211.
31. Dangovas, V., & Kuliesius, F. (2014). SDN-driven authentication and access control system. In *The International Conference on Digital Information, Networking, and Wireless Communications (DINWC2014)* (pp. 20–23). The Society of Digital Information and Wireless Communication.

32. Dargahi, T., Caponi, A., Ambrosin, M., Bianchi, G., & Conti, M. (2017). A survey on the security of stateful SDN data planes. *IEEE Communications Surveys & Tutorials, 19*(3), 1701–1725.
33. Desmedt, Y., & Shaghaghi, A. (2016). Function-based access control (FBAC): From access control matrix to access control tensor. In *Proceedings of the 8th ACM CCS International Workshop on Managing Insider Security Threats.* New York, NY: ACM.
34. Dhawan, M., Poddar, R., Mahajan, K., & Mann, V. (2015). SPHINX: Detecting security attacks in software-defined networks. In *NDSS* (pp. 8–11).
35. Di Maio, A., Palattella, M., Soua, R., Lamorte, L., Vilajosana, X., Alonso-Zarate, J., et al. (2016). Enabling SDN in VANETs: What is the impact on security? *Sensors, 16*(12), 2077.
36. Dong, X., Lin, H., Tan, R., Iyer, R. K., & Kalbarczyk, Z. (2015). Software-defined networking for smart grid resilience: Opportunities and challenges. In *Proceedings of the 1st ACM Workshop on Cyber-Physical System Security, CPSS '15* (pp. 61–68). New York, NY: ACM.
37. Erickson, D. (2013). The beacon openflow controller. In *Proceedings of the second ACM SIGCOMM Workshop on Hot Topics in Software Defined Networking* (pp. 13–18). New York, NY: ACM.
38. Feldmann, A., Heyder, P., Kreutzer, M., Schmid, S., Seifert, J. P., Shulman, H., et al. (2016). NETCO: Reliable routing with unreliable routers. In *2016 46th Annual IEEE/IFIP International Conference on Dependable Systems and Networks Workshop* (pp. 128–135). Piscataway, NJ: IEEE.
39. Feng, T., Bi, J., Yao, G., & Xiao, P. (2012). InSAVO: Intra-AS IP source address validation solution with OpenRouter. In *Proceedings of INFOCOM*.
40. Ferguson, A. D., Guha, A., Liang, C., Fonseca, R., & Krishnamurthi, S. (2013). Participatory networking: An API for application control of SDNS. In *ACM SIGCOMM Computer Communication Review* (Vol. 43, pp. 327–338). New York, NY: ACM.
41. Flauzac, O., Gonzalez, C., Hachani, A., & Nolot, F. (2015). SDN based architecture for IoT and improvement of the security. In *2015 IEEE 29th International Conference on Advanced Information Networking and Applications Workshops (WAINA)* (pp. 688–693). Piscataway, NJ: IEEE.
42. Fonseca, P., Bennesby, R., Mota, E., & Passito, A. (2012). A replication component for resilient openflow-based networking. In *2012 IEEE Network Operations and Management Symposium (NOMS)* (pp. 933–939). Piscataway, NJ: IEEE.
43. Foster, N., Harrison, R., Freedman, M. J., Monsanto, C., Rexford, J., Story, A., & Walker, D. (2011). Frenetic: A network programming language. *ACM SIGPLAN Notices, 46*(9), 279–291.
44. Gember, A., Dragga, C., & Akella, A. (2012). ECOS: Leveraging software-defined networks to support mobile application offloading. In *2012 ACM/IEEE Symposium on Architectures for Networking and Communications Systems (ANCS)* (pp. 199–210). Piscataway, NJ: IEEE.
45. Gharakheili, H. H., Exton, L., Sivaraman, V., Matthews, J., & Russell, C. (2015). Third-party customization of residential internet sharing using SDN. In *Telecommunication Networks and Applications Conference (ITNAC), 2015 International* (pp. 214–219). Piscataway, NJ: IEEE.
46. Giotis, K., Argyropoulos, C., Androulidakis, G., Kalogeras, D., & Maglaris, V. (2014). Combining openflow and sFlow for an effective and scalable anomaly detection and mitigation mechanism on SDN environments. *Computer Networks, 62*, 122–136.
47. Goransson, P., Black, C., & Culver, T. (2016). *Software defined networks: A comprehensive approach.* Los Altos, CA: Morgan Kaufmann.
48. Handigol, N., Heller, B., Jeyakumar, V., Mazières, D., & McKeown, N. (2014). I know what your packet did last hop: Using packet histories to troubleshoot networks. In *11th USENIX Symposium on Networked Systems Design and Implementation (NSDI 14)* (pp. 71–85).
49. Heller, B. (2009). *Openflow switch specification, version 1.0.0.* Open Networking Foundation.
50. Hong, S., Xu, L., Wang, H., & Gu, G. (2015). Poisoning network visibility in software-defined networks: New attacks and countermeasures. In *NDSS* (Vol. 15, pp. 8–11).

51. Hsu, H.-W., Huang, K.-L., Kao, Y.-C., Tsai, S.-C., & Lin, Y.-B. (2017). Deploying WLAN service with openflow technology. *International Journal of Network Management, 27*(3), e1970
52. Hu, H., Ahn, G. J., Han, W., & Zhao, Z. (2014). *Towards a reliable SDN firewall.* Presented as part of the Open Networking Summit 2014 (ONS)
53. Hu, H., Han, W., Ahn, G.-J., & Zhao, Z. (2014). FLOWGUARD: Building robust firewalls for software-defined networks. In *Proceedings of the Third Workshop on Hot Topics in Software Defined Networking* (pp. 97–102). New York, NY: ACM.
54. Jafarian, J. H., Al-Shaer, E., & Duan, Q. (2012). Openflow random host mutation: Transparent moving target defense using software defined networking. In *Proceedings of the First Workshop on Hot Topics in Software Defined Networks* (pp. 127–132). New York, NY: ACM.
55. Jo, H., Nam, J., & Shin, S. (2018). NOSArmor: Building a secure network operating system. *Security and Communication Networks, 2018*, 9178425.
56. Kalkan, K., & Zeadally, S. (2017). Securing internet of things (IoT) with software defined networking (SDN). *IEEE Communications Magazine*, (99), 1–7.
57. Karakus, M., & Durresi, A. (2017). Quality of service (QOS) in software defined networking (SDN): A survey. *Journal of Network and Computer Applications, 80*, 200–218.
58. Katta, N., Hira, M., Kim, C., Sivaraman, A., & Rexford, J. (2016). Hula: Scalable load balancing using programmable data planes. In *Proceedings of the Symposium on SDN Research* (p. 10). New York, NY: ACM.
59. Kazemian, P., Chang, M., Zeng, H., Varghese, G., McKeown, N., & Whyte, S. (2013). *Real time network policy checking using header space analysis.* Presented as part of the 10th USENIX Symposium on Networked Systems Design and Implementation (NSDI) (pp. 99–111).
60. Kazemian, P., Varghese, G., & McKeown, N. (2012). *Header space analysis: Static checking for networks.* Presented as Part of the 9th USENIX Symposium on Networked Systems Design and Implementation (NSDI 12) (pp. 113–126).
61. Khurshid, A., Zou, X., Zhou, W., Caesar, M., & Godfrey, P. B. (2013). VeriFlow: Verifying network-wide invariants in real time. In *Proceedings of the First Workshop on Hot Topics in Software Defined Networks* (pp. 49–54). New York, NY: ACM.
62. Khurshid, A., Zou, X., Zhou, W., Caesar, M., & Godfrey, P. B. (2013). *VeriFlow: Verifying network-wide invariants in real time.* Presented as Part of the 10th USENIX Symposium on Networked Systems Design and Implementation (NSDI 13) (pp. 15–27).
63. Kirkpatrick, K. (2013). Software-defined networking. *Communications of the ACM, 56*(9), 16–19.
64. Kloti, R., Kotronis, V., & Smith, P. (2013). Openflow: A security analysis. In *2013 21st IEEE International Conference on Network Protocols (ICNP)* (pp. 1–6). Piscataway, NJ: IEEE.
65. Koponen, T., Casado, M., Gude, N., Stribling, J., Poutievski, L., Zhu, M., et al. (2010). Onix: A distributed control platform for large-scale production networks. In *OSDI* (Vol. 10, pp. 1–6).
66. Kotani, D., & Okabe, Y. (2014). A packet-in message filtering mechanism for protection of control plane in openflow networks. In *Proceedings of the Tenth ACM/IEEE Symposium on Architectures for Networking and Communications Systems* (pp. 29–40). New York, NY: ACM.
67. Kreutz, D., Ramos, F., & Verissimo, P. (2013). Towards secure and dependable software-defined networks. In *Proceedings of the Second ACM SIGCOMM Workshop on Hot Topics in Software Defined Networking* (pp. 55–60). New York, NY: ACM.
68. Kreutz, D., Ramos, F. M., Verissimo, P., Rothenberg, C. E., Azodolmolky, S., & Uhlig, S. (2015). Software-defined networking: A comprehensive survey. *Proceedings of the IEEE, 103*(1), 14–76.
69. Krösche, R., Thimmaraju, K., Schiff, L., & Schmid, S. (2018). I did it my way! A covert timing channel in software-defined networks.

70. Lee, S., Wong, T., & Kim, H. S. (2006). Secure split assignment trajectory sampling: A malicious router detection system. In *International Conference on Dependable Systems and Networks, DSN* (pp. 333–342). Piscataway, NJ: IEEE.
71. Li, Q., Zou, X., Huang, Q., Zheng, J., & Lee, P. P. (2018). Dynamic packet forwarding verification in SDN. *IEEE Transactions on Dependable and Secure Computing*.
72. Lin, P.-C., Li, P.-C., & Nguyen, V. L. (2017). Inferring openflow rules by active probing in software-defined networks. In *2017 19th International Conference on Advanced Communication Technology (ICACT)* (pp. 415–420). Piscataway, NJ: IEEE.
73. Lindner, F. (2009). Cisco IOS router exploitation. *Black Hat USA*.
74. Liu, K., Deng, J., Varshney, P. K., & Balakrishnan, K. (2007). An acknowledgment-based approach for the detection of routing misbehavior in MANETs. *IEEE Transactions on Mobile Computing, 6*(5), 536–550.
75. Liu, X., Li, A., Yang, X., & Wetherall, D. (2008). Passport: Secure and adoptable source authentication. In *NSDI* (Vol. 8, pp. 365–378).
76. Liu, X., Xue, H., Feng, X., & Dai, Y. (2011). Design of the multi-level security network switch system which restricts covert channel. In *2011 IEEE 3rd International Conference on Communication Software and Networks (ICCSN)* (pp. 233–237). Piscataway, NJ: IEEE.
77. Mahajan, R., Rodrig, M., Wetherall, D., & Zahorjan, J. (2005). Sustaining cooperation in multi-hop wireless networks. In *Proceedings of the 2nd Conference on Symposium on Networked Systems Design & Implementation* (Vol. 2, pp. 231–244). Berkeley, CA: USENIX Association.
78. Marti, S., Giuli, T. J., Lai, K., & Baker, M. (2000). Mitigating routing misbehavior in mobile ad hoc networks. In *Proceedings of the 6th Annual International Conference on Mobile Computing and Networking* (pp. 255–265). New York, NY: ACM.
79. Matias, J., Tornero, B., Mendiola, A., Jacob, E., & Toledo, N. (2012). Implementing layer 2 network virtualization using openflow: Challenges and solutions. In *2012 European Workshop on Software Defined Networking (EWSDN)* (pp. 30–35). Piscataway, NJ: IEEE.
80. McBride, M., Cohn, M., Deshpande, S., Kaushik, M., Mathews, M., & Nathan, S. (2013). SDN security considerations in the data center. *Open Networking Foundation-ONF SOLUTION BRIEF*.
81. McKeown, N. (2009). Software-defined networking. *INFOCOM Keynote Talk, 17*(2), 30–32.
82. McKeown, N., Anderson, T., Balakrishnan, H., Parulkar, G., Peterson, L., Rexford, J., et al. (2008). Openflow: Enabling innovation in campus networks. *ACM SIGCOMM Computer Communication Review, 38*(2), 69–74.
83. Medved, J., Varga, R., Tkacik, A., & Gray, K. (2014). OpenDaylight: Towards a model-driven SDN controller architecture. In *2014 IEEE 15th International Symposium on World of Wireless, Mobile and Multimedia Networks (WoWMoM)* (pp. 1–6). Piscataway, NJ: IEEE.
84. Mehdi, S. A., Khalid, J., & Khayam, S. A. (2011). Revisiting traffic anomaly detection using software defined networking. In *International Workshop on Recent Advances in Intrusion Detection* (pp. 161–180). Berlin: Springer.
85. Meloni, S., Gómez-Gardenes, J., Latora, V., & Moreno, Y. (2008). Scaling breakdown in flow fluctuations on complex networks. *Physical Review Letters, 100*(20), 208701
86. Mendonca, M., Seetharaman, S., & Obraczka, K. (2012). A flexible in-network IP anonymization service. In *2012 IEEE International Conference on Communications (ICC)* (pp. 6651–6656). Piscataway, NJ: IEEE.
87. Monsanto, C., Foster, N., Harrison, R., & Walker, D. (2012). A compiler and run-time system for network programming languages. In *ACM SIGPLAN Notices* (Vol. 47, pp. 217–230). New York, NY: ACM.
88. Monsanto, C., Reich, J., Foster, N., Rexford, J., & Walker, D. (2013). Composing software defined networks. In *10th USENIX Symposium on Networked Systems Design and Implementation (NSDI 13)* (Vol. 13, pp. 1–13).
89. Moshref, M., Bhargava, A., Gupta, A., Yu, M., & Govindan, R. (2014). Flow-level state transition as a new switch primitive for SDN. In *Proceedings of the Third Workshop on Hot Topics in Software Defined Networking* (pp. 61–66). New York, NY: ACM.

90. Nadeau, T. D., & Gray, K. (2013). *SDN: Software defined networks: An authoritative review of network programmability technologies*. Sebastopol, CA: O'Reilly Media.
91. Naous, J., Walfish, M., Nicolosi, A., Mazières, D., Miller, M., & Seehra, A. (2011). Verifying and enforcing network paths with ICING. In *Proceedings of the Seventh Conference on Emerging Networking Experiments and Technologies* (p. 30). New York, NY: ACM.
92. Ng, E., Cai, Z., & Cox, A. (2010). *Maestro: A system for scalable OpenFlow control*. Rice University, Houston, TX, TSEN Maestro-Techn. Rep, TR10-08.
93. Nguyen, T.-H., & Yoo, M. (2017). Analysis of link discovery service attacks in SDN controller. In *2017 International Conference on Information Networking (ICOIN)* (pp. 259–261). Piscataway, NJ: IEEE.
94. Nippon Telegraph and Telephone Corporation, RYU network operating system. Retrieved June 1, 2018 from http://osrg.github.com/ryu
95. NIST: CVE-2014-9295 detail. Retrieved August 1, 2018 from https://nvd.nist.gov/vuln/detail/CVE-2014-9295, 2014.
96. Nobakht, M., Sivaraman, V., & Boreli, R. (2016). A host-based intrusion detection and mitigation framework for smart home IoT using OpenFlow. In *2016 11th International Conference on Availability, Reliability and Security (ARES)* (pp. 147–156). Piscataway, NJ: IEEE.
97. NSA Preps America for Future battle, Spiegel. Retrieved September 1, 2018 from https://goo.gl/PXMXeG, 2015.
98. OConnor, T. J., Enck, W., Petullo, W. M., & Verma, A. (2018). PivotWall: SDN-based information flow control. In *SIGCOMM Symposium on Software Defined Networking Research (SOSR)*. New York, NY: ACM.
99. Open Networking Foundation. The benefits of multiple flow tables and TTPs. Technical report, ONF Technical Report, 2015 [visited on 2018-07-01].
100. OpenFlow Switch Specification 1.5. 1(Protocol version 0x06), 2014.
101. OpenStack and network virtualization. Retrieved August 1, 2018 from http://blogs.vmware.com/vmware/2013/04/openstack-and-network-virtualization.html, 2013.
102. Open vSwitch. Retrieved August 5, 2018 from https://www.openvswitch.org/
103. Padmanabhan, V. N., & Simon, D. R. (2003). Secure traceroute to detect faulty or malicious routing. *ACM SIGCOMM Computer Communication Review, 33*(1), 77–82.
104. Pelekis, N., Kopanakis, I., Panagiotakis, C., & Theodoridis, Y. (2010). Unsupervised trajectory sampling. In *Machine learning and knowledge discovery in databases* (pp. 17–33). Berlin: Springer.
105. Perešíni, P., Kuźniar, M., & Kostić, D. (2015). Monocle: Dynamic, fine-grained data plane monitoring. In *Proceedings of the 11th ACM Conference on Emerging Networking Experiments and Technologies* (p. 32). New York, NY: ACM.
106. Pfaff, B., & Davie, B. (2013). *The Open vSwitch database management protocol*. Internet Engineering Task Force, RFC 7047 (Informational). http://vswitch.org
107. Phemius, K., Bouet, M., & Leguay, J. (2014). Disco: Distributed multi-domain SDN controllers. In *2014 IEEE Network Operations and Management Symposium (NOMS)* (pp. 1–4). Piscataway, NJ: IEEE.
108. Photos of an NSA upgrade factory show Cisco router getting implant. Retrieved September 1, 2018 from https://goo.gl/KNH6gD, 2014.
109. PicOS: One-of-a-Kind Open NOS. Retrieved September 1, 2018 from https://www.pica8.com/product/#sdn-edition
110. Porras, P., Shin, S., Yegneswaran, V., Fong, M., Tyson, M., & Gu, G. (2012). A security enforcement kernel for OpenFlow networks. In *Proceedings of the First Workshop on Hot Topics in Software Defined Networks* (pp. 121–126). New York, NY: ACM.
111. Porras, P. A., Cheung, S., Fong, M. W., Skinner, K., & Yegneswaran, V. (2015). Securing the software defined network control layer. In *NDSS*.
112. Qazi, Z. A., Tu, C.-C., Chiang, L., Miao, R., Sekar, V., & Yu, M. (2013). SIMPLE-fying middlebox policy enforcement using SDN. In *ACM SIGCOMM Computer Communication Review* (Vol. 43, pp. 27–38). New York, NY: ACM.

113. Salman, O., Abdallah, S., Elhajj, I. H., Chehab, A., & Kayssi, A. (2016). Identity-based authentication scheme for the internet of things. In *2016 IEEE Symposium on Computers and Communication (ISCC)* (pp. 1109–1111). Piscataway, NJ: IEEE.
114. Sándor, H., Genge, B., & Sebestyén-Pál, G. (2015). Resilience in the internet of things: The software defined networking approach. In *2015 IEEE International Conference on Intelligent Computer Communication and Processing (ICCP)* (pp. 545–552). Piscataway, NJ: IEEE.
115. Sasaki, T., Pappas, C., Lee, T., Hoefler, T., & Perrig, A. (2016). SDNsec: Forwarding accountability for the SDN data plane. In *2016 25th International Conference on Computer Communication and Networks (ICCCN)* (pp. 1–10). Piscataway, NJ: IEEE.
116. Schehlmann, L., & Baier, H. (2013). COFFEE: A concept based on OpenFlow to filter and erase events of botnet activity at high-speed nodes. In *GI-Jahrestagung* (pp. 2225–2239).
117. Scott-Hayward, S. (2015). Design and deployment of secure, robust, and resilient SDN controllers. In *2015 1st IEEE Conference on Network Softwarization (NetSoft)* (pp. 1–5). Piscataway, NJ: IEEE.
118. Scott-Hayward, S., Kane, C., & Sezer, S. (2014). OperationCheckpoint: SDN application control. In *2014 IEEE 22nd International Conference on Network Protocols (ICNP)* (pp. 618–623). Piscataway, NJ: IEEE.
119. Scott-Hayward, S., Natarajan, S., & Sezer, S. (2015). A survey of security in software defined networks. *IEEE Communications Surveys & Tutorials, 18*(1), 623–654.
120. Scott-Hayward, S., Natarajan, S., & Sezer, S. (2016). A survey of security in software defined networks. *IEEE Communications Surveys & Tutorials, 18*(1), 623–654.
121. Sezer, S., Scott-Hayward, S., Chouhan, P. K., Fraser, B., Lake, D., Finnegan, J., et al. (2013). Are we ready for SDN? Implementation challenges for software-defined networks. *IEEE Communications Magazine, 51*(7), 36–43
122. Shaghaghi, A., Kaafar, M. A., & Jha, S. (2017). WedgeTail: An intrusion prevention system for the data plane of software defined networks. In *Proceedings of the 2017 ACM on Asia Conference on Computer and Communications Security (ASIA CCS'17)* (pp. 849–861). New York, NY: ACM.
123. Shaghaghi, A., Kaafar, M. A., Scott-Hayward, S., Kanhere, S. S., Jha, S. (2016). Towards policy enforcement point of (PEPS). In *IEEE Conference on Network Function Virtualization and Software Defined Networks (NFV-SDN)* (pp. 50–55). Piscataway, NJ: IEEE.
124. Shaghaghi, A., Kanhere, S. S., Kaafar, M. A., Bertino, E., & Jha, S. (2018). Gargoyle: A network-based insider attack resilient framework for organizations. In *2018 IEEE 43rd Conference on Local Computer Networks (LCN)*. Piscataway, NJ: IEEE.
125. Shaghaghi, A., Kanhere, S. S., Kaafar, M. A., & Jha, S. (2018). Gwardar: Towards protecting a software-defined network from malicious network operating systems. In *2018 IEEE 17th International Symposium on Network Computing and Applications (NCA)* (pp. 1–5). Piscataway, NJ: IEEE.
126. Shang, A., Liao, J.,& Du, L. Pica8 Xorplus. http://sourceforge.net/projects/xorplus. [Online, visited on 2018-06-01].
127. Shin, S., & Gu, G. (2012). CloudWatcher: Network security monitoring using OpenFlow in dynamic cloud networks (or: How to provide security monitoring as a service in clouds?). In *2012 20th IEEE International Conference on Network Protocols (ICNP)* (pp. 1–6). Piscataway, NJ: IEEE.
128. Shin, S., & Gu, G. (2013). Attacking software-defined networks: A first feasibility study. In *Proceedings of the Second ACM SIGCOMM Workshop on Hot Topics in Software Defined Networking* (pp. 165–166). New York, NY: ACM.
129. Shin, S., Song, Y., Lee, T., Lee, S., Chung, J., Porras, P., et al. (2014). Rosemary: A robust, secure, and high-performance network operating system. In *Proceedings of the 2014 ACM SIGSAC Conference on Computer and Communications Security* (pp. 78–89). New York, NY: ACM.
130. Shin, S., Yegneswaran, V., Porras, P., & Gu, G. (2013). Avant-guard: Scalable and vigilant switch flow management in software-defined networks. In *Proceedings of the 2013 ACM SIGSAC Conference on Computer & Communications Security* (pp. 413–424). New York, NY: ACM.

131. Shin, S. W., Porras, P., Yegneswara, V., Fong, M., Gu, G., & Tyson, M. (2013). FRESCO: Modular composable security services for software-defined networks. In *20th Annual Network & Distributed System Security Symposium (NDSS)*.
132. Shirali-Shahreza, S., & Ganjali, Y. (2013). FleXam: Flexible sampling extension for monitoring and security applications in OpenFlow. In *Proceedings of the Second ACM SIGCOMM Workshop on Hot Topics in Software Defined Networking* (pp. 167–168). New York, NY: ACM.
133. Singla, A., & Rijsman, B. (2013). Contrail architecture. *Juniper Networks*, 1–44.
134. Skowyra, R., Bahargam, S., & Bestavros, A. (2013). Software-defined IDS for securing embedded mobile devices. In *2013 IEEE High Performance Extreme Computing Conference (HPEC)* (pp. 1–7). Piscataway, NJ: IEEE.
135. Smith, M., Dvorkin, M., Laribi, Y., Pandey, V., Garg, P., & Weidenbacher, N. (2014). OpFlex control protocol. *IETF*.
136. Snort—network intrusion detection & prevention system. Retrieved September 1, 2018 from https://snort.org, 2018.
137. Snowden: The NSA planted backdoors in Cisco products, InfoWorld. Retrieved August 1, 2018 from http://infoworld.com/article/2608141/internet-privacy/snowden--the-nsa-planted-backdoors-in-cisco-products.html, 2014.
138. Sonchack, J., Dubey, A., Aviv, A. J., Smith, J. M., & Keller, E. (2016). Timing-based reconnaissance and defense in software-defined networks. In *Proceedings of the 32nd Annual Conference on Computer Security Applications* (pp. 89–100). New York, NY: ACM.
139. Song, H. (2013). Protocol-oblivious forwarding: Unleash the power of SDN through a future-proof forwarding plane. In *Proceedings of the Second ACM SIGCOMM Workshop on Hot Topics in Software Defined Networking* (pp. 127–132). New York, NY: ACM.
140. Suresh, L., Schulz-Zander, J., Merz, R., Feldmann, A., & Vazao, T. (2012). Towards programmable enterprise WLANS with Odin. In *Proceedings of the First Workshop on Hot Topics in Software Defined Networks* (pp. 115–120). New York, NY: ACM.
141. SYNful Knock—a Cisco router implant—Part I. https://fireeye.com/blog/threat-research/2015/09/synful_knock-acis.html, 2015.
142. Tantar, E., Palattella, M. R., Avanesov, T., Kantor, M., & Engel, T. (2014). Cognition: A tool for reinforcing security in software defined networks. In *EVOLVE-A Bridge Between Probability, Set Oriented Numerics, and Evolutionary Computation V* (pp. 61–78). Berlin: Springer
143. Thimmaraju, K., Schiff, L., & Schmid, S. (2017). Outsmarting network security with SDN teleportation. In *2017 IEEE European Symposium on Security and Privacy (EuroS&P)* (pp. 563–578). Piscataway, NJ: IEEE.
144. Tootoonchian, A., & Ganjali, Y. (2010). HyperFlow: A distributed control plane for Open-Flow. In *Proceedings of the 2010 Internet Network Management Conference on Research on Enterprise Networking* (p. 3).
145. Tootoonchian, A., Gorbunov, S., Ganjali, Y., Casado, M., & Sherwood, R. (2012). On controller performance in software-defined networks. *Hot-ICE, 12*, 1–6.
146. Trevisan, M., Drago, I., Mellia, M., Song, H. H., & Baldi, M. (2017). Awesome: Big data for automatic web service management in SDN. *IEEE Transactions on Network and Service Management, 15*(1), 13–26.
147. Tsou, T., Yin, H., Xie, H., & Lopez, D. (2012). Use cases for alto with software defined networks.
148. Vault 7: CIA hacking tools revealed. Retrieved August 1, 2018 from https://wikileaks.org/ciav7p1, 2017.
149. VMware's network virtualization poses huge threat to data center switch fabric vendors. Retrieved August 5, 2018 from https://goo.gl/T2qDkL, 2013.
150. Voellmy, A., & Hudak, P. (2011). Nettle: Taking the sting out of programming network routers. In *International Symposium on Practical Aspects of Declarative Languages* (pp. 235–249). Berlin: Springer.

151. Voellmy, A., Kim, H., & Feamster, N. (2012). Procera: A language for high-level reactive network control. In *Proceedings of the First Workshop on Hot Topics in Software Defined Networks* (pp. 43–48). New York, NY: ACM.
152. Voellmy, A., & Wang, J. (2012). Scalable software defined network controllers. *ACM SIGCOMM Computer Communication Review, 42*(4), 289–290.
153. Wang, Y., Zhang, Y., Singh, V. K., Lumezanu, C., & Jiang, G. (2013). NetFuse: Short-circuiting traffic surges in the cloud. In *2013 IEEE International Conference on Communications (ICC)* (pp. 3514–3518). Piscataway, NJ: IEEE.
154. Wen, X., Chen, Y., Hu, C., Shi, C., & Wang, Y. (2013). Towards a secure controller platform for OpenFlow applications. In *Proceedings of the Second ACM SIGCOMM Workshop on Hot Topics in Software Defined Networking* (pp. 171–172). New York, NY: ACM.
155. Xing, T., Huang, D., Xu, L., Chung, C. J., & Khatkar, P. (2013). SnortFlow: A OpenFlow-based intrusion prevention system in cloud environment. In *Research and Educational Experiment Workshop (GREE), 2013 Second GENI* (pp. 89–92). Piscataway, NJ: IEEE.
156. Xing, T., Xiong, Z., Huang, D., & Medhi, D. (2014). SDNIPS: Enabling software-defined networking based intrusion prevention system in clouds. In *2014 10th International Conference on Network and Service Management (CNSM)* (pp. 308–311). Piscataway, NJ: IEEE.
157. Xu, T., Gao, D., Dong, P., Zhang, H., Foh, C. H., & Chao, H. C. (2017). Defending against new-flow attack in SDN-based internet of things. *IEEE Access, 5*, 3431–3443
158. Yao, G., Bi, J., Feng, T., Xiao, P., & Zhou, D. (2014). Performing software defined route-based IP spoofing filtering with SEFA. In *2014 23rd International Conference on Computer Communication and Networks (ICCCN)* (pp. 1–8). Piscataway, NJ: IEEE.
159. Yao, G., Bi, J., & Guo, L. (2013). On the cascading failures of multi-controllers in software defined networks. In *2013 21st IEEE International Conference on Network Protocols (ICNP)* (pp. 1–2). Piscataway, NJ: IEEE.
160. Yao, G., Bi, J., & Xiao, P. (2011). Source address validation solution with OpenFlow/NOX architecture. In *2011 19th IEEE International Conference on Network Protocols (ICNP)* (pp. 7–12). Piscataway, NJ: IEEE.
161. Yiakoumis, Y., Schulz-Zander, J., & Zhu, J. (2011). Pantou: OpenFlow 1.0 for OpenWRT. http://www.openflow.org/wk/index.php/Open_Flow1.0_forOpenWRT
162. Yin, H., Xie, H., Tsou, T., Lopez, D., Aranda, P., & Sidi, R. (2012). SDNi: A message exchange protocol for software defined networks (SDNS) across multiple domains. *IETF Draft, Work in Progress*.
163. Yoon, C., Lee, S., Kang, H., Park, T., Shin, S., Yegneswaran, V., et al. (2017). Flow wars: Systemizing the attack surface and defenses in software-defined networks. *IEEE/ACM Transactions on Networking, 25*(6), 3514–3530.
164. Yoon, C., Park, T., Lee, S., Kang, H., Shin, S., & Zhang, Z. (2015). Enabling security functions with SDN: A feasibility study. *Computer Networks, 85*, 19–35.
165. YuHunag, C., MinChi, T., YaoTing, C., YuChieh, C., & YanRen, C. (2010). A novel design for future on-demand service and security. In *2010 12th IEEE International Conference on Communication Technology (ICCT)* (pp. 385–388). Piscataway, NJ: IEEE.
166. Zaalouk, A., Khondoker, R., Marx, R., & Bayarou, K. M. (2014). OrchSec: An orchestrator-based architecture for enhancing network-security using network monitoring and SDN control functions. In *2014 IEEE International Conference on Network Operations and Management Symposium (NOMS)* (pp. 1–9). Piscataway, NJ: IEEE.
167. Zerkane, S., Espes, D., Le Parc, P., & Cuppens, F. (2016). Software defined networking reactive stateful firewall. In *IFIP International Information Security and Privacy Conference* (pp. 119–132). Berlin: Springer.
168. Zerkane, S., Espes, D., Le Parc, P., & Cuppens, F. (2016). Vulnerability analysis of software defined networking. In *International Symposium on Foundations and Practice of Security* (pp. 97–116). Berlin: Springer.
169. Zhang, P., Li, H., Hu, C., Hu, L., & Xiong, L. (2016). Stick to the script: Monitoring the policy compliance of SDN data plane. In *2016 ACM/IEEE Symposium on Architectures for Networking and Communications Systems (ANCS)* (pp. 81–86). Piscataway, NJ: IEEE.

170. Zhang, P., Li, H., Hu, C., Hu, L., Xiong, L., Wang, R., et al. (2016). Mind the gap: Monitoring the control-data plane consistency in software defined networks. In *Proceedings of the 12th International on Conference on Emerging Networking Experiments and Technologies* (pp. 19–33). New York, NY: ACM.
171. Zhang, P., Xu, S., Yang, Z., Li, H., Li, Q., Wang, H., et al. (2018). FOCES: Detecting forwarding anomalies in software defined networks. In *2018 IEEE 38th International Conference on Distributed Computing Systems (ICDCS)* (pp. 830–840). Piscataway, NJ: IEEE.
172. Zhang, P., Zhang, C., & Hu, C. (2017). Fast testing network data plane with RuleChecker. In *2017 IEEE 25th International Conference on Network Protocols (ICNP)* (pp. 1–10). Piscataway, NJ: IEEE.
173. Zhang, X., Jain, A., & Perrig, A. (2008). Packet-dropping adversary identification for data plane security. In *Proceedings of the 2008 ACM CoNEXT Conference* (p. 24). New York, NY: ACM.
174. Zhang, Z.-K., Cho, M. C. Y., Wang, C.-W., Hsu, C.-W., Chen, C.-K., & Shieh, S. (2014). IoT security: Ongoing challenges and research opportunities. In *2014 IEEE 7th International Conference on Service-Oriented Computing and Applications (SOCA)* (pp. 230–234). Piscataway, NJ: IEEE.
175. Zhou, Y., Chen, K., Zhang, J., Leng, J., & Tang, Y. (2018). Exploiting the vulnerability of flow table overflow in software-defined network: Attack model, evaluation, and defense. *Security and Communication Networks, 2018*, 4760632.
176. Zhu, S., Bi, J., Sun, C., Wu, C., & Hu, H. (2015). SDPA: Enhancing stateful forwarding for software-defined networking. In *2015 IEEE 23rd International Conference on Network Protocols (ICNP)* (pp. 323–333). Piscataway, NJ: IEEE.

Chapter 15
Survey on DDoS Attack Techniques and Solutions in Software-Defined Network

Tushar Ubale and Ankit Kumar Jain

Abstract Software-defined networking (SDN) introduces an innovative idea of "programmable network", which in turn provides flexibility and simplicity and speeds up the implementation. The core idea behind the SDN architecture is the separation of the control plane from the data plane. The data plane devices, such as switches, become simple packet forwarding devices, and the entire logic for handling the network traffic is moved into the controller which sits in the control plane. SDN adds flexibility, speeds the implementation, and simplifies management. However, this functionality of SDN also makes it as a target of one of the most popular type of attack known as distributed denial of service (DDoS) attack.

This chapter presents a concise survey of DDoS attacking techniques and solutions in SDN environment. Firstly, we present an overview of SDN and its advantages over traditional networks. Further, different vulnerabilities in SDN are being discussed along with DDoS attack. Then we present some characteristics that SDN poses to defeat this massive DDoS attack. Several taxonomies of DDoS attacks which affect the SDN environment are also discussed. Finally, we present future research directions that will be a crucial idea to defend such attacks in the near future.

The motivation behind this survey was to identify and examine various security drawbacks in the SDN architecture. We primarily focused on DDoS attack based on the recent statistics and increase of occurrence of DDoS attacks. Presenting the research challenges of this work gives us the direction to overcome the weakness that still needs to be addressed for the advancement of SDN.

Keywords SDN · DDoS attacks · Controller · Cyber attacks

T. Ubale · A. K. Jain (✉)
National Institute of Technology, Kurukshetra, Kurukshetra, India
e-mail: ankitjain@nitkkr.ac.in

© Springer Nature Switzerland AG 2020
B. B. Gupta et al. (eds.), *Handbook of Computer Networks and Cyber Security*,
https://doi.org/10.1007/978-3-030-22277-2_15

1 Introduction

Today's Internet has contributed to the formation of the digital society, where nearly every device is linked and reachable from anywhere [1, 2]. In spite of their extensive adoption, current networks such as data centres, enterprise networks, and cloud networks are increasing in terms of size and complexity [3]. Today's organizations are using advanced computing standards to meet their challenging needs that require more computing resources, planning, availability, and scalability [4, 5]. Such complex system processing cannot be satisfied by existing network technologies. In order to design such networks that can fulfil these proliferating demands, open source communities proposed a new networking design philosophy, "software-defined network (SDN)" [6]. SDN is a networking paradigm which makes the network programmable.

SDN is the essential outcome of extensive research efforts carried out in the past few decades towards transubstantiating the Internet to more open and programmable infrastructure [7].

Modern network elements are constrained in terms of hardware capacity. Due to this, scalability of the domain is limited. However, the concept of SDN is opposite because the hardware it runs on is specifically a server [8]. Automatic reconfiguration of devices according to traffic load is not possible. If we need to deploy an application, we need to modify each networking device manually. However, SDN deploys applications in the controller, which will distribute the resources properly to allow this application to function. SDN adds flexibility, simplifies management, and speeds up implementation. In addition, it provides the following characteristics:

- *Multi-tenancy*: Resource allocation and allowing much finer gain control
- *Quality of service (QoS)*: Allowing application to dynamically set QoS standards for, e.g. voice-over IP (VOIP) or video conferencing applications, to set high priority for user
- *Security*: Access control and resource allocation based on user identity

In this chapter, we analyse the security concerns in SDN in broad view. Firstly, we discuss in great detail the state-of-the-art programmable network (SDN) and then its architecture and finally present the security concerns which need to be addressed to overcome the weakness in the architecture. Our core idea of the survey is distinct in the sense that first we examine what are the different characteristics of SDN which help in defeating DDoS attacks in conventional networks. Then, we discuss various SDN planes and modules which can get affected when DDoS attacks happen. Finally, we examine some extensive newly attempted solutions which work for mitigation of DDoS attacks affecting different planes. We analyse various solutions along with their drawbacks which makes them inefficient for defeating DDoS attacks. We focused DDoS security issue in this chapter since the statistics shows the rapid occurrence of DDoS attack in recent years.

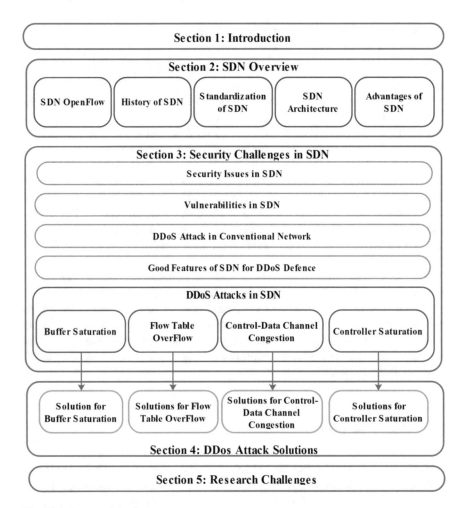

Fig. 15.1 Layout of the chapter

Figure 15.1 presents the overall structure of the chapter for better understanding of readers. Section 1 provides an introduction to the SDN field. Section 2 provides an overview of SDN including SDN's OpenFlow protocol, history of SDN, different working bodies for the standardization of SDN, its architecture, and advantages over traditional networks. Section 3 discusses security issues, vulnerabilities, and different DDoS attacks in conventional networks, along with some effective characteristics of SDN for defeating DDoS attacks and potential DDoS attacks that may happen in SDN itself. In Sect. 4, various defence mechanisms for the DDoS attacks in SDN are presented. Arrows in Fig. 15.1 indicate the different solutions that are proposed for DDoS attack. Section 5 discusses about several research challenges that need to be addressed to make SDN more influential. Section 6 presents the conclusion.

2 Software-Defined Networking Overview

Software-defined network is a physically distributed but logically centralized network that is centrally controlled by controller software [9]. Traditional networks have become more complicated and perplexed due to their growing size. Therefore, these networks cannot deal and satisfy networking requirements such as dynamic scalability, centralized management, networking cost, on-the-fly changes, handling network traffic, and server virtualization traffic in data centres. In addition, these traditional switches and routers have three layers, which are tightly coupled and interdependent with one another. Due to this coupling, evolution and innovation of each layer is hindered. Because of this interdependency, networking modifications such as configuring the device, limiting the rate of traffic, limiting the bandwidth, and tracking the network statistics need to be done individually and manually on each device [10]. Therefore, modifying a large number of networking devices becomes a tedious task.

The data plane networking devices such as switches become simple packet forwarding devices and the entire logic for handling the network traffic is moved to the controller, which is placed in the control plane. Thus, the controller abstracts the complexity of the network and switches become less expensive as they do not have to handle path computation and merely focus on traffic forwarding. Since the controller understands the construction of the network, it can communicate to the switches that are connected to it.

2.1 SDN OpenFlow

OpenFlow is a protocol which acts in southbound interface that allows a controller to instruct the switches for sending the packets [11]. In a conventional network, each switch has specific software to perform a particular task. This protocol helps the centralized controller to control special networking switches. Using this specific communication protocol, the two entities can communicate, but the messages inside the data plane are carried using existing protocols (i.e. TCP, IP).

The controller controls OpenFlow-enabled switches by writing commands directly to the switch flow table, also known as forwarding tables. The networking devices further act on information encoded in protocol headers (TCP ports and IP address) in order to decide the correct forwarding actions. Moreover, OpenFlow switches also support existing networking protocols. In the beginning OpenFlow protocol was designed for campus network. After some time, vendors showed keen interest and started investing in it. Alongside the protocol they began to see its use in data centres; by seeing the rising popularity done by the developers of protocol vendors, they began to create networking devices that have hardware support for this protocol as well. This leads to the creation of Open vSwitch, also sometimes abbreviated as OVS. Open vSwitch is licensed under Apache 2.0. Open vSwitch supports many traditional switch features such as VLAN tagging, standard spanning tree protocol (802.1D), port mirroring, flow export such as sflow and netflow, tunnelling (e.g. GRE, VXLAN, IPSEC), and QoS control.

2.2   History of SDN

The term software-defined networking was coined in 2009. The history of SDN proceeded in three stages, i.e. active networking, separation of control plane and data plane, and OpenFlow API. The idea behind active networking was to make network switches perform custom computations on packets. Active network helps in reducing the computing costs. Separation of control and data plane helped in more swift transformation as the control logic is not tied to hardware; it gave an easier network-wide view and gave more flexibility. The first instance of separation of planes was introduced by the Internet Engineering Task Force (IETF) working group in the form of ForCES [12] protocol in 2003. The standard essentially defined multiple control elements to control forwarding elements. In another way, the idea was to control switches through protocol interface. However, both approaches require standardization and deployment of new hardware.

Customizing the hardware potentially makes it easier to support a wider range of applications. Ethane project was the first project which elucidated a new architecture for business networks. The main focus of Ethane project was using the centralized controller to manage security and policy in network. The controller will compute the flow tables that must be installed in switches based on access control policies defined on domain controller. However, it requires custom switches that support Ethane protocol. Ethane laid the foundation of today's network which is known as "software-defined networking". SDN as a whole combines the concept of operating on existing protocol without modifying existing hardware. The idea here was to basically use the capabilities of existing hardware and control them through standard protocol. The protocol was named as OpenFlow, which communicates with the switch's flow tables to install forwarding instructions (entries) to control the forwarding behaviour of the network. Since switches already had flow tables, the only necessity was to encourage the switch vendors to open the interface for those flow tables so that a separate software controller would communicate with those flow tables.

2.3   Standardization of SDN

Figure 15.2 shows the working groups for the standardization of SDN. The Open Networking Foundation (ONF) is a non-profit association funded by companies such as Facebook, Google, Microsoft, Yahoo, Deutsche Telekom, and Verizon which is aimed for the development of SDN. International Telecommunications

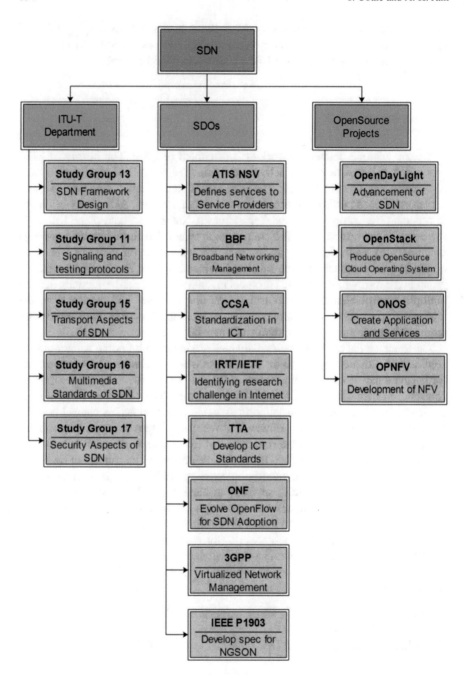

Fig. 15.2 SDN consortium

Union's Telecommunication sector (ITU-T) [13] is a United Nation agency that started the standardization of SDN in its study group (SG) 13. SG 13 is the leading study group that develops the framework of SDN. Another study group 11 started developing signals and protocols for SDN. ITU's ITU-D (Development) and ITU-R (Radio Communication) are coordinating with SG 13 and SG 11. The World Telecommunication Standardization Assembly (WTS-A) establishes the topic for ITU-T's study group, which in turn produces recommendations for these topics. Other study groups of ITU-T and their related area are study group 5 for energy efficiency and energy saving, study group 15 for generic information model, study group 16 for virtual content delivery, and study group 17 for security services of SDN. Other SDOs working for standardization of SDN are Alliance for Telecommunication Industry Solutions (ATIS), China Communication Standard Association (CCSA), Broadband Forum (BBF), Internet Research Task Force (IRTF), Internet Engineering Task Force (IETF), Open Networking Foundation (ONF), Third Generation Partnership Project (3GPP), European Telecommunication Standards Institute (ETIS), Open Cloud Connect, Telecommunication Technology Association (TTA), and IEEE P1903. Some open source software projects are OpenStack, OpenDaylight, Open Network Operating System (ONOS), ONF Atrium, and Open Platform for Network Function Virtualization (OPNFV).

2.4 SDN Architecture Model: Bottom-Up

ONF has proposed a reference model for SDNs. Compared to traditional network, this model separates the control plane, data plane, and application plane. By separating the control plane from the data plane, SDN brings the "power of abstraction". The data plane devices such as switches will become simple packet forwarding devices and the entire logic for handling the network traffic is moved into the control plane. Thus, the control plane represents the brain of a network, which controls the network behaviour. The switches become less expensive since they do not handle path computation and merely focus on traffic forwarding. Since the controller understands the structure of the network, it can intercommunicate with respective networking elements that are connected to it. Thus the controller hides the complexity of the network. The communication interface between the controller which belongs to the control plane and the data plane switches is carried out with the help of the OpenFlow protocol. OpenFlow is a standard application programming interface (API) [11]. Figure 15.3 represents the SDN architecture.

As shown in Fig. 15.3, the architecture consists of three layers separated from each other with some protocols acting as interface between these layers. In this chapter, we will use the word plane and layer interchangeably. The detail bottom-up layering specification of the above architecture is as follows:

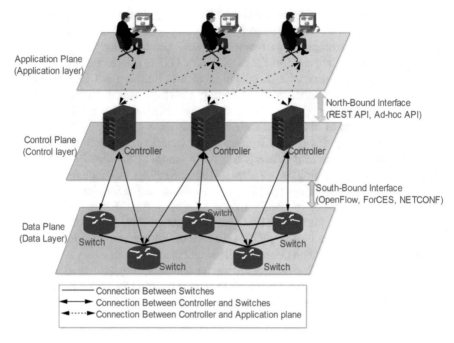

Fig. 15.3 SDN architecture

- *Data Plane*: Data plane includes forwarding devices such as routers, switches, wireless access point, and virtual switches. In SDN terminology, all these devices are named as switches or OpenFlow switches. Switches contain a flow table which represents the packet forwarding rule. Switches forward the traffic to the corresponding destination as stated by the control plane logic. The data plane devices such as switches will become simple packet forwarding devices and merely focus on traffic forwarding.
- *Southbound Interface*: Southbound protocols facilitate efficient control over the data plane. OpenFlow is the standardized and most well-known southbound protocol. Many vendors including HP, NetGear, and IBM produce their own switches which support OpenFlow. The open networking foundation is responsible for standardization of OpenFlow. The OpenFlow protocol uses a flow table to handle the network traffic expeditiously. Besides OpenFlow, there are several other protocols such as ForCES [12] and OpFlex [1], but more organizations are working for standardization of OpenFlow so it has become the de facto protocol.
- *Control Plane*: Control plane involves the controller which represents the brain of the entire network. The controller makes the packet forwarding decisions and installs the decisions in the switches. SDN represents physically distributed

but the logically centralized controller. Logical centralization simplifies the jobs of the network operators to configure and contend the network. The controller provides notifications, device management, and security mechanisms. Thus, the controller can intercommunicate with respective networking elements. A physically centralized controller can cause a single point of failure; therefore, it is hard to manage a huge network with a single controller. Contrary to this distributed controller can meet any requirement from small-scale to large-scale network.

- *Eastbound and Westbound*: Physically distributed controllers use east-westbound interface to communicate. Also, two complementing entities use east-westbound interface (e.g. SDN controller is communicating with VPN network). As a single controller may only handle a small network, so if one controller fails, it can inform the other controller to take over the traffic handling. Onix [14] and Hyperflow [15] have suggested these strategies.
- *Northbound Interface*: Northbound interface acts as middleware between control plane and application plane. The function of northbound interface is to hide the internal details of the network, permitting to program the network and to quest the services from it. This helps network operators to control the network accordingly, since SDN can be configured for various applications using single API to meet these demands. Therefore, it is likely that different protocols can exist. Current controllers provide their APIs such as rest API and ad hoc API to control the network.
- *Application Plane*: Application or management plane is the topmost plane in SDN architecture. Application plane involves applications which are written by software developers to manage the network. Application plane functionalities include fault monitoring and configuration management.

An SDN controller in control plane generates complex network functions such as computation of routing path, surveillance of network behaviour, and handling network access control. The bottom layer (i.e. data plane) handles packet build on high-level strategies defined in the application plane. The SDN allows its users to design and dispense new flow handling and control network algorithms conveniently. This adds much more flexibility and intelligence to the control plane. We can enforce protocols and new control functions just as writing an application similar to writing an app for Android OS or iOS. The OpenFlow protocol is a leading reference for communicating between the control plane and data plane. Before starting the message flow between the controller and switches, the switch must establish TCP connection with the controller.

Figure 15.4 shows how the switch does the packet processing when a packet is received [16]. When a new packet arrives in an OpenFlow-enabled switch, the switch checks for its highest priority match in the flow table. If a matching flow rule entry is found, the switch forwards the packet to the defined destination. Otherwise,

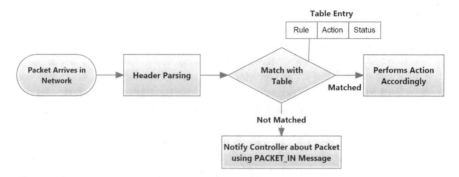

Fig. 15.4 Packet parsing in OpenFlow switch

Table 15.1 Comparison of SDN over conventional network

Characteristics	Conventional network	SDN
Network management	Difficult changes need to be done at each and every device	Separate data and control plane programmability
		Simplifies management and improves service delivery time
Performance	Devices have limited information and are relatively statically configured	Devices are dynamically globally configured along with cross-layer information
Configuration	Manual configuration	Automated configuration with centralized controller
Innovation	Limited hardware capacity Limited testing environment	Speedy deployment using upgrade of software
		Sufficient test environment with isolation

the switch sends Packet_In message to the controller asking for its destination address. The controller computes the path along with its destination and sends a Packet_Out message to the switch. The switch then modifies the existing flow rule or installs a new flow rule for further communication with the destination.

2.5 Advantages of SDN over Traditional Networks

The core idea behind SDN architecture is the separation of the control plane from the data plane. By separating the control plane from the data plane, SDN brings greater programmability in the network. This feature leads to improvement in traffic handling and easy configuration of SDN devices. In addition, this feature also gives the advantage of innovation in network design and operations. Table 15.1 presents the benefits of SDN over conventional network.

3 Security Challenges in Software-Defined Network

3.1 Security Issue in SDN

SDN security has become the most renowned topic in recent years. There are two major security challenges in SDN. One is towards solving conventional network security challenges using SDN technique. Another is securing SDN itself and fortifying SDN-enabled infrastructure. Considering the latter one, SDN itself is suffering from seven major threat vectors [17].

The threat vectors are listed below:

(a) Fake or spoofed traffic flow
(b) Attack on weakness in OpenFlow switches
(c) Attack on weakness in controllers
(d) Attack on control plane
(e) Lack of trust between control and management applications
(f) Vulnerabilities in administrative stations
(g) Lack of reliable sources for recovery of network

Among the well-known vulnerabilities, distributed denial of service (DDoS) attack on controllers has the most annihilating attack on the entire network.

3.2 Vulnerabilities in SDN

SDN provides strength and flexibility in networking. In addition to that, it also provides centralized control and brings down the deployment cost. This centralized control becomes vulnerable to some more attacks other than DDoS. Figure 15.5 depicts the representation of these vulnerabilities under different planes. Details about these attack scenarios are given as follows:

- *Network manipulation*: Centralization of the controller is the main theme of SDN. Once the controller is compromised, the attacker can program the network and manipulate the resources.
- *Data leakage*: Different commands for handling the packets include drop, forward, and send to the controller. The attacker can determine the packet processing time by analysing how packets are handled by the switch. If the attacker discovers the packets which are being sent to the controller, the attacker can generate similar types of packets which would be redirected to the controller causing the denial of service. In [18], authors explained how the DDoS attack can be launched through data leakage. Securing the storage of credentials for multiple logical networks is also one of the challenges faced in SDN. If logical network credentials are not isolated from each other, then this can lead to data leakage.

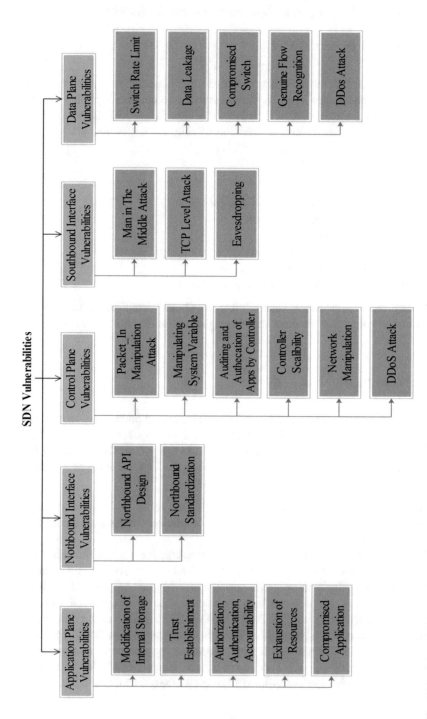

Fig. 15.5 Vulnerabilities in SDN

- *DDoS attack*: Separation of planes and protocols to communicate between different planes exploits the vulnerability of congestion. Southbound interface, northbound interface, switch hardware, and controller can all become the target of denial of service attack due to their limited capability [19, 20].
- *Compromised application*: SDN allows third-party application to supervise the network. Writing malicious applications can manipulate and exhaust the networking resources. Also writing an ambiguous application by developers exposes to vulnerabilities in software application that can be exploited by the attacker to conduct the attack.
- *Man in the middle attack*: The attacker modifies the communication among the communicating entities making the entities believe as if they are communicating with each other. This attack happens if there is no security between the communicating protocols. The OpenFlow switch description represents the use of TLS for secure communication between the controller and data plane switches. The lack of TLS adoption by OpenFlow vendors leads to man in the middle attack. In [21], the author studied about this attack and presented a feasible solution. In [22], authors have discussed various security solutions for this brutal attack.
- *Data modification*: As mentioned earlier, the controller programs the networking devices. If the attacker compromises the controller, then he/she could explicitly handle the complete system. From this site, the attacker can modify or insert fake flow rules inside the switch which would permit packets to mislead to different destinations.
- *Modification of internal storage of SDN*: The management plane applications have certain privileges for accessing the underlying system [23]. In other words, the controller shares some of its resources with third-party applications. Thus, the applications can access the internal database and manipulate it which can be further used for attack purpose.
- *Trust establishment*: SDN applications and controller must compel the trust mechanism since it has a centralized system architecture. Network devices' trust mechanisms exist, but for applications, trust mechanism does not exist [1].
- *Authorization, authentication, and accountability*: Attacks related to authorization can lead to illicit attacks to the controller. Authentication of applications due to its diversity is a major issue in SDN. There is no compelling mechanism that exists for the authorization and authentication of applications. Accountability of the third party is also a leading challenge considering the consumption of network resources [24].
- *Exhaustion of resources*: Performance of other applications is badly affected when all the system resources are consumed by malicious applications. Thus, the malicious applications can lead to memory consumption and CPU consumption and can also execute system command to dismiss the controller [25].
- *Northbound API design*: The dreadfully design of this API can be exploited by SDN applications to control the behaviour of other applications. For example, an application may evict an existing application session by manipulating northbound API.

- *Northbound API standardization*: There is no standard northbound API in the SDN architecture. So working with an open independent development environment is challenging and risky due to attack chances from skilled adversaries [26].
- *Packet_In controller manipulation attack*: Packet_In message is sent by the switch to the controller when incoming packets do not match the flow table entries of the flow table. At present, the control plane of SDN architecture has no integral security procedure that can circumvent the manipulation of Packet_In message even though the OpenFlow protocol is TLS enabled. Spoofed Packet_In messages can be sent by authorized switches to deprave the controller status [27, 28].
- *Manipulating the system variable*: The attacker needs to change the value of the system variable to deprave the controller status. For example, altering the system time may turn off the controller from linked switches.
- *Auditing and authentication of applications by the controller*: The controller is managed by third-party applications. Therefore, controller capabilities are used as a scale to measure the security of the control plane. For example, proper auditing and authentication of the applications help to keep track of how much resources are consumed by the applications [29].
- *Controller scalability*: The controller is the pivot element in the SDN architecture. It is responsible for decision making in the entire network. Due to lack of scalability, the bandwidth faces bottleneck, and this causes serious issues such as saturation attacks, delay constraints, and single point of failure [30].
- *TCP-level attack*: The specification of OpenFlow transport-level security is optional in the latest version of the OpenFlow protocol. Due to this, the southbound interface can be the target of TCP-level attacks [31].
- *Switch flow entry limit*: The SDN switch flow table is made of TCAM (ternary content addressable memory). The size of the flow table is kept limited as TCAM is costly. This limited capability becomes the target of saturation attack that leaves the switch in an unpredictable state [25].
- *Compromised SDN switch*: The attacker can compromise the SDN switch and fill up the targeted switch with fake flow entries which can subsequently forward the packet to a bogus destination. The attacker then analyses the packets which are being forwarded by the switch [32].
- *Genuine flow recognition*: The controller takes actions based on Packet_In message from the switch. If the attacker compromises the Packet_In message, then controller may take decisions which will send the packets to bogus destinations.
- *Eavesdropping*: The interface between the control plane and data plane can be the target of both passive and active eavesdrop. The attacker can learn about the network topologies by sniffing the currently flowing control messages.

3.3 DDoS Attacks in Conventional Networks

DoS attack is a cyberattack where a malicious user sends excessive fake requests to a server. The server does not find the return address of the attacker which causes the server to wait before closing the connection. Thus, the server keeps closing the connection of fake requests. This causes legitimate users to get the denial of service leading to DoS attack. The primary targets of DoS attack are popular websites and servers, making it unavailable to benign users. Sometime DoS attack may be launched on users too. The aims of this type of attacks are wastage of time, money, and resources of the victim. When this attack comes from several hosts (known as BOTS) that are managed by a malicious user, it is called distributed denial of service (DDoS) attack. In [20, 33] authors have discussed the countermeasures of these attacks. Figure 15.6 shows how the attacker uses bots for amplification of DDoS attack. DDoS attack provides many advantages to the attacker:

- The location of the attacker is difficult to identify due to randomly distributed attacking system.
- Attacker can use multiple systems to attack the victim unquietly.

Several types of DDoS attack affecting the victim or server [20, 33] are discussed below:

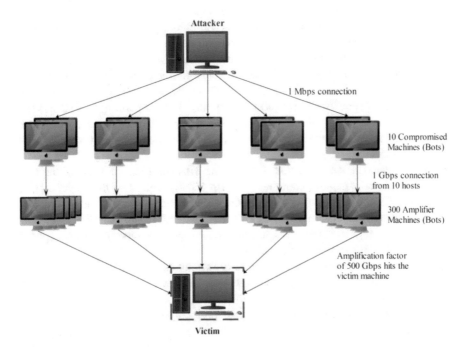

Fig. 15.6 Amplified DDoS attack

- *Email Bombing*: In this attack, a lot of spam emails are flooded into the victim's inbox by the attacker.
- *Ping of Death*: The attacker sends a larger packet than the victim's computer can handle. Ping command is use to check whether remote computer is communicating or not. This slows down the communication bandwidth of the server.
- *Smurf Attack*: In this attack, spoofed ICMP packets manipulate the IP address of the victim. ICMP packets are sent to share the network state information. The replies that are sent back towards the victim's computer are large in number congesting the network bandwidth.
- *Buffer Overflow Attack*: In this attack, a large amount of data is sent to the buffer, which has a temporary storage area. Such large data exceeds the buffer capacity and enters into another buffer which corrupts the data that is already presented in that buffer.
- *Syn Flood*: This is the most frequent DDoS attack. It occurs when client sends TCP Syn packets to the server, which opens up the connection between client and server. On receiving Syn packet, the server responds wo it and waits for acknowledgement but acknowledgement from the client side never comes. This keeps the server busy waiting.
- *UDP Flood*: This is very similar to Syn flood attack. In this attack, the client sends a large amount of UDP packets to the server. UDP flood consumes the bandwidth much faster as compared to Syn flood. The attacker uses botnet which consists of multiple systems and hence responding to each one becomes difficult.
- *HTTP GET Flood*: In this attack, the attacker sends a huge number of HTTP GET request messages to the server. The server replies to these requests and waits for acknowledgement, which keeps busy waiting because attacker never replies.
- *NTP Reflection Amplification Attack*: In network time protocol (NTP) attack, the attacker uses the traffic of a legitimate NTP server to overwhelm the target. The attacker uses spoofed IP to request the network time from multiple NTP servers. The response from these servers is targeted towards the victim. The packet size receiving from the servers will be larger, and the victim may get overloaded with the response.
- *DNS Reflection Amplification Attack*: The attacker forges the IP address of the client and sends domain name system (DNS) request to the servers. DNS is an IP address resolving mechanism which matches the IP address for the corresponding domain name and responds a particular IP back to the client. The attacker manipulates the DNS so that the maximum number of DNS response should be sent to the requesting client.
- *Zero-Day Attack*: The attacker exploits the vulnerability of the software that was undiscovered by the developers. Therefore, software users are at risk until the patch is being made.
- *ICMP Flood*: Internet control message protocol (ICMP) is an Internet layer protocol used for communication by networking devices. The network diagnostic tool ping and trace route both operate using ICMP. ICMP request and reply messages are used to ping a network device to check the connectivity between the sender and receiver. The IP address of the victim is spoofed by the attacker and

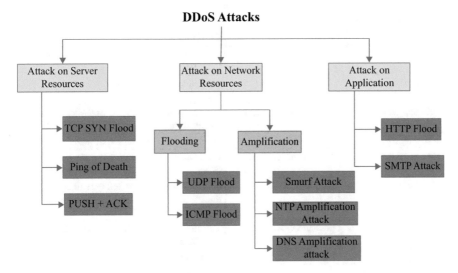

Fig. 15.7 Classification of DDoS attacks

abnormally numerous ICMP echo-request messages are sent to the networking devices. In response to this, these networking devices send ICMP echo-reply message to the target. The target IP address spoofs all the messages and is directed towards the victim. This in turn also leads to victim's bandwidth and resource consumption.

Figure 15.7 shows the classification of DDoS attacks under different resources. Major DDoS attacks that happened in the past few years are mentioned in Table 15.2. The attacks recorded in the table shows that government websites, banks, and military websites are the main target of attackers [34].

3.4 Effective Characteristics of SDN in Defeating DDoS Attacks

Unlike traditional network, SDN has some effective characteristics and these characteristics offer several advantages to subdue the DDoS attack.

- *Separation of control plane from data plane*: The researchers cannot perform experiments on a large scale over the traditional network. Moreover, the functioning of the newly designed algorithms cannot be examined and proved on the traditional network. SDN separates the bottom two planes, hence making it easier to test extensive defence experiments. The great advantage of SDN is its high configuration ability which permits experimentation in a real environment.

Table 15.2 DDoS attack in the past few years

Date	Aim	Description
28th February 2018	Github website	"Memcrashed"—Major amplification attacks from UDP port
8th November 2017	Boston Globe website	Interrupted its telephone's and editing system
30th September 2017	UK National Lottery	The attack targeted lottery website and its mobile app
24th August 2017	DreamHost DNS	DNS infrastructure was disrupted
13th April 2017	Melbourne IT DNS	Cloud hosting and mailing platforms broke down
21st October 2016	Dyn DNS	Dyn domain name system was attacked through a large number of DNS lookup requests
10th January 2016	Pakistan Govt website	The attack was launched on live radio of Pakistan government website
1st January 2016	BBC website	Over 500 Gbps of exhausting DDoS attack
1st December 2015	Green banks	Attack for ransom from green banks
30th November and 1st December 2015	DNS servers	Four different root servers were attacked with over five million queries per second
29th November 2015	Netherland public broadcaster	Public broadcaster named NPO was attacked
22nd October 2015	Thailand government website	Consequence of protest against Thailand's single gateway scrutiny program
30th March 2015	Github	http connections were hijacked using malicious JavaScript

The innovative ideas can be progressively deployed through a smooth change from trial phase to the working phase [35].

- *Global view of network*: The controller has the entire view of the network and monitors the traffic that can identify possible security threats. Centralization of SDN controller helps to dynamically isolate the compromised hosts and manifests benign hosts using the information obtained by the requesting end hosts.
- *Programmability of network*: SDN controller can be programmed by writing applications which can then control the network behaviour. The network is programmable, and we can manipulate the incoming traffic which blocks the malicious flows or hosts that disrupt the network. Moreover, intelligent scripts can be written for controller which can redirect the traffic towards intrusion detection systems (IDS).
- *Traffic analysis based on software*: Analysing traffic based on software allows innovation as it can be executed using different software tools, algorithms, and databases. Using software tools for traffic analysis reduces the burden of the switch to perform traffic parsing.
- *Dynamic network update policy*: Dynamic update of flow rules helps in immediate response to a DDoS attack [36]. Based on traffic analysis, innovative traffic

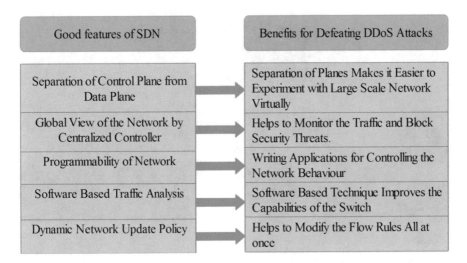

Fig. 15.8   Good features in SDN for defeating DDoS attack

blocking rule can be propagated across the network. In a traditional network, the rule for blocking the traffic is implemented only on target computers. In SDN the rule can be updated dynamically which can be placed in switches to block the traffic from attacker hosts or bots. In traditional network, each switch needs to be configured manually for changing policy, but in SDN, switch tables are updated dynamically all at once. This technique helps to keep track of all the switch flow tables. Figure 15.8 shows the features of SDN that helps to detect a DDoS attack.

3.5   Potential DDoS Attacks in SDN

As described in earlier section, the way the packet is processed by each module of the architecture attacker can exploit vulnerabilities of these modules on each layer for an attack. In the following subsections, we discuss how the attacker can make use of these modules to perform DDoS attack in SDN architecture. Figure 15.9 presents different SDN modules exploited during DDoS attack.

3.5.1   Buffer Saturation

The switch maintains a memory called as ternary content addressable memory (TCAM). When there is missing flow rule in the flow table, the switch stores part of the packet into buffer memory and sends the header as Packet_In message. When the buffer memory gets full, the switch sends the entire packet as Packet_In message. The attacker can send numerous packets whose entry does not match in the

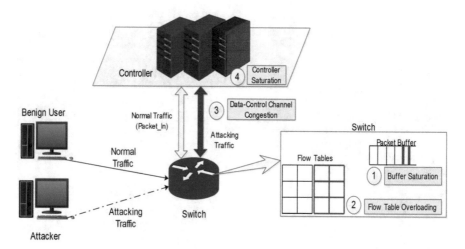

Fig. 15.9 DDoS attack in SDN

flow table, therefore forcing the switch to send the entire packet to the controller. A switch can send a limited number of Packet_In messages to the controller, for example, Hp Procurve [35] generates 1000 Packet_In messages. Thus, the limited capacity of buffer leads to buffer saturation.

3.5.2 Flow Table Overflow

The SDN switch sends miss packet entry to the controller and asks for a new flow rule. Each flow rule has a specific timeout value after which the entries will be replaced. The attacker takes advantage of this feature and generates new packets. Controller sends new flow rules to the switch for these packets. These new entries will replace the old entries, and after some time all entries will be replaced and the table gets filled up with fake entries. Therefore, the legitimate entries find no space in the flow table and hence get dropped. Pronto pica8 3290 [35] switch can hold 2000 flow table entries at a time.

3.5.3 Congestion of Control-Data Plane Channel

The SDN switch holds part of the packet in the buffer when the packet is sent towards the controller for processing. However, the buffer also has limited capacity and the SDN switch holds part of the packet in the buffer. Once the buffer gets full, the switch sends the entire packet to the controller as a Packet_In message for processing. Sending the entire packet towards the controller using the single bandwidth causes high constriction in the channel. Due to this, legitimate users also face high bottleneck for their request to get served.

3.5.4   Controller Saturation

Finally, as the flood requests arrive at the controller, the controller gets busy satisfying the fake request and these requests exhaust the throughput and processing capabilities of the controller. Infecting the controller downgrades the whole SDN architecture. To make this happen, an attacker only needs to create some significant amount of abnormal packets.

4   Defence Mechanism Against DDoS Attacks in SDN

DDoS mitigation in SDN environment is an active area of research; several explorations are carried out in various areas of SDN. Following are the defence mechanisms on the above discussed issues.

4.1   Solutions for Buffer Saturation Attack

Wang et al. [35] presented Scotch, a mesh of Open VSwitches that overlay the physical switches. When the physical switch gets overloaded because of new flow rules, these are forwarded to the Open VSwitches. Open VSwitches then forward the same to the controller as Packet_In message. The controller then installs a new flow rule either in the physical switch or Open VSwitch, which then forwards the packet to the destination. Thus, Open VSwitch acts as the buffer to store the new flow rules. The main drawback of this technique is that it is unable to distinguish between regular traffic and DDoS traffic. Thus, after a certain threshold, VSwitch drops the packet too.

Wang et al. [37] presented an entropy-based approach to defend against DDoS attack. The proposed approach involves statistics and analysis of the network traffic arriving to the network devices. Authors deployed their algorithm in the edge switch (switch near to the victim) for anomaly detection mechanism. The scheme calculates entropy based on IP and switch; when the entropy decreases beyond a specific threshold, the attack is detected. However, this solution needs to modify a switch which is not feasible.

Another similar work is done by Mousavi and St-Hilaire [38] where the randomness of the packet is measured. To detect the attack, two components were used, namely, window and entropy. The window represents the number of packets and entropy represents randomness. Sample entropy of normal traffic is decided as threshold. If traffic coming towards the controller exceeds the threshold, it is declared as attack traffic. If the traffic coming towards the controller varies in size, this method fails to detect it.

4.2 Solutions for Flow Table Overflow

Kandoi and Antikainen [39] proposed two methods—flow aggregation and optimal flow timeout value—to control DDoS attack. The flow aggregation method is used for matching several incoming packets for any one flow rule, and optimal flow timeout is used for replacing the flow rule after a specific time interval to prevent flow table overflow. In short, they suggested having an optimal timeout for flow rules. The drawback of this method is that it is not suitable for large area networks and, hence, cannot be used for heavy load traffic.

Dao et al. [40] detect DDoS attack based on IP filtering. As per analysis, an average user at least makes "k" number of connections and it sends at least "n" packets per connection. So, when a new packet arrives, its entry is made in the controller table. Then, it is checked if the average number of packet counter "s" is less than "n". If this is the case, then the drop rule is installed in the flow table. Otherwise, a timeout value of a particular source IP is increased indicating that it is a normal user. The disadvantage of this method is that it may install the drop rule for a false-positive user also.

You et al. [41] proposed a dynamic in/out balancing algorithm, known as DIOB/LFU algorithm to defend against the flow table overflow attack. The DIOB/LFU algorithm maintains the difference between rule-in and rule-out flow rules. The difference between rule-in and rule-out flow rule must always be less than or equal to zero. In addition, when "table full error" message is received from the switch, the controller evicts a certain amount of rules from the flow table whose idle timeout value is zero and counter value is zero. The algorithm tries to maintain the balance of flow rules in the table. The drawback of this algorithm is as the attack packets' incoming rate is much higher than balancing rate, it is difficult to deploy this algorithm in a real scenario.

Yuan et al. [42] executed a strategy known as peer support strategy. This quality of service (QoS)-aware peer support mitigation strategy is executed as an application in the controller. This application monitors status of each switch. When the switch flow table gets full, this application guides the traffic to other switches. Thus, the traffic loads get distributed across other switches. Peer switches support the targeted switch to manage the flow entries forwarded towards it. However, this method does not distinguish between legitimate traffic and attack traffic.

4.3 Solutions for Control-Data Plane Channel Congestion

In networking, when a client wants to communicate with the server or another client, they have to follow TCP handshake rules. In normal TCP handshake, whenever a packet comes in the switch and if switch entry does not match the packet, the switch directly forwards it to the controller and this is the cause of flooding attack. In Avantguard [43], the problem is solved with the help of the "migration module".

The migration module delays the handshake by making the switch work as a proxy server for TCP handshake and forwards only those connections to the controller who makes complete TCP handshake. The reason is, whenever an attacker tries for TCP handshake, it will never do complete handshake, meaning it never replies to packet sent by the server. Thus, this complete TCP handshake policy prevents the DoS attack. However, Avantguard can only defend TCP Syn flood attacks.

Piedrahita et al. [44] proposed the FlowFence mechanism to handle the network traffic. According to this scheme, the switches monitor their interfaces for congestion. Once congestion is detected, the switch notifies the controller. The controller requests the flow statistics from all the switches, and then the controller sends commands to the switch to limit the rate. However, this mechanism does not stop the attack entirely.

FloodDefender [45] presents a switch sharing mechanism to defend the channel congestion attack. In this mechanism, four modules, i.e. table-miss engineering module, packet filtering module, flow rule management module, and attack detection module, work together to defend the attack. Attack detection module keeps monitoring the switch for the attack detection. Once the attack is detected, it activates the other three modules. When a DDoS attack occurs, table-miss engineering module uses protecting rules to forward the traffic to neighbour switches. It uses average delay model to analyse how many neighbouring switches to involve in sharing. Table-miss packets are forwarded to neighbouring switches to save bandwidth between controller and victim switch. Packet filtering module filters the packet in two steps. Further, flow table management module installs the monitoring rules inside the victim switch to manage flow rules by removing the useless entries.

Wang et al. proposed FloodGuard [46], a lightweight, efficient, scalable, and protocol-independent defence framework for SDNs to avoid data to control plane saturation attack. It uses two techniques: proactive flow rule analyser module and packet migration module. The proactive flow rule analyser module sits in the controller as an application that generates flow rules based on the current status of the controller. Proactive flow rules belong to data plane. It represents the range of Packet_In messages, which can be handled by the control logic at this moment. Proactive flow rule analyser module uses symbolic execution engine, flow rule dispatcher, and application tracker to install flow rules. The packet migration module has two functions: First is to detect the saturation attack based on a particular threshold and second is to transfer the table-miss packets to data plane cache so that switch and controller do not get overloaded by packets. The data plane cache then sends flow requests as Packet_In message to the controller. The migration module executes the symbolic engine and generates flow rule to stop further flow requests. However, the symbolic execution cannot trace all execution paths.

In Flowsec [47] model, the author proposed a rate-limiting mechanism. Inside a switch, a meter is an element which measures the bandwidth utilization and number of packets passed through it. If packet rate exceeds the threshold, the meter band drops the packet. This packet drop mechanism filters out legitimate traffic too which is undesirable, and hence it is a drawback of this model.

4.4   Solutions for Controller Saturation

Avantguard [43] uses two modules, namely, "actuating trigger" and "connection migration", to overcome controller saturation. The actuating trigger enables the data plane to asynchronously report network status and payload information to the control plane. Moreover, actuating triggers can be used to activate flow rules under some predefined conditions to help the control plane manage network flow without delays. Connection migration module delays the handshake by allowing the switch work to as a proxy server for TCP handshakes and forwards only those connections to the controller who forms complete TCP handshakes. However, this approach defends only a particular type of DDoS attack. Switch hardware needs to be changed which is undesirable.

Zhang et al. [48] proposed a queue management technique for resource saturation attack. The controller schedules among the switches using weighted round robin (WRR) to serve the request of these queues for processing. If the size of switch queues increases beyond a threshold, then the queue is expanded to per-port queues of the each switch. When the traffic serving is accomplished, the queue size again becomes normal. The drawback of this technique is: for massive attack, multiple queues have to be maintained which becomes cumbersome.

Hsu et al. [49] proposed a solution based on hash value. A hash function operates in control plane which is used to assign incoming packets to queues in control plane. Round-robin model is used to schedule the queues. Whenever a new packet comes whose entries do not match, the controller extracts the essential information from the packet and calculates its hash value. From this hash value, packets are distributed to the queues, as a result sharing the services of the controller. However, this method does not detect the attack traffic.

FlowRanger [50] proposed a novel solution involving buffer prioritization to handle controller saturation attack. The mechanism derives the source identity based on the ranking algorithm and serves the requests using multiple priority buffers. FlowRanger has three components: trust management component, queuing management component, and request scheduling component. Trust management component computes the trust value of a new packet based on past requests. Queuing management component maps the request to the priority queue based on trust value. Request scheduling component analyses and serves the request based on length and priority level based on weighted round-robin strategy. There might be benign flows that may appear for the first time. So, blocking this request is not a good way to differentiate the users.

Braga [51] presented self-organizing maps (SOM), a neural network mechanism to control the controller traffic. SOM mechanism is used to classify normal traffic from attack traffic. It has three different modules that are feature extractor, flow collector, and classifier. Flow collector requests flow table entries periodically. Feature extractor modules collect these flow entries, extract the essential features, and organize them into six-tuples. To classify regular traffic from attacking traffic, SOM is initially fed with the broad set of six-tuples of attack traffic and normal traffic.

Table 15.3 summarizes the above discussed solutions; it also mentions which layers of SDN are protected against DDoS attack.

Table 15.3 Summary of defence mechanisms

Method	Focus	Proposed solution	Application plane	Northbound API	Control plane	Southbound API	Data plane
Scotch [35]	Open VSwitches	Open VSwitch acts as buffer for physical switches to store flow table	✓				✓
Entropy distribution [37]	Anomaly detection	Entropy of IP and switch is used as threshold to detect attack			✓		✓
Early detection [38]	Randomness of packet	Sample entropy of normal traffic is decided; traffic exceeding baseline is declared as attack traffic			✓		
Optimal timeout value [39]	Protection rule handling	Flow aggregation for matching flow rules and timeout value for flow rule replacement			✓	✓	✓
Limiting the connection rate [40]	IP filtering	If user sends less than "n" number of packets, it is considered as attacker					✓
Flow table overflow [41]	Dynamic in/out balancing algo	Difference between rule-in and rule-out must always be less than or equal to zero			✓	✓	✓
Flow table overloading [42]	Peer-support strategy	If flow table gets overloaded, direct the traffic to other switches			✓		✓
Avantguard [43]	Predefined policies	Connection migration component reducing data-control plane congestion	✓	✓		✓	
FlowFence [44]	Handling network traffic	Rate-limiting rules installed in switches					✓
FloodDefender [45]	Switch sharing mechanism	Table-miss packets are forwarded to neighbouring switches and further applying packet filtering			✓	✓	✓
FloodGuard [46]	Data-to-control plane saturation attack	Proactive flow rule analyser module installs flow rules and execution engine trace to generate suppressing rules			✓	✓	✓

(continued)

Table 15.3 (continued)

Method	Focus	Proposed solution	Application plane	Northbound API	Control plane	Southbound API	Data plane
Flowsec [47]	Rate-limiting mechanism	Switch meter drops the packet if packet rate exceeds threshold				✓	✓
Avantguard [43]	Tcp-Syn flooding	Connection migration modules delay the handshake and actuating trigger sends switch statistics to controller			✓		✓
Weighted round-robin strategy [48]	Switch queue management	Weighted round-robin strategy is used to schedule the switch queues to serve the request			✓	✓	
Design hashed-based control [49]	Hashed-based rate limiting	New packets' hashed value is calculated and assigned to queue to get service from controller			✓		
FlowRanger [50]	Buffer prioritization	Derives source identity based on ranking algorithm and serves the request according to priority			✓		
Lightweight DDoS [51]	Self-organizing map mechanism	SOM technique is used to differentiate normal traffic from attacking traffic			✓		

5   Research Challenges

As modern business communication systems are becoming more complex, the traditional network is unable to support this augmenting demand. SDN plays a vital role to satisfy these requirements along with speed and accuracy. SDN is still in its early adoption stage and security is the primary concern to make this transition to SDN. Centralization theme of SDN exposes too many weaknesses which should be examined for the better evolution of architecture. Such weakness includes:

Policy Conflict Resolution   Third-party applications must follow some policy rules to communicate with the controller; this maintains the integrity of the system. Since application written for handling the network has control over the entire SDN architecture, an attacker can take advantage of this policy and can write a malicious application. This helps to manipulate the network and direct the traffic. With respect to that authorization and authentication must be done before the application script starts managing the network [52]. In [53], authors have proposed a policy conflict technique.

Mutual Authentication   Controller communicates with both northbound and southbound interface. Authentication mechanism with the controller results in trust management and secure identification between the communicating entities. A role-based access control (RBAC) and audits must be done to look for unauthorised access to the controllers.

Application Development   Current application developments are controller dependent which hinders the evolution of the architecture. Hence independent third-party application must be developed. Besides these applications must be authenticated and authorized because they have access to controllers [54].

Optimization of Flow Tables   Optimal timeout values must be asserted for flow rules in switch flow tables [39]. In addition, TLS policy must be deployed to prevent eavesdropping between the switches. In order to improve traffic intelligence, some vital efforts need to be done in this area.

Attack-Tolerant System   A fault-tolerant system is designed to operate correctly even if there are some attacks on the system. For example, the system must offer service that fulfils the demands of a service-level agreement (SLA), so that during an attack an automatic triggering mechanism must be there to retrieve the compromised services and resources. As compared to traditional networks these attributes are easier to execute in SDN. Although some efforts are being made to bring this into action, still how to use features of SDN to handle attack tolerant system is an innovative path that needs to be tackled in future.

6 Conclusion

Software-defined networking brings the concept of "programmable network" in the networking domain, which in turn leads to flexibility and simplicity in terms of managing the network. The key idea behind this simplicity is decoupling control plane from the data plane and moving the logic of writing the applications to the application plane. In this chapter, we analysed the security concerns in SDN in broad view; however, we restrict the proposed solutions to defend distributed denial of service attack. This selection was based on recent statistics and considering the rapid increase in the DDoS attack incidents in recent years.

We surveyed the concept of software-defined networking (SDN) in detail. Particularly description of SDN architecture and functioning of each layer is provided. We also discussed how SDN came into existence and what benefits SDN have over traditional networks. Different solutions that are implemented at various modules of SDN architecture and their limitations to defend it are presented. In addition, various potential security issues of these solutions that we might face to deploy it in a large-scale environment are also analysed. Finally, we concluded with upcoming research challenges that need to be addressed to make SDN more influential.

References

1. Tewari, A., & Gupta, B. B. (2018). Security, privacy and trust of different layers in Internet-of-Things (IoTs) framework. *Future Generation Computer Systems.* https://doi.org/10.1016/j.future.2018.04.027.
2. Stergiou, C., Psannis, K. E., Kim, B. G., & Gupta, B. B. (2018). Secure integration of IoT and cloud computing. *Future Generation Computer Systems, 78,* 964–975.
3. Gupta, B., & Agrawal, D. P. (2016). In S. Yamaguchi (Ed.), *Handbook of research on modern cryptographic solutions for computer and cyber security.* Hershey, PA: IGI Global.
4. Wang, L., Li, L., Li, J., Li, J., Gupta, B. B., & Liu, X. (2018). Compressive sensing of medical images with confidentially homomorphic aggregations. *IEEE Internet of Things Journal, 6*(2), 1402–1409.
5. Gupta, B. B. (Ed.). (2018). *Computer and cyber security: Principles, algorithm, applications, and perspectives.* Boca Raton, FL: CRC Press.
6. Mousavi, S. M., & St-Hilaire, M. (2018). Early detection of DDoS attacks against software defined network controllers. *Journal of Network and Systems Management, 26*(3), 573–591.
7. Kim, H., & Feamster, N. (2013). Improving network management with software defined networking. *IEEE Communications Magazine, 51*(2), 114–119.
8. Zhu, L., Tang, X., Shen, M., Du, X., & Guizani, M. (2018). Privacy-preserving DDoS attack detection using cross-domain traffic in software defined networks. *IEEE Journal on Selected Areas in Communications, 36*(3), 628–643.
9. Bhushan, K., & Gupta, B. (2018). Distributed denial of service (DDoS) attack mitigation in software defined network (SDN)-based cloud computing environment. *Journal of Ambient Intelligence and Humanized Computing, 10*(5), 1–13.
10. Hausheer, D., Hohlfeld, O., Schmid, S., & Gu, G. (2018). Security and performance of software-defined networks and functions virtualization. *Computer Networks, 138,* 15–17.

11. Open Networking Foundation [Online]. Retrieved January, 2018, from https://www.opennetworking.org
12. Doria, A., Salim, J. H., Haas, R., Khosravi, H., Wang, W., Dong, L., et al. (2010, March). *Forwarding and control element separation (ForCES) protocol specification*. Internet Engineering Task Force [Online]. Retrieved from http://www.ietf.org/rfc/rfc5810.txt
13. ITU Telecommunication Standardization Sector's SDN Portal [Online]. Retrieved January, 2018, from www.itu.int/en/ITU-T/about/Pages/default.aspx
14. Koponen, T., Casado, M., Gude, N., Stribling, J., Poutievski, L., Zhu, M., et al. (2010). Onix: A distributed control platform for large-scale production networks. In *OSDI* (Vol. 10, pp. 1–6). Berkeley, CA: International Computer Science Institute.
15. Tootoonchian, A., & Ganjali, Y. (2010). HyperFlow: A distributed control plane for OpenFlow. In *Proceedings of the 2010 Internet Network Management Conference on Research on Enterprise Networking* (pp. 3–3). Berkeley, CA: USENIX Association.
16. OpenFlow Switch Specification [Online]. Retrieved February, 2018, from https://www.opennetworking.org/software-defined-standards/specifications/
17. Yan, Q., Yu, F. R., Gong, Q., & Li, J. (2016). Software-defined networking (SDN) and distributed denial of service (DDoS) attacks in cloud computing environments: A survey, some research issues, and challenges. *IEEE Communications Surveys & Tutorials, 18*(1), 602–622.
18. Shin, S., & Gu, G. (2013). Attacking software-defined networks: A first feasibility study. In *Proceedings of the second ACM SIGCOMM workshop on hot topics in software defined networking* (pp. 165–166). New York: ACM.
19. Gupta, S., & Gupta, B. B. (2017). Detection, avoidance, and attack pattern mechanisms in modern web application vulnerabilities: Present and future challenges. *International Journal of Cloud Applications and Computing (IJCAC), 7*(3), 1–43.
20. Zargar, S. T., Joshi, J., & Tipper, D. (2013). A survey of defense mechanisms against distributed denial of service (DDoS) flooding attacks. *IEEE Communications Surveys & Tutorials, 15*(4), 2046–2069.
21. Brooks, M., & Yang, B. (2015). A Man-in-the-Middle attack against OpenDayLight SDN controller. In *Proceedings of the 4th Annual ACM Conference on Research in Information Technology* (pp. 45–49). New York: ACM.
22. Akhunzada, A., Ahmed, E., Gani, A., Khan, M. K., Imran, M., & Guizani, S. (2015). Securing software defined networks: Taxonomy, requirements, and open issues. *IEEE Communications Magazine, 53*(4), 36–44.
23. Wen, X. (2013). Towards a secure controller platform for open flow applications. In *Proceedings of the ACM second ACM SIGCOMM workshop on Hottopicsin software defined networking*. New York: ACM.
24. Jain, A. K., & Gupta, B. B. (2018). A machine learning based approach for phishing detection using hyperlinks information. *Journal of Ambient Intelligence and Humanized Computing, 10*, 1–14.
25. Ubale, T., & Jain, A. K. (2018). SRL: An TCP SYNFLOOD DDoS mitigation approach in software-defined networks. In *2018 Second International Conference on Electronics, Communication and Aerospace Technology (ICECA)* (pp. 956–962). Piscataway, NJ: IEEE.
26. Nadeau, T. (2011, September 31). *Software driven networks problem statement*. Network Working Group Internet-Draft [Online]. Retrieved from https://tools.ietf.org/html/draft-nadeau-sdn-problem-statement-00
27. Hong, S., Xu, L., Wang, H., & Gu, G. (2015). Poisoning network visibility in software-defined networks: New attacks and countermeasures. In *NDSS* (Vol. 15, pp. 8–11). Ottawa: Health Canada.
28. Dhawan, M., Poddar, R., Mahajan, K., & Mann, V. (2015). SPHINX: Detecting security attacks in software-defined networks. In *NDSS*. Ottawa: Health Canada.
29. Hartman, S., Wasserman, M., & Zhang, D. (2013). Security requirements in the software defined networking model. In *IETF draft (draft-Hartman-sdnsec-requirements)*. Shenzhen: Huawei Technologies Ltd.

30. Sezer, S., Scott-Hayward, S., Chouhan, P. K., Fraser, B., Lake, D., Finnegan, J., et al. (2013). Are we ready for SDN? Implementation challenges for software-defined networks. *IEEE Communications Magazine, 51*(7), 36–43.
31. Liyanage, M., & Gurtov, A. (2012). Secured VPN models for LTE backhaul networks. In *Vehicular Technology Conference (VTC fall)* (pp. 1–5). Piscataway, NJ: IEEE.
32. Farhady, H., Lee, H., & Nakao, A. (2015). Software-defined networking: A survey. *Computer Networks, 81*, 79–95.
33. Specht, S. M., & Lee, R. B. (2004). Distributed denial of service: Taxonomies of attacks, tools, and countermeasures. In *ISCA PDCS* (pp. 543–550). Raleigh, NC: ISCA.
34. Akamai Solutions [Online] Retrieved January, 2018, from https://www.akamai.com
35. Wang, A., Guo, Y., Hao, F., Lakshman, T. V., & Chen, S. (2014). Scotch: Elastically scaling up sdn control-plane using vswitch based overlay. In *Proceedings of the 10th ACM International on Conference on emerging Networking Experiments and Technologies* (pp. 403–414). New York: ACM.
36. Ubale, T., & Jain, A. K. (2018). Taxonomy of DDoS attacks in software-defined networking environment. In *International Conference on Futuristic Trends in Network and Communication Technologies* (pp. 278–291). Singapore: Springer.
37. Wang, R., Jia, Z., & Ju, L. (2015). An entropy-based distributed DDoS detection mechanism in software-defined networking. In *Trustcom/BigDataSE/ISPA, 2015 IEEE* (Vol. 1, pp. 310–317). Los Alamitos, CA: Conference Publishing Services, IEEE Computer Society.
38. Mousavi, S. M., & St-Hilaire, M. (2015). Early detection of DDoS attacks against SDN controllers. In *Computing, Networking and Communications (ICNC), 2015 ₓInternational Conference on IEEE* (pp. 77–81). Piscataway, NJ: IEEE.
39. Kandoi, R., & Antikainen, M. (2015). Denial-of-service attacks in OpenFlow SDN networks. In *Integrated Network Management (IM), 2015 IFIP/IEEE International Symposium on IEEE* (pp. 1322–1326). Piscataway, NJ: IEEE.
40. Dao, N. N., Park, J., Park, M., & Cho, S. (2015). A feasible method to combat against DDoS attack in SDN network. In *Information Networking (ICOIN), 2015 International Conference on IEEE* (pp. 309–311). Piscataway, NJ: IEEE.
41. You, W., Qian, K., & Qian, Y. (2016). Software-defined network flow table overflow attacks and countermeasures. *International Journal of Soft Computing and Networking, 1*(1), 70–81.
42. Yuan, B., Zou, D., Yu, S., Jin, H., Qiang, W., & Shen, J. (2016). Defending against flow table overloading attack in software-defined networks. *IEEE Transactions on Services Computing, 12*(2), 231–246.
43. Shin, S., Yegneswaran, V., Porras, P., & Gu, G. (2013). Avant-guard: Scalable and vigilant switch flow management in software-defined networks. In *Proceedings of the 2013 ACM SIGSAC conference on Computer & Communications Security* (pp. 413–424). New York: ACM.
44. Piedrahita, A. F. M., Rueda, S., Mattos, D. M., & Duarte, O. C. M. (2015). FlowFence: A denial of service defense system for software defined networking. In *Global Information Infrastructure and Networking Symposium (GIIS), IEEE* (pp. 1–6). Piscataway, NJ: IEEE.
45. Shang, G., Zhe, P., Bin, X., Aiqun, H., & Kui, R. (2017). FloodDefender: Protecting data and control plane resources under SDN-aimed DoS attacks. In *INFOCOM 2017-IEEE Conference on Computer Communications* (pp. 1–9). Piscataway, NJ: IEEE.
46. Wang, H., Xu, L., & Gu, G. (2015). Floodguard: A dos attack prevention extension in software-defined networks. In *Dependable Systems and Networks (DSN), 2015 45th Annual IEEE/IFIP International Conference on IEEE* (pp. 239–250). Piscataway, NJ: IEEE.
47. Kuerban, M., Tian, Y., Yang, Q., Jia, Y., Huebert, B., & Poss, D. (2016). FlowSec: DOS attack mitigation strategy on SDN controller. In *Networking, Architecture and Storage (NAS), 2016 IEEE International Conference on IEEE* (pp. 1–2).
48. Zhang, P., Wang, H., Hu, C., & Lin, C. (2016). On denial of service attacks in software defined networks. *IEEE Network, 30*(6), 28–33.

49. Hsu, S. W., Chen, T. Y., Chang, Y. C., Chen, S. H., Chao, H. C., Lin, T. Y., & Shih, W. K. (2015). Design a hash-based control mechanism in vswitch for software-defined networking environment. In *Cluster Computing (CLUSTER), 2015 IEEE International Conference on IEEE* (pp. 498–499). Piscataway, NJ: IEEE.
50. Wei, L., & Fung, C. (2015). FlowRanger: A request prioritizing algorithm for controller DoS attacks in software defined networks. In *Communications (ICC), 2015 IEEE International Conference on IEEE* (pp. 5254–5259). Piscataway, NJ: IEEE.
51. Braga, R., Mota, E., & Passito, A. (2010). Lightweight DDoS flooding attack detection using NOX/OpenFlow. In *Local Computer Networks (LCN), 2010 IEEE 35th Conference on IEEE* (pp. 408–415). Piscataway, NJ: IEEE.
52. Jain, A. K., & Gupta, B. B. (2017). Two-level authentication approach to protect from phishing attacks in real time. *Journal of Ambient Intelligence and Humanized Computing, 9*(6), 1–14.
53. He, B., Dong, L., Xu, T., Fei, S., Zhang, H., & Wang, W. (2017). Research on network programming language and policy conflicts for SDN. *Concurrency and Computation: Practice and Experience, 29*(19), e4218.
54. Shin, S., Song, Y., Lee, T., Lee, S., Chung, J., Porras, P., et al. (2014). Rosemary: A robust, secure, and high-performance network operating system. In *Proceedings of the 2014 ACM SIGSAC Conference on Computer and Communications Security* (pp. 78–89). New York: ACM.

Chapter 16
Cooperative Mechanisms for Defending Distributed Denial of Service (DDoS) Attacks

Prachi Gulihar and B. B. Gupta

Abstract Distributed denial of service (DDoS) attack is one of the biggest challenges faced by the Internet community today. DDoS attack attempts to disrupt the availability of resources to the legitimate users by overwhelming the network and server resources. In this chapter, we discuss the importance of cooperative mechanisms over the centralised ones and various existing cooperative techniques to defend against DDoS attack. We also discuss their major drawbacks. The major disadvantage of centralised defence mechanism is single point of failure when the central kingpin node itself comes under attack. What we realise is that although these techniques have been developed, they are rarely deployed in the real world because the researchers have long ignored the economic incentive part in the working of cooperative DDoS mechanisms. Due to lack of incremental payment structures, the cooperation between the nodes fails. Sometimes the payment structures are non-existent, and in some cases, the payment structure is in place, but the incentives are not lucrative enough for the nodes to share their resources. The DDoS attack scenario can be divided into attack phase, detection phase and response phase. When the attacker machines perform in cooperation, then for the defence mechanism to be strong, it should also be in cooperation. This work gives an overview of the existing cooperative defence mechanisms at different layers of the Open Systems Interconnection (OSI) model and an overview of mechanism using third party for any of these three phases.

Keywords Distributed denial of service (DDoS) attack · Defence mechanisms · Cooperative third-party defence schemes

P. Gulihar (✉) · B. B. Gupta
Department of Computer Engineering, National Institute of Technology Kurukshetra, Kurukshetra, India

© Springer Nature Switzerland AG 2020   421
B. B. Gupta et al. (eds.), *Handbook of Computer Networks and Cyber Security*,
https://doi.org/10.1007/978-3-030-22277-2_16

1 Introduction

Distributed denial of service (DDoS) [1] attack is one of the biggest challenges faced by the Internet community today. They are performed by the slave machines which are a part of the botnet army and act on the commands of the master machine whose motive is to exhaust network and server resources like bandwidth and storage so that its services become unavailable to the legitimate clients. The largest reported DDoS attack was of volume 400 Gpbs in the year 2014 [2]. Since then, the DDoS attacks are growing in volume. Their efficiency and implementation techniques have become more sophisticated day by day, making it a big challenge for the security professionals. Recently, the study of economics of Internet has emerged as a fast emerging field of study for cyber defence. The workstations being distributed across the network along with the users having varied interests have made this study very important from the information security and policy designing point of view. The main purpose of any framework design is to keep up with the security standards of confidentiality, integrity and availability without being an overburden on the deployer.

The concept of "tragedy of the commons" plays an important role in distributing the limited resources of the Internet. In this, the users because of their own self-interest destroy the collective interest of a community sharing the resource. A sustainable pricing strategy is the one which is able to cater to the competitive advantage of different network providers offering the same set of services but on varied prices. A pricing mechanism will help in differentiating the services offered to the users, but another important task is of fixing the incentives. The pricing strategy plays a very important role in facilitating varied kinds of QoS requirements. Security professionals have realised that while designing any security mechanism, it is vital to keep in consideration the "theory of mind" which explains the way the attackers and benign users take decision to deceive or remain loyal to the system.

Distributed denial of service attacks are the ones in which the attacker gains control of the system by exploiting its vulnerabilities. In this manner, the attacker is able to compromise several machines which then together form an army of zombies who act as slave machines. The attacker or the master machine then commands the slave machines to begin the attack either by sending malicious packets to the victim's address or by flooding exhausting the connectivity bandwidth and server resources. When the attacker's target is connection bandwidth, then the attack takes place in network and transport layer, whereas when the target is on exhausting the server resources, then the attack takes place on the application layer. Figure 16.1 explains how distributed denial of service attack differs from the denial of service attack in a way that the former attack involves the execution of the attack by the coordination of numerous zombie machines and Internet connections whereas the latter only involved a single machine and a single connection in control of the attacker [3]. When the attacker performs the attack, it is doing that with the collaborative efforts of hundreds and thousands of machines; then why not defend

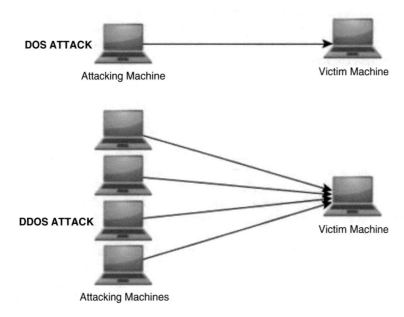

Fig. 16.1 DoS vs DDoS attack

the system in the similar way by achieving collaboration between several nodes which are ready to pool their resources in exchange for some economic incentive?

When combating DDoS attacks, the industry and the academia have always ignored the economic incentive part of the problem which has been the key aspect in defeating DDoS attacks. Incentives are the cornerstones of the race of humans. The problem is that although there are many distributed cooperative defence mechanisms, still the systems are being victims of DDoS attacks. This is because no solution has been able to lure ISPs to pool their free cache memories in order to perform collaborative defence. They have been rarely deployed on the Internet because their payment structure is either non-existent or it lacks an incremental pattern. This has led to failure of cooperation. Another closely related challenging problem is the deployment of the distributed solutions because detection and responses are scattered at different locations.

The DDoS attack defence mechanisms can be classified by the strategy used to detect the attack. It can be classified as anomaly-based, pattern-based and third-party detection. In pattern-based attack detection technique, the signatures of known attacks are stored in the database, and then the traffic is matched with the signatures stored; if the signature matches, then the DDoS attack is successfully detected. The main drawback of this approach is its vulnerability to zero-day attacks. Every now and then new attacks are launched and new viruses are made, so if the stored database is not updated in real time, then the system is bound to surpass many new attack types. In anomaly-based attack detection technique, an ideal model is defined, and the incoming traffic is then compared with that ideal model. If the deviations go beyond the defined acceptable limits, then the attack is detected. The advantage of this technique over pattern detection is that here the system can be trained to detect the new types of malicious traffic.

2 Motivation

The Internet Service Providers (ISPs) are facing a problem of increased volumes of illegitimate traffic. The main purpose of this malicious traffic is to exhaust the limited network resources like storage and bandwidth. The level of resources required to maintain the network performance falls short, and the quality of service (QoS) provided by the network degrades rapidly. A very large volume of malicious traffic is produced by misbehaving users who either knowingly or unknowingly launch flooding distributed denial of service attacks from their systems. Congestion control mechanisms are executed at network level to prevent the traffic from reaching its peak value by throttling mechanism. Throttling means regulating the rate of traffic being transferred over a network link to prevent it from collapsing due to traffic overload.

But this mechanism fails to maintain the required level of QoS. The ability of DDoS attack to generate massive volumes of unwanted traffic has made it one of the biggest threats the Internet is vulnerable to [4]. The main targets of DDoS attack are the websites. They attack the benign user's ability to access the website or server [5]. The primest marks of DDoS attack which went on for 2 days can be traced back to the year 1999 [6]. Since then, a lot of DDoS detection techniques and response strategies have been developed. A more advanced kind of DDoS attack is known as amplification attacks like Domain Name Server (DNS) amplification attack, NTP amplification attack, etc. in which these servers play the role of reflectors and create a stronger attack. In these attacks, the servers are not attacked directly, but instead these multiple servers are used to generate large traffic against small requests which is directed towards the spoofed IP address provided by the attacker who sent the request to these servers. The response data is used as unwanted traffic. As observed [7], there are two main characteristics because of which the DDoS defence mechanisms have been unable to provide reliable protection. First is the inability to distinguish between the malicious and benign traffic. There is no such mechanism which efficiently differentiates the traffic with minimum collateral damage to the legitimate requests. Second, DDoS attack sources are distributed across different sites which is why it becomes very difficult to trace them.

The reasons for failure of security in any system are twofold. First is the poor design and second is the poor incentive. Although the design part has been widely explored, the incentive part remains naïve. Computer systems are failing because the group of people responsible to protect them does not suffer from complete setbacks on failure. Just as the mathematics concepts came as a boon for security industry in the form of cryptography 25 years back, the same goes for theory of microeconomics now. The problem of incentives being misaligned has led to several frauds in the banking industry [8]. Construction and development of systems that promote fair behaviour among the users is a must to maintain the security standards and lower the system failure rates. The innovative concept of online auctions as a reputation system has motivated the researchers to explore more such options. This feedback mechanism gave a vent to the free riding problem faced by eBay [9]. A striking example of economic analysis was shown in January 2005 when the power of online music sharing shifted from music vendors to individual publishers [10].

3   Research Objective

This chapter presents various aspects of the security from DDoS attacks. This chapter gives a comprehensive view of how DDoS attack has evolved and the security challenges around it. Moreover, we have also presented various taxonomies on the types of DDoS attacks, the taxonomies of their defence mechanisms. This chapter also discusses in detail various payment structures and economic incentive schemes in the Internet. We conclude the chapter by discussing some of the existing research evaluation parameters. The main objective should be able to design a cooperative DDoS defence mechanism suitable for the Internet. However, the task is challenging due to the lack of degree of cooperation in network entities. The key factor to be considered while dealing with cooperative defence schemes is the motive of collateral profit which shall motivate the participating entities. For this, a multi-level defence scheme which combines anomaly-based and volume-based filtering of attack traffic using client puzzles as Proof of Work (PoW) which is further extended by using effective economic incentive scheme on the existing payment structures of the Internet will be beneficial like a DDoS mitigation framework which works in cooperation by proposing a solution to prevent DDoS attacks by transferring the risk to some third-party network entity like underutilised cache servers in the Internet by providing iterative economic incentives.

4   Statistics

The largest reported DDoS attack was of volume 400 Gpbs in the year 2014 [11]. Since then, the DDoS attacks are growing in volume. Their efficiency and implementation techniques are getting more sophisticated day by day, making it a big challenge for the security professionals. Figure 16.2 shows the distribution of various kinds of DDoS attacks the systems are prone to. The volumetric DDoS attack type is the most common one with 65% of the attacks being the volumetric attacks. They are performed by the slave machines which are a part of botnet and act on the commands of the master machine. The volumetric attacks are done by floods like User Datagram Protocol (UDP) floods, Internet Control.

Fig. 16.2 Types of DDoS attacks

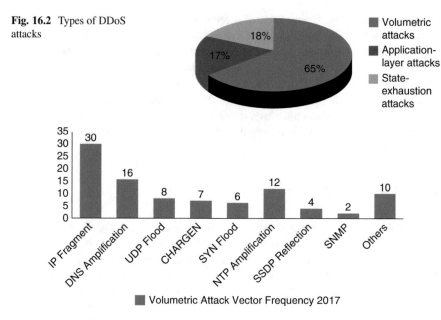

Fig. 16.3 DDoS attack vectors recorded

Message Protocol (ICMP) floods, etc. The second popular attacks are the state exhaustion attacks standing at 18%. This type of DDoS attack is also known as protocol attack because it exploits the vulnerability present in network protocols. Ping of Death exploiting buffer overflow has most instances in state exhaustion attacks.

The next kind of attacks are the application layer attacks standing at 17%. HTTP flood is the most popular kind in this subset. Figure 16.3 shows the various volumetric attack types prevalent in the year 2017 [12]. They include both infrastructure and application attack vectors. The percentage share of IP fragmentation is the most at 30 percent followed by amplification attack done using Domain Name Servers (DNS). A jump of 69 percent was recorded from August 2017 to December 2017 peaking in September. Probably the reason is that any person having a computer and Internet access is now able to generate volumetric DdoS attack from its location. The other vectors shown in the graph include PUSH, POST and GET floods.

5 Taxonomy of DDoS Attacks

The first kind of DDoS attack exploits the vulnerabilities in the network protocol and software [13]. And the second kind of DDoS attack focuses on exhausting the network resources by generating huge volumes of attack traffic. This kind of attack is known as flooding attack which is further divided into two types: simple

Fig. 16.4 Master slave
model

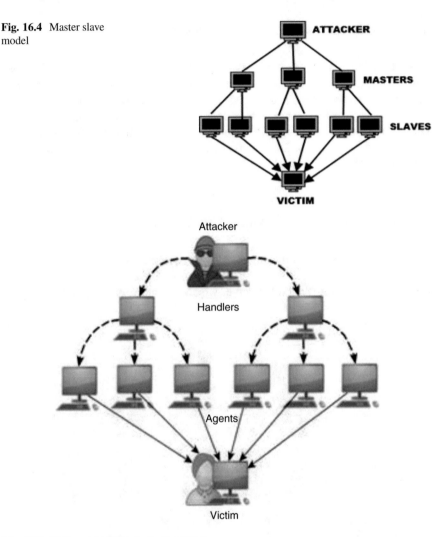

Fig. 16.5 IRC model of DDoS attack network

DDoS attack and amplified DDoS attack. Amplified DDoS attack is harder to defend because the sources of attacks are not traceable. In simple DDoS attack, an attacker makes an army of several zombie machines by exploiting the vulnerabilities in them as shown in Fig. 16.4. In amplified DDoS attacks, the use of reflectors is made. For example, a DNS server, web server and Network Time Protocol (NTP) server can behave as reflector nodes. They all return response packets based on the request packet. A DDoS network is comprised of attackers, agents, victim and control messages whose flow is denoted by dotted arrows in Fig. 16.5. It is via control messages that the attacker conveys the commands to the zombie army.

5.1   Architecture of DDoS Attack Network

The DDoS attack network is of three types [14]: agent-handler model, IRC and reflector-based model. The agent-handler model has three components: attacking machine, zombie machine and the agents. The attacker sends control messages to other zombie machines commanding them to send malicious traffic to the victim node. The Internet Relay Chat (IRC) model is the one in which the zombie machines are replaced by handlers. The function of handlers is to flood the victim on the command of the attacker machine.

5.2   Reflector-Based Flooding Attack

Figure 16.6 explains the reflector-based architecture of the DDoS attack. In this attack lies a big difference from the traditional DDoS attack scenario: the use of reflectors. A reflector is a kind of server which responds the client with the replies

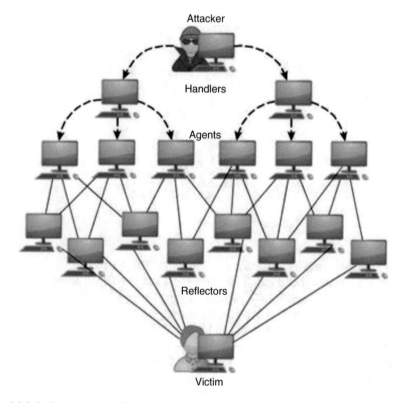

Fig. 16.6 Reflector model of DDoS attack network

in accordance with the queries received. The reflector-based DDOS attack is always diffused across the network and may further be of two types: amplified or non-amplified. Not all reflectors serve as amplifiers [15]. Reflectors are able to generate the attack traffic by catering to legitimate requests only.

5.3   IP Spoofing Based

IP Spoofing is the fundamental technique used in almost all kinds of DDoS attacks. It is done to prevent the location of the attacker from getting revealed. In the IP header, there is a field for source address, which is changed by the agent machines. In the reflecting DDOS attack, the attacking agent replaces its source address by the IP address of the victim machine. These victim machines may be existent or non-existent. For a DDoS attack to be successful, it is better to use existent IP addresses so that they can pass through ingress filtering defence mechanism. If the number of zombie machines in the attacker's army is large in count, then DDOS flooding attack can be performed without spoofing the IP address. This becomes more untraceable if the chain of zombie machines is spread across different geographical regions. The flooding-based DDoS attacks are broadly classified into direct attacks and reflector attacks [16].

5.4   Direct Flooding Attack

In direct flooding type DDoS attack, the architecture remains as of simple DDoS attack. The agent machine sends packets like Transmission Control Protocol (TCP), User Datagram Protocol (UDP) and ICMP directly to the victim machine, and the reply generated by the victim instead of going to the attacking machine goes to the IP address which the attacker had spoofed in the IP header. In the reflector flooding mechanism, the attacker spoofs its IP address as that of the victim. It then sends query packets to the reflector server, but the reply packets instead of coming to the attacking machine are diverted to the victim machine. The following are some typical flooding attacks.

5.5   Smurf Attack

This attack is also known as ICMP echo flooding attack. It aims to exhaust the bandwidth of the victim machine by sending multiple echo reply packets. This attack can also make use of amplifiers. The ICMP messages are used to get the status of the nodes in path. The amplifier will broadcast echo request message to the hosts in its subnet. So if its subnet is comprised of 100 nodes, then the victim will be getting echo reply message from 100 nodes. This is called amplification effect [17].

5.6 TCP SYN Attack

TCP SYN flood [18] is a kind of direct DDoS attack. In this attack, the attacker attacks the ability of the victim machine to accept any new TCP connections by leaving them in open state due to incomplete handshake protocol execution. In setting up of a TCP connection, the client initiates by sending TCP SYN packet to the server which replies with TCP SYN-ACK packet. The third step is when the client who requested the TCP connection sends back TCP ACK packet to the server, hence completing the three-way handshake. The server has only limited number of TCP connections; the attacker exploits this vulnerability and sends numerous TCP SYN packets without sending TCP ACK packets for the earlier requested connections, hence leaving open connections. This inhibits the server's ability to accept any TCP connection requests from the legit users.

5.7 UDP Flood Attack

UDP flooding DDoS attack aims at exhausting the bandwidth resource of the victim machine by diverting numerous UDP packets to it. The attacks which target the bandwidth are not completely curbed by increasing the bandwidth links of the victim machine; only its resistance can be increased. UDP protocol is a connectionless protocol. In a UDP flood attack, the victim receives numerous UDP packets at different ports. The victim machine then checks for the application on that port; finding none it replies back the sender with Destination Unreachable message packet. Due to absence of any kind of negotiation, spoofing a packet becomes much easier. Figure 16.7 explains the basic difference.

5.8 DNS Amplification Attack

Any network protocol which generates a reply to the query can be used in reflector flooding attack. But what empowers this characteristic is the technique of amplification. An amplifier is used to broadcast the query packet to all the servers in its range which aids the attacker to generate a bigger response to a small request as shown in Fig. 16.8. This way the volume generated as reply to the query becomes multi-fold, and using the technique of IP spoofing, this response is diverted to the victim machine which gets overburdened and hence cannot serve legitimate requests

Fig. 16.7 Direct vs reflective flooding mechanism

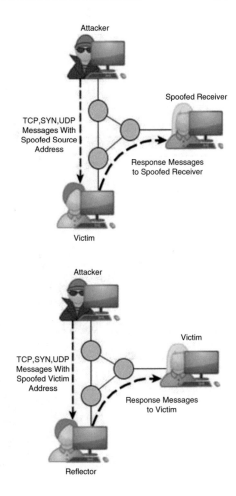

making the DDoS attack successful. Figure 16.9 illustrates the attack mechanism. The largest on record DDoS attack is caused by DNS amplification. The ratio of query to reply of DNS server is 1:70, whereas for NTP server, it ranges from 1:20 to 1:200.

DNS amplification attack is a recent type of reflector-based DDoS flooding attack. Complicated interaction mechanisms exist between clients and name servers. On comparing the smurf amplification attack with DNS amplification attack, one must notice the significant difference in their attacking mechanisms. In smurf attack, the echo request messages are broadcasted to multiple hosts in the subnet using amplifiers, because of which the amplification effect is achieved, whereas in DNS amplification, the server itself magnifies the volume of traffic diverted to the victim machine by generating larger response packets to very small query packets. Smurf attack performs flooding by generating multiple replies to a request, whereas DNS amplification generates a single big reply. This helps the attackers in getting more

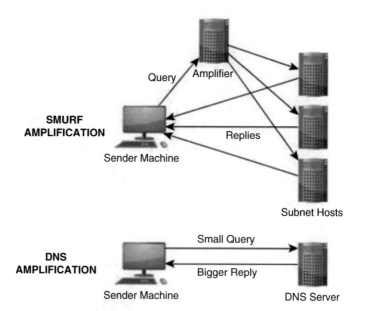

SMURF AMPLIFICATION

Query

Amplifier

Replies

Sender Machine

Subnet Hosts

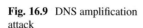

DNS AMPLIFICATION

Small Query

Bigger Reply

Sender Machine

DNS Server

Fig. 16.8 Smurf vs DNS amplification

Fig. 16.9 DNS amplification attack

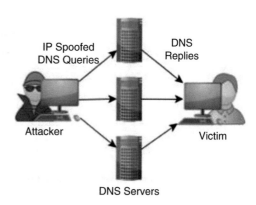

IP Spoofed DNS Queries

DNS Replies

Attacker

Victim

DNS Servers

work done in doing less efforts which is why this is a very popular and hard to defend flooding DDoS attack caused by DNS servers as amplifiers.

6 Taxonomy of Cooperative DDoS Defence Mechanisms

We can categorise DDoS defence mechanisms in two categories: centralised and distributed. This depends on whether the defence mechanism phases, detection, mitigation and response, are deployed at the same location or different locations. In the centralised mechanisms, the whole DDoS defence mechanism is either set up at

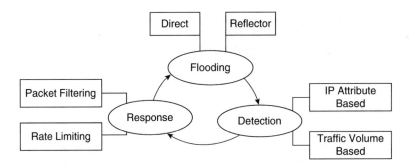

Fig. 16.10 DDoS attack scheme

source, destination or the intermediate network. But in centralised mechanisms, the detection might take place at the victim node, mitigation at the intermediatory nodes and response at the source of the attack traffic generation. This means that the whole process is scattered at various locations in the Internet, but to successfully combat against the DDoS attack, all these parties need to work together in collaboration with one another [19].

In this write-up, the focus is on several cooperative defence mechanisms available, but first we explain the need of such mechanisms when centralised ones are already in place. Figure 16.10 explains the action cycle. In centralised systems, the main issue is single point of failure. It means the whole of the defence system can crash if the only site where all its components are deployed comes under attack. The cooperative system is able to solve this problem by having multiple nodes in action for defence at different locations. These nodes have similar functionalities, so even if the nodes in one location are compromised, still we have numerous set of nodes in place to defend the victim site. Secondly, Internet does not have any central control authority over its autonomous systems, so a defence model which does not have a central authority in control will prove beneficial.

6.1 Pushback and Packet Marking

Chen and Park [20] proposed a cooperative mechanism by combining the techniques of pushback messages and packet marking. It is called Attack Diagnosis (AD) in which the victim machine first detects the DDoS attack and then sends AD commands to the upstream routers in the network. It is a reactive defence mechanism. It makes use of AD-enabled routers which then start marking each packet deterministically with the interface information it is passing through. The victim machine then uses this attached interface information to trace back the source of malicious packets.

The AD-related commands are authenticated using the Time To Live (TTL) field of the IP packet header. AD scheme is ineffective when the DDoS attack is performed at a large scale, so there exists an extension to AD which is called Parallel Attack Diagnosis (PAD). AD can stop the traffic from single router at a time, whereas PAD diagnoses and stops the traffic from multiple routers simultaneously.

6.2   IP Traceback and Port Marking

Chen et al. [21] have proposed one more distributed DDoS mechanism based on the concept of router port marking and packet filtering. These are presented as two modules used. The function of router port marking module is to mark the packets probabilistically by appending router's interface port number to the packets. It is a six-digit number which is locally unique. When the victim machine is flooded with the malicious packets, then it makes use of this appended information to trace back the source of the malicious packets.

The function of packet filtering module comes next which then filters the malicious incoming packets at the upstream routers. This mechanism has low computation and communication overheads. But it has two limitations. Firstly, as there is no authentication used, the attackers can forge the marking fields so that their actual location is never revealed. Secondly, although this technique effectively traces back the IP, it fails to identify the master behind the DDoS attack who is in control of the army of zombies or compromised machines.

6.3   Signature-Based Defence

Papadopoulos et al. [22] proposed Coordinated Suppression of Simultaneous Attacks (COSSACK) mechanism. It uses a software system called watchdog which is built on the edge routers. It is based on a critical set of assumptions like existence of attack signatures, edge router's capability to filter packets on the basis of these signatures and continuous connection availability. The watchdog software does ingress and egress filtering on the edge routers to stop DDoS attack flow, and it also sends multicast notifications to the source side. It is unable to withstand DDoS attack traffic generated from the legacy networks that have not deployed COSSACK.

6.4   Capability-Based Defence

Anderson et al. [23] have proposed distributed defence mechanisms based on the capabilities. In these mechanisms, firstly the sender has to obtain the rights to send from the receiver. These rights are kind of short-term contracts, tokens or authorisations. To understand this better, we can understand it through an analogy of sticking the postage stamp onto the letter before posting. The only difference here is that the postage stamp is bought from the post office whereas the sending rights will be obtained directly from the receiver. Another analogy will be of receiver defining the window size beforehand in sliding window protocol of data link layer. The major drawback of this scheme is that the capability setup channel is not secure. These mechanisms always have to be kept active, hence increasing the processing and memory overheads.

6.5   Datagram-Based Defence

Argyraki et al. [24] proposed an alternative to capability-based filtering mechanism which is datagram filtering mechanism in which instead of denying all the traffic by default, only the traffic that is denied is identified as malicious. This is called Active Internet Traffic Filtering (AITF). In this, the receiver is able to contact the misbehaving senders and ask them to stop. Every ISP polices its misbehaving nodes, or else they are at a risk of losing connectivity to the victim machine which may be an important point of access. So there lies as strong incentive for the participating ISPs to cooperate. AITF is affordable to be deployed by the ISPs because it preserves the receiver's bandwidth at per-connection cost. The legitimacy of the traffic is verified using three-way handshake which may not be completed because the handshake packets and the DDoS attack traffic are flowing through the same flooded link. This mechanism also has several deployment issues because it is not relying on edge routers for actual filtering. The routers used are placed in the middle of the network.

6.6   Anomaly-Based Defence

Liu et al. [25] proposed another distributed defence mechanism against network and transport layer DDoS attacks, namely StopIt. In this mechanism, each receiver installs a network filter which blocks the undesirable traffic. It makes use of Passport mechanism proposed by Liu for authentication purpose. It has made use of looped and third generation of telecom networks in its architecture. Every autonomous system has a StopIt server for sending and receiving StopIt requests. A filter is installed at the source and the filter requests are exchanged among the peer nodes. In this mechanism, the StopIt server can be attacked with packet floods and filter requests if the requests are allowed from neighbouring autonomous systems also. Moreover, StopIt mechanism needs complex detection mechanisms which make it hard to deploy.

6.7   Volume-Based Defence

Walfish et al. [26] proposed a distributed DDoS defence mechanisms to prevent application layer level attacks. In this paper, the concept of defence by offence is followed. It encourages the honest clients to speak up by increasing the volume of benign traffic it sends to the server being targeted by DDoS attack. This ensures that the percentage of bandwidth captured by the good clients is increased, hence out-crowding the one flooded by the attacker. In this work, it is not explained how will the server detect the attack. Speak-up mechanism is applicable only in session flooding attacks and not in request flooding or asymmetric attacks.

6.8   Hybrid Defence

Yu. et al. [27] proposed a Defense and Offense Wall (DOW) scheme. This is an extension to the speak-up work by Walfish et al. with addition of anomaly detection method. The anomaly detection method used is based on K-means clustering approach to detect asymmetric, request flooding and session flooding attacks. It has explained the mechanism using two models: the detection model and the currency model. The former's function is to drop suspicious packets, while the latter's function is to encourage the increase in session rates by legitimate clients. The major drawback of this mechanism is that it is too resource consuming to be implemented.

7   Literature Review

Mahajan et al. [28] proposed a distributed DDoS defence mechanism called Aggregate-based Congestion Control (ACC). Aggregates are a part of the network traffic which is identified as malicious. It is characterised by source IP addresses or destination ports. In this mechanism, the router detects the aggregates which are overloading its bandwidth rather than the IP sources. On detection of such samples, the router sends pushback message to the upstream routers in the network and then sends a rate limit. From then on, if the traffic from those upstream routers exceeds that rate limit, then the packets are dropped and multiple pushback messages are sent. This technique fails to be effective when the attack traffic is uniformly distributed in the network (Tables 16.1 and 16.2).

Mirkovic et al. [29] proposed a distributed framework called DEFensive Cooperative Overlay Mesh (DEFCOM). This framework supports information and service exchange among the cooperating nodes in the system. They have shown a distributed defence framework architecture of heterogeneous defence nodes which collaborate and cooperate with each other and work as a team to combat DDoS attack. By heterogeneous, what is meant is that all the defence nodes do not share the same

Table 16.1 Application layer cooperative DDoS defence mechanisms

Name of scheme	Author	Scheme description	Limitations
Aggregate congestion control and pushback (2002)	R. Mahajan et al.	ACC rate limits the aggregates rather than IP sources	Not effective against uniformly distributed attack sources
Attack Diagnosis and parallel AD (2005)	R. Chen, J.M. Park	Combines pushback and packet marking	AD is not effective against large-scale attacks
TRACK (2006)	R. Chen et al.	Combines IP traceback, packet marking and packet filtering	Not effective for attack traceback
Passport (2008)	X. Liu, A. Li, X. Yang, D. Wetherall	Makes use of symmetric key cryptography to put tokens on packets that verify the source	Attackers may get capabilities from colluders
			It only prevents the hosts in one AS from spoofing the IP addresses of other ASs
DEFensive Cooperative Overlay Mesh (2003)	J. Mirkovic et al.	Defence nodes collaborate and cooperate together	Classifier nodes require an inline deployment
			Unable to handle attacks from legacy networks
Stateless Internet Flow Filter (2004)	A. Yaar et al.	Capability-based mechanism	Always active
			Processing and memory costs overheads
StopIt (2011)	X. Liu, X. Yang, Y. Lu	Novel closed control and open service architecture for filters to be installed	Vulnerable to attacks in which attacker floods the router
			Needs complex verification/authentication mechanisms
			Challenging to deploy and manage in practice

functionality, like nodes near the victim will do the detection best, and the nodes near the source will cater to the response technique.

In this mechanism, the attack alerts from the generator nodes are flooded into the network after which the rate limits are sent to the upstream routers. From then on, all the resource requests that are sent to the downstream routers are first classified, and the malicious packets are dropped. This works in a P2P network scenario, just proper rate limits for both upstream and downstream routers need to be defined, and simultaneously the classifier nodes are at work to differentiate malicious traffic and benign traffic. The main disadvantage of this framework is that this is not compatible with the old or legacy networks, so if a large portion of the network is a legacy network, then the classifier nodes which are deployed in-line malfunction.

Table 16.2 Application layer cooperative DDoS defence mechanisms

Name of scheme	Author	Scheme description	Limitations
Active Internet Traffic Filtering (2009)	K. Argyraki, D.R. Cheriton	Misbehaving sources are policed by their own ISPs	Several deployment issues If the flooded link is outside victim's AS, the three-way handshake may not be completed
Speak-up (2002)	M. Walfish et al.	Encourages the good clients to out-crowd the bad ones	Not applicable against request flooding and asymmetric attacks
Defense and Offense Wall (2005)	J. Yu et al.	Encouragement method with anomaly detection	Very resource consuming to be implemented
CAPTCHA (2003)	L.V. Ahn et al.	Differentiates DDoS flooding bots from humans	More delay for legitimate users Disables web crawler's access to websites
Admission control and congestion control (2002)	M. Srivatsa et al.	Port hiding	Requires a challenge server which can be the target of DDoS attacks

Li et al. [30] addressed the drawback of the capability-based mechanism scheme by adding secure authentication systems to capability-based mechanisms. They called it a Passport system which uses symmetric-key cryptography to encrypt the tokens before appending them to packets being sent. This allows the routers in path to verify that the source address is genuine. Using this technique, the ISPs can protect their own addresses from being forged, so such schemes offer stronger incentive as compared to other filtering schemes.

This mechanism is vulnerable to colluding attacks in which the attackers get the capabilities from the cheating nodes or they can eavesdrop the packets of the node is honest. Another limitation of this scheme is that although the attackers cannot spoof the IP address of host belonging to other autonomous system, it can easily spoof the IP of some other host in the same autonomous system.

Kandula et al. [31] tried to differentiate the DDoS flooding done by humans and bots. They employed a mechanism called Completely Automated Public Turing test to tell Computers and Humans Apart (CAPTCHA). Although it is a good technique to differentiate robots and humans, the main disadvantage is that it requires the users to solve different puzzles to pass the authentication test having text and pictures which becomes an annoying task for the users.

Srivatsa et al. [32] proposed an admission control and congestion control scheme which limits the number of clients being served simultaneously. It works on the principle of port hiding which hides the port number on which the service requests are accepted, hence making the port invisible to the illegitimate clients. Then congestion control is performed to allocate more resources to good or legitimate set of clients.

8 Performance Evaluation Metrics

Although there is no any standard set of measurements used by the research community, the performance evaluation metrics for volumetric DDoS attack defence strategy can be divided into two according to the level of attack traffic experienced. The first category of the metrics is the ones which measure the performance evaluation under high traffic load, and the second one measures the performance under low traffic load. Some commercial products [33] also exist to measure the performance by evaluating a variety of results of the defence technique. They are discussed below.

8.1 Detection Rate

It measures the number of attacks that are detected from the number of attacks actually performed by the attacker.

8.2 False Positive Rate

It measures the number of times the legitimate user traffic is wrongly detected as DDoS attack traffic. A similar parameter is true negative which detects the attack even when it is absent. Similarly, false negative denotes the inability to find the malicious traffic.

8.3 Ratio Between Detection Rate and False Positive Rate

This metric is generated using Receiver Operating Characteristic (ROC) curves over detection rate and false positive rate. ROC curves are widely used to calculate the sensitivity and specificity of the evaluation parameters.

8.4 Failure Rate

It is an application layer level metric [34] which is calculated by finding the ratio of number of requests which go unresponded by the victim to the total number of requests received by the victim.

8.5 Average Latency

It is a measure of application level performance. It is the average of the time delays experienced between the sender initiating the request and the receiver receiving the response message at different instances.

8.6 Throughput

The throughput directly indicates the performance of any defence mechanism. It is the total amount of data transmitted in a unit time.

8.7 Bandwidth

It is the aggregate level of performance measure [35]. Bandwidth denotes the amount of traffic a link can carry under various states like normal state and attack state.

8.8 Malicious Packet Drop Rate

DDoS defence scheme on packet level aims to lower the volume of malicious packets by selectively dropping them from the whole traffic received. It reflects the capability of any defence mechanism to control the flooding traffic. It is calculated as the ratio of number of packets dropped before reaching the victim to the total number of packets destined for the victim.

8.9 Benign Packet Drop Rate

The main purpose of DDoS defence scheme is to maintain the level of QoS for the benign user traffic. The motive is to be able to forward as many benign packets as possible by preventing the bandwidth to collapse due to congestion. It is calculated as the ratio of number of benign packets dropped before reaching the victim to the total number of packets destined for the victim.

Adjusting the parameters of performance estimation is an important task. Selection of appropriate parameters to judge the performance of any scheme in the network depends on certain rules like the changes in the attack tragic load should be separated into two cases: first, when the variation in traffic rate is very slow and, second, when the attack traffic is changing at a rapid rate. The parameters of legitimate data traffic should be collected from the victim side when it is not under any kind of attack; then only a comparative analysis can be done when the developed scheme is enforced.

9 Conclusion

On analysis of various DDoS detection, mitigation and response frameworks, the common challenge faced by each one of them is to quicker the detection rate with sustainability of QoS for benign users. In all these techniques, the DDoS defence mechanism can be broken down into three parts: detection, mitigation and response. The mechanisms developed are not only victim-end defence or source-end defence mechanisms but a combination of both across the network. The backbone of these hybrid mechanisms remains a highly effective cooperative mechanism to ensure stable and rigid communication. So studying the incentive and payment structure used in any scheme from economic point of view is important. Like, Internet is comprised of several cache servers which may not be fully utilised and these unused cache capacities can be utilised in cooperative DDoS defence. The traffic flood can be diverted to these multiple servers each handling only a fraction of attack traffic, thus preventing congestion from the attack flood. This resource is already existing and will incur meagre costs to the parties involved, but management of network resources is one of the most essential issues of Internet. The heuristic techniques of optimisation have always been the backbone in solving economic engineering problems, and so the main task of the mechanisms like double auction is not only to increase the utility of free cache resources but also to promote sustainable individual profits in the long run.

10 Scope for Future Research

In the future research, the evaluation of these defence schemes on different topologies of Internet will be helpful in deployment of these mechanisms in broader technical areas. For any detection technique developed, setting the value of threshold is very important. Optimisation of threshold parameter for any network is an important research area. Inclusion of statistical features for calculating threshold value will enhance its precision. Timely detection of end of DDoS attack is also an important research area having future scope. In fighting against any kind of cyber attack, data plays a very crucial role. The recovery of the legitimate traffic should be very quick and must ensure integrity.

Over the past years, the research area of Internet economics has generated many useful works having an interdisciplinary approach. Long unknown things to the security professionals like incentives and market failure are now taken into consideration before designing any payment structure. The work being carried out in Internet domain field has spread across various other domains like algorithmic design, security and warfare, interconnected networks and dependability economics of these complicated networks. Psychology has proved to be an important consideration while developing practical schemes for Internet pricing. It gives a deeper understanding of fundamental user behaviour which helps in making the scheme more usable and secure.

References

1. Zargar, S. T., Joshi, J., & Tipper, D. (2013). A survey of defense mechanisms against distributed denial of service (DDoS) flooding attacks. *IEEE Communications Surveys & Tutorials, 15*(4), 2046–2069.
2. Srivastava, A., Gupta, B. B., Tyagi, A., Sharma, A., & Mishra, A. (2011). A recent survey on DDoS attacks and defense mechanisms. In *Advances in parallel distributed computing* (pp. 570–580). Berlin: Springer.
3. Mirkovic, J., & Reiher, P. (2004). A taxonomy of DDoS attack and DDoS defense mechanisms. *ACM SIGCOMM Computer Communication Review, 34*(2), 39–53.
4. Xu, K., Zhang, Z.-L., & Bhattacharyya, S. (2005). Reducing unwanted traffic in a backbone network. In *Steps to reducing unwanted traffic on the internet workshop (SRUTI)* (p. 915). Berkeley, CA: USENIX Association.
5. CERT Coordination Center. (2007, March). *Denial of service attacks.* Retrieved from http://www.cert.org/techtips/denial of service.html
6. Garber, L. (2000). Denial-of-service attacks rip the internet. *Computer, 33*(4), 12–17.
7. CERT Coordination Center. (2007, March). *CERT advisory CA-98.01 smurf IP denial-of-service attacks.* Retrieved from http://www.cert.org/advisories/CA-1998-01.html
8. Liu, X., Li, A., Yang, X., & Wetherall, D. (2008). *Passport: Secure and adoptable source authentication.* Renton, WA: USENIX.
9. Argyraki, K., & Cheriton, D. R. (2009). Scalable network-layer defense against internet bandwidth-flooding attacks. *IEEE/ACM Transactions on Networking (ToN), 17*(4), 1284–1297.
10. Liu, X., Yang, X., & Lu, Y. (2008). To filter or to authorize: Network-layer DoS defense against multimillion-node botnets. In *ACM SIGCOMM computer communication review* (Vol. 38(4), pp. 195–206). New York: ACM.
11. Retrieved March 21, 2018, from https://www.calyptix.com/top-threats/ddos-attacks-101-types-targets-motivations/
12. Retrieved March 21, 2018, from https://www.akamai.com/us/en/about/news/press/2017-press/akamai-releases-third-quarter-2017-state-of-the-internet-security-report.jsp
13. Molsa, J. (2006). *Mitigating denial of service attacks in computer networks.* PhD thesis, Helsinki University of Technology, Espoo, Finland.
14. Specht, S. M., & Lee, R. B. (2004). Distributed denial of service: Taxonomies of attacks, tools, and countermeasures. In *ISCA PDCS* (pp. 543–550).
15. Paxson, V. (2001). An analysis of using reflectors for distributed denial-of-service attacks. *ACM SIGCOMM Computer Communication Review, 31*(3), 38–47.
16. Chang, R. K. (2002). Defending against flooding-based distributed denial-of-service attacks: A tutorial. *IEEE Communications Magazine, 40*(10), 42–51.
17. CERT Coordination Center. (2007). *CERT advisory CA-98.01 smurf IP denial-of-service attacks.* Retrieved March, 2007, from http://www.cert.org/advisories/CA-1998.01.html

18. Mölsä, J. (2006). *Mitigating denial of service attacks in computer networks*. Espoo: Helsinki University of Technology.
19. Zargar, S. T., Joshi, J., & Tipper, D. (2013). A survey of defense mechanisms against distributed denial of service (DDoS) flooding attacks. *IEEE Communications Surveys & Tutorials, 15*(4), 2046–2069.
20. Chen, R., & Park, J. M. (2005). Attack diagnosis: Throttling distributed denial-of-service attacks close to the attack sources. In *Proceedings of the 14th International Conference on Computer Communications and Networks, ICCCN 2005* (pp. 275–280). Piscataway, NJ: IEEE.
21. Chen, R., Park, J. M., & Marchany, R. (2006). TRACK: A novel approach for defending against distributed denial-of-service attacks. In *Technical Report TR ECE—O6–02*. Blacksburg, VA: Department of Electrical and Computer Engineering, Virginia Tech.
22. Papadopoulos, C., Lindell, R., Mehringer, J., Hussain, A., & Govindan, R. (2003). Cossack: Coordinated suppression of simultaneous attacks. In *Proceedings: DARPA information survivability conference and exposition, 2003* (Vol. 1, pp. 2–13). Los Alamitos, CA: IEEE.
23. Anderson, T., Roscoe, T., & Wetherall, D. (2004). Preventing internet denial-of-service with capabilities. *ACM SIGCOMM Computer Communication Review, 34*(1), 39–44.
24. Argyraki, K., & Cheriton, D. R. (2009). Scalable network-layer defense against internet bandwidth-flooding attacks. *IEEE/ACM Transactions on Networking (ToN), 17*(4), 1284–1297.
25. Liu, X., Yang, X., & Lu, Y. (2008). To filter or to authorize: Network-layer DoS defense against multimillion-node botnets. In *ACM SIGCOMM Computer Communication Review* (Vol. 38(4), pp. 195–206). New York: ACM.
26. Walfish, M., Vutukuru, M., Balakrishnan, H., Karger, D., Karger, D., & Shenker, S. (2006). DDoS defense by offense. In *ACM SIGCOMM Computer Communication Review* (Vol. 36(4), pp. 303–314). New York: ACM.
27. Yu, J., Li, Z., Chen, H., & Chen, X. (2007). A detection and offense mechanism to defend against application layer DDoS attacks. In *Third International Conference on Networking and Services, 2007. ICNS* (pp. 54–54). Piscataway, NJ: IEEE.
28. Mahajan, R., Bellovin, S. M., Floyd, S., Ioannidis, J., Paxson, V., & Shenker, S. (2002). Controlling high bandwidth aggregates in the network. *ACM SIGCOMM Computer Communication Review, 32*(3), 62–73.
29. Mirkovic, J., Robinson, M., & Reiher, P. (2003). Alliance formation for DDoS defense. In *Proceedings of the 2003 workshop on New security paradigms* (pp. 11–18). New York: ACM.
30. Li, A., Yang, X., & Wetherall, D. (2008). *Passport: Secure and adoptable source authentication*. Renton, WA: USENIX.
31. Kandula, S., Katabi, D., Jacob, M., & Berger, A. (2005). Botz-4-sale: Surviving organized DDoS attacks that mimic flash crowds. In *Proceedings of the 2nd conference on Symposium on Networked Systems Design & Implementation-Volume 2* (pp. 287–300). Berkeley, CA: USENIX Association.
32. Srivatsa, M., Iyengar, A., Yin, J., & Liu, L. (2008). Mitigating application-level denial of service attacks on Web servers: A client-transparent approach. *ACM Transactions on the Web (TWEB), 2*(3), 15.
33. Hussain, A., Schwab, S., Thomas, R., Fahmy, S., & Mirkovic, J. (2006, June). DDoS experiment methodology. In *Proceedings of DETER Community Workshop* (pp. 8–14).
34. Ko, C., Hussain, A., Schwab, S., Thomas, R., & Wilson, B. (2006, June). Towards systematic IDS evaluation. In *Proceedings of DETER Community Workshop* (pp. 20–23).
35. Feibel, W. (2000). *The network press encyclopedia of networking*. San Francisco, CA: Sybex.

Chapter 17
Epidemic Modelling for the Spread of Bots Through DDoS Attack in E-Commerce Network

Biswarup Samanta

Abstract Cyber security is the protection of information systems from major criminal activities such as cyber warfare, cyber terrorism, and cyber espionage provided for the well-being of user's privacy. It is also known as IT security or computer security. The "information warfare" can hit and completely break down critical IT infrastructure of an organization or a country. Cybercrime has many types, but, in this chapter, we have focused on DDoS attack into an E-Commerce network to spread bots throughout the network. DDoS attack can be used to sabotage a service or as a cover for bot delivery. In this chapter, a dynamic SIS–SEIRS model is proposed to represent the propagation of bots in E-Commerce network through DDoS attack. A mathematical model is also formulated to represent the dynamism of the members of different compartments of the model. Numerical methods are employed to solve and simulate the system of equations developed. Results of numerical simulations are obtained using MATLAB.

Keywords E-commerce · Computer network · Cyber attack · Network security · Dynamic model · Epidemic model · Bots · Botnet · Malware · DDoS attack

1 Introduction

The growth of Internet technology has thrown several challenges in the form of requirement of a suitable cyber defense mechanism to protect the valuable business information stored in e-commerce systems and for information in transit over network. Toward this goal, it is very much necessary to understand the types of attack in the network and develop mathematical model to represent their behavior. In this chapter, we will be developing a mathematical model to understand DDoS attack while delivering bots within an e-commerce network.

B. Samanta (✉)
Department of Computer Science and Information Technology, Amity Institute of Information Technology, Ranchi, Amity University Jharkhand, Ranchi, Jharkhand, India

© Springer Nature Switzerland AG 2020   445
B. B. Gupta et al. (eds.), *Handbook of Computer Networks and Cyber Security*,
https://doi.org/10.1007/978-3-030-22277-2_17

A denial-of-service attack (DoS attack) or distributed denial-of-service attack (DDoS attack) is an attempt to make computer resources of a network unavailable to its legitimate user. In a DDoS attack, an attacker may use your computer to launch DDoS attack to another computer of your network or others by using various tools like Trinoo, Tribe Flood Network (TFN), Stacheldraht, Shaft, MStream, etc. Botnet is the popular medium to launch DoS/DDoS attacks. The term "Botnet" is used to refer to a group of compromised computers (also known as zombie computers) under the control of hackers, running malwares under a common command and control infrastructure [1]. A bot is an automated program for doing some particular task, often over a network. Bots have all the advantages of worms, but are generally much more versatile in their infection vector and are often modified within hours of publication of a new exploit (http://www.cisco.com/web/about/security/intelligence/virus-worm-diffs.html#8).

2 Literature Review

Tianhan Gao et al. have projected an innovative unspecified entree validation system grounded on proxy ring signature for CPS Wireless Mesh Network (CPS-WMN). A recognized safety immune of the projected procedure with SVO logic has been offered [2].

Lianwen Wang has described the outspread of the occurrence proportion of an SEIR endemic model, in their paper, through decline and changing whole inhabitants' scope to an overall nonlinear arrangement. The author has engrossed on launching the global stability of the SEIR model by submission of the renewed geometric approach built on the third additive compound matrix. Their implications are functional to two different incidence functions reflecting mass media effect [3].

Jinliang Wang et al. have examined the global asymptotic stability of multi-group SIR and SEIR age-structured models. These depictions allow the infectiousness and the death rate of susceptible entities to change and depend on the susceptibility, through which they measured the heterogeneity of population. They documented global dynamics and demonstrate that the heterogeneity does not change the dynamical construction of the basic SIR and SEIR with age-dependent vulnerability [4].

Kharchenko et al. have detailed in their paper that the industrial safety critical instrumentation and control systems (I&Cs) are facing additional information (in all-purpose and cyber, in specific) security oppressions and bouts. The goal of their paper was in depiction of the process and tools for condition-based security estimate of MV FPGA-based I&Cs [5].

Cyber battle benefits a foremost latent threat to critical infrastructures (CIs). Decision makers who want to cultivate tough CIs must deliberate both strategic and operational features of CIs as well as nonlinear dynamics describing such cyber-physical systems. Elisa Canzani and Stefan Pickl alliances System Dynamics (SD) through a game-theoretic method to realize cyber epidemics dynamics of

CI procedures created by attacker and protector strategic relations. Their research work was chastised on their previous work by surrounding a new block structure representing outline for turmoil impact study in networked CIs [6].

Kuldeep Kaur et al. studied that the data is harmless in banking organization for prolonged period and exposed any account after a prolonged time. The looming scope of the study of security is used to reduce threats. Security is used in the prolonged run which results in the reduction of number of branches, saying charges of linked and properties [7].

A Lyapunov function can address numerous purposes, e.g., it validates stability or termination of a system or permits building invariant groups, which in turn may be used to recommend safety and security. Eike Mohlmann and Oliver Theel suggested an upgrading to the putrefying technique, which decreases the graph structure before spreading the disintegration technique [8].

An improved SIRS model for examining dynamics of worm propagation in WSNs has been presented by Liping Feng. This model can define the technique of worm propagation through the energy feeding and unlike dispersed density of nodes. Grounded on this model, a control parameter R0 < 1 that entirely governs the global dynamics of worm proliferation has been developed by the explicit mathematical investigation. It has been observed that worm will be controlled in WSNs when R0 < 1, and they will be widespread otherwise. Lastly, grounded on R0, the author conferred the threshold of worm spread about communication circle and distributed densities of nodes in WSNs. Mathematical simulations endorse the accuracy of theoretical study [9].

Jinhua Ma is the first to examine the complicated communications between benign worms and malicious worms in dissimilar M2M network. Ma et al. demonstrated that the global dynamics are determined by the threshold value R0. In the absence of birth, death, and the treatment effect of users, they obtain the final size formula in varied vaccination schemes. The consequences establish that the nodes with higher node degrees are more vulnerable to contamination than those with lesser node degrees. Their paper delivers a strong theoretical basis to yield effective actions to control the large-scale spread of malicious worms in mixed M2M network [10].

The study on the prevailing body of literature in epidemiology by Canzani demonstrates the variety of practices used for exhibiting dynamics. The complexity of epidemics modelling augmented from compartmental SIR models that anticipate only organic pathogens to the numerous social network models. Traditional models and innovative outcomes, such as the Kermack–McKendrick threshold condition, have been enormously successful in informing public health policy. This review characterizes an initial work to discover high dynamics of catastrophe circumstances such as the spread of computer viruses in the cyber world and of the information dispersal on the IT infrastructure of a firm [11].

A fixing mechanism has been projected by Meng Wang, for benign worm spread based on the mobile network. In the discovery and mending mechanism, after gathering the difficulties of the entire mobile network, they place the effective benign worms into the mobile network atmosphere to advance the mending efficiency when malevolent worms outbreak. For benign worm spread mechanism, they first used the active mode of benign worm to quickly handle malicious worms, and later after the malicious worms are under control, they transferred to the passive mode and release mobile network resources further. Thus, they confirm the safety of mobile networks and also optimize the network correspondingly [12].

The paper written by Elisa Canzani et al. reports openly available information on IT security, its accessibility, and brilliance and offers an examination of openly accessible IT security information for mobile devices in Germany. They recognized that there are hardly any patterns in terms of timeliness, content, and quality [13].

Alomari E. et al. have presented a complete study, in their paper, to display the hazard of Botnet-based DDoS attacks on application layer, exclusively on the web server, and the augmented occurrences of such attacks that have obviously increased in recent times. Botnet-based DDoS attack occurrences and income fatalities of well-known companies and government websites are also described. This offers improved understanding of the problem, present solution space, and upcoming research opportunity to protect against such attacks efficiently [14].

In their paper, Suchacka et al. have presented the problem of modelling a realistic arrival process of bots' requests on an e-commerce web server. Based on real log data for an online store, sessions produced by bots were recreated and their key features were analyzed, including the inter-arrival time of bot sessions, the number of HTTP requests per session, and the inter-arrival time of requests in session. Using regression analysis, a mathematical model of the bots' traffic features was established and executed in a bot traffic generator. Their findings confirm the existence of a heavy tail in bot traffic features' distributions [15].

In their paper, Xu et al. have presented a competent method to perceive web bot traffic in a large e-commerce marketplace and then accomplished an in-depth analysis on the features of web bot traffic. Precisely, the authors projected bot detection approach consists of the following modules: (1) an Expectation-Maximization (EM)-based feature selection method to extract the most unique features, (2) a gradient-based decision tree to calculate the likelihood of being a bot IP, and (3) a threshold approximation mechanism targeting to recover a rational amount of non-bot traffic flow. The analysis results disclose their differences in terms of active time, search queries, item and store preferences, and many other aspects. These results deliver new understandings for public websites to further progress web bot traffic detection for protecting treasured web contents [16].

3 Modeling the System

Several mathematical models have been developed which give clear view of attacking behavior as well as the transmission of malicious codes in network [17–25]. In this section of our chapter, we will develop a model on DDoS attack to spread bots within an e-commerce network. DDoS attack paralyzes Internet systems by overwhelming servers, network links, and network devices like, routers,

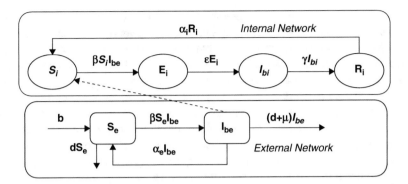

Fig. 17.1 Schematic presentation of SIS and SEIRS model

firewalls, etc., with bogus traffic (http://www.cisco.com/c/en/us/products/collateral/
security/traffic-anomaly-detector-xt-5600a/prod_white_paper0900aecd8011e927.
html). A network is composed of hosts and routers and it has an edge and a core.
The hosts live at the edge, while the core consists of an interconnected mesh of
routers [26]. Hosts are the interface between the organization's internal network
and external Internet. Hosts are the gateway of attacks to spread the bots into the
network.

Dynamic model for infectious diseases is mostly based on compartment structures that were initially proposed by Kermack and McKendrick [27–29] and
later developed by other mathematicians. We have divided the entire e-commerce
network into two sub-networks, viz., external network which basically consists of
host computers (SIS model) and internal network which consists of the remaining
nodes (SEIR model) of that network, which includes routers, servers, and other
devices attached to the network. We have represented the DDoS attack and spread
of malware into the network schematically by using an interactive epidemic SIS–
SEIRS model which consists of two sub-models as shown in Fig. 17.1.

Our entire SIS–SEIRS model consists of basically four types of nodes as a whole
which are discussed as follows:

The fraction of *Susceptible* class nodes of the total population at any time in
internal network and external network of the model is represented by S_i and S_e,
respectively. The fraction of *Exposed* class nodes of the total population at any time
in internal network of the model is represented by E_i. The fraction of *Infectious* class
nodes of the total population at any time in internal network and external network
of the model is represented by I_{bi} and I_{be}, respectively. The fraction of *Recovered*
class nodes of the total population at any time in internal network of the model is
represented by R_i.

Different transmission rates of the nodes among different compartments (classes)
in our proposed model are used to show the dynamism of the model are as
follows: β: transmission rate of the nodes from Susceptible class to Exposed class
in internal network and Susceptible class to Infectious class in external network;
c: transmission rate of nodes from Exposed class to Infectious class in internal

network; γ: rate of recovery in internal network, i.e., transmission rate of nodes from Infectious class to Recovered class in internal network; α_i: transmission rate of nodes from Recovered class to Susceptible class in the internal network due loss of immunity (e.g., due to outdated version of antivirus); b: birth rate of the susceptible nodes in external network; d: natural death rate of susceptible nodes and infectious nodes in external network (i.e., crashing of nodes due to the reason other than the attack of malicious codes); μ: death rate of infectious nodes in external network due to DDoS attack; α_e: rate of updated run of antivirus software which transfers the nodes from Infectious class of external network to its Susceptible class.

The corresponding system equations for the internal network of our proposed model are given in the following system Eq. (17.1):

$$
\begin{aligned}
\frac{dS_i}{dt} &= -\beta S_i I_{be} + \alpha_i R_i \\
\frac{dE_i}{dt} &= \beta S_i I_{be} - \varepsilon E_i \\
\frac{dI_{bi}}{dt} &= \varepsilon E_i - \gamma I_{bi} \\
\frac{dR_i}{dt} &= \gamma I_{bi} - \alpha_i R_i
\end{aligned}
\tag{17.1}
$$

For the above system (17.1), we may assume the following equation:

$$
\begin{aligned}
S_i + E_i + I_{bi} + R_i &= 1 \\
\Rightarrow R_i &= 1 - (S_i + E_i + I_{bi})
\end{aligned}
\tag{17.1.a}
$$

The corresponding system equations for the external network of our proposed model are given in the following system Eq. (17.2):

$$
\begin{aligned}
\frac{dS_e}{dt} &= b - \beta S_e I_{be} - d S_e + \alpha_e I_{be} \\
\frac{dI_{be}}{dt} &= \beta S_e I_{be} - \alpha_e I_{be} - (d + \mu) I
\end{aligned}
\tag{17.2}
$$

For the above system (17.2), we may assume the following equation:

$$
S_e + I_{be} = 1 \Rightarrow S_e = 1 - I_{be}
\tag{17.2.a}
$$

By using Eqs. (17.1.a) and (17.2.b), respectively, we may simplify the above-mentioned two system equations, viz., (17.1) and (17.2), into the following system (17.3) equation:

$$
\begin{aligned}
\frac{dS_i}{dt} &= -\beta S_i I_{be} + \alpha_i (1 - (S_i + E_i + I_{bi})) \\
\frac{dE_i}{dt} &= \beta S_i I_{be} - \varepsilon E_i \\
\frac{dI_{bi}}{dt} &= \varepsilon E_i - \gamma I_{bi} \\
\frac{dI_{be}}{dt} &= \beta (1 - I_{be}) I_{be} - \alpha_e I_{be} - (d + \mu) I_{be}
\end{aligned}
\tag{17.3}
$$

Let Z be used to represent the feasible region for the corresponding system (17.3) for the model given in Fig. 17.1. Hence, we may write Z as follows:

$$1Z = \Big\{ (S_i, E_i, I_{bi}, I_{be}) \in R^4 : S_i > 0, E_i \geq 0, I_{bi} \geq 0, I_{be} \geq 0,$$

$$S_i + I_{bi} + I_{be} \leq 1, I_{bi} + I_{be} < 1 \Big\}$$

4 Solution and Stability

In this section, we discuss the local stability at bots-free equilibrium as well as at endemic equilibrium as follows:

$$\frac{dS_i}{dt} = 0; \ \frac{dE_i}{dt} = 0; \ \frac{dI_{bi}}{dt} = 0; \ \frac{dI_{be}}{dt} = 0$$

4.1 Equilibrium Points

To calculate the equilibrium points for the proposed model, we set the right sides of the model equations of system (17.3) equal to zero, that is, using the above-mentioned four equations, the trivial bots-free equilibrium is obtained at point $E_1 \equiv \{1,0,0,0\}$, and the endemic equilibrium is found at point $E_2 \equiv \{S_i{}^*, E_i{}^*, I_{bi}{}^*, I_{be}{}^*\}$, where

$$S_i^* = \frac{\varepsilon}{\beta - \alpha_e - d - \mu} \cdot \alpha_i \cdot \frac{1}{\left(\varepsilon + \frac{\alpha_i \varepsilon}{\beta - \alpha_e - d - \mu} + \alpha_i + \frac{\alpha_i \varepsilon}{\gamma} \right)}$$

$$E_i^* = \alpha_i \cdot \frac{1}{\left(\varepsilon + \frac{\alpha_i \varepsilon}{\beta - \alpha_e - d - \mu} + \alpha_i + \frac{\alpha_i \varepsilon}{\gamma} \right)}$$

$$I_{bi}^* = \frac{\varepsilon}{\gamma} \cdot \alpha_i \cdot \frac{1}{\left(\varepsilon + \frac{\alpha_i \varepsilon}{\beta - \alpha_e - d - \mu} + \alpha_i + \frac{\alpha_i \varepsilon}{\gamma} \right)}$$

$$I_{be}^* = \frac{\beta - \alpha_e - d - \mu}{\beta}$$

4.2 Basic Reproduction Number

Number of infected node should increase to become endemic, i.e., $\frac{dI}{dt} > 0$. For system (17.1),

$$\frac{d\,I_{bi}}{dt} > 0$$

$$\Rightarrow \varepsilon E_i - \gamma I_{bi} > 0 \Rightarrow \frac{\varepsilon E_i}{\gamma I_{bi}} > 1$$

For system (17.2),

$$\beta S_e I_{be} - \alpha_e I_{be} - (d + \mu) I_{be} > 0$$
$$\Rightarrow \beta S_e I_{be} - (\alpha_e + d + \mu) I_{be} > 0$$
$$\Rightarrow \frac{\beta S_e}{(\alpha_e + d + \mu)} > 1$$

The above condition is satisfied, when the basic reproduction number

$$R = \frac{\beta}{\alpha_e + d + \mu} > 1$$

4.3 Stability of the System

Theorem 1 *The malware-free equilibrium E_1 of system (17.3) is locally asymptotically stable in Z if $R_{0e} < 1$ and is unstable if $R > 1$.*

Proof Linearizing system (17.3) around the malware-free equilibrium point $E_1 \equiv \{1, 0, 0, 0\}$, we obtain the following Jacobian matrix J_{E_1}:

$$J_{E_1} = \begin{bmatrix} -\alpha_i & -\alpha_i & -\alpha_i & -\beta \\ 0 & -\varepsilon & 0 & \beta \\ 0 & \varepsilon & -\gamma & 0 \\ 0 & 0 & 0 & \beta - (\alpha_e + d + \mu) \end{bmatrix}$$

The characteristic equation for the above matrix (J_{E_1}) is given as follows:

$$\{-(\beta - (\alpha_e + d + \mu) - \lambda)\}[-(\alpha_i + \lambda)\{(\varepsilon + \lambda)(\gamma + \lambda)\}] = 0$$

So, either,

$$\{-(\beta - (\alpha_e + d + \mu) - \lambda)\} = 0$$
$$\Rightarrow \lambda_1 = -(\alpha_e + d + \mu) + \beta \tag{17.4}$$

From Eq. (17.4), it can be found that the value of λ_1 will be negative if the following holds:

$$\beta < \alpha_e + d + \mu$$
$$\Rightarrow R < 1$$

Or

$$[-(\alpha_i + \lambda)\{(\varepsilon + \lambda)(\gamma + \lambda)\}] = 0 \tag{17.5}$$

From Eq. (17.5), we get the value of λ as follows:

$$\lambda_2 = -\alpha_i, \quad \lambda_3 = -\varepsilon \text{ and } \lambda_4 = -\gamma$$

Hence, all the eigenvalues of the Jacobian matrix J_{E_1} at equilibrium point $E_1 \equiv \{1, 0, 0, 0\}$ are negative when $R < 1$. So, it is proved that our proposed system is stable at equilibrium point $E_1 \equiv \{1, 0, 0, 0\}$ when $R < 1$.

But, when $R > 1$, we get

$$\frac{\beta}{\alpha_e + d + \mu} > 1 \Rightarrow \beta > \alpha_e + d + \mu$$

Now given the above condition, i.e., $\beta > \alpha_e + d + \mu$, it can be easily found from Eq. (17.4) that the value of λ_1 becomes positive; hence, our system becomes unstable. So, it is also proved that our proposed system becomes unstable at equilibrium point $E_1 \equiv \{1, 0, 0, 0\}$ when $R > 1$.

Theorem 2 *The endemic equilibrium E_2 of system* (17.3) *is locally asymptotically stable in Z if $R > 1$.*

Proof Linearizing system (17.3) around the endemic equilibrium point $E_2 \equiv \{S_i^*, E_i^*, I_{bi}^*, I_{be}^*\}$, we obtain the following Jacobian matrix J_{E_2}:

$$J_{E_2} = \begin{bmatrix} -\beta I_{be} - \alpha_i & -\alpha_i & -\alpha_i & -\beta S_i \\ \beta I_{be} & -\varepsilon & 0 & \beta S_i \\ 0 & \varepsilon & -\gamma & 0 \\ 0 & 0 & 0 & \beta - 2\beta I_{be} - (\alpha_e + d + \mu) \end{bmatrix}$$

From the characteristic equation for the above matrix (J_{E2}), we get either

$$-\beta + 2\beta I_{be} + (\alpha_e + d + \mu) + \lambda = 0$$
$$\Rightarrow \lambda_1 = -\beta(2I_{be} + 1) - (\alpha_e + d + \mu) \tag{17.6}$$

From Eq. (17.6), it is found that the value of λ_1 is negative. Or

$$-\varepsilon(0 + \beta I_{be}\alpha_i) - (\gamma + \lambda)[(\beta I_{be} + \alpha_i + \lambda)(\varepsilon + \lambda)$$
$$+ \alpha_i \beta I_{be}] = 0$$

$$\Rightarrow \lambda^3 + \lambda^2 \left(\beta I_{be} + \alpha_i + \varepsilon + \gamma \right) +$$

$$\lambda \left\{ \varepsilon \left(\beta I_{be} + \alpha_i \right) + \alpha_i \beta I_{be} + \gamma \left(\beta I_{be} + \alpha_i + \varepsilon \right) \right\} + \qquad (17.7)$$

$$\left\{ \gamma \varepsilon \left(\beta I_{be} + \alpha_i \right) + \gamma \alpha_i \beta I_{be} + \beta I_{be} \alpha_i \varepsilon \right\} = 0$$

Let λ_2, λ_3, and λ_4 are the roots of Eq. (17.7). From the theory of equation, it is found that the value of λ_2, λ_3, and λ_4 is negative. And from Eq. (17.6) above, it is already proved that the first eigenvalue λ_1 of J_{E2} is negative. So, all the four eigenvalues, viz., λ_1, λ_2, λ_3, and λ_4, of J_{E2} are negative when $R > 1$. Hence, the endemic equilibrium at E_2 is locally asymptotically stable if $R > 1$.

5   Numerical Discussion

In this section, we will show the result of numerical simulations using MATLAB to support the dynamism and stability of our formulated model using graphs. Here we have analyzed three cases as follows:

5.1   Case 1: All Classes of Nodes vs. Time When R < 1

Here in this case, we have plotted the different classes of nodes of our proposed model over time to show the dynamism and stability of the model when $R < 1$, as shown in Fig. 17.2 below.

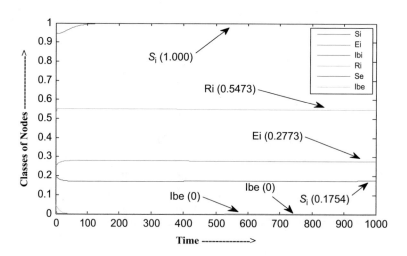

Fig. 17.2 Dynamic behavior of different classes of nodes over time *when R < 1*

Table 17.1 Value of various S, E, I, and R at different time frame when $R < 1$

$\beta < d + \mu + \alpha e; R < 1$							
β	μ	αe	αi	Υ	ε	d	b
0.245	0.11	0.169	0.00001	0.6	0.00001	0.03	0.03
	S_i	Ei	I_{bi}	Ri	Se	Ibe	Time interval
Initial	0.2000	0.2500	0.0500	0.5000	0.9500	0.0500	
Final	0.1732	0.2784	0.0000	05484	1.0000	0.0000	0–600
	0.1754	0.2773	0.0000	0.5473	1.0000	0.0000	0–1000
	0.2236	0.2534	0.0000	0.5230	1.0000	0.0000	0–10,000

We have done the said study for three different time periods (600, 1000, and 10,000) for the same initial condition $\{S_i, E_i, I_{bi}, R_i, S_e, I_{be}\} = \{0.2000, 0.2500, 0.0500, 0.5000, 0.9500, 0.0500\}$ and at the same value of β (0.246) and the same value for all other transmission rates to satisfy the condition, $R < 1$. And the results of the studies for those three cases are shown in Table 17.1 above.

The behavior of the nodes of the six classes is displayed in Fig. 17.2, and it shows that the values of number (fraction) of nodes at six different classes remain unchanged after the 100 units of time. From the above diagram, it is clear that our proposed model becomes stable after 100 time units and remains stable for longer times also for $R < 1$. The most interesting fact is that the stability of the model is due to the absence of viruses in our proposed system when $R < 1$, which is shown in Table 17.1 above, i.e., the fraction of infected nodes, I_{bi} and I_{be}, is zero (0.000) for all the three time frames.

5.2 Case 2: All Classes of Nodes vs. Time When $R > 1$

Here in this case, we have plotted the different classes of nodes of our proposed model over time to show the dynamism and stability of the model when $R > 1$, as shown in Fig. 17.3 below.

In this case, we have done the simulation for three different time periods (0–500, 0–1000, and 0–100,000 time units) for the same initial condition $\{S_i, E_i, I_{bi}, R_i, S_e, I_{be}\} = \{0.5000, 0.2500, 0.1500, 0.1000, 0.7500, 0.2500\}$ and at the same value of β (0.3612) and the same value for all other transmission rates to satisfy the condition, $R > 1$. And the initial and final observations of the studies for those three cases are shown in Table 17.2 below.

It is shown from the above graph (Fig. 17.3) that the proposed system becomes stable after the initial hiccup. But the final value of I_{bi} and I_{be}, which are given in Table 17.2, shows that the system is not virus-free. So unlike case 1, in case 2, although the system is stable, it contains infectious nodes when $R > 1$ for all the three time frames shown above. Another interesting observation from Table 17.2 is that the fractions of I_{be} is decreased by 0.0001 after first run, but remain same for the second and third run. But the fractions of infectious nodes for internal network,

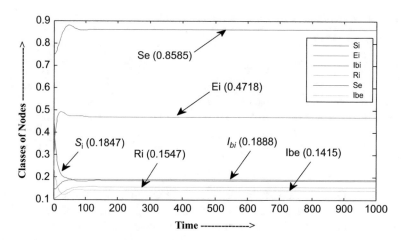

Fig. 17.3 Dynamic behavior of different classes of nodes over time when $R > 1$

Table 17.2 Value of various S, E, I, and R at different time frame when $R > 1$

$\beta > d + \mu + \alpha e; R > 1$							
β	μ	αe	αi	Υ	ε	d	b
0.3612	0.1101	0.17	0.061	0.05	0.02	0.03	0.04558
	S_i	Ei	I_{bi}	Ri	Se	Ibe	Time interval
Initial	0.5000	0.2500	0.1500	0.1000	0.7500	0.2500	
Final	0.1846	0.4719	0.1888	01547	0.8584	0.1416	0–500
	0.1847	0.4718	0.1888	0.1547	0.8585	0.1415	0–1000
	0.1848	0.4718	0.1888	0.1546	0.8585	0.1415	0–10,000

i.e., I_{bi}, remain same (non-zero) after the short-term (0–500 time units) as well as long-term (0–100,000 time units) execution of the system, and that indicates the local as well as global stability of the system.

5.3   Case 3. Comparative Study of S_i vs. I_{bi}

Here in this case, we have studied the behavior of I_{bi} with respect to S_i for our system Eq. (17.3) for the time frame 0–100, and the behavior is represented graphically in Fig. 17.4 below.

Here plotting is done for eight different cases with same initial condition $\{S_i, E_i, I_{bi}, I_{be}\} = \{0.5500, 0.1500, 0.1500, 0.1500\}$ and same value for μ, αe, αi, Υ, ε, d, and b for all the eight cases, but the value of β is increased by 0.01, i.e., we are making our system more infectious. The numerical result (final value) of this experiment is shown in Table 17.3.

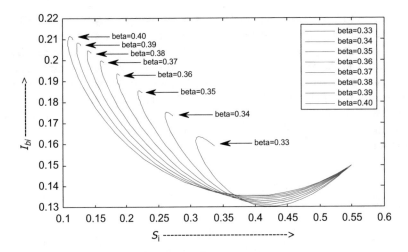

Fig. 17.4 Comparative study of S_i vs. I_{bi} while increasing β by 0.01 (time 0–100)

Table 17.3 Changes of S_i vs. I_{bi} while increasing beta by 0.01

μ	αe	αi	Υ	ε	d	b
0.11	0.17	0.07	0.05	0.02	0.03	0.25
Time: 0–100	S_i	I_{bi}			S_i-I_{bi}	
Case	β	0.5500	0.1500	Initial	0.4000	Diff.
1	0.33	0.3373	0.1592	Final	0.1781	Diff.
2	0.34	0.2727	0.1737	Final	0.0990	Diff.
3	0.35	0.2247	0.1848	Final	0.0399	Diff.
4	0.36	0.1896	0.1930	Final	−0.0034	Diff.
5	0.37	0.1637	0.1991	Final	−0.0354	Diff.
6	0.38	0.1441	0.2037	Final	−0.0596	Diff.
7	0.39	0.1286	0.2073	Final	−0.0787	Diff.
8	0.40	0.1162	0.2102	Final	−0.0940	Diff.

From the data shown in Table 17.3 above, it is observed that when $R > 1$, but the value of β increases, it leads to the increase in I_{bi}, which makes the system more infectious and unstable while decreasing the value of S_i, which is also shown in Fig. 17.4.

6 Conclusion

In this chapter, we have designed an interactive epidemic SIS–SEIRS model which consists of two interactive sub-models to represent the DDoS attack and spread of bots into an e-commerce network. It is mathematically proved that the proposed system is asymptotically stable at malware-free equilibrium point if the reproduction number is less than one and unstable if the reproduction number is greater than 1.

It is also proved mathematically that the proposed model is asymptotically stable at endemic equilibrium point if the reproduction number is greater than one.

It is also shown graphically that the stability of the model is due to the absence of malware in the system when the reproduction number is less than one. The comparison between S_i vs. I_{bi} shows that when β is increased by a fixed value (0.01), it decreases the value of S_i and increases the value of I_{bi} and hence makes the system more infectious. And the rate of increase in I_{bi} is more than the decrease of S_i. The limitation of our proposed model is that it does not allow inclusion of new node in internal network.

References

1. Godbole, N., & Belapure, S. (2015). Cyber security-understanding cyber crimes. In *Computer forensics and legal perspectives* (2015th ed., p. 14). Bengaluru: Wiley.
2. Gao, T., Wang, Q., Wang, X., & Gong, X. (2017). An anonymous access authentication scheme based on proxy ring signature for CPS-WMNs. *Mobile Information Systems, 2017*, 11.
3. Wang, L., Zhang, X., & Liu, Z. (2018). An SEIR epidemic model with relapse and general nonlinear incidence rate with application to media impact. *Qualitative Theory of Dynamical Systems, 17*(2), 309–329.
4. Wang, J., Liu, X., & Kuniya, T. (2017, September). Global stability for multi-group SIR and SEIR epidemic models with age-dependent susceptibility. *Discrete and Continuous Dynamical Systems – Series B (DCDS-B), 22*(7), 2795–2812. https://doi.org/10.3934/dcdsb.2017151.
5. Kharchenko, V., & Illiashenko, O. (2016). Diversity for security: Case assessment for FPGA-based safety-critical systems. In *20th International Conference on Circuits, Systems, Communications and Computers (CSCC 2016), Volume 76, 2016, MATEC Web Conference* (p. 02051).
6. Canzani, E., & Pickl, S. (2016). Cyber epidemics: Modelling attacker-defender dynamics in critical infrastructure systems. In *Advances in human factors in cyber security* (pp. 377–389). Cham: Springer.
7. Kaur, K., Pathak, A., Kaur, P., & Kaur, K. (2015, May). E-commerce privacy and security system. *International Journal of Engineering Research and Applications, 5*(5, Part-6), 63–73.
8. Möhlmann, E., & Theel, O. (2015). Breaking dense structures: Proving stability of densely structured hybrid systems. In *Electronic proceedings in theoretical computer science, 2015; 184 (Proc. ESSS 2015)* (pp. 49–63). https://doi.org/10.4204/EPTCS.184.4.
9. Feng, L. (2015). Modeling and stability analysis of worm propagation in wireless sensor network. *Mathematical Problems in Engineering, 2015*, 8. https://doi.org/10.1155/2015/129598.
10. Ma, J. (2015). Analysis of two-worm interaction model in heterogeneous M2M network. *Information, 6*, 613–632. https://doi.org/10.3390/info6040613.
11. Canzani. (2015). Insights from modeling epidemics of infectious diseases – A literature review. In *Proceedings of the ISCRAM 2015 Conference – Kristiansand*.
12. Wang, M. (2014). Spread and control of mobile benign worm based on two-stage repairing mechanism. *Journal of Applied Mathematics, 2014*, 14. https://doi.org/10.1155/2014/746803.
13. Canzani, E., Heldt, H.-C., Meyer, S., & Lechner, U. (2014). Towards an understanding of the IT security information ecosystem. In *Autonomous Systems 2014. Proceedings of the 7th GI Conference. VDI Reihe.*
14. Alomari, E., Manickam, S., Gupta, B. B., Karuppayah, S., & Alfaris, R. (2012, July). Botnet-based distributed denial of service (DDoS) attacks on web servers: Classification and art. *International Journal of Computer Applications, 49*(7), 24–32. arXiv preprint arXiv:1208.0403.

15. Suchacka, G., & Wotzka, D. (2017). Modeling a non-stationary bots' arrival process at an e-commerce web site. *Journal of Computational Science, 22*, 198–208.
16. Xu, H., Li, Z., Chu, C., Chen, Y., Yang, Y., Lu, H., et al. (2018, September). Detecting and characterizing web bot traffic in a large e-commerce marketplace. In *European Symposium on Research in Computer Security* (pp. 143–163). Cham: Springer.
17. Mishra, B. K., & Pandey, S. K. (2011). Dynamic model of worms with vertical transmission in computer network. *Applied Mathematics and Computation, 217*(21), 8438–8446.
18. Mishra, B. K., & Pandey, S. K. (2010). Fuzzy epidemic model for the transmission of worms in computer network. *Nonlinear Analysis: Real World Applications, 11*(2010), 4335–4341.
19. Mishra, B. K., & Pandey, S. K. (2012). Effect of antivirus software on infectious nodes in computer network: A mathematical model. *Physics Letters A, 376*, 2389–2393.
20. Biswarup, S., & Pandey, S. K. (2014, December). Attacking behaviour of computer worms on e-commerce network: A dynamic model. *International Journal for Research in Applied Science and Engineering Technology, 2*(XII), 2321.
21. Gelenbe, E., Kaptan, V., & Wang, Y. (2004). Biological metaphors for agent behaviour. In *Computer and information sciences ISCIS 2004, 19th international symposium* (Lecturer notes in computer science) (Vol. 3280, pp. 667–675). Cham: Springer.
22. Piqueira, J. R. C., Navarro, B. F., & Monteiro, L. H. A. (2005). Epidemiological models applied to virus in computer network. *Journal of Computer Science, 1*(1), 31–34.
23. Wang, Y., & Wang, C. X. (2003). Modelling the effect of timing parameters on virus propagation. In *2003 ACM workshop on rapid Malcode, ACM* (pp. 61–66).
24. Forest, S., Hofmeyr, S., Somayaji, A., & Longstaff, T. (1994). Self-nonself discrimination in a computer. In *Proceeding of IEEE symposium on computer security and privacy* (pp. 202–212).
25. Mishra, B. K., & Jha, N. (2010). SEIQRS model for the transmission of malicious objects in computer network. *Applied Mathematical Modelling, 34*, 710–715.
26. Shah, D. N. (2014). *Mark Stamp's information security principles and practices* (2014th ed., pp. 341–342). Bengaluru: Wiley.
27. Kermack, W. O., & McKendrick, A. G. (1927). Contributions of mathematical theory to epidemics. *Proceedings of the Royal Society of London. Series A, Containing Papers of a Mathematical and Physical Character, 115*(1927), 700–721.
28. Kermack, W. O., & McKendrick, A. G. (1932). Contributions of mathematical theory to epidemics. *Proceedings of the Royal Society of London. Series A, Containing Papers of a Mathematical and Physical Character, 138*, 55–83.
29. Kermack, W. O., & McKendrick, A. G. (1933). Contributions of mathematical theory to epidemics. *Proceedings of the Royal Society of London. Series A, Containing Papers of a Mathematical and Physical Character, 141*, 94–122.

Chapter 18
Physical Unclonable Function (PUF)-Based Security in Internet of Things (IoT): Key Challenges and Solutions

Mohammed Saeed Alkatheiri, Abdur Rashid Sangi, and Satish Anamalamudi

Abstract Security protocols play a pivotal role in transmitting the sensitive application data through packet switched and circuit switched data communication. State-of-the-art research comes up with the constrained IoT design to provide the connectivity in between things without any human intervention. Hence, IoT becomes a promising solution to provide the end-to-end connectivity through constrained network resources. Physical Unclonable Function (PUF) is a digital logic design that is incorporated in Integrated Circuit (IC). It is lightweight, unclonable, and simple to implement. Security mechanisms based on PUF can be an efficient way to provide security for resource-constrained IoT networks. This chapter describes different security aspects/scenarios of IoT that can use PUF-based mechanisms.

Keywords Internet of Things (IoT) · Security Physical Unclonable Function · IoT gateway · LLN nodes

1 Introduction

Recently, Internet of Things (IoT) is evolving as one of the promising and significant areas of the 5G communications. With 5G communication, millions of devices can be interconnecting around the globe where IoT can be considered as an integral part of several applications like smart cities, intelligent transportation services, smart grids, and many others. Each application of IoT promises to deliver an enhanced

M. S. Alkatheiri
University of Jeddah, Jeddah, Saudi Arabia

A. R. Sangi (✉)
Huaiyin Institute of Technology, Jiangsu Sheng, China

S. Anamalamudi
SRM University-AP, Amaravati, Andhra Pradesh, India

© Springer Nature Switzerland AG 2020   461
B. B. Gupta et al. (eds.), *Handbook of Computer Networks and Cyber Security*,
https://doi.org/10.1007/978-3-030-22277-2_18

quality of experience in day-to-day activities. For example, the real motivation behind the development of smart cities is to have control over the available resources which will in turn promote healthy economy and sustainable growth. To achieve the successful implementation of IoT, an interconnected network of IoT requires every device to be connected to its utility gateway (IoT gateway or LLN gateway) directly or indirectly. For that, these constrained devices are needed to be equipped with smart sensors (or actuators) to collect the application data and forward it into their network center for further processing. Different types of IoT networks that are being proposed are centralized and distributed networks. In addition, both random access-based packet switched and deterministic networks are being proposed to implement within the IoT networks. Some applications in IoT (e.g., Industrial and Medical Machine to Machine Communication) need to have end-to-end dedicated spectrum channels to support control/data streams for time-critical applications. For such applications, securing the data is most crucial to protect the end user safety. Thus, enabling security to the end-to-end communication in IoT is very significant to provide safety to the end users. The widespread use of mobile devices is systematically providing ease and further aids human tasks. For example, RFID is one of the most important technologies designed to have the capability to assist numerous human tasks. RFID can be used to identify and authenticate person, animal, or product and prevent counterfeiting and cloning of goods, drugs, and money. However, the pervasiveness of the digital and computing devices has raised the security risks and delivers new security challenges/threats. These security threats and challenges are increasingly becoming intricate and awaiting to be overcome. Because such devices have significant limitations in terms of energy, implementation, and physical tampering as well as side channel attacks. Numerous existing cryptography algorithms are powerful to prevent some security attacks, but require complex implementation, such as public key cryptography. Even though there are many lightweight encryption algorithms provided by researchers, these efforts are always based on the assumption that the secret keys stored in non-volatile memory are well protected. However, physical system attack can easily breach/crack this sensitive information. Therefore, the cryptography primitive, namely Physical Unclonable Functions (PUF), is designed to address the above issue and successfully prevent counterfeiting, cloning, and prediction. For security-sensitive applications, PUF provides a cost-effective solution, and it can address the problems of existing solutions.

PUF is a one way-function that is easy to evaluate by using physical system but difficult to predict as its output is perfectly random in nature. PUF is a logical circuit designed and implemented inside an integrated circuit (IC), which generates a response for a given challenge. The given challenge produces a different unpredictable response when it is applied to different chip. Moreover, PUF can generate unlimited amount of secret key for one chip and gives an ability to produce unique identifiers for each chip. Fabrication process of an IC leaves behind unique characteristic to these circuits. Due to some uncontrollable and unavoidable differences in the process at molecular scale of each chip, PUF takes the advantage of this uncontrollable randomness as its challenge, and response mapping (values are all binary strings) depends upon these variations. Therefore, PUF provides a unique challenge-response mechanism on each chip. As an example, the security related to the authentication process of the resource-constrained Internet of Things (IoT) devices is one of the major concerns as the conventional robust cryptographic solutions that are considered being powerful against some attacks but requires prohibitive cost and requires an increased power. These robust encryptions and security mechanisms are inhibited to be equipped in these devices which are not feasible as they have strict area and limited processing power. Thus, with the above concerns, the small size and limited processing power make these devices vulnerable to the attacker to reproduce the authentication protocol for the compromised nodes in IoT. Therefore, the attractive properties of PUF, i.e., lightweight, simplistic nature for authentication mechanisms, and reduced computational cost as compared to the requirements of existing cryptographic algorithms, make it a suitable candidate. Moreover, PUF provides us some features such as low cost computation, unpredictability, and unclonability. These features make PUF a promising candidate for resource-constrained IoT devices, and it is a very effective solution to solve the issues of secure communication in IoTs. PUFs have been proposed in [1] for device identify and authentication, and authors implemented PUF in IC to be used as anti-counterfeiting. Also it has been used as secure storage of cryptographic secrets [2], key-less secure communication [3], etc. Moreover, it is worth noting as stated in [4] that the conventional attack cannot be carried out if it is replaced by an ideal PUF.

This chapter is an effort to identify security issues in IoT that can best be resolved using PUF.

2 Overview of Security Issues in IoT

Different security bootstrapping methods are discussed in [3, 5], and this section covers what are the key security issues which can arise due to a failed security bootstrapping.

Before covering all security issues, we must understand that the term security covers a vast range of concepts, and here we are dealing with two broader key aspects of security in IoT, i.e., physical security and network security. An IoT network has to be protected mainly against following security aspects: authentication, access control, confidentiality, integrity, and availability.

Authentication process is used to validate communicating nodes before they share any secure information. Even the information of routing path is also important here. In IoT, authentication must be strong and highly automated. Access control is like verifying that the communicating node is not compromised. Confidentiality refers to the protection of vital information which is shared among communicating parties over open channel, e.g., wireless medium. Integrity confirms the data is unmodified and it is exactly as been sent by one party to the other, i.e., ensuring that no modification is done while data is in transit. Availability ensures that information is available when required [6].

When examining these threats, we found that under most of the IoT scenarios, the network is ultimately connected to public network whether it is comprised of hand-held mobile devices, number of static nodes, or a combination of both. So, the prime concern would be to look toward challenges posed under network security for IoT devices.

2.1 Physical Security

As we know, IoT networks are centralized with many remote nodes. Most of these nodes are in different locations like within ad hoc and sensor networks and have very less human intervention or attention. In this type of scenario, the attackers can seize and extract security information, keys, etc., from the device scattered in large area. Attacker can re-program the node or use physical or manufacturer info for their own needs. In case if common network key is used, then attack is more severe than the separate key in use [7]. DoS and DDoS attack can also be done in order to disrupt network communication, and these are very hard to detect [8, 9].

2.2 Network Security

2.2.1 Authentication Failure

This attack occurs at network layer; it aims the network route information and secure data. This type of attack happens when any of communicating node is compromised [7]. The prevention to this attack is authentication in the best possible way so that no illegitimate node is able to join the network.

2.2.2 Man in the Middle Attack (MitM)

MitM attacks are done by capturing information being sent between communicating nodes. This can be done by analyzing traffic, by which attacker is able to learn about the network. Such types of attacks can be mitigated by encrypting all data used for routing. It is mandatory to implement Advanced Encryption Standard (AES)-128 in Counter with CBC-MAC (CCM) mode for low power and lossy networks [10]. CCM combines the counter mode for encryption and the cipher block chaining message authentication code technique for authentication. MitM can also be done by analyzing traffic flow through network to successfully map traffic flow pattern; this happens in case the routing information remains unencrypted at data link and network layer [11]. These can be mitigated by using multi-path routing which requires more power consumption and is not very suitable for resource-constrained IoT networks.

2.2.3   Attacks on Data Integrity

Data integrity refers to unauthorized modification in a message or in stored data [12]. This attack can be mitigated by using access control for messages.

2.2.4   Spoofing

Spoofing is also known as identity theft; this means a communication node is not the one which it is pretending. This type of attack happens when an attacker gains access to a communicating node, either physically or via a network. If the attacker is able to create multiple false identities, then these are called Sybil attacks. By these attacks, the attacker can read secure data and send false routing information to disrupt normal routing process [13]. These attacks can be mitigated by applying correct authentication scheme at network layer.

2.2.5   Routing Information Replay Attacks

These attacks occur when the attacker records a message that is sent over a network and replays it multiple times to the network to disrupt operations [14, 15]. The IETF routing over low power and lossy networks (RPL) is designed to mitigate this attack. In RPL, repeated message or older messages are ignored by communicating parties [RFC6550].

2.2.6   Byzantine Routing Information Attacks

In this type of attacks, communicating node gets compromised by an attacker; that still contains a valid identity and security credentials. These attacks are very hard to detect; even authentication mechanisms could not counter such attacks.

2.2.7   Availability Attacks

Availability or selective forwarding attacks aim to routing paths and to disrupt communications among nodes. As seen in Fig. 18.1, the attacker can be able to send selected messages and creates confusion within the network. A situation where packets (msg1|msg2|msg3) are sent by Node A but the attacker node drops all the packets it receives is known as a black hole attack [16]. These types of attacks can be mitigated either by using end-to-end or hop-by-hop multipath routing protocols to send out the packets. Multipath method requires more energy; thus, it is not advised to be used in low power and lossy networks. Please refer to Table 18.1 for availability attacks in selective forwarding.

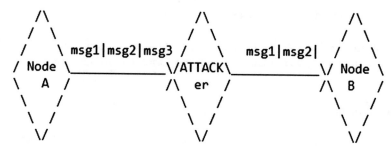

Fig. 18.1 Availability or selective forwarding

2.2.8 Wormhole Attacks

These attacks occur when two nodes with very short path among them get compromised. This attack forces nodes to recalculate network path. It is hard to detect but does not affect the data. In most of the cases, this attack is used in combination with other attacks like availability/selective forwarding to disrupt network communications [16]. Mitigating such attack is only possible with protecting the nodes to identity theft or false authentication.

2.2.9 Overload Attacks

Overload attacks are also referred to as denial-of-service (DoS) attacks, where compromised node fills the network with random traffic. These are aimed for exhausting network resources like routing and power, hence resulting in network breakdown. These attacks can be mitigated by limiting network usage to each node and also by isolating nodes which are sending excessive amount of traffic [17, 18].

3 Types of Physical Unclonable Function (PUF)

PUF is of various types and the following are two main types that can be suitable for resource-constrained IoT networks.

3.1 Arbiter PUF

Arbiter PUF is delay-based intrinsic silicon PUF which is based on number of switch blocks and an arbiter. It consists of switch block (MUXes) and an arbiter (flip-flop/latch). For "n" switch blocks, we have 2n "different delays." The circuit takes input in the form of multiple bits but gives single bit output based on the delay

Table 18.1 Overload attacks

Security issue type	Security issue description
	Based on the type of the security attack
Interception	The intruder intercepts the information through control/data signaling, but does not modify or delete; this kind of attack affects the privacy of the subscriber as well as the network operator
Reply attacks	The intruder can insert the unauthentic objects into the system that depend on the target and physical access type (e.g., spurious messages, fake service logic, or fake subscriber information)
Resource modification	The intruder creates the damage to the system by modifying the system resources
Interruption	The intruder tries to interrupt the operation by destroying the system resources (e.g., delete signaling messages and subscriber data, stop delivery, etc.)
	Based on methodologies used to cause the attack
Attacks based on data	The intruder targets the information stored in the IoT communication system and causes the damage by altering or inserting and/or deleting the data stored in the system
Attacks based on messages	The intruder targets the IoT system by adding, replacing, replaying, and dropping the control/data signaling flowing to and from the IoT network
Service logic attacks	The intruder tries to create the significant damages by simply attacking the service logic running in the various IoT network entities
	Based on the level of physical access
Class I	The intruder gains the access to the radio interface using a physical device and uses the modified mobile stations (eNodeB's) to broadcast the radio signal at higher frequency, eavesdrop, and execute "man-in-the-middle attacks"
Class II	The intruder gains the access to the physical cables connecting the IoT network switches and may cause considerable damage by disrupting the normal transmission of control/data signaling messages
Class III	The intruder will have access to some of the sensitive components of the IoT network and can cause important impairments by changing the service logic or modifying the subscriber information stored in the IoT network entity
Class IV	The intruder has the access to communication links connecting the Internet to the IoT network and can create a disruption through transmission of control/data signaling flowing between the link and adding some new control/data signaling messages into the link between the two heterogeneous networks
Class V	The intruder has an access to the Internet servers or cross network servers providing services to mobile subscribers connected to the IoT network and can cause the harmful damage by changing the service logic or modifying the subscriber data (profile, security, and services) stored in the cross network servers

(continued)

Table 18.1 (continued)

Security issue type	Security issue description
	Access of unauthorized sensitive data
Eavesdrop	The intruder intercepts the messages by continuously monitoring the operation of the communication network
Masquerading	The intruder frauds an authorized user by pretending that they are the legitimate users to obtain the confidential information from the end user or from the communication network
Analysis of the traffic flow	The intruder eavesdrops the traffic flow through length, rate, time, source, and destination of the traffic to trace out the user location
Browsing	The intruder search for data storage to trace out the sensitive information
Data leakage	The intruder obtains the sensitive information by exploiting the ways to access the legitimate user data
Inference	The intruder checks the reaction from a system by transmitting a query or control/data signal to the system
	Manipulation of sensitive data
Modification of user information	User information can be modified, inserted, replayed, or deleted by the intruder deliberately
	Unauthorized access to services
Access rights	The intruder will access the services through masquerading network entities or end user information
	Physical layer issues
Interference	The intruder intentionally creates the man-made interference onto a communication medium that causes the communication system to stop functioning due to high signal to noise ratio
Scrambling	One type of interference that is triggered based on short time intervals. With this, specific frame is targeted to disrupt a service. This kind of security attack is very complex to implement in communication network
	Medium Access Control (MAC) issues
Location tracking	The intruder monitors the presence of user equipment in a specific cell coverage or across multiple cell coverage
Bandwidth stealing	The intruder creates this kind of attack by inserting the messages during the Discontinuous Reception (DRX) period or through utilizing fake buffer status reports
Open architecture security issues	As IoT networks are IP-enabled networks with a high density of devices that are highly mobile and dynamic, an open architecture of an IP-based IoT results in increasing the number of security threats
Security issues at higher layers	The departure from proprietary operating systems for handheld devices to open and standardized operating systems and the open nature of the network architecture and protocols result in increasing number of potential security threats to the LTE wireless network, making it vulnerable to a wide range of security attacks including malwares, Trojans, and viruses

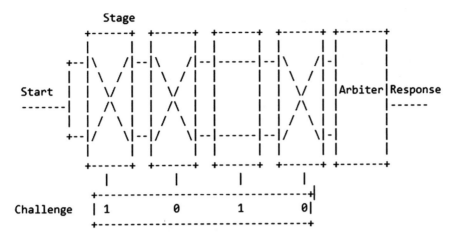

Fig. 18.2   Arbiter Physical Unclonable Function (PUF)

of two paths of equal length. The delay path is determined with respect to the input bits by controlling the MUXes. The MUXes pass through two delay signals from the left side if the input control bit is zero. Else, the top and bottom signals are switched. In this way, the circuit can create delay path for each input (Fig. 18.2).

The output is calculated based on the signal that is faster, and initially a signal is given to both paths at the same time. The signal moves through the path (facing variable delays), and an arbiter located at the end decides which signal is faster. The output is one if the signal from data input latch is faster; else output is zero. As there is more likelihood to get duplication due to precise timing, the output of PUF circuit can be obfuscated by XORing multiple outputs. There are different ways to construct k-bit response from 1-bit output in this delay-based PUF. At first, one circuit can be used k times with different inputs; a challenge is used as a seed for pseudo-random generator. Then, the PUF delay circuit is evaluated k times, using k different bit vectors from the pseudo-random number generator serving as the input X to configure the delay paths.

3.2   Ring Oscillator (RO) PUF

Ring oscillator PUF is based on ring oscillators (delay loops) and counters, rather than switch boxes and arbiter. Each ring oscillator is a particular circuit that oscillates with a particular frequency. Each oscillator oscillates with different frequency. These frequencies change with respect to environmental conditions such as temperature variation or power supply instability. Fixed sequence of oscillator pairs is selected to generate fixed bits, and oscillator frequencies are compared to generate output bit. Output bits vary from one chip to another even when compared

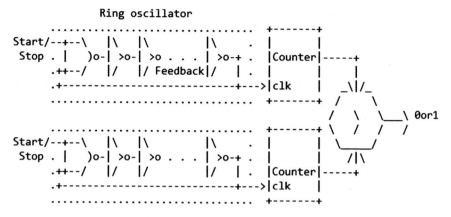

Fig. 18.3 Ring oscillator Physical Unclonable Function (PUF)

for the same sequence of oscillator pair. The output bit of oscillator is likely to be one or zero. The RO PUF has a strongly secure processor design and is more reliable than arbiter, but it is slower and consumes more power. On the other hand, we believe the arbiter PUF is more appropriate for resource-constrained platforms (refer to Fig. 18.3 above).

4 PUF Applicability

By reviewing survey on secure bootstrapping for IoT [10], viz., Managed, P2P or Ad-hoc, Opportunistic or Leap-of-Faith, Hybrid, and all security issues in IoT including both physical security issues and network security issues, we came to conclusion that the lack of physical security leads to other attacks, and if an attacker has the physical access, then it is much easier to crack down attack on network layer; hence, tampering with data and causing nuisance are eminent. To understand these facts in simpler words and going all at once, the opinion is divided in two parts: first going with security bootstrapping methods and then security in IoT. Finally, a discussion would provide some easier and real-time PUF usage example.

5 In Bootstrapping

When it comes to context of Managed security bootstrapping methods, the centralized server-based authentication is used to verify different nodes before communicating. A PUF can be used instead of putting long algorithms and programs to verify nodes with server. The basic idea of verifying nodes with server using PUF rather than pre-shared key will result in lesser demand of power, and authentication could be performed without executing more heavy algorithms, whereas in P2P or Ad-hoc methods where the node authentication is performed by using key exchanging program, a PUF-based mechanism to verify node-to-node authenticity would result in easier and safe authentication with less power consumption. In Opportunistic or Leap-of-Faith methods, the verification of node is done with an assumption that the network is not compromised. Even with above assumption, using PUF mechanism for authentication, which inherently is strong to break (the authentication schema), is more simple and cost-effective.

6 Securing Other IoT Aspects

In the case of security issues in IoT, again there are two parts, i.e., physical issues and network-related issues. Using PUF in IoT devices can remove all physical security issues as we had discussed earlier that output of PUF is random in nature and depends on physical factors and even if the attacker gains physical access to device or node, it is impossible to reverse engineer PUF, which proves its trustworthiness toward physical security of IoT. As regards network security issues, first, we must understand that most of the attacks are possible due to false authentication which is the beginning, and afterward other attacks are possible. To help mitigate network attacks, PUF-based mechanism is suitable.

Authentication failure can be mitigated by using PUF, as it will provide perfect authentication to legitimate devices only and false authentication is not possible while using PUF mechanism. If PUF-based authentication is in place, then there is no need to think about confidentiality attacks because there will always be the legitimate nodes communicating with one another. All other network attacks (except MitM and data integrity) are ultimately initiated with compromised nodes which can be done either by using physical attack or by using fake authentication to get inside a given network, and these all can be removed using single solution, a solution based on PUF. For MitM and data integrity over network, currently used methods, i.e., CBC-MAC, are better in terms of security as the data is encrypted using lighter encryption schemas and thus are good for resource-constrained devices.

7 More Examples

Nearly most of the security service providers offer hardware-based security solutions for software license authentication. This hardware contains PUF due to its low cost, unclonability, and security. Another example is related to the Government of India where PUF-based RFID tags are implemented for authentication system used in Fast-Tag automatic toll collection service. A renowned US based company, VERAYO, develops PUF-based IoT devices and serves well-reputed customers including US Department of Defense agencies. Moreover, a Dutch company,

"Intrinsic ID," also works in the field of developing PUF-based IoT devices and has reputed contracts including government and defense departments.

8 Conclusions

This chapter highlighted the applications of PUF in IoT and provided an insight of this fabulous technology that is believed to be suitable to use in any resource constrained environment, especially IoT. The inherent unique properties of an Integrated Circuit (every device holds at least one) can further affirm the suitability of PUF based security mechanisms in resource constrained network including IoT.

This lucrative and easy to implement technology could bring a revolution in adoptability in securing the IoT ecosystems. Further study in this regard is needed to more specifically devise novel security mechanisms based on PUF for IoT ecosystems.

Acknowledgment The authors hereby express their gratitude to the inventions of PUF and look forward to see its large scale adoption in securing IoT networks. Also, many thanks to the editor(s) of this book for providing a platform to introduce new security related concepts.

References

1. Garcia-Morchon, O., Kumar, S., Keoh, S., Hummen, R., & Struik, R. (2013, September). *Security considerations in the IP-based internet of things.* Draft-garcia-core-security-06 (work in progress).
2. Tsao, T., Alexander, R., Dohler, M., Daza, V., Lozano, A., & Richardson, M. (2014, October). *A security threat analysis for routing protocol for low-power and lossy networks (RPL).* Draft-ietf-roll-security-threats-11 (work in progress).
3. Sarikaya, B., Sethi, M., & Garcia-Carillo, D. (2018, September). *Secure IoT bootstrapping: A survey.* Draft-sarikaya-t2trg-sbootstrapping-05 (work in progress).
4. Ruhrmair, U., Solter, J., Sehnke, F., Xu, X., Mahmoud, A., et al. (2013). PUF modelling attacks on simulated and silicon data. *IEEE Transactions on Information Forensics and Security, 8*(11), 1876–1891.
5. Gupta, B., Agrawal, D. P., & Yamaguchi, S. (2016). *Handbook of research on modern cryptographic solutions for computer and cyber security.* Pennsylvania: IGI Global.
6. Edward Suh, G., & Devadas, S. (2007). Physical Unclonable Functions for device authentication and secret key generation. In *Proceedings of the 44th annual design automation conference* (pp. 644–654). ACM.
7. Meng-Day Y., M'Raihi, D., Sowell, R., & Devadas, S. (2011, October). Lightweight and secure PUF key storage using limits of machine learning. In *Cryptographic Hardware and Embedded Systems, CHES 2011—13th International Workshop, Nara, Japan* (pp. 358–373).

8. Gupta, B., Agrawal, D. P., & Wang, H. (2018). *Computer and cyber security: Principles, algorithm, applications, and perspectives* (p. 666). Boca Raton, FL: CRC Press, Taylor & Francis.
9. Shamim Hossain, M., Muhammad, G., Abdul, W., Song, B., & Gupta, B. B. (2018). Cloud-assisted secure video transmission and sharing framework for smart cities. *Future Generation Computer Systems, 83*, 596–606.
10. Winter, T., Thubert, P., Brandt, A., Hui, J., Kelsey, R., Levis, P., Pister, K., Struik, R., Vasseur, JP., & Alexander, R. (2012, March). *RPL: IPv6 routing protocol for low-power and lossy networks*. RFC 6550. https://doi.org/10.17487/RFC6550. Retrieved from https://www.rfc-editor.org/info/rfc6550
11. Bradner, S. (1997, March). *Key words for use in RFCs to indicate requirement levels*. BCP 14, RFC 2119. https://doi.org/10.17487/RFC2119. Retrieved from https://www.rfc-editor.org/info/rfc2119
12. Gupta, B. B., & Quamara, M. An overview of internet of things (IoT): Architectural aspects, challenges, and protocols. *Concurrency and Computation: Practice and Experience*, e4946.
13. Ruhrmair, U. (2012). SIMPL systems as a key less cryptographic and security primitive. *Lecture Notes in Computer Science, 6805*, 329–354.
14. Labrado, C., & Thapliyal, H. (2018). Design of a piezoelectric based physically unclonable function for IoT security. *IEEE Internet of Things Journal, 6*(2) 2770–2777.
15. O'Neill, M. (2016). Insecurity by design: Today's IoT device security problem. *Engineering, 2*(1), 48–49.
16. Kim, S. W. (2014). Physical integrity check in wireless relay networks. In: *2014 IEEE Conference on Communications and Network Security, San Francisco, CA* (pp. 514–515).
17. Kasmi, O., Baina, A., & Bellafkih, M. (2016) Multi level integrity management in critical infrastructure. In *2016 11th International Conference on Intelligent Systems: Theories and Applications (SITA), Mohammedia, Morocco* (pp. 1–6).
18. Zhang, X., Yang, X., Lin, J., Xu, G., & Yu, W. (2017, January). On data integrity attacks against real-time pricing in energy-based cyber-physical systems. *IEEE Transactions on Parallel and Distributed Systems, 28*(1), 170–187.

Chapter 19
Fog Computing: Applications and Secure Data Aggregation

Sudesh Rani and Poonam Saini

Abstract With the rapid increase in the number of internet of things (IoT) devices, a huge amount of data is generated which needs proper storage and analytical applications. However, the smart devices do not have adequate resources due to which the applications are mostly supported by cloud servers for providing on-demand and scalable storage as well as computation power using pay-as-you-go model. Despite the broad utilization of cloud computing, few applications such as health monitoring, real-time gaming and emergency response are latency sensitive to be deployed on cloud directly. Therefore, fog computing has emerged as a promising extension to cloud computing paradigm to provide better response time. In fog computing architecture, applications perform pre-processing near to the end user. The combination of fog and cloud can handle big data collection, secure aggregation, and pre-processing, thus reducing the cost of data transportation and storage. For example, in environmental monitoring systems, local data gathered can be aggregated and mined at fog nodes to provide timely feedback especially for emergency cases. The chapter presents the concepts of fog computing along with its characteristics. Furthermore, the chapter elaborates the applications of fog computing in various domains followed by discussion on secure data aggregation methods.

Keywords Cloud computing · Fog computing · Secure data aggregation

1 Introduction and Background

As everyone wants to access everything everywhere, IoT applications are usually supported by high-end servers which are mostly deployed on cloud. Since, smart devices have limited resources, therefore, cloud computing was introduced in 2000

S. Rani (✉) · P. Saini
Punjab Engineering College (Deemed to be University), Chandigarh, India
e-mail: sudeshrani@pec.ac.in; poonamsaini@pec.ac.in

B. B. Gupta et al. (eds.), *Handbook of Computer Networks and Cyber Security*,
https://doi.org/10.1007/978-3-030-22277-2_19

in order to meet the requirements of end users as it provides massive storage and computation resources on-demand using pay-as-you-go model. The user has to pay only for the resources which are being used and only for time the resources are allocated to the user. With the concept of cloud computing, data storage and application requirements are placed in the hands of cloud provider which essentially shifts the burden of IT management to the third party service provider. In this way, the organizations need not to purchase or acquire hardware/software, establish infrastructure and therefore get a cost-effective and on-premises IT solution. Despite the fact that cloud computing is extensively used in today's world, few applications such as health monitoring, emergency response system and real-time gaming are too much sensitive to latency such that the delay caused by massive amount of data transmission to cloud nodes and back to the application may not be acceptable. The data processing at cloud nodes fails to meet the time-constrained requirements as data sources are geographically distributed and low-latency is crucial. Also, it is not efficient to send all of the generated data to cloud for storage and processing as it consumes huge amount of network bandwidth and may not be scalable. To overcome these problems, edge computing was proposed which provides necessary resources near to the end-user devices for local storage and data processing. It decreases network congestion, accelerates data analysis and decision making. However, multiple IoT applications compete for limited resources at the same time due to which edge devices cannot handle the situation, thereby resulting in resource contention and increased processing latency.

1.1 Fog Computing

Cisco introduced a distributed computing paradigm called *fog computing* in order to address the limitations of cloud computing by providing services and resources at the edge of the network. The word "fog" in fog computing conveys the fact that cloud computing and its advantages are brought closer to the data source, similar as fog means clouds that are closer to the ground. In other words, fog acts as an intermediate layer in between the cloud data-centres and end-user devices to form a three-layer hierarchy as shown in Fig. 19.1.

Fog computing deals with IoT data locally to carry out computation and store data [26]. The aim is to enhance the overall efficiency by leveraging cloud resources, keeping data and computation closer to the end users at the network edge, thereby reducing the amount of data sent to cloud for analysis, storage and processing. Therefore, fog computing acts as a promising extension to cloud computing and provides an efficient solution to the problem of data processing in IoT. While fog computing is often chosen for efficiency purposes, it can also be used for security and compliance reasons. The devices called fog nodes provide cloud-like services on network edge and have more processing power than end devices but lesser than cloud servers, thereby reducing latency for applications. Fog nodes can be resource-rich machines like Cloudlets, IOx, etc. or resource-poor devices like routers, proxy

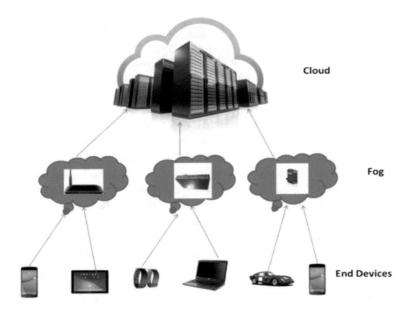

Fig. 19.1 Fog computing environment

servers, smart TVs, set-top boxes, gateways, etc. which enable diverse computing, storage and networking capabilities [39].

For an acceptable fog computing platform, there are various design goals like low-latency guaranteed applications and services, efficient utilization of energy and resources, generality, etc. However, there are several challenges to meet above-mentioned goals like choice of virtualization technology, fighting with latency imposed by data aggregation and resource provisioning, network management, security and privacy, enabling real-time analytics by dynamically determining which tasks need to be performed at fog layer and thereby, assigning rest of the tasks to cloud in order to minimize latency and maximize throughput. There are various applications which can benefit from fog computing paradigm such as smart home, smart city, smart grid, smart vehicle, health data management, augmented reality, and real-time video analytics [38]. Among the various applications of fog computing, heath monitoring and data management have been a very sensitive area. Since health data contains valuable and private information, therefore, security and reliability is of paramount importance. The delay of even few seconds in critical cases can cause serious impact on the life of a patient. The critical systems must operate securely even when there are interruptions in the Internet connectivity. The health monitoring system allows patients to share health data with doctor, monitor their health independently and notify the relevant caregivers quickly in emergency situations.

1.2 Data Aggregation

Data aggregation is defined as "the ability to summarize information" [17]. The data aggregation process enables the distribution of important system-wide properties in a decentralized manner. With the phenomenal increase in the number of geographically located IoT devices, lots of datasets are collected from multiple sources in various applications and sent to the cloud server. Such a process involves huge amount of bandwidth consumption because raw data may contain data which is meaningless. Hence, it becomes important to temporarily store data near to end devices, perform some sort of pre-processing on stored data, send notification alerts, etc. The pre-processing can be done by performing compression, aggregation, filtering, securing the data. The data aggregation technique involves collecting and aggregating data coming from different sources and finally transmitting to the base station for further processing. Whenever aggregation is performed, consolidated information is provided to the base station and redundant transmissions can be eliminated.

The data aggregation is often used in wireless sensor network (WSN) due to its limited power and communication capabilities, combined with the requirement of long network lifetime. The approach is a generic technique, which can also be used to improve accuracy of a system. Performing aggregation is a way to reduce the number of transmissions, reduce the error rate as more data transmitted implies more errors introduced in the system. In cloud computing, any event or data is transmitted to the cloud data centre inside core network and result will be sent back to the end user after a series of processing. Huge amount of burden is created by transferring large amount of data to the cloud. The combination of fog and cloud can handle big data gathering, aggregation and pre-processing, reducing data transportation and storage, etc. For example, in environmental monitoring systems, local data gathered can be aggregated and mined at fog nodes to timely provide feedback especially for emergency cases.

It has been observed that data processing at fog layer is a key technique to handle analytics on large scale of data generated by IoT applications. The objective of performing aggregation at fog layer is to minimize the total amount of data traffic which is sent over the network so as to utilize the resources in an efficient manner. Low latency data aggregation is considered for efficient data management. There are two approaches to aggregate data: with and without size reduction. The basic step to use various techniques of data aggregation in an efficient manner is to change continuous data transmission into buffered transmission based on local data pre-processing capabilities. With the help of aggregation, the number of transmissions is greatly reduced, therefore, aggregation may save network bandwidth and reduce the network congestion.

2 Applications of Fog Computing

Fog computing provides a wide range of applications. Some of the interesting applications that benefit from this emerging computing paradigm are as follows:

- **Smart Home:** With the rapid development of IoT, houses are getting equipped with various smart devices and sensors for enhanced living environment. However, devices from different vendors may not be compatible with each other and some tasks may require significant amount of storage and computation. Therefore, fog computing can be utilized to integrate such devices on one platform and provide smart home applications the required resources by leveraging cloud resources.
- **Smart Grid:** A significant change has to be brought in the field of electricity distribution network. Smart grid involves smart meters to be deployed at different locations so that status of electricity usage can be measured in real-time. Earlier, centralized server named SCADA is responsible for gathering and analysing the status information. The server responds to any demand change or emergency situation in order to stabilize power grid. But, with the concept of fog computing, decentralization of SCADA is done in which power grid is divided into fog-based micro-grids. The fog device will be in-charge of a micro-grid and will communicate with neighbouring fogs and higher tiers. Finally, SCADA will provide global coverage which is responsible for long-time repository and economic analytics.
- **Smart Vehicle:** Integrating fog computing in vehicular networks can be categorized into autonomous and infrastructure-based. In infrastructure-based, fog nodes are deployed along road-side which sends information to/from vehicles on road whereas autonomous system utilizes vehicles on-the-fly to support ad-hoc events.
- **Health Data Management:** The application is very sensitive since health data contains valuable and private information. With the advent of fog computing, users are allowed to monitor health independently, share health data to the respective doctor/physician in-charge, patients may take possession of health data locally. The health data can be stored at fog nodes and the data computation can be outsourced with keeping privacy preservation in mind, when patient seeks help from medical lab or physician's office.
- **Augmented Reality and Real-Time Video Analytics:** Popular applications on smart phones, tablets, etc. which overlay information on real-world view are based on augmented reality. Popular products based upon it are Google Glass, Microsoft HoloLens, etc. These applications need high computation power to process video streaming and high bandwidth for data transmission. A processing delay of more than 10 ms can ruin user experience and leads to a negative feedback. Therefore, these applications can benefit from fog computing for maximizing throughput and reducing latency in both processing and transmission.

Among various applications of fog computing, health monitoring and data management have been a sensitive area as a delay of even few seconds can cause a serious impact on the life of a patient.

2.1 Related Work

Akrivopoulos [2] presents health application that collects electrocardiogram (ECG) traces from a tailor-made device and uses patients' smartphone as a fog gateway to share information with doctor, monitor health status independently and notify authorities quickly in emergency situation. Historical data is available for further analysis, identifying patterns that may improve medical diagnosis in future. The working prototype evaluated parameters like storage, response time, etc. Integration of fog computing in cloud environment to implement military applications, border security and prisons is discussed by Lanka et al. [19]. Earlier, border is monitored by security forces, building miles of fences, etc. With the advancement of technology, cameras are deployed to monitor the borders. WSNs use cloud services to optimize information management, share monitored values and improve quality of service (QoS). Due to the inherent limitations of classical cloud computing, it may not be suitable in real-time scenarios. WSNs assisted with fog computing can control attacks at borders by spontaneous decision making and taking action in less time. Therefore, authors proposed to use fog nodes to assist cloud servers. The architecture is developed to provide high-end secure applications and the approach can be utilized to overcome vulnerabilities and help military officials to take decisions in real-time. Considering military as an enterprise stores all data on cloud servers, fog computing can help in early detection of danger or intrusion to make the situation better. The implementation should be fault-tolerant so that even if one node fails, it should not ruin the whole network.

A virtualized, decentralized emergency system based on fog computing for smart-enhanced living environment is presented by Nikoloudakis et al. [30]. The system uses positioning service to obtain received signal strength indicator (RSSI) between sensing device and wi-fi device. The service logic module updates user's location by probing profiling service. The profiling service maintains a database which contains personal, health and location information of user. The location-to-service-translation (LoST) service uses LoST protocol which is responsible for finding nearest authority responsible for emergency response. The system periodically calculates the position and identifies users out of predefined safety zone in order to inform concerned authorities and nearby volunteers quickly. The fog layer sends alerts in critical health conditions which require constant surveillance. Thereafter, system recalculates the user's outdoor position and sends distress messages containing user's information to concerned authorities as well as nearby volunteers. The proposed system enhances the quality of life, especially of elderly and dependent people.

Zao et al. [40] developed a brain computer interface (BCI) that detects different states of a user's brain in real life situation. Real-time synchronous data streaming is conducted with the help of message queuing telemetry transport (MQTT) publish/subscribe protocol assisted with fog computing. The users can search online data streams and their archives using semantic queries with linked data web. The system performs real-time classification of users' brain state with the help of cooperation between fog and cloud server. Meanwhile, the classification models are calibrated regularly in the cloud servers based on electroencephalogram (EEG) data and features extracted by fog servers. With fog computing, the computers nearer to end nodes are used to offload computational burden and speed up corresponding responses. Secure communication, multi-domain user authentication and authorization are provided to enhance the security of the system. The infrastructure collects datasets with users' approval.

A procedure to measure ultraviolet (UV) radiation through complementary metal-oxide semiconductor (CMOS) sensors in cameras of the smartphone is presented by Mei et al. [29]. The local fog servers aggregate the data which improves result accuracy and respond to the users requesting UV value in real-time. Experiments were conducted using light-weight, fast and effective android app called UV meter to validate and evaluate the correctness and accuracy of the procedure on both smartphones and smart watches. The authors proposed to use smartphones for computation of UV radiation directly from camera sensor reading in real-time. Since the general percentage of UV and solar radiations is different for different locations, seasons and time zones on the earth, history of UV levels is utilized to generate a specific percentage for a location at different times. An intelligent transportation system (ITS) assisted with fog computing to monitor driver's behaviour is presented by Aazam and Fernando [1]. The system performs data gathering, communication analysis, event detection, data storage, service creation and provisioning. The data is gathered by considering various factors such as driver's health, vehicle's condition, environmental, traffic and weather conditions. Based on gathered data, road safety algorithms are run at fog layer to determine any unusual condition. The fog layer performs urgent task scheduling and decision making, thereby generating alert or emergency notifications. Discrete event system specification (DEVS) simulation setup is used to provide results for cloud-only and fog-assisted scenarios and validate the usability of proposed architecture.

Craciunescu et al. [10] implemented fog computing system for e-health application. As the number of devices connected to Internet increases, cloud servers get overloaded which increases computational effort and network latency. The aim of paper is to introduce the concept of fog computing to decrease latency which is imposed by performing critical tasks on cloud. A fall detection and gas-leak detection algorithm is proposed with an aim to achieve an optimal balance between fog and cloud level operations so that maximum benefit can be reaped out of it. The paper demonstrated that fog nodes are used mainly for critical e-Health situations in order to speed up real-time processing as well as detection of unwanted events and cloud system for storing metadata and send to relevant caregivers. Also, fusion of data from multiple sources can prevent the system from giving false alarms so that user's condition can be correctly assessed at a given time. Therefore, fog nodes are used to speed up real-time processing for critical applications and cloud platform, to store patient history which can be retrieved whenever need arises. Ali and Ghazal [3] used smart watches to implement proposed real-time heart attack mobile detection service (RHAMDS) through voice and gesture control. The concept of fog computing is utilized to improve response-time of emergency aid for heart attack patients and prevent possible vehicle collision under vehicular ad hoc networks (VANETs). The system is implemented using smart watches to perform continuous real-time monitoring of voice command or gestures. Data fusion can be done for increased reliability and accuracy of the model. The use of mobile edge computing (MEC) server provides low latency and geographical awareness.

An e-health gateway called UT-GATE and a medical case study is presented by Rahmani et al. [33]. The authors proposed mobility support based on fog computing so that connectivity can be provided to mobile sensors. The gateway performs local data processing in order to provide real-time notification to doctors and physicians so that risk prediction can be done and complications can be reduced. The authors implemented Lempel–Ziv–Welch (LZW) compression algorithm. Sensitive medical data gathered by sensors is secured and preliminary data analysis is done to detect critical conditions before performing detailed analysis on cloud. Based on medical parameters, the therapy orders and recording intervals can be modified by medical staff.

Gia et al. [13] presented healthcare system architecture assisted with fog computing at smart gateways. The authors addressed a case study of electrocardiogram (ECG) where light-weight algorithms are used to extract features such as heart rate, P and T waves at smart gateways. Also, the effectiveness of algorithm is demonstrated for bandwidth utilization, quality of service (QoS) assurance and emergency notification. The paper also shows the real-time interaction in case of emergency and online analytics at fog layer. Also, the system can detect abnormalities of the heart.

Table 19.1 presents the summary of existing literature with observations.

3   Secure Data Aggregation

A survey on various distributed data aggregation algorithms is presented by Jesus et al. [17]. According to the authors, various global properties in an environment can be computed by determining them in a distributed way and then combining the results from different devices in order to execute an application. There are various computation functions such as COUNT, SUM, and AVERAGE, which can be used to determine network properties in a decentralized way. Due to energy constraints and for better resource utilization, aggregation needs to be performed. Sometimes, it becomes essential to reduce the amount of data transmitted over the network by establishing summaries through data aggregation. According to Jesus "There is no

Table 19.1 Existing work on applications of fog computing

S. no.	Title	Observations
1.	Exploiting smart e-Health gateways at the edge of healthcare Internet-of-Things: a fog computing approach [33]	• Proposed system is energy-efficient, reliable, secure, mobile and interoperable • Latency for sense-decide-act loop is reduced
2.	Real-time heart attack mobile detection service (RHAMDS): an IoT use case for software defined networks [3]	• Improves response time of emergency aid • Models incorporate sensors inside smart watches • Prevents vehicle collision • ECG sensors need to be incorporated in wearables for automatic detection of heart attacks
3.	Ultraviolet radiation measurement via smart devices [29]	• CMOS sensors improve cost efficiency • Results in suburban areas more accurate than urban areas • Brightness has strong impact on accuracy of results
4.	Application of fog computing in military operations [19]	• Decreased latency and power consumption • Spontaneous decision making • Additional algorithms enable sensors to themselves • Energy conservation needed by sensors to increase life of node
5.	Fog assisted driver behaviour monitoring for intelligent transportation system [1]	• Implementing fog has positive impact • Heterogeneous data gathered • Trade-off between delay and power consumption
6.	A fog-based emergency system for smart-enhanced living environments [30]	• Reduced response time • Enhances quality of life • Response time fluctuates due to network abnormalities • Health parameters not considered
7.	Fog-computing in healthcare internet of things: a case study on ECG feature extraction [13]	• Real-time interaction and online analytics in case of emergency and poor connection is possible with fog computing • Data transmission latency is minimized • Data transmitted over the network is reduced • Efficient utilization of network bandwidth using Fog Computing
8.	Implementation of fog computing for reliable E-health applications [10]	• Lower processing time with fog computing • 90% accurate algorithms • Less delay introduced by transmitting signal from sensors to fog node • Less delay introduced by transmitting signal from sensors to fog node • Additional h/w required to prevent false alarms • High heterogeneity of sensors requires complex algorithms
9.	Augmented brain computer interaction-based fog computing and linked data [40]	• Real-time responsiveness • Easy to use • Low data rate and transport latency • Online infrastructure highly scalable

ideal general solution to distributed computation of an aggregation function, as all the techniques have their own drawbacks and limitations to be applied in a particular environment".

Guan et al. [14] proposed a device-oriented anonymous and privacy-preserving data aggregation scheme (APPA) with authentication for applications in fog computing environment. The sensor devices and fog nodes are managed locally using multi-authority approach. Furthermore, in order to prevent the certificate forgery, pseudonym certificates are generated by trusted certificate authority (TCA) which are updated dynamically based on the node's requirements. The sensor node pseudonym certificate is used to encrypt sensed data before forwarding to the fog node for aggregation. Moreover, pseudonym matching also prevents malicious sensor nodes to upload data at fog node. The efficiency of the proposed scheme is evaluated based on parameters such as computational complexity and communication overhead. The computational complexity is analysed for registration phase, data encryption scheme, data aggregation and decryption scheme. The experimental analysis indicates that the scheme is suitable for resource-limited end user nodes. Huo et al. [16] proposed adaptive ω-event differential privacy-based data aggregation (Re-ADP) framework for real-time data generated by IoT devices in fog computing environment. The framework protects aggregated data sequence at fog nodes with window size of ω time stamp. The authors discussed a smart grouping approach to tackle perturbation errors while handling small statistics values in data collected from sensors. The grouping approach starts with segregation of sensors on the basis of statistics prediction using long short-term memory (LSTM) model. Afterwards, k-means clustering algorithm is used for grouping of sensor devices. Lastly, the aggregated data is perturbed using Laplacian mechanism. The results exhibit that the proposed framework improved data availability and utility in terms of mean absolute error (MAE) and quality of privacy (QoP) parameters.

Zhang et al. [42] presented a privacy-aware data collection and aggregation scheme for fog computing using homomorphic encryption-based technology. This has been used to reduce the overall communication overhead of any system along with privacy protection of IoT devices. The parameters viz. privacy protection, non-repudiation and unforgeability have been comprehended. Moreover, the authors ensure that data privacy will not be leaked. Furthermore, the authors studied an efficient batch verification mechanism in order to improve the efficiency of data integrity checking. The security and performance analysis indicates that the scheme is secure and efficient in terms of computation and communication cost. In 2018, data aggregation process has been used in smart grids and considered to be an essential requirement in terms of limiting packet size, data transmission amount and data storage. Okay and Ozdemir [31] presented a novel Domingo–Ferrer additive privacy-based secure data aggregation (SDA) scheme for fog computing-based SGs (FCSG). There is end-to-end confidentiality while ensuring low communication and storage overhead. Moreover, data aggregation is performed at fog layer that reduces the amount of data to be processed and stored at cloud servers, thereby achieving better response time and less computational overhead. The hierarchical architecture of FCSG and additive homomorphic encryption protects consumer privacy from third parties. The security analysis evaluates the packet size effect as well as cloud server storage. The dynamic analysis exhibited a significant improvement in terms of data transmission and storage efficiency.

Lyu et al. [24] addressed the constraints in IoT-based end devices, for example, in smart meter, data transmission is an energy-consuming operation. The novel smart metering aggregation framework, called as *PPFA*, enables the intermediate fog nodes to periodically collect data from nearby smart meters and derive aggregate statistics accurately. The Cloud/utility supplier calculates the overall aggregate statistics. The work uses concentrated Gaussian mechanism to distribute noise generation among parties in order to minimize the privacy leakage and mitigate the utility loss. Thus, the authors offered provable differential privacy guarantees of aggregate statistic on fog as well as Cloud level. Furthermore, a two-layer encryption scheme based upon OTP and public-key cryptography is performed for authentication. The real-world smart metering dataset has been used to confirm the theoretical analysis. The aggregation of sensed data from vehicles securely has become a challenge nowadays. Chen et al. [9] presented a light-weight and anonymous privacy preservation protocol for fog computing-assisted vehicle-to-infrastructure (V2I). Firstly, the protocol uses a certificate less aggregate signcryption (CL-A-SC) scheme based upon data collected by the vehicles and proves its security in random oracle model. Thereafter, an anonymous aggregation protocol is suggested. The security analysis shows that the protocol achieves desirable security properties. On the other side, the dynamic analysis for performance comparison exhibited that significant reduction in computation and communication overhead. It has been analysed that the work is more practical for road surface condition monitoring system.

Wang et al. [36] proposed anonymous and secure aggregation scheme (ASAS) in public cloud computing based on fog computing. In proposed scheme, fog nodes provided by public cloud server (PCS) aggregate data from terminal nodes and forward to it in order to save bandwidth. Also, fog nodes assist terminal devices to upload their data to PCS. After uploading the encrypted results, corresponding user processes the data by running some methods. The aggregation scheme is anonymous as it uses pseudonyms to protect identity of terminal devices so that data is sent in an anonymous and secure way via homomorphic encryption technique. A lightweight privacy-preserving data aggregation (LPDA) scheme to aggregate data coming from hybrid IoT devices using Chinese remainder theorem is proposed by Lu et al. [23]. The scheme performs filtering of false data injected at network edge itself through source authentication using one-way hash chain technique. Homomorphic Paillier encryption is used in the scheme which does not allow fog devices to view individual device's data during aggregation. A detailed security analysis and extensive performance evaluations are done.

A privacy-preserving data aggregation approach in mobile phone sensing is proposed by Zhang et al. [41]. The proposed approach protects participants' privacy by delinking the data from its sources and allows aggregator to get an exact distribution of data. Basically, the protocol receives a random permutation of all users' data without knowing the source of any particular piece of data. The authors provided an optimized grouping solution to the protocol when there are large numbers of users and have different source anonymity requirements. Therefore, the approach allows users in each group to execute protocol together and helps in reducing the bottleneck at the aggregator. The formal system model and security model presented for ASAS is instantiated based on linear pairings, short signatures and Castagnos–Laguillaumie cryptosystem. An aggregation scheme to aggregate data for MapReduce jobs in cloud is presented by Ke et al. [18]. When all the data is forward from map tasks to reduce tasks in traditional MapReduce framework, a huge amount of data was generated. Also, the data is many times redundant, which leads to wastage of computational resources as well as processing time. Therefore, the authors proposed architecture to perform aggregation in order to minimize data traffic during shuffle phase. The two modules, namely aggregator and aggregator manager, are integrated so that the existing Hadoop architecture can be enhanced and efficient aggregation can be facilitated in a virtual cloud data centre. The aggregators are located between map and reduce jobs which perform reduce-like operation to combine key-value pairs with the same key. On the other hand, aggregator manager deals with the placement of aggregator module and bandwidth assignment problem so that communication cost can be reduced. The prototype and simulation-based tests were performed to validate efficiency of the protocol in reducing network traffic.

Rout et al. [34] addressed the utility of network coding so that data aggregation can be optimized and the number of transmitted messages can be reduced, thereby reducing the network traffic in a WSN. The authors used a strategy to deploy the nodes in a network such that the topology formed supports many-to-many network flows (multiple sources and multiple sinks). Also, the proposed technique uses multicasting instead of flooding. In case, current sensed data is significantly different from previously transmitted data, it is transmitted to the aggregate node which saves a lot of energy and unnecessary transmissions can be avoided. A near optimal solution for maximum lifetime data aggregation (MLDA) problem was proposed by Dasgupta et al. [11]. The authors presented an efficient clustering-based heuristic for data gathering and aggregation for large-scale sensor networks termed as heuristic-GREEDY clustering-based MLDA (CMLDA) based on existing MLDA algorithm. The partitioning of sensors is done using proximity-based clustering algorithm and aggregation trees are created such that minimum residual energy among sensors is maximized. A 3-level hierarchical protocol proposed by Lindsey, Raghvendra and Sivalingam (LRS) is compared with the proposed protocol. LRS protocol is chain-based in which leader is chosen in a round-robin manner in each round. The experimental results demonstrate that "CMLDA achieves a factor of 2.27 increase in lifetime of large–scale sensor networks, when compared to the LRS protocol and incurs a small increase in the delay experienced by individual sensors" [11].

Table 19.2 presents the summary of existing secure data aggregation techniques with observations.

Table 19.2 Existing aggregation techniques in different environments

S. no.	Title	Observations
1.	APPA: an anonymous and privacy-preserving data aggregation scheme for fog-enhanced IoT [14]	• Node management using multi-authority approach • Pseudonym certificate is used to encrypt sensed data • Computational complexity and communication overhead is reduced • Suitable for resource-limited end user nodes
2.	Re-ADP: real-time data aggregation with adaptive ω-event differential privacy for fog computing [16]	• Improved data availability • Improved utility in terms of mean absolute error (MAE) and quality of privacy (QoP) parameters
3.	Privacy-aware data collection and aggregation in IoT enabled fog computing [42]	• Homomorphic encryption-based scheme • Secure and efficient in terms of computation and communication cost
4.	A secure data aggregation protocol for fog computing-based smart grids [31]	• Domingo–Ferrer additive privacy-based scheme • Provides end-to-end confidentiality • Low communication and storage overhead • Better response time
5.	PPFA: privacy-preserving fog-enabled aggregation in smart grid [24]	• Uses concentrated Gaussian mechanism to distribute noise generation • Offers differential privacy guarantees of aggregate statistic • **Dataset used:** real-world smart metering
6.	Privacy-preserving data aggregation protocol for fog computing-assisted vehicle-to-infrastructure scenario [9]	• Light-weight and anonymous privacy preservation protocol • Uses a certificate less aggregate signcryption scheme • Reduced computation and communication overhead • Suitable for road surface condition monitoring system
7.	Anonymous and secure aggregation scheme in fog-based public cloud computing [36]	• Saves bandwidth between fog node and PCS server • Secure and efficient scheme • Affordable execution times • PKI is indispensable
8.	A lightweight privacy-preserving data aggregation scheme for fog computing enhanced IoT [23]	• Communication overhead is reduced after aggregation • Efficient in terms of computational costs • Support fault-tolerance
9.	Privacy-preserving data aggregation in mobile phone sensing [41]	• Achieves n-source anonymity • Optimal grouping done to provide different privacy level to different users • Trusted authority required to establish key system • Focus is on privacy-preservation rather than performance

(continued)

Table 19.2 (continued)

S. no.	Title	Observations
10.	Aggregation on the fly: reducing traffic for big data in the cloud [18]	• Data redundancy is reduced by aggregation • Reduces in-cloud network traffic • Efficient bandwidth utilization • Extra overhead as appropriate selection of nodes performing aggregation needs to be for improved performance
11.	Network coding-aware data aggregation for a distributed wireless sensor networks [34]	• Robust and fault-tolerant • Better channel utilization • Scalable, hence, can be used in large networks • Static updation of table maintained at sink node is not easy in dense and large networks
12.	An efficient clustering- based heuristic for data gathering and aggregation in sensor networks [11]	• Significant improvement in system lifetime over existing protocols • Incurs small amount of delay but payback is significant • Clustering needs to be pre-computed • Centralized algorithm

4 Simulation Tools and Frameworks

Currently, iFogSim [15] is the standard tool to implement fog computing-based applications. However, few other simulation environments have been developed to support the analysis of fog computing-based protocols for energy efficiency and overall efficiency.

Table 19.3 summarizes various simulation tools and frameworks along with its characteristics to implement fog computing applications.

5 Conclusion

Past few years, there is a tremendous increase in the applications of IoT devices. Such applications generate huge amount of data that requires efficient data storage and computation ability. However, IoT devices have limited storage space and computational power. Moreover, cloud computing infrastructure provides huge storage capacity and computational power, although it leads to increased latency, especially in delay-sensitive IoT applications such as healthcare, military and e-business. To tackle such latency issues, fog computing environment has been developed that provides cloud-like facility near to end users. In this chapter, various applications of fog computing environment are discussed along with existing secure data aggregation techniques. As the process of data generation by IoT devices is very frequent, data aggregation plays an important role in efficient deployment of fog

Table 19.3 Simulation tools and frameworks for fog computing

S. no.	Simulator	Year	Based upon	Open source	Characteristics
1.	FogNetSim++ [32]	2018	OMNET++ (C++)	Yes	• Configurable based on application requirements • Customizable mobility models • Efficiency of simulator is analysed in terms of CPU and memory usage
2.	NetSim [35]	2018	C	No	• IoT module is used to implement fog computing application
3.	Yet another fog simulator (YAFS) [21]	2018	Python	Yes	• **Dynamic topology:** entities and network links can be created or removed along the simulation • Dynamic creation of messages sources: sensors can generate messages from different point access along the simulation
4.	iFogSim [15, 25]	2017	CloudSim [8] (Java)	Yes	• To model IoT, fog and edge environments • Measures the impact of resource management techniques in terms of latency, network congestion, energy consumption and cost • Case studies: latency-sensitive online game and intelligent surveillance through distributed camera networks are analysed
5.	EmuFog [28]	2017	MaxiNet [37], a multinode extension of the network emulator Mininet [20]	Yes	• Scalable and extensible docker-based fog emulation framework • Allows for user-defined constraints such as network latency thresholds or resource constraints • Case studies: dummy topology and a real-world topology are used for performance analysis
6.	FogTorch [5]	2017	Java	Yes	• **Input:** the specification of an infrastructure to be deployed, along with the related things binding and deployment policy; **Output:** eligible deployments • Automatically determine where to deploy each application component by satisfying the specified QoS constraints • **Extended simulators:** FogTorchPI [4, 6, 7], FogTorchPi-extended [27]

(continued)

Table 19.3 (continued)

S. no.	Simulator	Year	Based upon	Open source	Characteristics
7.	Discrete event system specification (DEVS)-based simulator [12]	2017	C++	No	• Performance is analysed for both cloud-only and cloud-fog scenarios in the context of processing delay and power consumption according to increasing number of users, on the basis of varying server load
8.	MyiFogSim [22]	2017	iFogSim	Yes	• Extension of iFogSim to support mobility through migration of virtual machines between cloudlets • The policy impact on application quality of service such as latency is analysed

computing applications. Lastly, simulation tools and frameworks used to implement fog computing-based applications have been discussed.

References

1. Aazam, M., & Fernando, X. (2017). Fog assisted driver behavior monitoring for intelligent transportation system. In *2017 IEEE 86th Vehicular Technology Conference (VTC-Fall)* (pp. 1–5). Piscataway: IEEE.
2. Akrivopoulos, O., Chatzigiannakis, I., Tselios, C., & Antoniou, A. (2017). On the deployment of healthcare applications over fog computing infrastructure. In *2017 IEEE 41st Annual Computer Software and Applications Conference (COMPSAC)* (Vol. 2, pp. 288–293). Piscataway: IEEE.
3. Ali, S., & Ghazal, M. (2017). Real-time heart attack mobile detection service (RHAMDS): An IoT use case for software defined networks. In *2017 IEEE 30th Canadian Conference on Electrical and Computer Engineering (CCECE)* (pp. 1–6). Piscataway: IEEE.
4. Antonio, B., Stefano, F., & Ahmad, I. (2017). Deploying fog applications how much does it cost, by the way? In *International Conference on Cloud Computing and Services Science*. Setúbal: SciTePress.
5. Brogi, A., & Forti, S. (2017). QoS-aware deployment of IoT applications through the fog. *IEEE Internet of Things Journal, 4*(5), 1185–1192.
6. Brogi, A., Forti, S., & Ibrahim, A. (2017). How to best deploy your fog applications, probably. In *2017 IEEE 1st International Conference on Fog and Edge Computing (ICFEC)* (pp. 105–114). Piscataway: IEEE.
7. Brogi, A., Forti, S., & Ibrahim, A. (2019). Predictive analysis to support fog application deployment. In *Fog and edge computing: Principles and paradigms* (pp. 191–222). Hoboken: Wiley.
8. Calheiros, R. N., Ranjan, R., Beloglazov, A., De Rose, C. A., & Buyya, R. (2011). CloudSim: A toolkit for modeling and simulation of cloud computing environments and evaluation of resource provisioning algorithms. *Software: Practice and Experience, 41*(1), 23–50.

9. Chen, Y., Lu, Z., Xiong, H., & Xu, W. (2018). Privacy-preserving data aggregation protocol for fog computing-assisted vehicle-to-infrastructure scenario. *Security and Communication Networks, 2018*, 1378583.
10. Craciunescu, R., Mihovska, A., Mihaylov, M., Kyriazakos, S., Prasad, R., & Halunga, S. (2015). Implementation of fog computing for reliable e-health applications. In *2015 49th Asilomar Conference on Signals, Systems and Computers* (pp. 459–463). Piscataway: IEEE.
11. Dasgupta, K., Kalpakis, K., & Namjoshi, P. (2003). An efficient clustering-based heuristic for data gathering and aggregation in sensor networks. In *Proceedings of the IEEE Wireless Communications and Networking Conference (WCNC)* (pp. 1948–1953). Citeseer.
12. Etemad, M., Aazam, M., & St-Hilaire, M. (2017). Using DEVS for modeling and simulating a fog computing environment. In *2017 International Conference on Computing, Networking and Communications (ICNC)* (pp. 849–854). Piscataway: IEEE.
13. Gia, T. N., Jiang, M., Rahmani, A.-M., Westerlund, T., Liljeberg, P., & Tenhunen, H. (2015). Fog computing in healthcare internet-of-things: A case study on ECG feature extraction. In *2015 IEEE International Conference on Computer and Information Technology; Ubiquitous Computing and Communications; Dependable, Autonomic and Secure Computing; Pervasive Intelligence and Computing (CIT/IUCC/DASC/PICOM)* (pp. 356–363). Piscataway: IEEE.
14. Guan, Z., Zhang, Y., Wu, L., Wu, J., Li, J., Ma, Y., & Hu, J. (2019). APPA: An anonymous and privacy preserving data aggregation scheme for fog-enhanced IoT. *Journal of Network and Computer Applications, 125*, 82–92.
15. Gupta, H., Vahid Dastjerdi, A., Ghosh, S. K., & Buyya, R. (2017). iFogSim: A toolkit for modeling and simulation of resource management techniques in the internet of things, edge and fog computing environments. *Software: Practice and Experience, 47*(9), 1275–1296.
16. Huo, Y., Yong, C., & Lu, Y. (2018). Re-ADP: Real-time data aggregation with adaptive ω-event differential privacy for fog computing. *Wireless Communications and Mobile Computing, 2018*, 6285719.
17. Jesus, P., Baquero, C., & Almeida, P. S. (2015). A survey of distributed data aggregation algorithms. *IEEE Communications Surveys & Tutorials, 17*(1), 381–404.
18. Ke, H., Li, P., Guo, S., & Stojmenovic, I. (2015). Aggregation on the fly: Reducing traffic for big data in the cloud. *IEEE Network, 29*(5), 17–23.
19. Lanka, D., Veenadhari, C. L., & Suryanarayana, D. (2017). Application of fog computing in military operations. *International Journal of Computer Applications, 164*(6), 10–15.
20. Lantz, B., Heller, B., & McKeown, N. (2010). A network in a laptop: Rapid prototyping for software-defined networks. In *Proceedings of the 9th ACM SIGCOMM Workshop on Hot Topics in Networks* (p. 19). New York: ACM.
21. Lera, I., & Guerrero, C. (2018). Yet another fog simulator (YAFS). Retrieved January 8, 2018, from https://pypi.org/project/yafs/
22. Lopes, M. M., Higashino, W. A., Capretz, M. A., & Bittencourt, L. F. (2017). Myifogsim: A simulator for virtual machine migration in fog computing. In *Companion Proceedings of the 10th International Conference on Utility and Cloud Computing* (pp. 47–52). New York: ACM.
23. Lu, R., Heung, K., Lashkari, A. H., & Ghorbani, A. A. (2017). A lightweight privacy-preserving data aggregation scheme for fog computing-enhanced IoT. *IEEE Access, 5*, 3302–3312.
24. Lyu, L., Nandakumar, K., Rubinstein, B., Jin, J., Bedo, J., & Palaniswami, M. (2018). PPFA: Privacy preserving fog-enabled aggregation in smart grid. *IEEE Transactions on Industrial Informatics, 14*, 3733–3744.
25. Mahmud, R., & Buyya, R. (2019). Modelling and simulation of fog and edge computing environments using iFogSim toolkit. *Fog and edge computing: Principles and paradigms* (pp. 1–35). London: Wiley.
26. Mahmud, R., Kotagiri, R., & Buyya, R. (2018). Fog computing: A taxonomy, survey and future directions. In *Internet of everything* (pp. 103–130). Berlin: Springer.
27. Maio, V. D. M. (2018). FogTorchPI-extended project repository. Retrieved Accessed: January 8, 2018 from https://bitbucket.org/vindem/fogtorchpi-extended/src

28. Mayer, R., Graser, L., Gupta, H., Saurez, E., & Ramachandran, U. (2017). EmuFog: Extensible and scalable emulation of large-scale fog computing infrastructures. In *2017 IEEE Fog World Congress (FWC)* (pp. 1–6). Piscataway: IEEE.
29. Mei, B., Li, R., Cheng, W., Yu, J., & Cheng, X. (2017). Ultraviolet radiation measurement via smart devices. *IEEE Internet of Things Journal, 4*(4), 934–944.
30. Nikoloudakis, Y., Panagiotakis, S., Markakis, E., Pallis, E., Mastorakis, G., Mavromoustakis, C. X., et al. (2016). A fog-based emergency system for smart enhanced living environments. *IEEE Cloud Computing, (6)*, 54–62.
31. Okay, F. Y., & Ozdemir, S. (2018). A secure data aggregation protocol for fog computing based smart grids. In *2018 IEEE 12th International Conference on Compatibility, Power Electronics and Power Engineering (CPE-POWERENG)* (pp. 1–6). Piscataway: IEEE.
32. Qayyum, T., Malik, A. W., Khattak, M. A. K., Khalid, O., & Khan, S. U. (2018). FogNetSim++: A toolkit for modeling and simulation of distributed fog environment. *IEEE Access, 6*, 63570–63583.
33. Rahmani, A. M., Gia, T. N., Negash, B., Anzanpour, A., Azimi, I., Jiang, M., et al. (2018). Exploiting smart e-health gateways at the edge of healthcare internet-of-things: A fog computing approach. *Future Generation Computer Systems, 78*, 641–658.
34. Rout, R., Ghosh, S., & Chakrabarti, S. (2009). Network coding-aware data aggregation for a distributed wireless sensor network. In *2009 International Conference on Industrial and Information Systems (ICIIS)* (pp. 32–36). Piscataway: IEEE.
35. Tayal, A. (2018). Fog computing in IoT. Retrieved January 8, 2018, from https://www.tetcos.com/file-exchange.html
36. Wang, H., Wang, Z., & Domingo-Ferrer, J. (2018). Anonymous and secure aggregation scheme in fog-based public cloud computing. *Future Generation Computer Systems, 78*, 712–719.
37. Wette, P., Draxler, M., Schwabe, A., Wallaschek, F., Zahraee, M. H., & Karl, H. (2014). Maxinet: Distributed emulation of software-defined networks. In *Networking Conference, 2014 IFIP* (pp. 1–9). Piscataway: IEEE.
38. Yi, S., Hao, Z., Qin, Z., & Li, Q. (2015). Fog computing: Platform and applications. In *2015 Third IEEE Workshop on Hot Topics in Web Systems and Technologies (HotWeb)* (pp. 73–78). Piscataway: IEEE.
39. Yi, S., Li, C., & Li, Q. (2015). A survey of fog computing: Concepts, applications and issues. In *Proceedings of the 2015 Workshop on Mobile Big Data* (pp. 37–42). New York: ACM.
40. Zao, J. K., Gan, T. T., You, C. K., Méndez, S. J. R., Chung, C. E., Te Wang, Y., et al. (2014). Augmented brain computer interaction based on fog computing and linked data. In *2014 International Conference on Intelligent Environments (IE)* (pp. 374–377). Piscataway: IEEE.
41. Zhang, Y., Chen, Q., & Zhong, S. (2016). Privacy-preserving data aggregation in mobile phone sensing. *IEEE Transactions on Information Forensics and Security, 11*(5), 980–992.
42. Zhang, Y., Zhao, J., Zheng, D., Deng, K., Ren, F., & Zheng, X. (2018). Privacy-aware data collection and aggregation in IoT enabled fog computing. In *International Conference on Algorithms and Architectures for Parallel Processing* (pp. 581–590). Berlin: Springer.

Chapter 20
A Comprehensive Review of Distributed Denial of Service (DDoS) Attacks in Fog Computing Environment

Bhumika Paharia and Kriti Bhushan

Abstract Cloud computing performs several functionalities, and one of the most important functionalities is the storage and processing of data or information. With day-by-day enhancement of technology, cloud has been overburdened, and to address this issue, the concept of fog computing has been introduced. Fog computing is an extension of the properties of cloud computing to the network's edge and additionally overcomes its limitations. Despite the growing fame of fog services, assuring the security and privacy of data is still a big challenge. Distributed denial of service (DDoS) attack is a well-known threat among the security concerns and an important research challenge when talking particularly about security of data in fog computing environment. Therefore, this chapter presents a survey which encompasses the various concepts of fog computing, DDoS attacks and some DDoS mitigation techniques, thus providing a comprehensive review. In addition, it beholds the future work in this domain. This chapter will attract new researchers and also strengthen the concept of fog computing.

Keywords Cloud computing · Fog computing · DoS · DDoS attack

1 Introduction

Cloud computing can be used as a utility by organizations to consume computing resources such as an application, or storage, or a virtual machine (VM). In a similar way, we use electricity at home instead of building and maintaining large infrastructures. Cloud computing allows its users to expand resources only on their core business without worrying about anything else. It provides global access to the configurable system. The system consists of shared pool of resources and higher-level services. In turn the management efforts are brought to minimal. Other than

B. Paharia · K. Bhushan (✉)
Department of Computer Engineering, National Institute of Technology, Kurukshetra, India
e-mail: k.bhushan@ieee.org

© Springer Nature Switzerland AG 2020
B. B. Gupta et al. (eds.), *Handbook of Computer Networks and Cyber Security*,
https://doi.org/10.1007/978-3-030-22277-2_20

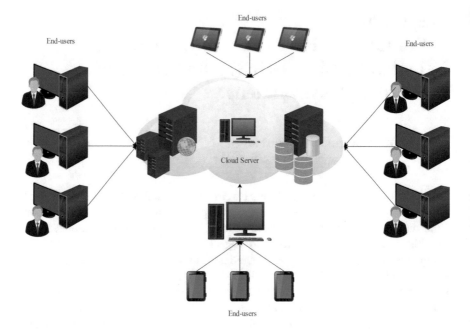

Fig. 20.1 Architecture of cloud computing

utility, it imports the economy of scale as well as coherence. It mainly delivers hosted services over the Internet [1].

Metaphorically, it is a group of networked elements (elements are not individually addressed or managed by user) that can share resources. It can be vague as an amorphous cloud. It has proposed a "pay-as-you-go" model enabling user to spend on the resources according to his needs [1]. Amazon EC2 (Elastic Compute Cloud) is a common example here. Cloud computing came into light around 1996.

In Fig. 20.1 the architecture of cloud computing is shown. Cloud server acts as centralized computing platform and provides services to various end users.

According to [2], cloud computing is used to store large data files on a platform. The use of cloud services eliminates the requirement of storage space on smart devices (phones, desktops, etc.); however, access of data is available [3–6]. Cloud architecture provides the following services:

- IaaS (Infrastructure as a Service) using applications like Amazon EC2, etc.
- PaaS (Platform as a Service) used in some environment like Django, etc.
- SaaS (Software as a Service) using applications like Google Docs, etc.

  Cloud computing has the following characteristics:

- On-demand self-service
- Broad network access
- Resource pooling
- Rapid elasticity
- Measured service

As explained in [7], initially "the cloud" had everything, but now a new concept called "fog computing" is getting attention. Fog computing extends cloud computing and provides services to the network's edge. It reduces cloud's workload as well as deals with services to the nearest of terminal devices [8]. Sometimes it is also termed as edge computing because it answers the query by keeping data proximate "to the ground", which means near end devices, instead of sending everything to data centre of the cloud.

In [9], OpenFog has reported that Business Matters mentioned fog computing to be in top five trends of innovations for 2018. In addition, Joe Kendrick, Forbes contributor, predicts that cloud would transform into fog. OpenFog came into the list of SDxCentral for its work which should be watched in edge computing's multi-access for creating standards. According to OpenFog [9], the marketing opportunity will outshine by $ 18 billion till 2022.

2   Fog Computing

This section consists of multiple sub-sections combinedly explaining fog computing. Section 2.1 gives a brief introduction to fog computing, and Sect. 2.2 describes its origin, i.e. history of fog computing. Section 2.3 explains the characteristics and applications used for fog computing. Sections 2.4 and 2.5 explain the security issues and challenges faced in fog computing, respectively.

2.1   Introduction to Fog Computing

Fog computing is a model in which the data is processed and applications concentrate on devices at the network's edge instead of transferring almost all load at cloud. It was termed by Cisco Systems as a "new model" to make reliable data transfer wirelessly to distributed devices in the network paradigm of IoT (Internet of Things). In this, the communication between devices is peer-to-peer which results in efficient sharing and storing of data while taking decisions locally [8].

Cisco Systems and IBM (who favour the word edge computing) both have open-ended actions which advance the current computing solutions to the network's edge devices. The devices such as routers and sensors [7] obscure the world with fog computing devices which have high reliable computing power and processing of data.

Concentration on fog computing is done in order to locally process data at smart devices instead of sending to the cloud for processing. Fog computing is an approach which deals with the increasing number of devices with Internet connections termed as IoT. Fog computing alternates the cloud property of establishing channels at cloud layer for storage and utilization. It simply is used to keep all the transactions at the edge of the network with the needed resources. The need for bandwidth is reduced

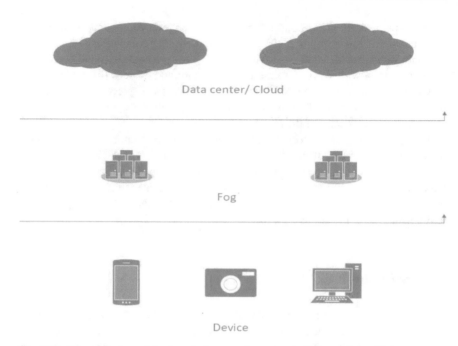

Fig. 20.2 The architecture of fog layer between end-user smart devices and cloud layer

by fog computing as it does not send every bit of information to the concerned cloud channels. It just aggregates the information at certain access points. By the use of this distributed technology, the overall cost can be reduced and efficiency is improved. The structure of the system is built in such a fashion so that the massive data and services are put very close to cloud system [8].

In Fig. 20.2 [8], all of the smart devices are interacting to cloud devices via fog devices. Each smart device is linked to the fog devices which further linked to cloud devices making the established communication. The key aspect of fog computing is to improve efficiency and lessen the supply of data transported to the cloud for analysis, processing and storage [10]. The advantages and limitations of fog computing must be considered in order to inculcate its use in businesses and research areas. Table 20.1 shows fog computing's advantages and limitations [10].

The hierarchical structure of fog computing comprises of three layers (shown in Fig. 20.3): the cloud layer, the fog layer and the end-user layer. All of these layers play a major role in the hierarchical architecture of fog computing so they are discussed further below [11]:

- The cloud layer, the core at one extreme end: It contains storage devices and high performance servers and also provides different application services like smart transportation, smart home, smart factory, etc. It is already a prominent storage of data in abundance. It also has the ability to do extensive analysis for computation support [12].

Table 20.1 Fog computing advantages and limitations

Advantages	Limitations
It reduces the amount of data sent to the cloud	Due to physical location, the benefit of the cloud of any data anywhere, anytime is affected
The overall cost is reduced and it also accelerates the process as well as computations	Introduces various security issues
The network bandwidth is conserved	There arise privacy issues
The response time of the system is improved	The availability of service is not met
Mobility is supported	Equipment used are costly
Network and Internet latency is minimized	Hardware failure is one of the threats
Efficiency of the network is increased	Trust is at stake because of third party communication
There is reduced congestion	Authentication is a major concern
Security is enhanced as data is kept closer to the edge	Wireless network security is at concern

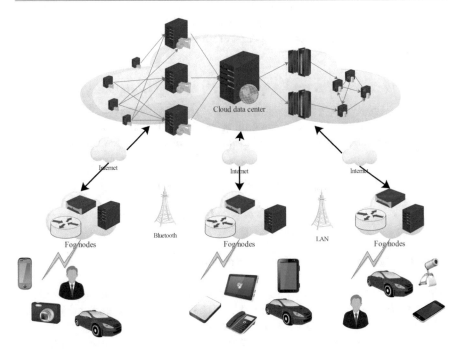

Fig. 20.3 Hierarchical architecture of fog computing

- The fog layer, the intermediate: This layer is on network's edge comprising of multiple fog nodes including routers, switches, gateways, etc. The fog layer is beneficial for applications which could be either latency-sensitive or real-time analysis required in nature. In addition to above functionalities, it also connects with data centre of cloud via IP core network. In order to gain more powerful storage and computing capabilities, it interacts and cooperates with cloud.

- The end-user layer, the other extreme end: It is closest to the physical environment comprising of different IoT devices. Devices such as smart cards, sensors, readers and so on. Especially smart vehicles and mobile phones which have computing power and can be utilized as smart sensing devices are important examples here. These are widely geographically distributed. They sense data of physical objects in the environment and then transmit to the upper layer for further processing and storage.

2.2   History

On November 19, 2015, Cisco Systems, ARM Holdings, Dell, Intel, Microsoft and Princeton University together founded the OpenFog Consortium. Their idea was to promote interests and develop the fog computing researches. Cisco Sr. Managing Director Helder Antunes became the consortium's first chairman, and Intel's Chief IoT Strategist Jeff Faders became its first president [8].

2.3   Characteristics and Applications of Fog Computing

There is a need to study fog computing in detail. It can be accomplished by describing its characteristics and applications which is done in the sub-sections.

2.3.1   Characteristics of Fog Computing

The following are the characteristics required when implementing a fog layer.

Proximity to End Users, Location Awareness and Low Latency

There is an indication of traditional approaches to fog. They provide the terminal nodes with services at the network's edge. They also support applications which require low latency or edge location such as video streaming, gaming, etc. [13]. In [12, 14], proof of low latency in fog computing compared to cloud computing is also explained.

Decentralized and Geographical Distribution

In contrast to centralized cloud, the fog computing needs distributed fog nodes geographically. They play some active roles while streaming quality data in excess which is needed for moving vehicles. The real-time applications are provided via access points and proxies located at tracks and highways [13, 15]. For example, Internet of Vehicle (IoV), fog computing can provide rich services based on interaction and connection of vehicle to vehicle as well as vehicle to access points [16].

Heterogeneity

Fog is considered to be a high virtualized platform located between cloud data centres and end devices. They provide storage, computing and processing network services (three building blocks of both fog and cloud) located at network's edge [13]. Being a virtualized platform, fog nodes can be used as virtual network nodes [16] or computing nodes, making them heterogeneous [17]. Heterogeneity continues not only with high speed links connected to data centres but also to the technologies which have wireless access like WLAN, Wi-Fi, etc., to end users [18].

Interoperability and Federation

Data streaming is considered as an example of services supported by fog. These services need cooperation of different providers, so fog nodes must provide interoperative and federated services across the domains [13, 16, 19].

Save Bandwidth and Low Energy Consumption

In face identification and resolution scheme [20], cloud computing requires transmission of raw face images to cloud. Some management policies for optimal energy and short-range communication mode of mobile nodes effectively decrease the energy consumption [21]. Sarkar and Misra [12] describes fog computing as greener computing. Some time and flow-based energy consumption model were suggested in [22].

Mobility Support

The essential requirements of fog are it should directly communicate with mobile devices. This will aid in supporting techniques for mobility like LISP protocol (LISP-MN) [23, 24]. The LISP protocol decouples location identity to host identity and requires a directory system which is distributed [13]. Fog nodes can be deployed in coffee shop, on airport (static fog nodes) and on trains and mobile vehicles (mobile fog nodes) [25–29].

Data Privacy and Comprehensive Security

Instead of sending sensitive data for analysis to the remote data centre, fog does within the building when necessary. Protection of fog nodes is done as same as done for other IT assets by security and cybersecurity solutions of Cisco. Firstly, fog can do encryption and isolation of data to protect it, and secondly, it mitigates the risks that arise during system upgrade [11].

Real-Time Applications

The data movement is reduced across the Internet and also provides terminals with rich services, which helps in meeting the demands of applications. These applications are generally time-sensitive in real world [18, 19]. Rather than using batch processing, it involves real-time interactions [13]. They in [20] have indicated the response time for face identification and resolution field was less when fog computing was used.

2.3.2 Applications of Fog Computing

Smart Grid

Load balancing applications of the energy may run on devices on edge of the network, for example, micro grids and smart meters [30]. The different energies like wind and solar are used on the basis of the demand of energy, requirements, availability and low cost [8]. In Fig. 20.4, the fog layer at the edge collects data generated and is processed by sensor grids and devices. The processed data is further assigned to the actuators of the control commands [31]. Fog supports volatile storage at the lowest layer to semi-fixed storage to the highest layer. Global insurance is issued by the cloud with the analysis of business intelligence [32].

Cyber Physical Systems (CPS) and IoT

IoT depicts a network which will append the physical objects with the identified network [33, 34]. CPS's trademark is a tight collaboration of system's physical and computational elements. In this context, fog computing is used in embedded systems as the computer and software programs are embedded in the devices not only for the purpose of computation.

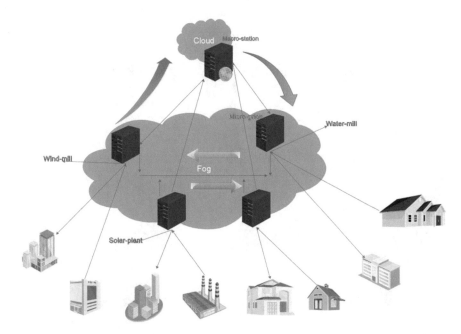

Fig. 20.4 Fog computing in smart grid

Smart Building

In this context, the sensors are employed in such way so that they can maintain the levels of various gases which can be harmful if increased. Also, they analyse the humidity and temperature of the building's atmosphere [32]. In case [8] if there is any problem in some house of the building, the sensor will read the data and will send signals to the authorized authority. By the time the appropriate action is taken, the system performs only basic necessary operations.

Smart City and Vehicular Network

By implying this if there is no traffic, the traffic lights will automatically change to indicate passing of an ambulance. Otherwise, if there is traffic present, the traffic light will change to stop, so no approaching vehicles interrupt the passing of the ambulance.

The smart street lights detect the presence of pedestrian and vehicles on the road and compute the speed and distance of the approaching vehicles to prevent accidents [8]. In Fig. 20.5, it is shown that when the sensor senses any movement, it switches on the light, and if there is nothing on the road, it switches off [31]. These applications are implemented by enabling interaction between Access Pont (AP) to AP, vehicle to vehicle, and/or vehicle to AP [32].

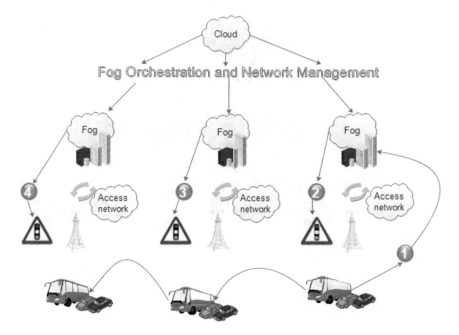

Fig. 20.5 Fog computing in connected vehicles and smart traffic lights

SDN

In Fig. 20.6, fog computing skeleton is proposed so that the concept of SDN could be applied in vehicular network. SDN is an emerging computer and network model and in vogue through the IT industry [35]. It divides data and control communication layers [36–40].

Wireless Actuator and Sensor Network

The typical wireless network sensors lag behind tracking and sensing applications but need wireless actuators to do physical activities such as carrying, opening and closing sensors [31]. The actuators act as fog computing devices to control the process's measurements itself. The stability of the process must be intact, and the oscillatory behaviour must be stable by building a closed loop system [8], for example, in this context, a rail system where there is a sensor provided that checks the heat of the system. If the sensor senses increase in the level of heat, it will automatically generate signals.

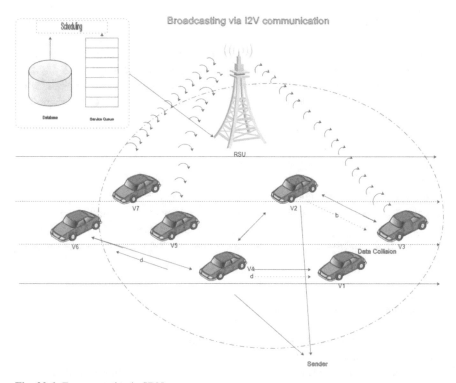

Fig. 20.6 Fog computing in SDN

2.4   Issues in Fog Computing

In this section, three important issues found in fog computing are discussed.

2.4.1   Security Issues

The concerning security issues are discussed below [41].

Authentication

A virulent user can either intrude with its own smart device or report false readings or can spoof IP address of legit users [42]. As solution, the work specifying Public Key Infrastructure should be placed in such a way that it provides multicast authentication. Some techniques like Diffie–Hellman cryptographic approach can be used. In smart meters after applying encryption, it is sent to the fog devices which are in home-area-network gateway (HAN).

Intrusion Detection Techniques

As there are restricted resources and computing, it is harder to analyse the rootkit in fog computing. Usage of hardware-based virtualization technology gives privilege to attacker for kernel level particularly the operating system which capitalizes on vulnerabilities. The information can be exported as they have more privilege than embedded hypervisor.

Detection Techniques of Malware in Fog Computing

In the fog environment, this technique uses hybrid detection techniques, consisting of behaviour-based [43] and signature-based techniques [44]. Doubtful vicious files in fog are sent to the cloud. If the detected vicious file is new for the system, it would be added to the database by the cloud and sent to the fog for its update as signature based.

Compromised Nodes in Fog Computing

Processing of data from the IOT devices is done at fog nodes. If the fog node has been compromised, it will be very difficult to protect the integrity of data. As a relevant solution to this problem, the fog node which has authentication from the cloud can only exist in the cloud environment.

Protection Needs for Data

Analysis should be done without exposing the content of data retrieved from IOT devices. When large amount of data needs analysis, it is distributed over multiple fog nodes and then merged. To solve the problem of protecting the integrity of data, the data obtained can be merged without any loss. But due to limited number of resources, the IOT data is difficult to encrypt and decrypt. To avoid and solve such problem, masking technique and lightweight encryption algorithm are required [45].

Data Management Issue

At different areas, the fog node may not provide services which were provided before. Due to duplication of files at some fog nodes, resources get wasted. Security issues related to personal information can happen on distributed nodes by vicious user by wrong approaches.

2.4.2   Privacy Issues

In these issues, the user control is absent, and there exists a secondary user which is unauthorized. There is some proliferation of data and data transmission can be seen. It also provides dynamic provisioning.

2.4.3   Legal Aspects

This issue arises when there is a weak trust relationship among the nodes as if the customer does not trust the enterprise. In context with these issues, there are some legal aspects also present. One more important legal aspect is SLA which is termed as service level agreement. It is an agreement between the customer or user and service provider. Another legal aspect is the cross-jurisdiction.

2.5   Security Challenges in Fog Computing

2.5.1   Identification/Authentication

With the growing number of devices, maintaining end user authenticity is a critical task. The security credentials of each and every end user must be efficiently managed and updated on regular intervals and also the security software [46–52]. Current scenario lacks any effective identification mechanism but works in fog computing [8]. The reachability of authentication server is not essential to authenticate end users resulting in lesser overhead for fog. They also help in authentication of data centres at the edge. Huang et al. [53] developed an authentication mechanism at user level which allows fog nodes and fog users authenticate mutually.

2.5.2   Systems with Access Controls

Here the access control list (ACL) is maintained which shows the privileges given to a particular user [54]. Unauthenticated user must be debarred of any access, as it will result in fabrication and breaching of information [46]. As suggested by authors in [8, 55], implementation of access control policies and rules based on attributes are done by utilizing Attribute based Encryption (ABE). The policy management framework in [56] has some policy-driven management modules supporting fog's orchestration layer.

2.5.3   Strained Resource Devices

The end user devices must have a security mechanism especially for the devices with longer life span. If their hardware or software gets compromised, it is infeasible to correct as no replacement or modification is possible. For example, for car manufacturers and customer who bought a car, if some hardware is being compromised, it cannot be replaced after it was sold [57].

2.5.4 Virtualization

It is one of the top research topics [58] which helps researchers by defining various mechanisms for security. Also, it explains the extension of security mechanisms to the fog. One scenario where it can be used at edge is virtual Trusted Platform Module (vTPM) which does secure the storage and also provide some cryptographic functions [59].

2.5.5 Privacy

If the security is being compromised, there are bigger chances of sensitive data to be breached [46]. There is an essentiality for protection if data is breached as it will have a drastic effect on performance of the system even leading to shut down. Many protocols of security like in [8] for authorization anonymously allow interaction between data centres at edge and other elements in the system.

2.5.6 Trust

In distributed fog computing where large number of nodes resides, both the scalability of network and a trustworthy environment are difficult to maintain. Taking some particular scenarios, firstly, like the one discussed in [60–62], many devices which are being compromised because they lack any security mechanism may give false positive results and, secondly, when cyber-physical systems are being compromised like the attack on Iran called Stuxnet [63–65] which leads to normal message exchanged in the forehand to the administrator but in backend nuclear reactor spins abnormally.

2.5.7 Rules and Network Security

There are many communication technologies which have their own security rules and mechanisms. As a result, when communication is established, one user's credentials are exposed to others. The security credentials of each and every end user must be efficiently managed and updated on regular interval with security software. Also, some sort of rules should be defined to maintain the security within the network [46]. As discussed in [55], earlier they have cryptographic attributes which helped in generating session keys by using its attributes as credentials.

2.5.8   Intrusion Detection System (IDS)

In [66], they proposed an infrastructure which assigns intrusion detection tasks to the centralized cloud computing services by employing 5G networks at mobile end users. There are various mechanisms and infrastructure as a solution to cloud-related problem which can further be extended to fog computing [67]. Some early warning systems like honeypots can be deployed for federated cloud computing which can be extended to fog computing [68].

2.5.9   Fog Forensics

Using digital forensics in fog environment can be termed as fog forensics. Cloud forensics has been described in [69]. Digital forensics can be seen as an application which identifies, collects and maintains data in a strict pattern [70]. It is considered to be challenging because fog has a large number of sensor nodes. To analyse and collect data from a large number of nodes, here, for example, keeping log for data makes acquisition difficult [71].

3   Security Threat Model for Fog Computing

By going through various technologies, viewing the attacker's intensity of attack, there are many security issues that may arise at different framework [72–77]. The security threat model is described as network framework, service framework, virtualized framework and end-user devices [54].

3.1   Network Framework

In preceding section, it was stated that fog computing interconnects edge devices using different networks for communication. The mode for communication could be the Internet, mobile end users and wireless networks. An attacker can target these vulnerabilities of communication framework [54]. The threats arising are discussed below:

- Man-in-the-middle (MiTM) attack—In this, the attacker fires attack once it gets control over some section of the network explained in [8]. Attacks like eavesdropping or traffic injections.
- Unavailability of service—It is commonly known as denial of service (DoS) or distributed denial of service (DDoS) attack. It is a threat to all communication networks. This attack has a limited scope; hence, it cannot completely affect the

core framework and will disturb the proximal devices in the network because of its design and defined protocols.

- Crooked gateway—In this scenario, the gateways are compromised by the attacker because of the open nature of some of the end-user devices. It produces the same result as of MiTM.

3.2 Service Framework

3.2.1 Data Centres at Edge

The data centres at edge anchor some management services and the virtualization servers [11]. It is favourable to attack the data centres at edge for an attacker considering multiple APIs to access points [54]. The serious security threat arising would be:

- Physically bruised—The constraints are not protected or guarded against physical damage, e.g. small businesses using fog nodes in cluster. In order to do this attack, the attacker needs to be proximal in the network; otherwise, it cannot destroy the devices. Hence, scope is limited to local as there may be many observers, so attack will only affect a particular area geographically.
- Privacy drained—In this scenario, some inside attacker and some attacker with non-harmful intensions may check the flow of information which breaches the privacy. Although this attack has limited scope, its effects can be dangerous if the information is further passed [78].
- Acceleration benefit—This attack allows access to various control over services of end devices to the external intruder (there may present an internal intruder as well). Thus, managed with restricted security which leads to either misconfiguration of framework or no proper maintenance.
- Service exploitation—The attacker can exploit the services once the intruder gains access to control over services. Access gained either by acceleration benefits or by taking advantage of internal knowledge or benefits.
- Crooked data centre—In the above scenario, the attacker has multiple benefits such as having complete control over services to be exploited next. In addition, it gives access to information travelling to crooked data centre and exploits all interactions with other outside system.

3.2.2 Core Framework

The core framework includes the centralized cloud and core management system which is mobile, and all interactions taking place with cloud provider cannot be trusted completely [54]. The reason behind this would be cyber-crimes [79] and/or intrusion by government [80]. A complete taxonomical study of cloud is given [81].

- Privacy drained—Privacy is drained because the terminal devices exchange information or data among the other layers in order to access service or resource.
- Service exploitation—Due to the distributed architecture of fog, not all the network is disrupted by the attack, but still some part of it is vulnerable which leads to fake true results.
- Crooked framework—Although the probability of this attack on some constraints of the network is low, it can have a drastic impact. If the attack is successful in taking down the whole network, some fault tolerance and security mechanism must be employed.

3.3   Virtualized Framework

It is responsible to deploy cloud computing services at network's edge where virtual machines came into picture which can be injected with some sort of malware [54].

- Unavailability of service—An attacker can try to restrict the use of resources by over-using it. Most of the edge data centres do not have all the resources like on other cloud framework.
- Resource exploitation—Rather than attacking the end devices, the attacker attacks local and remote constraints present in the network.
- Privacy drained—As the framework is not transparent, maybe implementation of different APIs occurs. It may give access to information about its logical and physical network such as status of the nodes. These APIs must have some security mechanism; otherwise, they are vulnerable to attack which in turn drains private information.
- Acceleration benefit—Virtual machines (VMs) injected with malware increases the probability of attack. There are some acceleration benefits where infected VM controls the constraints of the network or it fails to provide isolation, so infected VM alters the other VMs. This can be done due to the property of movement within the network of VMs.
- Manoeuvred VM—When the control of the network is with injected VMs, they can perform different attacks. The extraction and alteration of information occur and may also breach the security by injecting malware or logic bombs in the network.

3.4 End-Users Devices

They play an important part in the network as they are an alive player. These devour the services but may have some compromised end-user nodes which can make the whole system vulnerable [54].

- False positive result—If compromised at this level, there is no guarantee that the information/data travelling across the network is true which in turn gives false positive result (true result due to incorrect information). The information travelling can be due to aberration in internal sensor networks.
- Service exploitation—Here devices participate in supply of services such as in a network, a compromised VM controls assemblage of devices which acts as a distributed system. They are vulnerable as data can be manoeuvred.

4 DDoS Attack in Fog Environment

This section describes the DDoS attack briefly. Regardless of the growing demands for cloud services, it is a challenge to maintain the security and availability of data in the network [24, 82–85]. DDoS attack had a great impact on the overall performance of the network.

4.1 Taxonomy

Considering the advancements in technology increases the chances of more and more severe threats particularly DDoS attacks. The systems are controlled by the attacker by flooding the target with some malicious requests. This will in turn exhaust the services provided by the system [86]. Some consequences like service unavailability are shown in [87, 88]. The security threat model for fog computing is given in Fig. 20.7.

For DoS attack, a single connection or a single computer is enough to exhaust the target, but in DDoS, combination of multiple computers is required. Here multiple computers are infected and controlled by attacker, and they attack the target at the same time. These compromised systems are known as botnets. The attacker acts as the master for all the bots working for it as slaves.

4.2 Motive of Attackers

Behind each and every attack, there is a hidden motive. In [89], recognize vengeance, political issues, blackmailing, competitive environment, testing the

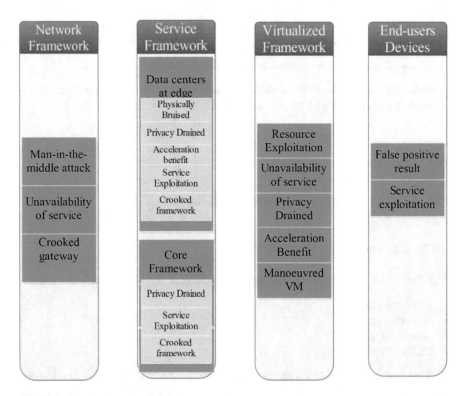

Fig. 20.7 Security threat model for fog computing

capability and sometimes just for fun, etc., are the motives hidden between the attacks.

4.3 Attack Modes

DDoS attack can be categorized into three different modes as explained:

- Restricted consumption of resources
- Connection within network

    The attacker prohibits legitimate user from any service through the network.

- Illegal use of the resources of end users without their knowledge
- Consumption of bandwidth
- Other resource usage
- Fabrication in exchanged information

Here the attacker could modify or alter the configuration of the system, making it inaccessible for legit users.

- Fabrication or physical damage to network components

After taking control of the system, the attacker can modify or even physically damage the components present in the network.

4.4 Types of DDoS Attack

Different types of DDoS attacks on fog are discussed below.

4.4.1 Application-Bug Level DDoS

This level attacks on the vulnerabilities pointed below [86]:

- System weakness
- Outdated patches
- Misconfiguration
- Protocol vulnerability

These types of attacks basically exhaust the application which leads to either crashing the system or temporarily shutting down. Some attacks such as HTTP POST, HTTP PRAGMA and ping of death can be performed here.

4.4.2 Infrastructural Level DDoS

The target of the attack is on bandwidth of the network, buffers, CPU and storage so that no legit user can use them. In this type of attack, the only requirement is the IP address of the victim. This attack is divided into two: direct attack and reflector attack [86].

Direct Attack

This attack is performed with the help of compromised systems or bots. It sends malicious requests to the target via bots to exhaust its resources, bandwidth and services, thus becoming unavailable to the legitimate users. This attack is further divided into two: network and application layer DDoS.

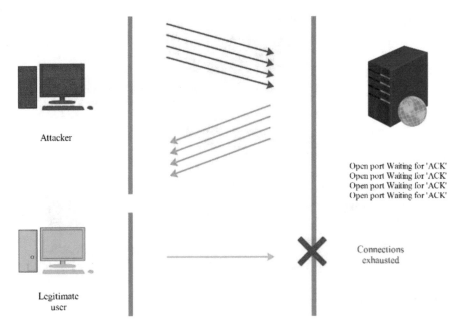

Attacker

Open port Waiting for 'ACK'
Open port Waiting for 'ACK'
Open port Waiting for 'ACK'
Open port Waiting for 'ACK'

Connections
exhausted

Legitimate
user

Fig. 20.8 TCP SYN DDoS attack

Network Layer DDoS

To perform DDOS attack here, the protocols existing in the network as well as transport layer can be used.

TCP SYN The Transmission Control Protocol (TCP) is very well-known to be a connection-oriented protocol located on the transport layer of TCP/IP model. The attack is demonstrated in Fig. 20.8.

UDP The attack is demonstrated in Fig. 20.9.

ICMP The attack is demonstrated in Fig. 20.10.

Application Layer DDoS

There is a significant use of HTTP flood traffic to exhaust the target located on the cloud. This type of attack is hard to detect, making more security concerns.

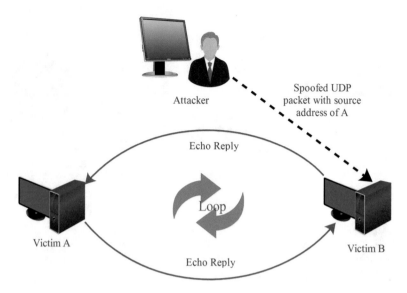

Fig. 20.9 UDP storm DDoS attack

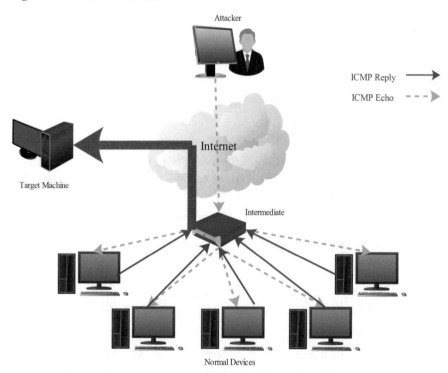

Fig. 20.10 ICMP smurf DDoS attack

HTTP   Here, some malicious HTTP packets such as HTTP GET or POST requests are sent to create extra traffic on web servers and applications. These attacks do not require abundant amount of traffic to exhaust the network.

XML   XML is a globally satisfied language and uses SOAP messages with HTTP to perform DDoS attack. The X-DoS, commonly known as Extensible Markup Language, has easier implementation because of freely available tools. An example of this attack on Amazon EC2 is known as DX-DoS being distributed version of XML.

Reflector Attack

Here IP is spoofed and requests are sent to multiple reflector hosts. After the requests are received, to flood the target, response is forwarded.

4.5   Strategies for Attack

After finding the vulnerabilities, an attacker needs to decide which attack strategies would be beneficial to saturate a network. The strategies needed are pointed down below:

- In order to perform the attack, the attacker needs to know which kind of traffic will be beneficial to exhaust the network.
- There is a need to know those resources which are limited and important for proper functioning of network. Their unavailability will create the needful.
- Once the attacker knows the resources, it is easier to plan the type of packets needed to perform the attack.
- The nature of data size must be known.
- The no. of packets sent per second is an important criterion.
- To perform the basic attack, general knowledge of Internet is enough.
- But for illegal activities, professional knowledge is required.

In order to understand these strategies, one example is needed. There exists a server performing on data sent by users, firstly the attacker plans to shoot abundant requests to saturate the target server. As a result, no request of legitimate user can be served.

4.6   Tools Used for DDoS Attack

4.6.1   LOIC

It is simple, popular, easy and freely available. This helps in performing effective DDoS attack on small server. LOIC is an open source network stress testing and denial-of-service attack application, written in C#. It sends enormous amount of TCP, UDP and HTTP requests to the target and has an additional feature that controls the bots to start the attack.

4.6.2   Bitnami

Bitnami is a library of installers or software packages for web applications and development stacks as well as virtual appliances. Bitnami stacks are used for installing software on Linux, Windows, Mac OS X and Solaris.

4.6.3   Wireshark

It is an open source packet analyser which is freely available. Its purpose is to do network troubleshooting, analysis, education, software and communication protocol development. Originally named Ethereal, the project was renamed Wireshark in May 2006 due to trademark issues. It administers the analysis of very large number of protocols. It has the capability to run on different platform and has live packet capturing with great graphical user interface (GUI).

4.6.4   Ettercap

Ettercap is a free and open source network security tool for man-in-the-middle attacks on LAN. It can be used for computer network protocol analysis and security auditing. It runs on various Unix-like operating systems including Linux, Mac OS X, BSD and Solaris and on Microsoft Windows.

5   Defence Mechanism

In this section, we discuss various defence mechanisms for security of fog computing and also the defence techniques used for DDoS attack detection and mitigation [78]. The following subsection discusses the defence mechanisms at different layers of network.

5.1   The Network

Wireless networking reigns the fog computing, so security of wireless network must be ensured from attacks. For example, in wireless networks attacks like Jamming attack and Sniffer attack can read or modify data if no encryption is applied on the data. Here fog node is at network's edge creating heavy load on the network management. It will cost a fortune to maintain the scalability of distributed cloud servers as fog nodes and also the accessibility is not at ease. One solution to this could be implementation of software-defined networks (SDN) in various conditions of fog environment. SDN is helpful to fog security in four different aspects which are discussed further below [78]:

- Monitoring the network with IDS—Monitoring the network is an essential aspect to protect it from DoS attacks. If the network is monitored regularly, then any malicious traffic coming to freeze the services can be detected and filtered. This is done at fog nodes, creating no problem to legit user in accessing the services. Some of the monitoring algorithms suggested by [90] are as follows:
  - Multipath-naive: in this, each security node is visited from beginning to end.
  - Shortest-through: where shortest route or path is analysed from beginning to end visiting intermediate nodes.
  - Multipath-shortest: like in first algorithm, multiple outports simultaneously receive network packets, and this function is supported by OpenFlow [91–93].

- Priority-based and isolated traffic—It refers to the prioritization of legitimate and malicious network traffic, thus dictating the use of resources which are shared for understanding like CPU or I/O [78]. SDN can disconnect the malicious traffic by isolating it using VLAN ID/tag.
- Access control mechanism for resources in the network—In order to protect against DDoS, an efficient access control mechanism must be introduced. In [94], discretionary scheme of access control for SDN was presented for protection against multiple applications or multi-tenants in flow of network. It is based on OpenFlow. This mechanism idealizes the traditional access control schemes of database management systems (DBMS) and operating system.
- Shared network—The critical situation is an open shared network where the security is at stake as anyone can get access to the network in it. If the security concerns are kept in mind while allowing guests to share network, then the fog-enhanced router can be open to guests wanting access in the network [78].

5.2   Access Control

It is needed to ensure some priorities to the entities participating in the fog environment in order to prevent any entity to perform some malicious actions or control actions without having authority to do that. The existing solutions based on symmetric key lack scalability for key management, but some solutions based on public key work on access control which is fine-grained [78].

For this approach of access control, an attribute-based encryption (ABE) scheme was constructed. Its main aim was to achieve confidentiality of data, scalability and fine-grain which was not achieved in the previous work. This work is achieved by capitalizing on PK-ABE integration with some techniques of proxy and lazy re-encryption exceptionally.

In fog environment, policy management is prerequisite for management of security. Talking about heterogeneous scenario, some threats like sharing security, reusing data and collaboration in policy management still exist. Some use-case scenarios are implied to give the proof of concept to demonstrate its usefulness and versatility.

5.3   Intrusion Detection

It is used to mitigate attacks like flooding attack or DoS, VM attacks, attacks from inside environment, hypervisors, etc. There is a need to make a log of measurements of power meters and detection of measurements. If these give abnormal results, make them vulnerable to get compromised by attackers. These are helpful if applied on fog nodes as it will make detection easier by analysing file logs, control policies for access and login information of user. It also monitors intrusive behaviour for attacks like port scanning and DoS.

6   Open Research and Future Work

This section increases the interests of researchers. It discusses the future work and open research issues existing in this domain. The security challenges need more attention. As this domain is still new, the security challenges will keep on increasing. Hence, there is a need for some efficient security mechanism for cloud computing.

Fog computing can also be used as a defence mechanism for cloud computing against attacks such as DDoS, MiTM, etc., as the location of defence techniques helps a lot. More solutions must be developed to detect and mitigate DDoS attack on cloud in terms of traffic rate, protocol used, etc., in order to determine DDoS attack to get optimal thresholds in already existing defence mechanisms. Some standard rules and policies must be deployed for both Internet (ISP) and cloud service provider (CSP). There should exist some up-to-date datasets for training and testing purposes which leads to increase in availability. The quality of datasets matters when ensuring security.

The performance metrics should be maintained in order to properly analyse the performance. The comparison with the existing mechanism will make it better if performance metrics are evaluated. The defence system must be dynamic in nature as it will guarantee to give better result according to the current scenarios. With the growing technologies, the new mechanism must have adaptability to new attacks. Pre-processing of datasets must be complex to make it less prone to attacks. The selection of the components is very crucial. Hence, it gives a very large area for further work in both research and industry.

7   Conclusion

In this chapter, we have presented a literature review for fog computing with DDoS attack in cloud and fog computing. It is a taxonomical representation of fog computing. Fog computing is explained with its characteristics and applications enriching the history of its origin. Fog computing can be seen as an aid to cloud computing not only to provide services at network's edge but also to ensure security. The technologies behind fog computing are described. Also, the security threat model is discussed in this chapter. This chapter also depicts the DDoS attacks in detail. The discussion goes with the motive behind the attack, modes, types, strategies of the attack and tools helpful in performing DDoS. Further some existing defence mechanisms have been enlightened. The chapter concludes by discussing some open research and future enhancements for fog computing.

References

1. *What is cloud computing? Definition from WhatIs.com.* Retrieved February, 2018, from http://searchcloudcomputing.techtarget.com/definition/cloud-computing
2. Xiao, Z., & Yang, X. (2013). Security and privacy in cloud computing. *IEEE Communications Surveys & Tutorials, 15*(2), 843–859.
3. Davey, R. P., Grossman, D., Rasztovitswiech, M., Payne, D. B., Nesset, D., Kelly, A. E., Rafel, A., Appathurai, S., & Yang, S. H. (2009). Long-reach passive optical networks. *Journal of Lightwave Technology, 27*(3), 273–291.
4. Zhang, W., Lin, B., Yin, Q., & Zhao, T. (2017). Infrastructure deployment and optimization of fog network based on microDC and LRPON integration. *Peer-to-Peer Networking and Applications, 10*(3), 579–591.
5. Bastug, E., Bennis, M., & Debbah, M. (2014). Living on the edge: The role of proactive caching in 5G wireless network. *IEEE Communications Magazine, 52*(8), 82–89.
6. Hassan, M. A., Xiao, M., Wei, Q., & Chen, S. (2015). Help your mobile applications with fog computing. In *Proceedings of the IEEE international conference on sensing, communication, and networking – workshop* (pp. 1–6). IEEE.
7. *What is fog computing? Why it matters in our big data and IoT world?* Retrieved February, 2018, from https://www.forbes.com/sites/bernardmarr/2016/10/14/what-is-fog-computing-and-why-it-matters-in-our-big-data-and-iot-world/2/
8. Stojmenovic, I., & Wen, S. (2014). The fog computing paradigm: Scenarios and security issues. In *Proceedings of the 2014 federated conference on computer science and information systems* (Vol. 2, pp. 1–8). Marlton, NJ: ACSIS. https://doi.org/10.15439/2014F503.
9. Just the facts: Insights of fog for 2018. *OpenFog Consortium.* Retrieved February, 2018, from https://www.openfogconsortium.org/just-the-facts-insights-of-fog-for-2018/

10. What is fog computing? (Fog networking or fogging). *WhatIs.com*. Retrieved February, 2018, from http://internetofthingsagenda.techtarget.com/definition/fog-computing-fogging
11. Hua, P., Dhelima, S., Ninga, H., & Qiu, T. (2017). Survey on fog computing: Architecture, key technologies, applications and open issues. *Journal of Network and Computer Applications, 98*, 27–42.
12. Sarkar, S., & Misra, S. (2016). Theoretical modelling of fog computing: A green computing paradigm to support IoT applications. *IET Networks, 5*(2), 23–29.
13. More, P. (2015). Review of implementing fog computing. *IJRET: International Journal of Research in Engineering and Technology, 04*(06), 335–338.
14. Oueis, J., Strinati, E.C., Sardellitti, S., & Barbarossa, S.. (2015). Small cell clustering for efficient distributed fog computing: A multi-user case, In *Proceedings of the IEEE 82nd vehicular technology conference (VTC Fall)* (pp. 1–5).
15. Zeng, D., Gu, L., Guo, S., Cheng, Z., & Yu, S. (2016). Joint optimization of task scheduling and image placement in fog computing supported software-defined embedded system. *IEEE Transactions on Computers, 65*(12), 3702–3712.
16. Kang, K., Wang, C., & Luo, T. (2016). Fog computing for vehicular ad-hoc networks: Paradigms, scenarios, and issues. *The Journal of China Universities of Posts and Telecommunications, 23*(2), 56–96.
17. Aazam, M., & Huh, E. N. (2016). Fog computing: The cloud-IoT/IoE middleware paradigm. *IEEE Potentials, 35*(3), 40–44.
18. Bonomi, F., Milito, R., Natarajan, P., & Zhu, J. (2014). Fog computing: A platform for internet of things and analytics. In N. Bessis & C. Dobre (Eds.), *Big data and internet of things: A roadmap for smart environments. Studies in computational intelligence* (Vol. 546, pp. 169–186). Cham: Springer.
19. Milito, R., Natarajan, P., & Zhu, J. (2014). *Fog computing: A platform for internet of things and analytics, in big data and internet of things: A roadmap for smart environments* (pp. 169–186). Cham: Springer.
20. Hu, P., Ning, H., Qiu, T., Zhang, Y., & Luo, X. (2017). Fog computing-based face identification and resolution scheme in internet of things. *IEEE Transactions on Industrial Informatics, 13*(4), 1910–1920.
21. Zhang, Y., Niyato, D., Wang, P., & Dong, I. K. (2016). Optimal energy management policy of mobile energy gateway. *IEEE Transactions on Vehicular Technology, 65*(5), 3685–3699.
22. Jalali, F., Hinton, K., Ayre, R., & Alpcan, T. (2016). Fog computing may help to save energy in cloud computing. *IEEE Journal on Selected Areas in Communications, 34*(5), 1728–1739.
23. Natal, A. R., Jakab, L., Portols, M., Ermagan, V., Natarajan, P., Maino, F., Meyer, D., & Aparicio, A. C. (2013). LISP-MN: Mobile networking through LISP. *Wireless Personal Communications, 70*(1), 253–266.
24. Natraj, A. (2016). Fog computing focusing on users at the edge of internet of things. *International Journal of Engineering Research, 5*(5), 1004–1008.
25. Varshney, P., & Simmhan, Y. (2017). Demystifying fog computing: Characterizing architectures, applications and abstractions. In *2017 IEEE 1st International Conference on Fog and Edge Computing (ICFEC)*. IEEE.
26. Luan, T. H., Gao, L., Li, Z., Xiang, Y., Wei, G., & Sun, L. (2016). Fog computing: focusing on mobile users at the edge. *arXiv:1502.01815v3*.
27. Hossain, M. S., & Atiquzzaman, M. (2013). Cost analysis of mobility protocols. *Telecommunication Systems, 52*(4), 2271–2285.
28. Gao, W. (2014). Opportunistic peer-to-peer mobile cloud computing at the tactical edge. In *Proceedings of the IEEE military communications conference* (pp. 1614–1620). Piscataway: IEEE.
29. Chen, X., Jiao, L., Li, W., & Fu, X. (2015). Efficient multi-user computation offloading for mobile-edge cloud computing. *IEEE/ACM Transactions on Networking, 24*(4), 974–983.
30. Wei, C., Fadlullah, Z., Kato, N., & Stojmenovic, I. (2014). On optimally reducing power loss in micro-grids with power storage devices. *IEEE Journal of Selected Areas in Communications, 32*(7), 1361–1370.

31. Bonomi, F., Milito, R., Zhu, J., & Addepalli, S. (2012). Fog computing and its role in the internet of things. In *Proceedings of the first edition of the MCC workshop on mobile cloud computing, ser. MCC'12* (pp. 13–16). New York: ACM.
32. *Research report on %year market sizing of Fog by OpenFog Consortium.* Retrieved February, 2018, from https://www.openfogconsortium.org/wp-content/uploads/451-Research-report-on-5-year-Market-Sizing-of-Fog-Oct-2017.pdf
33. Atzori, L., Iera, A., & Morabito, G. (2010). The internet of things: A survey. *Computer Networks, 54*(15), 2787–2805.
34. Ning, H., Fu, Y., Hu, S., & Liu, H. (2015). Tree-code modeling and addressing for non-id physical objects in the internet of things. *Telecommunication Systems, 58*(3), 195–204.
35. Liu, K., Ng, J., Lee, V., Son, S., & Stojmenovic, I. (2016). Cooperative data dissemination in hybrid vehicular networks: VANET as a software defined network. *IEEE/ACM Transactions on Networking, 24*(3), 1759–1773.
36. Kirkpatrick, K. (2013). Software-defined networking. *Communications of the ACM, 56*(9), 16–19.
37. Kim, H., & Feamster, N. (2013). Improving network management with software defined networking. *IEEE Communications Magazine, 51*(2), 114–119.
38. Kreutz, D., Ramos, F. M. V., Esteves Verissimo, P., Esteve Rothenberg, C., Azodolmolky, S., & Uhlig, S. (2014). Software-defined networking: A comprehensive survey. *Proceedings of the IEEE, 103*(1), 10–13.
39. Nunes, A., Mendonca, M., Nguyen, X. N., & Obraczka, K. (2014). A survey of software defined networking: Past, present, and future of programmable networks. *IEEE Communications Surveys and Tutorials, 16*(3), 1617–1634.
40. Bhushan, K., & Gupta, B. B. (2018). Distributed denial of service (DDoS) attack mitigation in software defined network (SDN)-based cloud computing environment. *Journal of Ambient Intelligence and Humanized Computing, 10*(5), 1985–1997.
41. Roman, R., Lopez, J., & Mambo, M. (2018). Mobile edge computing, Fog et al.: A survey and analysis of security threats and challenges. *Future Generation Computer Systems, 78*, 680–698.
42. Bhushan, K., & Gupta, B. B. (2017). Security challenges in cloud computing: State-of-art. *International Journal of Big Data Intelligence, 4*(2), 81–107.
43. Barbosa, P., Brito, A., Almeida, H., & Claub, S. (2014). Lightweight privacy for smart metering data by adding noise. In *Proceedings of the 29th annual ACM symposium on applied computing (SAC'14)* (pp. 531–538). New York: ACM.
44. Martignoni, L., Paleari, R., & Bruschi, D. (2009). A framework for behavior-based malware analysis in the cloud. In *Proceedings 5th international conference information systems security (ICISS 2009)* (pp. 178–192). New York: Springer.
45. Diro, A. A., & Chilamkurti, N. (2018). Distributed attack detection scheme using deep learning approach for internet of things. *Future Generation Computer Systems, 82*, 761–768.
46. Chiang, M., Fellow, I. E. E. E., & Zhang, T. (2016). Fog and IoT: An overview of research opportunities. *IEEE Internet of Things Journal, 3*(6), 854–864.
47. Bhushan, K., & Gupta, B. B. (2018). Hypothesis test for low-rate DDoS attack detection in cloud computing environment. *Procedia Computer Science, 132*, 947–955.
48. Liu, W., Nishio, T., Shinkuma, R., & Takahashi, T. (2014). Adaptive resource discovery in mobile cloud computing. *Computer Communications, 50*(13), 119–129.
49. Hu, P., Ning, H., Qiu, T., Song, H., Wang, Y., & Yao, X. (2017). Security and privacy preservation scheme of face identification and resolution framework using fog computing in internet of things. *IEEE Internet of Things Journal, 4*(5), 1143–1155.
50. Paharia, B., & Bhushan, K. (2018). Fog computing as a defensive approach against distributed denial of service (DDoS): A proposed architecture. In *2018 9th international conference on computing, communication and networking technologies (ICCCNT)* (pp. 1–7). Piscataway: IEEE.

51. Lee, K., Kim, D., Ha, D., & Rajput, U. (2015). On security and privacy issues of fog computing supported internet of things environment. In *Proceedings of the international conference on the network of the future* (pp. 1–3). IEEE

52. Lee, K., Kimy, D., Ha, D., Rajput, U., & Oh, H. (2015). On security and privacy issues of fog computing supported internet of things environment. In *Proc. 6th international conference on the network of the future (NOF), Montreal, QC, Canada* (pp. 1–3).

53. Huang, X., Xiang, Y., Bertino, E., Zhou, J., & Xu, L. (2014). Robust multi-factor authentication for fragile communications. *IEEE Transactions on Dependable and Secure Computing, 11*(6), 568–581.

54. Yi, S., Qin, Z., & Li, Q. Security and privacy issues of fog computing: A survey. In K. Xu & H. Zhu (Eds.), *Wireless algorithms, systems, and applications. WASA 2015* (Lecture notes in computer science) (Vol. 9204). Cham: Springer.

55. Dsouza, C., Ahn, G.-J., & Taguinod, M. (2014). Policy-driven security management for fog computing: Preliminary framework and a case study. In *Proceedings of the IEEE 15th international conference on information reuse and integration, IRI* (pp. 16–23). Piscataway: IEEE.

56. Gai, K., Qiu, M., Tao, L., & Zhu, Y. (2016). Intrusion detection techniques for mobile cloud computing in heterogeneous 5G. *Security and Communication Networks, 9*(16), 3049–3058.

57. Falliere, N., Murchu, L. O., & Chien, E. (2011). W32.stuxnet Dossier. Symantec Security Response, Ver. 1.4. Mountain View, CA: Symantec.

58. Berger, S., Cáceres, R., Goldman, K. A., Perez, R., Sailer, R., & van Doorn, L. (2006). vTPM: Virtualizing the trusted platform module. In *Proceedings of the 15th conference on USENIX security symposium (USENIX-SS'06)* (Vol. 15, Article No. 21). Berkeley: USENIX Association.

59. Wang, Y., Uehara, T., & Sasaki, R. (2015). Fog computing: Issues and challenges in security and forensics. In *Proceedings of the 39th IEEE annual computer software and applications conference, COMPSAC* (Vol. 3, pp. 53–59).

60. Zetter, K. (2014). *Countdown to zero day: Stuxnet and the launch of the world's first digital weapon.* New York: Crown.

61. Stuxnet. Retrieved January, 2017, from https://en.wikipedia.org/wiki/Stuxnet

62. Delgrossi, L., & Zhang, T. (2012). *Vehicle safety communications: Protocols, security, and privacy.* Hoboken: Wiley.

63. Zhang, T., Antunes, H., & Aggarwal, S. (2014). Defending connected vehicles against malware: Challenges and a solution framework. *IEEE Internet of Things Journal, 1*(1), 10–21.

64. Zhang, T., Antunes, H., & Aggarwal, S. (2014). Securing connected vehicles end to end. In *Proc. SAE World Congr. Exhibit., Detroit, MI, USA, Apr. 2014.*

65. Ibrahim, M. H. (2016). Octopus: An edge-fog mutual authentication scheme. *International Journal of Network Security, 18*(6), 1089–1101.

66. Iqbal, S., Kiah, M. L. M., Dhaghighi, B., Hussain, M., Khan, S., Khan, M. K., & Choo, K.-K. R. (2016). On cloud security attacks: A taxonomy and intrusion detection and prevention as a service. *Journal of Network and Computer Applications, 74*, 98–120.

67. Luo, W., Xu, L., Zhan, Z., Zheng, Q., & Xu, S. (2014). Federated cloud security architecture for secure and agile clouds. In K. J. Han, B.-Y. Choi, & S. Song (Eds.), *High performance cloud auditing and applications* (pp. 169–188). New York: Springer.

68. Lombardi, F., & Di Pietro, R. (2014). Virtualization and cloud security: Benefits, caveats, and future developments. In *Cloud computing: Challenges, limitations and R&D solutions* (pp. 237–255). Cham: Springer.

69. Zhang, M., Duan, Y., Yun, H., & Zhao, Z. (2014). Semantics-aware android malware classification using weighted contextual API dependency graphs. In *Proceedings of the 2014 ACM SIGSAC conference on computer and communications security (CCS'14)* (pp. 1105–1116). New York: ACM.

70. Simou, S., Kalloniatis, C., Kavakli, E., & Gritzalis, S. Cloud forensics solutions: A review. In L. Iliadis, M. Papazoglou, & K. Pohl (Eds.), *Advanced information systems engineering workshops. CAiSE 2014. Lecture notes in business information processing* (Vol. 178). Cham: Springer.
71. Kent, K., Chevalier, S., Grance, T., & Dang, H. (2006). Guide to integrating forensic techniques into incident response. *NIST Special Publication, 10*(14), 800–886.
72. Chaudhary, D., & Bhushan, K. (2017). DDoS attack defense framework for cloud using fog computing. In *2017 2nd IEEE international conference on recent trends in electronics, information & communication technology (RTEICT)* (pp. 534–538). Piscataway: IEEE.
73. Bhushan, K., & Gupta, B. B. (2017). Network flow analysis for detection and mitigation of fraudulent resource consumption (FRC) attacks in multimedia cloud computing. *Multimedia Tools and Applications, 78*(4), 4267–4298.
74. Paharia, B., & Bhushan, K. (2018). DDoS detection and mitigation in cloud via FogFiter: A defence mechanism. In *2018 9th international conference on computing, communication and networking technologies (ICCCNT)* (pp. 1–7). Piscataway: IEEE.
75. Bhushan, K., & Gupta, B. B. (2018). Detecting DDoS attack using software defined network (SDN) in cloud computing environment. In *2018 5th international conference on signal processing and integrated networks (SPIN)* (pp. 872–877). Piscataway: IEEE.
76. Paharia, B., & Bhushan, K. (2019). Fog computing: concepts, applications, and countermeasures against security attacks. In *Handbook of research on cloud computing and big data applications in IoT* (pp. 302–329). Hershey: IGI Global.
77. Hu, P., Ning, H., Qiu, T., Xu, Y., Luo, X., & Sangaiah, A. K. (2018). A unified face identification and resolution scheme using cloud computing in internet of things. *Future Generation Computing Systems, 81*, 582–592.
78. Choo, K.-K. R. (2016). Cloud computing: Challenges and future directions. *Trends and Issues in Crime and Criminal Justice, 400*, 1–6.
79. Landau, S. (2014). Highlights from making sense of Snowden, part II: What's significant in the NSA revelations. *IEEE Security and Privacy, 12*(1), 62–64.
80. Juliadotter, N. V., & Choo, K.-K. R. (2015). Cloud attack and risk assessment taxonomy. *IEEE Cloud Computing, 2*(1), 14–20.
81. Bureau of Transportation Statistics, U.S. Department of Transportation, Washington, DC, USA [Online]. Retrieved March, 2017, from http://www.rita.dot.gov/bts/sites/rita.dot.gov.bts/files/publications/national_transportation_statistics/html/table_01_26.html_mfd
82. Chen, M., Zhang, Y., Li, Y., & Mao, S. (2015). EMC: Emotion-aware mobile cloud computing in 5G. *IEEE Network, 29*(2), 32–38.
83. Amendola, D., Cordeschi, N., & Baccarelli, E. (2016). Bandwidth management VMs live migration in wireless fog computing for 5G networks. In *Proceedings of the IEEE international conference on cloud networking* (pp. 21–26). New York: IEEE.
84. Peng, M., Yan, S., Zhang, K., & Wang, C. (2015). Fog-computing-based radio access networks: Issues and challenges. *IEEE Network, 30*(4), 46–53.
85. Papagianni, C., Leivadeas, A., & Papavassiliou, S. (2013). A cloud-oriented content delivery network paradigm: Modeling and assessment. *IEEE Transactions on Dependable and Secure Computing, 10*(5), 287–300.
86. Osanaiye, O., Choo, K.-K. R., & Dlodlo, M. (2016). Distributed denial of service (DDoS) resilience in cloud: Review and conceptual cloud DDoS mitigation framework. *Journal of Network and Computer Applications, 67*, 147–165.
87. Chaudhary, D., Bhushan, K., & Gupta, B. B. (2018). Survey on DDoS attacks and defense mechanisms in cloud and fog computing. *International Journal of E-Services and Mobile Applications (IJESMA), 10*(3), 61–83.
88. Chaudhary, D., & Bhushan, K. (2017). DDoS attack mitigation and resource provisioning in cloud using fog computing. In *2017 International conference on smart technologies for smart nation (SmartTechCon)* (pp. 308–313). Piscataway: IEEE.
89. Bhushan, K., & Gupta, B. B. (2018). A novel approach to defend multimedia flash crowd in cloud environment. *Multimedia Tools and Applications, 77*(4), 4609–4639.

90. McKeown, N., Anderson, T., Balakrishnan, H., Parulkar, G., et al. (2008). OpenFlow: Enabling innovation in campus networks. *ACM SIGCOMM CCR, 38*(2), 69–74.
91. Mininet. *An instant virtual network on your laptop (or other PC)*. Retrieved March, 2017, from mininet.org
92. Sekar, A. G. V., Krishnaswamy, R., & Reiter, M. K. (2010). Network-wide deployment of intrusion detection and prevention systems. In *Proceedings of 6th international conference ACM Co-NEXT*. New York: ACM.
93. Klaedtke, F., Karame, G. O., Bifulco, R., & Cui, H. (2015). Towards an access control scheme for accessing flows in SDN. In *2015 1st IEEE Conference on Network Softwarization (NetSoft)* (pp. 1–6). IEEE.
94. Yap, K. K., et al. (2011). *Separating authentication, access and accounting: A case study with openWiFi. Technical report*. Menlo Park: Open Networking Foundation.

Chapter 21
Secure Machine Learning Scenario from Big Data in Cloud Computing via Internet of Things Network

C. L. Stergiou, A. P. Plageras, K. E. Psannis, and B. B. Gupta

Abstract The Cloud Computing (CC) technology refers to an infrastructure in which both data storage and data processing take place outside the mobile device. Furthermore, another new and fast growing technology called Internet of things (IoT) rises in the sector of networks and telecommunications with specific concern in the "modern" area of wireless telecommunication systems. Regarding our recent research, the main goal of the interaction and cooperation between things and objects sent through the wireless networks is to fulfill the objective set to them as a combined entity, with the aim to achieve a better environment for the use of Big Data (BD). In addition, counting on the technology of wireless networks, both CC and IoT could be developed rapidly and together. In this paper, we survey IoT and Cloud Computing technologies with focus on security problems that both technologies faced. Particularly, these two aforementioned technologies (i.e., Cloud Computing and IoT) have been compared, with the aim to examine the familiar characteristics and examine and discover the benefits of their integration to secure the use and transmission of Big Data. In conclusion, contributions of CC and IoT technologies and how the CC technology improves the operation of IoT as a base technology for Big Data systems have been presented.

Keywords Internet of things · Cloud Computing · Big Data · Security · Privacy

C. L. Stergiou · A. P. Plageras · K. E. Psannis (✉)
Department of Applied Informatics, University of Macedonia, Thessaloniki, Greece
e-mail: c.stergiou@uom.edu.gr; a.plageras@uom.edu.gr; kpsannis@uom.edu.gr

B. B. Gupta
Department of Computer Engineering, National Institute of Technology Kurukshetra, Kurukshetra, India
e-mail: bbgupta@nitkkr.ac.in

© Springer Nature Switzerland AG 2020   525
B. B. Gupta et al. (eds.), *Handbook of Computer Networks and Cyber Security*,
https://doi.org/10.1007/978-3-030-22277-2_21

1 Introduction

"Internet of things" (IoT) is a novel technology which operates in the sector of telecommunications. IoT could be defined by many researchers as "the network of devices, vehicles, buildings, and other items which are embedded with sensors, and these are connected to the network, permitting these objects to gather and interchange data" [1–3]. Over the next years, a flare in the number of connected devices as well as located sites and the functions they will perform are expected. Regarding the data used in a wireless network, there are security and privacy issues that need to be addressed. The problem with security and data privacy in everyday life could be solved or could be minimized with the use of BD analysis tools and services. BD is a new popular term, used to describe the surprisingly rapid increase in the volume of data in structured and unstructured form [4, 5]. BD usually uses CC as a base technology in order to operate. Similar to this, another technology that could be used as a base technology is the Edge Computing (EC).

IoT could be settled as a type of network of physical objects or things which are embedded with software, electronics, sensors, and connectivity that enables them. Due to that, IoT achieves greater rate and service by transmitting data with operators and various inter-connected devices [6–8].

An approach has been made by researchers in [9], in order to help other researchers who are interested in security issues. This approach provides an IoT security analysis of the recent security research activity and a novel IoT framework that is validated through a case study. The authors of this paper have shown through their work that the evolution of autonomous objects raises security threats.

Thus, the need of "cloud" support has become inefficient due to the intensive computations, the mass storage, and the security issues. Some examples include limited storage capacity, communication capabilities, energy, and processing. Inefficiencies like these have motivated us in order to find a model for the combination of CC and IoT. As a "base" technology, Cloud Computing consolidates various technologies and applications to get the maximum capacity and performance of the existing infrastructure [10–12].

On top of that, Mobile Cloud Computing (MCC) made its appearance, as a relative version of Cloud Computing, and it was improved by new developments in the field of "Cloud Computing." The latter aims provide access to data and information from anywhere at any time by obliterating the need for hardware equipment [2, 13–15]. More specifically, MCC is defined as an integration of cloud and mobile computing rendering mobile devices more resourceful. It is also a contemporary approach to innovative services for firms and institutions. CC can be used as a useful base for both Internet of Things and Video Surveillance technologies and provide improvements on their function [16–18].

Moreover, Cloud Computing aims to offer access to information and data from anywhere at any time, without the restrictions of the need for hardware equipment [11, 19–21]. As a result of the operations of CC, it could be used as a base technology for IoT and for several technologies in the telecommunication field and could also provide improvements on their functions.

In addition to this, CC additionally used to be a base technology for other technologies due to its types of services [11, 21, 22]. One of those is the Big Data. BD is a term used to describe the expected (due to the connection to the Internet devices) rapid increase in the volume of data production. Subsequently, these large amounts of data could be defined as "a broad term for data sets so large or complex that traditional data processing applications are inadequate" [12, 21]. Furthermore, BD is often associated to the use of predictive analytics or certain advanced methods to extract knowledge from the data. Rarely, it is also related to a particular size of set of data [4, 5]. Precision in BD could result in more confident decision making, and better decisions may drive in increased operational efficiency, reduced costs, and minimized risk [4]. From this scope, it can be observed that BD is now equally important both for business and Internet. This happens because more information drives to more accurate analysis [11]. The real problem is not that the large amounts of data have been obtained, but whether they have any value or not. Hopefully, by predicting that organizations would be able to acquire information from any source, harness the relevant data, and analyze them in a specific way in order to get quick answers, the following should be achieved: (1) reduce costs, (2) reduce time, (3) produce new items and optimize their offerings, and (4) take more ingenious decisions [7].

Last but not least, since we are talking about BD, IoT, and CC/MCC, many researchers tried to figure out ways for securing these sensitive/personal data. The security problems still remain a challenge since the new technologies are multiplied. Due to this, a security scheme for safe sensitive data transmission over the CC and the IoT devices has been proposed in [23]. Specifically, an alternative of RSA (Rivest–Shamir–Adleman) security has been deployed, namely MEMK ("Memory Efficient Multi Key") generation scheme, in order to provide support to the data transmitted from the IoT devices to the Cloud and back. This scheme has been also used by the authors of this paper [23] to boost the efficiency of the memory.

The rest of the paper is divided into sections as follows. Initially, in Sect. 2, a literature review related to the conjunction of the technologies mentioned in the introduction section (Sect. 1) of this paper has been presented. Subsequently, in Sect. 3, there is an illustration of issues related with BD and their privacy. In Sect. 4, the field of IoT and some of its major functions have been discussed in detail. Moreover, in Sect. 5, the CC technology and its basic characteristics have been presented and analyzed. Section 6 illustrates the integration of IoT and CC and surveys some of the benefits of their integration. Finally, Sect. 7 provides the conclusions of this paper and offers new possibilities for the development of future work.

2   Literature Review

To come through the proposed scenario, various related works that discuss the combination of the three afore-mentioned technologies (Big Data, Cloud Computing, and Internet of Things) have been studied. This section illustrates related work similar to this research. The main tumor of the related research studies is mainly related to previous work of our research team.

To start with, in [11], the authors aim in the interaction and the conjunction of Mobile Cloud Computing (MCC) and IoT through the integration of these technologies with the Big Data. This scenario, based on similar characteristics of MCC and IoT, and which of the benefits of these technologies could improve the use of BD applications. Also, in [11], an illustration has been presented of how the MCC and the IoT contribute to the BD technology, individually.

A region-based research [2] presents a survey research of IoT and CC focusing on the issues based on data privacy of both technologies. Particularly, the authors of [2] try to combine these technologies with the purpose to find and examine the familiar characteristics and then discover the profits of their integration. Additionally, the authors illustrate the contribution of CC in the field of IoT, and through this, it can be proved how the CC technology improves the operation of IoT.

In [7], the authors survey BD and CC technologies and their major features, focusing on security and data privacy issues. Particularly, a conjunction of the functionality of those two technologies has been done with the aim to consider the frequent characteristics and, in addition to this, to discover the profits which deal with security problems of their integration. Thus, a novel method of an algorithm has been presented in [7], which could be used for the purpose of upgrading the CC's security through the use of algorithms that can provide privacy of the large amounts of data.

Another research [8] focuses on a proposal of system integration between IoT and Video Surveillance (VS) technology, with the goal to indulge the requirements of the future needs of VS and to accomplish a better use of it. The VS data that have been transmitted through the network could be characterized as large-scale data and thus as BD. The basic outcome of the specific research [8] is an innovative topology paradigm which could offer a better use of IoT technology in VS and vice versa.

In [24] initially, an analytical study of IoT, CC, and BD to resolve various issues that face the health sector in regard to these technologies has been presented. In the proposed scenario, there is a collection of e-health data by sensor devices and actuators which has been transferred through an established network to a cloud server. These data could be processed in the cloud server in order to be analyzed, and by this analysis, there would be born what we call "data mining." Moreover, there is a research [24] that deals with security of medical data which constitute sensitive personal data and must be protected.

Moreover, in [3], the authors initially present a survey of the technologies IoT, BD, CC, and Monitoring with the aim to discover their common operations and to combine their functionality, in order to achieve beneficial scenarios of their use. The main objective of [3] is to propose a novel system which operates in IoT environment, within there will be collected and managed sensors' data. Additionally, the authors state that their proposed system will be energy efficient and it would be used in a "Green Smart Building."

In [12], the authors try to achieve and propose a type of network that will provide more intelligent media-data transfer. Thus, through the study of the use of various open source tools, the authors found the suitable for their experiments tool with the aim to measure the performance of their proposed model of network. At the end, the authors proposed the network topology that they have implemented from a small section of the script of CloudSim simulator with Cooja so that they could test a single network segment.

Stergiou et al. [25] surveys Social Networking (SNg), BD, and CC, focusing on their main features, by concentrating on the security problems of those technologies. In particular, the authors aim to combine the functionality of BD and SNg in CC environment so that they could analyze the common characteristics and ascertain the advantages of their integration related to security issues. The main outcome of [25] is the presentation of a novel system-framework-network in Cloud environment through which users of various Social Networks (SNs) will be able to exchange data and information and primarily large-scale data.

To summarize, the papers that deal with the security and privacy issues of management in MCC are illustrated [26–32]. As we can realize, there are several works in this field. More particular, in [26], the authors propose an entity-centric approach for an IDM model in Cloud environment. The proposed approach is based on two aspects: (a) active bundles and (b) anonymous identification. The active bundles include a payload of Personally Identifiable Information, privacy policies, and a virtual machine that enforces the policies, and additionally, the active bundles use a set of protection mechanisms in order to protect themselves. As regard the anonymous identification, they use it with the aim to mediate interactions between the entity and the Cloud services using entity's privacy policies. Moreover, the authors present the main characteristics of the approach which are the following: (a) independent of third party, (b) provides minimum information to the Service Provider, and (c) provides ability to use identity data on untrusted hosts. Then, [27] demonstrates the implementation of a mobile system that enables electronic healthcare data storage, update, and retrieval using Cloud Computing. The proposed mobile application is based in Google's Android OS and offers management of patient health records and medical images. This system was evaluated with the use of Amazon's S3 cloud service. Finally, the authors summarize the details of the implementation and then present initial results of the system in practice. Moreover, the authors of [28] survey the MCC technology, which could help the general readers to have an overview of the MCC including the definition, the architecture, and the applications. Also, [28] presents the issues, the existing solutions, and the recent approaches of the MCC technology. At the end, the authors discuss a number of future research directions of the MCC. Through [29], the authors propose a multi-faceted Trust Management system architecture for a Cloud Computing marketplace, with the aim to support the customers in reliably identifying trustworthy cloud providers. The proposed system offers means to identify the trustworthy cloud providers in terms of different attributes that assessed by multiple sources and roots of trust information.

Furthermore, [30] presents a sort survey of MCC evolution and additionally explains how Cloud Computing and mobile devices could be combined with good terms for future opportunities, implications, and legal issues for developing countries. In another research, the authors of [31] try to review the existing Distributed Application Processing Frameworks, also known as DAPFs, for SMDs in MCC domain. The main objective of [31] is to highlight issues and challenges to existing DAPFs in developing, implementing, and executing computational intensive mobile applications within MCC domain. Thus, through this work, the authors propose a thematic taxonomy of the current DAPFs, and then they review current offloading frameworks by using thematic taxonomy and analyze the implications and critical aspects of current offloading frameworks. Finally, [31] puts forward open research issues in distributed application processing for MCC that remains to be addressed. Also, [32] proposes a trust management approach by making an analysis of user behavioral patterns for a reliable Mobile Cloud Computing. So the authors suggest a method in order to quantify a one-dimensional trusting relation counting on the analysis of telephone call data from Mobile Cloud Environment. Subsequently, it is enhanced trustworthiness of data production, management, and overall application.

Finally, in [33], there is a proposal of an efficient algorithm for advanced scalable media-based Smart Big Data, such as 3D and Ultra HEVC, on Intelligent CC systems. The proposed encoding algorithm of [33] exceeds the conventional HEVC standard which has been demonstrated by the performance evaluations.

Also, related works of other research groups have been studied. Gnana Singh et al. [34] presents a survey on the BD and CC, with the importance to promote the research and development activities in the sector of the BD and the Cloud Computing. At the end, [34] introduces a method for storing the data on cloud using the CloudSim simulation software.

Then, [35] shows an analysis that focuses on the two key concepts, BD and CC, and some of the issues and possibilities which are innate with the deployment of CC and BD services. Through this study, it is shown which security challenges is among the most prominent problem in CC and BD services. Finally, after there is a consideration about some of the problems related to BD and CC, a number of solutions have been suggested in [35] toward improving the two key concepts that will go a long way in increasing the adoption rate of CC by organizations.

In [36], the authors survey on the effects of data processing and analyzing big healthcare data on a CC environment. Rallapallia et al. [36] proposes the use of the Hadoop, which is a system that could process large amounts of data sets on distributed environments, and also it can be deployed on a CC environment to process the big healthcare data.

The authors in [37] propose an IoT-based security system on smart building scenarios. By this, they are integrating coherent data as fundamental components. The aim of the integration is to drive the building management and security behavior of indoor services accordingly. A holistic platform named City Explorer, which offers security and discovery, is the component in which the proposed system is manifested.

In [38], an energy saving solution in buildings aiming to generate predictive models of energy consumption in buildings is illustrated. Moreover, the authors in [38] use a building as a reference, for which they have one year's unified data, in order to verify the proposed solution. At the end, the authors proposed strategies and control actions for energy saving in the building.

With the aim to take measurements about the temperature, the humidity, and the light in a building, the authors in [39] present an IoT-based sensing and monitoring system which is wirelessly connected. Also, in [39], there is a development of an Android application through which data is transmitted from the LabVIEW to a "smart" mobile device through which data are monitored remotely.

In [40], the authors analyze the problem of imperfection in smart city data. Additionally, the authors point on the management of these types of data and also create an evidential database with the use of the evidence theory, with the aim to improve the efficiency of the smart city. Moreover, in this paper, a special case of modeling imperfect data in the healthcare sector has been presented. Finally, a database which embraces both imperfect and perfect data was built up, and the different imperfect aspects in this database had been represented by the theory of beliefs and illustrated in this paper.

As an attractive service, the data sharing service in [41] has been characterized. As this paper informs us, the attribute-based encryption (ABE) is widely discussed and is the scheme on which the proposed scheme in this paper is based on. This scheme provides solutions for the resource-constrained IoT-mobile devices in the clouds. The feasibility and efficiency of the scheme have been proved through performance analysis and experiments which confirm that the scheme is also protected of adaptively chosen ciphertext attacks.

The widely and continuous deployment and use of novel technologies usually leads to threats that come from internal and external factors. A research [42] which deals with the personal mobile data privacy of mobile users provides a protection scheme that is based on the "Attribute-Based Access Control" (ABAC) and the data self-deterministic schemes. The "Attribute-based Semantic Access Control" (A-SAC) algorithm and the "Proactive Determinative Access" (PDA) algorithm have been used by the authors in [42] to support the proposed scheme. The benefits of the scheme are the constraining data accesses, the proactive prevention of the users' data threats on the cloud, and the increased level of secure sustainability.

Another region-based approach that deals with the data safety and the security mechanisms, in the healthcare sector this time, has been presented in [43]. The authors of this paper, through the blend of the RSA (Rivest–Shamir–Adleman) and the AES (Advanced Encryption Standard) algorithms, have been deployed a novel hybrid encryption scheme. The proposed scheme can protect the patients' personal information by concealment of them into a cover image. This image is characterized by high indistinctness, high capacity, and minimized distortion. The feasibility of the scheme is proved through the comparative analysis that was made between other state-of-the-art methods and the proposed one.

Moreover, the authors of [44] review the current research challenges and opportunities related to the development of secure and safe Intelligent Transport Systems (ITS) applications. Initially, they explore the architecture and main features of the ITS systems, and also they survey the key enabling standards and projects.

Likewise, the authors provide an analysis of a detailed ITS safety application case study and then evaluate in light of the European ETSI TC ITS standard.

Eventually, [45] states that the Internet of Things could enable innovations that enhance the quality of life; nevertheless, IoT generates unprecedented amounts of data that are difficult for traditional systems, Cloud Computing, and even Edge Computing to handle. Consequently, Fog Computing is designed to overcome these limitations.

Additionally, there are some "key"-related research works that deal with the security of the machine learning systems [46–51]. Specifically, [46] offers a framework for answering the major question "Can machine learning be secure?." The novel contributions of this work introduce (a) a taxonomy of different types of attacks on machine learning techniques and systems, (b) a variety of defenses against those attacks, (c) a discussion of ideas that are important to security for machine learning, (d) an analytical model giving a lower bound on attacker's work function, and (e) a list of open problems. Liao et al. [47] focuses to offer a brief overview on the current work toward the emerging research problem of secure machine learning. Furthermore, [47] presents a brief overview on secure machine learning and current progress on developing secure machine learning algorithms. Subsequently, [48] presents taxonomy which identifies and analyzes attacks against machine learning systems. In addition to this, the authors of [48] show how these classes influence the costs for the attacker and defender, and we give a formal structure defining their interaction. At the end, this work presents a discussion of how the proposed taxonomy suggests new lines of defenses. The authors of [49] design a novel, communication-efficient, failure-robust protocol for secure aggregation of high-dimensional data. Their proposed protocol allows a server to compute the sum of large, user-held data vectors from mobile devices in a secure manner and can be used, for example, in a federated learning setting, to aggregate user-provided model updates for a deep neural network. Through their work, the authors of [49] prove the security of their protocol in the honest-but-curious and active adversary settings and show that security is maintained even if an arbitrarily chosen subset of users drop out at any time. Also, the authors evaluate the efficiency of their protocol and show, by complexity analysis and a concrete implementation, that its runtime and communication overhead remain low even on large data sets and client pools. In [50], the authors rely upon a previously proposed attack framework to categorize potential attack scenarios against learning-based malware detection tools by modeling attackers with different skills and capabilities. Then, the authors of [50] try defining and implementing a set of corresponding evasion attacks to thoroughly assess the security of Drebin, an Android malware detector. As a result, the main contribution of this work is the proposal of a simple and scalable secure-learning paradigm that mitigates the impact of evasion attacks, while only slightly worsening the detection rate in the absence of attack. At the end, the authors argue that their secure-learning approach can also be readily applied to other malware detection tasks. Finally, the authors of [51] propose a DSQML protocol in which the client can classify two-dimensional vectors to different clusters, resorting to a remote small-scale photon quantum computation processor. The proposed protocol is secure without leaking any relevant information. Regarding the principle, the proposed protocol can be used to classify high dimensional vectors and may provide a new viewpoint and application for future "Big Data."

3 Big Data

Big Data is the concept of data where it is difficult to gather, store, handle, and process with classic tools and technologies. Over the last two decades, Big Data in the industry has grown enormously in various sectors and is growing exponentially. In 2011, the volume of data generated in the world was 1.8ZB, and this will double every 2 years in the near future [4, 5].

The concept of large data has been defined by the 3V model from Lenay [52] as "high volume, high speed and a wide variety of information items that require efficient and innovative forms of information processing for improved insight and decision making" [4, 11].

In 2012, Gartner [52] updated the definition as follows: "Big data is high-intensity, high-speed, and/or high-variety of information items that require new forms of processing to enable enhanced decision making, discovery of insight optimization of processing." The TechAmerica Foundation [53] defines the large data as follows: "Big data is a term describing high-speed, complex and variable high-volume data that requires advanced technologies and techniques to enable capture, storage, distribution, management and analysis of information."

3.1 Predictive Model of Big Data's 5V

For predicting Big Data's 5V, a real-time system is proposed that initially filters data from unreliable sources (honesty) and distinguishes the variety of data using the Bloom filter [54]. It then uses the Kalman filter to estimate the volume and speed of each data variety that arrives in the system; the data variability is incorporated, while the volume and speed are estimated. Kalman filter could be characterized as better filter than the other filters as it can be easily adapted to provide impartial estimates across a wide range of data streams even when the fluctuation is high. It is an effective retrospective filter, a mathematical toolkit capable of dynamically predicting future trends from incoming currents from sensor measurements with noise [21]. The Bloom filter is a probabilistic data structure that is used to filter data that does not belong to a set. Data streams consider it to be mainly text, audio, video, and video data [54].

3.2 Big Data Analytics

The creation of heterogeneous data from different physical devices requires quick real-time analysis. Incomplete data is a problem for real-time analysis, so we need algorithms that pre-process the data before analysis.

As production data continues and grows, the way in which Big Data can expand and follow this evolution is a challenge [3, 4, 21, 33].

One of the most important benefits of the Internet of Things technology is the creation of an unprecedented amount of data. Storing, holding, and completing data becomes critical. The Internet consumes up to 5% of the total energy produced today, and with these requirements, it will certainly increase even more. As a result, centralized devices and centralized data centers ensure both energy efficiency and reliability. The data must be stored and used intelligently for intelligent monitoring and activation. It is important to develop artificial intelligence algorithms that can collect or distribute depending on the current needs. New fusion algorithms need to be developed to understand the data collected. The modern non-linear, time machine learning methods are based on evolutionary algorithms, genetic algorithms, neural networks, and other artificial intelligence techniques needed for automated decision making. These systems present features such as interoperability, integration, and adaptive communications. They also have a modular architecture both in terms of hardware design and software development and are usually suitable for IoT applications. What is needed is the existence of a central infrastructure to support storage and analysis. This makes the IoT intermediate software level, and there are many challenges that are discussed below. Since 2012, the storage solutions based on Cloud are becoming increasingly popular in the coming years under analysis platforms based on the Cloud and data visualization platforms collected [3, 5, 12, 21].

Data analysis is the process of using algorithms that are executed on powerful platforms to discover hidden capabilities in large data such as hidden patterns or unknown associations, for example, the extraction of useful knowledge and their image [55]. This is done in the wording of the case, often based on conclusions gathered from the experience and the discovery of correlations between the variables [56]. According to Rajaraman [56], there are four types of data analysis:

Descriptive Analysis This deals with what has happened in the past and presents in a readily understandable form the data such as diagrams, graphs, pie charts, maps, spreadsheets, etc.; the display gives an insight into what the data imply. A typical example is the presentation of population census data that classifies the population in a country by gender, age, education, income, etc. [56].

Predictive Analysis It draws conclusions from the available data to say what is expected to happen in the near future. The tools used to collect data are time series analysis using statistical methods, neural networks, and engineering learning algorithms. An important use of predictive analysis is in marketing that understands the needs and preferences of customers [56].

Exploratory Analysis It finds unexpected relationships between parameters in large data collections. Collecting data from various sources and analyzing them provide additional opportunities for new ideas and random discoveries. One of the most important applications is to discover patterns in customer behavior from the feedback they get from tweets, blogs, Facebook, and emails to allow companies to predict customer actions such as renewing subscription to the magazine, changing a mobile phone service provider, canceling a hotel reservation, and so on [56].

Regulatory Analysis It identifies, based on the data gathered, opportunities to optimize solutions to existing problems, i.e., it tells us what needs to be done to achieve a goal. One of the common uses is the pricing of airlines based on data from travel models such as popular destinations, major events, holidays, etc., to maximize profit [56].

Moreover, Alexandrov et al. [57] present Stratosphere, which is an open source software for parallel data analysis. In addition, Kwon et al. [58] propose a research model to explain the intent to buy large analytical data, mainly from the theoretical approaches to data quality management and user experience.

3.3   Big Data Security Issues

New challenges and standards are developed and created in data security issues through the development and the use of BD technology. This creates a growing need for further research on security technologies in order to be able to handhold the large amount of data and to ensure effectiveness. Technologies for securing data are slow when applied to huge amounts of data [3, 12, 21, 33].

Regarding Table 21.1, we can conclude that even the most efficient algorithms give an encryption rate of 64.3 MB/s. So, in the sector of BD technology, in which large amounts of data need to be transferred, we can see a significant bottleneck for encryption of such large amounts of data. This is detrimental to the nature of BD which has real time processing and results.

Table 21.1 Encryption rates of popular algorithms

Algorithm	Key length (bits)	Megabytes processed	Block size (bits)	Rounds	Time taken	MB per second
3-DES	56, 112 or 168	128	64	48	6159	20,783
AES	128, 192, or 256	256	128	10, 12, or 14	4196	61,010
RSA	1024–4096	300	512	1	11,757,826	10,900

3.4   Big Data on Cloud System Scenario

Among all types of data in the cloud storage, large-scale data has occupied a significant part due to the explosive sharing on social networks and additionally video-on-demand services for movies, TV programs, etc. Moreover, to support users with various bandwidth requirements and device resolutions and full interactive playback in large-scale data demand, usually various versions at different bit rates are generated [3, 12, 21, 33, 59–61].

Schemes for large-scale data, named as Big Data, have shown good performances in cloud storage under different configurations. However, these codes treat all files as general data, in which one unrecoverable error will lead to permanent loss of the whole file. They do not consider the features of specific data types.

The Cloud Computing should provide its services with specific functions so that the IoT linked to it can support the smart city's turn. The Big Data, or large scale data, as it is described in the international literature is defined as the large quantity of data that specific scenarios described, related to the whole activity of the city.

In this work, we propose Cloud-based system for BD used and transmitted through an IoT network.

4   Internet of Things

The IoT could be characterized as "a network of devices that transmits, shares, and uses data from the physical environment to provide services to individuals, corporations, and society" [1, 8, 12], which was already defined in the introduction section. Also, IoT has multiple applications in health, transport, environment, energy, or types of devices such as sensors, devices worn/carried (wearable), watch, glasses, and home automation (domotics).

4.1   Advantages of the Data

Chances where the streaming data will produce novel markets with the aim to inspire positive change or to intensify existing services are examined by businesses. Some examples of fields that are at the heart of these developments are listed below [62]:

1. *IoT(a)*: Smart solution in the bucket of transport: With this, better solutions in transportation sector with the aim to provide a better way of living could be achieved.
2. *IoT(b)*: Smart power grids incorporating more renewable energy: With this, the system reliability could be achieved, and also the charges to consumers could be reduced, thus providing cheaper electricity.

3. *IoT(c)*: Remote monitoring of patients: With this, we could achieve a system which offers remote monitoring of patients. This system could offer a better and well-managed healthcare system by improving the quality of services, increasing the number of people served, and saving money.
4. *IoT(d)*: Sensors in homes and airports: With this, we could achieve safer places such as airports and houses by establishing a number of sensors in the field.
5. *IoT(e)*: Engine monitoring sensors that detect and predict maintenance issues: With this, we detect and predict maintenance issues, improve inventory replenishment, and even define priorities in scheduling maintenance work, repairs, and regional operations.

4.2 IoT Data

IoT is an example of networking where cyber-physical systems consisting of automatic sensors, actuators, and embedded systems are associated with the physical world including the human being for real-time support, security, personality, and high-level performance [1, 8]. IoT has great potential in manufacturing [3, 12].

Cyber-physical systems, smart devices, industrial instruments, sensors, actuators, and OPC Server are examples of IoT devices that produce heterogeneous data.

Data collected from the following IoT technologies play an important role:

1. *Radio-Frequency Identification (RFID)*: RFID technology uses electromagnetic fields for data transfer as well as automatic object detection [22]. It consists of tags and readers. Each device has a unique RFID tag. The reader detects objects by reading labels. Storing and managing RFID data is a challenge for large businesses as only certain items and products have RFID tags.
2. *Wireless Sensor Network (WSN)*: WSN is a network of distributed autonomous nodes connected to other nodes via wireless sensors in a limited environment [2, 22]. The sensor node is self-organizing and connected to other nodes to transmit its data back to the central grid. Some nodes have the ability to control actuators (physical devices) in the sense of automation. WSNs contain all the node information that have sensors and actuators to communicate and transfer their commands [3, 6].
3. *Cloud Computing*: Today, storage, computing power, infrastructure, platforms, and software can only be offered as a service by paying only as we use them. Infrastructure as a Service (IaaS), Platform as a Service (PaaS), and Software as a Service (SaaS) are the three main Cloud Computing models. The architecture of IoT Cloud Computing plays an important role for IoT data. They can be stored in Cloud and accessible from anywhere and anyone using an Internet browser or software [11].
4. *Industrial Internet*: The Industrial Internet, also known as the Industrial Internet of Things (IIoT), is the Internet of Things (IoT) only for industries. Smart machines link industrial world both internally and externally facilitating communication using advanced hardware and software [4].

4.3 Security

The security of IoT systems is one area of efforts to secure connected devices and networks on the Internet. The IoT involves the growing pervasiveness of objects and the entities provided with unique identifiers and the ability to automatically transmit data through a network. The major impact of the increased use of IoT communication came from computing devices and embedded sensor systems used in industrial machine-to-machine (M2M) communication and technologies such as smart energy grids, home and building automation, vehicle-to-vehicle communication, and wearable computing devices [2, 22, 63, 64].

The huge issue is that security has not always been considered in product design due to the idea of networking appliances and other objects were relatively new. Aiming to improve security and privacy issues, an IoT device that needs to be directly accessible through the Internet should be portioned into its own network and has limited network access. The network portion should be monitored in order to identify the potential abnormal traffic, and if there is any problem, action should be taken [2, 22, 63–65].

In the sector of IoT technology, there are system models. A wireless network model with a source-destination pair, N trusted relays, and J eavesdroppers ($J \le 1$) is considered. Suppose that the global CSE is available. The eavesdropper channel, source encoding schemes, decoding models, and accommodative protocol are admitted to be public; only source message is assumed to be confidential. In this work, the discussion is limited to two main accommodative models: Decode-and-Forward (DF) and Amplify-and-Forward (AF) [65–67].

4.3.1 Decode-and-Forward (DF)

Two are the main stages in DF model. In Stage 1, the source broadcasts its encoded symbols to its trusted relays using the first transmission slot. When the symbol x is transmitted, the received signals at the N relays are given by (21.1):

$$y_r = \sqrt{P_s} h_{SR}^* x + n_r \tag{21.1}$$

where P_s is the transmit power of source and n_r is the noise vector at relays [66].

In Stage 2, all the trusted relays that successfully decode the message re-encode the message and accommodatively transmit the re-encoded symbols to the destination by using the second transmission slot. Each relay transmits a weighted version of the re-encoded symbol. When transmitting the symbol $\tilde{x}$, the received signal at the destination is given by (21.2):

$$y_d = h_{RD}^{\dagger} w \tilde{x} + n_d \tag{21.2}$$

while the received signal at the listeners is expressed in vector form as (21.3):

$$y_e = H_{RE}^{\dagger} w\tilde{x} + n_e \qquad (21.3)$$

The transmit power budget for Stage 2 is considered to be $P - P_s$, where P is the total power for transmitting one symbol and P_s is the transmit power of source [66].

4.3.2 Amplify-and-Forward (AF)

The AF model is additionally a two-stage model just like the DF model. Stage 1 is similar for both AF and DF models, except that the transmit power can be different. The trusted relays forward the signals that are received during Stage 1 to the destination, using the second transmission slot in Stage 2. That is, each relay transmits a weighted version of the noisy signal that they received during Stage 1. The transmitted signals of all relays are denoted by the product of $diag\{w\}y_r$, where w is the weight vector and y_r is given by (21.1). The received signal at the destination is given by [66]:

$$y_d = \sqrt{P_s}h_{RD}^{\dagger}\text{diag}\{w\} h_{SR}^{*}x + h_{RD}^{\dagger}\text{diag}\{w\} n_r + n_d \qquad (21.4)$$

The received signals at the listeners, in a vector form, are denoted by [49]:

$$y_e = \sqrt{P_s}H_{RE}^{\dagger}\text{diag}\{w\} h_{SR}^{*}x + H_{RE}^{\dagger}\text{diag}\{w\} n_r + n_e \qquad (21.5)$$

Also, another security challenge in IoT is the encryption algorithm. The RSA algorithm is the most commonly used public key algorithm in the Internet, and it can be used in sensor networks by establishing a Trusted Platform Module (TPM), which costs less than 5% of a common sensor node [67]. So the memory has been measured for a fully authenticated handshake with 2048-bit RSA keys. This type of handshake has the largest memory requirements since it needs more code and buffer space for the client's Certificate and Certificate-Verify messages. The memory increased its use because the code basically contains hundreds of statements in the form buffer[x] = 0xff. The use of this encryption algorithm in IoT's security could offer better communication privacy in its functionality.

5 Cloud Computing

CC offers abilities and functions such as computing, storage, services, and applications over the Internet. In general, to render smartphones energy efficient and computationally capable, major changes to the hardware and software levels are required. This causes the cooperation of developers and manufacturers [68].

5.1 Features

Like all technologies, the CC technology has a number of characteristics which determine its operation. These characteristics are represented and outlined below.

CC(a): Storage Over Internet
Storage over Internet can be defined as "a technology framework that uses Transmission Control Protocol/Internet Protocol (TCP/IP) networks to link servers and storage devices and to facilitate storage solution deployment" [69, 70].

CC(b): Service Over Internet
The Service over Internet has a major objective: to "help customers all over the world in order to transform aspirations into achievements by harnessing the Internet's efficiency, speed and ubiquity" [69, 70].

CC(c): Applications Over Internet
Cloud Applications, or as scientific known as Applications over Internet, are the programs which have been written to do the job of a current manual task, or virtually anything, and which perform their job on the server through an Internet connection [69, 70].

CC(d): Energy Efficiency
Energy efficiency could be defined as "a way of managing and restraining the growth in energy consumption" [69, 70]. By delivering more services for the same energy input or for the same services for less energy input may be something more energy efficient [69, 70].

CC(e): Computationally Capable
The services of computational clouds are leveraging the computationally concentrated and ubiquitous mobile applications which have been enabled by the technology of MCC. Thus, a system can be considered as computationally capable when it meets the requirements to offer us the results we want by making the right calculations [69, 70].

5.2 Security on Cloud Computing

CC security is an evolving sub-domain of computer security, network security, and information security. It makes an allusion to a broad set of policies, technologies, and controls deployed to protect data, applications, and the associated infrastructure of CC.

CC technology offers through its storage solutions to users and industries various capabilities with the aim to store and process their data in third-party data centers [71]. Thus, by aiming to offer secure communication through the network, encryption algorithm plays a vital role. As regards the researches that have been made, an important encryption technique is the Symmetric Key Encryption. In Symmetric Key Encryption, only one key is used to encrypt and decrypt the data. In this encryption technique, the most used algorithm is the AES [72, 73].

AES (Advanced Encryption Standard) is the newest encryption standard and the more reliable, recommended by NIST to replace DES algorithm. The only effective scenario of attacking in AES is the brute force attack, in which the attacker tries to test all the character combinations to unlock the encryption. AES encryption model is fast and flexible, and in addition, it can be implemented on different platforms [74]. Below, a sample part of the AES encryption algorithm is represented.

Algorithm: Sample of AES

```
Cipher(byte[] input, byte[] output)
{
    byte[4,4] State;
    copy input[] into State[] AddRoundKey
    for (round = 1; round < Nr-1; ++round)
    {
        SubBytes ShiftRows MixColumns AddRoundKey
    }
    SubBytes ShiftRows AddRoundKey
    copy State[] to output[]
}
```

AES algorithm is characterized as better and safer than other algorithms for a number of reasons [75]:

- It performs consistently well in both hardware and software platforms under a wide range of environments. These include 8-bit and 64-bit platforms and DSPs.
- Its inherent parallelism facilitates efficient use of processor resources resulting in very good software performance.
- This algorithm has speedy key setup time and good key agility.
- It requires less memory for implementation, making it suitable for limited-space environments.
- The structure has good potential for benefiting from instruction-level parallelism.
- There are no serious weak keys in AES.
- It supports any block sizes and key sizes that are multiples of 32 (greater than 128 bits).
- Statistical analysis of the cipher text has not been possible even after using huge number of test cases.
- No differential and linear cryptanalysis attacks have been yet proved on AES.

5.3   Cloud Computing Trade-Offs

Cloud Computing has some disadvantages-limitations which should be eliminated over the years in order to achieve a better and more ideal use. Some businesses, especially the smaller ones, need to be aware of these limitations before going in for this technology.

CC(l-a): Security
One major issue of the Mobile Cloud Computing is the security issue. Before someone adopts this technology, they should know that all the company's sensitive information would be surrendered to a third-party Cloud service provider. This could potentially put the company in great risk. Hence, someone must be absolutely sure that they would choose the most reliable service provider, who will keep the information completely safe [11, 76, 77].

CC(l-b): Connectivity
Internet connection is critical to Cloud Computing. Thus, the user should be certain that there is a good result before opting for these services. Since someone having a mobile device which is connected to the Internet has become the norm in the wireless world of today, Cloud Computing has a very large potential user base [11, 78].

CC(l-c): Performance
Another major concern of the Cloud Computing pertains to its performance. Some users feel performance is not as good as in native applications. Thus, checking with one service provider and understanding their track record are advisable [11, 79, 80].

CC(l-d): Latency (Delay)
In Cloud Computing, latency (sometimes referred as turnaround time) is defined as the time involved in offloading the computation and getting back the results from the nearby infrastructure or cloud [11, 15].

CC(l-e): Privacy
Data privacy is important and is one of the main bottlenecks that restrict consumers from adopting Cloud Computing. Therefore, to gain consumers trust in the Cloud, the application models must support application development with privacy protection and implicit authentication mechanisms [11, 77, 81].

6   IoT and Cloud Computing Integration

Moreover, a new generation of services, counting on the concept of the "cloud computing," has made its appearance in the last few years with the purpose of offering access to services and the data from any place and at any time [82]. CC is a technology that can be set as a base technology in the use of IoT [68].

Table 21.2 Contributions of Cloud Computing in Internet of Things

Internet of Things characteristics	CC(a)	CC(b)	CC(c)	CC(d)	CC(e)
IoT(a)	X	X	X		X
IoT(b)	X	X		X	X
IoT(c)		X	X		X
IoT(d)	X	X	X	X	X
IoT(e)		X	X	X	X

A number of the major characteristics of the CC technology which relate to the features of IoT are (a) storage over Internet, (b) service over Internet, (c) applications over Internet, (d) energy efficiency, and (e) computationally capable. Table 21.2 presents the features of CC regarding the accessibility this technology provides when combined with the characteristics of IoT [68, 82].

Table 21.2 represents the characteristics of CC technology regarding the suitableness this technology provides. Furthermore, it enumerates the major features of the IoT technology. The main objective of Table 21.2 is to show which of the specific characteristics of CC technology relate more and improve the functionality of the characteristics of IoT technology. As we can observe from Table 21.2, the characteristic of IoT which is affected more by the characteristics of CC is "sensors in homes and airports." Regarding the CC, the features which are affected more are "service over Internet" and "computationally capable." As a general conclusion, we can observe that those two technologies contribute more each other in many of their features.

6.1   Security Issues in IoT and Cloud Computing Integration

There is a rapid and self-sufficient evolution taking into account the two technologies of IoT and CC. Initially, the virtually unlimited capabilities and resources of CC with aim to remunerate its technological constraints, such as processing, storage, and communication, could be a beneficial scenario for the IoT technology. In many cases, CC can offer the transitional layer between the things and the applications, hiding all the complexity and functionalities which are necessary to implement the latter [83].

Through the integration of IoT and CC, it could be observed that CC can fill some gaps of IoT such as the limited storage and applications over internet. On the other hand, IoT can also fill some gaps of CC such as the major problem of limited scope. Counting on motivations such those referred previously and the important issue of security in both technologies, we can consider some drivers for the integration. The security issue of this integration has a serious problem. When critical IoT applications move toward the CC technology, concerns arise due to the lack of trust in the service provider or the knowledge about service level agreements (SLAs) and knowledge about the physical location of data. Consequently, new challenges require particular attention as mentioned in surveys [84, 85]. Moreover,

Table 21.3 Effects of IoT and Cloud Computing security challenges

IoT and cloud computing security challenges	Internet of Things	Cloud computing
Heterogeneity		X
Performance	X	X
Reliability	X	
Big data	X	X
Monitoring	X	

public key cryptography could not be applied at all layers due to the computing power constraints imposed by the things [84]. These are examples of topics that are currently under examination in order to tackle the big challenge of security and privacy in CC and IoT integration [83].

Subsequently, some challenges about the security problem in the integration of those technologies are listed below [83].

1. *Heterogeneity*: A big challenge in CC and IoT integration is related to the wide heterogeneity of devices, operating systems, platforms, and services available and possibly used for new or improved applications [86].
2. *Performance*: Often CC and IoT integration's applications introduce particular performance and QoS requirements at several levels, and in some specific scenarios meeting requirements might not be easily achievable [87].
3. *Reliability*: When CC and IoT integration is adopted for mission-critical applications, reliability concerns typically arise [88].
4. *Big Data*: With an estimated number of 50 billion devices that will be networked by 2020, particular attention must be paid to transportation, storage, access, and processing of the large amount of data they will produce [89].
5. *Monitoring*: This is an essential activity in CC environments for capacity planning, for managing resources, SLAs, performance, and security, and for troubleshooting [90].

Table 21.3 shows the two technologies that we survey in this work and the challenges of their integration that arise from our study. These challenges are related to the security problem in the integration of the two aforementioned technologies, and they are listed in detail in Sect. 6.1. As we can observe from Table 21.3, both technologies have two common main challenges of their integration which are performance and Big Data. Additionally, we can observe that IoT technology is related to more challenges (4) than the CC technology (3).

6.2   Big Data Based on Cloud Server

In order to combine BD technology with CC technology and to achieve a beneficial operation of BD in Cloud environment, we have to study the relation of their basic features [3, 12, 22, 64].

Table 21.4 Correlation of BD and CC characteristics

Cloud computing features	Big data features				
	Volume	Velocity	Variety	Veracity	Value
Storage over Internet		X		X	X
Service over Internet	X		X	X	X
Applications over Internet	X	X	X	X	X
Energy efficiency	X	X			
Computationally capable		X	X		X

Initially, we have to define which are the basic features of BD, which are widely known as the 5 Vs of Big Data. In particular, the 5 Vs of BD are the following:

(1) *Volume*: the vast amounts of data created every second,
(2) *Velocity*: the speed at which new data is created and the speed at which data moves around,
(3) *Variety*: the different types of data we can now use. In the past we focused on structured data that neatly fits into tables or relational databases, such as financial data,
(4) *Veracity*: the messiness or trustworthiness of the data, and
(5) *Value*: all well and good having access to big data but unless we can turn it into value, it is useless [22, 64].

Table 21.4 demonstrates the basic features of BD (5 Vs) and how they are contributed by the major features of CC. As we can observe, there are two key features of BD technology which contribute more with the characteristics of CC technology: *Velocity* and *Value*. *Velocity* and *Value* contribute four from the five key features of CC. Also, another thing that we can observe from Table 21.4 is that the feature *Applications over Internet* contributed from all the key features of BD.

6.3 Proposed Efficient IoT and Cloud Computing Security Model

As we can infer, by taking advantage of the reasons which AES algorithm offers better security in CC and the two models that give benefits in security problems in IoT, we can propose a novel method that uses those benefits with the aim to improve the security and privacy problems in the integration of two technologies.

The AES algorithm offers the ability to have speedy key setup time and good key agility. So, if we use this algorithm in the functionality of DF model, we could have a trusted relay method with an encryption of a speed key setup. Therefore, instead the trust relay use that DF and AF methods offer we can seize additionally there no serious weak keys in AES and so we could have a beneficial security use of the encryption in the integrated new model. Moreover, we can take advantage of the less memory which AES needs for implementation that makes it for restricted-space environments. So we can seize the transmit power that the AF model offers, and as a result, we can have a better and more trusted transmission. In the way of transmission, when the symbol is transmitted with the use of DF model, the received signal at destination is given by Eq. (21.2), which was mentioned in the previous section.

With this proposed model, we can extend the advances of IoT and CC by developing a highly innovative and scalable service platform to enable security and privacy services. Through this research, we can propose the following part of algorithm which extends the security advances of both technologies. A proposal of this work could be this part of pseudocode algorithm which uses the original key consisting of 128 bits/16 bytes represented as a 6×6 matrix, as shown below.+

Algorithm 1: Pseudocode

```
input -> byte[]
byte[] + R.Key -> state[]
for 6 to 66
    W[i-1] -> T
    if i mod 6 = 0
            rotate T + 6
    W[i-6] / T -> W[i]
    R.Key+1
    i+1 -> i
Row +1 -> Row
state[] -> output[]
```

Algorithm 1 represents the procedure implemented in the server aiming to achieve better results of securing the data transmitted. Moreover, this procedure could be achieved in a limited number of loops of the algorithm. The algorithm takes as input data the transmitted signal and then with the use of AES algorithm and the key generated tries to decrypt the data by using the original key consisting of 128 bits/16 bytes which are represented as a 6×6 matrix. Through this procedure, we could achieve the less of loops of the algorithm, and in addition to this, we can achieve a more secure data decryption/encryption system for transmitting the data through the network.

Figure 21.1 shows the proposed pseudocode representation through a flowchart.

6.4 Experimental Results

Considering the benefits of the security models and algorithms of IoT and CC technologies, we can observe that we can have a beneficial use of their integration. Instead of the wide use of IoT, we can take advantage that CC security through the AES algorithm performs consistently well in both hardware and software platforms

Fig. 21.1 Flowchart of the
proposed procedure
implementation

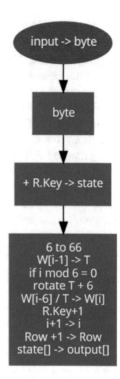

under a wide range of environments. This use could be possible for all types of platforms and DSPs. Furthermore, the novel integrated technology could have good potential for benefiting from instruction-level parallelism and will support any type of block sizes and key sizes that are multiples of 32 and used both of IoT and CC. Also, each transmitted signal through the new technology can be transmitted as a relay and trusted signal with a weighted version of the re-encoded symbol.

Through this integration, we can achieve some useful functions, i.e., we can use the Cloud-based IoT service with the aim to connect sensors and additionally make them capable to share the sensor readings with others, reducing the security issues. Furthermore, another useful operation is that we can use the HTTP protocol with the aim to send data between IoT and the CC applications. Moreover, some of the key advantages and challenges that can be defined from this integration are the following:

(1) Both the physical hardware manufacturing resource and software manufacturing can be intelligently perceived and connected into the wider networks with the support of IoT technologies.
(2) The collected information and data can be communicated and transmitted between M2M under the support of specific IoT technologies.
(3) The collected and transmitted information can be processed and computed according to particular requirements under the support of different CC service, and some useful data and decision information can be intelligently generated and obtained.

Table 21.5 exhibits the key features of the two encryption algorithms that are used with the aim to achieve integration of the technologies of IoT and CC concerning the security problem. Table 21.5 presents which of the key features of AES encryption algorithm contribute both IoT and CC technologies and at the end how completely contributes the integration model of IoT and CC.

Figure 21.2 shows the measurements that have been through time. As we can observe by this figure, the more often is the combined use of the algorithms, the higher level of security of the data usage we get every time. The upper line represents our proposed model of AES algorithm, and the other (down line) represents the existing AES algorithm.

Table 21.6 exhibits the key features of BD and which of those characteristics could be contributed by the integration method of the technologies IoT and CC concerning the security problem. Table 21.6 presents that all the characteristics of BD contributed by the integration model of IoT and CC technologies.

Table 21.5 AES contribution in IoT and Cloud computing

AES characteristics	Internet of Things	Cloud computing	IoT and CC integration
Key length	X	X	X
Rounds		X	X
Certifications	X	X	X
Speed	X		X

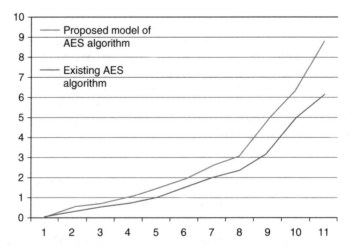

Fig. 21.2 Security level of encryption algorithms of measurement used for the study of AES model algorithm

Table 21.6 Correlation of BD characteristics with IoT and CC integration model

Big data features	Volume	Velocity	Variety	Veracity	Value
IoT and CC integration model	X	X	X	X	X

7 Conclusions

The CC technology provides a number of possibilities, but additionally places several limitations. Cloud Computing refers to an infrastructure where both the data storage and the data processing happen outside of the mobile device. Also, the IoT is a new technology which is growing rapidly in the field of telecommunications and especially in the modern sector of wireless telecommunications.

The main objective of the interaction and cooperation between things and objects sent through the wireless networks is to fulfill the objective set to them as a combined entity, with the aim to achieve a better environment for the use of Big Data. In addition, based on the technology of wireless networks, both the technologies of CC and IoT develop rapidly. In this work, we present a survey of IoT and CC with a focus on the security problems of both technologies. Particularly, we combine the two aforementioned technologies with the aim to examine the familiar characteristics and with the aim to discover the benefits of their integration in order to secure the use and the transmission of Big Data.

At the end, the security challenges of the integration of IoT and CC were surveyed through the proposed algorithm model, and additionally there is a presentation of how the two encryption algorithms which were used contribute in the integration of IoT and CC as base technologies for Big Data. This and additionally the security challenges surveyed in this work can be the domain of future research on the integration of those two technologies.

Acknowledgment The authors would like to thank the anonymous reviewers for their valuable comments and feedback which were extremely helpful in improving the quality of the paper.

References

1. Atzori, L., Iera, A., & Morabito, G. (2010). The internet of things: A survey. *Computer Networks, 54*(15), 2787–2805. https://doi.org/10.1016/j.comnet.2010.05.010.
2. Stergiou, C., Psannis, K. E., Kim, B.-G., & Gupta, B. (2016). Secure integration of IoT and cloud computing. *Future Generation Computer Systems, 78*, 964–975.
3. Plageras, A. P., Psannis, K. E., Stergiou, C., Wang, H., & Gupta, B. B. (2018). Efficient IoT-based sensor big data collection-processing and analysis in smart buildings. *Future Generation Computer Systems, 82*, 349–357.
4. Hilbert, M., & López, P. (2011). The world's technological capacity to store, communicate, and compute information. *Science, 332*(6025), 60–65.
5. Fu, Z., Ren, K., Shu, J., Sun, X., & Huang, F. (2015). Enabling personalized search over encrypted out-sourced data with efficiency improvement. *IEEE Transactions on Parallel and Distributed Systems, 27*(9), 2546–2559.
6. Mongay Batalla, J., & Krawiec, P. (2014). Conception of ID layer performance at the network level for internet of things. *Personal and Ubiquitous Computing, 18*(2), 465–480.
7. Stergiou, C., & Psannis, K. E. (2017). Efficient and secure big data delivery in cloud computing. *Multimedia Tools and Applications, 76*(21), 22803–22822.

8. Stergiou, C., Psannis, K. E., Plageras, A. P., Kokkonis, G., & Ishibashi, Y. (2017, June 19–21). Architecture for security in IoT environments. In *Proceedings of 26th IEEE International Symposium on Industrial Electronics*, Edinburgh, Scotland.

9. Sfar, A. R., Natalizio, E., Challal, Y., & Chtourou, Z. (2018). A roadmap for security challenges in internet of things. *Digital Communications and Networks (DCN), 4*(2), 18–137.

10. Kryftis, Y., Mastorakis, G., Mavromoustakis, C., Mongay Batalla, J., Pallis, E., & Kormentzas, G. (2016). Efficient entertainment services provision over a novel network architecture. *IEEE Wireless Communications Magazine, 23*, 14.

11. Stergiou, C., & Psannis, K. E. (2016). Recent advances delivered by mobile cloud computing and internet of things for big data applications: A survey. *International Journal of Network Management, 27*, 1–12.

12. Stergiou, C., Psannis, K. E., Plageras, A. P., Ishibashi, Y., & Kim, B.-G. (2018). Algorithms for efficient digital media transmission over IoT and cloud networking. *Journal of Multimedia Information System, 5*(1), 1–10.

13. Stergiou, C., Psannis, K. E., Plageras, A. P., Kokkonis, G., & Ishibashi, Y. (2017, June). Architecture for security monitoring in IoT environments. In *Proceedings of IEEE 26th international symposium on industrial electronics*, Edinburgh, Scotland.

14. Plageras, A. P., Psannis, K. E., Ishibashi, Y., & Kim, B.-G. (2016, October). IoT-based surveillance system for ubiquitous healthcare. In *Proceedings of IEEE/IECON 2016 - 42nd Annual Conference of the IEEE*, Industrial Electronics Society.

15. Li, J., Huang, L., Zhou, Y., He, S., & Ming, Z. (2017). Computation partitioning for mobile cloud computing in a big data environment. *IEEE Transactions on Industrial Informatics, 13*, 2009–2018.

16. Yu, R., Huang, X., Kang, J., Ding, J., Maharjan, S., Gjessing, S., & Zhang, Y. (2015). Cooperative resource management in cloud-enabled vehicular networks. *IEEE Transactions on Industrial Informatics, 62*(12), 7938–7951.

17. Agrawal, D., Gupta, B. B., Yamaguchi, S., & Psannis, K. E. (2018). Recent advances in mobile cloud computing. *Wireless Communications and Mobile Computing, 2018*, 5895817.

18. Ali, A. M. M., Ahmad, N. M., & Amin, A. H. M. (2014, December). Cloudlet-based cyber foraging framework for distributed video surveillance provisioning. In *2014 Fourth World Congress on Information and Communication Technologies (WICT)*, Bandar Hilir, Malaysia.

19. Rahimi, M. R., Ren, J., Liu, C. H., Vasilakos, A., & Venkatasubramanian, N. (2014). Mobile cloud computing: A survey, state of art and future directions. *Mobile Networks and Applications, 19*(2), 133–143.

20. Fremdt, S., Beck, R., & Weber, S. (2013, October) Does cloud computing matter? An analysis of the cloud model software-as-a-service and its impact on operational agility. In *46th Hawaii International Conference on System Sciences* (pp. 1025–1034).

21. Stergiou, C., & Psannis, K. E. (2017, July 24–26). Algorithms for big data in advanced communication systems and cloud computing. In *Proceedings of 19th IEEE Conference on Business Informatics 2017 (CBI2017)*, Doctoral Consortium, Thessaloniki, Greece.

22. Plageras, A. P., Stergiou, C., Psannis, K. E., Kim, B.-G., Gupta, B., & Ishibashi, Y. (2017, July 24–26). Solutions for inter-connectivity and security in a smart hospital building. In *Proceedings of 15th IEEE International Conference on Industrial Informatics (INDIN 2017)*, Emden, Germany.

23. Thirumalai, C., & Kar, H. (2018, April 21–22). Memory efficient multi key (MEMK) generation scheme for secure transportation of sensitive data over cloud and IoT devices. In *IEEE, Proceedings of 2017 Innovations in Power and Advanced Computing Technologies (i-PACT)*, Vellore, India.

24. Plageras, A. P., Stergiou, C., Psannis, K. E., Kokkonis, G., Ishibashi, Y., Kim, B.-G., et al. (2017, July 24–26). Efficient large-scale medical data (eHealth big data) analytics in internet of things. In *Proceedings of 19th IEEE International Conference on Business Informatics (CBI'17), International Workshop on the Internet of Things and Smart Services (ITSS2017)*, Thessaloniki, Greece.

25. Stergiou, C., Psannis, K. E., Plageras, A. P., Xifilidis, T., & Gupta, B. B. (2018, April 15–20). Security and privacy of big data for social networking services in cloud. In *Proceedings of IEEE conference on Computer Communications (IEEE INFOCOM 2018)*, Honolulu, HI.
26. Angin, P., Bhargava, B., Ranchal, R., Singh, N., & Linderman, M. (2010, October 31–November 3). An entity-centric approach for privacy and identity management in cloud computing. In *Proceedings of 29th IEEE International Symposium on Reliable Distributed Systems*, New Delhi, India. https://doi.org/10.1109/SRDS.2010.28.
27. Doukas, C, Pliakas, T., & Maglogiannis, I. (2010, August 31–September 4). Mobile healthcare information management utilizing cloud computing and android OS. In *Proceedings of 32nd Annual International Conference of the IEEE EMBS 2010*, Buenos Aires, Argentina.
28. Dinh, H. T., Lee, C., Niyato, D., & Wang, P. (2011). A survey of mobile cloud computing: Architecture, applications, and approaches. *Wireless Communications and Mobile Computing, 13*, 1587–1611. https://doi.org/10.1002/wcm.1203.
29. Habib, S. M., Ries, S., & Muhlhauser, M. (2011, November 16–18). Towards a trust management system for cloud computing. In *Proceedings of IEEE International Joint Conference TrustCom-11/IEEE ICESS-11/FCST-11*, Changsha, China.
30. Prasad, M. R., Gyani, J., & Murti, P. R. K. (2012). Mobile cloud computing: Implications and challenges. *Journal of Information Engineering and Applications, 2*(7), 7–15.
31. Shiraz, M., Gani, A., Khokhar, R. H., & Buyya, R. (2012). A review on distributed application processing frameworks in smart mobile devices for mobile cloud computing. *IEEE Communications Surveys & Tutorials, 15*(3), 1294–1313.
32. Kim, M., & Park, S. O. (2013). Trust management on user behavioral patterns for a mobile cloud computing. *Cluster Computing, 16*(4), 725–731. https://doi.org/10.1007/s10586-013-0248-9.
33. Stergiou, C., Psannis, K. E., & Gupta, B. B. (2019) Advanced media-based smart big data on intelligent cloud systems. *IEEE Transactions on Sustainable Computing, 4*(1), 77–87.
34. Gnana Singh, A. A., Tamizhpoonguil, B., & Jebamalar Leavline, E. (2016). A survey on big data and cloud computing. *International Journal on Recent and Innovation Trends in Computing and Communication, 7*(4), 273–277.
35. Awodele, O., Izang, A. A., Kuyoro, S. O., & Osisanwo, F. Y. (2016). Big data and cloud computing issues. *International Journal of Computer Applications, 12*(133), 14–19.
36. Rallapallia, S., Gondkar, R. R., & Ketavarapu, U. P. K. (2015, December). Impact of processing and analyzing healthcare big data on cloud computing environment by implementing Hadoop cluster. In *International Conference on Computational Modeling and Security (CMS2016)* (pp. 16–22).
37. Hernandez-Ramos, J. L., Moreno, M. V., Bernabe, J. B., Carrillo, D. G., & Skarmeta, A. F. (2015). SAFIR: Secure access framework for IoT-enabled services on smart buildings. *Journal of Computer and System Sciences, 81*(8), 1452–1463.
38. Moreno, M. V., Dufour, L., Skarmeta, A. F., Jara, A. J., Genoud, D., Ladevie, B., & Bezian, J.-J. (2016). Big data: The key to energy efficiency in smart buildings. *Soft Computing, 20*(5), 1749–1762.
39. Shah, J., & Mishra, B. (2016). Customized IoT enabled wireless sensing and monitoring platform for smart buildings. *Procedia Technology, 23*, 256–263.
40. Ben Sta, H. (2017). Quality and the efficiency of data in "smart-cities". *Future Generation Computer Systems, 74*, 409–416.
41. Li, J., Zhang, Y., Chen, X., & Xiang, Y. (2018). Secure attribute-based data sharing for resource-limited users in cloud computing. *Computers & Security, 72*, 1–12.
42. Qiu, M., Gai, K., Thuraisingham, B., Tao, L., & Zhao, H. (2018). Proactive user-centric secure data scheme using attribute-based semantic access controls for mobile clouds in financial industry. *Future Generation Computer Systems, 80*, 421–429.
43. Elhoseny, M., Ramirez-Gonzalez, G., Abu-Elnasr, O. M., Shawkat, S. A., Arunkumar, N., & Farouk, A. (2018). Secure medical data transmission model for IoT-based healthcare systems. *IEEE Access, 6*, 20596–20608.

44. Hamida, E. B., Noura, H., & Znaidi, W. (2015). Security of cooperative intelligent transport systems: Standards, threats analysis and cryptographic countermeasures. *Electronics, 4*(3), 380–423.
45. Dastjerdi, A. V., & Buyya, R. (2016). Fog computing: Helping the internet of things realize its potential. *IEEE Computer, 49*(8), 112–116.
46. Barreno, M., Nelson, B., Sears, R., Joseph, A. D., & Tygar, J. D. (2006, March 21–24). Can machine learning be secure? In *ACM, in Proceedings of the 2006 ACM Symposium on Information, Computer And Communications Security, ASIACCS '06*, Taipei, Taiwan (pp. 16–25).
47. Liao, X., Ding, L., & Wang, Y. (2011, June 27–29). Secure machine learning, a brief overview. In *IEEE, Proceedings of 2011 Fifth International Conference on Secure Software Integration and Reliability Improvement – Companion*, Jeju Island, South Korea.
48. Barreno, M., Nelson, B., Joseph, A. D., & Tygar, J. D. (2010). The security of machine learning. *Machine Learning, 81*(2), 121–148.
49. Bonawitz, K., Ivanov, V., Kreuter, B., Marcedone, A., McMahan, H. B., Patel, S., et al. (2017, October 30–November 3). Practical secure aggregation for privacy-preserving machine learning. In *ACM, Proceedings of the 2017 ACM SIGSAC Conference on Computer and Communications Security, CCS '17*, Dallas, TX (pp. 1175–1191).
50. Demontis, A., Melis, M., Biggio, B., Maiorca, D., Arp, D., Rieck, K., et al. (2017). Yes, machine learning can be more secure! A case study on android malware detection. *IEEE Transactions on Dependable and Secure Computing (Early Access), 16*(4), 711–724.
51. Sheng, Y.-B., & Zhou, L. (2017). Distributed secure quantum machine learning. *Science Bulletin, 64*(14), 1025–1029.
52. Bello-Orgaz, G., Jung, J. J., & Camacho, D. (2016). Social big data: Recent achievements and new challenges. *Information Fusion, 28*, 45–59.
53. Gandomi, A., & Haider, M. (2015). Beyond the hype: Big data concepts, methods, and analytics. *International Journal of Information Management, 35*(2), 137–144.
54. Kaur, N., & Sood, S. K. (2017). Dynamic resource allocation for big data streams based on data characteristics (5Vs). *International Journal of Network Management, 27*(4), e1978.
55. Hu, H., Wen, Y., Chua, T. S., & Li, X. (2014). Toward scalable systems for big data analytics: A technology tutorial. *IEEE Access, 2*, 652–687.
56. Rajaraman, V. (2016). Big data analytics. *Resonance, 21*(8), 695–716.
57. Alexandrov, A., Bergmann, R., Ewen, S., Freytag, J. C., Hueske, F., Heise, A., et al. (2014). The stratosphere platform for big data analytics. *The VLDB Journal, 23*(6), 939–964.
58. Kwon, O., Lee, N., & Shin, B. (2014). Data quality management, data usage experience and acquisition intention of big data analytics. *International Journal of Information Management, 34*(3), 387–394.
59. Müller, K., Schwarz, H., Marpe, D., Bartnik, C., Bosse, S., & Brust, H. (2013). 3D high-efficiency video coding for multi-view video and depth data. *IEEE Transactions on Image Processing, 9*(22), 3366–3378.
60. Shen, L., Liu, Z., Zhang, X., Zhao, W., & Zhang, Z. (2013). An effective CU size decision method for HEVC encoders. *IEEE Transactions on Multimedia, 2*(15), 465–470.
61. Ohm, J.-R., Sullivan, G. J., Schwarz, H., Tan, T. K., & Wiegand, T. (2012). Comparison of the coding efficiency of video coding standards – including high efficiency video coding (HEVC). *IEEE Transactions on Circuits and Systems for Video Technology, 12*(22), 1669–1684.
62. Batalla, J. M. (2015). Advanced multimedia service provisioning based on efficient interoperability of adaptive streaming protocol and high efficient video coding. *Journal of Real-Time Image Processing, 12*(2), 443–454.
63. Rouse, M. (2015, November 1). IoT security (internet of things security). *IoT Agenda* [Online]. Retrieved July 27, 2016, from http://internetofthingsagenda.techtarget.com/definition/IoT-security-Internet-of-Things-security
64. Plageras, A. P., & Psannis, K. E. (2017, July 24–26). Algorithms for big data delivery over the internet of things. In *Proceedings of 19th IEEE Conference on Business Informatics 2017 (CBI2017)*, Doctoral Consortium, Thessaloniki, Greece.

65. Dong, L., Han, Z., Petropulu, A. P., & Poor, H. V. (2010). Improving wireless physical layer security via cooperating relays. *IEEE Transactions on Signal Processing, 58*(3), 1875–1888.
66. Nair, A., Shaniba Asmi, P., & Aloor, G. (2016). Analysis of physical layer security via co-operative communication in internet of things. *International Conference on Emerging Trends in Engineering, Science and Technology (ICETEST - 2015), 24*, 896–903.
67. Hu, W., Tan, H., Corke, P., Shih, W. C., & Jha, S. (2010). Toward trusted wireless sensor networks. *ACM Transactions on Sensor Networks, 7*(5), 1–25.
68. Huang, D. (2011). Mobile cloud computing. *IEEE COMSOC Multimedia Communications Technical Committee (MMTC) E-Letter, 6*(10), 27–31.
69. Haque, M. N., Chowdhury, M. R. K., Gani, A., & Whaiduzzaman, M. (2014). A study on strategic provision of cloud computing services. *The Scientific World Journal, 2014*, 1–8.
70. Garg, S. K., Versteeg, S., & Buyya, R. (2013). A framework for ranking of cloud computing services. *Future Generation Computer Systems, 29*(4), 1012–1023.
71. Haghighat, M., Zonouz, S., & Abdel-Mottaleb, M. (2015). CloudID: Trustworthy cloud-based and cross-enterprise biometric identification. *Expert Systems with Applications, 11*(42), 7905–7916.
72. Kumar, Y., Munjal, R., & Sharma, H. (2011). Comparison of symmetric and asymmetric cryptography with existing vulnerabilities and countermeasures. *IJCSMS International Journal of Computer Science and Management Studies, 11*(3), 68–76.
73. Kaur, R., & Kinger, S. (2014). Analysis of security algorithms in cloud computing. *International Journal of Application or Innovation in Engineering & Management (IJAIEM), 3*(3), 171–176.
74. Singh, G., & Kinger, S. (2013). Integrating AES, DES, and 3-DES encryption algorithms for enhanced data security. *International Journal of Scientific & Engineering Research, 4*(7), 2058.
75. Sachdev, A., & Bhansali, M. (2013). Enhancing cloud computing security using AES algorithm. *International Journal of Computer Applications, 9*(67), 19–23.
76. Viswanathan, P. (2012, July 7). Cloud computing – is it really all that beneficial? *abouttech* [Online]. Retrieved May 24, 2017, from http://mobiledevices.about.com/od/additionalresources/a/Cloud-Computing-Is-It-Really-All-That-Beneficial.htm
77. Pfarr, F., Buckel, T., & Winkelmann, A. (2014, January 6–9). Cloud computing data protection – a literature review and analysis. In *Proceedings of 47th Hawaii International Conference on System Sciences*, Waikoloa, HI (pp. 5018–5027).
78. Almrot, E., & Andersson, S. (2013, May). *A study of the advantages and disadvantages of mobile cloud computing versus native environment.* Digitala Vetenskapliga Arkivet, Bachelor Thesis in Software Engineering, Blekinge Institute of Technology, Karlskrona.
79. Fremdt, S., Beck, R., & Weber, S. (2013, January 7–10). Does cloud computing matter? An analysis of the cloud model software-as-a-service and its impact on operational agility. In *Proceedings of 46th Hawaii International Conference on System Sciences 2013*, Wailea, Maui, HI (pp. 1025–1034).
80. Blog: Follow what's happening at Get Cloud Services. (2014, December 23). Mobile cloud computing – pros and cons. *GetCloud Services* [Online]. Retrieved December 24, 2017, from https://www.getcloudservices.com/blog/mobile-cloud-computing-pros-and-cons/
81. Shi, E., Niu, Y., Jakobsoon, M., & Chow, R. (2010, October 25–28). Implicit authentication through learning user behavior. In *ACM, Proceedings of ISC'10 13th International Conference on Information Security*, Boca Raton, FL (pp. 99–113).
82. Mell, P., Grance, T. (2011) *The NIST definition of cloud computing.* Recommendations of the National Institute of Standards and Technology, Special Publication 800–145. Computer Security Division, Information Technology Laboratory, National Institute of Standards and Technology, Gaithersburg. MD 20899–8930.
83. Botta, A., de Donato, W., Persico, V., & Pescapè, A. (2016). Integration of cloud computing and internet of things: A survey. *Journal of Future Generation Computer Systems, 56*, 684–700.
84. Bhattasali, T., Chaki, R., & Chaki, N. (2013). Secure and trusted cloud of things. In: *India Conference (INDICON), 2013 Annual IEEE* (pp. 1–6).

85. Simmhan, Y., Kumbhare, A. G., Cao, B., & Prasanna, V. (2011). An analysis of security and privacy issues in smart grid software architectures on clouds. In: *Cloud Computing (CLOUD), IEEE International Conference on IEEE* (pp. 582–589).

86. Grozev, N., & Buyya, R. (2014). Inter-cloud architectures and application brokering: Taxonomy and survey. *Software: Practice and Experience, 44*(3), 369–390.

87. Rao, B. P., Saluia, P., Sharma, N., Mittal, A., & Sharma, S. V. (2012). Cloud computing for internet of things and sensing based applications. In: *Sensing Technology (ICST), 2012 Sixth International Conference on IEEE* (pp. 374–380).

88. He, W., Yan, G., & Xu, L. D. (2014). Developing vehicular data cloud services in the IoT environment. *IEEE Transactions on Industrial Informatics, 10*(2), 1587–1595.

89. Dobre, C., & Xhafa, F. (2014). Intelligent services for big data science. *Future Generation Computer Systems, 37*, 267–281.

90. Aceto, G., Botta, A., de Donato, W., & Pescapè, A. (2013). Cloud monitoring: A survey. *Computer Networks, 57*(9), 2093–2115.

Chapter 22
Heterogeneous-Internet of Vehicles (Het-IoV) in Twenty-First Century: A Comprehensive Study

Richa, T. P. Sharma, and Ajay Kumar Sharma

Abstract Internet of vehicles (IoV) is considered one of the biggest innovations in the transportation world. IoV technology alludes to the advancement and deployment of an effective platform that takes into account the growth, expansion, integration of new technologies, and complex human interactions. The versatile mobile cellular systems are equipped for giving incredible coverage to vehicular clients, yet the prerequisite of stringent real-time security services cannot continuously be ensured in mobile systems. Consequently, the heterogeneous vehicular system (Het-VANET), which incorporates cellular systems with DSRC, develops as a promising answer to meet the correspondences necessities of the intelligent transportation system (ITS). In heterogeneous-IoV (HET-IoV), connectivity and near-field communications create enormous new interactive features which are presuming as to provide promising proposal to transform the operation and role for industrial systems such as transportation systems and manufacturing systems. The main motivation behind HET-IoV concept is to give advance connectivity, the pervasive presence of things and make efficient use of radio resources for these networks. Subsequently, the quick evolution of computing and communications technologies gives rise to vehicles with powerful computing abilities that are not limited to service recipients but also advocated service providers. This results with the idea of vehicular cloud computing (VCC) that collectively uses computational, communicative, and storage resources inside vehicle equipment, for example, on-board units, communications devices, or mobile user equipment arrived by passengers. Vehicular cloud computing (VCC) provides a new management mechanism for big data that enables the processing of data and the mining of valuable knowledge from it. Regardless, to the best of our knowledge, these works don't have a point by point examination of the new VCC perspective, which incorporates absolutely new applications, difficulties, and research issues. To associate this gap, this chapter gives an audit on the compromise

Richa (✉) · T. P. Sharma
CSE Department, NIT Hamirpur, Hamirpur, Himachal Pradesh, India
e-mail: teek@nith.ac.in

A. K. Sharma
CSE Department, NIT Jalandhar, Jalandhar, Punjab, India

© Springer Nature Switzerland AG 2020
B. B. Gupta et al. (eds.), *Handbook of Computer Networks and Cyber Security*,
https://doi.org/10.1007/978-3-030-22277-2_22

of Cloud and IoV. Starting by portraying fundamentals of IoV, heterogeneous vehicular access technologies and VCC analyze their characteristics, coordination, and challenges. In addition, it also provides a state-of-art picture of the heterogeneous vehicular communication model. Because of the reception of vehicular cloud, they both perform a powerful innovation by managing storage, on-demand retrieving of data, data dissemination in sparse environments, and security, with an attention on recent research challenges.

Keywords IoV · VCC · GPS · LTE-V · ITS

1 Introduction

Internet of vehicles (IoV) is another insurgency that is quickly developing in the field of the transportation world. The advent of the intelligent transportation system (ITS) has open doors for numerous studies related to vehicular communications. IoV is a network infrastructure of smart intelligent vehicles with self-configuring capabilities based on communication protocol and technologies, for example, sensing, Bluetooth, RFID, Wi-Fi, and global positioning system (GPS) that play a significant role for the development of ITS by increasing capacity of existing transportation network and roadside safety of travelers. IoV comprises of devices connected inside the vehicle car together or with networks, services, and devices outside the car that includes homes, infrastructure, offices, and many more. Overall, IoV has changed the transformational journey of emerging technologies and this will have a great impact on our daily transportation lives. These vehicles are no longer just a piece of machinery but a computerized system and highly sophisticated electronic devices with thousands of sensors embedded in them. The driverless vehicles are also gaining momentum around the globe for that an IoV paradigm is a must. Also, the mobility industry is bringing into light completely new business models to the transportation market [1]. Recently Qualcomm Connected Car Reference Platform is introduced by Qualcomm which aims to accelerate the advancements and complexity in connectivity among next-generation vehicles. The various automobile designed by Qualcomm equipped with latest advancements in 4G LTE, vehicle to everything (V2X), communication, Wi-Fi, Bluetooth which helps to resolve various challenges like future-proofing, wireless coexistence, and support for large number of in-car hardware architectures which further motivates the transportation industry to fill the gaps to resolve these issues which still requires further improvements. Qualcomm Snapdragon X12 and X5 LTE modems are the Qualcomm technologies automotive product for the platform which also features in vehicles networking technologies such as controller area network (CAN) interfaces and gigabit open alliance broad reach (OABR) Ethernet with automotive audio bus (A2B).

It is estimated that 10 billion IoV vehicles will be connected over the Internet by the year 2030 [2]. At present, many researcher, scientists, and engineers are more focusing on to developing smart environment applications, for example, smart parking, smart city, intelligent traffic management, security, and privacy for efficient dissemination of information to enhance and uplift the economic growth of the transport world. To achieve these, heterogeneous-vehicular networks are proposed that have the potential to supervise and guide vehicles and provide the necessary communication platform for unlimited Internet connectivity and access multimedia related applications. In addition, these networks feature low latency and high-reliability communications making this heterogeneous vehicular network vulnerable for safety-critical ITS applications. These developments in technology stimulate and motivate us to survey previous work, design new techniques, and find new applications of IoV. However, the most important barrier is that most organization and ventures don't know what to do with the Internet of vehicles. With the point of investigating HET-IoV communication paradigm and vehicular cloud computing designs, this study is conducted. Likewise, this work is impelled by the necessity for organizing communication models, as will be required later on to oblige trillions of vehicular gadgets.

The responsibilities of this study are numerous:

- Firstly, this chapter investigates the features and reports the premier research propels made in HET-IoV design recently.
- Secondly, it categorizes and classifies the IoV and HET-IoV communication structures and devises a scientific categorization.
- Additionally, it identifies and plots the key prerequisites for future vehicular cloud-based design issues and big data analytics concept in IoV.
- A few prominent case studies on smart vehicles pragmatic best practices are discovered and presented.

1.1 Evolution of Vehicular Paradigm from VANET toward IoV

During early 1991, in the USA, the Intermodal Surface Transportation Efficiency Act (ISTEA) generated the program for automated highway system (AHS) [2] and the concept demonstration was held in San Diego, California in late 1997. The major turnover in the field of the Internet of vehicles happened with the accretion of GPS enabled inside vehicle navigation devices combined with the mobile communication network in the early 2000s. The US Department of Transportation (DOT) has developed the vehicle-infrastructure integration program (VII) as a crucial part of intelligent transportation program. The motive of this program was to develop wireless vehicle to vehicle (V2V) and vehicle to infrastructure (V2I) communication to improve mobility and safety of nation's roadways [1]. The US DOT proposed dedicated short range communication (DSRC) to use V2I and V2V communication aimed to reduce crashes on roadways and congestion to improve mobility. Connections with traffic signals or any stationary devices lead to V2I communication whereas others just roll down into V2V. In 1999, the US FCC distributed 75 MHz of authorized spectrum in the 5.9 GHz band to DSRC. In addition,

USDOT appraises that V2V interchanges in view of DSRC can take out up to 82% of all accidents including healthy drivers in the USA, and around 40% of all accidents happened at crossing points [3]. These insights suggest the colossal potential for DSRC innovation to diminish crashes and to upgrade security for the driving open. In February 2014, US National Highway Traffic Safety Administration (NHTSA) proposed to start a V2V administer that monitors the life-saving communications technology properly introduced in every single new vehicle and light trucks [15].

It is estimated that 10 billion IoV vehicles will be connected over the Internet by the year 2030 [3]. As a consequence, there is a stringent need for the heterogeneous vehicular network vulnerable to safety-critical ITS applications. Heterogeneous vehicular networks use different radio access technologies (RATs) like LTE-V, 5G, Wi-Fi, WiMAX, LTE-D2D, vehicular cloud, and big data analytics that incorporated for communication in IoV. Various technology giants have been investing in IoV concept with the ultimate motive to develop an automated vehicular system with precisions; to this precision advancement in machine learning, computations made it possible to invent real-time image recognition systems that play a turning point in the development of connected vehicles [4]. The ultimate goal is to provide security and comfort to the passengers sitting in the vehicles, subsequently, there is a requirement of optimized solutions for efficient information dissemination algorithms for heterogeneous networks.

Next section will discuss the key aspects of IoV that are used to set up communication among vehicles along with another heterogeneous network. Furthermore, with the developing innovation, the IoV require quick wireless Internet access, for example, Wi-Fi and 4G-LTE to maintain the gadgets and network availability. 4G innovation is useful for current data dissemination situations; however, after 5 or 10 years, 4G innovation won't meet the future prerequisites, at that point, it will move to 5G innovation to meet the necessities, to give end to end idleness, enhance inclusion, and upgrade the information rate. This section also introduces the IoV integrating with cloud computing, characteristics, issues, system architecture, IoV enabling technologies, and communication protocols. Subsequently, we also discuss the research gaps and pragmatic best practices around the world that will ease understanding the evolution of the Internet of vehicles (Fig. 22.1).

2 Internet of Vehicles Vital Research and Innovation Motivation

We desire a world where connectivity is way simple like the air we breathe— ubiquitous, never failing, and ever-present. The US DOT appraises that DSRC-based V2V communications can limit up to 82% of all street crashes in the USA, possibly sparing a large number of lives and billions of dollars [5]. Previously in VANET, the items included are brief, irregular, and unstable, and scope of utilization is nearby and neglects to provide worldwide and reasonable services to clients. In addition,

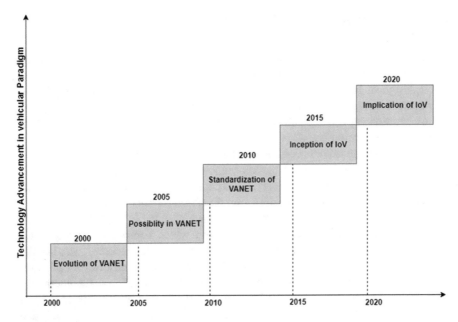

Fig. 22.1 Internet of vehicles paradigm

lack of processing capabilities in VANETs limit its use only to small services. To cope up with the limitations in VANET there is a room for advancements that lead to IoV. IoV focuses on the integration of human–vehicle–thing–environment. IoV technologies allude to the enormous advancement and deployment of an effective platform that takes into account the growth, expansion, integration of new technologies, and complex human interactions. The hardware engineering required for next era vehicles incorporates an extraordinary number of various gadgets (from the ECU controlling the conduct of the vehicles, to the man–machine interface gathering the driver's information), associated to each other through dedicated transports. The primary inspiration of IoV concept is to give advance connectivity and inescapable presence of things. In IoV, connectivity and near-field communications create enormous new intelligent features which are assuming as to give promising proposal to transform the operation and role for industrial frameworks, for example, transportation systems and manufacturing frameworks. Thanks to intelligent transportation system (ITS) for bringing advancement of IoV technology. In the interim, much consideration has been given to the appropriateness of portable cellular systems to help vehicular administrations, which can easily provide wide coverage and high data dissemination services to the vehicular clients. However, both heterogeneous cellular network and DSRC have their separate limitations when tested collectively in vehicular conditions that need to be addressed.

2.1 IoV Architecture and Background

Presently, there is no distinguished architecture for IoV in light due to the current different cognizance of IoV. A few analysts and researchers proposes the architectural design of IoV in view of IOT, which is equivalent as IoV and comprises of application layer, network layer, and sensing layer [6]. Regardless, IoV is not just an administration network for vehicle-to-vehicle or vehicle terminals communications, yet in addition a mind-boggling framework that has the element of human–vehicle–thing–environment complex planned collaboration in highly dynamic framework. During the coordination amid human–vehicle–thing–environment, IoV is essentially required to strengthen cognitive computing, information computing, and pervasive computing which desires traditional requirements of coordination in architecture and support heterogeneous networks with IoV [26]. The layered architectural design of a general vehicular system which incorporates heterogeneous systems is a very difficult errand. The preliminary challenge in a layered design architecture of IoV is the ideal number of layers and the capabilities for each layer, including: heterogeneous communication technologies (4G/LTE-V, Bluetooth, Zigbee, Wi-Fi, 5G, and so on), networking characteristics (versatility, interoperability, and reliability among vehicles), data security (authentication, integrity, and identification), and vehicle user interaction (audio, video, and sign identification) [5]. Some of the issues figured out include interconnectivity among vehicle onboard devices to other heterogeneous networks, cloud and Internet accessibility, adaptable advancement of new technologies, and application-oriented architecture. This design desires to recognize and viably group comparable functionalities and delegate components of heterogeneous networks con-sized in a layer.

To accomplish this objective, we incorporate the designs of IoV proposed by current scholarly world and industry and separated it into four layers as appeared in Fig. 22.2, that is, environment sensing layer, heterogeneous network layer, coordination control layer, and application service layer.

2.1.1 Environment Sensing Layer

The third party environment sensing layer is the recognition reason for IoV administrations, such as services of vehicle paradigms, autonomous cars, and intelligent traffic. The vehicle control dynamics and the traffic activity paradigm are the premises of IoV services implementation. The motivation behind detecting in the sense of a cyber-physical framework is to give the sensed information to elements outside the VANET continuously. From the point of view of vehicles, they sense data around the environment they are within by means of traffic jam framework, autopilot systems, and vehicle on-build sensor system for accomplishing assistant driving. In terms of environment sensing, this layer studies the technique to virtually monitor and extract various dynamic data of human, environment, and vehicle through sensing innovation techniques. This

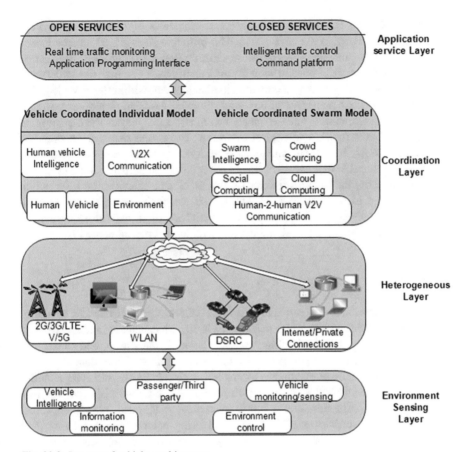

Fig. 22.2 Internet of vehicles architecture

corresponds to a system architecture where all the data of on-board sensed devices are initially collected, then execute the coordinated control instructions and afterward acknowledge the results to cooperative control. At the end, this layer actualizes the capacities of swarm detecting using swarm model and periodic sensing in individual model.

2.1.2 Heterogeneous Network Layer

During recent decades, researchers have been highly motivated to investigate the coordination of heterogeneous cellular networks with vehicular networks to cope up with the limitations related to IEEE 802.11p. By evaluating the characteristics of versatile access technologies, it is inferred that the heterogeneous cellular systems are the best decision as an alternative rather than IEEE 802.11p for supporting vehicular applications. Few of the numerous attributes related to long term evolution-vehicular (LTE-V) are high spectral efficiency, high data dissemination rate, and low latency in dynamic plane. The principle function of heterogeneous layer is to understand the system access, information handling, and information analysis and information transmission. In the meantime, it can likewise understand the remote monitoring and dynamic vehicle management within the IoV [13]. The fundamental idea of this layer is understanding the association among vehicles, information dissemination, and exchange, which also incorporates the transmission network, access network, and control networks. The access network provides the three-dimensional, real time, and consistent heterogeneous network access for vehicles associated in that network. On the other hand, the transmission and control network monitors the information access resources and balances the information load associated to this network. In addition, it establishes a stable information dissemination channel while providing quality information guarantee considering some stability metrics even in highly dynamic vehicular environment [14].

2.1.3 Coordination Control Layer

Vehicle coordination in IoV refers to integration of vehicle and driver as a solidarity that utilizes network technologies and alludes to the advancement in deep learning, swarm computing, artificial intelligence and cognitive computing, and so on. IoV can compute, gather, and manage the dynamic large-scale vehicular data of human, vehicle, and environment to enhance extensibility, sustainability, and computability of dynamic network and information structure. The ultimate objective for IoV is to improve coordination among human–vehicle–environment, reduce the social cost, improve the efficiency of transportation using heterogeneous network, and ensure that passengers are enjoying the latest comforts during traveling. This layer furnishes IoV applications with the network-wide ability of coordination and control among human–vehicle–environment, for example, information handling resource allotment, and swarm intelligence computing. From the point of view of vehicle coordinated individual model in IoV, this layer ought to provide the control and computing among human–vehicle paradigm in the IoV environment. On the other hand, the vehicle coordinated swarm model accomplishes the control and coordination management among multihuman and multivehicle that work together with one another and the environment they are within. Through crowd sensing, crowd sourcing, social computing, swarm intelligence, IoV can easily provide services/applications. Additionally, this model highlights the cooperation among human and human, vehicle and vehicle, and thing and thing. These all need an incorporated network to team up with one another and with the environment.

A computation platform has been provided by IoV to consider numerous decisions for whole network, and there are numerous virtual vehicular devices corresponding to physical vehicles and drivers. At that point, the virtual vehicle with driver is called as Autobot. In IoV, the Autobot can interface with one another by using swarm computing technologies and give the decision-making information for IoV in the computation platform. Moreover, to meet the coordinated control prerequisites, this layer ought to provide the capability for communication in a coordinated network.

2.1.4   Application Service Layer

The application layer of IoV gives different sorts of services to accomplish the necessities of human–vehicle–environment coordination. Moreover, the application layer ought to share data to help the novel administration and business operational modeling authority. This layer is firmly categorized into open services and closed services. The open services cover different existing open applications, for example, real-time traffic monitoring provided by various Internet service providers. An application-driven methodology and standardized APIs are fundamental for the acknowledgment of messages among vehicles. The key factors that affect the application approaches are security, privacy of the information, and integrity. To the extent the framework is concerned, an embraced architecture is crucial. These services seems to be appropriate like Bosch Auto Multimedia have developed a new software platform named APERTIS which understands the application-driven methodology and new developments worldwide. This platform runs on Linux operating system and other open-source services. These advancements will be available to empower a rich network of clients and contributors. Although the application layer administrators ought to provide the open services to third party vendors for more innovated ideas. The closed services are firmly identified with specific industry applications, such as the intelligent traffic control and command platform.

2.2   State-of-Art Technologies for IoV Communication

A worldwide network of wireless communication technologies (WCT) empowered vehicles includes Internet and different heterogeneous systems are proposed in IoV. The communication architecture is not limited to connections between vehicles and RSU, rather they also incorporate other communication gadgets. The heterogeneous incorporation of devices makes the architecture complex yet market oriented when contrasted with VANETs. The connected vehicles' market is expecting to surpass in the compound yearly growth rate (CYGR) of 35.54 and accomplish 37.7 million units by 2022, assessed to be 155.9 billion US dollars. The expansive scope of applications can be empowered by mainly two primary sorts of connectivity: infrastructure-based communications (intra vehicle connectivity or V2I) and direct communications between vehicles (inter-vehicle connectivity or V2V). V2V communications are fundamental for low latency applications, coverage enhancements. Concentrating on V2I correspondences, vehicles may convey to roadside units (RSUs) through short-range communication interface or even to a remote control system by exploiting wide range networks. With the rising of IoT innovations, vehicles are relied upon to communicate with any device based on the concept of vehicle-to-everything (V2X). Vehicles need to choose the perfect communication mode to fulfill the quality of service (QoS) request based on the system status. Each vehicular correspondence of IoV is empowered utilizing an alternate WCT. The various WCTs incorporated in V2X are Wi-Fi and 4G/LTE for V2I, CarPlay for V2P, IEEE WAVE for V2V and V2R, MOST/Wi-Fi for V2S, and vehicular cloud communication for V2C [21]. This segment is centered on the part of architecture relating connectivity and lists the different sorts of communication technologies guarantee in vehicular networks.

2.2.1 Intra Vehicle Connectivity or Vehicle to Sensor on Board Communication (V2S)

With the increase of smart wearables, vehicles are also equipped with large amounts of sensors like sensors for monitoring type pressure, detecting road conditions, driver ambiguous behavior, enhanced sensors for fully autonomous control unit, causalities in the engine if any, and many more. According to an estimate by 2020 sensors are forecasted to reach as many as 200 per vehicle. Earlier electronic equipment in cars comprises of very limited number of electronic control units (ECUs), each one dedicated to its individual function and fully uncoupled from the other one. The advancements in the exchange and interconnection of data between ECUs have become possible with the deployment of sophisticated communication architectures between them [7]. Nowadays, some motor vehicles equipped with 100 electronic control units with embedded microprocessors connected to five system buses, running hundreds of millions of lines of software code (100 MB of binary code) which is more than the line of code needed for MAC OS X "Tiger" and ten times the code written for Boeing 737 airplane devices. These systems manage mostly everything from braking to navigation, steering, entertainment, climate control, and many more. There exist various remote wireless technologies to build intra vehicular technologies like Bluetooth, RFID or 60GHz Millimeter Wave, ultra-wideband, and Zigbee which provide wireless connectivity between ECUs and sensors.

Zigbee is an enabling IEEE 802.15.4 standard used for V2S communication which requires low power utilization and adaptability for mesh network configurations [7]. Yet Zigbee supports data rate up to 250 Kb/s which can be insufficient for connected vehicles and also the interactions with the existing CAN is another major issue in Zigbee. Bluetooth is a short-range wireless innovation dependent on IEEE 802.15.1 standard with a frequency band of 2.5 GHz. It permits data rate over short distance of up to 3 Mb/s. Bluetooth transmission requires high power levels as it is not feasible for battery-driven sensors. Additionally, due to the poor scalability, Bluetooth system can only support eight dynamic gadgets (seven slave devices and one master devices) [8]. Ultra wideband (UWB) alludes to radio advancements that work in the frequency band of 3.1–10.6 GHz and with short range transmission at a data rate up to 480 Mb/s and with low energy levels. UWB frameworks work well for shadowing, fading factors in wireless channel, have low cost, appropriate for tracking and localization applications, and also have low processing nature.

2.2.2 Inter-Vehicle Connectivity or Vehicle to Vehicle Communication (V2V)

Information gathered from in-vehicle computer, on-board sensors, control system, or passenger can be efficiently disseminated from one vehicle to other vehicles in multihop gateway. V2V communication faces harsh challenges like fading of signals, shadowing, Doppler effect due to vehicular mobility, and lack of unified channel model for scenarios (urban, rural, and highway); within the scope of this work, we review various options for wireless technology for inter-vehicle communications. Some enabling technologies in V2V are DSRC including IEEE 1609 family for the higher layers, dynamic spectrum access (DSA) and IEEE 802.11p for physical, medium access control layer.

2.2.3 Vehicle to Internet Communication (V2I)

A must has feature for next-generation vehicles is Internet connectivity. The cellular networks like 3G and LTE-V and Wi-Fi are two promising candidates which provide reliable access services. Earlier in 1990, the concepts of Internet enable vehicles were theoretically proposed. Although, nowadays these Internet integrated vehicles are no longer conceptual identities, as numerous projects are initiated by electronic industry, automobiles, research community, and many more. These different manufactures categorized the vehicular-Internet connectivity into two domains:

- Build-in connections: These connections work for integrated cellular services in the on-board infotainment framework. The association of Internet relies on the build in mode rather than smartphone of the travelers. The recent build in connections are envisioned in BMW Connected Drive [3] which incorporates various applications like driver assistance, Internet connectivity to inside mobile devices, and emergency call center services. Audi Connect is another framework where build in is applied. Compared to cellular 3G services, LTE-V technology can offer ultra-high speed, lower cost, and high bandwidth connectivity. Recently, LTE-V projects are announced by Bosch, Huawei, and Vodafone which are taking place on the Autobahn highway in Germany. Verizon Wireless is also pursuing aggressively on the LTE connected car strategy. Yet some issues that can't be resolved once it become embedded.
- Brought-in connections: These connections cater to tethering of passenger smartphone to sink with the car. Popular tethering technology envisioned in brought-in connection is Mirror link powered by Car Connectivity Consortium (CCC) an organization which calls leading automobile (e.g., Toyota and Volkswagen) and ICT manufactures (Nokia, Sony, and Apple) together to create a phone-based car connectivity solution. Other connectivity systems like Toyota Touch,

CarPlay for iPhone users, and GM Oustar are also in demand. The advantage of secondary gadgets contraptions is that the vehicle does not require a pre-embedded infotainment structure.

2.2.4 Vehicle to Cloud Communication (V2C)

Vehicular cloud communication is another hybrid innovation that remarkably affects traffic administration and streets safety by quickly utilizing vehicular assets, for example, storage, computing, and using Internet services for instant decision making. Dash Express has reformed the navigation market in 2008 by using time and speed crowd sensing by its clients, that is, vehicles intermittently submit time and speed reports and routing directions to vehicles are refreshed utilizing clients reports. Current navigation systems are dependent on a similar group sourcing model. For instance, WAZE (by Google) is actualized in the Cloud and is assessed by means of V2I (DSRC, Wi-Fi, or LTE). The centralized cloud-based navigation system considers many propelled features such as traffic flow balancing, congestion control, and arrival time control on all preferred routes. The standalone advantage of vehicular cloud communication is data aggregation by utilizing cloud storage, where different private and government authorities can utilize the stored data in the cloud to function numerous investigations in minimal time. Although the cloud-based navigation systems lack in micromanaging traffic for most common issue of scalability (Fig. 22.3).

2.3   Applications of IoV

As depicted by the European Transportation Policy [3], the utilization of ITS is one of the key advances for enhancing the efficiency, safety, and closeness among vehicular society. ITS is grounded on refined communication networking getting information from various devices forming the traffic monitoring framework that combines the safe driving with infotainment services. Applications of IoV are perpetual like driver assistance for less congested network, secure roadways, faster terrain assistance, more effective utilization of the transportation framework, more proficient arranging of traffic monitoring and control, and more reliable traffic routings through centralized assistance. Broadly IoV applications can be categorized into two noteworthy classifications: safety applications and client infotainment applications. Applications that enhance vehicle security and increase the travelers safety on roads by notifying the vehicles about any perilous situations in their surrounding come in the category of safety applications. Applications that offer some entertainment and value-added services reside in the category of user infotainment applications. Although there is caboodle of challenges implementing IOVs in a real-time scenario, on the other side, IOVs offer some promising applications, which

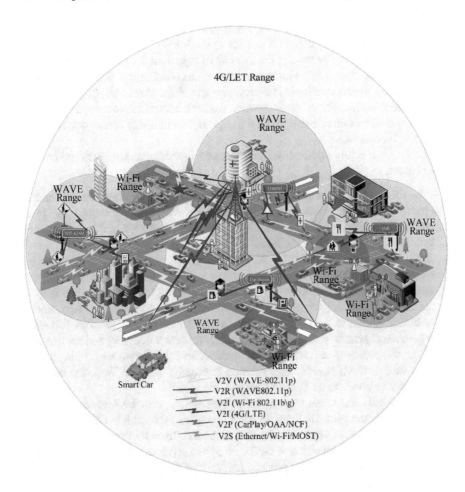

Fig. 22.3 Technologies for IoV communication

resolve many issues. The various advances in the area of vehicular networking applications are illustrated below:

Technologies to upgrade vehicular and traveler security are of incredible intrigue nowadays, and one of the critical applications is collision avoidance. Nowadays, collision avoidance techniques to a great extent belong to vehicular frameworks offered by transportation manufacturers which are comprehensively categorized into two functionalities: crash warning system and driver assistance system. Previously drivers were notified about the crash when it seems appearing and monitors the vehicles to take decisions to either come in a consistent state or emergency execution state. Specifically, collision warning incorporates notices about a chain vehicle collisions, alerts about road conditions like slippery roadways, steep turns, approaching highways, and emergency vehicle warnings. From other viewpoint, collision warnings should be imparted to vehicles instantly when collision occurs;

this leads to limit the possibility of any mishap and the early warning messages should also be utilized by drivers if there is a possibility of any collision. Mostly the intersections are complex among the most challenges that drivers face on roadways which need to be controlled. Moreover, the smooth coordination of vehicles through intersections will enhance fuel efficiency, efficient traffic flow, limit travel time, and vehicle coordination. We can easily switch from higher traffic movements to a more customary traffic control task without the requirement of traffic lights, stop symbols, or human interferences.

Some of the safety applications incorporated in vehicular networks are categorized below:

- Real-time traffic monitoring system: It depends on modern innovations in electronic, communication, computer, and network which monitor the route starting from the beginning to the end of that particular route and gather the real-time navigation information like humidity, visibility, and pollution constraints that helps to choose the optimal path. The attributes of the IoV traffic monitoring framework are incorporated among persons, vehicles, roads, and environment enhancing traffic movements by monitoring the movement of drivers and keep an activity log, conduct of vehicles stops, movements, and routes through sensors in build. Common traffic monitoring frameworks are comprised in following segments: (1) traffic data gathering unit, (2) the data processing and control unit, (3) traffic database server, (4) data communication transmission unit, and (5) inter-vehicle discharge: through vehicles terminal, radio, TV, Web, and on board units that release the on-board information.
- Road hazards and crash response: Next-generation vehicles can naturally send real-time information about an accident along with the vehicle GPS information to emergency relief squad nearby that can saves lives by providing emergency responses. The coordination of GPS with online services helps to react to drivers' inclinations toward routing, pricing, fuel accessibility, pricing, traffic alerts, and so on.
- Vehicle problem diagnosis: IoV vehicles can easily collect prognostic information that can foresee an issue before any vehicle part malfunctions or fails, which would prevent the passengers from any sort of inconvenience and help them to manage the planning of vehicle care. Preventive measures guarantees to decrease repair and guarantee costs [16].
- Upgraded safety: pilot programs for V2X communications are in progress that will warn drivers and passengers of possible collisions, hazardous road conditions, and different hindrances for safe travel. A scope of accident anticipation technologies are coordinated with heterogeneous communication technologies, for example, intersection monitoring system will likely to diminish the quantity of accidents in the upcoming years.
- Emergency calling: After the vehicle problem diagnosis, the emergency call framework for vehicles contacts the administrations, for example, police, fire, and family or companions in the event of emergency. It is both programmed and manual. This framework provides all the necessary present and past information

of the vehicle that incorporates number of travelers, speed, location, path, direction, reason for emergency calling, and so forth. This can be considered as the black-box of the vehicle.

- Route diversion: In case of road congestion, vehicles can redefine a new route for the same destination.

Client infotainment applications are very different, extending from providing both real time or nonreal time multimedia services and providing interactive communication platforms, for example, video-conferencing, weather forecasting data, or using Internet access services, for example, information exchange, Web browsing, music download, and playing interactive games to roadside benefit applications, for example, hospital blood group emergencies, prize list of various restaurants or gas stations nearby, and many more. User infotainment applications give two essential user related administrations: cooperative nearby services and worldwide Internet connectivity services. Cooperative nearby applications concentrating on infotainment that can be gathered from the locally based services, for example, point of intrigue notifications, neighborhood electronic commerce, and media downloading. Worldwide Internet administrations centers acquire the information from various services accessed by passengers like insurance and financial services, parking lot management, fleet management, and many more that focuses on software and data updates. In addition, client applications incorporate three kinds of utilization cases: first case gives the vehicle or the driver the opportunity to get to a data accessible on the Internet. The second kind permits neighborhood organizations, vacation attractions, or different vehicle dynamics to be advertised to neighboring vehicles in its vicinity. Furthermore, the third case permits an administration monitoring station to evaluate the condition of a vehicle without making a physical association with the vehicle. At the particular point when a vehicle enters the zone close to an administration garage or monitoring center, the administration center can question the vehicle for its diagnostic data to help the conclusion of the issue detailed by the client. Indeed, even as the vehicle approaches, the vehicle's previous history and the client's data can be recovered from a database and made accessible for the expert to utilize. Some of the client infotainment applications incorporated in vehicular networks are categorized below:

- Convenience services: The capacity to remotely access a vehicle providing services like remote door unlock and stolen vehicle discovery. IoV innovation can furnish transportation organizations with enhanced real-time activity, travel, and parking information, making it simpler to oversee transportation frameworks for limiting the traffic and congestion loads. Apple CarPlay, initially presented as iOS in vehicles, offers holistic autonomous coordination for Apple's Navigation and realistic navigation monitoring, cellphones, I-Message, and infotainment services. Like Google Android Auto, CarPlay gives a diversion free interface that permits drivers appreciate the services by associating android gadgets to the vehicle. Recently Chinese Tencent has propelled its homegrown navigation routing application namely Lubao that highlights client created contents with social functionalities.

- Connected driving: It is an on-board synchronization framework for vehicles. It interfaces vehicle's showcase unit to office or home PC, cell phone, and other online gadgets. The framework depends on remote login in various kinds of online gadgets with security accreditation. The framework would enhance productivity in driving term while maintaining a strategic distance from on-street fatalities. This is because of the use of already programmed applications for drivers in IoV.
- Cloud services: The cloud framework forms autonomous group of vehicles or connects the vehicles in a particular vicinity to traditional clouds. In either case, the assets of IoV are accessible for use as cloud services and also the vehicles simultaneously share smart cloud administrations. The framework would dispense with computational and storage impediments at vehicles which could open new action plans for connected vehicles.

3 Heterogeneous Vehicular Communication

A singleton remote communication innovation can't well help every one of ITS administrations especially in dense rush-hour traffic regions, traveler regions, and generous vehicular load stages. Consequently, the future development of vehicular systems is to deviate the focus from using single communication technology toward designing frameworks based on different advances. To support the concept of heterogeneous technologies, European Telecommunications Standards Institute (ETSI), US DOT, and the International Standards Organization (ISO) are examining the integral roles of IEEE 802.11p, LTE-V, 5G, and other cellular communication advances collectively. One of the key motivations for considering such heterogeneous vehicular frameworks is the board availability of LTE, DSRC, and other cell innovations. LTE is expected to assume a pivotal job supplementing the disadvantages of DSRC innovations for vehicular society. Some of the accompanying reasons for using LTE-V over basic DSRC are substantial coverage, centralized architecture, high capacity, high data penetration rate, and multicast/broadcast support. Many of the advancements have been operated in their own or within a closed system environment, so there is an urgent need to interoperate and communicate with other system too in order to provide better and safer traveling experience to migrate to next-generation intelligent transportation systems (ITS). For deploying Het-IoV, the challenging task is to select a reliable radio access methodology that fulfills all the QoS credentials of desired applications for vehicular clients. In addition, the challenges of supporting a dynamic vehicular environment, holistic composition of various networks in Het-IoV, and administrators to use radio assets in a productive and adaptable way require efficient management (Fig. 22.4).

Het-IoV is made from three principal parts, to be specific as radio communication network (RCN), a core network (CN), and a service station (SS). Service organizations can regularly supply an assortment of services to vehicular clients through the SS [9]. The CN is a key part of the Het-IoV that gives numerous vital capacities,

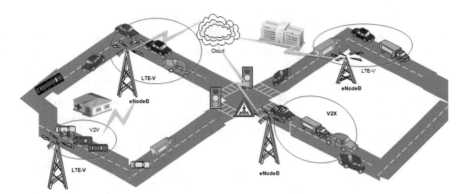

Fig. 22.4 Homogeneous vehicular framework

for example, data aggregation, validation, data dissemination, and switching. In the Het-IoV, there are two sorts of communication technologies, that is, V2V and V2I, which are like conventional vehicular systems upheld by just a solitary communication innovation. V2V contemplates short-and medium-go correspondence among vehicular customers, offering low organization costs and supporting constrained inertness message transport. Information gathered from in-vehicle computer, on-board sensors, control system, or passenger can be efficiently disseminated from one vehicle to other vehicles in multihop gateway. V2I empowers vehicles to associate with the Internet for reliable data dissemination and infotainment by means of an RSU.

3.1   V2I Communication

Concentrating on V2I correspondences, vehicles may convey to roadside units (RSUs) through short-range communication interface or even to a remote control system by exploiting wide range networks. Utilizing cellular networks is prudent to support V2I communication, that is, DSRC based on IEEE802.11p/1609 WAVE protocol. Some of the V2I communication technologies incorporated in heterogeneous vehicular networks are categorized below:

3.1.1   DSRC

DSRC is a wide-understanding remote advancement that is planned to help ITS applications in vehicular frameworks. The US DOT proposed DSRC to utilize V2I and V2V correspondence intended to diminish crashes on roadways and clog to improve portability. Connections with traffic signals or any stationary devices lead to V2I communication whereas others just roll down into V2V. In 1999, the US

FCC conveyed 75 MHz of approved range in the 5.9 GHz band to DSRC. The US DOT estimated that DSRC has capability to limit the road accidents by 82% of the estimated crashes every year in USA and estimated that 40% of those happens on intersections. These estimations recommend the huge potential for DSRC innovation to diminish crashes and to improve security for proficient driving. IEEE 802.11p has been received by DSRC to be utilized as its physical (PHY) and medium access control (MAC) layers, which is gotten from IEEE 802.11e with little changes in the quality of administration (QoS) perspectives. Advantages of DSRC are simple deployment and low expenses, and the ability to help V2V communications with the impromptu mode are its focal points compared with LTE systems. Although there are some disadvantages like unbounded delaying, scalability credentials, restricted radio range, brief V2I connectivity, and so on. However, DSRC has its very own disadvantages, for example, adaptability issues, unlimited postponements, constrained radio range, fleeting V2I network, and so on. Despite the way that the current DSRC development is given off an impression of being successful in supporting vehicular security applications in different field primers, and to hold the certification for diminishing accidents, gigantic troubles remain for using DSRC advancement in some undermining vehicular conditions. Vehicular communication may occur over extreme recurrence particular multipath and quick blurring channels, and additionally in thickly populated situations (Fig. 22.5).

In this manner, there is a huge opportunity to get better and upgrade in DSRC. Few issues in DSRC communication are highlighted like sparse pilot setup is lacking to minutely assess the channel state information and the main path is to improve the recipient execution to the detriment of usage complexities; channel blockage happens when the carrier sense multiple access (CSMA) mechanisms are utilized at the MAC layer of the DSRC organize the likelihood of impacts radically expands resulting huge end to end delays.

3.1.2 Cellular-Het-IoV Communications

Cellular frameworks offer two transmission modes for V2I interchanges: explicitly unicast and multicast/communicate. Unicast can be used for both uplink and downlink message scattering, which is point-to-point trades between a vehicle and the BS, generally called the evolved nodeB (eNB). Additionally, multicast/convey is used for the dispersal of downlink messages, which alludes to point-to-multi-point transmission.

LTE for V2I

LTE can provide uplink data rates to 50 Mbps, and downlink data rates up to 100 Mbps with an exchange speed of 20 MHz, and supports the outrageous flexible speed of 350 km/h. The design of the LTE system is credited to the low transmission inertia, for example, the round-trip time is lower than 10 ms, and the transmission

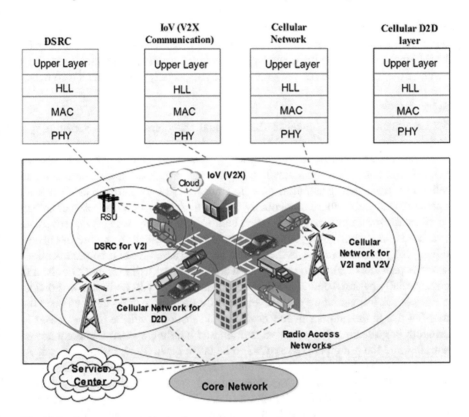

Fig. 22.5 Heterogeneous vehicular framework

latency in the RAN is up to 100 ms [3]. Along these lines, LTE is inserted to support V2I exchanges especially, in the hidden sending period of vehicular frameworks and LTE is required to expect a critical activity in supporting vehicular organizations. This could firstly occur in sparse locales where the vehicle thickness is low. Additionally, LTE frameworks are prepared for giving high utmost wide inclusion, for instance, LTE can support up to 1200 vehicles for each cell in rustic landscapes with an uplink delay under 55 ms and one CAM for consistency. Also, it can give an amazing framework to flexibility organization. Examinations of trialing LTE in vehicles to support distinctive applications, for example, infotainment, diagnostics, and route have been finished. The results exhibit that the LTE structure is able to give a data rate of 10 Mbps with quickening up to 140 km/h. LTE can be particularly valuable at combinations by enabling a strong exchange of cross traffic help applications [23].

Few issues should be settled before LTE frameworks can be broadly utilized for V2I correspondences. Initially, the MAC layer of LTE comes up with an effective planning system for legitimately mapping the vehicular traffic highlights. Despite the fact that it is essential to plot lightweight joining/leaving strategies for dynamic grouping of vehicles. The key challenge is to enhance the transmission adequacy while diminishing the overhead. In the interim, conventional applications offered by LTE frameworks may be impacted by different dimensions of potential impact as a result of the introduction of new sorts of action, especially the generous load ones.

5G

5G communication will enhance the potential outcomes of what versatile systems can do and extend out what services they can convey. 5G will give the establishment framework to building savvy IoV environment that will enhance vehicle communication dynamics like low latency, extremely high bandwidth and reliability. Each new generation aims to improve network performance for both operators and subscribers. Essentially, 5G will drive a new set of technology services, from autonomous cars to smart buildings. It will provide deeper coverage, enhanced connectivity, and constant data collaboration called for by the Internet of things (IoT). Gartner forecasts that 3% of network-based mobile communications services providers (20 to 30 mobile network operators) will launch 5G networks commercially by 2020 and 20.4 billion connected things will be in use worldwide. New network infrastructure will power the fully standardized 5G networks and the massive rise in the number of IoT devices and sensors. It will be the key driver in bringing large-scale IoT projects to fruition and building a steady, interconnected world. Amid the principal phase of 5G to be taken off in 2020, billions of gadgets will be associated with the fast portable networks. These sensor systems with higher speed and bigger ability to gather and analyze information will display smart facilities in urban territories. Higher speed and bigger ability to gather and break down information will exhibit brilliant offices in urban regions. 5G technology resolves this problem by dramatically reducing latency and providing smart cars with reliable, ultra-low latency bandwidth.

3.2 V2V Communication

V2V applications grant neighboring devices to exchange important information by communicating, which requires the user equipment (UE) to buy into a system official and secure endorsement. V2V applications anticipate UEs to transmit messages passing on V2V application information, for instance, traffic components, territory, and vehicle characteristics. To fit in with the fluctuating extent of V2V application information, the message payloads ought to be versatile. Also, 3GPP transport of messages can be unavoidably settled on conveying. If the immediate correspondence scope of V2V is constrained, the vehicular data can be sent by framework based V2V. V2V communication technologies incorporated in heterogeneous vehicular networks are categorized below.

3.2.1 LTE D2D Communications

Device to device (D2D) correspondences underlaying a cellular network have been proposed as a methods for exploiting the physical vicinity of conveying gadgets in LTE frameworks [10]. In the D2D mode, user equipment (UE) in nearness can specifically speak with one another. As a candidate system supporting V2V in Het-IoV, D2D interchanges in LTE confront a few difficulties. As, D2D communication with different connections in the LTE network shares similar radio assets which leads to interference which is a noteworthy issue while utilizing D2D in Het-IoV. For instance, in the FDD framework, when a D2D interface utilizes downlink assets, the donor eNodeB may make extreme obstruction for the D2D pair. Besides, the interference from neighboring cells is another issue confronting D2D interchanges. Besides, if a D2D consolidate uses uplink resources, the receiving end of the D2D pair may experience strong interference from a cellular UE using the similar uplink assets. Subsequently in numerous cases, the D2D revelation time is bigger than that distributed for message transmission, which isn't adequate for conveying security messages with strict QoS prerequisites.

3.3 V2X Communication

3GPP has been taking measures for the cell-based vehicle-to-everything (V2X) offering progressively powerful responses for vehicular correspondences. Contrasted with IEEE 802.11p, cell V2X can give better QoS support, greater consideration, and higher data rate for moving vehicles [6]. The V2X arrangement results in a higher spectral capability to serve more street customers. Despite the way that V2X organizations can exist together with IEEE 802.11p-based radio access in adjoining channels, V2X has the additionally preferred advantage of being adaptable and evolvable. This is because of the way that cell networks can manage all V2X application organizations with a comparative development in a start to finish way and V2X can give an advancement way from 4G LTE to 5G remote systems. The principal difference between V2X and IEEE 802.11p are outlined in Table 22.1. Also, D2D underlay correspondences in LTE can be used for cell V2X applications with high reliability and low latency. 3GPP determines the improvement of 3GPP help for V2X organizations (V2X) in the accompanying four zones: vehicles platooning, propelled driving, upgraded sensors, and remote driving. V2X incorporates network with different stages like distributed computing, enormous information investigation, and some more.

3.3.1 Vehicular Cloud

IoV and cloud computing have been a growing area in the field of research and innovations. It is a widely used area in many fields which provide intelligent

Table 22.1 Comparison of 802.11p and V2X communication

Parameters	802.11p	V2X communication
Scalability level	Low	High
Synchronization	Asynchronous	Synchronous
Waveform	Orthogonal frequency-division multiplexing (OFDM)	Single carrier frequency division multiple access (SC-FDM)
Channel coding	Conventional	Turbo
Resource multiplexing	TDM only	FDM and TDM possible
Retransmission technique	No HARQ	Hybrid automatic repeat request (HARQ)
Resource selection	Carrier sense multiple access with collision avoidance (CSMA-CA)	Semi persistent transmission with relative energy-based selection

perception, vehicle to vehicle (V2V) communication, and on demand use and sharing of resources. We are surrounded by mobile devices and smart devices through which we can communicate within the vehicle or outside side world. IoV able to provide advance level of service by connected with Internet anywhere, anyhow, and anytime [11]. The IoV is the application of IOT in the automobile industry [19, 20]. The IoV incorporates RFID innovation, satellite situating and route innovation, intelligent innovation, sensor innovation, and other innovation into the whole traffic management system. The board framework viable, makes vehicles, street, walker, and system interconnection, and turns into a remote portable system that capacities in a wide scope of territories [28]. There are many applications of IoV such as smart vehicles, smart transportation, smart parking, crash response, car problem diagnosis, integrated navigation, traffic management, infotainment, and so on shown in Fig. 22.6.

On the other hand, cloud computing provides cloud delivery services models such as infrastructure as a service (IaaS), platform as a service (PaaS), software as a service (SaaS), and private cloud and hybrid cloud for allowing clients to develop, run, and manage application functionalities [22, 24]. Vehicular cloud computing (VCC) is defined as a change in perspective from traditional VANET to the vehicular cloud in which vehicles utilize their onboard assets and cloud assets too [12]. Cloud computing and IoV have many advantages if both technologies are combined, they both will transform the way we disseminate information.

Yet some future challenges needed to be considered for VCC are large-scale implementation of VC, promoting reliability and availability in VCs, VC Support for Smart Cities, and many more.

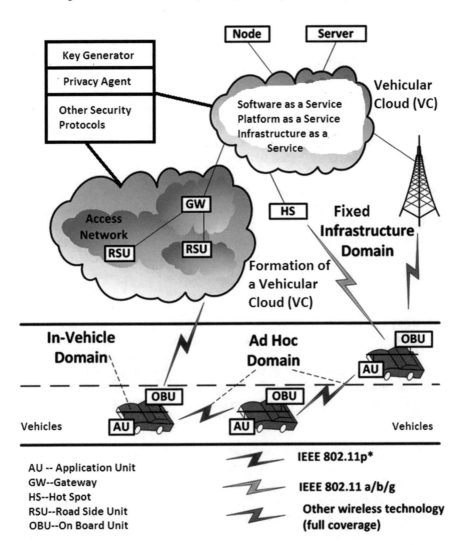

Fig. 22.6 Cloud-based architecture for IoV

4   Open Issues and Future Research Implications

VANET and Internet of vehicles (IoV) are the primary tools which help in aiming the concept of interaction of vehicles on roads into the reality. Although there is much advancement in this field, still there is the scope of improvement in oodles aspects. There are many open issues which demand to accept as challenges for the actualization of IOVs. These challenges are broadly classified into distinct categories based upon some specific issues. After completion of this section, the user can draw a broader view of open problems and issues related to VANETs.

4.1 Open Issues

4.1.1 Issues Related to the Management of Big Data

Vehicular communication requires many bandwidth spectrums. A huge amount of data are shared between the on roads vehicles and cloud servers associated between them. To conduct a smooth communication between these vehicles, addressing the problem of handling such big data effectively is required [17, 25]. This issue comprises many problems, which are listed as follows.

Bandwidth Allocation and Consumption

The larger the number of vehicles interacting with each other in a particular time the more significant is the requirement of the bandwidth. Therefore, an efficient technique is required to reduce the consumption bandwidth by smartly allocating memory. This needs proper management of accumulation, allotment, and validation of the data.

Smart Routing Protocols

Depending upon the network structure there may be an ample number of sensors are deployed for effectual vehicular connectivity and positioning. In this scenario, routing protocols must be robust and must be smartly designed to deliver the packets. It must improve the data decimation. Also, the routing protocol must be able to locate and recover the lost data packets when the network is massive. These expectations need a more impudent routing protocol. Hence this remains an open issue in VANETs.

Issues Related to the Location Verification and Positioning

Vehicular ad hoc networks constitute of lots of data gathered from different nodes. These data facilitate the information about the features of the vehicle like its current velocity, in which direction it is moving, heading to which direction, and what kind of vehicle it is. This information must be kept secret and need a privacy concern. There are some techniques which encrypt the data, but there are some areas which are vulnerable. As there is less traffic on the network, the pseudonym switching technique is susceptible and easily traceable. Another method, mix zone, applies to multiplane lanes, but it fails on one-way roads. Also, if the sensors and the vehicle are apart from each other, the delay is generated in the location query, and hence handover of the signals between the sensor and the server gets delayed. All these issues may lead to the leak of the information to the neighboring networks, which renders the problem of vehicle authentication and actual positions.

Security Concern of the Vehicular Communication

The vehicular network brought the revolution in the field of autonomous vehicles, but along with it also raises the issues related to the security of information shared between different vehicles. There are two types of attacks which affect the security of the network: one is attack on the user level and another one is attack on the system itself. Attacks on the former one leads to various congestion problems in the network. This may also drive a vehicle in the wrong direction and crashes [27]. As a result of it, a user will have less faith on the autonomous system and issues related to authentication and confidentially become an area of concern [18]. The problem increases when vehicle and server are at remote locations. Liability is also a major challenge related to security, for example, if government authorities want to identify a vehicle, after an accident, they must require access to the data associated with it [28]. This situation needs to handle proper instructions and security measures to maintain the secrecy of data. There is a need to encrypt the sensitive data from the attacks for reliable communication among the vehicles.

Support of Network Intelligence
One of the difficulties of future vehicular networks is that it needs to enhance network intelligence. In future heterogeneous systems, there will be an expansive number of sensors introduced in vehicles, and the edge cloud gathers and pre-processes the gathered information before offering them to different parts of the network, for instance, ordinary cloud servers.

4.1.2 Other Issues

Despite these significant issues, there are other notable areas which need a concern. It includes the robust transmission of data among vehicles which shares a radio medium in an efficient way. Secondly, there may be a situation in a real-time scenario, when an accident happens, or there is a traffic jam due to some unwilling reason. In this case, the traffic or the variation in the density of nodes increases abruptly. Also, a vehicular network must ensure quality of service (QoS) during an emergency situation, like an exchange of message without any delay. Here, message implies the précised information about the location, speed, and position of the vehicle. It must avoid the collision between the messages in a cloggy wireless environment. Lastly, there are many open challenges which are related to business point of view. For, example if there is a large number of sensors are distributed in a network, they need more roadside units (RSU) to acquire the real-time data. The more significant the amount of sensor and RSUs the higher will the cost of the network. This needs to be considered while designing a VANET.

4.2 Future Prospects

VANETs and IOVs possess applications with equal amount of challenges. Despite all issues and research challenges, IOVs promise a brighter future. The novelty of the IOVs leads to its various future aspects, which are mentioned as follows:

- Establishing a navigating system, which is more secure and précised.
- Security concerns need to be reviewed by attaining a balance between excogitation and security concerns.
- To tackle the issues related to the interfacing of data with cloud and its analysis. To conquer the different specialized challenges in cloud platform interface, network perception, convenient recovery, information mining, and investigation need to be considered.
- To acquire information (license, type, and so on) about the vehicle globally.
- Concept of online vehicles: Online vehicle implies that every vehicle will have its unique registration over cyberspace. It will also have information about its inspection report annually, the status of tax payment, record of services, and so on. Overall, this will reduce the cost related to vehicle management. Vehicles will have IDs on the Internet, making an online presence about the operation of falsely registered, smuggled, and illegally modified vehicles much more troublesome and increasing the overall security and credibility in Internet.
- RFID-based unique IDs with GPS-based location system will overcome the issues related to location and privacy.
- Internet facilities on the road with the help of RSUs. This also yields to new research problems related to confidentiality and regulating unique IDs.
- Heterogeneous VANETs over cloud if utilized in a productive mode can raise big data business to a new height. Big data business is not limited to automobile-Internet sector, insurance sector, cloud processing, and so on.
- M2M interactions can open the doors for the smart terminals which will provide service based on location in collaboration with IoVs.
- Information of the driver can be a substitute for mobile payment. The unique cloud ID can be utilized for vehicle-related payments in a secured manner.
- Lower down the hops of communication between the nodes.
- Novel algorithms must be designed to overcome the problem of overheads and must provide a solution to data dissemination at micro and macro level.

An expansive number of smart terminals will develop customized to the IoV, both in-vehicle and handset, with exceptional man-to-machine interfaces. With these terminals in hand, the IoV will be basic to the versatile world.

5   Pragmatic Encounters around the World

In perspective of the US DOT by 2025, IoV is a standout among the best gadgets for vehicular communication on the US interests. The amount of interconnected devices deployed beat the less number of devices deployed in 2011. This inclination was altogether creating as the amount of interconnected devices was around 9 billion out of 2012 and they will accomplish 24 billion until 2020 (Table 22.2).

Table 22.2 Approaches and systems of urban areas incorporated with smart vehicles

City	Experience
Barcelona	Execution of associated sensors has improved the utilization of information examination and advancement streams to structure a novel transport organization and helps in splendid development
Amsterdam	The success level has been increased by saving only the critical information and unnecessary data to be eradicated
Singapore	Completed a structure intended to overhaul traffic stream and keep street activity running thriving. A touch of the key exercises in the transportation part intertwine one watching, a general section serving all drivers and vehicle owners in the nation
Santa Cruz	Break down the information of violations to estimate the requirements of police "what's more" intensify the closeness of police in the required spots
New York City	The "One New York Design" reported in the year 2015 is an exhaustive arrangement for a practical and strong vehicle
Anyang (South Korea)	The vehicle has passed on a shrewd transport structure to give action organization and development information organization. Sensors send continuous action information to the control center, which uses the learning to offer information to general society by methods for the web and versatile application
Yinchuan (China)	Stipulated the association of a security cloud which includes 30,000 facilitated cameras. A section of this contains forefront HD cameras with shrewd examination abilities to ensure the security of the city and its occupants

6 Conclusions

The coordination of Het-IoV speaks to the accompanying huge future's jump head on the Internet. The new applications arising from this incorporation of cellular networks with DSRC known as Het-IoV open new directions for business and research. This section studied the literature remembering the true objective to recognize the comparing parts of IoV, heterogeneous systems, and vehicular cloud for organizing them into a special circumstance. In heterogeneous-IoV (HET-IoV), availability and close field correspondences make tremendous new intelligent highlights which are assuming as to give promising proposition to change the task and job for modern frameworks, for example, transportation frameworks and assembling frameworks. Since the gathering of the Cloud–IoV perspective engaged a couple of new applications, this chapter additionally inspected available stages and exercises by differentiating their principal viewpoints and perceived open issues and future research direction in the vehicular conditions. These works don't have a point by point examination of the new VCC perspective, which incorporates absolutely new applications, difficulties, and research issues. To associate this gap, this chapter gives an audit on the compromise of Cloud and IoV. Starting by portraying fundamentals of IoV, heterogeneous vehicular access technologies and VCC analyze their characteristics, coordination, and challenges. In addition, it also provides a state-of-art picture of heterogeneous vehicular communication model. Because of the reception of vehicular cloud, they both perform a powerful innovation by managing storage, on-demand retrieving of data, data dissemination in sparse environments, and security, with an attention on recent research challenges. These collaborations solves the critical research difficulties such like the heterogeneity of included gadgets and advancements; the required execution, unwavering quality, adaptability, and security; protection safeguarding; and legitimate and social perspectives.

7 Summary

- IoV introduction which was initially a VANET era is highlighted. In the first section, a brief introduction about the IoV, its evolution, dynamics, and evolution of IoV from VANET are discussed.
- Next section highlights IoV motivation and IoV layered architecture. Moreover, state of art technologies of IoV communication, that is, V2X is illustrated. This section categorizes various applications platforms in recent IoV.
- Integration means the ability to use the functionality of previous model's technology and integrate it with the new technology. Heterogeneous communication networks are incorporated in vehicular networks to meet the correspondence necessities of the ITS.
- Cloud–IoV covers the requirement of cloud computing, its elements, design issues, and architecture model.
- Pragmatic encounters of smart vehicles are described as a case study in the next section.
- In the last section, conclusion is summarized, which is evidently demanding of specific cloud and IoV requirement and new framework architecture for successful deployment of smart vehicular framework in the future.

Acknowledgments The authors would like to thank the anonymous reviewers for their valuable comments and feedback which was extremely helpful in improving the quality of the paper.

References

1. ITS Joint Program Office Research and Innovative Technology Administration (RITA). (2010, April 30). *Achieving the vision: From VII to IntelliDrive policy white paper*. Washington, DC: U.S. DOT.
2. Kaiwartya, O., et al. (2016). Internet of vehicles: Motivation, layered architecture, network model, challenges, and future aspects. *IEEE Access, 4*, 5356–5373. https://doi.org/10.1109/ACCESS.2016.2603219.
3. Fangchun, Y., Shangguang, W., Jinglin, L., Zhihan, L., & Qibo, S. (2015). An overview of internet of vehicles. *Communications China, 11*(10), 1–15.
4. Hossain, E., Chow, G., Leung, V. C., McLeod, R. D., Mišić, J., Wong, V. W., & Yang, O. (2010). Vehicular telematics over heterogeneous wireless networks: A survey. *Computer Communications, 33*(7), 775–793.

5. Gerla, M., Lee, E.-K., Pau, G., & Lee, U. (2014). Internet of vehicles: From intelligent grid to autonomous cars and vehicular clouds. In *2014 IEEE World Forum on Internet of Things (WF-IoT)* (pp. 241–246). Piscataway: IEEE.
6. Barbaresso, J., Cordahi, G., Garcia, D., Hill, C., Jendzejec, A., & Wright, K. (2014). *USDOT's intelligent transportation systems (ITS) ITS strategic plan 2015–2019. Report: FHWA-JPO-14-145*. Washington, DC: US Department of Transportation Intelligent Transportation Systems, Joint Program Office.
7. Hameed Mir, Z., & Filali, F. (2014). LTE and IEEE 802.11p for vehicular networking: A performance evaluation. *EURASIP Journal on Wireless Communications and Networking, 2014*, 89.
8. Bitam, S., Mellouk, A., & Zeadally, S. (2015). VANET-cloud: A generic cloud computing model for vehicular ad hoc networks. *IEEE Wireless Communications, 22*(1), 96–102.
9. Zheng, K., Zheng, Q., Chatzimisios, P., Xiang, W., & Zhou, Y. (2015). Heterogeneous vehicular networking: A survey on architecture, challenges, and solutions. *IEEE Communications Surveys & Tutorials, 17*(4), 2377–2396.
10. 3GPP TR 22.885. Study on LTE support for V2X Services.
11. Hossain, M. S., Muhammad, G., Abdul, W., Song, B., & Gupta, B. B. (2018). Cloud-assisted secure video transmission and sharing framework for smart cities. *Future Generation Computer Systems, 83*, 596–606.
12. Yu, R., Zhang, Y., Gjessing, S., Xia, W., & Yang, K. (2013). Toward cloud-based vehicular networks with efficient resource management. *IEEE Network, 27*(5), 48–55.
13. Céspedes, S., & Shen, X. S. (2015). On achieving seamless IP communications in heterogeneous vehicular networks. *IEEE Transactions on Intelligent Transportation Systems, 16*(6), 3223–3237.
14. Joshi, P., Kaur, J., & Gill, I. S. (2015). Heterogeneous configuration: A better approach to analyze VANET. *International Journal of Computer Applications, 118*(19), 26–30.
15. Zeadally, S., Hunt, Y. R., Irwin, A., & Hassan, A. (2012). Vehicular ad hoc networks (VANETs): Status, results, and challenges. *Telecommunication Systems, 50*(4), 217–241.
16. 3GPP TR 22.886. Study on enhancement of 3GPP support for 5G V2X services.
17. Sun, Y., Song, H., Jara, A. J., & Bie, R. (2016). Internet of things and big data analytics for smart and connected communities. *IEEE Access, 4*(1), 766–773.
18. Gupta, B., Agrawal, D. P., & Wang, H. (2018). *Computer and cyber security: Principles, algorithm, applications, and perspectives* (p. 666). Boca Raton: CRC Press, Taylor & Francis.
19. Ghazizadeh, P. (2014). *Resource allocation in vehicular cloud computing.* Ph.D. thesis, Old Dominion University.
20. M. Abuelela, S. Olariu, (2017). Taking VANET to the clouds. In *Proceedings of the ACM MoMM Paris, France*.
21. Abboud, K., Omar, H. A., & Zhuang, W. (2016). Interworking of DSRC and cellular network technologies for V2X communications: A survey. *IEEE Transactions on Vehicular Technology, 65*(12), 9457–9470.
22. Zheng, K., Meng, H., Chatzimisios, P., Lei, L., & Shen, X. (2015). An SMDP-based resource allocation in vehicular cloud computing systems. *IEEE Transactions on Industrial Electronics, 62*(12), 7920–7928. https://doi.org/10.1109/TIE.2015.2482119.
23. Cox, C. (2012). *An introduction to LTE: LTE, LTE-advanced, SAE and 4G mobile communications* (1st ed.). London: Wiley.
24. Gu, L., Zeng, D., & Guo, S. (2013). Vehicular cloud computing: A survey. In *Proc. IEEE Globecom Workshops (GC Wkshps), Atlanta, GA* (pp. 403–407).
25. Plageras, A. P., Psannis, K. E., Stergiou, C., Wang, H., & Gupta, B. B. (2018). Efficient IoT-based sensor BIG data collection–processing and analysis in smart buildings. *Future Generation Computer Systems, 82*, 349–357.
26. Vinel, A., Lan, L., & Lyamin, N. (2015). Vehicle-to-vehicle communication in C-ACC/platooning scenarios. *IEEE Communications Magazine, 53*(8), 192–197.

27. Tewari, A., & Gupta, B. B. (2018). Security, privacy and trust of different layers in internet-of-things (IoTs) framework. *Future Generation Computer Systems*. In press.
28. Gupta, S., & Gupta, B. B. (2017). Detection, avoidance, and attack pattern mechanisms in modern web application vulnerabilities: Present and future challenges. *International Journal of Cloud Applications and Computing (IJCAC), 7*(3), 1–43.

Chapter 23
A Systematic Review on Security and Privacy Issues in Mobile Devices and Systems

Mohamed Alloghani, Thar Baker, Dhiya Al-Jumeily, Abir Hussain, Jamila Mustafina, and Ahmed J. Aljaaf

Abstract The number of mobile devices that are getting connected to the Internet is on the rise and interconnectivity has brought together billions of devices in the cyber-sphere. The chapter focuses on security and privacy of mobile devices and systems for identifying security and privacy issues as well as the current measures of detecting and preventing such issues. The systematic review methodology will rely on the PRISMA checklist and flowchart to include and exclude papers in the review process. However, given the nature and debates around privacy and security in mobile systems, the search will be conducted in several databases which Digital library IEEE Xplore, Digital Library ACM, and the DBLP Computer Science Bibliography besides ProQuest Central and EBSCO. Given the number of databases that will be used to search for the articles, PICO will be used to prepare search strings and queries implemented in the databases. The results of the search will include descriptive statistics including distribution of articles per journal and year of publication as well as qualitative analysis of thematic areas emerging from the search string results. Finally, the findings and discussions will illuminate the problems identified, measures, and development in the provision of security and privacy in mobile systems. Probable research gaps and considerations for future studies will also be included in the conclusion section.

Keywords Mobile systems · Mobile systems security · Mobile systems privacy · Security in smart devices · Privacy in smart devices · Mobile health (mHealth) systems · Mobile cloud · Mobile networks · Digital forensics · Mobile applications and platforms · Smartphone devices · Big data cloud storage

M. Alloghani (✉) · T. Baker · D. Al-Jumeily · A. Hussain · A. J. Aljaaf
Applied Computing Research Group, Liverpool John Moores University, Liverpool, UK
e-mail: M.AlLawghani@2014.ljmu.ac.uk; t.baker@ljmu.ac.uk; D.Aljumeily@ljmu.ac.uk; A.Hussain@ljmu.ac.uk; A.J.Kaky@ljmu.ac.uk

J. Mustafina
Kazan Federal University, Kazan, Russia
e-mail: dnmustafina@kpfu.ru

© Springer Nature Switzerland AG 2020
B. B. Gupta et al. (eds.), *Handbook of Computer Networks and Cyber Security*,
https://doi.org/10.1007/978-3-030-22277-2_23

1   Introduction

Mobile security and privacy have increasingly become crucial in mobile computing, and there have been a lot of concerns regarding the security of business and personal information stored on mobile devices such as smartphones. Au and Choo explain that more users, as well as, businesses employ the use of smartphones not only to communicate but also to plan and organize the work of their users including private life [1]. These technologies within companies are resulting in profound changes specifically in the organization of information systems, and they have become the source of new encompassing risks. Au and Choo illuminate that the mobile devices collect and compile a huge amount of sensitive information hence their access must be controlled not only to protect the user's privacy but also the intellectual property of the organization [1, 2]. Au and Choo reiterate that smartphones have become the preferred attack targets as computers [1]. According to Tully and Mohanraj [3], such attacks often exploit weaknesses that are inherent in the smartphones that can emanate from the mode of communication such as short message service (SMS), multimedia messaging service (MMS), the world standard for mobile communication (GSM), Bluetooth, and Wi-Fi [4]. Tully and Mohanraj [3] elaborate that there are other exploits which target the vulnerabilities of software in either the operating systems or the browser [3]. Some of the malicious software depends on the weak knowledge more so of an average user. Rawat illuminate that the findings in 2008 by McAfee reveal that approximately 12% of the users heard of other individuals that had been affected by the mobile malware while only 2% had personal experience on that problem [4]. However, such numbers have been on an increasing trend in the last 10 years.

There are countermeasure security techniques that have been developed and applied to mobile devices such as smartphones ranging from security in various layers of software to information dissemination more so the end users. Rawat [4] argues that they are good practices that should be observed at every level from how they are designed to be used through to the development of software layers, operating system, and downloadable apps [4].

Tully and Mohanraj [3] argue that anonymity of the user in the digital age is crucial since the computers could be employed to infer the habits, lifestyle, association, and whereabouts of individuals from data or information collected in different day to day transactions [3]. But just removing explicit identifiers is not likely to provide enough protection. The main reason stems from the fact that the released information in combination with information that is publicly available has the potential of revealing an individual's identity. Huang and Zhou [5] add that the other great concern within the mobile setting is location privacy [5].

Gupta et al. [6] emphasized the importance of the Internet on daily life and the authors suggest that with increased usage of the Internet came the need for encipherment [6]. Some of the key areas of focus include securing mobile systems, detecting and preventing instructions, and security issues related to the Internet, botnet, local area network (LAN), Wireless Networks and their security issues, and emerging technologies such optical network security and the application of optics in cryptography. As for encryption, the authors focused on data encryption and public key infrastructure (PKI) alongside password-based authentication protocols.

In one of the latest publications, Gupta and Wang [7] explored and discussed computer and cyber security principles including algorithms and different perspectives. Given the rate of advances and sophistication of attacks, the author suggests advance security and highlighted ubiquity of machines as one of the challenges of computer and cyber security [7]. That is, most modern attacks leverage the fact that most devices including mobile systems operate in almost the same state. The mode of attacking a single host is applicable to millions of devices. In response, the authors suggested diversity and use of network automation as a technique of dealing with some of the attacks. Sandboxing and virtualization also emerged as the other recommended technique for avoiding ubiquity attacks. Besides these techniques, the author also discussed principles surrounding segregation of computing resources and its role in achieving system resilience against threats.

However, it is imperative to note that of discussion revolve around the computer and cyber security but rarely in the context of mobile platforms. Given emerging trends such Internet of things (IoT) and cloud computing, it is necessary and absolute requirement to address and focus on monitoring and protecting such systems. Akram et al. [8] explored security, privacy, and trust for all user-centered solutions. The authors considered the implications of the three thematic areas in healthcare and finance industries and discussed some of the techniques for detecting malware in mobile systems [8]. This paper discusses unlimited register machine of owners (URMO) model with capabilities of analyzing and defining operations of mobile devices. The authors also discussed other technologies including secure portable tokens (SPTs) alongside an anonymity-preserving mutual authentication protocol that is integrable in mobile operating systems and the design should protect some of the known attacks.

1.1 Novelty of the Research

The number of attack surfaces and entry points is fast increasing given the growth, adoption, and acceptance of the Internet of things. The number of objects connected as things is on the rise. As Sicari et al. [9] assert, IoT relies on heterogeneous technologies alongside heterogeneous innovative services for many application domains making it had to meet both security and privacy requirements [9]. The applications and use of mobile systems continue to demand for more novel security technologies. Sha et al. [10] identified security and privacy challenges based on the characteristics of IoT systems. Additionally, the study implemented three different architectural security designs based on the identified issues [10].

Despite the efforts and assertion of finding novel security approaches of handling security and privacy in IoT systems, minimal efforts and contributions are yet to be seen in mobile systems. In fact, different vendors use different technologies, and most of them lack operational synergy despite the interaction between the devices. As such, installing and enforcing independent security and privacy features may not prove to be effective especially in the context of IoT. Against this backdrop, the purpose of this paper was to conduct a systematic literature review targeting studies that address security and privacy in mobile systems. The study used a predefined search strategy and relied on the preferred reporting items for systematic reviews and meta-analyses (PRISMA) checklist to analyze the search results. The primary contribution of this article is to provide comprehensive information security and privacy issues and technologies that other researchers have reported.

2   Research Methods

The study uses systematic literature review (SLR) as the research methodology. Ferrari [11] explains that systematic literature review (SLR) is a method that entails ways of identification, analysis, and the interpretation of evidence that is available more so those related with the research question, phenomena, and area of interest [11]. Studies that lead to or contribute to the systematic review are usually referred to as primary sources though systematic review in this context is a form of secondary study. The research process that will be used in this chapter is summarized in the following figure.

In Fig. 23.1, the literature research area has been identified and the subsequent search requirements are also outlined in the proposal. The rest of the process, especially screening of documents and compiling a report on the findings of the review will ensue after the approval of the proposal. It is imperative to note that research process focuses on systematic literature review and the use of PRISMA checklist to include and exclude articles in the study.

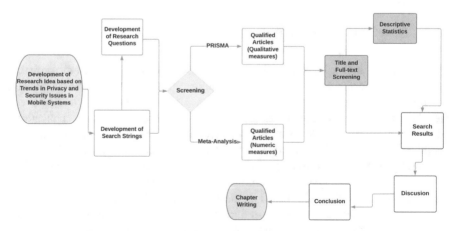

Fig. 23.1 The research process that will be used in completing the proposed chapter

Systematic literature review can also be referred to as a secondary form of study that seeks to identify, examine, and analyze researches which are relevant to the research question. Nie and Ma [12] highlight the characteristics of the SLR. The first feature is that at the start of the research, it must have a defined review protocol. It is this protocol that provides the definition for the research question for the research questions that are to be approached, as well as, the methods to be incorporated during the research [12]. For this chapter, the PRISMA protocol was used to review the papers retrieved from the database [13, 14].

Secondly, SLR proposes the creation of a research strategy that is well documented. Ferrari [11] reiterates that the strategy must be good enough to obtain the highest amount of primary studies with regard to the literature review that is relevant to the topic under study [11]. The author also advocates for additional exclusion and inclusion criteria the qualified primary sources of information or article retrieved from the search [11]. The planning including conducting and reporting results phases are followed during the SLR. The aim of the planning phase encompasses identifying the real need which is majorly the motivation for the execution of the SLR [15, 16]. Nie and Ma [12] reiterate that it consists of the major activities of not only defining the objective but also preparing of the protocol that guides the SLR to minimize biases that the research can commit [12]. In the conducting phase, the identification of the study entails the application of search strategy including the selected as per the defined protocol in the planning phase [17, 18]. Data are extracted for the selected works and synthesized to provide answers to the research questions. Eventually, this helps in facilitating analysis, as well as, synthesizing particularly for the creation of results. As for the reporting results phase, it is associated with SLR's documentation [12, 19]. It is where the results description gets executed, as well as, the answers to the research questions being prepared besides the results being disseminated to those interested. The state of art by systematic review (StArt) is employed in the provision of support for the performance of the SLR which helps in planning and the conduction phases of the SLR [20, 21]. The objective of conducting the SLR entails identifying and presenting issues regarding security and privacy in mobile systems [22].

The general outline flow diagram for the PRISMA technique and the subsequent number of papers included in the study is as summarized in Fig. 23.2.

As shown in the figure, the number of articles retrieved, eliminated, and retained were different at each stage and the subsequent analysis relied on the inclusion and not necessarily eligible for the study at identification stage. However, at screening stage, duplicates were removed, and titles screened to ensure relevance and suitability to area of interest. Besides the PRISMA checklist, full-text articles were qualified for the review and both qualitative and quantitative research papers were included. However, meta-analysis of the quantitative articles was not possible because different algorithms, numerical approaches, and novel techniques were presented in different paper. In ideal situations, meta-analysis is suitable and relevant when it is possible to identify the characteristics of the study. Furthermore, the ability identifies risk of biasness within each of the qualified and across them requires conformance in methods and uniformity in the representation of the results.

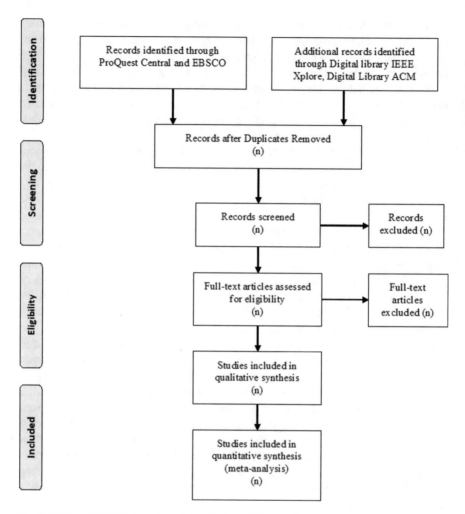

Fig. 23.2 The PRISMA flowchart diagram that will be used to implement the inclusion and exclusion criteria for the articles retrieved from the databases [13]

However, such characteristics were not easy to identify because of the different approaches used in addressing security and privacy issues in mobile systems.

3 Search Strategy

The search strategy employed encompasses the use of automatic search, which is commonly known as automatic lookup. It involves searching using search string that is in the electronic databases. The manual search then follows the automatic search through which the performances specifically for the works are through magazines, newspapers, and conferences [23, 24]. The databases for which the automating search is to be performed include Digital library IEEE Xplore, ProQuest Central, Digital Library Association for Computing Machinery (ACM), EBSCO, and the DBLP Computer Science Bibliography. Furthermore, manual search may be carried out in the conference Annals, as well as, periodicals that are specific to the area of e-governance and the pursuit of mobile systems [25].

The set criteria PICO provides the definition for the preparation of the search string. PICO consists of P-Population, I-intervention, C-comparison, and O-outcomes [26, 27]. The population, in this context, corresponds to the specific role more so within the lifestyle of the focus of the research [28]. It also includes the area of application, or the specific group of particularly of the industry. Intervention, on the other hand, delimits the focus of the research within the wider scope while comparison in the PICO not only identifies the alternatives but also compares with the delimitations carried out in the intervention [26, 29]. Finally, the outcomes from the PICO lists that which is intended to be accomplished, improved, measured, or even affected with regard to the population [30, 31]. The PICO criteria delimitation for this work is as illuminated below:

Population The definition of population is through the examination of various types of mobile systems. Keywords such as security and privacy are used to search the population.

Intervention The aim of intervention encompasses identifying and presenting the most relevant mechanisms, methods, and technologies that promote security and privacy of mobile systems. The keywords for this include technology, methods, and mechanisms.

Comparation The focus of this research study does not include comparative studies hence this technique has not been incorporated in the search strategy, as well as, the formation of the search string.

Search String Both automatic and manual search approaches will implement search strings created using Boolean operators constructed around the keywords and key concepts used described in the chapter. The search string will focus on Abstracts (AB), Document Texts (FT), Document Title (TI), and Publication Title (PUB). The Publication Title search string is an automatic lookup while the rest constitute manual search, although both will be implemented in an advanced search that illustrated in the figure below.

The search in Fig. 23.3 was implemented with limitations to full-text and peer-reviewed articles without specification of the publication. The general search string that will be implemented in search that is also used in Fig. 23.3 is shown below.

ab(security of mobile systems) AND ab(privacy in mobile systems) OR
ft(security of mobile systems) AND ft(privacy in mobile systems) OR
ti(security of mobile systems) AND ti(privacy in mobile systems) OR
pub(security of mobile systems) AND pub(privacy in mobile systems)

Advanced Search Command Line   Thesaurus   Field codes   Search tips

security of mobile systems			in	Abstract – AB	▾
AND	▾	privacy in mobile systems	in	Abstract – AB	▾
OR	▾	security of mobile systems	in	Document text – FT	▾
AND	▾	privacy in mobile systems	in	Document text – FT	▾
OR	▾	security of mobile systems	in	Document title – TI	▾
AND	▾	privacy in mobile systems	in	Document title – TI	▾
OR	▾	security of mobile systems	in	Publication title – PUB	▾

Look up Publications

| AND | ▾ | privacy in mobile systems | in | Publication title – PUB | ▾ |

Look up Publications

Fig. 23.3 An advanced search based on both automatic lookup and manual search implemented in ProQuest Central database

The same search string will be used in EBSCO, Digital library IEEE Xplore, Digital Library ACM, and the DBLP Computer Science Bibliography and the results collated and screened based on the algorithm represented in Fig. 23.2.

4   Data Synthesis

The studies included in the systematic review are heterogeneous (are not similar) hence different research designs have been included because of the diversity especially in the evidence base [32]. The data from these studies have been synthesized through descriptive or narrative synthesis process. Therefore, it is prudent to comprehend that due to the variety of methods employed in enhancing security and privacy of different mobile systems, it was relatively challenging to pull data for meta-analysis from the numerous studies that were examining or investigating this issue in discussion. Besides, the aim of each study differed in several aspects despite generally dealing with issues regarding privacy and security in mobile systems [33]. For instance, one of the studies focuses on security and privacy of mobile systems with in relation to mobile health while the others deal with: special issues on mobile networks and mobile systems, as well as, mobile could in the context of privacy, security, and digital forensics. The others, on the other hand, tackle privacy and security issues of mobile systems by examining not only the modern but also emerging mobile systems including the aspects of mobile applications and platforms [34]. Furthermore, there are also studies that examine security for smartphone devices using survey while another one provides a systematic review of cloud computing through the examination of databases and big data on the cloud [35, 36].

It was also noted that most of the articles discuss security and privacy but from the perspective of IoT [37–39]. The three articles focused on privacy and security in IoT as well as in the cloud. It is imperative to note that most mobile systems, including

IoT technology and concepts, are moving toward cloud computing. Furthermore, it emerged from the search results that "mobile systems" tend to be too generic and general because some of the articles address security and privacy in vehicular systems. Attempts of using "vehicular system" as exclusion criterion lead to a drastic reduction in the number of articles retrieved from the search process.

Before exploring the key concepts, it is important to note that most of the articles focused on encryption technologies, storage security, privacy and access management, and physical security of mobile systems. Given that there a lot of gray areas while addressing mobile systems, the focus was shifted to modern security techniques including satellite encryption as well as optical encipherments. For example, Khelifi et al. [40] focused on privacy and security issues in vehicular named data networks because of the growing likelihood of such networks becoming an important architecture in future [40]. According to the authors vehicular networks involve exchange of information via vehicle-to-vehicle or vehicle-to-infrastructure channels. The vehicle-to-infrastructure communication channels involve transmission of sensitive information between charging stations, satellites, smart grids, and pedestrians [40]. Hence, such systems are complex and have a larger attack exposure surface. Rauniyar et al. [41] also explored privacy and security for vehicular systems and identified network scalability, mobility and data transmission, data discrimination, time constraints, and privacy as the major concerns for the mobile systems [41]. It is important to note that vehicular network is growing fast and expanding rapidly without proper authority to oversee its expansion from a small town to a city. The lack of a governing boy is making it difficult to enforce security rules as well as standardize rules and policies for the industry [40, 41].

Given the amount of data exchanged between connected things within the vehicular network, integration with cloud systems is also critical and important for securing the systems [39, 42]. Adat and Gupta [43] also considered the challenges and security issues facing IoT and concluded that the levels of uncertainty when it comes to security of all levels and layers of IoT is worrying [43]. It is also imperative to note that both software as a service (SaaS) and platform as a service (PaaS) have innate risks and require protection. However, it is more practical and sensible to pursue security at infrastructure as a service (IaaS) level [43–45]. Chen et al. [44] identify four layers within IoT infrastructure and they include application, middle-ware layer, network layer, and perception layer. It is the application that contains modules for integration and data exchange between the hardware and software. The key challenge is its operation and handling of sensitive data with regard to illegal access, untheorized modification, and the duration of the granted access [44, 46]. As such privacy and security in mobile computing are serious issues that require involvement and engagement of different stakeholders [47, 48].

Most of the current attacks target middle-ware that integrates hardware and software system within the IoT framework. However, different research prospects have identified key technologies within the perception layer to have greater cyber threat risks compared to any other layer [49–51]. Hence, identifying the main point of attack in any system is critical in monitoring and preventing occurrences of such intrusions. It is also imperative to note that the above-discussed articles focused on IoT and its related security and privacy issues. However, the study aimed at exploring security and privacy issues in mobile systems and such article, despite providing critical security and privacy information, did not qualify under the auspices and thematic concern of the review. As such, additional filters based on key areas and concepts identified in the next section were used to make the search results more relevant and related to the objective of the research.

5   Key Concepts

The list of the concepts that this chapter will focus on include: vulnerability of systems, access control, threats and attacks on mobile systems, authentication technologies for mobile systems, and countermeasures and mitigation of threats and attacks of mobile systems, handling of personal data in mobile systems, privacy policies in mobile systems, security of mobile systems, and emerging trends in mobile systems.

Each of the concepts will be discussed independently and their contribution to the information and knowledge presented in the chapter discussed based on published peer-reviewed scholarly articles. It is also imperative to note the keyword filters focused on mobile systems with specific emphasis on smartphones and how connection within the IoT environment affects the security and privacy of the users within this context. Moreover, it is critical to recognize that mobile systems discussed.

6   Overview of Research Journal Articles

An implementation of the search string specified in the previous section returned 338 articles of which 300 were journal articles, 2 were reviews, 3 were general information, and the rest consisted of a case study, a correspondence article, and an interview. The eight articles were excluded from the search research results. Regarding subjects and the distribution of the search results-based field of study, the following chart summarizes the results. As per Fig. 23.4, most of the articles were published in Network Security Studies as well as journals dealing with Wireless Networks, Smartphones and Computer security. Other areas that predominantly featured in the search results include but not limited to privacy, Internet, authentication protocols, and computer information technology. Besides smartphone, cellular telephones and mobile communication networks, none of the articles expressed discussed the issue of security and privacy in mobile systems.

In Fig. 23.4, it should be noted that most of articles are counted in multiple subjects and as they do sum to 338 but more. Nonetheless, the search results will be screened by focusing security, privacy, and mobile related system studies. Some

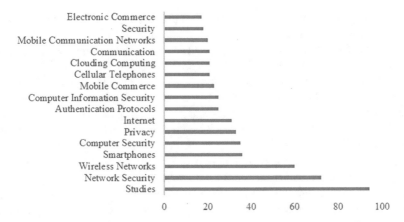

Fig. 23.4 Preliminary search results obtained by implementing the search string in

of the studies that are in the search results and will be used in the chapter are summarized as follows.

Arora et al. [52] seek to illuminate issues regarding the use of mobile technologies specifically for the problem of alcohol use [52]. The research emanates from the fact that the advancement of rapid technologies especially in mobile health has generated challenges and opportunities, as well as, ways of creating scalable systems that can collect or extracting unprecedented data amount besides conducting interventions while also protecting the privacy and security of the participants. There is little research literature in this area. However, there are things that can be borrowed from other communities such as Internet security or cyber security that provide several techniques that help in minimizing the risk and vulnerability of data breaches or even tampering in the mobile health as also observed in [53–58]. The proliferation of mobile health and wireless technologies provide scientists with the opportunity for collection of information and data in the real world through wearable sensors. Technologies of mobile health tend to produce data streams associated with the biological, behavior, psychology (cognition, attitudes, and emotions), biology, and daily environment of an individual [59–64]. Arora et al. [52] assert that research particularly in the mobile health helps in ensuring that critical behavioral, social, and environmental information are used to comprehend health determinants, as well as, improve health outcomes besides preventing development of alcohol use disorders (AUDS) and such observations are also found in [42, 65–69]. It is imperative to note that continued implementation of mobile services in healthcare is one of the reasons for pursuing security and privacy for mobile systems used within this domain. The health sector combines the intricacies of dealing with IoT application at individual level as well as coping and dealing with the need to integrate secure and private big data analytics for all electronic health record (EHR) applications [70].

Even though research in mobile health has been promising, progress has been relatively slow, and privacy and security issues remain a major concern for the researchers carrying out mobile health studies [52, 65, 67, 71]. The sensitivity of the data is an issue when it comes to security and privacy, especially with regard to the amount of information collected using mobile devices. Hauk [72] reiterate that since mobile devices such as sensors and phones are held by individuals, researchers have begun thinking concerning big data at individual level [72]. However, the article by Arora et al. [52] also provides detailed information regarding federal regulations that affect health information on privacy and security [52]. The regulators examined in this case include the HIPAA, the Common Rule, and the Code of Federal Regulations. HIPAA provides guidelines for privacy, as well as, security more so regarding personal information that is in use. This article beside other also defines the guidelines and policies for the maintenance of privacy and security of health information of a patient [52, 73–76]. The Common Rule, on the other hand, sets out guidelines and policies concerning informed consent, handling of biological data, adverse events, and vulnerable populations among others [52].

Lou et al. [77] alongside other researchers investigated security and private issues associated with mobile networks, mobile systems, and mobile cloud [62]. The articles were prompted by the fact that the use of mobiles devices and smartphones are increasingly becoming an integral part of lives of individuals [62, 77]. Crucial information such as medical and financial information, as well as, vital work-related data that are often processed on the mobile networks, mobile systems, and mobile cloud are vital to the advancement and development of secure mobile cloud, secure mobile operating systems, secure cellular networks, secure mobile devices, and applications [45, 46, 53, 78–82]. The scope of the article stems from the fact that special issues entails privacy, security, and digital forensics of mobile networks, mobile systems, as well as, mobile cloud inclusive of Androids, Windows Mobile Operating systems, iOS, applications and systems, design, the modeling, and testing of mobile networks, cloud, and systems with security and privacy in mind. In the article and related ones [50, 83–88], there are several submissions that the special issue has received, and the submissions have gone through rigorous process of peer review. All the submissions are jointly evaluated by the editors and they have also included seven high quality ones based on comments and ratings. Over the various mobile technologies and networks, the submissions include radio frequency identification (RFID), conventional mobile networks, Android mobile systems, near field communication (NFC), and millimeter-wave transmission of 45 GHz [89–92]. The findings of the research cover a relatively wide range of aspects related to privacy, security, and digital forensics inclusive of trade-off and balance between flexibility or efficiency and security of network protocols, private and secure Wi-Fi connections, mobile device authentication, digital forensics, mobile gaming security, and human security awareness [93].

Wang et al. [94] and Kaur and Chuchra [95] studied modern and emerging security and privacy options for mobile systems and provide the fundamentals of systems that are secure [94, 95]. The three cornerstones for the presentation of these fundamentals include integrity (which encompasses the inability to change or alter messages), authentication (entails trustworthiness particularly of the sender), and confidentiality (involves the inability more so to read messages for any individual other than the intended recipient) [94–97]. The author in this project programs an android application with the aim of sending geographical data particularly over a Bluetooth connection in a peer to peer manner that is secure [94]. The use of encryption, certificate validation, and digital signatures are the goals or objectives met in the application. The last application is featuring a user-interface with query parameters, and a Google Maps Interface, which the user is capable of setting when requesting data specifically concerning a certain position [98, 99].

Dmitrienko et al. [100] explored security and privacy aspects including the possibility of two-factor authentication on improving security. The research study examines privacy and security issues with regard to aspects of not only mobile platforms but also applications [100]. The research is prompted by the increasing trend where mobile devices are emerging as the most dominant platforms for computation among end users [100]. Such platforms store and process extensive amount of data and information concerning the users which may range from the location data of the user to credentials such as for online banking, as well as, enterprise virtual private networks (VPNs) [101]. Consequently, this has raised several issues of privacy and security concerns since the mobile platforms have become attractive targets particularly for attackers. This research study focuses on three parts in relation to privacy and security of mobile platforms. These areas include advanced attacks especially on mobile platforms, as well as, countermeasures; secure mobile services and applications; and online authentication security more so for mobile systems [100]. The results presented in the study encompass many peer-reviewed publications, as well as, extended technical reports. Some other papers that proved critical to the understanding of security and privacy issues are as follows [70, 102–104]. For instance, Hossain et al. [102] focused on security and privacy of video transmitted from the cloud to end users. Even though other authors would restrict and limit the insecurity incidences associated with video transmissions, the authors assert that the security is equally greater, especially in cases where private videos are leaked to the general public. The observation raises one of the major fundamental questions; how to enforce and implement big data transfer in open data sources. It is not apparent to identify the attributes that require regulations and those that do not require any regulation [105–109].

Das and Khan [46] focused on smartphone security technologies and related some of the current security and privacy challenges to the advancement of technology particularly in the mobile connectivity services such as GSM, GPRS, 4G, 3G, Bluetooth, Wi-Fi, and WiMAX have made mobile devices such as phones vital components of the lives of individuals [46] (Issue, 2015). However, the increase in the usage of such devices makes them vulnerable not only to malware attack but also other security breaching attacks. The diverse range of mobile device software platforms, mobile connectivity services, including standards makes it crucial to examine the holistic picture more so of the current development and advancement of research of smartphone security [46]. This journal article reviews issues such as threat, vulnerability, attacks, as well as, their solutions with the smartphone being the special focus. The authors further provide an analysis of the findings besides estimating the growth of different operating systems in the market for the smartphones.

7 Degree of Article Coverage

The articles highlighted in this chapter will be geared toward examining all the issues pertaining to privacy and security issues of mobile systems with regard to all devices. Some of the compelling issues discussed in the articles in the context of the topic under review include federal regulations that affect security and privacy in mobile health information, responsibility for the protection, the security risks, threats, and vulnerabilities of mobile systems, Internet security goals, mitigation and countermeasures to the security and privacy issues, the advancement of attacks on the mobile platforms and the development of their countermeasures, and authentication security specifically for mobile systems through the online platform. The other crucial issues illuminated in the articles are structure of operating systems (androids, iOS, Windows, and Symbian among others) of the mobile devices. The journal on security of the smartphones extends its survey by providing more and an extensive insight concerning the vulnerabilities, data protection and privacy, authentication, and attacks of smartphones devices. Besides these thematic areas, this chapter will address papers that were published in the last 5 years and address online security and privacy issues in mobile systems.

8 Findings/Results

Security and privacy issues in literature focus on specific aspects of security such as security requirements, security policies, access control mechanisms, authorization, and inter-organizational scenarios. Several security controls in areas of authorization, security concepts, verification, access control, and failure in handling software in mobile systems. Such factors are discussed at different levels and layers of security and privacy enforcement depending on the underlying system. Policies and fundamental principles vary from one mobile to the next but of importance is to consider the influence of the primary application and mobile vendor on the subsequent enforcement policy. Both security and privacy policies tend to vary from one vendor to the next and a good example is the differences between iOS and Android operating system. It suffices to acknowledge that Android supports user debugging and development while iOS do not and as such the security measures between the two operating systems are wildly different [61, 110, 111]. Hence, the difference in the operating systems and the policies implemented to enforce security and privacy need to be recognized and identified. For instance, it is apparent that Android system and its developer feature poses many security issues because with a portable memory and access to the target device, it is possible to install a malicious code and launch a stealth attack. However, the same is not possible with iOS-based systems and it becomes difficult for perpetrators to engineer and implement social engineering attacks on such systems.

Most of the articles also consider authorization and access control include issues related to online authentication security for the mobile systems, advanced attacks on the platforms of mobile systems and countermeasures, and secure mobile services and applications [90, 112–115]. However, it is imperative for such approaches to differentiate and identify different security threats for mobile systems and subsequently identify monitoring and prevention methods.

The findings demonstrate that the new mechanisms of security that were first developed on the mobile platforms such as the permission framework of Androids do not completely make these systems more secure and private. Instead, they are likely to introduce security vulnerabilities that can be exploited. However, such vulnerabilities may be mitigated using numerous mechanisms such as the deployment of additional security frameworks. The online authentication security for these systems, on the other hand, encompasses performing security analysis of two-factor authentication of mobile systems and investigation of the approaches more so for password-based authentication that is secure on the mobile systems. Besides the traditional password or login authentication credentials, the new schemes require an additional authentication stage/step as a way of confirming an online login attempt or banking transaction based on an one-time password (OTP). The OTP is usually generated either directly to the mobile device of the user or sent to user. From these results open research gaps and challenges are not only identified but also discussed with regard or respect to possible solutions.

Most of the techniques focus on controlling notifications and alerts that would otherwise exploit vulnerabilities within the mobile systems. As such, it is prudent to review logs and analyze all the probable points of entry [116]. One of the recommended approaches of dealing with some of these issues includes a holistic approach of monitoring and preventing attacks on the domains. Researchers recommend use of recommendation for alerts alongside correlation rules for identifying and eliminating activities that would otherwise be risky [117]. The other recommendations focus on reducing false-positive information feeds because it is difficult to scrutinize malicious information from a large volume of false positive information. For example, an alert that tends to control login failure is a policy that flags two failed login attempts. Such policies can also restrict the number of password resets and login attempts per day or per week, and for accountability purposes, it is prudent to record all the Internet protocol (IP) addresses of the computers or mobile devices attempting such logins [118, 119].

It is also customary to integrate and enforce thresholds for procedures that qualify as threats. In most cases, such information is aggregated into a single atomic variable for ease of visibility and ease of query results for monitoring inbound and outbound data transmission and communication. Further, it is recommended to consider the growth rate of the infrastructure as well as rates of penetration into different markets. It is factual that some regions have greater cyber threats compared to the rest and it is prudent for mobile service providers to be cognizant of this fact and take the required precautions [120].

9 Discussion

A systematic literature review will be performed for issues pertaining to privacy and security in mobile systems. As a result, a combination of manual and automatic search including primary studies had to be identified and the research questions of the studies analyzed. The evidences obtained from these research questions acted as guides to the identification gaps in research, as well as, incentives for future research. The distribution of the articles, quality of the papers, and biasness among the journals or publications are some of the areas that will require further attention.

However, based on the preliminary reviews of the articles retrieved from ProQuest Central database, several papers that address different aspects of privacy and security in mobile systems were found. Among them, journal articles with the emphasis on mobile networks, systems, and cloud within the context of security, privacy, and digital forensics were part of the main area of research interest.

The observation from the outcome of analysis from research journals of 2014–2018 focused on cloud computing, databases and big data on cloud, security of smartphone devices, aspects of mobile applications and platforms with regard to privacy and security, and privacy and security in mHealth due to increase in the technological automation of health services. The articles between 2017 and above focused on modern and emerging privacy and security issues of mobile systems, and special issues regarding mobile networks, systems, and cloud within the realms of privacy, security, and digital forensics. The bulk of these papers are from journals, research papers, surveys, and textbooks all in mobile systems, networks, and cloud within the context of security and privacy of users.

Moving forward, researchers and manufacturers will have to focus on hardware and software that render mobile system security and privacy compliant. As big data continues to develop, and different industrial application embrace the importance and role of mobile systems in IoT and Industrial 4.0 in general, it is imperative to source and pursue robust security and privacy systems. A practical application of mobile system is in mobile or e-health. The field of drug administration and management is one which could benefit from the use of mobile or IoT technologies. For instance, the elderly can benefit from an electronic reminder system but then again the system will have personal information that can be fraudulently be exploited and leveraged to make insurance claims or the same information sold leading to identity theft. As such, it is prudent to recognize the innumerable gray areas that exist in security and privacy in mobile systems.

10 Conclusion

The purpose of this chapter was to review articles on security and privacy in mobile systems. From the results, it emerged that the term "mobile systems" was ambiguous because the results of the search identified articles that addressed security and privacy in vehicular systems. Ideally, the term "mobile" refers to smartphones as well as moving smart vehicles and as the search results are sensible. However, based on the search results, the ensuing discussion and conclusion focused on security and privacy of smartphones and not vehicular network systems. Of importance and of future considerations is the application and enforcement of preventive, detective, and responsive techniques for ensuring security and privacy in mobile systems. It is undisputable that mobile systems, specifically smartphone systems, are fast growing and without proper central authority, it is not going to be possible and easy to enforce security and privacy laws. Finally, it imperative to note most of research articles are forced on IoT privacy and security and policy issues and it is necessary to focus on mobile systems because the number of devices going online are exponentially increasing and security is paramount, and vendors are obligated to do the same. The ideal condition requires involvement of both mobile vendors and service providers.

References

1. Au, M. H., & Choo, K.-K. R. (2017). Chapter 1 – Mobile security and privacy. In M. H. Au & K.-K. R. Choo (Eds.), *Mobile security and privacy: Advances, challenges and future research directions* (pp. 1–4). Boston: Syngress. https://doi.org/10.1016/B978-0-12-804629-6.00001-8.
2. Raggo, M. T., & Raggo, M. T. (2016). Chapter 3 – Mobile security countermeasures. In *Mobile data loss* (pp. 17–28). Boston: Syngress. https://doi.org/10.1016/B978-0-12-802864-3.00003-9.
3. Tully, S., & Mohanraj, Y. (2017). Chapter 2 – Mobile security: A practitioner's perspective. In *Mobile security and privacy* (pp. 5–55). Boston: Syngress. https://doi.org/10.1016/B978-0-12-804629-6.00002-X.
4. Rawat, D. B. (2013). *Security, privacy, trust, and resource management in mobile and wireless communications*. Hershey: IGI Global.
5. Huang, K., & Zhou, X. (2015). Cutting the last wires for mobile communications by microwave power transfer. *IEEE Communications Magazine, 53*(6), 86–93.
6. Gupta, B. B., Agrawal, D., & Yamaguchi, S. (2016). *Handbook of research on modern cryptographic solutions for computer and cyber security*. Hershey: IGI Publishing. https://doi.org/10.4018/978-1-5225-0105-3.
7. Gupta, B. B., & Wang, H. (2018). *Computer and cyber security: Principles, algorithm, applications, and perspectives*. Boca Raton: Auerbach Publishers. Retrieved from https://books.google.co.ke/books?id=rXBRuQEACAAJ.
8. Akram, R. N., Chen, H. H., Lopez, J., Sauveron, D., & Yang, L. T. (2018). Security, privacy and trust of user-centric solutions. *Future Generation Computer Systems, 80*, 417–420. https://doi.org/10.1016/j.future.2017.11.026.
9. Sicari, S., Rizzardi, A., Grieco, L. A., & Coen-Porisini, A. (2015). Security, privacy and trust in Internet of Things: The road ahead. *Computer Networks, 76*, 146–164. https://doi.org/10.1016/j.comnet.2014.11.008.

10. Sha, K., Wei, W., Andrew Yang, T., Wang, Z., & Shi, W. (2018). On security challenges and open issues in Internet of Things. *Future Generation Computer Systems, 83*, 326–337. https://doi.org/10.1016/j.future.2018.01.059.
11. Ferrari, R. (2015). Writing narrative style literature reviews. *Medical Writing, 24*, 230–235. https://doi.org/10.1179/2047480615Z.000000000329.
12. Nie, Y., & Ma, K.-K. (2002). Adaptive rood pattern search for fast block-matching motion estimation. *IEEE Transactions on Image Processing, 11*(12), 1442–1449.
13. Moher, D., Liberati, A., & Tetzlaff, J. (2009). PRISMA 2009 flow diagram. *The PRISMA Statement.* https://doi.org/10.1371/journal.pmed1000097.
14. Moher, D., Liberati, A., Tetzlaff, J., Altman, D. G., Altman, D., Antes, G., et al. (2009). Preferred reporting items for systematic reviews and meta-analyses: The PRISMA statement. *PLoS Medicine, 6*(7), e1000097. https://doi.org/10.1371/journal.pmed.1000097.
15. Kitchenham, B., & Charters, S. (2007). Guidelines for performing systematic literature reviews in software engineering. *Engineering, 2*, 1051. https://doi.org/10.1145/1134285.1134500.
16. Kitchenham, B., Pearl Brereton, O., Budgen, D., Turner, M., Bailey, J., & Linkman, S. (2009). Systematic literature reviews in software engineering – A systematic literature review. *Information and Software Technology, 51*(1), 7–15. https://doi.org/10.1016/j.infsof.2008.09.009.
17. Brereton, P., Kitchenham, B. A., Budgen, D., Turner, M., & Khalil, M. (2007). Lessons from applying the systematic literature review process within the software engineering domain. *Journal of Systems and Software.* https://doi.org/10.1016/j.jss.2006.07.009.
18. Budgen, D., & Brereton, P. (2006). Performing systematic literature reviews in software engineering. In *Proceeding of the 28th International Conference on Software Engineering – ICSE'06.* https://doi.org/10.1145/1134285.1134500.
19. Tarhan, A., Turetken, O., & Reijers, H. A. (2016). Business process maturity models: A systematic literature review. Information and Software Technology. https://doi.org/10.1016/j.infsof.2016.01.010.
20. Biolchini, J., Mian, P. G., Candida, A., & Natali, C. (2005). Systematic review in software engineering. *Engineering, 679*, 45. https://doi.org/10.1007/978-3-540-70621-2.
21. Cerchione, R., & Esposito, E. (2016). A systematic review of supply chain knowledge management research: State of the art and research opportunities. *International Journal of Production Economics.* https://doi.org/10.1016/j.ijpe.2016.09.006.
22. Pearson, F. (2014). Systematic approaches to a successful literature review. *Educational Psychology in Practice.* https://doi.org/10.1080/02667363.2014.900913.
23. Selby, A., & Smith-Osborne, A. (2013). A systematic review of effectiveness of complementary and adjunct therapies and interventions involving equines. *Health Psychology.* https://doi.org/10.1037/a0029188.
24. Wallace, B. C., Kuiper, J., Sharma, A., Zhu, M., Marshall, I. J., & Kuiper, J. (2016). Extracting PICO sentences from clinical trial reports using supervised distant supervision. *Journal of Machine Learning Research, 17*, 132.
25. Aslam, S., & Emmanuel, P. (2010). Formulating a researchable question: A critical step for facilitating good clinical research. *Indian Journal of Sexually Transmitted Diseases and AIDS, 31*(1), 47–50. https://doi.org/10.4103/0253-7184.69003.
26. Cooke, A., Smith, D., & Booth, A. (2012). Beyond PICO: The SPIDER tool for qualitative evidence synthesis. *Qualitative Health Research.* https://doi.org/10.1177/1049732312452938.
27. O'Sullivan, D., Wilk, S., Michalowski, W., & Farion, K. (2013). Using PICO to align medical evidence with MDs decision making models. In *Studies in health technology and informatics.* https://doi.org/10.3233/978-1-61499-289-9-1057.
28. Santos, C. M. d. C., Pimenta, C. A. d. M., & Nobre, M. R. C. (2007). The PICO strategy for the research question construction and evidence search. *Revista Latino-Americana de Enfermagem.* https://doi.org/10.1590/S0104-11692007000300023.
29. Rivas-Ruiz, R., & Talavera, J. O. (2012). *VII. Systematic search: how to look for medical documents.* Ciudad de México: Revista Médica Del Instituto Mexicano Del Seguro Social.

30. Shetty, S., Pitti, V., Babu, C. L. S., Kumar, G. P. S., & Deepthi, B. C. (2010). Bruxism: A literature review. *Journal of Indian Prosthodontist Society.* https://doi.org/10.1007/s13191-011-0041-5.
31. Timmins, F., & McCabe, C. (2005). How to conduct an effective literature search. *Nursing Standard.* https://doi.org/10.7748/ns2005.11.20.11.41.c4010.
32. Çoğaltay, N., & Karadağ, E. (2015). Introduction to meta-analysis. In *Leadership and organizational outcomes: Meta-analysis of empirical studies.* https://doi.org/10.1007/978-3-319-14908-0_2.
33. Khoury, B., Lecomte, T., Fortin, G., Masse, M., Therien, P., Bouchard, V., et al. (2013). Mindfulness-based therapy: A comprehensive meta-analysis. *Clinical Psychology Review.* https://doi.org/10.1016/j.cpr.2013.05.005.
34. Smith, B. R., & Blumstein, D. T. (2008). Fitness consequences of personality: A meta-analysis. *Behavioral Ecology.* https://doi.org/10.1093/beheco/arm144.
35. Hashem, I. A. T., Yaqoob, I., Anuar, N. B., Mokhtar, S., Gani, A., & Ullah Khan, S. (2015). The rise of "big data" on cloud computing: Review and open research issues. *Information Systems.* https://doi.org/10.1016/j.is.2014.07.006.
36. Hashem, I. A. T., Yaqoob, I., Badrul Anuar, N., Mokhtar, S., Gani, A., & Ullah Khan, S. (2014). The rise of "Big Data" on cloud computing: Review and open research issues. *Information Systems.* https://doi.org/10.1016/j.is.2014.07.006.
37. Ammar, M., Russello, G., & Crispo, B. (2018). Internet of Things: A survey on the security of IoT frameworks. *Journal of Information Security and Applications, 38,* 8–27. https://doi.org/10.1016/j.jisa.2017.11.002.
38. Kumar, P. R., Raj, P. H., & Jelciana, P. (2018). Exploring data security issues and solutions in cloud computing. *Procedia Computer Science, 125,* 691–697. https://doi.org/10.1016/j.procs.2017.12.089.
39. Stergiou, C., Psannis, K. E., Kim, B.-G., & Gupta, B. (2018). Secure integration of IoT and Cloud Computing. *Future Generation Computer Systems, 78,* 964–975. https://doi.org/10.1016/J.FUTURE.2016.11.031.
40. Khelifi, H., Luo, S., Nour, B., & Shah, S. C. (2018). Security and privacy issues in vehicular named data networks: An overview. *Mobile Information Systems, 2018,* 5672154:1–5672154:11. https://doi.org/10.1155/2018/5672154.
41. Rauniyar, A., Hagos, D. H., & Shrestha, M. (2018, 2018). A crowd-based intelligence approach for measurable security, privacy, and dependability in internet of automated vehicles with vehicular fog. *Mobile Information Systems,* 7905960. https://doi.org/10.1155/2018/7905960.
42. Volk, M., Sterle, J., & Sedlar, U. (2015). Safety and privacy considerations for mobile application design in digital healthcare. International Journal of Distributed Sensor Networks. https://doi.org/10.1155/2015/549420.
43. Adat, V., & Gupta, B. B. (2017). Security in Internet of Things: Issues, challenges, taxonomy, and architecture. *Telecommunication Systems, 67,* 1–19. https://doi.org/10.1007/s11235-017-0345-9.
44. Chen, K., Zhang, S., Li, Z., Zhang, Y., Deng, Q., Ray, S., & Jin, Y. (2018). Internet-of-Things security and vulnerabilities: Taxonomy, challenges, and practice. *Journal of Hardware and Systems Security, 2*(2), 97–110. https://doi.org/10.1007/s41635-017-0029-7.
45. Chen, X. M., & Zou, S. H. (2014). A secure mobile payments protocol based on ECC. *Applied Mechanics and Materials, 519–520,* 151–154. https://doi.org/10.4028/www.scientific.net/AMM.519-520.151.
46. Das, A., & Khan, H. U. (2016). Security behaviors of smartphone users. *Information and Computer Security, 24*(1), 116–134. https://doi.org/10.1108/ICS-04-2015-0018.
47. Elmaghraby, A. S., & Losavio, M. M. (2014). Cyber security challenges in smart cities: Safety, security and privacy. *Journal of Advanced Research.* https://doi.org/10.1016/j.jare.2014.02.006.
48. Kotz, D., Gunter, C. A., Kumar, S., Weiner, J. P., Arora, S., Yttri, J., et al. (2014). Privacy and security in mobile health (mHealth) research. *Alcohol Research: Current Reviews.* https://doi.org/10.1177/1357633X13487100.

49. Chin, E., Felt, A. P., Sekar, V., & Wagner, D. (2012). Measuring user confidence in smartphone security and privacy. In *Proceedings of the Eighth Symposium on Usable Privacy and Security – SOUPS'12*. https://doi.org/10.1145/2335356.2335358.
50. Kang, S., Kim, J., & Hong, M. (2013). Go anywhere: User-verifiable authentication over distance-free channel for mobile devices. *Personal and Ubiquitous Computing, 17*(5), 933–943. https://doi.org/10.1007/s00779-012-0531-4.
51. Martínez-Pérez, B., de la Torre-Díez, I., & López-Coronado, M. (2015). Privacy and security in mobile health apps: A review and recommendations. *Journal of Medical Systems*. https://doi.org/10.1007/s10916-014-0181-3.
52. Arora, S., Yttri, J., & Nilsen, W. (2014). Privacy and security in mobile health (mHealth) research. *Alcohol Research, 36*(1), 143–150. Retrieved from https://search.proquest.com/docview/1685862596?accountid=145382.
53. Garg, S. K., Lyles, C. R., Ackerman, S., Handley, M. A., Schillinger, D., Gourley, G., et al. (2016). Qualitative analysis of programmatic initiatives to text patients with mobile devices in resource-limited health systems. *BMC Medical Informatics and Decision Making, 16*, 16. https://doi.org/10.1186/s12911-016-0258-7.
54. Jiang, Y., & Liu, J. (2017). Health monitoring system for nursing homes with lightweight security and privacy protection. *Journal of Electrical and Computer Engineering, 2017*, 1360289. https://doi.org/10.1155/2017/1360289.
55. Mohit, P., Amin, R., Karati, A., Biswas, G. P., & Khan, M. K. (2017). A standard mutual authentication protocol for cloud computing based health care system. *Journal of Medical Systems, 41*(4), 1–13. https://doi.org/10.1007/s10916-017-0699-2.
56. Rakshitha, P., & Immanuel, A. (2017). A survey on context awareness security in healthcare. *International Journal of Advanced Research in Computer Science, 8*(3). Retrieved from https://search.proquest.com/docview/1901458446?accountid=145382.
57. Wazid, M., Zeadally, S., Das, A. K., & Odelu, V. (2016). Analysis of security protocols for mobile healthcare. *Journal of Medical Systems, 40*(11), 1–10. https://doi.org/10.1007/s10916-016-0596-0.
58. Yeh, K.-H. (2016). BSNCare+: A robust IoT-oriented healthcare system with non-repudiation transactions. *Applied Sciences, 6*(12), 418. https://doi.org/10.3390/app6120418.
59. Baig, M. M., Gholamhosseini, H., & Connolly, M. J. (2015). Mobile healthcare applications: System design review, critical issues and challenges. *Australasian Physical & Engineering Sciences in Medicine, 38*(1), 23–38. https://doi.org/10.1007/s13246-014-0315-4.
60. Chin-I, L., & Hung-Yu, C. (2015). An elliptic curve cryptography-based RFID authentication securing e-health system. *International Journal of Distributed Sensor Networks*. https://doi.org/10.1155/2015/642425.
61. Dong, Q., Guan, Z., Gao, K., & Chen, Z. (2015). SCRHM: A secure continuous remote health monitoring system. *International Journal of Distributed Sensor Networks*. https://doi.org/10.1155/2015/392439.
62. Jiang, S., Zhu, X., & Wang, L. (2015). EPPS: Efficient and privacy-preserving personal health information sharing in mobile healthcare social networks. *Sensors, 15*(9), 22419–22438. https://doi.org/10.3390/s150922419.
63. Watson, L., Pathiraja, F., Depala, A., O'Brien, B., & Beyzade, S. (2016). Ensuring safe communication in health care: A response to Johnston et al on their paper "Smartphones let surgeons know WhatsApp: An analysis of communication in emergency surgical teams". *The American Journal of Surgery, 211*(1), 302–303. https://doi.org/10.1016/j.amjsurg.2015.04.017.
64. Yang, H., Kim, H., & Mtonga, K. (2015). An efficient privacy-preserving authentication scheme with adaptive key evolution in remote health monitoring system. *Peer-To-Peer Networking and Applications, 8*(6), 1059–1069. https://doi.org/10.1007/s12083-014-0299-6.
65. Bloem, C. M., & Miller, A. C. (2013). Disasters and women's health: Reflections from the 2010 earthquake in Haiti. *Prehospital and Disaster Medicine, 28*(2), 150–154. https://doi.org/10.1017/S1049023X12001677.

66. Bloem, C., & Miller, A. (2011). (P1-20) disasters and women's health: The 2010 earthquake in Haiti. *Prehospital and Disaster Medicine, 26*(S1), s113. https://doi.org/10.1017/S1049023X11003529.
67. Lee, C., Hsu, C., Lai, Y., & Vasilakos, A. (2013). An enhanced mobile-healthcare emergency system based on extended chaotic maps. *Journal of Medical Systems, 37*(5), 1–9973. https://doi.org/10.1007/s10916-013-9973-0.
68. Safavi, S., & Shukur, Z. (2014). Conceptual privacy framework for health information on wearable device. *PLoS One, 9*(12). https://doi.org/10.1371/journal.pone.0114306.
69. Shin, M. S., Jeon, H. S., Ju, Y. W., Lee, B. J., & Jeong, S.-P. (2015). Constructing RBAC based security model in u-healthcare service platform. *The Scientific World Journal*. https://doi.org/10.1155/2015/937914.
70. Gupta, S., & Gupta, B. B. (2017). Detection, avoidance, and attack pattern mechanisms in modern web application vulnerabilities: Present and future challenges. *International Journal of Cloud Applications and Computing (IJCAC), 7*(3), 1–43.
71. Mendez, I., & VandenHof, M. C. (2013). Mobile remote-presence devices for point-of-care health care delivery. *Canadian Medical Association Journal, 185*(17), 1512–1516. Retrieved from https://search.proquest.com/docview/1476500625?accountid=145382.
72. Hauk, L. (2018). Benefits and challenges of remote video auditing in the OR. *AORN Journal, 107*(2), P7–P10. https://doi.org/10.1002/aorn.12078.
73. Belsis, P., & Pantziou, G. (2014). A k-anonymity privacy-preserving approach in wireless medical monitoring environments. *Personal and Ubiquitous Computing, 18*(1), 61–74. https://doi.org/10.1007/s00779-012-0618-y.
74. Chen, T., Chung, Y., & Lin, F. Y. S. (2012). A study on agent-based secure scheme for electronic medical record system. *Journal of Medical Systems, 36*(3), 1345–1357. https://doi.org/10.1007/s10916-010-9595-8.
75. Moorman, B. A., & Cockle, R. A. (2013). Medical device integration using mobile telecommunications infrastructure. *Biomedical Instrumentation & Technology, 47*(3), 224–232. Retrieved from https://search.proquest.com/docview/1366370612?accountid=145382.
76. Mulvaney, D., Woodward, B., Datta, S., Harvey, P., Vyas, A., Thakker, B., et al. (2012). Monitoring heart disease and diabetes with mobile internet communications. *International Journal of Telemedicine and Applications, 2012*, 12. https://doi.org/10.1155/2012/195970.
77. Lou, W., Liu, W., Zhang, Y., & Fang, Y. (2009). SPREAD: Improving network security by multipath routing in mobile ad hoc networks. *Wireless Networks, 15*(3), 279–294. https://doi.org/10.1007/s11276-007-0039-4.
78. Enenkel, M., See, L., Karner, M., Álvarez, M., Rogenhofer, E., Baraldès-Vallverdú, C., et al. (2015). Food security monitoring via mobile data collection and remote sensing: Results from the Central African Republic. *PLoS One, 10*(11). https://doi.org/10.1371/journal.pone.0142030.
79. Gheorghe, M. (2014). Mobile cloud computing for telemedicine solutions. *Informatica Economica, 18*(4), 50–61. Retrieved from https://search.proquest.com/docview/1649081693?accountid=145382.
80. Langovic, Z., Pazun, B., & Grujcic, Z. (2018). Processor systems security impact on business systems. In *Economic and social development: Book of proceedings* (pp. 443–449). Varazdin: Varazdin Development and Entrepreneurship Agency (VADEA). Retrieved from https://search.proquest.com/docview/2058257359?accountid=145382.
81. Sengupta, S., & Sarkar, P. (2015). An augmented level of security for Bluetooth devices controlled by smart phones and ubiquitous handheld gadgets. *International Journal of Information Engineering and Electronic Business, 7*(4), 58–75. https://doi.org/10.5815/ijieeb.2015.04.08.
82. Taylor, E. (2016). Mobile payment technologies in retail: A review of potential benefits and risks. *International Journal of Retail and Distribution Management, 44*(2), 159–177. Retrieved from https://search.proquest.com/docview/1767676353?accountid=145382.
83. Chen, H., Lo, J., & Yeh, C. (2012). An efficient and secure dynamic id-based authentication scheme for telecare medical information systems. *Journal of Medical Systems, 36*(6), 3907–3915. https://doi.org/10.1007/s10916-012-9862-y.

84. Chen, Y., & Chou, J. (2015). ECC-based untraceable authentication for large-scale active-tag RFID systems. *Electronic Commerce Research, 15*(1), 97–120. https://doi.org/10.1007/s10660-014-9165-0.

85. Gupta, A., Kalra, A., Boston, D., & Borcea, C. (2009). MobiSoC: A middleware for mobile social computing applications. *Mobile Networks and Applications, 14*(1), 35–52. https://doi.org/10.1007/s11036-008-0114-9.

86. Kokemüller, J., & Roßnagel, H. (2012). Secure mobile sales force automation: The case of independent sales agencies. *Information Systems and e-Business Management, 10*(1), 117–133. https://doi.org/10.1007/s10257-010-0157-x.

87. Yazji, S., Scheuermann, P., Dick, R. P., Trajcevski, G., & Jin, R. (2014). Efficient location aware intrusion detection to protect mobile devices. *Personal and Ubiquitous Computing, 18*(1), 143–162. https://doi.org/10.1007/s00779-012-0628-9.

88. Youn, T., Kim, J., & Lim, M. (2014). Study on two privacy-oriented protocols for information communication systems. *Journal of Intelligent Manufacturing, 25*(2), 339–345. https://doi.org/10.1007/s10845-012-0654-5.

89. Al-fayoumi, M. A., & Shilbayeh, N. F. (2014). Cloning SIM cards usability reduction in mobile networks. *Journal of Network and Systems Management, 22*(2), 259–279. https://doi.org/10.1007/s10922-013-9299-8.

90. Moon, S., & Yoon, C. (2015). Information retrieval system using the keyword concept net of the P2P service-based in the mobile cloud environment. *Peer-To-Peer Networking and Applications, 8*(4), 596–609. https://doi.org/10.1007/s12083-014-0265-3.

91. Spreitzenbarth, M., Schreck, T., Echtler, F., Arp, D., & Hoffmann, J. (2015). Mobile-sandbox: Combining static and dynamic analysis with machine-learning techniques. *International Journal of Information Security, 14*(2), 141–153. https://doi.org/10.1007/s10207-014-0250-0.

92. Wang, J., Floerkemeier, C., & Sarma, S. E. (2014). Session-based security enhancement of RFID systems for emerging open-loop applications. *Personal and Ubiquitous Computing, 18*(8), 1881–1891. https://doi.org/10.1007/s00779-014-0788-x.

93. Hennig, N. (2018). Assessing your security and privacy needs. *Library Technology Reports, 54*(3), 5. Retrieved from https://search.proquest.com/docview/2020766935?accountid=145382.

94. Wang, M., Yan, Z., & Niemi, V. (2017). UAKA-D2D: Universal authentication and key agreement protocol in D2D communications. *Mobile Networks and Applications, 22*(3), 510–525. https://doi.org/10.1007/s11036-017-0870-5.

95. Kaur, K., & Chuchra, R. (2017). Proposing enhanced Na Gaun Technique (Engt) for resource block allocation in Lte(long term evolution) systems for improving quality of service. *International Journal of Advanced Research in Computer Science, 8*(7). Retrieved from https://search.proquest.com/docview/1931114880?accountid=145382.

96. Caballero-Gil, C., Caballero-Gil, P., Molina-Gil, J., Martín-Fernández, F., & Loia, V. (2017). Trust-based cooperative social system applied to a carpooling platform for smartphones. *Sensors, 17*(2), 245. https://doi.org/10.3390/s17020245.

97. Militano, L., Orsino, A., Araniti, G., & Iera, A. (2017). NB-IoT for D2D-enhanced content uploading with social trustworthiness in 5G systems. *Future Internet, 9*(3), 31. https://doi.org/10.3390/fi9030031.

98. Sherkar, R. M. (2015). An extension to android security framework. *International Journal of Advanced Research in Computer Science, 6*(1). Retrieved from https://search.proquest.com/docview/1674900061?accountid=145382.

99. Su-Wan, P., Lim, J., & Kim, J. N. (2015). A secure storage system for sensitive data protection based on mobile virtualization. *International Journal of Distributed Sensor Networks*. https://doi.org/10.1155/2015/929380.

100. Dmitrienko, A., Liebchen, C., Rossow, C., & Sadeghi, A. R. (2014). On the (in)security of mobile two-factor authentication. In *Lecture notes in computer science (including subseries lecture notes in artificial intelligence and lecture notes in bioinformatics)*. https://doi.org/10.1007/978-3-662-45472-5_24.

101. Školc, G., & Markelj, B. (2018). Smart cars and information security TT – Pametni avtomobili in informacijska varnost. *Varstvoslovje, 20*(2), 218–236. Retrieved from https://search.proquest.com/docview/2095680841?accountid=145382.
102. Hossain, M. S., Muhammad, G., Abdul, W., Song, B., & Gupta, B. B. (2018). Cloud-assisted secure video transmission and sharing framework for smart cities. *Future Generation Computer Systems.* https://doi.org/10.1016/j.future.2017.03.029.
103. Plageras, A. P., Psannis, K. E., Stergiou, C., Wang, H., & Gupta, B. B. (2018). Efficient IoT-based sensor BIG data collection–processing and analysis in smart buildings. *Future Generation Computer Systems.* https://doi.org/10.1016/j.future.2017.09.082.
104. Wang, L., Li, L., Li, J., Li, J., Gupta, B. B., & Liu, X. (2018). Compressive sensing of medical images with confidentially homomorphic aggregations. *IEEE Internet of Things Journal.* https://doi.org/10.1109/JIOT.2018.2844727.
105. Bowen, K., & Pistilli, M. D. (2012). Student preferences for mobile app usage. *Research Bulletin.* https://doi.org/10.1002/pros.20492.
106. Homscheid, D., Kilian, T., & Schaarschmidt, M. (2015). Offen versus geschlossen-Welchen Zusammenhang gibt es zwischen Apple iOS-und Android-App-Entwicklern? In *Wirtschaftsinformatik* (pp. 1191–1205).
107. Hu, H., Bezemer, C. P., & Hassan, A. E. (2018). Studying the consistency of star ratings and the complaints in 1 & 2-star user reviews for top free cross-platform Android and iOS apps. *Empirical Software Engineering.* https://doi.org/10.1007/s10664-018-9604-y.
108. Saltaformaggio, B., Choi, H., Johnson, K., Kwon, Y., Zhang, Q., Zhang, X., et al. (2016). Eavesdropping on fine-grained user activities within smartphone apps over encrypted network traffic. In *Proceedings of the 10th USENIX Workshop on Offensive Technologies (WOOT 2016).* https://doi.org/10.1101/lm.529807.
109. Ubhi, H. K., Kotz, D., Michie, S., van Schayck, O. C. P., & West, R. (2017). A comparison of the characteristics of iOS and Android users of a smoking cessation app. *Translational Behavioral Medicine.* https://doi.org/10.1007/s13142-016-0455-z.
110. Barrera, D., & Van Oorschot, P. (2011). Secure software installation on smartphones. *IEEE Security and Privacy, 9,* 42–48. https://doi.org/10.1109/MSP.2010.202.
111. Han, J., Yan, Q., Gao, D., Zhou, J., & Deng, R. H. (2013). Comparing mobile privacy protection through cross-platform applications. In *Proceedings of the network and distributed system security symposium.*
112. Kodali, R. K., Jain, V., Bose, S., & Boppana, L. (2017). IoT based smart security and home automation system. In *Proceeding – IEEE International Conference on Computing, Communication and Automation, ICCCA 2016.* https://doi.org/10.1109/CCAA.2016.7813916.
113. Michalevsky, Y., Boneh, D., & Nakibly, G. (2014). Gyrophone: Recognizing speech from gyroscope signals. In *23rd USENIX Security Symposium (USENIX Security 14).* https://doi.org/10.1109/IEMBS.2009.5333489.Active.
114. Sivaraman, V., Chan, D., Earl, D., & Boreli, R. (2016). Smart-phones attacking smart-homes. In *Proceedings of the 9th ACM Conference on Security & Privacy in Wireless and Mobile Networks – WiSec'16.* https://doi.org/10.1145/2939918.2939925.
115. Yoon, H. S., & Occeña, L. (2014). Impacts of customers' perceptions on internet banking use with a smart phone. *Journal of Computer Information Systems.* https://doi.org/10.1080/08874417.2014.11645699.
116. Shukla, D., Kumar, R., Serwadda, A., & Phoha, V. V. (2014). Beware, your hands reveal your secrets! In *Proceedings of the 2014 ACM SIGSAC Conference on Computer and Communications Security – CCS'14.* https://doi.org/10.1145/2660267.2660360.
117. Younis, A. A., Malaiya, Y. K., & Ray, I. (2014). Using attack surface entry points and reachability analysis to assess the risk of software vulnerability exploitability. In *Proceedings – 2014 IEEE 15th International Symposium on High-Assurance Systems Engineering, HASE 2014.* https://doi.org/10.1109/HASE.2014.10.
118. Loukas, G. (2015). Cyber-physical attack steps. In *Cyber-physical attacks.* Oxford: Butterworth-Heinemann. https://doi.org/10.1016/B978-0-12-801290-1.00005-9.

119. Weber, J., Azad, M., Riggs, W., & Cherry, C. R. (2018). The convergence of smartphone apps, gamification and competition to increase cycling. Transportation Research Part F: Traffic Psychology and Behaviour. https://doi.org/10.1016/j.trf.2018.04.025.
120. Wang, X., Shi, J., & Guo, L. (2013). Towards analyzing and improving service accessibility under resource enumeration attack. *Procedia Computer Science, 17*, 836–843. https://doi.org/10.1016/j.procs.2013.05.107.

Chapter 24
Investigation of Security Issues in Distributed System Monitoring

Manjunath Kotari and Niranjan N. Chiplunkar

Abstract The distributed systems have a noteworthy role in today's information technology whether it is governmental or nongovernmental organization. Adaptive distributed systems (ADS) are distributed systems that can evolve their behaviors based on changes in their environments (Schlichting and Hiltunen, Designing and implementing adaptive distributed systems, 1998, http://www.cs.arizona.edu/adaptiveds/overview.html). For example, a constant monitoring is required in distributed system to dynamically balance the load using centralized approach (Sarma and Dasgupta, Int J Adv Res Ideas Innov Technol 2:5–10, 2014). A monitoring system or tool is used to identify the changes in the distributed systems and all the activities of the entire network systems. The monitoring of network may help to improve the efficiency of the overall network. However, the monitoring system may be compromised by the intruder by gathering the information from the distributed systems. The various secure and insecure monitoring mechanisms have been adopted by adaptive distributed systems. Most of the distributed systems nowadays use monitoring tools to monitor the various parameters of the networking system. The monitoring tool has been implemented to assess the performance overhead during monitoring. The Wireshark monitoring tool and JMonitor tool (Penteado and Trevelin, JMonitor: a monitoring tool for distributed systems. In Proceedings of international conference on systems, man, and cybernetics, COEX, Seoul, Korea, pp 1767–1772, 2012) have been used to monitor the communication between the various users and also to monitor the computational resources used in networked computers. The main concern of this chapter is to investigate the existing monitoring tools for finding the impacts of monitoring activities in the distributed network. The investigations result that, when the monitoring tool collects security-critical information, there is a high risk of information disclosure to unauthorized users. The second concern is that a secure communication channel

M. Kotari (✉)
AIET, Moodbidri, India

N. N. Chiplunkar
NMAMIT, Nitte, India
e-mail: nchiplunkar@nitte.edu.in

© Springer Nature Switzerland AG 2020   609
B. B. Gupta et al. (eds.), *Handbook of Computer Networks and Cyber Security*,
https://doi.org/10.1007/978-3-030-22277-2_24

can be implemented by using the Rivest, Shamir, and Adelman (RSA) algorithm to monitor the confidential information. This chapter illustrates the implementation and experimental results related to authors' research work and formulation of framework for security mechanisms in the context of adaptive distributed systems (Kotari et al., IOSR J Comput Eng 18:25–36, 2016).

Security issues for existing monitoring tool are investigated in detail here. In this connection, the chapter deals with the several security-related network scenarios experienced during monitoring with the help of Wireshark monitoring tool. The proper use of Wireshark monitoring tool helps to identify the possible security threats such as emerging threats of hackers, corporate data theft, and identifying threats due to viruses. The implementation of secure communication channel is discussed, which minimizes the above set of threats.

Keywords Distributed systems · Monitoring tool · Network management

1 Introduction

The monitoring may be exercised with the help of different monitoring tools available. These monitoring tools are indispensable for monitoring the entire network. In this chapter, monitoring security mechanism has been accomplished with the existing monitoring tool and various parameters over the distributed systems are studied. The foremost target of this chapter is to investigate the existing monitoring systems such as Wireshark monitoring tool and to develop a solution to secure communication channel to Wireshark monitoring tool [1] with improved security features. Thus, Wireshark monitoring tool is considered here and its advantages and disadvantages are discussed in detail.

1.1 Monitoring Systems

A system primarily used to keep track of other systems in a network is known as monitoring systems. The network monitoring expresses the usage of the system that continuously observes the networked computer in case of slow or failure and gives an alert message to network administrator [2]. The monitoring system usually comprises the following components such as monitoring module, event identifier, and monitoring hardware, detection of events, and processing of events. Specifically, monitoring is accomplished in two operations, namely detection of events that are relevant to program execution and storing or recording the collected data. The failure nodes [3] have been tracked by running monitoring application on network. Simple network management protocol (SNMP) agent accesses a monitor of another network to obtain current system status.

Monitoring system can be categorized into two types, namely internal monitoring system and external monitoring system [4]. In case of an internal monitoring system, the monitoring system is integrated with each client. Each client's monitoring system keeps track of program executions of the same system and records the data here. The recorded information is transmitted to central monitoring system. Whereas in case of an external monitoring system, the monitoring system resides outside the existing network and monitors the target system. Here the target system is usually present in the distributed system. The monitoring system helps security administrators to keep track of the attacker in the system. So the assessment technique allows monitoring the current attacker position and forecast his (her) path in the network [5].

In Software Defined Security Architecture (SDSA) monitoring system [6], the run-time environment associated with the security execution control module contains the security engine for supporting dynamic monitoring of systems and a set of (sub) modules for supporting security status monitoring, security task executions, and software developer managements, which are all on the top of the security engine. The responsibility of the security status monitoring module is to watch and control the running status of various security programs such as the status of processes, the status of memory stacks, the status of the file system, and the status of resources scheduling.

1.1.1 Monitoring Tools

The network monitoring tool helps to monitor the utilization of traffic, bandwidth availability and utilization, latency, central processing unit (CPU) utilization, responsiveness of CPU, and fault identification. These monitored parameters help the network monitoring tool to estimate the performance of distributed systems easily. Normally, network monitoring tool is a combination of software and hardware products. It completely tracks the network activities and raises an alert if required.

In energy manufacturing plant [7], it is very difficult to decide about how much capacity is required to get desired output. There is a chance of capacity review and capacity measurement techniques, but it should be associated with new machine with many functions. One of the solutions to measure capacity is use of multiple sensors. This solution has been used to quantify variations in power input throughout monitoring. It determines the amount of power input reduction during manufacturing. A monitoring tool has been used to identify and validate energy use reduction system.

1.1.2 Purpose of Network Monitoring Tools

The network administrators use monitoring tools for various purposes [8], viz.

- To detect the faults in routers as well as in the switches.
- To supervise the internet services as well as resources.
- To supervise the operations of several host in the network.

- To supervise the natural processes of the client server computing system.
- To monitor and supervise the operation of broadcast systems for achieving scalability.
- To monitor the bandwidth level like the usage of the distributed network.
- To monitor the exchange of messages among the users of the distributed network.

1.1.3 Features of Network Monitoring Tools

The network monitoring tool acts as eyes and ears of an organization to solve the problems. These tools monitor the server or system crash, running application, utilization of bandwidth, and utilization of CPU as well as memory. Monitoring tool has been included with following features, viz. automatic discovery, inventorying devices, warnings, and web-based interface [9]. The monitoring tool [7] should be able to diagnose both IPv4 and IPv6 traffics of traditional network. Most of the monitoring tools use sensors to collect information for the purpose of analysis. Some monitoring tools use agents to collect information, but their use affects the overall performance of the system. Hence, an agent-less monitoring tool may be considered as a little efficient product. One more important feature of the monitoring tool is that monitoring tools are able to monitor all applications and services, which run across the network. They enable the network administrators to analyze performance issues from either the network or application itself. This feature of monitoring tool lets network administrators to track response time of application such as processing of server request and response of networks. The following list provides the various features of the monitoring tools.

- *Auto discovery:* It is very awkward for system administrators to insert each healthy device manually. Most of the monitoring tools perform auto discovery of system. It helps system administrators to get a glance of IT infrastructure catalogue.
- *Network traffic status:* Apart from monitoring CPU, memory and disk utilization, monitoring tools may be used to monitor network bandwidth usage. It helps the network administrators to get an insight into the ISP's bandwidth utilization.
- *Log monitoring:* Monitoring tools manage the activity logs created by operating systems. It verifies the file size of activity log and performs configuration actions. This feature helps the system administrator to control the entire network infrastructure.
- *Alert management:* The monitoring tool provides alert signal alongside mere network monitoring activity. For example, if a firewall system drops more number of packets or if the CPU of a server crosses the 95% of utilization. In all these cases, the tool should generate alert message to network administrator.
- *Customizable Web dashboard:* The monitoring tool must be customizable in such ways that user can decide about what should be on the dashboard. It helps to decide how much manpower should be utilized to address monitoring activities.
- *Security monitoring:* Monitoring tool should be secure during monitoring. The possible attack on data link layer, network layer, and application layer should be

encountered with this tool. The network administrators must decide what needs to be monitored, rather than monitoring all parameters.

1.1.4 How Network Monitoring Works

For observing the issues of network connectivity, ping utility is sufficient for simple network. The Microsoft network monitoring provides analysis of network packets mainly to resolve network issues. Normally open-source network monitoring tool provides accuracy of data based on metrics, but these require additional utilities like automatic alert signals. The open-source monitoring tools are inexpensive. However, these monitoring tools are little inefficient.

The Wireshark monitoring tool captures traffic data in real-time environment [10]. It captures one packet for every 10 msec of one time slot. So, a very large number of packets have been stored in 1 h time slot. For every such capture, the Wireshark monitoring tool saves the elapsed time, capture number, protocol used for capturing, size of the packet, source IP address, and destination IP addresses for future reference purpose.

In [11] the authors presented a solution for limiting the security breaches during monitoring service. An enough security protection against nasty achievement of the monitoring has been provided through the SELinux OS. The security policy has been applied on the basis of new configuration of OS.

Basically there are two ways of capturing packet in networks [12], one is Macro Capturing, which deals with capturing of large amount of information and its analysis. Another type is Micro Capturing, which deals only with specific information as mentioned by a user. Here, in the Wireshark monitoring tool, the Micro-Capturing method is used. The live network data can be captured and examined in this tool.

1.1.5 Passive Monitoring Framework

Jeswani et al. [13] proposed a manual as well as automatic based approach for system monitoring. The authors present frameworks with probes for adjusting monitor levels. A typical requirement for any monitoring systems is a good quality of monitoring data. This monitoring framework is deployed to capture the activities of communication, computation, and storage components. Monitoring metrics needs to be calculated for different collected parameters of nodes. Many of the monitoring tools are able to collect large amounts of metrics as per needs.

The traditional approach of monitoring data leads to collect small amounts of data and the modern approach of monitoring leads to a huge amount of information [14, 15]. The second approach is complex and difficult to store. In addition, the analysis of large volumes of information is a difficult task. The authors are focused on how to merge the two methods to develop proficient solutions for balancing the two techniques.

1.1.6 Customized Process Monitoring Tool

Comuzzi and Martinez [16] developed a customized tool for process monitoring. The users can specify customization options through Customization Interface (CI), which is a part of Monitoring Customization Console (MCC). The users usually get access of customized monitoring data through Monitoring Console (MC). The architectural framework of the tool contains the following components, viz. Query Engine (QE), Management Engine (ME), and Notification Engine (NE). The QE helps to capture monitoring parameters as per the user-desired option. The ME manages the monitoring data as per the user's logic. The NE gives notifications to users about monitoring results.

The network management framework [17] for distributed systems is modular and extensible. The modules have been built and customized according to needs of users. The framework is based on SNMP and is meant for monitoring. Framework has been used to manage distributed systems by the help of multiple points' entry.

1.1.7 Secure Monitoring Framework for Distributed System

Chen et al. [18] present a monitoring framework for distributed information management systems in a unique way. This monitoring framework makes use of Web services and message queue techniques to collect log data. The collected information is used for business process monitoring. This tool is implemented to assess the performance overhead due to monitoring. Evaluation was conducted with and without monitoring under various loads in users. The investigation reports show that the monitoring mechanism does not change the performance of the system significantly. However, the monitoring framework is a kind of passive monitoring because it uses only one message queue. This tool is unable to visualize two unrelated events that appear during concurrent process. Multiple queues may be applied, but there is a chance of monitoring overhead.

Fonseca et al. [19] proposed a framework for gathering events of certain profiles of social network users. It also periodically collects profile-related activities and profile-based information. The framework helps to compute the average events of certain profiles and compares the collected values with latest collected profile values. These values will help to detect the variation in profile activities. In addition, these variations indicate that illegal profile usage or account has been hijacked. The framework also notifies the users about cancellation friendships of each other. It also detects the abnormal activities like user added or removed many other users.

The authors presented a framework with two components. One of the components is called core component, which calculates the user profile interactions. Another component is called web interface component, which is responsible for users profile metrics by visualizing and interacting. The start component is responsible for getting the occurrence of activities from various social networks. Once the start component finishes its data collection, the statistics component analyzes the collected information and generates a report. Based on the report generated by statistics module, the alert module processes the alert signals for appropriate suspicious activities. However, the proposed framework does not collect user-desired data from the social networks. Instead, the framework collects the bulk of data than it is necessary, in turn; it degrades the performance of the system.

Atighetchi and Adler [20] described new framework for remote monitoring. It supports largely security aspects by limiting unwanted users to access the monitoring elements. The framework also helps to cooperate in very congested distributed networks like temporary and low bandwidth networks. This remote monitoring resists spontaneous and passive attacks by the help of special sensor information.

In [21] a framework has been generated for specifying plans of monitoring parameters. Initially, the framework elaborates the process for stipulating plans and implementing them in both friendly and unfriendly environments. Then, it develops a model for execution of security policies.

1.1.8   Network Security Management

Agbogun and Ejiga [22] mentioned that different classes of intrusions, network tools, and procedures attackers are employed in networks hijack. The author presents how attacks prevented, minimized from the backend system. The following are the different steps used by intruders during exploitation of networks.

In scanning vulnerable systems, the intruders try to access network connection as well as scans IP address of a network. Once hackers are able to access IP address, then the hackers load Trojan viruses into the network. In addition, intruders use tools to identify vulnerabilities in the network and perform snooping or destroying operating system. The hacker tries to search the administrative passwords in computer system and thereby gain the access of the entire system.

The Access attack could be an external attacker. It uses different techniques to gain control of the network. An access attack may be classified into the following categories, namely Gaining Primary Access, Social Engineering; Password-based attacks, and IP Spoofing.

1.2   Problems in Monitoring Systems

According to Feyissa [23, 24] allowing the monitoring system to gather more data for the intention of adaptation may affect stern security problems. Because, sometimes, the monitoring system attacked by an intruder may misuse the information. The authors have also discussed the need to limit the monitoring system for the purpose of adaptation. They used security metrics for measuring the security criticality of data. These security metrics are helping in recognizing the malicious activities, which give security threats to distributed systems.

Aredo and Yildirim [4] discussed about the two main problems in adaptive distributed systems. Initially, system monitoring to collect information necessary for adaptation may cause security issues. Information about users, their activities, and message details gathered by the monitoring node typically take place outside the destination system. Such monitoring causes a significant security risk in the case, if an attacker overtakes the monitoring system. Finally, limiting the monitoring may hamper the capacity of the system to adapt to the varying environment and maintain the security mechanism. Aredo and Yildirim [4] do not address about how to achieve an adaptation through the minimal impact on its security mechanism. In addition, the authors do not discuss about what kind of data can be monitored and how to monitor without affecting the performance of the distributed monitoring architecture.

Aredo and Yildirim [4] presented the monitoring of adaptive distributed systems and security metrics for the adaptive distributed systems by using security metric functions. The basic mechanisms of ADS include monitoring, change detection, and reconfiguration in response to the changes in the environment [25]. A monitoring component is employed for collecting information on parameters, which are ana-lyzed later to detect changes in the environment of the target-distributed system. The intruder may overtake the role of a monitoring system and misuse the information.

There are two scenarios for monitoring the target systems, one is monitoring of module that is a part of the system and another monitoring that is outside the system. Here authors considered the scenario of monitoring outside the system because of following reasons. One of the reasons is that, if monitoring is part of the system then it is difficult in directly controlling the entire distributed system from centralized server. It requires additional chronological methods of monitoring. Whereas external monitoring, system is depending upon the existence of a single thread of control. In addition, the problem lies in direct monitoring the system in its total from a lone point of surveillance [26], which needs the compilation of locally observed activities in order to build global observations. Second, there is no central point of decision making when monitoring is part of the system. Thus, the method of making decisions in a distributed system may itself be distributed. The third reason is that, the dependencies between different programs in a distributed system are such that any alteration in the activities of one program can alter the behavior of the whole distributed system.

Figure 24.1 depicts a scenario of an external server monitoring the distributed system. An attacker may have the right of entry to the insecure communication channels and interrupts the user activities by collecting confidential data informa-tion.

Intrusiveness [27] is the effect of monitoring the network because during the sharing of resources with the monitoring system intrusions are entering into the system. Intrusive may modify the activities in a random manner. The problems of intrusive monitoring include, degradation of system performance, incorrect results, delay in execution, and masking or creating deadlock situations. The intrusiveness can be measured by identifying events in the monitoring systems. The monitoring systems can be of three categories, viz. software monitors, hardware monitors, and hybrid monitors.

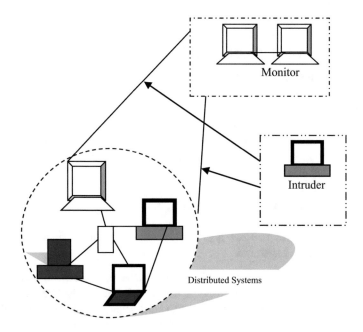

Fig. 24.1   External monitoring of distributed systems

1.3   Wireshark Monitoring Tool

Wireshark is a network packet analyzer tool, which has been used to capture the network packets [1]. The Wireshark tool could be used to monitor the online computers by using IP Address of the nodes.

1.3.1   Purposes of Wireshark

The Software developers, Network engineers, Network system administrators, and Researchers use Wireshark tool for various purposes, which include the following [4].

- Network System Administrators use this tool for troubleshooting the network problems.
- Network engineers use this tool for observing the security problems.
- Software developers are using it for debugging the protocol implementations.
- Researchers have been using this tool for studying the network protocol internals.

1.3.2 Characteristics of Wireshark

The following are the Characteristics of the Wireshark tool.

- By using the network interface, Wireshark tool captures live network packets.
- The complete protocol information can be displayed in each and every captured network packet.
- The captured packets could be saved and opened later. Also these captured packets could be filtered on the basis of some specific criteria and protocol.
- Wireshark tool colorizes the captured packets based on filtrations of packets.

1.3.3 Features Not Present in Wireshark Tool

The following features are not available in Wireshark tool when it is used in monitoring networked systems.

- Wireshark tool act as a packet analyzer, so it never detects any intrusions during monitoring. Hence it does not act as an Intrusion Detection System. For example, Wireshark tool does not provide any vigilant message if some other user changes the network bustle or performs unauthorized modifications in the network.
- By using Wireshark tool, it is very difficult to detect any kind of manipulation over the network.
- Wireshark tool gives the dump of information at a time. It is difficult to do the customization of data by using this tool.
- It is very difficult to implement and integrate with users connections, because Wireshark tool is an open source.
- It is very hard to keep track of the network activity of individuals, since it is not user-friendly.

However, the proper use of Wireshark tool helps to identify all of the above-mentioned activities, this will be discussed more in the section below.

1.3.4 Why Wireshark Tool?

In this chapter, Wireshark tool has been used to monitor the data. The Wireshark is better than other commercial tools because of the following reasons.

- It is an open source tool for monitoring.
- All other existing tools are not given attention to packet dissectors, which helps to count the packets and decoding it.
- In Wireshark tool, specialized hardware is not required to capture the packets and also, the packet capturing speed is high in Wireshark tool.
- The full documentation is available in Wireshark tool and protocols are not licensed like in other commercial tools.

The Wireshark tool has been selected for investigation of existing monitoring tool. When deploying the distributed nodes, captured network traffic [28] has been utilized. Captured network traffic may be utilized to ensure the good network connectivity. Also, the captured network traffic helps to locate the new nodes in a network. By passively capturing and analyzing packets facilitate deploying of new nodes, testing of existing nodes, and resolve the problems associated in distributed nodes. The system contains sniffer node and multiple user interfaces. The monitoring tool must have the following features, which includes

- Captured packets [29] should be stored according to its capture time.
- Captured packets should be interpreted as per human readable format in each protocol.
- Approximates the link qualities of the systems within the communication range.
- User interface shows only the selectively user required information.
- User interface shows the captured information in real time streams.
- Captured and analyzed information may be stored in file.

Apart from its good qualities, Wireshark tool has some drawbacks in terms of security breaches. The Wireshark tool is vulnerable to an attacker, which has been proved in this research work.

Wireshark tool identifies the viruses and worms traffic by looking at the raw data transmitted across the network. This has been viewed at the bottom of the Wireshark tool window. The suspicious packets are filtered using display filter. The display filter helps to identify traffics like, DCEPRC, NetBIOS, and ICMP. These traffics are not viewable under normal circumstances.

1.4 Algorithmic Procedure for Monitoring

A message that is transferring between the nodes of the distributed system as well as data related to that message could be monitored. The algorithmic procedure for monitoring of network using Wireshark tool has been explained in Fig. 24.2 [15].

As illustrated in Fig. 24.2, the monitoring node should start the Wireshark tool first. Select any one source node in the distributed system and create a new message for sending it to the destination node. Before sending this message to the target node, the source node has to select destination node IP Address. Upon selecting the IP Address of the target node, source node sends the created message. The message is received at the destination end. The monitoring node may capture these messages using the Wireshark tool and right click on the follow TCP stream to view the full message.

A simple chat application has been implemented to demonstrate the message passing between two users in a network. The following code snippet shows that, client1 and client2 should communicate through socket programming concepts.

```
client1 = New TcpClient (ComboBox1.Text, Port_No)
client2 = New TcpClient (TextBox2.Text, Port_No)
```

Algorithm_Monitor ()

{   Start Wireshark Software in Monitoring_Node

         Select Source_Node in developed application

         Source_Node creates a New_Message

         Source_Node locates the IPAddress of Destination_Node

         Send New_Message to Destination_Node

         Monitoring_Node capture the packet of New_Message for Analysis

         Right click on follow TCP Stream of captured packet

         Monitoring_Node now can monitor the full message transmitted over network.

}

Fig. 24.2 Algorithmic procedure for monitoring

The implementation of monitoring involves the Monitor_Node class. The Monitor_Node class consists of three constructors called Analyzer, Observer, and Capture. The Monitor_Node adds the requisite number of parameters and updates it for the intention of monitoring with a network.

The following code snippet demonstrates the working of Monitor_Node.

```
Monitor_Node ()
  {
  //Add parameters that need to be monitored
  //Update parameters at each time
  //Call Analyser ()
  // Call Observer ()
  // Call Capture()
  }
  // The Analyzer class
class Analyzer extends Monitor
  {
  Analyzer ()
  {
super();// call the parent class for analysis
        // Adding "listener" parameter to the class
        addAttr(new_Attribute("listener", false));
  }
  }
  // The_Observer_class
Class_Observer_extends_Monitor
```

```
        {
        observer ()
        {
super();// call the constructor of the parent class extends
            Monitor
        // Adding read-only "result" parameter
        addAttr(new_Attribute("result"));
            }
              }
```

The functionalities of Observer, Analyzer, and Capture have been depending on the monitoring rules of the networks. In this implementation, the analyzer collects the information and applies the monitoring rules and generates the results.

The observer fetches the results from the database, normally in the form of alarm signals generated by analysis.

```
      // Capture class captures the port number
 class Capture extends Monitor
      {
      Capture ()
      {
super();// call the constructor of the parent class
        // Capture port attribute
        capAttr(new Attribute("port_no"))
            }
      }
```

Wireshark tool should be specified by promiscuous mode before the commencement of capturing, otherwise Wireshark tool captures all incoming and outgoing packets of the LAN environment. In the promiscuous mode, the following parameters are required to be considered while capturing the packets.

- Limiting every packet to "n" bytes permits the user to denote the highest number of information that can be captured for every packet. The default limit of each packet will be 65,535.
- The fixed buffer size is used to capture the packets and it temporarily keeps the packets before writing it to the permanent memory.

In the case of monitor mode capturing, Wireshark tool captures all incoming and outgoing traffic packets. During this mode, the network adapter has been disassociated from the network. The following parameters need to be set during the capturing of packets, which includes host name, port_number, void authentication, and password authentication. The host name or IP Address has been selected to capture the packets. The port number has been set to capture the remote packets, 2002 being the default port number. The null authentication is considered as insecure capturing of packets. Credentials are required for password authentication to capture packets.

The libpcap engine of Wireshark tool captures the data packets from the network card and keeps all data packets in a kernel buffer. The kernel buffer has been read by the Wireshark tool. When the Wireshark tool deals with large file of capture, it slows down the network speed. Hence, multiple file option has been used to save the captured file. The following different methods have been used while saving the files.

Algorithm_Capture_Packet ()
// Get the Network Device information from the network
NetworkInterface [] devices = JpcapCaptor.getDeviceList ();
// Obtain the available list of network interfaces
// for each network interfaces do the following
// Display the name and description of network interface
// Display the name of data link and corresponding description
// Display the network interface MAC address
// Display the its IP address, subnet mask and broadcast address
// Capture the packets by calling openDevice method and set its interface information
openDevice (NetworkInterface intrface, int snaplen, boolean promics, int to_ms);
JpcapCaptor captor=JpcapCaptor.openDevice(devices[index], 65535, false, 20);
    captor.setFilter("icmp",true);
// Capture a single packet and display it.
End_Algorithm_Capture_Packet()

Fig. 24.3 Steps involved in packet capture procedure

A single temporary file has been created by default and saved. Multiple files with continuous mode have been used, if the file is more than threshold size. Multiple files with ring buffer, limit the maximum disk usage and keep only the latest captured packets.

The command ether_ [src|dst]_ host_ <ehost> allows monitoring tool to filter only Ethernet host addresses. The command [tcp|udp]_[src|dst]_ port_<port> allows the monitoring tool to filter only TCP and UDP port numbers with protocols.

The steps shown in Fig. 24.3 describe the process of packet capturing using Java API. The Jpcap is an API used in Java, it provides access to low level network information. Initially, jpcap.JpcapHandler interface class has been created and it allows processing the packets.

public class JpcapTip implements JpcapHandler.

```
{
    public void handlePacket(Packet packet)
    {
        system.out.println(packet);
    }
}
```

The Jpcap API provides a method jpcap.Jpcap.getDeviceList() to listen to the network device. This method returns an array strings as shown in the code snippet.

String[] devices = Jpcap.getDeviceList();

Once device names have been listed, then monitoring node must choose one device for listening.

String deviceName = devices[0];

Once device is selected and it has been open for listening by using method jcap,openDevice(). The method uses four parameters to open, which includes name of device, maximum number of bytes to read, status of promiscuous mode of the device, and timer value.

Jpcap jpcap = Jpcap.openDevice (deviceName, maxBytes, mode, timeout);

The openDevice method listens device packets by calling two possible methods such as processPacket() and loopPacket(). The processPacket method captures packet until it reaches the maximum number of specified.

Packets by user. The loopPacket method captures continuously.

jpcap.loopPacket(-1, new JpcapTip());

In this way, network packets have been captured by the monitoring node using Java API.

1.5   Implementation of Application for Message Exchange

In all kinds of networks like WAN or LAN users' exchange of messages between themselves with proper message formats. These message formats include IP Address as one of the key parameters. With the help of IP Address, any source systems or nodes present in the WAN or LAN can route the packets to the destination. The sending and receiving messages between two users' have been demonstrated in Figs. 24.4 and 24.5, respectively [15].

Initially, sender node locates DHCP server on the network. Then the sender node locates its IP Address by sending broadcast message to IP_Address 255.255.255.255. Upon receiving broadcast packet, the DHCP server sends a

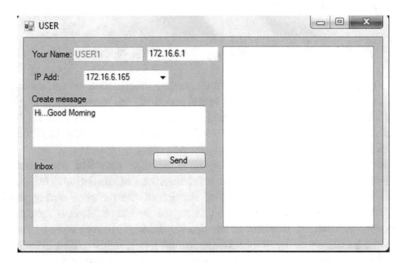

Fig. 24.4 Message sending process by Source_Node1

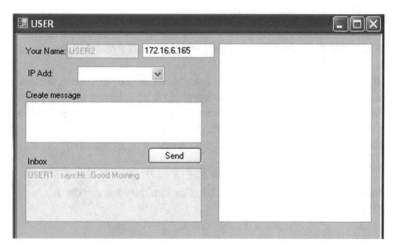

Fig. 24.5 Message receiving process by USER_Node2

response to the sender with packet containing IP address. After receiving this packet, the sender sends the request message to get the addressing information from DHCP server. In this way, sender locates the IP Address.

1.5.1 USER_Node1 is Sending a Message to USER_Node2

In this case, USER_Node1 is intended to send the message to USER_Node2, who may present in the same distributed network. Before transmitting the created message to USER_Node2, the USER_Node1 selects the destination IP Address (172.16.6.165) of the USER_Node2 as shown in Fig. 24.4.

1.5.2 USER_Node2 Received Message from USER_Node1

The USER_Node2, which is present in the same network, receives the message in its Inbox. In this way, USER_Node2 opens and reads the messages coming to its Inbox. This scenario has been illustrated in the Fig. 24.5. Similarly, USER_Node2 also creates a new message and sends it to USER_Node1 by selecting the IP Address (172.16.6.1) of USER_Node1.

Both cases are considered for exchanging of messages over distributed networks. These messages need to be monitored for the purpose of adaptation. The adaptive system helps to improve the quality of service of the message during sharing over distributed networking nodes. In this regard, one application is required for monitoring process. By the help of monitoring report, it is very easy to vary the bandwidth of the network. Also, this monitoring report helps to find existence of any node. The monitoring process has been explained in the next section.

1.6   Implementation of Monitoring Scenarios Using Wireshark Tool

The Sect. 1.5 describes the message passing procedure that uses IP_Address as a routing parameter. However, during this message transmission, IP_Address is disclosed to everyone. A third person who is present in the network may observe these messages with the service of monitoring tool with appropriate parameters. By using Wireshark monitoring tool, it is possible to view TCP packets. Instead of viewing in bunch of small chunks of data from client to server, the TCP stream sorts these chunks to make it easily viewable. Rather than taking in small packets and combining packets, the attacker may use follow TCP stream procedure to find the entire information. This scenario has been implemented in and presented in this chapter as shown in Fig. 24.6. As per the scenario, the user who is present in the network may right click on IP Address 176.16.6.165 and select follow TCP stream to get the entire information [15].

"Follow TCP stream" allows user to view all the packets on a TCP stream data between a pair of users. It is one of the most useful analyses in monitoring tool. The following TCP stream combines all the data pertaining to each packet. The TCP stream sorts all small packets and combines it for proper observation. The TCP-based method helps to view the data from the TCP stream, similar to what the application layer does. The type of data viewed may be passwords of Telnet stream or confidential messages communicated between the users. The size of the receiving TCP window decides the data transmission rates of the network. The TCP receive window updates about the packets that have been shared between the users during

Fig. 24.6 Monitoring using follow TCP stream

transmission of data. Based on this size, the data transmission speeds up or slows down.

In situation of monitoring node, any intruder node can view the full message transmitted over the broadcast web. As illustrated in the Fig. 24.6, the intruder may right click on the packet number 515 on Destination_Node2 IP Address 172.16.6.165 by using follow TCP stream. In this way, the monitoring tool like Wireshark may be misused by intruder to view the confidential messages. In this regard, a secure communication mechanism is required during the monitoring activities.

1.7 Implementation of Secure Way of Monitoring

Wireshark tool has been used to monitor the activities of suspected employees who belong to the same network. The tool initially captures the suspected employee packets and deciphers it to view the contents of the packets. The display filter has been used to filter out TCP packets. The packets have been examined by identifying small bits of text information during transmission. Every packet data has been copied individually and combined to see entire message being transmitted. The Wireshark tool fetches entire information by right clicking on each packet. In this way, the TCP stream window displays the complete chat, which is communicated between two suspected employees. This feature allows the user to view the chat just as the application layer views it. By using this feature, anyone can view the passwords of other users in a Telnet stream.

A distributed system contains a group of nodes associated together by a computer network in order to switch the data. With this implementation mechanisms "N" numbers of nodes are connected all over distributed systems, among which one node is considered as a monitoring node. The developed application is run on web server to get its services over the distributed systems. Any user who is present in the distributed system can access this application. However, to apply the developed application some configuration of authentication is needed on both positions of the users.

The intruder, who may be present within the distributed networks, may try to access the data, which is transmitted between two organizations or users. Intruder also can utilize the same Wireshark monitoring tool to capture the information. The intruder may follow the same procedure like, clicks on a "Follow TCP stream" option of Wireshark monitoring tool to get the exact message.

Security mechanism has been employed in order to protect the data, which shifts between the distributed systems and Monitoring Node. Sender Node should need to encrypt the information in RSA algorithm or other equivalent algorithm while sending. In this chapter, we have discussed RSA 1024-bit encryption procedure. On the receiving end, information is decrypted and displayed over the inbox of the recipient. When the intruder tries to access this information through existing

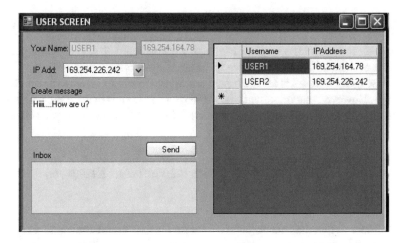

Fig. 24.7 GUI of the users in the network

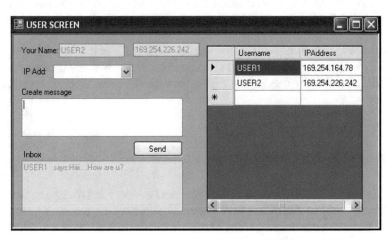

Fig. 24.8 Inbox of the User2

monitoring tool like Wireshark tool, only an encrypted message is displayed on the screen of the intruder.

Figure 24.7 shows the user screen of the sender process. In this, USER1 (169.254.164.78) has sent a created message to USER2 (169.254.226.242) by selecting an IP Address field. Username and its corresponding updated IP Addresses are displayed on the right side of the screen. Before broadcasting the message, the USER1 encrypts the message using RSA algorithm. The encryption process has been embedded along with send procedure, by clicking send button as shown in Fig. 24.8. The separate encryption button is avoided here to cut down the time delay of user interaction [15].

As evinced in Fig. 24.8, USER2 receives the message sent by USER1. The message is displayed over the inbox of USER2. On picking up the message, USER2 decrypts it and meets the original Message automatically. The decryption process has been embedded here to cut down the time delay of computation.

All the users' messages are encrypted and it provides a security to the monitored message. However, one important thing to be noticed here is that, all the parameters are encrypted; user is not having any option to bypass the encryption procedure.

1.8 Pseudo Code for Secure Transmission and Reception of Messages

Figure 24.9a shows the pseudo code of the sender process of the monitoring tool. While sending message to the user, sender process creates a string of message in line. These messages have been read line-by-line and encrypts entire message line-by-line using RSA algorithm. Also message has been displayed on the senders' screen.

Figure 24.9b depicts the receiver process. On the receiver side, the receiver process receives encrypted messages line by line and after reading it decrypts using RSA algorithm line by line. Also, original message has been displayed on screen of receiver.

2 Secure Way of Monitoring

As explained in the earlier section, massage can be supervised through the existing monitoring tool like Wireshark tool. Figure 24.10 shows the screen of Monitoring tool with an encrypted message. The Monitoring node may use "follow TCP stream" to look at the message. The coded message exposed on the cover of the Wireshark monitoring tool [15].

The implementation of secure way of monitoring has been done with RSA algorithm using Java programming. The pseudo code of RSA algorithm [30] is shown in Fig. 24.11. RSA is the widely used algorithm for secure encryption of data. In this algorithm, the USER_Node1 encrypts the information with the help of public key of USER_Node2 and the USER_Node2 decrypts the ciphertext with the help of private key of USER_Node2. The Java provides a BigInteger for the calculation of large prime numbers and uses 1024 bits of key length. Since 1024 bits provides more security for the messages, in terms of infeasibility for attackers to decrypt the messages.

The code snippet shown in the Fig. 24.11a explains about the generation of public key and private keys of RSA algorithm. In addition, code in the Fig. 24.11b explains how to encrypt or decrypt using these generated key pairs.

a
```
Sender_Process()

{

// User1 sends a message to User2

// while loop for sending messages to users

    while(true)

        try

        {

            pw.flush();

            String line = in.readLine();

                line =rsa.encrypt(line);

            pw.println(line);

        }

catch (Exception se) {//Connection Closes after sending otherwise gives exception}

}
```

b
```
    Receiver_Process()

    {

    // open reader to receive messages from other users

    // loop reading messages from server

            while(true)

            {

                String line = inFromUser.readLine();

                line= rsa.decrypt(line);

                System.out.println("From User" + line)

            }

        }
```

Fig. 24.9 (a) Sender process of monitoring. (b) Receiver process of monitoring

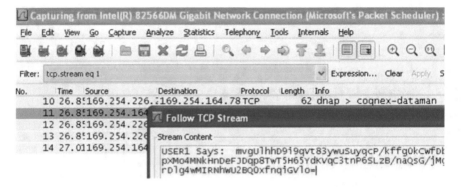

Fig. 24.10 Monitoring using Wireshark tool

a
```
RSA_Algorithm ()
{
//  Declaration of bit length of RSA using bit_length = 1024
//  Use of SecureRandom() function for getting random number
//  Select any 2 large prime using function BigInteger(bit_length / 2, 100, random)
//  Compute n by using   n = p.multiply(q)
//Calculate z
z = (p.subtract(BigInteger.ONE)).multiply(q.subtract(BigInteger.ONE));
//   Generation of key pairs, private and public keys
    en_key = new BigInteger("3");
    while (msg.gcd(en_key).intValue() > 1)
    {
        en_key = en_key.add(new BigInteger("2"));
    }
        dec_key = en_key.modInverse(z);
}
```

b
```
// Encryption of given message
    public BigInteger encrypt(BigInteger msg)
    {
    return msg.modPow(en_key, n);
    }

// Decryption of given message
    public BigInteger decrypt(BigInteger msg)
    {
    return msg.modPow(dec_key, n);
    }
```

Fig. 24.11 (**a**) Pseudo code of RSA algorithm. (**b**) Pseudo code of RSA encryption and decryption

The RSA algorithm has been used mainly for two purposes, namely it is a factor-based algorithm and its computing power increases constantly. RSA-1024 is considered as safe enough for protecting most of the vital information in the web. However, unencrypted messages take comparatively less processing time. On the other hand, these unencrypted messages are not confidential while transmission. During the experimental process, Public Key Infrastructure (PKI) has been adopted between the users with pairs of RSA 1024 bits asymmetric keys. To enable secure communication between the involved parties during the monitoring, each party must receive a list of the public keys of the other users that they will communicate with. In that case, each user receives the other user's public key for encryption process.

The PKI needs to perform in order to provide trust and security to electronic communication. The following functions are involved in working of PKI-based key management [31].

- Generating public key and private pairs for creating and authenticating digital signatures.
- Providing authentication to control access to the private key.
- Creating and issuing certificates to authenticate users.
- Registering new users to authenticate them.
- Maintaining history of keys for future references.
- Revoking certificates that are not valid.
- Updating and recovering keys in case of key compromise.

Cryptosystem techniques are proven safe. In this regard, the only analysis can be made to outline is how to decrypt a message without knowing the decryption key. Brute force methods are very simple, but lengthy to crack a message for attacker. However, attackers need not to crack entire encryption scheme to get portion of the message. In spite of several attempts, no one has been succeeded with 1024 bits of RSA algorithm. Such a resistance to attack makes RSA secure in practice. In RSA, it has been proved that it is very difficult for factorizing large prime numbers. Suppose, if large prime numbers p and q are having 100-digit numbers, then resulting n would be approximately 200 digits. The factorization of above case would take far too long time for breaking the code. Similarly, methods for determination of d are also difficult. Factorization of algorithm is still an age-old mathematical problem, contributed by Fermat and Legendre.

The RSA has been used widely in most of the application for following reasons: (1) RSA provides privilege of key revocation; (2) RSA provides distribution of new key during revocation of existing key; (3) RSA supports the spreading of the revocation; (4) RSA helps recovery from the leaked key.

The Wireshark tool decrypts the encrypted packets of Internet Key Exchange version 2 only. All other packets like Internet Key Exchange version 1 and Encapsulation Security Payload are decrypted with the help of ISAKMP (Internet Security Association Key Management Protocol). The following fields of the ISAKMP protocol have been used for encryption and decryption of packets. Initially length of 16 hex characters has been created for Senders Security Protocol Index (SPI). Similarly, length of 16 hex characters has been created for Receivers SPI.

The IKEv2 packets of sender to receiver have been encrypted/decrypted by using the key en_key. Similarly, the IKEv2 packets of receiver to sender have been encrypted/decrypted by using the key dec_key. The Integrity Checksum for receiver to sender has been calculated by the key en_key. Similarly, the Integrity Checksum for sender to receiver has been calculated by the key dec_key.

3 Summary

The framework for security mechanisms has been discussed in two ways. In the first, investigation of existing security mechanisms during monitoring and in the second, implementation of secure communication channel for monitoring.

Initially, existing Wireshark monitoring tool has been used for monitoring process. In this regard, a chat application has been developed for transferring messages between two users. The algorithmic procedure for monitoring has been explained in detail. The packet capture algorithm also has been discussed here. The impacts of monitoring scenarios have been discussed with help of implementation results. Finally, a secure way of implementation of monitoring mechanisms has been discussed with the help of RSA algorithm.

References

1. Sharpe, R., & Warnicke, E. (2014). *Capturing live network of data, Wireshark user's guide: For Wireshark 1.99*. https://www.wireshark.org/docs/
2. Mittal, H., Jain, M., & Banda, L. (2013). Monitoring local area network using remote method invocation. *International Journal of Computer Science and Mobile Computing, 5*(2), 50–55.
3. Moraes, D. M., & Duarte, E. P. (2011). A failure detection service for internet-based multi-as distributed systems. In *Proceedings of IEEE 17th International Conference on Parallel and Distributed Systems* (pp. 260–267).
4. Aredo, D., & Yildirim, S. (2006). Security issues in adaptive distributed systems. In *Proceedings of the Fourteenth European Conference on Information Systems (ECIS)* (pp. 2206–2215).
5. Kotenko, I., & Doynikova, E. (2014). Evaluation of computer network security based on attack graphs and security event processing. *Journal of Wireless Mobile Networks, Ubiquitous Computing, and Dependable Applications, 3*(5), 14–29.
6. Liu, Y., Xingyu, L., Jian, Y., & Xiao, Y. (2016). A framework of a software defined security architecture. *China Communications, 13*, 178–188.
7. Wiczer, J., & Wiczer, M. B. (2015). Improving energy efficiency using customized monitoring tools. In *Proceedings of 117th Metalcasting Congress, Modern Casting, Vernon Hills, IL* (pp. 36–39).
8. Wireshark Tutorial (http://www.wireshark.org/docs/wsug_html_chunked/), man pages (http://www.wireshark.org/docs/man-pages/), and a detailed FAQ (http://www.wireshark.org/faq.html) Retrieved April 2015.
9. Fuginia, M., Hadjichristofib, G., & Teimourikiaa, M. (2015). *A web-based cooperative tool for risk management with adaptive security, future generation computer systems* (pp. 1–16). Nicosia/Limassol: Frederick University.

10. Hernandez, C., Pedraza, L. F., & Salgado, C. (2013). A proposal of traffic model that allows estimating throughput mean values. In *Proceedings of 27th International Conference on Advanced Information Networking and Applications Workshops* (pp. 517–522). IEEE Computer Society.
11. Pop, F., Arcalianu, A., Dobre, C., & Cristea, V. (2011). Enhanced security for monitoring services in large scale distributed systems. In *Proceedings of International Conference on Intelligent Computer Communication and Processing (ICCP)* (pp. 549–556). IEEE.
12. Murugan, M., Kant, K., Raghavan, A., & Du, D. H. C. (2014). FlexStore: A software defined, energy adaptive distributed storage framework. In *Proceedings of 22nd International Symposium on Modelling, Analysis & Simulation of Computer and Telecommunication Systems* (pp. 81–90). IEEE Computer Society.
13. Jeswani, D., Natu, M., & Ghosh, R. K. (2012). Adaptive monitoring: A framework to adapt passive monitoring using probing. In *Proceedings of 8th International Conference on Network and Service Management (CNSM)* (pp. 350–356).
14. Penteado, M. G., & Trevelin, L. C. (2012). JMonitor: A monitoring tool for distributed systems. In *Proceedings of International Conference on Systems, Man, and Cybernetics, COEX, Seoul, Korea* (pp. 1767–1772).
15. Kotari, M., Chiplunkar, N. N., & Nagesh, H. R. (2016). Framework of security mechanisms for monitoring adaptive distributed systems. *IOSR Journal of Computer Engineering (IOSR-JCE), 18*(4), 25–36.
16. Comuzzi, M., & Martinez, R. I. R. (2014). Customized infrastructures for monitoring business processes. In *Proceedings of 8th International Symposium on Service Oriented System Engineering* (pp. 122–127). IEEE.
17. Oikonomou, G., & Apostolopoulos, T. (2007). A framework for the management of distributed systems based on SNMP. In *Proceedings of 22nd international symposium on Computer and information Sciences(ISCIS)* (pp. 78–83). IEEE.
18. Chen, S., Nepal, S., & Pandey, S. (2012). A unified monitoring framework for distributed information system management. In *Proceedings of 8th International Conference on Computing Technology and Information Management (ICCM)* (pp. 259–264). IEEE.
19. Fonseca, H., Rocha, E., Salvador, P., & Nogueira, A. (2014). Framework for collecting social network events. In *Proceedings of 16th International Conference on Telecommunications Network Strategy and Planning Symposium* (pp. 1–6). IEEE.
20. Atighetchi, M., & Adler, A. (2014). A framework for resilient remote monitoring. In *Proceedings of 7th International Symposium on Resilient Control Systems (ISRCS)* (pp. 1–8).
21. Jarraya, Y., Raya, S., Soeanua, A., Debbabia, M., Alloucheb, M., & Bergerb, J. (2013). Towards a distributed plan execution monitoring framework. In *Proceedings of 3rd International Symposium on Frontiers in Ambient and Mobile Systems (FAMS), Procedia Computer Science 19* (pp. 1034–1039). Elsevier.
22. Agbogun, J., & Ejiga, F. A. (2013). Network security management: solutions to network intrusion related problems. *International Journal of Computer and Information Technology, 4*(2), 617–625.
23. Feyissa, M. (2007). *Monitoring distributed systems for adaptive security*. Master thesis, Department of Computer Science, School of Graduate Studies of Addis Ababa University, Addis Ababa.
24. Zhou, Z. (2013). *Design and realization of distributed intelligent monitoring systems using power plant* (pp. 595–601). Berlin: Springer.
25. Schlichting, R. D., & Hiltunen, M. (1998). *Designing and implementing adaptive distributed systems*. University of Arizona, Arizona. Retrieved Feb, 2018, from http://www.cs.arizona.edu/adaptiveds/overview.html
26. Sarma, B., & Dasgupta, S. (2014). Dynamic load calculation in a distributed system using centralized approach. *International Journal of Advance Research, Ideas and Innovations in Technology, 2*(1), 5–10.
27. Falai, L. (2007). *Observing, monitoring and evaluating distributed systems*. Ph.D. Thesis, University of Lisboa, Portugal.

28. Hanninen, M., Suhonen, J., Hamalainen, T. D., & Hannikainen, M. (2011). Practical monitoring and analysis tool for WSN testing. In *Proceedings of International Conference on Design and Architectures for Signal and Image Processing (DASIP)* (pp. 23–32). IEEE.
29. Qadeer, M. A., & Zahid, M. (2010). Network traffic analysis and intrusion detection using packet sniffer. In *Proceedings of Second International Conference on Communication Software and Networks* (pp. 313–317). IEEE.
30. RSA elliptic curve cryptography. Retrieved November 30, 2017, from http://www.rsa.com/rsalabs/node.asp?id=2013
31. Choudhury, S., Bhatnagar, K., & Haque, W. (2002). *Public key infrastructure implementation and design*. New York: Hungry Minds.

Chapter 25
An Analysis of Provable Security Frameworks for RFID Security

Aakanksha Tewari and B. B. Gupta

Abstract Radio frequency identification (RFID) has become one of the most eminent commercial technologies in the last few years. The RFID tags are embedded or latched with any item for their unique identification. These tags can carry small amounts of data and have capability to perform simple computations. However, because of their simple architecture, the data these tags carry are not secure. This paper discusses some of the state-of-the-art authentication schemes that can secure RFID tags along with some security models that are used to verify whether an authentication scheme is secure against any potential security risks or not. This paper analyzes some authentication schemes and security models along with their strengths and weaknesses.

Keywords RFID tags · Hash-chain · Elliptic curve cryptography · Adversary · Unclonable function

1 Introduction

Radio frequency identification (RFID) technology has grown rapidly in the last few years having applications in the domain of retail and purchase passport issuing, railway tokens, etc. The maintenance of privacy of these tags has also become a primary concern. Here, security means that the adversary should not be able to impersonate a legitimate tag, and privacy ensures that any adversary cannot identify or locate a tag. In the last few decades various models ensured the security and privacy of RFID systems [1]. In this chapter, we perform a study of these models. Some of models, however, are not very easily applicable to any protocol.

The deployment of RFID system takes place in bulk and the systems comprised tags, transponders, and readers. RFID systems are rapidly replacing barcodes as they are more secure against tampering [2]. Using RFID has several advantages as

A. Tewari (✉) · B. B. Gupta
Department of Computer Engineering, National Institute of Technology Kurukshetra, Kurukshetra, India

© Springer Nature Switzerland AG 2020
B. B. Gupta et al. (eds.), *Handbook of Computer Networks and Cyber Security*,
https://doi.org/10.1007/978-3-030-22277-2_25

635

compared to barcodes; that is, the tags do not have to be in the line of sight of the reader for obtaining data. However, the low-cost requirement of RFID tags means that they have to have very limited resources. The RFID tags have capacity of few kbs and deploy around 5000–6000 gates out of which only a few hundreds can be devoted to security functions. The classical cryptography authentication protocols, however, required around 30,000–40,000 logic gates. In addition to that, we also have to consider the limited battery power [3].

However, in spite of these issues the use of RFID tags in various fields has been increasingly rapidly. Nevertheless, we cannot ignore the privacy issues related to these systems. The items deploying these tags may reveal confidential data such as location due to predictability. A very common solution to this issue is the use of random values as keys. There are many more issues such as above, which are faced by RFID systems. For example, various security models do not take into consideration that an adversary could be able to attack a tag physically, for example, tampering of the tag [4].

Although this situation must always be considered as products with low cost can be physically compromised very easily. Any adversary can carry out "reset" attacks and side-channel attacks by influencing the physical conditions of tags, that is, varying power and voltage. Some models, however, take this into consideration while examining a protocol's security [2, 4].

Many researchers have been working these past couple of years to ensure security and privacy of RFID systems. However, there is still no generic solution to this problem, and most of the existing solutions are specific to particular scenarios or provide security against certain types of attacks [3]. In addition to finding security solutions for RFID devices, researchers are also working on developing formal models that can be used to prove the strength of protocols. These models help in analyzing the design and working of RFID protocols; they also emphasize on the strengths and weaknesses of a protocol. However, these models also suffer from various deficiencies; for example, most of the frameworks do not fully comprehend the effects of functionalities and level of access provided to the adversary on the system [5].

In this chapter, our contributions are twofold. First, in Sect. 2 we provide an overview of various categories of authentication protocols for RFID systems along with their strengths and weaknesses. Second, in Sect. 3 we discuss some of the existing formal security models used to analyze the security of the above protocols. Section 4 gives a brief discussion of issues and defects in these models. Section 5 concludes this paper.

2   Existing RFID Security Protocols

In this section we discuss some categories of authentication protocols and their strengths and shortcomings. We present a detailed description of some state-of-the-art solutions.

2.1 Hash-Based Protocols

Hash-chain-based approaches deploy cryptographic mechanisms to secure passwords and other credentials. A hash-chain of length "N" is obtained by recursive application of one-way hash function [6] with an initial value "x": $h^N(x) = h(h(\ldots h(x) \ldots))$, such that if an adversary knows $h^N(x)$ and "x," it cannot obtain $h^{N-1}(x)$.

The first hash-based approach was proposed by Okhubo et al. [7], which used an identifier that was new for every session. This protocol did not use any random number generators. The parameters are renewed for every new session. They used a fresh tag identifier for every new session without using any random number generator. However, the protocol is vulnerable to replay attacks.

Weis et al. [8] proposed one-way hash function-based security scheme. Each tag has a temporary ID, which is the result of hash of a key "k." Each tag functions in either locked or unlocked state. During the locked state, the tag responds to all the requests with the temporary ID and no other action is taken.

Henrici et al. [9] proposed an authentication protocol, using one-way hash functions to ensure secure communication between the reader and the server. After the successful completion of every session, the tag ID is updated at both server's and tag's side in order to ensure location privacy and forward secrecy. The protocol also ensures anonymity; however, it fails to provide security against backtracking.

Molnar et al. [10] proposed another authentication protocol that used a hash tree approach instead of hash chains to distribute the cost of computations more evenly throughout the RFID system (among all the nodes). They also developed a new model library to store node details at the back-end server so as to prevent exhaustive search and ensure more security. The library architecture was very efficient in terms of searching speed; however, the authentication protocol failed to ensure anonymity.

2.2 ECC-Based Protocols

The current state-of-the-art authentication protocols for RFID systems include various categories of solutions such as mechanisms built up on public key cryptography or other mechanism to provide security at low cost by using simpler techniques to ensure tag security. Using public key cryptography for low-cost devices is not a very efficient idea as it requires a lot of resources and space. Similarly, if we attempt to use existing symmetric key solution with these devices, the protocols fail to work efficiently due to different network conditions and lesser resources [11].

Elliptic curve cryptography has been providing a very efficient substitute to public key cryptography for low-cost devices; it requires very small keys to provide security and privacy comparable to traditional public key cryptography-based schemes. The first ECC-based authentication protocol for RFID devices was proposed by Tulys and Batina [12] in the year 2006. However, Lee et al. [13] later on found out some weaknesses in the protocol and proposed a new solution to address those issues.

Liao et al. [14] proposed another ECC-based solution that did not use any hash functions or complex computations and hence was very simple to implement and suitable for passive tags also. Although Peter and Herman [15] proved that the aforementioned protocol is unable to ensure security against tracking, spoofing, and cloning. It also fails to ensure privacy. Liao et al. [16] proposed another authentication protocol that claimed to ensure privacy and anonymity; they also gave proofs that the protocol ensures security against tracking and tag cloning.

Tan et al. [17] proposed a three-factor-based key exchange mechanism for secure communication between low-cost devices, although the scheme was unable to secure the devices against denial of service and replay attacks. To overcome the vulnerabilities, Arshad et al. [18] presented an ECC-based authentication protocol. However, Lu et al. [19] showed that Arshad et al.'s protocol is vulnerable to password attacks that can make tags vulnerable to impersonation.

2.3   PUF-Based Protocols

A physically unclonable function (PUF) is used to map a set of challenge values to a set of response values based on a complex function. The complex function is based on a physical system and computes a response value for each challenge. PUFs provide a cost-effective security protocol. There are various ways to implement a PUF, for example, using silicon physical systems that hide timing and delay of ICs. PUFs are attached to the product and whenever there is a slight change in the host environment, for example, temperature and pressure. A different response value will be generated. Thus, PUFs are hard to predict because of the different response even with a slight change in challenge values [20].

The database stores a set of PUF-based challenge and response values. During an authentication session, a query message is sent to the database and it is accepted if the challenge value it contains has a matching response in the database [21]. Some other schemes used PUF approaches for generation of secret values for tokens, which can be used along with some classical authentication scheme. However, some literature [20–24] suggested that in order to obtain the secret value from the token the PUF has to deploy some error correction technique that increases the cost of computations.

Some other works have also explored various weaknesses to PUF-based functions. Most of the PUFs fail to ensure mutual authentication between the tag and the reader. PUF-based approaches also have scalability issues and are prone to denial of service attacks that can disrupt the connection and services between the server and the tag permanently [23].

2.4   HB Protocols

Hopper and Blum [25] proposed an authentication scheme in 2001, known as HB protocol. These protocols rely on Learning Parity with Noise (LPN) problem, which is a computationally hard problem.

LPN problem: Assume P to be a matrix with dimension $q\ k$, x be k-bit binary vector, υ is a vector such that $wt\ (\upsilon) \leq q.\ \eta$, where $\eta \in [0, \frac{1}{2}]$ and size of v is q-bits. Then, if we have $z = P.x \oplus \upsilon$, then the LPN problem is to obtain x_0 such that $|P.x_0 \oplus \upsilon| \leq q.\ \eta$ [26].

LPN has various applications in cryptography, as it is able to provide a stepping stone for provably secure solutions; that is, it can be mathematically shown that the solution is able to resist an active attacker in the existing environment. These schemes are very simple and take only a few steps; thus, they are very feasible for low-cost devices. The cryptographic schemes are mostly decisional, and for the LPN problem it can be shown that there is not a very significant difference between the decisional and the search approach. The cryptographic notions that can be derived from this problem can be collision resistant. The LPN problem is assumed to be collision resistant and remains a hard problem even for nonuniform noise values.

Juels and Weis [27] presented another HB-based approach for RFID systems referred to as HB+. They also demonstrated an active attack on [28] and added some other minor computations to improve the HB protocol. Later on, Gilbert et al. [29] proved that both HB and HB+ schemes are vulnerable man-in-the-middle attacks.

2.5   Ultra-Lightweight Protocols

The fourth class of protocols is the ultra-lightweight protocols that only use bitwise operations such as OR, AND, XOR, rotation, or permutation. These have the lowest overhead in terms of storage and computation.

In SASI [30], each tag has an ID and shares a pseudonym (IDS) and key value with the back-end database server. The length of each of them is 96 bits. SASI ensures strong authentication and integrity. It uses bitwise XOR ($\oplus$)($\oplus$), bitwise OR ($\vee$)($\vee$), bitwise AND ($\wedge$)($\wedge$), addition mod $2n$(+), and left rotate ($Rot(x, y)$) operation that left rotates the value of x with y bits. Complex operations such as hash functions are not used by this protocol. However, this protocol is susceptible to disclosure attacks and does not ensure untraceability.

Peris-Lopez et al. [31] proposed LMAP protocol that used simple bitwise operations XOR ($\oplus$)($\oplus$), bitwise OR ($\vee$)($\vee$), bitwise AND ($\wedge$)($\wedge$), and addition mod $2m$ (+). This protocol ensures mutual authentication and security from various attacks without the use of complex operations like hashing. This scheme uses an index pseudonym (IDS) that is 96 bits in length. Here the IDS is the index of the row where all the tag-related data are stored. Each tag has a key that is divided into four parts of 96 bits each. M2AP [32] protocol, which is very similar to LMAP, is also a lightweight mutual authentication protocol for RFID tags, where the index pseudonym updation procedure is different from LMAP, while key updating operations remain the same. Both LMAP and M2AP ensure anonymity and mutual authentication and provide security against various attacks such as replay attacks and man-in-the-middle attacks. However, both of these protocols are susceptible to de-synchronization and full-disclosure attacks. Another protocol EMAP [33] that is based on challenge–response mechanism is an authentication scheme for passive tags. Most of the complex computations in this protocol are performed by the reader and tags perform lightweight operations such as hash. It requires only one storage unit for the tag in addition to the ID for storing authentication related data. This protocol also ensures confidentiality, integrity, and untraceability.

Peris-Lopez et al. proposed the Gossamer protocol [34], which addresses the weaknesses of SASI [30] such as de-synchronization and disclosure attacks. It uses dual rotations and mixbits operation that is a lightweight function (combination of bitwise right shift and addition operations), although this protocol has low throughput.

3 Provable Security Models

Most of the authentication schemes these days turn out to be insecure, as they are developed solely based on previous experiences. But provable security has emerged as a new state-of-the-art model for verification and development of more secure protocols based on experience as well as cognitive reasoning. Provable security aims to provide concrete mathematical proof for ensuring protocol's security.

Modern cryptographic protocols deploy "game-based" security models that have an adversary (active or passive) that can carry out potential attacks over the concerned system. If there exists an adversary who can win the game, then the scheme is considered to be insecure.

3.1 Vaudeney's Model

This model [35] has the capability to affect all the ongoing communications between entities and is able to perform man in the middle attack on any entity accessible to the adversary. It also has the authority to get the output of a device authentication (0 or 1). The adversary in this model is able to select or deselect tags randomly, which are moving in and out of the range. The adversary has the ability to corrupt tags by extracting the details of their internal state. During any ongoing session, the adversary has temporary identifier for the tags within its range.

Oracles: The following oracles are defined by Vaudeney:

- *CreateTag()*: This oracle generates a tag with a unique identifier and updates the database.
- *DrawTag()*: The oracle selects or draws a set of fresh tags (which are to be sent to the adversary); it also identifies whether the drawn set of tags is legitimate or not.
- *Free()*: This oracle frees a virtual tag (vtag), which then becomes unreachable by the adversary.
- *Launch()*: The oracle launches a new protocol session.
- *SendReader()*: sends a message to the reader during a protocol run.
- *Result()*: On the completion of a protocol run, it generates the output 0 or 1.
- *Corrupt()*: This oracle returns tag status based on which tags are kept or destroyed.

Adversary: It is an algorithm that interacts with tags, has a public key, and requires oracles to carry out its operations. Vaudeney classified adversaries into the following categories:

- *Strong adversary*: has access to all the oracles without any limitations.
- *Weak adversary*: cannot corrupt tags; it can only listen the ongoing communications and interact with the oracle.
- *Forward adversary*: this adversary becomes active after a tag is corrupted after which no protocol interactions are allowed.
- *Destructive adversary*: it cannot interact with a corrupted tag; that is, tags are destroyed after being corrupted.

Vaudeney stated that $Strong^{Adv} \supseteq Destructive^{Adv} \supseteq Forward^{Adv} \supseteq Weak^{Adv}$

Security (Vaudeney's definition): if an adversary is able to identify a legitimate tag, then it wins the game. Thus, for a protocol to be secure, the probability of adversary's winning should be negligible.

Privacy (Vaudeney's definition): during the game, the adversary has a set of drawn tags among which it has to identify a legitimate tag by the result 0 or 1. If the output is 1, then adversary wins; therefore, for a scheme to ensure privacy, all such adversaries should be trivial.

Blinder: A blinder B for any adversary A is a *PPT* algorithm that observes all the messages sent and received by A. It can also simulate *Launch()*, *SendReader()*, *SendTag()*, *Result()* oracles. However, B is unable to access the reader's data.

An adversary is said to be blinded (denoted as A^B) if it does not use *Launch()*, *SendReader()*, *SendTag()*, and *Result()* oracles. Also, the adversary A^B is said to be trivial if after it is blinded, it produces the same output as before; that is, $|\Pr(A_{wins}) - \Pr(A^B_{wins})| \leq \epsilon$ where ϵ is a negligible function.

The game between the adversary A and the challenger C is divided into two phases (as shown in Fig. 25.1):

- Attack phase: during this phase, the adversary interacts with the system and queries with the oracle to gather information.

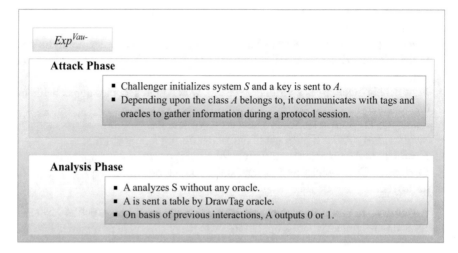

Fig. 25.1 Vaudeney's privacy experiment

- Analysis phase: during this phase the adversary is given a table of tags among which it has to identify which the legitimate and fake tags. A generates results as 0 or 1. If the output is 1, A wins.

Vaudeney's model discusses various aspects of security and includes most of the correctness and privacy aspects. However, it has some weaknesses. Vaudeney stated that wide-strong privacy is not possible to achieve which was later corrected by Ouafi [36] and Vaudeney [37]. Vaudeney stated that there exists an entity called Blinder, which answers the Result() oracle. Here, the adversary knows the selected tag, whereas Blinder doesn't. The blinder now knows the random coin flip.

3.2 Canard et al.'s Model

Canard et al. [38, 39] proposed a security model that is derived from Vaudeney [35, 37]. Canard's model utilizes strong, destructive, and weak adversaries and the use of oracles is also similar to that used by Vaudeney. However, unlike the notion of security and privacy in Vaudeney's model, Canard et al. ensure properties like soundness, correctness, and untraceability.

Some of the new properties introduced by Canrad et al. are:

Nonobvious link: a link between two virtual tags (v_1, v_2) is said to be nonobvious if (1) both tags refer to the same tag ID and (2) a "dummy" adversary that can call DrawTag, CreateTag, Free, Corrupt, oracle is unable to generate this link with probability $\geq 1/2$.

A nonobvious link can be categorized into the following classes:

(a) Standard: if both virtual tags are not corrupted by the adversary.
(b) Past: if v_1 is uncorrupted.
(c) Future: if v_2 is uncorrupted.

We have: *Future (Strongest Privacy)$\supseteq$Past$\supseteq$Standard.*
Canard et al. have dummy adversary A_D instead of a blinder B. Vaudeney had a blinder B, which was an entity on its own separate from the adversary A^B, whereas "dummy" adversary is a single entity having knowledge of all random choices that can be made.

Untraceability Experiment: Untraceability can be proved in a system if all the adversaries are unable to generate a nonobvious link with probability greater than the dummy adversary (probability $\geq 1/2$). It can be stated as:

$$\mathrm{Exp}^{\mathrm{UNT}} (S, A) = |\, \mathrm{Pr}\, (A_{\mathrm{wins}}) - \mathrm{Pr}\, (A_{D\ \mathrm{wins}})\, | \leq \epsilon$$

Canard et al. have most certainly overcome some of the demerits of Vaudeney by using A_D and nonobvious links but is still cannot be used with every scheme due to the use of nontrivial links and the limited scope within which untraceability is defined (as shown in Fig. 25.2).

Correctness: A scheme S is correct for any class of adversary A, if any A ϵ {Strong, Destructive, Weak} is a PPT algorithm where $\mathrm{Success}^{\mathrm{CORRECT}}$ (S, A) is negligible (as shown in Fig. 25.3). It can be stated as

$$\mathrm{Success}^{\mathrm{CORRECT}} (S, A) = \mathrm{Pr}\, |\, \mathrm{Exp}^{\mathrm{CORRECT}} (S, A) = 0\, |$$

3.3   Universal Composability Model

This framework [40] provides a very general methodology for executing and verifying protocol security. Since this framework ensures security under composition operation, here it is also referred as universal composition. The protocols that satisfy the notions of this framework are said to be universally composable (UC).

$Exp^{UNT}(S,A)$

- Challenger initializes system S and a key is sent to A.
- Depending upon the class A belongs to, it communicates with tags and oracles to gather information during a protocol session.
- A returns a link (v_1, v_2)

Fig. 25.2 Canrad et al.'s untraceability experiment

$Exp^{CORRECT}(S,A)$

- Challenger initializes system S and a key is sent to A.
- Depending upon the class A belongs to, it communicates with tags and oracles to gather information during a protocol session.
- A chooses an uncorrupted tag.
- A launches the attack phase. The experiment returns a bit 'b' as generated by the oracle.

Fig. 25.3 Canrad et al.'s correctness experiment

Universal Composition: The universal composition theorem states that running protocol π_ρ, with no access to F (where F is an ideal functionality), has essentially the same effect as running the original F-hybrid protocol π. More precisely, it guarantees that for any adversary A, there exists an adversary A_F such that no environment machine can tell with nonnegligible probability whether it is interacting with A and parties running π_ρ, or with AF and parties running π. In particular, if π UC-realizes some ideal functionality G, then so does π_ρ.

The UC framework is able to model: real world, ideal world, and an emulation (that models a real-world protocol into an ideal world protocol). It creates an interactive environment that captures the parameters values of algorithm at current time. The UC framework has the following components:

- In this framework, the adversary A interacts with environment Z, which comprises legitimate entities, each of which is PPT algorithms. Z generates initial input parameters and obtains the output parameters by performing random queries with the adversary.
- For an algorithm run for each adversary (PPT), there is a real-world simulation of the algorithm that can be modeled into an ideal-world scenario in the presence of a simulated adversary A in such a way that Z cannot be able to distinguish if it is interacting with the adversary and algorithm instance in the ideal world or the real world.

The adversary in the UC security model interacts with both real-world and ideal-world environments. The adversary can eavesdrop into any and all the communications and can schedule the activation sequence of the entities. Every session has an identifier "sid," which is shared by all the entities involved in the communication. During the session initiation, Z becomes active first, and it then activates the adversary. If Z stops, the whole simulation is aborted. Z may also allow more than one protocol sessions to run simultaneously.

In the ideal scenario the UC framework implements an anonymous authentication and anonymous key exchange functionality. To ensure anonymity in all the channels, anonymous wireless communications are involved. Figures 25.4 and 25.5 give a brief description of these functionalities.

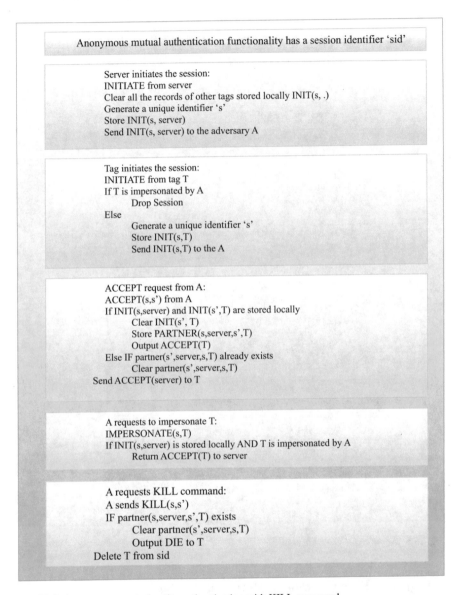

Anonymous mutual authentication functionality has a session identifier 'sid'

Server initiates the session:
INITIATE from server
Clear all the records of other tags stored locally INIT(s, .)
Generate a unique identifier 's'
Store INIT(s, server)
Send INIT(s, server) to the adversary A

Tag initiates the session:
INITIATE from tag T
If T is impersonated by A
      Drop Session
Else
      Generate a unique identifier 's'
      Store INIT(s,T)
      Send INIT(s,T) to the A

ACCEPT request from A:
ACCEPT(s,s') from A
If INIT(s,server) and INIT(s',T) are stored locally
      Clear INIT(s', T)
      Store PARTNER(s,server,s',T)
      Output ACCEPT(T)
Else IF partner(s',server,s,T) already exists
      Clear partner(s',server,s,T)
Send ACCEPT(server) to T

A requests to impersonate T:
IMPERSONATE(s,T)
If INIT(s,server) is stored locally AND T is impersonated by A
      Return ACCEPT(T) to server

A requests KILL command:
A sends KILL(s,s')
IF partner(s,server,s',T) exists
      Clear partner(s',server,s,T)
      Output DIE to T
Delete T from sid

Fig. 25.4 Anonymous mutual entity authentication with KILL command

There are many ways for combining more than one protocol together, for example, sequential or concurrent executions. The protocol executions can be run by one or more than one entity and have one or more inputs and outputs. All of the scenarios can be considered as special cases of UC framework by varying uses of synchronization, subsession, and inputs.

Anonymous mutual authentication functionality has a session identifier 'sid' shared by all
the entities

Server initiates the session:
INITIATE from server
Clear all the records of other tags stored locally INIT(s, .)
Generate a unique identifier 's'
Store INIT(s, server)
Send INIT(s, server) to the adversary A

Tag initiates the session:
INITIATE from tag T
If T is impersonated by A
    Drop Session
Else
    Generate a unique identifier 's'
    Store INIT(s,T)
    Send INIT(s,T) to the A

ACCEPT request from A:
ACCEPT(s,s') from A
If INIT(s,server) and INIT(s',T) are stored locally
    Clear INIT(s',T)
    Generate random key k
    Store PARTNER(s,server,s',T,k)
    Output ACCEPT(T,k)
Else IF partner(s',server,s,T) already exists
    Clear both PARTNER records
Send ACCEPT(server,k) to T

A requests to impersonate T:
IMPERSONATE(s,T)
If INIT(s,server) is stored locally AND T is impersonated by A
    Return ACCEPT(T) to server

Fig. 25.5 Anonymous key exchange

3.4 Juels–Weis Challenge–Response Model

The Juels–Weis model [41] is also a game-based framework where the system comprises one RFID reader R and n RFID tags. Each tag has its own key and pseudo key, which is reset after every session, this model uses the following messages:

- To assign a new secret key to the tag the *SetKey* message is used, when the tag receives *SetKey* message it discards the old key value and a new arbitrary secret is allotted to the tag.

- The *TagInit* message initializes the session key to a new value, discarding the current session details and issuing a new session key.
- The *ReaderInit* message is used by R to initialize a new session.

A is assumed to be an adversary that has the capability to generate any of the aforementioned messages. Once the tag is active, it is entitled to respond to any number of challenge–response, that is, (c_i, r_i) messages, which are based on the information from previous sessions parameters and challenges–response messages. The tag stores a log that details previous sessions and challenge–response message pairs.

Whenever the reader R receives the message (sid, r_i), it first evaluates a certain function based on its current status and all open as well-closed sessions. On the basis of this function, R outputs "accept" or "reject." A can corrupt any existing tag and issue any new tag as it is able to send any number of SetKey messages. Thus, if a tag receives SetKey message from A, it is said to be corrupted.

In this approach, it is assumed that the adversary A listens and controls all the ongoing communications and among the reader and the tags. Here, one reader R and a tags (T ∈ Tags), at the end of each session if one protocol party finds the other to be legitimate its outputs accept.

A has the ability to issue the following queries:

- *Execute(R,T,i)*: Here A eavesdrops on an actual execution of the protocol between reader (R) and tag (T) in session i. It is a passive attack.
- *Send(P₁,P₂, i,m)*: This query is the generalization of the challenge–response technique defined in Jules–Weis model along with the TagInit and ReaderInit messages. Here the adversary can impersonate a party P_1, which could be the reader or a tag during session "i" and sends m messages to some other party P_2.
- *Corrupt(T, K)*: This query is same as the SetKey query, here the adversary changes the secret key of the tag to K. This is more powerful attack as compared to Send query as the adversary has access to the tag.
- *Test(T₁, T₂, i)*: When the Test query is issued, in the session "i" depending upon b ∈ {0,1} an id ID_b is chosen from {ID_1, ID_2} and A has to guess the bit "b" correctly to succeed.

In the game that is to be played between the party and the adversary, the goal of the adversary is to identify the correct tag, and both of them must be fresh; that is, it has not been issued any corrupt queries. The following phases are considered in the game:

- *Phase I*: (learning phase) During this phase, A is able to send any number of Execute, Send, and Corrupt queries to learn about the tags and the reader.
- *Phase II*: (challenge phase) Here A chooses a new session and sends a Test message to the session. The session must be fresh and selects a random bit ∈ {0,1} depending on which it is given a tag to guess. A then continues making the queries, ensuring that the tags that are chosen for guessing remain fresh.

- *Phase III*: (guessing phase) the game terminates when A outputs a bit value b, A wins if it successfully guesses the tag ID and is able to distinguish between T_0 and T_1. The success of A is quantitatively represented as advantage of A and denoted as

$$\text{Adv}_A^{\text{UNT}}(k) = |\Pr[\text{A wins}] - \Pr[\text{random coin flip}]|$$

$$= \left| \Pr[b' = b] - \frac{1}{2} \right|$$

4 Issues With Security Models

In this section we will compare and contrast the models discussed in previous sections. Vaudeney's model and Canard et al.'s model try to define privacy as indistinguishability between real-time and ideal-world scenarios. Vaudeney has offered more categories of adversary, while other models consider ensuring privacy during authentication sessions. Vaudeney takes into account privacy of all ongoing sessions. Considering the real world and the ideal world, the UC model can also analyze more than one protocol at a time, where the environment is also interactive. However, it may sometimes be a shortcoming as some protocols that are insecure may remain undetected. Thus, the Vaudeney model must be used if we want to ensure strong privacy.

Considering Juels–Wies model privacy is ensured by the fact that adversary is unable to distinguish between two tags. Canard et al.'s model, which is built up on the Vaudeney model, provides same oracles and they can easily implement the privacy notions of Juels–Weis that fall under its future-privacy notion. Thus, if we consider indistinguishability of tags, Canard et al. can ensure better privacy as compared to Juels–Weis. Another issue with Juels–Weis is that if we have to test a system having only one tag, the model fails as it requires at least two tags to be in system for challenge phase.

Some models are designed to be applied to certain categories of protocols and they might not be able to model some other categories. For example, Vaudeney and Canard et al. can analyze authentication protocols well and they can also be adapted to model other, whereas the Juels–Weis and UC model allows all kind of protocols to be modeled easily and is not restrictive in nature.

Vaudeney and Canard et al. provide most categories of adversaries as compared to others, so in order to model a weak adversary that cannot corrupt a tag under any circumstances (possibility of this happening is very low) this model is feasible, whereas other models UC and Juels–Weis assume that a tag can always be corrupted. However, in the Juels–Weis challenge phase the adversary is unable to corrupt any of the tags. Vaudeney also provides adversary with the authority to corrupt tags at the end of the protocol run under the forward secrecy notion. However, the Juels–Weis model has some constraints, and it can also allow the adversary to corrupt a tag only to back-trace previous sessions that come under their notion of forward privacy.

Vaudeney and Canrad et al. define a strong adversary that has no restrictions on any kind of tag corruption. Initially, Vaudeney, however, failed to achieve the highest level of privacy that can be reached in all other models. However, Ouafi has extended the Vaudeney model to incorporate the notion of Strong privacy.

Vaudeney and Canrad et al. UC models allow more parallel and sequential runs of protocols and are able to incorporate all the tags present in the system at a time. However, Juels–Weis specify no tag at the initial stage; the adversary is allowed to study $(n - 1)$ tags at most.

5 Conclusion

In this chapter, we have shown various models along with their strengths and weaknesses that depend mainly upon the assumptions they make at the beginning, some of which are practically feasible and can be applied in real time. Some, on the other hand, are restrictive in nature and do not allow to incorporate all the RFID schemes. In this chapter, we have analyzed that Vaudeney and UC models incorporate most of the scenarios by providing a large number of oracles and adversaries. In order to analyze a protocol if we have to check for strongest privacy, Canrad et al.'s model is more suited. On the other hand, to analyze public key cryptography, Juels–Weis is a better choice. Further, if we can use more than one of these models as a combination or separately on any protocol, we can expect better results.

Acknowledgments This publication is an outcome of the R&D work undertaken under the project Visvesvaraya PhD Scheme of Ministry of Electronics & Information Technology, Government of India, and being implemented by Digital India Corporation.

References

1. Bu, K., Weng, M., Zheng, Y., Xiao, B., & Liu, X. (2017). You can clone but you can't hide: A survey of clone prevention and detection for RFID. *IEEE Communications Surveys & Tutorials, 19*(3), 1682–1700.
2. Buckley, J. (Ed.). (2006). *The internet of things: From RFID to the next-generation pervasive networked systems*. New York: Auerbach Publications.
3. Near Field Communications History. (2016). *Timeline of RFID technology*. Retrieved July, from http://www.nfcnearfieldcommunication.org/timeline.html
4. Edwards, C. (2016). RFID tags along with the Internet of Things. *Engineering and Technology Magazine 9*(8). http://eandt.theiet.org/magazine/2014/08/tagging-along.cfm.
5. Garfinkel, S. L., Juels, A., & Pappu, R. (2005). RFID privacy: An overview of problems and proposed solutions. *IEEE Security & Privacy, 3*(3), 34–43.

6. Lamport, L. (1981). Password authentication with insecure communication. *Communications of the ACM, 24*(11), 770–772.
7. Ohkubo, M., Suzuki, K., & Kinoshita, S. (2003). *Cryptographic approach to privacy-friendly tags*, RFID Privacy Workshop.
8. Weis, S. A., Sarma, S. E., Rivest, R. L., & Engels, D. W. (2004). Security & Privacy Aspects of low-cost radio frequency identification systems. *Security in Pervasive Computing, 2802*, 201–212.
9. Henrici, A., & Muller, P. (2004). Hash-based enhancement of location privacy for radio-frequency identification devices using varying identifiers. In *International Workshop on Pervasive Computing and Communication Security PerSec, Orlando, Florida, USA* (pp. 149–153).
10. Molnar, D., & Wagner, D. (2004). Privacy and security in library RFID: Issues, practices, and architectures. In *Conference on Computer and Communications Security—ACM CCS, Washington, DC, USA* (pp. 210–219). isbn:1-58113-961-6.
11. Kalra, S., & Sood, S. K. (2015). Secure authentication scheme for IoT and cloud servers. *Pervasive and Mobile Computing, 24*, 210–223.
12. Tuyls, P., & Batina, L. (2006). RFID-tags for anti-counterfeiting. In *Topics in cryptology (CT-RSA'06), LNCS 3860* (pp. 115–131). New York: Springer.
13. Lee, Y. K., Batina, L., & Verbauwhede, I. (2008). EC-RAC (ECDLP based randomized access control): provably secure RFID authentication protocol. In *IEEE International Conference on RFID* (pp. 97–104).
14. Liao, Y., & Hsiao, C. (2013). A secure ECC-based RFID authentication scheme integrated with ID-verifier transfer protocol. *Ad Hoc Networks, 18*, 133–146. https://doi.org/10.1016/j.adhoc.2013.02.004.
15. Peeters, R., & Hermans, J. (2013). *Attack on Liao and Hsiao's secure ECC-based RFID authentication scheme integrated with ID-verifier transfer protocol.* Cryptology ePrint Archive, Report 2013/399.
16. Liao, Y., & Hsiao, C. (2013). A secure ECC-based RFID authentication scheme using hybrid protocols. In *Advances in intelligent systems and applications* (pp. 1–13). Berlin: Springer.
17. Tan, Z. (2014). A user anonymity preserving three-factor authentication scheme for telecare medicine information systems. *Journal of Medical Systems, 38*(3), 1–9.
18. Arshad, H., & Nikooghadam, M. (2014). Three-factor anonymous authentication and key agreement scheme for telecare medicine information systems. *Journal of Medical Systems, 38*(12), 1–12.
19. Lu, Y., Li, L., Peng, H., & Yang, Y. (2015). An enhanced biometric-based authentication scheme for telecare medicine information systems using elliptic curve cryptosystem. *Journal of Medical Systems, 39*(3), 32. https://doi.org/10.1007/s10916-015-0221-7.
20. Delvaux, J., Gu, D., Verbauwhede, I., Hiller, M., & Yu, M.-D. (2016). Efficient fuzzy extraction of PUF-induced secrets: Theory and applications. In *Proceedings of the 18th International Conference on Cryptographic Hardware and Embedded Systems (CHES), vol. 9813. Santa Barbara, CA, USA* (pp. 412–431).
21. Akgun, M., & Caglayan, M. U. (2015). Providing destructive privacy and scalability in RFID systems using PUFs. *Ad Hoc Network, 32*, 32–42.
22. Aysu, E., Gulcan, D., Moriyama, P. S., & Yung, M. (2015). End-to-end design of a PUF-based privacy preserving authentication protocol. In *Proceedings of the 17th International Conference on Cryptographic Hardware and Embedded Systems (CHES), vol. 9293. Saint-Malo, France* (pp. 556–576).
23. Huth, A., Aysu, J., Guajardo, P. D., & Güneysu, T. (2017). Secure and private, yet lightweight, authentication for the IoT via PUF and CBKA. In *Proceedings of the International Conference on Information Security and Cryptology (ICISC)* (pp. 28–48).
24. Aysu, Y., Wang, P. S., & Orshansky, M. (2017). New maskless debiasing method for lightweight physical unclonable function. In *Proceedings of the 2011 IEEE International Symposium on Hardware-Oriented Security and Trust (HOST)* (pp. 134–139).

25. Hopper, N. J., & Blum, M. (2001). *Secure human identification protocols, Advances in cryptology – ASYACRYPT'2001, lecture notes in computer science* (Vol. 2248, pp. 52–66). Berlin: Springer.
26. Blum, M. L. F., Kearns, M. J., & Lipton, R. J. (1993). *Crypto-graphic primitives based on hard learning problems, advances in cryptology – CRYPTO'93, lecture notes in computer science* (pp. 278–291). Berlin: Springer.
27. Juels, S. W. (2005). *Authenticating pervasive devices with human protocols, advances in cryptology – Crypto2005, lecture notes in computer science* (Vol. 3621, pp. 293–308). Berlin: Springer.
28. Katz, J., & Shin, J. S. (2005). *Parallel and concurrent security of the HB and HB+ protocols,* Cryptology ePrint archive, Report 2005/461. http://eprint.iacr.org
29. Gilbert, H., Robshaw, M., & Silbert, H. (2005). *An active attack against HB+: A provable secure lightweight authentication protocol,* Cryptology ePrint Archive, Report 2005/237. http://eprint.iacr.org
30. Chien, H.-Y. (2007). SASI: A new ultralightweight RFID authentication protocol providing strong authentication and strong integrity. *IEEE Transactions on Dependable and Secure Computing, 4*(4), 337–340.
31. Peris-Lopez, P., Hernandez-Castro, J. C., Estevez-Tapiador, J., Ribagorda, A. (2006). *LMAP: A real lightweight mutual authentication protocol for low-cost RFID tags.* Printed handout of Workshop on RFID Security—RFIDSec 06 July.
32. Peris-Lopez, P., Hernandez-Castro, J. C., Estevez-Tapiador, J., & Ribagorda, A. (2006). *M2AP: a minimalist mutual-authentication protocol for low-cost RFID tags. Lecture notes in computer science* (pp. 912–923). Berlin: Springer.
33. Peris-Lopez, P., Hernandez-Castro, J. C., Estevez-Tapiador, J. M., & Ribagorda, A. (2006). EMAP: an efficient mutual authentication protocol for low-cost RFID tags. In *OTM Federated Conferences and Workshop: IS Workshop, IS'06, 4277. Lecture Notes in Computer Science* (pp. 352–361). Berlin: Springer.
34. Peris-Lopez, P., Hernandez-Castro, J. C., Tapiador, J. M. E., & Ribagorda, A. (2008). Advances in ultralightweight cryptography for low-cost RFID tags: Gossamer protocol. In *Proceedings of International Workshop on Information Security Applications* (pp. 56–68).
35. Vaudenay, S. (2007). On privacy models for RFID. In *Proceedings of 13th International Conference on the Theory and Application of Cryptology and Information Security (ASIACRYPT '07), vol. 4833 of Lecture Notes in Computer Science* (pp. 68–87). Kuching: Springer.
36. Ouafi, K. (2011). *Security and privacy in RFID systems.* Ph.D. thesis, EPFL, Lausanne, Switzerland.
37. Vaudenay, S. (2010). *Invited talk at RFIDSec 2010.*
38. Canard, S., Coisel, I., Etrog, J., & Girault, M. (2010). *Privacy preserving RFID systems: model and constructions.* Cryptology ePrint Archive, Report 2010/405.
39. Canard, S., Coisel, I., & Girault, M. (2010). Security of privacy preserving RFID systems. In *Proceedings of IEEE International Conference on RFID-Technology and Applications (RFID-TA10)* (pp. 269–274).
40. van Le, T., Burmester, M., & de Medeiros, B. (2007). Universally composable and forward-secure RFID authentication and authenticated key exchange. In *Proceedings of the 2nd ACM Symposium on Information, Computer and Communications Security (ASIACCS '07)* (pp. 242–252). Singapore: ACM.
41. Juels, A., & Weis, S. A. (2007). Defining strong privacy for RFID. In *Proceedings of the 5th Annual IEEE International Conference on Pervasive Computing and Communications Workshops (PerCom '07)* (pp. 342–347). New York, NY: IEEE.

Chapter 26
Computational Techniques for Real-Time Credit Card Fraud Detection

Sangeeta Mittal and Shivani Tyagi

Abstract With e-commerce becoming mainstream and a manifold increase in online transactions, security risks associated with these have become crucial concerns. In this chapter, we focus on the security issues arising out of online credit card usage. Literature in the last two and half decades has been reviewed to analyze the changing attack vectors and solution approaches to this problem. Most common attributes and open datasets of credit card transactions have been compiled to provide a starting point for new researchers. Existing fraud detection methods have been scrutinized for efficacy in addressing key challenges of fraud detection like real-time detection, concept drift, imbalanced datasets, and classifier adaptability. New directions in credit card fraud detection research have also been proposed.

Keywords Credit card fraud · Credit card fraud detection system · Machine learning · Computational models · Classifiers · Supervised and unsupervised learning

1 Introduction

Credit cards have been the main instruments for financial transactions in all online commercial activities since more than two decades. This makes credit card-based payment systems vulnerable to frauds. The history of credit card can be tracked down to 1958 when the first credit card was issued in USA, whereas in India the first credit card was issued in 1981. Since then credit card fraud has incurred losses of billions of credits and is increasing day by day. Credit card fraud is a serious growing problem that occurs as illegal/unauthorized usage of card information, unexpected transaction behavior, or any kind of transaction on an inactive card [1]. According to

S. Mittal (✉) · S. Tyagi
Department of Computer Science and Engineering, Jaypee Institute of Information Technology, Noida, India
e-mail: sangeeta.mittal@jiit.ac.in

© Springer Nature Switzerland AG 2020
B. B. Gupta et al. (eds.), *Handbook of Computer Networks and Cyber Security*,
https://doi.org/10.1007/978-3-030-22277-2_26

the Reserve Bank of India, in January 2018, a total of 36.2 million credit cards were operational. Major e-retailers like Amazon India, Flipkart, and Snapdeal have significantly captured the retail commerce in India. According to Statista portal, in 2018, the percentage of digital buyers has reached to about 60% (https://www.statista.com/statistics/261664/digital-buyer-penetration-in-india/ [Accessed on January 2, 2019]). Thus, the whole ecosystem is conducive to witness a manifold increase in credit card usage in an online transaction. Such usage is called "Card-Not-Present" as instead of physical card, only details of card are required.

The increase in digital payments is also giving rise to a manifold increase in online banking frauds in India. These frauds target banking facilities like credit, debit, and ATM cards, payment gateways, and other net banking techniques. However, a major chunk of frauds are launched on credit cards due to large credit limits offered by banks. An online credit card fraud leaves all the three parties, namely spender, issuing bank, and merchant, in a jiffy and causes economic loss to all of them. Without any specific proactive method being in place in the credit card company, the onus of fraud detection is on the cardholder/card user. The cardholder must report suspicious charges to the issuing bank. The bank then investigates the issue and if evidence of fraud is found then the process for reversing the credit for the transaction is initiated. The cardholder may not seem to be impacted because of fraud in credit card transactions as the issuing bank covers for many losses in fraud scenarios. However, this chargeback is conditional and not applicable in all frauds. Other indirect costs of inconvenience, time to follow-up are also involved. Merchants are also affected from losses due to fraud, particularly in online payments as they must accept full liability.

Even if the fraud loss is borne by the issuing bank, merchants may suffer losses due to unrecoverable costs like shipping cost, card association fees, merchant bank fees, and administrative cost. On the part of the credit card company also, a lot of resources are used in handling the dispute charges.

To address this problem, banks keep on issuing necessary advisories to its users about the secure usage of cards. However, the advisories do not always work against social engineering techniques used by the perpetrators. Thus, in case of an alleged fraud, banks must spend resources in detecting and retracing the source of fraud. The turnaround time for this detection has been several days, which does not prove useful to act as a deterrent against the frauds.

Common approaches suggested for securing smart card-based applications can be applied to credit card fraud detection also [2]. With credit cards issuance becoming easier and rise in buying options, the number of credit card transactions is increasing exponentially. About 130 million credit card transactions with total worth of 1365 crores took place in India in January 2018 (https://www.medianama.com/2018/03/223-india-credit-cards-and-debit-cards-january-2018/ [Accessed January 2, 2019]). Manual inspection of this huge number of transactions to uncover fraudulent ones is an infeasible task. Thus, credit card fraud is a good example of cases where machines can learn from past transactions to tell whether a current transaction is fraudulent or normal. The goal here is to obtain an automated *Fraud Detection System (FDS)* to detect all fraudulent transactions without raising a false alarm. A lot of machine learning-based computational models have been proposed to be used to automate this task [3–32].

In this chapter, computational methods to detect online credit card fraud specifically designed for "CARD-NOT-PRESENT" (CNP) fraud scenarios have been outlined and evaluated.

1.1 Research Contributions

The chapter is an amalgamation of a large body of literature in this area and contributes to the state of the art in the following ways:

1. Define a classification of credit card frauds
2. Outline major challenges in implementing a credit card FDS
3. Summarize the features of datasets used in studies related to credit card frauds and FDS
4. Provides a comprehensive summary of computational techniques proposed for FDS in last two and half decade
5. Critique the existing models with respect to their efficacy in addressing the challenges
6. Methodologically suggest approaches that can improve FDS performance while meeting the challenges

1.2 Chapter Outline

The chapter has been organized in six sections. First section introduces the significance of credit cards in today's commercial scenario. In Sect. 2, type of credit cards frauds and challenges towards designing computational models for fraud detection systems has been discussed. Section 3 discusses credit card datasets and their features. State of the art in categories of computational models proposed to be used for credit card fraud detection has been discussed in Sect. 4. Evaluation of the existing computational model approaches in addressing challenges of FDS has been done in Sect. 5. The chapter is concluded in Sect. 6.

2 Credit Card Frauds and Detection

A credit card is a small plastic card issued by a financial company that authorizes the cardholder to use it for payment of goods and services. The amount of purchase is recorded in the user's account and he has to repay the borrowed sum as well as any other charges agreed upon as understanding between the card company and the user (https://www.investopedia.com/terms/c/creditcard.asp [Accessed January 2, 2019]; Ways Criminal Steal Money: https://www.gadgetsnow.com/slideshows/15-ways-criminals-steal-money-from-your-debit/credit-card/public-wi-fi/photolist/55414129.cms [Accessed January 2, 2019]). These cards are used by presenting them physically at a Point of Sale (PoS) terminal as well as by furnishing card-specific information during online purchases. An unauthorized use in any of these two forms would be termed as *Credit Card Fraud*.

2.1 Types of Credit Card Frauds

Main motive of credit card fraud is to illegally obtain *physical possession* or *information of card*. However, the modus operandi may differ in various cases. On the basis of instances of frauds that have been discussed in financial information sources, they can be categorized into two main categories described in this section.

2.1.1 Obtaining Physical Cards Illegally

1. *Application Fraud*: Application fraud is when someone obtains a credit card using fake or false information by forging documents and providing fake telephone numbers of residence and place of employment.
2. *Lost and Stolen Card Fraud*: Physical security of credit card is an important factor. If a card is not adequately protected, then it can get accidently lost and fall in the hands of perpetrators. In some cases, an unattended card may be stolen with ill intention. These frauds can be used to launch other frauds.
3. *Counterfeit Cards*: Such frauds are committed through skimming actual credit card information and creating a forged magnetic tape having information about credit card.
4. *Mail Nonreceipt Fraud*: This fraud is also known as "never received issue" or "intercept fraud." It occurs when a user is expecting a new card or a replacement, but a criminal gets its possession before the actual user and starts using it.
5. *Assumed Identity*: All credit card issuance is checked for correct identification of the person to whom the card is being provided. In absence of fool-proof authentication mechanism, a fraudster may impersonate a naive person by obtaining and producing fake address proof and identity document.
6. *Doctored Cards*: One of the ways of fraud is to tamper information of an existing card with the help of a powerful electromagnet.
7. *Fake Cards*: Credit cards may be cloned by copying all the information encoded in magnetic strip and pasting into a new strip to get a fake card. Creation of fake cards can be done by someone who is skilled enough to forge the magnetic strip and the chip and break the complex security and even holograms of real credit cards.

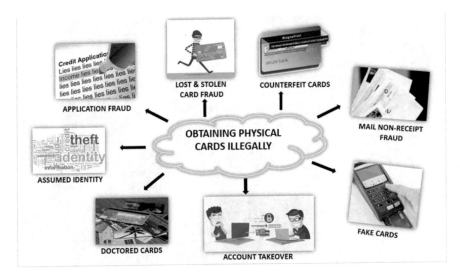

Fig. 26.1 Types of frauds by obtaining credit card illegally

8. *Account Takeover*: Such type of fraud is usually carried out online, where the fraudster talks to the credit card company to replace card by providing relevant documents and information. These attack vectors to physically obtain credit card in an illegal way have been summarized in (Fig. 26.1)

2.1.2 Obtaining Card Information Illegally

Another method to commit credit card fraud is to obtain card information illegally and various methods to do so have been summarized in (Fig. 26.2).

1. *Credit Card Imprints*: Credit card imprints are taken as a measure of security deposit for a service usage like hotel or car rentals. A dishonest service provider or its employee may skim the information, which can be used in fraudulent transactions.
2. *CNP (Card-Not-Present) Fraud*: Card-Not-Present is a type of credit card fraud executed by obtaining card information like a cardholder's name, billing address, account number, three-digit security code, and card expiration date. Such theft of credit card data may occur through online phishing, tampered swipe machines, or shoulder surfing. CNP is generally used in online transactions where the perpetrator does not have to be physically present.
3. *Card ID Theft*: It is the most difficult fraud to detect where the details of credit card become known to a criminal, and this information is used to take over a card account or open a new one. Identity theft constitutes 71% of the most common type of fraud.

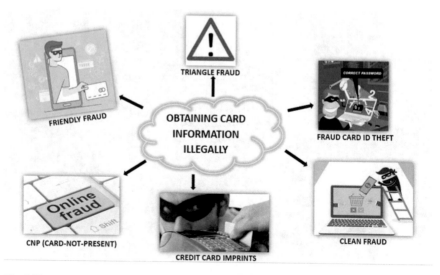

Fig. 26.2 Types of frauds by obtaining credit card information illegally

4. *Clean Frauds*: To commit this category of frauds, fraudster does a lot of home-work in collecting the user's actual details and working principles of underlying Fraud Detection System. The system does not suspect such a transaction and thus the fraud occurs in a clean manner.

5. *Friendly Fraud*: These frauds are about repudiation. In absence of proper online authentication mechanisms, actual user may deny making a purchase after doing it. The user claims that the card has been stolen before the said transaction.

6. *Triangle Fraud*: As the name suggests, this fraud takes place in three recursive steps. The first step is to create a fake ecommerce store or website that offers popular items at very low price. Users are tempted to make purchases at these sites and their credit card details are stolen. In the second step, goods are purchased from other merchants using previously stolen cards and delivered to the purchaser. The third step is to use the stolen information to make purchases elsewhere. This indirection can help the attack remain hidden for a long time.

First category of frauds, i.e., Illegal physical possession of card requires more resources and physical setup on part of perpetrator and riskier to commit as his/her physical identity can be revealed. These frauds are carried out generally by organized criminal groups. Therefore, these forms of frauds are not very attractive to individual fraudsters.

On the other hand, due to absence of physical identity disclosure, frauds committed by obtaining and misusing credit card information are rosier. With enormous Internet presence of credit card users, obtaining card information has become more feasible. Social engineering attacks as Phishing, Cloned website access due to Pharming attacks, Trojan and backdoor software, malicious insiders, shoulder surfing, and keyboard logging are few vectors by which credit card information can be allegedly obtained [33]. It can be inferred that information obtained by any of the methods would ultimately be used in online transactions.

From now onwards in this chapter, Card-Not-Present (CNP) will be used as an umbrella term to refer to any of these attacks. Thus, further discussion in this chapter is about second category of attacks.

2.2 Fraud Prevention/Detection System

Frauds aimed at obtaining credit card information can be committed through various vectors discussed in the previous section. These activities occur outside the credit card payment processing systems. An effective Fraud Prevention System (FPS) can contain these by using noncomputational measures like social awareness, proactive network security mechanisms like firewalls, and secure hardware [34]. However, prevention does not always succeed and there are instances of attacks taking place. Thus, the second layer of protection is to detect these frauds as soon as possible [35].

Fraud Detection System (FDS) has been, conventionally, manual where a sampled subset of transactions is audited to check for fraud. This system is neither effective nor scalable. To raise both of these performance parameters, automated computational based FDSs have been designed [36]. Goal of such system is to noninteractively check every transaction, regardless of the presence of prevention mechanisms, for the possibility of being a fraudulent one. Early automated FDSs were simple rule based, where rules were defined by financial experts. Also, these were used on archival data and time to detect was quite high [35].

With volumes of credit card transactions increasing widely, there is a pressing need to detect the fraudulent transaction in real time to prevent losses to the card user, card-issuing company as well as merchant. An ardent requirement is to assess each and every transaction to detect frauds in real time even in presence of dynamic attack vectors.

2.2.1 Heuristics to Identify Fraudulent Transactions

True information about a transaction being fraud can only be generated when the cardholder or the merchant files a complaint with the card-issuing company. To make FDS really effective, its designers use some heuristics to keep an eye on all transactions and raise an alert as soon as a suspicious transaction takes place. The most effective heuristics that can be included in the design model are:

1. A single IP address making multiple simultaneous transactions with different card numbers
2. Multiple IP and e-mail addresses using the same card
3. Large transactions being made than normal amount
4. Identity of user making transaction is not same as the identity of card holder

5. Country of the card usage is different from the country of card issuance
6. Payment made at odd hours according to the local time of the card holder

2.2.2 Challenges in Design of Credit Card Fraud Detection System

Building an effective, real-time, and scalable computation based automated FDS is subjected to several difficulties and challenges enumerated in Fig. 26.3:

1. *Concept Drift*—FDS targeting anomalous behavior suffer from the fact that in real world, profile of normal and fraudulent behavior changes with time. For computational techniques, this leads to a non-stationarity effect in modeling relation between dependent and target variables.
2. *Class Imbalance*—Credit card transactions data are a typical case of highly imbalanced data. In per unit of time, a large number of credit card transactions take place and most of them are genuine. Typically, out of each 10,000 transactions, only 1 has been found to be fraudulent. Traditional computational methods perform poorly in recognizing instances of rarely occurring class, which is actually the class of interest in FDS [37].
3. *Lack of Real-Time FDS*—Most of the existing FDS reported in literature work on archival data that can be used to drive future security policies and forensics. This analysis is effective in a limited manner to detect and block fraudulent transactions in real time [38].
4. *Fraud Detection Cost Overheads*—Many related studies conveniently ignore the overheads in implementing FDS. Cost is however important consideration while estimating the effectiveness of any solution.
5. *Lack of Domain-Specific Metrics*—Existing models have been evaluated on the basis of standard classifier metrics. No standard domain-specific metrics are available to particularly benchmark the performance of credit card FDS.
6. *Lack of Adaptability*—Behavior analysis-based fraud detection methods define normal behavior from past legitimate transactions of a user. Many a time user behavior may evolve due to external factors like family conditions, an increase or decrease in income, and frequent travelling. Existing supervised and unsupervised approaches used in fraud detection systems are not adaptive to changing datasets. Thus, efficiency of detecting new patterns of normal and fraudulent behaviors becomes difficult [39].
7. *Lack of Availability of Know-How*—Existing fraud detection methods are not made public due to apprehension of them being lesser effective. Thus, everyone has to re-invent the wheel and existing knowledge cannot be leveraged.
8. *Unavailability of Datasets*—Credit card companies do not release their labeled datasets for public scrutiny. Many computational methods are based on learning from datasets. Even a few datasets that are publicly available are actually a processed form of actual datasets to hide real variables and their relations.
9. *Lack of Aggregation Possibility to Leverage Cross User Data*—Optimally leveraging transaction data across card-issuing companies and types of cardholders is not possible due to lack of trust among card-issuing companies [28].

Fig. 26.3 Challenges in credit card fraud detection system

10. *Limited Up-to-Date Supervised Transaction Sets*—Computational models do not have at their disposal recent supervised transactions, provided in the form of investigators' feedback, to dynamically evolve learning models [37].

Challenges 1–6 can be handled computationally, but the remaining ones can be handled only by policy change and collaborative commitment towards fraud prevention. Thus, an effective computational FDS needs to meet these challenges. Particularly, first four are fundamental to the problems of modern-day credit card frauds. An ideal FDS should look for change in transaction patterns that are indicative of fraudulent transaction and produce a suspicion score about it. The score represents possibility of that transaction being fraudulent. If the score is available before the transaction is committed to databases, then it can save a lot of costs to all three stakeholders, namely user, credit card company, and merchant. It will lead to reduced human intervention as only probable frauds would be checked manually. Before discussing the computational models that have been proposed for designing FDS, we first elaborate on the data available in each credit card transaction and archive.

3   Information Available for Credit Card Fraud Detection

An automated FDS would be based on effective computational models. Each such model irrespective of its working principle requires a lot of domain data. In this section, we discuss the features of information that can be available to the models. The feature list has been compiled from the literature on FDS.

3.1   Labeled Credit Card Transaction Datasets

Information available as transaction datasets is input to computational models to solve the problem of fraud detection. A tabular representation of few such datasets and their cardinality has been compiled in Table 26.1. The datasets have been given Ids for ease of reference in further sections. In the dataset description column, the year of creation of data has also been mentioned. In few papers, actual period of data collection was not given. For such works, time of creation of data has been assumed to be some time prior to the publication of paper. Dataset cardinality has

Table 26.1 Summary of some datasets used in research

Dataset ID	Dataset description	Dataset cardinality
D1	European Card Holder Data (2013–2014) [37, 40–44]	284,807 transactions, 28 attributes
D2	Mellon Bank Credit Card Issuer Data (1990) [3]	1,100,000 transactions, 50 attributes
D3	Chase Bank & Union Bank Data (1995–1996) [6]	500,000 transactions
D4	US Bank Data (2000–2001) [14]	25,000 credit card records, 38 attributes
D5	Financial Institute Data (Webbiz-Ireland) (2004–2008) [16]	4 million transactions, 23 attributes
D6	Large European card-processing company Data (2012) [17]	80,000,000 individual transactions, 27 attributes
D7	Actual Fraud Transactions combined with the different number of normal transactions (before 2012) [18]	42 attributes with imbalanced ratios as 236, 23.6, and 4.7
D8	Australian Bank Data (2003) [20]	640,361 total transactions of 21,746 credit cards
D9	Vesta Corporation Data (before 2012) [21]	206,541 transactions
D10	Spanish Bank Dataset (2011–2012) [22]	180 million transactions, 10 attributes
D11	Major Financial Institution Data (before 2017) [24]	86 million transactions, 69 attributes
D12	E-tail Data (Jan 2015–Aug 2015) [26]	347,572 transactions, 70 attributes
D13	Retail Banking Data (before 2018) [30]	80 million transactions, 5 attributes
D14	Universo Online Inc. Data (2014) [31]	903,801 transactions

been mentioned to state the amount of information that has been used to study the problem of frauds in credit card-based payments. These datasets are highly imbalanced in ratios of fraudulent versus nonfraudulent transactions.

Most of the datasets have been obtained by the researchers from their industrial partners and, due to confidentiality commitment, have not been provided publicly. This restricts the usage of datasets in further researches as well as verification of existing results. Only Dataset "D1" is publicly available and is highlighted in bold. It is a publicly available and processed, and real dataset is available for free download at [45]. The dataset contains total 284,807 transactions made in September 2013 by cardholders of a European country. Out of these, only 492 transactions are fraud, which makes it highly imbalanced. The data have been made available as 28 principal components computed out of actual data, owing to confidentiality issues. Apart from that, there is "Time" attribute, which is the time elapsed since first transaction in the dataset. "Amount" attribute contains the sum of money involved in the transaction. This feature can be used to compute cost of an undetected fraud. Data have been labeled as "1" in case of fraud and "0" otherwise.

All the datasets mentioned in Table 26.1 have different credit card usage information attributes. On careful examination, these can be divided into three categories, namely customer's basic information, current transaction descriptors, and user-specific usage history.

1. Customer basic information descriptors

   (a) Whether card holder is male/female
   (b) Card holder's age—behavior of aged customers is more predictable
   (c) User identification information in terms of associated account number
   (d) Identification number of card, generally a 16-digit number
   (e) Type of card: Master, Visa, etc.
   (f) Encrypted customer ID: customer identifier
   (g) Date of birth
   (h) Registration date and time: the date and time the customer registered to open their account
   (i) Country of residence of the card holder

2. Current transaction descriptors.

   (a) Category of merchant assigned as code by card-processing company; for example, jewelers, electronics, etc.
   (b) Payment ID
   (c) Status of whether the transaction was successful or declined
   (d) Place of transaction
   (e) Currency
   (f) Quantity of current product ordered
   (g) Category of goods being purchased
   (h) Brand of goods
   (i) Is shipping country the card country
   (j) Payee account number

Table 26.2 Common attributes

S. no.	Attribute name	Description	Data set including attributes
1.	Transaction amount	Amount of money spent	D1–D3, D5–D6, D8, D10–D12
2.	Merchant code	Encoding categories of sold goods	D2, D6, D8, D11
3.	Transaction date	Date at which the transaction was performed	D2, D5–D6, D8
4.	Transaction time	Time at which the transaction was performed	D1–D2, D6, D10, D12
5.	Transaction place/recipient address	Geographical location of transaction determined by IP address	D5
6.	Fraud	1 if the transaction has been recognized as a fraud, 0 otherwise	D1, D6, D8, D10–D12
7.	Credit card number	The 16-digit unique credit card number	D8
8.	Current balance	Account balance after transaction	D5, D11
9.	Transaction type	Type of transaction: purchase/payment/transfer to other account	D5, D12
10.	Purpose	Car, real estate, life insurance, property, etc.	D2, D6, D12

(k) Transaction amount

(l) Country where the transaction took place

(m) Number of transactions in the last 48 h

(n) Accumulated amount of transactions in the last 48 h

(o) Number of terminals used in the last 48 h

3. History descriptors

(a) The payments made to the account in recent times

(b) Fraud rate: average rate of illegal operations, for all cards, in the last 50,000 transactions

Many of these attributes may not be directly available in each transaction but can be derived from other existing values. For example, Bahnsen et al. [17] derived 260 attributes from selected 14 original attributes in dataset. History and customer basic information descriptors are used to work out behavior-based fraud detection while current transaction-based descriptors can be used to find misuse [24]. On examining the body of work, it was found that the databases considered for this problem somewhat vary in the type of information considered to be available for designing the computation models. The common transaction attributes that were used in most of the datasets for credit card fraud detection have been presented in Table 26.2. Name of the datasets where the attributes were available for learning the models has also been mentioned in the last column.

Data types of the attributes are mixed and range from numerical to categorical and ordinal. For example, transaction size and current balance are real-valued and merchant code and country names symbolic.

4 Computational Techniques for Fraud Detection

Computational models proposed for credit card fraud detection date as long as the frauds themselves. A variety of statistical, machine learning and data mining tools have been utilized to obtain an automated fraud detection system in the presence of mixed data types. Table 26.3 summarizes five yearly snapshots of main techniques used against this problem from 1994 to till now.

Currently, the techniques used for credit card fraud detection can be classified into the following categories:

- *Fraud Analysis*: Deals with supervised learning for identifying misuse detection
- *User Behavior Analysis*: Deals with unsupervised learning for anomaly detection

If a large number of labeled transactions are available, then machine learning-based classifiers can be trained to distinguish future fraudulent and normal transactions. These classifiers use label information to model the two types of transactions. Various supervised learning methods like decision trees (DTs), back propagation neural networks, support vector machines (SVMs), random forests, and Bayesian networks (BNs) have been applied to obtain the desired result of detection [3–6, 14, 17, 30, 31, 37, 41]. They are effective only for detecting frauds following similar patterns as those identified as fraud in past.

However, these methods are unsuitable for recognizing new patterns of fraudulent transactions. Unsupervised class of methods is agile in adapting to novel frauds and thus can be used against an adaptive fraudster. Self-organizing maps, peer group analysis, break-point analysis, and competitive learning are few unsupervised methods applied for detection of frauds [8, 15, 21, 24, 46].

Another class of methods detects fraud according to individual behavior analysis of individual user, which was ignored in machine learning methods. These involve learning profile of normal transaction pattern for each user based on her or his normal transactions. Profile of current transaction is matched against this profile and a suspicion degree is assigned to each transaction based on the user's profile [22, 27, 44].

Pre-processing Transaction attributes are of mixed data type including categorical, ordinal, binary, numeric, and string. Binning, averaging, normalization, ordinal to numeric, categorical features to numeric, ranking, and ordering are few pre-processing methods applied to map input variables to a set of more descriptive features [5]. Pre-processing of data is a required step before applying many computational models based on machine learning.

Table 26.3 Summary of credit card fraud detection research using closed datasets

Study	Method used	Dataset_ID/description
[3] Credit Card Fraud Detection with a Neural-Network (1994)	Artificial Neural Network (ANN)	D2: 1,100,000 transactions over 2 months' period. Fifty attributes were mapped to 20 and used as input to the ANN
[4] Neural Networks Compared to Statistical Technique (1995)	Discriminant Model analysis	6-months data of real accounts with more than 50 million transactions
[5] Density-Based Clustering and Radial Basis Function Modeling to Generate Credit Card Fraud Scores (1996)	Radial Basis Function Network (RBFN) with Density-based clustering	Real data with 37 attributes
[6] Distributed Data Mining in Credit Card Fraud Detection (1999)	AdaCost algorithm	D3: a set of 20% fraud and 80% nonfraud transactions from Chase Bank
[7] Unsupervised Profiling Method for Fraud Detection (2001)	Behavioral outlier detection techniques used Peer Group Analysis and Break Point Analysis.	Per week spending data of 858 accounts over a period of 52 weeks
[9] Parallel Granular Neural Networks for Fast Credit Card Detection (2002)	Parallel Granular Neural Network (GNN)	Real transaction datasets, details not provided
[15] Real-Time Credit Card Fraud Detection Using Computational Intelligence (2007)	Self-organizing map-based clustering for Neural Network, Similarity functions: Euclidean-distance and Gravity function	Test database extracted from an actual banking database
[16] Identifying Online Credit Card Fraud Using AIS algorithm (2010)	Artificial Immune System (AIS) benchmarked against logistic regression model	D5: 4 million transactions from 462,279 different customers with 5417 fraudulent cases
[17] Cost Sensitive Credit Card Fraud Detection Using Bayes Minimum Risk (2013)	Cost-sensitive method based on Bayes minimum risk	D6: A set of 80,000,000 transactions with 27 attributes. Fourteen attributes were used. Ratio of frauds was 0.025%
[18] Detecting Credit Card Fraud by Genetic Algorithm and Scatter Search (2011)	Genetic Algorithm and Scatter Search	D7: Custom-defined datasets varying imbalance from 4.7 to 236
[20] Artificial Immune Systems for The Detection of Credit Card Fraud (2012)	Artificial Immune System (AIS)	D8: 640,361 total transactions, with 21,746 credit cards
[21] Improved Competitive Learning Neural Networks for Network Intrusion and Fraud Detection (2012)	Iterated Competitive Learning Network (ICLN) and Supervised Iterated Competitive Learning Network (SICLN)	D9: 206,541 transactions: 204,078 transactions are normal and 2463 are fraudulent

Title	Method	Dataset
[41] Credit Card Fraud Detection and Concept-Drift Adaptation with Delayed Supervised Information (2015)	Along with Balanced Random Forest (BRF), two traditional learning approaches for FDSs, namely, • classifier is retrained on daily data of most recent supervised samples • an evolving ensemble approach where older results are replaced by better ones	D1: 284,807 transactions, 28 attributes. Dataset was available from 2 years: 2013 dataset with 160k transactions and 304 frauds; 2014 dataset with 173k transactions and 380 frauds
[24] Adversarial Learning in Credit Card Fraud Detection (2017)	SMOTE for oversampling and Gaussian Mixture Models for classification	D11: 36 GB of data consisting of 86 million anonymized transactions. Eleven relevant attributes out of 69 actual were used
[27] A New Credit Card Fraud Detecting Method Based on Behavior Certificate (2018)	Behavior certificate (BC), which reflects cardholders' transaction habits	Synthetic data: normally distributed with mean $= 275$ and standard deviation $= 20$; 6-month period, amount is normally distributed for 10 cardholders, out of them for 5 cardholders, mean $= 50$ and standard deviation $= 10$. For other 5 ones, mean $= 1000$ and standard deviation $= 150$
[28] A Utilitarian Approach to Adversarial Learning in Credit Card Fraud Detection (2018)	Feed-forward Adversarial Learning Game Algorithm	8,000,000 transactions with 0.01% fraud cases
[30] Deep Learning Detecting Fraud in Credit Card Transaction (2018)	Deep learning or General Artificial Neural Network with built-in time and memory components such as Long Short-Term Memory	D13: 80 million transactions; 5 features were used
[31] A customized classification algorithm for credit card fraud detection (2018)	Fraud-BNC, a customized Bayesian Network Classifier (BNC)	D14: 903,801 transactions with 1.8% fraudulent ones described by 424 attributes
[22] Credit Card Fraud Detection through Parenclitic Network Analysis (2018)	Features for MLP-based classifier learnt from parenclitic network of transactions	D10: 15 million operations realized by 7 million cards, for a total of 250 GB of information
[37] Credit Card Fraud Detection: A Realistic Modeling and A Novel Learning Strategy (2018)	Proposed learning strategy using alert-feedback interaction	D1: 284,807 transactions, 28 features, frauds account for about 0.2% of all transactions
[44] Transaction Fraud Detection Based on Total Order Relation and Behavior Diversity (2018)	Logical graph of BP (LGBP)	D1: 284,807 transactions, 28 features
[46] Credit Card Fraud Detection Using Self-Organizing Maps (2018)	Self-Organizing Maps (SOMs)	Synthetic data simulated according to the Ukrainian credit card market

4.1 Computational Models Based on Supervised Machine Learning

This section summarizes the knowledge gathered from literature on the use of supervised methods for credit card fraud detection.

- *Discriminant Analysis*—In discriminant analysis, a set of independent features is selected to learn a model or mathematical equation to classify given data into two mutually exhaustive classes. In [4], fraudulent and nonfraudulent transactions were used to learn a statistical model of discriminant analysis to label good and bad accounts. The model, when run over more than 50 million transactions, gave good results of 4% false positives and 85% accuracy.
- *Decision Trees and Random Trees*—Decision Tree (DT) is a method of supervised classification in which root node is created first for one of the attributes. The node is split further according to all possible values of root attributes. This process of creating new nodes is repeated until a stopping criterion is met. All leaf nodes are associated with class labels to which most of the samples terminating to that leaf belongs to. Random tree is a decision tree that uses a random subset of attributes to create decision tree classifier. The subset size is defined using a subset ratio parameter [43].
- *Radial Basis Function Networks (RBFN)*—RBF model is learnt in two phases. Training includes learning cluster centers and scaling parameters. Centers can also be computed by vector quantization or tree classification algorithms. In the second phase, weights are computed according to cluster centers. One of the advantages of two-phase learning in RBF networks is the possibility of using unlabeled training data in the first phase. In [5], RBFN-based model has been trained to classify transactions as fraud and nonfraud. The results were claimed to be better than ANN with back propagation.
- *Meta-Classifier*—Meta-classifier, also known as ensemble learning, achieves strong classification results by combining results of multiple classifiers where each of the chosen classifier may be individually weak. In [6], AdaBoost learning was modified considering domain-specific misclassification cost as the main decision parameter. The algorithm has been named as AdaCost by the authors. Four base classifiers, namely C4.5, Classification and Regression Trees (CART), Ripper, and Bayes, were used to create the ensemble using class-combiner strategy. Authors were able to obtain 3% reduction in cumulative costs as compared to AdaBoost on Dataset D3.
- *Bayes Minimum Risk Classifier*: This classifier considers trade-offs between probability of a data sample falling into one class and cost associated with classification. In [17], Bayes minimum risk classifier was used and evaluated on cost-to-fraud metric suggested by them. It was seen that a 23% more saving could be obtained because of this method as compared to state of the art available then.

- *Random Forest*—Random forest is a result of applying a number of random tree-based classifiers and applying majority voting to determine classification result. Dal Pozzolo et al. [41] used balanced random forests of 100 trees to solve the problem of concept drift. Classifiers were updated on recent and delayed feedbacks. It was found that better results are obtained when recent feedbacks are given more weights than delayed ones.
- *Bayesian Network Classifier*—A Bayesian Network (BN) classification approach involves learning a Bayesian network of interdependencies between various independent attributes and probabilities to quantify each network link's strength in conveying the relation as conditional probability tables (CPT) for each node. Learning a BN is about learning the network structure as well as the probabilities. Authors in [31] applied BN-based classification approach to detect frauds in D14 database. For learning the network structure, they have suggested an evolutionary algorithm and named the obtained classifier as Fraud-BNC. Using this classifier, 98.31% of nonfraudulent transactions correctly classified against 71.87% with another classifier.
- *Artificial Neural Networks (ANN)*—ANNs are also known as Feed-Forward Neural Networks that use back propagation algorithm for training purpose. The connections between the units are acyclic. Information in terms of weights at each layer acts as input to next layer nodes. All intermediate layers, that is, those apart from input and output layer, remain hidden [43].

  In [3], neural networks were trained on labeled dataset and obtained model was used in real implementation in Mellon bank. The model was run every 2 h to verify transactions committed since the last commitment. Thus, making the time to detect was more than 2 h.
- *Deep Learning (DL)*—DL is recent popular concept based on the concept of a multilayer perceptron network. In this type of classification, each layer learns weight such as to reproduce the output itself. Stochastic gradient descent is the error function used to decide the direction to move in the state space. Various nonlinear activation functions like maxout activation, rectifier, and tanh have been used for approximation of complex functions. In [30], various deep learning models namely Artificial Neural Networks (ANNs), Recurrent Neural Networks (RNNs), Long Short-Term Memory (LSTMs), and Gated Recurrent Units (GRUs) were used to solve FD problem. Six hidden layer GRU architecture with 150 nodes produced the best performing model giving an accuracy score of 0.916.
- *Decision Tree-Based Classifiers*

  - *ID3*—Iterative Dichotomiser 3, popularly known as ID3, is the basic decision tree algorithm. At every step of tree creation, entropy of all remaining attributes is computed and one with minimum entropy is chosen [29]. Further nodes are creating by creating subsets of data values of chosen attribute. One of the drawbacks of ID3 is that it is disoriented because of presence of attributes with a large number of possible values [47].

- *C4.5*—Ross Quinlan, designer of ID3, extended his algorithm to C4.5 algorithm for serious commercial usage. To overcome the limitation of ID3, the stopping criterion used in C4.5 is normalized information gain instead of entropy. The attribute with the highest normalized information gain is chosen to make the decision [47].
- *C5.0*—It is immediate successor of C4.5 by the same designer. C5.0 improves its predecessor in many ways. It fares better in terms of speed, memory usage during runtime, lesser storage, and search complexity due to smaller trees. It also supports pre-classification tasks like winnowing, weighting, and postclassification like boosting.
- *CART*—Classification and Regression Trees (CART) is a type of decision tree. The tree is flexible such that if variables are categorical then output is classification and if the input is real valued output is real valued, that is, regression. Like basic decision trees, nodes are split on rules based on values of features. This splitting is recursively repeated until stopping criteria like no further information gain is achieved. For choosing attribute to split, the strategy is to choose the attribute whose gini Index is least after splitting [47].

Authors in [37] compared decision tree-based methods with computationally expensive Support Vector Machine (SVM)-based approaches. Results claim that decision tree methods are able to provide best 89% testing accuracy as compared to 83% by SVM.

- *Hybrid Supervised Approaches*—In these types of systems, accurate fraud detection has been obtained by applying multiple approaches in different phases. Authors in [14] apply three-stage FDS. In the first stage a rule-based filter is used to flag a suspicious transaction. This transaction is given a score on the basis of Dempster Shafer's theory of evidence. In the third stage, Bayesian learner that has been computed from transaction history database of user has been utilized to update the value of evidence and eventually term the transaction as fraud or nonfraud.

Supervised algorithms work by learning from true labels. But they need large training datasets [39]. ANNs give satisfactory classification rate even for large transaction datasets.

4.2 Computational Models Based on Unsupervised Machine Learning

Unsupervised learning is useful in studies that need to detect changes in behavior or unusual transactions. Actual labeled fraudulent and normal transactions are not available. An initial set of transactions considered as normal is used to start the classification process. Further transactions with any significant deviations from this set are considered to be fraudulent. Unsupervised techniques can be used to model user similarity. Some methods for unsupervised fraud detection in credit data have been explained below.

- *Peer Group Analysis (PGA)*: PGA is an unsupervised learning approach. It is about finding a set of peers by grouping similar objects over a time window and then calculating peer group statistics. Any object deviating from its peer group behavior is pointed out as suspicious. In [5], peer group analysis was used to form peer groups of fraudulent and nonfraudulent transactions. Authors propose to modify the method by changing the length of the time window used to determine the peer group. This change in window size caters to the need to detect short-term changes in spending behavior [8].

- *Break-Point Analysis*: In a set of observations, a break point is an observation or point of time where anomalous behavior is detected. As against supervised approaches that worked towards generalization of a normal versus fraudulent transaction, this method works for individual users. A transaction can be abnormal for one user but perfectly normal for any other user. Thus user-specific break-point analysis tracks its anomalous behavior and generates alarm when a break point is reached. In [8], BPA has been used to identify changes in spending behavior based on the transaction information of an account.

- *Self-Organizing Maps (SOM)*: It is an unsupervised learning method that configures the underlying neural network according to the topological structure of the input data. Weights of neurons are iteratively tuned to approximate the input data. Clustering method of SOM has been found to be appropriate for analyzing deviation in customer behavior in [46]. Self-organization is used to learn patterns from existing unlabeled transactions and keep them in different clusters according to similarity in patterns. Eventually two clusters representing legal card holder's and fraudster's behavior are found. Authors in [15] use SOM-based clustering to identify certain "suspicious" transactions that require further review.

- *Improved Competitive Learning Network (ICLN)*—It is type of neural network. Authors in [21] used unsupervised methods to learn natural clusters within the data. On applying their method on dataset D9, recall rate was only 57.4%. This metric was improved significantly when ICLN was modified to supervised ICLN, changing the recall rate to 79.1%.

- *Adversarial Learning*—The concept of adversarial learning is a specialized area of machine learning that learns the dynamic adversary behavior model and updates the classifier to adapt to the changed behavior. Modeling of adversarial scenarios makes varying assumptions on the amount of knowledge the adversary has about the classification system. Zeager et al. [24] investigated the method to model adversary's optimal strategy and update a logistic regression classifier, assuming that adversary can compare different strategies used by FDS. Gaussian Mixture Models (GMM) has been chosen as an unsupervised way to create three distinct strategies that the adversary can choose from [24]. Each transaction is assigned to the strategy it most likely belongs to. Best strategy is the one that gives adversary the highest false-negative rate. The classifier is retrained to counter this strategy. In this solution, the classifier was being checked for retraining in every game between adversary and FDS. Authors in [28] improved upon this approach by optimizing the retraining decision. They incorporated economic value into the decision to retrain and the selection of strategy. Results indicate that performance similar to [24] is obtained even when training is manifold reduced.

One of the advantages of using unsupervised neural networks over similar techniques is that these methods can learn from data stream. The more data passed to an SOM model, the more adaptation and improvement on result are obtained. More specifically, the SOM adapts its model as time passes. As a result, the fraudulent use of a card can be detected fast and effectively. However, neural networks have some drawbacks and difficulties that are mainly related to specifying suitable architecture on the one hand and excessive training required for reaching to best performance on the other hand.

4.3 Computational Models Based on Nature-Inspired/Biologically Inspired Computing

- *Genetic Algorithms (GA)*—Genetic algorithms are evolutionary algorithms that aim at obtaining better solutions as time progresses. The initial population selection process is random, which limits the probability of goodness of initial population to the random function chosen. In [18], genetic algorithm has been utilized to solve fraud detection problem. However, the initial population is selected by scatter search method. This method involves improving the random selection local improvement method like mutation. The algorithm works with 1050 fraud transaction and created three databases by varying number of normal transactions. The study concluded in finding the best set of variables that determine the transaction to be fraud or nonfraud.
- *AIS*—Artificial Immune Systems (AIS) are a recent branch of artificial intelligence based on the biological metaphor of the human immune system [48]. The immune system can distinguish between self and nonself, or more appropriately, between harmful nonself and everything else. Thus, AIS-based mathematical model assumes everything it has not seen as non-self. AIS can thus be constructed to flag "nonstandard" transactions without having seen examples of all possible such transactions during training of the algorithm. The technique has been used for identification of anomalous credit card transactions [16]. Authors implemented AIS to find frauds in Dataset D5. According to results, Artificial Immune System could achieve up to 98.96% accuracy. The misclassification of a large number of normal transactions makes this algorithm unsuited for fully automatic operation. However, potentially fraudulent transactions could be subjected to further automatic or human processing to reduce the number of

false negatives (FN). Authors in [20] also applied AIS to all types of credit card frauds namely lost, stolen, skimmed, and mail/phone fraud and achieved average detection accuracy up to 71% approximately.

4.4 Computational Models Based on Other Miscellaneous Approaches

Recently many other approaches have been explored as solution to the problem [22, 27, 44]. A hybrid data mining/complex network classification algorithm has been proposed in [22]. Complex networks were used to synthesize complex features from transaction logs. Specifically, parenclitic networks, a network reconstruction technique that works towards finding difference between a given data instance and a set of training instances, has been utilized. Network structure formation is based on finding topological features whose correlation strongly differentiates normal and abnormal transactions. About 5.9% increase in the Area Under the Curve (AUC) was observed when networks were trained with an objective of minimization of false positives.

A fraud detection method based on Behavior Certificate (BC) has been proposed in [27]. BC certifies the user's general as well as special case (festival/weekends) behavior features that FDS can verify. From the set of behavior features in transactions datasets, a binary behavior feature vector of 13 values, namely (1) "Weekday" (2) "Weekend" (3) "Festival" (4) "Normal Day" (5–8) "Interval$_i$" ($i = 1$–4) are four time-intervals (9) "Location"—area code (10–13) "Range$_i$" ($i = 1$–4) as transaction amount ranges. Interval and range values are user specific and learnt from his or her past spending behavior. On every new transaction, a risk value is computed on the basis of the cardholder's BC and an alert is generated if the risk is above threshold. The method performed well on a synthetic simulated dataset and gave specificity values of up to 92%.

Generally, the attributes of a transaction are totally ordered. For example, transaction_time $\rightarrow$ transaction_location $\rightarrow$ category_of_good $\rightarrow$ amount $\rightarrow$ shipping_address. Based on the total order relation and the transaction log of a user, we can construct a logic graph of BP (LGBP) for the user, which represents the dependent relations of all attribute values of this user's records and covers all transaction records [44]. In LGBP, path-based transition probability is computed. Based on this probability, recognization degree for a given transaction record and BP of user is calculated. Recognization degree of a transaction represents the probability of the transaction in the history even on considering user's transaction diversity. It has been reported that mean recall is about 95% and mean precision is about 85% on self-accumulated datasets. User's BP can be updated by event- or time-driven policies.

Telecommunication, computer intrusion, and money laundering share computational techniques for credit card detection [10, 12]. Fraudsters are adaptive to the protection mechanism in place. AIS and adversarial learning are tuned towards learning changing attacker profile. There is a dearth of published literature on fraud detection. Machine learning techniques based on supervised neural networks dominated the commercial fraud detection systems in the late nineties [10]. Outlier detection methods for behavioral outliers are an interesting line of approach in absence of a lot of labeled data [12]. Algorithms for adaptive pattern recognition and statistical modeling combined with rule-based expert systems also gave promising models [12]. With evolution in computational models in the first decade of the twenty-first century, other techniques for fraud detection were also explored. This included Hidden Markov Models, rule-induction techniques, fuzzy system, decision trees, Support Vector Machines (SVM), and K-Nearest Neighbor algorithms [19]. Among supervised methods, K2, TAN, Naïve Bayes, Logistic regression, and J48 decision trees were tried by few researchers [25]. A comparison between performance of logistic regression, random forests, and support vector machines was carried in [23]. Random Forest proved to be the most effective with highest 93.5 AUC. A study on hybrid methods that use AdaBoost and majority voting methods has been done in [43]. It was found that on single classifiers accuracy of fraud detection rates vary from 7.4% for Linear Regression (LIR) up to 100% for random forests, gradient-boosted trees, decision stump, neural network, multilayer perceptron, and logistic regression. AdaBoosting improved performance of naive Bayes, decision tree, and random tree. In LIR, the improvement was drastic from 7.4 to 94.1% fraud detection accuracy. Majority voting method further improved the results giving 95–100% fraud accuracy. A deep learning-based fraud detection model has been implemented in [33] and gives a good area under curve for preserving privacy of card parameters. In [49], a method to detect fraudulent transactions has been given by first shortlisting suspicious transactions using fuzzy c-means algorithm and based upon suspicion score a neural network-based classifier labels the transaction as fraud or nonfraud.

Despite having high accuracy, most of the machine learning methods suffer from high false-positive rates resulting in a nonreliable system, as too many resources are wasted verifying legitimate transactions instead of identifying anomalous ones.

5 Evaluation

In Sect. 2, major challenges faced by effective FDS were enumerated. In the previous section, many computational models were discussed with respect to their application as classifiers in fraud detection system. In this section, the extent to which the models are able to address the challenges has been analyzed.

5.1 Handling Class Imbalance

One of the biggest swinging blocks is the immense data and its distribution [50]. In almost all datasets, fraudulent transactions were significantly lower than normal healthy transactions accounting to around 1–2% of the total number of observations. The algorithms used for credit card fraud detection tend to produce unsatisfactory classifiers when faced with imbalanced datasets. The common methods used for dealing with unbalanced classification are:

- *Under sampling*—For large transaction datasets, some legitimate instances can be dropped to create a balanced dataset. This process of selectively choosing majority class instances is called under sampling [17] used under sampling approach to handle skewed class distribution. Five different databases S1, S5, S10, S20, and S50, each one having a different percentage of frauds 1%, 5%, 10%, 20%, and 50%, respectively, were created. Authors in [27] did undersampling to get 10:1 ratio.
- *Oversampling*—In cases where data are imbalanced as well as small in size, oversampling can be used. It involves synthetic creation of minority class samples sometimes by mere duplication. Bootstrapping and SMOTE (Synthetic Minority Over-Sampling Technique) are some more sophisticated techniques to create new samples [51]. A combination of over- and undersampling is often successful as well [21].
- *Synthetic Minority Over-Sampling Technique (SMOTE)*—It is a method to systematically create new synthetic samples of minority class transactions [52]. Depending upon the amount of oversampling required, neighbors from the k nearest neighbors are randomly chosen and their convex combinations are prepared to obtain new samples. SMOTE has been used for generating artificial fraud transactions for creating balanced datasets [52].
- *Stratified Sampling*—This method involves dividing the dataset based on some characteristics of data population. After dividing the population into the strata, one can randomly select samples from each subset [51].

In [6], with given 20:80 class distribution, four subsets are generated from each month for generating 32 datasets with 50:50 distribution. In [41], delayed samples and windowing were used to handle concept drift problem. In [16], Artificial Immune System (AIS)-based solution does not depend upon knowledge about fraudulent transactions. It learns normalcy from normal transactions and anything that is not normal is termed as fraudulent. Thus, skewness in the class distribution does not affect results. Supervised Incremental Competitive Learning Network (SICLN) performed very well on highly skewed data [21].

5.2   Handling Concept Drift/Adaptability

A fraudster tries to assimilate information about detection strategies by trying dummy attacks. It then tends to change fraud behavior like scale, frequency, and target, over time to avoid getting caught by an FDS. This problem is known as Concept Drift in FDS. The model should be able to detect and respond to it. Even if concept drift is detected early, an FDS still takes time before a new model is trained to use such information [41]. Another nonstationarity that can occur in FDS is due to variable behavior of card users caused by unknown, seasonal, periodical, trend-specific factors. Techniques that work towards adapting the classifier against concept drift adopted by fraudster are more successful in containing the frauds [42].

In practice, concept drift adaptation is achieved by combining ensemble methods and resampling techniques. In [41], concept drift adaptation is achieved by training a classifier over a sliding window and by using ensemble approaches by separating delayed supervised samples from feedback samples.

5.3   Ensuring Real-Time FDS

An ideal FDS aims to detect fraud before the transaction approval process. This real-time requirement is difficult to fulfill given the inherent delay in obtaining information about fraud occurrence due to verification latency [41]. Moreover, a detailed examination of every transaction in real time may not be possible as customers will not like to wait for this process. But during order processing period, fraud detection mechanism can be applied.

Towards this, authors in [15] demonstrated the use of clustering and filtering capabilities of SOM for marking the transactions that deviate away from the customer's cluster of behaviors as "suspicious" [15]. All transactions that are marked suspicious are put on hold and sent for extended authentication process. Other transactions were allowed to proceed without any delay. None of the studies have proved real-time behavior by discussing results of time to detection.

Concept drift and real time are conflicting requirements, as adapting to concept drift requires time. Both cannot be fulfilled by conventional supervised and unsupervised models described earlier.

For achieving a real-time Fraud Detection System computational models related to Streaming Analysis, Spark Streaming and Time Data Analytics can be explored [23]. These techniques will be useful in designing an FDS that learns from transaction streams in an unsupervised manner and thus is adaptive to both changing fraudster strategy and customer behavior.

5.4 Fraud Detection Cost Overheads

Many approaches of robust fraud detection involve a lot of pre-processing and complex model learning. However, in evaluation and performance comparison, these overheads have not been considered. A direct comparison between outcomes of methods without considering the model building effort would be unfair. This aspect has been ignored by all the works in FDS and can be a future line of research. Apart from that, when a transaction is refused, the investigators contact card holder to verify if it is the case of a false alert or a real fraud. This cost in terms of man hour or amount spent should also be considered as a cost-enhancing factor. Sometimes a false alert may lead to card being blocked (for example, as a preventive measure, if customer could not be contacted) then the inability to make transactions can translate into big losses for the customer.

For all these reasons, determining an all-inclusive cost measure is a challenging problem in credit card detection that has not yet been satisfactorily solved till now.

5.5 Lack of Domain-Specific Metrics

Credit card FDS has been seen as classification problem and metrics relevant to these problems, namely accuracy, confusion matrix, and Receiver Operating Characteristic (ROC) curve have been utilized for showing efficacy of the solutions. In fraud detection, recall rate is more important than the overall accuracy and precision. Accuracy alone cannot reflect the quality of the algorithms because by simply predicting that all transactions are good events and not detecting even a single fraud can still get high accuracy; for example, if the ratio of fraud against normal is around 1.2% in the data. The accuracy can be 98.8% if simply guessing every transaction is normal. Metric like balanced error rate (BER), which is average of FPR and FNR, is the mean of the errors on each class and would be more appropriate for skewed domain like this. Matthews correlation coefficient (MCC) is also a balanced metric for classification performance [43].

In conventional metrics, each misclassification has same cost. However, in domain of FDS, frauds of small and big amounts must not be treated with equal importance. Therefore, the cost of a fraud is often assumed to be equal to the transaction amount [53].

Along with, cost should also include the time taken by the detection system to react. The shorter is the reaction time, the larger is the number of frauds that it is possible to prevent.

In [6], a new metric "misclassification cost" (false-positive and false-negative error costs) has been defined. It has been used to modify AdaBoost learning algorithm's internal heuristics to cost instead of accuracy. Authors in [17] redefined "False Negatives (FN)" metric as amount of transaction that was misclassified. It has also been concluded that a false-negative error is usually costlier than a false-positive error in case of fraud detection. Another challenge in correctly defining metrics for fraud detection is that costs change from case to case and over time.

Therefore, there is still no standard evaluation criterion for assessing and comparing the results of fraud detection systems. Techniques proposed in literature focused on solving any one issue related with this problem; for instance, it may be either concept drift or imbalanced dataset. An ideal FDS need to address all the challenges discussed in Sect. 1.2. It should be able to provide empirical answers to questions like:

- What should be the training set size for a perfect computational model of FDS?
- What is the correct pre-processing method, if any, to be applied on raw data from any source?
- Which metric or set of metrics can best evaluate the FDS across all cases?
- What should be the frequency of retraining the computational model?
- Should give guaranteed upper bound on false alarm rates.
- Minimize false negatives.

5.6 Next-Generation Computational Model for Credit Card Fraud Detection

Much work has been done in developing techniques for the detection of frauds; however, there is still more to do. Learning from nonstationary data stream with skewed class distribution with real-time requirements along with low false positive and high true negatives ratio is a relatively recent domain. After critical examination of the body of work done on design of computational models for FDS, following are few directions in which further progress is required:

1. Support interactive dashboards to quickly spot anomalous transactions.
2. Support for traceback and postfraud evidence gathering.
3. Be agile to discover and resist emerging fraud strategies.
4. Adapt techniques from Big Data and streaming Analytics to combat fraud detection challenges.
5. Formal feature engineering models for building effective classifiers need to be designed.
6. Domain-specific "end-to-end" performance measures like time to detect and recovery percentages need to be related to standard detection metrics.

6 Conclusions

Credit card frauds are a problem of recent concern due to a rapid rise in credit card-based transactions. Many machine learning-based computational models have been proposed to design an effective credit card fraud detection system. In this chapter, most popular models proposed in last two and half decades have been analyzed. It was found that existing fraud detection systems suffer from problems like limited knowledge about credit card-based payment processing, nonexistence of standard algorithm, suitable metrics, and high rate of false-positive alarms. Over and above, there are no credit card benchmark datasets that can be tested for effectiveness of newer models. Technologies from streaming data and big data analytics have not yet been applied to this domain and can be explored.

References

1. Bhattacharyya, S., Jha, S., Tharakunnel, K., & Westland, J. C. (2011). Data mining for credit card fraud: A comparative study. *Decision Support Systems, 50*(3), 602–613.
2. Gupta, B. B., & Quamara, M. A. (2018). Taxonomy of various attacks on smart card–based applications and countermeasures. *Concurrency Computation Practice Experience*, e4993.
3. Ghosh, R. (1994). Credit card fraud detection with a neural-network. In *Proceedings of the Twenty-Seventh Hawaii International Conference on System Sciences*, Wailea, HI (pp. 621–630).
4. Richardson, R. (1997). Neural networks compared to statistical techniques. In *Proceedings of the IEEE/IAFE 1997 Computational Intelligence for Financial Engineering (CIFEr)*, New York City, NY (pp. 89–95).
5. Hanagandi, V., Dhar, A., & Buescher, K. (1996). Density-based clustering and radial basis function modeling to generate credit card fraud scores. In *IEEE/IAFE Conference on Computational Intelligence for Financial Engineering (CIFEr)*, New York City, NY (pp. 247–251).
6. Chan, P. K., Fan, W., Prodromidis, A. L., & Stolfo, S. J. (1999). Distributed data mining in credit card fraud detection. *IEEE Intelligent Systems and Their Applications, 14*(6), 67–74.
7. Hand, D. J., & Blunt, G. (2001). Prospecting for gems in credit card data. *IMA Journal of Management Mathematics, 12*(2), 173–200.
8. Bolton, R. J., & Hand, D. J. (2001) Unsupervised profiling methods for fraud detection. In *Conference on Credit Scoring and Credit Control*.
9. Syeda, M., Zhang, Y.-Q., & Pan, Y. (2002) Parallel granular neural networks for fast credit card fraud detection. In *IEEE World Congress on Computational Intelligence Proceedings* (Cat. No.02CH37291), Honolulu, HI (Vol. 1, pp. 572–577).
10. Bolton, R. J., & Hand, D. J. (2002). Statistical fraud detection: A review. *Statistical Science, 17*. https://doi.org/10.1214/ss/1042727940.
11. McCarty, B. (2003). Automated identity theft. *IEEE Security & Privacy, 99*(5), 89–92.
12. Kou, Y., Lu, C.-T., Sirwongwattana, S., & Huang, Y.-P. (2004) Survey of fraud detection techniques. In: *IEEE International Conference on Networking, Sensing and Control*, Taipei (Vol. 2, pp. 749–754).
13. Leung, A., Yan, Z., & Fong, S. (2004). On designing a flexible e-payment system with fraud detection capability. In *Proceedings. IEEE International Conference on e-Commerce Technology*, San Diego, CA (pp. 236–243).
14. Panigrahi, S., Kundu, A., Sural, S., & Majumdar, A. K. (2009). Credit card fraud detection: A fusion approach using Dempster-Shafer theory and Bayesian learning. *Information Fusion, 10*, 354–363.
15. Quah, J. T. S., & Sriganesh, M. (2007). Real time credit card fraud detection using computational intelligence. In *International Joint Conference on Neural Networks*, Orlando, FL (pp. 863–868).
16. Brabazon, A., Cahill, J., Keenan, P., & Walsh, D. (2010). Identifying online credit card fraud using artificial immune systems. In *IEEE Congress on Evolutionary Computation*, Barcelona (pp. 1–7).

17. Bahnsen, A. C., Stojanovic, A., Aouada, D., & Ottersten, B. (2013) Cost sensitive credit card fraud detection using Bayes minimum risk. In *12th International Conference on Machine Learning and Applications*, Miami, FL (pp. 333–338).
18. Duman, E., & Özçelik, M. (2011). Detecting credit card fraud by genetic algorithm and scatter search. *Expert Systems with Applications, 38*, 13057–13063. https://doi.org/10.1016/j.eswa.2011.04.110.
19. Zareapoor, M., Seeja, K. R., & Alam, A. (2012). Analysis on credit card fraud detection techniques: Based on certain design criteria. *International Journal of Computer Applications, 52*, 35–42. https://doi.org/10.5120/8184-1538.
20. Wong, N., Ray, P., Stephens, G., & Lewis, L. (2012). Artificial immune systems for the detection of credit card fraud: An architecture, prototype and preliminary results. *International Journal of Information Systems, 22*, 53–76.
21. Lei, O. Z., & Ghorbani, A. A. (2012). Improved competitive learning neural networks for network intrusion and fraud detection. *Neurocomputing, 75*(1), 135–145.
22. Zanin, M., Romance, M., Moral, S., & Criado, R. (2018). Credit card fraud detection through parenclitic network analysis. *Complexity*. Article ID 5764370, 9 pp.
23. Rajeshwari, U., & Babu, B. S. (2016). Real-time credit card fraud detection using streaming analytics. In *2nd International Conference on Applied and Theoretical Computing and Communication Technology (iCATccT)*, Bangalore (pp. 439–444).
24. Zeager, M. F., Sridhar, A., Fogal, N., Adams, S., Brown, D. E., & Beling, P. A. (2017). Adversarial learning in credit card fraud detection. In *Systems and Information Engineering Design Symposium (SIEDS)*, Charlottesville, VA (pp. 112–116).
25. Awoyemi, J. O., Adetunmbi, A. O., & Oluwadare, S. A. (2017). Credit card fraud detection using machine learning techniques: A comparative analysis. In *International Conference on Computing Networking and Informatics (ICCNI)*, Lagos (pp. 1–9).
26. Carneiro, N., Figueira, G., & Costa, M. (2017). A data mining-based system for credit-card fraud detection in e-tail. *Decision Support Systems*. https://doi.org/10.1016/j.dss.2017.01.002.
27. Zheng, L., Liu, G., Luan, W., Li, Z., Zhang, Y., Yan, C., et al. (2018). A new credit card fraud detecting method based on behavior certificate. In *IEEE 15th International Conference on Networking, Sensing and Control (ICNSC)*, Zhuhai (pp. 1–6).
28. Cody, T., Adams, S., & Beling, P. A. (2018). A utilitarian approach to adversarial learning in credit card fraud detection. In *Systems and Information Engineering Design Symposium (SIEDS)*, Charlottesville, VA (pp. 237–242).
29. Patil, S., Nemade, V., & Soni, P. K. (2018). Predictive modelling for credit card fraud detection using data analytics. In *International Conference on Computational Intelligence and Data Science*.
30. Roy, A., Sun, J., Mahoney, R., Alonzi, L., Adams, S., & Beling, P. (2018). Deep learning detecting fraud in credit card transactions. In *Systems and Information Engineering Design Symposium (SIEDS)*, Charlottesville, VA (pp. 129–134).
31. de Sá, A. G. C., Pereira, A. C. M., & Pappa, G. L. (2018). A customized classification algorithm for credit card fraud detection. *Engineering Applications of Artificial Intelligence, 72*, 21–29.
32. Dhankhad, S., Mohammed, E., & Far, B. (2018). Supervised machine learning algorithms for credit card fraudulent transaction detection: A comparative study. In *IEEE International Conference on Information Reuse and Integration (IRI)*, Salt Lake City, UT (pp. 122–125).
33. Wang, Y., Adams, S. C., Beling, P. A., Greenspan, S., Rajagopalan, S., Velez-Rojas, M. C., et al. (2018). Privacy preserving distributed deep learning and its application in credit card fraud detection. In *17th IEEE International Conference on Trust, Security and Privacy in Computing and Communications/12th IEEE International Conference on Big Data Science and Engineering* (TrustCom/BigDataSE), New York, NY (pp. 1070–1078).
34. Barker, K. J., D'amato, J., & Sheridon, P. (2008). Credit card fraud: Awareness and prevention. *Journal of Financial Crime, 15*(4), 398–410.
35. Abdallah, A., Maarof, M. A., & Zainal, A. (2016). Fraud detection system. *Journal of Network and Computer Applications, 68*, 90–113.
36. Dheepa, V., & Dhanapal, R. (2009). Analysis of credit card fraud detection methods. *International Journal of Recent Trends in Engineering, 2*(3), 126.

37. Dal Pozzolo, A., Boracchi, G., Caelen, O., Alippi, C., & Bontempi, G. (2018). Credit card fraud detection: A realistic modeling and a novel learning strategy. *IEEE Transactions on Neural Networks and Learning Systems, 29*(8), 3784–3797.
38. Subbulakshmi, T., Mathew, G., & Shalinie, S. M. (2010). Real time classification and clustering of ids alerts using machine learning algorithms. *International Journal of Artificial & Application, 1*(1), 20.
39. Sorournejad, S., Zojaji, Z., Atani, R. E., & Monadjemi, A. H. (2016). A survey of credit card fraud detection techniques: Data and technique oriented perspective. *ArXiv preprint*, arXiv:1611.06439.
40. Dal Pozzolo, A., Caelen, O., Le Borgne, Y.-A., Waterschoot, S., & Bontempi, G. (2014). Learned lessons in credit card fraud detection from a practitioner perspective. *Expert Systems with Applications, 41*, 4915–4928.
41. Dal Pozzolo, A., Boracchi, G., Caelen, O., Alippi, C., & Bontempi, G. (2015). Credit card fraud detection and concept-drift adaptation with delayed supervised information. In *International Joint Conference on Neural Networks (IJCNN)*, Killarney (pp. 1–8).
42. Dal Pozzolo, A. (2015). *Adaptive machine learning for credit card fraud detection* [online]. Retrieved from http://difusion.ulb.ac.be/vufind/Record/ULB
43. Randhawa, K., Loo, C. K., Seera, M., Lim, C. P., & Nandi, A. K. (2018). Credit card fraud detection using AdaBoost and majority voting. *IEEE Access, 6*, 14277–14284.
44. Zheng, L., Liu, G., Yan, C., & Jiang, C. (2018). Transaction fraud detection based on total order relation and behavior diversity. *IEEE Transactions on Computational Social Systems, 5*(3), 796–806.
45. Newman, D. J., & Asuncion, A. (2007) *UCI machine learning repository*. Transformed datasets are available at http://www.ulb.ac.be/di/map/adalpozz/imbalanced-datasets.zip.
46. Zaslavsky, V., & Strizhak, A. (2006). Credit card fraud detection using self-organizing maps. *International Journal Information & Security, 18*, 48–63.
47. Hssina, B., Merbouha, A., Ezzikouri, H., & Erritali, M. (2014) A comparative study of decision tree ID3 and C4.5. *International Journal of Advanced Computer Science and Applications* (Special Issue on Advances in Vehicular Ad Hoc Networking and Applications).
48. De Castro, L. N., & Timmis, J. (2002). *Artificial immune systems: A new computational intelligence approach*. London: Springer.
49. Behera, T. K., & Panigrahi, S. (2015) Credit card fraud detection: A hybrid approach using fuzzy clustering and neural network. In *Second International Conference on Advances in Computing and Communication Engineering*, Dehradun (pp. 494–499).
50. Heckerman, D. (1995). *A tutorial on learning with Bayesian*. Technical report, MSRTR-95-06. Redmond, WA: Microsoft Research.
51. Chawla, N. V., Bowyer, K. W., Hall, L. O., & Philip Kegelmeyer, W. (2002). SMOTE: Synthetic minority over-sampling technique. *Journal of Artificial Intelligence Research, 16*, 321–357.
52. Padmaja, T. M., Dhulipalla, N., Krishna, P. R., Bapi, R. S., & Laha, A. (2007). *An unbalanced data classification model using hybrid sampling technique for fraud detection* (Lecture Notes in Computer Science) (Vol. 4815). Berlin: Springer.
53. Elkan, C. (2001). The foundations of cost-sensitive learning. In *International Joint Conference on Artificial Intelligence*, Citeseer (Vol. 17, pp. 973–978).

Chapter 27
Requirements, Protocols, and Security Challenges in Wireless Sensor Networks: An Industrial Perspective

Bharat Bhushan and G. Sahoo

Abstract Wireless sensor networks (WSNs) have several application areas that also include the industrial automation systems where they are used for monitoring and controlling the industrial equipment. However, requirements in industrial wireless systems are different from general WSN requirements. Industries are benefitted a big deal by integration of sensors in industrial machinery, plants, shop floors, structures, and other critical places. This application of WSNs in industrial domain lowers the failure rates and improves the productivity as well as efficiency of the factory operations. Adequate security needs to be provided along with ensured reliability for integrating the wireless technology with the industrial domain. Industrial wireless sensor networks (IWSNs) are vulnerable to huge range of attacks owing to its hostile deployment location, open architecture, and insecure routing protocols. As sensors are resource constrained in terms of limited processing capabilities, constrained energy, short communication range, and storage capacity, WSNs become easy target for the adversary ensuring adequate security in the crucial services provided by WSNs reinforce its acceptability as a dependable and viable technology in the industrial and factory domain. In this chapter, the characteristic features of WSNs in factory automation are outlined along with the industrial application of WSNs. This chapter addresses several standards defined by various industrial alliances in the past few years. Then several reliability issues in industrial WSNs are explored along with various types of security attacks possible in IWSNs. It explores several security paradigms applicable for industrial wireless sensor networks. This chapter then presents a broader view toward WSN solutions and discusses important functions like medium access control (MAC). Some important design considerations for designing MAC protocols are also presented in this chapter. Finally, the chapter concludes with several open research topics and unsolved challenges that were encountered during the protocol design for further investigation.

B. Bhushan (✉) · G. Sahoo
Department of Computer Science and Engineering, BIT Mesra, Ranchi, India
e-mail: gsahoo@bitmesra.ac.in

© Springer Nature Switzerland AG 2020
B. B. Gupta et al. (eds.), *Handbook of Computer Networks and Cyber Security*,
https://doi.org/10.1007/978-3-030-22277-2_27

Keywords Medium access control · Security attacks · Factory automation · Security · Reliability · Cryptography · Routing · Resource availability · Wireless sensor networks (WSNs)

1 Introduction

Advancements in electronics and wireless communications over the years led to the evolution of wireless sensor networks (WSNs) [1, 2]. WSNs comprise distributed autonomous devices that are characterized by several distinct characteristics such as sensing, processing, and communicating data. The deployment of WSNs is enhanced due to its inexpensive, small, and smart sensors called sensor nodes (SNs), which are easily deployable. SNs are made up of small sensor component that measures the observed physical conditions and the microprocessor component that ensures the intelligently computed information [3, 4]. Also, SNs possess embedded wireless radio to facilitate communication between the neighboring nodes [5].

Industries, manufacturers, and companies face a major problem of increased and constant product supply because of the rapidly increasing demands for services. For delivering quality products, improving process efficiencies, ensuring accuracy, and timeliness of systems, low-cost automation of processes is crucial in industries. Industries are using sensors for providing real-time and control support but they are mostly based on complex and expensive wired solutions. Therefore, WSNs as compared to wired solutions bring an array of advantages in factory automation such as ease of deployment, elimination of expensive and complex installation of wired solutions, flexibility in sensor placements, decreased operational costs, large-scale deployment, data redundancy, packet errors, and so on. The self-organizing and self-configuring nature of WSNs makes them a better option for reliable management and energy-efficient services at high asset protection applications [6, 7]. A typical manufacturing plant or factory atmosphere is characterized uniquely by operations such as mobility, reflections, machinery rotations, metallic frictions, engine and boiler vibrations, temperature and humidity fluctuations, channel interference, presence of obstacles, and so on [8, 9]. Wired systems are impractical for these scenarios as there is demand for cable isolation. These though enhance reliability but add additional overhead and complexity. Therefore, wireless solutions are the most effective, viable, and attractive solution in this domain [10].

In this chapter, we focus on the industrial applications of WSNs [11, 12]. The aim of IWSN is to use low-cost and low-power nodes in order to reduce the OPerational EXpenditure (OPEX) [13] as well as CAPital EXpenditure (CAPEX) of the network. The efficiency and the productivity of IWSNs are enhanced by observing increased number of parameters and obtaining valuable feedbacks. The major characteristics of IWSN include self-organization, robust operation, low maintenance, and easy-deployment. IWSN, in general, comprises nodes, network managers, process controllers, and management console. Normal nodes sense and collect data and transmit it to the network manager called sink. The nodes communicate with the process controller or the actuators and also sometimes actuators may communicate among themselves. Such networks are called wireless sensor actuator networks (WSAN). These actuators can operate units such as a valve on the basis of data received from the sensors such as pressure and temperature. This chapter also focuses on one of the most important subclasses of IWSN. The most crucial factors that need to be addressed in IWSNs are accuracy, reliability, and time-criticality of the generated data. As these networks carry and share factory-specific, confidential, and sensitive data, it becomes necessary to guarantee the data accuracy and reliability. Meeting deadlines is of utmost importance in case of factory automation as communication failure or unwanted delay may cause havoc leading to disruptive service or even compromising the lives of workers. Also, transmitting or sharing of misread data may lead to similar impact as several machinery is controlled by accurately timed data [14].

Internet of Things (IoT) is defined as a system of interrelated mechanical, digital machines, and computing devices that are provided with data transfer ability and unique identifiers without the need of human–computer or human–human interaction [15, 16]. On the basis of this definition, such IoT environments can be used to establish transmission networks for data and information generated by various applications. IoT is a fast-growing technology that can find several industrial applications. IoT changes the day today life of individual as it improves the way of moving, transforming, and working in industrial applications. All industrial operations become smarter since devices communicate with each other carrying out independent works, measurement displays, and results. Industrial associations are generally funded by government academy and authority for the purpose of enhanced cooperation and development thereby providing better services to the industry and government ally. In the current scenario, major driving force behind industry alliances of IoT includes manufacturers, service providers, government, vendors, telecom operators, etc. [17, 18].

The adoption of a wide range of technologies integrated in one single network is gaining importance today as these networks are routinely connected to the internet web services as well as the backend software enterprise. The open nature of wireless medium throws several issues such as privacy, security, and reliability. The traditional defense mechanisms for threats and attacks that exist for wired networks may also be applicable for WSNs if only the energy consideration of WSNs is not a primary concern. Security, privacy, and reliability are all interlinked and enhancing of reliability requires interaction, cooperation, and involvement of trusted surrounding sensors [19]. As the networks share and transmit sensitive data, appropriate security schemes are required to ensure that the transmitted data are protected and secured since the adversary can interfere, eavesdrop, or even disrupt communication. Sensors can be captured, reprogramed, and made to communicate false data readings such as temperature, pressure, vibrations, movements of machinery parts leading to disastrous consequences such as explosions or endangered lives. Also, in case of lack of security, energy of sensors can be depleted by continuously keeping them busy sensing and transmitting false data leading to disabled networks. For providing complete security solutions to the network, means of security needs to be integrated to each and every SN else even a single insecure network component can serve as the entry point of the attack thereby rendering the entire system inoperable. Therefore, there is a need of security prevailing in every design aspect of WSN applications [20–23].

In comparison to the already discussed articles, the major contribution of this chapter is to:

- View and present the industrial perspective of WSN domain. The chapter categorizes the industrial applications into several classes along with their application examples. Systems that possess similar goals and requirements are grouped into a single category.
- Review the essential requirements of industrial WSNs and also highlight several less treated requirements of IWSNs. In addition, this chapter also reviews various industrial standards such as WirelessHART, WIA-PA, ISA100.11a, and GINSENG.
- Concentrate on three most important aspects of IWSNs, namely security, reliability, and MAC. Various aspects of these along with their design requirements that support industrial systems are discussed in detail.
- Address the security aspect of IWSNs in brief. The chapter presents the various types of attacks that can be launched in an IWSN and also presents a brief about implementation of security standards in industrial domain.
- Highlight the importance of MAC protocols in IWSNs. Several design considerations involving MAC protocols are discussed highlighting the paradigm shift in designing of MAC protocols. The chapter also presents a brief overview of few MAC protocols along with their applicability in IWSNs.

This chapter is organized as follows. Section 2 of this chapter explores the sample WSN industrial deployments. It outlines the characteristic features of WSNs in factory automation such as resource constraints, dynamic topology, harsh environments, and so on. Section 3 of this chapter explores the various IWSN requirements such as minimal cost and compactness, interoperability, energy consumption, fault tolerance, low delay, quality of service, dynamic topology, resource constrained nature, data aggregation, and so on. The industrial applications of WSNs such as safety systems, monitoring systems, and control systems are also detailed in this section. The wireless standards designed specifically for industrial WSNs such as wirelessHART, ISA100.11a, WIA-PA, and GINSENG are explained in this section. Section 4 of this chapter explores several reliability issues in industrial WSNs such as handling interference, diversity technique, multipath technique, identification technique, synchronization, redundancy, and so on. The need for security in IWSNs is explored in Sect. 5 where first the security objectives such as confidentiality, integrity, authentication, freshness, and availability are outlined. Further, this section throws light on various types of attacks such as eavesdropping attack, denial of service attack, selective forwarding attack, node compromise attack, physical attack, and identity attack. In order to control the medium access and decide the communication schedule, MAC protocols are necessary. The designed schedule must be on the basis of the application requirements. Section 6 highlights the advantages of time division multiple access (TDMA) in IWSN and also explores the advantages of TDMA over CDMA. Some important design considerations for designing MAC protocols are also presented in this section. Finally, we provide a summary of our study and conclude this chapter in Sect. 7 along with several open research topics and challenges for further research.

2   Sample WSN Industrial Deployments

Manufacturing plants, companies, and industries are depending majorly on information received through the network of sensors that are installed on key points in the entire field or factory. Hence, the technology is getting a boost as it does not require any complex infrastructure for handling, sensing, and data measuring of inaccessible areas. A vast range of industries like refineries or oil pipelines, beverage or food manufacturers, and chemical companies are using wireless communication systems to handle activities that are nontrivial like air pressure, weight load, electric current, corrosion, and temperature.

This is the technology that allows to access real-time data and remotely acquire control and even make decisions based on the data received by detecting unusual or random processes, collecting and studying periodic data, generating alarms, calculating and tracking machine states, equipment's and instruments, etc. [24, 25]. Even the existing management systems as well as other wireless and wired devices could be successfully merged with sensor networks and even be combined with internet to easily manipulate and control systems anytime and anywhere. Some major applications of WSNs include the straightforward replacement of wired sensors to make room for vibrations and measurement of temperature [13, 26], motor vibration monitoring sensor because certain places make wiring very difficult and sometimes even require cable isolation. WSNs are useful for generally enabling the condition monitoring systems like reporting periodic information of tiny machines performance statistic. The sensor mainly supports machinery maintenance by finding rare and unusual conditions and also generates alarms to take immediate actions if any unwanted events occur. WSNs also enable in situ motor analysis [27]. Complex systems like the heavy power plants also exploit merits of the WSNs for a more appropriate and balanced prognostics monitoring and multisensor machinery diagnosis. Ramamurthy et al. [28] also mention the application of such networks in RF identification tags that enable a very safe access to equipment's for technician using mobile computers. Various applications of WSNs including the temperature measurement sensors for vibration-based condition monitoring and end-mill inserts for tool breakdown have been seen in [27] and [29], respectively. Also, these networks offer new chances like multisensory data fusion methods for calculating tool wear utilizing vibration handling of work piece and spindle.

A very efficient technique for enhancement of throughput and reliability of industrial networks is proposed in [30]. Authors have exploited frequency and time diversity included in IEEE 802.15.4 industrial network with an aim of guaranteeing real-time throughput and reliability. Miskowicz and Koscielnik [31] assume the reliability in data transfer by probabilities of analytical modeling of failure probabilities of transmission in industrial domain. Whereas Fischione et al. [32] ensured a required package delivery and delay probability while reducing energy requirement of the IWSN. The protocol is solely based on medium access control, duty cycling, and randomized routing combinedly managed for efficient energy utilization. So, the design approach falls mainly on constrained optimization, whereby main function is energy consumption and delay.

3   Industrial WSN: Requirements, Applications, and Standards

Requirement needs is a standard to differentiate between IWSN and traditional WSN. Being a huge field, IWSN is divided into various classes based on services and functional requirements. This section describes the cataloguing of industrial systems, WSN functions in these structures, listing significant industrial designing needs along with proposed hi-tech standards. Industrial systems are categorized into five classes grounded onto operational requirements and data criticality in accordance with the International Society of Automation [33, 34]. These five classes are elaborated in the section below.

- *Safety systems.* This includes usage wherein events require instant actions, that is, in the order of seconds or milliseconds. Systems of fire alarm are an example for the same. Nodes are positioned consistently all through the concerned area so as to involve the entire area.
- *Closed loop regulatory systems (CLRS).* Here usage of feedbacks is incorporated for system control. In a desired topology, installation of nodes is done in the concerned field and periodically controller is sent the measurement that are crucial for smooth system operation. Such systems might consist of timing requirements stricter than safety systems. Controller takes a decision depending on these results gathered. It then sends this conclusion to the actuators to act upon the data. A new procedure set has been planned for these set of classes [35].
- *Closed loop supervisory systems (CLSS).* Just like regulatory structures, in CLSS the measurements are not estimated periodically instead they depend on some happening of events. Such feedbacks are not so detailed. Supervisory system is an example for the same that collects data and responds only on the observation of specific trends relating to some action.
- *Open loop control systems (OLCS).* A human operator operates such control systems. Collection of data and transmission of the gathered data to key database are done by WSN. The data are thus analyzed by the operator and appropriate measures are taken as and when required.

Table 27.1 Comparison of various classes of industrial systems

Classes		Protocols		
		Transport	Routing	MAC
1	Safety systems	ER-MAC	MMSPEED	ER-MAC
2	CLRS	RBC	RPL	GinMAC
3	CLSS	ART	RPL	PEDAMACS
4	OLSS	ART	TEEN	PEDAMACS
5	Information gathering system	None	HEED	HEED (clustering)

- *Information gathering systems.* These are deployed for data gathering and dispatching it to server. The most common paradigm is the installation of WSN nodes in an area to collect data like moisture content and temperature for specific time interval. This collected information then can be used as a means for longstanding designs of moisture and temperature management.

Table 27.1 above compares these five classes in terms of the protocols used for transport, routing, and as MAC.

In a temperature supervising system, the alert function is not critical. It is used for signaling temperature on various phases so as to depict the finishing of some activities. This alerting system gets converted to a safety system whenever temperature goes beyond a certain limit. Hence, certain classes of systems can perform many roles.

3.1   IWSN Requirements

Various industrial domain requirements are satisfied using wireless standards designed for IWSN. Brief about these requirements is presented in the section below.

3.1.1   Minimal Cost and Compactness

Increased productivity, increased profit, and decreased cost are the main objectives of industrial WSN. The shift to usage of wireless solutions from wired ones has been majorly due to smaller cost needs for installation and implementation. According to [36], rate of wired solutions is $200 per sensor. Lowering space necessities for installation along with the cost savings are the additional advantage of compact node size. Thus, solutions of IWSN are estimated to cut cost and consists of nodes of small sizes.

3.1.2 Interoperability

Wired systems incorporating sensors are used in the current industries for several operations. Latest wireless solutions need to collaborate with legacy systems. Some wireless standards require interoperability, which can be sourced for certain function.

3.1.3 Noise Resistance and Its Coexistence

A standard industrial location consists of several communication systems with wireless networks, which are capable of creating interference across the radio signals thereby intensifying the path loss [37]. WSN standards effectively endure the interference. Such existent industrial scientific-medical band (also called ISM band) has been studied in several networks with 2.4 GHz of operational frequency.

3.1.4 Energy Consumption

Energy consumption has two aspects: efficient energy consumption and low energy consumption. As far as low energy consumption is concerned, battery powering WSN nodes and the nodes itself also must be energy-efficient so that network lives longer. The energy efficiency of entire network can be increased by balancing the load over the entire network. This load balancing requires energy-aware techniques and routing protocols, which enhances the overall network lifetime.

3.1.5 Self-Organizing

WSNs are developed to be organized and configured by themselves. Sensor nodes get mostly positioned in deliberate locations that are not easily accessible. Hence, they need operation without human involvement for longer time intervals, therefore, autonomous operations are a major requirement. WSN nodes in harsh circumstances such as severe cold climates are some of its examples.

3.1.6 Robustness/Fault-Tolerance

WSNs must be robust and fault-tolerant. SNs might stop operating after a certain time duration due to its limited energy. Hence, there is need of such a network, wherein the failure of a single node does not lead to the failure of the whole network. For this reason, routing protocols are desired to be fault-tolerant and must be receptive to active changes in topology.

3.1.7 Link-Reliability and Low Delay

In comparison to the traditional networks, WSN nodes with less power have lesser link reliability. Because of which high delay and packet loss is seen leading the WSNs to be used less in the industries. Appropriate technique needs to be incorporated to resist the failures of link with the usage of effective techniques of retransmission at link layer and transport layer or with the help of routing protocols involving replication. Out of all the systems, control systems are sensitive to delays. These need predictable behavior of WSN transmission and expect present guarantees.

3.1.8 Service Differentiation

IWSN have a combination of distinct sensors and are complex. Data produced by these sensors entail distinct treatments in networks and require service differentiation, which is present at various levels, for example, packet level and node level. Within alike nodes, certain values are significant than others. Priority assignment is done for the service differentiation and distinct nodes are given different priorities in the node level priority. Just because sensor to actor communication and actor to actor or sensor to sensor communications differ, service differentiation becomes a crucial requirement.

3.1.9 Quality of Service (QoS)

IWSNs focus on applications and each application differs depending on its requirements. Such requirements are quantified in terms of service needs, which forms basis of determination of QoS. Data to be relocated between two points within 25 ms are an example for the same. Separately at each function, applications enforce specific requirements in the communication system. Application specific and network QoS are two perspectives defined by Dazhi and Varshney [38]. At the application level, there is higher level of abstraction, for example, least active sensors, minimum coverage area, and precision of measurement. Latency, reliability, and availability are major QoS needs of network. QoS is a need to be considered in all functions.

3.1.10 Resource Constraints

WSN nodes are typically battery constrained possessing limited computational and processing capabilities along with lesser memory availability. These constraints always force the researchers to find varied ways, unlike traditionally designed measures of secure systems, to implement security techniques and algorithms in WSNs.

3.1.11   Dynamic Topology and Harsh Environments

In an industrial environment, connectivity and topology of deployed network are sometimes not stable due to the probability of node or link failure. Nodes sometimes malfunction and lose their connectivity due to the worse conditions of industrial environment like the presence of obstruction, vibrations by motors, RF interference, variations in temperature and humidity levels, dust, and dirt, etc. Moreover, they are also prone to physical damage and mishandling if deployed in the secure area.

3.1.12   Scalability

There are two different perspectives to view scalability. First is the design perspective in which the standards and protocols need to be accessible and also various industrial applications need to be matched with it. The second outlook is that the IWSN installations should adapt changes for adding or removing various nodes. Functionalities have to be incorporated with sensor nodes for every function. IWSN must be able to hold newer nodes without QoS degradation. Scalability also requires the self-organizing needs.

3.1.13   Multiple Source and Multiple Sinks

Probability of usage of many applications across one WSN has proliferated with the constant advancement of WSN. Usage of many sinks in a single network is the result of it. WSAN (wireless sensor actuator networks) is an example for such a topology. They consist of multiple actors behaving like separate sinks. It is common in complex industrial systems.

3.1.14   Predictable Behavior

Industrial systems are said to be complicated and large that impose certain requirements which have to be met with. Solutions must possess a predictable behavior to realize the requirements efficiently. Solutions desirable for IWSN and mainly for WSAN must be trustworthy because the complexity involved with these systems adds to huge costs. Thus, to ensure that a correct solution is being used, it has to be analyzed before its installation as well as implementation.

3.1.15   Application-Specific Protocols

IWSN standards are reusable in many application cases. However, protocols contained in these standards majorly target specific applications. Each industrial application has its own distinct requirement. Therefore, specific protocols are required for satisfying the necessities.

3.1.16 Data Aggregation

Data are sensed by the sensors continuously but these data may sometimes be redundant. Identical data may be sensed by the sensors deployed in a specific area. This sensed data's significance is dependent on the requirements of the applications and is categorized as data from the same sensor or data from sensor group. Thus, the number of packets sent gets minimized thereby increasing the energy efficiency. Data aggregation is hence majorly an application layer function.

Gungor and Hancke [39] can be referred to know more about the IWSN requirements, technical approaches, and challenges. IWSN is determined on actual implementations and expects the planned protocols to be grounded on truthful assumptions. Ramon and Gerhard [40] is one such study that discusses fallacies regarding WSNs timeliness. It is usually to design a protocol and intensify it across many available network simulators mainly due to unavailability of resources and time so that its usefulness can be proved [41]. On the other hand, analysis and performance modeling can be performed analytically. Owing to several assumptions made because of the system's complexity, such models can prove to be negative to some extent. Due to imprecision persisting in the replication models, these proposals might not be accurate [42]. For the correct estimation of protocols proposed for IWSN, eventual implementation and real-world testing deployment are necessary. Another major problem is the time sensitivity requirement meaning that the time-critical data must reach BS on time mainly depending on urgency levels like unusual events or machine failures. Due to frequent node and link failures in WSNs, ensuring the timeliness in reporting data to sink is definitely an issue. Along with this, sensors physical proximity and redundancy usually arise due to data compilation by sensors nearby. This kind of situation affects the unique behavior of collected data if a proper aggregation technique is not followed to remove it. Moreover, the important thing is that the information that will be received by the base station will be the only criteria for taking actions if there is a case of emergency.

3.2 Industrial Applications

Extensive industrial applications deploy WSNs abolishing human need in various places comprising hazardous arenas. It cuts industrial charges, which previously had wired solutions because wiring encompasses extra cost. Wire use can even invite more costs such as insulations for protection from dangerous physical effects including high temperature. Wire placement needs to be replaced or arranged whenever current system arrangements need removal thereby posing further problems. As far as moving objects are concerned, they are a threat when wiring has to be implemented around them since it restricts mobility. A robot is an example for the same. In all such cases, wireless devices prove out to be very advantageous, where insulation of the device for extreme conditions is the only requirement. Another classification for the class of systems discussed above is: safety systems, control systems, and monitoring systems. [43, 44] include various applications with WSN deployment. Certain applications for these categories are discussed below.

- *Safety systems.* The most crucial safety systems applied by WSN is fire safety. WSN provides features like close monitoring, fire fighters examining (such as police), and web-enabled facility giving real-time information external to disaster site location. This real-time examining keeps fire fighters up-to-date. Potentially hazardous applications including nuclear power plants make use of safety systems incorporating WSN. Due to the improper monitoring, the problems arise because of old elements used in such works [45, 46].
- *Control systems.* Control systems are the main category of industrial application of WSN. At the first place, closed loop control systems that examine several modules in system and act correspondingly upon observation of changes. These systems can be categorized as factory automation systems and process control systems. Also, such systems are grounded on actuation and monitoring and have certain delay requirements approximately <100 ms and comparably not stricter than automation systems. Second, open loop systems are just like closed loop systems having an additional feature of incorporating a human operator [47, 48].
- *Monitoring systems.* The classes, information gathering systems and alerting systems continue to use traditional WSNs with minimal needs. These systems serve an extensive range of applications such as industrial monitoring, environmental monitoring, military monitoring to name among a few [49]. Such systems perform data collection in a region for a considerable duration, which is studied meticulously for collecting results.

3.3 Industrial Standards

High reliability, low power requirement, easy administration, deployment, and maintenance are the rudimentary qualities required by IWSN. These requirements form the basis of design goals for such devices. Wireless Networking Alliance, Zigbee Alliance, the Chinese Industrial Wireless Alliance, HART Communication Foundation (HCF), and the International Society of Automation are standards founded for IWSN. The standards thereby introduced grounded on IEEE 802.15.4 standard are wirelessHART, Zigbee [50], ISA100.11a [51], and WIA-PA. Project of GINSENG, not a wireless standard but useful for controlling performance in control systems that are closed looped with WSN, has also been discussed in this article. Because of the merits that time division multiple access (TDMA) has over carrier sense multiple access (CSMA), all the above-mentioned are based on TDMA. Various types of industrial standards are detailed in the section below.

- *WirelessHART.* It is grounded on IEEE 802.15.4 physical layer with 2.4 GHz of operational frequency and exercise 15 channels that are distinct. This practices time synchronized mesh protocol (TSMP) [52] that was established by the Dust Networks. TDMA is used by TSMP for channel access, channel blacklisting, and channel hopping at network layer. Technique wherein data transfer occurs at various frequencies and at distinct periods of time is called Channel hopping. Almost 15 channels are supported by this standard. Interference and noise have been reduced because of TDMA employed with channel blacklisting and hopping. Star and Mesh are the topologies supported by wirelessHART.

- *ISA100.11a*: For providing robust and safe communication for applications in course automation, ISA100 group established this standard. Physical layer is grounded on IEEE 802.15.4. Interference effects are controlled by this and also use channel blacklisting and channel hopping. It capitalizes merits in both systems. At network layer, IPv6 provides opportunities to users to use Internet thereby giving varied options thereby promoting integration. Interface with wirelessHART is made possible. Star and Mesh topologies are supported.

- *WIA-PA:* It was proposed by Chinese Industrial Wireless Alliance. Objective was to come up with a high reliability, intelligent multihop, and energy efficient WSN solution. It is well matched with the standards of IEEE 802.15.4 and is developed to give a mesh network that could organize itself and is receptive to changes in network conditions. IEEE 802.15.4 is MAC layer compatible with blend of FDMA, TDMA and CSMA is deployed for medium access. It stands for wireless networks for industrial automation process automation (WIA-PA).

- *GINSENG:* GINSENG project [53] has an objective of proposing a method for performance checks aided by WSN for time-defined applications and presenting a MAC protocol capable of meeting needs of applications. The protocol of GinMAC [54] is based on TDMA and grounds on tree, which provides services like consistency and on time data delivery. The main techniques incorporated in this scheme were exclusive TDMA, off-line dimensioning, and delay confirm reliability control. Solutions here are applied in present systems to show usage and functioning [55].

Grounded on brief of ultramodern wireless standards, the article mentions about certain fresh advancements. WirelessHART and ISA100.11a are top standards present today. Hart Communication Foundation (HCF) and International Society of Automation (ISA) have settled to join forces and create single criterion originated from wirelessHART and ISA100.11a, in spite of the competition. To investigate the possibilities of convergence, a subcommittee called ISA100.12 is developed [56]. This union can provide worldwide standard with boons of both standards and thus provide better IWSN solutions.

4 Reliability Issues Related to the Industrial Domain

The accuracy, efficiency, and reliability are the major serious factors that need to be considered in deployed industrial environment. Since the network shares and transfers factory-specific confidential data, it is important to ensure accurate data measurement and secured data transmission and reception is ensured by destination

Table 27.2 Interferences in IWSNs

Broad-band interference	Narrow-band interference
Motors	Cell telephones
SCR and inverter circuits	TV and radio transmitters
Electric contacts switch	Power-line hum
ESD, computer	Signal generator
Ignition systems	UPS system, local oscillator
Voltage regulators	Test equipment
Electromagnetic lightning pulses	Ultrasonic and microwave equipment
Vapor/arc lamps	Electronic ballasts
Pulse generators	Medical equipment
Welding apparatus	Pager transmitters
Thermostats	Microprocessor equipment
Frequency converter	High frequency generators

at specified time. Holding to the deadlines is a very crucial aspect in industrial automation, wherein failure or unwanted delay can lead to machine failures, havoc in production, and disrupted services. Misreading and illegal sharing of data can also have similar impacts as the machinery is assumed to be properly controlled.

- *Characteristic features of Industrial environment:* Wireless networks that come into play in industries are expected to operate smoothly under very few stringent operations [57, 58]. Interference is a huge issue in Industrial WSNs. It is generally generated by multitude of sources; thus, it can very easily degrade the network by breaking communication in the wireless technologies. Interference occurs when generated signal from a node is damaged by another signal from varied source. Some common narrow band and broad band signals in factory domain are illustrated in Table 27.2.

In the section below, we elaborate the possible measures that are in use to enhance data communication reliability of the WSNs:

- *Handling Interference:* The signal bandwidth is intentionally distributed over the frequency domain in the case of spread spectrum modulation techniques. These are the most common ways to handle interference as they are not affected from jamming and interference and offer more access capability and secure communication. In the wireless communication technique, there are two spectral techniques. One is direct sequence spread spectrum (DSSS) and the other is frequency hopping spread spectrum (FHSS). DSSS is capable of providing higher capabilities than FHSS. DSSS is affected by various environmental factors and is best suited with large data package in narrow band interference environments, whereas FHSS is robust and is capable of resisting interference better than DSSS. As a result, FHSS is perfect for heavy interference environment.
- *Multipath technique*: It is a very robust technique that increases reliability at the cost of high energy requirements. Data that are sent by the sender are sent through

various paths with increased probability that one of them at least will definitely reach the receiver. If data are blocked from one of the many paths then also the data can be sent to the user through various other paths. Mesh paths use multiple options to deliver data with reliability rate of 99.9.

- *Diversity Technique:* Many radios can be used to operate on different ranges with a view of switching to various frequencies in case some frequencies fail because of these interferences.
- *Redundancy*: It could play a very reliable role in establishing a good communication system by ensuring that there is stand-by sensor which replace the others when not in use or in case of failure. Nodes can be controlled with more transmission capabilities. Let's say, for example, they possess the capability of switching toward a transmission mode of high speed in order to send direct messages or by hop of a controller. This will help in avoiding delays while rerouting data or if it is interrupted by end of the obstacles. Healthy and responsive measures can be considered to carry out certain node failures that occur in turn of normal network functioning. Several countermeasures have been proposed in [59] that include replacement of damaged or dead nodes, formatting new paths for routing and adjusting transmission power and sampling rate.

5 Sensor Network Security

5.1 Need for Secure IWSNs

The open nature of wireless medium brings forth several reliability and security issues. Thus, the traditional security attacks as well as the existing defense mechanisms that have been proposed for wired networks can also be considered for wireless networks. All the three terms accuracy, security, and reliability are intertwined and therefore in order to increase the reliability of the system, guaranteeing information security and privacy is of utmost importance. Enhancement of reliability basically demands more interaction and cooperation of the surrounding sensors, which itself are not trustworthy. As the industrial wireless network must be capable of storing and transmitting sensitive data, ensuring data protection in absence of appropriate security measures is a challenging task as the adversary can interfere, disrupt, or eavesdrop on the wireless communication. In absence of proper security standards, the network may malfunction, introduce delay, halt production, halt product delivery, or degrade the overall QoS. Moreover, the sensors can be reprogrammed and captured by the attackers to inject false data readings such as temperature, vibrations, movement, and rotations of parts, which can severely damage the machinery, endanger lives, and cause explosions. Also, the sensors energy can be made exhausted by the adversary by keeping them busy for continuous period of time by transmitting false data. For providing enhanced security to IWSNs, security mechanisms need to be incorporated into each and every node as even one single weak and inefficient point in the entire network may be exploited by the adversary. While dealing with the security in IWSNs, several security objectives must be kept into considerations such as confidentiality, availability, nonrepudiation, integrity, data freshness, and authenticity.

5.2 Attacks in IWSNs

Although the security targets specified beforehand are applicable to both wireless and wired applications, the wireless medium between the devices and the sensors pose increased vulnerability. Based on the function and their specific needs, industrial environments select their security objectives that need to be ensured. Here in this below section, few possible attacks in wireless sensor networks are elaborated [60].

- Eavesdropping attack: It is type of attack in which an attacker may choose to eavesdrop willingly on the communication of network and try to steal the data. These types of attacks are difficult to detect because the attacker seemingly eliminates their presence in the network. The main purpose of this attack is to infringe the confidentiality by inhibiting the network and listening or sniffing to routing the data packages and subsequently read using cryptographic tool. An eavesdropper may use latest techniques instead of purely being inactive to get the valuable information. With help of jamming, disrupting, or modifying the packets of network, an attacker can actively affect the communication channel. In order to prevent eavesdropping—new techniques of encryption can be done, encryption basically refers to scrambling the data before sending it to receiver and building more secure networks, contributing to digital literacy.
- Denial of service: It aims at shutting down a network or machine thereby causing issues for its intended users. Such attacks take place when adversaries use laptops or PCs to allow signal with a view to interfere with radio frequencies, which is presently used by the network to disrupt communication protocols. DoS attacks can achieve this by sending triggered information leading to crash or flooding of the traffic toward the target. This crash leads to exhausting battery power, valuable computational power, processing time due to in extensive and improper retransmitting message signals. Some of Dos attacks include Buffer overflow attacks, ICMP flood, and SYN flood [61, 62].
- Node compromise: It is crucial problem in WSNs, which boosts the inside attacks. It is a type of attack through which means are reprogrammed by an attacker, in unfeasible situations for an attack to reprogram nodes and physically capture the network. Mainly, this type of malicious activity is carried out by a compromised node including stealing secrets from the data, which are encrypted, reporting wrong data, launching various type of routing attacks, and so on [63, 64].

- Selective forwarding: Despite other than the attacks in the network layer mentioned above, WSNs are also vulnerable to another attack known as Selective Forwarding. This attack is characterized by the forwarding of data by certain malicious or reprogrammed nodes in the form of the packets ensuring that they are camouflaged. This malicious activity further results in the production of unpredictable network behavior. The main target of this attack is the sensor network due to their multi-hop nature. Major drawback of this attack is increase in node power consumption as there exist several routes for every message transfer. Another distributed detection scheme presented by Yn and Xiao uses multiple-hop acknowledgements for raising alarms in network. It identifies intermediate malicious nodes and thereby avoids such attack [65, 66].

- Physical attacks: It refers to the node itself being subject to physical attacks. It associates with the attacker's ability to seize physical access to the nodes. This makes the way for huge range of attacks that includes stealing or destroying of the nodes, dislocating them, reclaiming confidential information's like cryptographic keys and injecting malicious code, etc. Another sensor protection mechanism can be Tamper proofing the hardware, but this is a big ticket and may not be very effective against the attackers [63, 67].

- Identity attack: Identity attack facilitates a malicious user in the network to hijack application requests and assumes application components responsibility. Adversaries can use identity attacks to launch two types of attacks: Sybil attack and Spoofing attack. In Sybil attack, malicious nodes forge many identities in order to trick the network. Malicious nodes obtain several identities and behave like several independent nodes in the network. Such attacks can potentially disrupt the normal network functioning. Due to multiple identities, adversary can defeat the routing protocols that use multiple disjoint paths. These disjoint paths hops through the attacker's fake identities. One node can participate only for one time in the activities such as reputation calculation and polling but the fraud node can participate for several number of times thereby can win the voting. The network performance is significantly reduced by defeating fault-tolerant and group-based voting schemes such as distributed storage, redundancy mechanism, and multipath routing. Whenever a legal node distributes a certain task among other network nodes, the adversary node executes the assigned task alone utilizing multiple identities and delays the results. Also, an identity forged node can collaborate with various other attacks and hamper the network performance. These attacker nodes can also behave as a black-hole thereby dropping packets using several identities. Even after being detected, these adversaries still continue to hamper the network using its acquired fake identities. Therefore, a single malicious node may introduce multiple network threats. Also, for an adversary, it is necessary to maintain same identity group for a considerable amount of time so as to gain some reputation for its fake identities from other nodes. Also, multiple adversaries can collaborate together and launch even more stronger attacks such as node isolation from the network or manual overlay partition.

6 Medium Access Control

Medium access control (MAC) is a category of protocols that control the medium access and decide the fundamental scheduling pattern of the sensor nodes for communication. Planning of schedule should be done in accordance with some application specific requirements. For solving scheduling problems, these methods can be categorized into following main classes [68, 69].

- *Fixed Assignment Protocols.* Resources that are available are subdivided suitably among various sensor nodes. The validity of this subdivision is time restricted and any sort of alteration cannot be done for a specific time duration because of the allocation of resources to specific nodes. On the basis of medium access control mechanisms protocols are subdivided into following categories: TDMA, CDMA, and FDMA (Time Division Multiple Access, Code Division Multiple Access, and Frequency Division Multiple Access, respectively). In MAC protocol based on TDMA, time is subdivided in the group of sensor nodes, which needs synchronization of time. In MAC protocols based on FDMA, various subchannels are made from the subdivision of frequency medium. In MAC protocols based on CDMA, spread spectrum technology is used to send signals and along with this, transmission of multiple signals is allowed via same passage-by applying a special encoding scheme [70, 71]. Fixed assignment protocols can be classified into distributed as well as centralized control. Generally, schedule is defined by the sink, in the case of centralized control. Network nodes can categorize the scheduling control, in case of distributed control. Schedule for the set of nodes is defined by some specific selected nodes.
- *Demand Assignment Protocols.* In these, only on demand, resources are given to a node. Allocation, in this case, is restricted by the duration of time, which will be required for communication of data. The resources are returned after the data communication gets finished. In this case, protocols depend on the changes made in conditions of the network and adjustment of their performance is made in accordance with the level of traffic. Protocols may be based on distributed as well as centralized control.
- *Random Access Protocols.* Distributed control is intended by these protocols and the random arrangement of resources forms the basis of gaining some advantages of randomness. This category is suitable for busty traffic and topology change (happening dynamically). ALOHA [72] is one among the earliest and significant random-access protocols. Pure ALOHA's nodes access the medium as well as transmit when the data are available for communication. CSMA operates on ALOHA's principle, but it is modest as compared to ALOHA because it only sends data when it senses that the channel is free for transmission.
- *Hybrid Protocols.* Many protocols are combination of more than one kind of protocols, that is, it can use demand, or fixed, or random-access protocols. TDMA and CSMA are combined in order to use them advantageously. For instance, Z-MAC [73], TDMA, and CSMA can be combined in following ways.

1. TDMA slot scheduling: This can be done by allowing contention within the slots scheduled.
2. Define schedule with a contention-free period.

The subsections listed below will discuss—significance of TDMA (in IWSN) and its benefits over CSMA, design considerations significant for MAC protocols would probably be skipped, which have been discussed previously under the discussion of IWSN requirements. Classification of MAC protocols would also be discussed. Lastly, some of the significant representative protocols (satisfying IWSN requirements) are discussed.

6.1 CSMA vs TDMA

Most proposals that include MAC functions in WSNs use either TDMA or CSMA. TDMA is based on reservation while CSMA is based on contention. The basic TDMA and CSMA procedures are shown in Figs. 27.1 and 27.2, respectively. Studies reported by [74] prove the TDMA based protocols to be more energy efficient in comparison to its counterparts. According to [75], this behavior is shown because of two major reasons. First, there is significant number of collisions in the CSMA methods, which results in huge energy consumption due to retransmission of data. Second, there is efficient bandwidth utilization in TDMA methods under high load thereby leading to enhanced energy efficiency.

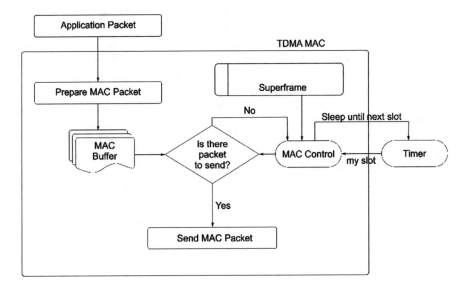

Fig. 27.1 Simple TDMA procedure

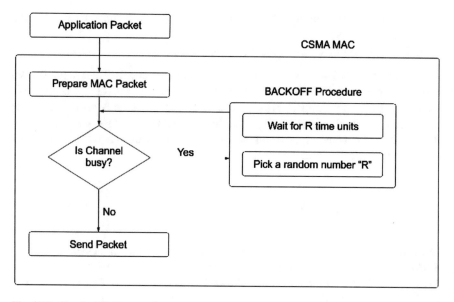

Fig. 27.2 Simple CSMA procedure

Same as above, comparison between TDMA and CSMA can be proposed only on the basis of conditions of operations as CSMA is more advantageous over TDMA [76, 77]. In this chapter, delay sensitivity, predictability, and reliability are the most issues for industrial applications that have been discussed. TDMA schemes are capable of handling these issues in an efficient manner and moreover, the TDMA that work on fixed slots is more predictable in comparison to the CSMA thereby making it suitable for use in closed loop regulatory systems. Since there is less collision in TDMA-based protocols and also, they ensure predefined bandwidth allocation, therefore it achieves better reliability. Even if the TDMA schemes are collision free and energy efficient, several issues such as efficient slot allocation and synchronization require attention. In order to ensure interference-free and collision-free channel access, there is a need of proper slot allocation schemes. Also, TDMA faces scalability issues due to its time synchronization requirement and fixed time allocation [78, 79].

In order to illustrate the performance variation between CSMA and TDMA, we explore a simulation study by Kulkarni [80], who simulated and analyzed various scenarios (that includes local gossip, converge cast, and broadcast scenarios) in order to differentiate between the CSMA and TDMA schemes. We focus on the second scenario that is the converge cast scenario that includes network setup of 10×10 sensor grid and widely used by industrial WSNs. Sensors in the sub-grid transmit messages to the BS. CSMA-based scenario accounted for 10–15% collision with a subsequent increase in the number of grid nodes. The major observation of this finding was that it accounted for 50% of lost messages due to collision in case

Table 27.3 Comparison of CSMA and TDMA

Serial number	Condition	CSMA	TDMA
1	Reliability	Low	High
2	Delay incurred under high traffic	High because of collisions	Under control
3	Performance prediction	No	Yes
4	Throughput under high traffic	Decreases	Increases

of 25 nodes simultaneously transmitting messages. CSMA mechanisms suffer lower delay than TDMA.

However, it had increased throughput because of the entire message finally reaching the BS. There was a severe impact on throughput as well as reliability in the case of CSMA-based schemes. Choosing among the TDMA and CSMA schemes is application dependent. TDMA-based solutions provide more healing to the industrial requirements thereby proving itself to be more suitable for industrial domain.

Table 27.3 above compares TDMA and CSMA in terms of their reliability, delay under high traffic, performance prediction, and throughput.

6.2   Design Considerations

Several design considerations involving MAC protocols are detailed in the section below.

- *Node Deployment.* Different topologies are associated with different application scenarios for deployment of nodes according to their requirements. This topology is considered by the communication part to effectively utilize the constrained node resources. In order to design an efficient protocol, a number of deployed nodes need to be considered.
- *Control Packet Overhead.* Due to several reasons such as setting up of schedules, routes, and time synchronization, there is a need to control the communication. This is necessary for the WSN functioning. However, this consumes energy, time, and bandwidth, and thus may amplify delay in data communication. The MAC protocols must support restricted overhead of control packets so as to be able to satisfy QoS requirements such as high reliability, high energy efficiency, and low delay.
- *Time Synchronization.* In the hybrid schemes and reservation-based schemes, node synchronization needs to be ensured. Maximum number of features and functions in TDMA-based WSN work on the basis of time stamp, initiating with slot reservation and communication. Hence efficient time synchronization techniques need to be employed. It can be further categorized into two levels: *global synchronization* and *local synchronization*. The nodes in a region are synchronized in *local synchronization* whereas in *global synchronization* involves

entire network synchronization. Therefore, synchronization category depends on the designing of the protocol.

- *Slot Scheduling.* The mechanism of allocation of slot for MAC is referred as slot scheduling. Hybrid protocols that utilize CSMA and TDMA are better than those protocols that are completely based on TDMA. The standards such as ISA100.11a, WIA-PA and wireless HART utilize hybrid MAC scheduling. Therefore, selection from TDMA or hybrid protocols is most critical issue.
- *Duty-Cycling.* It is the scheme of SNs that are controlled by MAC function, which defines SNs sleep period, which remains inactive during communication. Due to duty-cycle tuning, the overall energy consumption can be decreased. However, latency is affected by the duty-cycle. A low-duty cycle consequence in high latency but low energy usage. Therefore, there is a trade-off between energy and latency. The most suitable duty cycling needs to save energy and at the same time maintains the required level of latency.
- *Multichannel.* It utilizes a number of channel and selects the channel with minimum interference and therefore, consequently helps in reduction of interference occurring on wireless medium. This is the reason why it is considered as an effective method. Latest sensor nodes support this method. ISA100.11a and wirelessHART are incorporated with this method. Probability of concurrent communication increases with this method. It is quite challenging to switch channels as well as simultaneously taking care of maintenance of coordination and remove overlaps.
- *Cross-Layer Support.* In this class, effective decisions are made because information is exploited from different layers and consequently, it is better than traditional approaches. Interdependence of different layers adds up the complexity of protocol and therefore it becomes difficult for protocols to analyze. In order to support cross layer communication, formation of generic APIs at various layers is required and this is a challenging task.
- *Channel Utilization.* The amount of bandwidth that the protocol utilizes effectively in order to transfer data is defined as channel utilization. TDMA-based protocols can help in achieving efficient utilization of channel at higher data rates. Energy has to be conserved in order to have low traffic and this can be achieved by ensuring that MAC protocol only functions when application needs minimal transfer of data, for instance, communicating and sensing temperature in every 60 s. If an application is considered which are getting implemented by common protocols and which consists of heterogeneous nodes in a network, such that data of temperature and pressure should be sent in every 5 and 1 s, respectively. Equal time slot will be provided to the node in case of TDMA approach and henceforth is not considered an effective method whereas CSMA or intelligent TDMA slot scheduling (which provides large number of slots for transferring more data) or grouping of TDMA with CSMA, would be more preferable as compared to TDMA approach.
- *Node Priority.* Nodes are arranged in a level of priority and according to their priority, at MAC function, service differentiation is given. In TDMA, nodes with higher priority can get the allotment of more than one slot in order to enforce

reliability. In case of hybrid protocol, nodes having greater priority can access channel first for the CSMA. In case of clustering protocols, highest priority belongs to cluster head and lower priority is given to its participants. Generally, node prioritization is accomplished statically, but changes in priority order can be made dynamically too.

- *Collision Avoidance.* Contention mechanism is utilized in hybrid protocols, that is, channels are accessed randomly, which consequently results in collision. There are many demerits associated with collision, such as: packets might be lost, subsequent packets might get delayed, increment in retransmission, and decrement in lifespan of the network. Henceforth, collision affects performance of protocols severely. Collision avoidance techniques must be applied in order to eradicate the contention of nodes.

6.3 MAC Protocols and Classification

On the basis of design goals, protocols can be categorized as in [81–83]. Formerly efficiency of energy used to be the chief concern and best effort for delivery of data used to be sufficient. MAC protocol's design has been evolving gradually through various techniques, design goals, and various other criteria. In industries, needs such as low-delay, reliability, and robustness gets equal priority as that of energy efficiency. Henceforth, a paradigm shift has been made in designing of MAC protocols. Main classes of protocols are QoS-Aware protocols, energy-efficient protocols, and real-time protocols. Main objective of energy efficient protocols is to expand the lifespan of network and to support communication of data up to its maximum limit. Studies have been done for mechanisms for saving energy for MAC as well as for WSN. QoS-Aware protocols provide network QoS along with application specific QoS. Studies have been done on QoS-Aware protocols appropriate for WSAN scenario. Real-time protocols come under the category of QoS-Aware protocols but now they have become a separate category for research. This type of protocols is for time-critical applications. They are preferable for WSAN class of system. Some of the MAC protocols are discussed in the section below.

- *GinMAC:* GinMAC protocol possesses tree topology and is based on TDMA. The main objective behind designing GinMAC was time-critical delivery of data. It was a part of GINSEC project and in the form of oil refinery, it aims on a specific application domain. Chief techniques utilized are Delay Conform Reliability Control, Exclusive TDMA, and Off-line Dimensioning. Low-duty cycling conserves energy. Cross-layer communication is supported by GinMAC. When GinMAC is implemented then, characteristics of channel and patters of traffic are already known and all complex calculations are done offline. Protocols have more predictable performance because of offline dimensioning. It is generally intended for small scale network because up to 25 nodes can be supported at maximum. TDMA slots cannot be reused and are exclusive in GinMAC. This results in limited protocol's scalability but this does not pose an issue because GinMAC is used in GINSEC project as an application specific protocol.

- *QoS-MAC:* It provides deterministic bounds for reliability and delay. The goals of designing are suitable for needs of IWSN classes along with QoS needs [84]. A collision-free scheme based on TDMA has been proposed in which time axis is subcategorized into epochs (which are fixed length slots). For deployment of node, tree topology is assumed. This protocol ensures lower and upper bounds on delay among nodes for converge-cast network pattern. Cross-layer support includes a scheme of retransmission, which is implemented to get improvised transport reliability. It implements some methods for energy efficiency by utilizing various duty cycling for various nodes based on their positioning in the tree.
- *PEDAMACS*: Delay Aware along with Power Efficient MAC for Sensor Networks: PEDAMACS is a protocol based on TDMA and aims to delay guarantee along with achieving energy efficiency [85]. It was constructed for applications, which may require periodic communication. A sink with uninterrupted supply of power which can reach any node with a single hop is assumed. The sink performs synchronization of time, scheduling of slots, and discovery of tree topology. Data are transmitted via intermediate hops to the sink by the nodes. PEDAMACS provides bounded delay guarantee and tries to eradicate network congestion. At every node, traffic data are generated, which is then transmitted to the sink and thus helps in management of traffic.
- *ER-MAC:* It stands for Emergency Response MAC. It was proposed by Lanny for serving applications, which need urgent response. It is a combination of CSMA and TDMA MAC protocol [86]. It was constructed in order to provide higher levels of adaptivity. It is scalable because it gives topology as well as traffic adaptability. It first uses CSMA to communicate along with collision avoidance, then it constructs a data gathering tree and lastly allots TDMA schedules. It subdivides the frame into contention period along with contention-free slots. Addition of new nodes is supported by contention period. Nodes that do not possess any data to transmit on their allotted slots do not turn on their radio's switch, this conserves energy. ERMAC employs normal and emergency mode for normal operation and to facilitate emergency response, respectively. Highest priority is assigned to the nodes in emergency mode. Each child synchronizes with its parent's time, in order to employ local time synchronization.

7 Conclusion and Future Works

Our aim with this book chapter was to highlight the industrial perspective of WSNs. We classified industrial systems into various classes and in this article we provide a survey on issues of security and reliability of WSNs in factory automation.

These factors focus on carefully designing secure and robust protocols useful for manufacturing processes, industrial plants, and factories. Several important industrial system requirements are explored along with its future aspects. Extensive industrial applications deploy WSNs abolishing human need in various places comprising hazardous arenas. The chapter explores various applications areas related to industry domain and employ WSNs. Huge number of existing standards useful for industrial applications are explored along with their attack defense techniques that they employ against various threats and attacks. Several security issues and reliability problems prominent in WSNs are discussed considering the unique nature of industries including interference, work flow, process management, and equipment movements. Due to these factors, secure and robust protocols need to be designed that is suitable for manufacturing processes and factories. Several existing industry standards are studied along with mechanisms to deal with attacks in IWSNs. Security functions in industrial standards are discussed and then various driving forces in satisfying the IWSN requirements such as routing, transport, and medium access control are explored. The chapter explores various types of MAC protocols and compares CDMA and TDMA in terms of several metrics. The chapter also explores several design considerations involving MAC protocols.

8   Future Research Trends

WSANs are rapidly growing and developing area in the field of research. Several interesting problems are also discussed and left wide open for future research and investigations. These open research topics are as follows.

- The specific as well as orthogonal requirements of WSAN needs to be fulfilled as the hardware used by WSANs is very much different from IWSNs. Therefore, creation of standards for this kind of network requires new protocols to be developed.
- Creation of industrial standards from scratch is a time consuming as well as tedious task therefore applicability of industrial standards such as wirelessHART needs to be studied for WSAN.
- Existing complex cryptographic algorithms due to its high complexity are not suitable for IWSNs as these possess less processing and power capabilities. Therefore, future research in this field may focus on developing new protocols for countering the security issues effectively.
- Considering the resource constraint nature and demanding deployment environments of WSNs, makes ensuring adequate security a challenging task. The physical level security needs to be enhanced in order to make the nodes resistant and tamper proof to withstand severe conditions such as high temperature, pressure, and humidity.
- Resilience and robustness of WSNs need to be considered as an important issue. This is because the networks strength to guarantee acceptable level of security

B. Bhushan and G. Sahoo

in case of node failures and the ability of network to remain functional even in presence of attacks is of utmost concern.

- Transmitting sensitive data to the BS becomes difficult in unfavorable conditions therefore mechanism for storing the data in the current node for a reasonable period of time is necessary. This is even more essential in an industrial system as each and every bit of condition information is significant. Thus, there is a need of secure distributed data storage system.

References

1. Low, K. S., Win, W. N. N., & Meng, E. (2005). Wireless sensor networks for industrial environments. In *International Conference on Computational Intelligence for Modelling, Control and Automation and International Conference on Intelligent Agents, Web Technologies and Internet Commerce (CIMCA-IAWTIC'06)* (Vol. 2, pp. 271–276). https://doi.org/10.1109/CIMCA.2005.1631480.
2. Akyildiz, I., Su, W., Sankarasubramaniam, Y., & Cayirci, E. (2002). Wireless sensor networks: A survey. *Computer Networks, 38*(4), 393–422. https://doi.org/10.1016/s1389-1286(01)00302-4.
3. Gutierrez, J., Villa-Medina, J. F., Nieto-Garibay, A., & Porta-Gandara, M. A. (2014). Automated irrigation system using a wireless sensor network and GPRS module. *IEEE Transactions on Instrumentation and Measurement, 63*(1), 166–176. https://doi.org/10.1109/tim.2013.2276487.
4. Jan, N., Ondrej, K., & Radislav, S. (2014). A distributed fault detection system based on IWSN for machine condition monitoring. *IEEE Transactions on Industrial Informatics, 10*, 1118–1123. https://doi.org/10.1109/TII.2013.2290432.
5. Zafar, I., Heung-No, L., & Saeid, N. (2018). Highly reliable decision-making using reliability factor feedback for factory condition monitoring via WSNs. *Wireless Communications and Mobile Computing, 2018*, 1–9. https://doi.org/10.1155/2018/8058624.
6. Stergiou, C., Psannis, K. E., Kim, B., & Gupta, B. (2018). Secure integration of IoT and cloud computing. *Future Generation Computer Systems, 78*, 964–975. https://doi.org/10.1016/j.future.2016.11.031.
7. Hackmann, G., Guo, W., Yan, G., Lu, C., & Dyke, S. (2010). Cyber-physical codesign of distributed structural health monitoring with wireless sensor networks. In *Proceedings of the 1st ACM/IEEE International Conference on Cyber-Physical Systems – ICCPS 10.* https://doi.org/10.1145/1795194.1795211.
8. Boubrima, A., Bechkit, W., & Rivano, H. (2017). Optimal WSN deployment models for air pollution monitoring. *IEEE Transactions on Wireless Communications, 16*(5), 2723–2735. https://doi.org/10.1109/twc.2017.2658601.
9. Stergiou, C., & Psannis, K. (2017). Efficient and secure BIG data delivery in Cloud Computing. *Multimedia Tools and Applications, 76*(21), 22803–22822. https://doi.org/10.1007/s11042-017-4590-4.
10. Wang, C., Li, J., Ye, F., & Yang, Y. (2016). A mobile data gathering framework for wireless rechargeable sensor networks with vehicle movement costs and capacity constraints. *IEEE Transactions on Computers, 65*(8), 2411–2427. https://doi.org/10.1109/tc.2015.2490060.
11. Tsang, K. F., Gidlund, M., & Åkerberg, J. (2016). Guest editorial industrial wireless networks: Applications, challenges, and future directions. *IEEE Transactions on Industrial Informatics, 12*(2), 755–757.
12. Guck, J. W., Reisslein, M., & Kellerer, W. (2016). Function split between delay-constrained routing and resource allocation for centrally managed QoS in industrial networks. *IEEE Transactions on Industrial Informatics, 12*(6), 2050–2061. https://doi.org/10.1109/tii.2016.2592481.

13. Krishnamurthy, L., Adler, R., Buonadonna, P., Chhabra, J., Flanigan, M., Kushalnagar, N., et al. (2005). Design and deployment of industrial sensor networks. In *Proceedings of the 3rd International Conference on Embedded Networked Sensor Systems – SenSys 05.* https://doi.org/10.1145/1098918.1098926.
14. Tanwar, S., Kumar, N., & Rodrigues, J. J. (2015). A systematic review on heterogeneous routing protocols for wireless sensor network. *Journal of Network and Computer Applications, 53*, 39–56. https://doi.org/10.1016/j.jnca.2015.03.004.
15. Begum, K., & Dixit, S. (2016, March). Industrial WSN using IoT: A survey. In *International Conference on Electrical, Electronics, and Optimization Techniques (ICEEOT)* (pp. 499–504). Piscataway: IEEE.
16. Gupta, B. B., & Quamara, M. (2018, October). A dynamic security policies generation model for access control in smart card based applications. In *International Symposium on Cyberspace Safety and Security* (pp. 132–143). Cham: Springer.
17. Christos, S., Kostas, P., Andreas, P., Yutaka, I., & Byung-Gyu, K. (2018). Algorithms for efficient digital media transmission over IoT and cloud networking. *The Journal of Multimedia Information System, 5*(1), 27–34.
18. Plageras, A., Psannis, K., Stergiou, C., Wang, H., & Gupta, B. B. (2017). Efficient IoT-based sensor BIG data collection-processing and analysis in smart buildings. *Future Generation Computer Systems, 82*, 349–357. https://doi.org/10.1016/j.future.2017.09.082.
19. Lin, X., Huang, L., Guo, C., Zhang, P., Huang, M., & Zhang, J. (2016). Energy-efficient resource allocation in TDMS based wireless powered communication networks. *IEEE Communications Letters, 21*, 1. https://doi.org/10.1109/lcomm.2016.2639484.
20. Hoang, T. M., Duong, Q., Vo, N.-S., & Kundu, C. (2017). Physical layer security in cooperative energy harvesting networks with a friendly jammer. *IEEE Wireless Communications Letters, 6*(2), 174–177. https://doi.org/10.1109/LWC.2017.2650224.
21. Hitesh, S., Ravinder, K., Boncho, B., & Peter, P. (2017). Cloud attenuation issues in satellite communications at millimeter frequency bands-state of art. *International Journal of Scientific and Engineering Research, 8*, 851–857.
22. Zou, Y., Zhu, J., Wang, X., & Hanzo, L. (2016). A survey on wireless security: Technical challenges, recent advances, and future trends. *Proceedings of the IEEE, 104*(9), 1727–1765. https://doi.org/10.1109/jproc.2016.2558521.
23. Bhushan, B., & Sahoo, G. (2017). Recent advances in attacks, technical challenges, vulnerabilities and their countermeasures in wireless sensor networks. *Wireless Personal Communications, 98*(2), 2037–2077. https://doi.org/10.1007/s11277-017-4962-0.
24. Zhao, F., & Guibas, L. (2004). *Wireless sensor networks: An information processing approach.* Amsterdam: Elsevier.
25. Kevan, T. (2005). Upgrading a steel mill – Wirelessly. *Wireless Sensors, 22*, 3–6.
26. Kevan, T. (2006). Shipboard machine monitoring for predictive maintenance. In *Wireless sensors magazine.*
27. Sundararajan, V., Andrew, R., William, W., & Paul, W. (2004). *Distributed monitoring of steady-state system performance using wireless sensor networks* (p. 15). California: American Society of Mechanical Engineers, Manufacturing Engineering Division, MED. https://doi.org/10.1115/IMECE2004-59884.
28. Ramamurthy, H., Prabhu, B. S., Gadh, R., & Madni, A. (2005). Smart sensor platform for industrial monitoring and control. In *Sensores* (p. 4). Irvine: IEEE. https://doi.org/10.1109/ICSENS.2005.1597900.
29. Muhammad, R., Jaharah, G., Mohd, N., & Haron, C. (2014). A review of sensor system and application in milling process for tool condition monitoring. *Research Journal of Applied Sciences, Engineering and Technology, 7*, 2083–2097. https://doi.org/10.19026/rjaset.7.502.
30. Kunert, K., Jonsson, M., & Uhlemann, E. (2010). Exploiting time and frequency diversity in IEEE 802.15.4 industrial networks for enhanced reliability and throughput. In *2010 IEEE 15th Conference on Emerging Technologies and Factory Automation (ETFA 2010).* https://doi.org/10.1109/etfa.2010.5641347.

31. Miśkowicz, M., & Kościelnik, D. (2010). Modeling end-to-end reliability in best-effort networked embedded systems. In *2010 IEEE 15th Conference on Emerging Technologies and Factory Automation (ETFA 2010)*. https://doi.org/10.1109/etfa.2010.5641118.
32. Park, P., Fischione, C., Bonivento, A., Johansson, K. H., & Sangiovanni-Vincent, A. (2011). Breath: An adaptive protocol for industrial control applications using wireless sensor networks. *IEEE Transactions on Mobile Computing, 10*(6), 821–838. https://doi.org/10.1109/tmc.2010.223.
33. Zand, P., Chatterjea, S., Das, K., & Havinga, P. (2012). Wireless industrial monitoring and control networks: The journey so far and the road ahead. *Journal of Sensor and Actuator Networks, 1*, 123–152. https://doi.org/10.3390/jsan1020123.
34. Zheng, L. (2010). Industrial wireless sensor networks and standardizations: The trend of wireless sensor networks for process automation. In *Proceedings of SICE Annual Conference 2010* (pp. 1187–1190). Piscataway: IEEE.
35. Akyildiz, I., & Kasimoglu, I. (2004). A protocol suite for wireless sensor and actor networks. In *Proceedings of 2004 IEEE Radio and Wireless Conference (IEEE Cat. No.04TH8746)*. https://doi.org/10.1109/rawcon.2004.1389058.
36. Rabaey, J., Ammer, M., Silva, J. D., Patel, D., & Roundy, S. (2000). PicoRadio supports ad hoc ultra-low power wireless networking. *Computer, 33*(7), 42–48. https://doi.org/10.1109/2.869369.
37. Willig, A., Matheus, K., & Wolisz, A. (2005). Wireless technology in industrial networks. *Proceedings of the IEEE, 93*(6), 1130–1151. https://doi.org/10.1109/jproc.2005.849717.
38. Dazhi, C., & Varshney, P. K. (2004). QoS support in wireless sensor networks: A survey. In *Proceedings of the International Conference on Wireless Networks, ICWN'04* (Vol. 1, pp. 227–233).
39. Gungor, V., & Hancke, G. (2009). Industrial wireless sensor networks: Challenges, design principles, and technical approaches. *IEEE Transactions on Industrial Electronics, 56*(10), 4258–4265. https://doi.org/10.1109/tie.2009.2015754.
40. Ramon, S. O., & Gerhard, F. (2010). Timeliness in wireless sensor networks: Common misconceptions. In *Proceedings of the 9th International Workshop on Real-Time Networks RTN*.
41. Imran, M., Said, A. M., & Hasbullah, H. (2010). A survey of simulators, emulators and testbeds for wireless sensor networks. In *2010 International Symposium on Information Technology*. https://doi.org/10.1109/itsim.2010.5561571.
42. Halkes, G., & Langendoen, K. (2009). Experimental evaluation of simulation abstractions for wireless sensor network MAC protocols. In *2009 IEEE 14th International Workshop on Computer Aided Modeling and Design of Communication Links and Networks*. https://doi.org/10.1109/camad.2009.5161468.
43. Li, H., & Savkin, A. V. (2018). Wireless sensor network based navigation of micro flying robots in the industrial internet of things. *IEEE Transactions on Industrial Informatics, 14*(8), 3524–3533. https://doi.org/10.1109/tii.2018.2825225.
44. Sinha, P., Jha, V. K., Rai, A. K., & Bhushan, B. (2017). Security vulnerabilities, attacks and countermeasures in wireless sensor networks at various layers of OSI reference model: A survey. In *2017 International Conference on Signal Processing and Communication (ICSPC)*. https://doi.org/10.1109/cspc.2017.8305855h.
45. Nikoletseas, S., Yang, Y., & Apostolos, G. (2016). *Wireless power transfer algorithms, technologies and applications in ad hoc communication networks*. Cham: Springer. https://doi.org/10.1007/978-3-319-46810-5.
46. Nurul, F., Samsul, H., Eko, P., Udin, A. R., Choirur, R., & Unggul Pamenang, M. (2017). A prototype of monitoring precision agriculture system based on WSN. In *2017 International Seminar on Intelligent Technology and Its Applications (ISITIA)* (pp. 323–328). Piscataway: IEEE. https://doi.org/10.1109/ISITIA.2017.8124103.
47. Nelofar, A., Kewen, X., Ahmad, A., & Saleem, U. (2017). Adaptive TCP-ICCW congestion control mechanism for QoS in renewable wireless sensor networks. *IEEE Sensors Letters, 1*, 1. https://doi.org/10.1109/LSENS.2017.2758822.

48. Bayindir, R., & Yucel, C. (2010). A water pumping control system with a Programmable Logic Controller (PLC) and industrial wireless modules for industrial plants—An experimental setup. *ISA Transactions, 50*, 321–328. https://doi.org/10.1016/j.isatra.2010.10.006.
49. Sisinni, E., Saifullah, A., Han, S., Jennehag, U., & Gidlund, M. (2018). Industrial internet of things: Challenges, opportunities, and directions. *IEEE Transactions on Industrial Informatics, 14*(11), 4724–4734. https://doi.org/10.1109/tii.2018.2852491.
50. Alliance, Z. (2008). Zigbee specification (document 053474r17). Luettu. 21.
51. I. W. W. Group. (2008, May). Draft standard ISA100. 11a. In *Internal working draft*. North Carolina: International Society of Automation.
52. Kristofer, P., & Lance, D. (2008). TSMP: Time synchronized mesh protocol. In *IASTED International Symposium on Distributed Sensor Networks, DSN 2008*.
53. O'Donovan, T., Brown, J., Roedig, U., Sreenan, C., Adam, D., Klein, A., Sá Silva, J., Vassiliou, V., & Wolf, L. (2010). GINSENG: Performance control in wireless sensor networks. In *2010 7th Annual IEEE Communications Society Conference on Sensor, Mesh and Ad Hoc Communications and Networks (SECON)* (pp. 1–3). https://doi.org/10.1109/SECON.2010.5508206.
54. Petcharat, S., James, B., & Utz, R. (2010). Time-critical data delivery in wireless sensor networks. In *International Conference on Distributed Computing in Sensor Systems* (pp. 216–229). Berlin: Springer. https://doi.org/10.1007/978-3-642-13651-1_16.
55. Büsching, F., Pöttner, W.-B., Brökelmann, D., von Zengen, G., Hartung, R., Hinz, K., & Wolf, L. (2012). A demonstrator of the GINSENG-approach to performance and closed loop control in WSNs. In *Ninth International Conference on Networked Sensing Systems (INSS)*. https://doi.org/10.1109/INSS.2012.6240572.
56. Stig, P., & Simon, C. (2011). WirelessHART versus ISA100.11a: The format war hits the factory floor. *IEEE Industrial Electronics Magazine, 5*, 23–34. https://doi.org/10.1109/MIE.2011.943023.
57. Duan, Y., Li, W., Fu, X., Luo, Y., & Yang, L. (2018). A methodology for reliability of WSN based on software defined network in adaptive industrial environment. *IEEE/CAA Journal of Automatica Sinica, 5*(1), 74–82. https://doi.org/10.1109/jas.2017.7510751.
58. Taylor, J., & Sayda, A. (2005). An intelligent architecture for integrated control and asset management for industrial processes. In *Proceedings of the 2005 IEEE International Symposium On, Mediterranean Conference on Control and Automation Intelligent Control, 2005*. https://doi.org/10.1109/.2005.1467219.
59. Zhao, G. (2011). Wireless sensor networks for industrial process monitoring and control: A survey. *Network Protocols and Algorithms, 3*, 43–63. https://doi.org/10.5296/npa.v3i1.580.
60. Bhushan, B., & Sahoo, G. (2018). Routing protocols in wireless sensor networks. In *Computational Intelligence in Sensor Networks Studies in Computational Intelligence* (pp. 215–248). Berlin: Springer. https://doi.org/10.1007/978-3-662-57277-1_10.
61. Thai, J., Yuan, C., & Bayen, A. M. (2018). Resiliency of mobility-as-a-service systems to denial-of-service attacks. *IEEE Transactions on Control of Network Systems, 5*(1), 370–382. https://doi.org/10.1109/tcns.2016.2612828.
62. Kumar, R., Chandra, P., & Hanmandlu, M. (2016). A robust fingerprint matching system using orientation features. *Journal of Information Processing Systems, 121*, 83–99.
63. Tomic, I., & Mccann, J. A. (2017). A survey of potential security issues in existing wireless sensor network protocols. *IEEE Internet of Things Journal, 4*(6), 1910–1923. https://doi.org/10.1109/jiot.2017.2749883.
64. Kumar, R., Hanmandlu, M., & Chandra, P. (2014). An empirical evaluation of rotation invariance of LDP feature for fingerprint matching using neural networks. *International Journal of Computational Vision and Robotics, 4*(4), 330–348.
65. Zhu, J., Zou, Y., & Zheng, B. (2017). Physical-layer security and reliability challenges for industrial wireless sensor networks. *IEEE Access, 5*, 5313–5320. https://doi.org/10.1109/access.2017.2691003.
66. Pu, C., & Lim, S. (2018). A light-weight countermeasure to forwarding misbehavior in wireless sensor networks: Design, analysis, and evaluation. *IEEE Systems Journal, 12*(1), 834–842. https://doi.org/10.1109/jsyst.2016.2535730.

67. Wang, G., Wang, B., Wang, T., Nika, A., Zheng, H., & Zhao, B. Y. (2018). Ghost riders: Sybil attacks on crowdsourced mobile mapping services. *IEEE/ACM Transactions on Networking, 26*(3), 1123–1136. https://doi.org/10.1109/tnet.2018.2818073.
68. Ripudaman, S., Brijesh, R., & Sanjay, B. (2017). A low delay cross-layer MAC protocol for k-covered event driven wireless sensor networks. *IEEE Sensors Letters, 1*, 1–4. https://doi.org/10.1109/LSENS.2017.2776303.
69. Fatima, Z. D., & Djamel, D. (2016). MAC protocols with wake-up radio for wireless sensor networks: A review. *IEEE Communications Surveys and Tutorials, 19*, 587–618. https://doi.org/10.1109/ COMST.2016.2612644.
70. Liu, J., Li, M., Yuan, B., & Liu, W. (2015). A novel energy efficient MAC protocol for wireless body area network. *Communications China, 12*, 11–20. https://doi.org/10. 1109/CC.2015.7084398.
71. Chi-Han, L., Ching-Ju, L. K., & Chen, W.-T. (2017). Channel-aware polling-based MAC protocol for body area networks: Design and analysis. *IEEE Sensors Journal, 17*(9), 2936–2948. https://doi.org/10.1109/JSEN.2017.2669526.
72. Solic, P., Radic, J., & Rozic, N. (2016). Early frame break policy for ALOHA-based RFID systems. *IEEE Transactions on Automation Science and Engineering, 13*(2), 876–881. https://doi.org/10.1109/tase.2015.2408372.
73. Rhee, I., Warrier, A., Aia, M., Min, J., & Sichitiu, M. (2008). Z-MAC: A hybrid MAC for wireless sensor networks. *IEEE/ACM Transactions on Networking, 16*(3), 511–524. https://doi.org/10.1109/tnet.2007.900704.
74. Hannachi, A., & Bachir, A. (2017). Distributed cell scheduling for multichannel IoT MAC protocols. In *2017 13th International Wireless Communications and Mobile Computing Conference (IWCMC)*. https://doi.org/10.1109/iwcmc.2017.7986450.
75. Nguyen, V., Oo, T. Z., Chuan, P., & Hong, C. S. (2016). An efficient time slot acquisition on the hybrid TDMA/CSMA multichannel MAC in VANETs. *IEEE Communications Letters, 20*(5), 970–973. https://doi.org/10.1109/lcomm.2016.2536672.
76. Chingoska, H., Hadzi-Velkov, Z., Nikoloska, I., & Zlatanov, N. (2016). Resource allocation in wireless powered communication networks with non-orthogonal multiple access. *IEEE Wireless Communications Letters, 5*(6), 684–687. https://doi.org/10.1109/lwc.2016.2615616.
77. Kim, J., Lee, H., Song, C., Oh, T., & Lee, I. (2017). Sum throughput maximization for multi-user MIMO cognitive wireless powered communication networks. *IEEE Transactions on Wireless Communications, 16*(2), 913–923. https://doi.org/10.1109/twc.2016.2633471.
78. Kurt, S., & Tavli, B. (2017). Path-loss modeling for wireless sensor networks: A review of models and comparative evaluations. *IEEE Antennas and Propagation Magazine, 59*(1), 18–37. https://doi.org/10.1109/map.2016.2630035.
79. Kumar, R. (2017). Hand image biometric based personal authentication system. In *Intelligent techniques in signal processing for multimedia security* (pp. 201–226). Cham: Springer.
80. Kulkarni, S. (2004). TDMA service for sensor networks. In *Proceedings of 24th International Conference on Distributed Computing Systems Workshops, 2004* (pp. 604–609). https://doi.org/10.1109/ICDCSW.2004.1284094.
81. Singh, R., Rai, B. K., & Bose, S. K. (2017). A low delay cross-layer MAC protocol for k-covered event driven wireless sensor networks. *IEEE Sensors Letters, 1*(6), 1–4. https://doi.org/10.1109/lsens.2017.2776303.
82. Siddiqui, S., Ghani, S., & Khan, A. A. (2018). ADP-MAC: An adaptive and dynamic polling-based MAC protocol for wireless sensor networks. *IEEE Sensors Journal, 18*(2), 860–874. https://doi.org/10.1109/jsen.2017.2771397.
83. Kumar, A., Zhao, M., Wong, K., Guan, Y. L., & Chong, P. H. (2018). A comprehensive study of IoT and WSN MAC protocols: Research issues, challenges and opportunities. *IEEE Access, 6*, 76228–76262. https://doi.org/10.1109/access.2018.2883391.
84. Hu, Y., Gao, A., Xu, T., & Li, L. (2017). Cascade self-tuning control architecture for QoS-aware MAC in WSN. *IET Wireless Sensor Systems, 7*(5), 146–154. https://doi.org/10.1049/iet-wss.2016.0092.

85. Ergen, S., & Varaiya, P. (2006). PEDAMACS: Power efficient and delay aware medium access protocol for sensor networks. *IEEE Transactions on Mobile Computing, 5*(7), 920–930. https://doi.org/10.1109/tmc.2006.100.
86. Sitanayah, L., Sreenan, C. J., & Brown, K. N. (2010). ER-MAC: A hybrid MAC protocol for emergency response wireless sensor networks. In *2010 Fourth International Conference on Sensor Technologies and Applications*. https://doi.org/10.1109/sensorcomm.2010.45.

Chapter 28
Privacy Preservation of Electronic Health Record: Current Status and Future Direction

Anil Kumar and Ravinder Kumar

Abstract Recent developments in health sector have made it possible to collect, store, manage, and share medical data in large scale. Managing and sharing of health record is primarily requirement in electronic health record software, however, reusability of electronic health records in distributive environment or access by third party must maintain principle of database system and implement the guidelines of international privacy policy standards and regulations. Privacy preservation is the major concern while dealing with real-time datasets in health sector. Privacy preservation algorithms have to ensure protection of sensitive information related to patients' diagnoses and diseases. Privacy preserving data mining (PPDM) deals with data perturbation, anonymities, and modification as per the requirement of the system. Data perturbation is one of best PPDM techniques that basically deals with numeric values and focuses on privacy implementation. In this chapter, we will select and review different articles that are related to electronic health records (EHRs), their privacy standards, challenges, and regulations currently adopted in different countries. This chapter mainly reviews the current status of privacy preservation polices used in EHR, privacy techniques and analysis, and future scope of privacy in global scenario.

Keywords Privacy · Security · Electronic health record (EHR) · Privacy preserving data mining (PPDM)

A. Kumar
USICT, GGSIPU, Delhi, India

R. Kumar (✉)
Skill Faculty of Engineering, SVSU, Dudhola Palwal, India

© Springer Nature Switzerland AG 2020
B. B. Gupta et al. (eds.), *Handbook of Computer Networks and Cyber Security*,
https://doi.org/10.1007/978-3-030-22277-2_28

1 Introduction

Privacy is not a clearly defined concept, being subject to a number of culturally dependent variables. Rapid development of information communication and technologies has changed the classical way of maintaining healthcare record. Since the last two decades, information communication and technologies (ICTs) have been integrated with other multidisciplinary areas. Like other sectors of developing and under developing countries, ICT directly or indirectly was involved and healthcare domain is not escaped from drastic advancement of ICT. In our daily routine tasks, social and professional work technologies impact the lot. The patient-related sensitive data such as heart failure status, heart rhythms, blood pressure, and oxygen-related problems, must be secured in eHealth domain.

The key motivation factors from the above discussion is that an individual as well as an organization deep concerned and put it in higher priority level. The protection from the individual information, accessibility of data, and the way the data are stored in the database system are known in the research areas to make an efficient mechanism. Different users of the system will have anxiety of leakage of personal information and they want to secure electronic health records, which must provide information security, more access rights to the owner of information, data privacy, and secure database management. The proposed chapter provides the mechanisms to maintain privacy of patient electronic health records by disclosing minimal information in electronic health domain. A sensitivity, data privacy, task-based access control, and minimal data storage will be evaluated and applied to machine learning (ML) algorithms for electronic health records using Python or in Weka tool in future.

This chapter is organized as follows: Sect. 2 presents the literature survey of PPDM and EHR, Sect. 3 illustrates the basics of privacy and EHRs. Section 4 discusses the privacy models and techniques. Section 5 presents the data protection and privacy laws in different countries. Privacy preserving data mining applications are presented in Sect. 6. Chapter is concluded along with future direction in Sect. 7.

2 Literature Survey

Privacy can be defined as *"the claim of individuals, group, or institutions to determine for themselves when, how and to what extent information about them is communicated to others."* Presently, there are around 9.6 billion Internet-connected devices and around 1.3 billion mobile broadband connections. As presented in every 2 days, these connected devices create and share roughly fivefold Exabyte of dataset of different areas. The resultant huge data creation and sharing is called data revolution and big data digital world also exposes many risks during communication when people surf the web, online banking activities, or communicate via email, instant messaging. Hacker can access electronic health record (EHR) on eHealth domain from the Internet and can misuse the user data for his or her own behalf. Today rapid development in the technology also affects the healthcare organization. Hospitals, clinical centers used the ICT (information and communication technology) in the large scale. Many countries around the world emerges has public–private partnership (PPP) policy to adopt eHealth infrastructure in health sector which facilitates online health advise and true enable health information, however there are chances of patients sensitive information leakages in this types of distributes environment. Health information technology (HIT) services through Internet and Intranet facilitate the demand of services like other sector of the economy and directly reduce cost of services to different stakeholders and user. Doctor, pathological staffs, and medicine clinics get the patient electronic records using eHealth anytime and anywhere. Patient's health records may be distributed in different hospitals and clinics for better treatments of particular disease and tests, and this scattered information might be leaked and create problem for the patient in terms of his/her data privacy. The eHealth domain contains different types of patient records that have been extendedly studied by researchers within relevant field. Privacy and effective data storage have become the major challenges in eHealth domain. It had been described [1] that privacy is a fundamental right. Supreme Court of India has also verdict that privacy is also now the fundamental right of citizen. Electronic health record stores demographical and sensitive data, and these data are distributed between different stakeholders. Consistency, completeness, accuracy, data privacy, and security are essential requirements of electronic health records. EHRs have joined the block of most confidential data like personal information of the patient. Using fine-grained data access control method and patient centric approach [2] has described a secured personal health record. However, when the data are communicated through Internet, it imposes the risk of privacy exposure and heavy computation overhead to system. Holomorphic encryption has been proposed as a novel model [3] to design a secure communication.

As described in the literature, the electronic health record provides levels of privacy that are mandatory and should be managed properly. Far spread medical facilities and related personnel are disseminated within the eHealth domain. Many approaches had been put forward to increase privacy by the researches using various encryption techniques such as hashing, AES (advanced encryption standard), DES (data encryption standard) algorithms, and access control methods. Despite these techniques, when data are disseminated across the medical facilities, these are not able to offer patients with anonymity. This leads to a situation in which the patients' data are required to be accessed by different medical authorities that are concerned with the treatment of the given patient. The trust-based privacy methods had been described in literature to decrease the privacy risk in the electronic health record. This approach divided the role of users to maintain the privacy of data. Although the limitation of the security and privacy risk is overcome by this approach, yet it restricts the application to be utilized by other users. It requires more computations, resulting in increase of applicable cost. On the basis of content and orientation, privacy and security policies can be applied. Somehow, the degree of privacy level increases as diseases become so complex that they require inputs from many expert physicians for diagnose and treatment. How to maintain the privacy level and to what extent is not crystal cleared by this research. To improve data mechanism in eHealth domain research work had been carried out as illustrated in [4] and few of them apply data protection during the process and residing storage. Time efficient and reliable privacy technique for electronic health record was proposed presented in [5]. As per [6] eHealth record requires huge amount of space while in [7] it is described that the wireless sensor techniques can decrease the space complexity and also require automatic process mechanism for data management. Leakage of information directly from the database during communication or when data are shared imposes higher level of risk. Authors in [8] described privacy and security—two different concepts, but without applying security on the data, data privacy cannot be achieved.

Privacy and security are correlated and sometimes interchangeable to each other. RSA, DES, and Diffie–Hellman key exchange algorithms are some of the different encryption techniques that can be used to secure data. Federal approach had been used in the past, which mainly concerns the risks and benefits of service providers, but at the same time ignores the privacy issues of individual customer. On the basis of federal approach many research projects had been addressed in the western countries. Different PPDM algorithms have been proposed in the past to preserve privacy of health records, but some of them use only prosper classification and clustering before analysis on that specific area. The authors in [9] have presented the new anonymity problem due to classification and proposed a genetic algorithm on real-time dataset. The anonymity algorithm to integrate data of multiple stakeholders is proposed in [5]. The algorithm described in [10] apply horizontal partitioning method of data distribution can be integrated with privacy algorithms for security of data, while disclosing data from one party to another and presented a model for medical research using pseudonymous mechanism. Various cryptographic and noncryptographic privacies preserve approaches used in eHealth domain. Some of them protect the eHealth data used by public key encryption and symmetric key encryption methods of information security. An encryption method was proposed in [11] on the basis of attribute-centered approach to access control of health data by multiple parties and multiple accessibilities of different owners in multiuser environment. Attribute revocation approach is used to manage in case of user identity verification instead of attribute-centered approach. The attribute-based approach is considered as more expensive because of bilinear computation for data decryption. In health record data are [12] encrypted and decrypted through Lagrange multipliers in creation of symmetric key encryption, and owners of data can generate and share the key providing the automatic revocation feature; however, it is costly in terms of computations. It had been described in [13] that the role-based permission approach is only for the legitimate user to access electronic health records for specific period of time, but this approach reduces the utility of data, creates complexity when a user plays the different roles in a given span of time. The smart card- and pin-based [14] data security is presented for the patient health record during communication. A biometric authentication approach is illustrated in [15] for patient health record security and privacy. The cryptographic key management system is encrypted and the same key is again decrypted at the other end so that only authorized user can access the relevant data as demonstrated by Jafari et al. [16]. In [17] raised various significant privacy problems due to authorized device connectivity in the electronic health records system. Information and communication technologies have led to a situation in which patient's health data are facing a new privacy and security threats as presented in [18]. Three fundamental security goals are confidentiality, integrity, and availability (CIA), which also play the major role in the privacy of electronic health record. CIA principles are the primary requirements for privacy preservation of EHR, because EHRs may be seriously threatened by hackers, viruses, and worms.

Individual data are shared and used by the researchers or by third party and they guarantee that data will not be reidentified by the user. k-anonymity protection is a formal model, invented by Aggarwal and Philip [19] and Sweeney [20] who had described that k-anonymity protection on the shared data applied only if each member in the released information cannot be identified distinguishably until $k - 1$ individual information is available in the shared list. This paper basically focuses to find out the identification attacks in releasing information.

Electronic health record (EHR) software stores and processes several data types such as images, textual, numerical, and many more. Various papers are available in the privacy and security literature that show that individual identification can be released using quasi-identifier disclosure even if direct identification-related attributes were removed from the list. Statistical data disclosure control has been proposed in [21] to maintain the quasi-attributes for protecting the privacy of individual data. SDC applied on clinical dataset with nonnumerical data type. In literature many theoretical concepts had been presented by researchers. They had also used open dataset to apply randomization and k-anonymity-based techniques on horizontal and vertical data partitioned. The survey in this paper contained privacy preserving data mining and different algorithms available in the literature, used in different domains. Various enterprises provided offers to EHR systems to maintain the records. Microsoft HealthVault, Google Health, and other openEHR software provided data protection, but they were fail to satisfy the customer privacy requirements, as described in [22], as per rules and regulations stated in the constitution in privacy and security standards available in different countries. Security and privacy in EHRs can be hacked, impose viruses and worms to destroy the personal information [23]. Current state of electronic health record has been explored and analyzed in [24]. Disseminating the individual information in distributed system required more attention in the context of security and privacy issues. Now, with the advancement in ICT, Cloud computing is an emerging GenNext technology. This paper focuses on retrieving EHRs after encryption on the other side and sending the encrypted EHRs. In this paper, authors emphasized on Diffie–Hellman key exchange algorithms for data privacy and security [25]. In recent study, authors illustrated that machine learning can be used for proper implementation of security and privacy. ML can fill the gap between data regulation, standard, and technology. The machine learning-based data de-identification is proposed in [26] and automated NPL-based de-identification model has also been proposed and tested in [26]. In distributed environment, data are stored in different servers at various places. Linked data are stored separately from clinical data, thus, sensitive data values are secured in EHRs, but these are not fully secured that they can maintain and manage the privacy of individual [27]. Authors designed a framework on the basis of "privacy by design," the standard proposed in European 2020.

EHRs store different types of patient's data, some are related to demographic values such as DOB, name, and age, while some are related to quasi-identifier and others contained sensitive values. Linked data are still associated even after the identifier data are removed. It has been presented in [28] that how to disassociate the linked data after specific time span. It had been proposed in [29] that the new automatic method of a sanitization for textual medical documents, which was done manually earlier, is time consuming and costly. Large sum is used in statistical and small sum is used nonstatistical data values. SPLU is a new statistical framework of privacy, which allows releasing data. Framework used data-randomized perturbation for sensitive data privacy. The SPLU is basically using sanitized data for query processing and auditing methodology. Framework imposed maximum utility for large sum querying. The framework included privacy protection through small sum querying mechanism [30]. Today, EHR data availability can be used for secondary purpose. The clinical data can be used for privacy protection, but it is very tedious task to convert clinical data into existing EHR system. This model converts the clinical text content information into EHRs and applies privacy algorithms to de-identification of sensitive data as described in [31]. Traditionally, statistical methods are used to fulfill CIA principles that use only traditional database system. This system is not applied on GWAS (genome-wide association study) data values. Scalability of the system can be measured when it provides best data privacy [32]. The authors in [33] present that privacy preservation could be provided in two phases. First phase implements privacy preserving algorithms and sanitize the data and second phase uses expert analytics view for further filtering. Health ubiquitous computing uses WSN data collection and processing automatically. WSN-based ubiquitous health can be hacked and breach individual's personal data privacy, therefore, it required more data security and privacy implementation. Proposed framework recognized user activities and monitoring the action accordingly from sensor actuators [34]. In [35] survey paper, most relevant PPDM techniques and challenges are focused. Advancement of ICT also impacts the healthcare sector. Improvement in this sector provides best facilities, better treatments to patients, reduces cost and quality of services, but healthcare sectors are also facing the problem of privacy breaches when data are shared in the distributed system. Personal identity can be identified and might affect its life or business. This paper provided a scheme, in which shared data are transformed in different formats and encrypted accordingly after a fixed interval of time as described in [36].

In cloud computing, data are easily updated, processed, and shared to multiple users in the distributed environment and accessible without any privacy breaches. Sharing database causes serious issues related to its security and privacy. Publishing sensitive data of a person can affect his/her life. It is observed in [37] that new CPGEN algorithms were developed and implemented multi-objective, optimization

Table 28.1 Security and privacy differentiation

S. no.	Security	Privacy
1	Security relate to CIA	Privacy is related to user information
2	Encryption and decryption algorithms are used for security	Third party cannot use data without permission of data owners
3	Confidentiality is provided in security	Concerned the data owner to maintain its data confidentiality
4	Security offers the capability of being confident, the decisions are honored	Privacy offers to decide what and to whom information be shared and at what extent

and multiple privacy constraints policies for implementation of algorithm. The transactional data can be used for secondary purpose such as for insurance companies. Graph-based manifold model used for data privacy is described in [38]. Further a new fuzzy system-based model was used for security and preserving privacy. Big healthcare data have potential uses in different ways. Data can be used for prediction, decision making, etc. Data are available in public cloud and not stored in the way that could be easily secured and implement privacy algorithms. The above paper mainly focuses on recent anonymization and encryption algorithms for securing and providing privacy in the best ways. EHRs provide different facilities, but these also compromise the privacy of patients' data. In this paper, authors implemented balanced $p+$- and k-anonymity. The method is analyzed and tested in SMT-Lib, Z3 Solver, and HLPN (high level petri Nets) model testing and verification [39]. Support vector machine classification is used for predicting the relationship, and it also shows that there exits an attribute based on rest of the attributes. SVM uses binary attribute in the work [40]. How the privacy preservation can be achieved with the help of decision tree classifier when our data are stored in distributed environment is described in [41, 42]. Various architectures are used for making EHR system. In electronic health records, authors [43] proposed a new three-tier architecture for healthcare system. The security and privacy of EHRs and WBAN (wireless body area network) can be implemented using ML and ANN on the data stored and implemented in the distributed system.

Table 28.1 shows the basic difference between security and privacy. In information and security area, both terms are sometimes interchanged. Still, it is necessarily to know the basic difference between them.

3   Basics of Privacy and Electronic Health Records

3.1   Privacy

There is no universal acceptable definition of "privacy," different people use their own privacy definition. Privacy has come to the notice when it became an important issue in the world. Though in 1948, under the Universal Declaration of Human Rights section privacy was recognized as a right, but to a confined scope such as

Table 28.2 Identifier discloser

ID	Age	Zip code	Country	Disease
1	27	14248	USA	HIV
2	28	14207	Canada	HIV
3	26	14206	USA	Cancer
4	25	14249	Canada	Cancer
5	41	13053	China	Phthisis
6	48	14064	Japan	Hepatitis
7	45	14062	India	Obesity
8	42	14248	India	Asthma
9	33	14204	USA	Flu
10	37	14205	Canada	Flu
11	36	14248	Canada	Flu
12	35	14248	USA	Indigestion

home and in correspondence. Its definition is very difficult to achieve as the privacy is applied in broad areas where data are shared and concerned to various types of information, so it is not easy to give a common definition.

The privacy preserving categories are mainly of three types:

1. Information: Relates to identification-based data attributes such as personal data.
2. Bodily: Deals to store invasive procedural.
3. Communication: Refers travelling of data from one end to another.

Privacy protection sometimes calls for the protection of individual personal data only, but for an organization and individual, apart from personal data, some sensitive data elements need to be secured as compared to personal information. This is especially for the celebrities of the society. So, the distribution data elements according to their categories are very important. On the bases on concrete and accurate dataset analyst can be able to provide a well and good prediction. In the information scope, Westin defined privacy as "the claim of individuals, groups, or institutions to determine for themselves when, how, and to what extent information about them is communicated to others." As defined in literature privacy is "the right of an individual to be secured from unauthorized disclosure of information about oneself that is contained in an electronic repository." Similar definitions have been proposed on the bases of monitoring and security of sensitive information. Privacy breaches can be understood with the help of Table 28.2. Table 28.2 shows that some data values are hidden after applying privacy mechanism on original data values as shown in Table 28.3.

3.2 Privacy Threats

Privacy threats are correlated to attributes and their type. Privacy threats are mainly of three types. The threats those affect the individual identification data such as

Table 28.3 Applied generalization on the original table

ID	Age	Zip code	Country	Disease
1	(27–28)	142**	America	HIV
2	(27–28)	142**	America	HIV
3	(27–28)	142**	America	Cancer
4	(27–28)	142**	America	Cancer
5	41	130**	Asia	Phthisis
6	48	140**	Asia	Hepatitis
7	45	140**	Asia	Obesity
8	42	142**	Asia	Asthma
9	33	142**	America	Flu
10	37	142**	America	Flu
11	36	142**	America	Flu
12	35	142**	America	Indigestion

**indicates hidden values

Table 28.4 Privacy threats

S. No	Privacy threat types	Attributes
1	Individual identification	Age, sex, phone number
2	Quasi-identification	Gender + DOB
3	Sensitive identification	Critical illness

name, age, sex, phone no., and email address are known as direct identification threats. The threats that related and affected the combination of attributes are dependable attributes and are known as quasi-identifiers such as combination of gender and date of birth and zip code can be able to disclose the identity of a person. Direct identifier attributes are mainly concerned to demographical data values. Sensitive data elements are the attributes such as HIV, cancer, hepatitis etc. which contains data value, data owner and are not willing associate these attributes, like if a person has been affected from affected sharply. Table 28.4 shows the different types of privacy threats. These threats are directly related to data stored in the databases as described in the above discussion.

3.3   EHR (Electronic Health Records)

EHRs (Electronic Health Records) are the software that are used for collecting, maintaining, and retrieving the data from EHR software by health professional and patients. Our EHRs are may be in centralized or distributed in nature. Database management in the EHR can design the scheme of horizontal or vertical data storage system. The EHR scheme is used in this fashion. Centralized electronic health records accumulate medical data of patients and provide the availability and accessibility 24 × 7. EHRs are not tied to a single medical institution. Now many enterprises are involved in this area. Google Health and Microsoft Vault

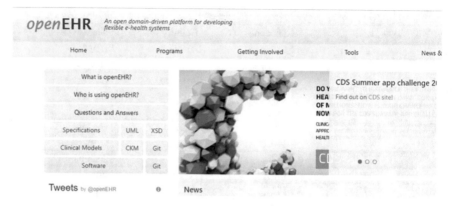

Fig. 28.1 OpenEHR

provided almost each and every function related to health record. OpenEHR is a well-known available software for health, insurance companies, and hospital management system all together to get the electronic database of providers of centralized EHR/PHR systems. Figure 28.1 shows the basic operation in EHR system.

OpenEHR is an open source software for storing, retrieving, and managing of electronic health record.

3.4 Requirements of Data Privacy in Electronic Health Records

The individual's privacy is among the most worried challenges about EHR data. In data stored in healthcare system, information loss can put a high impact of an individuals' personal and professional life. Healthcare data are increasingly being digitized as electronic health records, medical images, and physician notes. Data redundancy has two sides in EHRs, one that it is of great help to healthcare sector, and the second one is that it poses a high threat on patient's data privacy because of its easy accessibility.

Data Partitioning Models: In the era of Internet and cloud storage and computing, data are stored and collected from various resources. If data are stored centralized then privacy mechanism is not required. In distributed environment data are stored at various storage areas and collection of these data are ubiquitous, require more privacy preserving mechanism for protection of individual privacy. In collaborating companies' model, privacy preservation mainly focused on the key question that how control is distributed when data are stored and shared among different parties. In the concern of privacy preserving point of view, the easiest way to solve is to divide the control of data ownership. From privacy point of view the access of data reside at a single site and at different site, requires different accessibility algorithms and more attention for proper privacy preserving mechanism. For these data partitioning models are required. There are basically two data partitioning or data distribution models:

1. Horizontal partitioning
2. Vertical partitioning

In general, a dataset D is known as set of entities and information are stored in each entity. Thus $D = (E, I)$, where E is entity set and I denotes the information feature set related to that entity.

Horizontal Partitioning: Horizontal partitioning is also known as homogenous distribution of data, where we assume that different sites have collected similar information set for different entities. For example, in banking system, all banks collect same set of information from different sites.

Vertical Partitioning: Vertical partitioning is also known as heterogeneous distribution data, where we assume that different sites collect different feature sets for same entities. Vertical partitioning used joining mechanism for linking information. For example, Tata Motor collects the vehicle manufacturing information and Maruti Suzuki collects the tire information. Vehicle information is joined with tire information, in this case it is known as vertical portioning distribution and linked data.

4   Privacy Models and Privacy Techniques

4.1   Privacy-Preserving Data Mining Models and Algorithms

Privacy Model: In privacy model, we will discover those models that are used in transforming the data from one end to other destination point and to ensure the privacy protection. Although these methods reduce the granularity of representation in order to reduce the privacy. The granularity reduction can change the loss of information or in a file that is in sharing mode, data can be hidden. These reductions sometimes granulate information or provide less utility services, so there are some cases when information could be lost. There exists trade-off between privacy persevering and information loss. Privacy model-based techniques and examples are as follows.

4.1.1   The Randomization Method

The randomization is a technique used in a classical way to manage the data privacy. This technique is used to hide the data after overlapping probability distribution. The method of randomization can be understood in the following.

Suppose X is an original dataset containing different attributes

$$X = \{x1, x2, x3 \ldots xn\} \tag{28.1}$$

and a distorted component such as noise is added in dispute mask $[nv]$, then database X becomes

$$X = \{X = x1 + x2 + x3 + xn\} + nv. \tag{28.2}$$

4.1.2 The Anonymity Model

The k-anonymity model was developed by Latanya Sweeney. In quasi-identifier, this is basically a combination of attributes. The leakage of this attributes' values is known as attack on it and disclosure of the privacy of dataset. k-anonymity can be defined as

$$\text{Let } RT = (a1, a2, , a3..an) \tag{28.3}$$

RT is a relation and $Q1$ (list of attributes) associated with RT (table).

Now k-anonymity satisfied condition if and only if sequences of values of $RT(qi)$ and occurrence of items are as

$$K = RT(qi). \tag{28.4}$$

Anonymity is calculated in Eq. (28.4). k-anonymity is good algorithm. It can be applied in two ways:

1. Generalization
2. Suppression

However, k-anonymity can be attacked by unsorted matching attacks on the database.

4.1.3 Distributed Privacy Preservation

In many cases, data are stored in distributed environment e.g., in various cities, countries or available over internet. To access the quasi-identifier and individual entities may become a cause of attack if not managed properly. Distributed privacy presentation is used to manage the privacy preservation. The final result will be the aggregated result.

Table 28.5 summarizes the privacy model available in the literature. Each model has its own benefits and drawbacks. Some models used only numeric values, while some models use only nonnumeric attribute values. The selection of model is dependent upon the requirements of the cases. The hybrid model provided a best

Table 28.5 Summary of privacy model

Model	Technology	Algorithms used	Attacks
k-joint anonymity model	Generalization, suppression	k-joint anonymity	Linkage attack + background knowledge attacks
L-diversify	Domain generalization	Based on k-anonymity algorithms	Skewness attacks + similarity attacks
T-closeness	Domain generalization, sensitive value distribution	EMD measurement	Similarity attacks
P+, k-anonymity	Generalization,		Homogeneous attacks + linkage attacks
P-sensitivity, k-anonymity, neighborhood search	Clustering	Nearest neighbor search	Background + homogenous attack
Adaptive utility based	Association mining	Adaptive utility based anonymization	Background + homogenous attack

result as combination of k-anonymity, p+ algorithms is used for sensitive data privacy, while l-diversity is used for best in de-identification and if both are used the k-anonymity presented best results instead of individual execution of the algorithms.

As discussed earlier that privacy has no common definition yet various metrics have been proposed in the context of PPDM. Since the privacy has to pass through multiple parameters, no single metric is enough for evaluation. There are three main categories of metrics related to privacy, and they totally depend upon what to measure. Privacy level metrics are used to measure and specify the security of data disclosure, thus, data quality metrics quantify the loss of information/utility and complexity metrics measure efficiency and scalability of the different techniques.

4.2 Privacy Metrics Level and Data Quality

1. *Privacy Metrics*: Data metrics and result metrics are two subsets of privacy metrics. In data metrics various privacy algorithms such as randomization or perturbation are used and the resultant obtained in secure data form. Result metrics evaluates in the similar way, but applies classifiers for data mining and stores it in transformed data. Preserving a certain level of privacy and maintaining the maximum utility of data are the main aims of PPDM, as discussed earlier. The

Table 28.6 Original data

Age	Sex	Zip code	Disease
21	M	53909	Anemia
26	M	53909	Flu
32	F	53810	Cancer
36	F	53710	Toen ACL
48	M	52100	Flu
56	F	52100	Whiplash

Table 28.7 Generalized data
$k - 2$

Age	Sex	Zip code	Disease
21–30	M	53909–53920	Anemia
26–30	M	53909–53920	Flu
32–40	F	53710–53810	Cancer
36–40	F	53710–53810	Toen ACL
48–60	M	52100–52108	Flu
56–60	F	52100–52108	Whiplash

privacy metrics' level quantifies the data security at given possible attacks. In this scenario, data privacy metrics measures sensitive information hide front the original data and results metrics shows how much data disclosed to the original data.

Table 28.7 shows that how the value in range available in Table 28.6 is changed, so that individual data of patient will not be predicted and thus the rule of privacy is maintained on the basis of k-anonymity.

First privacy metrics measures confidence. Confidence used additive noise-based randomization method. This method estimates how much the values are changed using randomization and how the original value changed after applying randomization. Suppose, the original value lies in between an interval of [$x1$; $x2$] and $c\%$ is confidence level, then the interval $x2$ with respect to $x1$ is called the amount of privacy at $c\%$ confidence. This method also fails to solve in the distribution of original data in confidence level in a smaller interval than [$x1$; $x2$] with the same $c\%$ confidence.

In multiplicative noise, randomization method is used to maintain the privacy of information and the differences between original data and perturbation data can be measured. Suppose x is the attribute storing single value and variable z distorted value. Then Var (x & z) shows the variance between original values and perturbation values in dataset. For perturbation, k-anonymization techniques can be applied. k-anonymization techniques include various algorithms such as l-diversity and t-closeness for suppressed and generalized data. The different privacy techniques estimate certain level of privacy and hide the prime- or quasi-based disclosure and sensitive data disclosure from the original dataset. In broad metrics specify following techniques.

2. *Data Quality*: Privacy preservation may degrade data quality. Applying data quality metrics may loss the important data values and thus degrade its functionality and force to adopt the utility loss. In general, result is compared

with original dataset and privacy-preserved transformed dataset after applying privacy preserving techniques. The data quality metrics mainly have three parameters: accuracy, completeness, and consistency. Accuracy shows how much transformed data are closed to original dataset and completeness calculates the loss of individual data value and data stored in the new data while consistency deals with quality of loss in sanitized data from original dataset.

4.3   Privacy Techniques

4.3.1   Algorithms Against Identity Disclosure

Preventing the identity disclosure needs that quasi-identifier applies privacy methods in a way that data utility could not degrade. However, most privacy preserving techniques are failed to maintain the utility optimization in transformed dataset. The possible solution to maintain identity disclosure effectively is to use heuristic strategies on individual prime identity attribute. Based on this, algorithms are classified further.

Transforming Quasi-Identifiers: Three main techniques are used to transform quasi-identifiers for preventing identity disclosure:

1. Microaggregation
2. Generalization
3. Suppression

Microaggregation techniques replace a group of values in a Quasi-identifiers (QID) using a summary statistics (e.g., centroid or median for numerical and categorical QIDs, respectively). This technique has been applied mainly on demographics effectively but not in diagnosis codes.

On the other side, generalization applied the QID value replacement on the basis of semantic consistency. There are two generalization models used for privacy preservation, one is called global and the other is known as local recoding.

1. Global recoding involves mapping the domain of QIDs into generalized values. These values correspond to aggregate concepts (e.g., British instead of English, for Ethnicity) or collections of values (e.g., English or Welsh for ethnicity, or 18–30 for age). Thus, all occurrences of a certain value (e.g., English) in a dataset will be generalized to the same value (e.g., European).
2. Local recoding works on group basis for mapping of individual record into generalized records. Like value stored in Americans English in two different records, can be replaced in one record for preventing identity disclosure.

Thus, in existing methods, data utility can be preserved by following general strategies:

1. Quantify the loss of information using an optimization measure.

2. Assuming data to be used in specific analysis tasks and attempting to preserve its accuracy on published data.
3. Accounting utility requirements specified by data owners only and generating that data as per their requirements.

In this way, capturing data utility by measuring the information loss is incurred by data transformation.

5 Data Protection and Privacy Preserving Laws

1. *Canada*: Canada government has formulated the (PIPEDA) law for the safety of its citizen The Personal Information Protection and Electronic Documents Act (PIPEDA) describes complete rules for data collection, uses, and disclosure of the individual information by the third party. The PIPEDA clearly defines the necessity of laws in the health sector and Canadian people can easily understand the requirements and reason of this important law that how the individual data are protected by laws.
2. *Morocco*: In morocco, PDPA, the personal data protection act (09-08 act), saves the individual information and maintains the privacy of data while using personal and sensitive data. Data controllers are responsible for maintaining and controlling the safety of individuals' privacy by restricting the personal disclosure that specifies the sensitive data during the operation.
3. *European-Union*: European Convention on Human Rights article 8 provided "right to privacy" in private and family life. Medical data might be disclosed at EHR's side, therefore, EU government provided a strong privacy law. European commission, every year, announces the data protection directive for data protection and privacy. All European Countries adopted its IT a data protection law.
4. *United States*: HIPAA, The Health Insurance Portability and Accountability Act (HIPAA) is a law passed by the president Obama, which states that an individual identity could not be breached and identifiable health information should have the following:

   (a) HIPAA included almost all privacy and security laws and applied them in all 50 states.
   (b) If it is necessary to disclose the individual information, then it is mandatory to authorize the data from the owner of the laws.
   (c) Only owner has the right to disclose individual data if required for further execution in health-related issues.

5. *India*: Personal information is stored in UID. UID is used with health record to identify personal and demographic information while linking this information with medical artifacts. Thus, it is easy to attack on identity and sensitive data if improperly linked on EHR systems. All health record systems must therefore

adhere to the following standards for capturing information related to patient demography and identifiers. In broad sense, Indian IT2012, act:

(a) ISO/TS 22220:2011 Health Informatics—Identification of Subjects of Health Care
(b) MDDS—Demographic (Person Identification and Land Region Codification)

Some directives are proposed by the Government of India for implementing the strategy on privacy and security of health record:

1. It is the responsibility of implementers to ensure that all data- related fields are subjected to the health record application as discussed in above two standards.
2. The implementors should ensure that system is able to receive all information when required in MDDS compliant format as per that standard. Where codes related to location, authority, type of organization, etc., are required, they should be taken from the MDDS-demographic standard.

A health record system must have provision to include patient identifiers of following types:

1. UIDAI Aadhaar Number (preferred where available)
2. In case Aadhaar is not available:

(a) Local identifier (as per scheme used by HSP)
(b) Any Central or State Government issued Photo Identity Card Number

Carrying out Guidelines of data protection and privacy are as follows (Table 28.8):

1. Aadhaar number must serve as unique health identifier that is to be ensured and mandatory for implementers. In the absence of Aadhaar number, system must allow the user to insert at least two other identifiers. Sometimes, there is a situation where no identifier is available, then a temporary identifier may be set and later confirmed identifier should replace in a given span of time. In situations where identity of patient cannot be obtained or ascertained, temporary identifiers may be used (as per scheme used by HSP) and later confirmed identifiers may be inserted (while making earlier ones as inactive).
2. Patient's identification on EHRs: Aadhaar number (UID) is not mandatory for keeping record of patients in electronic health record system, thus, it becomes difficult to match patient's record when required to exchange the records on distributed EHR system. The consequence is that identity of a person can be used at different locations by different peoples for unusual purposes.

Table 28.8 Data protection laws

Country	Law	Salient features
EU	Data Protection Directive	Protect peoples' fundamental rights and freedom and particular right to privacy
UK	Data Protection Act (DPA)	Individual can control their information themselves. Freedom to right and protection levels
Russia	Russian federal law of personal data	Required data operators to take preventive action against the unlawful action
Moracco	09-08 Act, in 2009	CNDP authority will ensure the protection of sensitive and personal data by data controllers
Brazil	Constitution	Private life, honor, and image of people are inviolable right
India	IT Act and IT Amendment Act "right to privacy" Act	Implement reasonable partial security, secure the personal data Make a law on "right to privacy" also known as fundamental right No
USA	HIPPA ACT and PSQIA HITECH ACT	Make national health standards, patients' safety work product Protect privacy and security of EHRs

6 Privacy Application

Privacy-preserving data mining (PPDM) has numerous applications. In almost every field of area weather it is related to science, arts, and commerce, data mining is required the most. In general PPDM is used in multidisciplinary area; some of them are presented in this chapter. As discussed above in various sections, privacy is now known as "right of an individual.". Protected individual data privacy is applied in almost every sector area. In this section, we will discuss a number of different applications of privacy-preserving data mining methods.

Application of PPDM can be classified in different ways. The main areas of application are further sectioned in groups such as Cloud computing, WSN (Wireless Sensor Network), and LBS (Location Based Services).

6.1 Cloud Computing PPDM

The U.S. National Institute of Standards and Technology (NIST) defined the cloud computing as "a model for enabling ubiquitous, on-demand network access to share pool of configurable computing resources that can be rapidly provisioned and realized with minimal management effort or service provider integration.". In other words, cloud uses distributed infrastructure accessible through Internet. In cloud architecture, everything is working as a service. Cloud computing development models are based on location. It can be public cloud, private cloud, or community cloud, it totally depends on the requirement of the organization. Cloud architectures use SaaS, PaaS, and IaaS terminology which means software as a service, platform as a service, and infrastructure as a service, respectively. In cloud computing, our data are stored anywhere in the world and as we have discussed in previous sections that every country has its own privacy standards, regulation, and laws regarding privacy preservation; thus, it is necessarily to protect our data on the cloud that require more attention. The privacy preserving techniques are required mainly when the data are shared or stored in distributed computing. Privacy preserving auditing control and query control techniques play a stringent role for data protection.

6.2   EHR Databases

In EHRs data are stored in distribution partitioning way. Two most important medical systems The scrub and Datafly are used by various clinics for maintaining clinical data. Scrub data system is used to deidentify clinical notes and letters as most of clinical data are in the form of text and images. Clinical reports mostly use abbreviations. These abbreviations are either understood by the algorithms or the persons who know the medical terminology. So on the basis of clinical data, a person's identification is not easy and a maximum of 30–40% data can be identified. The different algorithms are used by the scrub system when a block of text corresponded to address, phone number, and name. These algorithms compete with each in scrub system. The local knowledge sources are used by the scrub system for finding the results on the basis of their values comparing with each other. The scrub system success rate of removing the identifiable information from the data is more than 97%.

The Datafly systems are well-known systems for privacy preservation of transformations of electronic health records. Datafly systems are used to store and design the multidimensional formats. The multidimensional format stores different data and some of them are used indirectly or directly for identification. Information is identified directly from SSN and indirectly from the combination of age, zip code, and sex.

The Datafly system assumes that removing of direct identification variable is not only guaranteeing the privacy preservation of any individual data. Datafly stem uses anonymity method such as k-anonymity and l-diversity for maintaining the privacy of medical data. k-Anonymity method can be used for preventing from linked attacks. The suppression method of k-anonymity is applied on outlier values for preventing the identification. In Datafly system, users set the anonymity level on the basis of recipient queries. In general, anonymity levels are between 0 and 1, where 1 denotes the maximum level generalization and 0 indicates that Datafly system provides only original data.

6.3   Biological Terrorism

Biological terrorism is related to biological agents such as virus, toxins. EHRs stored patient's information related to diagnoses, medical reports, and other demographical data. Sometimes biological agents such as fungi affect the patient's medical data that are displaced on the databases and reflect that patients are facing critical illness, and on the basis of these biological agents, privacy of patients' information is leaked. Other common symptoms like anthrax used in many diseases. Common symptoms may be the cause of disclosing the sensitive data. The sharing of data from different stakeholders of these patients records those are affecting by this symptoms may violated privacy preserving rule therefore best way to find the solution is that selective portion of data are allowed to access to authorized user.

6.4   Household Security

There are number of applications used in home security because of its nature of surveillance. The main concern is to implement the household security system for preventing privacy of the individual. Credential identification, verification problem, and identity theft come in this category. In this, system should match the identification credential of a person presented in the home site. For example, the theft of SSN poses a serious threat. The SSN is semantically associated with other attributes to validate the credential of the person and justify that these data truly own it. A new technology identity theft is used to avoid the identity theft. Advanced intelligent identity angel is used to crawl cyberspace, and identify the persons who are at alarming risk of losing identity.

6.5   Web Camera Based Surveillance

Today, a common technology is used for publicly surveillance, that is, web camera. With the help of webcam unusual activities are easily analyzed and detected. Webcam surveillance works on images and finds out the features of a persons' information. It is an invasive approach used for surveillance. The method used in webcam can store sensitive information for extracting facial count from the images and comparison of data detects the unusual activities. It makes an assumption that unusual activities are monitored to detect on the basis of facial feature count instead of a specific particular of a person. The webcam surveillance is mostly used in specific domain. This strategy downgrades the privacy of sensitive information.

6.6   The Watch List Problem

The government has a list of terrorists and suspected activists, and it needs a method to track their activities. The watch list approach provides a strategy to monitor this problem effectively. The watch list approach is applied to carry out monetary transitions in different areas such as hospitals, hotels, airlines, and store purchases. It is a very tedious task to monitor the transactional data, because transactional data are private and concerned privacy is subjective, and it even does not appear in the record list, therefore, it needs a stringent action to protect these transactional data for maintaining privacy of sensitive information. Hence, the transactional behavior of suspected activists may be identified with the help of watch list.

6.7   Genomic Privacy

In the last three decades DNA sequencing and forensic analysis have changed as advancement of biotechnology and data sciences. Medical record database has grown up at fast rate and preserving the privacy of medical data is facing difficulty to manage properly. DNA data are considered very sensitive, because these identify a person uniquely. When data are stored in multi dimensions and in distributed system, simply removing a unique attribute is not sufficient in preventing the re-identification of the person. One of the popular software such as Clean Gene has capabilities to identify a person independently. DNA identification is not necessarily dependent on other demographical attributes. The clean gene identifies the person's particular disease on the basis of available knowledge in the system. The software relies on publicly available medical data and knowledge of particular diseases in order to assign identifications to DNA entries. It has been reported that 98% of individual are identified easily using this approach. Genome approach works on the basis of DNA sequencing and then constructing a genetic profile of the individual with other attributes such as sex, age, and disease. This approach is more effective in small scale of grouping. k-anonymity method can be applied on genetic profile for securing the personal identification. Anonymity methods such as generalization and suppression are quite effective to prevent re-identification of a person. With the help of k-anonymity individual data are not distinguished in $(k - 1)$ entities. Second approach used in genome is to construct synthetic data adding noise on original data. The patients' data, when admitted in the hospital, are saved in the local or remote server and these genomic data can be used in near future for different purposes such as research, insurance companies, and government projects and policy making. Whatever action has been taken by the patient or doctor, the data patterns are encoded in the portal and released in the distributed system. The patients' published data at public domain can be further combined with genomic profile to reidentify the uniqueness of a person.

6.8   Location Based Services PPDM

Global position system (GPS) is a new pervasive technology used to find out the accurate location of a device. LBS uses spatial temporal data for searching the device or a person carrying those devices. Location information of a person can be leaked and thus it violates the privacy standards and regulations. To protect the location privacy, PPDM techniques such as anonymity and data perturbation can be applied with query control and audit control techniques for persons' privacy.

7   Conclusion and Future Directions

In the past few years, the field of privacy preserving data mining in domain of EHRs has suitable techniques to address privacy preserving tasks. The future direction is mainly related to adopting EHRs. Privacy preservation is applied in every field and electronic health record is not escaped from this technology. PPDM techniques have not fully adopted in real-world applications such as EHRs, WBSN (Wireless Body Area Network), WSN (Wireless Sensor Networks), Smart Grid Security, Forensic investigation, Biomedical Information and technology, Smart Metering system, and many more. The adoption of privacy preservation in these fields is required in priority bases.

In the last two decades the adoption of EHR increased drastically and required new safety measures for patient's information. For this, technologies should implement privacy preserving data mining techniques with machine learning, deep learning, and artificial intelligence in its EHRs. Other route for adoption is to integrate the PPDM with existing application so that existing system can be protected and its stakeholder data are secured. Personalized privacy is challenging to implement. On one side it emphasizes to ownership right to control the data. The different standards and regulation guidelines show that users have to control over the specifics of their data. This might affect the full utilization of data for fruitful results and this tends to trade-off between privacy preservation and utility. Thus, it is also harmful when user is aware of privacy risks of data disclosure. On the other hand, if user is not directly or indirectly involved in privacy preserving mechanism, then sensitive data can be hacked and misused by the third party without the consent of patients. So, personalized data control can create privacy and utility trade-off. Therefore, a proper context-based data personalized control access from patient's side is required for further research. Homogeneous encryption and various transfer protocols are used for privacy preserving data mining, but many of them create the trade-off between functionality efficiency. There is scope of developing effective and more efficient protocol to increase the technological application of security and privacy preservation. Today, ubiquitous computing is used in many areas for data collection, processing, and operating the action. WSN, WBAN, and Smart Grid are different areas that require more scope of data privacy and security. Context-based privacy can be accomplished and applied in these areas. Context-based privacy takes action when states of its agents are changed and its new or changeable policies are applied accordingly. However, it is very difficult to make policies for every ubiquity.

References

1. Bos, J. W., Lauter, K., & Naehrig, M. (2014). Private predictive analysis on encrypted medical data. *Journal of Biomedical Informatics, 50,* 234–243.
2. Li, M., Yu, S., Ren, K., & Lou, W. (2010, September). Securing personal health records in cloud computing: Patient-centric and fine-grained data access control in multi-owner settings. In *International Conference on Security and Privacy in Communication Systems* (pp. 89–106). Berlin: Springer.
3. Fan, L., Buchanan, W., Thummler, C., Lo, O., Khedim, A., Uthmani, O., & Bell, D. (2011, July). DACAR platform for eHealth services cloud. In *Cloud Computing (CLOUD), 2011 IEEE International Conference on* (pp. 219–226). Los Alamitos: IEEE.
4. Squicciarini, A. C., Hintoglu, A. A., Bertino, E., & Saygin, Y. (2007, June). A privacy preserving assertion based policy language for federation systems. In *Proceedings of the 12th ACM Symposium on Access Control Models and Technologies* (pp. 51–60). New York: ACM.
5. Jurczyk, P., & Xiong, L. (2009). Distributed anonymization: Achieving privacy for both data subjects and data providers. In E. Gudes & J. Vaidya (Eds.), *Data and applications security XXIII. DBSec 2009* (Lecture notes in computer science) (Vol. 5645). Berlin: Springer.
6. Abbas, A., & Khan, S. U. (2014). A review on the state-of-the-art privacy-preserving approaches in the e-health clouds. *IEEE Journal of Biomedical and Health Informatics, 18*(4), 1431–1441.
7. Goldman, J., & Hudson, Z. (2000). Virtual exposed: Privacy and eHealth. *Health Affairs, 19,* 140–148.
8. Clifton, C., & Anandan, B. (2013, December). Challenges and opportunities for security with differential privacy. In *International Conference on Information Systems Security* (pp. 1–13). Berlin: Springer.
9. Mohammed, N., Chen, R., Fung, B., & Yu, P. S. (2011, August). Differentially private data release for data mining. In *Proceedings of the 17th ACM SIGKDD International Conference on Knowledge Discovery and Data Mining* (pp. 493–501). New York: ACM.
10. Pommerening, K., & Reng, M. (2004). Secondary use of the EHR via pseudonymization. In *Medical care compunetics on system sciences* (pp. 441–446). Amsterdam: IOS Press.
11. Li, M., Yu, S., Ren, K., & Lou, W. (2010). Securing personal health records in cloud computing: Patient-centric and fine-grained data access control in multi-owner settings. In S. Jajodia & J. Zhou (Eds.), *Security and Privacy in Communication Networks. SecureComm 2010. Lecture Notes of the Institute for Computer Sciences, Social Informatics and Telecommunications Engineering* (Vol. 50). Berlin: Springer.
12. Chen, T. S., Liu, C. H., Chen, T. L., Chen, C. S., Bau, J. G., & Lin, T. C. (2012). Secure dynamic access control scheme of PHR in cloud computing. *Journal of Medical Systems, 36*(6), 4005–4020.
13. Zhang, R., Liu, L., & Xue, R. (2013). Role – Based and time bound access and management of HER data. *Security and communication Networks, 7*(6), 994–1015.
14. Ueckert, F., & Prokosch, H. U. (2002). Implementing security and access control mechanism for an healthcare record. In *Proceedings of the AMIA Symposium* (pp. 825–829). Bethesda: American Medical Informatics Association.

15. Hu, J., Chen, H. H., & Hou, T. W. (2010). A hybrid public key infrastructure solution (HPKI) for HIPAA privacy/security regulations. *Computer Standards & Interface, 32*(5–6), 274–280.
16. Jafari, M., Safavi-Naini, R., Saunders, C., & Sheppard, N. P. (2010). Using digital rights management for securing data in a medical research environment. In *Proceedings of the Tenth Annual ACM Workshop on Digital Rights Management* (pp. 55–60). New York: ACM.
17. Rothstein, M. A. (2007). Health privacy in the electronic age. *The Journal of Legal Medicine, 28*(4), 487–501.
18. Farzandipour, M., Sadought, F., Ahmadi, M., & Karimi, I. (2010). Security requirement and solutions in electronic health record: Lessons learned from a comparative study. *Journal of Medical Systems, 34*(4), 629–642.
19. Aggarwal, C. C., & Philip, S. Y. (2008). A general survey of privacy-preserving data mining models and algorithms. In *Privacy-preserving data mining* (pp. 11–52). Boston: Springer.
20. Sweeney, L. (2002). K-anonymity: A model for protecting privacy. *International Journal of Uncertainty, Fuzziness and Knowledge-Based Systems, 10*(05), 557–570.
21. Martínez, S., Sánchez, D., & Valls, A. (2013). A semantic framework to protect the privacy of electronic health records with non-numerical attributes. *Journal of Biomedical Informatics, 46*(2), 294–303.
22. Fernández-Alemán, J. L., Señor, I. C., Lozoya, P. Á. O., & Toval, A. (2013). Security and privacy in electronic health records: A systematic literature review. *Journal of Biomedical Informatics, 46*(3), 541–562.
23. Ghazvini, A., & Shukur, Z. (2013). Security challenges and success factors of electronic healthcare system. *Procedia Technology, 11*, 212–219.
24. Gkoulalas-Divanis, A., Loukides, G., & Sun, J. (2014). Publishing data from electronic health records while preserving privacy: A survey of algorithms. *Journal of Biomedical Informatics, 50*, 4–19.
25. Wang, H., Wu, Q., Qin, B., & Domingo-Ferrer, J. (2014). FRR: Fair remote retrieval of outsourced private medical records in electronic health networks. *Journal of Biomedical Informatics, 50*, 226–233.
26. Deleger, L., Lingren, T., Ni, Y., Kaiser, M., Stouten borough, L., Marsolo, K., & Solti, I. (2014). Preparing an annotated gold standard corpus to share with extramural investigators for de-identification research. *Journal of Biomedical Informatics, 50*, 173–183.
27. Randall, S. M., Ferrante, A. M., Boyd, J. H., Bauer, J. K., & Semmens, J. B. (2014). Privacy-preserving record linkage on large real world datasets. *Journal of Biomedical Informatics, 50*, 205–212.
28. Loukides, G., Liagouris, J., Gkoulalas-Divanis, A., & Terrovitis, M. (2014). Disassociation for electronic health record privacy. *Journal of Biomedical Informatics, 50*, 46–61.
29. Sánchez, D., Batet, M., & Viejo, A. (2014). Utility-preserving privacy protection of textual healthcare documents. *Journal of Biomedical Informatics, 52*, 189–198.
30. Fu, A. W. C., Wang, K., Wong, R. C. W., Wang, J., & Jiang, M. (2014). Small sum privacy and large sum utility in data publishing. *Journal of Biomedical Informatics, 50*, 20–31.
31. Meystre, S. M., Ferrández, Ó., Friedlin, F. J., South, B. R., Shen, S., & Samore, M. H. (2014). Text de-identification for privacy protection: A study of its impact on clinical text information content. *Journal of Biomedical Informatics, 50*, 142–150.
32. Yu, F., Fienberg, S. E., Slavković, A. B., & Uhler, C. (2014). Scalable privacy-preserving data sharing methodology for genome-wide association studies. *Journal of Biomedical Informatics, 50*, 133–141.
33. Gursoy, M. E., Inan, A., Nergiz, M. E., & Saygin, Y. (2017). Privacy-preserving learning analytics: Challenges and techniques. *IEEE Transactions on Learning Technologies, 10*(1), 68–81.
34. Mendes, R., & Vilela, J. P. (2017). Privacy-preserving data mining: Methods, metrics, and applications. *IEEE Access, 5*, 10562–10582.
35. Majeed, A. (2018). Attribute-centric anonymization scheme for improving user privacy and utility of publishing e-health data. *Journal of King Saud University-Computer and Information Sciences.* In press.

36. Kulkarni, Y. R., & Senthil Murugan, T. (2016). Genetic grey wolf optimization and C-mixture for collaborative data publishing. *International Journal of Modeling, Simulation, and Scientific Computing, 9*(06), 1850058.
37. Wang, L. E., & Li, X. (2018). A graph-based multifold model for anonymizing data with attributes of multiple types. *Computers & Security, 72*, 122–135.
38. Abouel mehdi, K., Beni-Hessane, A., & Khaloufi, H. (2018). Big healthcare data: Preserving security and privacy. *Journal of Big Data, 5*(1), 1.
39. Anjum, A., Choo, K. K. R., Khan, A., Haroon, A., Khan, S., Khan, S. U., & Raza, B. (2018). An efficient privacy mechanism for electronic health records. *Computers & Security, 72*, 196–211.
40. Kamateri, E., Kalampokis, E., Tambouris, E., & Tarabanis, K. (2014). The linked medical data access control framework. *Journal of Biomedical Informatics, 50*, 213–225.
41. Yu, H., Vaidya, J., & Jiang, X. (2006, April). Privacy-preserving SVM classification on vertically partitioned data. In *Pacific-Asia Conference on Knowledge Discovery and Data Mining* (pp. 647–656). Berlin: Springer.
42. Brickell, J., & Shmatikov, V. (2008, August). The cost of privacy: Destruction of data-mining utility in anonymized data publishing. In *Proceedings of the 14th ACM SIGKDD International Conference on Knowledge Discovery and Data Mining* (pp. 70–78). New York: ACM.
43. Wang, J., Zhang, Z., Yang, X., Zuo, L., & Kim, J. U. (2013). *Data security and privacy of e-healthcare in electronic medical environment* (Vol. 22, pp. 92–98). ASTL SIA.

Chapter 29
QKD Protocols Security Between Theory and Engineering Implementation

Hicham Amellal, Abdelmajid Meslouhi, Abderahim El Allati, and Anass El Haddadi

Abstract Quantum cryptography is proposed as a big revolution in IT security, even some theoretical studies considered that the exploitation of quantum physics features can enable us to get unconditional security. With the passage of time, appeared the quantum cryptanalysis which includes in the beginning a collection of theoretical quantum hacking strategies. However, the implementation of quantum key distribution protocols (QKD) showed several vulnerabilities in quantum cryptography scheme, which exploited to spy on the quantum communication. Therefore, the engineering implementation of QKD protocols showed a significant difference between the theoretical promises and experiment results. In order to make QKD protocols more applicable in real security solutions, we analyze in this contribution the variation of the security level of QKD protocols between the quantum theory and the implementation phase. In the same context, we focus on the quantum attacks via exploiting the vulnerabilities of classical devises using in the implementation phase and these impact on the security level of QKD.

Keywords Information security · QKD protocols · Quantum hacking strategies · Vulnerabilities

H. Amellal (✉)
Department of Computer Science, Faculty of Science, University Mohamed 5, Rabat, Morocco

A. Meslouhi
Department of Physics, Faculty of Science, University Mohamed 5, Rabat, Morocco

A. El Allati
Department of Physics, FST El-hoceima, University Abdelmalek Essaadi, Tétouan, Morocco

A. El Haddadi
DSCI Team - NSAS Al-Hoceima, University Abdelmalek Essaadi, Tétouan, Morocco

DSCI Team - NSAS Al-Hoceima, Morocco

University Abdelmalek Essaadi, Tétouan, Morocco

© Springer Nature Switzerland AG 2020   741
B. B. Gupta et al. (eds.), *Handbook of Computer Networks and Cyber Security*,
https://doi.org/10.1007/978-3-030-22277-2_29

1 Introduction

Currently, IT security requirements are growing and the trend is definitely not down. In fact, all aspects of our modern life depend on information technology and their security: smart cities, cloud computing, IoT, and in various other areas [1–10]. Since antiquity, the cryptography is considered a very effective way to secure the information. Historically, the cryptography is developed with the intersection of mathematics, computer science, and currently quantum physics, especially after the entry of quantum key distribution in modern cryptography. Unfortunately, in turn the quantum communication has not escaped from quantum attacks. Recently emerged different quantum hacking strategies against quantum cryptography protocols, serving as the basis for the exploitation of vulnerabilities in protocols and devices used in quantum communication [11–15]. In fact, the quantum cryptography proposes a new technique to protect communication based on the physics of information instead of various mathematical solutions employed in classical cryptography [16–18]. Accordingly, quantum security based on some principles of quantum mechanics such as entanglement, superposition, no-cloning theorem, and the quantum measurement[19, 20]. In quantum process, to transfer and to store data is always based on physical means; this includes photons in optical fibers or electrons in electric current. Therefore, all attempts to penetrate quantum communication by a spy Eve can be viewed as measurements on a physical means, which makes the hacking process detectable. This is because measurements on the quantum carrier of information disturb it and so leave traces. All these quantum phenomena have made the theoretically cybersecurity closer than ever before to arrive at unconditional security level. Recently, the promises of quantum cryptography, it began to fade with the appearance of the quantum version of crypt-analysis science. Accordingly, many quantum hacking strategies have developed such as intercept and resend, entanglement-based attacks, and individual attacks in a realistic environment. Moreover, each hacking strategy includes different attacks, which increased the number of menaces in quantum communication [21–25]. The implementation of QKD protocols appeared other weakness specially in the classical material used in the communication scheme [26, 27].

The chapter is organized as follows: In Sect. 2, security analysis of quantum cryptography. In Sect. 3, vulnerabilities of QKD protocols in the implementation scheme. Finally, conclusions are drawn in the last section.

2 Security Analysis of Quantum Cryptography

Quantum cryptography or more precisely quantum key distribution is a new generation of encryption based on some quantum phenomena to develop a cryptosystem, which outperforms all present classical algorithms regarding the security level proposed. Accordingly, to take advantage of quantum cryptography was proposed a set of protocols to realize the quantum key distribution implementation, where the first quantum cryptographic protocol to appear in the literature was introduced by Charles Bennett and Gilles Brassard in 1984, which known for its acronym BB84 [28].

2.1 Some Examples of Implementation

The first implementation of the quantum key distribution is carried out by the Swiss company "id Quantum," which transmitted in 2004 a large financial transaction. In 2007 the same company transmitted the results of the national elections in Geneva. QKD is also of interest to the US Agency for Advanced Military Research "Darpa" and the European Union which has developed the project "Secoqc." Recently, several missions, with varying scopes, are bringing space-based QKD closer to reality. The Chinese quantum satellite Micius was brought into orbit in August 2016 and carries a series of quantum-optical experiments by Shanghai Engineering Center for Microsatellites. Micius involved a huge platform carrying a technology demonstrator, whereas missions aiming to commercialize satellite-based QKD will need to target a miniaturized, more cost-effective approach. In the same context, in 29 September 2017, the first intercontinental video conference using Micius, between the presidents of the Austrian and Chinese academies of science. The cryptographic key pair used by the stations in Vienna and Beijing had been generated using an optical QKD payload aboard the Chinese satellite mission. Accordingly, this experience was of more than just academic interest, because a space-based QKD infrastructure could prove an important approach indeed, perhaps the only really viable long-term solution to secure worldwide communications. However, this experience provides an overview of QKD's principles and engineering challenges, and how a satellite-based QKD network might roll out in the coming years, which made it possible to establish new standards in quantum cryptography.

2.2 Quantum Cryptography Security Basis

QKD is based on several quantum principles. It exploits the fact that an attacker cannot clone a set of non-orthogonal states, and hence cannot measure them without going detected. Generally, QKD security based on some quantum phenomena such as: entanglement, no-cloning theorem, the measurement theory, and the superposition.

2.2.1 Entanglement

Entanglement is a quantum phenomenon, highlighted in the years 30 [29–35]. Generally, it is said that two or more objects are "entangled" when they form an inseparable entity, so that the state quantum of the two objects must be described globally, without being able to separate an object from the other. Subsequently, any measurement on one of the systems affects the second system, regardless of the distance between them. Accordingly, in the engineering approach, the entanglement implemented based on the protocol of teleportation, which considered as a protocol of quantum communication, to transfer the quantum state of a system to another system similar and spatially separated from the first, putting profit the quantum entanglement. The principle of the transfer of quantum information consists in using a pair of entangled particles, for example two polarized photons. Moreover, the photons are shared between two interlocutors Alice and Bob, who can be separated by an arbitrary distance, where Alice has a third polarized photon, in an unknown quantum state. Thus, it performs a measurement that leads simultaneously to form a quantum system by the two photons in its possession. This instantly causes the teleportation of the unknown quantum state of the third photon, while destroying it. At this level, Bob cannot access the teleported quantum state. So, he has to wait for Alice to send him the result of her measurement. Finally, Bob can make a measurement of Alice's result photon, which will give him the information contained in the photon which was not entangled. We can describe the mathematical process of quantum teleportation as follows: We can represent a state whose total spin is zero where each element of global system to a $spin^{\frac{1}{2}}$ depending on the basis of calculation by:

$$|\psi\rangle = \frac{|0\rangle\,|1\rangle - |1\rangle\,|0\rangle}{\sqrt{2}} \tag{29.1}$$

We can do a Z measurement on the first particle, leaving the second particle alone with the help of the operator $Z \otimes I$. If we measure 0 for the first particle, the state of the second particle must be $|1\rangle$. Similarly, if we measure 1 for the first particle, the state of the second particle must be $|0\rangle$. We rewrite this state in terms of eigenvectors of the operator of X in the bases $|^{+}_{-}\rangle$. Recall that:

$$|0\rangle = \frac{|+\rangle\,|1\rangle + |-\rangle\,|0\rangle}{\sqrt{2}} \tag{29.2}$$

and

$$|1\rangle = \frac{|+\rangle\,|1\rangle - |-\rangle\,|0\rangle}{\sqrt{2}} \tag{29.3}$$

The first term of the preceding formula can be written as follows:

$$
\begin{aligned}
|0\rangle\,|1\rangle &= \left(\frac{|+\rangle + |-\rangle}{\sqrt{2}}\right)\left(\frac{|+\rangle - |-\rangle}{\sqrt{2}}\right) \\
&= \frac{1}{2}\left(|++\rangle + |-+\rangle - |+-\rangle - |--\rangle\right)
\end{aligned}
\tag{29.4}
$$

And the second term by:

$$|1\rangle\,|0\rangle = \left(\frac{|+\rangle - |-\rangle}{\sqrt{2}}\right)\left(\frac{|+\rangle + |-\rangle}{\sqrt{2}}\right)$$

$$= \frac{1}{2}\,(|++\rangle - |-+\rangle + |+-\rangle - |--\rangle)$$

$$= -\frac{|+-\rangle - |-+\rangle}{\sqrt{2}} \tag{29.5}$$

Therefore:

$$|\psi\rangle = \frac{|0\rangle\,|1\rangle - |1\rangle\,|0\rangle}{\sqrt{2}}$$

$$= \frac{1}{\sqrt{2}}\frac{1}{2}\,(|++\rangle + |-+\rangle - |+-\rangle - |--\rangle - |++\rangle + |-+\rangle - |+-\rangle + |--\rangle)$$

$$= -\frac{|+-\rangle - |-+\rangle}{\sqrt{2}} \tag{29.6}$$

If we measure the operator X for the first particle and get the result "+", the second particle must be in the state $|-\rangle$ and vice versa. Thus, several measures to determine the entanglement of a state $|\phi\rangle$. Accordingly, different measurement methods to determine the entanglement of a state are proposed, but the most used is the quantum concurrence, which represented mathematically by the following expression:

$$C\,(\phi) = \left|\left\langle \phi | \tilde{\phi} \right\rangle\right| \tag{29.7}$$

where $\left|\tilde{\phi}\right\rangle = Y \otimes Y$ and $|\phi^*\rangle$ the conjugate complex of the state $|\phi\rangle$. Teleportation protocol takes place in a series of stages. We start by creating an entangled EPR pair.

Step 1: Alice and Bob Share a Pair of Entangled Particles

Alice and Bob create the intricate state:

$$|\beta_{00}\rangle = \frac{|0_A\rangle\,|0_B\rangle + |1_A\rangle\,|1_B\rangle}{\sqrt{2}}$$

$$= \frac{|00\rangle + |11\rangle}{\sqrt{2}} \tag{29.8}$$

It is considered that the first pair member belongs to Alice and the second pair member belongs to Bob. Now, Alice and Bob physically separate. Alice decides that she wants to send a quantum state to Bob. It can do this by letting it interact with the first peer EPR.

Step 2: Alice Applies a CNOT Gate

Let's start by writing $|\chi\rangle$ the state of the whole system which is the product of the unknown state and the pair EPR:

$$|\chi\rangle = |\phi\rangle \, |\beta_{00}\rangle = (\alpha \, |0\rangle + \beta \, |1\rangle) \otimes \left(\frac{|00\rangle + |11\rangle}{\sqrt{2}} \right)$$

$$= \frac{\alpha \, (|000\rangle + |011\rangle) + \beta \, (|100\rangle + |111\rangle)}{\sqrt{2}} \tag{29.9}$$

The first two qubits in this state belong to Alice and the third qubit belongs to Bob. So Alice has a 01 and Bob at a 1. After the EPR pair interaction with the unknown state of the first qubit of Eq. (29.9) by applying a CNOT gate, Alice uses the unknown state $|\phi\rangle$ like a control qubit and its EPR pair member as a target qubit. We recall that if the control qubit is 0, nothing happens and if the control qubit is 1, the target qubit has freaked out.

$$|00\rangle \longmapsto |00\rangle \,, |01\rangle \longmapsto |10\rangle \,, |00\rangle \longmapsto |11\rangle \,, |11\rangle \longmapsto |10\rangle \tag{29.10}$$

So, when Alice applies the CNOT gate to Eq. (29.9), the state becomes:

$$\left|\chi^{'}\right\rangle = U_{CNOT} \, |\chi\rangle$$

$$= \frac{\alpha \, (U_{CNOT} \, |000\rangle + U_{CNOT} \, |011\rangle) + \beta \, (U_{CNOT} \, |100\rangle + U_{CNOT} \, |111\rangle)}{\sqrt{2}}$$

$$= \frac{\alpha \, (|000\rangle + |011\rangle) + \beta \, (|110\rangle + |101\rangle)}{\sqrt{2}} \tag{29.11}$$

Step 3: Alice Applies a Hadamard Gate

Alice applies a Hadamard gate to the first qubit as follows:

$$H \, |0\rangle = \frac{|0\rangle + |1\rangle}{\sqrt{2}}, H \, |1\rangle = \frac{|0\rangle - |1\rangle}{\sqrt{2}} \tag{29.12}$$

We rewrite the state (Eq. (29.11)) as:

$$\left|\chi^{'}\right\rangle = \frac{\alpha \, |0\rangle \, (|00\rangle + |11\rangle) + \beta \, |1\rangle \, (|10\rangle + |01\rangle)}{\sqrt{2}} \tag{29.13}$$

Alice transforms the state into:

$$\left|\chi^{''}\right\rangle = H \left|\chi^{'}\right\rangle = \frac{\alpha H \, |0\rangle \, (|00\rangle + |11\rangle) + \beta H \, |1\rangle \, (|10\rangle + |01\rangle)}{\sqrt{2}}$$

$$= \alpha \left(\frac{|0\rangle + |1\rangle}{\sqrt{2}} \right) \left(\frac{|00\rangle + |11\rangle}{2} \right) + \beta \left(\frac{|0\rangle - |1\rangle}{\sqrt{2}} \right) \left(\frac{|10\rangle + |01\rangle}{2} \right) \tag{29.14}$$

We recall that Bob is in possession of the third qubit.

Step 4: Alice Measures Her Pair

Alice chose one of the possible next measures: $|00\rangle$, $|01\rangle$, $|1\rangle$, and $|1\rangle$ on these two qubits. Therefore, we can write (Eq. (29.14)) as follows:

$$\left|\chi''\right\rangle = \frac{1}{2}\left(\alpha\,|0\rangle + \beta\,|1\rangle\right) + |01\rangle\left(\alpha\,|1\rangle + \beta\,|0\rangle\right) + |10\rangle\left(\alpha\,|0\rangle - \beta\,|1\rangle\right)$$
$$+ |11\rangle\left(\alpha\,|1\rangle - \beta\,|0\rangle\right) \tag{29.15}$$

Step 5: Alice Informs Bob of His Result via a Classic Channel

Alice informs Bob the result of his measurement through a classic channel, for example, the telephone, the internet, or other traditional means of communication. For example, if Alice got 01, Bob applies her X door to get the state sent by Alice. Nothing about this state is communicated on the classic channel, Bob can get it because they share an EPR pair of entangled particles.

2.2.2 Superposition

Quantum mechanics postulates that the states of a given physical system form a vector space (a Hilbert space). Consequently, any linear combination of possible states is itself a possible state. The state of a quantum object is represented by the linear combination of several fundamental states. Schrodinger's cat was conceived to explain the superposition phenomenon in the microscopic state. The cat is both dead and alive, that is to say a superposition of state. The superposition is the ability of a quantum system to be in a linear combination of the states $|0\rangle$ and $|1\rangle$ at the same time until it is measured. Therefore, the qubit can exist in the state $|0\rangle$ or the state $|0\rangle$, but it can also exist in what we call a superposition state, unlike the classical bit which can be in the state 0 or in the state 1 (Fig. 29.1).

The superposition of a quantum state $|\psi\rangle$ is given by:

$$|\psi\rangle = C_1\,|\alpha_1\rangle + C_2\,|\alpha_2\rangle + \ldots + C_n\,|\alpha_n\rangle \tag{29.16}$$

C_i is the complex coefficient of the linear combination and $|\alpha_i\rangle$ the vectors of the chosen base (which depends on the observable).

Fig. 29.1 The impact of superposition

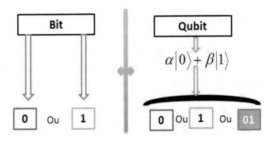

2.2.3 No-Cloning Theorem

The no-cloning theorem was enunciated in 1982 by Wootters and Zurek. The theorem is a result of quantum physics that forbids the identical copy of an unknown and arbitrary quantum state. For example, classically we can download files from the internet and copy them onto our own computers, conversely in quantum theory copying is impossible. Therefore, the attacker cannot do a perfect copy to the quantum states used by Alice to create the key, and send the originals to Bob.

We consider the next two states $|\psi\rangle$ and $|\phi\rangle$, and we suppose that there is a unit operator U such that:

$$U\left(|\psi\rangle \otimes |\chi\rangle\right) = |\psi\rangle \otimes |\psi\rangle \tag{29.17}$$

and

$$U\left(|\psi\rangle \otimes |\chi\rangle\right) = |\phi\rangle \otimes |\phi\rangle \tag{29.18}$$

For some target states $|\chi\rangle$ we take the tensor product of $\left(|\psi\rangle \otimes \langle\chi| U^{\dagger}\right)$ and $U\left(|\Psi\rangle \otimes |\phi\rangle\right)$, and we consider that $UU^{\dagger} = I$. We get next expression:

$$\left(|\psi\rangle \otimes \langle\chi| U^{\dagger}\right) U\left(|\Psi\rangle \otimes |\phi\rangle\right) = \langle\Psi|\phi\rangle \langle\chi|\chi\rangle \tag{29.19}$$

We take the tensor product of $|\Psi\rangle \otimes |\Psi\rangle$ and $|\phi\rangle \otimes |\phi\rangle$:

$$\left(|\Psi\rangle \otimes |\Psi\rangle\right)\left(|\phi\rangle \otimes |\phi\rangle\right) = \left(\langle\Psi|\phi\rangle\right)^2 \tag{29.20}$$

Therefore:

$$\langle\Psi|\phi\rangle = \left(\langle\Psi|\phi\rangle\right)^2 \tag{29.21}$$

This equation can only be corrected in two cases: if $\langle\Psi|\phi\rangle = 0$ in this case, the states are orthogonal. The second case is realized only when $\langle\Psi| = |\phi\rangle$. This result means that there is not a unitary operator U that can be used to clone a arbitrary quantum states, so we cannot make a perfect copy of a quantum state in general.

2.2.4 Quantum Measurement Theory

The measurement theory is a series of operations that allows access to information, with a high probability or even with certain success. Thus the measurements can be specified to define a finite set or infinite possible events and select an event between them according to a predefined parameter. Accordingly, the quantum measurement is considered as the third postulate of quantum mechanics, which showed that the results of possible measurements of a physical quantity A are the eigenvalues of the operator A corresponding to this quantity. Moreover, any quantum measure can be described by a set of operators M_m, where m is the possible measurement result. The probability of measuring m knowing that the system is in the state $|\Psi\rangle$ is:

$$P\left(m|\,|\Psi\rangle\right) = \left\langle\Psi|M_m^\dagger M_m|\Psi\right\rangle \qquad (29.22)$$

The system after the measure m is represented by the state $\left|\Psi'\right\rangle$:

$$\left|\Psi'\right\rangle = \frac{M_m|\,|\Psi\rangle}{\sqrt{\left\langle\Psi|M_m^\dagger M_m|\Psi\right\rangle}} \qquad (29.23)$$

According to classical probability theory we have:

$$\sum_m P\left(m|\,|\Psi\rangle\right) = \sum_m \left\langle\Psi|M_m^\dagger M_m|\Psi\right\rangle \equiv 1 \qquad (29.24)$$

Therefore:

$$\sum_m M_m^\dagger M_m \equiv 1 \qquad (29.25)$$

Unlike the classical computing, the quantum measurement perturbs the system in a fundamental way. When we make a measure the qubit will be existed into the state $|\Psi\rangle \longmapsto |0\rangle$ or in the state $|\Psi\rangle \longmapsto |1\rangle$. Therefore, after the measurement the original state is lost. Accordingly, we will not be able to find the values of α and β which are mentioned in Eq. (29.9).

2.3 QKD Protocols

The implementation of quantum key distribution protocols is based on two communication channels to connect Alice and Bob. The first is a quantum channel on which the quantum key is distributed and second is a classic channel used to send encrypted messages and must be unconditionally secure (see Fig. 29.2).

2.3.1 The Standard BB84 Protocol

To implement the quantum communication we based on several quantum key distribution protocols. In this sense, several quantum protocols have emerged, including the best known, the BB84 protocol introduced by Bennett and Brassard in 1984 [28], E91 protocol proposed by Artur Ekert in 1991 [36–38], and the

Fig. 29.2 The standard
scheme of quantum
communication

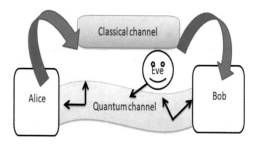

protocol announced by Bennett in 1992 (B92) [39]. Accordingly, in this study, we
consider that Alice and Bob share information with the standard BB84 protocol
using coherent states as an encoding basis. In fact, in the BB84 protocol each
signal is transmitted by a single qubit sent by Alice and received by Bob. The qubit
encrypted a key bit in one of the two conjugate orthonormal bases. When Alice uses
the horizontal/vertical (H=V) basis, her signal states are given by:

$$|H\rangle = \frac{1}{\sqrt{2}} (|0_z\rangle + |1_z\rangle)$$

$$|V\rangle = \frac{1}{\sqrt{2}} (|0_z\rangle - |1_z\rangle) \tag{29.26}$$

When Alice uses the diagonal/anti-diagonal D=A basis, the signal states will have
the form:

$$|D\rangle = \frac{1}{\sqrt{2}} (|0_z\rangle + i |1_z\rangle)$$

$$|A\rangle = \frac{1}{\sqrt{2}} (|0_z\rangle - i |1_z\rangle) \tag{29.27}$$

The BB84 algorithm can be resumed by the following steps:

- **Step 1:** Alice forwards a random sequence of states to Bob by choosing 0 or 1
  encrypted in the basis H=V or D=A.
- **Step 2:** Bob makes a measurement on the received states by choosing randomly
  one basis H/V or D/A.
- **Step 3:** Alice and Bob communicate through a classical channel the chosen basis
  for measuring. After that, they remove from the generated key those bits for
  which they have used different basis (see Table 29.1).
- **Step 4:** In the remaining bits, they exchange a fraction of bits through a classical
  channel in order to augment the security of the generated key.

In the case when a attacker Eve tries to discover the secret key that Alice and Bob
are going to exchange using the BB84 protocol. Whatever the strategy of attack
used, Eve will have to make a transformation on the photons or a measurement of

Table 29.1 Protocol BB84: key exchange

Alice polarizes	$\frac{\pi}{4}$	0	$\frac{\pi}{4}$	$\frac{\pi}{2}$	$\frac{\pi}{4}$	$\frac{\pi}{4}$	$\frac{-\pi}{4}$	$\frac{\pi}{2}$	$\frac{-\pi}{4}$
Bit sequence	1	0	0	1	0	0	1	1	1
Bob polarizes	$0/\frac{\pi}{4}$	$\frac{\pi}{4}/\frac{-\pi}{4}$	$0/\frac{\pi}{2}$	$\frac{\pi}{4}/\frac{-\pi}{4}$	$0/\frac{\pi}{2}$	$\frac{\pi}{4}/\frac{-\pi}{4}$	$0/\frac{\pi}{2}$	$0/\frac{\pi}{2}$	$\frac{\pi}{4}/\frac{-\pi}{4}$
Bob's measurements	1	1	0	1	0	0	1	1	1
Bits retained	1	–	–	1	0	0	–	1	1

the polarization of the photons, thus inducing a disturbance of the quantum system, which facilitates the detection of the attack by Alice and Bob. If Eve measures on the same basis as Alice, she will not be detected in a real environment, where an attacker Eve threatens the quantum communication, the attacker must intercept and measure the polarization of the photons sent by Alice according to one of the two bases H/V or D/A and finally send a new photon polarized to Bob for each intercepted photon, to obtain information about the secret key that is shared between Alice and Bob. In fact, just like Bob, Eve has to decide for each intercepted photon to measure its polarization according to one of the two bases. Therefore, based on Heisenberg uncertainty principle and the fact that the two bases form a pair additional properties, any attacker leading this attack course the risk of introducing inconsistencies in the Alice and Bob data. In fact, Eve by intercepting and measuring the polarization of photons sent by Alice will make an average of 2 times the wrong choice for the base. The polarization then behaves randomly and even if Eve sends Bob a polarization photon in accordance with the result of his measurement, it will send 1 time out of 2 to measure the wrong photon. Thus, Eve introduces an error in Bob's data once in 4 because Bob will measure this bad photon in the correct base (the one chosen by Alice) 1 time out of 2. If Eve intercepts all the photons sent by Alice, there will be inconsistency between Alice and Bob's data in 25% of the data exchanged. By comparing a subset of their data, Alice and Bob are able to determine with near certainty whether there was espionage on the quantum channel. If the attacker is detected, Alice and Bob must restart the protocol.

2.3.2   BB84 Protocol Security Analysis

The security of BB84 is based on three principles of quantum mechanics:

- The no-cloning theorem: Eve cannot intercept the states quantum that are used to create the secret key to make copies,
- The measure disrupts the quantum system,
- The measures are irreversible.

To analyze the security level of the protocol, we based on the mutuel information variation between Alice and Bob I_{AB} and between Alice and Eve I_{AE}.

$$I_{AB} = H(A : B) = \sum_{a,b} p(a, b) \log_2 \frac{p(a, b)}{p(a)p(b)} \tag{29.28}$$

where $p(a) = \sum_b p(a, b) = \frac{1}{2}$ and $p(b) = \sum_a p(a, b) = \frac{1}{2}$ and $p(a, b) = p(a)p(a|b)$.

The Mutual Information I_{AE}

We consider the four possible measurement probabilities:

1. $p(a = 0|e = 0)$ the probability that Eve measures 0 knowing that Alice sent a 0,
2. $p(a = 0|e = 1)$ the probability that Eve measures 1 knowing that Alice sent a 0,
3. $p(a = 1|e = 0)$ the probability that Eve measures 0 knowing that Alice sent a 1,
4. $p(a = 1|e = 1)$ the probability that Eve measures 1 knowing that Alice sent a 1.

For the four probabilities of measurement there are two cases: Eve measures the photon, or Eve ignores the measure as follows:

$p(a = 0|e = 0)$:

– If Eve makes the measurement:

She has a probability β to choose to measure, a probability $\frac{1}{2}$ to choose the right base. If Eve chooses the right base, she has a probability 1 of having a 0. If she chooses the wrong base, she has a probability of $\frac{1}{2}$ to get a 0. So we have:

$$p(0|0) = \frac{1}{2}\beta \left(1 + \frac{1}{2}\right) = \frac{3}{4}\beta \tag{29.29}$$

$p(a = 0|e = 0)$:

$$p(1|1) = \frac{1}{2}\beta \left(1 + \frac{1}{2}\right) = \frac{3}{4}\beta \tag{29.30}$$

– If Eve ignores the measure:

She have a probability $(1 - \beta)$ to ignore the measurement and a probability $\frac{1}{2}$ to choose the base 0 in its bit string. So we have:

$$p(0|0) = p(1|1)(1 - \beta)\frac{1}{2} \tag{29.31}$$

$p(a = 1|e = 0)$:

– If Eve makes the measurement:

She have a probability β to measure, and a probability $\frac{1}{2}$ to choose the right base. If she chooses the right base, she have a probability 0 to have a 1 or if she chooses the wrong base, she has a probability $\frac{1}{2}$ to get a 1. So we have:

$$p(1|0) = \frac{1}{2}\beta\left(0 + \frac{1}{2}\right) = \frac{1}{4}\beta \qquad (29.32)$$

The same for $p(a = 0|e = 1)$

$$p(1|0) = \frac{1}{2}\beta\left(0 + \frac{1}{2}\right) = \frac{1}{4}\beta \qquad (29.33)$$

– If Eve ignores the measure:

She have a probability $(1 - \beta)$ to ignore the measurement and a probability $\frac{1}{2}$ to choose 1 in its bit string. So we have:

$$p(1|0) = p(0|1) = \frac{1}{2}(1 - \beta) = \frac{1}{2} - \frac{1}{2}\beta \qquad (29.34)$$

Therefore:

$$p(a = 0|e = 0) = p(a = 1|e = 1) = \frac{1}{2} + \frac{1}{4}\beta \qquad (29.35)$$

and

$$p(a = 1|e = 0) = p(a = 0|e = 1) = \frac{1}{2} - \frac{1}{2}\beta \qquad (29.36)$$

So, we calculate I_{AE} by:

$$
\begin{aligned}
I_{AE} &= \sum_{a,b} P(a, b) \log_2 \frac{P(a, b)}{P(a)P(b)} \\
&= \frac{1 + \beta}{2} \log_2(1 + \beta) + \frac{1 - \beta}{2} \log_2(1 - \beta) \qquad (29.37)
\end{aligned}
$$

The Mutual Information I_{AB}

The four possible measurement probabilities are:

1. $p(a = 0|b = 0)$ the probability that Bob measures 0 knowing that Alice sent a 0,
2. $p(a = 0|b = 1)$ the probability that Bob measures 1 knowing that Alice sent a 0,
3. $p(a = 1|b = 0)$ the probability that Bob measures 0 knowing that Alice sent a 1,
4. $p(a = 1|b = 1)$ the probability that Bob measures 1 knowing that Alice sent a 1.

We calculate now each probability separately as follows:

– If Eve makes the measurement:

$p(a = 0|b = 0)$:

She have a probability β to choose to measure, and a probability $\frac{1}{2}$ to choose the correct base. If she chooses the correct base, she has a 0 chance of having a 1. If she chooses the wrong base, she has a $\frac{1}{2}$ probability of getting a 1. Therefore, she has a probability w of choosing to measure, and to choose the right base. If she chooses the right base, she returns the right photon and Bob will have a probability equal to 1 to have a 0. If she chooses the wrong base, she has a probability $\frac{1}{2}$ of getting a 0 and $\frac{1}{2}$ to get a 1. In each of these cases Bob will have a probability of $\frac{1}{2}$ to receive a 0.

$$p(0|0) = \frac{1}{2} - \frac{1}{8}\beta \tag{29.38}$$

– If Eve ignores the measurement:

She have a probability $(1-\beta)$ to ignore the measurement and Bob have a probability of 1 to get a 0. Therefore:

$$p(0|0) = 1 - \beta \tag{29.39}$$

Therefore:

$$p(a = 0|b = 0) = (1 - \beta) + \frac{3}{2} \times \frac{\beta}{2} = 1 - \frac{\beta}{4} \tag{29.40}$$

Now, we can calculate I_{AB} as follows:

$$I_{AB} = \sum_{a,b} P(a, b) \log_2 \frac{P(a, b)}{P(a)P(b)}$$

$$= \log_2 \left(2 - \frac{\beta}{2}\right) - \frac{\beta}{4} \log_2 \left(\frac{1}{\beta} - 1\right) \tag{29.41}$$

It's clear from Fig. 29.3 that the mutual information I_{AB} is bigger than I_{AE}. Also, the legitimate receiver gained more information compared to the Eavesdropper, which prove the effectiveness of the BB84 protocol even in the presence of the spy.

In spite of all quantum principles and the proposed QKD protocols, appeared various quantum hacking strategies which menace the quantum communication. In the next subsection, we discuss the famous quantum attacks.

2.4 Quantum Hacking Strategies

Similarly to classical computing, since the birth of quantum information theory, various threats have begun to appear. In the beginning, these attacks were introduced theoretically only, before becoming practical strategies with the development of technical tools necessary for their implementation. Generally, quantum attack

Fig. 29.3 Mutual information I_{AB} (blue), I_{AE} (red)

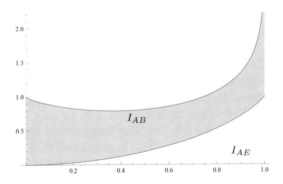

strategies are classified in two types: individual attacks and collective attacks. In fact, the first type is considering very simple and is the most studied type of quantum attack strategies. The key point of an individual attack is that Eve interacts separately with each signal from Alice. Accordingly, some attacks are based on the fact that Eve is able to postpone her interaction with the Alice's signal until after the security phases of the classical channel to get more information about the public discussion between Alice and Eve. Alternatively, Eve measures the state instantly and uses the information in the "sifting" and error correction phases. Contrary to the first type, in collective attacks Eve prepares a state and interacts it with each Alice's signal. Then, Eve sends the signal to Bob and keeps the state he has. When all signals are transferred, Eve waits to get as much information as possible from public communication to make the best measurement on the saved states. The most general version of the collective attacks is the coherent attacks. In this kind of attack, Eve is allowed to perform any quantum operation on the signal in transit and use any possible state. In this study we focus on quantum hacking strategies which exploiting the vulnerabilities of classical devices using in the engineering implementation, where we concentrate on the weaknesses in the classical channel and detectors. Accordingly, many kind of attacks have been proposed but most importantly have shown a practical possibility to hacking the quantum communication network, in spite of the aforementioned physical postulates. Mainly, the faked state attack and the blinding detectors attack are realistic scenarios where Eve performs her operations, on the quantum channel to gain information in the first strategy and blinding Bob's detector in the second one. In this study, we classified quantum hacking strategies in two big families: attack strategies in an ideal environment and individual attacks in an realistic environment.

2.4.1 Theoretical Hacking Strategies Against QKD Protocols

The hacking strategies is considered as a theoretical attacks, where realized on ideal quantum conditions. The most powerful kind of this family is the intercept and resend attack. The main idea in this strategy is that Eve trying to intercept each photon coming from Alice and measure it in a predefined base. Then, according to her result Eve prepares a new photon and transmits it to Bob. Alice's qubit will be encrypted either in "$H = V$" or "$+ = -$" such as:

$$|+\rangle = \frac{1}{\sqrt{2}}\left(|H\rangle + |V\rangle\right), |-\rangle = \frac{1}{\sqrt{2}}\left(|H\rangle - |V\rangle\right) \tag{29.42}$$

If Alice sends a 0, she will either encode in $|H\rangle$ or in $|V\rangle$ with a equal probability. Similarly, Eve will choose randomly either the base "$H = V$" or "$+ = -$". Generally, Eve obtains a correct result in two cases: the first is if Alice sends $|H\rangle$ and Eve makes her measurement in the base "H=V " and the second case if Alice sends $|+\rangle$ and Eve makes her measurement in the base "$+ = -$". Accordingly, any other combination will give random results of measurement. We assumed that Eve cannot listen to the classic communication between Alice and Bob. Therefore, she will not know if her measurement is wrong. To analyze the effective of this attack, we based on the calculus of the conditional probabilities $p(b|a)$ for the four possible outcomes, which are given as follows:

$$p\left(b = |H\rangle \,|a=0\right) = p\left(b = |+\rangle \,|a=0\right) = \left(\frac{1}{2}\right)^3 + \left(\frac{1}{2}\right)^2 \times 1 = \frac{3}{8}. \tag{29.43}$$

$$p\left(b = |V\rangle \,|a=0\right) = p\left(b = |-\rangle \,|a=0\right) = \left(\frac{1}{2}\right)^3 + \left(\frac{1}{2}\right)^2 \times 0 = \frac{1}{8}. \tag{29.44}$$

where "a" is the bits sent by Alice and "b" is the result of Eve's measurement. Similar expressions are also obtained in the case of $p(b|a = 1)$. For conditional probabilities $p(a|b)$ we have: $\sum_s p(a|b) = \frac{1}{2}$, therefore we obtained $p(a|b) = 2p(b|a)$. In addition, the collision probability which represents the probability that Eve gets the same result as Alice is:

$$P_c\left(a|b = |H\rangle\right) = \left(\frac{3}{4}\right)^2 + \left(\frac{1}{4}\right)^2 = \frac{5}{4}. \tag{29.45}$$

similarly for $b = |V\rangle$, $b = |+\rangle$ and $b = |-\rangle$. Then, the average collision probability is given by:

$$\langle P_c\rangle = \sum_b \frac{1}{4}p(a|b) = 4\left(\frac{1}{4}\right)\left[\left(\frac{1}{4}\right)^2 + \left(\frac{3}{4}\right)^2\right] = \frac{5}{4} \tag{29.46}$$

Another important question is how many bits need to be canceled to minimize Eve's information on the secret key. This parameter is noted τ and calculated based on the collision probability as follows:

$$\tau = 1 + \log \langle P_c\rangle^{\frac{1}{n}} \approx 0,322 \tag{29.47}$$

where n is the number of bits.

Consequently, we have to reject only one-third ($\tau \approx 0.322$) of the key to prove that Eve has less than one bit of information on the key. Looking at the Renyi entropy for $b = |H\rangle$, we obtain:

$$R\,(A|B) = \sum_b \frac{1}{4} R\,(A|B = b) = 4\left(\frac{1}{4}\right)(1 - \log 5) = 3 - \log 5 \quad (29.48)$$

Then, we calculate Shannon's conditional entropy:

$$\begin{aligned} R\,(A|B = |H\rangle) &= -\frac{3}{4}\log\frac{3}{4} - \frac{1}{4}\log\frac{1}{4} = -\log\frac{5}{8} \\ &= 5 - \log 5 \\ &= 0.811 \end{aligned} \quad (29.49)$$

which is equal to the four entropies $H(A|B = |V\rangle)$, $H(A|B = |+\rangle)$, and $H(A|B = |-\rangle)$ where:

$$H\,(A|B) = \sum_b \frac{1}{4} H\,(A|B=b) = 4\left(\frac{1}{4}\right)\left(-\frac{3}{4}\log\frac{3}{4} - \frac{1}{4}\log\frac{1}{4}\right) = 0.811 \quad (29.50)$$

The total information that Eve will have about each bit is $1 - H(A|B) \approx 0.2$, which is a low rate for her. Therefore, Eve will develop this strategy to gain more information. In fact, she can use another basis of measurement, such as the basis of "Breidbart" which make Eve get $1 - H(A|B) \approx 0.4$.

2.4.2   Hacking Strategies in the Engineering Implementation

Is the hacking strategies realized in the implementation phase, via exploiting the vulnerabilities of classical devices which used in quantum communication scheme. In fact, many attacks of this kind are appeared such as: Trojan horse attack, the photon number splitting attack (PNS), and faked state attack, which considered one of the very dangerous menaces on QKD implementation. Faked state attack is a special form of "Intercept/Resend" attacks, exploiting the weaknesses embedded in quantum key distribution devices. In fact, the spy Eve profited the vulnerability in Alice's detector using a particular approach. Eve intercepts Alice's signal and measures the polarization on a randomly chosen basis. Then, she prepares her measurement results on new photons and sends them to Bob, at the same time; she controls the detectors of Bob and accommodates them to work in linear mode. If Bob choices the same basic as Eve, the attacker pulses will deliver enough power to trigger Bob's detector, so Bob's results will be similar to Eve's values. On the other hand, if the basis chosen by Eve and Bob is different, the attacker's pulses are separated by the modulator and the measured intensity is insufficient to trigger Bob's detectors. Accordingly, Eve's interference introduces an acceptable error rate and generates an identical key sequence as that of legitimate users. Moreover, Alice and Bob recognize the validity of the generated key and do not pay attention to Eve's presence. Thus, another strong point of this type of attack is that even if Bob does a measure in a different base than Eve, the attacker will remain undetectable because Bobs detectors will be blind in this case. In addition, "QKD" system includes a large selection of detectors using Bob in the measurement phase. Therefore, Eve cannot excite a specific detector in a specific base of her choice, without disturbing the other detector(s) [23, 25, 40]. We can summarize the faked state attack in the following steps:

- Eve blocks the quantum channel between Alice and Bob wholly,
- Eve clones Bob's setup to measure Alice's sent qubits, choosing a randomly detection basis.
- Eve obliges Bob to make a similar measurement as her choice by causing a click in Bob's detector corresponding to her basis only and with the same bit value as she has just detected.
- Eve prepares a specific faked quantum state which will be sent to Bob.
- Eve blinds Bob's detectors, depending on her measurements, and keeps them operational only for her choice.
- Bob's detectors receive the signal sent by Eve, and then Bob makes a measurement according to his basis choice. So if Bob chooses the same basis as Eve, then the operational detector will click; otherwise, the blinded detectors will not click. In this case, we can conclude that Eve not only gains the same shared information but also remains undetectable.

3 Vulnerabilities of QKD Protocols in the Implementation Scheme

We mentioned previously that quantum cryptography implementation scheme includes some classical devices such as classical channel and detectors. In this section we analyze the effect of classical ingredients on security level proposed by the quantum key distribution protocols.

3.1 Analysis of Public Channel Security

The first classical device used in QKD implementation is a public channel, which is just a classic communication link, may be internet, telephone, or other conventional means of communication. In fact, we use the classic channel to send encrypted messages. Therefore, they must be as unconditionally secure. Therefore, the following security phases must be respected (see Fig. 29.4)

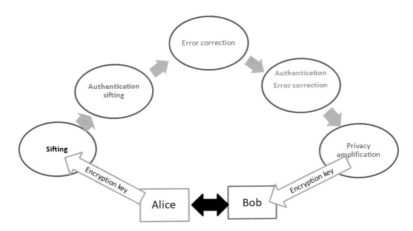

Fig. 29.4 Security phases of the public channel

- **Sifting:** Alice and Bob negotiate the bits that are used and the bits that are rejected. This message exchange must be authenticated to secure the channel against "man-in-the-middle" attacks.
- **Authentication sifting:** This operation is based on the principle of unconditional security, for example, the WegmanCarter schema.
- **Error correction:** this phase is divided into two parts: in the beginning they estimate the error and find the correct rate error. Then, they correct the error for fixing the public channel errors.
- **Authentication error correction:** Alice and Bob verify that the outputs of the error correction phase are the same. In other words, they authenticate the whole communication during the phase of the conciliation, because any error means the presence of Eve.
- **Privacy amplification:** It is the distillation of secret information that is shared, to use it as a encryption key.

3.2   Analysis of Detectors Weaknesses

We consider the following simple implementation scheme of quantum cryptography. The scheme includes a quantum channel (fiber optic channel) and a classical detector used by Bob in the measurement phase.

We remark from the scheme (see Fig. 29.5) that the quantum communication based on another classical device is represented by the detectors. Accordingly, the QKD protocols which proposed are settled in an ideal environment. The photon sources emit single-photon signals only and the detectors are 100% efficient. However, in engineering implementation, based on today's technology it is impossible to have detectors that are highly sensitive and often detect a signal even if none

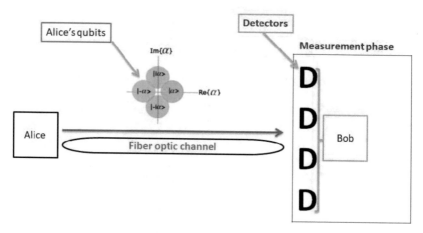

Fig. 29.5 Simple QKD implementation scheme

was sent. This has to be considered when performing the error correction and privacy amplification. In fact, quantum laws will not be applied on a classical tools. Therefore, the security discussion concerned the detectors must be treated classically. In Sect. 2 we discussed various quantum hacking strategies, which attack the detectors to disable the work of QKD protocols. Consequently, Eve hacked the quantum communication without broken the quantum security. That is why, the detectors are a very danger vulnerabilities which menace the quantum communication security in the engineering implementation.

From the above, it turns out that the use of the actual scheme to implement the quantum key distribution to secure the communication is not enough to protege the quantum network. Accordingly, similar to the classical network, we should strengthen the security of classical devices by the proposition of the other quantum solution such as the quantum firewall [40].

4 Conclusion

In this contribution, we analyzed the security level of QKD protocols between theory and the engineering implementation. In fact, we showed that the classical devices used in quantum communication implementation make the QKD protocols weakly. However, the eavesdropping exploiting this weakness to broke the quantum security. Accordingly, we discussed the effectiveness of the classical channel in real implementation, where we showed how difficult it is and how is expensive to get unconditional secure classical channel, which greatly limits to implement QKD protocols in the commercial use. Moreover, we analyze the weakness of classical detectors, which represent a very important part in the implementation scheme, where the measurement phase is based 100% on the efficiency of detectors. Therefore, we referenced many quantum attacks, which are based on detectors vulnerabilities to menace quantum communication. Consequently, the QKD is just a theoretical revolution in the IT security, where we need to get rid of classical devices to exploit all advantages of quantum cryptography to real engineering implementation.

References

1. Gupta, B. B., Agrawal, D. P., & Yamaguchi, S. (2016). *Handbook of research on modern cryptographic solutions for computer and cyber security.* Hershey: IGI Global.
2. Gupta, B. B. (2018). *Computer and cyber security: Principles, algorithm, applications, and perspectives* (Vol. 666). Boca Raton: CRC Press.
3. Wang, L., Li, L., Li, J., Li, J., Gupta, B. B., & Liu, X. (2018). Compressive sensing of medical images with confidentially homomorphic aggregations. *IEEE IoT Journal, 6,* 1402–1409.
4. Tewari, A., & Gupta, B. B. (2018). *Security, privacy and trust of different layers in internet-of-things (IoTs) framework. Future generation computer systems.* Amsterdam: Elsevier.
5. Stergiou, C., Psannis, K. E., Kim, B. G., & Gupta, B. (2018). Secure integration of IoT and cloud computing. *Future Generation Computer Systems, 78,* 964–975.
6. Adat, V., & Gupta, B. B. (2018). Security in Internet of Things: Issues, challenges, taxonomy, and architecture. *Telecommunication Systems, 67*(3), 423–441.
7. Gupta, S., & Gupta, B. B. (2017). Detection, avoidance, and attack pattern mechanisms in modern web application vulnerabilities: Present and future challenges. *International Journal of Cloud Applications and Computing, 7*(3), 1–43.
8. Plageras, A. P., Psannis, K. E., Stergiou, C., Wang, H., & Gupta, B. B. (2018). Efficient IoT-based sensor BIG Data collection–processing and analysis in smart buildings. *Future Generation Computer Systems, 82,* 349–357.
9. Gupta, B. B., Gupta, S., & Chaudhary, P. (2017). Enhancing the browser-side context-aware sanitization of suspicious HTML5 code for halting the DOM-based XSS vulnerabilities in cloud. *International Journal of Cloud Applications and Computing, 7*(1), 1–31.
10. Hossain, M. S., Muhammad, G., Abdul, W., Song, B., & Gupta, B. B. (2018). Cloud-assisted secure video transmission and sharing framework for smart cities. *Future Generation Computer Systems, 83,* 596–606.
11. Bruss, D. (1998). Optimal eavesdropping in quantum cryptography with six states. *Physical Review Letters, 81*(14), 3018–3021
12. Scarani, V., Acin, A., Ribordy, G., & Gisin, N. (2004). Quantum cryptography protocols robust against photon number splitting attacks for weak laser pulse implementations. *Physical Review Letters, 92,* 057901.
13. Qi, B., Fung, C.-H. F, Lo, H.-K., & Ma, X. (2007). Time-shift attack in practical quantum cryptosystems. *Quantum Information and Computation, 7,* 73–82.
14. Amellal, H., Meslouhi, A., Hassouni, Y., El Baz, M., & El Allati, A. (2017). Cryptanalysis on a scheme to share information via employing discrete algorithm to quantum states. *Journal of the Korean Physical Society, 70,* 449–453. https://doi.org/10.3938/jkps.70.449
15. Amellal, H., Meslouhi, A., Hassouni, Y., & El Allati, A. (2017). SQL injection principle against BB84 protocol. *International Journal of Computers and Communications, 11.* ISSN: 2074-1294.
16. Dirac, P. A. M. (1947). *The principles of quantum mechanics* (3rd ed.). Oxford: Clarendon Press.
17. Dieks, D. (1982). Communication by EPR devices. *Physics Letters A, 92*(6), 271–272.

18. Nauerth, S., Fürst, M., Schmitt-Manderbach, T., Weier, H., & Weinfurter, H. (2009). Information leakage via side channels in freespace BB84 quantum cryptography. *New Journal of Physics, 11*, 065001.
19. Dirac, P. A. M. (1947). *The principles of quantum mechanics* (3rd ed.). Oxford: Clarendon Press.
20. Wootters, W. K., & Zurek, W. H. (1982). A single quantum cannot be cloned. *Nature, 299*, 802–803. https://doi.org/10.1038/299802a0
21. Lamas-Linares, A., & Kurtsiefer, C. (2007). Breaking a quantum key distribution system through a timing side channel. *Optics Express, 15*, 9388393.
22. Lütkenhaus, N. (2000). Security against individual attacks for realistic quantum key distribution. *Physics Letters A, 61*, 052304.
23. Makarov, V., & Hjelme, D. R. (2005). Faked states attack on quantum cryptosystems. *Journal of Modern Optics, 52*, 69105.
24. Makarov, V. (2009). Controlling passively quenched single photon detectors by bright light. *New Journal of Physics, 11*, 065003.
25. Makarov, V., & Skaar, J. (2008). Faked states attack using detector efficiency mismatch on SARG04, phase-time, DPSK and Ekert protocols. *Quantum Information and Computation, 8*(67), 92–93.
26. Makarov, V., Anisimov, A., & Skaar, J. (2006). Effects of detector efficiency mismatch on security of quantum cryptosystems. *Physical Review A, 74*, 022313.
27. Scarani, V., Acin, A., Ribordy, G., & Gisin, N. (2004). Quantum cryptography protocols robust against photon number splitting attacks for weak laser pulse implementations. *Physical Review Letters, 92*, 057901.
28. Bennett, C. H., & Brassard, G. (1984). Public key distribution and coin tossing. In *Proceedings of the IEEE International Conference on Computers, Systems, and Signal Processing* (pp. 71, 79, 92). New York: IEEE Press.
29. Zhao, Y., Fung, C.-H. F., Qi, B., Chen, C., & Lo, H.-K. (2008). Quantum hacking: Experimental demonstration of time-shift attack against practical quantum-key-distribution systems. *Physical Review A, 78*, 042333.
30. Nauerth, S., Fürst, M., Schmitt-Manderbach, T., Weier, H., & Weinfurter, H. (2009). Information leakage via side channels in freespace BB84 quantum cryptography. *New Journal of Physics, 11*, 065001.
31. Lydersen, L., Wiechers, C., Wittmann, C., Elser, D., Skaar, J., & Makarov, V. (2010). Hacking commercial quantum cryptography systems by tailored bright illumination. *Nature Photonics, 4*, 686–689. https://doi.org/10.1038/nphoton.2010.214
32. El Allati, A., El Baz, M., & Hassouni, Y. (2011). Quantum key distribution via tripartite coherent states. *Quantum Information Processing, 10*, 5589–5602.
33. Eleuch, H., & Bennaceur, R. (2004). Nonlinear dissipation and the quantum noise of light in semiconductor microcavities. *Journal of Optics B: Quantum and Semiclassical Optics, 6*, 189.
34. Curado, E. M. F., Rego-Monteiro, M. A., Rodrigues, L. M. C. S., & Hassouni, Y. (2006). Coherent states for a degenerate system: The hydrogen atom. *Physica A, 371*, 16.
35. Glauber, R. J. (1963). Coherent and incoherent states of the radiation field. *Physical Review, 131*, 2766 (1963).
36. Ekert, A. (1991). Quantum cryptography based on Bell's theorem. *Physical Review Letters, 67*(6), 661–663.
37. Greenberger, D., Horne, M. A., & Zeilinger, A. (1989). Going beyond Bell's theorem. In M. Kafatos (Ed.), *Bell's theorem, quantum theory and conceptions of the universe* (Vol. 80, pp. 69–72). Dordrecht: Kluwer.
38. Li, C., Wang, Z., Wu, C., Song, H. S., & Zhou, L. (2006). Certain quantum key distribution achieved by using Bell states. *International Journal of Quantum Information, 4*(6), 899–906.
39. Bennett, C. H. (1992). Quantum cryptography using any two nonorthogonal states. *Physical Review Letters, 68*, 3121.
40. Amellal, H., Meslouhiy, A., Hassouni, Y., & El Baz, M. (2015). A quantum optical firewall based on simple quantum devices. *Quantum Information Processing, 14*, 2617–2633. https://doi.org/10.1007/s11128-015-1002-4

Chapter 30
Survey of Security and Privacy Issues on Biometric System

Priyanka Datta, Shanu Bhardwaj, S. N. Panda, Sarvesh Tanwar, and Sumit Badotra

Abstract A biometric system is a high-tech system that uses the data about the individual, already stored in the database to identify the individual. Biometric system is gaining popularity since it provides security and privacy to the data so that no one can misuse the data of the individual. But still, the system is not fully secure because the pattern can be recognized by the third party with the help of the remote application like antireply attacks or liveliness detection over the Internet to access the biometric data. This paper presents a survey of security and privacy issues on the biometric system and discusses the various case studies such as E-passport and Aadhaar identification, followed by the threats and issues. So, in this paper it is concluded that there must be some techniques or protocols that are based on the signal processing and the cryptography mechanism that would protect the biometric data from the intruders.

Keywords Biometric · GDPR · IT Act · Aadhaar · E-Passport · Security in biometric · Privacy in biometric

1 Introduction

A biometric system is the system which is basically pattern recognition systems that is operated by collecting the biometric data from an individual, via extracting a set of data from the collected data, and compare the extracted set of data with the saved data in the database [1]. Biometrics system is used to measure individuals' unique behavioral or physical characteristics to authenticate or recognize their identity [2]. There are two modes on which biometric system can operate, depending on the application context. The two modes are verification modes and identification

P. Datta · S. Bhardwaj (✉) · S. N. Panda · S. Tanwar · S. Badotra
Chitkara University Institute of Engineering and Technology, Chitkara University, Rajpura, Punjab, India
e-mail: priyanka.datta@chitkara.edu.in; shanu.bhardwaj@chitkara.edu.in; snpanda@chitkara.edu.in; sarvesh.tanwar@chitkara.edu.in; sumit.badotra@chitkara.edu.in

© Springer Nature Switzerland AG 2020
B. B. Gupta et al. (eds.), *Handbook of Computer Networks and Cyber Security*,
https://doi.org/10.1007/978-3-030-22277-2_30

modes. In verification modes, biometric system already stores the user template in a database; while validating the user, the system compares the collected information with the stored information, and if they match, then the user is a valid user, else not. Another mode is identification mode in which the system recognizes a user by comparing its data with all the saved template in the database; that is, one to many comparisons take place for establishing an individual identity.

Since biometric-based authentication has many benefits over conventional methods, there is a significant rise in the use of biometric systems in the recent years. It is very important that a biometric system must be designed in such a way that it can tolerate attack when used in security critical applications, mainly in unattended distant application like e-commerce [3].

Nowadays almost every citizen is using Internet as a source of communication, transaction, registration, and for many more. They are sharing their vital data such as Aadhaar number, PAN number, bank account number, and personal photographs over the Internet, being unaware that their data can be misused by an intruder.

This paper is organized as follows: Section 2 of the paper discusses the literature review. Case study is defined in Sect. 3 of the paper followed by limitation and future scope in Sect. 4.

2   Literature Review

2.1   GDPR and IT Act

General Data Protection Regulation (GDPR) is the act of European Union law on privacy and protection of data for all the citizens of the European economic area and European Union. This act was implemented from May 25, 2018. Similarly in India, Information Technology Act 2000 (IT Act) is the primary law that deals with electronic commerce and cybercrime. This act provides legal structure for the recognition to digital signatures as well as records that are electronically saved.

This section provides the difference and similarity between notable features of the IT Act and GDPR for data protection.

2.2   Difference Between GDPR and IT Act 2000

The objective of GDPR is to provide protection to each and every citizen while processing data. GDPR works on the following principles:

- DATA INTEGRITY: It means the consistency and accuracy of data.
- FAIRNESS: It means the optimization of data.
- TRANSPERENCY: It means the data be clear.
- ACCOUNTABILITY: It means the discipline and the presentation of data.

Table 30.1 Differentiation of GDPR and IT Act

Principle	Article and section	Difference
Objective	–	• GDPR provides protection to individual's rights and freedom for data processing • IT Act 2000 does not express it
Processing of data	• GDPR: Article 5 • IT: Rule 5 of 2011	• GDPR listed the following principles: – Data integrity – Protection from illegal processing – Fairness – Accountability – Transparency • IT Act applies only for the collection of data and its uses and does not express processing
Law of processing	• GDPR: Article 6 • IT: Rule 5 of 2011	• GDPR consists of five additional conditions of processing • IT Act does deal with the law of processing
Delicate personal data	• GDPR: Article 9 • IT Act 2000: Sec. 43A • IT Act 2011: Rule 3	• IT Act and GDPR of this particular category have mentioned different laws
Rights	• GDPR – Article (14-18) – Article (20-22) – Article 7(3) • IT Rules, 2011 – Rule 5(6) – Rule 5(3) – Rule 5(7)	• IT Act had not used the word "RIGHT" • In GDPR, important rights are mentioned such as right to restrict processing, right to access, and many more
Security	• GDPR – Article 32 – Article 35 – Article 37 – Article 30 – Article 33 • IT Rules 2011 – Rule 4	• GDPR consists of the security measures for data processing in detail. These include the assessment of maintaining the records of data processing by security officer • IT Act does not mention in detail

Table 30.1, given below, highlights the key principle used for the differentiation of GDPR and IT Act.

2.3   Similarity Between GDPR and IT Act 2000

The objective of both the laws is to facilitate the transferring of data for the advantage of electronic commerce. According to the GDPR rules, the collection of data should be lawful and related data should be collected. It is also mentioned that data cannot be held for longer period than required for data-processing purpose. Same thing had also been mentioned in the IT Act. Minor exception is present in the GDPR with respect to the data retention. Under IT Act and GDPR, "consent" of data provider or subject of information is a vital criterion for lawfulness. Similarly biometric data, sexual orientation, and health records are considered as sensitive data by both the Rules and the Act. Again both the Act and GDPR had made it mandatory that before collecting someone's personal data, consent should be taken. In addition, the provider of data has the privilege of withdrawing the consent. Adoption of security audit and internal policies for protecting data are required by both IT Act and GDPR. Protection of data practices also includes approved certification and voluntary compliance. According to the IT Act and GDPR, the data transfer to another country or body can take place only if the level of protecting data is same for both of them. Still the benchmark for protecting data is very high in case of GDPR; IT Act had to revise more its ACT to achieve this benchmark (Table 30.2).

Table 30.2 Similarity between GDPR and IT Act

Principle	Article and section	Similarity
Objective	–	• Transferring of data for GDPR and IT Act are same in case of electronic commerce
Processing of data	• GDPR: Article 5 • IT: Rule 5 of 2011	• Laws required for are – Data should be collected lawfully – It should be specified purposely
Law of processing	• GDPR: Article 6 • IT: Rule 5 of 2011	• For both the data provider should be prerequisite for the collection of data
Delicate personal data	• GDPR: Article 9 • IT Act 2000: Sec. 43A • IT Act 2011: Rule 3	• Both laws consist of – Biometric data – Sexual orientation – Health records
Rights	• GDPR – Article (14-18) – Article (20-22) – Article 7(3) • IT Rules, 2011 – Rule 5(6) – Rule 5(3) – Rule 5(7)	• Few rules under IT Act, Sec. 43A are loosely similar to the GDPR rights
Security	• GDPR – Article 32 – Article 35 – Article 37 – Article 30 – Article 33 • IT Rules 2011 – Rule 4	• Some of the data security for protection are similar for both of them. They are – Security audit – Absorption of internal policies – Certification mechanism

2.4 Related Work

Prabhakar et al. [4] presented the view that the biometric system was much more efficient than that of the tradition system for recognition purpose. So the security of this authentication perspective was greater concern. According to the authors, for making the authentication a secure platform, the basic requirements were:

- Universality: The characteristic should be universal that every person must have the particular characteristic.
- Distinctiveness: The characteristics of every person should be unique or differ from each other.
- Permanence: The characteristics of each person must be permanent.

By keeping all these factors in mind, there was a possibility that for allowing access in the record, the fingerprint of one person matches with the fingerprint of another person. Therefore, it was the great need to secure the system more to avoid replication or to enhance the biometric system [4].

Jain et al. [1] had proposed a scheme whose objective was to ensure that the services were used by the genuine user only. Examples of this application are ATM, laptop, access to buildings securely, computer system, and cellular phones. These systems are insecure, in the lack of strong scheme for personal recognition. Biometric recognition means the process of automatic identification of a person, based on his or her behavioral and physiological features. It is also possible to either confirm or establish a person's identity, which is centered on "who she is" than by "What she have" or "what she remembers" [1].

Juels et al. [5] had explained the security and privacy effects of the forthcoming worldwide experiment in authentication technology. They also explained security and privacy issues that can be applied to e-passports and then analyze the issues with respect to ICAO (International Civil Aviation Organization) ethics for e-passports. They had identified privacy and security threats for e-passports and then estimate developing and future of e-passport types in respect to this threat. They had primarily analyzed the standard of ICAO and the reason for being adopted by some nations. Some principles had been identified for the protection of biometric identity cards and analyzing those principles with respect to the e-passport standard of ICAO, Malaysian e-passport, and ICAO deployments. They had drawn some conclusions like:

- The privacy data needed for biometric information mean illegal reading of e-passport information, which is a privacy risk and security risk too. If biometric authentication is done without supervision, then risk can grow.
- At least basic access and Faraday cage control must be applied in ICAO deployments for preventing remote unauthorized access of e-passports data. They had cited an example of the USA where deployment of ICAO e-passport does not deliver enough protection for its biometric information.
- Since the active authentication used by the US deployment, users data are essential to supply to the US deployment according to ICAO spec for combining

the capability of optically scan e-passport, which was sufficient for elementary access control in the US deployment for ICEO e-passport, but are not convincing.

According to the author, e-passport deployment is in the first part of coming-generation identification devices. E-passport might provide important knowledge for how to build more private and secure identification platform in the coming future [5].

Faundez-Zanuy [6] described that biometric offers superior deposits of advantages than that of making "password" but it was not adopted yet. The disadvantage of the biometric system was that the data are not to be used as secret, not be able to replace or in case of elder people or manual workers who do not have fingerprints. There were many remote applications like antireply attacks or liveliness detection over Internet to access the biometric data by third party (intruder). According to the author, there must be constant update to keep the data protected [6].

Lai et al. [7] discussed security system of biometric under the framework of privacy–security trade-off. Two different conditions had been identified, either the attacker had side information related to the biometric measurement or not, and had been considered. In the situation where the attacker/hacker does not have information, the author considered the two cases of perfect privacy and perfect security. In both cases, the region had been identified for the complete privacy–security trade-off. More precisely, that an outer bound on the privacy–security pair was achievable by any system had been derived. Furthermore, a system had been proposed to attain this upper bound. In the situation when the hacker has information about the biometric measurements, outer and inner bounds on the privacy and security portion have been derived [7].

Huang et al. [8] had defined different types of resources allocated in the form of network services managed and provided by servers. The mostly used method is remote authentication, which is used to define the identity of remote user. There are three types of authentication factors that were:

- Passwords: This is known by the client.
- Smart card: It is with the client.
- Biometric characteristics like iris scan, voice print, and fingerprint.

Conserving privacy and security was a thought-provoking matter in distributed network. This research paper had shown a movement toward solving this matter by suggesting a general framework for three types of authentication factors to safe resources and services from unauthenticated usage. An authentication was created on biometrics, password, and smart card. The author's framework not only explains how to get secure three-layer authentication from two layers, but it also mentions several prominent matters of biometric authentication in a network that was distributed [8].

Meng et al. [9] had revealed the survey reports on various biometric user authentication techniques, which can be developed on the touch-enabled mobile phones. Some of the points on biometric authentication were as follows:

- The taxonomy of the existing biometric authentication on the mobile phones as well as it had analyze, what would be the feasibility if they are implemented on mobile phones which are touch enabled.
- Systematic characteristics of any generic biometric authentication system had been described highlighting and their countermeasures on touch-enabled mobile phones.
- A system for implementing a reliable authentication framework by establishing a multimodal user authentication of biometric in a proper way, for validating the framework experimental results had been provided. The results show that biometric with multimodal can be implemented on the touch-enabled mobile that can significantly decrease the false rate of a single biometric system.
- Lastly, various challenges were identified in these areas. It had suggested that explained dynamics could become the mainstream object for designing user authentication on the touch-enabled mobile phones [9].

Natgunanathan et al.'s [10] biometric characteristics are linked with individuals if these data are leaked, then it will violate individual privacy, and may cause serious and continuous issues, since the biometric data of individual are irreplaceable. The privacy-preserving biometric schemes (PPBSs) had been developed over the past decade for protecting the biometric data, but they too had some drawbacks. The main objective was to provide a brief summary of the existing PPBSs, including encryption-based biometric schemes, hybrid and multimodal based schemes, concealable biometric based schemes, and SC-based schemes. It had also explained the functional mechanism of PPBSs. The drawbacks associated with PPBSs were also discussed and summarized. The analysis can help to develop more efficient and effective PPBSs in the future [10].

Memon [11] narrated that biometric was also used to access the data from the personal devices that overcome the limitation of commonly used password-based mechanisms as biometric was easy and more convenient but there were also the chances of stolen of biometric data with the help of malicious ways. The author presented the idea that there must be some techniques or protocols that were based on the signal processing and the cryptography mechanism that would protect the biometric data from the intruders [11].

Kumar et al. [12] proposed a privacy-preserving-based biometric authentication system in the field of healthcare. There was a huge impact of the recent technologies such as Internet of Things in the healthcare and medical sector. The patients were treated much better than that of the traditional approaches. But with the recent development, the patient's data travelled a lot from one area to another. So there might be a great need to provide complete authentication to the data. Biometric system was considered to be the best and low-cost system to secure the patient's parameters as well as the authentication to the patient when there was a case of sensor data [12].

Jaronde et al. [13] proposed a low-cost biometric system for newborn infants not to get swapped in the hospital. Swapping of newborns in the hospitals was a challenging issue that occurred all over the globe. The traditional DNA procedure was very expensive. To overcome the limitation, a low-cost method was implemented, which involved the scanning and matching of infant's footprints and mother's hand impressions using biometric system. In case the infant got swapped in the hospital, recognize the infant with the help of data that are being stored. So by this way, biometric identification system was considered a great and low-cost tool [13].

Osadchy and Dunkelman [14] traced that the existing authentication system discard the center of attraction that was privacy protection. In the traits of biometrics such as fingerprint and face detection, there must be a system that was well trained for its users. There was a need to develop a system for preserving the privacy with great accuracy [14].

2.5 History of Biometric System

Year	Description
2000	The vendor test of face recognition held first time
2000	Consists of the vascular patterns used for the recognition purpose published first time
2000	Program on biometric degree was established at the University of West Virginia
2001	In Florida, face recognition process was used for the first time at Super Bowl
2001	Subcommittee of ISO/IEC on biometrics was established
2002	Technical committee of M1 on Biometrics was formed
2002	Palm Print Paper was submitted to ISC (Identification Services Committee)
2002	Formal US Government coordination of biometric activities begins
2003	ICAO adopted blueprint to merge biometrics to machine-readable documents
2003	Forum of European biometrics was established
2004	Program of US-VISIT becomes operational
2004	DOD implemented ABIS
2004	In the USA, database of first state automate palm print was deployed
2004	The grand challenge of face recognition begins
2005	Iris recognition patent filed by the USA

2.6 Existing Authentication Techniques

Methods	Examples	Properties
The user knows	• Username • Password • PIN code	• Forgotten password/PIN • Many passwords • Can be shared
The user has	• Cards • Keys	• Duplicity • Lost • Stolen • Can be shared
The user has and the user knows	• ATM card • PIN	• Password (weak link) • Can be shared
Unique about the user	• Face • Fingerprint • Iris • Voice	• Can never be shared • Can never be lost • Can never be stolen

3 Case Study

3.1 Aadhaar Card

When there was a need for the authentication approach, the model that comes under consideration was "Aadhaar." Aadhaar is basically a 12-digit number for the unique identification given by a governmental agency of India called Unique Identification Authority of India, commonly known as UIDAI. It is based on the information of biometric and demographic [15]. UID, that is, Universal Identification, is the largest program of biometric identification in the world having more than 200 million people enrolled [16]. Aadhaar provides a very strong authentication in different services such as in the field of e-health care, voting mechanism, commercial, and many more. In the case of voting mechanism, finger printing for the identification plays a vital role. So, to access the finger print, the database of Aadhaar card is used [17].

In Aadhaar card authentication, UIDAI members collect the following data for the enrolment in the Aadhaar service:

- Iris scanning of both eyes
- Fingerprinting of all fingers including thumbs
- Digital photograph

This multimodal is very advantageous because various biometrics suit best for different fields. The scanning of iris provides much more than that of finger printing but in the same phase fingerprinting is cheaper than the iris. Aadhaar card holders use smart phones with personal identification number, that is, PIN or can use

 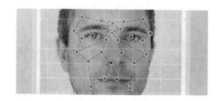

Face

Fig. 30.1 Face recognition (https://www.nec.com/en/global/solutions/safety/Technology/FaceRe cognition/index.html)

biometric to verify the identity of individual. The Aadhaar data in the centralized database can be accessed by anyone, such as bank, employers, law, and many more in real time.

But the security risks are always a controversial part in the Aadhaar system. There is a valid proof that the system like Aadhaar is having some security issues. One of the journalists found that the description of many of the enrollees with their Aadhaar number was posted online in the Indian governmental website [18].

3.2 E-Passport

According to the US Government, within few years, travelers from different nations would carry a new type of passport that is e-passport. It will deploy two new technologies like biometric and RFID (Radio Frequency Identification) (Figs 30.1, 30.2, and 30.3).

Almost all computer-oriented biometrics, which include face recognition, finger-print, and irises, are used for deployment in e-passport.

- *Face Recognition:* It means photographic imaging of face. Essentially, it is the automated analog of the human process for face recognition.
- *Fingerprint Recognition:* It depends on an imaging. Criminal investigation used fingerprint, which is often based on different type of features available in fingerprint. Fingerprint scanner can be silicon sensor or optical form.

Fig. 30.2 Fingerprint
recognition

Fig. 30.3 Iris recognition
(https://en.wikipedia.org/
wiki/Iris_recognition)

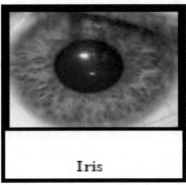

- *Iris Recognition:* Noninvasive scanning which is deployed with high-precision
  camera is used for iris scanning in biometric system. In a biometric system the
  device that collects the user data is called sensor.

3.3   Biometric Authentication Process

Biometric authentication process is nearly similar to other systems. An authenticated user can register initially by presenting a good-quality image to sensor. The
system can store the data in the data structure known as template. Template is used
as a reference for user authentication. Matching is the process where currently
presented biometric data will be compared to the saved data contained in the
templates for the authorized user.

It seems to be simple, but in reality the process of biometric authentication is
surrounded with security and privacy complication.

3.4   The Biometric Threat of E-Passport

If the biometric data are leaked, than an e-passport will have the following risk:

• Security for e-passport deployment will be compromised.
• Compromised security for external biometric system also.

Biometric data play a very important role in the e-passport system. A digitized facial image is allocated as the "global interchange feature," which means that it will serve as international standard for biometric authentication.

Optional fields are fingerprint and iris information, which might be used at the issuing country's discretion. In biometric system, data secrecy is a subtle issue.

Two trends badly affecting security by the mean of public disclosure of biometric information:

1. Automatic
2. Spillover

• *Automation:* As biometric authentication is an automation process, so it normally leads to relaxation of oversight. This is the case with e-passport.

At the Malaysian airport, whenever an individual places an e-passport in front of the gate, it will automatically be opened and the individual with the help of fingerprint scanner can authenticate himself, without any intervention of other human being. If the fingerprint data match with the e-passport data, then he or she can board the flight. Australia is also planning to implement "Smart Gate" technology in its airport with face recognition.

It will minimize human oversight for user authentication but will increase the chance of spoofing of biometric systems.

• *Spillover:* Biometric data stored in one system are used to authenticate user in multiple areas but can threaten the integrity with others or unrelated ones.

Many systems used for fingerprint recognition can be fooled when gelatin "fingers" are presented in them with ridges copied from the image of fingerprints. Biometric data are very important for individuals, so secrecy should be maintained so that unauthorized access of data can be prohibited.

3.5   Smart Card

In a system like client-server, smart card with the authentication scheme based on password is mostly used for validating a user residing at the remote location. Simple password can easily be hacked, to solve this type of problem secret keys of cryptographic and password is used for authentication purpose of the user located at the remote area [19]. This also had problem like long cryptographic keys are hard to remind and it leads confusion to identify the actual user.

Some merits of biometrics are as follows:

- Keys of biometrics are unforgettable.
- These types of keys are difficult to share or copy.
- It is very difficult to share or copy biometric keys.
- Difficult to guess easily.
- It is not easy to break someone's biometric information.

Thus authentication of remotely located user by biometric system is highly secured and reliable than the traditional authentication scheme [20].

4 Limitation and Future Scope

The biometric framework was significantly more efficient than traditional framework for recognition patterns. But still there are several issues that are mentioned below:

- The data are not to be used as secret.
- The data are not able to replace, or in case of elder people or manual workers, they do not have fingerprints.
- If the database of the biometric data anyhow gets corrupted, then the whole system fails.
- The secrecy requirements for biometric data imply that unauthorized reading of e-passport data is a security risk as well as a privacy risk. The risk will only grow with the push towards unsupervised use of biometric authentication.

To overcome these limitations, the future work for these problems will be:

- It is the great need to secure the biometric system more to avoid replication done by different hacking algorithms like antireply attack or to enhance the biometric system.
- There must be some techniques or protocols that were based on the signal processing and the cryptography mechanism that would protect the biometric data from the intruders.
- The future work is to identify all the practical threats on authentication and develop more secure authentication protocols with better results.
- There must be constant update to keep the data protected.

References

1. Jain, A. K., Ross, A., & Prabhakar, S. (2004). An introduction to biometric recognition. *IEEE Transactions on Circuits and Systems for Video Technology, 14*(1), 4–20. https://doi.org/10.1109/TCSVT.2003.818349.
2. Liu, S., & Silverman, M. (2001). Practical guide to biometric security technology. *IT Professional, 3*(1), 27–32. https://doi.org/10.1109/6294.899930.

3. Bolle, R. M. (2001). Enhancing security. *IBM Systems, 40*(3), 614–634. https://doi.org/10.1147/sj.403.0614.

4. Prabhakar, S., Pankanti, S., & Jain, A. K. (2003). Biometric recognition: Security and privacy concerns. *IEEE Security & Privacy Magazine, 1*(2), 33–42. https://doi.org/10.1109/MSECP.2003.1193209.

5. Juels, A., Molnar, D., & Wagner, D. (2005). Security and privacy issues in E-passports. Security and privacy for emerging areas in communications networks, 2005. In *SecureComm 2005. First International Conference on* (pp. 74–88). https://doi.org/10.1109/securecomm.2005.59

6. Faundez-Zanuy, M. (2006). Biometric security technology. *IEEE Aerospace and Electronic Systems Magazine, 21*(6), 15–26. https://doi.org/10.1109/MAES.2006.1662038.

7. Lai, L., Ho, S. W., & Poor, H. V. (2011). Privacy–Security trade-offs in biometric security systems—Part I: Single use case. *IEEE Transactions on Information Forensics and Security, 6*(1), 122–139. https://doi.org/10.1109/TIFS.2010.2098872.

8. Huang, X., Xiang, Y., Chonka, A., Zhou, J., & Deng, R. H. (2011). A generic framework for three-factor authentication: Preserving security and privacy in distributed systems. *IEEE Transactions on Parallel and Distributed Systems, 22*(8), 1390–1397. https://doi.org/10.1109/TPDS.2010.206.

9. Meng, W., Wong, D. S., Furnell, S., & Zhou, J. (2015). Surveying the development of biometric user authentication on mobile phones. *IEEE Communications Surveys and Tutorials, 17*(3), 1268–1293. https://doi.org/10.1109/COMST.2014.2386915.

10. Natgunanathan, I., Mehmood, A., Xiang, Y., Beliakov, G., & Yearwood, J. (2016). Protection of privacy in biometric data. *IEEE Access, 4*, 880–892. https://doi.org/10.1109/ACCESS.2016.2535120.

11. Memon, N. (2017). How biometric authentication poses new challenges to our security and privacy [in the spotlight]. *IEEE Signal Processing Magazine, 34*(4), 194–196. https://doi.org/10.1109/MSP.2017.2697179.

12. Kumar, T., Braeken, A., Liyanage, M., & Ylianttila, M. (2017). Identity privacy preserving biometric based authentication scheme for Naked healthcare environment. *IEEE International Conference on Communications*. https://doi.org/10.1109/ICC.2017.7996966.

13. Jaronde, P. W., Muratkar, N. A., Bhoyar, P. P., Gaikwad, S. J., & Nagrale, R. B. (2018). Review on biometric security system for newborn baby. *International Journal of Scientific Research in Science and Technology, 4*(2), 907–909.

14. Osadchy, M., & Dunkelman, O. (2018). It is all in the system's parameters: Privacy and security issues in transforming biometric raw data into binary strings. *IEEE Transactions on Dependable and Secure Computing, 5971*(c), 1–10. https://doi.org/10.1109/TDSC.2018.2804949.

15. Srivastava, S., Agarwal, N., & Agarwal, R. (2013). Authenticating Indian E-health system through "Aadhaar" A unique identification. *International Journal of Scientific & Engineering Research, 4*(6), 2412–2416.

16. Kataria, A. N., Sharma, A. K., & Zaveri, T. H. (2013). *A survey of automated biometric authentication techniques* (pp. 1–6).

17. Hemalatha, T., Krishna, D., Krishna, K. B., & Subhramanyam, V. B. (2014). Aadhar based electronic voting system and providing authentication. *International Journal of Engineering and Advanced Technology, 4*(2), 237–240.

18. Dixon, P. (2017). A failure to "Do No Harm" – India's Aadhaar biometric ID program and its inability to protect privacy in relation to measures in Europe and the U.S. *Health and Technology, 7*(4), 539–567. https://doi.org/10.1007/s12553-017-0202-6.

19. Wen, F., Susilo, W., & Yang, G. (2015). Analysis and improvement on a biometric-based remote user authentication scheme using smart cards. *Wireless Personal Communications, 80*(4), 1747–1760. https://doi.org/10.1007/s11277-014-2111-6.

20. Li, C. T., & Hwang, M. S. (2010). An efficient biometrics-based remote user authentication scheme using smart cards. *Journal of Network and Computer Applications, 33*(1), 1–5. https://doi.org/10.1016/j.jnca.2009.08.001.

Chapter 31
A Novel Session Key Generation and Secure Communication Establishment Protocol Using Fingerprint Biometrics

Arpita Sarkar and Binod Kumar Singh

Abstract Security of information is provided by various cryptographic techniques. Symmetric key cryptography is one of such methods which require a shared secret key between two parties to communicate. Distribution of such secret key is the main challenge in symmetric key cryptography. Efficient and reliable techniques are needed to distribute the shared secret key between communicating parties. To defeat the problem of key management and key distribution this chapter proposes a cancelable fingerprint biometric based session key generation and secure communication establishment protocol. In this proposed technique two users generate a 128 bit session symmetric key in their end, with the help of their combined cancelable fingerprint templates and a random shuffle key provided to them by a trusted authentication server. Authentication server is located in between the communicating parties. Cancelable templates of both users are securely transmitted to each other using public key cryptography. There is no need to share the secret key through the insecure channel as the communicating parties generate the same session key in their end. This session key is valid for only one communication session. In this approach session key is generated from fingerprint and privacy of the fingerprint is protected by the cancelable transformation of fingerprint template of both communicating parties. An overview of the proposed protocol in cloud environment is also discussed in this chapter.

Keywords Cryptography · Cryptographic key · Session key · NIST · Symmetric key cryptography · Key management · Key distribution · Cloud computing

A. Sarkar (✉) · B. K. Singh
Deparment of CSE, NIT, Jamshedpur, Jharkhand, India
e-mail: asarkar.cse@nitjsr.ac.in; bksingh.cse@nitjsr.ac.in

© Springer Nature Switzerland AG 2020
B. B. Gupta et al. (eds.), *Handbook of Computer Networks and Cyber Security*,
https://doi.org/10.1007/978-3-030-22277-2_31

777

1 Introduction

Digital information transmitted over communication channel are need to be stored somewhere. Security of this digital information and a protected transmission of data become very significant. In Internet technology the number of devices connected to the Internet, those with a digital identity, is increasing day by day. With the developments in the technology, Internet of Things (IoT) becomes important part of human life. Various security issues are considered as major problems for a full-fledged IOT environment. [1] Cryptographic techniques for example [2, 3] encryption–decryption algorithms are used to provide information security. These prevent the attacker to trap data and steal information stored in a computer. According to the Kerckhoffs' principle security of cryptography depends on secrecy of cryptographic key. Cryptographic techniques are broadly categorized in symmetric key cryptography and asymmetric key cryptography. In symmetric key cryptography shared secret key is used for encryption as well as for decryption. Examples of symmetric key cryptography systems include the Data Encryption Standard (DES) and Advanced Encryption Standard (AES). Symmetric key cryptography is more efficient for enciphering large messages compared to asymmetric key cryptography as well as symmetric-key cryptosystems are fast and suitable for real-time applications. An asymmetric key cryptography is working faster for enciphering short messages. Symmetric key cryptography needs a shared secret key between two parties. Number of keys required in this symmetric key is one of the problems. Suppose Alice want to communicate with N number of people, then she must have N no of different keys. So if N no of people want to communicate with N no of people, then total N(N-1) no of keys are required. Now if a key is to be used for both directions, then N(N-1)/2 keys are needed. So, if one million people need to correspond with each other, each person has almost one million different keys and in total one trillion keys are required. This problem is known as N^2 as for N entities number of required key is N^2. Distribution of symmetric key is another problem. Because both parties who want to communicate using symmetric key cryptography need to be exchanged and must be protected from unauthorized access. Shared cryptographic key is changed for every session of communication in order to prevent the amount of message compromised. Therefore, strength of symmetric cryptography depends on transmission of symmetric key among communicating parties who want to exchange data in a secured manner. Both communicating parties have same impact on the shared key which is agreed upon. For distribution of these shared secret key we need an efficient way to maintain and distribute secret keys. Key distribution center (KDC) takes the charge to distribute these shared secret keys. To reduce the number of keys each person establishes a shared secret key with the KDC. KDC creates a secret key for each member. This key can be used only between the member and the KDC. If user A wants to communicate with user B, there needs a shared secret key between A and B. KDC can create a session key between A and B using their key with the KDC. The shared session key of A and B is used to authenticate themselves with the center and to each other before the session key is established. This shared session key is used between two parties only for once. Needham–Schroeder [4] protocol is one of such protocol which uses multiple challenge–response interactions between parties to achieve a flawless protocol. Kerberos is also a similar kind of authentication protocol and at the same time a KDC. Difficulties with these types of protocols are that strong link between secret key and its owner is not established. On the other hand, symmetric key cryptographic algorithms involve a pair of mathematically related cryptographic key, a public and a private key. This cryptosystem is designed such that computation of the private key from the public key is computationally hard. This public key is announced publicly and used for encryption. The private key, which is required for decryption must be kept secret. Few examples of public-key cryptosystems are Diffie–Hellman key exchange protocol, the RSA (Rivest, Shamir, Adleman) algorithm, elliptic curve cryptography, etc. [4]. This public-key cryptosystems does not need any additional key management techniques. A secure channel is not required for sharing the secret key since the only shared key is the public key which is publicly announced. But the public-key cryptosystems are computationally expensive and not suitable for practical purposes. Therefore, in practice a symmetric key is shared with the help of a public-key cryptosystem. The symmetric key is used for encryption/decryption in a symmetric-key cryptosystem. There are so many authentication-based session key exchange protocols in literature but none of them are able to establish a strong link between the user and the secret key. To overcome such problem biometric data based key management techniques have been proposed to establish a strong link between the person's identity and the associated cryptographic keys. In this technique biometric data is integrated with cryptography to provide strong security and known as crypto-biometric systems (CBS). Crypto biometric systems are used to combine biometric data with cryptography to provide strong security. Standard hash function or user defined algorithms can be used to produce cryptographic key from biometric data. A message communication between two users can take place by combining biometric data of both users along with traditional cryptography. The main demanding task is to combine the biometric data of both users and at the same time maintain privacy of both user biometric data. Because biometric data is inborn and if someone hacked the biometric data it can't be revocable like a pin number or passwords. To overcome this situation and also maintain the privacy of biometric data idea of cancelable template has been proposed in literature. Cancelable template is a one-way transformation of original biometric template. So instead of generating cryptographic keys directly from original biometric template it is preferable to generate keys from cancelable template of user. In this chapter a session key based protocol has been proposed. The fingerprint templates of communicating parties are used to generate 128 bit session key with the help of a shuffle key provided by an authentication server. The original biometric data of the user are first transformed into cancelable template before sharing it with the other party. So, the privacy of biometric data is also preserved here. The session symmetric key is generated by both parties in their end so there is no need to share the secret session key in order to start the communication between both parties. The main key feature of the proposed work is as follows:

- Privacy of biometric data:

Both communicating parties generate cancelable template which secures privacy and provides irrevocability of revocable biometric data.

- Authentication server:

There is an authentication server in between the communicating parties. Users register themselves with the authentication server and get a shared secret key between the user and the authentication server. Server sends a random key encrypted by that shared secret key. After decryption of the message user can get the random key which will be used for generating final session key.

- No trust to the server:

The random key generated by server is not used as a final key for communication between two parties. If the key provided by the server is compromised still it will not help the attacker to get the message exchange between both parties. User will not share any kind of biometric data with the server as there is no trust between server and user.

- Revocable key generation:

In this work revocable key can be generated in every session for better security reasons. If previous key is compromised, then it will not affect the next session anymore.

There is a mutual authentication maintained by authentication server and the users because there is no trust between server and user. So for authentication each other user here uses nonce and sends it to the other party. The other party also sends the nonce encrypted with the shared secret key between them. This way the user and the authentication server mutually authenticate each other by multiple challenge and response interactions between them.

- Shuffle key update at server side:

For every session server will provide a new random shuffle key. The proposed algorithm to generate random shuffle key at server side is able to update the random shuffle key in every session by the authentication server.

1.1 Motivation

Information exchange through the network is increasing day by day. Transmission of data through the network is not only an important thing, storage of data is also important. While sharing of information through public network, network security becomes an important aspect so that data must be protected from unauthorized access. Network security means not only the security in the computers at each end of the communication chain, but also depends on the transmission security of data through the communication link which is vulnerable to attack. An adversary can target the communication channel in order to get the data and modify it. Hence network security is as essential as securing the computers and encrypting the message. While developing a secure network the following three security services need to be achieved.

Availability This component of security aspect guarantees that only authorized entities are eligible to access the particular communication channel.

Confidentiality It is the most common aspect of security goal. Confidential information need to be protected which ensuring that no one can read the message except the intended receiver of the message. Confidentiality not only applies to the storage space of information but also needed during the transmission of information.

Integrity Information changes need to be done only by authorized entities. This security aspect ensures the receiver that the received message has not been modified in any way from the original.

Cryptography plays a major role in information security by hiding information which can be revealed only by authenticated users. It is used to transmit the data in a secure and confidential way over an insecure channel and prevent eavesdropping and data tampering. Cryptographic algorithms like public key or asymmetric key and private key or symmetric key algorithms are designed to achieve security goals. However this private key or symmetric key cryptography suffers from the problem of key sharing and key distribution. Symmetric cryptography requires key management which involves key sharing, maintaining key secrecy, and key distribution. As same key is used in encryption and decryption algorithms, it demands key sharing between the communicating parties before any communication. Larger bit cryptographic keys are hard to remember. In this current scenario integration of biometrics with cryptography can be one probable solution where the keys are generated and shared through some insecure channel. Moreover, in biometric based cryptography, biometrics of both communicating parties can be used in cryptographic key generation to associate both users with the key which can satisfy the non-repudiation of users for the communication. Deriving of cryptographic keys directly from biometric feature is also challenging. This is because if the biometric data is compromised somehow it is not revocable like a password or PIN number. Cryptographic key derived from biometrics must be non-invertible such that the reverse computation will not be feasible. In other words, if the key is compromised somehow, hackers would not be able to compute the user's biometrics from the cryptographic key. For this reason the idea of cancelable biometric is adopted in the present research work for generation of cryptographic key directly from user's cancelable fingerprint biometric. Many schemes have been proposed to use biometrics for designing session key generation and authentication protocol, but none of the scheme utilizes the full potential of the biometrics in all respects. These all current security issues formed the motivation to design a session key generation protocol that is not vulnerable to security attacks, to develop an enhanced mechanism to protect the user template and minimize the storage required for storing biometric template.

1.2 Objectives

This chapter sets out to design a fingerprint based session key generation protocol with some objectives which are as follows:

- Firstly to generate a revocable but non-invertible session key from fingerprint features of sender and receiver for symmetric cryptography.
- Secondly to preserve privacy and security of the fingerprint data of both communicating parties. At the same time exchange the fingerprint data of both users securely using cryptographic technique such that attacker cannot get the user's biometric data.
- Thirdly revocable key can be generated in every session for better security reasons. If previous key is compromised, then it will not affect the next session anymore.

1.3 Contribution of the Chapter

The major research contribution of this chapter can be summarized as following components:

- A detailed literature survey on network security, issues related to network security, various cryptographic techniques, and biometrics, key derivation techniques from biometrics, and session key generation and authentication protocol has been discussed.
- Develop a formal model of the proposed protocol. Then design and implementation of the proposed fingerprint based session key generation protocol from fingerprint data of sender and receiver are done. This proposed model is able to revoke the key easily.
- Design an approach to generate cancelable template from fingerprint template. Then the cancelable templates of both users are used to generate session key. This approach is also able to generate revocable key from irrevocable fingerprint data.
- Design an approach to generate session key from cancelable templates of both fingerprint template of sender and receiver.
- Validate the performance of the protocol's security goals. For this purpose NIST randomness testing is done.
- Comparison of performance with existing protocol.
- Application of the proposed protocol in cloud scenario.

1.4 Organization of the Chapter

The organization of chapter takes the following form:

A review of associated research work is discussed in Sect. 2. Problem formulation has been discussed in Sect. 3. Section 4 deliberates about the proposed work. This includes the architecture of the proposed system and its various phases. The experimental findings are presented in Sect. 5. Security analysis of this method is discussed in Sect. 6. Comparison with some existing works is discussed in Sect. 7. Application of the proposed protocol in cloud scenario with some security issues in cloud computing is discussed in Sect. 8. And finally, there is a conclusion in Sect. 9.

2 Background

Discussions about previous works related to protocols that are explicitly designed for sharing the crypto-bio keys or protocols which establish biometric based secure authenticated sessions are shown here. Boyen et al. [5] proposed a biometric based remote authentication protocol using fuzzy extractors. The problem with this protocol is that it stores the reference biometric template along with the protected crypto-biometric template. Although this reference biometric template is not shared, it can still be considered as a privacy compromise. Ueshige and Sakurai [6] suggested one-time biometric authentication protocol which generates biometric authentication based secure sessions but it requires storage of classical biometric templates. In this protocol, a one-time transformation is produced which is unique to the session. This transformation is applied to the stored templates as well as the fresh biometric data. An authentication protocol based on fuzzy extractor is described by Tang et al. [7]. This protocol offers security by employing the ElGamal public-key cryptosystem [8]. Fan and Lin [9] proposed a three-factor remote authentication scheme using smart cards, passwords, and biometrics in 2009 where fuzzy sketch is used for securing a key and using the key regeneration on a smart card. Abid and Afifi [10] suggested a protocol for ePassport authentication based on elliptic curve cryptography. They used fingerprint biometrics to securely generate the parameters of the elliptic curve. These parameters are used for the ePassport bearer's authentication. This proposal is hypothetical and no experimental evaluation is reported because it requires a stable, constant input from biometrics which is almost not possible. Barni et al. [11, 12] proposed a scheme for privacy preserving authentication based protocol on fingerprints. This scheme employs the ElGamal cryptosystem which facilitates biometric comparison in encrypted domain. Upmanyu et al. offered a blind authentication protocol [13, 14] based on homomorphic encryption. Few authentication protocols [6, 11, 12, 14, 15] are only able to authenticate the subject. But they are unable to produce the cryptographic keys required for secure communication. Some protocols in [5, 7, 10] can share same keys for all the sessions. Thus it is vulnerable to replay attacks. In present day scenario most of the practical systems, e.g., the transport layer security (TLS) protocol [7] recommends a session specific symmetric key for secure communication. This session keys are generated for every session. Public-key cryptographic protocols are used to share this key. Scheirer and Boult proposed

[16, 17] an idea of "bipartite biotokens," where they combined their earlier proposal of revocable biotokens [18] with fuzzy vaults [19] which enables to securely share keys using biometrics. In this scheme, a series of transformations is shared between the client and the server. A new transformation is applied in every communication session. The bipartite biotokens are session specific and make it possible to share session specific data between two parties. Buhan et al. [20, 21] proposed a protocol "Secure Ad-hoc Pairing with Biometrics: Safe" which can be used to establish a secure link between two parties. Keys are obtained from biometrics with the help of the fuzzy extractor scheme. The drawback of this protocol is that it shares the biometric data between the two parties and requires mutual trust among them and need secure channel for swapping the biometric data. Barman et al. [22] proposed a novel secure key exchange protocol using biometrics of the sender and receiver. But in this protocol problem of key distribution in symmetric cryptography remains same as the biometric based key needs to be shared through some communication channel. Sarkar et al. proposed a model for biometric cryptosystem where they generate symmetric key from user's biometric. But the recommended randomness testing is not done for generated symmetric key. Moreover the generated key is fixed for all communication sessions [23]. Very few works have been done in past for generating symmetric as well as asymmetric cryptographic keys from fingerprint biometric based cancelable templates for secure communication between two users. In this proposed approach biometric templates are first transformed into cancelable one and then both user's cancelable template are combined. After that cryptographic keys are generated from that cancelable template [24]. An approach of biometric based cryptographic key sharing has been proposed by Barman et al. [25, 26]. Few work has been done for cancelable fingerprint template generation using Cartesian transformation techniques has been proposed by Chakraborty et al. [27]. Several approaches have been proposed by Barman et al. for generation of revocable cryptographic key from combined cancelable biometric data of sender and receiver. And use of this biometric based key for symmetric cryptography established a secure communication between communicating parties [28–30].

3 Problem Formulation

The major challenge in symmetric key cryptography is sharing of secret key. Parties who want to communicate using symmetric key cryptography use same key which must be protected from unauthorized access. Shared cryptographic key is changed for every session of communication in order to prevent the amount of message compromised if an attacker compromised the key somehow. Therefore, strength of symmetric cryptography depends on transmission of symmetric key among communicating parties who want to exchange data in a secured manner. Key distribution center takes the charge to distribute these shared secret keys. Present day knowledge based or smart card based authentication is used to confirm privacy of key exchange protocol. But the problem with these types of protocol is strong link between secret key and its owner is not established. Crypto biometric systems are used to combine biometric data with cryptography to provide strong security and also established a link between the user and the key. Standard hash function or user defined algorithms can be used to generate cryptographic key from biometric data. The main demanding task is to combine the biometric data of both users and at the same time maintain privacy of both user biometric data. Because biometric data is inborn and if someone hacked the biometric data it can't be revocable like a pin number or password. Cancelable template is one of the probable solutions which are a one-way transformation of original biometric template. So instead of generating cryptographic keys directly from original biometric template it is preferable to generate keys from cancelable template of user to ensure privacy of user biometrics.

In this chapter fingerprint template of communicating parties is used to generate session key with the help of a shuffle key provided by an authentication server. The original biometric data of the user are first transformed into cancelable template before sharing it with the other party. So, the privacy of biometric data is also preserved here. Each of the communicating parties generate same session symmetric key. Therefore, the communicating parties do not need to share the session symmetric key. Server plays a vital role here. User A and B before exchanging their cancelable template with each other authenticate themselves with each other and send their public key certificate to each other. Server sends a random shuffle key to one of the parties say A. User A then passes the random shuffle key to B. If user A and B are authenticated users then only they will have the key sent by the server and will able to generate the final session key. This random shuffle key generated by the server is valid for only one session. It helps both the parties to authenticate each other with the server and prevent impersonating either of them and also randomize the elements of the combined template. Security efficiency of the proposed approach is also analyzed in this chapter.

4 Proposed Methodology

In this section a fingerprint biometric based session key generation protocol is proposed. The proposed protocol is described in Fig. 31.1. In this protocol it is assumed that two users named as user A and B is the communicating party who wants to communicate with each other. There is an authentication server which is located in between two users and authenticates the communicating party. In this section the proposed protocol which includes three phases, that is, the registration phase, authentication phase, and communication, is discussed in detail.

Registration Phase
Each user registers with the authentication server and is granted a user identity and a shared secret key between the user and the server. The authentication server maintained a database with these identities. A and B have a shared secret key with the authentication server, namely $K_{A\text{-}AS}$ and $K_{AS\text{-}B}$.

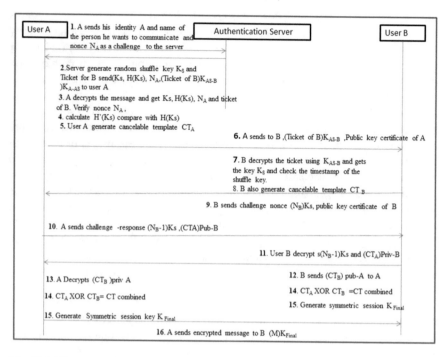

Fig. 31.1 The proposed model for biometric based session key generation protocol

Authentication Phase

User A sends a request message by sending his registered identity and the name of the person he wants to communicate with. Authentication server verifies user and issues a shuffle key and encrypts it with the shared secret key between them. Authentication server also generates a ticket to share the shuffle key for user B with whom A wants to communicate and send it to A. Although A gets the ticket for B but he is unable to open it as it is encrypted by the shared secret key between server and B. Both parties also exchange their cancelable template after mutually authenticating themselves.

Communication Phase

With the help of combined template and the shuffle key provided by the server they produced final session key and communicate with each other. Biometric data of the user is used here not for any kinds of biometric authentication of the user but for the purposes of increasing the randomness in the generated session key. This proposed protocol uses multiple challenge–response interactions between parties to achieve a flawless protocol.

Different symbols used to describe the work flow of the proposed protocol are listed in Table 31.1

Table 31.1 Different symbols used to describe the work flow of proposed protocol

Symbol	Description	Symbol	Description
A, B	Registered ID of users	$K_{AS\text{-}B}$	Shared secret key between server and user B
N_A, N_B $(N_A\text{-}1), (N_B\text{-}1)$	Nonce generated by A and B as a challenge Response generated by server and A	$K_{A\text{-}AS}$	Shared secret key between server and user A
Ks	Shuffle key generated by server	CT_A, CT_B	Cancelable template of user A and B
$H(Ks)$	Hash of shuffle key	$CT_{Combined}$	Combined cancelable template of A and B

The protocol works as follows:

Authentication Phase

Step 1. User A sends a request to the authentication server that he wants to send a confidential message to user B. The message contains her registered identity and the name of B and a nonce N_A.

Step 2. A random shuffle key K_S is generated by the server, which generates a hash code $H(K_S)$. This shuffle key is valid for only one session. To check the validity of the session key one timestamp is also attached with the key. Server generates a ticket for user B which is encrypted by $K_{AS\text{-}B}$, shared secret key between server and user B. This ticket contains Ks, $H(K_s)$, and a timestamp T. Server now sends a reply to user A's request containing ticket for user B, nonce $(N_A\text{ -}1)$ as a response to challenge N_A sent by A, shuffle key K_s, hash of shuffle key $H(K_S)$. All these messages are encrypted by $K_{A\text{-}AS}$ (shared secret key between user A and authentication server).

Step 3. User A upon receiving the message decrypts it with the shared secret key $K_{A\text{-}AS}$. A now first checks that the nonce sent by the server is same as the nonce sent by him before with the first request message. If both are same, then user A and server can both mutually authenticate themselves and the message received by A is actually coming from server.

Step 4. User A now have the key K_S from server. User A applies the same hash function on the K_S and output is $H'(K_S)$. A has now $H(K_S)$ sent by the server and $H'(K_S)$ that A has generated. If $H(K_S)$ and $H'(K_S)$ are equal, then it proves beyond doubt that the value of Ks is authenticated and genuinely sent by server. If both $H(K_S)$ and $H'(K_S)$ are same, then A now has the shuffle key K_S which can be used to generate final symmetric key.

Step 5. User A now generates cancelable template CT_A using the algorithm described in Sect. 4.2.1.

Step 6. User A now sends two items to user B. The first is ticket received from the server and second is his public key certificate.

Step 7. User B received the message sent by A and decrypts the ticket using K_{AS-B} and gets the key K_S. Now user B checks the timestamp of the key. This timestamp prevents replay attack. B can check the validity of K_S.

Step 8. B also generates a cancelable template CT_B.

Step 9. B now generates a nonce N_B as a challenge and encrypts it with K_S and sends it to A along with his public key certificate.

Step 10. A proves that she possesses the shuffle key sent by the server K_S and sends (N_B-1) as a challenge–response by encrypting it with K_S. Along with this message A also sends his cancelable template CT_A encrypted with B's public key.

Step 11. B decrypts the message and checks the value (N_B-1). If the value is verified means A is an authenticate user. B also decrypts the cancelable template with its private key.

Step 12. B sent his cancelable template CT_B encrypting it with public key of A.

Step 13. User A decrypts the cancelable template CT_B using his private key. User A and B both have the cancelable template of one another.

Step 14. User A and B combined their template by applying XOR function and generate a combined template denoted as $CT_{combined}$. Now both A and B have the same combined template and same random key K_S provided by the server.

Step 15. Both parties now generate the secret session symmetric key K_{Final} by applying the proposed algorithm described in Sect. 4.2.4. As the both parties generate same symmetric secret key in their end this key is no longer needed to share through the insecure channel.

Communication Phase

Step 16. A and B now start communication. A sends a message to B encrypted with K_{Final}.

Different tasks in this approach are discussed in detail in the following section. Different task involved in the proposed protocol is shown in Fig. 31.2.

4.1 Feature Extraction from Fingerprint of User A and B

In this tactic minutia points are extracted from the given fingerprint image of A and B. The steps involved in minutia extraction are as follows:

- Image enhancement: Image enhancement is done to improve the eminence of the obtained biometric feature. The biometric features like fingerprint being gained need to be enhanced so that they can be used for further analysis. This process is done to eliminate redundant pixels from an image and achieve the brightness and contrast.
- Image binarization: The goal of this step is to obtain a binary image. One can choose a threshold value and choose all the pixels above that value as white and below that value as black. This process is one of the modest for binarization.

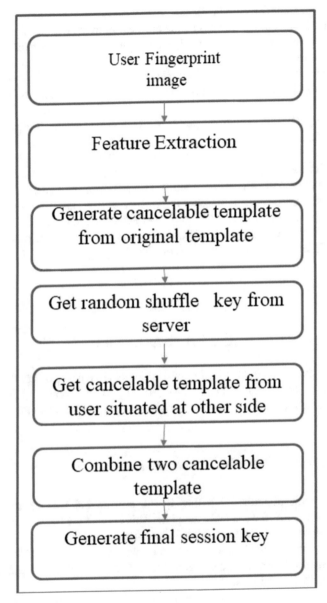

Fig. 31.2 Different tasks involved in the proposed protocol

- Morphological operation: Morphology involves processing images based on shapes. Each pixel in the output image is result of processing the equivalent input image with its adjacent pixels. Dilation and erosion are examples of morphological operations. Dilation involves adding pixels, while erosion involves excluding pixels from boundaries. The rules for dilation and erosion are as follows: in dilation the value of the output pixel is the maximum of all adjacent pixels, while for the erosion the rule is accurately same with the maximum being substituted by minimum.

- Thinning: Thinning is used to eliminate selected image from binary sources and is particularly used for skeletonization. All lines will be condensed to a single pixel thickness.
- Minutiae extraction: Minutiae points are take out from the fingerprint image. Bifurcations, ridge ending, and other features are found in this method. In this method principal curve algorithm is used to detect minutia points of a given input fingerprint image of the sender and receiver. This algorithm returns (x, y, θ, q) as a minutiae point, where (x, y) denote (x, y)-coordinate value, θ represents the alignment angle, and q represents the quality of a minutiae point. Only (x, y) coordinate values are measured as the extracted minutiae points. These values are kept in two vectors (X, Y). Vector F_x encompasses x-coordinate values and vector FY holds y-coordinate values of minutiae points.

$$F_x = [x_i], \text{ where } i = 1 \text{ to } n$$

$$F_y = [y_i], \text{ where } i = 1 \text{ to } n$$

For example, assume that eight minutiae points are extracted. Let the points be $(33, 3)$, $(12, 6)$, $(67, 11)$, $(76, 11)$, $(3, 34)$, $(20, 47)$, $(20, 49)$, and $(87, 65)$. Then X and Y coordinate values can be represented as shown in Fig. 31.3.

4.2 Cancelable Template Generation

In this phase the fingerprint template of the user A and B is altered into non-invertible forms, called cancelable template. This is for if the unique biometric data is compromised, the biometric traits will no longer be in use. So, it is compulsory to change the irrevocable biometric data into revocable one before it is practiced in cryptography. Both A and B parties generate their own cancelable template.

The process is as follows:

From the X and Y arrays bred in previous step, a template is created.

Fig. 31.3 X and Y coordinate values

4.2.1 Proposed Algorithm to Generate Cancelable Template

```
Cancelable Template Generation Algorithm:-
 Inputs:-
 A[]= integer array of length 32 each of 2 bytes to hold random
   469 values ranging from 1 to 32
 X[]= integer array of length 32 each of 2 bytes to hold x
   coordinate values of minutiae points
 Y[]= integer array of length 32 each of 2 bytes to hold y 473
   coordinate values of minutiae points
 N= total number of minutiae points read from file
 Output:-
 T[]=integer array of length 32 to hold Cancelable templates
 Steps involved in algorithm are as follows:-
 Create an array A to hold 32 random short integer values
 ranging from 0 to 31.
 Read file containing extracted minutiae (x,y) points.
 Store first 32 x-coordinate values in array x[]
 Store first 32 y-coordinate values in array Y[]
 If (I is even)
   T[A[I]]= (x-coordinate MOD 256) +1;
 Else
   T[A[I]]= (y-coordinate MOD 256) -1;
 END If
 Pseudo code:-
 BEGIN
 //Read minutia points from image file one by one.
 FOR(I=1 and I<=N)
         X[I]=read X coordinate from file 497
         Y[I]=read Y coordinate from file 498
 END FOR
 FOR(I=1 and I<=N)
  A[I]=call RANDOM()
 END FOR
 Inputs:-
 A[]= integer array of length 32 each of 2 bytes to hold random
   values ranging from 1 to 32
 X[]=integer array of length 32 each of 2 bytes to hold x
   coordinate values of minutiae points
 Y[]=integer array of length 32 each of 2 bytes to hold y
   coordinate values of minutiae points
 N= total number of minutiae points read from file
 Output:-
 T[]=integer array of length 32 to hold Cancelable templates
 Steps involved in algorithm are as follows
 Create an array A to hold 32 random short integer values
 ranging from 0 to 31.
 Read file containing extracted minutiae (x,y) points
 Store first 32 x-coordinate values in array X[]
 Store first 32 y-coordinate values in array Y[]
 Calculate each element of T[] using formula
 If(I is even)
         T[A[I]]= (x-coordinate MOD 256) +1
```

```
Else
        T[A[I]]= (y-coordinate MOD 256) -1
End IF
```
Pseudo code
BEGIN
```
//Read minutia points from image file one by one.
FOR(I=1 and I<=N)
        X[I]=read X coordinate from file
        Y[I]=read Y coordinate from file
END FOR
//create a set of random numbers
FOR(I=1 and I<=N)
        A[I]=call RANDOM()
END FOR
//create cancelable template
FOR(I=1 and I<=N)
        IF(I MOD 2=0)
                    T[A[I]]=(X[I] MOD 256) +1;
        ELSE
                    T[A[I]]=(Y[I] MOD 256) +1;
        END IF
END FOR
RETURN T[]
```

4.2.2   Combined Template Generation

A after generating his/her own cancelable template send it to B by encrypting it with B's public key. The same is done by B. After generating his/her own cancelable template B sends the same to A by encrypting it with A's public key. Let the templates be CT_A and CT_B. A new template $CT_{Combined}$ is created by concatenating both templates in by both A and B. Therefore now both the parties A and B have the same combined cancelable template with them.

$$CT_A \oplus CT_B = CT_{Combined}$$

Inputs:-
$CT_A = 32$ short integers each of 2 byte (total 64 bytes template from A)
$CT_B = 32$ short integers each of 2 byte (total 64 bytes template from B)
$CT_{Combined} = CT_A \oplus CT_B$
RANDOM(X) = generate unique RANDOM number within range 0 to X.
Output:-
KEY [] = 16 byte array holding the new generated value from CT_A and CT_B

$$CT_A \oplus CT_B = CT_{Combined}$$

Algorithm to generate combine template is as follows:

Combined Template Generation Algorithm :-
```
Perform XOR operation to combine templates CTB and CTA in
CTcombined
Randomly choose and place 16 bytes from CTcombined into KEY[]
```

```
Pseudocode
-----------------
J=0;

For (I =0;I<16++I)
{
    T=RANDOM(32);
        KEY[I]=CT_combined[T];
}
```

4.2.3 Symmetric Session Key Generation

In this proposed protocol session symmetric key is generated from the combined cancelable template of both communicating party A and B. As the key is generated from cancelable biometric template of both user A and B there is no need to store, remember, or share the secret key. Fingerprint biometric traits are used to generate cryptographic key. These biometric traits are used only to increase the randomness in the symmetric key and not for any biometric authentication purposes. For every communication session server will generate a new shuffle key. With the help of that key both users will generate a new symmetric key. The algorithm to generate session key is as follows:

Session Key Generation Algorithm:-
      Input:-
      SHUFFLE_KEY=Random shuffle key sent from Server. This is of
16 bits.
      KEY[]= 16 byte array holding the new generated value from
CT_A and CT_B
      Output:-
      K_{Final}[] = 16 BYTE array to hold new key value
      Steps involved in generating session key are

      1. Use Server generated SHUFFLE_KEY
      2. Inspect each bit of SHUFFLE_KEY left to right.
      3. If SHUFFLE_KEY bit is zero then
                  Fill value of left most KEY[0]to K_{Final}[0]
            ELSE
                  Fill value of right most KEY[15]to K_{Final}[0]
      4. Continue step 3 for16 times ranging from 0 to 15.

Pseudocode:-

```
FOR(I=0;I<=16;++I)
{
    If (SHUFFLE_KEY.BIT(SHUFFLE_KEY.BIT[I]==0)
    {
        K_Final[X]= KEY[I];
            X=X+1;
    }
    ELSE
```

```
{
        K_Final [J] = KEY [I] ;
            J=J-1;
}
}
```

K_{Final} is generated.

This K_{Final} now is the final session key of 128 bit. It will be used to establish a secure communication between user A and B.

4.2.4 Shuffle Key Update from Server

For better security reasons an algorithm is proposed to change the shuffle key in each session. In the proposed approach final session key generation is depends on two factors. First factor is that cancelable biometric templates of users and secondly the random shuffle key (KS) provided by the authentication server. The revocability of the session key is accomplished with not only cancelable template but also with the random shuffle key. Present approach in the proposed protocol has a provision to update the shuffle key time to time. The proposed algorithm generates session wise, new shuffle key. Session wise shuffle key generation process is as follows:

```
Shuffle Key Generation Algorithm From Server:-
Input:- current system time in milliseconds
Output:-
SHUFFLE_KEY
Time= get current system time in milliseconds
SHUFFLE_KEY= Time MOD 32000

Pseudocode:-
RANDOM()
A[]= Integer array of 32 elements
INTEGER I
FOR I=1 AND I<=32

    T=System current time in nanoseconds
    N= T MOD 32
    A[I]=N
END FOR
RETURN A[]
```

5 Experimental Results and Analysis

Database In this work publicly accessible fingerprint database FVC 2002 DB1 is used.

Experimental Setup This work is executed with Intel® Core ™ i7 processor with 2.4 GHZ clock speed in MATLAB12 successively with Windows 10OS and JAVA 1.8 sdk has been used for NIST test purposes.

Experimental Findings Two unlike fingerprint images are taken from the database as an input fingerprint of user A and user B. The minutia points or features are taken out from the fingerprint images using the principal curve analysis algorithm in MATLAB. In this current research work fingerprint data is taken only to resolve arbitrariness and not for verification of the user. Therefore, only x and y coordinates value of minutia points are measured as the features of fingerprints. After generation of cancelable template, values for user A and B are as follows:

Cancelable_template_userA (CT_A):
{294,320,223,219,205,215,347,215,190,234,92,358,123,318,188,188,188,193, 243,228,324,246,343,190,232,103,241,332,283,220,203,190}

Cancelable_template_userB (CT_B):
{203,343,188,190,193,190,215,188,92,358,103,123,294,223,190,219,205,215, 246,332,320,243,232,347,228,324,234,283,220,318,188,241}

After exchange of cancelable template at both side of user A and B they concatenate the template using XOR function and generate a combined template $CT_{Combined}$.

The value of concatenated cancelable template is as follows:

Combined_cancelable_template ($CT_{Combined}$):
{493,23,99,101,12,105,396,107,226,396,59,285,349,481,2,103,113,22,5,424, 4,5,447,485,12,291,27,87,455,482,119,79}

Now the sender and receiver both have the same combined cancelable template and the same random shuffle key provided by the authentication server. After that 128 bit key is generated from the combined cancelable biometric template of both user.

Shuffle key provided by server: 1011110100001000

For a single session the final key is (K_{Final}):
00000100000011000000011001110001001101011011101110100111110111111.

If user A wants to communicate user B for the next time the authentication server will send a new random shuffle key. And the user with their combined cancelable template and the random shuffle key will be able to generate a fresh new final key for communication. So for every session a fresh key will be generated, thus the protocol is not vulnerable to replay attack.

5.1 Randomness Testing of 128 Bit Final Key with the NIST Statistical Test Suite

The NIST statistical test suite [31] consists of 15 experimental tests specially designed to analyze binary sequences (bit streams). The tests examine randomness of data according to various statistics of bits or statistics of blocks of bits. All NIST STS tests examine randomness for the whole bit stream. The NIST recommendation says that if P-value ≥ 0.01, the bit sequence is random. Generated session key must be random. Randomness is required for cryptographic purposes. In this proposed protocol total 50 different session key each 128 bit is generated for 50 different communication sessions. The NIST test results show that the proposed protocol is

Table 31.2 Randomness test for the proposed biometrics-based key exchange protocols based on the NIST statistical test suite

No.	Name of the statistical test	P-value	Results
1	The frequency (Monobit) test	0.87	PASS
2	Frequency test within a block	1.69	PASS
3	The runs test	0.00	FAIL
4	Tests for the longest-run-of-ones in a block	0.18	PASS
5	The binary matrix rank test	1.37	PASS
6	The discrete Fourier transform (spectral) test	1.57	PASS
7	The non-overlapping template matching test	1.16	PASS
8	The overlapping template matching test	2.61	PASS
9	Maurer's universal statistical test	1.61	PASS
10	The linear complexity test	0.00	FAIL
11	The serial test	0.00	FAIL
12	The approximate entropy test	0.00	FAIL
13	The cumulative sums (Cumsum) test	0.03	PASS
14	The random excursions test	1.12	PASS
15	The random excursions variant test	2.58	PASS

Table 31.3 Randomness test for the proposed biometrics-based key exchange protocols based on the NIST statistical test suite

No.	Name of the statistical test	P-value	Results
1	The frequency (monobit) test	1.58	PASS
2	Frequency test within a block	1.75	PASS
3	The runs test	1.70	PASS
4	Tests for the longest-run-of-ones in a block	1.36	PASS
5	The binary matrix rank test	0.97	PASS
6	The discrete Fourier transform (spectral) test	1.20	PASS
7	The non-overlapping template matching test	3.28	PASS
8	The overlapping template matching test	0.06	PASS
9	Maurer's universal statistical test	2.92	PASS
10	The linear complexity test	0.00	FAIL
11	The serial test	2.04	PASS
12	The approximate entropy test	1.84	PASS
13	The cumulative sums (Cumsum) test	0.03	PASS
14	The random excursions test	1.67	PASS
15	The random excursions variant test	2.18	PASS

successful in 11 out of 15 tests every time. In the remaining four tests, the outcomes of protocol are close to the expected recommendation. Therefore, the cryptographic session key generated by the current approach satisfies the NIST recommendations for random and pseudorandom patterns for cryptographic applications. Average p-Values are calculated and documented in Table 31.1, 31.2 and represented in Fig. 31.4.

Fig. 31.4 Chart shows name of the tests and their corresponding P-value

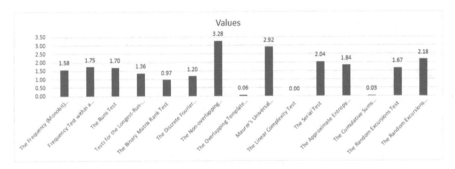

Fig. 31.5 Chart shows name of the tests and their corresponding P-value

5.2 Randomness Testing of Shuffle Key from Server with the NIST Statistical Test Suite

In this proposed protocol server is sending a 16 bit shuffle key on request of the user. For cryptographic purposes, this key should be random and unpredictable. Both communicating party will get this random shuffle key which is actually working as a transformation key. With the help of this key and the combined template final session key can be generated. This shuffle key is generated by the server randomly for every session. In this proposed protocol a total of 50 different 16 bit shuffle keys are generated for 50 different sessions. The NIST test results show that the proposed protocol is successful in 14 out of the 15 tests every time. Therefore, the shuffle key is generated by server satisfying the NIST recommendations for random and pseudorandom patterns for cryptographic applications. Average p-value are calculated and documented in Table 31.3 and represented in Fig. 31.5.

Computation time is also calculated for different tasks involved in the proposed protocol for a single session and listed in Table 31.4.

Table 31.4 Computation time for different operations in the proposed protocol

Operations	Time (in s)
Cancelable templates generation	0.007
Combined cancelable template generation	0.003
Final session key generation	0.000001208

6 Security Analysis

This section discusses about the security of the proposed biometric based authentication protocol. Here the entire security analysis of the proposed approach is divided into following sections.

6.1 Privacy of Fingerprints

A and B exchange their fingerprint template after transforming those into cancelable template and encrypt the cancelable template into public key of each other. So for an attacker it is impossible to get the cancelable template because it does not have the private key of A and B.

Both A and B communicating party are not able to derive the original minutia points of each other from cancelable template. By transforming original minutia points into cancelable one it is guaranteed that the fingerprint identity of one party is not disclosed with other.

The cancelable template (CT_A, CT_B) are concatenated and the combined template is generated. For a particular session if the cancelable template is compromised it won't affect the next session as template is completely revocable.

6.2 Security of 128 Bit Cryptographic Key

In this approach 128 bit session key is generated to initiate a communication between A and B. This key is generated from the combination of cancelable template of two fingerprints of A and B. The key is not shared by them but generated at their end independently. There is no need to store the key for decryption.

6.3 Prevention Against Replay Attack

This approach prevents replay attack because in every individual session of communication a unique session key is used to establish a secure communication between A and B. This session key is destroyed after every session and a fresh session key is generated using proposed session key generation algorithm in this paper. So if an attacker wants to make a replay attack by using a previously transmitted message by legal users, then it will make no sense to the legitimate user as the cryptographic key has been changed already.

6.4   Prevention Against Man-in-Middle Attack

In this approach fingerprint of communicating parties is transmitted over communication channel by encrypting with the public key of both sender and receiver. If the man in middle eavesdrops the cancelable template of both parties, then also he will be not able to generate genuine key without the knowledge of the shuffle key sent by the server.

6.5   Known Key Attack

In this case if the 128 bit cryptographic key and the key sent by the server are compromised somehow by the attacker for one session it does not affect the previous or next session. In this proposed approach both final 128 bit key and the key generated and sent by the server are updated in every session. At the end of the session both the keys are destroyed.

6.6   Known Fingerprint Attack

Two different kinds of attacks are possible within category of "known fingerprint attack". First let us consider the case that fingerprints of user A or user B have been compromised. This is possible even if the users have not stored their original template anywhere in biometric system. The attacker still will not be able to generate combined cancelable fingerprint template as he must have access to cancelable templates of user A and user B together at the same time. Similarly, while generating original cryptographic key adversary should know about the random shuffle key sent by server. In second case even if attacker is able to generate cancelable template but without the shuffle key sent by the server, he or she cannot generate the final cryptographic key.

6.7   Known Server Key Attack

An adversary may get access to the random key sent by the server, then also he will be not able to generate final cryptographic key as he need the cancelable template of both A and B to generate the final key.

7 Comparison with Few ExistingWork

In this section the work is compared with few existing methods. The safety of the cryptographic key depends on the biometric template only in [32, 33]. But in this proposed work session key is constructed not only from the biometric template but also with the shuffle key provided by server. So if an attacker gets the biometric template he must have the shuffle key to generate the session key. In some of the existing works [34–37] single user's biometric data is used to protect the secret key. The proposed work combined biometric data of both users, then generated key from the combined biometric data. In the proposed protocol, an attacker has to determine the shuffle key along with a user's biometric template to compromise the session key, but in an existing protocol [25, 26] the security of the secret key can be cracked with the information about the template only. Nandakumar [36] proposed a methodology for key sharing in which the key is safe by the biometric template of the client. In this scheme, secret key K_{ss} is merged with the transformation key of the server K_{sr} and the client's biometric template. This key K_{ss} is used to authenticate the client, and the session key is transmitted to the server by encoding it with the client specified nonce, K_{sr} and the corrected code word. This protocol uses only one sample of biometric data and the other user is a server which uses knowledge-based authenticator to provide session key security. In every session, the same biometric data and server transformation key are used. But in the proposed scheme fresh session key is used in every new session. Nandakumar uses only one sample of biometric data of the client, but in the current approach, the biometric templates of two communicating users are used to improve security of the protocol.

8 Application of the Proposed Protocol in Cloud Scenario

Cloud computing [38] provides shared services and computing resources over the Internet. In last few years, usage of Internet is increasing very rapidly which increases cost of hardware and software. To decrease overall cost cloud computing has come up with an idea of sharing resources. The cloud computing network can be of four types. These are private, public, hybrid, and community cloud. Community cloud is shared between multiple organizations which fit only to a specific community. Private cloud contains private data of a user and is not shared, highly secure. Hybrid cloud is both public and private depending on their purpose. Public cloud is a platform where whole computing resource is located at a cloud computing company which offers cloud services. Along with decrease of cost, cloud computing also has some security risks [39] as explained below.

Misuse and Reprehensible Use of Cloud Computing External hackers find advantage of simple registration, procedures, and comparatively unspecified access to cloud services to launch various attacks like cracking password.

Insecure Application Programming Interfaces (API) Cloud services are made available to consumers through interfaces or APIs. Cloud service providers must ensure that security is integrated into their service models. At the same time end users should be aware of security threats.

Wicked Insiders Malicious insiders create a greater threat in cloud computing environment. This is because consumers do not have a clear idea of policies and procedures. Insiders with bad intent can gain unauthorized access into cloud computing resources.

Shared Technology Issues/Multi-Tenancy Nature Multitenant architecture poses security risks as same cloud database might contain share of data of different users.

Data Crash Comprised data may include deletion or editing of data without taking a backup. Unlinking a record from a larger environment might cause loss of an encoding key. Again, illegal access of sensitive data may lead to great loss to consumer.

Account, Service, and Traffic Hijacking Attackers can access critical areas of cloud computing services like integrity, confidentiality, and availability of services. Examples of such attacks are phishing, fraud, and exploitation of software vulnerabilities.

The proposed protocol can be safely applied in cloud environment. Here one authentication server is used to authenticate the user. This authentication server and the users can be part of hybrid cloud platform. When biometric data is exchanged between the communicating parties the data is highly encrypted with RSA public key encryption. Moreover the exchanged data is cancelable biometric; hence, the security issues of cloud environment does not affect the message exchange.

The implementation of authentication protocol in cloud is as follows:

Authentication/Registration Phase
In registration phase a user has to register himself with the authentication server. If he has already registered, then he need not require further registration. Otherwise authentication server gives a new ID. After registering itself then the transaction will become secure and the process become authenticated. After authentication is done with the server, a username and password are provided for accessing the cloud by the authentication server. In this process the user registered himself for accessing data. At the same time authentication server sends the username to cloud provider. Overall framework is designed in Fig. 31.6.

8.1   User Request to Cloud Provider to Data

User requests for access data to the cloud provider. Cloud provider checks the user name and password to cloud directory. If it is valid access is granted to the user.

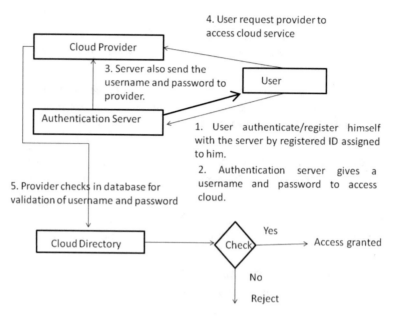

Fig. 31.6 Overall framework for implementation of the proposed protocol in cloud scenario

Further Observations from the Proposed Protocol

Data security for cloud based applications is increased by using RSA keys of 1024 bit while exchanging cancelable biometric data. Cancelable biometric data of the user is encrypted with 1024 bit RSA key. When the user logins to the cloud web portal, accesses the applications but does not log out and in fact just leaves the session idle, then in this case if an attacker breaks in to the user system attempting to download and access the biometric data from the user system, then the attacker would be required to enter the private key. Suppose the attacker in his attempt to break in to the biometric system becomes successful, or, somehow able to guess the private key and then obtain encrypted data. The attacker will still not be able to access the original biometric data as it is not stored anywhere.

9 Conclusions

Key sharing and key management techniques are major cause of cryptographic key management techniques. In this proposed biometric based session key protocol, combination of cancelable templates of communicating parties is used along with use of random shuffle key provided by trusted authentication server to generate final session key. There is no requirement of the user to remember or store cryptographic key in any device. Both communicating parties do not need to share the session key through not so secure channels. Communicating parties generate the same session key in their end without any need of exchange of final session key. The session key generated remains valid only for one single session. This protocol therefore resolves the issue of key management and key distribution. The generated key is random in each session due to use of cancelable template of both users along with added shuffle key from authentication server. Testing of randomness of the generated session key is done using test procedures stated by National Institute of Standards and Technology (NIST). The way the proposed protocol can be transferred to cloud scenario is also discussed in this chapter. Other biometric data, for example, irises, faces, could be easily implemented using this proposed protocol in near future.

References

1. Vipindev, A., & Gupta, B. (2018). Security in internet of things: Issues, challenges, taxonomy, and architecture. *Telecommunication Systems, 67*(3), 423–441.
2. Gupta, B. (2018). *Computer and cyber security: Principles, algorithm, applications, and perspectives* (p. 666). Boca Raton, FL: CRC Press, Taylor & Francis.
3. Gupta, B., Agrawal, D. P., & Shingo, Y. (2016). *Handbook of research on modern cryptographic solutions for computer and cyber security.* Pennsylvania: IGI Global.
4. Stallings, W. (2010). *Cryptography and network security: Principles and practice* (5th ed.). Upper Saddle River, NJ: Prentice Hall.
5. Boyen, X., Dodis, Y., Katz, J., Ostrovsky, R., & Smith, A. (2005). Secure remote authentication using biometric data. In *Eurocrypt.* https://doi.org/10.1007/11426639_9
6. Ueshige, Y., & Sakurai, K. (2006). A proposal of one-time biometric authentication. In: H. R. Arabnia, & S. Aissi, (Eds.) *Security and Management.*
7. Tang, Q., Bringer, J., Chabanne, H., & Pointcheval, D. (2008). A formal study of the privacy concerns in biometric-based remote authentication schemes. In *Information Security Practice and Experience Conference (ISPEC).* https://doi.org/10.1007/978-3-540-79104-1_5
8. Elgamal, T. (1985). A public key cryptosystem and a signature scheme based on discrete logarithms. *IEEE Transactions on Information Theory, 31*(4), 469–472. https://doi.org/10.1109/TIT.1985.1057074.
9. Fan, C., & Lin, Y. (2009). Provably secure remote truly three-factor authentication scheme. With privacy protection on biometrics. *IEEE Transactions on Information Forensics and Security, 4*(4), 933–945. https://doi.org/10.1109/TIFS.2009.2031942.
10. Abid, M., & Afifi, H. (2009). Towards a secure e-passport protocol based on biometrics. *Journal of Information Assurance and Security (JIAS), 4*(4), 338–345.
11. Barni, M., Bianchi, T., Dario Catalano, M., di Raimondo, R. D. Labati, P. Failla, D. F., et al. (2010a). Privacy-preserving fingercode authentication. In: *The 12th ACM Workshop on Multimedia and Security (MM&Sec10), Rome, Italy, Sept.* https://doi.org/10.1145/1854229.1854270
12. Barni, M., Bianchi, T., Catalano, D., di Raimondo, M., Labati, R. D., Failla, P., et al. (2010b). Privacy-preserving finger code authentication. In *The12th ACM Workshop on Multimedia and Security (MM&Sec10), Rome, Italy.* https://doi.org/10.1145/1854229.1854270
13. Upmanyu, M., Namboodiri, A. M., Srinathan, K., & Jawahar, C. V. (2009). Efficient biometric verification in encrypted domain. In *International Conference on Biometrics (ICB).* https://doi.org/10.1007/978-3-642-01793-3_91
14. Upmanyu, M., Namboodiri, A. M., Srinathan, K., & Jawahar, C. V. (2010). Blind authentication: a secure crypto-biometric verification protocol. *IEEE Transactions Information Forensics and Security, 5*(2), 255–268. https://doi.org/10.1109/TIFS.2010.2043188.

15. Bringer, J., Chabanne, H., Izabachène, M., Pointcheval, D., Tang, Q., & Zimmer, S. (2007). An application of the Goldwasser-Micali cryptosystem to biometric authentication. In *The 12th Australasian Conference on Information Security and Privacy (ACISP'07)*. https://doi.org/10.1007/978-3-540-73458-1

16. Scheirer, W. J., & Boult, T. E. (2008). Bio-cryptographic protocols with bipartite biotokens. In *Biometric Symposium*. https://doi.org/10.1109/BSYM.2008.4655516

17. Scheirer, W. J., & Boult, T. E. (2009). Bipartite biotokens: Definitions, implementation, and analysis. In *International Conference on Biometrics (ICB)*. https://doi.org/10.1007/978-3-642-01793-3_79

18. Boult, T. E., Scheirer, W. J., & Woodworth, R. (2007). Revocable fingerprint biotokens: Accuracy and security analysis. In *IEEE Conference on Computer Vision and Pattern Recognition*. https://doi.org/10.1109/CVPR.2007.383110

19. Juels, A., & Sudan, M. (2002). A fuzzy vault scheme. In A. Lapidoth, & E. Teletar (Eds.) *Proceedings of IEEE International Symposium Information Theory* (p. 408). Piscataway, NJ: IEEE Press

20. Buhan, I., Doumen, J., Hartel, P., & Veldhuis, R. (2007). *Secure Ad-hoc pairing with biometrics SAFE*. Technical report, University of Twente. https://doi.org/10.1504/IJSN.2009.023424

21. Buhan, I. (2008). *Cryptographic keys from noisy data*. Ph.D. thesis, University of Twente, Enschede, Netherlands.

22. Barman, S., Chattopadhyay, S., Samanta, D., & Gaurang, P. (2016). A novel secure key-exchange protocol using biometrics of the sender and receiver. *Computer and Electrical Engineering, 64*, 65. https://doi.org/10.1016/j.compeleceng.2016.11.01.

23. Sarkar, A, & Singh, B. (2018). Cryptographic key generation from cancelable fingerprint templates. In *Proceedings of 4th IEEE International Conference on Recent Advances in Information Technology Proceedings of RAIT* (Vol. 1).

24. Sarkar, A., & Singh, A. (2017). Cancelable biometric based key generation for symmetric cryptography. In *IEEE International Conference on Inventive Communication and Computational Technologies* (pp. 404–409). https://doi.org/10.1109/ICICCT.2017.7975186.

25. Barman, S., Chattopadhyay, S., & Samanta, D. (2014). In *An Approach to Cryptographic Key Distribution Through Fingerprint Based Key Distribution Center, Advances in Computing, Communications and Informatics (ICACCI), 2014 International Conference on IEEE, 24–27 Sept. 2014, Delhi, India* (pp. 1629–1635). https://doi.org/10.1109/ICACCI

26. Barman, S., Samanta, D., & Chattopadhyay, S. (2014b). An approach of biometric based cryptographic key sharing. In *International Conference on Communication and Computing (ICC), Bengaluru, India* (pp. 151–158).

27. Chakraborty, A., Datta, A., Nandi, P., Bar, P., Begum, S., & Barman, S. (2014). A proposed approach to generate revocable fingerprint template using Cartesian transformation. In *Proceedings of 1st International Science and Technology Congress (IEMCONGRESS 2014), Kolkata, India* (pp. 196-201).

28. Barman, S., Samanta, D., & Chattopadhyay, S. (2015a). Approach to cryptographic key generation from fingerprint biometrics. *International Journal of Biometrics, 7*(3), 226–248.

29. Barman, S., Samanta, D., & Chattopadhyay, S. (2015b). Revocable key generation from irrevocable biometric data for symmetric cryptography. In *2015 Third International Conference on Computer, Communication, Control and Information Technology (C3IT)* (pp. 1–4, 7–8 Feb). https://doi.org/10.1109/C3IT.2015.7060182

30. Barman, S., Samanta, D., & Chattopadhyay, S. (2015c). Fingerprint-based crypto-biometric system for network security. *EURASIP Journal on Information Security, 1*, 3. https://doi.org/10.1186/s13635-015-0020-1.

31. Andrew, R., Juan, S., James, N., Miles, S., Elaine, B., Stefan, L., et al. (2010). *A statistical test suite for random and pseudorandom number generators for cryptographic applications*. National Institute of Standards and Technology Special Publication 800-22 revision 1a National Institute of Standards and Technology Special Publication 800- 131 p.

32. Kanade, S., Camara, D., Petrovska-Delacrtaz, D., & Dorizzi, B. (2009). Application of biometrics to obtain. High entropy cryptographic keys. In *Proceedings of World Academy on*

Science, Engineering, and Technology, Hong Kong
33. Kanade, S., Petrovska-Delacretaz, D., & Dorizzi, B. (2010). Generating and sharing biometrics based session keys for secure cryptographic applications. In *BTAS: IEEE International Conference on Biometrics: Theory, Applications and Systems* (pp. 1–7).
34. Hao, F., Anderson, R., & Daugman, J. (2006). Combining crypto with biometrics effectively. *IEEETransComputer, 55*(9), 1081–1088.
35. Nandakumar, K., Jain, A., & Pankanti, S. (2007). Fingerprint-based fuzzy vault: Implementation and performance. *IEEE Transactions Information Forensics Security, 2*(4), 744–757.
36. Nandakumar, K. (2013). BioSAKE: Biometrics-based secure authentication and key exchange. In *Proceedings of 2013 International Conference on Biometrics (ICB)* (pp. 1–8). Madrid, Spain: IEEE.
37. Nandakumar, K., & Jain, A. K. (2008). Multibiometric template security using fuzzy vault. In *IEEE Second International Conference on Biometrics: Theory, Applications and Systems* (pp. 1–6).
38. Christos, S., Psannis, K. E., Kim, B.-G., & Gupta, B. (2016). Secure integration of IoT and cloud computing. *Future Generation Computer Systems, 78*, 964–975.
39. Gupta, S., & Gupta, B. B. (2017). Detection: Avoidance, and attack pattern mechanisms in modern web application vulnerabilities: Present and future challenges. *International Journal of Cloud Applications and Computing (IJCAC), 7*(3), 1–43.

Chapter 32
Trees, Cryptosignatures, and Cyberspace Mobile Agent Interfaces

C. F. Nourani

Abstract A basis for agent computing with intelligent languages and crypto-signatures trees is presented with applications to WWW interfaces. We present intelligent syntax and put forth intelligent tree computing. Multiagent signatures are defined and applied to define the basis for tree information-theoretic computing and agent cyberspace applications. The project is applicable to design multiagent protocol and has been applied to put forth cryptosignatures. The project has further led to foundations to computing with intelligent trees. Intelligent game trees are defined with chess playing examples and applications to cyberspace computing. Techniques for generating intelligent models are developed with soundness and completeness theorems abbreviated here with basis in our papers. The models can be applied as a basis to authentication on cyberspace computing. The WWW applications are summed by an authentication proposition. Agent computing has been applied in our papers and colleagues elsewhere to business and cyberspace commerce.

Keywords Intelligent tree computing · Multiagent AI · Agent cryptosignatures · WWW intelligent interfaces · Agent language processing · Agent standards · Runtime cybersecurity · Signature protocol · Block chain

1 Introduction

Cybersecurity is not a seat belt to safeguard us on cyber processes or damages; it is a key in the success supporting our new digital economy. People and businesses need to rely on the security of digital technologies. Signing for Trust with basic principles for a secure digital world with digital signatures is in more sense than one responsibility for cyber and IT security, the responsibility in the digital

C. F. Nourani (✉)
Berlin Institute of Technology, AI Labs, Berlin, Germany
e-mail: cyrusfn@alum.mit.edu

© Springer Nature Switzerland AG 2020   807
B. B. Gupta et al. (eds.), *Handbook of Computer Networks and Cyber Security*,
https://doi.org/10.1007/978-3-030-22277-2_32

supply chain, or based on the needs of users. Significant research is currently conducted on dynamic learning and threat detections for cybersesurity. While actually collecting and labeling more of the exercise data are comparatively easy to address in exercise planning, the process is by definition limited by resource availability. There is a considerable gap in validation basis to ensure cybersecurity. This gap is addressed by the agent computing basis for cybersecurity presented in this chapter. For network security [1] a complementary approach is to create realistic data sets on demand in emulated/simulated testbeds capable of supporting arbitrary network topologies, sufficiently real hardware, real OS/application/attack/defense software, and a combination of synthetic and real actors. An example is the Cyber Defense Technology Experimental Research Laboratory (DETERLab) or Virtual Assured Network (CyberVAN). Cybersecurity has to be responsible for cyber and IT security, digital supply chain, and cybersecurity factors for a focus on the needs of system users. To prelude agent computing for cybersecurity that is the theme for this chapter let us preview a NATO 2017 [2] research group report on the topics for Intelligent Autonomous Agents for Cyber Defence and Resilience. The report states that the future cyber defense must involve extensive use of partially autonomous agents that actively patrol the "friendly" networks, and detect and react to threat activities rapidly before the hostile malware is able to inflict major damage, evade friendly agents, or destroy friendly agents. That implies having cyber defense agents with a significant degree of intelligence, autonomy, self-learning, and adaptability. The report focuses on what the tactical environments would such an agent operate. On what data would be available for the agent, what actions would the agent be able to take, how would agents plan a complex course of actions. What would the agent learn from its experiences, and how. How would the agent collaborate or interact with humans. How are we to ensure that the agent will not take undesirable destructive actions.

This chapter is a foundation for agent computing techniques that can support cybersecurity with a forward to validation structures. The term "agent" has been recently applied to refer to AI constructs that enable computation on behalf of an AI activity [3]. It also refers to computations that take place in an autonomous and continuous fashion, while considered a high-level activity, in the sense that its definition is hardware and software independent, therefore implementation independent [4]. The present paper develops the techniques and theory of computing with trees on signatures that bear agent functions on trees. Our results for computability of initial models by tree rewriting are developed further as a foundation for computing on trees to be applicable to intelligent tree computing [5]. The concepts of intelligent syntax and intelligent languages are presented. The present applications are tree computing, agent authentication, intelligent WWW interfaces, and multiagent protocol. Tree rewriting is defined on intelligent trees by presenting the concepts and definition of algebraic tree intelligence content and mutual tree intelligence content within a forest. At the forest suddenly a tree information theoretic theorem had presented itself, defining a correspondence between intelligent tree rewriting and tree intelligence preservation. Models for intelligent theories emerge from the algebraic intelligent tree rewriting. Intelligent algebraic tree completion theorems and initial model rewrite theorems are put forth for intelligent trees. To bring the techniques to a climax a soundness and completeness theorem is proved for intelligent tree rewriting as a formal model basis. A proposition sums the applications to WWW. The first author and others had suggested intelligent agents can be applied to Web Browsers a few years ago. An article in Computer World, January 1997, features "WBI" and quotes "the most productive internet tools. ... you don't waste time looking for things that you don't need." It has been claimed agents can help us at the sea of information that grows and surrounds us every day. However, it is not appropriate to have WWW agents wandering astray carrying on unpredictable and unknown exchanges returned to us as puzzles.

2   Computing on Trees

2.1   A Logical View

In order to present some motivation for the methods proposed certain model-theoretic concepts are reviewed and some new techniques are presented. The Hendin style proof for Godel's completeness theorem is implemented by defining a model directly from the syntax of theories. A model is defined by putting terms that are provably equal into equivalence classes, then defining a canonical structure on the equivalence classes [6]. The computing enterprise requires more general techniques of model construction and extension, since it has to accommodate dynamically changing world descriptions and theories. The models to be defined are for complex computing phenomena, for which we define generalized diagrams. The techniques in [7–9] for model building as applied to the problem of AI reasoning allow us to build and extend models through diagrams. This required us to focus attention on generalized diagrams for models. The first author had created generic diagrams, abbreviated, G-diagrams [7–9] to build models with a minimal family of generalized Skolem functions. The minimal set of function symbols is the set with which a model can be inductively defined. The models are initial and computable [5]. The G-diagram methods allowed us to formulate AI world descriptions, theories, and models in a minimal computable manner. Thus models and proofs for AI and computing problems can be characterized by models computable by a set of functions.

It allows us to program with objects and functions "running" on generic model tableaux diagrams. To allude to our AI planning techniques as an example, the planning process at each stage can make use of GF-diagrams [9], G-diagrams with free Skolemized trees, by taking the free interpretation, as tree-rewrite computations for the possible proof trees that correspond to each goal satisfiability. Suppose there are some basic Skolem functions $f1, \ldots, fn$ that define a G-diagram. During planning or proof tree generation a set of Skolem functions g1, ..., gn could be introduced. While defining such free proof trees, a set of congruence relations relates the g's to the f's. The proofs can make use of the tree congruence relations or be carried out by tree rewriting.

2.2 Tree Computation

The computing and reasoning enterprise require more general techniques of model construction and extension, since it has to accommodate dynamically changing world descriptions and theories. The techniques in [8, 9] for model building as applied to the problem of AI reasoning allow us to build and extend models through diagrams. This requires us to focus on the notion of generalized diagram. A technical example of algebraic models defined from syntax had appeared in defining initial algebras for equational theories of data types [10, 11]. In such direction for computing models of equational theories of computing problems are presented by a pair $(\sum, E)$, where $\sum$ is a signature (of many sorts, for a sort set S) [10] and E a set of $\sum$-equations. Let $T<\sum>$ be the free tree word algebra of signature $\sum$. The quotient of $T<\sum>$, the word algebra of signature $\sum$, with respect to the $\sum$-congruence relation generated by E, will be denoted by $T<\sum,E>$, or $T<P>$ for presentation P. $T<P>$ is the "initial" model of the presentation P.

The $\sum$-congruence relation will be denoted by $\equiv P$. One representation of $T(P)$ which is nice in practice consists of an algebra of the canonical representations of the congruence classes, abbreviated by $\sum$-CTA. It is a special case of generalized standard models we had defined (see [5], for example). Some definitions are applied from our papers that allow us to define standard models of theories that are $\sum$-CTA's. The standard models are significant for tree computational theories that we had presented in [5] and the intelligent WWW interface models applied by the present paper. We apply generic diagrams, Definitions 1 and 2 to define canonical standard models in the same sense as set theory. These definitions are basic to sets and in defining induction for abstract recursion and inductive definitions. We had put forth variants of it with axiomatizations in our papers. The definitions were put forth by the first author for the computability with initial models. The canonical models are applied to multiagent computing during the last several years by Nourani [5, 12].

2.3 G-Diagrams for Initial Models

The G-diagrams for models [8, 9] are diagrams in which the elements of the structure are all represented by a minimal set of function symbols and constants, such that it is sufficient to define the truth of formulas only for the terms generated by the minimal set of functions and constant symbols. Such assignment implicitly defines the diagram. This allows us to define a canonical model of a theory in terms of a minimal family of function symbols. The minimal set of functions that define a G-diagram is the function set with which a standard model could be defined. Formal definition of diagrams is stated here, generalized to G-diagrams, and applied in the sections to follow.

Definition 1 Let M be a structure for a language L, call a subset X of M a generating set for M if no proper substructure of M contains X, i.e., if M is the closure of X U {c(M): c is a constant symbol of L}. An assignment of constants to M is a pair <A,G>, where A is an infinite set of constant symbols in L and G: A →M, such that {G(a): a in A} is a set of generators for M. Interpreting a by g(a), every element of M is denoted by at least one closed term of L(A). For a fixed assignment <A,G> of constants to M, the diagram of M, D<A,G>(M) is the set of basic (atomic and negated atomic) sentences of L(A) true in M. (Note that L(A) is L enriched with set A of constant symbols.)

Definition 2 A generic diagram for a structure M is a diagram D<A,G>, such that the G in Definition 1 has a proper definition by minimal specific functions.

For planning applications Nourani 1991 [8] had presented some specific example functions. Thus initial standard models are models definable from their G-diagrams. Further practical and the theoretical characterization of models by their G-diagrams are presented by this author in [9]. It builds the basis for some forthcoming formulations that follow, and the tree computation theories that we had put forth. Method of constructing initial models by algebraic tree rewriting for the intelligent languages is to be developed from our approach in [13, 14]. We showed how initial algebras can be defined by subtree replacement and tree rewriting [5]. The G-diagram for the model is also defined from the same trees.

3   Intelligent Languages and Models

3.1   *Intelligent Syntax and Agent Language Processing*

By an intelligent language we intend a language with syntactic constructs that allow function symbols and corresponding objects, such that the function symbols are implemented by computing agents. Sentential logic is the standard formal language applied when defining basic models. The language L is a set of sentence symbol closed by finite application of negation and conjunction to sentence symbols. Once quantifier logical symbols are added to the language, the language of first order logic can be defined. A model A for L is a structure with a set A. There are structures defined for o such that for each constant symbol in the language there corresponds a constant in A.

For each function symbol in the language there is a function defined on A; and for each relation symbol in the language there is a relation defined on A. For the algebraic theories we are defining for intelligent tree computing in the forthcoming sections the language is defined from signatures for a language of many-sorted equational logic. The signature defines the language by specifying the function symbols' arities. The model is a structure defined on a many-sorted algebra consisting of S-indexed sets for S a set of sorts. A set of function symbols in the language, referred to by AF, is the set modeled in the computing world by AI agents with across and/or over board capability.

Thus the language defined by the signature has designated function symbols called AF. For the specific foundations we refer to [14], for example. The AF function symbols define signatures that have specific message paths defined for carrying context around an otherwise context free abstract syntax. A set of function symbols in the language, referred to by AF, is the set of agents with nontrivial capability. The computation is expressed by an abstract language that is capable of specifying modules, agents, and their communications. We have put together the AI concepts with syntactic constructs that could run on the tree computing theories we are presenting in brief. We have to define how the syntactic trees involving functions from the AF are to be represented by algebraic tree rewriting on trees. This is the subject of the next section, where free intelligent trees are defined. An important technical point is that for agents there are function names on trees.

Definition 3 We say that a signature $\sum$ is intelligent iff it has intelligent function symbols. We say that a language has intelligent syntax if the syntax is defined on an intelligent signature.

Definition 4 A language L is said to be an intelligent language iff L is defined from an intelligent syntax.

Intelligent languages and signatures allow us to present computational theories with formulas on terms with intelligent function symbols.

3.2 Agent Authentication

By Definition 3 agent signatures are carried by the intelligent signature. Computing with intelligent trees might embed automatic agent signature authentication. The basis for the computing is a signature match to start agent messages. Basic authentication is automatic when the intelligent computing interface to WWW is cranked up. Further encoding can be embedded when the agent signatures are designed. For example, the agent signature can specify what the agent types are with which it can engage exchange at all. The signature might specify the class of messages and/or transactions allowed. Basic agent protocol can also be encoded by the agent signatures. The Cyberdocking project Nourani 1997 [13] has specific modular docking facilities at the cyberspace.

3.3   Abstract Intelligent Syntax

It is essential to the formulation of computations on intelligent trees and the notion of congruence that we define tree intelligence content. A reason is that there could be loss of tree intelligence content when tree rewriting because not all intelligent functions are required to be on mutual message exchanges. Theories are presented by axioms that define them and it is difficult to keep track of what equations not to apply when proving properties. What we have to define, however, is some computational formulation of intelligence content such that it applies to the present method of computability on trees. Once that formulation is presented, we could start decorating the trees with it and define computation on intelligent trees. It would be nice to view the problem from the stand point of an example. The examples of intelligent languages we could present have <O,A,R> triples as control structures. The A's have operations that also consist of agent message passing. The functions in AFS are the agent functions capable of message passing. The O refers to the set of objects and R the relations defining the effect of A's on objects. Among the functions in AFS only some interact by message passing. Furthermore, one must be aware that the functions could affect objects in ways that affect the intelligence content of a tree. There you are: the tree congruence definition thus is more complex for intelligent languages than those of ordinary syntax trees. Let us define tree intelligence content for the present formulation.

Definition 5 We say that a function f is a *string function*, iff there is no message passing or information exchange except onto the object that is at the range set for f, reading parameters visible at each object. Otherwise, f is said to be a *splurge function*. We refer to them by string and splurge functions when there is no ambiguity.

Remark: Nullary functions are string functions.

Definition 6 The tree intelligence degree, TID, is defined by induction on tree structures:
   (0) the intelligence content of a constant symbol function f is f;
   (i) for a string function f and tree f(t1,...,tn) the TID is defined by
   U TID (ti::f), where (ti::f) refers to a subtree of ti visible to f;
   (ii) for a splurge function f, TID is defined by U TID (f:ti), where f:ti
   refers to the tree resulting from ti upon information exchange by f.

There are implicit mobile object computing principles at Definition 6, for example, the concept of a subtree being visible to a function, and of course, agents. The theorem below formalizes these points. Thus out of the forest of intelligent trees there appears an information theoretic rewrite theorem.

Theorem 1 *A preview to Theorem 2 is that trees rewriting on intelligent syntax trees, guided only by what equations state, might cause a loss of intelligence content onto the resulting set of trees.*

Proof [5] Thus rewriting computing with agent trees is irreversible and at times nonterminating. Let us now define computing with intelligent equational theories.

Definition 7 We say that an equational theory T of signature $I\sum$ is an intelligent $I\sum$ theory iff for every proof step involving tree rewriting, the TID is preserved. We state T<IST> |- t=t' when T is an $I\sum$ theory.

Definition 8 We say that an equational theory T is intelligent, iff T has an intelligent signature $I\sum$, and axioms E, with $I\sum$ its intelligent signature. A proof of t=t' in an intelligent equational theory T is a finite sequence b of $I\sum$-equations ending in t=t' such that if q=q' is in b, then either q=q' in E, or q=q' is derived from 0 or more previous equations in E by one application of the rules of inference. Write T <IST>|- t=t' for "T p proves t=t' by intelligent algebraic subtree replacement system."

By definition of such theories proofs only allow tree rewrites that preserve TID across a rule. These definitions have been applied to prove the theorems, set up the foundations for what could make intelligent tree rewriting TID, and define intelligent tree computation [5].

Thus the essence of intelligent trees will not be lost while agent tree computing. Next, we define a computing agent function's intelligence content from the above definition. This is not as easy as it seems and it is a matter of the model of computation applied rather than a definition inherent to intelligent syntax. Let us present it as a function of intelligent syntax only, because we are to stay with abstract models and build models from abstract syntax. The definition depends on the properties of intelligent trees [5] to be defined in the following section.

4 Intelligent Trees

4.1 Embedding Intelligence

Viewing the methods of computation on trees presented in the sections above we define intelligent trees here.

Definition 9 A tree defined from an arbitrary signature $\sum$ is intelligent iff there is at least one function symbol g in $\sum$ such that g is a member of the set of intelligent functions AFS, and g is a function symbol that appears on the tree.

Definition 10 We define an intelligent $\sum$-equation, abbreviated by $I\sum$-equation, to be a $\sum$-equation on intelligent $\sum$-terms. A $I\sum$ congruence is a $\sum$-congruence with the following conditions:

1. the congruence preserves $I\sum$ equations;
2. the congruence preserves computing agents intelligence content of $\sum$-trees.

Canonical models are definable with canonical sets C on the carriers with <function,base-set> pair by recursions such that C with a set of tree rewrite rules R represents T<$I\sum$,~R>, where ~R is the set R of axioms for P viewed as $I\sum$-rewrite rules.

Theorem 2 *Trees rewriting on intelligent syntax trees, guided only by what equations state, might cause a loss of intelligence content onto the resulting set of trees.*

Proof Trees with AFS functions by definition affect TID, thus a rewrite from a tree formed by a function g in AFS to a tree that does not have g as a function symbol causes an intelligence loss. For example, a harmless looking equation of the form f-1(f(t)) = t, where f in AFS causes an intelligence loss to the resulting set of trees, from the left-hand to the right-hand tree t.

Thus computing with arbitrary rewriting is irreversible and at times nonterminating. And we are facing a computing wilderness at the present time. Let us now define computing with intelligent equational theories.

Definition 11 Let $\sum$ be an intelligent signature. Then a canonical term I$\sum$-algebra (I$\sum$-CTA) is a $\sum$-algebra C such that

1. |C| is a subset of T<$\sum$> as S-indexed families.
2. gt1...tn in C implies ti's are in C and

   gC (t1,...,tn) = gt1...tn, where gC refer to the operation in algebra C corresponding to the function symbol g.
   For constant symbols (2) must hold as well, with gC = g.

3. gt1...tn in T<AFS> implies ti's in C and

   gC(t1,...,tn) = gt1...tn; for constant symbols it must hold as gC=g.

Definition 12 Let C be an I$\sum$-algebra. Let P = ($\sum$,E) be a presentation. Then C is $\sum$-isomorphic to T<P>, iff

(1) C satisfies E
(2) gC (t1,...,tn) $\equiv$ P g.t1...tn
(3) gC(t1,...,tn) $\equiv$ P gt1...tn, with gt1...tn in T<AFS> whenever ti's are in T<AFS> and gC is in AFS.

Note: (2 and 3) must also hold for constants with g.C = g; $\equiv$ refers to the I$\sum$-congruence generated by E.

4.2 Intelligent Rewrite Models

Term rewrite model theorems for intelligent syntax

Lemma 1 *Let R be a set of I$\sum$-equations. Let R be the set of algebraic I$\sum$-rewrite rules obtained by considering each equation l =r in Ro as a rule l => r, then for t,t' in T<$\sum$>, t =>$_*$ t' iff T(R) <IST>|- t = t'.*
Recall that a presentation ($\sum$,E) defined an equational theory of signature $\sum$ and axioms E. Next we show how canonical models can be constructed by algebraic

subtree replacement system. A definition and what we have done thus far get us to where we want to go: the canonical algebraic intelligent term rewriting theorems $\sum$ <s1,,,sn,s> denotes the part of the signature with operations of arity (s1,...,sn) and coarity s, with Csi the carrier of algebra C of sort si. FTP refers to finite termination property and UTP to the unique termination property of tree rewriting.

Definition 13 Let R be a convergent set of $\sum$-rewrite rules, i.e., T <$\sum$,R> h as the FTP and UTP properties, let [t] denote the R-reduced form of t in T<$\sum$>. Let |C| be a subset of |T<$\sum$>|, for g in $\sum$ <s1...sn,s> and ti in C si, define gC (t1,...,tn) = [g(t1,...,tn)]. If this always lies in C, then C becomes a I$\sum$-algebra, and we say that (C,R) represents a I$\sum$-algebra A iff the I$\sum$-algebra so defined by (C,R) is I$\sum$-isomorphic to A.

The following intermediate theorem gives sufficient conditions for a recursive algebraic tree characterization of an initial model for an I$\sum$ equational presentation. It is the mathematical justification for the proposition that initial models with intelligent signature can be automatically implemented (constructed) by algebraic subtree replacement systems. The normal forms are defined by a minimal set of functions that are Skolem functions or type constructors. Thus we have the following canonical intelligent model theorems. The theorems provide conditions for automatic implementation by intelligent tree rewriting to initial models for programming with objects.

Theorem 3 Let $\sum$ be an S-sorted signature, R a convergent set of $\sum$-rewrite rules. Let |C| be a subset of |T<$\sum$>|. Define gC(t1,...,tn) = [g(t1,...,tn)]. Furthermore, assume that [f] = f for all f in $\sum$(l,s). If there exists a subset CF of $\sum$ such that |C| = |T<CF>| and the following conditions are satisfied for g with nontrivial arity (s1,...,sn):

1. gC(t1,...,tn) in C whenever ti in C, for ti of sort si;
2. for all g, ti in C, and g in CF,
gC(t1,...,tn) = gt1,...tn; in particular for a constant g, gC = g;
3. for g in $\sum$—CF, gC(t1,...,tn)=t, for some t in T<CF>;
4. for g in AFS, gC(t1,...,tn) = t for some t in T<CF ∩ AFS>.
Then: (1) C is a canonical term I$\sum$-algebra; and
(2) (C,R) represents T <$\sum$,R>, R is R viewed as a set of I$\sum$ equations.

Proof First prove by induction on complexity of terms that (C,R) defines a $\sum$-algebra structure on C. The basis is given by the assumption that constant symbols are trivially R-reduced, because we define σ (C). = [σ] in C, for each σ of 0 arity. Now define σ<C> (t1,...,tn) = [σ(t1,...tn)], where [t] denotes the R-reduced form of T. It is readily seen from the definitions that (C,R) defines a $\sum$-algebra. Now since each t in C is R-reduced by (1) and (2) we have σ<C>(t1,...,tn) = σ(t1,...,tn), where σ is in CF. We have already seen that for constant symbols σ, σ <C> = σ. By (3) and (4) the trees formed with function symbols apart from CF are reduced to CF terms that are AFS preserving. Thus (C,R) defines a canonical term I$\sum$-algebra C. This gives us (1). To show that C is isomorphic to T<Σ,R> we apply the CTA representation theorem for IΣ presentations. C satisfies $\underline{R}$ because all t in

C are R-reduced, and the Σ-algebra structure on C is defined by R. Furthermore, $\sigma{<}C{>}(t1,...,tn) <I\sum> \equiv [\sigma\ (t1,...,tn)]$—because $\sigma\ {<}C{>}(t1,...,tn) = [\sigma\ (t1,...,tn)]$ and since C is a CTA Σ-algebra $\sigma\ (t1,...,tn) = \sigma\ t1...tn$, therefore, $\sigma\ {<}C{>}\ (t1,...,tn) = [\sigma\ t1...tn]$, while preserving AFS terms. Thus we have the conditions for CTA representation. By Theorem 6, C is isomorphic to $T{<}\sum,R{>}$.

Theorem 4 *Let $\sum$ be an S-sorted signature, and R a convergent set of rewrite rules such that [g] = g. Define a $\sum$-algebra structure C on $T{<}\sum{>}$ by $gC(t1,...,tn) = [g(t1,...,tn)]$. Let C_* be the smallest sub $I\sum$-algebra of C. Then C is a canonical term algebra consisting of R normal forms and (C,R) represents $T{<}\sum,R{>}$.*

Proof Similar to proof of Theorem 3.

Thus an initial free model with signature $I\sum$ is formed. The model can be implemented by algebraic subtree replacement systems.

Definition 14 The mutual intelligence content, MIC, of an intelligent function f, a member of the intelligent signature AFS, is determined by the $I\sum$-congruence on T<AFS> relating the functions in AFS. It is union of the TID over the trees that are a member of the congruence class of the free T<AFS> with respect to the $I\sum$-congruence defined on the $T{<}\sum, w{>}$, where w is the arity of f.

4.3 Intelligent Rewrite Models

Term rewrite model theorems for intelligent syntax
We have proved how to obtain canonical intelligent models in [5]. The theorems provide conditions for automatic implementation by intelligent tree rewriting to initial models for programming with objects.

Theorem 5 *(The MIC Theorem) Let P be a presentation with intelligent signature $I\sum$ for a computing theory T with intelligent syntax trees. Then T is*

a. *A sound logical theory iff every axiom or proof rule in T is TID preserving;*
b. *A complete logical theory iff there is a <function,base-set> pair defining a canonical set C and a G-diagram, such that C with R represents $T{<}I\sum,{\sim}R{>}$, where ~R is the set R of axioms for P viewed as $I\sum$-rewrite rules.*

Proof By Definition of MIC, theorems above, completeness theorems for the first order logic, and completeness of induction for algebraic structures [5].

It is the logical foundations MIC theorem for intelligent syntax algebraic theories. At some further forthcoming research we might take a brief walk in the consequent fields and present new areas for computing. There are further MIC theorems that are relevant to computing and the model theory of computing with intelligent trees. Some of these applications appear in double vision computing [2].

5   Computing on Intelligent Trees

We present a brief overview of the applications of our methods to AI planning problems [4, 8, 9], as yet another exciting application areas for intelligent tree computing. Our planning process at each stage can make use of GF-diagrams by taking the Skolemized trees and tree-rewrite compute possible proof trees that correspond to each goal satisfiability [4, 7]. We have proposed [9] method that can be applied to planning with GF-diagrams with applications to current directions in AI for multiagent computing appears in [5]. The techniques can be applied to implement planning and reasoning for AI applications. While planning with GF-diagrams that part of the plan that involves free Skolemized trees is carried along with the plan goal proof tree. The idea is that if the free proof tree is constructed, then the plan has a model in which the goals are satisfied. The model is the initial model of the AI world for which the free Skolemized trees were constructed [9, 15]. How are these applications affected by our intelligent language formulation is to be addressed by forthcoming papers. The applications to multiagent AI computing is presented here and by the papers referenced [16–22].

6   Intelligent Game Trees

A Multiagent chess playing paradigm is defined by Nourani [12]. By defining spheres on boards and strength degrees for pieces winning strategies on games can be defined. The new intelligent tree computing theories we have defined can be applied to present precise strategies and prove theorems on games. The present computational model for multiagent system provides a formal basis for single agent moves. For each agent function there is a way to determine mutual information content with respect to the decision trees connected to it. The foundations to intelligent game tree computing started around 1993 by the first author with the concepts of tree information content and mutual information among trees [5]. Let us view an abstract chess player as we defined [12] by a pair <P,B>. *The player P makes its moves based on the board B it views. <P,B> might view chess as if the pieces on the board had come alive and were autonomous agents communicating* by messages, as in Alice in Wonderland.

6.1   Intelligent Game Trees and AND/OR Trees

The chess game trees can be defined by AND/OR trees [23]. For the intelligent game trees and the problem solving techniques defined, the same model can be applied to the game trees in the sense of two-person games and to the state space from the single agent view. The two-person game tree [24] is obtained from the intelligent tree model, as is the state space tree for agents. To obtain the two-person game tree the cross-board-co-board agent computation is depicted on a tree. Whereas the state-space trees for each agent is determined by the computation sequence on its side of the board-co-board. We have defined an abstract notion of information on intelligent game trees corresponding to what Shannon might have defined for games. The way the intelligent game trees are defined, a tree information theoretic theorem presents itself, corresponding intelligent tree rewriting to tree information content preservation. AND/OR trees Nilsson [23] are game trees defined to solve a game from a player's stand point. Formally a node problem is said to be solved if one of the following conditions hold.

1. The node is the set of terminal nodes (primitive problem—the node has no successor).
2. The node has AND nodes as successors and the successors are solved.
3. The node has OR nodes as successors and any one of the successors is solved.

A solution to the original problem is given by the subgraph of AND/OR graph sufficient to show that the node is solved. A program which can play a theoretically perfect game would have task like searching and AND/OR tree for a solution to a one person problem to a two-person game. An intelligent AND/OR tree is and AND/OR tree where the tree branches are intelligent trees. The branches compute a Boolean function via agents. The Boolean function is what might satisfy a goal formula on the tree. An intelligent AND/OR tree is solved iff the corresponding Boolean functions solve the AND/OR trees named by intelligent functions on the trees. Thus node m might be $f(a1,a2,a3)$ & $g(b1,b2)$, where f and g are Boolean functions of three and two variables, respectively, and ai's and bi's are Boolean valued agents satisfying goal formulas for f and g. Agent and/or trees were devised by (Nourani 1992) on.

```
        g      is on OR agent
       / | \
          |
      b1 | b2
        f   f is an AND agent
       /_|_\
      /  |  \
```

6.2   Intelligent Game Trees and the WWW

When it comes to intelligent interfaces to the WWW the basic applications for intelligent game trees are in managing to acquire and complete a critical business transaction at minimal time when there are agents competing on the WWW. Intelligent game tree strategies are not always based on ordinary game principles.

Without further investment it is not prudent to elaborate on the details here. Starting with basic authentication as presented in Sect. 2.3, where authentication is an abstract term referring to matching signatures to some specified signatures, with authentication encoded onto the signatures. Let us state a proposition as a basis to WWW intelligent computing. The proposition may be proved from what we have stated thus far.

Authentication proposition WWW intelligent interface computing incorporates basic agent authentication via intelligent tree signatures.

At the present stage it might sound ludicrous to think agents play games at WWW, but AI computing is on the brink onto agent computing and marketing via virtual communities [1, 25].

7 Practical Areas

For multiagent multi_kernel designs with many kernels running in parallel we are really in a bind to compose definitions such that it forms a tight computing system. To make that problem tractable, we have to set some game rules for agent message passing within kernels and without, and some rules for object sharing across kernels. Let us for the sake of an example of how the definition could look like, set the following rules. Then it will be obvious where the arbitrary choices were made if we were to offer alternative definitions. We could also show how the well-known notions of computing security are definable for the present formulations such that formalization and validation could be presented. Let us suppose that objects are sharable between a pair of kernels defining functionality provided the function invoking the object application has authenticated access codes to the object and there are no locking synchronization problems. We refer to this as *vertical sharing* of objects. Further, let us assume that agents only communicate with mutually predefined agent functions across kernels once authenticated and that object sharing is via a function local to the kernel at which the object resides. We shall refer to this as *horizontal sharing* of objects.

We could start stating some obvious principles for the aerodynamics of computing with multiagent systems such that the cyberspace journeys are proved safe. With the prerequisites stated it is easy to see that the formulation of privacy and security could be structured. Let Kn be the pair of kernels <kn,kn'> defining a functionality. We refer to such pair as *mates* in the sense that they are coupled in a vertical structure with shared objects defining a functionally. Let us state basic design principles for private and secure AI systems that we refer to by **PSAIS**.

7.1   Basis Soundness

A design has a *sound basis* iff each Kn satisfies PSAIS principles once restricted to functions and agent communications local to its vertical structure.

7.2   Structural Soundness

a. Authentication is certified for access to objects.
b. Mutual exclusion is synchronized for shared objects.
c. External object sharing is authenticated by designated agents.

7.3   Mutual Horizontal Soundness

For every pair Km and Kn that are neighbors with communicating agents, <Km,Kn> are said to have mutual horizontal soundness iff:

a. Km and Kn share objects by message passing to agents that have names visible across kernels; and by observing the structural soundness principles for shared objects.
b. Mutual exclusion principles are applied to vertical structure sharing by two external pairs Km and Kn of vertical structures.
c. Horizontal operations preserve each kernel's vertical soundness.

Theorem 6 *AI systems designed by multiagent multi_kernel techniques have PSAIS iff the designs satisfy the soundness principles.*

The above formulation could be applied to prove that an autonomous system has integrity in terms of the well-known concepts and methods for basic security of operating systems. Various security rules could be formulated for each of the kernels by applying the structural formulation out forth in the present paper. The actual implemented system does not have to run on a kernelized operating system. The methods we are presenting are abstract and conceptual computing techniques. The practice and the formalisms for transforming the various well-known properties for security rules are to await a future report from this project. But we have presented the basic methodology thus far to prove viability of our techniques. There does not appear to be any alternate formulation for multiagent AI systems at the present time. Thus we could call it ours and then see what its value is to be over the next generation of computing with AI systems. Let us raise a flag where our turbo-jet landed, and then decide how much the frontier living covered by our flight is to be valued.

8 New Realistic Areas

Example application newer areas are [2] on IOT and cyberphyscial systems worth reviewing [26]. These systems are usually composed of a set of networked agents, including sensors, actuators, control processing units, and communication devices. The proliferation of wireless embedded sensors and actuators is creating new challenges for cybersecurity. Furthermore, new application in areas such as medical devices, automotive, and smart infrastructure with increasing throle that the information infrastructures play in existing control systems—such as in the process control industry or the power grid. Many cyberphysical applications are safety-critical: their failure can cause irreparable damage to the systems under control and to the people depending on it. In particular, the protection of critical infrastructures that rely on CPS, for example, electric power grids, industrial control systems, oil and natural gas systems, water and waste-water treatment plants, healthcare devices, and transportation networks plays a fundamental role in society.

9 Concluding Comments

What is accomplished thus far is the basis for a cybersecurity with multiagent computing with basic automatic authentication on agent intelligent tree automata. The chapter has developed cybersecurity principles that enable validation on cyberspace, authentication that counter cyberthreats. The chapter further defined the basis for tree information-theoretic computing with agent cryptosignature encoding applications. Further mathematical foundations are defined by [13, 14]. Last but not the least, we have soundness and completeness theorems for the intelligent tree logic [5]. Intelligent game trees and multiagent games are presented in brief. We have applied the formulation to computing with intelligent functions alluding to forthcoming application areas. A start to mobile computing applications to the WWW interface applications is stated.

References

1. Thompson, B., & King, J. M. (2018). An agent-based modeling framework for cybersecurity in mobile tactical networks - cybersecurity in mobile tactical networks. *The Journal of Defense Modeling and Simulation, 15*, 205–218.
2. NATO. (2017). *Intelligent autonomous agents for cyber defence and resilience organized by the North Atlantic Treaty Organization (NATO) research group IST-152-RTG. Prague, Czech Republic, on 18–20 October 2017.*
3. Genesereth, M. R., & Nilsson, N. J. (1987). *Logical foundations of artificial intelligence.* Burlington, MA: Morgan-Kaufmann.
4. Nourani, C. F. (1997). *Intelligent Tree Computing, Decision Trees and Soft OOP Tree Computing September 2, 1997 Frontiers in Soft Computing and Decision Systems Papers from the 1997 Fall Symposium, Boston Technical Report FS-97-04 AAAI.* www.aaai.org/Press/Reports/Symposia/Fall/fs-97-04.html

5. Nourani, C. F. (1994). Slalom tree computing - A computing theory for artificial intelligence. *AI Communications, 4*(4), 207–213. Revised December 1995, December 1996.
6. Thatcher, J. W., Wagner, E. G., & Wright, J. B. (1978). Data type specification: Parameterization and the power of specification techniques. In *Proc. 10th Annual Symposium on Theory of Computing (STOC), San Diego, CA* (pp. 119–132). New York, NY: ACM.
7. Nourani, C. F., & Fähndrich, J. (2015, August). *A formal approach to agent planning with inference trees.* Trieste: NAEC.
8. Nourani, C. F. (1991). Planning and plausible reasoning in AI. In *Proc. Scandinavian Conference in AI, May 1991, Denmark* (pp. 150–157). IOS Press.
9. Nourani, C. F. (1995). *Free proof trees, model-theoretic planning and nondeterministic algebraic plan computation with G-diagrams.* Sheffield, UK: AISB.
10. Goguen, J. A., Thatcher, J. W., Wagner, E. G., & Wright, J. B. (1973). *A junction between computer science and category theory (Parts I and II)* (N.Y. research report, RC4526). Yorktown Heights, NY: IBM T. J. Watson Research Center.
11. Nourani, C. F. (2004). *Intelligent tree computing, cryptosignatures and cyberspace interfaces* (ICAI-02). Monte Carlo Resort, Las Vegas, NV: CSREA Press.
12. Nourani, C. F. (2017). *A new cryptosignature block chain protocol algorithm* (Technical report on research gate).
13. Nourani, C. F. (1996). *Cyberdocking. A business plan on a venture sent Microsoft.*
14. Nourani, C. F. (1997). Intelligent languages. A preliminary syntactic theory. In A. Kelemenová (Eds.) *Proceedings of the Mathematical Foundations CS'98 Satellite Workshop on Grammar Systems.* Silesian University, Faculty of Philosophy and Sciences.
15. Nourani, C. F. (1999). Agent computing, KB for intelligent forecasting, and model discovery for knowledge management, June 1998. In *AAAI Workshop on Agent Based Systems in the Business Context Orlando, Florida, July 1999* (AAAI Press technical report WS-99-01).
16. Nourani, C. F. (1997). Modelling, validation, and hybrid design of intelligent systems February 5, 1997 KMEL98, Karlsruhe, Germany, January 1998. In *8th Workshop Knowledge Engineering Methods and Languages.* Institut fur Angewandte Informatik und formal Beschreibungsverfhrn, Karlsruhe University, Germany, January 1998.
17. Brazier, F. M. T., Dunin-Keplicz, B. M., Jennings, N. R., & Treur, J. (1997). DESIRE: Modeling multi-agent systems in a compositional formal framework. *International Journal of Cooperative Information Systems, 6*(1), 67–94.
18. Nourani, C. F. (2003). A sound and complete agent logic paradigm, 2000. In *Parts and Abstract Published at ASL, and FSS, AAAI Symposium 2003.*
19. Brazier, F. M. T., Jonker, C. M., & Treur, J. (1997). Formalization of a cooperation model based on joint intentions. In *Lecture notes in computer science* (Vol. 1193, pp. 141–155). Berlin: Springer.
20. Nourani, C. F., & Schulte, O. (2013). *Multiagent decision trees, competitive models, and goal satisfiability.* Ostrava, Czech Republic: DICTAP.
21. ACM. (1998). *The mobile object papers, ACM October 98* (vol 41, no. 10).
22. Nourani, C. F. (1992). A multi-agent AI approach to fault free and fault tolerant AI, FLAIRS-93. In D. D. Dankell II, (Eds.) *Proc. Florida AI Symposium, April 18 1993, Florida. Florida Artificial Intelligence Research Symposium.* St. Petersburg, FL: Florida Research Society.
23. Nilsson, N. J. (1969). Searching, problem solving, and game-playing trees for minimal cost solutions. In A. J. Morell (Ed.) *IFIP 1968, Amsterdam, North-Holland* (Vol 2, pp. 1556-1562).
24. Gale, D., & Stewart, F. M. Infinite games with perfect information. In: *Contributions to the theory of games, annals of mathematical studies, vol. 28, Princeton.*
25. Nourani, C. F. (1998). *Intelligent trees, thought models, and intelligent discovery: Model based reasoning in scientific discovery (MBR'98), Pavia, Italy, December 17–19, 1998.*
26. Cardenas, A., & Crispo, B. (2016). Cyber-physical security and privacy. In: IEEE internet computing, vol. 20, no. 5. Intelligent Cybersecurity Agents [Guest editors' introduction] - IEEE Journals & Magazine. https://ieeexplore.ieee.org/document/75793973/7

Chapter 33
Permutation–Substitution Based Image Encryption Algorithms Using Pseudorandom Number Generators

Kishore Bhamidipati and Soorya Annadurai

Abstract This chapter introduces the concept of Random Number Generators, and how they can be used to effectively, quickly, and securely encrypt data in the form of an image. The structure of an image is also explored as a preliminary, and different tests that are exclusive to image encryption were analyzed for two different works of image encryption research.

Keywords Random number generation · Image encryption · Histogram analysis · Correlation coefficient · Cryptanalysis · Entropy · Differential Analysis · Mean squared error · PSNR

1 Preliminaries

The field of image encryption can be considered as both a science and an art. The scientific component of this field of cryptography involves the usage of different components to enforce a secure encryption algorithm in different ways, such as a random number generator, a permutation schematic, a substitution schematic—all of which are elaborated in this chapter. Along with these tools, other mechanisms like the usage of chaotic systems (chaos theory applications), digital signatures (asymmetric cryptography applications), or even mathematical applications (like the usage of the digits of the irrational number "pi" or the sequence generated by a Fibonacci sequence) can be applied to a crypto-system. Each mechanism has its own merits and shortcomings; the science is to understand each of them and to apply it accordingly to the situation and application at hand. The art, however, lies in the way these different tools and mechanisms are applied. For instance, the permutation–

K. Bhamidipati (✉)
Manipal Institute of Technology, Manipal Academy of Higher Education, Manipal, India
e-mail: kishore.b@manipal.edu

S. Annadurai
Microsoft IDC (R&D) Pvt. Ltd., Bangalore, India

© Springer Nature Switzerland AG 2020
B. B. Gupta et al. (eds.), *Handbook of Computer Networks and Cyber Security*,
https://doi.org/10.1007/978-3-030-22277-2_33

substitution architecture (which is yet to be elaborated) is a proven mechanism that enforces both the scrambling of data in pixelated form and the transformation of that data into an inscrutable form.

As a trivial example, consider a completely white image. As always, the ultimate goal of image encryption is to convert an image with meaningful visual data into a form where no data, indications, or inferences can be extrapolated from.

In a nutshell, the act of encryption through permutation is intended to scramble any possible meaning that can be inferred from an image. And the act of substitution is intended to eliminate any true source of logical meaning in the image by transforming the data, or pixels, from one form to another. However, let us consider one possible usage of these techniques individually.

If we perform strictly permutation without substitution, the image will remain as it is, since the shuffling of a set of white pixels will result in the same set, as any two white pixels are indistinguishable from one another. However, if we perform strictly substitution (assume substitution to be an operation where a one-to-one conversion mapping between two independent pixel values is used to convert one pixel to another in place), the entire white image will be transformed into another image of a random color (assume it to be yellow, for the sake of this discussion). This is because every individual white pixel will be identically transformed into the target yellow pixel. From the perspective of the cryptanalyst, while this will not divulge the true, original color of the sensitive (completely black) image, it will give an indication that all the pixels of the original image are identical. This effectively defeats the aforementioned goal of image encryption.

To this effect, the combination of techniques in addition to permutation and substitution (such as the appropriate use of a random number sequence) can be used in order to combat the above limitations. Some example methodologies are discussed in subsequent sections of this chapter.

However, we must first understand the implications of what images really are, what properties they possess, and how this can have varied effects on security of data as a whole—not only from a binary perspective, but also from a visual perspective.

2   Image Fundamentals

An image encryption algorithm deals with pixels that have a visual significance as well as binary significance. Images have certain general intrinsic properties such as a comparatively high level of data redundancy, and a larger bulk of data compared to the amount of logical data represented. The first aspect can be explained by observing that in the average image of a specific subject (such as a scenery, a person, or anything else), there is a higher probability that any two pixels that are adjacent to one another will have a similar color, when compared to an image with completely random pixels. The second aspect can be explained by observing that if some amount of information needs to be transmitted from one entity to another (such as a password, or the name of people in a crowd), that data is much better represented in binary form than visual form (in the same analogy, a picture of the password written on a surface or a picture of a crowd of people in an audience) if the primary interest is to save transmission bandwidth. So, it can be said that the logic-to-space density is significantly lower in images than typical binary data streams.

Of course, these are mere generalizations, and describe only the average image. While these should not be interpreted as hard-and-fast rules for all image encryption algorithms, they can be taken as guidelines to understand the different implications of images and pixel structures (Fig. 33.1).

2.1 Image Structure

In general, we consider three different categories of images—namely grayscale images, RGB images, and RGBA images.

Visually, the distinction between these image categories is simple. Grayscale images represent pixels as a degree of blackness and whiteness, and these pixels are arranged in a grid format to visually represent data. RGB images have three layers, or channels, of pixels arranged in a grid format that are superimposed upon one another in order to provide a combined effect of color. Each channel possesses varying degrees of red, green, and blue, respectively (hence the name RGB). This system works because it is a well-known fact that any color can be produced by mixing appropriate amounts of red, green, and blue. RGBA images add an extra level of detail to the standard RGB image by including an Alpha channel, which combines the image with a background to create the visual appearance of partial or full transparency.

In Fig. 33.2, bpp stands for bits per pixel.

From a visual perspective, all images are two-dimensional in nature. This is because, to the human eye, any image has a given length and a given breadth. This perception is independent of the type of image that is observed, i.e., grayscale, RGB, RGBA, or any other format specification.

The fundamental unit of this perceived two-dimensional image is known as a pixel.

In a grayscale image, a pixel is required to display only a degree of whiteness or blackness. In practice, this pixel can assume a value ranging from 0 to 255 or 0b00000000 to 0b11111111 (in binary representation). Therefore, this pixel representation is 8 bits in size or 8 bpp (bits per pixel). This holds true for any single-channel representation of an image.

In an RGB image, a pixel is required to display three individual and superimposed degrees of redness, greenness, and blueness (owing to the three individual color channels). Each sub-pixel in every channel is again represented by 8 bits. Therefore, the overall pixel in an RGB image requires $3 \times 8 = 24$ bits for its representation.

An RGBA image consists of 4 independent channels. Therefore, using a similar logic, every pixel representation requires $4 \times 8 = 32$ bits per pixel.

Fig. 33.1 Visualization of gray, color, and alpha-based images. (**a**) A grayscale image. Here, the background of the image is purely white, and the tick mark is filled in with a shade of gray. (**b**) An RGB image. Here, the green color can be observed filling the tick mark in the image. (**c**) An RGBA image. The checkered background can be observed behind the RGB image, which is a standard visualization for transparency effects

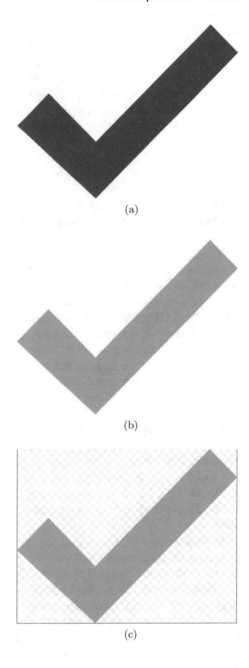

Use of Alpha Channel to create Transparent Image

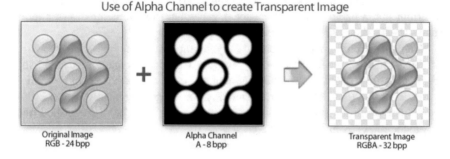

| Original Image | Alpha Channel | Transparent Image |
| RGB - 24 bpp | A - 8 bpp | RGBA - 32 bpp |

Fig. 33.2 Creation of a transparent image with an Alpha channel

These different forms of pixel representations need to be considered while developing an image encryption algorithm, as these data structures need to be handled appropriately and are not considered during simple bit manipulations in other standard encryption algorithms like AES, DES, and others.

2.2 Random Number Generation Fundamentals

While this chapter does not focus on the history, development, and theory behind random number generations, it is extremely critical to understand the importance of [pseudo] random numbers.

Consider the previous example of encrypting a completely white image. As observed, a purely permutation-based image encryption algorithm is insufficient, as the encrypted image will remain white. A purely substitution-based image encryption algorithm will also remain insufficient, as no matter how much confusion is applied to transform one pixel value to another, it will be identical for all pixels of the completely white image. By extension of this example, the combination of permutation and substitution in another image encryption algorithm will also not suffice for generating an encrypted image that provides no indication or implications about the original image.

Random numbers can play an extremely vital role here. If a random number were to be used to assist in the substitution process (as a primitive example, by simply XOR-ing the random number with the resultant pixel after a round of permutation and substitution), then all the final encrypted pixels would be dissimilar from one another. This removes (to some extent) the ability of the cryptanalyst to determine that all the pixels were originally of the same color—an ability which could be exploited in a pure substitution, or permutation combined with direct substitution, based image encryption algorithm.

The term "PRNG" stands for "pseudorandom number generator" which implies that a sequence of numbers (bits, bytes, blocks, or any other form) is produced from an algorithm which looks random from a basic external analysis, but is in fact deterministic in nature (as the sequence is generated from some unknown internal state). Hence, this sequence is "pseudorandom" in nature.

Such pseudorandomness is termed "cryptographically secure" (also known as CSPRNGs) if no other entity other than the intended recipient[s] can reliably distinguish the output from true randomness, even if the PRNG algorithm is perfectly known (but not its internal state). A non-cryptographically secure PRNG would pass basic statistical tests for randomness—but it can be distinguished from true randomness by an intelligent attacker.

For instance, consider the following generator:

1. There is an internal state

$$s,$$

   which is a sequence of 20 bytes.
2. The generator produces a long sequence of bytes by 20-byte chunks.
3. To produce the next chunk, the algorithm is

$$output \ s, \ then \ set \ s \ to \ SHA - 1(s).$$

This PRNG will be very good statistically, but it is trivial to distinguish from true randomness: just take two consecutive 20-byte chunks in the output, and see if the second is the result of SHA-1 over the first. This is not a *cryptographically secure PRNG*.

Of course, every CSPRNG is a PRNG, but not every PRNG is a CSPRNG. Some non-CS PRNG like the Mersenne Twister can achieve quite high a performance and be adequate in non-cryptographic situations where there is no intelligent attacker to defeat (e.g., physics simulations). Although there also are some known high-performance CSPRNG (e.g., Rabbit stream cipher or Trivium stream cipher), a non-CSPRNG may give an edge in contexts where the lack of cryptographic security is not an issue, and/or performance is more critical.

In subsequent sections of this chapter, we describe some techniques where both CSPRNGs and PRNGs can be used in order to achieve extremely high security in image encryption algorithms.

3   Proposed Schemes

In this chapter, we consider two different methodologies of employing permutation, substitution, and PRNGs in order to achieve highly secure image encryption standards. We also demonstrate the ability to prove the high security standards of these algorithms in the next section of this chapter.

The two works we are considering are:

1. A New Direction Towards Image Encryption Using Pixel Intensity Modification and Pixel Swapping—Ann Mathews, Jayesh Khattar, Manvi Gupta, Nishith Sinha
2. A Novel Self-transforming Image Encryption Algorithm Using Intrinsically Mutating PRNG—Soorya Annadurai, Manoj R., Roshan David Jathanna

3.1 Work 1: Pixel Intensity Modification and Pixel Swapping

This work utilized a combination of two individual pseudorandom number generators, namely the Linear Feedback Shift Register and the Compound Inverse Congruential Generator.

3.1.1 Stage 1: Varying Color Intensities

This stage focuses on the varying of the color intensities of each pixel value. The pixels of the image are subjected to a function where each value in one row is added to a random number generated by LFSR. A seed that is input into the LFSR generator is converted to binary and the 8th, 19th, and the 32nd bits are XOR'd, the result of which is stored in the leftmost bit of the binary sequence, after right-shifting the original sequence by one bit position. This process is repeated 8 times, with the value generated in the preceding iteration as the seed for the next one. The XOR'd result is stored in an array each time, and this value is returned as the pseudorandom number for the encryption process. The RC4 is then used to generate a single random number to be added to each row of the pixel matrix.

Algorithm 3 ultimately implements the function that varies the color intensity of each pixel. The variable val is loaded with each pixel intensity. Note that the function may have to be repeated for each intensity value in a pixel for the corresponding RGB values in some cases. The pseudorandom number generated by the LFSR algorithm is added to each row value. Also, note that a random number is added to each column value. In python, the randint function of the random library that uses the Mersenne Twister algorithm to generate random numbers may be used for this purpose.

3.1.2 Stage 2: Varying Pixel Position

This stage comprises of the modification of the pixel matrix by swapping values from one vertical half of the matrix to random positions in the other half of the matrix. The random positions are determined by the pseudorandom numbers generated by the Compound Inverse Congruential Generator, known as CIG for short. The CIG code inputs a list of unique prime numbers greater than or equal to 5. It returns a list of pseudorandom numbers within the range of 0 and the product of the primes given as input. The list thus obtained consists of each number in the specified range in a random order. The image is horizontally divided into two halves. The least prime numbers greater than the value of width and half the height of the image are passed as input to CIG. On modifying this result, we obtain a list which is inclusive of all the pixel positions in the first half of the image (assuming numbering of pixels in row-wise order). That is, we obtain all pixels within the range 0 to (width × height)/2 in random order. Using the generated list, each pixel in the second half of the image is swapped with a pixel in the location specified in order in the list. We thus obtain a highly secure encrypted image. The swapping is further clarified using algorithms specified below.

Since the primes may exceed the width and height of the first half of the image, the list obtained using Compound Inverse Congruential Generator may contain values that exceed pixel positions in the first half of the image (they may exceed width × height/2). Hence, it is essential to use the following algorithm to limit the values obtained within the list.

Assuming numbering of pixels in row-wise order, we need a mechanism to find the position of the pixel in (row, column) order since the pixels in most image processing environments are stored in the form of a pixel access matrix.

Ultimately, using the above preliminary algorithms, we can define an algorithm to swap pixels from one half of the image to another as demonstrated in Algorithm 11.

Combining the two levels of encryption on the same image one followed by another, the basic algorithm to encrypt an image can be presented as follows in Algorithm 13.

Algorithm 1 LFSR

Require: Shifts the initial value by one bit and XORs the 8th, 19th, and 32nd bits, which is then returned.
Require: INPUT: Integer seed value.
Require: OUTPUT: A 32-bit value that becomes the next seed, and the result of an XOR of 3 bits.
1: **procedure** LFSR(INTEGER SEED)
2:     $bin[0 \ldots 31] \leftarrow 32 - bit\ binary\ representation\ of\ seed\ value$
3:     $x \leftarrow bin[7]$
4:     $y \leftarrow bin[18]$
5:     $z \leftarrow bin[31]$
6:     $x_1 \leftarrow 1 - x$
7:     $y_1 \leftarrow 1 - y$
8:     $z_1 \leftarrow 1 - z$
9:     $xor \leftarrow x * y * z + x_1 * y_1 * z + x_1 * y * z_1 + x * y_1 * z_1$
10:     **for** $i \leftarrow 0 : 30$ **do**
11:         $bin[i] \leftarrow bin[i + 1]$
12:     $bin[31] \leftarrow bin[i + 1]$
13:     $num \leftarrow$ decimal representation of the binary value bin
14:     **return** num, xor

Algorithm 2 LFSR_Use

Require: Implement the linear feedback shift register.
Require: INPUT: Integer seed value.
Require: OUTPUT: A 8-bit pseudo-random number.
1: **procedure** LFSR_USE(INTEGER SEED)
2:     $x \leftarrow LFSR(seed)$
3:     $s \leftarrow x + x[1]//x[1]$ is 2nd value returned by LFSR
4:     $p \leftarrow x[0]//x[0]$ is 1st value returned by LFSR
5:     **for** $i \leftarrow 0 : 7$ **do**
6:        $z \leftarrow LFSR(p)$
7:        $s \leftarrow s + z[1]$
8:        $p \leftarrow z[0]$
9:     $new \leftarrow z[0]$
10:    $n \leftarrow$ decimal representation of the binary value s
11:    **return** n, new

Algorithm 3 RC4_Use

Require: Random number generation that can be used as many times as required.
Require: INPUT: Integer values m and n to aid random number generation.
Require: OUTPUT: Random number and the next values for m and n.
1: **procedure** RC4_USE(INTEGER M, INTEGER N)
2:     $m \leftarrow (m + 1) \mod 256$
3:     $n \leftarrow (n + S[m]) \mod 256$
4:     $S[m], S[n] \leftarrow S[n], S[m]$
5:     $key \leftarrow S[(S[m] + S[n]) \mod 256]$
6:     **return** key, m, n

This effectively demonstrates how a combination of permutation and substitution with the assistance of a combination of pseudorandom number generations can assist in an overall secure image encryption algorithm.

3.2 Work 2: A Novel Self-transforming Image Encryption Algorithm Using Intrinsically Mutating PRNG

This work uses a simple substitution-only schematic without permutation. This work has been included in this chapter to show the power of the appropriate usage of PRNGs in order to achieve high degrees of image encryption security.

Assume the dimensions of the image to be (m; n; o). Each pixel value has range [0, 255], and uses 1 byte of memory.

Algorithm 4 RC4(k)

Require: Initialization of S.
Require: INPUT: A key of length 1 to 256 bytes.
Require: OUTPUT: An initialized S array used for stream generation.
1: **procedure** RC4(K)(INTEGER SEED)
2:     $keylen \leftarrow \lfloor log_2 k \rfloor$
3:     **for** $i \leftarrow 0 : keylen$ **do**
4:         $K[i] \leftarrow k \mod 256$
5:         $k \leftarrow k/256$
6:     **for** $i \leftarrow 0 : 255$ **do**
7:         $S[i] \leftarrow i$
8:         $T[i] \leftarrow K[i \mod keylen]$
9:     $j \leftarrow 0$
10:    **for** $i \leftarrow 0 : 255$ **do**
11:        $j \leftarrow (j + S[i] + T[i]) \mod 256$
12:        $S[i], S[j] \leftarrow S[j], S[i]$
13:    **return** S

Algorithm 5 Encrypt_Color

Require: Varies the pixel intensity of each pixel in a pixel matrix for a given image.
Require: INPUT: Integral seed value, number of rows in the pixel matrix, no. of columns in the pixel matrix.
Require: OUTPUT: A color encrypted pixel matrix.
1: **procedure** ENCRYPT_COLOR(INTEGER KEY, INTEGER HEIGHT, INTEGER WIDTH)
2:     $x \leftarrow key$
3:     $k \leftarrow (0, 0, 0)$
4:     $n_r \leftarrow LFSRUse(x)[1]$
5:     **for** $i \leftarrow 0 : height$ **do**
6:         $n_C \leftarrow LFSRUse(n_r)[0]$
7:         **for** $j \leftarrow 0 : width$ **do**
8:             $val \leftarrow pix[i][j] + n_c$ //pix matrix contains the pixel intensities
9:             $pix[i, j] \leftarrow val$
10:            $r \leftarrow RC4Use(k[1], k[2])$
11:            $n_c \leftarrow (n_c + r[0]) \mod 256$
12:        $n_c \leftarrow LFSRUse(n_r)[1]$

Algorithm 6 is_prime

Require: To check whether the given number is prime or not.
Require: INPUT: Integer number.
Require: OUTPUT: Returns True if the number is prime, else False.
1: **procedure** IS_PRIME(INTEGER NUMBER)
2:     **for** $i \leftarrow 2 : number$ **do**
3:         **if** $number$ mod $i == 0$ **then return** False
4:     **return** True

Algorithm 7 prime

Require: Searches for a prime number greater than the number given.
Require: INPUT: Integer number.
Require: OUTPUT: Returns a prime number greater than the input value.
1: **procedure** PRIME(INTEGER NUMBER)
2:     **for** $i \leftarrow number : 2 * number$ **do**
3:         **if** $is\, prime(0)$ **then return** i

Algorithm 8 CIG

Require: Implements CIG to obtain a list of pseudo-random numbers.
Require: INPUT: List of unique primes greater than or equal to 5.
Require: OUTPUT: Returns a list of pseudo-random numbers.
1: **procedure** CIG(INTEGER PRIMES[])
2:     Define integer list[], integer t[]
3:     $T \leftarrow 1$
4:     **for** $x \in primes$ **do**
5:         $T \leftarrow T * x$
6:     **for** $x \in primes$ **do**
7:         $Append(T/x)$tot
8:     **for** $i \leftarrow 0 : T$ **do**
9:         $S \leftarrow 0$
10:         **for** $j \leftarrow 0 : length\, primes$ **do**
11:             $S \leftarrow S + t[j] * (i \mod p[i])$
12:             $S \leftarrow T$
13:         Append s to list
14:     **return** list

Algorithm 9 CIG_Use

Require: Deletes all values exceeding the limit.

Require: INPUT: A list of pseudo-random numbers generated by CIG and the limit to which they may exceed.

Require: OUTPUT: A list of pseudo-random numbers generated by CIG within the limit.

1: **procedure** CIG_USE(INTEGER LIST[], INTEGER LIMIT)
2:    **for** $x \in list$ **do**
3:       **if** $x > limit$ **then** Delete x

Algorithm 10 Find

Require: Finds the (row, column) position in pixel matrix.

Require: INPUT: Position in the form of sequenced pixels in row-wise order, height and width of image.

Require: OUTPUT: Returns two integers one specifying row value and another specifying column value.

1: **procedure** FIND(INTEGER POSITION, INTEGER HEIGHT, INTEGER WIDTH)
2:    **return** $position/width, position \bmod width$

Algorithm 11 Swap

Require: Swaps the pixels in the second horizontal half of the image with the pixels in locations specified by the list.

Require: INPUT: A list of pseudo-random numbers obtained after call to CIG and CIG_Use, height and width of image.

Require: OUTPUT: A pixel matrix with the swapped values.

1: **procedure** SWAP(INTEGER LIST[], INTEGER WIDTH, INTEGER HEIGHT)
2:    $C \leftarrow 0$
3:    **for** $i \leftarrow height/2 : height$ **do**
4:       **for** $j \leftarrow 0 : width$ **do**
5:          $Position \leftarrow list[c]$
6:          $C \leftarrow C + 1$
7:          $X \leftarrow Find(position, height, width)$
8:          Swap pixel at [i,j] with pixel at [X[0], X[1]]

Algorithm 12 Encrypt_Position

Require: Implements algorithm 11.
Require: INPUT: Height and width of image.
Require: OUTPUT: Encrypted image.
1: **procedure** ENCRYPT_POSITION(INTEGER HEIGHT, INTEGER WIDTH)
2:     $Limit \leftarrow height * width/2$
3:     $H \leftarrow least\ prime > height/2$
4:     $W \leftarrow least\ prime > width$
5:     $CIG([H, W])$
6:     $CIGUse(List, Limit)$
7:     $Swap(List, height, width)$

Algorithm 13 Encryption

Require: Implements two-level encryption on the image.
Require: INPUT: Encryption key which is confidential to the user.
Require: OUTPUT: The encrypted image.
1: **procedure** ENCRYPT_POSITION(INTEGER HEIGHT, INTEGER WIDTH)
2:     $Height \leftarrow$ Heightofimage
3:     $W \leftarrow$ Widthofimage
4:     $EncryptColor(key)$
5:     $EncryptPosition(Height, Width)$

First, we describe the encryption procedure. It consists of three independent steps:

1. PRNG Generation
2. Self-XOR transform
3. Transforming the image with the PRNG

The novelty of this encryption lies in the usage of the custom PRNG. The generation of large prime numbers is a relatively computationally intensive procedure. However, prime numbers are known to increase security standards by a large extent (due to other mathematically "hard" problems that are out of the scope of this chapter). Ideally, it would be preferable to have a unique prime number corresponding to each pixel value of the image. However, this is not feasible in real-time applications (as this requires $m * n * o$ prime numbers to be generated for the encryption algorithm to proceed). So, an advantageous compromise is reached wherein a small sequence of random primes is generated in a custom algorithm described below, which is then recycled and modified with assistance from the original pixel sequence after usage, thus creating a mutation. This creates a truly random and dynamic random number sequence that cannot be replicated without exquisite knowledge of the pixels of the original image or knowledge of the key. The former is assumed to be impossible, and the latter is considered to be out of the scope of cryptography (key management). Therefore, this algorithm is both novel and secure in nature.

Assume the dimensions of the image to be (m, n, o). Each pixel value has range [0, 255], and uses 1 byte of memory.

3.2.1 Encryption Procedure

PRNG Generation Let $\Omega(n)$ be a function to return the last 8 bits of n, $\Theta(n)$ be a function to return the largest prime factor, and $\oplus$ be the XOR operation.

- A random number, α is passed as a seed.
- μ is generated by manipulating the current system time.
- Let the array (to hold the PRNG) be rarr[1:256].
- For i = 1:256: $\mu = \mu + \alpha$, rarr[i] = $\Omega(\theta(\mu) * \mu)$.
  The array with the new PRNG, rarr[1...256], is returned, with each element of the random array rarr[ ] using 1 byte of memory.

Self-XOR Transform

- Take the middle element of PRNG, x, and obtain $r = x\%(m * n * o)$.
- Arrange the pixels of the image in a cyclic, one-dimensional order. Start from the rth position in the linear array, and XOR it with the previous element in the logical circular array. Continue for all pixels in the image.

Transforming the Image with the PRNG Arrange all the pixel values of the image in a linear, one-dimensional order. Let this array be called encr[m*n*o].

- Initialize index i = 0 for the iterations, and c = 0 for the PRNG index.
  Calculate encr[i] = encr[i] $\oplus$ rarr[c] Modify rarr[c] = $((rarr[c]^2 rarr[c+1]) \% 255)$ $\oplus$ encr[i], c = (c+1) % 255.
  Perform this transformation for all pixel values by incrementing i.
- Initialize index i = m*n*o, and c = 0.
  Calculate encr[i] = encr[i] $\oplus$ rarr[c] Modify rarr[c] = ((rarr[c]2 * rarr[c+1])%255) $\oplus$ ((encr[i]+(i/(n*3))) * (encr[i] + (i%(n*3))/3) * (encr[i]+(i%(n*3))%3)). Then increment c in a cyclic order, i.e., c = (c+1) % 255.
  Perform this transformation for all pixel values by decrementing i.
- Store the transformed image as the final encrypted image.

3.2.2 Decryption Procedure

PRNG Generation The PRNG is generated in the same manner as in the encryption procedure. The same random number α is passed as a seed, along with the previously generated μ. The generated PRNG array, rarr[1...256], is returned, with each element using 1 byte of memory.

Transforming the Encrypted Image with the PRNG

- Arrange all the pixel values of the image in a linear, one-dimensional order.

- Initialize the index i = m*n*o, and c = 0. For every ith pixel value in the linear image, XOR it with the cth element in the generated PRNG, rarr[ ].
  Before continuing the iteration, modify rarr[c] = ((rarr[c]^2 rarr[c+1])%255) $\oplus$ ((encr[i]+(i/(n*3))) * (encr[i]+(i%(n*3))/3) * (encr[i]+(i%(n*3))%3)).
  Then increment c in a cyclic order, i.e., c = (c+1) % 255.
  Perform this transformation for all pixel values by decrementing i.
- Initialize i = 0 for the iterations, and c = 0 for the PRNG index. XOR the ith pixel value in the linear image with the cth element in rarr[ ]. Store the resultant value in another array encr[ ].
  Modify rarr[c] = ((rarr[c]^2 rarr[c+1])%255) $\oplus$ encr[i], c = (c+1) % 255.
  Perform this transformation for all pixel values by incrementing i.

Self-XOR Transform

- Take the middle element of PRNG, x, and obtain $r = x\%(m * n * o)$.
- Arrange the pixels of the image in a cyclic, one-dimensional order. Start from the rth position in the linear array, and XOR it with the previous element in the logical circular array. Continue for all pixels in the image.
- Store the generated image as the final decrypted image.

4 Experimental Results

The process of analyzing the results is slightly different when comparing standard data encryption algorithms and image encryption algorithms. This is due to the added dimension of visual interpretation based on the spatial arrangement of pixels in an image. This property is not immediately apparent in other data encryption algorithms.

4.1 Visual Test

Visual observation is an important factor in an image encryption. The lesser the resemblance between the encrypted and original images, the better the encryption scheme. This also implies that no information should be deduced by comparing the original and encrypted images.

Clearly, as shown in Fig. 33.3, there are no visual resemblances between the original and encrypted images. This indicates a successful visual test.

4.2 Histogram Analysis

Statistical attacks can be used to derive conclusions from the encrypted forms of images. These attacks are especially effective when a known-plaintext attack is

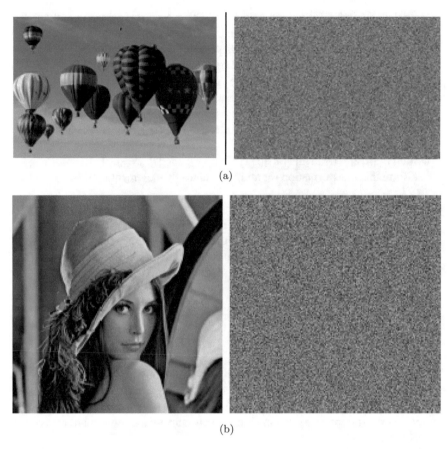

Fig. 33.3 Visual test of described encryption algorithms. (**a**) Encryption of image by method in Work 1. (**b**) Encryption of image by method in Work 2

executed. To prevent the leakage of information by such attacks, it must be ensured that the original and encrypted forms of the image do not exhibit any statistical similarity. A histogram analysis provides information about the distribution of the number of pixels in an image for each value of a pixel's intensity. In this test, three histograms have been plotted for each color plane of the three-dimensional color image. If in the encrypted histogram, there is an equal probability of generating pixels of all intensities, there is a higher degree of encrypted symmetry, as there is no possibility of eliminating attack options. Moreover, if the histograms of the original and encrypted images show no statistical resemblance, an attack based on the histogram analysis of the encrypted image will not deterministically provide information about the original image. Claude E. Shannon, the father of modern information theory, suggests that several cryptographic ciphers can be broken by an appropriate statistical analysis. Here, the resistance to statistical attacks has been demonstrated by means of histogram and correlation tests.

Figures 33.4 and 33.5 indicate the histogram analysis for the original and encrypted images generated by the first method described in this chapter.

The original image has a non-uniform histogram, implying that data can be visually extracted. However, in the encrypted image analysis, the histograms

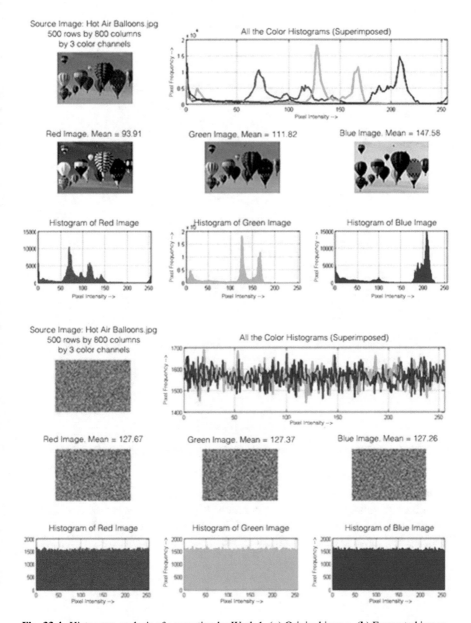

Fig. 33.4 Histogram analysis of encryption by Work 1. (**a**) Original image. (**b**) Encrypted image

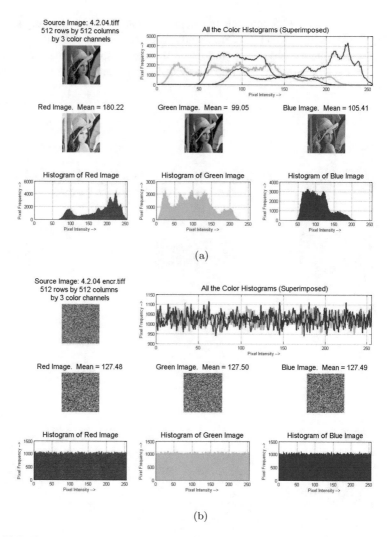

Fig. 33.5 Histogram analysis of encryption by Work 2. (**a**) Original image. (**b**) Encrypted image

resemble a straight line. This shows that every pixel intensity in the encrypted image has a nearly equal probability of generation. It can also be observed that there is no similarity between the histograms of the original and encrypted images, thus showing resistance to a known-plaintext attack.

4.3 Correlation Coefficient Analysis

In an ordinary image, adjacent pixels will generally be related to each other, in all directions: horizontally, vertically, and diagonally. However, the pixels of an encrypted image should show minimal correlation to its neighbors. The correlation test performed here considers all pairs of adjacent pixels in the horizontal, vertical, and diagonal axes.

$$E(x) = \frac{1}{n}\sum_{i=1}^{N} x_i, \; E(y) = \frac{1}{n}\sum_{i=1}^{N} y_i$$

$$V(x) = \frac{1}{n}\sum_{i=1}^{N}(x_i - E(x)^2), \; V(y) = \frac{1}{n}\sum_{i=1}^{N}(y_i - E(y)^2)$$

$$cov(x, y) = \frac{1}{n}\sum_{i=1}^{N}(x_i - E(x))(y_i - E(y))$$

$$\gamma_{xy} = \frac{cov(x, y)}{\sqrt{V(x)}\sqrt{V(y)}}, \; with\, V(x) \neq 0, \, V(y) \neq 0$$

Here, x_i and y_i are the values of two adjacent pixels in a particular color plane. N denotes the number of pixel pairs (x_i, y_i) in the test image. (x) and (y) are the expectation/mean values of all the x_i and y_i values. $V(x)$ and $V(y)$ are the individual variances of all of the x_i and y_i values. $cov(x, y)$ is the covariance of the distributions of all x_i and y_i values. γ_{xy} represents the correlation between the x_i and y_i distributions.

In a statistical analysis, the correlation coefficient can range from -1.00 to $+1.00$. A positive correlation is exhibited when one variable increases with the increase in another, and vice versa. Likewise, a negative correlation exists when one variable decreases as another increases, and vice versa. When the value of the correlation coefficient is 0.00, the two variables are independent of each other. This implies that the covariance between x and y, $cov(x, y)$ is equal to zero. Here, the two variables considered are the intensities of any two adjacent pixels in a particular axis. In this test, all three axes were considered for the three color planes of the RGB image.

Table 33.1 shows the correlation results for the second encryption algorithm described in this chapter.

Figure 33.6 gives an indication of the correlation plots of the original and encrypted images generated by the second algorithm. The 9 on the left shows a generic 45-degree line for all plots, indicating that the pixels of the original image are generally closely related to each other in each axis. However, for the encrypted image, there is no correlation whatsoever (as is indicated by the

Table 33.1 Correlation coefficients of two adjacent encrypted pixels by Work 1

	Correlation coefficient of adjacent pixels		
Lena (4.2.04.tiff)	Horizontal	Vertical	Diagonal
Original image	0.9502767042	0.9654508326	0.9372732083
Proposed algorithm	−0.0009676951	0.0009016908	0.0022480862

completely scrambled plots for each axis). This is the desired behavior of a secure image encryption algorithm.

4.4 Entropy Analysis

Entropy is a measure of the randomness of the occurrence of a particular pixel value. Entropy can range from 1 to 8, where 8 is the ideal value for the encrypted image.

In 1949, Shannon introduced the concept of information entropy as a quantifiable measure of data in a source. Entropy is the expected value (mean) of information contained in a message. For calculating entropy in this test, entropy is defined as:

$$H(s) = -\sum_{i=1}^{3N} P(s_i) \times \log_2(P(s_i))$$

Here, $3N$ is the total number of symbols (color planes per pixel), and $P(s_i)$ is the probability of the occurrence of the symbol s_i. In this case, a color plane of a pixel is 8 bits in size. Thus, s_i can result in 2^8 different outcomes. If we assume these to be generated by the encrypting algorithm with equal probability, then the entropy of the set of symbols is 8. Entropy can range from 1 to 8. If the entropy value is less than 8, then the probability of predicting the original symbols increases, which compromises encryption strength.

The near-ideal value of entropy by the second work in Table 33.2 shows that the predictability of encrypted pixels by the proposed algorithm is negligible, and is thus capable of resisting against entropy-based attacks. This is significant, as the high entropy value indicates the pixel values in all three color channels cannot be determined in computationally feasible time.

4.5 Differential Analysis

The encrypted image should be sensitive to small changes introduced in the original image. If not, then many concurrences can be observed in the encrypted forms of two original images with small differences, and a series of known-plaintext attacks can relate the original and encrypted forms of an image. Moreover, this type of

Fig. 33.6 Correlations plots
(three color planes) in
horizontal, vertical, diagonal
axes. (**a**) Original image. (**b**)
Encrypted image

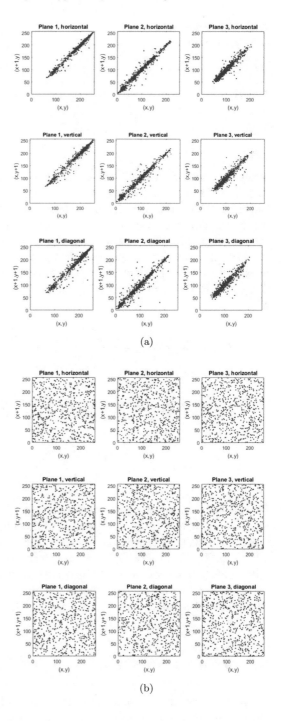

Table 33.2 Entropy values of encrypted images

Lena (4.2.04.tiff)	Entropy value
Original image	7.7501974797
Proposed algorithm	7.9997980997

Table 33.3 NPCR and UACI values of encrypted images

Lena (4.2.04.tiff)	NPCR value of images	UACI value of images
Proposed algorithm	0.9948659261	0.3344753151

attack facilitates the determination of the keys used during the encryption process (μ and α). Two measures were considered: NPCR (Number of Pixels Change Rate), and UACI (Unified Average Changing Intensity). NPCR gives an indication of how many encrypted pixel values exhibit a change when exactly one pixel of original image is changed. UACI measures the average intensity of the differences between the original image and the encrypted image. If two plain images P_K and $\overline{P_K}$ differ in exactly one color plane of exactly one pixel, let their encrypted forms be C_K and $\overline{C_K}$. For an RGB image of height M, width N, and number of planes O, UACI and NPCR are

$$UACI = \frac{1}{M \times N \times O} \sum_{X=1}^{M} \sum_{Y=1}^{N} \sum_{Z=1}^{O} \left[\frac{C_K(X, Y, Z) - \overline{C_K}(X, Y, Z)}{255} \right]$$

$$NPCR = \frac{1}{M \times N \times O} \sum_{X=1}^{M} \sum_{Y=1}^{N} \sum_{Z=1}^{O} D_K(X, Y, Z)$$

$$D_K(X, Y, Z) = \begin{cases} 0 & \text{if } C_K(X, Y, Z) = \overline{C_K}(X, Y, Z) \\ 1 & \text{if } C_K(X, Y, Z) \neq \overline{C_K}(X, Y, Z) \end{cases}$$

For this test, six separate encryptions were generated, where one encryption was made on the image in its intact form, and five others were made upon changing exactly one plane of exactly one pixel in random locations. High NPCR (ideally 100%) and UACI (ideally 33%) values indicate that the encryption algorithm will reflect large differences on minor changes in the original image.

Table 33.3 shows that the proposed algorithm in work 2 is highly sensitive to changes in the original image.

4.6 Mean Squared Error

A reliable encryption algorithm must ensure not only resistance to external attacks, but accuracy in decryption by the intended recipient. If there are differences between the original and decrypted forms of a test image before and after transmission (encryption), then there is loss in data. To measure the loss in data after an encrypted transmission, mean squared error (MSE) was considered as a measure. MSE is the average squared difference between a reference image and a distorted image. It is computed pixel-by-pixel by adding up the squared differences of all the pixels and dividing by the total pixel count.

If two RGB images A and B are to be considered as the original and decrypted forms of the transmitted image, where $A = a_1 \ldots a_M$, $B = b_1 \ldots b_M$, and M is the number of pixels, then MSE can be defined by the formula:

$$MSE(A, B) = \frac{1}{3M} \sum_{3M}^{i=1} (a_i - b_i)^2$$

Since the difference of the pixel plane values at a particular position is squared, large differences are heavily penalized, thus drastically increasing the error quantity.

The MSE value for the red, green, and blue planes of the decrypted image (when compared to the original image) was found to be zero in both works, implying that all pixels of the original and decrypted images were identical. The same results were found for all test images.

4.7   Peak Signal-to-Noise Ratio

PSNR indicates the change between the original pixels and the distorted pixels, calculated in decibels. It can be used for either encryption or decryption tests. The ideal PSNR value between the original and encrypted image is 0 (implying complete introduction of "noise" into the image), and the ideal value between the original and the decrypted image is infinity (implying complete recovery of data).

For both works, the PSNR value was infinity for decrypted images, implying no loss in data, and the value for the encrypted image in the second work was significantly low (8.643746373387632).

5   Conclusion

In this manner, two new encryption algorithms were described. One used a combination of two pseudorandom number generators in order to assist a round of substitution, along with a round of permutation with a custom logic. The other used a key to generate a list of random primes, and consecutively using every list to generate another list. This procedure ensures singularity in the encryption mapping schematics.

Both these techniques had been tested by several techniques, and a detailed explanation of testing tools like visual testing, histogram analysis, correlation coefficient analysis, entropy analysis, differential analysis, mean squared error, and peak signal-to-noise ratio was also provided.

For both algorithms, the entropy tests show results as high as the current industry standards. The correlation tests show almost no similarity between the original and encrypted images, and the histogram analysis verifies this assessment. Several empirical tests have been conducted to show that the proposed algorithm is stronger than several other candidate algorithms, and in conclusion, the results show that these algorithms, along with variants of the permutation–substitution architecture along with pseudorandom number generators, can be expected to find many applications in the real world.

Chapter 34
Recent Trends in Text Steganography with Experimental Study

Ravinder Kumar and Hitesh Singh

Abstract There have been pressing needs for securing a document and its content, either in electronic form or printed form. This is because counterfeiting and forgeries are extremely widespread all over the world, causing tremendous damage to individuals, industries, societies, and even national security. This is the main reason why people think about to protect their work and prevent such illicit activities. Because of these various methods like cryptography, steganography, and coding have been used. Steganography is the best-suited technique that allows user to hide a message in another message (cover media). Most of steganography research uses cover media as pictures, video clips, and sounds. However, text steganography is not normally preferred due to the difficulty in finding redundant bits in text document. To embed information inside a document, its characteristics have to be altered. These characteristics can be either insertion of spaces or non-displayed characters, deliberate misspellings distributed throughout the text, resizing of fonts, and so on. But due to slight change in the document it will be visible to the third party or attacker. To overcome this problem there is a need to alter the document in such a way that it will not visible to the human eyes yet it is possible to decode it with computer. The present chapter highlights the technique for reconstruction of the printed document using text-based steganography. This technique may be used if the original document (e.g., bank checks, legal documents, and certificates) is torn out and the important information is lost. Extracting the information from the torn part of the document and recreating the document will help in regaining the lost information. This method will first extract the text information present in the document and encode it into symbols. Then embed these symbols into the document multiple numbers of times without affecting the integrity of the document. For recreating the document, the hard copy of the document can be processed in order

R. Kumar (✉)
Skill Faculty of Engineering, SVSU, Dudhola Palwal, India

H. Singh
Department of CSE/IT, Shri Vishwakarma Skill University, Gurugram, India

Department of Computer Science and Engineering, HMRITM, Delhi, India

© Springer Nature Switzerland AG 2020   849
B. B. Gupta et al. (eds.), *Handbook of Computer Networks and Cyber Security*,
https://doi.org/10.1007/978-3-030-22277-2_34

to retrieve the embedded information. Thus, the information is regained from the original printed text document. This method will help in reconstruction of printed document from its part or whole.

Keywords Text steganography · Data hiding · Cover object · Stego object · Information security

1 Introduction

Steganography is derived from Greek word "stegauw" meaning covered writing. Steganography is the art and science of hiding message in such a way that secret message cannot be detected in the process of communication. Steganography methods are used since 2500 years. It has been used in military, personal, diplomatic, and IPR (intellectual property rights) applications. As shown in Fig. 34.1 steganography can be divided into two directions, protection against detection and protection against removal. In protection against detection modifications are done in such a way that it is not visible by the human or any form of digital media. Protection against removal on the other hand is further divided into two parts: water marking and finger printing. In it modification can be detected but technique is used for the protection of the integrity of the document [1].

2 History of Steganography

One of the earliest uses of steganography was documented in histories of Herodotus. He used to shave the head of his most trusted slave. Then make a tattoo using black ink in order to write the secret message. Then allow him to regrow the hair. Then send him to the destination. Then his head is again shaved in order to read the message. For the reply same procedure is applied but on another slave [2].

The first book written in the field of steganography was "Steganographia" by Johannes Trithemius. He was a German abbot. His work describes the methods to

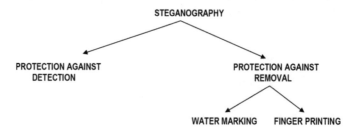

Fig. 34.1 Types of steganography

communicate with the sprits which were published in Latin in three parts. First two parts were based on cryptography which described the methods of hiding message in writing. The third part of his book was based on occult astrology [2].

A combination of cryptography and steganography methods was used to hide the message by Queen of Scot, Mary. She used to hide letters in the bunghole of a beer barrel, which freely moved in and out of her prison [3].

Many steganographic techniques were used in World War II. Nazis in Germany used a technique called Microdots. These are microchips which were created at the high magnification of over 200×. These microchips are the size of tiny dots on a standard typewriter. Those chips contain lot of information about a size of page, drawing, and so on [1].

Different methods were used at the time of civil war in the USA in order to provide secret message to slave in order to aid them in their escape. Different patterns were printed in quilt and hung from the window in order to spread the message. In Vietnam War the US soldiers used various hand gestures in photo shoot when they were captured. Those messages were spread when they were published in newspapers. Another method used by them was eyelid method. In this method eyelid was blinked using Morse code. It was the unique method of that time [2].

3   Text-Based Steganography

Text-based steganography is the method of hiding text message within the text document. It is the most difficult type of steganography technique because of the unavailability of redundant bits as compared to other files like image, video, and audio. It has been observed that structure of text is identical to what is observed by human eye, while the structure of other files like image, video is different from what has been observed. So, it is very easy to hide information in these types of documents as no changes are observed by the humans. On the other hand, if slight changes are done at text document, then it can be easily detected by the human eye. Different methods have been designed for hiding text within the text of text-based steganography. The possible implementation areas of text-based steganography are copyright protection, document authentication, prevention of e-document forging, and so on [4, 5].

Various researchers have done researches in the field of text-based steganography. Different methods have been used in order to hide message in text. Some has used the white spaces in order to hide information. In this method if there is one space then it is assumed that bit 1 is hidden and if there is double space it is assumed that bit 0 is hidden. The major disadvantages of this method are that it can be used only in electronic documents. Once documents are printed the information is lost. Some has used line spacing method. By just shifting the positions of lines up and down the message is embedded in the documents. Some of them also used the linguistic methods by replacing some symbols with another one like commas with and etc. but in this method major disadvantages are the embedding capacity.

Text-based steganography can be broadly classified into two main categories: format-based and linguistic steganography. Format-based method is further divided into word shift encoding, line shift encoding, white space encoding, and feature encoding methods. Linguistic method is further divided into syntax method and semantic method.

3.1 Format-Based Steganography

In the format-based steganography physical features of text symbols are compromised. In this approach the features are modified in such a manner that it cannot be detected by naked human eye. In some cases, lines are shifted up and down in order to hide information bits 0 and 1. In some cases, words are shifted left of right or just up or down. In other cases white spaces between the words or between the lines or paragraphs are compromised. In feature-based encoding physical feature of the words is modified in order to hide the information. It totally depends on the languages and the symbols [6] (Fig. 34.2).

In line shifting encoding the position of the text lines is shifted up or down, respectively, in order to hide the information bit [7]. This can be done in such a way that it cannot be detected by human eye only specific computer program can detect it. Special code words are assigned in this case. Information bit 1 is assigned if line is shifted up and 0 is assigned if line is shifted down. In some cases, $+1$ is assigned for shifting the line upwards and -1 for shifting the line downwards and 0 for no changes of lines. This method uses differential encoding techniques for robustness

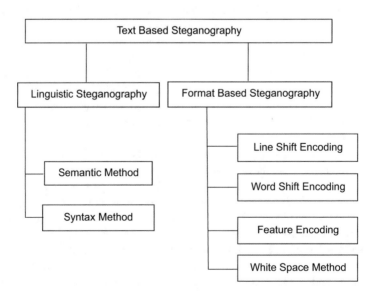

Fig. 34.2 Types of text-based steganography

and performance achievements. The embedding capacity is considerable in this type of techniques. For example, having a page with 40 lines, that is, 220 = 1,048,576 distinct code words per page. In order to hide the message the encoder has to shift the line up or down according to the bit has to be embedded. In order to decoding the information decoder has to measure the distance between the neighboring lines. This can be archived by two different methods. One is by measuring the distance between the baselines of two different neighboring lines and another by measuring the distance the centroids of two distinct lines. A base line is described as a logical line on which character resides. On the other hand, centroid is a center of mass of a text line. The text lines $i - 1$ and $i + 1$ are the lines which is not shifted and the line i is shifted either up or down. In a text file which is unaltered the distance between the baselines of two adjacent lines is constant. Now suppose si − 1 and si are the distances between baselines $i - 1$ and i and between baselines i and $i + 1$, respectively. In case of centroids the decision is based on the difference between centroid spacing in the original document and in the altered document. To calculate the position of centroids, we can use the following formula:

$$ci = \frac{\sum_{f=ti}^{bi} [j \cdot n(j)]}{\sum_{f=ti}^{bi} n(j)} \tag{34.1}$$

where $i = 1 \ldots N$ is the current line, ci is the position of centroid, N is the number of lines on the page, ti and bi are top and bottom limits of the line i, n is a function that counts how many pixels are ON ($f(k, j) = 1$, $k = 0 \ldots W$, see (34.1)). The next step is to calculate the distance between the centroids of the lines $i - 1$ and i, and i and $i - 1$, let it be si − 1 and si. Figure 34.3 shows a fragment of a document encoded using line shifting coding. In the second part, the second line was moved with 0, 1 mm (Fig. 34.3).

One of the methods for hiding text is explained in [8]. In this method Persian language characteristics are utilized as described in Fig. 34.4, as Persian language

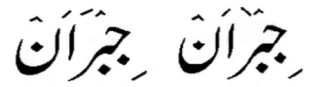

Fig. 34.3 Example of Arabic language

Fig. 34.4 Points in Persian
language

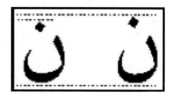

contains lot of points. In this method first of all a document written in Persian language is taken. Then by reading the binary bits of message algorithms are run. Suppose first bit is 0 then first alphabet is containing point is unchanged. Then next alphabet is read. If 1 has to be hiding then point of Persian alphabet is slightly moved upwards. In this manner entire message is hidden in the cover text document. The major advantages of this method are presence of higher embedding capacity due to the availability of lot of points. But disadvantage is that information may be lost while retyping and due to unavailability of OCR software it is difficult to retrieve the information from the printed text.

In another method [9] Arabic language is used to hide information in text document. Since Arabic language also consists of lot of points. Some alphabets contain points and some other alphabets are there which do not contain points. The message is hiding in such a manner that 0 is hidden in letters without points and 1 in letters without points. Extensions of letters are done of the letters by using Unicode 0640. In order to identify in which letter information is hidden the extension is performed before and after the cover letter. This scheme is also very useful and powerful as Arabic languages also consist of lot of points.

After utilizing Persian and Arabic texts another method was introduced in text steganography by using Thai Texts [10]. In these methods redundancies present in Thai text vowels, diacritical, and tonal symbols are compromised. This method is blind as original text message is not required for extraction of original message. Embedding capacity of text is increased I this method with other proposed methods. In this 2.2 bytes are embedded per kilobytes.

An improved version of Arabic text steganography was introduced [11]. An Arabic character kashida is introduced. The advantages of using this symbol are that they can be justified easily without affecting the integrity of the document. A bit 1 is hiding with replacing the symbol by extension version of letter and 0 is hiding by leaving the symbol as it is. The results are compared with other method. It has been observed that results of proposed method are far better than other methods.

Microsoft Excel is also used for hiding text information [12]. A lot of organizations use Excel sheets for their official purposes. In this approach the information is hiding by rotating the letters with a certain angles. The information is retrieved by again measuring the angle of letter presents in every cell. The method has high embedding rate as compared with previously discussed methods.

Another method was introduced for hiding text within text by using English alphabets [13]. They use reflection symmetry of the alphabets. In this, some alphabets are divided horizontally and have reflection symmetries like B, D, E, H, I, K, O, S, X, whereas other remaining alphabets do not have this symmetry. Bit 1 is embedded by using reflection symmetry symbols, whereas bit 0 is embedded by using other symbols. The embedding capacity is also higher in this type of document as lot of English texts are found in English newspapers, magazines, websites, and so on.

After MS Excel, MS Word can also be used to hide text within the text by utilizing the word document properties [14]. In this method fonts are replaced by some similar fronts in such a way that human eye cannot determine them. This method is very powerful method for hiding text. The major advantage of this method is that it can be printed after embedding the secrets message as printers are more sensitive to the font's types.

Arabic language letter Kashida is further utilized in the text-based steganography [15]. In this the properties of Arabic language are further utilized in order to enhance the security features of text-based steganography. As discussed previously the Arabic language contains pointed letter and letters which do not contain points. So, four scenarios are used in this method. In first scenario kashida is entered after pointed letter to embed 1 otherwise 0. In second scenario kashida is entered after non-pointed letters in order to embed 1 otherwise 0. In third scenario kashida is entered after letter to encode 1 otherwise 0. In the last scenario kashida is entered after letter to encode 0 otherwise 1. These four scenarios are used to hide the information. This enhances the embedding capacity of the document.

In the previous Arabic text-based steganography only one diacritic is used but in another method two diacritics are used Fathah and Kasrah to hide the message [16]. In this approach two diacritics are replaced with each other in order to hide the information. These methods tremendously increase the embedding capacity of the document.

Another method for hiding text is by utilizing the white space within the text documents. The main reason for utilizing the white space is that changing the number of trailing spaces has little chance of changing the meaning of a phrase or sentence. Another reason is that a casual reader is unlikely to take notice of slight modifications to white space. Three methods of white space encoding have been described. The methods exploit inter-sentence spacing, end-of-line spaces, and interword spacing in justified text [4, 17].

The work done in [18] has utilizes the white space of Holy Quran. The method uses extended format of later called kashida and white space between words. Suppose if the secret bit 1 is embedded then kashida is added between the letters of Arabic language. Then before moving to the next word white space present should be also used. If 1 is to be embedded then add whose consecutive white space between words otherwise add one white space in order to embed 0. Thus, secret bit represents one inserted kashida followed by two white spaces. This method further enhances the embedding capacity of the document.

Another method was proposed for hiding the information using white space [19]. The method hides the secret message present in the MS Word document into the white space characters by doing certain changes in font type and style. The changes made in white space are invisible to the users and thus maintain the integrity of the document. These methods have better embedding capacity and efficiency as compared with other methods. Their capacity is to hide 7 bits of information into each interword and intersentence white space as compared to other methods like UniSpaCh that can hide only 2 bits per space.

A method called UniSpaCh is proposed in [20]. In this method selected Unicode space character is analyzed. Then selected Unicode symbol is inserted into intersentence, interword, end of line, and end of paragraph white space. This method improves the embedding capacity of the document. The various experimental results suggest that this method has higher embedding capacity and greater imperceptivity of white space manipulation as compared to other methods.

3.2   Linguistic Steganography

In this method linguistic steganography is used for hiding secret message in text document [21]. Vedic Numeric Code is used in this method. Frequency of English letters in alphabets in conjunction with new Vedic Numeric Codes is used in this method to hide the information.

Another method for hiding text within the text is introduced by using Oriya language which is an Indian language [22]. A quantum truth table is used in this method for the purpose of mapping. It also uses two special symbols lie inverted commas, open and closing in Oriya language in order to hide the information. In this method stego and cover objects length should remain same. Satisfactory results are depicted by experimentation.

Another method of text-based steganography is proposed in [23]. This method utilizes Malayalam language which is again an Indian language. This method uses Unicode symbols of Malayalam language. In this approach the secret message can be encoded into Malayalam text by matching the Unicode symbols of Malayalam text. The results suggest that the proposed method is more precise as compared to other methods in encoding and decoding of the messages.

Recent studies have been conducted in the areas of linguistic steganography and security [24–40]. These research show that there are still more scope for text-based steganography especially in the field of linguistics. As it is very hard to detect the message from naked eyes of human and even from software.

3.3   Other Methods in Text-Based Steganography

Various methods have been discussed in the field of text-based steganography. One of them is based on random characters and word sequences [41]. In this method, the characters or words sequence is random; therefore, it is meaningless and attracts the attentions too much.

In another method [5], some specific characters from certain words are selected as hiding place for information. In the simplest form, for example, the first words of each paragraph are selected in a manner that by placing the first characters of these words side by side, the hidden information is extracted. This has been done by classic poets of Iran as well. This method requires strong mental power and takes a lot of time. It also requires special text and not all types of texts can be used in this method.

One of the features of HTML documents is their case insensitivity of tags and their members as discussed in [41]. For example, the three tags <BR>, <Br>, and <br> are equally valid and are the same. As a result, one can do information steganography in HTML documents by changing the small or large case of letters in document tags. The information has been extracted by comparing these words with words in normal case and by using the appropriate function. However, in the WML, all tags should be written in lowercase letters and, as a result, this method cannot be employed.

The paper [17] utilizes special features of a text document of its space pattering. In that work, the inward spaces of different text lines are slightly modified. After that modification, the average space of various lines has the characteristics of a sine wave and a wave constitutes a mark.

The work done in optical watermarking for printed document authentication [42] describes a novel visual information concealment technique. The optical watermark is constructed by the superposition of multiple two-dimensional binary images (referred to as layers), each with different carrier structural patterns embedding various hidden information. The hidden information is embedded into each layer using phase modulation. Based on the properties of the human visual system and modulation principle, the hidden information becomes visible to the human eyes only when a right key is positioned on top of the optical watermark with the right alignment. These keys play the similar role as keys in encryption that is to decode hidden information. Thus, such a lock and key approach improves the security level of optical watermark. In addition, multiple layer structure of optical watermark makes it more robust structure against reverse engineering attacks.

In the method of information hiding in Microsoft Word document by changing tracking technique [43], the data embedded is disguised such that the stegodocument appears to be the product of the collaborative writing effort. Text segment in the document is degenerated, mimicking to be the work of the author with inferior writing skills, with the secret writing skills, with the secret message embedded in the choice of degenerations. The degenerations are then revised with the changes being tracked, making it appear as if a cautious author is correcting a mistake. The change tracing information contained in the stegodocument allows the original cover, the degenerated document and hence the secrete message to be recovered.

In the method of hiding data in a kind of PDF text [44] first points out the secret channel in a kind of PDF English text, which is generated from the document that makes the text justified to occupy the full line, width, and position of each character individually. In succession it describes steganographic system PDFstego in which several strategies are applied to improve security, such as making use of redundancy to compliment security, constituting two chaotic maps to meet the Kirchhoff's principle and to prevent statistical attacks, and applying the secure hash algorithm to enable integrity service.

A theoretical framework for the problem of data hiding in the text document has been explained, as how that problem can be seen as an instance of well-known Gel and Pinker problem. Costas setup and the family of quantization-based method have been considered in order to show how it can be applied in text data hiding applications. The main idea was to consider a text character as a data structure consisting of multiple quantifiable feature, such as shape, position, orientation, size, and color, they showed that previous data hiding techniques, namely open space method and character feature method, are particular case of general quantization-based text data hiding techniques. Finally, we presented the color quantization as a new method for semi-fragile data hiding in digital and printed text document [45].

4   Recent Trends in Text-Based Steganography

New approach with number system-oriented text steganography for short messages is the outcome for preventing such purpose [46]. The combination of mathematical, computation rules, and knack of us hides the data from view. The approach used to hide data is innovative among data transfer protocols as word to word or rather alphabet to alphabet including numbers and special characters is derived. This approach makes data invisible when moving in any one of the ways, such as SMS, WhatsApp, Email, or Facebook messenger. Good mixtures of any number, characters form a pair of sets that can be used to hide information. Security agencies like navy, army, or air force can use such kind of techniques transferring data from one node to another for sake of setting aside their native soil.

Another technique implants secret information into the shelter media for searching novel probabilities for occupying a language Hindi which is apart from English. The proposed approach namely Indian Script Encoding Technique (ISET) will work by implementing the linguistic attributes of Hindi language [47]. In this approach, there is no difference between vowels and consonants. In this new approach, we worked with random and Hindi texts where Hindi text is used as a secret message and random text as a cover medium. Secret message will be hidden in cover medium. Our aim to propose this new ISET method is to increase robustness of the data and also increase in capacity of hidden data.

In another method [48], combined with the recurrent neural network (RNN) and reinforcement learning (RL), a real-time interactive text steganography model (RITS) is designed and implemented. The proposed model can automatically generate semantically coherent and syntactically correct dialogs based on the input sentence, through the reasonable encoding of the text in the dialog generation process to realize secret information hiding and transmission. We trained our model using publicly collected datasets which contains 5808 dialogs and evaluated the proposed model from several perspectives. Experimental results show that the proposed model can be very efficient to implement the embedding and extraction of information. The generated dialog texts are of high quality which shows high concealment.

An innovative text steganography approach is proposed which uses natural language text as cover as well as secret message [49]. The concept of shared key is also used here, that holds the count of each parts-of-speech of secret message. This key is RSA encrypted and shared with communicative parties. Stego created by this method also is in natural language text. This method is successful as the stego keeps the original meaning of the text in gross which makes it robust and undetectable. It shows good result in capacity ratio; also, the similarity index has been assessed by Jaro–Winkler distance and Generalized Levenshtein distance.

A simple and novel approach for steganography through transliteration is proposed in [50]. A phonetic keyboard layout is very popular for writing languages having non-roman alphabets. Bengali, a language spoken by 230 million people, is a fair example and in this work we utilize Bengali digital text for data hiding by the proposed technique. For several characters in the Bengali alphabet, there are multiple options to represent a character in its equivalent roman form using a phonetic keyboard layout. The main idea of the proposed method is to exploit this special feature of Bengali phonetic keyboard layouts to hide secret information in form of bits. One of these options can be used to represent the bit "0" and the other option can represent the bit "1" in a document without any risk of understanding by any intermediate user. The results show that the proposed method is very prominent to be a successful steganography technique. Steganalysis results show that the capacity of the method is 1.2%, which is adequate for a text steganography system with very low risk of machine detection. This method can be easily adapted and applied for any other language having non-roman alphabet.

Various novel methods are proposed in the last year [8–16, 18–38, 47, 51–66]. The models are proposed to secure transfer of messages from sender to receiver. The security techniques are applied to Text only. Some has utilized the format of the texts by just manipulating the different symbols of different languages. Lots of work are done in Arabic texts because of the fact that this language contains lots of points which can be manipulated very easily. Some has done the work in Indian languages also. Some has done the linguistic-based methods.

As text-based steganography is a widely used secure technique for secure transmission. A novel method has been designed while using text-based steganography. In this method symbols are retrieved and converted into other symbols and embedded in the same text by doing certain manipulations. This can be used to recreate the documents after printouts, even when certain harm is done to the documents.

An approach for printed document authentication has been done by using concepts of text-based steganography. This is done by extracting the information from the printed document and embedding its converted form in same document. In this method text present in the document was first extracted and converted into encoded symbols. These encoded symbols were embedded into the background or along the boundary of the document multiple numbers of times by utilizing RTF file properties. This is how the text is present in the form of symbols multiple number of times in the document without affecting the integrity of the document. In order to retrieve the information from the hard copy of document, the document was scanned. The scanned image was converted into document file with the help of OCR software. Then the embedded symbols were extracted from the document file followed by conversion of symbols into text. Then this text is matched with the original text present in the document. This is how document is authenticated.

This method for document authentication is very useful tool for authenticating both electronic and printed documents. Nowadays various cases are coming for illegal documents like fake degrees, mark sheets, and tempered legal documents. It is a challenging issue for the governments to come with an idea or mechanism in order to prevent such illegal activities without intervening the integrity of the documents.

5 Implementation of Text-Based Steganography

In a modern era of Information Technology, illicit copying and distribution accompany the adoption of widespread electronic distribution of copyrighted material. This is the main reason why people think about how to protect their work and how to prevent such illicit activities. For this purpose, various methods including cryptography, steganography, coding, and so on have been used. Steganography is the best-suited technique that allow user to hide a message in another message (cover media). Most of steganography research use cover media as pictures, video clips, and sounds. However, text steganography is not normally preferred due to the difficulty in finding redundant bits in text document. To embed information inside a document, its characteristics should be altered. These characteristics can be either the text format or characteristics of the character. But the problem is that if slight change has been done to the document then it will become visible to the third party or attacker. The key to this problem is to alter the document in such a way that it is simply not visible to the human eye yet it is possible to decode it with computer.

In the proposed method, an approach for document reconstruction using text-based steganography is introduced. This is done because if somehow the document is torn out then the important information will be lost. So, in order to get that information, we have to recreate the document. This can be done by extracting the information from the torn part of the document and recreating the document. RTF file format is used as a cover object to embed text information by exploiting text document properties. The textual information is embedded in document not once but multiple number of times. This repeated information will help us to recreate the printed document even from the small portion. For extracting data, hard copy is scanned and scanned image is converted into editable document file with the help of OCR software, followed by extraction of information from the document.

The objective of this project is to develop a system based on the concepts of text-based steganography, which helps in reconstruction of printed document from its part or whole.

The scope of the project is:

- The RTF file is to be used as a cover object.
- Only textual information can be embedded.
- Texts are placed in such a way that they will not create any distortion to the original text and they can be scanned out at the time of information retrieval.
- Document should be printed after embedding data in it.
- A4 size paper is used for printout.

High quality scanner and OCR software are required.

An approach for document reconstruction using text-based steganography has been made by extracting the information from the torn part of the document and

Table 34.1 Tabular analysis of results obtained after embedding symbols into the background and along the boundary

Result #	Type	No. of times embedded	Total words present	Total words retrieved	% Retrieval
1	Symbols into background (* and #)	4	43	43	100
2	Symbols along border (* and #)	4	43	43	100
3	Symbols into background (A and B)	4	43	43	100
4	Symbols along border (A and B)	4	43	43	100
5	Symbols into background (O and X)	4	75	75	100
6	Symbols along border (O and X)	4	75	75	100

recreating the document. In this method text present in the document was first extracted and converted into binary followed by the replacement of binary digits with certain sets of two symbols, e.g., 0 with "A" and 1 with "B." These encoded symbols were embedded into the background or along the boundary of the document multiple numbers of times by utilizing RTF file properties. Figure 34.6 shows the symbols embedded into the background of the document, and Fig. 34.7 shows the symbols embedded around the boundary of the document. This is how the text is present in the form of symbols multiple number of times in the document without affecting the integrity of the document. In order to retrieve the information from the hard copy of document, the document was scanned. The scanned image was converted into document file with the help of OCR software.

Then the embedded symbols were extracted from the document file followed by conversion of symbols into binary and then to text. One of the drawbacks shown by the results in Table 34.1 is that the embedding capacity of the document is very less only two or four times symbols are embedded. This creates problem at the time of information retrieval. So, if the embedding capacity is increased then it will be proved beneficial for better retrieval of information. Embedding capacity plays a significant role because suppose in A4 size paper any text is present. With the help of proposed method that text is transformed into the stream of symbols. Take an example of character "a" its ASCII value is 97 now when it is converted to binary its value is 01100001. It means that for each character there is 8 bit binary information. So according to the proposed method any text is transformed into binary and then replaces 1s and 0s with symbols. Which means 8 units is required to represent one single alphabet. Suppose in A4 size paper if there are 20 characters then after transformation 160 symbols (combination of two symbols) are required to represent those 20 characters. This is the main reason why issue of embedding capacity is important. So in order to increase the embedding capacity of document, text is converted into binary followed by replacement of group of two binary digits with unique symbols. As there are four different combinations of binary groups like 00, 01, 10, and 11, four different symbols are required to replace those groups. After replacement of symbols a stream of combination of four symbols is obtained. From this stream of symbols again group of two symbols are selected. In that 16 different combinations of group are obtained which are replaced with 16 different unique symbols, which results in formation of stream of symbols? These replacement of symbols result in 1/4th reduction of space in document which helps in increasing the embedding capacity of document. Figure 34.6 shows the symbols embedded into the background of the document, and Fig. 34.7 shows the symbols embedded around the boundary of the document after implementation of discussed method for improving embedding capacity of document. The results shown in Table 34.1 clearly show that the embedding capacity of the document is very less. But with the help of proposed method for increasing embedding capacity of document results in Table 34.2 shows that the embedding capacity is increased to much extent. Now symbols are embedded 9–19 times which is much more as compared to the results of Table 34.1. Suppose the document is accidentally damaged, or torn then some of the information is lost. By utilizing the above discussed methods information is regained. Figure 34.7 shows the torn part of the document and Table 34.1 shows the implementation results obtained.

An approach for document reconstruction using text steganography has been proposed. The text of the document file is first extracted and encoded into the symbols, which are then embedded into the document multiple numbers of times without affecting the integrity of the document. The information can then be retrieved from hard copy of the document by scanning and converting the scanned image into document file with the help of OCR software. Then the embedded symbols are extracted from document file and processed to get information.

Three different algorithms are introduced, one for embedding symbols into the document, second for extraction of symbols from hard copy of the document and another for improving the embedding capacity of the document.

Algorithm for Embedding Text in the Document File

Step 1: Open the input.rtf file containing text

Step 2: Convert all text information of RTF file into binary

Step 3: After converting text into binary, replace 0 with O and 1 with o (symbols can vary)

Step 4: The information got in Step III will be stored in the output.txt file

Step 5: By utilizing RTF file properties open the input.rtf file and embed the text present in outout.txt file multiple number of times in to the input.rtf file

Step 6: After embedding the text, store the output in finaloutput.rtf file.

Step 7: Take printout of finaloutput.rtf file

Algorithm for Retrieving the Text From the Document

In order to retrieve the information from the hard copy of document, following algorithm is used.

Step 1: Hard copy of the document is scanned with the help of scanner

Step 2: Scanned image is converted into editable.doc file with the help of OCR software

Step 3: Extract the embedded symbols from document file

Step 4: Retrieved symbols are converted into binary

Step 5: Binary is converted into text (ASCII) format

Step 6: Compare the retrieved text from the original text present in the document.

Algorithm for Improving the Embedding Capacity of the Document

The increased embedding capacity will be beneficial for better retrieval of information. This can be explained further. Suppose, we have some text present in A4 size paper. With the help of proposed method, the text is transformed into the stream of symbols. Take an example of character "a," its ASCII value is 97 now when it is converted to binary its value is 01100001. It means that for every one character there is 8 bit binary information. Thus, the method transforms any text first into binary and then replaces 1s and 0s with symbols. This means 8 units are required to represent one single alphabet. Suppose in A4 size paper if there are 20 characters then after transformation 160 (8×20) symbols (combination of two symbols) are required to represent those 20 characters. This is the main reason why issue of embedding capacity is important.

Algorithm for Improving Embedding Capacity

Step 1: Convert text into binary

Step 2: After receiving binary stream enter space after every two digit

Step 3: Now replace binary digit with symbols, e.g.:

00 – A
01 – B
10 – C
11 – D

Step 4: After receiving the stream of symbols remove the space between each symbol

Step 5: Now enter space after every two symbols

Step 6: Now replace these group of digits with another set of symbols

EXAMPLE:

AA – E   BA – I   CA – M   DA – Q
AB – F   BB – J   CB – N   DB – R
AC – G   BC – K   CC – O   DC – S
AD – H   BD – L   CD – P   DD – T

Step 7: After replacing new symbols we have got stream of symbols

Step 8: Remove the space between the streams of symbols

Step 9: END

Fig. 34.5 Image embedded as background

The results of implementation of proposed algorithm are shown. A module is designed for the implementation of the algorithm for embedding the text into the document file. The first part of the module converts the text into binary and then into symbols and store them in separate file. This part of the module can also be used for reverse purpose, i.e., conversion of symbols into binary and then into text. Second part of module embeds the symbols into the text document file multiple number of times without affecting the integrity of the document. Another module is designed for improving the embedding capacity of the document.

For taking printouts of the document, high quality laser printer is used. For the purpose of scanning and conversion of image into document file, HP Scanjet 8390 scanner cum OCR has been used. Another OCR, Abby Fine Reader v 9.0.0.724 also has been used for the purpose of converting image into document file (Fig. 34.5).

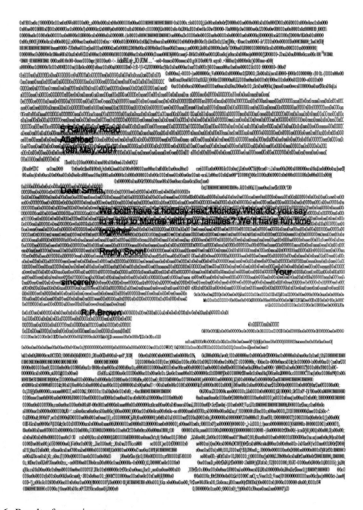

Fig. 34.6 Result of experiment

Results obtained after scanning and converting the scanned image into document file using OCR software (Fig. 34.6).

Symbols embedded along the boundary and document torn vertically (Fig. 34.7).

The information retrieved after implementation of retrieval algorithms are like that "The Crystal Gazer I shall gather myself into myself again, I shall take my scattered selves and make them one. I shall fuse them into a polished crystal ball Where I can see the moon and the flashing sun. I Shall sit like a sibyl, hour after hour intent. Watching the future come and the present go - And the little shifting

Fig. 34.7 Text as a border, file: crystal

The Crystal Gazer

her myself into myself again,
/ scattered selves and make them
one.
:hem into a polished crystal ball
:e the moon and the flashing sun.
: a sibyl, hour after hour intent.
future come and the present go -
shifting pictures of people rushing
self-importance to and fro.

- Sara Teasdale

pictures of people rushing In tiny self-importance to and fro. - Sara Teasdale." This shows that the results are 100%, which mean that as such all the information is retrieved which are lost.

The present work proposed a method for reconstructing printed document using text-based steganography. This has been done by converting text into symbols and encoding them into document multiple numbers of times. From the hard copy of the document encoded symbols have been extracted. As results shown in Table 34.2 complete retrieval of information is achieved in some cases. Results of algorithm for increasing embedding capacity of document shown in Table 34.3 more retrieval of information is achieved as compared with the results of Table 34.2. Even when

Table 34.2 Tabular analysis of results obtained after embedding symbols into the background and along the boundary

Result #	Type	No. of times embedded	Total words present	Total words retrieved	% Retrieval
1	Symbols into background (* and #)	2	43	0	0
2	Symbols along border (* and #)	4	43	0	0
3	Symbols into background (A and B)	2	43	43	100
4	Symbols along border (A and B)	4	43	30	69
5	Symbols into background (O and X)	2	75	75	100
6	Symbols along border (O and X)	4	75	52	69

Table 34.3 Tabular analysis of results obtained after implementation of method for improving embedding capacity of document

Result #	Result type	No. of times embedded	Total no. of words	Total no. retrieved words	% Retrieval
1.	Crystal (background)	9	75	75	100
2.	Eclipse (background)	15	49	49	100
3.	Mother (background)	6	104	61	58
4.	Year (background)	11	59	57	96
5.	Letter (background)	17	40	40	100
6.	Crystal (boundary)	7	75	75	100
7.	Eclipse (boundary)	11	49	49	100
8.	Mother (boundary)	6	104	104	100
9.	Year (boundary)	8	59	59	100
10.	Letter (boundary)	11	40	40	100

Table 34.4 Tabular analysis of results obtained after implementation of method for the retrieval of information from the torn part of the document

Result	Result type	No. of times symbol embedded	Total words present in document	Total no. of words retrieved	% Retrieval
1	Document torn vertically (symbols embedded as background)	9	75	0	0
2	Document torn horizontally (symbols embedded as background)	9	75	75	100
3	Document torn zigzag (symbols embedded as background)	9	75	75	100
4	Document torn diagonal (symbols embedded as background)	9	75	0	0
5	Document torn vertically (symbols embedded along boundary)	7	75	75	100
6	Document torn horizontally (symbols embedded as boundary)	7	75	75	100
7	Document torn zigzag (symbols embedded as boundary)	7	75	75	100
8.	Document torn diagonal (symbols embedded as boundary)	7	75	62	86.66

document is torn, information is retrieved from its torn parts successfully as shown in results in Table 34.4 which helps in recreating document.

6 Conclusion

As steganography becomes more widely used in computing, there are issues that need to be resolved. There are a wide variety of different techniques discussed in previous sections with their own advantages and disadvantages. Many currently used techniques are not robust enough to prevent detection and removal of embedded data. The use of benchmarking to evaluate techniques should become more common and more standard definition of robustness is required to help overcome this problem.

Data hidden in text has a variety of applications, including copyright verification, authentication, and annotation. Making copyright information inseparable from the text is one way for publishers to protect their products in an era of increasing electronic distribution. Annotation can be used for tamper protection. For example, if a cryptographic hash of the paper is encoded into the paper, it is a simple matter to detect.

The present work proposed a method for reconstructing printed document using text-based steganography. This has been done by converting text into symbols and encoding them into document multiple number of times. From the hard copy of the document encoded symbols can be extracted for recreating the document. The results show that complete retrieval of information is achieved in some cases. Even when document can be torn, information is retrieved from its torn parts to some extent as shown in results in Table 34.3 which helps in recreating the document.

The method has some limitations. RTF file is used as a cover object. Only texts are used for embedding purpose. A4 size paper is used for printout. High quality scanner and OCR like HP Scanjet G4050A4 scanner with OCR Software C1957A are preferred. For original text 12 font size is preferred and 8 font size for embedded symbols. When the symbols are embedded along the boundary area, its width is taken slightly larger than normal one, i.e., 2 in. from left and right margins and 3 in. from top and bottom margins.

The discussed method is used only for text data. This can further be extended for other forms, such as tabular data, images, and logos. The embedding capacity of the document can further be improved so it provides room for large amount of data. This will help in extracting the data even from small part of the document.

References

1. Popa, R. (1998). *An analysis of steganographic techniques*. The Politehnica University of Timisoara, Faculty of Automatics and Computers, Department of Computer Science and Software Engineering.
2. Kahn, D. (1996, May). The history of steganography. In *International Workshop on Information Hiding* (pp. 1–5). Berlin: Springer.
3. The Science of Secrecy, Steganography. Last visited May 6, 2009, from http://www.arch.columbia.edu/DDL/cad/A4S13
4. Bender, W., Gruhl, D., Morimoto, N., & Lu, A. (1996). Techniques for data hiding. *IBM Systems Journal, 35*(3.4), 313–336.
5. Johnson, N. (2009). *Steganography*. George Meson University. Last visited May 4, 2009, from http://patriot.net/~johnson/html/neil/stegdoc
6. Rabah, K. (2004). Steganography-the art of hiding data. *Information Technology Journal, 3*(3), 245–269.
7. Alattar, A. M., & Alattar, O. M. (2004, June). Watermarking electronic text documents containing justified paragraphs and irregular line spacing. In *Security, Steganography, and Watermarking of Multimedia Contents VI* (Vol. 5306, pp. 685–696). International Society for Optics and Photonics.
8. Bhaya, W., Rahma, A. M., & Al-nasrawi, D. (2013). *Text steganography based on font type in MS-Word documents*.
9. Odeh, A., Elleithy, K., & Faezipour, M. (2013, May). Steganography in Arabic text using Kashida variation algorithm (KVA). In *2013 IEEE Long Island Systems, Applications and Technology Conference (LISAT)* (pp. 1–6). IEEE.

10. Kumar, K. A., & Pabboju, S. (2018). An optimized text steganography approach using differently spelt English words. *International Journal of Pure and Applied Mathematics, 118*(19), 2113–2125.
11. Mandal, K. K., Koley, S., & Mondal, S. (2018). Number system oriented text steganography in English language for short messages: A decimal approach. In *Intelligent Computing and Information and Communication* (pp. 183–193). Singapore: Springer.
12. Khairullah, M., & Ratul, M. A. S. (2018). Steganography in Bengali unicode text. *SUST Journal of Science and Technology.*
13. Ahmadoh, E. M., & Gutub, A. A. A. (2015). Utilization of two diacritics for Arabic text steganography to enhance performance. *Lecture Notes on Information Theory, 3*(1), 42.
14. Al-Nofaie, S., Fattani, M., & Gutub, A. A. A. (2016, February). Capacity improved Arabic text steganography technique utilizing 'kashida' with whitespaces. In *The 3rd International Conference on Mathematical Sciences and Computer Engineering (ICMSCE2016)* (pp. 38–44).
15. Por, L. Y., Wong, K., & Chee, K. O. (2012). UniSpaCh: A text-based data hiding method using Unicode space characters. *Journal of Systems and Software, 85*(5), 1075–1082.
16. Kumar, R., Malik, A., Singh, S., Kumar, B., & Chand, S. (2016, April). A space based reversible high capacity text steganography scheme using font type and style. In *Computing, Communication and Automation (ICCCA)* (pp. 1090–1094). IEEE.
17. Huang, D., & Yan, H. (2001). Interword distance changes represented by sine waves for watermarking text images. *IEEE Transactions on Circuits and Systems for Video Technology, 11*(12), 1237–1245.
18. Roy, S., & Venkateswaran, P. (2013). A text based steganography technique with Indian root. *Procedia Technology, 10*, 167–171.
19. Banerjee, I., Bhattacharyya, S., & Sanyal, G. (2012). A procedure of text steganography using Indian regional language. *International Journal of Computer Network and Information Security, 4*(8), 65.
20. Vidhya, P. M., & Paul, V. (2015). A method for text steganography using Malayalam text. *Procedia Computer Science, 46*, 524–531.
21. Yang, Z., Guo, X., Chen, Z., Huang, Y., & Zhang, Y. J. (2018). RNN-Stega: Linguistic steganography based on recurrent neural networks. *IEEE Transactions on Information Forensics and Security, 14*, 1280.
22. Xiang, L., Wu, W., Li, X., & Yang, C. (2018). A linguistic steganography based on word indexing compression and candidate selection. *Multimedia Tools and Applications, 77*, 28969.
23. Zhang, L., Wang, S., Gan, W., Tang, C., Zhang, J., & Liang, H. (2018, June). SLIDE: An efficient secure linguistic steganography detection protocol. In *International Conference on Cloud Computing and Security* (pp. 298–309). Cham: Springer.
24. Mandal, K. K., Koley, S., & Mondal, S. (2018). Number system oriented text steganography in English language for short messages: A decimal approach. In *Intelligent Computing and Information and Communication* (pp. 183–193). Singapore: Springer.
25. Naqvi, N., Abbasi, A. T., Hussain, R., Khan, M. A., & Ahmad, B. (2018). Multilayer partially homomorphic encryption text steganography (MLPHE-TS): A zero steganography approach. *Wireless Personal Communications, 103*, 1563–1585.
26. Kaur, A., Kaur, S., & Sethi, G. (2018). A study on text based steganography using email platform and color mapping. *International Journal of Computer (IJC), 29*(1), 1–12.
27. Ditta, A., Yongquan, C., Azeem, M., Rana, K. G., Yu, H., & Memon, M. Q. (2018). Information hiding: Arabic text steganography by using Unicode characters to hide secret data. *International Journal of Electronic Security and Digital Forensics, 10*(1), 61–78.
28. Sanghi, A., Chaudhary, S., & Dave, M. (2018). Enhance the data security in cloud computing by text steganography. In *Smart Trends in Systems, Security and Sustainability* (pp. 241–248). Singapore: Springer.
29. Siahaan, R. F., Zarlis, M., & Nasution, B. B. (2018, September). Performance analysis of steganography alphanumeric text in the text based on Indonesian linguistic. In *IOP Conference Series: Materials Science and Engineering* (Vol. 420, No. 1, p. 012123). IOP Publishing.

30. Zuo, X., Hu, H., Zhang, W., & Yu, N. (2018, June). Text semantic steganalysis based on word embedding. In *International Conference on Cloud Computing and Security* (pp. 485–495). Cham: Springer.
31. Fateh, M., & Rezvani, M. (2018). An email-based high capacity text steganography using repeating characters. *International Journal of Computers and Applications*, 1–7. https://doi.org/10.1080/1206212x.2018.1517713
32. Xiang, L., Li, Y., Hao, W., Yang, P., & Shen, X. (2018). Reversible natural language watermarking using synonym substitution and arithmetic coding. *Computers, Materials and Continua, 55*(3), 541–559.
33. Ashraf, Z., Roy, M. L., Muhuri, P. K., & Lohani, Q. D. (2018, July). A novel image steganography approach based on interval type-2 fuzzy similarity. In *2018 IEEE International Conference on Fuzzy Systems (FUZZ-IEEE)* (pp. 1–8). IEEE.
34. Bhushan, B., & Sahoo, G. (2017). Recent advances in attacks, technical challenges, vulnerabilities and their countermeasures in wireless sensor networks. *Wireless Personal Communications, 98*(2), 2037–2077. https://doi.org/10.1007/s11277-017-4962-0.
35. Kumar, R., Chandra, P., & Hanmandlu, M. (2016). A robust fingerprint matching system using orientation features. *Journal of Information Processing Systems, 12*(1), 83–99.
36. Kumar, R., Chandra, P., & Hanmandlu, M. (2012). Fingerprint matching based on orientation feature. In *Advanced Materials Research* (Vol. 403, pp. 888–894). Trans Tech Publications.
37. Gupta, B. B., & Samir, K. B. (2013). A DWT method for image steganography. *International Journal of Advanced Research in Computer Science and Software Engineering, 3*, 983.
38. Shi, S., Qi, Y., & Huang, Y. (2016, December). An approach to text steganography based on search in internet. In *Computer Symposium (ICS), 2016 International* (pp. 227–232). IEEE.
39. Kumar, R., Chandra, P., & Hanmandlu, M. (2013, December). Local directional pattern (LDP) based fingerprint matching using SLFNN. In *2013 IEEE Second International Conference on Image Information Processing* (ICIIP-2013) (pp. 493–498). IEEE.
40. Sinha, P., Rai, A. K., Jha, V. K., Bhushan, B. (2007, July) Security vulnerabilities, attacks and countermeasures in wireless sensor networks at various layers of OSI reference model: A survey. In *International Conference on Signal Processing and Communication - ICSPC'17*, Coimbatore, Tamil Nadu, India.
41. Bennett, K. (2004). *Linguistic steganography: Survey, analysis, and robustness concerns for hiding information in text.*
42. Al-Hamami, A. H., & Al-Shamkhy, R. A. *Using natural features of letters in text information hiding.*
43. Huang, S., & Wu, J. K. (2007). Optical watermarking for printed document authentication. *IEEE Transactions on Information Forensics and Security, 2*(2), 164–173.
44. Liu, T. Y., & Tsai, W. H. (2007). A new steganographic method for data hiding in Microsoft word documents by a change tracking technique. *IEEE Transactions on Information Forensics and Security, 2*(1), 24–30.
45. Shirali-Shahreza, M. (2008, February). Text steganography by changing words spelling. In *10th International Conference on Advanced Communication Technology, 2008. ICACT 2008.* (Vol. 3, pp. 1912–1913). IEEE.
46. Gupta Banik, B., & Bandyopadhyay, S. K. (2018). Novel text steganography using natural language processing and part-of-speech tagging. *IETE Journal of Research*, 1–12. https://doi.org/10.1080/03772063.2018.1491807
47. Khairullah, M. (2018). A novel steganography method using transliteration of Bengali text. *Journal of King Saud University - Computer and Information Sciences.*
48. Samphaiboon, N., & Dailey, M. N. (2008, May). Steganography in Thai text. In *5th International Conference on Electrical Engineering/Electronics, Computer, Telecommunications and Information Technology, 2008. ECTI-CON 2008.* (Vol. 1, pp. 133–136). IEEE.
49. Al-Azawi, A. F., & Fadhil, M. A. (2010). Arabic text steganography using kashida extensions with Huffman code. *Journal of Applied Sciences, 10*, 436–439.
50. Yang, B., et al. (2011). Steganography in MS Excel document using text-rotation technique. *Information Technology Journal, 10*(4), 889–893.

51. Shirali-Shahreza, M. H., & Shirali-Shahreza, M. (2006, July). A new approach to Persian/Arabic text steganography. In *5th IEEE/ACIS International Conference on Computer and Information Science, 2006 and 2006 1st IEEE/ACIS International Workshop on Component-Based Software Engineering, Software Architecture and Reuse. ICIS-COMSAR 2006* (pp. 310–315). IEEE.

52. Gutub, A., & Fattani, M. (2007). *A novel Arabic text steganography method using letter points and extensions.*

53. Chaudhary, S., Dave, M., Sanghi, A., & Sidh, H. (2018). Indian script encoding technique (ISET): A Hindi text steganography approach. In *Information and Communication Technology for Sustainable Development* (pp. 393–401). Singapore: Springer.

54. Yang, Z., Zhang, P., Jiang, M., Huang, Y., & Zhang, Y. J. (2018, June). RITS: Real-time interactive text steganography based on automatic dialogue model. In *International Conference on Cloud Computing and Security* (pp. 253–264). Cham: Springer.

55. Ahvanooey, M. T., Li, Q., Hou, J., Mazraeh, H. D., & Zhang, J. (2018). AITSteg: An innovative text steganography technique for hidden transmission of text message via social media. *IEEE Access, 6,* 65981.

56. Fateh, M., & Rezvani, M. (2018). An email-based high capacity text steganography using repeating characters. *International Journal of Computers and Applications,* 1–7. https://doi.org/10.1080/1206212x.2018.1517713

57. Bala, B., Kamboj, L., & Luthra, P. (2018). Secure file storage in cloud computing using hybrid cryptography algorithm. *International Journal of Advanced Research in Computer Science, 9*(2), 773.

58. Walke, A., Bhanushali, J., Rajgor, A., & Jain, J. (2018). Enhanced password processing scheme using visual cryptography and steganography. *International Journal on Recent and Innovation Trends in Computing and Communication, 6*(4), 35–37.

59. Baawi, S. S., Mokhtar, M. R., & Sulaiman, R. (2018, June). Enhancement of text steganography technique using Lempel-Ziv-Welch Algorithm and two-letter word technique. In *International Conference of Reliable Information and Communication Technology* (pp. 525–537). Cham: Springer.

60. Din, R., Utama, S., Hanizan, S. H., Hilal, M. M., Hanif, M. A., Zulhazlin, A., & Fazali, G. M. (2018). Evaluating the feature-based technique of text steganography based on capacity and time processing parameters. *Advanced Science Letters, 24*(10), 7355–7359.

61. Wu, Y., Chen, X., & Sun, X. (2018). Coverless steganography based on English texts using binary tags protocol. *Journal of Internet Technology, 19*(2), 599–606.

62. Azeem, M., Yongquan, C., Ditta, A., Rana, K. G., & Rajpoot, F. A. (2018). Information hiding: A novel algorithm for enhancement of cover text capacity by using unicode characters. *International Journal of Information and Computer Security, 10*(4), 437–453.

63. Taha, A., Hammad, A. S., & Selim, M. M. (2018). A high capacity algorithm for information hiding in Arabic text. *Journal of King Saud University-Computer and Information Sciences.*

64. Hu, H., Zuo, X., Zhang, W., & Yu, N. (2018, June). Covert communication by exploring statistical and linguistical distortion in text. In *International Conference on Cloud Computing and Security* (pp. 288–301). Cham: Springer.

65. Kamat, S. D., Patil, S. S., & Mali, A. S. (2018). Implementation of steganographic model using inverted LSB insertion. *International Journal of Engineering and Management Research (IJEMR), 8*(4), 59–62.

66. Majumder, A., & Changder, S. (2013). A novel approach for text steganography: Generating text summary using reflection symmetry. *Procedia Technology, 10,* 112–120.

Chapter 35
Machine Learning Based Intrusion Detection Techniques

Kishor Kumar Gulla, P. Viswanath, Suresh Babu Veluru, and R. Raja Kumar

Abstract Nowadays the usage of Internet has being increased exponentially due to the reason of keeping most sensitive data in on-line. It leads vulnerabilities on the data that is available in on-line like intruders can raise any kind of attacks. Therefore, intrusion detection helps a computing environment or computer system to deal with such kind of attacks. Intrusion detection is also an important supplement as well as component in the traditional computer security mechanism. It can be considered as a typical classification problem. Therefore to develop an effective intrusion detection method, the machine learning methods can be used. This chapter briefs the current state of the art in the intrusion detection domain using the supervised learning approaches of machine learning.

Keywords Machine learning · Intrusion detection · Classification

1 Introduction

Denning proposed the first intrusion detection model in 1987 with an aim to build an effective and accurate detection model. Later between late 1980s and early 1990s the expert systems and statistical approaches together applied to build the effective detection model. At last during the period mid 1990s and to late 1990s the process of acquiring the information of normal and abnormal behavior is changed from manual to automatic system. Therefore to make the process as automatic, the techniques such as artificial intelligence and machine learning techniques can be used. The

K. K. Gulla (✉) · R. R. Kumar
Rajeev Gandhi Memorial College of Engineering and Technology, Nandyal, India

P. Viswanath
Indian Institute of Information Technology-Chittoor, Sri City, India
e-mail: viswanath.p@iiits.in

S. B. Veluru
AI Lead, ServisBOT, Waterford, Republic of Ireland

© Springer Nature Switzerland AG 2020   873
B. B. Gupta et al. (eds.), *Handbook of Computer Networks and Cyber Security*,
https://doi.org/10.1007/978-3-030-22277-2_35

categorization of intrusion detection system (IDS) is based on its characteristics. Therefore, IDS can be classified as audit source location, behavior on detection, detection method, and usage frequency.

This chapter focus on the classification of detection method. Furthermore, the detection method is categorized into two classes such as misuse detection and anomaly. There is a diversity of attacks or misuses that are predefined. For each attack or class a set of example feature vectors are identified and stored in a database. To classify the given test feature vector into one of the attacks or classes, it can be compared with the stored feature vectors of each attack or class. For anomaly detection, the normal user behavior is stored into a feature database and it can be used to compare the current connection feature vector. It can be classified as anomaly or possibly an attack if it deviates too much with each of connections in the database.

Furthermore, the misuse based detection approach is categorized into various classes such as data mining based methods, signature based methods, state transition based analysis methods, and rule based methods. Similarly, the anomaly based detection techniques are categorized as distance based methods, model based methods, profiling methods, rule based methods, and statistical methods.

As an intrusion detection system is a typical classification problem, therefore the measure called confusion matrix can be used for evaluation of an intrusion detection system. It is shown in Table 35.1. The entries in this matrix are false positives (FP), true positives (TP), false negatives (FN), and true negatives (TN). These entries are framed based on the actual class label of the examples and the predicted class label of the examples by a classifier. The projects such as mining audit data for automated models for intrusion detection (MADAM ID) and intrusion detection using data mining (IDAM) are the example projects that show the emphasis on the data mining methods towards the intrusion detection application.

The remaining sections brief about various existing methods for intrusion detection application.

An intrusion detection is a typical classification problem, so any classification algorithms can be used. There are various classification algorithms such as decision tree classifier, Bayesian classifier, nearest neighbor classifier, rule based classifier, support vector machines, and neural network classifier. However, each classifier is having its own merits and de-merits. No classifier is the best classifier. However, the decision tree classifier has been used for a variety of applications due to

Table 35.1 A Confusion matrix

| | | Predicted class labels | |
		Positive class (Normal)	Negative class (Attack)
Actual class labels	Positive class (Normal)	True positives (TP)	False negatives (FN)
	Negative class (Attack)	False positives (FP)	True negatives (TN)

its advantages such as simplicity, interpretability, and performance. The major functionalities in the machine learning/data mining are classification and clustering. Classification is a supervised learning approach which uses to train a model using the data in which the class label is also associated with each pattern. Furthermore, this model is used to classify the given network connection is a normal connection or anomaly. Alternatively, clustering is an unsupervised learning approach which uses the data in which only the feature values of objects will be considered.

The data mining methods such as association rules and frequency episodes are used to extract the normal user patterns from audit data [8], further that uses for the network traffic analysis. The rough set based decision tree algorithm is proposed for intrusion detection application [16]. In this approach, the decision tree is induced based on the uniformity of an attribute which gives its goodness value. The rule based expert systems [4] such as SRIs IDES [12] and LANLs, NADIR [14] have become popular for intrusion detection systems. Artificial intelligence (AI) techniques played a vital role in intrusion detection domain. The AI techniques are used for data reduction and also classification of data. AI techniques such as state transition analysis, rule based expert systems, and genetic algorithms are also applied for intrusion detection application [2].

The fuzzy logic systems and data mining methods together are applied for intrusion detection to improve its flexibility [13]. For detecting intrusions in the multi-user Air Force computer system environment a prototype is developed [15]. It consists of two methods such as signature based detection and anomaly detection. IDES [1] is a classic intrusion detection system which further merged to next-generation intrusion detection expert system (NIDES). In IDES, the behavior of users is recorded and summarized time to time when they are doing various activities in the system. Furthermore, this statistics are used to determine whether the current users behavior is intrusions behavior if any deviations found with the stored statistics and profile.

The rest of the chapter discusses various state-of-the-art methods of machine learning based intrusion detection methods. Section 2 discusses the decision trees and also various types of decision trees. Section 3 discusses the core of the chapter, i.e., ensemble techniques and also its varieties for decision trees. The datasets used for various experiments are given in Sect. 4. Section 5 gives the experimental results of various methods discussed in this chapter. The conclusions are given in Sect. 6.

2 Decision Trees

This section discusses various decision trees like conventional or standard decision trees, soft or fuzzy decision trees in which fuzzy set theory principles are incorporated, randomized soft decision trees in which the parameters such as attribute and cut point can be randomly chosen at the nodes in the induction process of a tree and rough set based decision tree in which rough set theory principles are incorporated such as lower approximation and upper approximation in the design process of a tree.

2.1 Conventional Decision Trees

A decision tree is a directed decision tree which has zero or more internal nodes along with one or more leaf nodes. A node in a decision tree called root node if it does not have an incoming edge. The nodes which have incoming edge and one or more outgoing edges are called internal nodes. The nodes which have only incoming edges are called leaf nodes. The internal nodes split the input space into two or more subspaces based on the given expression at that node. If the expression can be evaluated using only a single attribute, then that type of decision tree is called univariate decision tree or axis parallel decision tree. Alternatively, if the evaluated expression is having several attributes, then it is called multivariate decision tree or oblique decision tree.

There are two phases in decision tree induction such as growing phase and pruning phase. The decision tree is allowed to fully grown until each leaf node becomes pure in growing phase. Because of this the decision tree sometimes may be over fitted, which can be resolved in pruning phase.

Let $\mathcal{X}$ be the dataset which consists of data instances along with class label. More formally $\mathcal{X} = \{(X_i, y_i) \mid i = 1, 2, \ldots n\}$, where each X_i is described with d-dimensional feature vector and also associated a class label y_i. Let $\mathcal{A} = \{A_1, A_2, \ldots, A_j, \ldots, A_d\}$ be the set of attributes or features which are assumed as continuous attributes. To construct a decision tree each attribute will be evaluated using any of the attribute selection measures such as information gain, gini index, and gain ratio. The attribute which gives more information among all attributes that can be chosen as the good splitting attribute at the node in the growing phase of a decision tree. This process will be repeated to the remaining nodes until the end of the growing phase. To describe the induction of a decision tree an information gain is chosen as the attribute selection measure. In this process first entropy of dataset $\mathcal{X}$ can be calculated as follows:

$$Entropy(\mathcal{X}) = \sum_{i=1}^{c} -p_i \log_2(p_i) \tag{35.1}$$

where c indicates number of class labels, p_i indicates the probability of samples belong to the class i. Weighted average of the entropy over the attribute A_i can be calculated as follows:

$$Info(A_i, \tau_k) = \frac{n_1}{n} Entropy(\mathcal{X}_1^{(i)}) + \frac{n_2}{n} Entropy(\mathcal{X}_2^{(i)}) \tag{35.2}$$

where $\mathcal{X}_1^{(i)}$ and $\mathcal{X}_2^{(i)}$ indicate the two resulting blocks of the data $\mathcal{X}$ over the attribute A_i by choosing the threshold or cut point τ_k. Finally, the information gain G over the attribute A_i can be calculated as

$$G(A_i, \tau_k) = Entropy(\mathcal{X}) - Info(A_i, \tau_k) \qquad (35.3)$$

If $\mathcal{A}$ is categorical data, then the information gain of the attribute can be computed as follows:

$$G(\mathcal{X}, A_i) = Entropy(\mathcal{X}) - \sum_{j=1}^{v} \frac{|\mathcal{X}_j|}{|\mathcal{X}|} \times Entropy(\mathcal{X}_j) \qquad (35.4)$$

where X_j is the subset of the instances of $\mathcal{X}$ in which the attribute A_i is having a value j.

Similarly, the decision tree can be built using the other measures such as *Gain ratio* and *Gini index*.

2.2   Soft Decision Trees

The construction of soft decision trees is similar to the conventional decision trees but differs in the computation of goodness measures of the attributes. The fuzzy membership values are used in the construction process of a soft decision trees.

Let the attribute B represent a continuous valued attribute. Let τ be the threshold or cut point. Conventional decision trees follow hard partition or crisp partition, whereas soft decision trees consider soft partition. The definitions of crisp partition and fuzzy partition are given in [7]. As shown in Fig. 35.1, in case of hard partition if the attribute B value is greater than threshold τ, then it will be assigned to block B_2 otherwise it is assigned to block B_1. Contrary to hard partition in case of soft partition the assignment of attribute B value uses fuzzy concept. In case of soft partition, if the attribute B value is less than or equal to $\tau - w/2$, then it will be

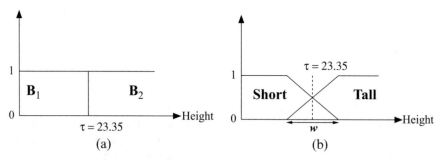

Fig. 35.1 (a) Hard partition vs (b) soft partition

assigned to a fuzzy block B_1 which is named with a linguistic variable called "short," if B value is greater than or equal to $\tau + w/2$, then it will be assigned to fuzzy block B_2 which is called with a linguistic variable "tall." Otherwise it belongs to both "short" and "tall" with some membership degree. "w" represents the width of overlapping of fuzzy sets "short" and "tall" as shown in Fig. 35.1b.

Let x_i be the instance and its fuzzy membership value $\mu_{short}(x_i)$ can be computed as follows if it assigns to fuzzy block "short."

$$\mu_{short}(x_i) = \begin{cases} 1 & \text{if } x_i \leq \tau - w/2, \\ \frac{(\tau+\frac{w}{2})-x_i}{w} & \text{if } \tau - \frac{w}{2} < x_i < \tau + \frac{w}{2}, \\ 0 & \text{if } x_i \geq \tau + w/2. \end{cases}$$

Similarly, $\mu_{tall}(x_i)$ is the membership value of an instance x_i and it will be calculated as follows if it assigns to fuzzy block "tall."

$$\mu_{tall}(x_i) = \begin{cases} 0 & \text{if } x_i \leq \tau - w/2, \\ \frac{x_i-(\tau-\frac{w}{2})}{w} & \text{if } \tau - \frac{w}{2} < x_i < \tau + \frac{w}{2}, \\ 1 & \text{if } x_i \geq \tau + w/2. \end{cases}$$

In the process of constructing a soft decision tree, fuzzy information gain of each attribute A_i in $\mathcal{X}$ can be computed as follows:

$$G_F(A_i, \tau_k) = Entropy_F(\mathcal{X}) - Info_F(A_i, \tau_k, \mathcal{X}) \tag{35.5}$$

where $Entropy_F(\mathcal{X})$ is the fuzzy entropy of a $\mathcal{X}$ which is a training set and it can be computed as follows:

$$Entropy_F(\mathcal{X}) = \sum_{k=1}^{c} -(\mu_{p_k}, \mathcal{X}) \log_2(\mu_{p_k}, \mathcal{X}) \tag{35.6}$$

where μ_{p_k} represents fuzzy proportion of data instances in fuzzy set $\mathcal{X}$ that belong to class c_k. Similarly, the other term $Info_F$ represents fuzzy entropy for fuzzy partition of tuples in $\mathcal{X}$ over the attribute A_i values that can be computed as follows:

$$Info_F(A_i, \tau_k, \mathcal{X}) = \frac{N_F^{\mathcal{X}_1}}{N_F^{\mathcal{X}}} Entropy_F(\mathcal{X}_1) + \frac{N_F^{\mathcal{X}_2}}{N_F^{\mathcal{X}}} Entropy_F(\mathcal{X}_2) \tag{35.7}$$

where τ_k be the optimal threshold. $Entropy_F(\mathcal{X}_1)$ and $Entropy_F(\mathcal{X}_2)$ represent fuzzy entropy of the subsets $\mathcal{X}_1$ and $\mathcal{X}_2$, respectively.

The above process is repeated for each attribute A_i in $\mathcal{A}$. The attribute can be chosen as good splitting attribute if it has high fuzzy information gain among all attributes at the root node. To enhance the decision tree from the root node the above process is repeated on the obtained child nodes.

To classify an unseen instance in this soft decision tree model the matching fuzzy membership values of the instance to each node from root to leaf are calculated. To classify an unseen instance x_i to either of the class labels C_1 or C_2 its membership values will be considered. Let P_{i1} be the fuzzy membership value of x_i to assign to class label C_1. Similarly, P_{i2} be the fuzzy membership value of x_i to assign class label C_2. For final classification of x_i, class C_1 will be assigned to x_i if $P_{i1} > P_{i2}$ otherwise class C_2 will be assigned.

2.3   Randomized Soft Decision Tree

In order to induce a decision tree for continuous valued attribute the single cut point that leads the optimal partition will be taken up in the conventional method of decision tree. Alternatively to design the randomized soft decision tree several cut points will be considered. At each node in the decision tree construction process the parameters such as the cut point and attribute chosen randomly from the distributions as given below.

Let the maximum information gain be $G_F^{max}(A_i)$ of the attribute A_i among its all possible cut points. The probability distributions are formulated over all attributes in the A as given below, from which the attribute is chosen randomly.

$$P(A_i) = \frac{G_F^{max}(A_i)}{\sum_{k=1}^{d} G_F^{max}(A_k)} \tag{35.8}$$

Similarly, the cut point τ_k can also be chosen randomly from the distribution obtained over possible cut points of attribute A_i as shown below.

$$P(\tau_k) = \frac{G_F(A_i, \tau_k)}{\sum_{\forall l} G_F(A_i, \tau_l)}. \tag{35.9}$$

where $G_F(A_i, \tau_k)$ is the fuzzy information gain of the attribute A_i with respect to the threshold τ_k.

Therefore, at each node in the induction process of a decision tree the above procedure is considered for choosing the splitting attribute and the threshold or cut point.

2.4   Rough Set Based Decision Tree

In this section, the design of rough set based decision tree is discussed. The basic concepts are explained clearly in [6]. Let IS be the information system which is also called a dataset and it is defined as $IS = (O, A, D)$, where O represents the Universe of objects for the set of instances such as $\{x_1, x_2, \ldots, x_n\}$, similarly A

represents the set of condition attributes such as $\{A_1, A_2, \ldots, A_d\}$ and D be the set of decision attributes. The lower approximation and upper approximation are the two concepts in the rough set theory that are very useful for data analysis.

The popular heuristics to find the goodness of the attributes in the induction of decision trees are information gain, gain ratio, and gini index. However, the goodness of the each attribute A_i can be evaluated as shown below in the rough set based decision tree.

$$RA_i = \sum_{k=1}^{c} \frac{|A_i X_k|}{\sum_{j=1}^{c} |X_j|} \tag{35.10}$$

where $|A_i x_k|$ is the cardinality of the boundary set or rough set $A_i x_k$, which can be determined as follows:

$$A_i X_k = \overline{A_i X_k} - \underline{A_i X_k}$$

where $\underline{A_i X_k}$ and $\overline{A_i X_k}$ are the lower approximation and upper approximation of the subset x_k with respect to the attribute A_i, respectively. The above process will be repeated recursively on the obtained subset of the instances from parent until any of the following conditions are true.

- If the node becomes pure
- If the ratio of number of elements in the node and the number of elements in the O is less than the predefined threshold τ.

3 Ensemble Techniques

This section describes various ensemble of decision trees. In the ensemble of decision trees how each component can be built is also discussed. The different types of ensemble of decision trees like ensemble of standard decision trees, ensemble of soft decision trees, and ensemble of rough set based decision trees are discussed in this section.

3.1 *Ensemble of Standard Decision Trees*

This section discusses the two methods of ensemble of standard decision trees. In the first method k-Means and ID3 methods are used to derive each component, whereas in the second ensemble—k-Prototype and C4.5 methods are used.

3.1.1   *k*-Means + ID3

This method *k-Means + ID3* method [3] is proposed by Gaddam et al. Each X_i in the dataset $\mathcal{X}$ is described with a d-dimensional features and also associated a class label y_i (0 for normal and 1 for anomaly). This method is developed using two steps such as training and testing. In the training phase the given dataset is partitioned into k-clusters such as $S_1, S_2, \ldots, S_k$ using k-Means clustering algorithm. The ID3 decision tree is derived on each cluster S_i. Furthermore, f candidate clusters are considered instead of k clusters. The considered f clusters are based on the nearness of the given query pattern. In the second phase, i.e., testing again two stages are defined such as *candidate selection* and *candidate combination* for f candidate clusters. The decisions of k-Means and ID3 are extracted for a given query pattern in the candidate selection phase. These extracted decisions are combined using any of the following two rules in the candidate combination phase. The two rules are *nearest neighbor rule (NC)* and *nearest consensus rule (NC)*. In *NN* rule, the classification decision of a given query pattern is based on the decision of ID3 decision tree in association with the nearest candidate clusters. In *NC* rule, the classification decision is based on the decisions of both methods, i.e., k-Means and ID3 which are agreed. This method is experimented on the DARPA intrusion detection datasets that have a combination of numeric and non-numeric attributes.

3.1.2   Limitations of *k*-Means + ID3

The above method is having few limitations which are given as follows.

- The k-Means clustering algorithm cannot applied on the non-numeric data.
- The ID3 decision tree is biased to the attributes which have many values.

3.1.3   k-Prototype + C4.5

This method is proposed by Kumar et al. [5]. In this method k-Prototype clustering method is used for clustering. The k-Prototype is a method that can be applied for mixed data, i.e., combination of both numeric and non-numeric features or attributes. First the given data $\mathcal{X}$ is partitioned into k clusters such as $S_1, S_2, \ldots, S_k$ using k-Prototype clustering method. On each cluster S_i the decision tree T_i is built using C4.5 decision tree. Each cluster S_i is represented with a centroid r_i. To classify the given query pattern as either *normal* or *anomaly* an anomaly score P_i is considered. For this only f candidate clusters are considered out of k-clusters. Evaluation of P_i is given as follows:

$$P_i = \sum_{i=1}^{f} \omega_i y_i \tag{35.11}$$

where for each cluster S_i the weightage w_i is given and it is calculated as follows:

$$w_i = \frac{1/d_i}{\sum_{j=1}^{f} 1/d_j} \tag{35.12}$$

where d_i is the distance of a query pattern to a cluster G_i. The query pattern Q is classified using a threshold rule, i.e., if the anomaly score P_i is greater than the threshold τ (which value is set to 0.5) then it is an anomaly otherwise it is normal.

3.2 Ensemble of Randomized Soft Decision Trees

In this section "Ensemble of Soft Decision Trees" is discussed which is proposed by Kumar et al. [7]. The subset X_i is derived from the given data $\mathcal{X}$ using bootstrap method. The method discussed in Sect. 2.3 is used to derive the decision trees $T_1, T_2, \ldots, T_l$ on each subset $X_1, X_2, \ldots, X_l$, respectively. The threefold cross validation is used for the parameter l from the set $\{1, 3, 5, 7, 9, 11, 13, 15\}$.

To classify the given query pattern Q using this ensemble method the majority voting from the outputs of each decision tree T_i is considered.

3.3 Ensemble of Rough-Fuzzy Set Based Decision Trees

The method discussed in this section, i.e., "Ensemble of Rough-Fuzzy set based decision trees" is proposed by Kumar et al. [6]. The two popular concepts in rough set theory are *lowerapproximation* and *upperapproximation*. The definitions of various terms such as *lowerapproximation, upperapproximation, reduct, positiveregion*, and *fuzzyequivalenceclass* are given in [6]. For any particular task, to use the information effectively a single reduct is not enough. There are few limitations if a single reduct is chosen for any data. For example, due to noise in the data that effects the reduct and further it effects the method (classification) also. Therefore choosing several reducts gives better solution for a task.

The authors in [6] proposed an approach to generate multiple reducts from the data. To build an ensemble of rough-fuzzy set based decision trees multiple reducts are derived. On each reduct the rough set based decision tree which is discussed in Sect. 2.4 is built. For a given query pattern Q each decision tree in the ensemble of decision trees gives an output. From this output the majority voting is considered for the final classification of a query pattern.

4   Datasets

In this section, various datasets used for experiments for methods presented in this chapter are discussed. Table 35.2 gives the details of the datasets used for various experiments.

5   Experimental Results

In this section, the experimental results that are done by respective authors are given.

5.1   *k-Means + ID3 and k-Prototype + C4.5 Results*

Figures 35.2 and 35.3 show the performance of the two methods, i.e., k-Means + ID3 and k-Prototype + C4.5 over the datasets NAD-1998 and NAD-1999, respectively. In these two figures, NN rule and NC rule indicates k-Means + ID3 method with nearest neighbor rule and nearest consensus rule, respectively. Similarly, ensemble in these two figures indicates k-Prototype + C4.5 method. From the experimental results, it is shown that k-Prototype + C4.5 method performed better than k-Means + ID3 method.

5.2   *Ensemble of Randomized Soft Decision Tree Results*

To show the performance of this method it is compared with the other related methods such as standard decision tree, soft decision tree, and randomized soft decision tree over the datasets such as *1999 KDDCUP, SPAM MAIL*, and *PIMA*. Tables 35.3 and 35.4 show the experimental results over these three datasets. Table 35.4 shows the robustness of the method "Ensemble of Randomized Soft Decision Tree Results" compared to all remaining methods mentioned in the table.

Table 35.2 Datasets used for experiments of all methods

S. No	Name of the dataset	#instances	#attributes	References
1	NAD-98	7500	12	[10, 11]
2	NAD-99	7500	10	[10, 11]
3	1999-KDDCUP	10, 000	41	[10, 11]
4	Spam mail	4601	57	[9]
5	Pima	768	8	[9]
6	Iris	150	4	[9]

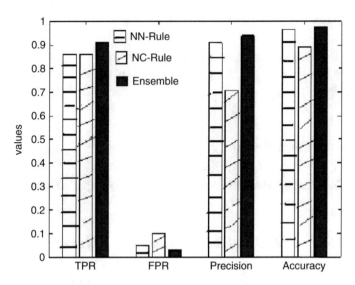

Fig. 35.2 Results over NAD-1998 for k-Means + ID3 and k-Prototype + C4.5

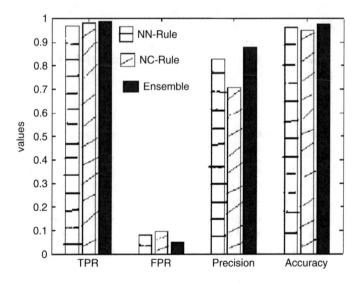

Fig. 35.3 Results over NAD-1999 for k-Means + ID3 and k-Prototype + C4.5

To show the effectiveness of the randomized soft decision trees noise is injected with various levels of percentage in the datasets. The results are shown in two different ways, i.e., before injecting noise and after injecting noise. The randomized and also its ensemble are outperformed the other related methods. For the comparisons the *accuracy* metric is used with standard deviation.

Table 35.3 Experimental results before injecting noise

	1999 KDDCUP	SPAM MAIL	PIMA
Standard decision tree	94.67% ± 2.59	93.72% ± 0.53	72.44% ± 2.51
Soft decision tree	95.94% ± 2.1	94.98% ± 0.46	73.66% ± 2.1
Randomized soft decision tree	96.98% ± 1.21	96.26% ± 0.27	74.89% ± 1.62
Ensemble of randomized soft DTs	98.23% ± 0.91	98.14% ± 0.26	76.96% ± 1.21

Table 35.4 Experimental results after injecting noise

	1999 KDDCUP	SPAM MAIL	PIMA
Standard decision tree	91.61% ± 2.77	91.25% ± 1.71	71.125% ± 2.27
Soft decision tree	93.55% ± 2.03	92.54% ± 1.36	72.84% ± 1.87
Randomized soft decision tree	94.87% ± 1.56	93.92% ± 1.23	74.97% ± 1.18
Ensemble of randomized soft DTs	97.68% ± 0.89	97.56% ± 0.73	76.26% ± 0.67

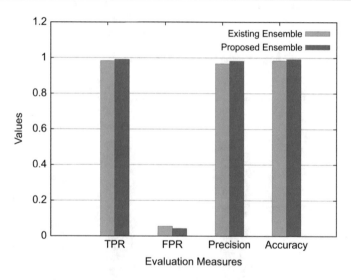

Fig. 35.4 Results over 1999 KDDCUP for Ensemble of Rough-Fuzzy Decision Trees and k-Prototype + C4.5

5.3   Ensemble of Rough-Fuzzy Set Based Decision Trees Results

Figures 35.4, 35.5, 35.6, and 35.7 show the comparative results between the two ensemble of methods that are discussed in Sects. 3.3 and 3.1.3 over various datasets such as 1999 kddcup, Iris, NAD-1998, and Spam mail datasets, respectively. The proposed ensemble and existing ensemble in Figs. 35.4, 35.5, 35.6, and 35.7 indicates Ensemble of Rough-Fuzzy Set Based Decision Trees and k-Prototype +

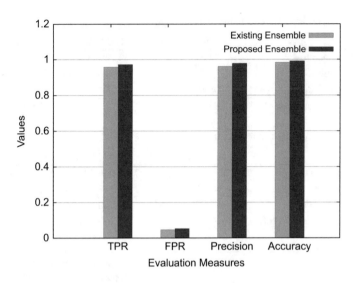

Fig. 35.5 Results over Iris for Ensemble of Rough-Fuzzy Decision Trees and k-Prototype + C4.5

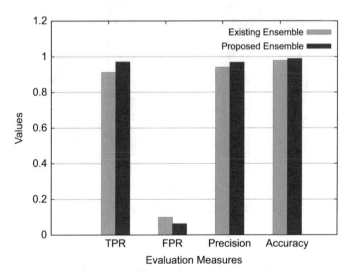

Fig. 35.6 Results over NAD-1998 for Ensemble of Rough-Fuzzy Decision Trees and k-Prototype + C4.5

C4.5, respectively. The experimental results of these two methods show that the performance of Ensemble of Rough-Fuzzy Set Based Decision Trees is better than k-Prototype + C4.5 in terms of *TPR*, *FPR*, *Precision*, and *Accuracy*.

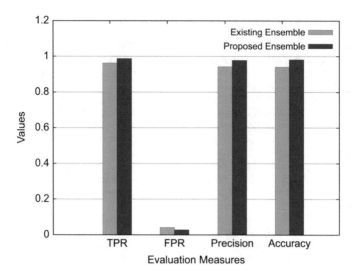

Fig. 35.7 Results over Spam mail for Ensemble of Rough-Fuzzy Decision Trees and k-Prototype + C4.5

6   Conclusion

This chapter mainly focused on various machine learning based intrusion detection methods. To show the effectiveness of discussed methods various experiments are carried out on several standard datasets. Furthermore, the optimization techniques can be applied on the discussed methods to get the optimal decision tree as the future work.

References

1. Axelsson, S. (2000). Intrusion detection systems: A survey and taxonomy.
2. Frank, J. (1994). Artificial intelligence and intrusion detection: Current and future directions. In *Proceedings of the 17th National Computer Security Conference*.
3. Gaddam, S. R., Phoha, V. V., & Balagani, K. S. (2007). K-Means+ID3: A novel method for supervised anomaly detection by cascading k-means clustering and ID3 decision tree learning methods. *IEEE Transactions on Knowledge and Data Engineering, 19*(3), 345–354.
4. Ilgun, K., & Kemmerer, A. (1995). State transition analysis: A rule-based intrusion detection approach. *IEEE Transaction on Software Engineering, 21*(3), 181–199.
5. Kumar, G. K., Viswanath, P., & Rao, A. A. (2011). Intrusion detection using an ensemble of decision trees. In *Indian International Conference on Artificial Intelligence* (pp. 382–392).
6. Kumar, G. K., Viswanath, P., & Rao, A. A. (2015). Ensemble of soft decision trees using multiple approximate fuzzy-rough set based reducts. *International Journal of Information Processing, 9*(2), 36–46.
7. Kumar, G. K., Viswanath, P., & Rao, A. A. (2016). Ensemble of randomized soft decision trees for robust classification. *Sadhana, 41*(3), 273–282.

8. Lee, W., & Stolfo, S. J. (1998). Data mining approaches for intrusion detection. In *7th USENIX Security Symposium.*
9. Lichman, M. (2013). UCI machine learning repository. http://archive.ics.uci.edu/ml, University of California, Irvine, School of Information and Computer Sciences.
10. Lincoln Laboratory MIT.DARPA intrusion detection data sets. http://www.ll.mit.edu/mission/communications/ist/corpora/ideval/data/index.html.
11. Lippman, R. P., Fried, D. J., Graf, I., & Zissman, M. A. (2000). Evaluating intrusion detection systems: The 1998 DARPA off-line intrusion detection evaluation. In *Proceedings of DARPA Information Survivability Conference and Exosition* (pp. 12–26).
12. Lunt, T., & Jagannathan, R. (1994). A prototype real-time intrusion-detection expert system. In *Proceedings of 1988 IEEE Computer Society Symposium on Research in Security and Privacy* (pp. 59–66). Washington: IEEE Computer Society Press.
13. Luo, J. (1999). Integrating fuzzy logic with data mining methods for intrusion detection.
14. Mukherjee, B., Heberlein, L., & Levitt, K. (1994). Network intrusion detection. *Computer Networks, 8*(3), 26–41.
15. Smaha, S. (1998). Haystack: An intrusion detection system. In *Proceedings of the Fourth Aerospace Computer Security Applications Conference* (pp. 37–44).
16. Zhou, L., & Jiang, F. (2011). A rough set based decision tree algorithm and its application in intrusion detection. In *4th International Conference on Pattern Recognition and Machine Intelligence* (pp. 333–338). Berlin: Springer.

Chapter 36
Feature Selection Using a Machine Learning to Classify a Malware

Mouhammd Al-Kasassbeh, Safaa Mohammed, Mohammad Alauthman, and Ammar Almomani

Abstract Generally, malware has come to be known as one of the biggest threats, so malware is a program which operates malicious actions and steals information, to specifically identify it as software which is designed specifically to through breaking the system of a computer without consent from the owner. This chapter aimed to study feature selection and malware classification using machine learning. The identification of such features was done through the intuition that various parts of the PE files' features can correlate with one another less than with the class files, being clean or dirty. Such features are implemented as algorithms in machine learning to help classify the malware, resulting in such classification to be properly implemented in antivirus programs to help enhance the rate of detection.

Keywords Malware · Machine learning · Classification · Feature selection

M. Al-Kasassbeh
King Hussein Faculty of Computing Sciences, Princess Sumaya University for Technology, Amman, Jordan
e-mail: m.alkasassbeh@psut.edu.jo

S. Mohammed
College of Information Technology, University of Mutah, Mutah, Jordan

M. Alauthman (✉)
Department of Computer Science, Zarqa University, Zarqa, Jordan
e-mail: malauthman@zu.edu.jo

A. Almomani
Department Information Technology, Al-Huson University College, Al-Balqa Applied University, Irbid, Jordan
e-mail: ammarnav6@bau.edu.jo

© Springer Nature Switzerland AG 2020   889
B. B. Gupta et al. (eds.), *Handbook of Computer Networks and Cyber Security*,
https://doi.org/10.1007/978-3-030-22277-2_36

1 Introduction

In the world of the fast-growing in Internet usage, malware has come to be known as one of the biggest threats, so malware is a program which operates malicious actions and steals information, to specifically identify it as software which is designed specifically to break into the system of a computer without consent from the owner. This term is also used to refer to any threat on computers in general. Also, it can be classified as file infections or a malware of stand-alone nature. In addition, we can sort it by using the action which is used to perform, such as worms, adware, spyware, or Trojans [1].

Moreover, to develop a malware, the skill required for this has decreased. This is because of the vicious tools which are now available on the Internet, and there is software of automated detection, and the ability to purchase malware easily will allow anyone to become an attacker easily regardless of their skill level. Researchers demonstrate the attacks are becoming more automated and used by script kiddies [2].

Therefore, protecting the computer system is one of the most important things which should be done by companies and users because a small attack can lead to huge informational and financial damage. Since the current methods and procedures do not offer enough protection, one is ought to use techniques which are machine based. This research investigates the advantages and disadvantages of machine learning-based detection for malware in order to identify the appropriate method and its features to produce a perfect algorithm which can separate and identify the various malware types [3].

The accuracy is measured based on the file is infected or legitimate and then separated it to its malware family, if the file it was infected. The results obtained will be discussed using Cuckoo Sandbox scoring to find the suitable method in order to create a similar module. It should be noticed that implementing this module would not be discussed further [4].

2 Literature Review

Mohammed et al. [1] identified malware as a computer security issue used to avoid the normal detection methods which rely on signature matching. Those that contain identical malware variants and patterns are used for the machine techniques in order to identify others. Comparative study of various selection methods used by the KNN algorithm to classify the malware based on the n-grams analysis, resulting in the use of "principal component analysis (PCA)" feature selection in addition to the "support vector machines (SVM)" classification to provide the best classification with the minimum features. In this study, the dataset used includes the 1156 malware files in addition to 984 benign files of different formats; the obtained accuracy in this paper is equal to 93%.

As for Gavrilut et al. [2], the authors suggested a framework of the Perceptron Training Subroutine algorithms in order to separate the clean or malware files to lower the chance of false positives. The authors utilized three datasets, which are a training dataset, a test dataset, as well as a "scale-up" dataset, as illustrated in Table 36.1.

After further successful testing on datasets of medium sizes, it can be concluded that this framework was very useful in providing the user with a scaling process to allow the user to work on larger datasets of similar nature.

Chumachenko [3] provided a research to identify what is the best feature extraction and representation in addition to a classification which would lead to appropriate accuracy using the Cuckoo Sandbox. "Naive Bayes and random forest, k-nearest-neighbors in addition to decision trees, and not to mention the support vector machines," where they were assessed. The dataset contained 1156 malware files belonging to 9 different families where 984 contained different formats. The results provided us with suggestions to put the random forest method to use on multi-class classification since it provided the best accuracy possible. It should be noticed that though the previous method was successful, they are ought to use the support vector machines instead.

Liu et al. [4] suggested a learning malware system analyzed through machines to contain three parts. One is the data processing and malware detection. The other is decision-making. The first deals with Opcode n-gram and the gray-scale images in addition to importing functions to extract the malware features. The latter tends to implement the features to classify and identify the files which are suspicious of malware. The dataset in this paper includes "20000 malware instances" that had been collected by Anubis, Kingsoft, as well as ESET NOD32. Lastly, the detection part would put to use "shared nearest neighbor (SNN) algorithm" to identify the new malware family, resulting in this system classifying with a percentage of 98.9% accuracy and 86.7% identifying the specific malware.

Raman [5] considers malware as a menace for computing since there is a gap between the malware appearing on the computer and the development of signs which are used to identify that specific malware. The dataset in this algorithm includes 100,000 pieces of malware in addition to 16,000 clean programs. Therefore, the author uses data mining algorithm to provide seven features within the formatting of the Microsoft PE, which is provided to machine learning's algorithm

Table 36.1 The datasets

Database	Files		Unique combinations	
	Malware	Clean	Malware	Clean
Training	27,475	273,133	7822	415
Test	11,605	6522	506	130
Scale-up	Approx. 3M	Approx. 180M	12,817	16,437

to classify that malware to result in a model which uses more features and classifies it by comparing it to existing research; the accuracy of malware classification was 92%.

Vinod et al. [6] extracted features of n-gram from a series of files, where they found various sizes of two, three, four, and five containing two selection procedures. One is the principal component analysis (PCA), and the other is the minimum redundancy-maximum relevance. They came to use and implement six classifiers, "Naive Bayes, AdaBoostM1, Instance-Based Learner (IBK), Sequential Minimal Optimization (SMO), and the random forest algorithm, and datasets include 6000 samples. Majority of them were portable executable (PE)" and the others were simply binge samples resulting in high accuracy of 94.1%, which can be obtained from the 2-g size containing both previous samples. However, one setback was the fact that extracting the code of n-grams was a bit difficult since some were not easily separated.

Another researcher, Ismail et al. [7], extracted that n-gram from packet payloads finding malware at the infrastructure level of a network to later suggest that there is a similar pattern used to detect solely based on the idea that the malware would carry certain features of the old one. The dataset included 2507 training flows as well as the test dataset of 3470 flows in addition to 27,491 training flows, and the used algorithm was Kernel method algorithm. Then later incorporated this domain knowledge which he derived from the SNORT signatures using a Naive Bayes classifier, by using this information they came to find that their experiment work which used only a few features of only 90,000 features put to utilize, therefore to reduce the processing time from 53 h to only 3 by solely optimizing the number of those features.

One more researcher, Moskovitch et al. [8], had the ability to extract various n-gram sizes which were not only two, three, and four but also six using the binary codes. They also revised three specific selection methods. One is the Fisher Score (FS), the other is the document frequency (DF), and the last one is the Gain Ratio (GR) using various classifiers such as "Naïve Bayes (NB), SVM in addition to the artificial neural networks (ANN), and the decision trees (DT)" using datasets containing 7000 malicious files and 22,000 of binge sets. The results provided evidence that the Fisher Score came to be the best used for the selection method since it had a significantly high level of accuracy when compared with the other classifiers, a whopping percentage of 95%.

Moskovitch et al. [9] also extracted identical sizes of the n-gram out of two codes using only two methods of selections, those being the GR and FS, and by four machine classifiers being the DT, the NN, and the SVM in addition to the NB and a dataset which contained 30,000 files precisely to report a high level of accuracy of 95% when the size of the gram was five being used along the other classifiers.

Reddy and Pujari [10] managed to extract various sizes of the n-gram, those being the two, three, and four, and implemented the previous document frequency when it came to the selection feature stage where they used three classifiers. One is the SVM, the other is IBK, and the last one is the decision tree and applying the theory of the Dempster–Shafer. It can be noticed that the dataset contained 2500 samples of viruses and 2500 of begin codes, and the results provided an accuracy of 95%.

Liangboonprakong and Sornil [11] extracted the sequential pattern features of the n-gram, two, three, four, and one using the sequential floating forward selection (SFFS) procedures alongside three classifiers. In this paper, a dataset of "9448 cases by 682,936 feature vectors" is used. One was the multilayer perceptron; the others were C4.5 and the SVM, providing a result of 96.64% accuracy when it came to the 4-g using the SVM classifier.

Lin et al. [12] using n-grams features from dynamic and static features. Also, the authors used approximately 790,000 n-grams and proposed a genetic algorithm to classify malware. They implemented feature reduction and selection, and also they obtained an accuracy equal to 90% using 10 features as well as 96% using 100 features. In this paper, the dataset was 389 benign samples in addition to 3899 malware. Feature reduction and selection had been performed on the determined number of n-grams; it is not strictly associated with the number of features, which is needed in order to read from the behavior of dynamic and static from the files.

Gavriluţ et al. [2], they developed a system of detections based on rule induction algorithms that are known as **RIPPER**, and the utilized dataset included 4266 files, 3265 of them were malicious and the rest were 1001 benign programs. However, they achieved an accuracy of 69.90–96.18%. It should be noticed that those algorithms also provided a high percentage of false positives in which the best accurate one held a number of 84 false positives. The most appropriate algorithm held a rate of 93.01% in terms of high accuracy in addition to the low number of false positives.

Singhal and Raul [13] analyzed the method used to detect using two algorithms; one was the "random forest combined with information gain" which provides a better representation of features. It should be noticed that the dataset compiled had files which included 5000 executables where the 12 feature extraction was easier to result in an accuracy of the 97% while holding a very small percentage of false positives up to 0.03.

Baldangombo et al. [14] suggested a method of extraction which would be based on the API in addition to the DLLs and the PE and using various methods of SVM. The dataset in this paper included 4500 malware files and 1000 benign programs. In addition, they using the J48 decision trees, and Naive Bayes in order to provide a high level of accuracy using the first algorithm with a 99% using the PE header and a combination of the header with the API function. Lastly, the API solely provided 99.1%.

Alazab et al. [15] the methodology employed in this paper involved the collection of large datasets included "29580 binary executables" in order to train the classifiers. They adopted many data mining algorithm such as KNN, SMO and NB in order to achieve high-performance results. The advantages of one data mining algorithm in order to accurately detect zero-day malware can be analyzed and evaluated successfully. The obtained results showed a high accuracy of 98.5%.

Siddiqui et al. have data mined in order to detect Trojans [16], where the author mined for mine from the body of the Trojans to extract n-grams. The dataset contained approximately 5000 PE files where 3000 were Trojans and the others were completely clean, and using the principal component analysis and the random forest algorithms in addition to the latter and the SVM when classifying leads to an increase in detection reaching to 94%.

Schultz et al. provided a framework for data mining in order to detect new executables [17]; the dataset included 1000 malicious files in addition to 1000 clean files. The author implemented three algorithms. One was a multi-classifier, the other was a probabilistic predictor, and the last one was a learner based on inductive rules to then later be deport them into an algorithm of signature-based nature providing 97.76% success rate.

Shafiq et al. provided the framework titled "PE-Miner" [18], where the author extracted several features in order to detect malware on the spot; all this was done by using SVM algorithm to analyze the aggregate values of the PE header files to conclude 189 specific features. They also revised the system by using the datasets of Malfease and VX Heavens and get a 99% detection rated less than 0.5% of false positives.

Finally, the researcher Kong et al. [19] provided a structure using malware which was automated and solely based on the informational structure of that specific malware. The dataset included 526,179 malwares, and the used algorithms are KNN and SVM in addition to the decision tree. Upon extracting the features using the cell graphs of each one, the authors came to conclude that there were similarities in the two programs of malware. All this is by implementing the distance metric learning to cluster them and sort them depending on family and maintaining the different ones at a margin; then they finally assembled those using an ensemble in order to classify the malware and include them in the family which they belong to (Table 36.2 summarize of malware detection methods).

However, there are many researcher use feature selection on field of network security such as [20, 21] they utilized and evaluate feature selection method for intrusion detection, Alauthman et al. [22] applied the feature selection with neural network in order to detect P2P Bot, and Altaher et al. [23] used information gain method as feature selection approach with evolving clustering technique to detect malware.

3 Experiment

The clean documents are taken from the Windows 7 and Windows XP's installation base. As for the dirty documents, those would be taken from the Vx Heavens archive's subset existent at the vx.netlux.org. The experiments were conducted for purposes of the classification and selection of features or attributes by the implementation of a machine learning workbench named as WEKA, as this would put to use algorithms specific to machine learning. This is specifically scripted for

Table 36.2 Comparison between related works

Paper	Algorithm	Datasets	Results and accuracy
[1]	KNN and SVM	1156 malware files in addition to 984 benign files	93%
[3]	Naive Bayes, random forest, k-nearest-neighbors, and decision trees	1156 malware files belonging to 984 files contained different formats	The results provided us with suggestions to put the random forest method to use on multi-class classification since it provided the best accuracy possible
[4]	Shared the nearest neighbor (SNN) algorithm	20,000 malware instances	Resulting in this system classifying with a percentage of 98.9% accuracy and 86.7% identifying the specific malware
[5]	Data mining algorithm	100,000 pieces of malware in addition to 16,000 clean programs	The accuracy of malware classification was 92%
[6]	Naive Bayes, AdaBoostM1, IBK, SMO, and the random forest algorithm	6000 samples	High accuracy of 94.1%, which can be obtained from the 2-g size containing both previous samples
[7]	Kernel method algorithm	2507 training flows as well as the test dataset of 3470 flows in addition to 27,491 training flows	Reduce the processing time from 53 h to only 3 by solely optimizing the number of those features
[8]	NB, FS and SVM, ANN, and DT	7000 malicious files and 22,000 of binge sets	FS came to be the best used for the selection method since it had a significantly high level of accuracy of 95%
[9]	DT, the NN, and the SVM in addition to the NB	30,000 files	A high level of accuracy of 95% when the size of the gram was five being used along the other classifiers
[10]	SVM, IBK, and the decision tree	2500 samples of viruses and 2500 of benign codes	The results provided an accuracy of 95%
[11]	SVM	9448 cases by 682,936 feature vectors	The result of 96.64% accuracy when it came to the 4-grams using the SVM classifier
[12]	Genetic algorithm	389 benign samples in addition to 3899 malware	They obtained an accuracy equal to (90%) using 10 features as well as 96% using 100 features

(continued)

Table 36.2 (continued)

Paper	Algorithm	Datasets	Results and accuracy
[2]	Rule induction algorithms that are known as Ripper	4266 files, 3265 of them were malicious and the rest were 1001 benign programs	The most appropriate algorithm held a rate of 93.01% in terms of high accuracy in addition to the low number of false positives
[13]	Random forest combined with information gain	5000 executables	12 feature extraction was easier to result in an accuracy of the 97% while holding a very small percentage of false positives up to 0.03
[14]	SVM, decision trees, and Naive Bayes	4500 malware files and 1000 benign programs	A high level of accuracy using the first algorithm with a 99% using the PE header
[15]	KNN, SMO, as well as NB	29580 binary executables	The obtained results showed high accuracy of 98.5%
[16]	Random forest algorithms in addition to the SVM	5000 PE files where 3000 were Trojans and the others were completely clean	Increasing detection reaching to 94%
[17]	Probabilistic predictor, a learner based on inductive rules and signature-based nature	1000 malicious files in addition to 1000 clean files	Providing 97.76% success rate
[18]	SVM	Malfease and VX Heavens	Get a 99% detection rated less than 0.5% of false positives
[19]	KNN and SVM in addition to the decision tree	526,179 malware	Authors came to conclude that there were similarities in the two programs of malware

those that "need an environment in which they can easily manipulate data and run experiments themselves" [14].

According to Witten et al., features that are irrelevant would affect negatively the machine learning. So omitting those would fasten and make the algorithms perform better, in addition to representing the issue more appropriately and speeding it up, and finally shed light on the attention of the user regarding the significant variables. Those would note that "The best way to select attributes is manual, based on a deep understanding of the learning problem and what the attributes actually mean" [15].

The use of experience in the analysis of malware had allowed a selection of 100 features in a set, all out of the 645 features, then those metadata features would be entered in the PE header, in addition to data that would contain information regarding all of those 10 sections, and their features related to the exports and import ones. A dataset was created containing 3722 clean files and 5193 dirty files in order to evaluate the 100 features by operating the random forest algorithm 100 times with 1 feature being implemented at a time [16]. The classifier of random forest that applied the Debug Size feature by itself presented 92.34% accuracy. In Table 36.3, 13 features containing the best accuracy are presented there in a decreasing

Table 36.3 Feature
evaluation

Features name	Accuracy
Debug Size	0.9234
DebugRVA	0.9224
ImageVersion	0.8898
OperatingSystemVersion	0.8850
SizeOfStackReserve	0.8837
LinkerVersion	0.8599
DllCharacteristics	0.8273
lateRVA	0.8249
ExportSize	0.8146
ExportRVA	0.8122
ExportNameLen	0.8084
ResourceSize	0.8025
ExportFunctionsCount	0.8001

order. One must note that a few of those features were highly correlated with
another, therefore placing those in the exact PE file. The features were divided in a
descending order regarding their accuracy when classified to then be grouped into
seven buckets depending on the original location of the PE file. This operation was
done to separate highly correlated features. A new bucket would be defined, upon
discovering a feature existent in the list from another part regarding the PE file. This
resulted in seven buckets that are stated as FileHeader, Sections, Resources, Exports
and imports, and finally the OptionalHeader and data directory.

3.1   *Feature Selection Algorithm*

In order to discover the minimum feature set, their intuition guided them in terms of
features that are more significant and less correlated to those that would contain
a high level of accuracy out of each of the seven buckets. The features here in
those buckets were as follows: NumberOfSections, VirtualSize2, ResourceSize,
ExportSize, IatRVA and ImageVersion, and, finally, Debug Size.

Thirteen experiments were conducted using various classifiers of machine learning nature, specifically six in order to discover the features by the implementation
of this algorithm:

Allow n to be the feature number in the iteration. Where F is the feature set that
would contain the features with the most accuracy (Debug Size) out of the bucket
containing the most accurate one (Data directory). The iteration would be defined
as follows:

1. Run the Ridor, Random Forest, J48 Graft, PART, and the J48 in addition to the
   IBk.
2. Move on to the next bucket existent in the order:

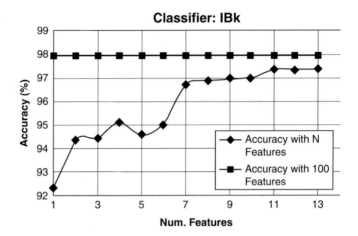

Fig. 36.1 Classification using IBk

(a) Run IBk, J48, and classifiers using FNote accuracy of model Sections, Resources, Exports, Imports, OptionalHeader, and FileHeader.
(b) Upon every bucket being visited, do wrap this around reaching the bucket of Data Directory and then follow this order

3. Select the feature of the individual containing the most accuracy out of the existing bucket, which wasn't selected before. Add such a feature to the F, where F would contain features of $n + 1$.

Move to step 1. This is finished after the 13 iterations. The results of the above experiments are graphed in Figs. 36.1, 36.2, 36.3, 36.4, 36.5, and 36.6.

The graphs provide a step gaining the accuracy regarding iterations reaching to the eighth iteration, as this is where it gets to be small. The features implemented in the experiment, specifically the seventh, were NumberOfSections, VirtualSize2, ResourceSize, ExportSize, IatRVA, and the ImageVersion and finally the Debug Size since those contained the most level of accuracy out of all the seven buckets provided previously. An explanation is attempted to describe as to why such features are considered to be related to the good classification out of such fields' definition, in addition to looking closely at the data post-hoc as follows:

1. Debug Size. Provides the debug-directory table size that is often files of Microsoft-related executables containing a debug directory. Therefore, various programs that are cleaned would contain a non-zero value regarding the Debug Size.
2. ImageVersion. Provides the files' version, as it can be defined by the user, in addition to not relating to the program's function; various programs that are clean would contain more versions in addition to a bigger set of image version since the majority of malware would have a 0 value of the ImageVersion.

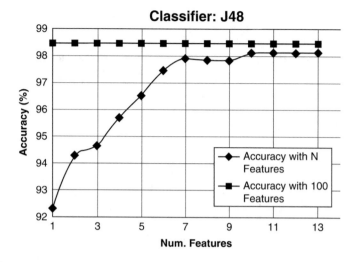

Fig. 36.2 Classification using J48

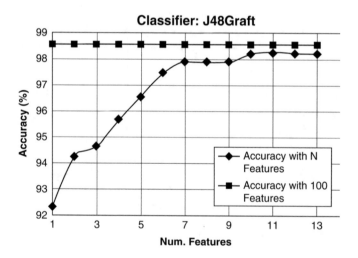

Fig. 36.3 Classification using J48 Graft

3. IatRVA. Provides the relative virtual address regarding the table import address; such feature is valued at 4096 of the cleanest files with a value that is very large, 0 of virus files. Various malware would not implement the import functions or simply may just obfuscate the import tables of such [5].

4. ExportSize. Provides the export table's size, since not the executable programs, but the DLLs would solely contain export tables. Therefore, such value feature could be a non-zero for clean files that would have various DLLs in addition to virus files having 0.

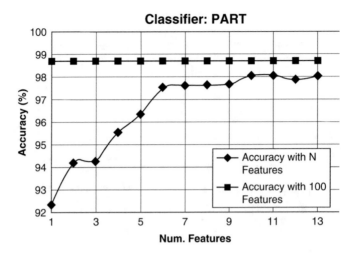

Fig. 36.4 Classification using PART

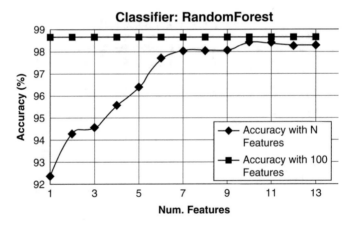

Fig. 36.5 Classification using random forest

5. ResourceSize. Provides the resource selection size as various files containing viruses would not contain any resources when compared to clean ones that have bigger ones.
6. VirtualSize2. Provides the second section size as various viruses contain a sole section with a value of 0, in that field.
7. NumberOfSections. Provides the sections numbered, where the value for this would be different in clean and files containing a virus; one must note that such feature is still unclear in the way that it helps to separate the clean files and those containing malware.

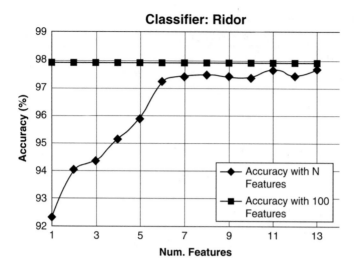

Fig. 36.6 Classification using Ridor

Table 36.4 Evaluating classifiers fed seven features

Classifier	TP rate	FP rate	Accuracy
IBK	0.9730	0.0936	0.9730
Random forest	0.9822	0.0670	0.9821
J48	0.9856	0.0568	0.9854
J48 Graft	0.9856	0.0592	0.9855
Ridor	0.9792	0.0738	0.9791
PART	0.9822	0.0670	0.9821

3.2   Classifying by the Use of the Lower Feature

The dataset containing 16,000 clean files and 100,000 malware were divided into 5 groups where the 7 features were implemented, those that were chosen in their experiment simply as input to be the Ridor, random forest, PART, J48 Graft and J48, and IBk. The evaluation of classifiers are based on cross-validation approach, However, in this research, we used estimated the average results of five-folds to As shown in Table 36.4. Metrics applied were as follows:

- True Positives (TP): Dirty files that were regarded as dirty in numbers.
- True Negatives (TN): Clean files that were regarded as clean in numbers.
- False Positives (FP): Clean files that were regarded as dirty in numbers.
- False Negatives (FN): Dirty files that were regarded as clean in numbers.

The rates of true positive would be as follows:

$$TP/(FN + TP) \qquad (36.1)$$

Table 36.5 Comparison to related research

Paper	No. features used	TP rate (%)	FP rate (%)
Shafiq et al. [11]	189	99	0.5
Siddiqui et al. [9]	84	92.4	9.2
Khan et al. [14]	42	78.1	6.7
This paper	7	98.56	5.68

The rate of false positive would be as follows:

$$FP/ (FP + TN) \tag{36.2}$$

The level of accuracy would be as follows:

$$TP + TN/ (TP + TN + FP + FN) \tag{36.3}$$

4 Discussion

The most appropriate classification algorithm data was the J48, out of the classifiers that were put to the test. The features here containing a key data regarding the various parts of the PE file are as follows: NumberOfSections, VirtualSize2, ResourceSize, ExportSize, IatRVA, ImageVersion, and Debug Size; upon the implementation of them as input in the machine learning classifiers, results would be evaluated and compared to the projects conducted previously.

The classification rules of the Ridor, PART, J48 Graft, and J48 as a Python script were implemented in order to allow others to study them. The script would be prototypical malware classifier, as comparing the classifiers offered a result related in the research regarding the number of features implemented for the classification which was provided as follows (Table 36.5).

5 Conclusion

Here, a presentation of seven key features was provided to aid in separating the programs that are clean or have malware. The identification of such features was done through the intuition that various parts of the PE files' features can correlate with one another less than with the class files, being clean or dirty. Such features are implemented as algorithms in machine learning to help classify the malware, resulting in such classification to be properly implemented in antivirus programs to help enhance the rate of detection.

References

1. Khammas, B. M., Monemi, A., Bassi, J. S., Ismail, I., Nor, S. M., & Marsono, M. N. (2015). Feature selection and machine learning classification for malware detection. *Jurnal Teknologi, 77.* https://doi.org/10.11113/jt.v77.3558.
2. Gavriluţ, D., Cimpoeşu, M., Anton, D., & Ciortuz, L. (2009). Malware detection using machine learning. In *International Multiconference on Computer Science and Information Technology, 2009. IMCSIT'09* (pp. 735–741). IEEE.
3. Chumachenko, K. (2017). *Machine learning methods for malware detection and classification.* XAMK University of Applied Science.
4. Liu, L., Wang, B.-S., Yu, B., & Zhong, Q.-X. (2017). Automatic malware classification and new malware detection using machine learning. *Frontiers of Information Technology & Electronic Engineering, 18,* 1336–1347.
5. Raman, K. (2012). Selecting features to classify malware. In *InfoSec Southwest 2012.*
6. Vinod, P., Laxmi, V., & Gaur, M. S. (2012). Reform: Relevant features for malware analysis. In *26th International Conference on Advanced Information Networking and Applications Workshops (WAINA), 2012* (pp. 738–744). IEEE.
7. Ismail, I., & Elektrik, F. K. (2013). *Naive Bayes classification with domain knowledge for new malware variants and stateless packet level detection.* Skudai, Malaysia: Universiti Teknologi Malaysia.
8. Moskovitch, R., Stopel, D., Feher, C., Nissim, N., Elovici, Y. (2008). Unknown malcode detection via text categorization and the imbalance problem. In *IEEE International Conference on Intelligence and Security Informatics, 2008. ISI 2008* (pp. 156–161). IEEE.
9. Moskovitch, R., Stopel, D., Feher, C., Nissim, N., Japkowicz, N., & Elovici, Y. (2009). Unknown malcode detection and the imbalance problem. *Journal in Computer Virology, 5,* 295.
10. Reddy, D. K. S., & Pujari, A. K. (2006). N-gram analysis for computer virus detection. *Journal in Computer Virology, 2,* 231–239.
11. Liangboonprakong, C., & Sornil, O. (2013). Classification of malware families based on n-grams sequential pattern features. In *8th IEEE Conference on Industrial Electronics and Applications (ICIEA), 2013* (pp. 777–782). IEEE.
12. Lin, C.-T., Wang, N.-J., Xiao, H., & Eckert, C. (2015). Feature selection and extraction for malware classification. *Journal of Information Science and Engineering, 31,* 965–992.
13. Singhal, P., & Raul, N. (2012). Malware detection module using machine learning algorithms to assist in centralized security in enterprise networks. *International Journal of Network Security & Its Applications, 4,* 61.
14. Baldangombo, U., Jambaljav, N., Horng, S.-J. (2013). *A static malware detection system using data mining methods.* arXiv preprint arXiv:13082831.
15. Alazab, M., Venkatraman, S., Watters, P., & Alazab, M. (2011). Zero-day malware detection based on supervised learning algorithms of API call signatures. In *Proceedings of the Ninth Australasian Data Mining Conference* (Vol. 121, pp. 171–182). Australian Computer Society, Inc..
16. Siddiqui, M., Wang, M. C., & Lee, J. (2008). Detecting Trojans using data mining techniques. In *International Multi Topic Conference* (pp. 400–411). Springer.
17. Schultz, M. G., Eskin, E., Zadok, F., & Stolfo, S. J. (2001). Data mining methods for detection of new malicious executables. In *2001 IEEE Symposium on Security and Privacy, 2001. S&P 2001. Proceedings* (pp. 38–49). IEEE.
18. Shafiq, M. Z., Tabish, S. M., Mirza, F., & Farooq, M. (2009). PE-Miner: Mining structural information to detect malicious executables in realtime. In *Recent advances in intrusion detection* (pp. 121–141). Berlin: Springer.
19. Yan, G., Brown, N., & Kong, D. (2013). Exploring discriminatory features for automated malware classification. In *International Conference on Detection of Intrusions and Malware, and Vulnerability Assessment* (pp. 41–61). Springer.

20. Alkasassbeh, M. (2017). An empirical evaluation for the intrusion detection features based on machine learning and feature selection methods. *Journal of Theoretical and Applied Information Technology, 22*, 95.
21. Almseidin, M., Alzubi, M., Kovacs, S., & Alkasassbeh, M. (2017). Evaluation of machine learning algorithms for intrusion detection system. In *2017 IEEE 15th International Symposium on Intelligent Systems and Informatics (SISY), 14-16 September 2017* (pp. 000277–000282). https://doi.org/10.1109/SISY.2017.8080566.
22. Alauthaman, M., Aslam, N., Zhang, L., Alasem, R., & Hossain, M. (2018). A P2P Botnet detection scheme based on decision tree and adaptive multilayer neural networks. *Neural Computing and Applications, 29*, 991–1004.
23. Altaher, A., ALmomani, A., Anbar, M., & Ramadass, S. (2012). Malware detection based on evolving clustering method for classification. *Scientific Research and Essays, 7*, 2031–2036.

Chapter 37
DeepDGA-MINet: Cost-Sensitive Deep Learning Based Framework for Handling Multiclass Imbalanced DGA Detection

R. Vinayakumar, K. P. Soman, and Prabaharan Poornachandran

Abstract Contemporary malware families typically use domain generation algorithms (DGAs) to circumvent DNS blacklists, sinkholing, or any types of security system. It means that compromised system generates a large number of pseudorandom domain names by using DGAs based on a seed and uses the subset of domain names to contact the command and control server (C2C). To block the communication point, the security organizations reverse engineer the malware samples based on a seed to identify the corresponding DGA algorithm. Primarily, the lists of reverse engineered domain names are sink-holed and preregistered in a DNS blacklist. This type of task is tedious and moreover DNS blacklist able to detect the already existing DGA based domain name. Additionally, this type of system can be easily circumvented by DGA malware authors. A variant to detect DGA domain name is to intercept DNS packets and identify the nature of domain name based on statistical features. This type of system uses contextual data such as passive DNS and NXDomain. Developing system to detect DGA based on contextual data is difficult due to aggregation of all data and it causes more cost in real-time environment and moreover obtaining the contextual information in end point system is often difficult due to the real-world constraints. Recently, the method which detects the DGA domain name on per domain basis is followed. This method doesn't rely on any external information and uses only full domain name. There are many works for detecting DGA on per domain names based on both manual feature engineering with classical machine learning (CML) algorithms and automatic feature engineering with deep learning architectures. The performance of

R. Vinayakumar (✉) · K. P. Soman
Center for Computational Engineering and Networking (CEN), Amrita School of Engineering, Amrita Vishwa Vidyapeetham, Coimbatore, India
e-mail: r_vinayakumar@cb.amrita.edu

P. Poornachandran
Centre for Cyber Security Systems and Networks, Amrita School of Engineering, Amrita Vishwa Vidyapeetham, Amritapuri, India
e-mail: praba@amrita.edu

© Springer Nature Switzerland AG 2020
B. B. Gupta et al. (eds.), *Handbook of Computer Networks and Cyber Security*,
https://doi.org/10.1007/978-3-030-22277-2_37

methods based on deep learning architectures is higher when compared to the CML algorithms. Additionally, the deep learning based DGA detection methods can stay safe in an adversarial environment when compared to CML classifiers. However, the deep learning architectures are vulnerable to multiclass imbalance problem. Additionally, the multiclass imbalance problem is becoming much more important in DGA domain detection. This is mainly due to the fact that many DGA families have very less number of samples in the training data set. In this work, we propose DeepDGA-MINet which collects the DNS information inside an Ethernet LAN and uses Cost-Sensitive deep learning architectures to handle multiclass imbalance problem. This is done by initiating cost items into backpropogation methodology to identify the importance among each DGA families. The performances of the Cost-Sensitive deep learning architecture are evaluated on AmritaDGA benchmark data set. The Cost-Sensitive deep learning architectures performed well when compared to the original deep learning architectures.

Keywords Cyber security · Cybercrime · Multiclass imbalance · Cost-Sensitive learning · Deep learning · Domain fluxing · Domain generation algorithm · Malware · Botnet · Malicious domain name

1 Introduction

Contemporary malware families installed on infected computers typically use domain generation algorithms (DGAs) [17]. As stated by DGArchive,[1] there are 72 different DGA families. The DGA families might increase in the near future because it can oppose the botnet takedown mechanism [17]. A malware family which uses DGAs is called as domain fluxing [19]. DGAs support to generate many pseudo-random domain names and a subset of the domain names is used to establish a connection to command and control (C2C) server. To make a successful communication, an author has to register only a small subset of domain names. Based on the successful establishment of communication, the malicious author can start executing malicious activities while the entire information is passed to the botmaster. Then the botmaster issues instructions to bots and sometime even to update the malware family itself. Analysis of DNS traffic provides a way to detect malicious activities hosted by botnet. In recent days, botnet has been used as a primary approach to countermeasure many malicious activities [26].

Recent days, botnet has remained as a serious threat to the Internet service community. Thus detecting DGAs has been a significant problem in the domain of cyber security [11]. DNS blacklisting is the most commonly used method for detecting DGA domain name in earlier days. The significance of DNS blacklisting

---

[1] https://dgarchive.caad.fkie.fraunhofer.de/.

method for DGA analysis is studied by Kührer et al. [11]. The study used both public and private blacklists. Private blacklisting is prepared by vendors and the experimental results show that the private blacklisting survived better than the public blacklisting. The results of public blacklisting performance varied for DGA malware families. They suggest that the DNS blacklisting is very useful and can be used along with the other approach to provide a more appropriate level of protection. Another approach is to reverse engineer the malware along with its DGA to identify the seed. Once the seed is known, then subsequent domain names can be registered and those registered domain names act as an impersonator C2C server to seize botnets. This type of process is typically called as sinkholing [23]. Once the botnet is seized, an adversary has to redeploy new botnet with revised seeds to further continue the process to do malicious activities. Both blacklisting and sinkholing methods consume more time and resource intensive approaches. More importantly blacklisting completely fails to detect new types of domain name or variants of existing domain name. Sinkholing has low success rate in detecting new types of DGA domain and variants of existing DGA domain name. Later, DGA classifiers are built using machine learning (ML) algorithms. This type of DGA classifier stays in the network and captures the DNS requests and looks for the DGA domain name. Once the DGA domain name is detected, it gives an alert to the network admin to further examine the foundation of a DGA. The existing works on ML based detection are classified into retrospective and real-time. Retrospective detection methods follow clustering and estimate the statistical properties for each cluster for classification [3, 43, 44]. To enhance the system detection rate, retrospective methods use other contextual information WHOIS information, NXDomain, HTTPheaders. Most of the existing methods belong to retrospective detection and contain several issues in deploying in real-time systems [10, 43, 44]. On the other side, real-time detection method acts on domain name only to detect the DGA domain name. Most of the ML based real-time detection methods are based on feature engineering. These methods are easy to evade and require extensive domain knowledge to extract significant features to distinguish the domain name into either legitimate or DGA domain name [20]. In recent days, to avoid feature engineering phase, the application of deep learning is leveraged in the field of cyber security [25, 27–32, 34, 35, 37, 39]. In [42] the authors proposed LSTM based DGA detection and categorization and the method can be deployed in any environment. Generally, the deep learning architectures are prone to multiclass imbalance problems. There are a few DGA families that contain few samples of domain name. Thus the deep learning architectures bias towards the classes which have more number of samples and as a result DGA families which contain very few samples remain undetected. Additionally, deep learning based DGA detection stays safe in an adversarial environment when compared to CML based DGA detection. To handle multiclass imbalance problem, [24] proposed Cost-Sensitive LSTM which performed better than the Cost-Insensitive LSTM architecture. Consequently, in this work we use Cost-Sensitive LSTM and additionally other Cost-Sensitive deep learning based architecture are considered to evaluate the performances on AmritaDGA[2] data set. The main contributions of the proposed work are given below:

- This work proposes DeepDGA-MINet, which uses Cost-Sensitive deep learning based architectures which can handle the multiclass imbalance in DGA family categorization. The performances of various Cost-Sensitive deep learning based architectures are shown on AmritaDGA data set.
- A detailed experimental analysis of various Cost-Sensitive deep learning based architectures is shown on two different types of testing data sets. These data sets are completely disjoint and include time information. Thus models evaluated on these data sets facilitate to meet zero day malware detection.

The rest of the part of this chapter is organized as follows: Sect. 2 discusses the background details of DNS, botnet, DGA, Keras embedding, deep learning architectures, and Cost-Sensitive deep learning architectures. Section 3 discusses the related works on application of deep learning on DGA analysis. Section 4 discusses the description of data set. Section 5 discusses the statistical measures. Section 6 includes the proposed framework. Section 7 includes experimental results and observations. At last, conclusion, future work, and discussions are presented in Sect. 8.

2 Background

2.1 Domain Name System (DNS)

Domain name system (DNS) is a critical component in an Internet service system. It maintains a distributed database that facilitates to translate domain name to Internet protocol (IP) address and vice versa. Thus DNS is a main component for nearly all network services and has been a main target for attackers. Domain name is a name of a particular application in an Internet service system which follows naming convention system defined by DNS. The maximum length of the domain name is 63 and parts of the domain name are separated by dots. Generally, the right most element in a domain name is root and left most element is the host label. DNS maintains a hierarchy to manage the domain name named as domain name space. The domain name space is divided into different authorities called as DNS zone. The hierarchy is shown in Fig. 37.1 and it represents the organizational structure. The domain name with the host label and root is called as fully qualified domain name (FQDN). Primarily, there are two types of DNS server, they are recursive and non-recursive. Recursive server contacts the nearby DNS server if the requested

---

[2]https://vinayakumarr.github.io/AmritaDGA/.

Fig. 37.1 An overview of domain name system

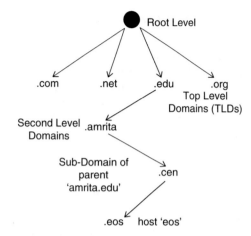

information doesn't exist. Thus there may be a possibility for various attacks such as denial of service (DoS), distributed denial of service (DDoS), DNS cache poisoning, etc.

2.2 Botnet

Botnet is a network of compromised computers that is remotely controlled by botmaster or bot herder. The compromised computers use same malicious code and each compromised computer in a network is called as bot. Botmaster frequently updates the code of bot to evade the current detection methods. A bot uses DGAs to establish a communication channel to a command and control (C2C) server. Recently, botnet behavior is discussed in detail by Alomari et al. [2]. Botnet has been most commonly used by cyber criminals nearly to inject various types of malicious activities and has become a serious threat in the Internet service. Recent botnets use fluxing approach to establish a communication point between bot and C2C server. Mostly, two types of fluxing are used. They are IP flux and domain flux. This work is towards domain flux and domain flux uses the DGA. The DGA algorithm is shared between the botmaster and bots. To establish a connection to C2C server, there may be possibility that DGA generates many failed DNS queries.

Based on the architectures, botnets are grouped into three categories [6]. They are centralized, decentralized, and hybrid. In centralized architecture a botmaster controls all the connected bot in a single point called command and control server (C2C server). Centralized botnet architecture uses star and hierarchical topology and Internet relay chat (IRC) and Hyper Text Transfer Protocol (HTTP) protocols. Decentralized architecture contains more than one C2C server and peer-to-peer protocol. Hybrid architecture is a combination of centralized and decentralized architecture.

2.3 Domain Generation Algorithms (DGAs)

Mostly, recent malware families use DGA instead of hardcoded addresses [17]. This is due to the fact that the DGA is an algorithm which generates large number of pseudo-random domain names based on a seed and appends a top level domain (TLD) such as .com, .edu, etc. to the pseudo-random domain names. A seed can be anything mostly used are data and time information and a seed is shared between the botmaster and bots.

2.4 Domain Name Representation Using Keras Embedding

In this work, Keras embedding is used for domain name representation. In the beginning, a dictionary is formed for the DGA data set which contains only unique characters. Generally, it includes an extra position to handle an unknown character in the testing phase. Each character in a domain name is replaced by a particular index of the dictionary. This transforms the index value in a domain name vector into N dimensional continuous vector representation. The N acts as hyperparameter. This type of representation captures the similarity among the characters in a domain name. The Keras embedding takes the following parameters as input:

- **Dictionary-size:** The number of unique characters
- **Embedding-length:** The size of the embedding vector dimension
- **Input-length:** The size of the input vector

We used Gaussian distribution to initialize the weights during beginning phase in training. The weights are fine-tuned during backpropogation and it coordinatively works with other deep learning layers.

2.5 Deep Learning Architectures

Deep learning is an advanced model of classical machine learning (CML) [13]. They have the capability to obtain optimal feature representation by taking raw input samples. Generally, there are two types of deep learning architectures, one is convolutional neural network (CNN) and another one is recurrent structures (RSs) such as recurrent neural network (RNN), long short-term memory (LSTM), and gated recurrent unit (GRU). Primarily CNNs are used on data which includes spatial properties and RSs are used on data which includes time or sequence information. Basic information along with mathematical details for RNN and CNN is discussed below.

Recurrent neural network (RNN), enhanced model of RNN named as long short-term memory (LSTM) [13], minimized version LSTM named as gated recurrent

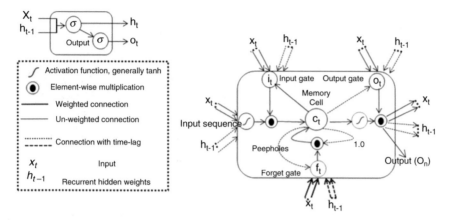

Fig. 37.2 Architecture of recurrent neural network (RNN) unit (left) and Long short-term memory (LSTM) memory block (right)

unit (GRU) [13] belong to the family of RSs. They are most commonly used on sequential data tasks. The structures of RSs look similar to classical feed-forward networks (FFN) and additionally the neurons in RSs contain a self-recurrent connection. All RSs are trained using backpropagation through time (BPTT). RNN in RSs generates vanishing and exploding gradient issue when the network is trained for longer time-steps [13]. To handle vanishing and exploding gradient issue, LSTM was introduced. It replaces the simple RNN unit with a memory block. This has the capability to carry out the important information across time-steps. A memory unit contains a memory cell and gating functions such as input gate, output gate, and forget gate. All 3 different gating functions control a memory cell. However, LSTM contains more parameters. Later a minimized version of LSTM, named as GRU is introduced. GRU achieves the same performance as LSTM and additionally it is computationally inexpensive. A basic unit in RNN, LSTM, and GRU is shown in Figs. 37.2 and 37.3, respectively. The computational functions for RNN, LSTM, and GRU are defined mathematically as follows:

Generally RSs take input $x = (x_1, x_2, \ldots, x_T)$ (where $x_t \in R^d$) and maps to hidden input sequence $h = (h_1, h_2, \ldots, h_T)$ and output sequences $o = (o_1, o_2, \ldots, o_T)$ from $t = 1$ to T by iterating the following equations:

Recurrent Neural Network (RNN)

$$h_t = \sigma(w_{xh}x_t + w_{hh}h_{t-1} + b_h) \tag{37.1}$$

$$o_t = sf(w_{ho}h_t + b_o) \tag{37.2}$$

Fig. 37.3 Architecture of
unit in gated recurrent unit
(GRU)

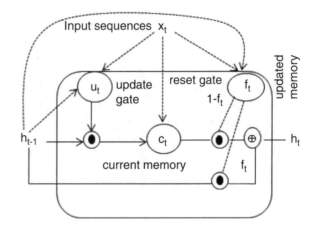

Long Short-Term Memory (LSTM)

$$i_t = \sigma(w_{xi}x_t + w_{hi}h_{t-1} + w_{ci}c_{t-1} + b_i) \tag{37.3}$$

$$f_t = \sigma(w_{xf}x_t + w_{hf}h_{t-1} + w_{cf}c_{t-1} + b_f) \tag{37.4}$$

$$c_t = f_t \odot c_{t-1} + i_t \odot \tanh(w_{xc}x_t + w_{hc}h_{t-1} + b_c) \tag{37.5}$$

$$o_t = \sigma(w_{xo}x_t + w_{ho}h_{t-1} + w_{co}c_t + b_o) \tag{37.6}$$

$$h_t = o_t \odot \tanh(c_t) \tag{37.7}$$

Gated Recurrent Unit (GRU)

$$u_t = \sigma(w_{xu}x_t + w_{hu}h_{t-1} + b_u) \tag{37.8}$$

$$f_t = \sigma(w_{xf}x_t + w_{hf}h_{t-1} + b_f) \tag{37.9}$$

$$c_t = \tanh(w_{xc}x_t + w_{hc}(f \odot h_{t-1}) + b_c) \tag{37.10}$$

$$h_t = f \odot h_{t-1} + (1 - f) \odot c \tag{37.11}$$

where w terms for weight matrices, b terms for bias, σ is the *sigmoid* activation
function, sf at output layer denotes the *softmax* activation function, *tanh* denotes

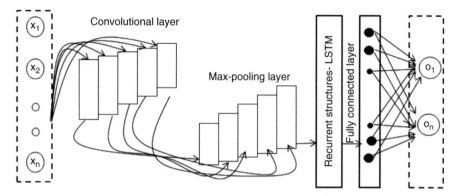

Fig. 37.4 An overview of combination of convolutional neural network (CNN) and long short-term memory (LSTM) architectures

the *tanh* activation function, i, h, f, o, c denotes the input, hidden, forget, output, and cell activation vectors, in GRU input gate and forget gate are combined and named as update gate u.

Convolutional neural network (CNN) is a type of deep learning architecture which is most commonly used in spatial data analysis [13]. Primarily, CNN is composed of three different sections, they are convolution, pooling, and fully connected layer. Convolution operation is composed of convolution and filters that slide over the domain name vector and extracts the features. The collection of features of convolutional layer is called as feature map. The feature map is huge and to reduce the dimension pooling is used, pooling can be max, min, or average pooling. Finally, the reduced feature representation is passed into fully connected layer for classification. Moreover, the pooling layer can also be passed into RSs to extract the sequence information among the character in the domain name. This type of hybrid architecture is shown in Fig. 37.4.

2.6 Employing Cost-Sensitive Model for Deep Learning Architectures to Handle Multiclass Imbalance Problem

All deep learning architectures focus on minimizing the cost function of the network by considering the true output y^l and a target t^l, where l defines the number of neurons and let's define the cost function for *softmax*.

$$E(t) = - \sum_{S \in samples} \sum_{l} t^l(t) \log y^l(t) \qquad (37.12)$$

Generally gradient descent with truncated version of real-time recurrent learning (RTRL) is used to minimize the cost function [13]. As Eq. (37.12) indicates that the deep learning architectures consider all the samples of each class equally. Thus, deep learning architectures are more prone to class imbalance problem. This type of architectures biased towards the classes which has more number of samples and shows less performance for detecting DGA families which contains less representation in training data set [42]. Cost-Sensitive learning is an important approach in many of the real-time data mining applications and capable to handle multiclass imbalance problem [18].

There are various methods exist to convert the Cost-Insensitive LSTM to Cost-Sensitive method [48]. One of the most commonly used methods is to accommodate the balanced training samples via following oversampling or under sampling [49]. In [48] the authors reported the resampling approach is not an efficient method in dealing with class imbalance on multiclass applications. Later, several methods were introduced based on threshold. In [12] the authors proposed Cost-Sensitive based neural networks to handle multiclass imbalance problem by using the error minimization function with the aim to achieve the expected costs. They haven't mainly targeted the class imbalance problem in their experiment. Following [24], introduced Cost-Sensitive LSTM which incorporates the misclassification costs into the backward pass of LSTM. Each sample S is coupled with a cost item $c[class(S), k]$, where k and $class(S)$ define the predicted and actual class, respectively. A cost weight is assigned based on the frequency of samples of a class. Generally, the cost items indicate the classification importance.

$$E(t) = - \sum_{S \in samples} \sum_{l} t^l(t) \log y^l(t) c[class(S), k \qquad (37.13)$$

Based on Eq. (37.13), the basic equations for all deep learning architectures are changed by including the cost item. A cost item typically controls the magnitude of weight updates [9].

Initially for an input data samples the cost matrix is not known. Application of genetic algorithm can be used to identify the optimal cost matrix. However, it requires more time and considered as a difficult task [41]. Let's assume the data samples in one type of class are equal cost. $C[i, i]$ indicates the misclassification cost of the class i, which is produced using the class distribution as

$$c[i, i] = \left(\frac{1}{n_i}\right)^{\gamma} \qquad (37.14)$$

where $\gamma \in [0, 1]$ is a hyperparameter, if $c[i, i]$ is inversely proportional to the class size n_i, then $\gamma = 1$ amd $\gamma = 0$ indicate the deep learning architectures are Cost-Insensitive.

3   Related Works on Domain Generation Algorithms (DGAs) Analysis

A detailed review of detecting malicious domain names is reported by Zhauniarovich et al. [47]. In earlier days, blacklisting is the most commonly used method. These methods completely fail to detect new kinds or variants of DGA based domain name. Later, many approaches have been introduced based on machine learning (ML). These ML based solutions are mostly retrospective which means the methods build clusters based on the statistical properties [3, 43, 44]. These methods are not efficient in real-time DGA domain name detection. Additionally, the retrospective methods take advantage of additional information obtained from HTTP headers, NXDomains, and passive DNS information. Later, real-time detection based on ML is introduced. These methods act on a per domain information which means extract different features from domain name and pass into ML algorithms for classification [20]. However, these ML based solutions rely on feature engineering. This is considered as one of the daunting tasks and these solutions are vulnerable in an adversarial environment.

Recently the application of deep learning is leveraged for DGA detection which completely avoids feature engineering [33, 42]. In [42] the authors proposed a method for DGA detection and categorization. The method uses LSTM which looks for DGA domain name on per domain bases. The method performed well when compared to the benchmark classical methods based on HMM and also results are compared with the feature engineering methods. In [33] the authors proposed a method to collect DNS logs inside an Ethernet LAN and to analyze the DNS logs the application of deep learning architectures such as RNN and LSTM was used. The results are compared with the classical method, feature engineering with Random Forest classifiers. A detailed experimental analysis is shown for various data sets collected in real-time and public sources. The application of various deep learning architectures such as RNN, GRU, LSTM, CNN, and CNN-LSTM is evaluated for DGA detection and categorization [40]. For comparative study bigram with logistic regression and feature engineering with Random Forest classifier is mapped. In all the experiments, the deep learning architectures performed well when compared to the classical methods. In [26] the authors developed a cyberthreat situational awareness framework by using DNS data. They showed a method to collect the DNS logs at an Internet service provider level and application of deep learning architecture is used for DNS data analysis with the aim to detect the DGA domain names. In [45] the authors proposed a method to automatically label the data into DGA or non-DGA and used deep learning architecture for DNS data analysis. For comparative study, 11 different feature sets are extracted based on the domain knowledge and passed into Random Forest classifier. A detailed study of all the different models was evaluated on very large volume of data set which was collected from both the public source and real-time DNS streams. The deep learning model particularly CNN performed well when compared to feature based approach and the system performance has been shown on live stream deployment. In [14] the authors evaluated the performance of recurrent networks on very large volume of data set which consists of 61 different DGA malware families. In recent days, many deep learning architectures based on character level embedding are introduced for many text applications in the field of NLP. To leverage the application of these models [46] evaluated the performance of various benchmark deep learning architectures with character based models for DGA detection and compared with classical methods, feature engineering with Random Forest and multilayer perceptron (MLP) classifiers. The methods based on deep learning with character level embedding performed better than the classical methods. The application of various Image Net models such as AlexNet, VGG, SqueezeNet, InceptionNet, ResNet are transformed for DGA detection by Feng et al. [7]. They followed preprocessing approach to convert the domain name into image format and followed transfer learning approach. In [15] the authors evaluated the performance of various supervised learning models such as LSTM, recurrent SVM, CNN with LSTM, and bidirectional LSTM and compared it with the classical methods HMM, C4.5, ELM, and SVM on the 38 DGA families data set which was collected in real-time. In [5] the authors proposed a method which uses recurrent networks for DGA detection. The method takes the benefit of side information from WHOIS database. This is due to the fact that the DGA families with a high average Smashword score are very difficult to detect based on the domain information alone in the case of a per domain basis method. Smashword score defines the average of n-gram (n ranges [3–5]) intersection with words from an English word dictionary. Generally, it is the measure that gives the measure of closeness between DGA and English words. In [24] the authors proposed Cost-Sensitive LSTM to handle multiclass imbalance in DGA families detection. The proposed method showed 7% improvement in both precision and recall when compared to the Cost-Insensitive LSTM. Additionally, the Cost-Sensitive LSTM showed better performance in detecting 5 additional DGA based bot families. In [22] the authors evaluated the performance of various benchmark character based models for DGA detection and categorization. These models are based on ensemble of human engineered and machine learned features. The importance to time and seed is given while selecting the data set for train and test. Thus this type of methodology allows effectively to evaluate the robustness of the trained classifiers for identifying domain names initiated by the same families at various times or even seed changes. They also state that their method performed well for detecting DGA in the case of time dependent seed when compared to time invariant DGAs. They also evaluated the best performed model on real-time DNS traffic and showed that many of the legitimate domain names are flagged as legitimate. This is mainly due to the reason that Alexa is not completely a non-malicious domain name in real-time DNS traffic. In [16] the authors proposed a unique deep learning architecture typically called as spoofnet which correlates both DNS and URL data to detect malicious activities. Following, the spoofnet architecture is evaluated on various types of data sets of DGA and URL and additionally employed for spam email detection [38]. To meet zero day malware detection, [37] incorporated the time information in generating the data sets for train and test. To leverage the application of various character based benchmark models, [35] transformed these approaches to DGA analysis.

4   Description of Data Set

To measure the performance of Cost-Sensitive based deep learning architectures, we have used the AmritaDGA[3] data set [36]. This data set has been used as part of DMD-2018 shared task. Along with the data set, baseline system[4] is publically available for further research. This data set contains domain names which are collected from publically available sources and real-time DNS traffic inside an Ethernet LAN. Additionally, the data set has been designed by giving importance to the time information. Thus, the trained models on this type of data set have the ability to meet zero day malware detection. The data set is composed of two types of testing data sets. Testing 1 data set is formed using publically available sources and Testing 2 data set is formed using DNS traffic inside an Ethernet LAN. The statistics of AmritaDGA is shown in Table 37.1. The data set was used for two tasks, one is binary and other is multiclass classification. Binary class classification

Table 37.1 AmritaDGA data set used in DMD-2018 shared task

Class	Training	Testing 1	Testing 2
benign	100,000	120,000	40,000
banjori	15,000	25,000	10,000
corebot	15,000	25,000	10,000
dircrypt	15,000	25,000	300
dnschanger	15,000	25,000	10,000
fobber	15,000	25,000	800
murofet	15,000	16,667	5000
necurs	12,777	20,445	6200
newgoz	15,000	20,000	3000
padcrypt	15,000	20,000	3000
proslikefan	15,000	20,000	3000
pykspa	15,000	25,000	2000
qadars	15,000	25,000	2300
qakbot	15,000	25,000	1000
ramdo	15,000	25,000	800
ranbyus	15,000	25,000	500
simda	15,000	25,000	3000
suppobox	15,000	20,000	1000
symmi	15,000	25,000	500
tempedreve	15,000	25,000	100
tinba	15,000	25,000	700
Total	397,777	587,112	103,200

[3]https://vinayakumarr.github.io/AmritaDGA/.
[4]https://github.com/vinayakumarr/DMD2018.

aims at classifying the domain name as either legitimate or DGA and multiclass categorizes the domain name to their families.

5 Statistical Measures

To measure the performance of trained models of various deep learning architectures, we adopted the various statistical measures. These various measures are approximated based on the positive (PD) : legitimate domain name, negative (NG): DGA domain name, true positive (T_{PD}) : legitimate domain name that is predicted as legitimate, true negative (T_{ND}) : DGA domain name that is predicted as DGA domain name, false positive (F_{PD}) : DGA domain name that is predicted as legitimate, and false negative (F_{ND}) : legitimate domain name that is predicted as DGA domain name. Using confusion matrix T_{PD}, T_{ND}, F_{PD}, and F_{ND} are obtained. Confusion matrix is represented in the form of matrix where each row denotes the domain name samples of a predicted class and each column denotes domain name samples of actual class. The various statistical measures considered in this study are defined as follows:

$$Accuracy = \frac{T_{PD} + T_{ND}}{T_{PD} + T_{ND} + F_{PD} + F_{ND}} \tag{37.15}$$

$$Recall = \frac{T_{PD}}{T_{PD} + F_{ND}} \tag{37.16}$$

$$Precision = \frac{T_{PD}}{T_{PD} + F_{PD}} \tag{37.17}$$

$$F1-score = \frac{2 * Recall * Precision}{Recall + Precision} \tag{37.18}$$

$$TPR = \frac{T_{PD}}{T_{PD} + F_{PD}} \tag{37.19}$$

$$FPR = \frac{F_{PD}}{F_{PD} + T_{ND}} \tag{37.20}$$

Accuracy estimates the fraction of correctly classified domain name, *Precision* estimates the fraction of DGA domain name which is actually DGA domain name, *Recall* or *Sensitivity* or *TPR* estimates the fraction of DGA domain names that are classified as DGA domain name, and *F*1-score estimates the harmonic mean of precision and recall.

6 Proposed Architecture: DeepDGA-MINet

The proposed architecture named as DeepDGA-MINet is shown in Fig. 37.5. A
detailed overview of DeepDGA-MINet is shown in Fig. 37.6. This contains mainly
3 different sections: (1) data collection, (2) Cost-Sensitive deep learning layers, and
(3) classification.

In data collection, the system collects the DNS logs inside an Ethernet LAN in
a passive way. The data has been passed into NoSQL database. Further, the domain
name information is extracted from the DNS logs and passed into the Cost-Sensitive
deep learning layers. This implicitly composed of character level embedding layer
which helps to map the domain name characters into domain name numeric

Fig. 37.5 Proposed
architecture:
DeepDGA-MINet

Fig. 37.6 A detailed
overview of
DeepDGA-MINet

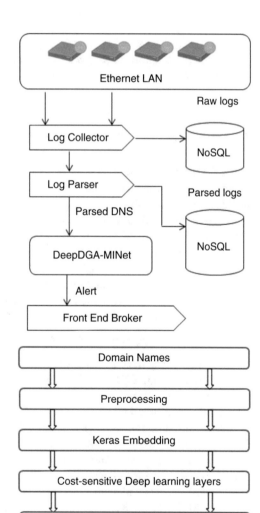

representation. The character level embedding layer works with Cost-Sensitive deep learning layers to extract the similarity among characters during backpropogation. Further, Cost-Sensitive deep learning layer extracts significant features from the character level embedding vectors. Finally, the feature set is passed into the fully connected layer for classification. This composed of *softmax* activation function which uses categorical cross-entropy loss function. The *softmax* and categorical cross-entropy loss function are defined mathematically as follows:

$$Soft \max (x)_i = \frac{e^{x_i}}{\sum_{j=1}^{n} e^{x_j}} \tag{37.21}$$

$$loss(p, e) = - \sum_x p(x) \log(e(x)) \tag{37.22}$$

where x denotes an input , e and p denote true probability distribution and predicted probability distribution, respectively. To minimize the loss function *adam* optimizer is used. Finally, the classification results are displayed in Front End Broker.

7 Experiments, Results, and Observations

The detailed configuration details of deep learning architectures are reported in Table 37.2. In this research all the deep learning architectures are implemented in TensorFlow [1] with Keras [4] higher level library and various experiments of deep learning architectures are run on GPU enabled TensorFlow inside Nvidia GK110BGLTeslak40. All deep learning architectures are trained using AmritaDGA data set. To control the train accuracy across the more number of epochs, we have used validation data set that was from 20% of train data set taken randomly. The domain name samples are transformed into numeric vectors using Keras embedding. Keras embedding implicitly builds a dictionary which contains 39 unique characters. The character list is given below:

abcdefghijklmnopqrstuvwxyz0123456789._ -

Using dictionary the characters of a domain name are transformed into indexes. The maximum length of the domain name is 91. Thus the domain name which contains less than 91 is padded with 0s. The index vector is passed into Keras embedding. It takes 3 different parameters such as Dictionary-size is 39, Embedding-length is 128, and Input-length is 91. Keras embedding follows deep learning layers and the detailed configuration details of deep learning layers are reported in Table 37.2. The deep learning layers follow fully connected layer for classification. All the trained models of various deep learning architectures are tested on the two types of AmritaDGA data set and the detailed results are reported in Tables 37.3, 37.4, 37.5, and 37.6. All DMD-2018 shared tasks submitted systems have used Cost-Insensitive deep learning architectures. The proposed deep learning architectures based on

Table 37.2 Detailed configuration of deep learning architectures

Layer (type)	Output shape	Param #
RNN		
embedding_1 (Embedding)	(None, 91, 128)	5120
simple_rnn_1 (SimpleRNN)	(None, 128)	32,896
dropout_1 (Dropout)	(None, 128)	0
dense_1 (Dense)	(None, 21)	2709
activation_1 (Activation)	(None, 21)	0
Total params: 40,725		
LSTM		
embedding_1 (Embedding)	(None, 91, 128)	5120
lstm_1 (LSTM)	(None, 128)	131,584
dropout_1 (Dropout)	(None, 128)	0
dense_1 (Dense)	(None, 21)	2709
activation_1 (Activation)	(None, 21)	0
Total params: 139,413		
GRU		
embedding_1 (Embedding)	(None, 91, 128)	5120
gru_1 (GRU)	(None, 128)	98,688
dropout_1 (Dropout)	(None, 128)	0
dense_1 (Dense)	(None, 21)	2709
activation_1 (Activation)	(None, 21)	0
Total params: 106,517		
CNN		
embedding_1 (Embedding)	(None, 91, 128)	5120
conv1d_1 (Conv1D)	(None, 87, 64)	41,024
max_pooling1d_1 (MaxPooling1)	(None, 21, 64)	0
dense_1 (Dense)	(None, 21, 128)	8320
dropout_1 (Dropout)	(None, 21, 128)	0
activation_1 (Activation)	(None, 21, 128)	0
dense_2 (Dense)	(None, 21, 21)	2709
activation_2 (Activation)	(None, 21, 21)	0
Total params: 57,173		
CNN-LSTM		
embedding_1 (Embedding)	(None, 91, 128)	5120
conv1d_1 (Conv1D)	(None, 87, 64)	41,024
max_pooling1d_1 (MaxPooling1)	(None, 21, 64)	0
lstm_1 (LSTM)	(None, 70)	37800
dense_1 (Dense)	(None, 21)	1491
activation_1 (Activation)	(None, 21)	0
Total params: 85,435		

Table 37.3 Detailed Testing 1 data set results of DMD-2018 shared task participated systems [36]

Team name	Accuracy (%)	Recall (%)	Precision (%)	F1-score (%)
UWT	63.3	63.3	61.8	60.2
Deep_Dragons	68.3	68.3	68.3	64
CHNMLRG	64.8	64.8	66.2	60
BENHA	27.2	27.2	19.4	16.8
BharathibSSNCSE	18	18	9.2	10.2
UniPI	65.5	65.5	64.7	61.5
Josan	69.7	69.7	68.9	65.8
DeepDGANet	60.1	60.1	62	57.6

Table 37.4 Detailed Testing 2 data set results of DMD-2018 shared task participated systems [36]

Team name	Accuracy (%)	Recall (%)	Precision (%)	F1-score (%)
UWT	88.7	88.7	92.4	90.1
Deep_Dragons	67	67	67.8	62.2
CHNMLRG	67.4	67.4	68.3	64.8
BENHA	42.9	42.9	34	27.2
BharathibSSNCSE	33.5	33.5	22.9	22.3
UniPI	67.1	67.1	64.1	61.9
Josan	67.9	67.9	69.4	63.6
DeepDGANet	53.1	53.1	65.3	54.1

Table 37.5 Detailed Testing 1 data set results of AmritaDGA baseline system for multiclass classification [36]

Architecture	Accuracy (%)	Precision (%)	Recall (%)	F1-score (%)
RNN	65.8	63.6	65.8	62.6
LSTM	67.2	66.3	67.2	62.2
GRU	64.9	65.5	64.9	60.1
CNN	60.4	62.9	60.4	56.8
CNN-LSTM	59.9	61.5	59.9	55.6

Table 37.6 Detailed Testing 2 data set results of AmritaDGA baseline system for multiclass classification [36]

Architecture	Accuracy (%)	Precision (%)	Recall (%)	F1-score (%)
RNN	66.2	62.7	66.2	60.9
LSTM	66.9	69.5	66.9	62.7
GRU	66.5	71.8	66.5	63.7
CNN	64.3	69.1	64.3	59.6
CNN-LSTM	65.8	67.6	65.8	62.5

Table 37.7 Detailed Testing 1 data set results of the proposed method—deep learning architectures based on Cost-Sensitive data mining concept

Architecture	Accuracy (%)	Precision (%)	Recall (%)	F1-score (%)
Cost-Sensitive-RNN	65.8	63.6	65.8	62.6
Cost-Sensitive-LSTM	68.3	65.8	68.3	64.0
Cost-Sensitive-GRU	68.3	65.8	68.3	66.0
Cost-Sensitive-CNN	62.8	63.8	62.8	59.5
Cost-Sensitive-CNN-LSTM	64	64.3	64	62

Table 37.8 Detailed Testing 2 data set results of the proposed method—deep learning architectures based on Cost-Sensitive data mining concept

Architecture	Accuracy (%)	Precision (%)	Recall (%)	F1-score (%)
Cost-Sensitive-RNN	65.8	63.6	65.8	62.6
Cost-Sensitive-LSTM	67.3	69.9	67.3	63.1
Cost-Sensitive-GRU	67.6	67.6	67.6	63.9
Cost-Sensitive-CNN	67.1	74.8	67.1	65.6
Cost-Sensitive-CNN-LSTM	67.1	70.7	67.1	64.7

Cost-Sensitive performed better than the baseline system of DMD-2018 and all the submitted entries of DMD-2018 shared task, as shown in Tables 37.7 and 37.8. The detailed results for Testing 1 AmritaDGA data set are reported in Tables 37.9 and 37.10 for Testing 2 AmritaDGA data set. All baseline system of DMD-2018 and all the submitted entries of DMD-2018 shared task methods are based on Cost-Insensitive models. The Cost-Sensitive models can even perform well in detecting real-time DGA. This is due to the reason that most of the data set in real-time are highly imbalanced. This work has given importance only to achieve the best performance when compared to the baseline system and other submitted system entries of DMD-2018 shared task. However, the proposed method can perform well in any other data set and real-time detection of DGA domain name. Mostly, the results obtained by all the models are closer in nature. Moreover, the LSTM model has outperformed other deep learning architectures. However, the reported results can be further enhanced by following parameter tuning method. This is due to the reason that the optimal parameters implicitly have direct impact on getting the best performance in deep learning [13].

8   Conclusion, Future Works, and Discussions

This work proposes DeepDGA-MINet tool which provides an option to collect a live stream of DNS queries and checks for DGA domain name on a per domain basis. It uses the application of Cost-Sensitive deep learning based methods to handle multiclass imbalance problem. Each class or DGA family is associated with cost items and these are directly initiated into backpropogation learning algorithm. The

Table 37.9 Class-wise test results of the proposed method for Testing 1 data set of AmritaDGA

Classes	Cost-Sensitive RNN		Cost-Sensitive LSTM		Cost-Sensitive GRU		Cost-Sensitive CNN		Cost-Sensitive CNN-LSTM	
	FPR	TPR	FPR	TPR	FPR	TPR	FPR	TPR	FPR	TPR
benign	0.056	0.906	0.069	0.947	0.016	0.864	0.057	0.937	0.048	0.855
banjori	0.004	0.0	0.001	0.0	0.001	0.0	0.0	0.0	0.001	0.0
corebot	0.001	0.996	0.004	1.0	0.008	0.999	0.002	0.998	0.004	0.999
dircrypt	0.036	0.712	0.029	0.817	0.045	0.767	0.035	0.594	0.066	0.631
dnschanger	0.052	0.988	0.051	0.994	0.053	0.993	0.082	0.863	0.061	0.993
fobber	0.009	0.0	0.008	0.0	0.008	0.0	0.024	0.0	0.02	0.0
murofet	0.075	0.0	0.061	0.0	0.067	0.0	0.003	0.006	0.009	0.0
necurs	0.004	0.839	0.004	0.86	0.009	0.857	0.021	0.762	0.015	0.644
newgoz	0.001	0.99	0.001	0.999	0.0	1.0	0.017	1.0	0.002	1.0
padcrypt	0.001	0.99	0.0	1.0	0.0	1.0	0.0	0.999	0.001	1.0
proslikefan	0.018	0.673	0.014	0.689	0.022	0.71	0.013	0.633	0.022	0.506
pykspa	0.034	0.738	0.033	0.886	0.034	0.771	0.031	0.663	0.031	0.712
qadars	0.001	0.764	0.0	0.119	0.001	0.892	0.0	0.302	0.0	0.528
qakbot	0.036	0.426	0.043	0.605	0.021	0.372	0.058	0.486	0.061	0.309
ramdo	0.0	0.998	0.0	1.0	0.0	1.0	0.001	0.999	0.0	1.0
ranbyus	0.004	0.854	0.003	0.874	0.003	0.842	0.008	0.711	0.002	0.75
simda	0.001	0.001	0.0	0.001	0.0	0.0	0.0	0.35	0.002	0.309
suppobox	0.005	0.742	0.002	0.812	0.005	0.95	0.002	0.823	0.008	0.612
symmi	0.0	0.176	0.0	0.601	0.0	0.613	0.0	0.152	0.0	0.585
tempedreve	0.018	0.124	0.015	0.135	0.035	0.131	0.023	0.178	0.025	0.114
tinba	0.008	0.922	0.003	0.97	0.003	0.886	0.017	0.573	0.005	0.966
Accuracy (%)	65.8		68.3		68.3		62.8		64.0	

proportion of cost is a hyperparameter and selected based on hyperparameter tuning method. The performance obtained by Cost-Sensitive based deep learning architectures is good when compared to the Cost-Insensitive deep learning architectures. Moreover, the performance shown by various Cost-Sensitive deep learning based architectures is almost similar. Hence, a voting methodology can be employed to enhance the DGA domain detection rate. This remains as one of the significant direction towards future work. This work has considered only 20 DGA families. The performance is shown for classifying a domain name into corresponding DGA family. Therefore, the further research on investigating the performance of Cost-Sensitive deep learning architectures on more number of DGA families remain as a significant direction towards future work. As well as in this work the hyperparameter tuning is not followed for deep learning architectures. Hyperparameters have direct impact on the performance of deep learning architectures. Thus investigation of proper hyperparameter tuning remains as another significant direction towards future work.

Table 37.10   Class-wise test results of the proposed method for Testing 2 data set of AmritaDGA

Classes	Cost-Sensitive RNN		Cost-Sensitive LSTM		Cost-Sensitive GRU		Cost-Sensitive CNN		Cost-Sensitive CNN-LSTM	
	FPR	TPR	FPR	TPR	FPR	TPR	FPR	TPR	FPR	TPR
benign	0.192	0.956	0.106	0.984	0.106	0.978	0.088	0.944	0.098	0.979
banjori	0.001	0.0	0.0	0.0	0.0	0.0	0.0	0.336	0.0	0.0
corebot	0.0	0.229	0.0	0.228	0.0	0.228	0.0	0.227	0.0	0.228
dircrypt	0.058	0.7	0.101	0.797	0.092	0.767	0.055	0.45	0.105	0.41
dnschanger	0.011	0.988	0.01	0.994	0.01	0.99	0.022	0.901	0.012	0.987
fobber	0.001	0.0	0.001	0.0	0.002	0.0	0.006	0.0	0.003	0.0
murofet	0.003	0.0	0.001	0.0	0.002	0.0	0.001	0.001	0.001	0.0
necurs	0.029	0.838	0.023	0.857	0.024	0.854	0.015	0.662	0.011	0.619
newgoz	0.008	0.99	0.05	1.0	0.055	1.0	0.06	0.999	0.064	0.999
padcrypt	0.017	0.99	0.0	1.0	0.0	1.0	0.001	0.997	0.0	0.999
proslikefan	0.007	0.332	0.004	0.33	0.005	0.4	0.019	0.542	0.012	0.679
pykspa	0.033	0.735	0.031	0.89	0.029	0.882	0.038	0.78	0.022	0.65
qadars	0.001	0.497	0.0	0.049	0.0	0.183	0.002	0.117	0.0	0.391
qakbot	0.032	0.399	0.029	0.601	0.025	0.516	0.016	0.328	0.01	0.376
ramdo	0.0	0.996	0.0	1.0	0.0	1.0	0.0	0.968	0.0	1.0
ranbyus	0.001	0.848	0.001	0.87	0.001	0.872	0.008	0.684	0.003	0.756
simda	0.001	0.0	0.0	0.017	0.0	0.0	0.003	0.001	0.0	0.224
suppobox	0.003	0.787	0.001	0.89	0.002	0.918	0.005	0.935	0.003	0.521
symmi	0.0	0.956	0.0	0.974	0.0	0.998	0.0	0.994	0.0	0.968
tempedreve	0.013	0.17	0.014	0.16	0.017	0.17	0.016	0.1	0.024	0.17
tinba	0.004	0.129	0.001	0.283	0.001	0.279	0.012	0.386	0.004	0.657
Accuracy (%)	65.8		67.3		67.6		67.1		67.1	

Acknowledgements This research was supported in part by Paramount Computer Systems and Lakhshya Cyber Security Labs. We are grateful to NVIDIA India, for the GPU hardware support to research grant. We are also grateful to Computational Engineering and Networking (CEN) department for encouraging the research.

References

1. Abadi, M., Barham, P., Chen, J., Chen, Z., Davis, A., Dean, J., et al. (2016). TensorFlow: A system for large-scale machine learning. In *OSDI* (Vol. 16, pp. 265–283).
2. Alomari, E., Manickam, S., Gupta, B. B., Anbar, M., Saad, R. M., & Alsaleem, S. (2016). A survey of botnet-based DDoS flooding attacks of application layer: Detection and mitigation approaches. In *Handbook of research on modern cryptographic solutions for computer and cyber security* (pp. 52–79). Pennsylvania, PA: IGI Global.
3. Antonakakis, M., Perdisci, R., Nadji, Y., Vasiloglou, N., Abu-Nimeh, S., Lee, W., et al. (2012). From throw-away traffic to bots: Detecting the rise of DGA-based malware. In *USENIX Security Symposium* (Vol. 12).
4. Gulli, A., & Pal, S. (2017). Deep Learning with Keras. Packt Publishing Ltd.

5. Curtin, R. R., Gardner, A. B., Grzonkowski, S., Kleymenov, A., & Mosquera, A. (2018). Detecting DGA domains with recurrent neural networks and side information. arXiv preprint arXiv:1810.02023.

6. Eslahi, M., Salleh, R., & Anuar, N. B. (2012). Bots and botnets: An overview of characteristics, detection and challenges. In *2012 IEEE International Conference on Control System, Computing and Engineering (ICCSCE)* (pp. 349–354). Piscataway, NJ: IEEE.

7. Feng, Z., Shuo, C., & Xiaochuan, W. (2017). Classification for DGA-based malicious domain names with deep learning architectures. In *2017 Second International Conference on Applied Mathematics and Information Technology* (p. 5).

8. Freund, Y., & Schapire, R. E. (1996). Experiments with a new boosting algorithm. In *ICML* (Vol. 96, pp. 148–156).

9. He, H., & Garcia, E. A. (2008). Learning from imbalanced data. *IEEE Transactions on Knowledge & Data Engineering, 21*(9), 1263–1284.

10. Krishnan, S., Taylor, T., Monrose, F., & McHugh, J. (2013). Crossing the threshold: Detecting network malfeasance via sequential hypothesis testing. In *2013 43rd Annual IEEE/IFIP International Conference on Dependable Systems and Networks (DSN)* (pp. 1–12). Piscataway, NJ: IEEE.

11. Kührer, M., Rossow, C., & Holz, T. (2014). Paint it black: Evaluating the effectiveness of malware blacklists. In *International Workshop on Recent Advances in Intrusion Detection* (pp. 1–21). Cham: Springer.

12. Kukar, M., & Kononenko, I. (1998). Cost-sensitive learning with neural networks. In *ECAI* (pp. 445–449).

13. LeCun, Y., Bengio, Y., & Hinton, G. (2015). Deep learning. *Nature, 521*(7553), 436.

14. Lison, P., & Mavroeidis, V. (2017). Automatic detection of malware-generated domains with recurrent neural models. arXiv preprint arXiv:1709.07102.

15. Mac, H., Tran, D., Tong, V., Nguyen, L. G., & Tran, H. A. (2017). DGA botnet detection using supervised learning methods. In *Proceedings of the Eighth International Symposium on Information and Communication Technology* (pp. 211–218). New York, NY: ACM.

16. Mohan, V. S., Vinayakumar, R., Soman, K. P., & Poornachandran, P. (2018). Spoof net: Syntactic patterns for identification of ominous online factors. In *2018 IEEE Security and Privacy Workshops (SPW)* (pp. 258–263). Piscataway, NJ: IEEE.

17. Plohmann, D., Yakdan, K., Klatt, M., Bader, J., & Gerhards-Padilla, E. (2016). A comprehensive measurement study of domain generating malware. In *USENIX Security Symposium* (pp. 263–278).

18. Qiu, C., Jiang, L., & Kong, G. (2015). A differential evolution-based method for class-imbalanced cost-sensitive learning. In *2015 International Joint Conference on Neural Networks (IJCNN)* (pp. 1–8). Piscataway, NJ: IEEE.

19. Schiavoni, S., Maggi, F., Cavallaro, L., & Zanero, S. (2014). Phoenix: DGA-based botnet tracking and intelligence. In *International Conference on Detection of Intrusions and Malware, and Vulnerability Assessment* (pp. 192–211). Cham: Springer.

20. Schüppen, S., Teubert, D., Herrmann, P., & Meyer, U. (2018). FANCI: Feature-based automated NXDomain classification and intelligence. In *27th USENIX Security Symposium (USENIX Security 18)* (pp. 1165–1181).

21. Seiffert, C., Khoshgoftaar, T. M., Van Hulse, J., & Napolitano, A. (2010). RUSBoost: A hybrid approach to alleviating class imbalance. *IEEE Transactions on Systems, Man, and Cybernetics Part A: Systems and Humans, 40*(1), 185–197.

22. Sivaguru, R., Choudhary, C., Yu, B., Tymchenko, V., Nascimento, A., & De Cock, M. (2018). An evaluation of DGA classifiers. In *2018 IEEE International Conference on Big Data (Big Data)* (pp. 5058–5067). Piscataway, NJ: IEEE.

23. Stone-Gross, B., Cova, M., Gilbert, B., Kemmerer, R., Kruegel, C., & Vigna, G. (2011). Analysis of a botnet takeover. *IEEE Security & Privacy, 9*(1), 64–72.

24. Tran, D., Mac, H., Tong, V., Tran, H. A., & Nguyen, L. G. (2018). A LSTM based framework for handling multiclass imbalance in DGA botnet detection. *Neurocomputing, 275*, 2401–2413.

25. Vinayakumar, R., Barathi Ganesh, H. B., & Anand Kumar, M., Soman, K. P. DeepAnti-PhishNet: Applying deep neural networks for phishing email detection cen-aisecurity@iwspa-2018 (pp. 40–50). http://ceur-ws.org/Vol2124/#paper_9
26. Vinayakumar, R., Poornachandran, P., & Soman, K. P. (2018). Scalable framework for cyber threat situational awareness based on domain name systems data analysis. In *Big Data in Engineering Applications* (pp. 113–142). Singapore: Springer.
27. Vinayakumar, R., & Soman, K. P. (2018). DeepMalNet: Evaluating shallow and deep networks for static PE malware detection. *ICT Express, 4(4)*, 255–258.
28. Vinayakumar, R., Soman, K. P., & Poornachandran, P. (2017). Applying convolutional neural network for network intrusion detection. In *2017 International Conference on Advances in Computing, Communications and Informatics (ICACCI)* (pp. 1222–1228). Piscataway, NJ: IEEE.
29. Vinayakumar, R., Soman, K. P., & Poornachandran, P. (2017). Evaluating effectiveness of shallow and deep networks to intrusion detection system. In *2017 International Conference on Advances in Computing, Communications and Informatics (ICACCI)* (pp. 1282–1289). Piscataway, NJ: IEEE.
30. Vinayakumar, R., Soman, K. P., & Poornachandran, P. (2017). Evaluation of recurrent neural network and its variants for intrusion detection system (IDS). *International Journal of Information System Modeling and Design, 8(3)*, 43–63.
31. Vinayakumar, R., Soman, K. P., & Poornachandran, P. (2017). Long short-term memory based operation log anomaly detection. In *2017 International Conference on Advances in Computing, Communications and Informatics (ICACCI)* (pp. 236–242). Piscataway, NJ: IEEE.
32. Vinayakumar, R., Soman, K. P., & Poornachandran, P. (2017). Secure shell (SSH) traffic analysis with flow based features using shallow and deep networks. In *2017 International Conference on Advances in Computing, Communications and Informatics (ICACCI)* (pp. 2026–2032). Piscataway, NJ: IEEE.
33. Vinayakumar, R., Soman, K. P., & Poornachandran, P. (2018). Detecting malicious domain names using deep learning approaches at scale. *Journal of Intelligent & Fuzzy Systems, 34(3)*, 1355–1367.
34. Vinayakumar, R., Soman, K. P., & Poornachandran, P. (2018). Evaluating deep learning approaches to characterize, signalize and classify malicious URLs. *Journal of Intelligent and Fuzzy Systems, 34(3)*, 1333–1343.
35. Vinayakumar, R., Soman, K. P., Poornachandran, P., Alazab, M., & Jolfaei, A. (in press). Detecting domain generation algorithms using deep learning. In *Deep learning applications for cyber security*. Cham: Springer.
36. Vinayakumar, R., Soman, K. P., Poornachandran, P., Alazab, M., & Thampi, S. M. (in press). AmritaDGA: A comprehensive data set for domain generation algorithms (DGAs). In *Big Data Recommender Systems: Recent Trends and Advances, Institution of Engineering and Technology (IET)*.
37. Vinayakumar, R., Soman, K. P., Poornachandran, P., & Menon, P. (2019). A deep-dive on machine learning for cyber security use cases. In: *Machine Learning for computer and cyber security: Principle, algorithms, and practices*. Boca Raton, FL: CRC Press.
38. Vinayakumar, R., Soman, K. P., Poornachandran, P., Mohan, V. S., & Kumar, A. D. (2019). ScaleNet: Scalable and hybrid framework for cyber threat situational awareness based on DNS, URL, and email data analysis. *Journal of Cyber Security and Mobility, 8(2)*, 189–240.
39. Vinayakumar, R., Soman, K. P., Poornachandran, P., & Sachin Kumar, S. (2018). Detecting Android malware using long short-term memory (LSTM). *Journal of Intelligent & Fuzzy Systems, 34(3)*, 1277–1288.
40. Vinayakumar, R., Soman, K. P., Poornachandran, P., & Sachin Kumar, S. (2018). Evaluating deep learning approaches to characterize and classify the DGAs at scale. *Journal of Intelligent & Fuzzy Systems, 34(3)*, 1265–1276.
41. Wang, S., & Yao, X. (2012). Multiclass imbalance problems: Analysis and potential solutions. *IEEE Transactions on Systems, Man, and Cybernetics, Part B (Cybernetics), 42(4)*, 1119–1130.
42. Woodbridge, J., Anderson, H. S., Ahuja, A., & Grant, D. (2016). Predicting domain generation algorithms with long short-term memory networks. arXiv preprint arXiv:1611.00791.

43. Yadav, S., Reddy, A. K. K., Reddy, A. L., & Ranjan, S. (2010). Detecting algorithmically generated malicious domain names. In *Proceedings of the 10th ACM SIGCOMM Conference on Internet Measurement* (pp. 48–61). New York, NY: ACM.
44. Yadav, S., Reddy, A. K. K., Reddy, A. N., & Ranjan, S. (2012). Detecting algorithmically generated domain-flux attacks with DNS traffic analysis. *IEEE/ACM Transactions on Networking, 20*(5), 1663–1677.
45. Yu, B., Gray, D. L., Pan, J., De Cock, M., & Nascimento, A. C. (2017). Inline DGA detection with deep networks. In *2017 IEEE International Conference on Data Mining Workshops (ICDMW)* (pp. 683–692). Piscataway, NJ: IEEE.
46. Yu, B., Pan, J., Hu, J., Nascimento, A., & De Cock, M. (2018). Character level based detection of DGA domain names. In *2018 International Joint Conference on Neural Networks (IJCNN)* (pp. 1–8). Piscataway, NJ: IEEE.
47. Zhauniarovich, Y., Khalil, I., Yu, T., & Dacier, M. (2018). A Survey on malicious domains detection through DNS data analysis. *ACM Computing Surveys, 51*(4), 67
48. Zhou, Z. H., & Liu, X. Y. (2006). Training cost-sensitive neural networks with methods addressing the class imbalance problem. *IEEE Transactions on Knowledge and Data Engineering, 18*(1), 63–77.
49. Zhou, Z. H., & Liu, X. Y. (2010). On multi-class cost-sensitive learning. *Computational Intelligence, 26*(3), 232–257.

Chapter 38
ABFT: Analytics to Uplift Big Social Events Using Forensic Tools

Priyanka Dhaka and Bharti Nagpal

Abstract Researchers and analysts are rapidly going through with large even terabyte- and petabyte-sized data sets when carrying digital investigation, which is becoming one of the major challenges in digital forensics. With invariably rising network bandwidth, it can be highly difficult to operate and store network traffic. To have a control over this, new algorithmic approach and computational methods are needed; even though Big Data is a challenge for forensic researchers, it effectively helps them in investigating patterns to prevent or detect and resolve crime. This chapter brings up care toward challenges in forensic investigation related to Big Data and possible ways to help a forensic investigator figure out large data sets in order to carry out forensic analysis and investigation. World is intent across big social events which even raises a concern toward criminal activities involved there in and there by bounding across Big Data. There are many practical applications where one can process large amount of data, and this data comes moreover in unstructured form. Right from various events that are considered about big communities, there are various real-life postulates where large quantity of data is produced and processed which is required to be mined (Hambrick et al., J Anxiety Disord 18:825–839, 2004). Big Data analytics has provided a striking growth that has shown up as a result of the accessibility of large sum of data that is fitting across a varied range of application domains all so in the region of science, business, and government. This chapter has also paid attention toward different aspects of commerce with analytics mentioning Big Data in social events.

Keywords Big Data · Social events · Digital forensics · HDFS · MapReduce · MongoDB

P. Dhaka (✉)
Maharaja Surajmal Institute, New Delhi, India

B. Nagpal
Ambedkar Institute of Advanced Communication Technologies and Research, New Delhi, India

© Springer Nature Switzerland AG 2020   929
B. B. Gupta et al. (eds.), *Handbook of Computer Networks and Cyber Security*,
https://doi.org/10.1007/978-3-030-22277-2_38

1   Introduction

Everything in the business world is influenced by analytics today. On the arrival of new and modern techniques for analytics and potentially to mine Big Data processes, it is now becoming essential to uplift the analytics in an improved way. The digital forensic field is getting intensive importance and adverting at a time when data warehouse requirement are increasing rapidly; because of this exponential growth, it is not exceptional for big corporations and law enforcement agencies to look into digital investigation with data sets larger than terabytes. Current digital investigation tools have not been able to handle terabytes of data in an effective manner; therefore, Big Data techniques need to be considered at this point. Big Data analytics is the method of examining Big Data to reveal hidden patterns, unmapped correlations, and some other usable information that can facilitate to make better decision [1]. With Big Data analytics, data scientists can analyze large volume of data that conventional analytics failed to touch. It typical deals with huge size of data with different prospects; this may include data processed through big social events, Internet of things and social networking sites, or from worldwide fundamental events. Since data is so large and coming from many different sources, it is becoming a miscellaneous mixture of semi-structured and unstructured data. The quantity of data produced across the globe and that continue to grow at an accelerating rate causes the servers to overflow with log files, message streams, transaction records, business records, and mobile device data records which need to be effectively analyzed through some major analytical processing where "Big Data" is commonly known. To manage this huge amount of data, some alternative methods of data management are also used which are further referred to as NoSQL that provides a variety of methods to manage information without dealing with the complexities of queries by speeding up the query response and providing graph database for social network analytics [2]. The elongation of Big Data to the computer forensic field will have some of the following benefits:

1. Makes better information standard and quality related to data analysis
2. Cuts down the system and human processing time
3. Reduces monetized costs included in digital forensics

Concerning with a recent survey carried out by the American Institute of CPA, "Big Data is named as the issue at the peak facing forensic and evaluation professionals in next 3–5 years" [3].

1.1   Big Data Analytics and Digital Forensics

In digital forensics data is in both structured and unstructured format, is noisy and not noisy, and is in homogeneous and non-homogeneous form which usually indulges into large data set cases; this large data set research needed to be elongated to digital forensics up to a considerable extent.

2   Aspects of Big Data Analytics

All enterprises are capturing data about their costumers, sales, products, financial transactions, profits, and many more. Processing and storing this data by using various tools and techniques including data mining process seems to be quite much satisfactory, whereas manipulating, applying, and utilizing this unstructured data involves various challenges ranging from data size to data types. In order to maintain this huge size and large variety of data with more security, accuracy, and privacy, various technologies arrive and contact with each other and converge into the category called Big Data analytics. Big Data analytics basically deals with large amount of data sets which are of different sizes from terabytes to petabytes and zettabytes, and this methodology is basically used to process the data with reduced latency. It follows one of the following features: high levels of volume, velocity, and variety. Moreover, this data arrives from videos/audios, log files, social media, the Internet, peripheral devices, satellites, and sensors—which are randomly generated on a real-time basis at huge scale [2, 4, 5].

Analyzing Big Data requires analysts and researchers to take improved and quicker decisions for data that was formerly unserviceable and outback. Big Data requires high-performance analytics which is generally processed by specialized software tools and applications for data mining, data optimization, text mining, and predictive analysis and forecasting. Applying Big Data tools on highly large volume of data sets helps the organization to find which data is relevant and can be analyzed to get good business decisions for future events.

3   Challenges: Big Data Analytics

Considering the large volume of data and various formats of data which are collected across entire organization, Big Data is becoming very complex to manage. Big Data analytics provides patterns and associations between diversities of data with business results. The challenges related with analytics require more efficient algorithms to receive the perfect outcome. Big Data faces various challenges because it deals with heterogeneous data sets and there is also a difficulty that all sorts of data cannot be obtainable at the same time [6].

The increasing volume of data is one more challenge for Big Data analysis as there is always a call for timely response with acknowledgment to distributed processing of data. To take full advantage of Big Data analytics, organizations will need to address several challenges related to Big Data. Some of those key challenges are as follows.

3.1 Meeting the Requirement for Speed

In today's business need, companies are curious to determine not only how much data they require but also how quickly they can search and analyze the relevant amount of data; the challenge is passing with the extensive volume of data and getting the level of details required along with a very high speed. The challenge rises with the degree of granularity upraises. One of the better solutions is availability of hardware, a hardware which is highly reliable with high memory and effective in parallel processing to compact large volume of data very quickly [7]. One other option is assigning data into memory, i.e., using a high reliable hardware to keep the information about data and using some of the commodity hardware to solve a problem. Both of the methods permit the organization to examine large data volumes and derive business perspectives in the real world.

3.2 Intellection with Data

It yields a great perspective to acquire data into correct shape so that it can be visualized as a piece of data analysis. For this there is a need to visualize data in form of context coming thereafter from different types of customer requirements; this challenge can be solved by having proper domain expertise in place. Insuring what kind of data people are analyzing, they should have a profound knowledge about where the data comes from, what audience will be taking in that data, and in what form [8].

3.3 Computing Data Quality

Even after analyzing data speedily and placing it into appropriate context for the audience, who are there ready to use the information, the quality of the data for deciding all the intends and purposes will be endangered, if the data is not precise or opportune. This is the challenge for almost all the data analytics and even more noticeable and marked if perceiving more information for Big Data projects. Here data visualization is only considered to be an important tool if data quality is to be checked. To compute this problem, organizations must have a data governing body or information management team in order to insure the data is accurate and up to date. It should ever be good to have a descriptive method to refer data quality issues so that the conflicts wouldn't arise later.

3.4 Exhibiting Significant Results

Plotting points on a graph for analysis of highly significant databases becomes difficult when handling extreme amount of information. This problem can be solved by clustering data into a higher-level view, where smaller groups of data get visual. By converting data into discrete sets with similar values which is also termed as binning, data can be more effectively visualized.

3.5 Transacting with Outliers

Outliers generally correspond to 1–5% of data, but while working with extremely high amounts of data, viewing 1–5% of data is kind of difficult. Feasible solution is to make a distinguishable chart for the outliers and the result can also be binned into both the views the statistical distribution of the data and seeing the outliers. While the outliers may not be the interpreter of the data, they may also bring out potentially important perspectives.

The accessibility of new in-memory technologies and high-performance analytics that requires data visualization is giving a great way to analyze data very much faster than ever. Visual analytics enables business organizations to use raw data and represent it in a meaningful way [9, 10].

4 Big Data Analysis with Parallel Computing

Big Data analysis in the era of parallel computing defines a comparison between distributed processing and MapReduce technology. Due to the enhancement of the data size in zettabytes, the current sequential methodologies and data mining tools for a single personal computer are becoming inefficient to handle such a vast amount of data. It is becoming essential to handle daily Internet traffic with zettabytes of data with the help of Big Data tools and techniques, in which most of the techniques involve parallel computing to service their needs. The parallel and cloud computing methods are counted to be better solution for Big Data mining.

The process of parallel computing is centered on distributing a large problem into minor ones, and every one of them is conceded out by one solo processor independently. These processes are accomplished simultaneously in a distributed and parallel manner [11]. There are two conjoint methodologies used to confront the Big Data problem. The first one is where the distributed procedure centered on the data parallelism paradigm, where a particular Big Data set can be manually distributed into n subsets and n algorithms are correspondingly accomplished for the corresponding n subsets. The final result can be acquired from a group of the outputs generated by the n algorithms. The second one is the MapReduce designed technique under the cloud computing platform. This method consists of the map and reduces procedures, in which the first performs filtering and sorting and the far along executes a summary operation in order to produce the final result. The organization performances of the MapReduce-based technique are quite constant no problem how many computer nodes are used, smarter than the baseline single machine and distributed processes excluding for the class uneven data set. In addition, the MapReduce procedure needs the minimum computational cost to practice these Big Data sets.

4.1 Hadoop Distributed File System (HDFS) and MapReduce: An Approach Processing Parallel Computing

Hadoop Distributed File System is an open-source framework given by the Apache Software Foundation; it is used for storing huge amount of data sets with clusters of commodity hardware and streaming access pattern. Streaming access pattern means "write ones, read any time, but don't change the content of the file," where MapReduce is used to process data which is stored in HDFS (Fig. 38.1).

HDFS consist of five series:

1. Name Node: Node that supervises the Hadoop Distributed File System (HDFS)
2. Master Node: Node where JobTracker runs and which receives job requests from clients
3. Job Tracker: Schedules jobs and tracks the allocated jobs to task tracker
4. Data Node: Node where data exists in progress before any processing takes place
5. Task Tracker: Tracks the task and informs status to JobTracker

Here, name node, master node, and job trackers act as masters, and data node and task tracker act as slaves; every master server can communicate with each other and every slave node can communicate with each other. HDFS is installed on the top of a normal file system with a block size of 64 MB.

A MapReduce divides a large data set into small independent chunks and classifies them into key and value pairs for parallel processing. This method of parallel processing recovers the speed and reliability of clusters and returning a solution more speedily. The main benefit of MapReduce is that it easily scales data processing over numerous computing nodes. Beneath this model, the data

Fig. 38.1 Hadoop distribution

processing origins are called mappers and reducers [11–13]. Disintegrating a data processing application into mappers and reducers sometimes becomes nontrivial. But, when one writes an application in the MapReduce form, scaling the application to route over hundreds or thousands of machines in a cluster is simply a configuration change. This simple scalability is what has engrossed many computer scientists to practice the MapReduce model.

The *Mapper*'s job is to process the input data, mostly the input data is in the form of file or directory and is stored in HDFS, and the *Map* function splits the input data into small chunks by the InputFormat and generates a map task for each chunk in input. The job tracker allocates those tasks to the data nodes. The output of each Map task is divided into group of key-value pair for every reducer.

The *Reducer*'s job is to process the various results of data that comes from mapper and combines them to answer the big problem that a master node wants to resolve, and after processing the data, it writes the output back into HDFS. Thus the reducer is capable of collecting the data from all of the mappers for the keys and syndicates them to answer the problem (Fig. 38.2).

MapReduce is beneficial for parallel processing on terabytes or petabytes of data kept in Apache Hadoop (Fig. 38.3).

The following table defines some of MapReduce's main benefits:

1. *Scalability*: MapReduce can process petabytes of data, kept in HDFS on one cluster.
2. *Least Data Motion*: MapReduce moves computed procedures to the data on HDFS and not the additional approach round. Processing tasks are present on the data nodes which knowingly moderate the input-output patterns and subsidize to Hadoop processing speed.
3. *Simplicity*: Developers can write applications in their language of selection, like Java, C++, or Python, and MapReduce jobs are simple to process.
4. *Speed*: Parallel computing means that MapReduce can proceed problems that take days to solve by solving them in minutes.

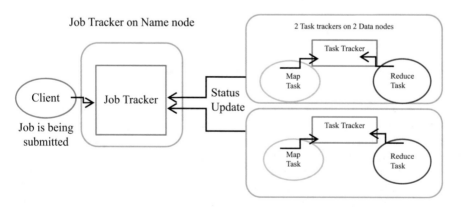

Fig. 38.2 HDFS architecture

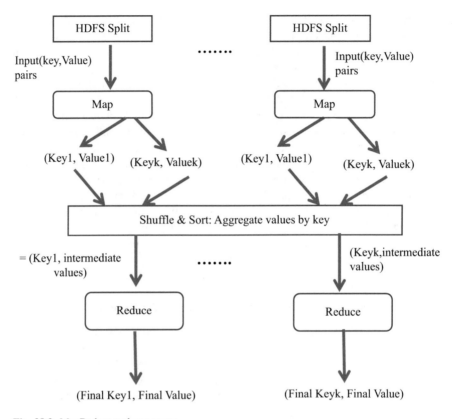

Fig. 38.3 MapReduce task processes

5. *Recovery*: MapReduce prevents from failure. If a machine with one copy of data is inaccessible, another machine has a copy of the same key-value pair which can be utilized to resolve the similar sub-task, and the JobTracker keeps the record of it all.

5 Text Analytics: The Next Genesis of Big Data

A huge amount of textual information is generated day by day and even in an unstructured format. All sort of mail, messages, notification, and documents are generated in a text format. Many times the information comes partially and may represent certain kind of bias facts, and this information is heterogeneous which comes from many different sources [14, 15]. The purpose of text analysis is to drive superior quality of structured data from unstructured data set. Text analysis is also known as text mining. A great reason of performing text analysis is to determine opinion about product and services or to improve customer superior data.

Text analysis is measured to construct an association between texts in the shape of subject model, which one can figure out in given context. The main objective of text analysis is to understand the meaning of words in a given context and with reference to context. Specifying the "who," "what," "where," "when," "why," and the view of the conversation changes the unstructured data into structured data and makes the businesses capable to listen to every information exchanged between the organization and other social activities. Perfect text analytics systems are commercializes as social media supervising results. The hospitals and restaurants also get benefited by the use of text analytics in order to listen to the conversation. A large volume of customer feedback for resorts and restaurants gets into mark outside the customer-business conversation. Text analytics can also be used to germinate a finer understanding of likes and dislikes of the customers and upraises the motivation of the customers which improves the customer loyalty and improves sales.

Leading companies have made broad moves screening the importance of text analysis. For example, IBM has been driving their Watson platform truly tough and as of late adopted AlchemyAPI to augment the analytics side of Watson. In addition, Microsoft bought Equivio, a text analytics company centering on eDiscovery. Moreover, text mining is basically a procedure of converting unstructured data into usable form. There are many ways and forms in which text analysis can be conducted which are discussed as follows.

5.1 Subject Recognition

This process brings up the collection of unstructured data, recognizing the particular topic and then clustering them based on the subject or topic. This process also involves association topics and gives a very big impression for organizational-level decision-making. It basically deals with sentiment analysis and opinion mining.

5.2 Concept Mining

The main thought behind this is that the concept can be utilized to know the relationship within documents. Visitant conducts are inherently sensitive to the concept, which can be outlined as an accumulation of external factors. Concept awareness permits incorporative external explanatory information into the learning process and adapting user behavior accordingly [5]. It is being carried out with the use of contextual information, metadata, and associations to describe the procedure (Fig. 38.4).

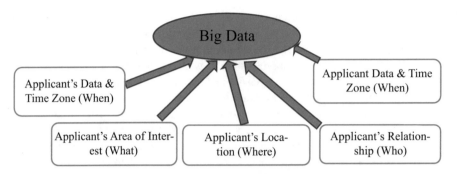

Fig. 38.4 Various forms of data that can be utilized as contextual information

5.3   Recognizing Context in User Data

Big Data contains large amount of information regarding reports, reviews, newspaper articles, social chats, and many more in the form of documents which are present in the form of sentences and paragraphs. These data sets contain punctuation marks and labels and utilize standardized spellings and different ways of writing any context and some short text data from social networking sites which never used to follow any standard way of writing and have less character representation. Due to huge difference in the way of writing and context size, this text needs to be mined through text analytics [6]. When a text file is written, it is segregated into three logical portions—introduction, details, and conclusion. One should be familiar with the idea that the introduction part describes the topic and provides the context, the succeeding paragraph carries the detailed information, and the conclusion closes the topic. The context of big unstructured documents can be recognized in two ways.

5.3.1   Intra-document Information: Utilizing Information Regarding the Words in the Document

Information for the word formatting can be utilized to find context. Word is counted to be most valuable if it occurs in a particular title or at the very beginning of a document. In this method, the resemblance between the sentence and the title is recognized. Contextually important word can be detected using its position in the sentence, sentence location in a paragraph, and paragraph view or position in text.

The first position in a sentence in a paragraph of text document can be given highest priority. An important word is mostly distributed throughout the document and thereby given with more importance than the other words in a particular document [12].

5.3.2   Inter-document Information: Utilizing Information Regarding Document

Unstructured text documents traverse from a couple of sentences to some pages; in such instances, the best method to find a context is to notice the author of the document. The language in which the document is written, the quality of written language that makes it easy to read, index, agenda, writing style, and many more facts could be considered.

Activities like what other kind of documents the user reads, how has he configured all the documents with in smartphones, tablets or in system. On utilizing such kind of information, it is becoming easy to recognize child, sibling, and parent folders within the document itself in order to predict user's area of interest. These two methods together make use of environmental information.

5.4   Type of Context

Using text analytics with Big Data helps the organization to attain big success, provides opportunities to work upon big social events by propagating real-time contextual analysis which discovers patterns in real-time data streams, and examines trends from social media flow. Here it comes up with useful outputs and events with higher-quality models and strengthens knowledge (Fig. 38.5).

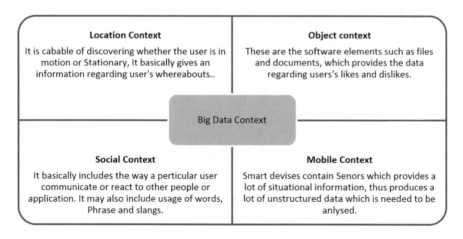

Fig. 38.5 Big Data context

6 Management of Big Data Analytics with NoSQL Tools

NoSQL databases are becoming popular and widely admired. These not only SQL databases are capable of storing all sets of data including unstructured data. The traceability of NoSQL databases like MongoDB, Cassandra, and HBase makes them a significant option for Big Data analytics [15–17]. The business analytics programs are becoming capable to provide business users to simply examine data in NoSQL databases by means of the following factors:

- *Rich visualization*—Interactive web-based interfaces for ad hoc reporting and charting
- *Flexible exploration*—Seeing data over dimensions like time, product, and geography and over measures like gross and quantity
- *Predictive analysis*—Effective predictive analytics abilities by employing hi-tech statistical algorithms such as classification, regression, clustering, and association rules

6.1 Limitations of Traditional Databases for Big Data

A large variety of databases are RDBMS solution types. In such types of databases, the data entered into the table is based on rigid schema, as a SQL-based query is required to read/write data to such databases. Because of having a rigid schema, the data stored into the table is not flexible enough making it difficult to scale very large databases. Here the large queries are solved manually which makes these traditional databases not feasible for Big Data solutions.

6.2 Why NoSQL?

NoSQL puts a different path to figure out the Big Data problem. Key-value document-based storage is taken into account in most of the NoSQL databases, which are the basic unit of information in NoSQL databases providing superior performance, high availability, and simplified scalability which aggregates documents and functions as in relational database table.

6.2.1 Detailed Study About the NoSQL Tool: MongoDB

MongoDB was developed by Dwight Merriman and Eliot Horowitz, and the database was liberated to open source in 2009 and is accessible in terms of the Free Software Foundation's GNU AGPL Version 3.0 commercial license [18].

MongoDB is an open-source database that uses document-oriented model and pre-eminent NoSQL database which is written in c++. Instead of using tables and rows like in a relational database, it comprises key and value pairs which are the basic unit of information in MongoDB providing superior performance, high availability, and simplified scalability which aggregates documents and functions as in relational database table [14]. MongoDB endorses a dynamic schema design which enables a document to have different fields and structures. This database uses a Binary JavaScript Object Notation (BSON) format for document storage which is a binary-encoded serialization of JavaScript Object Notation (JSON)-like documents. Binary JSON (BSON) is lightweight, traversable, and efficient to be used in MongoDB. MongoDB, a Big Data tool, is designed to assure data security and also provides role-based access control, encrypted communication, and robust auditing [16]. It provides easy to use integrated key management and protects the data within a given directory, it provides a clear structure of a single object and has no complex joins, and it also uses internal memory for keeping the working sets and capable of providing faster access of data. MongoDB is also adequate to assign index on any attribute.

6.2.2   Why to Employ MongoDB on Data Set

- *Document-Oriented Storage*: Data is stored in the form of Binary JavaScript Object Notation (BSON) format; the maximum BSON format size is 16 Mb. This maximum size assures that a single document cannot use maximum amount of RAM and during transmission inordinate amount of bandwidth.
- *Indexing*: Practice index on any attribute which reduces the problem of scanning each and every document in MongoDB because it supports effective resolution of queries. Indexes keep a small part of data set in a simple to traverse form. Index stores the value of set of fields sequential to value of field as nominal to index.
- *Replication*: It is the process of synchronizing data around multiple servers; it enhances the availability of data by providing multiple copies of data on different data servers, hence offering redundancy; it protects the database from the deprivation of single server; and it keeps the data safe and provides disaster recovery and replica set which is transparent to application.
- *MapReduce Command*: MapReduce function initially queries the collection and then maps the result document to give out key-value pair, which is then reduced on the basis of keys having multiple values [19].
- *Auto-sharding*: Sharding is the process of storing data records over multiple machines as the machines may not be suitable to store large amount of data and unable to provide an acceptable read-write throughput. Sharding provides all rights of replication to master node. Single replica set has a limitation of 12 nodes, so there is a need to apply sharding. Sharding is necessary because memory size cannot be sufficient enough when active data set is large and vertical scaling is very large. The sharding process is explained in the following figure.

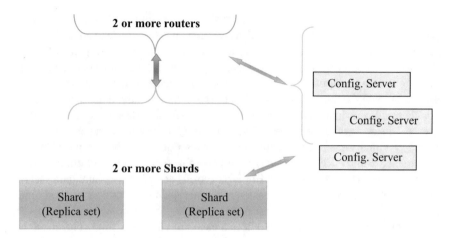

Fig. 38.6 Sharding in MongoDB using sharding clusters

In Fig. 38.6, there are three primary elements which are described as follows:

A. *Query Router*: The query routers process the operations to shards and then return result to the clients. A sharded cluster may carry multiple query routers to split up the client request load.
B. *Shards*: Shards are employed to store consistent data on different machines providing high availability of requirements; basically, each shard is a distinguished replica set.
C. *Config Server*: Config. server contains cluster's metadata which carries mapping of cluster's data set to shards, and query routers utilize this metadata to object operations to a particular shard; basically, sharded clusters contain three config. servers.

Basically MongoDB consists of 16 MB namespace file which can support approximately 24,000 namespaces, and a namespace file cannot be larger than 2047 MB. MongoDB stores not more than 100 levels of nesting for Binary JavaScript Object Notation (BSON) documents, and maximum document must be $<2^{32}$ documents. The maximum size of MMAPV 1 (original storage engine) of MongoDB based on memory mapped files is 32 TB.

In Fig. 38.7, it is being demonstrated that mongod command is running with a directory of gave and place storage information examining that the database is running correctly and waiting for connection at port 27017.

6.2.3 Limitations

- Every document in MongoDB consists of a field name which makes the data size usually higher.
- Only small operations are subsidized at a single document level.
- MongoDB provides less flexibility as it has no JOINs.

Fig. 38.7 Running mongod command

- Less up-to-date information is available.
- At a particular point in time, the aggregation and data analysis process, i.e., mapping and reducing process, is not very fast, so faster configurations are required by adding Hadoop into admixture.

6.2.4 Case Study: Healthcare Analysis

A better health care system requires a strong financing procedure, reliable data sets for building proper decisions, and better healthcare facilities, but this procedure is going tough while maintaining huge data sets by database management tools; there is a requirement to gather and analyze the healthcare data by employing Big Data tools like MongoDB; this could improve treatment trials and also lows down the cost of taking unnecessary trials by analyzing data set deployed in the tool [3, 20]. MongoDB also minimizes the total time and resources in conducting clinical research. In this chapter the worldwide data set of various healthcare diseases is collected and analyzed using MongoDB.

The desired information obtained from world health statistics was inserted into MongoDB as key-value pairs, and after inserting the desired data, one can find all the required information as described in Fig. 38.8.

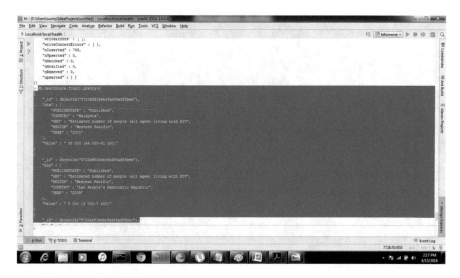

Fig. 38.8 Tool snapshot with records

The information was inserted in MongoDB. Now obtaining information by using OR criteria:

```
Record 1:
db.HivClusters.find({
$or:[
{"Estimated number of people (all ages) living with HIV 2013":
{"Initial Cluster 1":6300000,
"Initial Cluster 2":100}},
{"Estimated number of people (all ages) living with HIV 2013":
{"Final Cluster 1":3866667,
"Final Cluster 2":163431}
}
]
}).pretty()
```

The result obtained is:

```
{
"_id": ObjectId("57109650974247ccc76987ef"),
"Estimated number of people (all ages) living with HIV
2013":
{
"Initial Cluster 1": 6300000,
"Initial Cluster 2": 100
}}
{"_id": ObjectId("57109650974247ccc76987f4"),
"Estimated number of people (all ages) living with HIV
2013":
{"Final Cluster 1": 3866667,
"Final Cluster 2": 163431}
}
```

7 Big Social Data Correlating Big Events

An increase in popularity of Big Data and its awareness on social media leads to its great extent of involvement in many big social events like in healthcare and biomedicine conferences, rethinking data privacy, born digital data in the humanities, artificial intelligence and data science, smart cities innovation, and many more events. The data which is constantly accumulating from these events is termed as Big Social data. In today's world, society constantly interacts with each other, and this interaction is commonly mediated by information technology in a digital form. The social data explosion has resulted in a complete deep study of emerging new topics in Big Social data.

The Big Social data is basically a combination of many different forms like:

- *Big Data Science* that provides tools to operate and supervise social data including social media and social networking.
- *Big Data Analytics* capable of extracting the inner nature of social data.
- *Social Computing* provides technology-intercede social services.

Big social events are generally processed to uncover the most interesting and inspirational work from various organizations whether related to businesses, ethical data, leading industries, or even new game processing methodologies; through some planned strategies, one can understand attendee behavior, a primary concept to design the event layout and a thoughtful process to attain varieties. There are many hosts that are capable of engaging the events with relevant data and information to their marked hearings. These types of hosts are:

1. *Google I/O*: The tech describes how to regenerate an event to serve attendees.
2. *Social Media Marketing World*: The conference uses Slack as the new tool in its big network strategy.
3. *Institute of Food Technologists Annual Meeting and Food Expo*: The food Industry events are conducted in order to understand how to get a deeper knowledge of attendee and display behavior.
4. *Code Conference*: The conference ensures the diverse audience. Re/Code builds its attendee list.

7.1 Types of Big Social Data

In the area of digital human interactions, there are both machine-generated and human-generated data which likely change the state into social insight. Human-generated content needs more intelligent solution to decode the semantics of people's opinion and behavior. Big Data is now capable of predicting what is their changing in social interaction and how it is changing [10]. Human-generated data is basically a content that is produced through social technology-mediated interactions of people in social media platforms. This type of data is basically categorized into

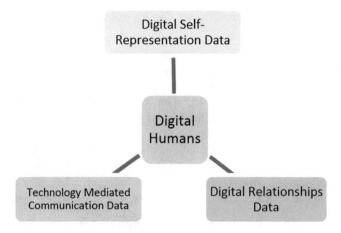

Fig. 38.9 Types of social data in the current digital environment

three types of data containing digital-self representation data, technology-mediated communication data, and digital relationships data. These three types of data are utilized as social data in the current digital environment (Fig. 38.9).

7.2   Classification of Big Social Data Types

1. *Digital-self representation data*: It consists of data corresponding to identity categorization and communicative structure in the digital environment, for example, profile data that consist of information about login data like name, nickname, email address, and password; mandatory data which consist of service- and application-required data—full name, contact number, birthday, and many more; and extended data which comprises profile pictures, education, and qualification.
2. *Technology-mediated communication data*: It consists of data that is related to two-way communication, knowledge innovation and dispersion by technology. It consists of data types like public communication data, private communication data, and collaborative communication data.
3. *Digital relationships data*: It consists of data that provides digital social relationships pattern. Digital relationships data consist of explicit data and implicit data, and these data are revealed through technology-mediated communication data, for example, message posts and tweets can be analyzed through interconnections among individuals.

8 Conclusion

Everything is derived from analytics today. Starting from the decisions at small businesses to decision-making at large companies, certain type of analytics is required. With the emergence of new techniques for analytics and ability to mine more about Big Data, it is now a time to strategize analytics to uplift big social events in a better way. Data states the level and brings out hidden facts. With so much of tools and techniques, this data can be addressed more confidently. Business analytics requires deriving values from Big Data in order to organize various big events. Event planning using big social data is one of the major areas of interest, and it is mainly derived through text analytics processes where prediction of attendees' behavior can help in a great way. Business analytics comes with challenges, and with efficient text analytics and data correlation, it can help one get over from these challenges.

References

1. Rashidi, P., et al. (2011). Discovering activities to recognize and track in a smart environment. *IEEE Transactions on Knowledge and Data Engineering, 23*(4), 527–539.
2. Arora, R., & Aggarwal, R. R. (2013). Modeling and querying data in MongoDB. *International Journal of Scientific & Engineering Research, 4*(7), 141–144.
3. World Health Organization. (2008). *The global burden of disease: 2004 update*. Geneva: WHO Press.
4. Sun, J., Wang, F., Hu, J., & Edabollahi, S. (2012). Supervised patient similarity measure of heterogeneous patient records. *SIGKDD Explorations, 14*(1), 16–24.
5. Singh, N., Garg, N., & Mittal, V. (2013). Big data – Insights, motivation and challenges. *International Journal of Scientific & Engineering Research, 4*(2), 2172–2175.
6. Tuli, P., & Sahu, P. (2013). System, monitoring and security using keylogger. *International Journal of Computer Science and Mobile Computing, 2*(3), 106–111.
7. Shinde S. R., Shinde, R., Shanbhag, S., Solanki, M., Sable, P., & Kimbahune, S. (2014). mHEALTH-PHC - Application design for rural Health care. In *Canada international humanitarian technology conference - (IHTC)*. Piscataway: IEEE.
8. Kaur, R., & Kaur, A. (2012). Digital forensics. *International Journal of Computer Applications, 50*(5), 5–9.
9. Duggal, P. S., & Paul, S. (2013). Big data analysis: Challenges and solutions. In *International conference on cloud, big data and trust 2013, RGPV, November 2013*.
10. Shilpa, & Kaur, M. (2013). BIG data and methodology-A review. *International Journal of Advanced Research in Computer Science and Software Engineering, 3*(10), 991–995.
11. Monteith, S., Glenn, T., Geddes, J., & Bauer, M. (2015). Big data are coming to psychiatry: A general introduction. *International Journal of Bipolar Disorders, 3*, 21.
12. Colombo, P., & Ferrari, E. (2015). Enhancing MongoDB with purpose-based access control. *IEEE Transactions on Dependable and Secure Computing (TDSC), 14*(6), 591–604.
13. Saini, A., Ubriani, J., Minocha, J., & Sharma, D. (2016). New approach for clustering of big data: DisK-Means. In *International conference on computing, communication and automation (ICCCA 2016), April 2016*. Piscataway: IEEE.
14. Grover, P., & Johari, R. (2015). BCD: Big data, cloud computing and distributed computing. In *IEEE global conference on communication technologies (GCCT −2015) Kanyakumari, Tamil Nadu, April 2015*. IEEE.

15. Bhardwaj, V., Johari, R., & Bhardwaj, P. (2015). Query execution evaluation in wireless network using MyHadoop. In *4th IEEE international conference on reliability, infocom technologies and optimization (ICRITO 2015), AMITY University, September 2015*. IEEE.
16. Grover, P., & Johari, R. (2016). MVM: MySQL Versus MongoDB. In M. Pant, K. Deep, J. Bansal, A. Nagar, & K. Das (Eds.), *Proceedings of fifth international conference on soft computing for problem solving. Advances in intelligent systems and computing* (Vol. 436). Singapore: Springer.
17. Kang, Y.-S., Park, I.-H., Rhee, J., & Lee, Y.-H. (2016). MongoDB-based repository design for IoT-generated RFID/sensor big data. *IEEE Sensors Journal, 16*(2), 485–497.
18. Aghi, R., Mehta, S., Chauhan, R., Chaudhary, S., & Bohra, N. (2015). A comprehensive comparison of SQL and MongoDB databases. *International Journal of Scientific and Research Publications, 5*(2), 1–3.
19. Hasan, M. (2014). Genetic algorithm and its application to big data analysis. *International Journal of Scientific & Engineering Research, 5*(1), 1991–1996.
20. Newton-Howes, G., Weaver, T., & Tyrer, P. (2008). Attitudes of staff towards patients with personality disorder in community health teams. *The Australian and New Zealand Journal of Psychiatry, 42*(7), 572–577.

Chapter 39
HackIt: A Real-Time Simulation Tool for Studying Real-World Cyberattacks in the Laboratory

Palvi Aggarwal, Cleotilde Gonzalez, and Varun Dutt

Abstract Computer-based simulation tools have an important role to play in helping us understand the behavior of people performing as attackers (people who launch cyberattacks) and defenders (people who protects computer networks against cyberattacks) in complex cyber situations. In this paper, we introduce a simulation tool called HackIt that could be used to build dynamic cyberattack scenarios. We used the HackIt tool to investigate the influence of timing of deception strategies involving honeypots (computers that pretend to be real, but those that are actually fake) on the decisions of participants performing as attackers. In a lab-based experiment, participants performing as attackers were randomly assigned to two between-subjects conditions, each involving six repeated games: early ($N = 20$) and late ($N = 20$). In early condition, deception was present via honeypots on the second and third games, whereas in late condition, deception was present via honeypots on the fourth and fifth games. Presence of deception meant that the honeypots were easy to exploit in deception rounds. In both conditions, the goal of attacker was to steal credit-card information for computers on the network. Results revealed that the proportion of honeypot attacks were higher in late condition compared to early condition. Similarly, we found that the proportion of regular attacks were lower in late condition compared to early condition. We highlight the potential of using the HackIt tool for creating realistic cyberscenarios and evaluating the effectiveness of different deception strategies in reducing cyberattacks.

Keywords Deception · Honeypots · Cyberattacks · Cybersecurity tools · Deception strategies

P. Aggarwal (✉) · C. Gonzalez
Carnegie Mellon University, Pittsburgh, PA, USA
e-mail: coty@cmu.edu

V. Dutt
Indian Institute of Technology Mandi, Mandi, India
e-mail: varun@iitmandi.ac.in

© Springer Nature Switzerland AG 2020
B. B. Gupta et al. (eds.), *Handbook of Computer Networks and Cyber Security*,
https://doi.org/10.1007/978-3-030-22277-2_39

949

1 Introduction

Cyberattacks are targeting government, industries, banking, and e-commerce business at an alarming rate. The cyber criminals use advanced cyberattacks, e.g., SQL injection, phishing, Trojans, ransomwares, rootkits, and malware, to breach the network and gain access to information [1]. The growing threat of cyberattacks on critical cyber organizations reveal the urgent need for finding methods that enhance network security. Presently, there are numerous cyber defense mechanisms available to fight against various cyberattacks, but very few of these solutions can prevent zero-day cyberattacks, attacks that target publicly known but still unpatched vulnerabilities [2]. Deception is an art of persuasion where defenders intentionally mislead the hackers to something which is not true [3], and it may provide a promising real-time solution against cyberattacks [4, 5]. Deception technology may help reduce cyberattacks by shifting the cognitive, economic, and time costs of cyberattacks back onto the attacker. The objective of this chapter is to investigate how deception tools may help reduce cyberattacks.

The principles of deception have been around for years, and recently, they have become a secret weapon of purple teams and threat hunters worldwide [4–6]. Deception may involve communication between a target and a deceiver, in which the deceiver tries to convince target to trust the fake explanation of ground truth [3]. Deception can be implemented with existing tools, e.g., firewalls with blacklists, intrusion prevention, and URL filtering [7]. Several researchers have proposed deception's use via honeypots [8–10]. Honeypots are servers that mimic real server, but they are actually fake [11].

Prior research has proposed a number of tools for using deception in cybersecurity. Some of these tools include the deception tool kit (DTK), honeynets, honeytokens, thug, TrapX, and smokescreen [8–11]. The DTK is one of the earliest tools that applied deception methods for cyber protection. Using TCP wrappers, DTK process the incoming malicious requests that are usually blocked in the network. Researchers have also proposed honeynets [11], which are a group of honeypots that are used for real-time applications. The client-side honeypots were proposed to detect malicious Web-based activities that try to breach client application vulnerabilities [12].

Furthermore, some researchers have proposed noncooperative dynamic deception games for understanding hackers' cyberattack decisions via experimentation and mathematical modeling [13–15]. For example, Aggarwal et al. [16] investigated the role of the amount of deception and the timing of deception in a cyberattack scenario using a noncooperative deception game (DG). The DG involved two phases: probe and attack. During probe, participants performing as hackers could probe webservers, some of which were honeypots. Once hackers probed the network, they could attack one of the webservers for real. Results revealed that using late timing of deception and high amount of deception helped in reducing cyberattacks.

The focus of the past research was on developing tools for deception and understanding human factors in abstract environments. The results of lab-based experiments as part of the past research were based on abstraction of choices and outcomes, which may not be realistic enough to capture how computers are attacked by hackers in the real world. The primary objective of this research is to develop a cybersecurity tool which helps us understand the human factors influencing hacker's decisions in complex cyber situations involving deception. To accomplish the above objective, we developed a HackIt tool, i.e., a tool to simulate complex cyber situations and showcase the potential of this tool via certain cyberattack scenarios involving deception.

Using HackIt tool, we simulate two deception scenarios where the timing of deception is either early or late. The goal of the hacker in these scenarios is to steal the credit-card information from the network. The network consists of two webservers where one of the webservers is a real webserver and the other one is a fake honeypot webserver. In this chapter, using the HackIt game, we investigate whether an early or late timing of deception is effective in trapping hackers into honeypots. Furthermore, we compare our results with the findings presented by Aggarwal et al. [16].

In what follows, we first discuss the functioning of the HackIt tool. Next, we explain the methods of an experiment run using the HackIt tool. Furthermore, we detail the results from HackIt tool and discuss the implications of our results for decision-making of hackers in the real world.

2 HackIt Tool

Hacking websites generally may involve two phases: searching for vulnerabilities (probing) and attacking computer workstations (attacking). HackIt is a cybersecurity tool that allows researchers to create various cyber situations and to map real-world cyberattack scenarios by involving two phases: probe phase and attack phase. The probe phase involves scanning of webservers in the network for vulnerabilities, whereas the attack phase involves gaining access to different computers and stealing information or compromising computer systems. For example, using the HackIt tool, one can create networks of different sizes, use deception and configure different webservers as honeypots, and create any number of fictitious ports, services, fake operating systems, and fake files on honeypots. The HackIt tool can run various network commands that include nmap, use_exploit, ls, and scp. Nmap is a network utility that shows the open ports, operating system, and services on the specified webserver. The nmap utility provides the list of vulnerabilities on the corresponding webservers. The use_exploit command exploits vulnerabilities of a system and helps hacker to gain access to a webserver. Next, the ls command lists the files currently on the file system of the machine. The scp command transfers files to the remote machine. The probe phase involves scanning of webservers in the network using nmap command. Using nmap command, hacker may collect information about the open ports, services, and vulnerabilities available in the network. Furthermore, the attack phase involves exploiting vulnerabilities and stealing information. To exploit any webserver, the hacker may use use_exploit command and gain access of the webserver. Next, the hacker could steal information from computer systems using the scp command. In the next section, we perform an experiment with the HackIt tool, where we evaluated the effectiveness of timing of deception via honeypots on reducing cyberattacks.

3 Experiment

3.1 Experiment Design

In this chapter, we analyzed the effect of timing of deception on hacker's actions. The timing of deception was manipulated across two between-subjects conditions: early deception ($N = 20$) and late deception ($N = 20$). In both conditions, participants playing as hackers were given 6 game rounds in a sequence (end point unknown to participants), where 2-game rounds possessed deception. Figure 39.1 shows the experimental design of the deception game implemented in HackIt tool. In this experiment, if the timing of deception was early, then deception was present on the second and third rounds in the sequence. However, if the timing of deception was late, then deception was present in the fourth and fifth rounds in the sequence. Presence of deception meant that the honeypots were easy to exploit via popular ports and vulnerability in the deception rounds compared to the nondeception rounds (more details ahead in this chapter). However, participants were not told that honeypots will involve easy-to-attack configurations in deception rounds. Also, participants were not disclosed of the number of rounds and on which deception was involved. Participants were told that there would be repeatedly interacting in games with different websites containing two new computer systems. To analyze human data, we looked at the proportion of honeypot attacks and proportion of regular attacks at the attack stage by the hacker across six rounds in each condition.

Condition/ Rounds	1	2	3	4	5	6
Early Deception	-	D	D	-	-	-
Late Deception	-	-	-	D	D	-

Fig. 39.1 Experiment design using deception game with six rounds and two conditions, i.e., early deception and late deception. *D* deception present; - deception not present

3.2   HackIt Task

In this chapter, we simulated a network of two webservers in HackIt tool where the objective of the hacker was to steal real credit-card information located on one of these webservers. Figure 39.2 shows the step-by-step HackIt task procedure. Step 1 of Fig. 39.2 shows a simulated network with two webservers where one of the webservers acts as a honeypot webserver and another one acts as a real webserver. Table 39.1 shows the information about the configuration of easy-to-attack and difficult-to-attack systems. For example, a system with Windows XP operating system, port 80/tcp, and service http will be easily exploitable. However, a system with Linux operating system, port 22/tcp, and service ssh will be difficult to attack. In deception rounds, honeypot webservers were configured in such a way that hackers could easily attack them. However, the regular webserver was difficult to attack in these deception rounds. In the experiment, participants were informed about the easy-to-exploit and the difficult-to-exploit configurations in Table 39.1.

Next, the hacker probes the network using nmap command to gain information about both the webservers. For example, in step 2 and step 3, the hacker probes webserver 1 and webserver 2, respectively (Fig. 39.2). Probing both the webservers gave the information about the operating system, open ports, services, and vulnerabilities. For example, probing webserver 1 gave the information to the hacker that webserver 1 is running on Solaris operating system. The open ports on webserver 1 are 80, 135, 21, and 111, where SQL injection, DOS attack, brute force attack, and DDOS attack are possible. The information provided to the hacker as a result of probing the systems gave him an idea of the possible success of an attack on that system. Once the hacker collects information about open ports and services, he/she could attack a webserver by using the "use_exploit" command. The use_exploit command exploits vulnerabilities of a system and helps the hacker to gain access to that webserver. For example, in step 4, the hacker used the use_exploit command to gain access of webserver 1 using DoS_attack vulnerability. Once the hacker exploited a system and gained access, he/she lists all the files by using the "ls" command. After this command, the hacker transfers required file, i.e., "pin.txt," using the "scp" command (step 5, Fig. 39.2). Once the hacker copies the file from the exploited system, he/she is informed whether he/she was successful or not in stealing a real credit-card file from the computer. Once the task is complete, the hacker is given the textual feedback about the success or failure of his action to copy the real credit-card file (step 6, Fig. 39.2).

3.3   Participants

A total of 40 participants were recruited through an e-mail advertisement to participate in an online cybersecurity study conducted using HackIt tool. About 68% of participants were males. The age of participants ranged from 18 years to 32 years

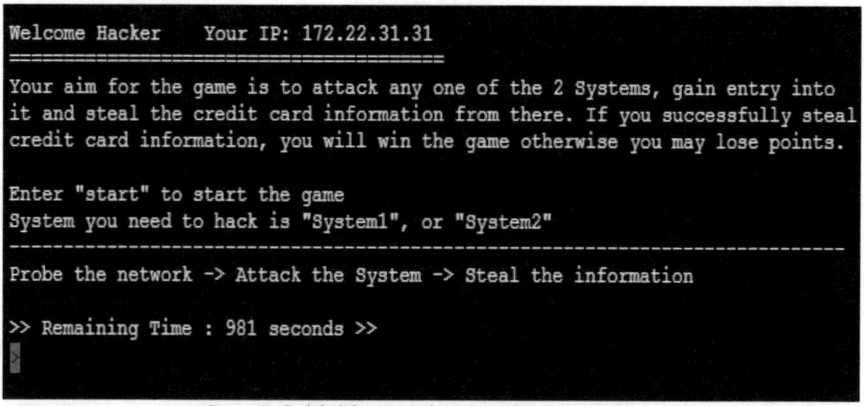

```
Welcome Hacker      Your IP: 172.22.31.31
========================================
Your aim for the game is to attack any one of the 2 Systems, gain entry into
it and steal the credit card information from there. If you successfully steal
credit card information, you will win the game otherwise you may lose points.

Enter "start" to start the game
System you need to hack is "System1", or "System2"
------------------------------------------------------------------------------
Probe the network -> Attack the System -> Steal the information

>> Remaining Time : 981 seconds >>
```

Step 1: Initial instructions to the participants

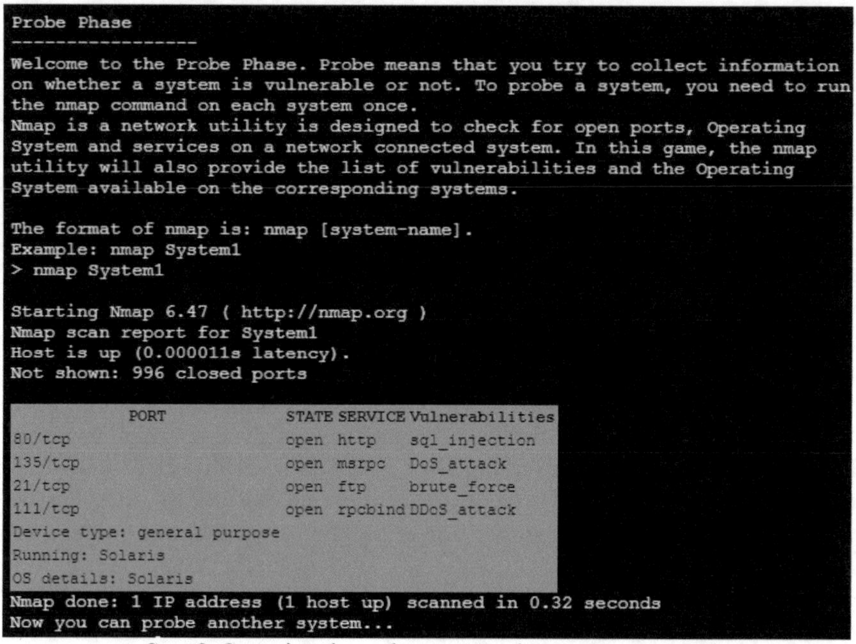

```
Probe Phase
-----------
Welcome to the Probe Phase. Probe means that you try to collect information
on whether a system is vulnerable or not. To probe a system, you need to run
the nmap command on each system once.
Nmap is a network utility is designed to check for open ports, Operating
System and services on a network connected system. In this game, the nmap
utility will also provide the list of vulnerabilities and the Operating
System available on the corresponding systems.

The format of nmap is: nmap [system-name].
Example: nmap System1
> nmap System1

Starting Nmap 6.47 ( http://nmap.org )
Nmap scan report for System1
Host is up (0.000011s latency).
Not shown: 996 closed ports
```

PORT	STATE	SERVICE	Vulnerabilities
80/tcp	open	http	sql_injection
135/tcp	open	msrpc	DoS_attack
21/tcp	open	ftp	brute_force
111/tcp	open	rpcbind	DDoS_attack
Device type: general purpose			
Running: Solaris			
OS details: Solaris			

```
Nmap done: 1 IP address (1 host up) scanned in 0.32 seconds
Now you can probe another system...
```

Step 2: Scanning the webserver 1 using nmap command

Fig. 39.2 HackIt game environment

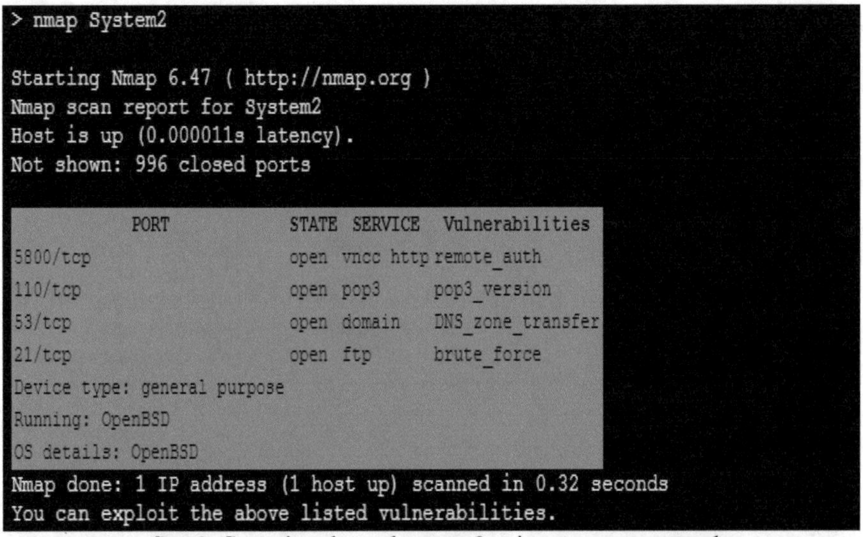

```
> nmap System2

Starting Nmap 6.47 ( http://nmap.org )
Nmap scan report for System2
Host is up (0.000011s latency).
Not shown: 996 closed ports

          PORT            STATE SERVICE   Vulnerabilities
5800/tcp                  open  vncc http remote_auth
110/tcp                   open  pop3      pop3_version
53/tcp                    open  domain    DNS_zone_transfer
21/tcp                    open  ftp       brute_force
Device type: general purpose
Running: OpenBSD
OS details: OpenBSD
Nmap done: 1 IP address (1 host up) scanned in 0.32 seconds
You can exploit the above listed vulnerabilities.
```

Step3: Scanning the webserver 2 using nmap command

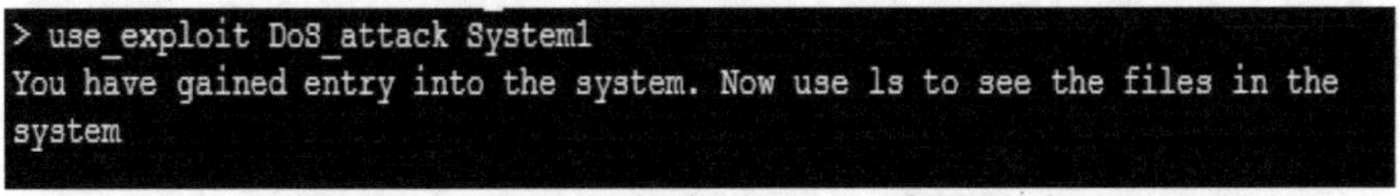

```
> use_exploit DoS_attack System1
You have gained entry into the system. Now use ls to see the files in the
system
```

Step 6: Scores Step 4: Exploiting one of the Webservers

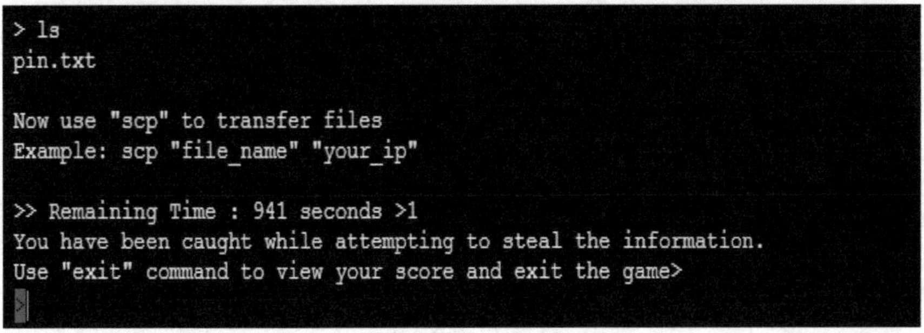

```
> ls
pin.txt

Now use "scp" to transfer files
Example: scp "file_name" "your_ip"

>> Remaining Time : 941 seconds >1
You have been caught while attempting to steal the information.
Use "exit" command to view your score and exit the game>
>
```

Step 5: File transfer

```
You played as a hacker !

Your Score : -5
Winner of Game : Analyst
```

Enter Trial No. 2

Fig. 39.2 (continued)

Table 39.1 Configuration of honeypot and regular systems

Easy to attack	Difficult to attack
Operating systems: • Windows Server 2003 • Windows XP • HP-UX 11i • Solaris	*Operating systems*: • OpenBSD • Linux • Mac OS X • Windows 8
Services and ports: • 21/tcp—ftp • 25/tcp—smtp • 80/tcp—http • 111/tcp—rpcbind • 135/tcp—msrpc	*Services and ports*: • 22/tcp-ssh • 53/tcp-domain • 110/tcp-pop3 • 139/tcp-netbios • 443/tcp-https • 445/tcp-microsoft-ds • 3306/tcp-mysql • 5900/tcp-vncc http • 6112/tcp-dtspc • 8080/tcp-apache

(Mean = 22; SD = 4). About 60% of participants possess 4-year undergraduate college degree, and 40% participants have a graduate or a professional degree. Hackers were remunerated INR 50 for participation in the study. In addition, they won INR 5 for transfer of a real credit-card file and lost INR 5 for transfer of a fake credit-card file.

3.4 Procedure

Participants were given instructions about their objective in the HackIt task, and they were informed about their own action's payoffs. Specifically, human hackers were asked to maximize their payoff by stealing the real credit-card file from the network over several rounds of play (participants were not aware of the end point of the game). Each round had two stages: probe stage and attack stage. The hacker could probe two webservers in the network using "nmap" utility. After probing the webservers, he/she received information about open ports, operating systems, services, and vulnerabilities associated with each webserver. Next, the hacker had two alternatives to choose during attack stage: exploit webserver 1 or exploit webserver 2. Hacker participants had to choose between these alternatives presented to them and exploit one of the webservers using "use_exploit" command. Once the webserver was exploited, hackers transferred the credit-card file to their remote computer.

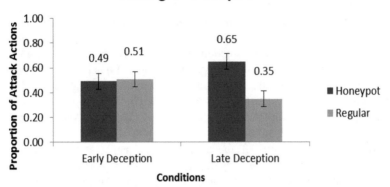

Fig. 39.3 Proportion of honeypot-/regular-attack actions for different timing of deception, early deception, and late deception

4   Results

We ran an experiment involving human participants and different between-subject conditions where deception occurred early or late in the HackIt environment. Figure 39.3 shows the proportion of regular-attack and honeypot-attack actions when the timing of deception was early and late.

The results revealed that the proportion of regular attacks was lower for late deception compared to early deception condition ($0.35 < 0.51$; $t(238) = 2.50$, $p < 0.05$, $\eta^2 = 0.21$). Thus, the simulated experiment conducted using HackIt tool helped us to validate the lab-based findings from the deception game obtained by Aggarwal et al. [16].

5   Discussion

In this chapter, we discussed HackIt, a simulation tool with a great potential to help cybersecurity researchers to investigate the decision-making of hackers and analysts in real-world cybersecurity scenarios. HackIt tool could provide a more realist task scenarios where the hackers were able to use real commands for network probing, exploiting, and transferring the information. Thus, the development of the HackIt tool could provide us a platform to migrate from abstract decision-making tasks to more applied and complex decision-making task. We showed a concrete research example of using HackIt to evaluate the effects of timing of deception on hacker's decisions. Results revealed that late timing of deception was more beneficial compared to early timing of deception in trapping hackers in honeypots. We believe that HackIt tool would be helpful in creating other cybersecurity scenarios involving dynamic network sizes, dynamic network configurations, and various deception strategies.

In this chapter, we simulated the information-stealing scenario in HackIt tool where the hacker was supposed to steal a credit-card file from a regular webserver system. Researchers simulated a deception strategy in HackIt, which varied in time. We found that the proportion of honeypot attacks were higher when deception was late compared to early. Similarly, we found the proportion of regular attack actions were lower when deception was late compared to early. These results obtained using the HackIt tool agree with the findings obtained by [16]. The likely reason for this finding is that the hacker did not have any clue about the presence of deception in early rounds. According to IBLT, the recency and frequency of events play a role in decision-making. In the case of early deception condition, no instances were created in memory that tells about the presence of honeypots. Thus, the hackers attacked regular webservers more frequently. Due to trust build in early rounds, hacker's started relying on feedback in later rounds as well. Thus, they end up attacking more on honeypots compared to regular webservers.

In addition, results from the HackIt tool suggest that it would be beneficial for analysts to use deception late in a repeated cyberattack on a computer network. Thus, initial rounds of attack that lack deception will likely make hackers believe in the information provided by the network. Furthermore, late deception will likely help analysts to trap hackers effectively.

Currently, we investigated only one factor involving deception using HackIt tool, i.e., timing of deception. The network size was also limited to two webservers where one computer was acting as honeypot webserver and the other one was acting as regular webserver. In future, we wish to perform a series of experiments involving participants performing as hackers in other simulated network scenarios. We wish to extend our existing research work on creating deception in HackIt tool to investigate the effectiveness of deception in networks of different sizes. A network can be classified as small, medium, or large sized based on the number of computer systems present. The effectiveness of honeypots may vary with the network size. HackIt tool provides the flexibility to configure any number of webservers as honeypots and regular webservers. Honeypots are costly, and their installation and maintenance are also costly not only in terms of money and manpower but also in terms of time. Furthermore, we plan to investigate what proportion of honeypots in a network will be effective to trap hackers successfully in different ways. We also wish to investigate the effectiveness of deception technology via different cost models on hacker's probing actions and against other cyberattack types (like SQL injection, denial of service (DoS), and zero-day attacks).

Acknowledgment Palvi Aggarwal was supported by Visvesverya Ph.D. Scheme for Electronics and IT (IITM/DeitY-MLA/ASO/77), Department of Electronics and Information Technology, Ministry of Communication and IT, Government of India. Cleotilde Gonzalez was supported by the Army Research Laboratory under Cooperative Agreement Number W911NF-13-2-0045 (ARL Cyber Security CRA) to Cleotilde Gonzalez. Varun Dutt was supported by the Department of Science and Technology, Government of India award (award number: SR/CSRI/28/2013(G)) to Varun Dutt. The views and conclusions contained in this document are those of the authors and should not be interpreted as representing the official policies, either expressed or implied, of the Army Research Laboratory or the Indian or U.S. Government.

References

1. Trustwave global Security Report. (2015). Retrieved from https://www2.trustwave.com/rs/815-RFM-693/images/2015_TrustwaveGlobalSecurityReport.pdf
2. Symantec Corporation. (2014). *Internet security threat report*. Retrieved from http://www.symantec.com/content/en/us/enterprise/other_resources/bistr_main_report_v19_2129 1018.en-us.pdf
3. Whaley, B. (1982). Toward a general theory of deception. *Journal of Strategic Studies, 5*(1), 178–192.
4. Denning, D. (1999). *Information warfare and security*. New York: Addison Wesley.
5. Mitnick, K. D., & Simon, W. L. (2011). *The art of deception: Controlling the human element of security*. Indianapolis, IN: John Wiley & Sons.
6. Glantz, D. (1989). *Military deception in the second world war* (Cass series on soviet military theory and practice). London: Routledge. isbn:ISBN 978-0-714-63347-3.
7. Rowe, N. C., & Custy, E. J. (2008). Deception in cyber-attacks. In *Cyber warfare and cyber terrorism*. Hershey, PA: Information Science Reference.
8. Cohen, F. (1998). The deception toolkit. *Risks Digest, 19*.
9. Rowe, N. C. (2003, June). Counter planning deceptions to foil cyber-attack plans. In *IEEE Systems, Man and Cybernetics Society Information Assurance Workshop, 2003* (pp. 203–210). IEEE.
10. Heckman, K. E., Walsh, M. J., Stech, F. J., O'boyle, T. A., DiCato, S. R., & Herber, A. F. (2013). Active cyber defense with denial and deception: A cyber-wargame experiment. *Computers & Security, 37*, 72–77.
11. Spitzner, L. (2003). The honeynet project trapping the hackers. *IEEE Security & Privacy, 99*(2), 15–23.
12. Qassrawi, M. T., & Zhang, H. (2010). Client honeypots: Approaches and challenges. In *4th International Conference on New Trends in Information Science and Service Science (NISS) 2010* (pp. 19–25). IEEE.
13. Aggarwal, P., Gonzalez, C., & Dutt, V. (2017, June). Modeling the effects of amount and timing of deception in simulated network scenarios. In *2017 International Conference on Cyber Situational Awareness, Data Analytics and Assessment (CyberSA 2017)*, London, UK (pp. 1–7). IEEE.
14. Aggarwal, P., Gonzalez, C., & Dutt, V. (2016a, June). Looking from the hacker's perspective: Role of deceptive strategies in cyber security. In *2016 International Conference on Cyber Situational Awareness, Data Analytics and Assessment (CyberSA 2016)*, London, UK (pp. 1–6). IEEE.
15. Garg, N., & Daniel, G. (2007). Deception in honeynets: A game-theoretic analysis. In *IEEE SMC Information Assurance and Security Workshop. IAW'07*. IEEE.
16. Aggarwal, P., Gonzalez, C., & Dutt, V. (2016b). Cyber-security: Role of deception in cyber-attack detection. In D. Nicholson (Ed.), *Advances in human factors in cybersecurity* (pp. 85–96). Cham: Springer.

Printed in the United States
by Baker & Taylor Publisher Services